THE CARLISLE MILLENNIUM PROJECT
EXCAVATIONS IN CARLISLE, 1998-2001

Volume 2: The Finds

Christine Howard-Davis

With contributions by

Andrew Bates, Mike Bishop, Paul Booth, Jeremy Bradley, Dana Challinor,
Sharon Clough, Kate Cramp, Richard Darrah, Brenda Dickinson, Denise Druce, Emma-Jayne Evans,
Anna Gannon, Jennifer Gilpin, Frances Graham, Erika Guttmann-Bond, Kay Hartley,
Gunnar Hellström, Martin Henig, Elizabeth Huckerby, Claire Ingrem, Jennifer Jones, Lynne Keys,
Ray McBride, Richard MacPhail, Ian Miller, Quita Mould, Julian Munby, Susan Pringle, Ruth Shaffrey,
David Shotter, David Smith, †Vivien Swan, Emma Tetlow, Roger Tomlin, Cathy Tyers, Ian Tyers,
Penelope Walton Rogers, Margaret Ward, Susan Winterbottom, Anne-Sophie Witkin, and John Zant

Illustrations by Adam Parsons

LANCASTER IMPRINTS 15

2009

Published by
Oxford Archaeology North
Mill 3
Moor Lane Mills
Moor Lane
Lancaster
LA1 1GF
(*Phone:* 01524 541000; *Fax:* 01524 848606)
(*website:* http://thehumanjourney.net)

Distributed by
Oxbow Books Ltd
10 Hythe Bridge Street
Oxford
OX1 2EW
(*Phone:* 01865 241249; *Fax:* 01865 794449)

Printed by
Information Press, Oxford, UK

ISBN 978-0-904220-57-5
ISSN 1345-5205

Series editor
Rachel Newman
Indexers
Marie Rowland and Adam Parsons
Design, layout, and formatting
Marie Rowland

Front cover: Plan of Carlisle, produced *c* 1560 © British Library; Military fitting in the form of an eagle.

Rear Cover: X-ray of scale armour neck protection from Period 4B (mid-second century)

LANCASTER IMPRINTS Lancaster Imprints is the publication series of Oxford Archaeology North. The series covers work on major excavations and surveys of all periods undertaken by the organisation and associated bodies.

Contents

List of Illustrations v
Abbreviations xiii
Contributors xiv
Summary xvii
Phasing Summary xix
Acknowledgements xx

15 A SYNTHESIS 483
    Setting the Stage: the Original Appearance of the Site. 483
    Painting the Backdrops: Roads and Buildings 484
    Putting Actors on the Stage 490
    There's No Place Like Home 502
    Discard and Disposal 520
    Putting Food on the Table 520
    Health and Happiness 526
    From Roman to Norman: the 'Dark Earths' of Period 7 528
    Medieval Occupancy of the Site 529
    In Conclusion 537

16 ROMAN AND POST-ROMAN POTTERY 539
    The Samian 539
    The Coarse Pottery (including amphorae and mortaria) 566
    The Medieval and Post-medieval Pottery 660

17 THE COINS, MILITARIA, AND OTHER METALWORK 679
    Introduction 679
    The Roman Coins 679
    The Post-Roman Coins 686
    The Goldwork 686
    The Roman Militaria 687
    Other Copper-alloy Objects 725
    Other Objects of Iron 745
    The Lead Objects 761
    The Iron Slag 764

18 THE GLASS AND OTHER FINDS 767
    Introduction 767
    The Roman and Later Vessel and Window Glass 767
    Other Objects of Glass 774
    The Ceramic Objects 777
    Jet and Amber Objects 777

19 THE STRUCTURAL WOOD AND OTHER WOODEN ARTEFACTS 781
    The Structural Wood 781
    The Wooden Artefacts 805

20 THE LEATHER AND OTHER ORGANIC ARTEFACTS 817
    The Roman Stitched Sheet Leather 817
    The Roman Shoes 831
    The Medieval Leather 841
    The Textiles and Cord 858
    The Worked Bone 858

21 THE STONEWORK AND OTHER BUILDING MATERIALS..869
    The Roman Sculptural Stone 869
    The Building Stone 873
    The Other Worked Stone 873
    The Ceramic Building Materials 887

22 PALAEOECOLOGICAL EVIDENCE 903
    The Human Skeletal Remains 903
    The Animal Bone 903
    Fish Remains 920
    Insect Remains 921
    Waterlogged and Charred Plant Remains 926

BIBLIOGRAPHY xxiii
INDEX..li

Volume 3: DVD-ROM

A 1   CONTEXT LISTING.. 937

A 2   THE CERAMICS 1095

A 3   THE ROMAN COINS 1103

A 4   CONSERVATION 1115

A 5   THE FINE METALWORK 1131

A 6   THE IRONWORK.. 1189

A 7   THE LEAD.. 1309

A 8   THE GLASS AND OTHER FINDS.. 1325

A 9   THE WOOD.. 1365

A 10   THE LEATHER AND OTHER ORGANIC ARTEFACTS.. 1387

A 11   THE STONEWORK AND OTHER BUILDING MATERIALS 1433

A 12   THE HUMAN AND ANIMAL BONE 1451

A 13   THE INSECTS 1481

A 14   THE PALAEOENVIRONMENTAL MATERIAL 1489

A 15   THE SOILS 1525

A 16   ABSOLUTE DATING... 1535

List of Illustrations

Figures

261	Period 2 features, with the layout of the first timber fort (Period 3A) superimposed	484
262	The Period 3 timber fort	485
263	The Period 4 timber fort	488
264	The Period 6 stone fort	489
265	The layout of the fort in Period 3A	503
266	Excavated part of Building *7400*, with probable metalworking hearth *7435*	505
267	Excavated buildings attributed to Period 3B	507
268	Depiction on a tombstone showing a three-legged table	507
269	The intersection of the main roads of the fort, with the new buildings of Period 3C	509
270	Excavated buildings attributed to Period 4A	510
271	Excavated buildings attributed to Period 4B	514
272	Excavated buildings attributed to Period 5	516
273	Excavated buildings attributed to Period 6	517
274	Period 6 Buildings *2301*, *2302*, and *5200*	518
275	A provincial butcher's shop, showing different cuts of meat, from a tombstone from Dresden	521
276	The handle of a bronze jug from Carlisle, showing the sacrifice of a pig	522
277	Amphora from Building *7392*, labelled as containing top-quality fish sauce from Tangiers	523
278	The excavated medieval features in relation to the castle and its defences	529
279	Period 8A Structure *7653* and its Period 8B successor, Building *7399*	531
280	Tenements *1234* and *1235*	534
281	A family dinner, as depicted in the Luttrell Psalter	536
282	All vessels (maximum numbers) by date of production	540
283	Histogram of decorated and stamped samian vessels by half decade	545
284	Samian from Period 3A	553
285	Samian from Period 3B	554
286	Samian from Period 3C	555
287	Samian from Period 4A	556
288	Samian from Period 4A/B	557
289	Samian from Period 4B	558
290	Samian from Period 4C	558
291	Samian from Period 5	560
292	Samian from Period 6 and unstratified	562
293	Samian reused as counters and spindle whorls	565
294	The core range of vessel forms used by the Roman army for food preparation	570
295	Dressel 20 and Dressel 23 amphorae with stamps and graffiti	574
296	Gaulish and 'black sand' amphorae	576
297	Spanish, carrot, and North-African amphorae	577
298	Stamped mortaria, *1-14*	587
299	Stamped mortaria, *15-19, 21*	589
300	Vessels from Periods 2 and 3A	610
301	Period 3A vessels	612
302	Period 3B vessels	614
303	Period 3C vessels	616
304	Periods 3D-3E vessels	617
305	Period 4A vessels, *76-104*	619
306	Period 4A vessels, *105-27*	621
307	Periods 4A and 4A/B vessels	623
308	Period 4A/B vessels	625
309	Period 4B vessels, *167-93*	627
310	Fragment of jar *194* with appliqué leaves	628
311	Period 4B vessels, *195-221*	630
312	Period 4B vessels, *225-49*	632
313	Period 4B vessels, *250-67*	634

314	Period 4B vessels, *268-82*	635
315	Period 4C vessels	636
316	Period 4D vessels	637
317	Period 5 vessels	638
318	Period 5A vessels	639
319	Period 5B vessels	640
320	Period 5C vessels	641
321	Period 5D vessels	642
322	Period 6A vessels, *360-86*	645
323	Period 6A vessels, *387-401*	646
324	Period 6B vessels, *405-30*	648
325	Period 6B vessels, *431-5*	649
326	Period 6C vessels, *436-68*	651
327	Period 6C vessels, *469-84*	653
328	Period 6D vessels	655
329	Period 6E vessels	656
330	Period 7 vessels	658
331	Periods 8 and 9 vessels	659
332	Quantification of the medieval pottery from each excavation trench	661
333	Medieval vessels, *1-23*	672
334	Medieval vessels, *24-37*	673
335	The goldwork	686
336	Scale mail fragment *2722*	690
337	Scale mail fragment *2885*	691
338	Scale mail fragment *2657*	691
339	Iron and copper-alloy scales from mail	692
340	Fittings from Corbridge-type armour	692
341	Newstead-type backplate *2721*	693
342	Fittings from Newstead-type armour	694
343	Fragments of plate armour	694
344	Arm-guard *2883A*	695
345	Arm-guard *2883B*	697
346	Arm-guard *2886*	698
347	Iron arm-guard fragments	699
348	Iron greave *2724*	700
349	Iron helmet cheekpiece *2723*	701
350	Copper-alloy helmet fittings 1	701
351	Copper-alloy binding for cheekpiece	701
352	Copper-alloy helmet fittings 2	702
353	Complex fitting (Copper Alloy 223)	702
354	Suggested scheme of leathering on the *manicae*	704
355	Copper-alloy suspension loops and split pins	705
356	Iron shield fittings	706
357	Copper-alloy military belt and apron fittings	707
358	Copper-alloy studs and strap terminals	708
359	Other copper-alloy military fittings	708
360	Bone and ivory sword grips	709
361	Iron arrowheads	710
362	Iron artillery bolts	711
363	Wooden rack *25*	712
364	Possible *ballista* mechanisms, oak bound with iron	713
365	Possible *pila*	713
366	Iron spearhead *444*	714
367	Iron spearheads and ferrule	715
368	Possible standard *2898*	716
369	Caltrops	716
370	Ceramic slingshot	717
371	Lead slingshot	718

372   Iron tent peg *1374*......718
373   Iron turf cutter *2706*......719
374   Copper-alloy horse harness *340*......719
375   Copper-alloy harness clips......720
376   Copper-alloy harness decorations......721
377   Copper-alloy harness pendants......722
378   Dome-headed studs......723
379   Copper-alloy saddle plates......723
380   Saddle plates *363* and *1258*......724
381   Bow (*1-6*), crossbow (*7-10*), and plate brooches (*11-12*)......726
382   Penannular brooches......727
383   Brooch or buckle pins and chains......728
384   Bangles and an anklet......729
385   Earrings and finger rings......730
386   Hair pins......731
387   Other pins......732
388   Elements of buckles......733
389   Button-and-loop fasteners......734
390   Toilet, surgical, or pharmaceutical instruments......734
391   Weaving tablet......735
392   Spoons and vessels......736
393   Enamel disc *77*......736
394   Locks and keys......737
395   Baluster-shaped knobs......737
396   Possible candlestick *509*......738
397   Seal boxes......738
398   Knife guards......738
399   Studs and pins......739
400   Studs......739
401   Copper-alloy bell *225*......740
402   Rein trace *580*......740
403   Medieval harness fitting *40*......741
404   Metalworking scrap......742
405   Escutcheon from Period 4A Building **3376**......743
406   Tubes and objects of unknown purpose......744
407   Objects of unknown purpose......744
408   Undiagnostic objects......745
409   Brooch *774*......745
410   Needles......746
411   Razors and knives......747
412   Knives of Roman and early medieval date......747
413   Knives of medieval date 1......748
414   Knives of medieval date 2......748
415   Shears *316*......749
416   Flesh hooks......749
417   Chain fragments......750
418   Bucket handles and escutcheon......750
419   Lamp holder *3283*......750
420   Latch lifter, elements of locks, and keys......751
421   Fish hook *3285*......751
422   *Styli*......752
423   Snaffle bit *293*......753
424   Horseshoes......753
425   Holdfasts and a carpenter's dog......754
426   Iron wallhooks......754
427   Hinges......755
428   Spiked loops and rove bolt......755
429   Tools, Period 3......756

430   Tools, Period 4 757
431   Tools, Period 5 757
432   Tools, Periods 6 and 7 757
433   Tools, Period 8 758
434   Unstratified tools...758
435   Suspension loops..758
436   Looped pins 759
437   Reaping hook *3020* 759
438   Agricultural objects 759
439   Unidentified objects...760
440   Vessel (or lid) *91* 760
441   Scale pan *286*..761
442   Weights 762
443   Gallet *7* 762
444   Tools and fasteners..763
445   Unidentified lead objects 763
446   Pillar-moulded bowls 768
447   Colourless vessels, cups...769
448   Blue-green blown vessels...770
449   Square storage bottles 771
450   Melon beads, Period 3 773
451   Beads, Periods 4-7 and unstratified...774
452   Glass bangles 775
453   Glass gaming counters 776
454   Medieval spindle whorl 777
455   Shale bangles 778
456   Shale spindle whorl 778
457   Jet objects..779
458   Techniques for the conversion of oak by splitting, hewing, and sawing to shape...............780
459   Examples of radially cleft timbers 782
460   W1426, showing the sawn knot 784
461   W1665, inner radially split section of oak, surviving as a complete pile............................784
462   Sill-beam fragment W1013, probably from a long timber 785
463   Widths of the planks and boards used in Period 3 drain *4463*...785
464   Period 3A Building *4653*, the west wall of which may have been a rebuild 787
465   Comparison of the cross-sectional areas of posts in Buildings *3772*, *3376*, and *5689* 790
466   Comparison of cross-sectional areas of posts in adjacent Period 4 buildings, *5688* and *5689* 790
467   Comparison of the size of posts used in three walls of the Period 4 *principia*, Building *5688*...........791
468   Comparison of post sizes used in Period 4 Building *3376*...792
469   The internal wall of Building *3376*, which may have supported the roof ridge.......................792
470   Oak weather-board shutter, from Building *3688*..793
471   Distance between the lowest slot and the bottom of the posts in Building *3772* 794
472   The construction of the north wall of Period 3C Building *7200*...795
473   Reconstruction of proposed shutter system on the south wall of Building *5689*...............796
474   Frame forming structure of Period 4A drain *6781* 797
475   Framed drain cover of drain *6781*, with nailed planks allowing access to the drain beneath 798
476   Part of Period 4A plank drain *6362*, made from high-quality oak..799
477   The way in which pipes were joined changed through time 800
478   Roman, and possibly medieval, combs 806
479   Coarser combs, perhaps for grooming horses 807
480   Wooden spindle whorls..807
481   Round oak base of a stave-built vessel 808
482   Partial reconstruction of barrel *24* 808
483   Boxwood pyx, *40*..809
484   Turned bowl and the base of a basket..810
485   Other utensils 811
486   Table leg *9*..812
487   Ruler *28*..812

488 Writing tablets, possible wheel spoke, and shingle 813
489 Lock housing *18* 814
490 Plasterer's float *15* 814
491 Fragment of saddle frame *21* 814
492 Wooden pegs 815
493 Wooden objects of unknown purpose 815
494 Possible bow *1* 816
495 Reconstruction of the standard Roman army tent 821
496 Hem types and other conventions used 823
497 Seam types 824
498 Attachment points on leather *34* 824
499 Panel *23* and gable reinforcing patch *24* 825
500 Reconstruction of the insertion of the eaves flap 826
501 Percentage of different seam types over time 826
502 Saddle cover *43* 827
503 Elements of saddle cover *43* 828
504 Panel *46* 829
505 Bardings *47* and *48* 830
506 Pouch *68* 830
507 Styles of shoes from the forts at Carlisle 832
508 Sole types, thonging, and nailing patterns 834
509 Nailed shoes and boots of first- to mid-second-century date 836
510 Nailed shoes of mid-second-century date 838
511 One-piece shoes, possible toe strap, and a wooden sole 839
512 Shoe styles from the medieval deposits 844
513 Turnshoes 846
514 Toggle-fastening and front-fastening shoes and ankle boots 847
515 Front-fastening and side-lacing boots and shoe 848
516 Shoes with low throat, and divided tie-strap fastening 850
517 Shoe with divided tie-strap, slip-on shoe with high throat, and ankle boots 851
518 Girdle and straps 853
519 Sheath, panels, and archer's bracer 854
520 Roman hairpins 859
521 Probable early medieval comb case 859
522 Spindle whorls and weaving combs 860
523 Possible weaving accessories 861
524 A spoon and scoops 862
525 Fragment of bone inlay 863
526 Bone counters 864
527 Tuning peg 864
528 Toggles, possibly cheekpieces 864
529 Bone tools and knife handle 865
530 Small cap or terminal 865
531 Antler tools 866
532 Medieval hammer-head 866
533 Off-cuts and plaques 867
534 Objects of unknown purpose 868
535 Building stone from the Period 6 *principia* 873
536 Histogram showing distribution of quern lithology by century 874
537 Imported style of 'kerbed' querns 876
538 Possible millstones *32* and *33* 878
539 Possible millstone *10* and millstone *41* 879
540 'Cake tin' quern 879
541 Beehive querns 880
542 Disc querns 880
543 Primary whetstones 881
544 Possible shaft straightener 882
545 Secondary-use and natural whetstones 882

546 Projectiles 883
547 Pot lids 883
548 Loomweight, spindle whorl, and pestle 884
549 Possible lamp or lampholder *49* 885
550 Lamp or lampholder *37* 885
551 Counters 886
552 Stone vessel 886
553 Writing implement 886
554 Signatures and tally marks 892
555 *Pila* brick and material with graffiti 893
556 Kiln flooring-block *16* 894
557 Flue tiles 895
558 Water pipe *22* 896
559 Water pipes, or possibly vaulting tubes 897
560 Fragments of chimney 898
561 Legionary stamps 899
562 Joining fragments of water pipe with star graffito 900
563 Average height at the withers of cattle and sheep/goat 906
564 Scattergram of Roman and medieval cattle distal metacarpi (Periods 3-8) 909
565 Anatomical part representation of cattle in rank order, Periods 3-5 911
566 Anatomical part representation of cattle within road and non-road construction layers, Periods 6B and 6C..912
567 Anatomical part representation of cattle in rank order from Period 8........912
568 Anatomical part representation of sheep/goat from Period 6 and Period 8 913
569 Anatomical part representation of pig in rank order from Periods 3-6.........914
570 The proportions of the ecological groups of Coleoptera................................922
571 The proportions of the synanthropic species..923

Plates

151 The low bluff on which the fort, and later castle, was built...........................483
152 A wattle wall panel associated with Period 4B Building *5689*......................486
153 Laser-scanned image of part of a panel of nailed weather-boarding 486
154 Foundations of the second-century military workshop at Ribchester 487
155 Period 5 ceramic water pipe, *in situ* 487
156 A legionary stamp on a tile from the Scalesceugh tilery................................489
157 A reconstruction of a late Iron Age farm 490
158 Bone weaving comb from Period 3A Building *4658* 491
159 A well-worn dagger frog, lost in the early days of the fort 492
160 A smithing hearth within Period 4 Building *5689*, to the east of the *principia*...........493
161 A fragment of plate armour with a square hole, probably from an arrow strike............493
162 A caltrop, which would have been scattered on the ground to hinder the movement of horses..........494
163 An unusual figure-of-eight brooch, probably with 'native' origins................494
164 Fragments of a gold necklace lost in Period 6 Building *2302* 495
165 An almost complete military boot from one of the many waterlogged deposits 495
166 A small fragment of plate armour which appears to have been painted black............497
167 Scale armour, showing iron and copper-alloy scales used together to add decoration..........497
168 A plain iron greave, found with the deposit of armour from Period 4 Building *5689* 498
169 A copper-alloy strip preserves the outline of the cheekpiece it once bound 498
170 A modern re-enactor dressed as an auxiliary 499
171 A modern Indian border guard wears headgear that increases his height to over 2 m...........499
172 A high-quality saddle plate decorated with niello, a black inlay made from silver...........500
173 Part of the wooden sub-frame of a saddle found in Period 3A Building *4658* 501
174 A decorative element from a horse harness 501
175 A large rein trace, from Building *5689* 502
176 Small off-cuts of copper-alloy sheet, found in Building *4658*.........................503
177 Hairpin from Period 3B Building *7394* 508
178 Repoussé stud, possibly a campaign badge, from Building *3796*....................512
179 Antler-handled knife from Building *2059* 512

180 A possible baker's peel, and a wooden base from a large basket, *in situ* in Building *5689* 513

181 Lunate pendant, part of the trappings of cavalry horse harness, from Building *5689* 515

182 Small fragment of a possible wooden ruler, from Building *5689* 515

183 Fragment of an Ebor-ware candlestick, made in York, from Building *2302* 518

184 Enamelled disc from floor *2186*, in Period 6C Building *2301* 519

185 Mask of Silenus, from a large beaker imported from Northern Gaul or the Rhineland 525

186 Delicate bone spoon from Period 5A 526

187 Part of a wooden-soled bath shoe 526

188 A small ivory-handled razor 527

189 Chinese barbers working in the open air, where the light is best 527

190 One of several medieval shoes found in medieval outer ward ditch *1231* 532

191 A medieval knife blade with a maker's mark 535

192 A small pair of iron shears, now bent, but originally used in household needlework 535

193 The preserved black pitch 'waterproof' lining on an amphora neck 567

194 An almost complete ring-neck flagon..568

195 A flat-rimmed bowl with the distinctive lattice of Black-burnished ware vessels........................570

196 The distinctive form of a North African wine amphora 573

197 The stamped mortarium from Elginhaugh 581

198 Examples of products from the Brampton kilns 590

199 Fine rouletted beakers from Carlisle..594

200 A mica-dusted indented beaker 599

201 Locally produced dish imitating a Black-burnished ware form 603

202 A red-slipped Wilderspool vessel..605

203 Gritty-ware rims..664

204 Large fragments of green-glazed jugs..667

205 Zoomorphic jug handle..671

206 Reduced greyware jar base..674

207 Group of five *denarii* from layer *3447*, overlying Buildings *3772* and *4006* 680

208 Gold necklace from Kirby Thore 687

209 Layer *6419*, containing armour, during excavation 688

210 Fragment of scale mail, from Building *5689* 689

211 Newstead-type backplate *2721* 693

212 X-ray of arm-guard *2883A* 696

213 Possible *ballista* mechanisms 713

214 Object *340*, showing the clumsy repair..719

215 The blade of knife *386*, showing an inlaid maker's mark..749

216 X-ray of knife *387*, showing struck maker's mark..749

217 The remains of wattle panelling in the east wall of Building *3772*..795

218 Water pipe of alder, the originally circular bore having been flattened by the weight of soil above....799

219 Period 4B pipes and junction boxes *in situ* 800

220 Base of barrel *24* 808

221 Brand on barrel *24*..809

222 Red pigment on peg *42* 815

223 Inscriptions and stamp C C M; S D V 831

224 Example of two-ply cord 858

225 Wooden haft within bone tool *71* 865

226 *Genius 1*..869

227 *Genius 2*..869

228 *Genius 3*..870

229 Fragment *4*, either a garment or mural crown 870

230 Female head *5*..870

231 Male figure *6* 871

232 Building stone *7* 871

233 Pedimental stone or *aedicula 8*..871

234 Altar *9*..872

235 Column base, building stone *106* 873

236 Traces of leather wrapped around a water pipe..897

237 Stone *pilae* in the hypocaust of the Period 6 *principia*, obviating the need for brick....................901

238 Natural holes in the parietal bone, a common trait in both ancient and modern cattle skulls 906
239 Deformation of the proximal articulations, in contrast to a normal bone of cattle 907
240 Cattle scapula, showing hook-related damage 914
241 Glenoid of a horse scapula, with eburnation and pitting associated with osteoarthritis 915
242 Cereal grain, germinated 927
243 Alder seed 930
244 Fragments of hazelnut shell 930
245 Alder pollen, shown under an electron microscope................................931
246 Modern alder carr in Cumbria........................932
247 Sedge rhizome bases 933

Tables

11 Quantification of samian vessel classes by percentage of weight, sherd-count, and EREs.....................538
12 Quantification of sources of samian vessels by site period 542
13 Quantification of samian vessel types by fabric................................543
14 Quantification of South Gaulish samian vessels retaining identifiable moulded decoration, by epoch..544
15 Numbers of Central and East Gaulish vessels with moulded decoration attributable to specific potters...546
16 Summary of graffiti and marks on samian ware 563
17 Repaired samian vessels.....................564
18 Reused samian ware (counters and spindle whorls)........................565
19 Quantification of Roman coarse pottery by excavation area........................567
20 Stratified Roman pottery by period........................568
21 Amphorae for main stratified periods, post-Roman, and unstratified, by sherd count...................572
22 Totals of all amphorae by fabric (stratified and unstratified)........................573
23 Quantities of mortaria by period 580
24 Stratified mortaria for Periods 1-3........................580
25 Stratified mortaria for Period 4........................582
26 Stratified mortaria for Period 5........................584
27 Stratified mortaria for Period 6........................585
28 Stratified major coarse wares by period 592
29 Stratified Black-burnished wares by period 593
30 Stratified fine tablewares for Periods 1-3 596
31 Stratified tablewares for Period 4 597
32 Stratified tablewares for Period 5 599
33 Stratified tablewares for Period 6 600
34 Quantification by sherd count and weight of the medieval pottery 661
35 Quantification by sherd count and weight of the post-medieval pottery 661
36 Amounts of medieval and post-medieval pottery in MIL 1 and MIL 5........................664
37 Amounts of medieval and post-medieval pottery in MIL 3 and MIL 4........................668
38 Roman coins until the death of Hadrian 681
39 Carlisle: early Flavian coins........................682
40 Distribution of coins by denomination........................685
41 Originating mints of the fourth-century coins 685
42 The chronological distribution of brooch types 725
43 Distribution of ironwork between trenches........................745
44 Roman and medieval smithing-hearth bottom statistics........................766
45 The sections and species used to make posts for buildings in Periods 3 and 4........................786
46 Size and function of timbers made from inner sections of large trees in AD 83 or later........................786
47 Growth rates and average annual ring widths of posts from drain 6781........................788
48 Characteristics of the slow-grown timber from drain 5925........................788
49 Characteristics of the fast-grown timber from drain 5925, ordered by growth rate........................789
50 Sizes and spacings of post centres for Buildings 3772, 5688, 5689, and 7392........................790
51 Details of complete water pipes, and those with a recorded bore diameter........................799
52 Evidence for the carpenter's toolkit........................801
53 Details of evidence of coopered vessels 809
54 Approximate distribution of Roman stitched leather by period 817
55 Distribution of stratified stitched leather finds according to context type........................818

56	Variation in levels of the reworking of stitched leather	822
57	Tent panels with complete length or width preserved	825
58	Number of instances of the three main seam types	826
59	Roman scrap/waste (sheet) leather in medieval contexts	841
60	Leather straps from medieval contexts	852
61	Sheet leather from medieval contexts	856
62	Summary of the total building material assemblage	887
63	Chronological distribution by weight	887
64	The proportions, by weight, of the main tile types in Periods 4, 5, and 6	888
65	Distribution of fabric types by period, giving weight in kilograms	890
66	Percentage of main tile types in each fabric group (securely identified forms and fabrics only)	890
67	Main tile types as percentage of fabric groups 1-5 (securely identified forms and fabrics only)	890
68	The stamped tiles	891
69	Condition of the animal bone, expressed as a percentage of the total number of fragments	904
70	Total number of fragments by species	905
71	Principal stock animals by phase expressed as a percentage of the sum of cattle, sheep/goat, and pig fragments (n)	908
72	Quantification of cut marks identified as from the dismemberment, filleting, or skinning of animals	910
73	Quantification of chop and cut marks in the three main species	910
74	Incidences of hook-related damage to cattle scapulae	914
75	Aged maxillary and mandibular teeth of horses	915
76	Representation of taxa according to phase (NISP)	921
77	The proportions of the ecological groups of Coleoptera	923
78	The proportions of the synanthropic species	924
79	Samples producing carbonised cereal grains	926

Abbreviations

BP	Before Present
BS	Body sherd
CAU/CAL	Carlisle Archaeological Unit/Carlisle Archaeology Ltd
CIL	*Corpus Inscriptionum Latinarum*
GIS	Geographic Information System
GPR	Ground Penetrating Radar
GSB	Geophysical Surveys of Bradford
IT	Information Technology
NGR	National Grid Reference
NISP	Number of individual species
OA	Oxford Archaeology
OD	Ordnance Datum
OS	Ordnance Survey
RIB	*The Roman Inscriptions of Britain*
RIC	*The Roman Imperial Coinage*
SM	Scheduled Monument

Contributors

Andrew Bates
Oxford Archaeology North, Mill 3, Moor Lane Mills, Moor Lane, Lancaster, LA1 1GF

Mike Bishop
Braemar, Kirkgate, Chirnside, Duns, Berwickshire, TD11 3XL

Paul Booth
Oxford Archaeology South, Janus House, Osney Mead, Oxford, OX2 0ES

Jeremy Bradley
Oxford Archaeology North, Mill 3, Moor Lane Mills, Moor Lane, Lancaster, LA1 1GF

Dana Challinor
Charcoal Specialist, Oxford

Sharon Clough
Oxford Archaeology South, Janus House, Osney Mead, Oxford, OX2 0ES

Kate Cramp
Oxford Archaeology South, Janus House, Osney Mead, Oxford, OX2 0ES

Richard Darrah
Riven Oak, 79 Park Lane, Norwich, NR2 3EQ

Brenda Dickinson
(Formerly of) Department of Classics, University of Leeds, Leeds, LS2 9JT

Denise Druce
Oxford Archaeology North, Mill 3, Moor Lane Mills, Moor Lane, Lancaster, LA1 1GF

Emma-Jayne Evans
(Formerly of) Oxford Archaeology South, Janus House, Osney Mead, Oxford, OX2 0ES

Anna Gannon
Department of History of Art, St Edmund's College, University of Cambridge, Cambridge, CB3 0BN

Jennifer Gilpin
(Formerly of) University of Reading, Whiteknights, PO Box 217, Reading, Berkshire, RG6 6AH

Frances Graham
Leasyke, 1 Crosshills Road, Cononley, BD20 8JZ

Erika Guttman-Bond
Institute for Geo and Bioarchaeology, IGBA, Faculty of Earth and Life Sciences, Vrije Universiteit, De Boelelaan 1085, 1081 HV Amsterdam, The Netherlands

Kay Hartley
Flat 2, 27 Hanover House, Leeds, LS3 1AW

Gunnar Hellström
Oxford Archaeology North, Mill 3, Moor Lane Mills, Moor Lane, Lancaster, LA1 1GF

Martin Henig
Institute of Archaeology, Oxford University, 36 Beaumont Street, Oxford, OX1 2PG

Christine Howard-Davis
Oxford Archaeology North, Mill 3, Moor Lane Mills, Moor Lane, Lancaster, LA1 1GF

Elizabeth Huckerby
Oxford Archaeology North, Mill 3, Moor Lane Mills, Moor Lane, Lancaster, LA1 1GF

Claire Ingrem
Department of Archaeology, School of Humanities, University of Southampton, Highfield, Southampton, SO17 1BJ

Jennifer Jones
Department of Archaeology, Durham University, South Road, Durham, DH1 3LE

Lynne Keys
267 Weedington Road, London, NW5 4PR

Ray McBride
Tyne and Wear Museums, Discovery Museum, Blandford Square, Newcastle Upon Tyne, Tyne and Wear, NE1 4JA

Richard Macphail
Institute of Archaeology, University College London, 31-34 Gordon Square, London, WC1H 0PY

Ian Miller
Oxford Archaeology North, Mill 3, Moor Lane Mills, Moor Lane, Lancaster, LA1 1GF

Quita Mould
Eastmoor Manor, Eastmoor, Kings Lynn, Norfolk, PE33 9PZ

Julian Munby
Oxford Archaeology South, Janus House, Osney Mead, Oxford, OX2 0ES

Susan Pringle
Museum of London Specialist Services, 46 Eagle Wharf Road, London, N1 7EE

Ruth Shaffrey
Oxford Archaeology South, Janus House, Osney Mead, Oxford, OX2 0ES

David Shotter
Centre for North-West Regional Studies, Lancaster University, Fylde College, Lancaster, LA1 4YF

David Smith
Institute of Archaeology and Antiquity, University of Birmingham, Edgbaston, Birmingham, B15 2TT

†Vivien Swan

Emma Tetlow
School of GeoSciences, University of Edinburgh, Geography Building, Drummond Street, Edinburgh, EH8 9XP

Roger Tomlin
Wolfson College, Oxford University, Linton Road, Oxford, OX2 6UD

Cathy Tyers
Department of Archaeology, University of Sheffield, Northgate House, West Street, Sheffield, S1 4ET

Ian Tyers
Dendrochronological Consultancy Ltd, 65 Crimicar Drive, Sheffield, S10 4EF

Penelope Walton Rogers
The Anglo-Saxon Laboratory, Marketing House, 8 Bootham Terrace, York, YO30 7DH

Margaret Ward
2 Woodfields, Christleton, Chester, CH3 7AU

Susan Winterbottom
48 Lyndhurst Street. Stoke-on-Trent, ST6 4BP

Anne-Sophie Witkin
Department of Archaeology and Anthropology, University of Bristol, 43 Woodland Road, Clifton, Bristol, BS8 1UU

John Zant
Oxford Archaeology North, Mill 3, Moor Lane Mills, Moor Lane, Lancaster, LA1 1GF

Summary

Between 1998 and 2001, major excavations were undertaken immediately to the south of Carlisle Castle, in advance of construction works associated with Carlisle City Council's Gateway City (Millennium) Project. The investigation comprised five main trenches, the positions of which were determined by the development footprint. Several geophysical surveys associated with, but completed prior to, the main phase of excavation, were also carried out, together with a limited excavation in which no significant archaeological remains were encountered. Previous excavations had demonstrated the archaeological significance of the area; it was known that the site lay within the multi-phase Roman fort and the medieval castle's outer ward, and it was anticipated that the ditch separating the castle from the medieval city would be encountered beneath Castle Way.

Evidence for pre-Roman activity was restricted to cultivation marks, the remains of a field system of possible Iron Age date. The arrival of the Roman army saw the construction of a turf-and-timber fort during the autumn/winter of AD 72–3, a date known from the dendrochronological dating of timbers recovered from the south rampart in the 1980s. The Millennium excavations fixed the position of the west rampart and located the junction of two major roads, and in the southern part of the fort, the remains of barracks, workshops/stores, and external areas were investigated. A small part of the central range, including fragments of what may have been the *principia* and the *praetorium*, was also exposed.

An extensive internal reconstruction undertaken in the autumn/winter of AD 83-4 saw the replacement of almost all the original buildings with new structures. The barracks were rebuilt to a slightly larger specification, but otherwise the layout remained essentially unchanged; the fort defences do not appear to have been modified at this time. Following a minor episode of refurbishment *c* AD 93–4, the fort was demolished around AD 103–5. The break in occupation appears to have been a short one, however, and rebuilding, again in timber, occurred *c* AD 105. The excavations uncovered barrack blocks in the southern part of the second fort and fragments of two central-range buildings: the *principia* and an adjacent structure that might possibly have been a workshop. A shift in the character of occupation during the Hadrianic period suggests that the fort may have evolved from a conventional base into something like a works-depot, a change precipitated, perhaps, by the construction of Hadrian's Wall and the fort at Stanwix less than 1 km to the north. In the possible workshop in the central range, an important cache of articulated armour fragments was deposited towards the end of this period.

The fort was again demolished in the mid-second century, perhaps as a consequence of the Antonine re-occupation of southern Scotland in the early AD 140s. The status of the site during the second half of the century remains obscure. Intermittent occupation occurred, but the site does not seem to have been used as a conventional fort. The early third century saw extensive rebuilding in stone, but it is not clear whether the new installation was a conventional fort or something else, although for the most part the new layout followed that of the earlier forts. What was probably the west curtain wall lay inside the Flavian rampart, the *principia* was constructed on the site of the earlier headquarters buildings, the position of the major roads was maintained, and barracks were erected to the south. A building stone in the east wall of the *principia* suggests that the reconstruction was the work of *Legio VI Victrix*, although epigraphic evidence from elsewhere suggests that the fort was garrisoned by detachments from the other two British legions.

Thereafter the site was occupied to the end of the Roman period, with occupation certainly extending into the fifth century. Heavy coin loss outside the *principia*, associated with large quantities of animal bone and an increase in items of personal ornament, suggest that the fort may have taken on a market function in the late fourth century. Eventually, the excavated buildings were levelled and their remains covered by 'dark earths', although parts of the *principia* probably remained upstanding for centuries. Any activity in these centuries cannot, however, be characterised. Intensive activity recommenced in the mid-twelfth century, when most of the site was incorporated into the castle's outer ward. On the west, the city wall was constructed, whilst further east a road or track running north towards the castle's main gate was flanked to the west by a probable timber building, from which a palisade trench extended westwards. Following the construction of another timber building of particularly substantial construction, a layer of soil accumulated across this part of the site. Subsequently, activity within the outer ward was limited principally to the digging of a few pits, although at some stage an earthwork was constructed across the southern part of the ward in an east to west direction. The latest surviving levels, which need date no later than the thirteenth century, comprised a further accumulation of soils suggestive of gardening activity. The earliest cartographic information relating to this area, from the sixteenth century, clearly shows the main area of excavation as gardens and orchards.

To the south, a near-complete section was obtained across the large defensive ditch beneath Castle Way. This feature probably originated in the second half of the twelfth century but was recut, perhaps during the early fourteenth century, after becoming choked with earth and debris, seemingly largely as a result of rubbish disposal from the direction of the castle. From the late fourteenth century, the ditch was no longer maintained and encroachment occurred from tenements on the north side of Annetwell Street. All later medieval and most post-medieval deposits in this area had been removed when Castle Way was constructed.

Exceptional preservation of waterlogged organic materials, including the remains of timber buildings, and outstanding artefactual and environmental assemblages, were a feature of the late first-century to mid-second-century levels over the greater part of the site, and of the medieval deposits within the ditch. As a consequence, the Millennium excavations yielded evidence rarely found on archaeological sites in Britain, the study of which has greatly enhanced our understanding of daily life in Roman and medieval Carlisle.

Phasing Summary

Pre-Roman (Period 1)

1	Agricultural activity represented by plough-marks overlain by a buried soil horizon (Iron Age?)

Roman (Periods 2–6)

2	Earliest Roman activity; pre-fort or (more probably) associated with first fort construction (c AD 72–3 or shortly before?)
3A	Construction and primary occupation of the first fort (AD 72–3 to AD 83–4)
3B	Extensive internal refurbishment, perhaps associated with the arrival of a new garrison (AD 83–4 to c AD 93–4)
3C	Less extensive refurbishment, including construction of some new buildings (c AD 93-4 to c AD 103-5)
3D	Demolition of the first fort (c AD 103–5)
3E	Activity immediately post-dating the demolition of the first fort (c AD 103–5)
4A	Construction and primary occupation of the second fort (c AD 105 to c AD 125)
4B	Internal reorganisation of the second fort, possibly associated with a (partial?) change of use to a more industrial function (c AD 125 to c AD 140s)
4C	Demolition of the second fort (c AD 140s)
4D	Activity immediately post-dating the demolition of the second fort (c AD 140s)
5A	Abandonment or near-abandonment of the fort site, characterised by the accumulation of dark soils, but also slight evidence for continued activity (c AD 140s to c AD 160+?)
5B	Occupation of indeterminate nature characterised by the construction of a few small timber structures and associated external surfaces. Site probably not occupied by a conventional fort at this time (second half of the second century)
5C	Similar activity to Period 5B (second half of the second century)
5D	Continued evidence for low-level activity on some parts of the site, but probable abandonment of other areas characterised by accumulations of dark soils (late second to early third century)
6A	Rebuilding in stone and primary occupation within a conventional fort or some other type of military installation (early third century to late third/early fourth century)
6B	Second phase of occupation within the stone fort, characterised by alterations to some buildings and changes in external areas (late third/early fourth century to mid- late fourth century)
6C	Third and final phase of occupation within the stone fort, characterised by changes to some external areas, particularly those adjacent to the *principia*. Internal alterations to some buildings also apparent (mid- late fourth century to early fifth century or later)
6D	Demolition and robbing of most of the excavated stone fort buildings (early fifth century or later)
6E	Slight evidence for occupation post-dating the demolition of some fort buildings (early fifth century or later)

Post-Roman (Periods 7–9)

7	Accumulation of early medieval dark soils sealing almost all late Roman levels. Excavated areas probably largely unoccupied, though the taphonomy of the dark soils and the presence of a small artefactual assemblage suggest pre-Norman activity in the vicinity of the site (later fifth century? to late eleventh/early twelfth century)
8A	Early Norman occupation within the outer ward of the medieval castle, characterised by the construction of a timber structure and a road or track leading to the gatehouse, and by the construction of the city wall on the western edge of the site (approximately second half of twelfth century)
8B	Construction of a large timber building within the outer ward (approximately late twelfth century)
8C	Accumulation of dark soils over the excavated areas in the outer ward, indicative of a major change in the character of occupation (gardens?; approximately late twelfth-early thirteenth century)
8D	Localised activity in the outer ward, characterised by pits and small clay-lined hearths (approximately thirteenth century)
8E	Construction of a possible east to west-aligned earthwork on the southern edge of the outer ward (approximately thirteenth century)
8F	Accumulation of possibly cultivated soils over much of the outer ward (thirteenth/early fourteenth century)
8i	Construction and subsequent infilling of the large ditch on the southern edge of the castle's outer ward (mid-twelfth century to thirteenth century)
8ii	Recutting of the ditch, followed by further silting (approximately late thirteenth/early fourteenth century to late fourteenth century)
8iii	Encroachment of medieval tenements into the partially filled ditch, characterised by the construction of timber buildings and fences (approximately late fourteenth century to fifteenth century)
8iv	Similar activity to Period 8iii (approximately end of fourteenth century to fifteenth century)
9	Activity from the sixteenth century to the present day

Acknowledgements

As with any large archaeological project undertaken over a protracted period, the success of the Carlisle Millennium excavations and of the subsequent post-excavation programme has been due to the expertise, enthusiasm, and hard work of a large number of people, far too numerous to list individually. Sincere thanks are offered to all who, in one way or another, have contributed to the project in the period of over a decade that has elapsed from the earliest stages of planning to the publication of this volume.

We would particularly like to thank the many staff of Carlisle Archaeological Unit/Carlisle Archaeology Ltd (CAU/CAL) who, together with a number of volunteers, were involved in the excavations themselves, or who dealt with the huge artefactual and environmental assemblages generated by the fieldwork. From its inception to the early stages of the post-excavation programme, the Millennium project was managed by Mike McCarthy, Principal Archaeologist with Carlisle City Council and Director of CAU/CAL, who was responsible for planning and developing the excavation programme as part of Carlisle City Council's Millennium project team. The excavations of 1998-2001 were directed by John Zant and Gerry Martin, whilst the 1997 excavation on the south abutment of the Castle Way (Irish Gate) footbridge was supervised by Bill Barkle. Many field staff and volunteers worked on the project, and those who saw the programme through from the beginning, or who were part of the team responsible for the main 2000-1 campaign, include Jamie Armstrong, Simon Bailey, Mick Boyle, Tom Burns, Cath Chisman, Jo Cook, Iain Cumming, Pat Daniel, Stanley Darke, Frank Giecco, Aaron Goode, Rachel Grahame, Paul Hetherington, Maureen Kilpatrick, Gill Kirkly-Allsop, Mark Littlewood, Faye Minter, Julian Newman, Martin O'Hare, Claire Shaw, Richard Sims, Kerry Tyler, Neil Wigfield, and Don Wilson. Many of these individuals continued to work on the project during the initial stages of post-excavation.

Responsibility for the initial cleaning, cataloguing, recording, and stabilising of the enormous artefactual assemblage was shouldered by Gill Scarlett, assisted by Celia Harding, Stephen Wadeson, and Fiona Wooler. In addition to helping out with the excavation, Neil Wigfield was also responsible for supervising the collection, recording, and storage of all environmental and timber samples, and was heavily involved in the selection and sub-sampling of the timber for dendrochronological dating and other analyses. There is little doubt that the day-to-day running of the excavations would have been considerably more onerous without the administrative expertise and cheerful efficiency of Angela Farren and Judy Page. Regular pottery viewings undertaken by Cathy Brooks and Louise Hird, together with provisional coin identifications provided throughout the project by David Shotter, assisted with the establishment of a broadly dated occupational sequence from the earliest stages of the excavation. David also participated in a number of in-house seminars conducted by Oxford Archaeology North (OA North) to discuss various aspects of the stratigraphic sequence. The final report has unquestionably benefited from his unrivalled knowledge of the Roman period in north-west England.

Officers of Carlisle City Council closely involved with the development of the Millennium project, and whose input to various aspects of the archaeological works is gratefully acknowledged, included Mike Battersby, Director of Environment and Development, Duncan Fone, Head of Design, Richard Majewicz, Project Architect, and Bob McCormack, Clerk of Works. Thanks are also due to the staff of Laings Ltd, and in particular to Keith Little, Project Manager, and Construction Managers Dave Ely and John Osbourne.

In view of the fact that the excavations were conducted, for the most part, within the area of two Scheduled Monuments, the project would have been impossible without the advice, assistance, and co-operation provided by English Heritage staff, in particular David Sherlock, then Guardianship Inspector, Andrew Davison, North-West Regional Inspector, Henry Owen-John, Assistant Regional Director at the time of the excavations, Dave Mullings, Carlisle Castle Facilities Manager, and Ian Power, the Castle's Head Custodian. The progress of the excavations was monitored on behalf of Carlisle City Council by Philip Holdsworth and Helena Smith of Cumbria County Council's Archaeology Service.

It is impossible to see how the post-excavation phase of the project would have progressed as smoothly as it did without the hard work, assistance, and co-operation provided by John Egan, Carlisle City Solicitor and Secretary, and the goodwill and professionalism shown both by John and by other Officers of Carlisle City Council at what was a crucial time in the project's history. For OA North, the post-excavation assessment and the early stages of analysis were managed by Carol Allen, whose efficiency and professionalism in dealing with a variety of thorny issues and an almost overwhelming quantity of archaeological material was key to the successful completion of this stage of the project. Latterly, the reins of management and administration were taken up by Rachel Newman, who steered the project through analysis to publication, and who was responsible for editing this publication. The project database was constructed by Jo Cook, who also provided vital IT support throughout the post-excavation programme. Provisional phase drawings were compiled by Emma Carter and Mark Tidmarsh; the published illustrations were prepared by Adam Parsons and Marie Rowland; Adam was also responsible for the design of the report covers, and Marie for typesetting this volume. Much of the artefactual and environmental data included in the first volume were made available by Chris Howard-Davis, who also provided much useful advice, and Nick Johnson supplied invaluable support in the editing and organisation of the *Appendices* (Volume 3).

The post-excavation programme was monitored on behalf of Carlisle City Council by Richard Newman, Jeremy Parsons, and latterly Mark Brennand of Cumbria County Council's Historic Environment Service. A post-excavation Advisory Panel, comprising members of the OA North project team and representatives from Carlisle City Council, Cumbria County Council's Historic Environment Service, Tullie House Museum and Art Gallery, and English Heritage, met at regular intervals in order to monitor progress, exchange ideas and information, and to provide advice. Panel members, who are thanked for providing continuing support throughout the post-excavation programme, included John Egan, Peter Messenger, and Mark Beveridge (Carlisle City Council), Richard Newman, Mark Brennand, and Jeremy Parsons (Cumbria County Council), Tim Padley, David Clarke, and Hilary Wade (Tullie House Museum and Art Gallery), Andrew Davison (English Heritage), and Rachel Newman, Christine Howard-Davis, Adam Parsons, and John Zant (OA North).

Ian Caruana is thanked for providing a copy of the report on the Annetwell Street excavations of 1973-84 and 1990 in advance of publication, and for subsequent comments on the interpreted stratigraphy. Without this, our understanding of the development of the Roman and medieval sequence would have been so much the poorer. Thanks are also due to the staff of Tullie House Museum and Art Gallery in Carlisle, and in particular to Tim Padley, Keeper of Archaeology, for his advice, generosity with information, and co-operation throughout the project.

Lindsay Allason-Jones (Newcastle University), David Breeze (then of Historic Scotland), Ian Caruana, Richard Newman (Cumbria County Council), Peter Salway (chairman of Oxford Archaeology's Academic Advisory Committee), David Shotter, and Tim Padley (Tullie House Museum and Art Gallery) deserve special thanks for consenting to act as academic readers, and for making a number of valuable comments and suggestions. The report has greatly benefited from their knowledge and expertise; any errors that remain are of course, the authors' own.

Many specialists contributed to this report, either directly, or indirectly by the generous gift of their time in answer to enquiries. Thanks are due to them all, and without their contributions, this report would have been the poorer.

Margaret Ward wishes to thank Brenda Dickinson and Roger Tomlin for their help and information over and above that provided by their reports on the samian stamps and graffiti respectively. Joanna Bird, Geoff Dannell, and Felicity Wild are also thanked for their help with details incorporated in the report; Hilary Cool, Jerry Evans, and David Shotter generously provided information on finds from other sites, and Andrew David, of English Heritage, supplied access to unpublished information on survey work at Scalesceugh.

Ian and Cathy Tyers would like to thank Richard Darrah for information on the reuse of timber on the site, and John Zant for stratigraphic information. They would also like to recognise English Heritage's financial contribution towards the dendrochronological work. David Small and Emma Tetlow would like to thank Mark Robinson of the Oxford University Museum of Natural History for access to his conclusions from the original assessment of environmental samples from the site.

Elizabeth Huckerby and Denise Druce would like to extend particular thanks to Neil Wigfield for the original recording and ordering of the environmental bulk samples and for the preliminary processing of samples from MIL 1- MIL 4. They would also like to thank the Oxford Archaeology South environmental team for their valuable work in processing the large number of samples required for this analysis. Frances Graham is to be thanked for sorting the samples and helping with the identification of the plant remains. She was assisted by Sandra Bonsall, who looked especially at samples from the medieval period. They would also like to acknowledge the help of Allan Hall, University of York, and Charlotte O'Brien, of the Bio-Laboratory of the Department of Archaeology, University of Durham, who gave generously of their time to identify unknown plant taxa. In addition, they would like to thank the Department of Archaeology, University of Durham, for allowing them access to the modern seed reference collection, and the Hohenheim Botanical Gardens, Stuttgart, for supplying modern examples of several seeds. Finally, they would like to give special thanks to Jacqui Huntley, the English Heritage regional science advisor for the North East, for her unstinting advice, assistance, and support. Elizabeth Huckerby would also like to thank Frances Graham for preparing the pollen samples, and the Department of Biology at the University of Lancaster for the use of their laboratory facilities.

Carlisle City Council is thanked for permission to reproduce photographs from a number of CAU/CAL excavations and material from the collections of Tullie House Museum and Art Gallery. Thanks are also due to the following organisations for permission to reproduce photographs and other images from their collections: The estate of the late Barri Jones (Pl 151); the British Library (front cover); and Tullie House Museum and Art Gallery (Pl 208). Thanks are also due to the following persons for their permission to reproduce photographs: Phillip Barker of Lancaster University (Pl 245); Christine Howard-Davis (Pls 171 and 189); Tom Huckerby (Pls 246 and 247); Joe Jackson of COH I TUNGRORUM (The Tungrians) (Pl 170); and Wendy Smith (Pls 242, 243, and 244).

The authors, and all those involved in the production of this volume, wish in particular to acknowledge, and pay tribute to, the supreme generosity of the late Vivien Swan, who struggled against severe and often debilitating illness to complete her enormous contribution to this report. Her death, as she achieved this, has saddened us all, and it is sincerely hoped that our minor amendments have done justice to her intent.

The Millennium excavations formed part of Carlisle City Council's Gateway City (Millennium) Project, which was jointly funded by the Millennium Commission and a partnership between Carlisle City Council and local businesses. In addition, Carlisle City Council provided substantial funding for the post-excavation and publication programme, which included the provision of a popular booklet and a teachers' resource pack, in addition to the academic report. Considerable assistance in kind was also provided by English Heritage, which undertook the expensive and time-consuming task of conserving the large and important assemblage of Roman and medieval leather generated by the excavations, and funded the conservation of the armour. English Heritage also set up and funded a highly successful exhibition at Carlisle Castle, which presented the results of the excavations to the general public during the course of what was inevitably quite a long period of post-excavation analysis.

15

SYNTHESIS

This volume is intended to complement the detailed stratigraphic interpretation (*Chs 1-14*), and present the finds, both artefacts and ecofacts, in the light of that analysis. It provides syntheses of the material, which can illustrate the lives and occupations of the many individuals who have lived and worked on the site throughout its existence. The rich archaeological context, much enhanced by the widespread waterlogging which fostered the unusual survival of organic materials, resulted in huge numbers of finds being recovered. Their range and abundance means that they can be used, more than at many sites, to attempt to reconstruct the appearance of the successive Roman forts, the day-to-day activity that went on within them, and also later, medieval activity, both within the castle and the growing town immediately beyond it.

Roman material forms overwhelmingly the greatest part of the assemblage, but as James (2002, 35) has pointed out, the vast resource of finds from Roman sites has regularly been almost entirely neglected in favour of detailed discussion of installations and texts:

'The shift of focus from army-as-institution to soldiers-as-people is, I think, fundamental for understanding all aspects of the Roman military' (*op cit*, 43). This neglect is not confined to Roman material, however, but pervades the whole gamut of British archaeology to a greater or lesser degree. It has been an important aim of the Carlisle Millennium Project to attempt to redress this, at least in terms of Carlisle.

Setting the Stage: the Original Appearance of the Site

The strategic value of the bluff on which the primary fort was built is clear (Pl 151), even though it is possible that fitting the fort comfortably onto it involved a certain amount of drainage, and even modification. The area had at some time been cultivated, but had fallen into disuse (*Ch 22*), although it is not obvious how long it had been abandoned before the army took up residence. Evidence seems to point towards

Plate 151: The low bluff on which the fort and later castle were built

the abandonment of arable agriculture in the Iron Age (*Ch 2; Appendix 15*), with perhaps a return to pastoralism and some reforestation. In short, the site seems to have been boggy rough pasture and scrubby mixed woodland, including alder, oak, birch, and hazel. It is not unreasonable to assume, on present evidence, that the woodland continued to the banks of the Rivers Eden and Caldew, at the confluence of which the site lies.

Painting the Backdrop: Roads and Buildings

The foundation of the fort must have involved substantial land clearance. It is not clear whether or not the site itself was wooded, but the considerable amount of alder (and lesser amounts of ash) used in the Period 3A buildings (*Ch 3*) implies that the wider surroundings were quite heavily wooded. There is little to indicate whether or not any formal buildings were put up during the earliest Roman occupation, for instance, as temporary accommodation whilst the ground was being prepared for building (Period 2; Fig 261). Thus, it seems most likely that the first troops to arrive would have been accommodated in tents, as was normal practice on campaign (Vegetius: *Epitome of military science III*, 8 (Milner 1993, 78)). Several panels from the typical 'no frills' eight-man army tent are known from the site (*Ch 20, p 822*; Winterbottom in prep a) and from the putative annexe at Castle Street (Padley and Winterbottom 1991). Interestingly, no

wooden tent pegs survived, perhaps suggesting that the tent fragments were discarded during subsequent repair, as broken or unwanted tent pegs would most probably have been thrown away at an earlier stage, when the tents were being taken down. Tents would have provided reasonably warm and weather-proof accommodation, and were presumably where both kit and personal possessions were stored during the early days of the fort. A second, more elaborate, type of tent is now being recognised from Carlisle and elsewhere (*Ch 20, p 822*), which might represent somewhat more luxurious temporary accommodation for officers, and for the many administrative obligations which were a permanent part of Roman army life.

The stratigraphic footprint of a tent or tents would be ephemeral in the extreme and would be difficult to recognise, although it might be possible to interpret the layout from the distribution of finds. There is no doubt, however, that a tented camp was arranged with care and system, as Vegetius describes (Milner 1993), and whether in tent or well-built barrack block, pots and glasses would still get broken, and hobnails lost from boots. Whilst in a barrack-block, these objects would have been likely to have been cleared and deposited outside the buildings, it is surely more probable that within a tent, in muddy weather at least, they would simply have been trodden into the ground.

The nature of the timber used in the earliest buildings (Period 3A) is of interest. Whilst substantial post-in-trench structures, they were constructed mainly from

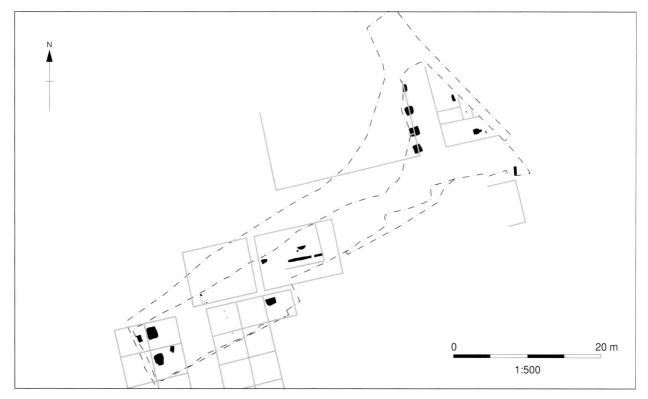

Figure 261: Period 2 features, with the layout of the first timber fort (Period 3A) superimposed

alder and ash, although more oak was used in the most southerly parts of the fort, and the ramparts were entirely of oak (Caruana in prep). Small trees were used either whole, or halved and quartered, providing timber uprights no more than 100 mm square, and often less. This may have been a matter of using the locally available timber (*Ch 19, p 787*), as there is no indication that it was brought into the fort from any distance, or that larger trees or more durable wood, like oak, was sought out. It seems that getting buildings erected within the new fort was most important, and the fact that both alder and ash would probably have rotted within five to ten years seems to imply that there was perhaps little view of the long term, and that these were effectively temporary buildings, intended to house men and horses as quickly as possible, especially as the felling dates from the primary rampart imply winter activity (Caruana in prep). Indeed, it was not long before a wall in Building *4653* (Fig 262; barracks) needed to be shored up by driving in supporting posts alongside the originals (*Ch 3*). This seemingly winter construction timetable might mean that the defences, at least, were erected as soon as the fighting season ended (*Ch 12*). It must, however, be borne in mind that winter was then, as now, the preferred time for felling (Latham 1957, 19), and thus the dates could be taken to imply systematic felling and stockpiling over the winter, for use later.

Evidence for the above-ground appearance of the first buildings is more disparate. Surviving timbers indicate that wattle panels were used (*eg* Period 3C Building *3772*), probably made to measure rather than having been prefabricated. These were sealed with daub, and on external walls (such as in Period 3C Building *4657*), the timber framing was completely hidden, the surfaces being rendered with mortar, presumably for a finer and more weatherproof finish. Indeed, a wooden implement, resembling a modern plasterer's float, was found in Period 3A Building *4653* (*Ch 19, p 814*) and could well have been used to apply mortar in the manner seen in a fresco from Sens in Northern France (Ling 2000, fig 54). Internal wattle walls are implied by the impressions in fragments of daub, as well as occasionally surviving intact (Pl 152) or as demolished waste. Some internal doors may also have been of wattle (*Ch 19, p 796*), although whether or not these were coated with daub is not clear. Large numbers of nails, which might have suggested that they were widely used in construction at this period, were not found, and most important structural timbers were probably jointed. The nails found are relatively small (40–80 mm) and can only have been used in smaller-scale carpentry, like the Period 4 nailed weather-boarding (Pl 153), or even in cabinet-making. In later periods, wooden thresholds testify that doors opened outwards, onto the roads, being harr-hung. Several Period 3 buildings appear to

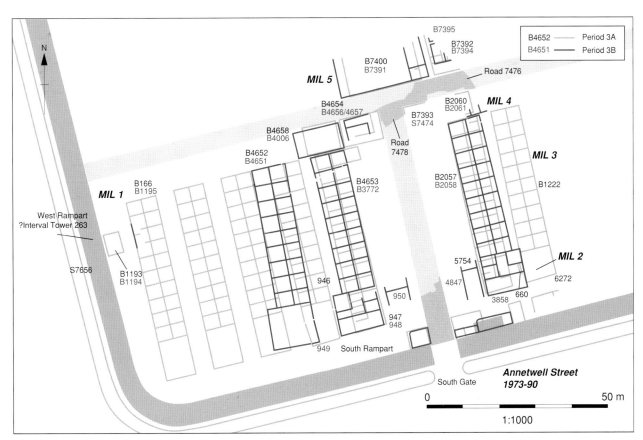

Figure 262: The Period 3 timber fort

485

*Plate 152: A wattle wall panel associated with Period 4B Building **5689***

Plate 153: Laser-scanned image of part of a panel of nailed weather-boarding

have had earthen floors, and it is possible that other materials were also used.

Several periods of demolition and rebuilding have guaranteed that none of the walls have survived to anything like their original height, but evidence from elsewhere (*Ch 19*; Goodburn 1991) suggests that the walls might well have stood to some 2 m, or more. It is likely that most structures were a single storey, with pitched roofs. Most of the buildings probably had windows, but it is unlikely that any of the Period 3 buildings investigated were glazed, although the small amount of window glass from contemporary contexts might imply some glazing elsewhere in the fort. It is possible that Roman glazed lights were removable, and thus could be reused in later structures, although it is perhaps more likely that the embrasures were closed by wooden shutters.

There is less evidence to suggest how these buildings might have been roofed, although the lack of ceramic or stone roofing materials from the first fort could point to a less durable material. Shingles are known from Vindolanda (Birley 1994, 77, fig 23) and, although associated with the second fort, a single oak shingle

with apple and pear wood pegs (*Ch 19, p 813*) was found in a Period 4B posthole. Reed thatch must also have been a possibility, although sods or heather have been used as roofing materials until recently and would presumably have been readily available. There must be some possibility that ceramic tiles or stone roofing were used, but efficiently stripped from the buildings on demolition, although this seems unlikely, as ceramic tiles are relatively fragile, and some breakage might have been expected, the fragments being discarded with other demolition debris. In the event, only a single roof tile was recovered from Period 3A deposits, and this does not seem enough even to hint at tile reclamation. The tilery at nearby Scalesceugh seems to have provided tiles for the Period 4 buildings, but it seems unlikely that the tilery was in production in the AD 70s (*Ch 16, p 590; Ch 21, p 901*). Occasional soot-blackened flue tile fragments point to rooms heated by a hypocaust, but there is nothing to suggest that any of the buildings excavated were heated in this way at this time, the most likely source being a bath-house associated with the fort.

The apparent lack of glazing and the use of organic roofing material might be significant, echoing the use of less durable woods in the structures, and adding to the sense that these were in effect interim buildings, erected as quickly as possible during the initial military push northwards, and perhaps signifying no intent to remain in Carlisle for any length of time. It was not until some time later, when more permanent occupation became a probability, that supplies of good wood were organised, together with the infrastructure to produce tiles, and import more specialist building requisites, such as sheet glass.

In the ten or so years between the building of the fort and its major refurbishment (Periods 3A and 3B), it is clear that the Romans had reconnoitred the locally available resources and organised supplies. Buildings in Periods 3B and 3C were made largely of good-quality oak, with posts split from relatively large trees of around 1 m in diameter (*Ch 19*). Indeed, the growth patterns of the trees are so similar to those of contemporary timber used at Vindolanda, little more than 20 km to the east, that a common local origin may be argued (*Appendix 9*), although not a specific source. It does, however, provide evidence that timber was not imported, ready-dressed and cut, from supplies stock-piled elsewhere. Indeed, it might be taken to suggest some local collaboration, but whether by civilian dealers or Roman quartermasters is unclear. It has been suggested (Bowman 1994, 43) that important resources like timber were under military control, and evidence from Vindolanda (Bowman and Thomas 1994, 215.7.3) makes it clear that at least some supplies were bought in; perhaps the builders in Carlisle were using the same supplier. Most buildings were still of post-in-trench construction, and buildings of sill

Plate 154: Foundations of the second-century military workshop at Ribchester

beam construction, for example **7200**, were confined to Period 3C (*Ch 4*). The reason for this change is not clear, neither is its significance. Both construction techniques can be seen in a contemporary building (**4657**), and elsewhere in the North, for example the workshop at Ribchester (Buxton and Howard-Davis 2000), where both methods can be seen in a single structure (Pl 154), which was by no means uncommon (Hanson 1982). At Ribchester, it might simply have been a response to unstable ground, as one of the walls was built over the waterlogged and poorly compacted fills of an earlier ditch.

The primary fort was built in conventional fashion, the buildings facing onto, and often flanked by, metalled roads or other hard-standing. These roads were reasonably well-drained, with substantial roadside drains from Period 3B onwards, and, on occasion, they incorporated below-ground water pipes, presumably supplying water to various points in the fort. In Period 4, these were made from hollowed alder logs, jointed into oak blocks, and later (Period 5) they were replaced by ceramic water pipes (Pl 155). Both were capable of conducting water under pressure, and the two-way pipe junction seen in Period 4B (*Ch 6*) suggests that water was piped to the centre of the fort, where there was perhaps a trough, or faucet. Vegetius (*Epitome of military science III*, 2 (Milner 1993, 64)) makes it clear that a Roman commander should be well aware of the benefits of well-regulated and clean water-supplies, as well as the constant threat of sickness. It would be difficult to imagine that such things were not taken into account

Plate 155: Period 5 ceramic water pipe, in situ

in the layout of a fort. Thus, this was probably a highly managed environment, kept largely clear of rubbish, and with well-built and relatively well-appointed accommodation and work-space.

It is unlikely that the buildings in the second fort (Period 4) differed much in appearance, or in raw

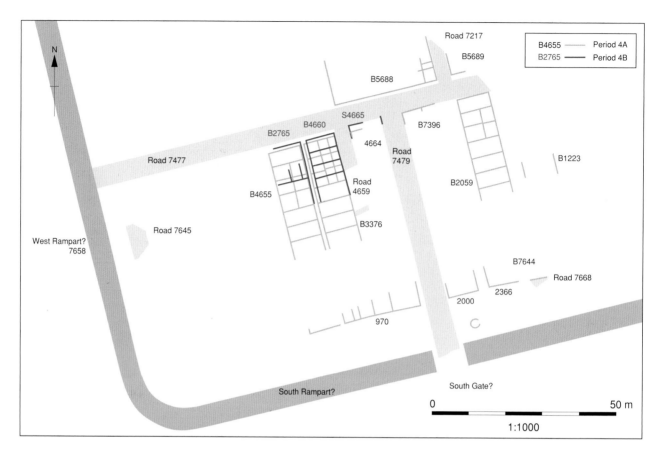

Figure 263: The Period 4 timber fort

materials, although it seems that the oak used was perhaps of poorer quality, possibly as local supplies of good timber had been depleted. Internal walls continued to be of wattle and daub, as attested in Buildings **3376**, **4655**, and **4660** (*Ch 19*; Fig 263), and a significant increase in the amount of tile and brick (albeit in demolition deposits and hardcore) points to the likelihood that some of the buildings within the fort now had roofs clad with tiles, both *imbrices* and *tegulae* being found (*Ch 21*). Building **5689**, possibly a workshop associated with the commander's house (*praetorium*), if the fort has a conventional layout, had what might have been shuttered entrances opening onto the main east to west road (**7477**). These seem to imply some potential to have an open frontage, either in order to present a shop-like display area, or perhaps to allow extra light for workshops, or even that work was undertaken outside, under cover, to take advantage of daylight. The timbers of the *principia* (Building **5688**) were consistently larger than other contemporary structures, including its neighbour **5689**, and imply that it was a two-storey structure. This was probably a reflection of its enhanced status, and the small amount of grey and white-painted wall plaster, found in demolition layers, hints at some interior decoration. In addition, it was possibly weather-boarded, with feathered boards nailed to the outside walls (Pl 153). This would have changed its external appearance considerably,

again setting it apart from its neighbours and drawing attention to its importance. It might well have been glazed, but at this date Roman window glass was not transparent, intended to admit light rather than to allow a view (*Ch 18, p 773*), and the windows could have been quite high in the walls. The largest fragments of window glass from the site came from a robber trench disturbing minor road **7217**, to the east (*Ch 18, p 773*), although all but a few of the fragments from this period came from in and around its neighbour, Building **5689**, suggesting that this, rather than Building **5688**, was glazed, adding weight to its interpretation as the commanding officer's accommodation. In view of the possibility, however, that at least the excavated part of Building **5689** was something of a general storeroom, it might rather suggest that either unused glass was kept there for issue, or that broken glass was collected for recycling, a possibility which does not, however, seem to be supported by any particular corresponding concentration of vessel glass.

Following the demolition of the second fort in the mid-second century, activity is difficult to characterise (*Ch 7*), although the ceramic water pipe (Pl 155) might well imply continued occupation somewhere within the fort site (possibly serving the large courtyard building seen at Annetwell Street (Caruana in prep)), with the already sophisticated Period 4 system of

488

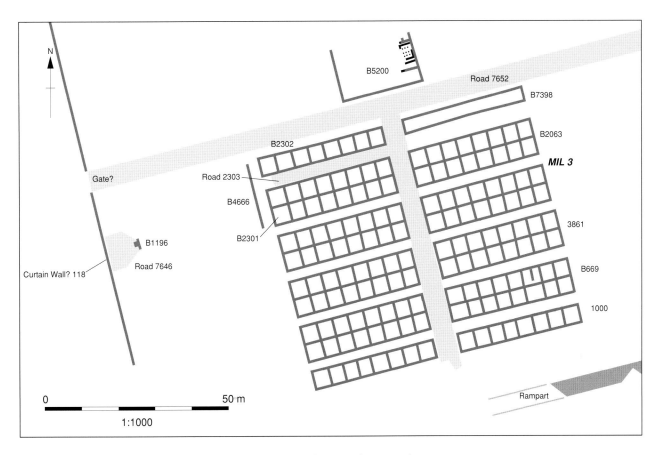

Figure 264: The Period 6 stone fort

water supply (*Ch 6*) being upgraded. Similarly, there are indications of insubstantial buildings, but, in terms of the finds, there only seems to have been disturbance and large-scale dumping. The amount of residual brick and tile in the deposits of this period might imply that there was a considerable amount of demolition and recycling going on, much of the waste finally entering the stratigraphic record, in make-up or levelling deposits, early in Period 6A.

In Period 6, the fort was rebuilt in stone, although internal walls were probably less substantial, perhaps timber on dwarf stone walls. Some of the buildings, especially a possible barracks, Buildings *2301* and *2302* (Fig 264), could have had their walls faced with grey limestone, whilst, more generally, others were built from red sandstone (*Ch 21, p 873*). If, however, the walls were subsequently rendered, they might well have looked little different from their timber predecessors. There is little evidence for the timber component of these structures, as the site was no longer waterlogged and organic materials did not survive. There were, however, considerably more nails from Period 6 structures than from earlier ones (*Appendix 5*). Some of these would be residual, deriving from earlier buildings, but if, for instance, the upper parts of the walls were rendered and weather-boarded, like the Period 4 *principia*, then far more nails than previously would have been used in their construction. Evidence

strongly suggests that the buildings had tiled roofs, many having been made at the Scalesceugh tilery and some bearing legionary stamps (*Ch 21; Pl 156*). Several of the curving *imbrices* appear to have reduced surfaces (*Ch 21, p 892*), suggesting a deliberate attempt to produce bi-coloured roofs, with the *imbrices* forming grey stripes on the largely orange terracotta roofs. There is, in addition, evidence for stone roofing tiles. It is possible that the Period 6A *principia* (Building *5200*) might have had chimneys (*Ch 21, pp 897-8*), possibly adding to the impression, from the hypocaust inserted in Period 6B (*Ch 9*), as well as from flue tiles, that it was relatively luxurious. Evidence for glazed windows is not so clear-cut, as the diagnostically Roman matt-glossy window glass was going out of

Plate 156: A legionary stamp on a tile from the Scalesceugh tilery

489

production by the third century, to be replaced by completely transparent, cylinder-blown sheet (Boon 1966), which, in small fragments, cannot easily be distinguished from vessel glass.

Putting Actors on the Stage

The Roman army that erected the fort in Carlisle in the early AD 70s did not arrive in a blank and empty land. The Iron Age background of the region is not well-known and remains under-researched (Hodgson and Brennand 2006; 2007), but there were local inhabitants, presumably scattered across the countryside in small dispersed settlements, farms, and small-holdings, and following a lifestyle rooted in that of their ancestors (Pl 157), originating at least in the neolithic period (Higham 1986; Bewley 1994, 84). Their presence is reflected in the handful of mesolithic, neolithic, and Bronze Age flints from later contexts at this site (*Appendix 11*) and throughout Carlisle (*eg* Fell 1990). It was a lifestyle grounded in farming and stock-raising, but it was also possibly highly stratified and hierarchical, with local elites acting as the opinion-leaders and policy-makers who would have heavily influenced the nature of local reactions to the arrival of Rome. Current knowledge of the opinions of local rulers is filtered through the account of Tacitus (*Agricola* (Mattingly 1948)), which, as propaganda, was intended to tell the story with a slant favourable to his father-in-law, Agricola, and consigns the indigenous inhabitants to literary oblivion.

One of the features of the Iron Age in north-west England is the almost complete absence of an archaeologically visible material culture (Hodgson and Brennand 2006). This does not for one moment suggest that the indigenous inhabitants of the area were culturally impoverished, simply that the things that mattered to them were made from largely perishable materials that have not survived. In particular, they do not seem to have favoured the use of pottery, presumably preferring wooden or leathern vessels. It is this lack of an identifiable cultural assemblage that has made it extremely difficult to get any idea at all of the initial relationships between the local population and the Roman army (McCarthy 2005, 49). The unsettled politics of the time, with factional rifts within the Brigantes and, in Venutius, a leader thought to have generated considerable resistance to Rome (Shotter 2004a), perhaps suggest that the occupation was not entirely welcome. The sandstone bluff upon which the fort was built is undoubtedly a strong and easily defensible situation, which would have been an important tactical consideration. The possibility, however, that the fort might have been built on abandoned agricultural land could suggest that Rome also sought compromise, and was hoping to avoid direct confrontation, or that the army wished for increased security by distancing itself from contemporary local settlement.

The lack of artefactual evidence for local late Iron Age indigenous groups has meant that it is effectively impossible to gauge the extent of their physical interaction with the newly arrived army in any concrete way. In addition, there has always been an acknowledged difficulty in identifying an indigenous material culture at Roman military sites (Clarke 1999, 42). Over and above this, it is now being understood that attempts to recognise or define such categorical divisions as Roman and 'native' are somewhat unhelpful (Gosden 2005, 208). There would, however, have been contact, local goods and services being bought and sold, friendships and other more commercial relationships developed; in addition,

Plate 157: A reconstruction of a late Iron Age farm

slaves would have been bought and sold, and the fluidity of individual relationships would soon merge and blur, not only the fine detail, but the entire picture. It is possible that most of this interaction took place outside the fort, perhaps in the large enclosed annexes which many of them, including perhaps Carlisle, seemed to have had. These might be thought of as liminal areas, providing a degree of insulation between the highly Romanised interior of the fort, and the outside, foreign, and implicitly threatening, world. It would not be difficult to see these enclosures providing the context for a range of relatively intangible services, from freight depot to overnight stops, where men and women of all ranks and origins could well have met and fraternised in the course of day-to-day employment.

If a degree of isolation is, then, assumed for at least the early occupation, it could have been the case that few artefacts of indigenous origin actually entered the fort precinct. There is little or no evidence for more ephemeral objects, like textiles, withy baskets, foodstuffs, and so on, which might, given the favourable depositional conditions in the fort, have survived. Only one artefact might point to a local presence in Period 3A, a single bone weaving comb (Pl 158), an object type frequently associated with 'native' activity as a result of its relatively common appearance in late Iron Age assemblages elsewhere

Plate 158: Bone weaving comb from Period 3A Building **4658**

in Britain and north-western Europe (Tuohy 1992). Its presence inside a Roman building (**4658**) suggests some interaction, but a second example was found within an occupation layer in Building **5689** (Period 4A), alongside a vast amount of other stored material, and it is possible that both were brought to the site in Roman household luggage (even by 'natives' from other tribal areas) rather than by locals visiting the site.

The amount of evidence for the physical presence of Roman soldiers is in great contrast to that for the indigenous population, even if only indisputably military objects, like armour and weapons, are considered. There are, however, major questions as to what constitutes a military assemblage (Allason-Jones 1999a, 4), since on the one hand military equipment can be found in contexts as unlikely as a cow burial in a Meroitic pyramid in the Sudan, and on the other, as is the case in many overtly military sites, the assemblage is that of well-to-do and relatively comfortable domesticity, with little to suggest the unequivocal presence of soldiers (op cit, 2).

It is perhaps fitting to start a review of the evidence from the successive Carlisle forts with the most personal of evidence. Documents from excavations at Annetwell Street name a number of cavalry officers, probably serving in the ala Gallorum Sebosiana, and stationed within the fort (Tomlin 1998, 44), and in consequence it is possible to list a number of individuals, whose voices were heard in Carlisle during the first century AD: officers include Agilis, Albinus, Gentilis, Peculiaris, Pacatus, Sodalis, Docilis, Sollemnis, Mansuetus, Martialis, Genialis, and Victor. All of these men seem likely, from their names, to have had their origins in the Rhineland (op cit, 45). Verecundus, Docca, Pastor, Felicio, Victorinus, Festus, and Maior served within their units (op cit, 58), and to these can now be added Primus, Clemens, and Maglus, all of whom scratched their names on their personal belongings, in this case samian bowls (Ch 16, p 563).

The number of weapons and obviously military fittings, such as the nielloed dagger frog from Period 3A external layer 7182 (Ch 17), makes it clear that there were soldiers aplenty, but, interestingly, the range, quality, and quantity of more domestic items, such as glassware and pottery, from buildings identified as possible barracks, also make it clear that they valued their creature comforts (Allason-Jones 1999a). Ultimately, therefore, it could be more ephemeral and possibly subjectively defined traits such as these that allow differentiation between soldiers and others resident in a fort.

There are some interesting differences between the distribution and make-up of militaria from the sequence of forts, although again these can only be seen

Plate 159: A well-worn dagger frog, lost in the early days of the fort

as general trends. They do appear to reflect differences in activity, which could therefore be of importance to an understanding of life within the fort. In the first fort, there are few, if any, weapons except for a cache of baked-clay slingshot associated mainly with the demolition of possible workshop *4006* in Period 3B (*Ch 4*). All the other objects are the kinds of small items that might be expected to fail or be lost in the course of day-to-day wear and tear. The dagger frog (Pl 159; *Ch 17, pp 706-7*), probably well-worn before arriving in Carlisle, had been lost from a belt, a hinge had failed on plate armour, or a few scales had become detached from scale mail. All of these would be matters of minor maintenance, and it is unlikely that any of the items lost on roads or within buildings would have been searched for with any particular assiduity. It is, perhaps, of interest that an ivory sword handle and a jet sword pommel were lost or stored within probable Period 3A *praetorium* *7392* (*Ch 3*).

The loss of part of another ivory sword grip (*Ch 17, pp 708-9; Ch 20, p 858*) in a barrack, Building *3772*, might also suggest the presence of an officer or officers, and, in addition, two of the four horse-harness strap fittings from this period also derive from this building. The fittings are not particularly ornate, and could point to the accommodation of cavalry at this time, as suggested by the layout of barracks (*Ch 5*), although it must be borne in mind that infantry officers were also mounted. Even if their horses were maintained by a slave or other personal attendant, as is suggested on the gravestones of cavalrymen from the Rhineland (see, for instance, Feugère 2002, pls 181, 184), it seems likely that they would have kept their tack close by, perhaps in their personal quarters.

The more easily detached items of harness, like decorative pendants, appear consistently on roads and other external surfaces, and must frequently have been lost and then trampled into the surface, or swept or washed into nearby drains. Being of little monetary worth, either as objects or as recycled metal, it is extremely unlikely that they would have been systematically searched for by the loser, or even scavenged by the poorer elements of the fort's society.

The situation in Period 4 is somewhat different. There are, again, large numbers of fired-clay slingshots, but as many of these were in construction trenches cut into earlier workshop *4006* (*Ch 4*), it seems reasonable to suggest that they in fact derived from the earlier cache. In this period, the finds of militaria show a marked concentration on the central range, in the *principia* (*5688*) and Building *5689*, and on roads *7217* and *7477*. The *principia* must have formed a focus of activity in any fort, its central position acting as a hub both in day-to-day activity and in any more ceremonial congress that took place (Goldsworthy 2003, 83). Again, the military items lost on nearby roads are more personal, comprising belt fittings, harness pendants, and so on.

The amount of armour from Building *5689* marks it out as exceptional, and it seems likely that damaged equipment was stored and repaired within the building. Indeed, a hearth (*Ch 4*; Pl 160) and industrial residues appear to confirm this, being typical of low-temperature blacksmithing of the sort that might have been necessary to rework plate armour (*Ch 17, p 765*). There was a clear 'make-do and mend' nature to the repairs to the arm-guards (*manicae*) and other large items of armour (*Ch 17, p 704*), and one fragment at least appears to have been punctured by an arrowhead (Pl 161). On the other hand, there is a marked concentration of arrows and other small projectile points around the *principia* (*5688*), with over 20 within the building and associated layers, whilst only eight were associated with Building *5689*, more than half of them from external layers associated with the demolition of the building. What this means is not entirely obvious, but it might be the case that the *principia* was involved with the storage and issue of consumables such as arrows, and the regulation of issue of other weaponry and military equipment. Indeed, broadly contemporary written records from a pit elsewhere in the fort list troopers with missing lances, as recorded by Docilis in a letter to his prefect Augurinus (Tomlin 1998), making it clear that, as might be expected, there was a regular audit. Such activity originating in the *principia* might also explain the presence of a turf cutter (*Ch 17, p 719*) amongst the finds from this structure. Interestingly, two wooden objects, tentatively identified as parts of a projectile launcher not dissimilar to a ballista, came from the demolition layers of the same building (*Ch 17, p 712*).

The distribution of spearheads is also of interest; of the nine examples from the Period 4 fort, three were from intervallum road *7645* or nearby, perhaps suggesting that the road was used as a practice field, and two from Building *2765*, with one from R4, in pit *2914*. The outstanding quality of the spear from Building *2059* might again suggest that it was the property of an officer, and its presence at the northern end of a possible barrack block, facing onto the main east to west road, might suggest that officers were

Plate 160: A smithing hearth within Period 4 Building **5689**, *to the east of the* principia

Plate 161: A fragment of plate armour with a square hole, probably from an arrow strike

accommodated close to the *principia*, which was certainly the case in temporary camps (Feugère 2002, 45), although not necessarily in permanent forts. The position of the officers' quarters, however, remains a matter of debate (*Ch 12*). The remainder came from demolition and robbing layers associated with the *principia* (**5688**), Building **5689**, and others.

The much smaller group of militaria from Period 5 was, for the most part, associated with external areas, in part simply because few buildings are known. It is likely that some items, at least, were residual, and this is perhaps reflected in their poor preservation. It is interesting that almost all the fragments of armour are scale mail, which was presumably prone to shed small numbers of scales if snagged, or if the wire fixings failed, and thus their loss might be contemporary, as it is clear that, despite apparently large-scale clearance elsewhere in the fort site, life went on (Caruana in prep).

Direct evidence for soldiers increased again with the construction of the stone fort (Period 6; *Ch 8*), but did not reach the quantities seen in the second timber fort (Period 4), even though the purposes of the buildings corresponded broadly to those of earlier periods. As many of the smaller items of weaponry were essentially utilitarian, few changes in their design appear through time, and it is in consequence difficult to know whether, for instance, arrowheads found in Period 6 contexts were in fact contemporary with these deposits, or were residual. A few objects actually derived from occupation layers within barracks, Buildings **2301** and **2302**, and were thus probably contemporary; both produced examples of cast-lead slingshot, which appeared in the fort for the first time at a date normally regarded as marking the cessation of its use in Roman warfare, although it has been

Plate 163: An unusual figure-of-eight brooch, probably with 'native' origins

Plate 162: A caltrop, which would have been scattered on the ground to hinder the movement of horses

found in Scotland in Antonine contexts (Bishop and Coulston 1993, 115; *Ch 17, p 718*). Of most interest, perhaps, is the fact that caltrops, designed as an anti-cavalry defensive weapon (Pl 162), are almost entirely confined to Period 6, and must presumably reflect an introduction marking some change in the manner of warfare or defence.

A fort was also home, or at least workplace, to many other personnel. Lower-status groups such as slaves, probably present in some numbers, are effectively archaeologically invisible, using the same objects as their masters, or hand-me-downs, rather than having any separate and obvious artefact set of their own. In addition, they are unlikely to have had separate accommodation, but would probably have lived in and about the barracks and stables, again reducing the likelihood that their presence would be recognised from artefact distribution patterns, as has sometimes been the case with enslaved groups elsewhere (Bishop and Coulston 1993, 163).

Similarly, it would be difficult to discern the presence of civilians, as much of the material assemblage that might accompany them, brooches, belt plates, and so on, would be effectively indistinguishable from those of soldiers, and indeed some civilians were probably retired soldiers from elsewhere. In recent years, it has been suggested that certain day-to-day items, most specifically brooches, might have held a covert symbolism of resistance and anti-Roman feeling for some civilian groups (Jundi and Hill 1998; Gosden 2005, 205), and their presence might thus be an indication of indigenous individuals,

although this linkage is perhaps somewhat simplistic. The unusual figure-of-eight-style brooch (Pl 163), from an occupation layer (*7442*) in Building **7400**, the probable Period 3A *principia*, echoes the simple wound wire brooches produced to the south-east at Victoria Cave, near Settle, in Yorkshire, which are thought to represent a native Brigantian strand in the development of Dragonesque brooches (Olivier 2000). Its presence might therefore indicate either the presence of an indigenous individual, or small-scale trade at a personal level.

Although it was customary in the Roman army that soldiers were expected to have other skills, and therefore act as smiths, potters, farriers, and leather-workers, it appears certain that many other, more menial, tasks were undertaken by slaves or hired hands, and it is likely that slave ownership permeated the entire military hierarchy (James 2002, 43). The Vindolanda correspondence makes clear reference to male slaves within the households of senior officers (Bowman 1994, 57-8) and it is not impossible that a reference to fetters amongst the letters from Carlisle (Tomlin 1998), whilst probably heavy sarcasm regarding the late arrival of some troops from London and not a direct reference to slaves, makes it clear that fetters for slaves or prisoners were a common item. None have been found in Carlisle, however.

It is increasingly accepted that women, like slaves, are difficult to discern archaeologically, yet there would have been at least some within the fort. Many of the artefacts previously taken as indicators of female presence are no longer regarded as valid; beads, for instance, can be (and are) worn by either gender, and it has become increasingly obvious that melon beads, especially, are closely associated with horse tack rather than humans (Birley and Greene 2006, 39). There are, however, a few items that are more likely, as far as modern knowledge allows, to be associated with women. Romanised men do not appear to have worn earrings or the more decorative forms of necklace (Allason-Jones 1995, 25), although it is possible that the men of auxiliary units followed in part the traditional fashions of their homelands. Hairpins seem to be almost exclusively associated with the complex feminine hairstyles which only appear in Britain after the arrival of Rome, and are well-known throughout

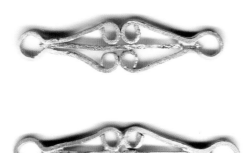

*Plate 164: Fragments of a gold necklace lost in Period 6 Building **2302***

the Empire (Allason-Jones 1989a, 137). It is of interest, but not entirely surprising, that the hairpins from this site are largely confined to Period 6, after the Severan reforms at the end of the second century, which allowed soldiers to form legal relationships (Goldsworthy 2003, 102–3). These items were found mainly on external surfaces, perhaps implying that women were visitors rather than residents, living more comfortably in the town to the south. Fragments of gold necklace (Pl 164), however, without doubt belonging to a woman of some wealth, are from a Period 6 building (**2302**).

Physical size may be a relatively reliable indicator of gender, and it has been suggested that, in the past, sexual dimorphism was more marked than it is at the present day (van Driel-Murray 1995, 3). This is particularly useful in the more personalised items of clothing, such as shoes, where, if they do not indicate the presence of adolescent boys, smaller shoe-sizes are likely to indicate the presence of women, and, in the case of the smallest, children. The survival of organic materials within the forts is, however, unsystematic, and little can be made of the distribution of such objects. Very few shoe soles survived in sufficiently good condition to make an accurate estimate of their original size, but there seems to be enough evidence to suggest the presence of individuals with relatively small feet in the first and second centuries. Whether these were women or adolescent males cannot now be ascertained, although a single goatskin shoe of unusual construction and high quality from Period 3A Building *1222* may have belonged to a woman (*Ch 20, p 840*). Although there is no evidence amongst the leather shoes for the presence of small children, there was a single small-sized shoe amongst the assemblage from Annetwell Street (Winterbottom in prep a).

For the most part, however, the shoes found were those of adult men and, in the main, unsurprisingly military in style, although the small number of one-piece shoes might have been favoured by civilians. The earliest shoes are a well-known type, similar, but not identical, to the military boot or *caliga (Ch 20; Pl 165)*, enclosing the foot and rising above the ankle, thereby affording some protection in rough country, especially when worn, as seems to be the case, with socks (see, for instance, a small knife handle from Piercebridge, which shows this clearly (Worrell 2005,

Plate 165: An almost complete military boot from one of the many waterlogged deposits

452)). Even soldiers were not immune to changes of fashion, and the style seems to have gone out of favour in the AD 120s, later styles being lower at the ankle. There is, however, a restricted range of styles amongst the assemblage (Ch 20, Fig 507), and although this might simply be an artefact of preservation, it is possible that the shoe-makers working within the fort were only turning out a utilitarian range of military footwear, and that there was little scope to order and buy more luxurious shoes. It is perhaps not surprising, given Carlisle's climate, that other styles were rare; for instance, there was only a single sandal, and one or possibly two wooden-soled bath shoes, perhaps adding to the largely conjectural evidence for a bath-house in the vicinity of the fort.

There is very little evidence to suggest the use of leather for clothing other than shoes, although logic would suggest that it was widely used. One fragment of a possible baldric from the Period 3B *principia* (Building **7391**) has been recognised (Ch 20, p 829), and the numerous copper-alloy and iron buckles make it clear that belts and other items were made of leather or possibly textile (Ch 17, p 706). There is no evidence for other items of clothing, most presumably being of woollen or linen textiles; the only other evidence comes from the small group of brooches. Used to fasten clothes or fix looser coverings like cloaks in place at the shoulder, surprisingly few were recovered, and there seems to be a roughly equal split between simple penannular brooches, plate, and bow brooches, which does not particularly add to any understanding of the range of clothing worn. From the later second century onwards (Periods 5 and 6), the small group was dominated by penannular and crossbow brooches (Ch 17, pp 725-8). The latter are often suggested to have been used as indicators of rank (Swift 2000, 88), and this certainly seems to have been the case with those of precious metals, but whether it was a practice that ran down through the ranks is seldom explored. They do, however, appear to have had a close link with military activity, and they may well have been made in Pannonia, specifically for the military market, and even have been a standard issue (Swift 2003, 7–8).

Thus almost all that remains to illustrate the clothing and appearance of soldiers billeted in or visiting the fort is the large assemblage of armour and other military fittings (Ch 17). This was not, of course, worn all the time, but must provide a good impression of the 'public face' of the garrison. It must be borne in mind that the armour recovered from Period 4 Building **5689** was scrap, and thus perhaps a little out of date by the time it was set aside for recycling, but it nonetheless provides a vivid illustration of the armour worn by soldiers billeted at the fort in the late first and early second centuries, and, perhaps better than any other group of finds, gives an impression of what would have been seen by the local population during the relatively early years of occupation. The basic purpose of armour is to protect the body and limbs of a soldier in battle, but it is not difficult to progress from that fundamental necessity to a range of other purposes, not least as a uniform, reinforcing the unity and exclusivity of a group of soldiers and signalling their strength and preparedness to the outside world. The metal-studded *cingulum* (or probably more correctly *balteus*; Bishop and Coulston 1993, 96), or military belt, from which the sword was suspended, seems to have been of particular personal importance, identifying a man both to the outside world and to his colleagues as a soldier (Feugère 2002, 175). Although largely fragmentary, several belt plates were recovered, coming mainly from external layers and roads, which might confirm their casual piecemeal loss. This seems more likely than deliberate discard as, certainly in the early Empire, loss of the *cingulum* was regarded as a matter of disgrace, and its confiscation was used as a symbolic punishment (Bishop and Coulston 1993, 100).

Roman armour was intended to protect the most vulnerable parts of the human body, and covered principally the torso and the head. Best known is the plate armour (*lorica segmentata*), long associated with the Roman legionary, which comprised a series of articulated plates which enclosed the torso and shoulders. This changed through time, allowing some dating; most of the plate armour from the fort is of the Corbridge type, characteristic of the mid-first to mid-second century AD, or the Newstead type, characteristic of the mid-second to mid-third century (Ch 17, pp 692-3, 703). Made from hammered or rolled iron sheet, it would originally have been silvery grey in appearance, but would presumably have changed its colour through time and, depending on circumstance, could have been a range of colours, from a metallic grey to rust red. Copper-alloy fittings would, of course, originally have been pinkish or brassy in colour, but would have dulled and, in their most neglected state, become green. Conservation has suggested that some fragments of armour were painted black (Pl 166), which adds a new element to their appearance; it might simply have stopped it from rusting, but also raises the possibility that there were times when it was not prudent to stand out in the landscape.

A second, more flexible form of body armour was made of small copper-alloy and (considerably more rarely) iron scales, wired to a textile backing or latterly to each other, again forming a substantial defence against penetrating weapons. Unusually, iron scales predominate within this assemblage. It has become clear that scale mail became a medium for decoration, and patterns were introduced, either by varying the scale size, or by alternating iron and copper-alloy

Plate 166: A small fragment of plate armour which appears to have been painted black

scales, in this case to pick out patterns in copper-alloy on an iron background (Pl 167). Sometimes, copper-alloy scales were coated with white metal in order to produce a silvery surface, and evidence from Carlisle suggests that some, at least, of the rivets were silvered (*Ch 17*). In addition, evidence from this site suggests composite armour, with scales wired to embossed plates at neck openings. Although these plates are known elsewhere in copper-alloy, the iron example from this set is currently unique (*Ch 17, p 703*).

Articulated laminar arm-guards (*manicae*) were introduced in the later first century AD, protecting the sword arm from slashing blows (Bishop and Coulston 1993). Three such garments have been found, all clearly repaired and refashioned from other cannibalised examples. The lower legs were protected with greaves, a rare almost complete iron example (Pl 168), like the *manicae*, being amongst the armour from in and around Period 4 Building **5689**. Greaves were most commonly associated with cavalry, whose legs were less protected, but there is evidence from the Adamklissi metopes, which show them also to have been worn by legionaries (*Ch 17, p 703*). It is possible that their use might otherwise have been restricted to officers, representing a left-over Classical Greek tradition, although they are generally not well-known (Feugère 2002, 106).

Further body protection was provided by a large shield, which most soldiers would have carried. Evidence from Carlisle for these is very limited, with only scraps of iron reinforcing bars, copper-alloy edge binding, and a few fragments of leather shield covers. All of these point to sub-rectangular rather than oval or round shields, similar to the first-century example from Doncaster (Buckland 1978a). Of course, it is likely that these were painted with insignia, as shown by the well-known rectangular example from Dura Europos (James 2004, 176–86), and possibly the name and cohort number of its bearer, as is mentioned by Vegetius (*Epitome of military science II*, 18 (Milner 1993, 50)), which would have added to the general impression of colour. What is often overlooked is that

Plate 167: Scale armour, showing iron and copper-alloy scales used together to add decoration

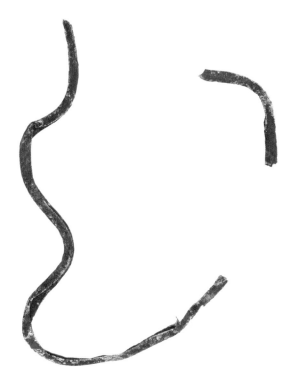

Plate 169: A copper-alloy strip preserves the outline of the cheekpiece it once bound

Plate 168: A plain iron greave, found with the deposit of armour from Period 4 Building **5689**

shields were also regarded as an offensive weapon (Tacitus: *Annals, XIV*, 36 (Jackson 1937)), and would have added spectacularly to the aggressive image.

Evidence for headgear is less copious, although fragments of a cheekpiece and ear protector were found. A copper-alloy binding strip for a cheekpiece can be shown to have bound leather, instead of metal (Pl 169), presumably raising the possibility of *cuir boulli* face protection, rather than the iron or copper-alloy plates that are more normally found (see, for instance, Robinson 1975, 53). There is also a range of other fittings, perhaps the most important being the dagger frog (Pl 159) and other belt plates and studs of tinned or silvered copper-alloy, inlaid with niello (*Ch 17, p 707*). This expensive and showy equipment is typically of first- to early second-century date, falling

from fashion under the Antonines (Bishop and Coulston 1993, 119), and has, on occasion, been associated with legionary officers. The frog (Period 3A layer *7182*) is paralleled at early sites like Hod Hill (Brailsford 1962, pl 1, A97), and is quite likely to have been well-used when it was finally lost in Carlisle in the early AD 70s. It has been suggested that, to the south, at Ribchester, the first, pre-Agricolan, Roman troops to arrive were somewhat more showy than their successors (Buxton and Howard-Davis 2000, 48), possibly because they were legionary troops with higher expectations, even on campaign, or because they were attempting to smooth their path by 'putting on a show for the natives', and the same might well be the case at Carlisle.

Whilst much has been written about Roman armour, little comment seems to have been made on its public appearance. It is clear from finds from Carlisle that armour in good condition was bright and colourful, a point emphasised by modern re-enactment groups, and would have made a considerable impression on spectators, especially if the other, less often preserved, elements of military display, trumpets, banners, crests, and, of course, the Eagles, are taken into account (Pl 170). There is no evidence from the site for the colours of tunics and cloaks, and it is possible that most were white, possibly natural undyed wool (Goldsworthy 2003, 121; Croom 2002, 28); it seems they were worn shorter than in civilian life, and frequently over breeches. Similarly, it is not clear whether colour varied with rank or units, crests, or banners, except that

Plate 170: A modern re-enactor dressed as an auxiliary
(J Jackson)

Plate 171: A modern Indian border guard wears headgear
that increases his height to over 2 m (C Howard-Davis)

Pliny records that scarlet was the preserve of generals (*Natural History* 22.3.3 (Jones 1951)), and other officers might well have worn cloaks of duller hue (Croom 2002, 28*)*, but it is obvious from this assemblage that the body armour itself was intentionally patterned, and of course, depending on the weather and the time of day, would have shone and glittered as men moved. The cheekpieces of helmets, when tied in place, had the effect of hiding faces and throwing eyes into shadow, both dehumanising soldiers as individuals, distancing them from onlookers, and by making eye-contact difficult if not effectively impossible, enhancing their threatening aspect, an effect taken to extremes by the totally enclosed facemask-type cavalry helmets, seen for instance at Newstead (Curle 1911), which would have added an extremely disconcerting, if not almost supernatural, aspect.

The different forms of body armour must have had a discernible effect on the manner in which men moved; it would seem difficult, if not impossible, to slump or slouch when wearing *lorica segmentata*, for instance, and rigid scale mail had to be quite well tailored to the individual, or it would have seriously impeded movement (*Ch 17, p 702*). This might well have had the effect of making men appear unusually tall or upright, especially when wearing their helmets, a factor that other martial groups have deliberately exploited as an added fear-inducing factor (Pl 171).

What is less evident is the noise that a century, or even an individual soldier, must have made. The many pendants and strap ends, including studded military aprons worn by most soldiers, must surely have produce a cacophany of sound when troops moved *en masse* (Bishop and Coulston 1993, 99), especially when added to the rhythmic strike of iron hobnails as they marched, especially on surfaced roads.

There is epigraphic evidence to show that at various times there were both legionary troops and auxiliaries (both infantry and cavalry) stationed at Carlisle (*Ch 12*), and literary evidence from Vindolanda and elsewhere makes it quite clear that individuals ranged quite widely, often being detached from their troop for extended periods (Goldsworthy 2003, 144). In addition, a handful of pottery vessels in Ebor ware, and Wilderspool red-slipped ware, both made expressly for their local military markets (York and Chester respectively) and seldom sold elsewhere, points to the presence of individuals or small groups of legionaries from the Sixth (York-based) and Second (based at Caerleon) legions, or the Twentieth Legion (from Chester), possibly in conjunction with the various phases of building work (*Ch 16, p 605*). It is, however, impossible to deduce the nature of the garrison from finds themselves, beyond a few generalisations, in that rectangular shields, *lorica segmentata,* and niello-decorated military fittings are

Plate 172: A high-quality saddle plate decorated with niello, a black inlay made from silver

often associated with legionaries, and scale mail more frequently with auxiliary troops. The decorative scheme on a silvered and niello-decorated saddle plate (Pl 172; *Ch 17, pp 723-4*) seems, if only tentatively, to point to its use by an infantry officer, rather than cavalry.

The types of weaponry cannot help to distinguish between them, spearheads especially being workaday weapons used by all, and seldom richly decorated. The presence of a relatively large number of arrowheads has been cited at other sites (see, for instance, Potter 1979, with regard to Watercrook near Kendal) as indicating the presence of units of *sagittarii*, but they are also found in small numbers on many military sites, both legionary and auxiliary (J L Davies 1977, 265). Even at Carlisle, where a relatively large quantity was recovered, they still comprise little more than a few quivers-worth of arrows, mainly from Period 4. Most of the goose bones from Roman deposits on the site are from the wing (*Appendix 12*), and might possibly represent the collection of flight feathers for fletching (unless used for dusting!). If pointing to specialist troops, it would seem more likely to be a small number of men on detachment, and at a similar or slightly later date, the presence of at least one archer is attested at Housesteads, where a tombstone portrays him carrying a typical re-curved bow and with a quiver of arrows over one shoulder (Smith 1968a, 284). Similarly, the clay, lead, and stone slingshot might suggest the presence of specialist slingers, but equally it must have been a skill developed by others, not least as it was useful for bringing down small game to supplement rations.

There is, however, a considerable amount of material which can be associated with horses, most likely cavalry, and the *ala Gallorum Sebosiana* is attested at Carlisle in the first century (*Ch 12*). Of course, the most direct evidence for the presence of horses comes from their bones, which were found in relatively small numbers from Period 3 onwards (*Ch 22, p 919*). Whilst it cannot be certain that these all derived from riding

horses, rather than those used for traction, it is of note that most animals were full grown, and mainly between eight and eleven years of age at death, none had skeletal changes associated with heavy traction, and there were no bones of immature animals. There were insufficient long bones to allow valid conclusions as to the height at the withers of the Roman horses, but there is no real reason to believe that they would have been different in stature from those at Ribchester (Stallibrass 2000a, 95), being the size of large ponies, at between 12 and 14 hands. Although the quantities of bone are not great, it seems unlikely that horses were being bred in the vicinity, and unlike Ribchester, where it has been suggested that animals might have been brought to the fort relatively young for training, with the unsuitable mounts later culled (*op cit*, 382), horses coming to the Carlisle forts were already trained.

Some of the horse bones from Roman layers show signs of butchery, with skinning marks, and even bones split to retrieve the marrow (*Ch 22, p 915*). It is conventional to assume that horsemeat was not consumed by Romanised troops (Tacitus: *Histories IV*, 60 (Moore and Jackson 1931)), but there is no real reason to avoid the possibility that this might have been an ethnic preference, perhaps reflected in a different means of preparation, which did not usually leave obvious signs of butchery (King 1991, 17), or economic expediency, or even a gesture of contempt towards slaves or prisoners (Dixon and Southern 1992, 180). It is, however, possible that the evidence of butchery on these bones simply reflects the economic use of resources, with animals, slaughtered for other reasons, being utilised for a number of purposes, not least the hide, although no horse-hide was noted amongst the leather attributable to species. A concentration of horse foot bones within drip gully *3762*, associated with Period 3B Building *4006*, has been linked to the possible removal of hides, as, at a later date (Period 6), has a group of articulated foot bones found on road *2303* (*Appendix 12*). Horsemeat has often been used to feed hounds, and several dogs were amongst the bone assemblage. Considering the number of wild species represented in the animal bone, it would be surprising if hunting with dogs was not a favoured pastime amongst officers stationed within the fort, and the average height at the withers for dogs in the stone fort (0.41 m) indicates that they were of a suitable size for hunting. An altar found at Birdoswald (Raybould 1999, 11; Collingwood and Wright 1983) was dedicated by a group of hunters (*venatores Banasses*), and the amount of deer bone from Roman deposits at Carlisle (*Ch 22, p 917*) makes it clear that hunting was part of daily life.

The most direct evidence for riding was the two leather saddle covers from Period 3C Building *4657* (pit fill *4144*; *Ch 20, p 819*), and a small wooden fragment, tentatively identified as part of a wooden

*Plate 173: Part of the wooden sub-frame of a saddle
found in Period 3A Building* **4658**

saddle frame, from an occupation layer (*4165*) within
Period 3A Building *4658* (Pl 173; *Ch 19, p 814*). Marked
differences in the standard of workmanship of the
saddles might point to a difference in status between
their respective owners (*Ch 20, p 823*). A small group of
tinned and niello-decorated saddle plates gives some
impression of the extent of decoration which could
be applied to the saddle (*Ch 17, p 723*). In addition,
there are parts of several bardings, large loose leather
'garments', which were draped over the back and
head of a horse; to what end remains obscure: they
may simply have served to protect unsaddled horses
from the weather. A coarse wooden comb from
Period 3B external layer *999* (*Ch 19, p 807*) would
have been ideal for grooming. A single element of
an iron snaffle bit was also found, and, in Period 6,
fragments of horseshoe (*Ch 17, p 753*).

There are also large numbers of copper-alloy fittings
which can be directly associated with horse tack,
comprising mainly the multitude of small pendants
with which it was decorated, and the buckles and
clips which were used to connect harness straps.
Whilst the functional aspect of horse tack means
that many components of military and civilian
harness must have been very similar, the consistent
and predictable range of fittings which seem to be
associated with cavalry at a number of forts must
surely suggest that this, too, was subject to military
control in some manner. No doubt the decorative

element must have added to the general glittery, noisy
impression given by passing troops. On the whole, the
objects recovered do not stand out as unusual, and
individual items can be paralleled at a number of sites
in Britain, along the western *limes*, and further afield.
There was, however, a single unusually decorative
harness fitting, from the chest or shoulder (*Ch 17,
p 719*), which must have come from an impressive
set of harness, brought to Carlisle during the early
AD 70s and lost in the construction trench (fill *4240*)
for Period 3A Building *4654* (Fig 262). Whilst quite
well-used and frequently repaired (Pl 174), this object
is clearly large enough to have been missed as a
casual loss; indeed, if it had been lost in use, it would
have caused a significant and presumably noticeable
failure of the harness. This leads to the possibility
that it was in fact a deliberate deposition, a valuable
and symbolic item placed in the construction trench
of one of the first buildings on the site. This would
perhaps have seemed more obvious if it could have
been shown to be a foundation deposit linked to the
headquarters, but Building *4654* has been identified
as a possible workshop (*Ch 3*), and it was perhaps
the craftsmen for whom the structure was erected,
and who would have had easy access to such fittings
in the course of their day-to-day employment, who
chose to make the gesture.

There must surely have been a considerable amount
of 'show' involved in the deployment of troops, in
an attempt to impress the locals with the superiority
of the arriving forces. One final object can add to
this visual impression, providing almost the only
evidence, apart from bone, for the use of traction
animals, in this case probably mules, which were
favoured for heavy vehicles (White 1970, 300), but not
necessarily so. A large rein trace (Pl 175), surmounted
by the figure of an infant deity in completely Classical
style (*Ch 17, p 741*), was found in occupation debris
within Period 4 Building *5689* (Fig 263). Whilst little
is known of the appearance of official vehicles at this
time, it is difficult to believe that this did not come
from a fairly impressive vehicle, perhaps in this case,
garaged, or dismantled and in store.

Plate 174: A decorative element from a horse harness, found in the construction trench of one of the earliest buildings

*Plate 175: A large rein trace, probably from a cart or carriage of some magnificence, from Building **5689***

There's No Place Like Home

The multiple renewal of buildings, effectively within the same footprint, inevitably causes problems of residuality, and it is therefore impossible to be certain of the precise date of deposition of many of the objects from them. Those from floor or other occupation deposits inside individual buildings are of most direct relevance, as they are likely to have been in contemporary use, but occasionally material from construction trenches or later demolition layers can contribute to an understanding of the use of specific buildings.

Period 3A

The substantial amount of disturbance and redeposition makes it difficult to assess pottery use at a building-by-building level within the first fort, especially since there might have been systematic and repeated use of pottery and tile as hardcore when levelling the site (*Ch 16, p 572*). Not surprisingly, the first arrivals brought their own supplies with them, reflecting a mixture of acquisition from established sources of supply (for instance mortaria from Verulamium) and, presumably, centralised issue; in the tablewares especially, there was a wide range of fabrics and forms reflecting piecemeal personal acquisition (*Ch 16, p 571*). It is obvious, however, that the establishment of a source of good-quality pottery was a priority, with relatively large-scale production beginning almost as soon as the troops arrived. A basic set of crockery can be recognised, which presumably reflected the needs of the individual soldier, with food preparation and cooking vessels, storage vessels, and tablewares. The latter were of unusually high quality, and were presumably made at the nearby Fisher Street kilns (*Ch 16, p 593*), perhaps reflecting the fact that the range of imported wares reaching the fort in its early days was poor.

Neither the purpose of the earliest rampart-back building (*1193*) nor of possible barrack, Building *166*, in the south-west quadrant (Fig 265) could be interpreted from the finds, although the presence of locally made rusticated jars in the latter might suggest occupation. Building *1194* replaced *1193* at an early stage (*Ch 3*) and an occupation layer (*472*) within the former produced a stack of fabric-wrapped coins, approximating to one day's pay for a legionary soldier, and dated to *c* AD 77-8 (*Ch 17, p 679*). It produced few other artefacts, beyond locally made pottery jars and bowls, but there were several fragments of fine table glass, probably including a flagon (*Appendix 8*), within the occupation layers. A small amber bead from floor *1110* could reflect a feminine presence, as amber was often accorded a special affinity with women during the Roman period (*Ch 18, pp 777-8*), but it is quite possibly a residual object of considerably earlier (perhaps prehistoric) date. Animal bone from the same period includes evidence for the butchery and skinning of cattle, and the consumption of domestic fowl and hare (*Ch 22*).

Two smaller buildings, *4658* and *4654*, lay to the south of the main east to west road (*7476*) and to the west of the main north to south road, the latter standing at the intersection, facing both roads (Fig 265). The assemblage from within *4658* included part of a pillar-moulded bowl in brown glass, and a lid in Dorset Black-burnished ware, presumably brought to the site in personal baggage long before the large-scale supplies resulting from second-century military supply contracts (*Ch 16, p 601*). A range of locally made flagons, jars, and bowls undoubtedly reflect breakage during the day-to-day occupation of the building. There were no weapons,

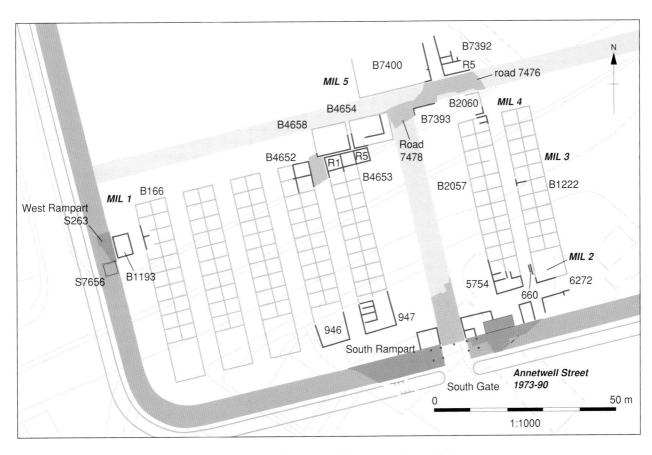

Figure 265: The layout of the fort in Period 3A

and only a single stud, similar to those seen on some of the armour, hints at the presence of military kit (two more were found in disturbed contexts; *Ch 17, p 687*); heavily worn, and thus, presumably, discarded, military footwear was found in post-trench fill *4088* (*Ch 20, p 837*). Like many of the buildings in the fort, there were several small fragments of copper-alloy sheet, probably off-cuts (Pl 176), which might have been used casually in a range of activities, in the way that today some items, for instance, masking tape, can be used for anything from home decorating to first aid. Two large possible buckle pins were also found, although they were not securely provenanced (*Ch 17, p 733*).

Building *4658* was one of only four structures from this period to produce lead spills, and also produced one of only two fragments of unprocessed galena from the site (*Ch 17, p 763*). In the absence of any evidence for lead slags, this cannot be cited as evidence for lead-refining or any related process in the fort, although this was being undertaken elsewhere in Carlisle in the first half of the second century (Zant *et al* in prep). If correctly identified, the wooden saddle fragment might indicate some connection with horses, but whether as a workshop or stabling cannot be determined (*Ch 19, p 814*). A small amount of fine glassware might suggest that men were living within the building, a dark blue flagon fragment from floor *4010*, and the pillar-moulded bowl from fill *4088* of a

Plate 176: Small off-cuts of copper-alloy sheet, found in Building 4658

503

construction trench, implying some aspiration, as both would have been expensive items (*Ch 18, p 768*). One of the two so-called weaving combs came from this building, and it is tempting, if there was a connection with horses, to see this possibly put to another use, perhaps grooming (*Ch 21*). A small copper-alloy lidded container was also recovered from construction trench fill *4088*, although what it might once have contained cannot now be determined (*Ch 17*).

Finds associated with Building *4654* differ from those found in its neighbour (*4658*). Stitched leather and shoe-making waste raise the strong possibility that this was a leatherworking shop (*Appendix 10*), and a large needle, substantial enough to have been used for leatherworking, or perhaps as a baling needle, was found in the same structure, albeit in a construction trench (*Ch 17, p 746*). Not surprisingly, as it seems that shoes were being made in this building, there were also a few loose hobnails. A few cattle and sheep/goat mandibles and foot bones from pit *4565* have been characterised as butchery waste (*Ch 22, p 912*), but could well derive from untrimmed, unprocessed hides, and thus be associated with its use as a workshop. Some sense of organisation or regulation might be drawn from the presence of two styli (*Ch 17, p 753*), both from drain fills, although they could easily have been lost whilst the building was in use.

No less than three glass gaming counters were found in the building, although only one came from a floor, the others again coming from drain and gully fills (*Ch 18, p 776*). The presence of gaming counters might suggest an element of free time, and it is not difficult to imagine a corner workshop close to the *principia* soon becoming a focus for gossip, the number of pottery beakers perhaps reflecting this social element (*Ch 16, p 608*). The single niello-decorated stud from floor *4279* might possibly be associated with the leatherworking, but might equally have been lost by a visitor come to share the news. There were few objects which could be linked to day-to-day living, the one fragment of a glass storage vessel coming from a make-up layer (*4239*), and thus possibly imported from elsewhere; mussel shell from the same deposit suggests that, as was often the case, midden deposits were used for this purpose. There was also a slight connection with horses, in the form of the single ornate copper-alloy harness fitting (*Ch 17, p 719*), although this was from a construction trench, and may have been a deliberate, possibly votive, deposit (*p 501*) and thus have had little to do with what was going on in the building after its construction.

A further small building, *7393*, on the other side of road *7478* from *4654* (Fig 265), also produced a small amount of leather, fragments of tent and saddle, but from an associated external layer. It also produced fragments of a repaired late Neronian samian bowl (*Ch 16, pp 541, 553, 564*), alongside a range of coarse pottery vessels, but otherwise there was almost no metalwork or glass, the latter only storage vessels. This might raise the possibility that the samian vessel, no longer of use as tableware, might have been found some other, *ad hoc*, use. In addition, it bore considerable similarity to a vessel from the Castle Street excavations (Dickinson 1991a), showing that, even at an early date, imported vessels were being dispersed throughout the wider settlement. Only a small part of Building *2060* to the east was examined, producing very few finds.

Immediately behind all these buildings lay long narrow blocks, aligned north to south and probably extending to the south rampart of the fort (Fig 265), seemingly the northern ends of buildings identified as barrack blocks in the Annetwell Street excavations (Caruana in prep). The most westerly examined was *4652*; this produced remarkably few finds other than pottery, most being fragments of glass storage bottles and other table vessels. A concentration of mortaria, distinctive vessels associated with the preparation of food, makes a strong case for this building providing accommodation for soldiers. There was also some samian ware, most notable being an unusual and little-worn Hermet form 9 bowl of later Neronian/early Flavian date, which was presumably exceptional even when originally purchased (*Ch 16, p 553*). There is a strong chance that this vessel was in fact one of a pair, the other being found almost on the same spot, but residual in Period 6 Building *2302*. Although subjective, this assemblage gives the impression that the building was kept relatively clean or was cleared before demolition, and it is of note that only a single animal bone was recovered. The high-quality samian, the number of coins lost, and the presence of good-quality stored meat, suggested by perforated scapulae (*Ch 22, p 913*), might suggest a fairly ordered, almost domestic, context.

Like Building *4652*, *4653* to the east produced a ceramic assemblage notable for the concentration of mortaria, and the composition of the other finds was broadly similar, but with a few small, easily lost items from armour (most notably a cuirass hinge from demolition layer *4101* (*Ch 17, p 703*). Floor *3954* (R1) produced glass gaming counters and a single harness fitting, echoing the finds from apparent workshop *4654* to the north. There was good organic preservation within this building, resulting in the survival of leather tentage and shoemaking waste (*Ch 20, p 818*), part of a possible wheel spoke, and fragments of two illegible wooden writing tablets (*Ch 19, pp 752-3*). The latter might imply some administrative function for this building, but, alternatively, in a milieu where literacy was relatively widespread, might reflect personal letters or orders, belonging to any one of the individuals living within. A wooden tool resembling a plasterer's float came from layer *4083* (R1), but there was nothing to suggest its actual purpose. Again, like Building **4652**, there was little animal bone, although it included evidence for the consumption of venison, often regarded as a high-status meat. At Vindolanda, letters link its consumption with the household of Cerialis, the commanding officer at the turn of the first century AD (Bowman 1994, 69). Unless reflecting the presence of an officer, the venison might imply that, if not living off the land, the barrack-blocks' first-century inhabitants lived rather well. Whilst presumably comprising dumped imported material, a layer in R5 (*4106*) produced a significant number of fragments of scrap iron, especially cut sheet. It may well be that this represents the use of midden deposits for levelling, and it seems reasonable to suggest that they originated from an early smithy or workshop elsewhere in the fort.

To the east of the main north to south road, small parts of two more putative barrack blocks were investigated (**2057** and **1222**). No finds other than ceramics were recovered from the former, and the group from the latter was mainly from the fills of a drain and a gully. These included the largest group of stitched leather from Period 3A, comprising mainly tentage, but also a horse barding (*Ch 20, p 818*). It was the waterlogged conditions in these features that enhanced preservation, and pit fill *1075* also produced a complete double-sided wooden comb, clearly a personal possession (*Ch 19*), and a fragment of glass bangle (*Ch 18*). Hobnails came from the floor, and it is perhaps salutary that, without the waterlogged conditions, these would have been the only artefacts other than pottery and the bangle. The animal bones indicated some primary butchery of cattle, sheep/goat, and pig, and their consumption, along with estuarine fish (*Ch 22, p 921*). Interestingly, there was some evidence of the butchery of dogs, but whether this was the opportunist collection of dog skins, or the animals were being cut up as food for other hounds, cannot be determined. It seems unlikely, though not impossible, that they were used as human food, unless at a time of severe stringency, but evidence from elsewhere suggests a strong link between the deposition of dog carcasses and ritual (Merrifield 1987, 32; King 2005, 360), and it is not beyond reason that this butchery in fact hints at sacrifice.

Finally, to the north of road **7476**, two significant buildings, **7400** and **7392**, were examined. Building **7400** stands out from the others, in producing, during the last phase of activity, evidence for a probable metalworking hearth (Fig 266), and a large number of small fragments of copper-alloy sheet, a possible casting sprue, and solidified spills of molten copper alloy, some found within timber-lined silos sunk into

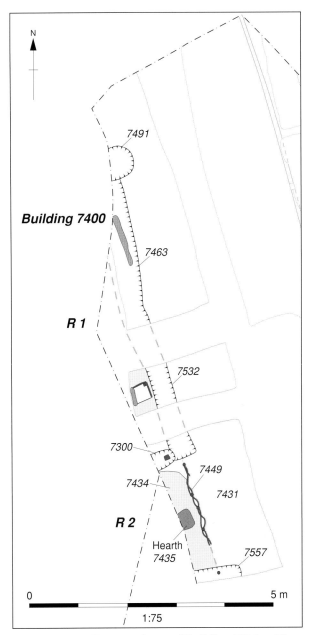

Figure 266: Excavated part of Building **7400**, *with probable metalworking hearth 7435*

the floor (*Ch 3*). Although the quantities were small, there was also more melted lead from this building than any other in this period, and it is possible that it was used for the production of trial pieces, although none of these survived. This seems to present good evidence that the building was used, in part at least, as a workshop, and what appears to be an imperfectly made metal hairpin from possible floor *7487* might give a clue to the range of small items which could have been produced alongside military necessities (*Ch 17, pp 730-1*). One of the few other finds from the building, however, was a weaving tablet, of the kind normally used to produce narrow ribbons and braids, and an unusual brooch likely to be of indigenous origin (Pl 163), raising the possibility of a local person, possibly female, and probably of low status, living or working there. In terms of its position, however, this building is likely to have been the *principia*, and thus this assemblage is somewhat at odds with the conventional roles attributed to such a structure (see *Ch 3, pp 97-8*).

Building **7392** is thought to have been the *praetorium* (*Ch 3*), at least part of which would have formed the domestic quarters of the commanding officer and his household. The impression given by finds other than the pottery is, however, far from one of domestic activity. There are several hundred small fragments of copper-alloy sheet, some made into rivets, alongside short fragments of copper-alloy wire, of similar size to that used for wiring together scale mail, and an obvious suggestion is that the debris represents the production and / or repair of mail; indeed, a small fragment of mail came from circular pit *7541* (fill *7542*), as did a small decorative fitting, and a larger, somewhat enigmatic, object, which was possibly associated with helmet reinforcement (*Ch 17, p 744*). Most of this material derived from occupation layers, and the remainder from pit *7570* (fill *7569*), in R5.

The composition of the metalwork assemblage from this building is very similar to that from the putative *principia* to the west and might well imply that activity within them was closely linked. Indeed, there is considerably more secondary metalworking debris in **7392** than in its neighbour, and it could perhaps be the case that the more noxious procedures were carried out in **7400**, and that it was acceptable to carry out 'cleaner' elements, perhaps assembly, within the *praetorium* complex. There are no diagnostic tools amongst the ironwork to give any clue as to what was being done, although three wooden-handled points (perhaps awls or punches) might well have been the kind of tool used in making copper-alloy scales. There was, in addition, an unused pottery crucible in a locally made fabric, presumably intended for melting lead or copper alloy for casting. Again, there was a small amount of lead spillage and a few fragments of cut sheet. The impression that this might in part have served as a workshop for armour is perhaps added to by the presence of a broken ivory sword grip from floor *7573* in R5, and a possible jet pommel from occupation layer *7548* in the same room, the latter being found with a large jet ring, both relatively unusual and probably high-status objects (*Ch 17, p 708*).

A small amount of shoe-making waste was also recovered from Building **7392**, suggesting that some leatherworking was going on, but what is probably most important is the marked lack of domestic items other than the ubiquitous pottery. A single damaged penannular brooch was found, but the presence of what appear to be part-made pins might suggest that these were being produced, or repaired, there. Otherwise, there was only a single small fragment of a glass storage bottle from an occupation layer (*7497*). The earliest samian vessel from the site came from the fill (*7381*) of a construction trench for this building; dating to the period AD 45–65, its context might suggest that it was broken and discarded in the earliest days of the fort.

Period 3B

Locally made material still dominated the pottery supply during Period 3B, although the appearance of Brampton ware seems to indicate, as has been suggested for other important materials, that sources of supply were being organised, and supply routes secured (*Ch 16, p 591*). A change in the range of decoration used on the local products can be recognised, with an increased emphasis on techniques like barbotine decoration, which perhaps implies that the highly skilled and sophisticated potters associated with the fort could have learnt their skills in the Rhineland or North Gaul, perhaps recruited to the *ala Gallorum Sebosiana* (*Ch 16, pp 612-13*). Supplies of imported pottery continued to reach the fort in small amounts, presumably mainly as individual acquisitions or small orders, most being of North Gallic origin. Unusual mortaria from Wroxeter and Elginhaugh seem to point to contact at an individual level, perhaps troops seconded to the fort, or on the move, carrying their own equipment with them.

Rampart-back building **1194** (Fig 267) seems to have continued in existence during this period, although only one artefact relating to it was recovered, a penannular brooch from pit *376* (fill *441*). The building was also singularly devoid of animal bone, perhaps suggesting that it was kept relatively clean at this time. Building **1195** was erected to the immediate east; probably a barrack block, it, again, produced few finds other than pottery. The presence of high-quality glass, including a facet-cut drinking cup and a dark blue ribbed vessel (*Ch 18, p 769*), may imply that it was not necessarily poorly appointed.

During this period, the main east to west road was flanked by a small building, **4006**, which replaced **4658**. Like its predecessor, it produced a considerable amount of scrap copper alloy. Some, from construction trenches, presumably originated from earlier activity, but there were sufficient amounts from floors and occupation deposits to suggest that whatever activity it was that generated this scrap during Period 3A continued in the new building, which also contained a small oven or kiln. A buckle fragment from occupation deposit *3802* appeared to have been deliberately cut through, and might hint at the recycling of scrap metal (*Ch 17, p 733*). A small amount of leatherworking waste lay upon the floor, suggesting some shoe-making, and sawn antler also suggests some bone-working; amongst the animal bone, articulated bovine foot bones from an external gully seem to imply some acquisition or storage of hides.

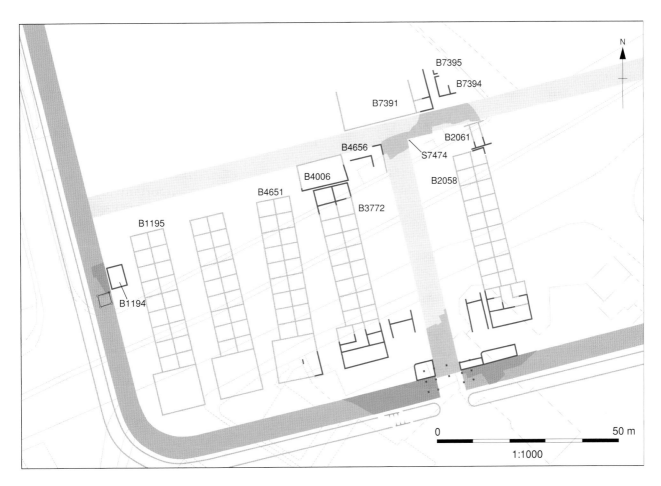

Figure 267: Excavated buildings attributed to Period 3B

There were, within the building, torn leather tent panels, and sewn sheet-leather fragments which might have been parts of bags (*Appendix 10*), implying storage, or even the stowage of kit. There were, in addition, fragments of one, or possibly two, brown glass pillar-moulded bowls, which, as relatively fine (but not best-quality) tableware, again suggest a certain level of disposable income and, unless standard issue, some aspiration to comfort. It is not, however, impossible that these distinctive vessels were in fact residual, with a single fragment also coming from underlying Building **4658** (*Ch 18, pp 767-8*). Building **4006** also produced an unusually large amount of ceramic eating and, particularly, drinking vessels (*Ch 16, p 613*), suggesting that those using the building were accustomed to live well. The distribution of this material, spreading out onto the road, raises the possibility that it served in some manner as a social gathering place. The extremely rare survival of a carbonised fragment from the leg of a small three-legged wooden table (*Ch 19, pp 810-11*) gives an unusual glimpse of the furniture available at the time, but whether it was used in this building, or ended its days as firewood, is not clear. It is, however, of interest that some of the German cavalry tombstones which show slaves or grooms exercising horses (for instance Goldsworthy 2003, 115) also show the deceased

reclining, glass in hand, with a small three-legged table within reaching distance, upon which stand his drinking vessels (Fig 268). Presumably, this shows the deceased pursuing a preferred pastime, and would not have been an unacceptable way to while away off-duty evenings within the fort at Carlisle. A feature of the (Period 3D) demolition deposits above this building was the large group of fired clay slingshot (*Ch 18, p 777*). A single example was recovered from floor *3805*, and most of the later examples were probably residual, having originated earlier in the life of the building.

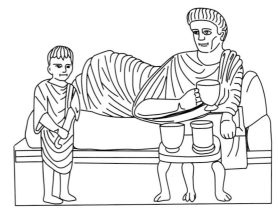

Figure 268: Depiction on a tombstone showing a three-legged table (after Goldworthy 2003)

To the east, small building *4656* had been badly disturbed (Fig 267), which, to an extent, resulted in the very small numbers of finds from associated occupation layers. Indeed, most of the finds could be residual, and actually from its predecessor, including a small group of glassware. Although the storage vessels would not have been out of place in its predecessor (Building *4654*), several fragments of a dark blue glass flagon stand out as somewhat more luxurious. Of the finds from occupation layers, two are iron nails, and the third is a bone gaming counter or tally, perhaps echoing the three glass examples found within Building *4654*. Two melon beads, now increasingly associated with horse tack (*Ch 18, p 775*), came from demolition deposits. Despite its position, there is little in this assemblage to suggest the function of the building.

To the east of the main north to south road, small building *2061* produced more finds than its predecessor, *2060*, including two more bone counters like that from Building *4656* to the west, and a few studs of the kind that might have come from armour or other military leatherwork. A broken and burnt samian dish, found in occupation layer *1882*, again gives an indication of the extent of subsequent disturbance, with most of this vessel being recovered from later demolition (Period 3D) deposits. Presumably, a battered fragment of glass pillar-moulded bowl also had its origins in the earlier building (*2060*, Period 3A).

An apparent barracks, Building *4651*, produced few finds. To the east, Building *3772* again produced very few objects from floors or occupation levels, only two frit melon beads, a fragment of sword grip, and a small bone collar. As reasonable numbers of finds came from the construction fills and later demolition deposits, this might well give the impression that the building was kept clean whilst in use, the objects lost being small, easily kicked aside and hidden. Waterlogged conditions in one of the construction trenches preserved a boxwood hair comb (*Ch 19, p 806*), probably a personal possession, and other objects included several copper-alloy fittings from cavalry tack, and a ballista bolt, again from construction trenches and thus perhaps more properly associated with the preceding structure. Two more melon beads and a bone cheekpiece from a bridle were amongst finds from the demolition levels, giving this building perhaps a stronger association with horses than any others (*Ch 4, pp 138-9*). A small stack of silver coins from the same demolition deposits could point to the presence of higher-paid cavalry at this point, although all the army was paid in silver (*Ch 17, pp 679-80*).

In the south-east quadrant, immediately to the south of Building *2061*, small parts of a barracks, Building *2058*, were examined. Finds other than pottery were restricted to a single fragment of glass from a demolition level, and leather tentage and horse bardings from an associated external layer.

North of the main east to west road, the putative *principia*, *7400*, was replaced by Building *7391*. Other than pottery, the finds from floors and other occupation layers were very restricted, and there was little indication of the metalworking that had been carried out before, except in the group of copper-alloy off-cuts from make-up layers and the fills of construction trenches, all of which could be residual. A single small fragment of plate armour was found on possible floor *7455*, but the material does not aid an interpretation of the possible functions of the building.

Building *7392* to the east seems to have been replaced by two smaller structures, *7394*, and to the north, *7395* (*Ch 4*). Again, floors and occupation levels within *7394* produced little, the only finds of note being a bone counter, a stylus, and an iron lamp-holder. Material from construction trench fills did, however, shed further light on earlier activity. A smithing hearth bottom and hammerscale must presumably derive from the earlier activity within *7392*, identifying at least some of the work undertaken as blacksmithing, alongside the copper-alloy working, although this might challenge the suggestion that the work undertaken in *7392* was marginally 'cleaner' than that in its neighbour, the putative *principia*, *7400*. There was, in addition, a metalworking punch (*Ch 17, p 756*). Other finds from the same fills also included personal objects, amongst them a very fine hairpin topped by a female head complete with earrings (Pl 177), another boxwood comb, and a

*Plate 177: Hairpin from Period 3B Building **7394***

plate brooch, possibly intended to be enamelled, but apparently unfinished. A small, and unusual, sidelight was shed onto day-to-day food provision, by the presence of a single small barbed iron fishhook from construction trench fill *7315*, and the proximity of the fort to what was presumably then, as now, a salmon river, raises a charming image, not often associated with Roman military activity. One of the few salmonid head bones from the excavations was from the predecessor building, **7392**, its presence implying that small whole fish were, on occasion, brought to the building (*Ch 22, p 920*). Only two finds other than pottery were recovered from Building **7395** to the north, both small fragments of sheet off-cut, both from construction trench fills.

Period 3C

During Period 3C, there seems to have been little substantive change in the nature of the pottery supply, with regard to both locally made and imported wares. It is of interest, however, that there was an increase in the supply of North Gaulish grey ware. Usually represented by relatively large biconical beakers, they are thought to be associated with beer-drinking rather than the consumption of wine (*Ch 16, p 598*). Again, they can be linked to the presence of the *ala Gallorum Sebosiana*, perhaps reflecting a cultural preference for beer. Its is not clear whether the beakers were supplied systematically by the garrison quartermasters, or were brought in personal baggage, but as there is nothing to suggest that the locally supervised potteries were catering for this very specific requirement, it seems most likely to have been the latter.

In this period, only two fragmentary buildings were recognised as undergoing change (*Ch 4*); both faced the main east to west road, but lay one to each side of the main north to south road (Fig 269). To the west, Building **4657** has provided an unusually large and varied assemblage, a large proportion of which came from a substantial pit (*4130*, especially fill *4144*) within the building, and associated with its final phase, with the few finds other than pottery from the floors and occupation layers. These were remarkably similar to those from other buildings, for instance **3772** (Period 3B) to the west (Fig 267), and suggest that, whilst in use, they were kept more or less clean, the few small objects lost being hidden by furniture and fittings. The contents of pit *4130* are of considerable interest, and perhaps represent a process of triage for armour and other equipment at times of substantial troop movement and the temporary abandonment of sites (*Ch 17, p 705*). It included a considerable amount of leather, including large parts of two saddles, horse bardings, and the waste from manufacturing these items, shield covers, and tent panels, all having been cut up in the course of recycling (*Ch 20, p 820*). There were, in addition, no less than nine substantially complete and probably quite old samian vessels,

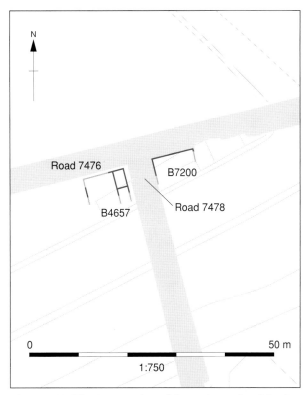

Figure 269: The intersection of the main roads of the fort, with the new buildings of Period 3C

including unusual forms such as Dr 67, a very worn and repaired bowl of form Dr 29, and other cups and dishes (*Ch 16*). As ever, scrap copper alloy and iron were present, but also a headstud brooch (*Ch 17, p 725*) and a small knife blade. It has been claimed (see, for instance, Fulford 2001) that structured deposition took place within apparent disposal pits at a number of sites, most spectacularly at Newstead (Clarke 1997), but there seems little obviously 'special' within this group except for the leather. Domestic waste within the pit included three cattle scapulae (one hook-damaged) and a number of lower limb bones, as well as partial cattle and pig skulls (*Ch 22*). A few of the bones had been gnawed, presumably by dogs, but whether this implies that some at least of the rubbish had lain exposed for a while, or that the inhabitants kept and fed dogs within the building, is not clear. Glass gaming counters from the construction trench fills, both abraded and fragmentary (*Ch 18*), echo those of the preceding building (**4654**), perhaps a leather workshop, which stood on the spot in Period 3A (Fig 265), and should therefore probably be seen as residual.

Building **7200** stood on the other side of the main north to south road, directly opposite **4657**. Like its neighbour, it produced a large collection of finds, with most coming from floors and occupation layers, and, again like Building **4657**, many had been deposited in a large pit (*6808*, fill *6809*). Unusually, in this case, there were very few finds other than pottery from the construction trenches. This was one of the few Period 3 structures which did not appear to have been kept particularly clean, though, again, most of the objects were small, easily lost items. They included an iron finger ring from floor 6879 (Ch 17, p 730), and a turned boxwood container from occupation layer 6897 (Ch 19, p 809), along with bone and glass gaming counters and small fittings from armour, for instance the buckle from floor 6655 (Ch 17, p 692). Many of these must have been personal possessions, as, perhaps, were the two iron styli, possibly suggesting an element of record-keeping or administration. There was, in addition, a small group of worn nailed shoes, and the only sandal from the site (Ch 20, p 839), along with single hobnails within the debris on the floor. The sandal and some of the shoes were mainly from make-up layer 6818, and might thus have originated elsewhere. Like other structures, there was a significant background noise, comprising small fragments of copper-alloy sheet, wire, and rivets, and in this case several large but insubstantial possible buckle pins made from rolled sheet. There was also a cold-chisel, probably used in iron-working, and the small number of sheet-iron off-cuts seems to reflect such activity. Pit 6808 also seems to have been used for the disposal of scrap metal, including fragments of sheet iron tentatively identified as plate armour (Appendix 6), and it is possible that this represents the same process of triage seen in Building 4657 to the west. Finally, a fragment of ceramic crucible, presumably for melting

copper alloy, was amongst objects from demolition debris 6673 (Appendix 8; Ceramic Object 53), its presence reinforcing the general air of widespread small-scale metalworking which runs throughout this part of the site during Period 3.

Period 4A

The first fort was demolished at the end of Period 3, and the buildings fronting onto the main east to west road, **7476**, were constructed anew in the early second century (Period 4A). The two best-preserved buildings to the south, **4655** and **3376** (Fig 270), seem to have fronted onto the road, and would appear to have been large buildings aligned north to south, which were almost certainly barracks.

During Period 4A, there seems to have been a sustained and thriving local pottery industry, probably still under military control but, possibly as a result of a garrison change, with different potters, who were producing a new and innovative range of vessels alongside the military staples (Ch 16, p 618). The changes were echoed in the mortaria, where makers stamping their wares showed strong links with Wroxeter and Wilderspool. The Brampton kilns continued as a favoured source of supply, but little pottery produced at other British sites was reaching the fort, the thriving local suppliers presumably making it unnecessary to

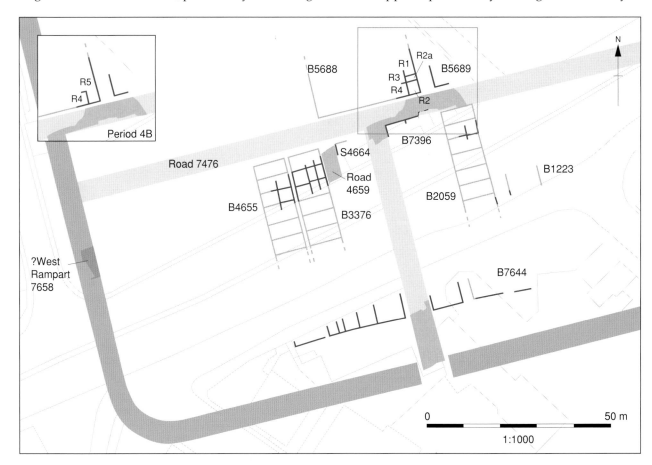

Figure 270: Excavated buildings attributed to Period 4A

510

import anything but specialist vessels and exotica. Apart from samian ware, continental imports, often drinking vessels, continued to show strong links with the Rhine and North Gaul, and could well continue to reflect regional preferences and, by extension, give some faint indication of the tribal affinities of auxiliary troops in garrison at the time (*Ch 16, p 598*).

Like earlier buildings in the south-west quadrant, the lack of artefacts in floor and occupation layers within Building *4655* is an obvious feature. These produced only a few tiny scraps of iron and copper alloy, and a handful of fragments of glass storage bottles, although there was a range of pottery, including Gallo-Belgic wares and part of a triple jar (*Ch 16, p 618*). A large amount of the material associated with this structure derived from construction trenches and almost certainly should be considered with the earlier buildings on the site; it includes what is, in the fort, an unusually large number of fragments of glass storage vessels and tablewares (*Ch 18*). There was, in addition, a single baked clay slingshot, probably associated with the group found a little to the east, centred on Period 3B Building *4006*, although the added presence of at least one stone projectile (*Appendix 11*) might mean that it was in fact contemporary with the building. Demolition deposits again contained fragments of glass storage vessels, and a shallow lead pan of unknown purpose (*Ch 17, pp 761-2*). A fragment of galena came from demolition layer *3366*, and there was a considerable amount of burnt clay and other industrial debris, like hearth bottoms, in the same layers (*Ch 17, p 763*). Again, it seems likely that, rather than reflecting activity within the building, these deposits were in fact dumped from somewhere else in the fort or extramural settlement, as seems to have been the case in the last days of the *fabrica* at Ribchester (Buxton and Howard-Davis 2000, 139).

Building *3376*, to the immediate east, produced considerable numbers of pottery vessels associated with eating and drinking, much of it from the Brampton kilns. This concentration seems to have spilled out onto the road to the east (*4659*), where amphora fragments and a wine cooler were found along with yet more drinking vessels (*Ch 16, pp 575; 629*). This is in considerable contrast to the dearth of other finds from within the building, where floor levels produced only a single fragment of glass, most finds other than pottery deriving from construction trenches and posthole fills. These include at least 13 examples of baked clay slingshot (*Ch 17, pp 717-18*), as well as one of red sandstone (*Appendix 11*), and a very worn silvered military apron fitting (*Ch 17, pp 721-2*), all harking back to activity within earlier buildings in this position. It is, perhaps, of significance that there were a further six baked clay slingshot in demolition debris over this structure, possibly suggesting that they continued to be used or stored there. Demolition layers also included a moderate amount of lead, including solidified spills, and a possible trial-casting (*Ch 17, p 763*).

To the east of the main north to south road, Building *7396* (Fig 270) was unusual in that most of its associated finds were from floors and occupation layers. Although the nature of the assemblage has been, to an extent, influenced by the survival of a number of organic objects, it seems to be somewhat different in composition from its predecessor and from those of Period 3 in general. There is, as in its predecessors, a significant amount of evidence for leatherworking; it produced over 1000 fragments (70% of the waste leather from the site), strongly suggesting that this served at least in part as a shoe-makers' workshop (*Appendix 10*). The presence of two small knives, one with a typical Roman-style bone handle, the other with a simple wooden one (*Ch 17, p 748*), is unusual for the site, perhaps implying that they were associated with the work undertaken there, rather than being personal possessions, especially as it seems clear that in other parts of the site knives had been carefully looked after. For example, throughout the entirety of Period 3, only one example came from a building. Neither knife, however, seemed to have served a specialist purpose and might just have been used around the workshop. There were also tools which seem more appropriate to woodworking, such as a saw (from occupation layer *6660*), and textile manufacture (two wooden spindle whorls), or even agriculture (a reaping hook). It is possible, perhaps, to link some of these to leatherworking, especially saddlery (or, more speculatively, other upholstery), with the saw blade used in the production of the wooden sub-frames, and the whorls used to spin linen thread for sewing. The same layer (*6660*) also produced a scale pan (*Ch 17, pp 761-2*); the large lead weight fixed to this object (as a tare?) seems to imply that it was intended to weigh heavy but relatively small objects, and might perhaps have been used with a steelyard. More usual items included gaming counters, both bone and glass, and a few fragments of glass cups. There was a marked lack of the scrap metal that had characterised many of the earlier building assemblages, and nothing that could be linked with metalworking.

It is of interest that this very different assemblage, with, at a subjective level, a more rural feel to it, was one of the few to produce identifiably non-military dress items, with an enamelled dress-fastener coming from layer *6660*, although there was also a repoussé stud of a kind sometimes suggested as a sort of campaign badge (Pl 178), making it clear that soldiers were also present (*Ch 17, p 707*). It is, however, possible to see, within this building, a trade that might of necessity have had more contact with civilians. Literary evidence from Vindolanda (Bowman 1994, 44) reflects dealings

Plate 178: Repoussé stud, possibly a campaign badge, from Building 3796

with the leather trade, and it is obvious that hides were probably moved over considerable distances by civilian contractors, presumably reflecting the specialised, if noxious, nature of the tanning industry. Indeed, it has been suggested that the tannery at Catterick in North Yorkshire could have serviced much of the military North (*ibid*).

Further east again, Building *2059*, in contrast, produced almost no finds other than pottery from floors or occupation layers, and nothing can be deduced from the assemblage of what might have gone on within it, except that, as might be expected, there was a considerable amount of eating and drinking. Similarly, almost no finds came from construction trenches, except for an antler hoe from posthole *1757*, which might have broken during the excavation of this feature (*Ch 20, pp 865-6*). There were, however, substantially more artefacts associated with its demise. Amongst the latter, the most impressive was a spearhead of unusually high quality, heavily decorated, and clearly a valuable object (from layer *1725*; *Ch 17, p 714*). Other objects from demolition layers include the lid of a copper-alloy jug, again presumably a relatively valuable object, an antler-handled knife (Pl 179; *Ch 17, p 748*), and fragments of glass storage vessels and

samian, which might have originated in Period 3A or 3B contexts. Some of the finds from this building originated in robber trenches rather than demolition debris, and it is not impossible that these were intrusive, rather than residual, although nothing obvious stands out.

To the north of the main east to west road, it seems likely that Building *5688* served as the *principia* during Period 4. Like its neighbour to the east (Building *5689*), it stood throughout the entire period. It produced a large assemblage of finds in Period 4A, although more than half of these were from construction trench fills, and are thus likely to be residual material deriving more-or-less from the last days of its predecessor. Several rooms were recognised within the excavated part of the building (R1-5; Fig 270), each perhaps housing different activities, or used to store different types of item, although this does not seem particularly represented in the assemblage. All the rooms produced small numbers of iron nails, presumably deriving from the structure and its fittings.

Amongst the finds from R1 and R2, the most common artefacts, other than pottery, were glass and bone gaming counters or tallies (*Ch 18, p 776; Ch 20, p 863*). Other finds hinted at fixtures or furniture, with a single copper-alloy knob, and an iron latch-lifter from R1 and a slide bolt from R2 (*Ch 17, p 763*). The latter are amongst the very few objects from the site reflecting any need for security. Presumably, the *principia* was a place where there was some need to restrict access to documents and / or objects, which was not, perhaps, so necessary elsewhere. A single *lorica* tie hook reflects the presence of soldiery, and there was also part of a broken cavalry harness fitting (*785; Appendix 5*). Both R1 and R2 produced small amounts of stitched sheet leather tentage (*Ch 20, p 819*), perhaps reflecting their use for storage. A single example of a caltrop was also recovered from R2 (all other examples coming from Period 6 contexts), as well as a single socketed ballista bolt (*Ch 17, p 712*). Hobnails on the floors were presumably lost in passing, although there was also a small amount of leather scrap from shoes found throughout the building.

Plate 179: Antler-handled knife from Building 2059

Occupation layers in R4 produced three dome-headed studs and a strap junction, all probably associated with horse harness, and yet more gaming counters, this time four of bone and one of glass, from the fill (*6528*) of slot *6525*. More studs and a small knife guard were amongst the few finds from R5, which also produced a possible leather sheath (*Ch 20, p 855*).

During this period, the part of Building *5689* examined was confined to a single room. It produced significantly fewer finds than other Period 4 buildings, the majority from construction trench fills, reducing the likelihood that they were contemporary with the structure. Organic finds add to the importance of the assemblage, with what might well be a baker's peel, the solid wooden base of a basket (Pl 180; *Ch 19, pp 809-10*), and a decorated bone weaving comb (*Ch 20, p 861*). There was, in addition, a single *ligula* (*Ch 17, pp 734-5*). Tent leather from this period was confined to possibly residual material from construction trenches, as was the copper-alloy and iron scrap so familiar from Period 3.

A comparison between the finds from these two central-range buildings (*5688* and *5689*) is of interest. Although both assemblages are small, and some of the artefacts from *5688* are clearly residual, they

Plate 180: A possible baker's peel, and a wooden base from a large basket, in situ *in Building* **5689**

appear to have had different characters, with military equipment and a large number of gaming counters scattered throughout the putative *principia*, *5688*, and more practical and perhaps more homely objects in the possible *praetorium*, *5689*, perhaps reflecting its use as a residence for the commanding officer and his household.

Period 4B

Evidence from the pottery suggests that Period 4B saw the peak of deposition of rubbish in those parts of the successive forts examined during the Millennium Project (*Ch 16, p 868*). This does not seem, particularly, to be borne out by other types of material, but presumably implies that the fort was a crowded, bustling, and above all busy place, the growing evidence for industry perhaps reflecting the demands made by the construction of Hadrian's Wall. The sources of supply for the pottery were little different, with most needs catered for locally, by the military workshop at Fisher Street (*Ch 16, p 593*), but with an increase in material from Brampton, the products from the two centres being largely complementary. Although not a large component of the assemblage, there was an increase in the amount of Black-burnished ware reaching the site, its origin from more than one West-Country producer perhaps reflecting a shortage of supply; this might also be deduced from the rapidity with which local producers started to produce good-quality imitations, and also increased their repertoire of reduced (greyware) pottery forms (*Ch 16, p 570*). They were also producing imitation samian vessels, especially Dr 37 and, significantly, Dr 29, a form which had largely gone out of production in the late first century, but seemed to be finding a renewed vogue in this period at Carlisle at least (*Ch 16, p 541*). Local mortarium production appears to have continued, but at a reduced level, with an increasing reliance on imports from a range of sources, including, for the first time, the major kiln site of Mancetter-Hartshill (Swan 1984).

Facing the main east to west road during this period, Buildings *2765* and *4660* appear to be direct replacements for those demolished at the end of the preceding phase (Fig 271), although it is clear that their intended purpose was somewhat different. Samian wares seem to be largely residual, with very few vessels (between 10 and 18) found within Building *2765*. There was, however, a good range of other pottery: mortaria; jugs; flagons; storage and cooking vessels. Graffiti on at least one implies a need to assert ownership at some level (perhaps that of the *contubernia*) and strongly suggest that the building was at least in part accommodation (*Ch 16, pp 563-4*). With the exception of several fragments of glass storage vessels and an undoubtedly residual pillar-moulded bowl, Building *2765* was singularly devoid of anything non-ceramic

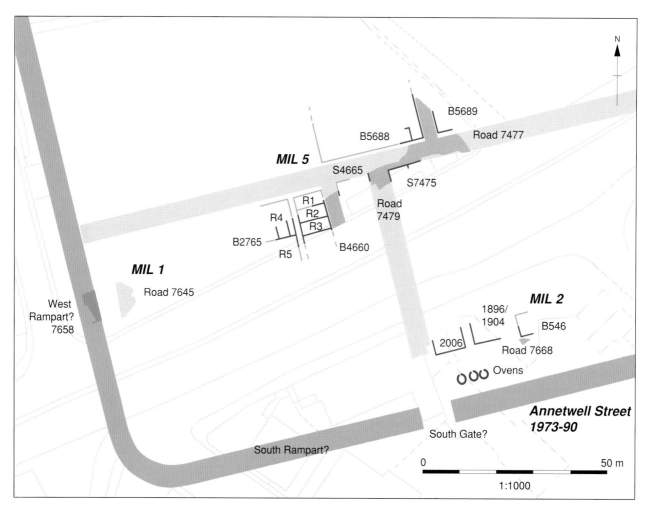

Figure 271: Excavated buildings attributed to Period 4B

(including animal bone) which might reflect the nature of activity within, except for the amounts of iron slag and oak charcoal throughout the building, especially from R4, which indicated its use as a smithy (*Ch 6*). There are, however, no tools amongst the ironwork to confirm this, although a large whetstone was recovered from one of the floors. Changing depositional conditions mean that no leather survived, whilst the copper-alloy sheet reflects the 'background noise' of general use; nails and other small fragments of iron, and a small amount of lead, seem most likely to be from the structure itself. Pits and slots within the structure produced two spearheads (*Ch 17, pp 714-15*), and there were three slingshots, again from gully fills, which might also have originated in Period 3 deposits, along with most of the other shot.

The neighbouring building, *4660*, was similar in having almost no finds other than pottery and metalworking debris from floors or occupation layers, although the considerable amount of pottery included a segmental bowl and a biconical jar, both of North Gallic origin, and a range of beakers (*Ch 16, p 618*). In R2, the fill of an oven or hearth (*2768*) produced a nail cleaner, probably part of a personal chatelaine set. Vessel glass

from construction layers was almost certainly residual, including strong-coloured vessels that would have gone out of production some time before, alongside the common square storage bottles (*Ch 18*). Demolition layers produced sufficient amounts of the latter to suggest that they were in fact contemporary with the building, and perhaps used inside. Other finds from these layers included melon beads, more baked-clay slingshot, and a second-century trumpet brooch (*Ch 17*), again likely to have been contemporary with the last days of the building. There was only one other structure evident in the south-east quadrant. Building *546*, in the south of the fort, produced almost no finds other than pottery, although the presence of five cattle scapulae with a distinctive hole to allow them to be hung from a hook, and deer bone, amongst the animal bone assemblage (*Ch 22, pp 913-14*) suggests the storage and consumption of good-quality meat.

In the central range, although some changes were made to the room layout, the *principia* (*5688*) was largely unaltered (*Ch 6*). Pottery from the building included a full range of preparation, cooking, and eating vessels, although other finds had a strong military theme, with arrowheads and ballista bolts, and strips of copper-

514

*Plate 181: Lunate pendant, part of the trappings of cavalry horse harness, from Building **5689***

alloy edge-binding, like that for a helmet cheekpiece (*Ch 17, p 701*) seen in a contemporary layer (*6280*) in Building *5689* to the east. Lead weights appeared for the first time during this period (*Ch 17, pp 761-2*), and, alongside yet another stylus, seem to reinforce the sense of regulation and record-keeping associated with this building.

Building *5689* was remarkable for the amount of armour and other associated militaria from occupation levels, especially, but not exclusively, *6419* (*Ch 6*). At this time, if not before, this part of the building seems to have served for the repair of armour, much reconstructed from parts scavenged from other items beyond repair (*Ch 17, p 688*). A large amount of scrap copper-alloy and iron sheet may relate to the manufacture and/or repair of scale mail, and a possible iron punch would have been used in the same activity (*2951; Appendix 6*). In addition, a group of three small lunate pendants from cavalry harness might point to the manufacture of such simple and easily made objects (Pl 181).

It is, however, clear that not all the items in the building were related to the manufacture of arms and armour; a short length of fine copper-alloy chain might be from a joined pair of brooches, whilst a small copper-plated bell could have been made for an animal. The impressive rein trace from layer *6280* hints at the storage of vehicles or vehicle fittings (*Ch 17, p 741*). There was, in addition, an appreciable amount of glass from storage vessels, as well as more window

*Plate 182: Small fragment of a possible wooden ruler, from Building **5689***

glass than from anywhere else on the site (*Ch 18, p 773*). Although an obvious reason for the presence of this material would be glazed windows, it might have been stored within the building, but intended for use elsewhere. Organic finds included part of a wooden rule (Pl 182), fragments of plied withy, and what appear to be pads of felted moss, perhaps intended as wadding (*Ch 20*). None was found in close association with the plate armour, but it is possible that it served as padding within a textile undergarment, worn beneath the armour and intended to soften the impact of blows during combat. Despite this overtly industrial impression, the building also produced a range of pottery, amongst it a number of high-quality beakers in Argonne ware (*Ch 16, p 548*).

Periods 4C and 4D

Period 4C encompasses the demolition of the second fort, and it is highly likely that many of the finds are residual, deriving from the disturbance of earlier deposits. Thus, those from Period 4C debris associated with the *principia* (Building *5688*) were presumably, in the main, from Period 4B, having been disturbed by the act of demolition. Most of the finds from Building *5689* came from associated external layers rather than demolition debris, and included considerable amounts of window glass, as had the same building in the previous period. Its presence in late external layers might, however, suggest that the building stood in a state of decay for long enough for windows to fall out or be smashed, although it is also possible that it had served as a store for window glass. One of the layers (*6248*) also produced one of the few hairpins found before the construction of the stone fort in Period 6 (*Ch 8*), its presence suggesting a woman or women in or around the fort at this time. The commanding officer's family, or female slaves associated with his household, would seem obvious candidates.

Pottery from Periods 4C and 4D derives, in the main, from deposits associated with the decay and demolition of the fort buildings. It is perhaps of interest that the vessels from the demolition of Buildings *4660* and *5688* include better-quality wasters from the local kilns, presumably sold at a reduced price, alongside good-quality vessels (*Ch 16, p 593*). It is not clear what this might suggest, except that at a time when most of the buildings were in decline and on the verge of demolition, it could well have been the case that the elite households of the commander and senior officers were no longer in residence, the wasters being purchased by a more frugal regime.

Period 5

Although Period 5 is difficult to characterise, with a substantial amount of residual pottery, what appear to be significant changes in the sources of the contemporary vessels can be recognised (*Ch 16, pp 637-8*). The Brampton potteries had gone out of production, as had the original, Fisher Street, kilns in Carlisle. Both were replaced, however, by a new kiln in Carlisle, a considerable distance from the fort, at English Damside (*Ch 16, pp 594-5*). The removal of this activity to the far side of the extramural settlement might well imply that large-scale pottery-making was no longer under direct military control, perhaps because the fort had a much-reduced, or even no, garrison at this point. Although imported Black-burnished ware was still reaching the site, pottery use was dominated by imitations produced at the new

kiln, which could also reflect an interruption in the military supply chain. At the same time, there was an increase in imported mortaria, with vessels coming to the site from Corbridge (another military producer), and in increasing numbers from Mancetter-Hartshill (*Ch 16, p 583*). Another significant development was a change in emphasis for the supply of drinking beakers, with Cologne and Colchester being the dominant suppliers, the reliance on North Gaul perhaps falling away as troops with close affinities to that area left the fort.

Few buildings can be associated with Period 5 (Fig 272). The small group of finds other than ceramics from Building **2764** (Period 5B) derived entirely from construction-related features, and is confined mainly to nails and other amorphous fragments of iron. In Period 5C, Building **7397** produced only a single glass bead and a plain copper-alloy ring. The assemblage from a third structure, **7473**, also from Period 5C, is similarly sparse, producing, amongst other things, a single copper-alloy scale from mail.

Period 6A

Period 6A was one of considerable change, with the fort being rebuilt in stone, and the buildings in the

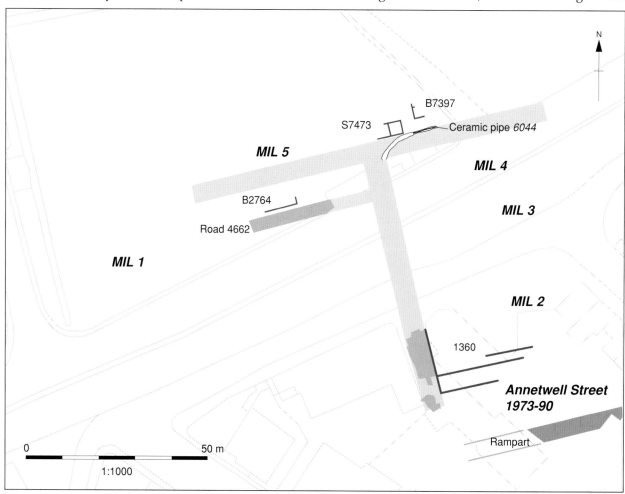

Figure 272: Excavated buildings attributed to Period 5

516

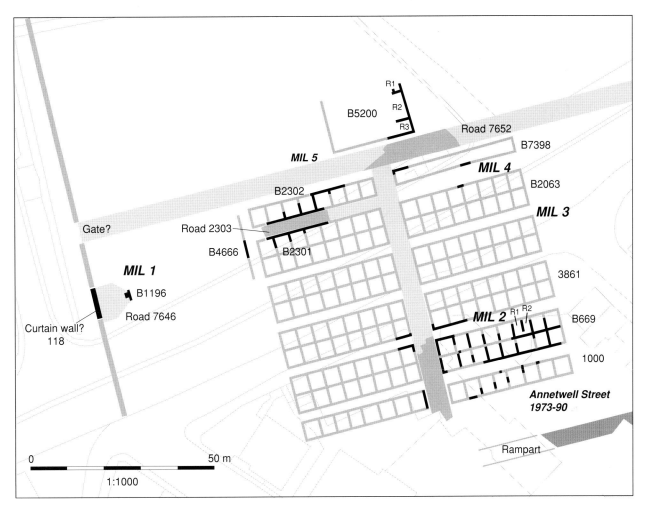

Figure 273: Excavated buildings attributed to Period 6

south-west and south-east quadrants being realigned (Fig 273). In addition, these levels were not subject to the extensive waterlogging that had characterised many of the earlier deposits and, in consequence, the organic component of the assemblages is much diminished, reducing the likelihood of recognising activities like leatherworking, which clearly comprised a significant proportion of the industry in earlier periods. Had its recognition been reliant only on the identification of specialist tools amongst the metalwork, however, it would have gone undetected.

The pottery assemblage also reflects a substantial change in sources of supply. Within a few years, the English Damside potteries had gone out of production and, for the first time, the pottery supply to Carlisle more closely resembled the norm for northern military sites (*Ch 16, p 595*). Supply was dominated by Black-burnished ware Fabric 1, with some supplementary material arriving from lesser producers. In addition, there is evidence to show the beginnings of trade with the East Yorkshire producers, who would later dominate the market, although it was late in the period before Crambeck or East Yorkshire calcite-gritted wares made any significant impact (*Ch 16,*

p 643). At the same time, the Nene Valley became the dominant supplier for tablewares, in part filling the space in the market left by the decline in samian production; this again reflects a restructuring in the sources of supply, with both Colchester and Cologne products disappearing, and only a trickle of fineware beakers reaching the site from Central Gaul. The presence of Ebor ware early in the third century was of particular interest, probably associated closely with troops of *Legio VI* from York. These are known to have been involved in the rebuilding of the fort, a stone inscribed LEG VI being recovered from the Period 6 *principia* (*Ch 21, p 871*). Many of the pottery vessel forms reflected the North African origins of these troops (*Ch 16, pp 578-9*).

A small part of a building (*1196*) tentatively identified as a granary (*Ch 8*), was investigated in the far western part of the fort. It produced no finds other than pottery, but this included Ebor ware, and the animal bone assemblage suggested that pig, cattle, and red deer were being consumed nearby. To the east, Building *2302* lay alongside the main east to west road. Whilst producing considerable amounts of residual pottery, as construction disturbed the underlying layers, there is

Plate 183: Fragment of an Ebor-ware candlestick, made in York, from Building **2302**

of the finds other than pottery were in R3, with R1, R2, and R4 (Fig 274) producing almost nothing, although it is perhaps of significance that R2 produced a single item of weaponry (a spearhead) and part of a glass storage vessel.

Considerably more objects were recovered from R3, from the earliest floor and the Period 6B occupation layers above. They had a wide range, from scrap copper alloy to two links of a valuable and highly fashionable gold necklace, which must surely have been worn by a woman of some wealth (*Ch 17, pp 686-7*). It might be that the increased number of finds implies that this was a more public area than the other rooms investigated, and the presence of at least one tool (an iron awl), and a knife blade, might hint at its use as a workshop or even for retail. Although there is nothing in the plan of this room to reinforce this conclusion, it faced the main east to west road, and would have been a prime location.

little unusual about the more contemporary material, except that it included a well-used and repaired candlestick (Pl 183), again in Ebor ware, perhaps implying (albeit tentatively) that men of *Legio VI* might have been billeted nearby. If nails are excluded from the assemblages from floors and occupation layers within this building, there was very little to indicate any activities that were going on inside. The majority

Building **2301** was parallel and to the immediate south, and associated pottery included a grey ware tankard and a Cologne beaker, implying its use as accommodation (*Ch 16, p 646*). In Period 6A, its floors were singularly devoid of finds, and, as elsewhere, finds from the construction trenches and make-up layers were largely residual. An iron punch from occupation layer *2554* in R2 is the only item that can

Figure 274: Period 6 Buildings **2301**, **2302**, *and* **5200**

be associated with any specialised activity, although its nature remains uncertain (*Ch 17, p 757*).

To the east of the main north to south road, only a small fragment of Building *2063* (Fig 274) was investigated, the few finds other than ceramics all coming from the single surviving construction trench. Further to the south, Building *669* (Fig 273) is thought to have been part of a barrack (*Ch 8*), but produced very few finds other than ceramics. Although by this date much of it was residual, samian pottery from floor *527* included an inkwell, again reflecting the general air of literacy, both personal and administrative, that seems to pervade fort life both at Carlisle and other sites on Hadrian's Wall.

In the central range, Building *5200* is thought to have been the *principia* (Fig 274). Its status could well be reflected in the animal bone assemblage, with cattle and pig supplemented by roe deer, goose, and domestic fowl (*Appendix 12*). As the group includes butchery waste alongside that from more domestic activity, it might be the case that the absence of sheep / goat bone shows a genuine preference amongst the occupants of the building at this time. Finds are limited to a few fragments of iron nails and other iron and copper-alloy scrap. Material from the construction trenches reflects the Period 4 activity to the east, in Building *5689* (*Chs 5* and *6*), and includes copper-alloy armour binding strips (*Ch 17, p 702*).

Period 6B
Pottery supplies reaching the site during this period were effectively unchanged, with Crambeck greywares and calcite-gritted wares becoming steadily more important. Mancetter-Hartshill vessels still dominated the mortarium supply, and products from the Nene Valley, the finewares (*Ch 16, pp 605-6*).

Material from make-up layers within Building *2302* (Fig 274) presumably reflects activity elsewhere in the fort, and includes caltrops, and a single lead slingshot, continuing a long-standing tradition, which might point towards specialist troops. Material from floors was largely confined to R4, with an awl, a quern, and a few iron structural fittings; there is also a single ballista bolt (*1041; Appendix 6*). The material from within Building *2301* is notable for its almost complete lack of copper-alloy objects, the apparent profligacy shown towards this material during Period 4, in particular, having disappeared. The vast majority of the ironwork was structural fittings and nails, which are most likely to have come from the building itself. A small fragment of an emerald green glass bead, a type typical of the third or fourth century, was found in R2 (floor *2184*), and is an all too small suggestion that women might have frequented this building (*Ch 18, p 775*). A stone-lined pit within R3

contained several narrow strips of iron, reminiscent of the arm-guards from Period 4 (*1091; Appendix 6*), and although they lacked any distinctive features that might have confirmed their identification, their deposition within pit *2294* (fill *2296*) echoes the circumstances of the finds of armour from Period 4 (*Ch 6*). Glass and bone gaming counters had been a feature of earlier groups of finds from within some of the buildings, but those associated with Buildings *2301* and *2302* were for the first time all reworked from samian sherds, perhaps reflecting a more *ad hoc* arrangement than before (*Ch 16, p 565*).

Period 6C
Distinct sources of pottery supply can be discerned into the fourth century, when there was an apparent decline in Black-burnished ware reaching the fort, matched by an increase in calcite-gritted wares from East Yorkshire; mortaria derived mainly from the Crambeck kilns (*Ch 16, p 585*). There was a noticeable increase in the variety of sources of supply for finewares, which, when linked to other evidence, may suggest that by this time the main east to west road (*7652*) and the area to the east of the *principia* were serving as a market. Not only would this mean that traders would have brought a range of wares to sell, but also purveyors of food and drink would have brought the 'tools of their trade', with storage and serving vessels on occasion being dropped in the street. In addition, there were a few fragments of North African amphora (*Ch 16, p 573*), the contents of which were likely to have been sold in the market.

There was little change to the layout throughout the life of the fort, Buildings *2301* and *2302* differing little, and still giving the impression of having been kept clean and clear of rubbish. One exception was the large enamelled disc (Pl 184) found on floor *2186* within *2301* (*Ch 17, pp 735-6*). It is not clear what purpose these discs served, but they were occasionally used as sword chapes, and could well reflect the less standardised military dress and

Plate 184: Enamelled disc from floor 2186, *in Period 6C Building* **2301**

equipment of the fourth century (Goldsworthy 2003). A stone carving of a female head (*Ch 20, p 870*), possibly a deity, was recovered from the fill (*2317*) of slot or gully *2308*, but seems likely to have been residual in rubble from that feature.

Although not copious, the finds from Building **669** (Fig 273) are of interest; floor *519* within R1 produced part of a snaffle bit, suggesting the proximity of horses, or perhaps the storage of tack (*Ch 17, p 753*), whilst possible floor *518* in the neighbouring room (R2) produced two bone hairpins, strongly suggesting a feminine presence (*Ch 20, p 859*), and raising the possibility of women living within the fort, perhaps as wives, subsequent to the Severan reforms of the late second century (Goldsworthy 2003, 102–3). Animal bone from this structure seemed to incorporate a considerable amount of domestic rather than butchery waste, perhaps suggesting more cookery and/or consumption in this building.

Floors within the *principia*, Building **5200** (Fig 274), again produced little, fragments of a colourless glass cup and a small knife blade within R3 hinting at a fairly domestic context, and there was a flesh hook (used in cooking) from a make-up layer (*5440*) in the same room (*Ch 17, pp 749-50*). To the east, a timber lean-to (Structure **7651**) produced the same sparse range of objects. Like R3 in Building **5200**, it had a slight air of domesticity, with a knob (probably from furniture), a knife blade, and another bone hairpin. The same preponderance of small fragments of ironwork, largely structural, dominated the fills of associated features, including pits, one of which produced two caltrops, an object largely confined to Period 6 (*Ch 17, p 716*). The animal bone from a pit associated with this structure seems to confirm an unusual status for it and, by extension, the building, with evidence for red deer, goose, heron, and swan, and for bone/antler working (*Ch 22, p 917*).

Periods 6D and 6E
Material from demolition layers and subsequent robbing is almost all residual, and the only crossbow brooch (typical of the late third or fourth century) associated with a structure came from demolition layer *2204*, associated with Building **2301**. Similarly, an openwork belt plate of a late type (*Ch 17, pp 706-7*) came from the fill of a robber trench associated with the same building, possibly implying interest in scavenging from the site. Fragments of a stone sculpture representing a *Genius* also came from the demolition deposits associated with Building **2302** (*Ch 21, p 870*). Scant evidence for late occupation within Building **2301** (Period 6E) comprised only iron nails and a crudely made penannular brooch (*Ch 17, pp 727-8*), which might reflect impoverished circumstances.

Discard and Disposal

It can be seen that, without the survival of organic artefacts, there is little to differentiate the assemblages from individual buildings or to indicate specialist activity. One slight difference, perceived at a fairly subjective level, is that, in all periods, the buildings thought to have been barrack accommodation were markedly cleaner that those thought to have been workshops. The explanation for this is not clear. It must be accepted that although cultural perceptions of what comprises unacceptable living conditions can vary quite considerably, most people endeavour to keep track of their personal possessions and to keep their living quarters in a fairly sanitary condition, in order to avoid sickness. Perhaps corroborating this, it is noticeable that more tools, including ordinary knives, were apparently lost or abandoned in the workshops, especially immediately before their demolition, than elsewhere, perhaps reflecting the possibility that some of the tools used were held in common, or were of army issue, and therefore their discard or loss was not regarded as a personal matter, and they were casually abandoned in the workshops when they fell empty.

The question of where rubbish was disposed of is a difficult one. Floors within the buildings were largely clean, but there was substantially more material on the roads. It is, however, difficult to imagine that casual dumping was sanctioned on the principal roads, and rubbish there might well derive from loss and casual trample in the course of day-to-day use, if not from the use of midden waste for levelling. This does not, however, seem to be the case with the minor roads, where evidence suggests that large amounts of butchery and industrial waste of one sort or another were allowed to accumulate. This could well have been cleared fairly regularly, of course, with the surviving deposits being the last in the sequence, not cleared when adjacent buildings were due for refurbishment or demolition. Indeed, make-up layers and dumps associated with the clearance and renewal of buildings often seem to incorporate industrial and other debris from elsewhere, perhaps indicating that midden deposits were cleared and used for levelling on a regular basis throughout the lifetime of the forts.

Putting Food on the Table

It has become a widely accepted truism that an army marches on its stomach, and supplying the inhabitants of the forts with food would have been a major logistical exercise. Josephus, writing at the end of the first century AD, described even a tented camp on campaign as 'an improvised city… with its market place, its artisan quarter…' (*The Jewish war III*, 71–107 (Williamson 1972)) and there is no reason to believe that a permanent fort was any different, bustling with soldiers and their retainers, as well as civilians, most, if not all, of whom would have required one or more meals a day. Thus the acquisition and distribution of provisions must have been a vital facet of army maintenance (Davies 1971, 122).

The provision of meat is the easiest element to chart, and the large amount of animal bone from the site is an obvious guide to the amount and range of animals consumed. There was, at all times, a marked preference for beef, with pork and mutton consumed in substantially lesser amounts (*Ch 22, p 908*), and there is no doubt that most of it arrived at the fort on the hoof, as was probably normal practice (King 1991, 16). The slaughter and butchery of animals was not only a part of daily life, but also a significant part of religious activity, and the finer sensibilities of modern westerners, which regard such activities as shocking or offensive and tend to hide them from public view, simply did not pertain. The dispatch of a large animal, however, is not without risks, and it seems likely that beasts were confined, if only to avoid the damage caused by frightened or injured animals running amok. The means of death remain unknown, but as none of the skulls showed any sign of the use of a poleaxe, it seems most likely that animals were killed by severing an artery in the neck, as remains common today outside of industrial abattoirs, and seems to have been the case in Roman sacrifice (see, for instance, the numerous depictions of Mithras sacrificing the bull (for instance, Henig 1984, pl 40).

Assuming that midden rubbish was not routinely spread over the site, the widespread distribution of bone with evidence of butchery and dismemberment seems to imply that, in the parts of the fort examined, there was no specific place for these tasks. It seems unlikely, however, that such a messy activity would have been undertaken in living quarters, and the concentration of bone in external layers might point to it being done outside buildings, perhaps at the edge of the road. In this circumstance, it would not be difficult to see a certain number of carcasses issued to a barrack block, and butchered for distribution to *contubernia* or individuals, on the road outside. Evidence from gravestones (Fig 275) suggests that in some circumstances butchery (or perhaps more likely the retail sale of meat) was a specialist occupation (Kemkes *et al* 2002, 220, fig 255) and it is possible that there were specialist slaughterers and butchers amongst the garrison, undertaking the task when and where required.

Figure 275: A provincial butcher's shop, showing different cuts of meat, from a tombstone from Dresden, Germany

Processing the carcass obviously starts with the removal of the hide, often with the head and feet still attached, and this was probably passed on for tanning. The carcass was then dismembered, cut into manageable-sized pieces, and processed as desired. A feature of the cattle scapulae from all Roman periods at the site was a hole caused by suspending it from a hook, presumably to smoke, dry, or salt sides of beef, thereby considerably extending their shelf-life (*Ch 22, p 913*). As a specialist product intended for storage, it is not impossible that some beef was actually brought to the fort in this form. The flesh would also have been removed from other joints, and the bones, especially the long bones, were chopped and split to remove marrow. Horn and bone are both useful by-products, although the former rarely survives within the archaeological record. Tallow and sinew are equally important, and it is likely that little was wasted. Apicius' recipes (Flower and Rosenbaum 1958) make it clear that offal was consumed with enthusiasm, and whilst his recipes are clearly those of late Classical middle- and upper-class Rome, there is no reason to believe that the ordinary soldier ate much differently (less expensive spices, perhaps), and officers, originating from the same elite, would probably have expected similar food on the many high days and holidays of the Roman calendar.

Like those from other contemporary military sites in the North West, for instance Ribchester (Stallibrass 2000a), during Periods 3–5 the animals purchased for meat were not prime beef cattle, which are usually slaughtered as they reach adulthood (*Ch 22, p 908*). The presence of older females, presumably sold for slaughter as their value as dairy animals declined, and animals which had been used for traction, presumably mainly castrated males, make it clear that quartermasters purchased what they could, rather than the best. A first- or early second-century document from Frisia, now the northern Netherlands, records the sale of a single cow, witnessed, for the army, by no less than two senior centurions (Lewis and Reinhold 1966, 516), with the cow delivered to the fort by the vendor, and it is quite possible that the same piecemeal acquisition was the norm in Britain. The situation seems to have changed in the stone fort (Period 6), however, when the age at death profile of cattle became closer to that expected in the consumption of prime beef, and beasts were being processed in significantly larger numbers, suggesting a considerable change in the livestock available and the manner of their procurement (*Ch 22, pp 908-9*).

Without doubt, sheep, goats, and pigs were treated in the same manner. Evidence from a number of sites in Britain (King 2005, 331) has led to the conclusion that the consumption of sheep/goat was governed by some cultural preference, being more popular in the late pre-Roman Iron Age and amongst groups more likely to be indigenous, whilst the eating of beef and pork was more allied with a Gallic and/or German tradition closely associated with military establishments and adopted more widely in the course of Romanisation (*op cit*, 332). Interestingly, despite the amount of evidence for its presence amongst the bone assemblage, there is no mention of mutton or lamb in the Vindolanda documents, although, goat meat is specifically listed, even though the Gallic officers of Vindolanda seem to have preferred beef and pork (Bowman 1994, 68). Whilst sheep/goat was clearly consumed within the fort at Carlisle, the lack of juvenile bone, which might have indicated the consumption of elite dishes such as young lamb, might suggest that its presence in the diet of the common soldier was confined to mutton.

Bacon is mentioned relatively frequently as a constituent of the rations carried by those on active service (Davies 1971, 124), presumably as it keeps well, and must therefore have been consumed in some quantity. Similarly, there is little doubt from the pages of Apicius (Flower and Rosenbaum 1958) that pork was consumed with enthusiasm in Rome, and the written record from Vindolanda (Bowman 1994, 68) makes it obvious that pork and ham played a significant role in the diet of the senior officers at least. Pork fat is listed separately, and might, as lard, have replaced olive oil in the northern diet (Davies 1971, 124). There is little or no evidence amongst the animal bone from the Carlisle forts to suggest the consumption of sucking pig, and it seems that, until Period 6, it is highly unlikely that breeding pigs were kept in or close to the fort.

In addition to their important place in the Roman diet, cattle and, to a lesser extent, sheep and pigs, were the principal animals of sacrifice (White 1970). Literary evidence from Dura Europos dated to the early third century included a list of sacrifices carried out on official religious holidays by the local garrison (Lewis and Reinhold 1966, 567–8),

and it is clear that this included the sacrifice of at least one, and on occasion more than seven, bulls or cows almost every week. Without doubt, most of this meat would have been consumed by the garrison, and if religious activity at Carlisle was at a similar scale, sacrificial animals would have made a significant contribution to the weekly supply of meat, possibly in the form of shared feasts (Henig 1984, 90). The notional requirement of certain physical attributes in animals destined for sacrifice (White 1970, 276) might well account for the small but significant numbers of prime beef cattle seen in the archaeological record alongside elderly draught animals (seen also in the animal bone assemblage from Annetwell Street (Stallibrass 2000b, 64)). A scene of the sacrifice of a pig, and including the presence of a uniformed soldier, is depicted on the handle of a bronze jug from Carlisle, now in the British Museum (Henig 1984, 132; Fig 276), implying that Classical practice was well known and understood in the settlement.

Figure 276: The handle of a bronze jug from Carlisle, showing the sacrifice of a pig

It is also clear that wild resources made an appreciable contribution to the diet of the Carlisle garrison. Venison is the most obvious case, with red deer, roe deer (seen from Period 3 onwards), and fallow deer (in Period 6), the latter also present in many late villa assemblages (King 1991, 17) and thought to have been introduced, in small quantities, by the Romans (*Ch 22, p 917*). It is possible that, in the case of red deer, the evidence was skewed by the deliberate collection of shed antler for other purposes, but it is clear from evidence elsewhere that hunting was a significant pastime amongst the officers of a fort. For instance, the existence is known of a brotherhood of hunters at Birdoswald (Raybould 1999), whilst a request appears for hunting nets amongst the Vindolanda archive (Bowman 1994, 75), and an altar was found at Stanhope in Weardale, recording the successful taking of a wild boar (*ibid*), by an officer of the *ala Gallorum Sebosiana*. In the medieval period, the distribution of meat from deer carcasses was a highly ritualised and stratified procedure (Cummins 1988) and it seems likely that Roman officers would have distributed or received their venison within the system of clientage which governed much Roman behaviour. Several hare were noted amongst the Period 3 bone assemblage, and it is likely that these, too, were hunted, probably with dogs, as can be seen as a frequent motif on decorated samian bowls, for instance on examples from Blackfriars Street (Dickinson 1990, figs 176.23, 176.25).

Chicken, geese, and duck were all consumed in small amounts, but it is not possible to differentiate between wild and domesticated fowl, and all three could have been kept for eggs as well as meat. In addition, white goose feathers seem to have had a monetary value which made them worth collecting (Davies 1971, 130), and there was a thriving trade in feathers for cushions and quills, between Rome and the tribes of northern Gaul (Applebaum 2002, 515). The changing pattern of consumption in Period 6 is emphasised by the presence of more unusual birds, swan and heron, both of which were prized additions to the elite medieval table (Woolgar 1999, 114), and their appearance in the rubbish accumulated in and about the *principia* (Building **5200**) might point to the same situation during the third and fourth centuries AD. It must, however, be noted that the heron was only represented by wings, which might have been collected for other reasons. It is not clear whether the pigeon found in a Period 4C demolition layer over Building **5688** was eaten, although Apicius gives several recipes (Flower and Rosenbaum 1958).

The presence of several species of fish in Period 3 buildings, including members of the cod and salmon families, and flatfish, add more to the impression of gourmet tastes, as do the small numbers of oyster and mussel shells in all periods (*Appendix 12*). Containers for fish sauce, including the highest quality tunny fish sauce (Fig 277), were seen amongst the amphorae from Period 3 (*Ch 16, pp 577-8*). Fish sauce was used widely in Roman cooking as a salty condiment, not dissimilar to Thai *nam pla* sauce (Parker 2002, 638),

*Figure 277: Amphora from Building **7392**, labelled as containing top-quality fish sauce from Tangiers (modern Morocco)*

and modern tastes preserve this, in recipes such as that for Worcestershire sauce, where a principal ingredient is anchovy.

Evidence from the bone assemblage also suggests that the cows and sheep/goat supplied to the fort probably came from herds managed for dairying as well as meat. It is probable that the principal dairy product was cheese, which can of course be stored for considerable amounts of time without apparent deterioration, as well as being highly nutritious. Although there is ample literary evidence for the consumption of cheese by soldiers (Davies 1971, 124), it does not survive well in the archaeological record. The only clue to its production is the presence of specialist pottery vessels, such as cheese presses, although none were recognised in the Millennium assemblage. These dishes are, however, all rather small and would seem to be more appropriate for the production of cheeses intended to be eaten young (for example a whey cheese like ricotta), and there is no archaeological evidence as to whether or not larger, more durable hard cheeses, similar to parmesan or sheep-milk peccorino, were made.

Grain, consumed as bread or as a form of porridge, was the staple carbohydrate. Evidence from the site attests to the presence of barley, emmer/spelt wheat, bread wheat, and oats (*Ch 22, p 927*), although the latter might have been wild, getting into the stored grain as a weed infestation. It is generally thought that barley was used predominantly as animal feed (Huntley 2000a, 351), but as beer seems to have played a significant part in the life of the fort at Vindolanda, where Atrectus the brewer is mentioned by name (Bowman 1994, 45), and Celtic beer (*cervesa*) appears on household lists (*op cit*, 68), it is not impossible that it was also used for brewing. A document recovered from earlier excavations within the Carlisle fort lists the distribution of barley and wheat to the officers of cavalry units (Tomlin 1998, 44), but in this case it seems obvious that the barley was intended for horse feed, and the wheat for the men.

There is ample evidence, in the form of chaff, for the processing of emmer/spelt within the fort, for example in the burnt material from the oven/hearth in Period 3B workshop *4006* (*Ch 22, p 927*). Presumably this was grown locally, as it appears to have been normal practice to process grain intended to be transported over any distance, thereby reducing the weight of the load. It is estimated that the Roman soldier might have been given an allowance of 3 lb of grain per day (Davies 1971, 123), and Tacitus records that it was Agricola's intention, in the AD 70s, to ensure that every fort had a year's supply in store (*op cit*, 122). The buttressed appearance of Building *1196* (Period 6A; Fig 273) suggests that it might have been a granary (*Ch 8*), and further evidence for stored grain within the fort is supplied by the copious presence of insect grain pests (*Ch 22, p 924*) and sprouted grain within Building *4655* (Period 4A; Fig 270), although presumably charred sprouted grain could also be a waste product of the malting process.

Literary evidence seems to imply that a Roman soldier ground his own grain when on campaign (Davies 1971, 126), but it seems reasonable to suggest that, whilst in quarters, some of the grain allowance was distributed as fresh bread or, whilst in the field, as the Roman equivalent of Ship's Biscuit (hard tack). Considerable numbers of fragments of rotary millstones and querns were found during the excavations (*Ch 21, pp 877-81*). Although few were in their primary place of deposition, fragments from beneath material generated by the demolition of Building *3772* (Period 3D; Fig 267) seem to imply that some grain was ground whilst in barracks. Bread would, presumably, have been baked daily, and a wooden peel from Building *5689* (*Ch 19, p 810*; Pl 180) must suggest the presence of at least one large bread oven. Evidence for the consumption of grain is most graphic in the presence of bran in several deposits thought to have incorporated human cess, and confirm that the whole grain was eaten, wholemeal bread being regarded, even then, as more wholesome and good for the digestion (Davies 1971, 126; Tannahill 1988, 77–8).

Evidence for other vegetable foods is relatively restricted, fig seeds and grape pips indicating that these two exotic imports were consumed on site, both presumably in their dried form, as neither grow well in the modern climate of Carlisle. Palestinian carrot-shaped amphora, used to transport figs and dates, were noted in the early part of Period 3 (*Ch 16, p 578*), and indicate the range and distance of trade contacts that were regarded as normal for the military supply network. There is a little evidence for the consumption of cultivated plums (again possibly reaching the site as prunes) and considerably more for the collection and consumption of sloes (*Ch 22, p 932*), which grow abundantly in present-day Cumbria (Halliday 1997). There is, in addition, some evidence for the consumption of apples or pears. Hazelnuts were eaten and possibly also stored in one of the buildings (*4653*, a barrack) late in its life. There were also a few fragments of walnut, presumably again an import, as the tree is not thought to have been introduced into Britain until the medieval period, possibly during the fifteenth century (Harrison *et al* 1981, 28). The seeds from blackberries, wild strawberries, elderberries, and rowan were also present within the assemblage and could have been gathered from the wild to supplement the available foodstuffs; alternatively, they might have simply grown in neglected corners of the fort.

Coriander, dill, and wild celery were found amongst the seeds from waterlogged deposits on the site, and were almost certainly used as flavourings (*Ch 22, p 930*). Poppy seeds (both field and opium) can also be used as a flavouring, and opium poppy seems to have had at least a medicinal use, if not a recreational one, as does wild celery (Allason-Jones 1999b, 139). Many of the other seeds come from plants with known medicinal uses, for instance henbane, and may well have been used as such, although some, like mallow, were also eaten for their glutinous leaves (Flower and Rosenbaum 1958, 79), and continue to be valued in North African cookery to this day (der Haroutunian 1985, 64). The remaining plant varieties recognised are most likely to have been brought to the site as hay for animal feed, or to have grown on waste ground. It must, however, be remembered that a much wider range of greenstuff was consumed in the past than today, with, for example, a late medieval garden manual listing no less than 78 different herbs, including chickweed and fat-hen (both found in Carlisle), to be used in flavourings and medicines (Drummond and Wilbraham 1994, 21).

Olive oil was also used in substantial amounts, even though it had to be imported from the Mediterranean. It would have reached the site in amphorae of Dressel 20 type, found in considerable quantities, and imported from the large-scale producers in Spain (*Ch 16, p 572*). Radish oil, pressed from seeds, was a widely used substitute for olive oil (Davies 1971, 134), and a large deposit found at Ribchester, in Lancashire, was thought to have been raised in garden plots associated with workshops just outside the fort (Buxton and Howard-Davis 2000, 125). There is ample evidence that soldiers stationed in Egypt grew at least some of their own foodstuffs (van der Veen 1998, 107) and it is not unreasonable to suggest that they did so at Carlisle as well, with radish seeds recovered from a number of contexts (*Ch 22, p 928*), although it is possible that these represent wild plants growing locally as a weed.

The most obvious drink available to the inhabitants of the fort was water, presumably supplied in part by the succession of complex systems of pipes (*Chs 19 and 21*). It was not, however, necessarily the safest drink, and must on occasion have carried considerable risks, a possibility well-known to Vegetius (*Epitome of military science* (Milner 1993, 64)). The Vindolanda archive (Bowman 1994) makes it clear that beers and wines were consumed with some enthusiasm, the former probably brewed locally, and probably more to the taste of local and Germanic troops than those from further afield. A wooden barrel made from silver fir, sunk into the floor of a Period 4B structure (**7475**), would have started its life in the Rhine wine trade (see, for instance, Earwood 1993, 80 and fig 49), and many of the amphorae from the site would have contained wine, imported first from Campania and, after the wine trade there was destroyed by the eruption of Vesuvius in AD 79, from Gaul (*Ch 16, p 576*). There

seems to have been an habitual differentiation between sour wine, usually substantially watered and a day-to-day drink, and what would today be regarded as vintages, undoubtedly more expensive, their consumption largely confined to officers. Presumably some milk was available, both of cow and sheep / goat, but neither would have kept well, and it appears that cow's milk was not drunk routinely (Applebaum 2002, 50); although the *Edict of Diocletian* lists ewe's milk, it makes no mention of that of cows (*op cit*, 509).

Most of the pottery and glass vessels from the site can be associated with the preparation and consumption of food and it may be that there was a basic standard issue of food preparation and cooking vessels (*Ch 16, p 571*), but that plates, dishes, and drinking cups were rather more a matter of personal preference, which might account for the increased occurrence of graffiti on these, all apparently indicating personal or possibly group (perhaps at *contubernium* level) ownership. Mortaria from almost all of the buildings interpreted as barracks are a fairly certain indication that food was being prepared within them. Glass, pottery, and copper-alloy flagons would have served as containers for wine, and although there are few drinking vessels amongst the glass from the site (*Ch 18, p 767*), samian pottery forms Dr 27 and Dr 33 are both small cups (Webster 1996) of a size suitable for wine-drinking, and a range of beakers was identified, at least one decorated with an image of the satyr Silenus (Pl 185), notorious for his drunkenness. These were either made locally for this specific market, imported from Northern Gaul and the Rhinelands in bulk, or carried by individuals. A potential enthusiasm for beer, probably amongst garrisons with North Gallic affiliations, seems to be strongly supported by the presence of large biconical drinking vessels, of a type well known in northern *Gallia Belgica* (amongst the coarse pottery of Period 3; *Ch 16, p 615*).

Plate 185: Mask of Silenus, from a large beaker imported from Northern Gaul or the Rhineland

The specific use of a number of other items of ceramic and glass tableware is not always obvious, although many would have served as plates and dishes, and the North African origins of Severan legionaries in *Legio VI* are reflected in the range of distinctive (and presumably traditional) vessel types that can be associated with them (*Ch 16, p 577*). The use of some of the more unusual samian forms is open to question, and it is possible that some were in fact purely decorative, and others, for instance those displaying pornographic motifs, were probably intended as much as talking points than tableware. Glass jars and bowls are often shown full of fruit in Roman wall-painting (see, for instance, Henig 1983, pl 5), and this is one obvious use for them, even though to modern minds eating fruit might not immediately be associated with a soldier's life. It could be the case that the illustration of glass, capturing its translucency and the naturalistic depiction of its contents, might have been as much to display the skills of the artist as to give an accurate illustration of the tableware in use. In general, it is probable that food was eaten with the fingers, although some of the small knives from the site were probably used at table, and the delicate bone spoon (Pl 186) from Period 5A (external layer *5997*) may well have been used in the commanding officer's household (*Ch 20, pp 862-3*), as might the metal example lost on the main east to west road in Period 6A (*Ch 17*).

Plate 186: Delicate bone spoon from Period 5A

It is notable that the quality of the tablewares in use during Period 3 was outstanding, and this could well point to the presence of better-paid troops, possibly legionaries, whose expectations, even on campaign, seem to have been consistently high. These men may have been seasoned hands, perhaps coming north from Exeter, or north-west from York, bringing with them both products made locally, and those of the relevant legionary kilns (for instance a lamp in Ebor ware from York; *Ch 16, pp 615-16*).

Health and Happiness

In any standing army, there is a concern for health and morale, as problems with either can be debilitating. The Classical Roman tradition was one of personal cleanliness and it seems that soldiers would have been encouraged or obliged to maintain standards (James 1999, 16) that were perhaps new to some of them. Some of the ceramics from the site (*Ch 21, p 901*) hint at the presence of a bath-house, which, although it has not been located, was probably to the west of the fort, close to the River Caldew. There is otherwise little in the material assemblage to confirm its presence, except for a single wooden-soled bath shoe (Pl 187; *Ch 20, pp 839-40*).

Plate 187: Part of a wooden-soled bath shoe

As might be expected in an establishment full of men, there are distinctive blades thought to be razors (*Ch 17, pp 746-7*), the conventional fashion being, until the reign of Hadrian, who was bearded, to remove facial hair, either by shaving or plucking. As the latter was a painstaking and lengthy business, often done by skilled personal slaves, it seems reasonable to assume that ordinary soldiers favoured the razor. There might well have been specialist barbers (Boon 1991), but there is little evidence for this within the forts, except that the most distinctive example of a razor (Pl 188) was found in a roadside drain (*Ch 17, p 746*). To this day, barbering remains a specialist occupation, and in many places, where the climate is suitable, is carried out in the street, where the light is better (Pl 189). Similarly, throughout the Roman period in Britain, it was the convention to wear hair cut short (Croom 2002, 66), although presumably there was some regional or ethnic variation in this, and several double-sided boxwood combs from

Plate 188: A small ivory-handled razor

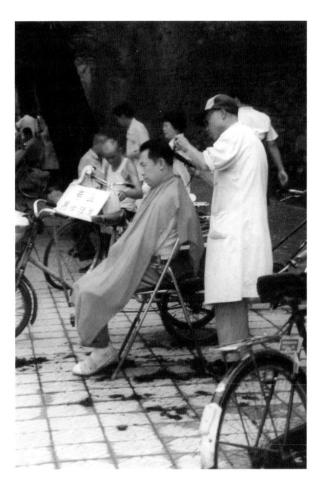

Plate 189: Chinese barbers working in the open air, where the light is best (C Howard-Davis)

the site bear witness to its maintenance (*Ch 19, p 806*). The narrowly-spaced teeth characteristic of one side of these combs allowed them to be used for the removal of head lice, and the remains of a complete louse still adhered to the teeth of one from a foundation trench for Period 3B Building *7394* (*Ch 19*). A small fragment of mirror, probably residual in Period 5 (from layer *2782*), also seems to reflect a concern for appearance (*Ch 17, p 735*). Other aspects of camp hygiene are more nebulous, although some features seem to have accumulated human cess and/or animal waste on a fairly casual basis, along with moss, frequently used for personal cleaning (*Ch 22, p 929*). The Period 6 *principia* seems to have had a well-constructed latrine inserted in Period 6B (*Ch 9*), but no large communal latrines, of the type seen at Housesteads (Collingwood and Richmond 1976, 38) on Hadrian's Wall, were encountered. Environmental evidence suggests that the large numbers of flies and other insects breeding in what appear to have been puddles of rotting waste in some parts of the site, could have been significant vectors in the spread of disease. Some of the species are known to carry pathogens and the eggs of internal parasites into human housing. In particular, the two commonest, the house fly, *Musca domestica,* and the stable fly, *Stomoxys calcitrans*, can

spread salmonella, typhoid, diarrhoea, and possibly even poliomyelitis (*Ch 22, p 926*).

The presence of herbs with potentially medicinal uses perhaps indicates medical treatment, a likelihood confirmed by the presence of an altar to Asclepius, the god of health (*Ch 21, p 872*). However, it seems that altars to Asclepius might be particularly associated with central-range buildings, particularly the commanding officer's accommodation (*praetorium*) and the *principia* (Tomlin and Hassall 2001, 390 n 20), perhaps offering a more general protection for the health of the fort, rather than that of the individual. Although it is likely that the inhabitants of the fort held religious beliefs, both at a personal and institutional level, nothing other than a few fragments of statuary were found (*Ch 21*) that might illuminate this facet of their daily lives.

Recreation is an essential human need, and most of a soldier's life was probably rather boring. Glass and bone gaming counters make it obvious that gambling was one pastime, their distribution implying that workshops and the main road outside the *principia* were favoured spots, both presumably providing a focus for gossip. It has been suggested (*Ch 20, pp 863-4*) that the numbers scratched on the back of some bone counters might mean that they were the equivalent of tallies or even gambling chips, rather than pieces in a board game, and betting would almost certainly have taken place. In addition, large numbers of eating and drinking vessels were found on or close to the main roads (*Ch 16, p 616*), perhaps again indicating that much of the social life of the fort took place outside, at least in good weather. Very few lamps were found amongst the pottery and metalwork, this absence perhaps emphasising the problems in providing good light at night, especially in the winter, when northern days are very short, whilst in the summer, when they are long, the area around the *principia*, the main focus of the fort, would seem an obvious place to gather. Other more strenuous activities would have included hunting, which clearly provided a significant pastime for officers at least, and fishing, hinted at in both timber forts (Periods 3 and 4).

Basic literacy and numeracy seem to have been a requirement for most in the army, certainly by the second century AD (Raybould 1999, 129). A few wax writing tablets were recovered, although they had become illegible. A small archive of ink tablets was, however, recovered from the Annetwell Street excavations, reflecting a life dominated by regulation and administration (Tomlin 1998). There was, in addition, a relatively large number of iron styli (*Ch 17, pp 751-2*), found in ones or twos, and at least two samian inkwells, all implying that the need to read and write percolated down the ranks; indeed, it was not unusual for slaves and freedmen to be literate, and it is becoming increasingly clear that senior officers and their families maintained a lively correspondence (Bowman 1994), either in their own hand or through a scribe, evidence suggesting that the situation was little different amongst the lower ranks.

The extramural settlement that grew rapidly to the south of the fort would have provided a range of less tangible services, including taverns for drinking and eating, prostitutes, or more respectable young women to woo. None of these activities can be attested archaeologically at Carlisle, but literary references from second-century Syria paint a vivid contemporary picture:

> The soldiers from Antioch were wont to spend their time applauding actors, and were more often found in the nearest tavern garden than in the ranks. Horses shaggy from neglect, but every hair plucked from their riders... Withal the men were better clothed than armed, so much so that Pontius Laelianus, ... a disciplinarian of the old school, in some cases ripped up their cuirasses with his finger tips, he found horses saddled with cushions, and by his orders the pommels on them were slit

open and the down plucked from the saddles of the cavalry as from geese... Gambling was rife in camp, sleep night-long, or if a watch was kept, it was over the wine cups (Fronto: *Letter to Lucius Verus xix*; Lewis and Reinhold 1966, 511–12).

From Roman to Norman: the 'Dark Earths' of Period 7

The long period from the apparent abandonment of the fort during the fifth century to the appearance on the site of clearly medieval activity in the late eleventh or twelfth century is not easy to characterise in terms of its artefact assemblage. There is no doubt that deposition continued, although in precisely what manner is a matter for debate (*Ch 14*). There are hints, in the form of imported amphora sherds of late fourth- or fifth-century type (*Ch 16, p 573*), that rubbish was still being deposited, at least in the immediate post-Roman period. A single hairpin from layer *5199* could be of seventh- to ninth-century date and thus also broadly contemporary with Period 7 activity (*Ch 17, p 732*). In addition, there was possibly continued deposition of ostensibly late Roman material, like bangles, beads, and other occasional personal items (suggesting they were still being worn), perhaps alongside more drastic disturbance (presumably anthropogenic) which continued to turn over the earlier Roman deposits, bringing objects like a later first- or second-century glass bangle and a second- to early third-century knee brooch (from Period 7 layers *5296* and *2139* respectively) up from considerably earlier levels. It seems probable that the situation was really somewhere between the two, with highly Romanised groups continuing to exploit the area, perhaps doing no more than using it as a quarry to be scavenged and turned over for recyclable goods, or as a dump for their own waste, or even to exploit the (presumably) nutrient-rich soils as agricultural land.

The large proportion of some objects, most notably iron nails (*Ch 17, p 754*), might point towards this continued mixing, as, though these objects are effectively undatable, they can be associated closely with Roman building techniques, and are considerably more likely to have derived from decaying Roman buildings than from later structures. In all, 653 nails or fragments were recovered from Period 7 deposits. Comprising 16.5% of the nails from the site, this would seem to imply some considerable disturbance, as these were found throughout the succession of Period 7 deposits. The animal bone assemblage from the period was large but in poor condition (*Ch 22, p 904*), much presumably redeposited from disturbance of the large Period 6C deposits seen around the *principia*, although a substantial element of new material was still entering the deposits, as is shown by radiocarbon dates on bone from pit *5375* (*Ch 11; Appendix 16*).

A few fragments of 'wavy-edge' horseshoes and fiddle-key horseshoe nails (*Ch 17, pp 753-4*), sometimes, but not exclusively, associated with pre-Norman activity (Clark 1995, 95), were also noted amongst the finds from this period, although they continued to appear in medieval levels (Period 8). It is, however, increasingly evident that these were probably coming into use during the late Roman period, and continued with little change in their appearance into the twelfth century, when their numbers in the Carlisle assemblage increased significantly. What is clear, however, is that this disturbance was frequent and continued, with the few typically early medieval artefacts, dating to the

ninth to twelfth centuries, being themselves found as residual objects in Period 8 layers. As a result of this prolonged disturbance, it is impossible to create a clear picture of the changing life and activities of people living in the area at this time.

Medieval Occupancy of the Site

Medieval buildings

Continued disturbance, and the restricted area available for excavation, has made it difficult to reconstruct the appearance of Period 8 buildings within the curtilage of the medieval castle, although later buildings erected over the backfilled ditch (*1231*) marking its southern boundary were better preserved (Fig 278). The earliest evidence for medieval buildings comes from within

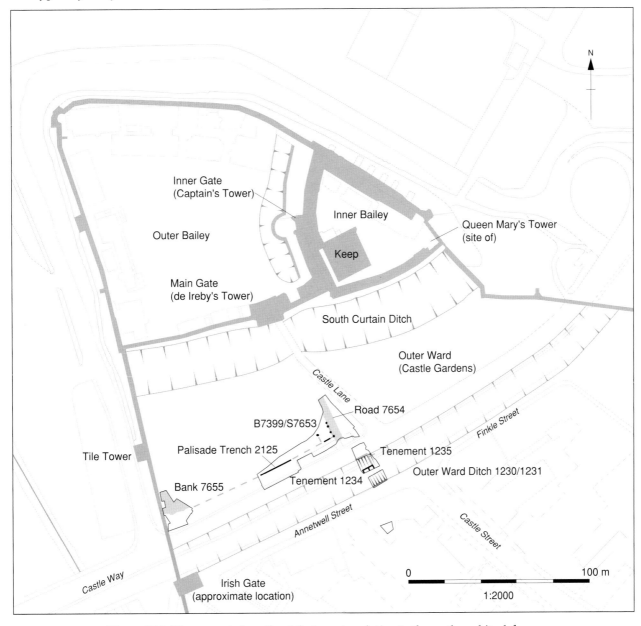

Figure 278: The excavated medieval features in relation to the castle and its defences

the outer ward of the castle (Buildings **7653** and **7399**), where massive postholes make it clear that they were at least in part timber-built, with earthfast posts, and, in the case of Period 8B Building **7399**, extremely large (*Ch 11*). At this level in the stratigraphic sequence within the castle, the associated deposits were not waterlogged, and so no timbers survived to help with precise dates, or contribute to any analysis of the appearance or status of the buildings. Waterlogged timbers from the later buildings to the south (those encroaching on ditch **1231**) appear to suggest that there was little difference between the medieval treatment of timbers, and the nature of the above-ground framing, from their Roman predecessors, and without dendrochronological analysis, they would have been impossible to differentiate.

Most of the timbers from Period 8iii tenements **1234** and **1235** were of oak, from relatively small trees (0.3–0.4 m in diameter), and where it could be determined, they were radially split (*Ch 19, p 803*). Within the castle, however, the post pipes within some of the postholes of an earlier building (**7399**) point to considerably larger timbers, *c* 0.6 m in diameter (*Ch 11; Fig 279*) There is no evidence to suggest that any of the medieval buildings were roofed with ceramic or stone tiles, and only one, extremely small, fragment of window glass was associated with tenement **1234** (Period 8iv, layer **1313**; *Ch 18, p 773*). Conventionally, medieval window glass has only been associated with high-status and / or ecclesiastical buildings (Oakley and Hunter 1979). It is not impossible that this tiny fragment was residual, having been dumped in the upper fills of the ditch, coming from high-status accommodation within the castle. It has become apparent, however, that glass windows were also to be found in good-quality town houses (*ibid*), and it is as likely that the glass was actually from the house that probably stood on the tenement from the late fourteenth century (*Ch 11*).

The problems of residuality were as rife in the medieval assemblage as they had been in the Roman; indeed, they increased rather than diminished with regard to medieval buildings. There is a strong possibility that some fragments of the Period 6 buildings stood for several hundred years (*Ch 10*), and there seems to have been a continued and possibly systematic disturbance of the site as a whole during Period 7. Inevitably, this brought a great number of Roman finds up into the 'dark earth' layers. The intensity of this disturbance might well have abated by the end of the eleventh century, when a coin of William II (AD 1087-1100) was lost on what was probably the contemporary ground surface (*Ch 17, p 686*). The twelfth century would have seen renewed large-scale disturbance of the site, by clearance and building, as the castle was enhanced (*Ch 11*). This would have been compounded by the

excavation of the massive ditch (**1230**, later recut as **1231**), cutting a deep swathe (*c* 20 m wide and *c* 4.5 m deep) through waterlogged Roman deposits, and marking the southern limits of the castle (Fig 278). As a result, significant amounts of Roman timbers and leatherwork were redeposited within dumped medieval deposits. In addition, there is evidence to suggest that the medieval builders and road-workers on the site sought out Roman tile and stonework to use as hardcore and levelling on road **7654**, apparently leading up towards the castle's gatehouse.

Period 8A

Timber building **7653** (Fig 279) seems to have been the earliest medieval structure on the site, and associated red gritty wares would point to occupation in the twelfth century (*Ch 16, p 665*). As there were no surviving floors or any of the occupation deposits that must have accumulated upon them, contemporary finds cannot help in refining the dating, or in giving any indication of what might have gone on within. The likelihood of an arcaded front (*Ch 11*), based on earth-set posts, unlike the other walls, which were unbonded dwarf stone walls, presumably supporting a timber frame, and the wide (2 m) doorway, might suggest an agricultural or similar use. There were few associated finds, although an iron horseshoe fragment came from post-pit **5121** inside the building, and other fragments were associated with the cobbled road, **7654**, onto which it opened, showing clearly that shod mounts passed along it. Not surprisingly, pit **5282**, also associated with the road, produced recognisable residual Roman material, but no medieval finds (*Ch 11*). Whilst the dating of Building **7653** is imprecise, the presence of two copper-alloy hairpins, both possibly of ninth- to tenth-century date (one from cobbles **5205**, associated with the building, the other from layer **5137**) might add weight to the likelihood of activity pre-dating the Norman Castle. It should be remembered that the *Anglo-Saxon Chronicle* recorded the expulsion of one Dolfin from Carlisle in 1092 (Earle and Plummer 1892), although the precise site of his residence is unknown.

Period 8B

Building **7653** was demolished and replaced by a considerably larger structure, Building **7399** (*Ch 11*). Again, apart from the ground plan, showing it to have been constructed from massive earthfast timbers (Fig 279), there is little evidence for its appearance, or for what might have gone on inside, as no floors or occupation deposits survived. Pottery suggests a late twelfth- or early thirteenth-century date for its construction (*Ch 16, p 665*), although it should be noted that, given the size of the building, there were very few fragments, and as they were small and from posthole fills, they are unlikely to have been in their original place of deposition.

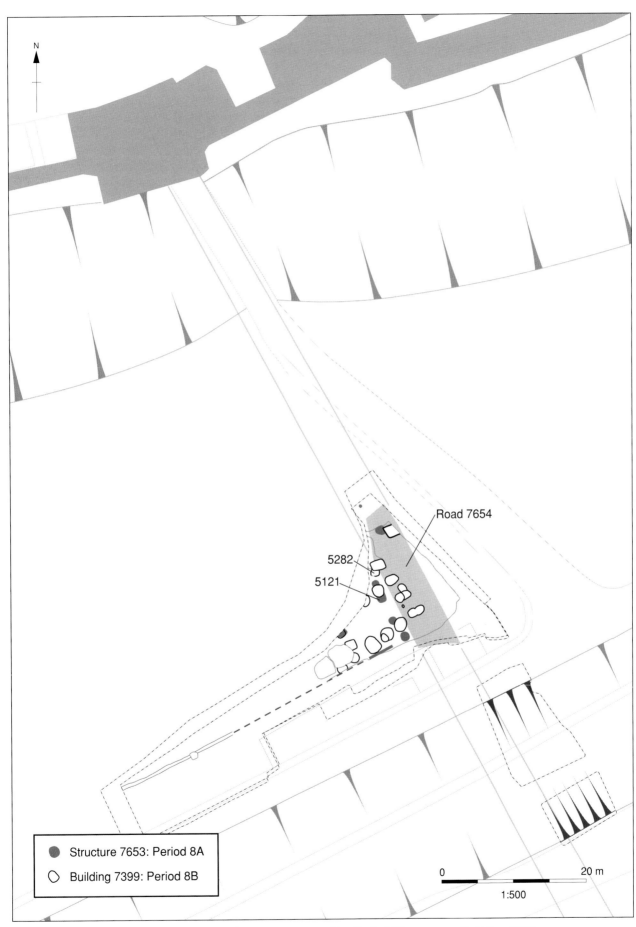

N

Road 7654

5282

5121

Structure 7653: Period 8A

Building 7399: Period 8B

0   20 m

1:500

*Figure 279: Period 8A Structure **7653** and its Period 8B successor, Building **7399***

531

The sheer size of the building might suggest that it was of considerable importance, a hall, or perhaps a barn, but there were no finds that could be linked directly with activity inside. Like the pottery, other finds came from the postholes, and could thus be either residual or associated with its demolition. Simple bone knife handles and a toggle or bobbin were made from almost unmodified sheep metapodials, and are effectively undatable (*Ch 20, p 863*). Other finds include horseshoes, and a flat-bladed socketed arrowhead came from posthole *5164* (fill *5166*). The latter is a long-lived type, but whether it was linked with hunting or military activity cannot be determined.

Period 8E

A denuded earthen bank, **7655** (Fig 278), possibly originated in Period 8E. Finds do little to elucidate either its purpose, or the date of its construction, and inevitably they included an element of redeposited Roman material. There was, however, a group of medieval pottery, within which Fully Reduced wares were probably intrusive (*Ch 16, pp 666-7*), and the presence of eighteenth- to twentieth-century glass vessels (*Ch 18, p 772*) seems to confirm some post-medieval disturbance.

Period 8i

There proved to be no stratigraphic links between the structures within the castle ward and the creation of the outer defences (*Ch 11*; Fig 278). Finds from the fills of the original massive ditch (**1230**), which cut deep into the Roman layers beneath, are inevitably very mixed; and apart from the pottery, dated to the twelfth to thirteenth centuries (*Ch 16*), nothing amongst the inorganic finds can be regarded as unequivocally medieval in date. A small and mixed group of leather, including Roman tentage, but with six medieval shoes (*Ch 20, p 840*), suggests that infilling began quite soon after its construction, with a sole of late eleventh- to early twelfth-century type giving the earliest date. The shoe was quite worn, however, and possibly quite old when discarded. The remainder of the shoes can be dated to the mid-thirteenth century or later, but it is possible that the latest was introduced when the ditch was recut (**1231**).

Period 8ii

It seems probable that ditch **1230**, having been allowed to silt, was recut, probably in the late thirteenth century, possibly as a result of Scottish attacks in AD 1296-7 (*Ch 14*), although it was almost immediately allowed to fill again. Stratigraphic evidence suggests that most of the material entered the ditch from the north side, suggesting that the inhabitants of the castle regarded it as a convenient repository for waste. The finds from the recut ditch (**1231**) are again very mixed, and include a considerable amount of residual Roman material. The dating of the associated pottery is not particularly conclusive, but considered alongside dating evidence from the shoes (Pl 190), confirms a largely fourteenth-century date for the fills. Extensive waterlogging meant that there was a considerable assemblage of leatherwork (*Ch 20*), originating, presumably, from households of all ranks associated with the castle. Objects amongst the leatherwork include a decorated knife sheath and the suspension straps for hanging a knife or sword from the waist, leather from a possible bellows, and a range of shoes, the fashionable nature of some suggesting their original owners were of fairly high status,

Plate 190: One of several medieval shoes found in medieval outer ward ditch **1231**

although it is also likely that they passed down the social scale through a succession of wearersm (*Ch 20, p 843*). There are, in addition, two typically medieval knives, both much-used, with worn triangular blades (*Ch 17, p 748*), and a spindle whorl made from a Fully Reduced green-glazed potsherd (*Ch 18, p 777*).

Period 8iii

The growth of Carlisle during the fourteenth century presumably began to put pressure on available space, and it can be attested historically that the tenements facing onto the north side of Annetwell Street began to encroach on Crown land, their boundaries soon extending over the fills of ditch *1231* (*Ch 11*), despite the fact that these were demonstrably wet and presumably unstable.

Tenement 1234

Building *1492* (Fig 280) stood within tenement *1234*, and was represented by a series of ground-laid oak sill beams, probably dating to the fourteenth century (*Ch 11*). There is, however, nothing amongst the timber to illustrate the appearance of the building or what went on inside, although a small fragment of window glass from layer *1313* might hint at one or more glazed windows. A few trampled sherds of Partially Reduced ware vessels came from floors *1668* and *1671*, but no other finds were associated with the building itself. The material assemblage from elsewhere within the tenement is equally uninformative, comprising a single harness fitting, a bent dress or hairpin, and a few nails. Waterlogging preserved a group of leather, mainly shoes, which also suggest a mid-thirteenth- to mid-fourteenth-century date, presumably discarded by the occupants of Building *1492*, along with cobbling waste, suggesting the repair and modification of footwear. This is quite likely to have been an everyday domestic activity, rather than evidence for a skilled tradesman (*Ch 20, p 842*). An archer's bracer was found in the construction trench (*1788*) for the northern boundary fence (*2065*), one post in which had a felling date of spring/summer AD 1385 (*Appendix 16*). This implies the use of a bow, but in what social context cannot now be determined, although the somewhat *ad hoc* nature of the object, being made from a worn shoe sole, might suggest that it was a fairly workaday item. A decorated leather panel, from a smallish container, possibly a quiver, might add to this evidence for archery (*Ch 20, p 842*).

Tenement 1235

No building survived on the neighbouring property (tenement *1235*; Fig 280) and thus none of the finds can be directly linked to contemporary activity. Pottery from Period 8iii comprised a similar range to that found within *1234* (*Ch 16, p 669*), whereas most of the other finds were relatively featureless fragments of iron nails.

Period 8iv

The two tenements and the remains of the structures upon them were eventually overlain by a series of soil deposits (*Ch 11*). The range of pottery fabrics within these suggests a considerable amount of residuality and, as in Period 8iii, the range of other material was limited, although more recognisable artefacts, including knife blades with maker's marks (Pl 191), a pair of small shears, probably for needle-working (Pl 192), and a bone tuning peg, were also found (*Ch 17, p 749; Ch 20, p 864*). Such objects seem to indicate households of some pretension, but whether they represent the rubbish of the Period 8iii inhabitants, or were dumped from elsewhere, is unknown. Both tenements produced more leatherwork, mainly shoes, of late fourteenth- to early fifteenth-century date, and cobbling waste, but also including part of a small leather ball (*Ch 20, p 857*), suggesting that at least some members of the household had time for leisure.

People and pastimes

There is only a restricted range of evidence for the appearance of the medieval occupants of either the castle, or the tenements that encroached on the part-filled outer ditch (*1231*) in the fourteenth and fifteenth centuries. Only their footwear survived in any quantity, that of the former dumped in ditch *1231*, and that of the latter deposited within the confines of the tenements which expanded from Annetwell Street northwards over the backfilled ditch (*Ch 11*). It is again a salutary lesson that, without these waterlogged deposits, there would have been little left of the personal lives of the many people who passed through the site.

Whilst there were undoubtedly women of both high status and low living and working in and around the castle, very little survives to illustrate their appearance. There were three decorative hair or dress pins, all from Period 8A contexts, along with three smaller dress pins, often used to fix the complex folds of veils or other garments (Egan and Forsyth 1997), amongst the later finds from ditch *1231*. Carved bone comb cases, like the fragment from Period 8D pit *5072* (*Ch 19*), are also regarded as female possessions, and a plain wooden double-sided comb came from the boundary between tenements *1234* and *1235*.

The situation is not much clearer for the male inhabitants during the medieval period. Amongst the leather dumped in the outer ditch there were knife sheaths and the suspension straps for fitting either these or a sword to a belt, as well as the archer's wristguard (*Ch 20, p 855*). Three iron arrowheads were also found, one each in Periods 8A, 8B, and 8C (*Ch 17, p 710*); alongside the leatherwork, these seem to suggest the presence of armed men in and around the castle and the later tenements, which is not surprising.

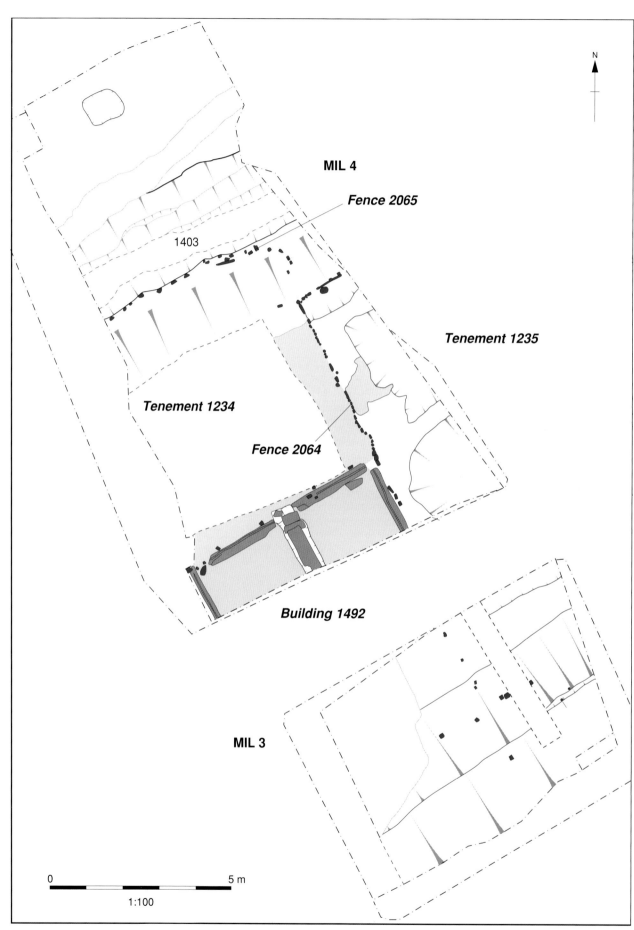

N

MIL 4

Fence 2065

1403

Tenement 1235

Tenement 1234

Fence 2064

Building 1492

MIL 3

0   5 m

1:100

*Figure 280: Tenements **1234** and **1235***

Plate 191: A medieval knife blade with a maker's mark

The range of footwear, dating from the late eleventh/twelfth to the early fifteenth centuries, suggests that some inhabitants, at least, were keen followers of fashion, but it is clear, from the amount of remodelling and repair, that boots and shoes which started life on the feet of relatively wealthy members of (presumably) elite households, ended, some time later, cut down, patched, and repaired, on the feet of rather more humble people. The wear patterns of several shoes imply painful foot problems, with one seeming to imply that the wearer, if not a child, was club-footed (*Ch 20, p 852*). Otherwise, there is remarkably little evidence to indicate the appearance of the medieval inhabitants, a few small fragments of a coarse woollen fabric, perhaps from a garment with leather trimmings, coming from ditch *1231*. The presence, amongst the animal bone assemblage, of cats (both adult and kittens) skinned for their fur (*Ch 22, p 916*), throws a sidelight on clothing, and it seems likely that, on occasion, catskin provided fur trimmings for the clothes of the medieval inhabitants of Carlisle.

Horses, some of them quite elderly, would have provided transport or served as draught animals. Men and, on occasion, women of high social status would have ridden to the hunt (Woolley 2002), accompanied by large dogs, those from the site being between 0.55 m and 0.70 m to the shoulder (*Appendix 12, p 1470*). More or less contemporary illustrations, like the fifteenth-century Devonshire hunting tapestries (Woolley 2002), give a good indication of the wealth and conspicuous display of a formal hunt, little of which survives in the archaeological record.

Evidence for what might be described as more 'refined' pastimes is restricted to the Period 8iv layers within tenements *1234* and *1235*. The small pair of iron shears (Pl 192) were probably used in needlework, a

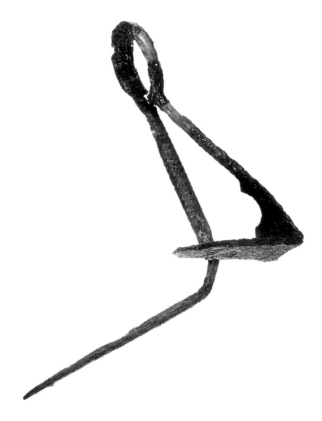

Plate 192: A small pair of iron shears, now bent, but originally used in household needlework

well-known occupation for the medieval lady and her retinue (Girouard 1989, 24), and the single bone tuning peg hints at musical accompaniment. A leather ball from tenement *1235* perhaps suggests more boisterous games (*Ch 20, p 857*).

Putting food on a later table

It is not entirely clear from what kinds of household the food remains from Period 8 derived, and it is possible that they reflect the consumption patterns of a fairly wide social range. What is likely, however, is that much of it, deposited in the outer ward or dumped in the outer ward ditch (*1230/1231*), derives from provisioning the castle household over an extended period from the late twelfth to the mid-fourteenth centuries. As a royal castle, Carlisle was governed by a constable (Summerson 1990, 130), who would have headed a large and wide-ranging establishment capable of accommodating the royal household. It would have comprised a considerable number of people, of all social stations, and a wide range of skills, who would all need to be fed (Fig 281). To this end, evidence for food consumption should range from the most humble to sumptuous meals fit, quite literally, for a king. Indeed, it seems to have been the case that food was the largest expenditure of the aristocratic budget (Dyer 1989, 55). Later material (Periods 8iii and 8iv) can be associated with the domestic arrangements of tenements *1234* and *1235*, which appear to have been occupied by moderately well-to-do citizens.

Figure 281: A family dinner, as depicted in the Luttrell Psalter

As in the Roman period, the most obvious information about what people on the site were eating, and how it was raised, came from the animal bone assemblage, which was better preserved in the medieval period than in Period 7. Inevitably, the assemblage was dominated by the bones of the three principal meat-providing species and, as in the Roman period, cattle predominated, but with the importance of sheep/goat marginally outweighing that of pig (*Ch 22, p 920*). It is clear that beef was by far the favoured meat of medieval households, frequently comprising 50% of the flesh consumed, and much of it came from older animals (often used for traction) at the end of their useful lives (Dyer 1989, 60). This can be seen amongst the material examined, where there was a marked incidence of deformity of the feet, as a result of being used to pull heavy loads (*Appendix 12, p 1466*).

There seems little difference in the manner in which animals were processed in the Roman and medieval periods, with both butchery and food waste amongst the material examined. It is interesting, however, that there was a marked increase in the medieval period in the number of metapodials that had been split longitudinally, which may represent a greater interest in producing raw material for bone working (*Appendix 12, p 1461*). This possibility is perhaps reinforced by an apparent decline in the presence of sawn red deer antler, perhaps implying that the latter was declining in importance or in availability as a raw material, a phenomenon that may have been connected with the restriction of red deer to royal parks, where they were the prerogative of the King, from the Norman Conquest onwards (MacGregor 1985, 32).

An increase in the numbers of female cattle, and the occasional occurrence of neonates, might well suggest that the beef was being drawn from herds kept principally for dairying (*Ch 22, p 909*). A rise in the number of adult sheep/goat could, in the same light, suggest that these were being kept for

wool, although there was also an increase in juvenile individuals, possibly implying increased interest in meat and milk (*Ch 22, p 909*). Although there is no corroborative evidence, it is perhaps possible that this dichotomy implies animals brought to the site for two different tables, with elderly mutton for the common man, and lamb for the social elite. Indeed, debris from the butchery and preparation of meat for the elite table is an obvious component of the medieval assemblage, apparently pertaining to consumption within the castle. The evidence seems to imply that pigs were smaller than hitherto, and an age at death which ranges from neonate to elderly adult has been taken to imply that many of these animals could have been kept within the town, possibly by individuals, in the manner widespread in the post-medieval period (*Appendix 12, p 1458*). To this end, the pig is cheap to feed on kitchen waste and produces copious returns in the form of large and frequent litters. Enamel hypoplasia seen in the teeth of one medieval individual might imply a poor or restricted diet, as might be the case in a confined animal (*Ch 22, p 908*).

Considerable numbers of domestic fowl were noted amongst the medieval bone assemblage, a mixture of mature and immature individuals perhaps suggesting that they were locally kept, for eggs and a ready supply of meat for the table. Goose and mallard were also noted, all adult birds, but it is unclear whether these were domesticated or taken in the wild. Swan and grey heron, both served at the elite medieval table (Woolgar 1999), were probably hunted, herons being a favoured game for falconers (Woolley 2002, 31), but swans were also bred for the table, swanneries being tightly controlled by the Crown (*ibid*). Hare was also present, presumably provided by hunting.

Wild resources are well represented by red, roe, and fallow deer, the former in the greatest quantities. There is some doubt as to whether fallow deer failed to thrive after their introduction late in the Roman period, being reintroduced by the Normans (MacGregor 1985, 34), and certainly both this species and roe deer were not present in large quantities. Red deer was regarded as the principal animal of the chase, its taking being restricted to the King and his associates. The amount of deer consumed by an elite household seemed to vary considerably with circumstance, but it is clear that venison played an important role in the gift exchange that reinforced relationships within and between elite households (Dyer 1989, 60–1). It is thus without doubt that the butchered red deer in Period 8A Building *7653*, and Period 8B Building *7399*, both in the outer ward, and in the fills of the outer ward ditch, had been destined for the tables of nobility, and possibly only that of the most senior (*ibid*). That is not to say that it was necessarily consumed within the buildings where it was found, and the presence of butchery waste might imply that these were service buildings of some kind, or that it had been kept for some secondary use. Similarly, its presence in the ditch presumably indicates that waste from the castle kitchens was being dumped outside, presumably as far away from elite accommodation as possible.

Although the evidence is restricted to a few bones from the outer ward ditch, it seems likely that large cod were on occasion consumed (*Ch 22, p 921*). Although seldom recovered archaeologically, fish played a large part in the medieval diet, its consumption being associated with the two or three days of ritual abstinence expected of the laity every week (Dyer 1989, 61), and these few bones make it clear that deep-sea fish were getting to the site, presumably as dried or salted stockfish. Alongside this, small amounts of oysters, mussels, and whelks were found in the outer ward ditch fills and on the later tenements (*Appendix 12*).

Seeds from a limited number of medieval pits seem to reflect a remarkably similar range of material to that of the Roman period, especially within the stone fort (Period 6), with cereals (wheat and oats) and wild fruits, such as strawberry and blackberry. Material from the primary fills of ditch *1230* (Period 8i) suggests the consumption of apple/pear, hazelnuts, and bilberry, implying once again that wild fruits and nuts were a welcome addition to the diet (*Ch 22, p 934*).

Pottery gives some illustration of the range of kitchen and tablewares used for cooking and serving food.

The range was restricted, and differed little from that seen elsewhere in Carlisle (McCarthy and Brooks 1988; 1992). In the twelfth and thirteenth centuries, unglazed jars, usually with sagging bases, were used for cooking, extensive sooting suggesting that they were placed in the embers of the hearth. As the most commonly found form amongst the medieval pottery from the site (*Ch 16, p 663*), it seems likely that most (those from the outer ward and its defensive ditch) came from the castle kitchens. Jugs were the second most common form and were used mainly for the storage and serving of liquids, although these were not the only uses to which jugs could be put (McCarthy and Brooks 1988, fig 45). It is a feature of Carlisle pottery during the medieval period that it was relatively plain (*Ch 16, p 663*), and it is likely that such simple vessels were used not only in the kitchen, but also at table, even at an elevated social level, although it is possible that metal vessels were used in such circles. The repertoire of other pottery forms is very limited, probably reflecting the widespread use of wooden vessels, like that found in ditch *1231*, at table (*Ch 19, p 810*).

In Conclusion

The huge range of finds from the site demonstrates, on occasion quite startlingly, the very special nature of archaeological deposits in Carlisle. The extensive waterlogging has preserved a wealth of organic objects, mainly of wood and leather, that do not normally survive in the archaeological record. It is a salutary lesson that, without this organic survival, the assemblage would have been half the size, and our understanding of the site much more fragmentary.

It can thus be seen that, draped over the framework of the stratigraphic succession, analysis of the finds can add depth and detail to an archaeological reconstruction of the site. The information available is inevitably patchy and inconsistent, the conclusions drawn often subjective, but it is this more holistic approach that starts to 'bring things alive' and perhaps allows a fuller picture to be painted of the lives of the men and women whose abandoned buildings and jettisoned rubbish, accumulated over almost 2000 years, was examined by the Carlisle Millennium Project.

Period	No vessels	No sherds	Weight (g)	% Burnt sherds
0	1	1	4	0
2	1	1	2	0
3A	134	200	1326	11
3B	73	121	1027	29
3C	57	118	1034	11
3D	23	56	232	45
3E	22	30	185	14
4A	209	304	2158	9
4A/B	82	172	2059	16
4B	237	349	2583	9
4C	34	50	461	8
4D	9	29	174	0
4-5	6	10	156	20
5	29	49	423	14
5A	64	105	1135	12
5B	88	164	944	7
5C	51	87	1055	4
5D	58	76	852	9
6A	125	176	1275	7
6B	58	73	513	12
6C	46	64	518	9
6D	19	23	119	0
6E	13	14	179	15
7	58	62	521	16
8	163	204	1517	3
9	33	43	266	6
Unstratified	64	81	714	14
Total	**1757**	**2662**	**21,432**	**289**

Table 11: Quantification of samian vessel classes by percentage of weight, sherd-count, and EREs

16

ROMAN AND POST-ROMAN POTTERY

The Samian

M Ward

The samian assemblage comprised 2662 sherds, weighing 21.43 kg in total, and representing a maximum of 1757 vessels (48.8 EVES). It was in a relatively good state of preservation, although most vessels were represented by only small or medium-sized sherds (average weight 8 g), with as much as 24% of the material unattributable to form; in contrast, at least 36 vessels presented complete or near-complete profiles. There was a maximum of 442 moulded bowls (326 retaining decoration) and one rouletted example; up to 26 beakers were recorded (18 of them from South Gaul), of which ten retained decoration.

The greater part of the assemblage (60%) was produced in South Gaul, 38% in Central Gaul, and only 2% in East Gaul. At least 13% of the assemblage was burnt, comprising vessels that ranged across all dates and periods (see Table 11). Around 12% of the collection showed evidence of wear or secondary use, including graffiti, repairs, reworking, and reuse (see *Appendix 2* for a catalogue of the graffiti).

The collection bears close comparison with those from other sites excavated in Carlisle, at Blackfriars Street, Castle Street, Tullie House, and Annetwell Street (Dickinson 1990; 1991a; 1992; in prep). Parallels were drawn with eight vessels from the published corpus (see *2, 18–19, 20, 23, 35, 40, 43, pp 553, 556, 559-61*), and further examination would doubtless reveal an even closer relationship between individual sites.

Terminology and methodology

The products of the samian industry were highly standardised and, as a result, their study and publication have developed along similar lines across the whole of western Europe; the internationally accepted terminology is employed here. The abbreviations 'SG', 'CG', and 'EG' denote vessels which were produced in South Gaulish, Central Gaulish, and East Gaulish workshops. Hartley and Dickinson's numbering system for the *Names on* terra sigillata: *an index of makers' stamps and signatures in*

Gallo-Roman sigillata *(samian ware)* (2008a; 2008b; forthcoming) has been employed, using Roman numerals in lower case following the potter's name. Vessel types are Dragendorff's form numbers unless otherwise stated; for an explanation of this and other terminology, see Webster (1996).

All the material was examined and quantified by sherd-count, sherd-weight, and EVE (estimated vessel equivalents: Orton 1989), data being recorded on a Microsoft Access database. Full details of sherds and numbers of vessels, including weights and measurements of rims for EVEs, were recorded. Decorated vessels were selected for illustration on the basis of intrinsic interest or significance to the site. Date-ranges, such as *c* AD 70-110, or *c* AD 120-200, have generally been given in preference to epochs (*eg* Flavian-Trajanic or Hadrianic-Antonine), but the date-ranges should not be regarded as any more precise.

Although measurements for EVEs were recorded, this manner of recording has been so little employed in samian reports that comparisons are currently impossible (Willis 1998, 94). Estimated maximum numbers of vessels are given here. The estimation of minimum numbers is, however, considered very misleading, especially with such a large collection, containing many small fragments of the same date, origin, and form. It is, for instance, impossible that the 145 South Gaulish fragments of indeterminate form, in varying fabrics but dated loosely within the wide date-range of *c* AD 70-110, belonged to only one vessel. In fact, the number of vessels represented will have been far closer to the maximum of 145 than to the minimum of one. However unsatisfactory such estimation is, maximum numbers of vessels may be thought to be closest to the truth in the specific case of samian ware. Taking the wider view, provision of measurements for EVEs will facilitate the integration of the samian ware into the pottery assemblage as a whole.

Nature of the assemblage

The stratified material comprised 2581 sherds, representing a maximum of 1694 vessels, found in approximately 800 contexts and averaging just over three sherds per context. The remaining 81 sherds (a maximum of 64 vessels), found in all five sites, were not closely phased or unstratified (Table 11). The distribution of the pottery between the sites by vessel count was: MIL 1, 13%; MIL 2, 2%; MIL 3, 3%; MIL 4, 6%; MIL 5, 76%.

As might be expected, most of the material was recovered from Periods 3 (18%), 4 (32%), and 5 (17%), which together encompass the years during which samian pottery is known to have been produced (Table 11). In Period 6 (producing 15% of the total assemblage), it can be presumed that the later vessels, at least, were in use during Period 6A. Period 7 contexts, dating to a time when the samian industry had long ceased production, contained 3% of the assemblage; 9% was found in medieval contexts (Period 8), and 2% was recovered from the few post-medieval contexts (Period 9). Material from Period 7 onwards can be regarded as residual with complete confidence.

In general, the sherds were thinly distributed; 378 contexts contained only single sherds and 75% of all contexts produced three or less. There was, however, a group of 13 contexts, which had 20 sherds or more. For instance, Period 3D demolition layer *1809* (in Building **2061**) contained 26 fragments, although these represented only seven vessels, of which four were probably residual, the fragments deriving from vessels first recorded in Period 3B. The assemblage consisted mainly of small- to medium-sized fragments, averaging *c* 8 g per sherd. Average sherd weight was, however, markedly greater in some periods than in others, partly as a result of the presence of a small number of large sherds in some (for example Period 8C). Some 36 vessels (2% of the total), found throughout the Roman periods and later, presented complete or near-complete profiles: two were found in Period 8 (fill *1698* of outer ward ditch **1231** and fill *1409* of ditch *1403*), including Stamp *25* dated to *c* AD 115-40. A Flavian cup of form 27g was recovered from Period 9 (*2103*, the fill of a construction trench for the modern subway).

A maximum of 442 moulded bowls was recognised, forming 25% of the total assemblage, of which 326 bowls (74%) retained some part of their decoration. Although it is difficult to compare collections which have been quantified differently, this appears to be a substantially larger proportion than the 10% suggested as average (Dickinson 2000, 204), but lower than the proportion of 30% quoted for Ribchester (*ibid*).

Moulded bowls made up 28% of the South and East Gaulish vessels, in comparison with only 20% of

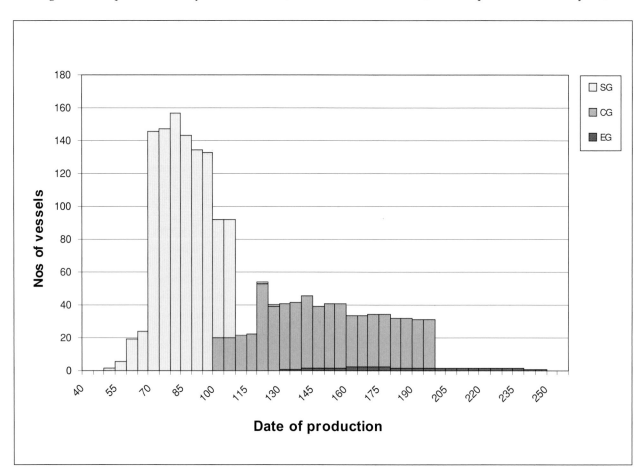

Figure 282: All vessels (maximum numbers) by date of production

those from Central Gaul. As is considered usual, the proportion amongst the products of Les Martres-de-Veyre was larger (31%; cf Darling 1998, 176). Whilst the large proportion of moulded vessels seen amongst the South Gaulish material is predictable, that seen within the East Gaulish vessels could indicate either an increased availability of moulded vessels in the Carlisle market, or perhaps a local preference. On the other hand, it could be an artefact of analysis, and simply reflect the fact that small, undiagnostic fragments of East Gaulish plainwares are difficult to differentiate, and often go unrecognised.

There were 54 stamps and one mould signature (3% of the total assemblage; pp 549-51). Of these, at least five of the stamps were by potters who might be termed illiterate, and 14 were unattributable.

Context and date
South Gaulish products
South Gaulish wares formed 60% of the total assemblage, most being produced during the Flavian period, particularly in the earlier years; they included just over half of the moulded bowls. They comprised, with very few exceptions, products of the La Graufesenque kilns, and 28 of the 29 stamped vessels in the group (53% of the total assemblage) were attributable to La Graufesenque producers. The possible exception, in a slightly unusual fabric, was a dish stamped by Roppus i (Stamp 24), perhaps produced at a pottery in the Lot Valley (Polak 2000, 28ff); a similar fabric was possibly present amongst the unstamped material, but in the absence of chemical analysis this cannot be confirmed. In addition, there was at least one vessel from Banassac (in production c AD 110–50), which was unstratified. This tiny fragment of bowl form 37 showed the same ovolo as one recorded at Old Penrith (Dickinson 1991b, fig 53.72), and Banassac products have been found at other North Western sites, including Lancaster (Dickinson forthcoming) and elsewhere in Carlisle (for example Annetwell Street, Dickinson in prep). Three small, plain fragments from Periods 4A, 5A, and 5C have provisionally been attributed to Montans, although this remains uncertain. In general, Montans products were more common in the North West than those of Banassac, and have been recorded at sites ranging from Wilderspool and Chester to Watercrook, as well as elsewhere in Carlisle (Dickinson 2000, 210).

The large proportion of South Gaulish ware is an outstanding feature of this collection (Fig 282) and reflects the amount of material recovered from early contexts, particularly of Periods 3-4A (Table 12). It includes at least 16 pre-Flavian vessels; although there were none of the exclusively pre-Flavian cup forms (24/25, Ritterling 8, or Ritterling 9; Table 13),

there were at least two fragments from bowls of the predominantly pre-Flavian form Ritterling 12, which can be contrasted with 15 examples of Curle 11, produced in the Flavian or Flavian-Trajanic period. There was also a stamped dish of Crestio that must have been produced as early as c AD 45-65, and around 70 vessels produced in the late-Neronian to Flavian years. The presence of unequivocally pre-Flavian vessels and the large number of Neronian-Flavian products is entirely consistent with the suggested foundation date for the first fort in the early AD 70s.

There were up to 40 vessels of form 29, of which 24 retained some decoration (Table 14), representing 14% of all South Gaulish moulded bowls from the site. At least five are likely to be pre-Flavian products (eg 2, 46, pp 553, 561) and another nine could be (eg 3-4, p 553). Of the eight form 29 vessels recorded in Period 3A contexts (eg 2-5, p 553), one, probably a late-Neronian product, had already seen repair-work by the time it was deposited in demolition debris overlying the remains of Building 7393 (Fig 265), a structure of uncertain purpose (demolition layer 7108). Both the decoration and the repair of this bowl can be compared with an example from period 2 at Castle Street (Dickinson 1991a, fig 287.1).

An early date is also supported by the ratio of form 29 to other decorated forms, most importantly form 37. If only those bowls with surviving moulded decoration are considered, the ratio of form 29 to form 37 is 1:8, but if those without surviving decoration are included, then the ratio becomes 1:6. The same ratio was noted in the Lancaster extramural settlement, although in a much smaller collection (Ward forthcoming a). In contrast, at Walton-le-Dale, an industrial site on the River Ribble near Preston, only one form 29 was present in an assemblage of over 2000 vessels (F Wild pers comm). It is generally held that the original South Gaulish version of form 29 was produced before c AD 85 or AD 90, the latter being the terminus ante quem generally favoured by specialists. The large number of bowls of this form, together with the evidence of the potters' stamps and the plain wares, again supports a pre-Agricolan foundation for the fort, as has also been argued for activity at Castle Street (Dickinson 1991a, 344).

Nine of the stamps fell within the range c AD 70-85/95, including two each by Secundus ii and Calvus i. Two were on moulded bowls of form 29 (Stamps 35, 44, c AD 70–85, both lacking decoration). Of the four stamps dated c AD 80/5–110, the latest were those of Mercator i and L Tr--Masculus.

Much of the unstamped South Gaulish ware appears to have been produced in the earlier Flavian period,

Period	South Gaul	Central Gaul	East Gaul	Total vessels
0	1			1
2	1			1
3A	133	1		134
3B	73			73
3C	55	2		57
3D	22	1		23
3E	21	1		22
4A	188	21		209
4A/B	81	7		88
4B	155	82		237
4C	25	9		34
4D	9			9
5	23	6		29
5A	42	20	2	64
5B	22	64	2	88
5C	7	43	1	51
5D	7	49	2	58
6A	49	70	6	125
6B	12	42	4	58
6C	11	35		46
6D	1	17	1	19
6E		13		13
7	6	43	9	58
8	20	26	1	47
8A	1	12	2	15
8A/B	1			1
8B	1	3	1	5
8C	4	28	1	33
8D	3	9		12
8E	5	3		8
8F	2	7	2	11
8i	7	10		17
8ii	4	5		9
8iii	2			2
8iv		3		3
9	21	11	1	33
Not closely phased	39	23	2	64
Total	**1054**	**666**	**37**	**1757**

Table 12: Quantification of sources of samian vessels by site period

and there are numerous bowls of form 37 in styles associated with such potters as Germanus, Frontinus, and Paullus. One very large bowl shows an ovolo devolved from one used by Frontinus; the moulding is very poor and its general appearance suggests a date after *c* AD 85/90 (see *27, pp 557-8*). A large part of this bowl (26 fragments, including the worn footring), was found incorporated into probable intervallum road *7645* (surface *256*, Period 4A/B). There are several instances of that distinctive ovolo, with a long trident tip turned left, which was used by the group of potters including Albanus iii, Amandus,

and Coii Bass[. Their main period of activity is currently thought to have been from the AD 80s into the Trajanic period. There were also moulded bowls in the style of Mercator i (contemporary with his plainware stamp), and that of L Tr-- Masculus, which have been dated to *c* AD 85–110 (Stamps *17, 34*). In contrast, there were few bowls attributable to the styles of potters such as Masculus and Biragillus, working after *c* AD 85, and such as there were survived as mere fragments. A sherd of form 37 from this latter period was found in occupation layer *2800* (Building *2765*; a smithy workshop of

Form	South Gaul	Central Gaul	East Gaul	Total
Hermet 9	2			2
Curle 11	17	3		20
Curle 15	2	1		3
Curle 21		1		1
Curle 23		1		1
15/17	14			14
15/17 or 18	47			47
15/17 or 15/17R	5			5
15/17R	1	1		2
15/17R or 18R	13			13
18	98			98
18 or 18/31	9			9
18 or 18R	76			76
18R	33			33
18R or 18/31R	6			6
18/31	2	35	2	39
18/31 or 18/31R		19		19
18/31 or 31		24	2	26
18/31R		40		40
18/31R or 31R		18		18
31		14		14
31 or 31R		10		10
31R		23		23
31(R) group			7	7
27	147	40		187
27g	15			15
27 or 35	1			1
29	38			38
29 or 37	2			2
30	14	6		20
30 or 37	8			8
37	226	130	11	367
33	7	63	2	72
35	13	1		14
35 or 36	1	1		2
36	11	6		17
38		5	1	6
40		1		1
43		1		1
43 or 45		3	1	4
45		9	4	13
46		1		1
54		1		1
67	18			18
72		6		6
79		2		2

Table 13: Quantification of samian vessel types by fabric

Form	South Gaul	Central Gaul	East Gaul	Total
79R		1		1
79 or Tg		1		1
80		1		1
81		1		1
Vd			1	1
O&P pl 55.13		1		1
Bowl	5	5		10
Cup	3	1		4
Dish	11	14		25
Inkwell	1	1		2
Closed		2		2
Indeterminate	208	172	6	386

Table 13: Quantification of samian vessel types by fabric (contd)

Form/Epoch	Total vessels
Dragendorff 29	
Neronian	1
Neronian-earlier Flavian	14
early Flavian	9
Dragendorff 29 or 37	
Late Neronian-early Flavian	2
Dragendorff 30	
Neronian-early Flavian	3
Flavian	3
Flavian-Trajanic	1
Dragendorff 30 or 37	
Flavian	1
Flavian-Trajanic	1
Dragendorff 37	
early Flavian	7
Flavian	76
Flavian-Trajanic	60
c AD 110-50 (Banassac ware)	1
Indeterminate moulded bowl	
Flavian	2
Hermet 9	
late-Neronian or early-Flavian	2
Déchelette 67	
earlier-Flavian	1
Flavian	3
Flavian-Trajanic	2
Maximum vessels	**189**

Table 14: Quantification of South Gaulish samian vessels retaining identifiable moulded decoration, by epoch

Period 4B; Fig 271), where it was associated with a coin of Trajan, c AD 103–17. Its decoration is as on a bowl from Ribchester (Dickinson 2000, 207, fig 45.15), said to be in the style of Biragillus.

Central Gaulish products
Central Gaulish products accounted for a further 38% of the total assemblage, ranging in date from the Trajanic products of Les Martres-de-Veyre through to the late-Antonine products of Lezoux (Table 12). No first-century Lezoux ware was identified, nor were there any of the distinctive products from the Chantier Audouart. There were 22 stamped vessels in Central Gaulish fabrics, representing 40% of the total.

Les Martres-de-Veyre
Les Martres-de-Veyre products accounted for 17% of the Central Gaulish products (6% of the total; cf 3.6% at Lancaster; Ward forthcoming a). The group included 30 moulded bowls, decorated in the styles of the Potter of the Rosette, Igocatus (X-4), Drusus i, etc (Table 15), and 27% of the second-century stamps are on vessels which can be attributed to the Les Martres kilns. Secundinus ii (style III), Potter X-12, and Potter X–13 were amongst the group who moved from Les Martres to Lezoux c AD 125, and all three are represented in this assemblage by vessels from both production centres. Interestingly, although there were contemporary stamps, there were no bowls of Cettus, the prolific potter of the later-Hadrianic to early-Antonine period at Les Martres, yet examples of his work were found nearby in Castle Street (Dickinson 1991a).

The earliest occurrence of a Central Gaulish product was in Period 3A (road **7478**, primary surface *6670*), where a single Hadrianic fragment was certainly intrusive. There were also two sherds in Period 3C Building **4657** (floor layer *4162*), a possible workshop (Fig 269), one stamped by Roppus ii-Rut[, and dating

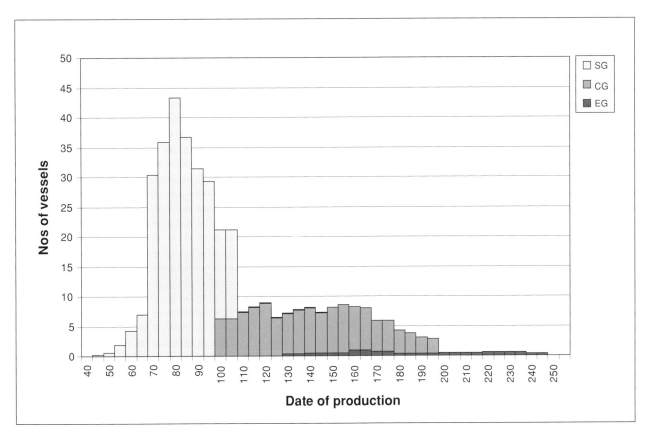

Figure 283: Histogram of decorated and stamped samian vessels by half decade (maximum 388)

c AD 115-40; these are also considered to be intrusive. In Period 3D demolition layer *3377* (associated with Buildings *3772* and *4006*), there was a badly burnt fragment of a Trajanic form 27 cup from Les Martres-de-Veyre, and a fragment of form 37 in the style of Potter X–3, *c* AD 100-20, was found in Period 3E layer *620* (MIL 2).

Evidence seems to suggest that the so-called 'Trajanic gap' in the samian supply does not appear to the degree seen at neighbouring sites in Carlisle, or elsewhere (Dickinson 1990, 213; 1991a, 344). Indeed, the chronological distribution of stamped and decorated samian appears to reflect a high level of use during the Trajanic to very early-Hadrianic period, at the time when the workshops at Les Martres-de-Veyre were at their peak (Fig 283). Seven stamped vessels came from Les Martres (30% of the Central Gaulish stamps and 27% of all the second-century and later examples). Admittedly, only two of these were dated to the period *c* AD 100–20/5; four were dated *c* AD 115–35/40, and one, a late product of Sacerus ii, was as late as *c* AD 140-60 (*pp 549-51*). Of the four produced there during the period *c* AD 115–35/40, one was by Roppus ii and two were by Roppus ii-Rut[. One of the Roppus ii-Rut[dishes was found in an occupation layer in Building *4657*; the fill (*4144*) of a contemporary pit (*4130*) in this building contained the dish stamped by Roppus i, in an unusual South Gaulish fabric (Stamp *24*). It seems likely that there are more Hadrianic vessels

amongst the unstamped material from Les Martres, and allowance was made for this possibility by giving indeterminate sherds a broad date-range in the earlier second century. Nevertheless, the great bulk of Les Martres ware from the Millennium project will surely have been produced *c* AD 100–20/5, as suggested by the evidence of the moulded bowls. Almost a third (32%) of the attributable Central Gaulish bowls could have been made at Les Martres during that period (Table 15).

Lezoux
Lezoux products accounted for 83% of the Central Gaulish products (32% of the total). Of the group of potters that moved from Les Martres-de-Veyre to Lezoux early in the Hadrianic period, the workshops of Secundinus ii (style III), Potters X–12, and X–13 seem to have continued to supply moulded bowls to the fort after the move.

Similarly, Ioenalis and Tasgillus ii are represented by stamps on plainware vessels produced at Lezoux, *c* AD 120/5-40. Six moulded bowls (13%) were certainly produced at Lezoux in the period *c* AD 120-45 or AD 125–50; another five bowls lie within the range *c* AD 135–60/5, but are not closely datable. Besides the four stamps from Les Martres that were dated *c* AD 115–35/40, there are five from Lezoux dated before *c* AD 150. Thus, 36% of the second-century and later stamped vessels are possibly Hadrianic

Period	Fabric	Potter	No vessels	Stamp No
Trajanic	Les Martres	Drusus i	3	
		Secundinus ii	1	
		Igocatus	3	
		Potter of the Rosette	1	
		Potter of the Rosette or X-13	1	
Trajanic to early-Hadrianic		X-12/X-13	2	
		X-13	2	
		Libertus/Butrio (perhaps at Les Martres)	1	
Hadrianic or early-Antonine	Lezoux	Secundinus ii	1	
		X-12 / X-13	1	
		X-13 / Sacer	1	
		X-6	2	
	(EG)	[La Madeleine potter]	[1]	
		Criciro v (*c* 135-60)	1	
		Paternus iv	1	
		early Cinnamus group	3	5, 6
Early- to mid-Antonine		Maccirra / Maccius?	1	
	(EG)	[Blickweiler potter]	[1]	
		Criciro v (*c* 150-70)	3	55
		Cinnamus, early or standard?	1	
Mid-Antonine		Cinnamus standard style	1	
		Cinnamus developed style	1	
		Divixtus?	1	
		Albucius/Paternus etc	1	
	(EG)	[Reginus vi, style I]	[2]	15
Mid- to late-Antonine		Mercator iv?	1	
		Iullinus ii	1	
		Casurius	2	
		Paternus v	1	
		Do(v)eccus i	2	11
Third-century	(EG)	[Afer group]	[1]	
Total no of attributable bowls			**45 [5 EG]**	

Table 15: Numbers of Central and East Gaulish vessels with moulded decoration attributable to specific potters

products, and there is a slight peak in the very early Hadrianic period before the supply levels off (Figs 282 and 283). A marked upsurge of activity under Hadrian has been noted at other sites in Carlisle (Dickinson 1990, 214), as well as at Lancaster (Hird and Howard-Davis in prep) and Walton-le-Dale (Hird forthcoming a), but most notably after *c* AD 125; at Ribchester there was a slightly later peak in the supply (*c* AD 135; Dickinson 2000, 203). It is possible, however, that the relatively high level of activity in the early years of the second century (until *c* AD 125) appears exaggerated as a result of its juxtaposition with the ensuing dearth of Antonine material (Fig 283).

Evidence from the Millennium assemblage seems to point to a relative reduction in the samian supply to the fort after *c* AD 125. Indeed, it failed to pick up noticeably thereafter, and remained at much the same level throughout the Antonine period (Fig 282). Inspection of the plain wares confirmed that the usual peak of supply seen in the Antonine period is simply not present (*cf* Bulmer 1980a, fig 3, for Chester). Interestingly, there was no such shortfall outside the fort, at Blackfriars Street (Dickinson 1990, 214, diagram 3), or at Castle Street, to judge from the seriograph there (Dickinson 1991a, 7). This raises a number of questions as to whether the site was occupied at the same level of consumption during the Antonine period as it had been before, or whether activity was of a very different nature (see *Ch 7*). The evidence drawn from both the stamped and decorated Antonine vessels seems to confirm the suggestion of considerable change.

Looking at the Antonine samian as an isolated group, certain trends can be noted. Six moulded bowls were probably produced in the period *c* AD 130/40–60; three stamps were dated *c* AD 135–60, two *c* AD 140–60/5, and one *c* AD 140–70, together constituting 23% of the second-century and later stamps. Two (8%) belonged to the earlier career of Cinnamus (Stamps *5, 6*), both on moulded bowls, there are, in all, no more than four bowls in his earlier style (*36, 47, 53,* and possibly *42, pp 559-62*). This is a far smaller proportion than that quoted for sites in Scotland in particular (Hartley 1972a, 33), and more generally for others on the northern frontiers and hinterland (although it is unclear whether Hartley was giving proportions based on the total number of samian vessels from these sites, or on the stamped and/or decorated vessels). At Blackfriars Street, there was a contemporary decline (Dickinson 1990, 213–14) and at Birdoswald, there was a sharp fall-off in the samian supply in this period (*c* AD 140/5–60; Dickinson 1997, fig 177). In the Carlisle fort, however, the fall-off in the period *c* AD 145–50 is less obvious (Fig 283), as the samian supply to the site was apparently greatly reduced throughout the Antonine period.

There are only two, or possibly three, bowls in Cinnamus's standard and developed styles, produced in the early-to mid-Antonine period, after *c* AD 150 and *c* AD 155 respectively. These form only 4% of the second-century material. At Castle Street, too, the earlier style was preponderant (Dickinson 1991a, 344) and both sites are in marked contrast to those from the northern frontiers and hinterland analysed by Brian Hartley (1972a, table V), where the later products of Cinnamus outnumbered his earlier products by more than 2:1 (if, again, Hartley's figures are indeed comparable). Their virtual absence from the Millennium Project might be explained by a period of abandonment just after the middle of the second century, but on the other hand, the collection did contain up to four bowls by Criciro and two by Casurius, who were contemporaries of Cinnamus at Lezoux, working in the period before *c* AD 170 and after *c* AD 160 respectively (*see 39, 40, 43, 44, 49, 52*). The signature of Criciro (Mould signature *1, p 551*) and a stamp of Peculiaris (Stamp *20, p 550*) were dated to the period *c* AD 150/5–70.

The reduction in the contemporary supply of stamped and decorated samian is also reflected in the plainwares (Table 13), which show an absence of forms such as 31R or 79, produced after *c* AD 160. The former is usually abundant on sites with steady occupation at this time. Not surprisingly, a similar shortfall was also noted in the southern part of the fort, at Annetwell Street, where the supply seemed to decline after *c* AD 155 (Dickinson in prep). Three stamps from the Millennium assemblage were dated *c* AD 160–80/5 (15% of the second-century material). Only two Central Gaulish stamps were firmly dated to after *c* AD 160, those of Regulianus and Do(v)eccus i, found in Periods 5D and 6D respectively. The single East Gaulish stamp of certain Antonine date was Mammilianus's rim-stamp on a bowl in the style of Reginus vi (II), found in Period 5D. Even these three were probably mid-Antonine products (Stamps *23* and, on moulded bowls, *11* and *15*); another of Reginus's bowls was found in Period 6A (see *48, p 551*). The specifically mid-Antonine bowls comprised only 13% of the second-century material, compared with 22% at a site in Lancaster (Ward forthcoming a).

The potter Do(v)eccus is generally considered to have been active rather later in the Antonine period (*c* AD 165 or *c* AD 170+ according to current dating), and a form 30 bowl in his style appears late (*51, p 551*). However, the stratigraphical evidence of the stamped bowl (*52*) suggests that his mould-making career started slightly earlier, perhaps *c* AD 160 (see Stamp *11*). Ten decorated Central Gaulish bowls (22% of the second-century material) were firmly dated to the period *c* AD 160–200. They were decorated in the styles of potters such as Iullinus, Mercator iv, and Paternus v, but most were mere fragments; in addition, the styles of Casurius and Do(v)eccus i were represented by two vessels each. The presence of all these later Central Gaulish bowls, together with that of the East Gaulish wares, could suggest renewed activity in or after the AD 160s, although, in view of the small numbers of vessels involved, this must still have been very limited in scale.

The presence of samian mortaria is regarded as a good indicator of late-Antonine activity, as the initial appearance of form 45 on sites in Roman Britain cannot have been before *c* AD 170. The conventional British dating for the form is followed here, although continental scholars consider the form to have been an even later introduction, and even in some British collections they have been considered to be third-century products (*eg* Bird 1986, 178–81; *cf* Ward 2008, 178): the dating still awaits confirmation from well-stratified British deposits. Whatever the precise date of introduction, the mortarium forms rapidly increased in popularity. The earliest form 45 in this assemblage is represented by a fragment of a Lezoux vessel, found in a Period 6A gravel surface (*5870*), external to the *principia*, Building **5200**, and in all, 18 mortaria were recorded. In Periods 6A-6C, the mortaria composed 4% of the total assemblage.

East Gaulish products
The East Gaulish wares made up only 2% of the total assemblage, ranging in date from the Hadrianic

period to the middle of the third century, although the later products were surprisingly few. In all, 37 East Gaulish vessels were recognised; one bowl from Blickweiler (3%); four vessels from La Madeleine (11%); at least six from the Argonne (16%); 11 from Trier (30%); and up to 12 from Rheinzabern (32%). A further three were of unknown origin (8%). Of the three East Gaulish stamps, that from La Madeleine (Stamp 53) found in Period 5A was not closely datable within the Hadrianic-Antonine period; the stamp of Mammilianus in Period 5D (Stamp 15) occurred on a bowl from a mould of Reginus vi (I) made at Rheinzabern c AD 160–80, and a fragment of swallow-tailed stamp of late second- to mid-third-century date (Stamp 54) also came from Rheinzabern. The presence of the latter in the Period 7 'dark earths' might point to its being a third-century product.

The general scarcity of East Gaulish wares on the western side of Britain is well known (Dickinson 2000), and at only 2% of the total, the proportion of East Gaulish wares at this site contrasts strikingly with the 17% seen at the putative *vicus* and third-century fort at Piercebridge in the North East (Ward 2008, 170). Even so, for a site that certainly saw considerable activity in the third century, the proportion of East Gaulish wares in this collection is very much lower than at other sites in the North West, including Lancaster (4–8% Dickinson forthcoming; Ward forthcoming a), Ribchester (Dickinson 2000), and Chester (Bulmer 1980a, 87). Nonetheless, samian ware was certainly in use in the fort in the third century, and possibly beyond, albeit on a reduced level. The evidence of reworking in the collection could suggest longer-term survivals.

The three stamps were on vessels produced at La Madeleine (one) and Rheinzabern (two). Their proportion (5%) is very much lower than the abnormally high figure of 20% quoted for Carlisle (Dickinson and Hartley 1971, 141), on the basis of which it was suggested that the fort was supplied overland from the Tyne (see also Dickinson 1990, 214). More recent evidence must challenge this, with the proportion of East Gaulish stamps from the Millennium Project (5%) and elsewhere in Carlisle (*eg* Annetwell Street, *c* 10%; Dickinson in prep) now seeming much lower.

La Madeleine
The earliest stamped or decorated vessels represented are those of the La Madeleine potteries, which were at their peak of production in the Hadrianic-early Antonine period. However, a mortarium found in Period 6B is also thought to have been produced there, presumably after *c* AD 170 at the earliest (see also Goury 1939, fig 3). The proportion of La Madeleine vessels in this collection is relatively low at 11%,

compared with that at Castle Street and Annetwell Street, where it comprised 25% (Dickinson 1991a; in prep).

Blickweiler
The single Blickweiler product is not easily dated, but may have been produced in the early or even the mid-Antonine period. Although never frequent, the apparent absence of Blickweiler products may sometimes reflect the similarity of the ware, when lacking diagnostic decoration, to some products of Les Martres-de-Veyre.

Argonne
Argonne wares are usually more distinctive and, at Carlisle, they are strikingly common. Despite the absence of stamped or decorated wares, the proportion of Argonne ware in this assemblage (16%) is, as at other Carlisle sites, much higher than elsewhere in the North West. At Blackfriars Street and Annetwell Street (Dickinson 1990; in prep) it represented 13% of the East Gaulish assemblage, but at Castle Street, only 6%, where it was said to be unusually low for Carlisle (Dickinson 1991a, 344). The six or more vessels from the Millennium Project are again most likely to be Antonine products, apart from the mortaria, which are probably of third-century date (see Bird 1993, 12). The lack of stamps and decorated pieces underlines the importance of the plain wares in analysis of the contribution of different sources of samian supply, despite the difficulties involved in their recognition.

Rheinzabern
Rheinzabern wares first appear on the site in Period 5D on the final surface (*2500*) of road **4662**, with one of two bowls in the style of Reginus vi, which was stamped by the bowl-maker Mammilianus. Stamps of Reginus have already been recorded at Castle Street and Blackfriars Street (Dickinson 1991a; 1990). This potter is known to have moved from Heiligenberg to Rheinzabern in the middle of the second century, and is known to have been producing moulds at Rheinzabern in the period *c* AD 160–80 at least (see Mees 2002, 325), making these bowls contemporary with the mid-Antonine vessels from Lezoux. None of the stamped or decorated vessels from Rheinzabern have been attributed to the next generation of potters, and most of the plainware can be dated only broadly within the later second- to third-century range.

Trier
The latest samian vessel recorded on the site is a bowl from Trier in the style of, but apparently, judging by its general appearance (fabric, slip, and general modelling), later than, the Afer group (see *50, p 561*). The bowl is likely to have been produced in the second quarter of the third century, perhaps as late

as *c* AD 245/50. A single, abraded sherd was found in Period 6B (layer *5575*; *Ch 9, p 317*), in association with a coin of Tetricus I (AD 271–3) and a radiate (*Appendix 3*). Several other vessels were thought to be third-century in date, but only five were assigned a firm date, probably before *c* AD 250. These were all relatively small parts of vessels, including a late form 45 mortarium, two deep dishes (the East Gaulish version of form 31R), and a beaker (Ludowici Vd). All appeared to be from Trier. Although all the late East Gaulish material was very fragmentary, the Trier products appeared in general to be later than those from Rheinzabern, and were most likely to be third-century products. The presence of only one moulded bowl, and the complete absence of stamps from Trier, does not reflect the evidence of the unstamped vessels, and in fact Trier wares formed 30% of the East Gaulish assemblage. It should be borne in mind, however, that plainwares from Trier can be confused with certain Rheinzabern and particularly Lezoux products.

Catalogue of samian potters' stamps
Brenda Dickinson

Each entry (not illustrated) gives excavation number; potter (i, ii *etc*, where homonyms are involved); die; form; reading; reference to published drawing (where available); pottery of origin; date.

Superscript a, b, and c indicate:

a A stamp attested at the pottery in question.
b Not attested at the pottery, but other stamps of the same potter used there.
c Assigned to the pottery on the evidence of fabric, distribution, *etc*.

Ligatured letters are underlined.

1. Balbinus 2a. Form 18/31. IINIB[INI·M] (Vanvinckenroye 1968, 26, 7) Les Martres-de-Veyre[a]. The deterioration of the letters has led to some examples having the first B as II, followed by a vertical stroke (scratch?) joining the Λ.
    MIL 1, *327*, Period 4A/B, *c* AD 100–20, Road *7645*, road surface

2. Calvus i 5o. Form 15/17 or 18. [OFCΛL]VI La Graufesenque[a].
    MIL 5, *2179*, Period 6A, *c* AD 70–90, Building *2301*, fill of construction trench *2187*

3. Calvus i 5cc. Form 27. OFCALVI (Polak 2000, pl 5, C36) La Graufesenque[a].
    MIL 5, *3190*, Period 3C, *c* AD 75–95, Building *4657*, R3.3, occupation layer

4. Cetias 1a. Form 18/31. [CETI]AS·FC Lezoux[a]. The potter worked earlier at Les Martres-de-Veyre.
    MIL 2, *504*, Period 8, Hadrianic or early Antonine, fill of medieval pit *503*

5. Cinnamus ii 5a. Form 37. [CIN]NAMI retr, stamped in the mould (Juhász 1935, Taf 45, 73); Lezoux[a].
    MIL 1, *243*, Period 6A, *c* AD 135-60, Road *7646*, soil layer

6. Cinnamus ii 5d. Form 37. CINNAMI retr, stamped in the mould, Lezoux[a].
    MIL 5, *2628*, Period 5B, *c* AD 140-65, Road *4662*, external layer

7. Cocuro 1a. Form 33. [CO]CVRO·F (Hartley 1972a, fig 82, 136), Lezoux[a].
    MIL 5, *2667*, Period 5A, *c* AD 130-50, fill of gully *2712*

8. Cotto ii 1c. Form 18. OFCOTTO (Curle 1911, 234, 31) La Graufesenque[b].
    MIL 5, *3244*, Period 4A, *c* AD 70–100, Building *4655*, fill of construction trench *3241*

9. Crestio 5a. Form 18 or (less probably) 18R. [O]F CRESTIO (Dickinson 1984, fig 70, 3), La Graufesenque[a].
    MIL 5, *7381*, Period 3A, *c* AD 45–65, Building *7392*, fill of construction trench *7380*

10. Crestus 3a. Form 15/17 or 18. OΓ[·CRES] (Nash-Williams 1930, 173, 30), La Graufesenque[b].
    MIL 2, *623*, unstratified, *c* AD 70–85

11. Do(v)eccus i 13a. Form 37 (mould-stamp in the decoration). D[OIICCVS] retr (Stanfield and Simpson 1958, pl 147, 2) Lezoux[b].
    MIL 5, *2140*, Period 6D, *c* AD 160-85, Road *2301*, demolition layer

12. Flavius Germanus 5a. Form 18. OF·FL[ΛGE·], La Graufesenque[a].
    MIL 5, *2806*, Period 5A, *c* AD 80–110, external layer

13. Ioenalis 2a. Form 18/31. [IO]ENALIS (Vanvinckenroye 1968, 26, 28), Lezoux[a]. The potter worked earlier at Les Martres-de-Veyre. Burnt.
    MIL 5, *6381*, Period 4B, *c* AD 125-40, Road *7477*, road surface

14. Malluro 3e. Form 18/31 or 31. [MA]LLVROF (Knorr 1907, Taf 31, 245), Lezoux[a].
    MIL 5, *5075*, Period 8D, *c* AD 135-60, fill of medieval pit *5072*

15. Mammilianus 4b. Form 37 rim. [MΛMMIL]IΛNVS, between guide-lines (Ludowici 1927, 220), Rheinzabern[a]. The bowl is from a mould in the style of Reginus vi (Style I).
    MIL 5, *2500*, Period 5D, *c* AD 160?-80, Road *4662*, road surface

16. Marcellinus i 1c. Form 27. MARCIILL[INI] (Hartley 1972a, fig 82, 142), Les Martres-de-Veyre[a].
    MIL 5, *2824*, Period 4B, *c* AD 115-35, Building *4660*, R1.1, occupation layer

17. Mercator i 1a. Form 18. OFM[ERC] (Polak 2000, pl 14, M65), La Graufesenque[a].
    MIL 5, *2921*, Period 4B, *c* AD 85–110, Building *4660*, R4.1, floor

18. Ortius Paullus 1a. Form 18. ORTI·PΛVLLI (Polak 2000, pl 17, P56), La Graufesenque[a].

MIL 5, *2790* and *2806*, Periods 4D and 5A, *c* AD 80–100, external layers

19. Patricius i 3d. Form 27. OF.PATRICI (Hartley 1972a, figs 81–82), La Graufesenque[a].
MIL 5, *7104* and *5727*, Periods 3C and 6B, *c* AD 70–85, Building *7200*, fill of robber pit *7105* and fill of pit *5668*

20. Peculiaris ii 5a. Form 33. PECVLIAR·F (Curle 1911, 238, 72), Lezoux[a]. Slightly burnt.
MIL 5, *6098*, Period 5C, *c* AD 155–70, fill of pit/posthole *6097*

21. Primus iii 12g. Form 18. OFPRIMI (Wheeler 1926, fig 24, 16), La Graufesenque[a].
MIL 5, *4106*, Period 3A, *c* AD 60–75, Building *4653*, R5.1, floor

22. Primus iii 21b or 21b′. Form 27g. OFPRM or OFPRM (Polak 2000, pl 18, P115), La Graufesenque[a]. Heavily burnt.
MIL 1, *267*, Period 5, *c* AD 55–70, external layer

23. Regulianus 2a. Form 33. REGVLIΛ I? Lezoux[a].
MIL 5, *2427*, Period 5D, *c* AD 160-85, Road *4662*, road surface

24. Roppus i 5a. Form 18. ROPPVS·FEC (Polak 2000, pl 19, R12), South Gaulish. The fabric does not quite fit the La Graufesenque range, and the piece may have been made at one of the potteries in the Lot Valley.
MIL 5, *4144*, Period 3C, *c* AD 70–90?, Building *4657*, R1.3, fill of pit *4130*

25. Roppus ii 3a. Form 18/31R. ROPPVS·F, Les Martres-de-Veyre[b].
MIL 4, *1409*, Period 8iii, *c* AD 115-40, fill of medieval ditch *1403*

26. Roppus ii- Rut- 1a. Form 18/31. [ROPPI·RV]T·M (Dickinson 1984, fig 70, 44), Les Martres-de-Veyre[a]. The top of the T does not register.
MIL 5, *4162*, Period 3C, *c* AD 115-40?, Building *4657*, R1.1, floor

27. Roppus ii- Rut- 1a″. Form 15/17R or 18/31R. [RO]PPI·RV (Terrisse 1968, pl 54), Les Martres-de-Veyre[a]. The stamp is from the second modification of the die that was used for Stamp *25*, above.
MIL 5, *3318*, Period 4B, *c* AD 115-40?, Road *4659*, fill of roadside ditch *3014*

28. Sacerus ii 1a. Form 18/31R. [SACERI·M]AN, Lezoux[c].
MIL 5, *2150*, Period 6A, *c* AD 140-60?, Building *2302*, fill of construction trench *2297*

29. Secundinus i 5a. Form 18R. SECVNDINI (Polak 2000, pl 21 S64), La Graufesenque[a].
MIL 1, *283*, Period 4A/B, *c* AD 80–110, possible rampart *7658*, rampart layer

30. Secundus ii 12c. Form 27g. OFSEC (Knorr 1907, Taf 31, 230), La Graufesenque[b].

MIL 4, *1950*, Period 3B, *c* AD 70–90, Building *2061*, R4.1, floor

31. Secundus ii 30c. Form 18. SECVND retr, La Graufesenque[b].
MIL 5, *3572*, Period 4A, *c* AD 70-90, Building *3376*, fill of construction trench *3442*

32. Senonius 4a. Form 18/31R. [SE]NONI, Lezoux[a].
MIL 5, *2827*, Period 6A, *c* AD 135-60, external layer

33. Tasgillus ii 2b. Form 27. TASGILLVS·F, Lezoux[a]. A stamp of a potter who began work at Les Martres-de-Veyre under Trajan, and moved to Lezoux in the Hadrianic period.
MIL 5, *2792*, Period 5A, Hadrianic, external layer

34. L. Tr–Masculus 5a. Form 18. OFMASCVI (Polak 2000, pl 13, M49), La Graufesenque[a].
MIL 5, *3027*, Period 5A, *c* AD 85–110, external layer

35. Virtus i 1a. Form 29. OFVIRTVTIS, La Graufesenque[a].
MIL 5, *6869*, Period 4A, *c* AD 70–85, Building *5688*, fill of construction trench *6866*

36. IΛI· I\. Form 27g. South Gaulish.
MIL 5, *3372*, Period 4A, Neronian or early-Flavian, Building *4655*, fill of construction trench *3300*

37. +……+. Form 15/17 or 18. South Gaulish.
MIL 1/MIL 5, *327* and probably *6583*, Periods 4A/B and 4B, Flavian, Road *7645*, road surface and Road *7477*, fill of drain *5925*

38. ·Λ·I·I·Λ·II. Form 27g. South Gaulish.
MIL 1, *267*, Period 5, Flavian, external layer

39. IV[. Form 27g. South Gaulish. Slightly burnt.
MIL 1, *106*, Period 6A, Flavian, Wall *118*, fill of construction trench *105*

40. IΛ·Λ·I. Form 27. South Gaulish.
MIL 3, *901*, Period 4A, Flavian, external layer

41. Form 27. South Gaulish.
MIL 3, *910*, Period 4B, Flavian or Flavian-Trajanic, external surface

42. .A[?. Form 27. South Gaulish.
MIL 5, *3272*, Period 4A, Flavian or Flavian-Trajanic, Road *4659*, road surface

Unidentified

43.]V F. Form 18 or 18R. South Gaulish.
MIL 5, *5966*, Period 5D, Neronian or early Flavian, fill of gully *5964*

44.]EN. Form 29. South Gaulish.
MIL 5, *7258*, Period 3B, *c* AD 70–85, Road *7476*, fill of drain *7100*

45. I[or]I. Form 15/17 or 18. South Gaulish.
MIL 3, *960*, Period 3B, Flavian, external layer

46. OF[?. Form 15/17 or 18. South Gaulish.
MIL 5, *3333*, Period 4B, Flavian, Building *4660*, R2.1, floor

47. OF[. Form 18. South Gaulish.
MIL 1, *326*, Period 5, Flavian, external layer

48. V[or]M?. Form 18/31. Central Gaulish (Les Martres-de-Veyre). Overfired.
MIL 4, *1563*, Period 4B, Trajanic, external surface

49. O\[. Form 18/31. Central Gaulish.
MIL 5, *2605*, Period 5C, Hadrianic or early Antonine, external layer

50.]A·F. Form 18/31 or 31. Central Gaulish.
MIL 5, *9994*, unstratified, Hadrianic or early Antonine

51.]A. Form 18/31 or 31. Central Gaulish.
MIL 5, *5334*, Period 6C, Hadrianic or Antonine, Building *5200*, R5.2, make-up layer

52.]M·. Form 33. Central Gaulish.
MIL 5, *3240*, Period 4A, early-to mid-Antonine, Building *4655*, fill of construction trench *3241*

53. VI[or]IΛ. Form 18/31. East Gaulish (La Madeleine).
MIL 5, *2667*, Period 5A, Hadrianic-Antonine, fill of gully *2712*

54. The swallow-tail end of a stamp label, East Gaulish (probably Rheinzabern).
MIL 5, *2110*, Period 7, late second or first half of third century, post-Roman 'dark earth'

Mould-signature

55. Criciru retr below the decoration of form 37, from a mould signed before firing: Criciro v of Lezoux.
MIL 5, *5989*, Period 5B, *c* AD 150-70, fill of posthole *6007*

Form and function
Moulded vessels

Most of the moulded bowls were represented by mere fragments, many lacking identifiable decoration. The 40 vessels of form 29 were restricted to South Gaulish products (*p 541*) and there were very few examples of form 30 in the collection (14–22 South Gaulish and six Central Gaulish examples). At least 83% of all moulded vessels were hemispherical bowls of form 37. Their quality was variable; some of the earlier vessels were finely moulded and well finished but, in contrast, the moulding of two or three South Gaulish bowls of Flavian-Trajanic date, found in Periods 4A/B and 4B, was poor enough to suggest that they might have been seconds (*cf* Bulmer 1980b, 87).

A small Central Gaulish bowl, apparently from the workshop of Criciro, might have been the work of an apprentice (*44*, *p 561*). Such bowls are often Hadrianic-early Antonine products, as is this example. Small bowls of form 37 have been noted before at Carlisle, for example at Castle Street (Dickinson 1991a, 364), whilst to the south, at Walton-le-Dale, there were ten small bowls out of 63 Central Gaulish vessels (F Wild *pers comm*). Frequently not attributable to any specific potter's style, it seems most likely that these bowls are the work of apprentices. There were perhaps four bowls from the workshop of Criciro v (*39*, *40*, *44*, *49*, *pp 559-61*), up to three of which showed the same composition, and one of which bore his moulded signature. The same composition was noted in a vessel from Castle Street (Dickinson 1991a, 354, fig 293.61) and it seems possible that this could represent a bowl from the same mould (if not the same vessel), although this cannot be confirmed without inspection. The new find has, however, clarified some uncertainties concerning the decoration of the Castle Street bowl.

A large part of a vessel of the unusual moulded form, Hermet 9, was recovered from a primary floor in Period 3A barrack Building *4652* (*3538*; *1*, *p 553*). This small bowl (or cup) has an everted-rim and is less angular than Knorr's form 78 (Hermet 1934, pl 4.8–9); a similar vessel was found at Richborough (Pryce 1932, pl 26.8). Various compositions, none identical to the Carlisle scheme, are illustrated by Hermet (1934, pl 91.11–44), although the vertical rows are also recorded on form 67. Pryce (*loc cit*) suggested that Hermet's form 9 was the forerunner of Knorr's form 78, whilst Mees (1995, 58) notes the presence of form 78 in the Hofheim earth-fort. The foot of this neat little vessel was scarcely worn at the time of its breakage and deposition in Period 3A. The Carlisle vessel may indeed be considered a late-Neronian forerunner, or perhaps a very early Flavian product. However, four coins from the reign of Vespasian were also recovered from the same floor (*3538*, R3, Phase 1; *Appendix 3*), perhaps calling a very early date for this floor into question. Another sherd of form Hermet 9 was recovered from the fill of a Period 6D robber trench (*2154*) in Period 6 barrack Building *2302*. Though the basal wreath is identical, this fragment appears to be thinner-walled, and must be presumed likely to represent a second vessel, however rare the find. If this is the case, they can be assumed to be a pair, found within a few metres of each other, even though their final deposition was centuries apart.

There were also between 10 and 18 South Gaulish beakers of form Déchelette 67. This quantity appears to represent a much higher proportion (9%) of the decorated South Gaulish vessels than that regarded as being unusual at Ribchester (5%; Dickinson 2000, 204). Most examples from the site were moulded (Table 14), with the exception of between one and three decorated *en barbotine*. One moulded example in Period 4A (*3341*, an occupation layer in Building *3376* (R2, Phase 1)) showed only plain, vertical lines (*cf* Hermet 1934, pl 4.8 *etc*), and scrolls were popular on others (see *11, 16, pp 554-5*). These vessels are not attributable to specific potters, but all were produced in the early-Flavian or Flavian-Trajanic period. They were distributed throughout the life of the forts at Carlisle, although there were more examples in Period 4A (Period 3A: one; Period 3B: two; Period 3C: two; Period 4A: seven; Period 4B: two; Periods 4C, 5A, 6A: one in each; Period 8: one). As an indication of the level of disturbance, several sherds of identical appearance and decoration, and conceivably from the same vessel (see *11, p 554*), were found in contexts dating to Periods 3B, 4A, and 4B in both MIL 3 and MIL 5, though these trenches were admittedly some 25 m apart.

Vessels with other than moulded decoration included a rouletted bowl of form 30 from Les Martres-de-Veyre, found in Period 4A/B (*320*, fill of pit *319*) adjacent to road *7645*. There were up to six beakers of Central Gaulish form 72 (at least one of which had 'cut-glass' decoration) produced after *c* AD 160 and found in Period 5D road *4662* (*2541*, external deposit). Plain examples were also suspected: a large part of an apparently undecorated example was recovered from a fill associated with Period 6A road *7652* (*5774*). Apparently the sole East Gaulish beaker, a plain form Ludowici Vd from third-century Trier (*cf* Bird 1993, 10*f*), was found in the Period 7 'dark earths' (*2126*). One fragment of Central Gaulish form 54, found in Period 8, was decorated *en barbotine*. The same type of decoration adorned the rim and (very unusually) the external wall of a Central Gaulish form 36 dish, of which fragments were found in Periods 5D (fill *2410*, of roadside ditch *2409*, associated with road *4662*) and 6B (floor *2384*, barrack Building *2301*). This was probably a one-off product by a Hadrianic-early Antonine potter with extra clay, or time, to spare. Lion-headed *appliqué* spouts are usually frequent in late assemblages containing mortaria of form 45; in the Millennium assemblage, however, only one mortarium, from third-century Trier, showed the vestiges of the large ears of a lion or bat, even though mortaria made up 16% of all East Gaulish vessels.

Plain vessels
Plain forms of interest included two inkwells: although not the standard form Ritterling 13, one was probably a South Gaulish product of Flavian-Trajanic date, found in a Period 4A layer (*6674*), associated with road *7477*. The other, from Hadrianic-Antonine Lezoux, was found in Period 6A make-up deposit *527*, in barrack Building *669*. Both showed traces of what is presumed to be ink.

The information provided by the more standardised forms is integrally linked with their dating. The array

of dish forms 15/17, 18, 18/31, 31, and their rouletted versions, probably reflects the chronological pattern of availability rather than local tastes. The scrappy nature of the fragments, many lacking rims or the distinctive junction of wall and base, meant that many could only be identified as either form 15/17 or form 18, or their rouletted versions. The likelihood is that many were of form 18, which became more popular than 15/17 as the Flavian period progressed. Twenty examples of form 18 or 18R had the pronounced external offset at the wall/base junction commonly recorded on vessels at early sites, such as the Neronian fortress at Usk (Tyers 1993, 133); this feature may suggest production in the Neronian period or perhaps the very early AD 70s. The Hadrianic-early Antonine forms 18/31 and 18/31R were found in profusion on the site, although deep dish form 31R and its generally unrouletted East Gaulish equivalents produced after *c* AD 160, Ludowici form Sb *etc*, constitute only 1.6% of the total. Even the typically Antonine form 38 flanged bowl was in short supply, there being only six examples in the entire collection. There were very few of the later-Antonine forms which might be regarded as typical of a later Roman collection: five vessels of the form 79 or 80 set; one cup of form 40; and no dishes (or shallow bowls) of form 32.

Amongst the cups, there were substantially more of form 27 than there were of form 33, in the ratio of almost 3:1. Indeed, there were only seven South Gaulish examples of form 33. At Usk (Tyers 1993, 134), all the footrings of form 27 were of the grooved variety (form 27g), while amongst the 162 South Gaulish form 27 cups noted in the Millennium assemblage, 18 footrings survived and only two or three lacked the groove that characterises the earlier form, 27g. In the second century, form 27 was, as usual, outnumbered by the increasingly popular form 33 amongst both Central and East Gaulish wares, but only in the ratio 2:3. Form 27 was out of production after *c* AD 160, and thus the relative shortage of form 33 again reflects the apparent shortfall in the samian supply in the second half of the second century.

Catalogue of decorated samian ware
Abbreviations: SG - South Gaulish; CG - Central Gaulish; EG - East Gaulish; Déch - Déchelette 1904; Cala Culip - Nieto and Puig 2001; S and S - Stanfield and Simpson 1958; Osw - Oswald 1936; Rogers - Rogers 1974.

The fragments have been drawn in conventional style, and rubbings placed in the archive. Entries are listed in order of chronological period on the site and date of manufacture, almost all coming from MIL 5. Figure-types as they appear on bowls are frequently smaller than Oswald's illustrated types (Dannell *et al* 1998, 71 and 87). Where this discrepancy occurs, it is not noted in the catalogue, unless considered particularly significant.

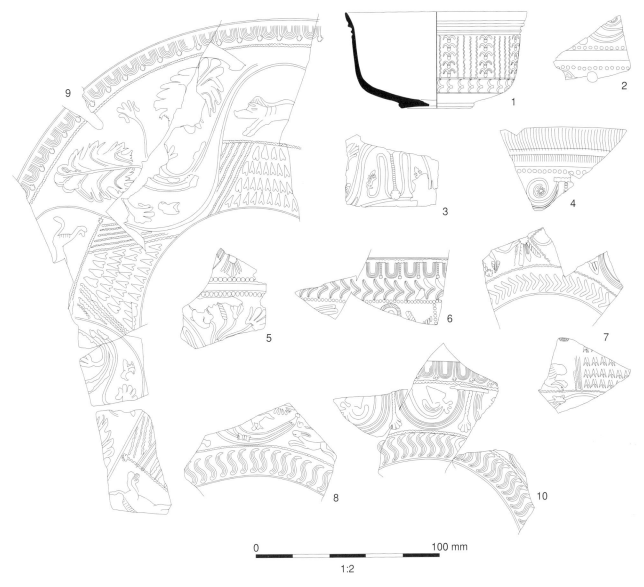

Figure 284: Samian from Period 3A

1. **SG**, Hermet 9, rim diameter 100 mm (Fig 284). A small moulded bowl or cup, with vertical rows of bifid motifs and wavy lines, as recorded on form 67 (Hermet 1934, pl 4.8). Below is a wreath of bifid leaves as on form Hermet 9 in the Guildhall Museum (Stanfield 1936, fig 3 no 9); the rim is everted as on Stanfield's no 8 and, with vertical wavy lines, no 10. Probably late-Neronian or very early Flavian. A single fragment of an identical basal wreath found in Period 6D (2154) is presumed to represent a second, thinner-walled vessel. Seven sherds form an almost complete profile; the flat foot, as moulded, is little worn, if at all.
   MIL 5, *3538*, Period 3A, Building **4652**, R3.1, floor

2. **SG**, Dr 29 (Fig 284). Winding scrolls in both zones of a straight-walled vessel, probably late-Neronian. Broken at a round rivet hole drilled through the lower scroll; *cf* the repaired form 29 at Castle Street (Dickinson 1991a, fig 287.1).
   MIL 5, *7108*, Period 3A, Building **7393**, demolition layer

3. **SG**, Dr 29 (Fig 284). A fragment only of the lower zone: a winding scroll with ornament, Cala Culip type Cc 67. *Cf* Knorr

1952, Taf 51.B, OFPRIMI. Probably *c* AD 60–80.
MIL 5, *4584*, Period 3A, Building **4654**, R3.2, fill of pit/trench *4583*

4. **SG**, Dr 29, rim diameter 200 mm (Fig 284). Two adjoining, glossy rimsherds: the upper zone contained festoons terminating in neat rosettes (as occurred also on a second, very similar bowl in Period 4A *7152* and *7159*), with pendant Cala Culip type Ed 11. *Cf* perhaps Dickinson 1992, fig 6.3 from the nearby putative annexe ditch. *c* AD 65–80/5 and probably Flavian.
   MIL 5, *7524*, Period 3A, external area adjacent to Building **7392**, demolition deposit

5. **SG**, Dr 29 (Fig 284). A scroll in the lower zone with indistinctly moulded and badly abraded leaves, including Cala Culip type Ed 14. In the upper zone, a motif (Nieto and Puig 2001, type Ee 18) most probably hanging between festoons (*op cit*, no 258, form 29 VIRTHV). Probably *c* AD 70–80/5.
   MIL 5, *7450*, Period 3A, fill of external gully/slot *7488*

6. **SG**, Dr 37, rim diameter 180 mm (Fig 284). A very glossy and finely-moulded small bowl. This has an ovolo with a small rosette terminal recorded on bowls of Germanus, above a wreath of bifid motifs and panelling with beaded borders, ring-rosette, and hare (Déch 949?). *c* AD 70–80/5. Two sherds in *7459* and a fragment in Period 4A *6869*.

    MIL 5, *7459*, Period 3A, fill of external gully/slot *7488*; *6869*, Period 4A, Building *5688*, fill of construction trench *6866*

7. **SG**, Dr 37 (Fig 284). Badly blurred decoration: an indistinct ovolo overlaps arrowheads next to a lion (Osw 1397?) noted on form 29 of Mommo at Pompeii (Atkinson 1914, no 14), above a winding scroll. The composition was influenced by form 29, *c* AD 70–80/5. A small fragment in *3458* adjoins a sherd in Period 3B (*3477*). Other sherds in Period 3B (from deposit *3477* and fill *3547* (hollow *3978*), both in road *4661*) display a bifid wreath below a scroll and saltire (though not certainly from the same bowl).

    MIL 5, *3458*, Period 3A, Building *4652*, R4.1, fill of gully *3370* (one sherd); also joins *3477*, Period 3B, Road *4661*, external layer

8. **SG**, Dr 37 (Fig 284). A glossy bowl with basal S-shaped godroons below a winding scroll with a tendril binding (bow with two beads); in the interstices, an indistinct hare and goose (*cf* Osw 2129 and 2232?). The decoration was influenced by form 29, *c* AD 70–85.

    MIL 5, *3911*, Period 3A, Building *4653*, demolition layer

9. **SG**, Dr 37, rim diameter 200 mm (Fig 284). An indistinct ovolo with a large rosette, devolved from one associated

with Paullus. The leaf is type Ca 112 on Cala Culip, no 341; Dannell (G Dannell *pers comm*) notes that it occurs on a bowl at La Graufesenque (G73 85) with a mould signature PAS (Passienus); *cf* Mees 1995, Taf 161.1. In the interstices, a boar and hound (*cf* Osw 1696N and 2015) and an indistinct bird. Probably *c* AD 75–90. It has the almost complete profile of the bowl; the footring is slightly worn and burnt.

MIL 5, *4088*, Period 3A, Building *4658*, fill of construction trench *4087*; also joins *3802*, Period 3B, Building *4006*, occupation layer (nine sherds), and *3971*, Building *4006*, fill of construction trench *3970* (one sherd); *3272*, Period 4A, Road *4659*, road surface (two sherds), and *3343*, Road *4659*, make-up layer (one sherd)

10. **SG**, Dr 37 (Fig 284). A small bowl whose ovolo with trident tongue is perhaps that on form 30, with a mould-stamp of Cobniddus at La Graufesenque (1953D; G Dannell *pers comm*). Below is a single zone of festoons and a basal wreath of S-shaped godroons. Probably *c* AD 75-95. A slightly burnt piece in *7562* adjoins two sherds in Period 3B.

    MIL 5, *7562*, Period 3A, external layer; also joins *6824*, Period 3B, Road *7476*, external layer, and *7453*, Building *7395*, fill of construction trench *7598*

11. **SG**, Déchelette 67 (Fig 285). Glossy, but blurred decoration: a scroll with Nile goose (*cf* Osw 2226?) and an indistinct hare. Below are filling motifs commonly used on form 37 (*cf* Dickinson 1991a, fig 291.39), possibly Cala Culip type Cd 6a. The small leaf is type Ca 68 on vessel no 683 there. For the use of such scrolls on this form, see that from Aislingen (Knorr in

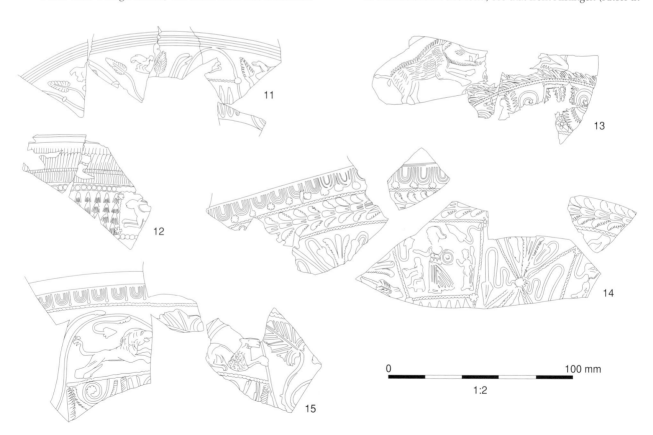

Figure 285: Samian from Period 3B

554

Ulbert 1959, Taf 73.1). Probably c AD 70–80/5. As the sherds were found scattered in both MIL 3 and MIL 5, it is possible that two vessels are represented, but as their decoration and appearance are identical, they are illustrated together. Four fragments in Period 3B, two in Period 4A, and four in Period 4B.

MIL 3, *999*, Period 3B, external layer; MIL 5, *3479*, *3509*, *3517*, Road *4661*, road surface and external layers; also joins MIL 3, *901*, Period 4A, external layer; MIL 5 *3231*, Period 4B, Building *2765*, R4.1, fill of posthole *3232*

12. **SG**, Dr 29, rim diameter 200 mm (Fig 285). The upper compartment contains an indistinct hare (*cf* Osw 2105?) in a composition popular on form 29; *cf* Dickinson and Hartley 2000, no 1049 at Castleford, and, with the same fillers, Atkinson 1914, pl 12.7 at Pompeii). Probably c AD 65-80. Three adjoining sherds of a slightly burnt, but glossy, vessel.

MIL 5, *4204*, Period 3B, Building *4656*, fill of construction trench *4205*

13. **SG**, Dr 37 (Fig 285). Zonal decoration: the lower zone contains festoons flanking pendant grapes (*cf* Mees 1995, Taf 90.1, Germanus); in the upper zone, a boar (*cf* Osw 1636) and a lion (Déch 752?) over grass. c AD 70–85/90. Four adjoining sherds.

MIL 5, *3195*, Period 3B, Building *4656*, construction trench for sill beam

14. **SG**, Dr 37, rim diameter 220 mm (Fig 285). Decoration blurred: an ovolo associated with Frontinus above a wreath of leaf-and-bud motifs, which often occurs with this ovolo. Panelling: Minerva (a small variant of Osw 133A), flanked by a seated figure (Oswald's 'bird-catcher;' Cala Culip Ab 26) and a diminutive draped figure. Another sherd shows only the wineskin of a drinker (*cf* Osw 623). Dannell (G Dannell *pers comm*) notes a bowl with a devolved

version of this ovolo and the seated figure, wreath, corner tendril, and a smaller version of Osw 623, at La Graufesenque (G66?[46]); two pieces at La Graufesenque (G78? U54) with an identical figured panel, saltire, and leaf tips probably came from the same mould as the Carlisle vessel. c AD 75–90. Single sherds in *3971* and *4204*, five sherds in *4207*, two sherds with some burning in Period 3E; one in Period 5B.

MIL 5, *3971*, Period 3B, Building *4006*, fill of construction trench *3970*; *4204*, *4207*, Building *4656*, fill of construction trench *4205*; also joins *3177*, Period 3E, external layer; *3186*, Period 5B, external layer

15. **SG**, Dr 37, rim diameter at least 220 mm (Fig 285). Ovolo associated with C Val Albanus and M Crestio above a bead row and a scroll with leaf (see Cala Culip type Ca 99) and two badly blurred lions (Déch 732 and 747). At Colchester, a date of c AD 75-90 was proposed for bowls with this ovolo (Dannell 1999, 74). A single sherd came from *3412*, three in Period 4A, and a rim sherd in Period 4B.

MIL 5, *3412*, Period 3B, Building *4651*, floor?; also joins *3285*, Period 4A, Building *4655*, R1.1, occupation layer; *3120*, Period 4B, Building *2765*, R2.1, floor

16. **SG**, Déchelette 67, rim diameter 70 mm (Fig 286). Fragments of a scroll with lotus (Cala Culip type Cc 35 or 40?). The lotus was a popular motif in scrolls on form 29 in particular (*cf* Dannell 1999, 62, no 41). c AD 70–85/90. Two sherds in *4144* and one in Period 5B.

MIL 5, *4144*, Period 3C, Building *4657*, R1.3, fill of pit *4130*; also joins *3186*, Period 5B, external layer

17. **SG**, Dr 37, rim diameter 200 mm (Fig 286). A blurred ovolo whose tongue terminates in a blob, above a scroll. The ovolo, leaf, and

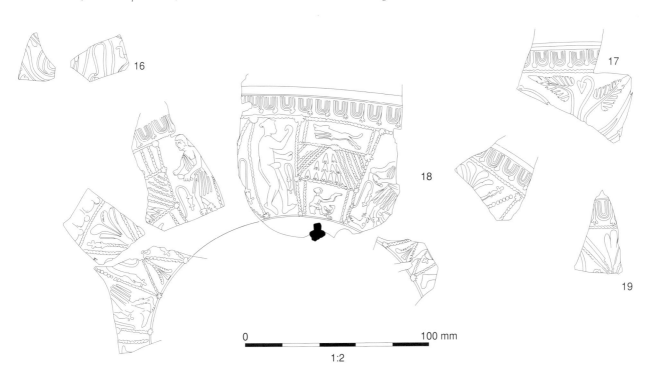

Figure 286: Samian from Period 3C

small heart-shaped leaf are probably those on a bowl from Old Penrith (Dickinson 1991b, no 42), dated *c* AD 75–95. The presence of similar scrolls on form 29 at Cala Culip (*eg* no 123 OF.IVCVNDI) might suggest a date before *c* AD 85/90 at the latest.

MIL 5, *4144*, Period 3C, Building *4657*, R1.3, fill of pit *4130*

18. **SG**, Dr 37, rim diameter 200 mm (Fig 286). A badly blurred ovolo recorded with the mould-stamp of M Crestio (Mees 1995, Taf 47.3) and found commonly at Cala Culip. Divided panelling with hound (Osw 2004?), a bird-catcher (Osw 961; bird-tamer?), satyr facing right, and Peleus facing left. The last two figures are smaller than both the Déchelette and Oswald types (*cf* Déchelette nos 336 and 510; Osw 635 and 883). The satyr has shorter legs than at Cala Culip, where type Aa 19 occurs with this ovolo on vessel no 629. Peleus may be Cala Culip type Aa 21; he is shorter than Hermet 1934, pl 20 no 134; *cf* Hermet's type 133 as noted on a bowl with the same decoration from Castle Street (Dickinson 1991a, 346 no 17). The bead rows forming the main panel borders on both are unusual. Probably *c* AD 80–100. The footring is worn from use and the bowl has broken at two rivet holes of the dove-tailed (cleat) variety: one through the decoration, the other below it, retaining a lead rivet. The complete profile is formed by two sherds from layer *3190* and seven from pit fill *4144*, with five from Period 4A.

MIL 5, *3190*, Period 3C, Building *4657*, R1.3, occupation layer; and *4144*, Building *4657*, R1.3, fill of pit *4130*; also joins *4460*, Period 4A, Structure *4664*, floor

19. **SG**, Dr 37 (Fig 286). A burnt fragment showing that long-tongued ovolo whose large trident tip turns left, associated with Albanus iii, Amandus, Coii Bass[, and other potters at La Graufesenque (see Dickinson 1991a, fig 291.42 from Castle

Street). Below, a saltire with indistinct central motif; *cf* Mees 1995, Taf 1.8 ALBA[. Probably *c* AD 80–100.

MIL 5, *6878*, Period 3C, Building *7200*, floor

20. **SG**, Déchelette form 67 (Fig 287). Slightly blurred panelling: a saltire with a leaf-and-bud motif and rosette fillers. For a similar composition, see that from Castle Street, Dickinson 1991a, fig 289.20. Flavian.

MIL 5, *3240*, Period 4A, Building *4655*, fill of construction trench *3241*

21. **SG**, Dr 37, diameter perhaps 240 mm (Fig 287). A large bowl with slightly orange slip. Ovolo with a blurred trident-tipped tongue above a frieze of opposing stags (Cala Culip types Bb 15 and 18), separated by a composite grass plant. Similar stags were used on form 29 (*eg* Knorr 1919, Taf 74C, OFSECVND) and on form 37 of Mercator at Richborough (Pryce 1928, pl 27.11), and are known to occur with this ovolo. *c* AD 80–95/100. Four sherds and two flakes.

MIL 5, *3240*, Period 4A, Building *4655*, fill of construction trench *3241*

22. **SG**, Dr 37 (Fig 287). Blurred ovolo, with a faint tongue and stronger trident tip, associated with Mercator; panelling with saltires, Diana and Victory (*cf* Osw 104 and 814). The two figures appear to be those on a bowl in the Bregenz Cellar, with a similar ovolo (Jacobs 1913, taf 3.19), and also on form 29 at Rottweil (Knorr 1919, taf 68, OFPVDENT). A date in the range *c* AD 80–100/10 is suggested.

MIL 5, *3211*, Period 4A, Building *3376*, demolition layer

23. **SG**, Dr 37 (Fig 287). Divided panelling: saltires and composite grass plants on a smudged leaf-and-bud base; a stag (Cala Culip

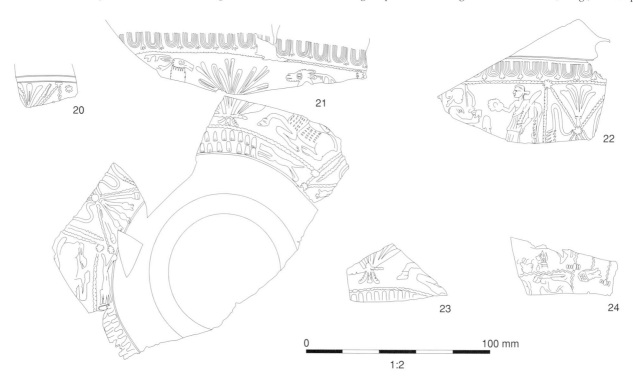

Figure 287: Samian from Period 4A

556

type Bb 19) and hound (Osw 2004). A similar stag occurs on the Richborough form 37 of Mercator noted above (*22*), and Mercator used the poppy-headed motif (*cf* Dickinson 1991a, fig 290.29 from Castle Street). Probably *c* AD 85–100/10. Eleven sherds, including the worn and slightly burnt footring: six from *1562*; two from *1605*; two in Period 4B; one in Period 8. MIL 4, *1562*, Period 4A, Building **2059**, R3.3, demolition layer; *1605*, Building **2059**, fill of robber trench *1730*; also joins *1561*, Period 4B, external layer; *1493*, Period 8iii, fill of medieval ditch *1403*

24. **CG**, Dr 37, from Les Martres-de-Veyre (Fig 287). Panels with blurred and reduplicated wavy-line borders and astragaloid ornaments (Rogers R25): a hare (*cf* Osw 2116 or 2117, blurred), a bear (?), and various poorly moulded motifs, including a lyre (Rogers U229) recorded for the Potter of the Rosette and for X–13. No parallels have been found for the two indistinct motifs (baskets of flowers?). *c* AD 100–20/5.
MIL 5, *3341*, Period 4A, Building **3376**, R2.1, occupation layer

25. **SG**, Dr 37 (Fig 288). A small fragment of ovolo with trident tip above animals including a boar (Osw 1636?) between trees

characteristic of the school of Germanus (see also *27*). The grass tufts (Cala Culip type Ef 20) may suggest Mercator's group, who favoured the wreath of S-shaped godroons. *c* AD 80–95/100.
MIL 1, *361*, Period 4A/B, Road **7645**, external layer

26. **SG**, Dr 37, rim diameter 200 mm (Fig 288). Badly blurred ovolo, perhaps that with a faint tongue and stronger trident associated with Mercator. For the general composition with trees, see Knorr 1952, taf 28F, GERMANI. Very similar to *25*, but with a bifid basal wreath; the grass tufts suggest Mercator's group. A smudged figure with half a spear (*cf* Déch 161) rides a bullock(?) rather than the horse of Oswald's type 255; see Dannell 1978, fig 10.10, no 10, form 78 at Chichester. Perhaps *c* AD 80–95/100. One sherd each from *361* and *1168*, and two from *1169*.
MIL 1, *361*, *1168*, *1169*, Period 4/B, Road **7645**, external layers

27. **SG**, Dr 37, rim diameter 260 mm (Fig 288). A very large bowl whose upper decoration is very poorly moulded. The ovolo is devolved from one with a large rosette associated with Frontinus. The basal wreath of leaf-and-bud motifs had poppy-

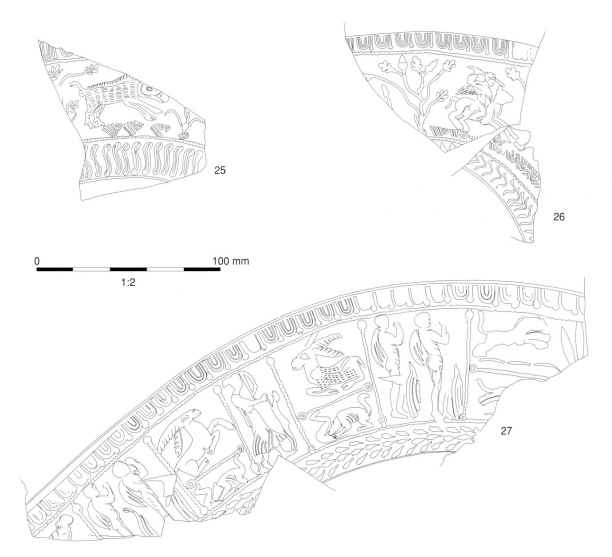

Figure 288: Samian from Period 4A/B

557

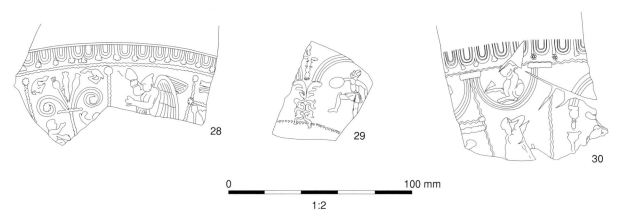

100 mm

1:2

Figure 289: Samian from Period 4B

headed arms. Divided panelling is perhaps repeated in the same order on the opposite side of the bowl with indistinct figures: a large figure with shield (type Ac 20 as on Terrisse 1968, pl 49.1202) is repeated in pairs; Diana (Déch 63a?) flanked by two stags (Cala Culip type Bb 15 and one lacking the front leg of type Bb 19), each over a large cat devouring a victim (type Aa 27); a lion (type Ba 14) leaps at a grass plant and another animal, above a hound (?). *c* AD 80–110, but the general appearance suggests a date after *c* AD 85/90. An almost complete profile, with worn footring, formed by 26 sherds from road surface *256*, and a fragment from Period 5. Another in *209*, the Period 6C fill of a robber trench, has the same basal wreath and probably belonged to the same bowl.

MIL 1, *256*, Period 4A/B, Road **7645**, road surface; also joins *245*, Period 5, external layer; *209*, Period 6C, Road **7646**, fill of robber trench *208*

28. **SG**, Dr 37, rim diameter 200 mm (Fig 289). An ovolo with rosette tip associated with Calvus i and Mercator i, but devolved. Two indistinct figures include Osw 646; the small Nile geese (Cala Culip types Bf 2 and 36?) occur above spirals at Prestatyn (Ward 1989, fig 76.39) and Rottweil (Knorr 1952, Taf 27.1). Dannell (G Dannell *pers comm*) notes the Victory (Osw 808B) with a devolved version of the ovolo at La Graufesenque (R2059). *c* AD 80/5–110. Adjoining sherds in make-up deposit *3113* and slot *3229*.

MIL 5, *3113*, Period 4B, Building **2765**, R1.1, make-up layer; *3228*, Building **2765**, R1.1, fill of slot *3229*

29. **CG**, Dr 37, from Les Martres-de-Veyre (Fig 289). A gladiator in arcades (Osw 1063, *cf* Terrisse 1968, pl 2.112) with astragali based on vertical stacks of double dolphins. *cf* S and S, fig 4.4 and 15, in the style of Drusus i (X–3), *c* AD 100–20. There were small flakes of a second bowl with the same arrangement of dolphins but in a different fabric. Main piece from *3085*, flakes from surface *6000* of Road **7477**.

MIL 5, *3085*, Period 4B, Building **2765**, R1.1, fill of posthole *3086*; *6000*, Road **7477**, road surface

30. **CG**, Dr 37, rim diameter 200 mm (Fig 289). Ovolo Rogers B29 above A24, festoons and arcades on composite uprights (S and S, pl 19.241). Figures, all badly blurred, include a sea-bull, Asclepius, and a seated figure (see Osw 42, 905 and 949). *Cf* S and S, pl 17.217, 18.228 and Romeuf 2001, pl 14.1051 in the style of Igocatus (X–4), who worked at Les Martres-de-Veyre, *c* AD 100–20. Fourteen sherds, mostly adjoining: five from *6207*; three from *6381*; two from *6412*; and a flake from *6324*; also one each from Periods 4C and 5D. It is uncertain whether a fragment of ovolo B29 from *5985* (Period 5C fill of posthole *5984*) is from the same bowl.

MIL 5, *6207*, Period 4B, Building **5688**, R5.3, floor; *6381*, Road **7477**, road surface; *6412*, Road **7217**, road surface; *6324*, Road **7217**, road surface; also joins *5998*, Period 4C, Building **5688**, demolition deposit; *5945*, Period 5D, external deposit

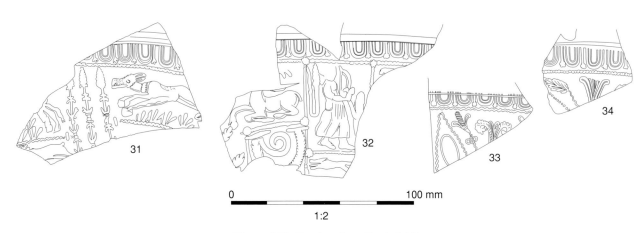

100 mm

1:2

Figure 290: Samian from Period 4C

31. **SG**, Dr 37 (Fig 290). Ovolo with trident tip turned slightly right, above divided panelling: hound (Osw 1995, its head indistinct as here) over plants with sets of vertical motifs (Cala Culip type Ca 72; see Knorr 1919, Textbild 7). *c* AD 80–100/10. Five sherds from Building *4660*, demolition deposit *3175*, one of which was burnt; there were two burnt fragments from Period 5A and one unburnt in Period 5B.
MIL 5, *3175*, Period 4C, Building *4660*, demolition layer; also joins *2709*, Period 5A, fill of gully *2712*; *2547*, Period 5D, Road *4662*, external layer

32. **SG**, Dr 37, rim diameter 220 mm (Fig 290). A heavy bowl with a brownish slip and poorly moulded decoration: a devolved trident-tipped ovolo above divided panelling with a small Diana (Déch 63). A stag (Cala Culip type Bb 19) sits right of a stylised tree (*cf* Dannell 1999, 41.157 at Colchester). The general appearance suggests a date of *c* AD 80/5–110. Four sherds, unburnt.
MIL 5, *3175*, Period 4C, Building *4660*, demolition layer

33. **CG**, Dr 37, rim diameter 200 mm (Fig 290). Ovolo Rogers B44 above A23 and a saltire with double-D motif (U182), leaf-and-buds (G169?) and rams' horns (G345). *Cf* Terrisse 1968, pl 17.312 in the style of the Potter of the Rosette, who worked at Les Martres-de-Veyre in the Trajanic period. Unburnt.
MIL 5, *2794*, Period 4C, Building *4660*, demolition layer

34. **CG**, Dr 37 (Fig 290). A blurred ovolo (Rogers B20) above a saltire with plant motif (G18) and leaf (H115). The style of Secundinus ii (Rogers' Secundinus I) who moved from Les Martres to Lezoux, where this bowl was produced, *c* AD 20–35. Unburnt.
MIL 5, *6175*, Period 4C, Building *5688*, R5, demolition layer

35. **CG**, Dr 37 (Fig 291). Slightly burnt: an indistinct ovolo (Rogers B231) above panelling with bead rows (A2) and six-dotted rosette terminals (C280) and trifid motif (G67); the saltire to the left included an acanthus (K22?). The caduceus, U103, repeated in a vertical stack, is characteristic of Paternus iv (style III, Rogers 1999, pl 80) and is used with this ovolo on a bowl at Catterick (Dickinson 2002a, fig 198.54). The dog may be an unidentified type recorded at Castleford (Dickinson and Hartley 2000, fig 26.498). The decoration is very similar to that on a bowl from Blackfriars Street (Dickinson 1990, fig 181.57) with the same saltire and indistinct acanthus, but only the hindquarters of an animal. Style of Paternus iv (III) and probably *c* AD 135–65.
MIL 2, *560*, Period 5A, external layer

36. **CG**, Dr 37 (Fig 291). Badly abraded decoration: a scroll with the leaf Rogers H22 used by Sacer (see Simpson and Rogers 1969, fig 2.7, from Corbridge) and Cinnamus (Karnitsch 1959, Taf 72.1). Stamped intra-decoratively in the mould: CINNAMI retrograde, Die 5d of Cinnamus ii, attested at Lezoux, *c* AD 140–65 (Stamp *6*). Two adjoining pieces; the footring is very worn from use, and the exterior is extremely abraded.
MIL 5, *2628*, Period 5B, Road *4662*, road surface

37. **EG**, Dr 37 (Fig 291), La Madeleine. The same motifs occur in VIRTVS-ware at Butzbach: an upper wreath of opposed trifid motifs (*cf* Müller 1968, Taf 11.260) and a lower wreath of the same motif; an arrow (Taf 11.255) and bird (Taf 11.257); the runner is Ricken 1934, Taf 7.88 in the Saalburg list. This figure is now recorded for VIRTVS (Bemmann 1985, Taf 1.44, *cf* Abb 1.10). Hadrianic-early Antonine, and probably *c* AD 130–60. Two sherds.
MIL 5, *2614* and *2492*, Period 5B, Road *4662*, road surface/deposit

38. **EG**, Dr 37 (Fig 291). Grooved around part of the internal wall on a level with the ovolo. An excellent ware similar to some from Les Martres-de-Veyre, identified by Joanna Bird as being from Blickweiler: the ovolo is Knorr and Sprater 1927, Taf 82.32. Below an indistinct bead row (Taf 82.39?) are grapes (Taf 81.22), leaf (Taf 81.59), astragalus (Taf 81.58), birds (Taf 80.9–10), hare (Taf 80.1), and bush with emerging animal (Taf 81.27). The ovolo, grapes, bird, and bush appear at Butzbach on a bowl listed as '*Ware mit Eierstab Knorr-Sprater 1927, Taf 82.32*' (see Müller 1968, Taf 25.668). This bowl is not easily dated, but may have been produced in the early- or even the mid-Antonine period. The ovolo occurs with grapes and birds in the Verulamium fire deposit of *c* AD 155–60, where the bowl was said to represent one of the later Blickweiler styles (Hartley 1972b, fig 98, D139). One sherd from *2618*, and two from *2617*, adjoin three sherds in Period 5C external deposit *2605*, adjacent to Road *4662*.
MIL 5, *2617*, *2618*, Period 5B, Road *4662*, external layers; also joins *2605*, Period 5C, external layer, adjacent to Road *4662*

39. **CG**, Dr 37 (Fig 291). Panelling with rosette terminals (Rogers C132): Apollo (larger than Déch 55) above a panther (Déch 799), and hare (Osw 2061). The details and composition are those of the bowl signed by Criciro (see also *40, qv*); even the vertical bead rows are similarly reduplicated very faintly. However, the fabric and surfaces are not identical and this sherd must represent another bowl; see also *49*. *c* AD 150–70.
MIL 5, *2710*, Period 5B, external surface adjacent to Road *4662*

40. **CG**, Dr 37 (Fig 291). Ovolo Rogers B204, with its tassel degraded. Panelling: bead rows, faintly reduplicated in places, with rosettes (Rogers C132). In the lower compartments, a panther (Déch 799); a fragment of hare facing right; a trifid motif (Rogers G67); and an erotic group smaller than Oswald pl XC, type B. Above, Apollo and cupid (larger than Déch 55 and 255), and a bird (Osw 2295A) in a festoon with acanthus tips (Rogers K10). For the same motifs at Castle Street, see Dickinson 1991a, fig 293.61. All these motifs occur in the same composition on a bowl influenced by Attianus and signed similarly by Criciro, in a pit of *c* AD 150–60 at Alcester (Hartley *et al* 1994, fig 50.278). However, if the Alcester illustration is accurate, slight differences in the spacing might indicate that this bowl was not from the same mould. The signature is retrograde below the decoration, as the mould was signed before firing, by Criciro v, *c* AD 150–70 (Mould signature *1*).

Figure 291: Samian from Period 5

Seven sherds and flakes, including the complete and very worn footring from posthole *6007* (fill *5989*). Two sherds adjoin, one slightly burnt, from Period 6A Building **5200**. See also *39* and *51* in Periods 5B and 6B respectively.

MIL 5, *5989*, Period 5C, fill of posthole *6007*; also joining *5657*, Period 6B, Building **5200**, R4.1, fill of construction pit *5677* and *5834*, Period 6A, Building **5200**, fill of construction trench *5270*

41. **CG**, Dr 37, perhaps 230 mm (Fig 291). A large bowl with ovolo Rogers B103 above beaded panelling and well-spaced decoration: an indistinct head of Minerva (Osw 126 or 126A), warrior (Osw 215, not listed for any named potter) and gladiator (Osw 1061A). The ovolo and motifs indicate the work of Divixtus or Advocisus, *c* AD 150/60–90. The use of Minerva suggests Divixtus, who liked such heads (S and S, pl 116). Probably *c* AD 150–80. Three non-joining sherds.
MIL 5, *5876*, Period 5C, fill of trench *5875*; *5956*, Structure *7473*, fill of feature *5957*; also *5868*, Period 5D, external layer

42. **CG**, Dr 37 (Fig 291). A large scroll containing a medallion with warrior (Osw 204), from a bowl, probably in the later style of Cinnamus (*cf* Karnitsch 1959, Taf 76.6), *c* AD 150/5–80. Three adjoining pieces.
MIL 5, *5956*, Period 5C, Structure *7473*, fill of feature *5957*

43. **CG**, Dr 37, rim diameter 170 mm (Fig 291). A small bowl with ovolo Rogers B208 above panels with bead rows (A3). An indistinct medallion (E25) contains a triton (Déch 16), as on a bowl in the style of Casurius at Bewcastle (Stanfield 1935, pl 1.1). A distinct version of the vine-scroll M22 lies over a long-eared hare (Osw 2116). A pigeon-like bird (Déch 1037) struts above an acanthus (probably Rogers K16; S and S, pl 135.38). A very faint leaf-tip was obscured by the superimposed festoon probably intended to enclose it, as on the Bewcastle bowl (*qv*). Ovolo B208 is probably the same as B176, known for Casurius. The ovolo, pigeon, and acanthus occur on another bowl by Casurius from Blackfriars Street (Dickinson 1990, fig 179.38). Three adjoining rimsherds. *c* AD 160–90.
MIL 5, *2589*, Period 5C, Road *4662*, fill of trench *2590*

44. **CG**, Dr 37 (Fig 291). A poorly moulded, small bowl with squashed details. The blurred ovolo is most likely to be Rogers B47. Below a bead row are freestyle figures: a nude man (Osw 684A), lion (Osw 1450), and hound (see S and S, pl 87.20 by Attianus), and probably the lion Osw 1424; *cf* S and S, pl 118.12. Repetitive snake-and-rock motifs (Osw 2155) were used by Attianus or Criciro and the ovolo indicates the latter. Its poor quality, together with its small size, suggests that, rather than being a second, it was the work of an apprentice in the workshop of Criciro. The style of this bowl is so close to that of Attianus that it may have been a contemporary product, perhaps *c* AD 135–60. The footring is very worn.
MIL 5, *2427*, Period 5D, Road *4662*, road surface

45. **EG**, Dr 37 (Fig 291). Reddish gloss on an orange-buff fabric heavily flecked with yellowish inclusions. The plain band is stamped diagonally and upside down [MAMMIL]IANVS between guidelines (Stamp *15*): Die 4b of Mammilianus, attested at Rheinzabern, *c* AD 160?–80. The bowl is from a mould in the style of Reginus vi (style I): ovolo (Ricken and Fischer 1963, E 58) with guideline above roundels and perhaps a smaller ring. The roundels are not exactly the same as Ricken and Fisher (1963), O 121 or 122. Type O 121 is listed in Ricken-Fischer for the work of Ianu(arius I) and is ascribed there as '*auf der schwäbischen Reginus-Ware: Knorr Cannstatt (1905),*

Taf 18, 4'. The roundels on the Cannstatt and the Carlisle bowls have a plain outer ring and a central blob, unlike O 121 and a second Cannstatt bowl (Knorr 1905, Taf 18, 5). *Cf* Ricken 1948, Taf 16.10: Reginus vi (style I) at Rheinzabern, probably *c* AD 160–80. Two adjoining sherds.
MIL 5, *2500*, Period 5D, Road *4662*, road surface

46. **SG**, Dr 29 (Fig 292). In the lower zone, a winding scroll with neat leaves, a six-beaded tendril-binding, and a nine-petalled rosette terminal, all motifs used by Labio: the segmented leaf and binding are on a stamped form 29 at London (Knorr 1952, Taf 32B). Dannell noted the frilled leaf and rosette on a stamped form 29 previously found at Carlisle (see Dannell *et al* 2004, no 2744). Probably *c* AD 55–70.
MIL 5, *5800*, Period 6A, Building *5200*, fill of construction trench *5193*

47. **CG**, Dr 37 (Fig 292). The composition and details resemble those of Rogers 1999, pl 30.17. The ovolo is Rogers B144 above astragaloid borders (A9); panther (Déch 799?) in a festoon (Rogers F35), Apollo with lyre (Osw 83), and two types of Venus (Osw 278 and 286). To the left of this last type was stamped in the mould, [CIN]NAMI retrograde (Stamp *5*): Die 5a of Cinnamus ii, attested at Lezoux, *c* AD 135-60. Seven adjoining sherds.
MIL 1, *243*, Period 6A, Road *7646*, external layer

48. **EG**, Dr 37, rim diameter 220 mm (Fig 292). Reddish gloss on a reddish orange fabric with few inclusions. Two fragments of rim whose addition to the bowl cut off a row of uneven rings (apparently in place of an ovolo; *cf* Ricken 1948, taf 18.14). A third sherd belongs to the same bowl, showing a plant (Ricken and Fischer 1963, P 50) used only by Reginus vi (I) while working at Heiligenberg and Rheinzabern; *cf* Wild 1988, fig 2.18, from Ribchester. The Carlisle bowl was a Rheinzabern product of the later second century, probably *c* AD 160–80.
MIL 5, *2567*, Period 6A, Road *2303*, road surface

49. **CG**, Dr 37 (Fig 292). A blurred and abraded ovolo, Rogers B204 with a smudged terminal. Panels with rosettes C125, pediment U269, bird, and Diana (Déch 1019 and 64). The style of Criciro, *c* AD 150–70. This is the same composition as *39* and *40*, but the impression of the ovolo is dissimilar and may not be from the same bowl, although in a similar fabric. The ovolo occurs with other of the motifs at Castle Street, showing the other side of the pediment and the opposing bird (Dickinson 1991a, fig 293.61).
MIL 5, *5330*, Period 6B, Building *5200*, R4.1, make-up layer

50. **EG**, Dr 37 (Fig 292). A badly abraded sherd with a poor, brownish slip on a heavily flecked, pinkish buff fabric from Trier. Poorly moulded decoration: the arcades (Gard 1937, type KB 68, and Fölzer 1913, Taf 32.953) occur on a bowl at York (Hartley and Dickinson 1990, fig 109.1113). The small, indistinct roundel on the edge of the Carlisle sherd is Gard's type M 1, originally containing a mask. This roundel occurs on one bowl, and the overlapping festoons and arcades occur on another, from the London waterfront (Bird 1986, 2.77–78), although there the

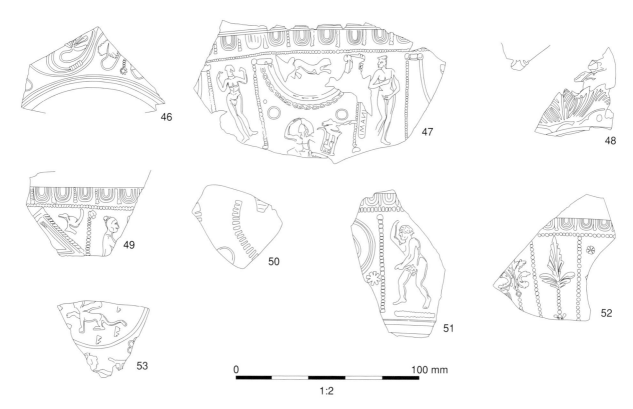

Figure 292: Samian from Period 6 and unstratified

festoons were more closely impressed. Bowl *50* is in the style of Afer, who worked at Trier in the early third century, but Joanna Bird notes that the fabric, slip, and general modelling suggest a later date. The bowl was certainly produced in the third century, probably in the second quarter, and possibly as late as *c* AD 245/50. It is now clear that a poorly made bowl from Catterick with overlapping festoons and arcades (Dickinson 2002b, fig 157.120) has the same indistinct roundel, along with an ovolo used by Afer (Gard's type 18).
MIL 5, *5575*, Period 6B, external layer adjacent to Building *5200*

51. **CG**, Dr 30 (Fig 292). A small, indistinctly modelled ovolo above panelling with Rogers A3 borders and an indistinct twist. The cupid is Déch 251 (considerably smaller than Osw 442); it was used by Do(v)eccus i along with this same rosette (C170) on a bowl from Papcastle (S and S, pl 148.22). *c* AD 165/70–200 (a date after *c* AD 170 having been proposed by 2009). Slightly burnt.
MIL 5, *5377*, Period 6C, Structure *7651*, fill of pit *5378*

52. **CG**, Dr 37 (Fig 292). The fragment of mould-stamp in the decoration reads D[OIICCVS] retrograde, Die 13a of Do(v)eccus i (Stamp *11*). The indistinct ovolo, if Rogers B160, seems exclusive to him (*cf* S and S, fig 44.2) and the roundly-beaded borders are associated with his ovolo B160 and with Die 13a. The borders, unusually for Do(v)eccus but not for Casurius, have no junction-masks. Brenda Dickinson (*pers comm*) notes the larger leaf (Rogers H68?) on a bowl stamped by Casurius at Littleborough. Do(v)eccus, however, did use this rosette (C131; here with a central dot) whereas Casurius did not favour rosettes or junction-masks. Do(v)eccus certainly used the small leaf (H101) and the bifid motif, as well as beads terminating in leaves (*cf* Rogers 1999, pl 40.7). The acanthus is not a Rogers type, but has been noted

with the same stamp at the Brougham cemetery (Dickinson *et al* 2004) and at Benwell (B Dickinson *pers comm*). The Carlisle bowl appears to have been a hybrid piece. As Casurius began work before Do(v)eccus, it probably represents one of Do(v)eccus' earliest moulds. Dickinson suggested a date of *c* AD 160–85 for Stamp *11* in 2004. Two adjoining sherds, unburnt.
MIL 5, *2140*, Period 6D, Road *2303*, demolition layer

53. **CG**, Dr 37 (Fig 292). A festoon with a sphinx (Osw 857) and indistinct leaf-tips above Apollo (Osw 83); *cf* Knorr 1905, Taf 2.2 from Cannstatt. The rosette filler is Rogers C53, recorded at Catterick with the sphinx (as on S and S, pl 157.12) and the unusual filling motifs, apparently the tip of a fan- or wedge-shaped motif (see Dickinson *et al* 2002, 317, no 10). The style is that of the Cerialis ii – Cinnamus ii group, *c* AD 135–60.
MIL 1, *9991*, unstratified

Discussion

In addition to its significance as a dating tool, samian provides other important detail about the site and its occupation. Despite an awareness that evidence for the use, repair, reworking, and reuse of samian ware is of value (Bulmer 1980b, 89; Marsh 1981, 227f), it is still not widely discussed and thus the scope for comparison with other sites remains limited, despite continuing calls for the full publication of such data (Willis 1998, 121; 2005, 8.7.1). More than 10% of the collection showed signs of wear from primary use, almost all on footrings, but only one vessel, a deep dish probably of form 31R from Period 6E (*5306*, the fill of robber trench *7650* associated with road *7652*), had suffered extreme scouring of its interior.

Site	Context	Period	Fabric	Form	Stamp No	Potter	Vessel date	Same as	Graffito
MIL 5	7587	3A	SG	15/17 or 18			70-100		Erased
MIL 5	3244	4A	SG	18	8	Cotto ii	70-100		X V
MIL 5	3572	4A	SG	18	31	Secundus ii	70-90		V
MIL 1	1169	4A/B	SG	18	47	OF[	70-100	326	X X
MIL 1	327	4B	SG	15/17 or 18	37	+.....+	70-100	6583	X
MIL 3	910	4B	SG	27	41	IAI[?	70-110	815	A
MIL 5	2767	4B	SG	15/17 or 18			50-80		Fragments
MIL 5	2800	4B	SG	18 or 18R			70-110		Three nicks
MIL 5	2800	4B	SG	33			70-100		III
MIL 5	3218	4B	SG	18			70-110		Three nicks
MIL 5	3315	4B	SG	15/17 or 18			70-110		Erasure and secondary fragments
MIL 5	5918	4B	SG	27 or 35			70-100		AP
MIL 5	6207	4B	SG	15/17 or 18			70-100		[…]CLII[…]
MIL 5	6153	4C	SG	15/17 or 18			70-100		V[…]
MIL 5	2790	4D	SG	18	18	Ortius Paullus	80-100	2806	I x I
MIL 1	326	5	CG	18/31			100-25		PRIM[…]
MIL 5	2605	5C	CG	18/31	49	O\[?	120-50		A
MIL 5	6098	5C	CG	33	20	Peculiaris i.	155-70		Accidental damage?
MIL 5	5883	6A	SG	18			70-100		MAGL[…]
MIL 5	5325	6C	CG	31R			160-200		Accidental damage?
MIL 5	2107	7	CG	18/31			100-40		[…]V
MIL 5	2110	7	CG	79 or Tg			170-200		X

Table 16: Summary of graffiti and marks on samian ware

Graffiti

Graffiti occur particularly frequently on samian ware (Evans 1987, 202), and often give information about the individuals who owned and used specific vessels. In this assemblage there were 20–2 instances (1.3%; Table 16; *Appendix 2*). All the graffiti were made after firing and are thus likely to be marks of ownership. They were not confined to the products of any particular period or producer: 16 were on South Gaulish vessels of the Neronian-Flavian to Domitianic-Trajanic periods; and four to six were on Central Gaulish vessels ranging from the Trajanic to the late-Antonine periods (two Central Gaulish dishes in Periods 5C and 6C may have suffered accidental damage). All the vessels were plain forms, four being cups (two Central Gaulish) and 16-18 dishes (two to four, Central Gaulish). Their restriction to plain forms is of interest, and raises the possibility that decorated vessels were thought sufficiently distinctive to be recognised without further identification. At least eight of the graffiti were simple marks of identification, including four 'crosses' (X) and two vessels with incised nicks (as well as the two dishes which may have suffered accidental damage to their footrings). Ten probably signified personal ownership; three were fragmentary names, restored most probably as Primus, Clemens, and Maglus; in a further three, or possibly four, cases, names may have been abbreviated to only a letter or two. Two of the marks, which presumably also signified ownership, had subsequently been deleted; one had been re-inscribed, presumably when the vessel changed hands. It is almost always samian vessels which show evidence of such changes (Tomlin 2002a, 504 on the graffiti from Catterick). Another vessel was inscribed III and one (or possibly two) read X V.

Only one graffito was found in an early context (Period 3A (7587)), and this, on a Flavian dish, had been erased. In contrast, 14 examples were recovered from Period 4 levels (Table 16), half of which were in Period 4B, including three that signified ownership. Three others, found in Period 5 contexts, included one perhaps accidentally damaged; two, from Period 5 soil deposit 326, and 2605, a Period 5C external deposit adjacent to road 4662, signified ownership. In Period 6A, a Flavian dish from construction trench fill 5883 (Building 5200) belonged to an individual with a Celtic name (probably Maglus or a derivative). The late-Antonine dish of form 31R, found in Period 6C road surface 5325 (road 7652), had probably suffered accidental abrasion. The two instances in Period 7 were on dishes produced in the early second century and in the period c AD 170-200. The lack of graffiti on second-century Central Gaulish vessels might well reflect the general shortage of Antonine samian on the site.

Repairs

Only six vessels, four of which were bowls, had seen repair work, comprising 0.3% of the samian ware (Table 17). This proportion may be compared with 0.7% recorded at Prestatyn (Ward 1989, 154), 1.4% at Piercebridge and 3% in the Tofts Field area (Ward 2008, 193), 1.6% at Lancaster (Ward forthcoming a), and 2.8% at Worcester (Ward forthcoming b). For whatever the reason, repairs were not common in the sample from this part of the Carlisle fort. It is of interest to compare the incidence of repaired bowls (here only four vessels, but comprising 67%), with that from sites of differing status. At Walton-le-Dale, their proportion was much higher (c 88%; Evans and Ratkai forthcoming); in contrast, at one site in Lancaster, they comprised only 30% (Ward forthcoming a).

Three of the repaired vessels were from South Gaul, one from Les Martres in the Trajanic period, and two

from Lezoux, and came from many periods of the site. Two of the repairs were of the round, drilled variety, three of the cut variety (dove-tailed or cleat-type), and one was indeterminate. The evidence of this very small sample may not accord with the theory that dove-tailed rivets were a later method, preferred in the second century (Marsh 1981, 227). On the other hand, whatever their date of production, it remains unclear when these vessels were repaired.

It is difficult to judge the success of repair work, particularly when the vessel finally broke through the rivet hole and lacks rivets, as, for example, in the probably late Neronian fragment (2, p 553) from Period 3A demolition deposit 7108 (Building 7393). Lead was traced or suspected in several cases, and two bowls retained lead rivets or fragments thereof. The success of the repairs, even of those retaining their rivets, is uncertain. For instance, a large part of a moulded bowl (18, p 556), produced c AD 80-100 and worn in use, had been repaired with, and retains, lead rivets in dove-tailed holes, but the vessel had broken again at the rivet holes, either during or following the repair work. It seems unlikely that the bowl was in use for long, if at all, after its repair and before its deposition in Period 3C Building 4657, by which time it was in at least nine pieces (a further five being residual in a possible floor (4460) in Period 4A Structure 4664). The latest vessels showing evidence of repair were both plainware dishes of Antonine date, one from Period 6B road 2303 (2350), the other from the Period 7 'dark earths' (2227). The latter was repaired with round-holed rivets; the former may also display a round hole, but this is uncertain.

The repair, successful or otherwise, of the bowl found in a Period 3A occupation layer in Building 7393 might gain in significance if that building was a workshop (Ch 3, pp 103-4). Similarly, another of the repairs was found in Period 4B Building 2765, which has been identified as a smithy (Ch 6). Repaired samian vessels have been found in association with metalworking elsewhere, for example at Prestatyn

Site	Context	Period	Fabric	Form	Vessel Date	Same as	Type of repair	Comments
MIL 5	7108	3A	SG	29	60-70		Round	Fig 284.2
MIL 5	4144	3C	SG	37	80-100	Period 3C (3190), Period 4A (4460)	Cut; lead rivet	Fig 286.18
MIL 5	6289	4B	CG	30	100-25		Cut	
MIL 5	3000	4B	SG	37	70-110		Cut	
MIL 5	2350	6B	CG	18/31R or 31R	140-200		Uncertain	
MIL 5	2227	7	CG	31R	160-200		Round; lead riveting	

Table 17: Repaired samian vessels

Site	Context	Period	Fabric	Form	Vessel Date	Item	Diameter	Comments
MIL 5	2605	5C	CG	37	140-70	counter	30 mm	Ovolo B143 or 144? not drawn
MIL 1	259	6A	SG	67	70-110	counter	18 mm	Fig 293.1
MIL 5	2177	6A	CG	33	120-200	spindle-whorl	30 mm Hole 4 mm	Fig 293.2
MIL 5	2325	6B	CG	ind	120-200	disc	40 mm	Obtrusive fingerprint. Fig 293.3
MIL 5	5497	6C	CG	ind	140-200	counter	20 mm	Fig 293.4
MIL 2	512	6D	CG	ind	100-60	counter	25 mm	Possibly Trajanic Les Martres ware. Fig 293.5
MIL 5	2143	6D	CG	ind	120-200	counter	20 mm	Fig 293.6
MIL 5	2216	6D	CG	ind	120-200	disc	40 mm?	Fig 293.7
MIL 5	2105	7	EG	37	160-240	counter	20 mm	Rheinzabern ware. Possibly same bowl in (2103)? Fig 293.8
MIL 5	5272	8A	CG	37	140-200	counter	30 mm	Basal line of the decoration. Fig 293.9
MIL 5	5051	8C	CG	33	140-200	spindle-whorl	35 mm Hole 7 mm	Broken at the hole. Fig 293.10
MIL 5	5102	8C	CG	33	120-200	spindle-whorl	34 mm Hole 7 mm?	Broken at the hole. Fig 293.11
MIL 5	2103	9	EG	37	160-240	disc	35 mm	Top of an ovolo from Rheinzabern Fig 293.12

ind= indeterminate

Table 18: Reused samian ware (counters and spindle whorls)

and Piercebridge (Ward 1989, 154; 1993, 19-20). In the northern '*vicus*' at Piercebridge, the metalworking carried out in a workshop may have been associated with the repair and reworking of samian ware (Ward 2008, 193).

Secondary use

The 'working life' of a samian vessel could be extended by reuse. Fourteen vessels (0.8% of the assemblage) had been cut down or reworked as counters or discs, and spindle-whorls (Table 18; Fig 293). The quantity of repaired, reworked, and reused samian is far smaller than that recorded at Piercebridge, where a workshop was presumed to have operated in the Roman period (*above*). In the Millennium assemblage, 71% of the repaired or reworked pieces were recovered from Roman levels. There were several types of reuse: two vessels were sawn or filed down (Period 5B, *559*, the fill of gully *558*, and Period 6B, *5838*, the fill of ditch *5839*); two fragments found in Periods 5B (*326*, external layer) and 6D (*2216*, demolition deposit in Building *2302*) may have been filed down or rubbed. The latter, a sub-rectangular item, might perhaps have been used as a rubber, but only a flake survived (in the same context as one of the discs (Table 18)). There were no bases showing signs of use for mixing or grinding purposes, or of reuse upside down (Marsh 1981, 229; Ward 2008, 192).

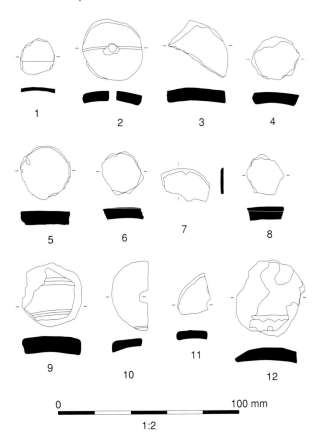

Figure 293: Samian reused as counters and spindle whorls

Ten counters or discs were found, three of them probably too large to be gaming counters (Table 18). Batches of counters were also found at Old Penrith (24 or more; Dickinson 1991b, 135) and Piercebridge (25 or more; Ward 2008, 192). In this group, their diameters varied from 18 mm to 40 mm, the three large discs in Periods 6B, 6D, and 9 measuring 35-40 mm. One small counter was worked from a thin-walled South Gaulish beaker of form 67. At least half of the examples derived from bowl forms, and three showed fragments of decoration; one bore the bowl-maker's fingerprint clearly detailed. The vessels ranged in date of production from the Flavian period to the third century, but the earliest context in which a counter was found was an external layer (*2605*) in Period 5C. There were eight examples in Period 6, one in Period 7, and two in medieval and later contexts (Periods 8 and 9). At least three of the remaining items were recovered from contexts associated with a possible barrack, Building **2302**, in Periods 6B and 6D. It is conceivable that a rough counter and a large disc, found in Periods 7 and 9 respectively, could represent the same East Gaulish bowl. That in Period 9 shows the top of an ovolo, suggesting a bowl produced at Rheinzabern in the later second or earlier third century.

There were three probable spindle-whorls, one in Period 6A and two in Period 8C. Their central holes accord in size with those attributed to Roman spindles, ranging here from 4 mm to 7 mm. The discs themselves were 30–35 mm in diameter (Table 18; Fig 293) and were fashioned from Hadrianic-Antonine or Antonine products. Each was taken from the cup form 33, whose shape presumably best suited the purpose (fragments of cups being a less common find than dishes on the site). None of the spindle-whorls showed clear evidence of wear in their secondary use, but both Period 8 examples were broken. It is significant that the example found in Period 6A, along with three of the counters, must have been reworked when East Gaulish samian ware was still in production and when some late Central Gaulish vessels could still have been in use. This spindle-whorl was found in the fill (*2177*) of a wall construction trench (*2178*) in Building **2301**, a barrack, of the stone fort. This lies immediately south of Building **2302**, in which three of the counters were found.

It has been noted (Cool 2000, 53) that in a sample from various sites, including Birdoswald and South Shields, only one context contemporary with samian production produced a spindle-whorl. At Carlisle, however, it seems that such items were being deposited in the first half of the third century (*op cit*, fig 30), when the Rheinzabern and Trier workshops were still in operation. Cool has suggested that spindle-whorls found in late

contexts may not have been redeposited, but may have been reworked during the late-Roman or post-Roman periods. On the other hand, the counter and spindle-whorls found in Periods 8 and 9 could have been part of the group found, already reworked, in earlier phases. The bowl, or bowls, from which the roughly worked disc from Period 9 and counter from Period 7 came could not have been produced, or reworked, before the late second century, and Rheinzabern wares are not noted before Periods 5D and 6A. Nonetheless, it remains unclear whether reused samian items found in post-Roman contexts represent the redeposition of material reworked during the Roman period, or reworking at a much later date.

The higher proportion of East Gaulish wares in Period 7 'dark earth' deposits (16%) may be thought to represent rubbish derived from Period 6 activity rather than survival in use, but there has been little research into residuality (*cf* Hartley and Dickinson 1985, 82, on samian ware at Saxon West Stow). Individual pieces such as the counter in Period 7, if not merely fragments of residual rubbish, could have been reworked in the sub-Roman period or else could have survived in secondary use.

The Coarse Pottery
(including amphorae and mortaria)

V G Swan, R M McBride, and K F Hartley, with contributions by R S O Tomlin and P Booth

The fine and coarser wares recovered during the excavations (stratified and unstratified) comprised some 15,460 sherds, weighing 343.892 kg, and with an equivalent vessel estimate (EVE) of 227.09. When the samian totals are added, some 18,128 sherds of pottery, weighing 364.84 kg, with an EVE total of 275.94, were recovered from deposits containing material discarded during the life of the forts. The coarsewares (including amphorae) recorded in deposits of the Roman period (Periods 2-6) comprised 87.4% of the total number of sherds and 88.4% by weight. From the same deposits, amphorae accounted for only 1135 sherds (8.4% of total), weighing 12.464 kg (41% of total), with an EVE of 7.63 (3.7% of total EVEs). These last clearly represent packaging for foodstuffs, rather than vessels in use, and they are thus documented separately.

The coarsewares were generally in a good state of preservation, and often excellent in the first-century deposits, where the anaerobic conditions had, for example, permitted the preservation of the internal lining and sealing (around the mouth) of black

Plate 193: The preserved black pitch 'waterproof' lining on an amphora neck

pitch 'waterproofing' on several of the amphorae (Pl 193) and their lids (*eg* amphora *17, 11, 12, 14*). A rare sequence of pen-and-ink *dipinti* on an amphora (*16*) also owed their survival to these exceptional conditions.

Methodology

All the stratified pottery was examined and quantified by sherd-count, sherd-weight, and EVEs (Orton 1989; these are strictly rim equivalents and are therefore referred to as EREs hereafter). The fabrics have been divided into two groups: A) those described and illustrated in the *National Fabric Reference Collection* (Tomber and Dore 1998); and B) other fabrics, less well known and not included in the above. A fabric type-series was established (*Appendix 2*), incorporating the categories of information on a *proforma* record sheet, as established by Peacock (1977; Orton *et al* 1993). The fabrics were identified by eye or with the aid of a x10 or x20 hand lens or binocular microscope. Data recorded on an Access database comprised information on the excavated area, phasing, context, vessel-part, fabric, diameter, functional class, detailed vessel-form or type and decoration, sherd-joins (where obvious), and other features such as burning, wear, and repair. Unstratified sherds and those in medieval and later contexts (Phase 8 onwards) were identified, counted, and weighed only. Vessels for illustration were chosen mainly for chronological and typological reasons, coupled with the need to expand the published repertoire of forms found at Carlisle, particularly those relating to the changing sequences of local production.

Context and chronological variation

There was considerable variation between trenches with regard to the amount of pottery recovered (Table 19), with that from MIL 5 (including amphorae) comprising over 81% of the total by sherd count, weight, and EREs. In part, this is due to the size of MIL 5, but more significantly, it was the only area which had a continuous stratigraphic sequence from AD 72/3 into the post-Roman period, the others having been truncated. There were also significant differences in the amounts of pottery recovered from each period (Table 20), but because of the uneven survival of later deposits in different trenches, the material from MIL 5 is often the main source for the comparison of pottery usage.

Consideration of pottery usage can be affected by a number of factors, and although the relative amount of pottery recovered might be expected to increase through time, as a result of the accrual of redeposited rubbish alongside freshly discarded material, there were significant deviations from this pattern, which only partly relate to the scope and intensity of activity on the site. The relatively high levels of rubbish in the first two periods of significant occupation (Periods 3 and 4) probably resulted in part from the waterlogged nature of the terrain and the character of the buildings. It can be suggested that Roman timber buildings with earth or timber floors are often associated with more rubbish than stone buildings, presumably in part because material can be trodden into earth floors or fall through the floorboards. Indeed, it might be further suggested that, during the life of the timber forts, waste was not always cleared away, with larger fragments and sometimes semi-complete vessels left lying around (Pl 194), probably deliberately, in order to contribute

Trench	Weight (g)	% Weight	No Sherds	% Sherds	Rim EREs	% Rim EREs
MIL 1	36,385	10.6	1602	10.4	21.01	9.3
MIL 2	12,469	3.6	385	2.5	6.34	2.8
MIL 3	6059	1.8	180	1.2	1.97	0.9
MIL 4	9596	2.8	430	2.8	3.33	1.5
MIL 5	279,383	81.2	12,863	83.2	194.44	85.6
Total	**343,892**		**15,460**		**227.09**	

Table 19: Quantification of Roman coarse pottery by excavation area

Period	Weight (g)	% Weight	Sherds	% Sherds	EREs (%)	% Rim EREs
1, 2, and 3A	23,113	7.6	527	3.9	8.84	4.3
3B	19,027	6.3	415	3.1	7.04	3.4
3C, 3D, and 3E	16,304	5.4	434	3.2	5.57	2.7
4A	25,618	8.4	1255	9.3	17.40	8.4
4A/B	11,892	3.9	595	4..4	10.35	5.0
4B, 4C, and 4D	59,775	19.7	2925	21.7	45.86	22.1
5	8683	2.9	402	3.0	4.89	2.4
5A	7384	2.4	399	3.0	10.61	5.1
5B	12,479	4.1	465	3.4	9.82	4.7
5C	11,152	3.7	606	4.5	10.16	4.9
5D	12,547	4.1	665	4.9	8.56	4.1
6A	37,814	12.4	1545	11.4	21.31	10.3
6B	17,626	5.8	1006	7.5	13.47	6.5
6C	20,515	6.8	1243	9.2	17.96	8.7
6D	7251	2.4	516	3.8	9.18	4.4
6E	8194	2.7	471	3.5	5.61	2.7
Total	**304,119**		**13,512**		**207.19**	

Table 20: Stratified Roman pottery by period

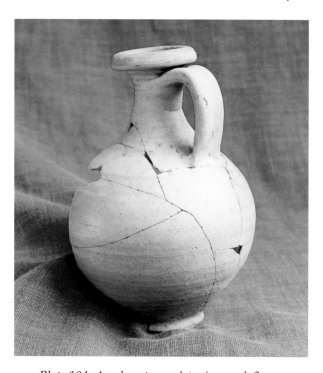

Plate 194: An almost complete ring-neck flagon

to the build-up and gradual raising of ground level. This seems particularly to have been the case with regard to some of the earlier alterations. Period 3A (*Ch 3*), lasting only about a decade, stands out as having a surprising amount of discarded pottery, even in comparison with Period 3B. This must, in part at least, reflect the density of occupation; evidently large quantities of basic provisions (particularly amphorae and mortaria) were brought to the site at, and immediately after, its foundation, despite the

likelihood that pottery production began in the area immediately (*p 593*). It is also possible that rubbish-disposal was less well-organised in the early days of the fort. A further reduction in the quantity of pottery disposed of in the decade or so beginning with Period 3C (Periods 3C-3E; *Ch 4*) partly reflects the absence of a garrison for the latter part of the period. Even so, there is probably more pottery than might be expected, and this perhaps reflects the fact that when the fort was demolished in the early years of the second century, considerable numbers of vessels seem to have been left within the buildings on demolition, and these were sealed by the construction of the second timber fort (Period 4A; *Ch 5*).

Ceramic discard levels were even higher in the early days of the second timber fort (Period 4A) than they had been in Period 3A. Whilst residual material may have been a contributory factor, this could well reflect a greater availability of pottery in general, and for personal purchase in particular. It was in Period 4B (*Ch 6*), however, that there was a peak in relative quantities of this material (see Table 20). It is possible that the more industrial character of the late Hadrianic occupation meant that even less attention was paid to the disposal of rubbish. The exact nature of the garrison at this time remains unclear, although evidence suggests the temporary presence of legionaries, presumably during the erection of Hadrian's Wall. It might well be the case that a succession of temporary occupants were less concerned with maintenance and waste disposal, partly because constant change would have made it difficult to establish an orderly routine. Moreover, this relatively unchecked accumulation seems to have been compounded by deliberate episodes of levelling, which included laying of clay floors directly over the debris of industrial activity (*eg* Buildings *5689* and *2765*).

In Period 5 (*c* AD 140/50-200/10), the lower levels of pottery discarded (little more than one third of those seen previously) provide a strong contrast to the preceding periods. This seems to reflect the absence of a resident garrison, following the demolition of the fort, and thereby a relatively low level of activity (*Ch 7*), which was probably sporadic and certainly more informal than it had been for at least 50 years. In fact, the generally smaller average sherd size for this period suggests that the greater part of the material is residual, mainly from dumping, at least some of which had probably been brought in from elsewhere for levelling.

The construction of the stone fort in Period 6 caused significant disturbance to earlier deposits. Although a permanent garrison was now in residence, the relative amount of contemporary rubbish disposed of during Period 6A (lasting approximately a century) was significantly less per decade than in Periods 3 and 4, despite increased levels of residual material. This probably reflects greater general tidiness and more systematic rubbish disposal, a characteristic of the interior of forts with stone buildings. In addition, there was probably less need to raise the ground-level of the site because, over the preceding 130 years, the terrain had gradually been raised above the water table by the demolition and levelling of earlier buildings, and the insertion of drains. An apparent reduction in intensity of occupation might have been another significant factor in the overall decrease of stratified pottery for this period. Certainly, at this date, the buildings seem to have been less tightly packed than before, and, as units in the late Roman army decreased in size, the barracks probably accommodated fewer soldiers to use and discard pottery (Hodgson and Bidwell 2004). It is difficult to calculate the precise duration of the various phases of later activity (Periods 6B-6E); nevertheless, there seems to be a somewhat higher level of ceramic disposal in Period 6C (*Ch 9*), and (residual material aside) this may reflect the presence of a market in the centre of the fort from about the middle of the fourth to the early fifth century (*Ch 13*; *pp 463-5*). Thereafter, pottery deposition declined sharply, mirroring the cessation of the supply of coinage (*Appendix 3*), the demolition of the fort, and the near abandonment of the parts of the site investigated, although it is possible that material continued to be dumped on the site.

General dating: the impact of the ceramic evidence

In the earliest periods of Roman activity (Periods 2-4), the establishment of a site chronology was rightly reliant on the precision of dendrochronological dates (*Appendix 16*), with additional refinement from the coins (*Ch 17*) and the decorated samian. In this situation, the greatest contribution of the coarse pottery lay in providing other types of information, in particular with regard to the composition and origins of the garrison, for example the presence of non-local builders, and larger scale troop movements. In addition, it provided valuable information on the rapid development of local pottery production, other sources of supply, and long-distance trade. For Period 5 (lacking both dendrochronological dates and significant numbers of coins) and Period 6A (when most samian is residual and coinage is very scarce), the coarse pottery assumed a more significant role in dating. Indeed, dating the construction of the stone fort (Period 6A), is entirely dependent on the coarse pottery. The increased amounts of late third- and fourth-century coinage complements and occasionally refines the ceramic dating of the final phases of Roman occupation (Periods 6B-6E).

Interpretation of the assemblage
The basics of institutional supply

In recent years, the interpretation of pottery in a Roman military context has become an increasingly complex field. It has been appreciated for some time that, during the first and early/mid-second centuries, forts or fortresses built in regions where the indigenous population was aceramic (or had little established ceramic tradition) relied significantly on pottery made locally by soldier-craftsmen drawn from within the garrison (probably *immunes*; Breeze 1977), or by civilian contractors working under supervision of the army in the immediate vicinity of individual military installations, the latter probably not common until the early second century (Swan 2002). Pottery workshops set up in such circumstances were often (but not always) an adjunct of the fort tilery, particularly when building-work requiring tiles was taking place (Swan and McBride 2002). At Carlisle, the marked absence of tiles in Period 3A buildings, and the reliance on wooden water pipes (*Ch 3*), suggests that the garrison's first potteries made only pottery. However, local tile manufacture seems to have begun, albeit at a small scale, by the beginning of Period 3B (AD 83-4; *see Ch 20*).

Probably partly as a result of its distance from the well-used trade routes of the eastern seaboard, and the apparent reluctance of western producers to send their products northwards in any quantity, the import of pottery in any significant amounts seems to have remained a long-term problem for Carlisle. Indeed, military-controlled kilns just outside the fort and nearby works-depots (*p 590*) served as the principal suppliers to the fort until at least the

Plate 195: A flat-rimmed bowl with the distinctive lattice of Black-burnished ware vessels

mid-second century, when there might have been a break in occupation (Period 5). After this, from *c* AD 160 until well into the third century, another local, but presumably by this time civilian, enterprise (*pp 594-5*) became the main supplier, not only to the newly rebuilt fort, but also to the wider extramural settlement. Indeed, it is notable that for almost the first 70 years of the fort's existence, imported vessels of most types remained relatively scarce, particularly fine tablewares. The only exception to this was the supply of Black-burnished ware cooking vessels from the South West (Pl 195), although these did not begin to be shipped northwards until the AD 120s, initially arriving only in small quantities (Tyers 1996, 185). It was not until the third century that changing circumstances, possibly improvements in communication and travel overland, and changes in policy with regard to military supply, allowed Carlisle to shed its dependency on local producers. By the middle of the fourth century, however, the movement of Black-burnished ware up the west coast had ceased, and Carlisle, like many other military sites in northern Britain, became dependent on pottery from north of York and the East coast (*ibid*).

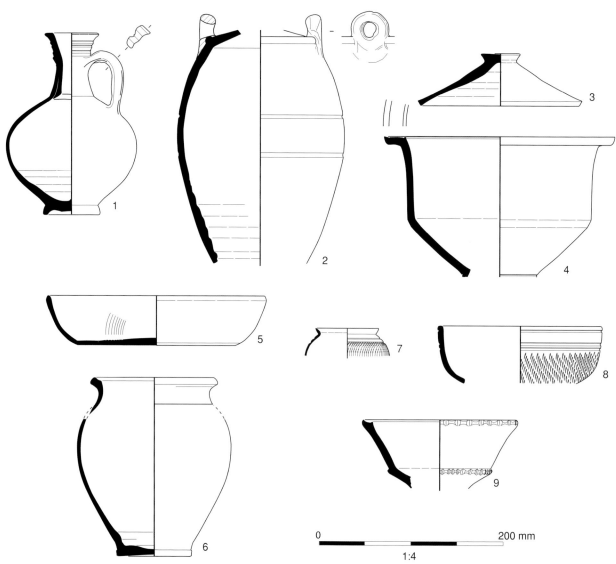

Figure 294: The core range of vessel forms used by the Roman army for food preparation, cooking, storage, and consumption in the first and second centuries

Evidence from Carlisle, and other first- and second-century military sites, seems to suggest that the Roman army required its potters to make a core-range of vessels (Fig 294), which may well have constituted a 'kit-issue' (for food-preparation, cooking, storage, eating, and drinking), and which were intended essentially for daily use in the barracks, but were also used in the officers' quarters (Swan 2002). It would usually have comprised: flagons (in relatively standard sizes for the wine ration (Fig 294.1)); storage-vessels (Fig 294.2); multi-purpose mortaria; carinated cooking-bowls with flat or reeded rims and matching lids (Fig 294.3-4); shallow cooking-dishes for the flat-bread ration, designed to be pushed into the hot ash of the bread oven (Fig 294.5); tall cooking-jars with an out-splayed rim sometimes used for boiling water (Fig 294.6); and small wine beakers (Fig 294.7), eating- or serving-bowls, and dishes (Fig 294.8). The potters seem to have been allowed more discretion in the basic forms of the tablewares than in other vessels, as well as in vessels intended for special functions such as costrels, tazze (Fig 294.9), triple vases, and crucibles. Indeed, whilst some of these products may have been official military issue, others could have been available for purchase by individual soldiers, though it is highly unlikely that local opportunities for personal purchases were available immediately after the foundation of Carlisle's first timber fort, as it lay in newly conquered, relatively isolated, and probably hostile, territory, and secure supply lines would not have been established. It is important to stress the relative uniformity of the basic range of vessels commissioned by the fort and produced by the local military-controlled workshop, because the recognition of additional, often non-standard, forms produced by the same workshops can provide evidence for the origins of the potters, and, by implication, of the origins of, and transfers and recruits to, the garrison.

Such local products would have been supplemented, whenever possible, by pottery acquired through more long-distance institutional arrangements, this being particularly the case for table- and drinking vessels (eg samian, colour-coated, and other finewares), and also specialist forms such as mortaria. The organisation of these acquisitions may well have been undertaken by the military, sometimes centrally, and sometimes by the individual unit or in collaboration with other units, perhaps through specific contracts and allied arrangements made through *negotiatores* and other middlemen. However, in recent years it has become increasingly obvious that not all the pottery found on military sites derived from supplies commissioned and issued in bulk by the resident quartermaster. Some vessels may well be personal purchases, made by soldiers from merchants operating in the vicinity of their current garrison, or brought with them on transfer from somewhere else.

In addition, it is now known that, on transfer, some units may well have brought with them the surplus pottery from their previous posting (Swan and Bidwell 1998), or arranged for stocks to be transported to them in order to bridge the gap in supplies until a pottery was up and running at the new posting. Again, such *ad hoc* provisioning might well reflect the geographical and cultural origins of the troops, and the ancestry of incoming potters might similarly be mirrored in their products.

Evidence for troop origins

A second factor requires consideration in the interpretation of the pottery at Carlisle (and, indeed, elsewhere). The mobility of the Roman army is well-documented, but more recent research has shown that, on transfer, detachments took their utilitarian communal pottery with them, this often being the military-made pottery which had been made and issued to them at their base of origin. Examples of this include the early Flavian transfer of Exeter Fortress ware from the West Country to Camelon in southern Scotland, and to York (Swan and Bidwell 1998, 22-3, n3), and also the later movements of Ebor-ware vessels, of North African type but made at York, to various military establishments in northern Britain, including Hadrian's Wall (Swan 1992; 1997). In addition to these large-scale institutional transfers, it is likely that new recruits, and serving soldiers who travelled to a new posting, took with them their own personal pottery (particularly drinking vessels), which had been acquired at their place of origin.

It is sometimes difficult to determine with any certainty how much material in a military assemblage represents personal possessions arriving in the baggage of transfers or recruits, and how much of it was purchased from traders operating in the vicinity. Sometimes it is more obvious; for instance, distinctive finewares that appear to be well outside their normal regions of production and distribution are less likely to have been acquired locally. It is also reasonable to assume that coarseware vessel types which are not local, and which are not normal components of military supply, are less likely to have been shipped long distances as items of trade and are more likely to have travelled in the baggage of individuals, or small groups of men. Such vessels can sometimes be linked to specific alien traditions of eating and drinking, or to other facets of a non-local lifestyle (Swan 1992). The recognition of such phenomena may, in turn, aid the identification of troop transfers or help to pinpoint regions of recruitment, matters for which epigraphic sources are often sparse or totally lacking. Carlisle is particularly suited to these lines of analysis. Being a strategic location on a major road, sometimes well behind the frontier of the province, and sometimes a key component of the frontier itself, or serving as an industrial establishment supporting frontier installations, made it more susceptible to changes in garrison and the presence of soldiers moving to or from the frontier zone, both often preceded by alterations to the accommodation and the attendant arrival of temporary demolition and building detachments.

Location and functional interpretation

The repeated levelling-up of deposits within the late-first- and early to mid-second-century forts, and the relatively frequent renovation and modification of the buildings, ensured that a considerable amount of pottery entered the stratigraphic record at its point of use. Since the purpose of many of these buildings can be suggested with relative confidence, this provided an unparalleled opportunity to interrogate the associated pottery, and to determine which functional classes of vessels could be related to specific locations, and whether the disparate status of the builders and occupants of different buildings was mirrored by the contents. For this reason, the catalogued data for each phase are usually arranged by building and its immediate environs, or by groups of buildings sharing the same function.

The amphorae

(with a contribution on the graffiti and a titulus pictus, *by RSO Tomlin)*

Some 136.472 kg of amphorae sherds were recovered (1247 fragments, 9.19 EREs), of which 86% came from stratified Roman levels (Periods 2-6; Table 21). They are dominated by plain body sherds and have been classified by form and fabric using mainly the typologies of Dressel (1899), Laubenheimer (1985), and Peacock and Williams (1986).

The Flavian period to the late second/mid-third century (Periods 2-6A) was characterised by a very limited, and steadily diminishing 'package' of amphora types (Table 22), which contained various bulk commodities, including wine, oil, fish-products, and dried fruit. These comprised, in chronological order of their appearance: Dressel 20 (south Spanish olive oil); Dressel 2-4 and Camulodunum 139 black sand amphorae (Italian wines); Camulodunum 186 (south Spanish fish sauce and allied products); small Palestinian carrot amphorae (dates and other dried fruits); Gauloise 3, 4, and 5, and Dressel 9 *similis* (Gaulish wines). This narrow range of vessel forms occurs frequently, both at Carlisle and on other northern military sites, and was most probably the result of institutional supply, organised by the Roman army (Funari 1996).

From the third century onwards, most of the amphorae from the site were residual in the contexts from which they were recovered, and the supply of other, contemporary, types was probably no more than episodic, confined to the early third and the mid-late fourth centuries; quantities in each were very small. In the latter period, the amphorae are more likely to have arrived as a result of civilian trading than as institutional supply.

It is clear that the builders of the first fort (Period 3A; *Ch 3*) brought with them a range of amphora-borne comestibles. A fish-sauce amphora was trodden into the old ground surface (Period 1), and a Dressel 20 found its way into the fill of a Period 3A foundation trench. Inevitably, the incidence of different amphora types varies from building to building, which might give some indication of the changing status of various

Period	Dressel 20	Gauloise 4	Black sand	CAM 186	Small carrot	North African	Carrot-bodied	Intermediate	Total
1-3A	115 (9.2)		5 (0.4)	1 (0.1)	1 (0.1)				**133 (10.7)**
3B	115 (9.2)	3 (0.2)	3 (0.2)	1 (0.1)				1 (0.1)	**123 (9.9)**
3C-3E	79 (6.3)			1 (0.1)				1 (0.1)	**81 (6.5)**
4A	83 (6.7)	24 (1.9)	1 (0.1)	15 (1.2)				1 (0.1)	**123 (9.9)**
4B-4D	139 (11.2)	15 (1.2)	28 (2.3)	30 (2.4)				3 (0.2)	**215 (17.3)**
5	150 (12.0)	4 (0.3)	7 (0.6)	11 (0.9)				5 (0.4)	**177 (14.2)**
6A	103 (8.3)	19 (1.5)	15 (1.2)	3 (0.2)		17 (1.4)		2 (0.2)	**159 (12.8)**
6B	51 (4.1)	13 (1.0)		6 (0.5)				2 (0.2)	**72 (5.8)**
6C-6E	30 (2.4)		2 (0.2)	4 (0.3)		10 (0.8)	3 (0.2)	2 (0.2)	**51 (4.1)**
Post-Roman/ unstrat	91 (7.2)	2 (0.2)	1 (0.1)	10 (0.8)			7 (0.6)	1 (0.1)	**112 (9.0)**
Totals	**956 (76.7)**	**80 (6.4)**	**62 (5.0)**	**93 (7.5)**	**1 (0.1)**	**27 (2.2)**	**10 (0.8)**	**18 (1.4)**	**1247**

Table 21: Amphorae for main stratified periods, post-Roman, and unstratified, by sherd count and percentage of total sherd count (in brackets) for each fabric or category (excludes MIL 1 from Period 4 onwards)

Fabric	Weight (g)	% Weight	Sherds	% Sherds	EREs	% EREs
Dressel 20	117,876	85.8	956	76.7	5.19	56.5
Gauloise 4	3753	2.7	80	6.4	1.91	20.8
Black sand (Periods 1-5)	4229	3.1	44	3.5	1.00	10.9
Black sand (Period 6-unstratified)	948	0.7	18	1.4	0.05	0.5
South Spanish (including CAM 186)	7186	5.2	93	7.5	0.56	6.1
Small carrot (Palestinian)	5	<0.1	1	0.1		
North African	2082	1.5	27	2.2	0.48	5.2
Carrot-bodied (Palestinian)	118	0.1	10	0.8		
Indeterminate	1275	0.9	18	1.4		
Total	**137,472**		**1247**		**9.19**	

Table 22: Totals of all amphorae by fabric (stratified and unstratified)

Plate 196: The distinctive form of a North African wine amphora

parts of the site. For example, during Period 3A, rubbish that may have derived from the commanding officer's accommodation (Building **7392**) contained more amphorae than elsewhere, and clearly indicated a taste for luxury products, including high-quality tunny-fish relish in a vessel of form Camulodunum 186 (Fig 277), and imported dried fruits in a Palestinian small carrot amphora (a type not seen elsewhere in the fort at that time). In addition, the more usual Campanian wine amphorae (Dressel 2-4) were supplemented by a smaller and much rarer Campanian jug-amphora (Camulodunum 139), perhaps containing a special vintage. Interestingly, although oil amphorae (Dressel 20) and fish-sauce containers (Camulodunum 186) occurred quite widely in the barracks and associated buildings of Period 3A, wine amphorae were rarer (except in the probable *praetorium* (Building **7392**) and its close vicinity), perhaps suggesting that its issue to troops was under tighter control, with a daily ration decanted from the bulk containers.

From the third century onwards, most amphorae were recovered from residual contexts. Presumably, this does not presage a cessation in the supply of basic goods, but indicates that they were being transported in other, largely organic, containers, for example wine in barrels or skins. The disappearance of anaerobic conditions on the site from the third century onwards means that such containers have not survived. Unusually, there were two instances of late amphorae reaching the site; the first of these, in the early third century (Period 6A; *Ch 8*), saw the arrival of small numbers of North African oil amphorae, possibly being brought by legionary detachments involved in rebuilding the fort at that time. The second, and much later instance, in the mid-late fourth century (Period 6C; *Ch 9*; Pl 196), saw the arrival of North African wine amphorae, Palestinian carrot-bodied amphorae, and other probably Eastern Mediterranean amphorae, their contents perhaps being sold on, piecemeal, in the market postulated at this time.

The following abbreviations are used in catalogue entries:

Beltràn 00: amphora types in Beltràn 1970
Callender 00: numbers of amphora stamps in Callender 1965
Camulodunum 00: vessel types in Hawkes and Hull 1947
Dressel 00: amphora type-numbers in Dressel 1899
Funari 00: amphora stamp numbers in Funari 1996
Gauloise 00: amphora types in Laubenheimer 1985
Peacock and Williams 00: amphora types in Peacock and Williams 1986
Pélichet 00: amphora types in Pélichet 1946
Remesal 00: amphora stamp numbers in Remesal Rodíguez 1997.

Dressel 20 and Dressel 23: Peacock and Williams Class 25

Dressel 20, the well-known globular oil amphora with a distinct, but slightly variable fabric, from Baetica in southern Spain, was by far the most abundant type found in the fort (and indeed elsewhere in the military North and Roman Britain more generally; Funari 1996). It accounted for some 76.7% of sherds by weight, and 56.5% EREs (Table 22). In total, 18 Dressel 20 rims were recorded, and where sufficient survived, they have been dated from the Augst (Switzerland) typology and chronology (Martin-Kilcher 1987). These vessels were present from the establishment of the first fort; it is likely that absolute supply levels were relatively stable, but relative percentages inevitably rose (Table 21), as other amphora types ceased to be

imported. Although there is some reduction to the total amounts recorded in third-century deposits (Period 6A; *Ch 8*), the quantities are rather more than might be expected from residual material, and it is likely that Dressel 20s continued to reach the fort, as a trickle, during the first half of the third century. A single battered rim (in a Severan context) might be attributable to Dressel 23, the smaller third-century successor of Dressel 20, which has only recently been recognised in Britain and elsewhere (Martin-Kilcher 1987, 58-9; Carreras Monfort and Williams 2003), but their fabrics are very similar and, in the

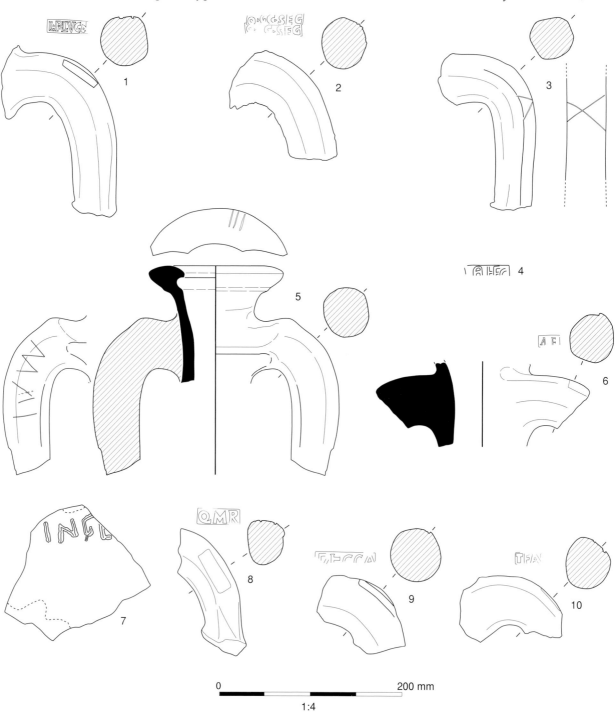

Figure 295: Dressel 20 and Dressel 23 amphorae with stamps and graffiti

574

absence of diagnostic rim sherds, they are difficult to distinguish.

Also of interest is the apparent chronological change from the use of the coarser, paler Baetican fabrics (Tomber and Dore 1998; BAT AM1) to the slightly finer, more pinkish (*op cit*; BAT AM2) fabrics. From the stratigraphic evidence it seems that the coarser BAT AM1 fabric was pale buff until the middle/late Antonine period, when a deeper buff colour became more usual. The finer BAT AM2 fabric first appeared in the last quarter of the second century (Period 5C), initially in the same deeper buff, but with a pale greyish core. In third-century contexts (Period 6A), however, this finer fabric is deeper pinkish-buff with a mid-grey core.

Catalogue (including stamps and graffiti in chronological sequence)

1. Handle, stamped L.P.LVCA with carefully executed letters (Fig 295). No exact parallels are known, but possible variants may include Callender 885, L.LVCI or Callender 913, L.P.L. MIL 5, *3402*, Period 3A, Building *4652*, R1.2, floor

2. Handle with double-impressed (overlapping) stamp (Fig 295): Q.I.C.SEG : Callender 1461 (a); Funari 122; Remesal 162 (1). MIL 5, *3763*, Period 3B, Building *4006*, fill of gully *3762*

3. Handle with *ante-cocturam* incised 'X', presumably a production tally mark (Fig 295). MIL 5, *3495*, Period 3B, Road *4661*, road surface

4. Handle with incomplete stamp (Fig 295): A.?L.FO: Callender 37; Funari 141. This stamp has previously been assigned to the mid-second century, but the present context suggests a slightly earlier date. MIL 5, *6381*, Period 4B, Road *7477*, road surface

5. Rim, neck, and handle (Fig 295). The rim has a typical Flavian profile (Martin-Kilcher 1987, abb 28, type 3). There is a fragment of a faded and illegible *titulus pictus* on the lower part of the neck, and two incised *post-cocturam* graffiti on the rim and handle.
   Roger Tomlin writes (2002b, 361, no 8 and figs 7a and b): 'From the position of the *titulus pictus* I would expect a numeral (weight empty or full, presumably), or the name of a firm (shippers, presumably), but this is not the usual distinctive lettering of numerals (verticals very narrow, horizontals very broad), nor is it like the lettering for firms' names, which is itself distinctive.
   Two conjoining sherds preserve most of one handle and two conjoining rim-sherds preserve about three-quarters of the circumference. There are two graffiti incised after firing:
   (i) On the handle: MΛI, presumably for M VI: *m(odii) VI*
   (ii) On the rim: III, presumably *(sextarii) III*.
   Taking the graffiti together and assuming that V was cut inverted, this would be a note of capacity:
   m(odii) VI (sextarii) III, 'Six *modii*, three *sextarii*.'
   For numerals cut after firing on the rim and handle of Dressel 20, sometimes explicitly beginning with M, see *RIB* II.6, 33-4

(Collingwood and Wright 1994). Capacity is about seven *modii*, more or less.'
MIL 5, *3341*, Period 4A, Building *3376*, R2.1, occupation layer; also *3739*, Building *3376*, R3.1, fill of pit/posthole *3738*

6. Fragment of neck and upper part of a handle (Fig 295) with a stamp broken off at the end: AE[. MIL 4, *245*, Period 5, external layer

7. Body-sherd with graffito (Fig 295).
   Roger Tomlin writes (2002b, 362, no 9, fig 8): 'from a late second-century context, deeply incised after firing: INGE[...], *Inge[nuus]*.
   The name is common, and has already occurred at Carlisle (*RIB* II.7, 2501.240; Collingwood and Wright 1995).'
   MIL 5, *5797*, Period 5D, external layer

8. Handle with the stamp QMR (Fig 295). This is a common stamp: Callender 1481; Funari 153; Remesal 209. It has been dated to the mid-second century, which suggests that the present example may be residual in its early third-century context. MIL 5, *2577*, Period 6A, Building *2301*, R1.1, make-up layer

9. Part of handle with stamp: ?D?ECCA ; no parallels known, residual (Fig 295). MIL 5, *5377*, Period 6C, Structure *7651*, fill of pit *5378*

10. Part of handle with stamp (Fig 295): TFA[; no parallels known; residual. MIL 5, *5242*, Period 7, post-Roman 'dark earth'

Gaulish amphorae

These were the most common wine amphorae found at Carlisle (2.7% of total weight of amphorae, 6.4% by count and 20.8% EREs; Table 22), as is the case elsewhere in the military North and Roman Britain in general. Produced at a number of sources in southern Gaul, Provence, and the middle Rhone valley (including Lyons; Laubenheimer 2003), the fabrics and forms are, as a result, somewhat variable, but typological differences suggest some evolution through time, with the rims becoming more drooping and the lid-seating deeper in the Antonine period.

A minimum of eight vessels were recognised, comprising at least four amphora types: Gauloise 3 (four examples); Gauloise 4 (one example); and Gauloise 5 (one example), all flat-bottomed wine containers. The fourth type, Dressel 9 *similis*, perhaps with a hollow toe, probably carried fish sauce or a similar preserve. Most examples can be attributed to the two fabrics defined by Tomber and Dore (1998), the second, pinkish-tinged fabric (GAL AM2) being more common. It is almost certain that these amphorae do not occur at Carlisle until after AD 83-4 (Period 3B; Table 21); a single amphora-lid, in a fabric similar to that of Gauloise 4, was attributed to Period 3A external deposit *7182*, but may have been trampled into the surface during the rebuilding of Period 3B.

This evidence is compatible with the suggestion that Gaulish wines were imported to fill the gap left by the demise of the Campanian wine industry in AD 79 (Widemann 1987; see 'black sand' amphorae). Moreover, although Gauloise 4 amphorae do not appear to be prominent until after c AD 105 (Period 4A), some of the examples are probably residual and displaced from late in Period 3, having been found in foundation trenches, drains, and road-surfaces of the second fort. The quantitative evidence (Table 21) suggests that such amphorae probably continued to arrive in Carlisle until at least the late third century, though levels of residuality in subsequent phases of activity make it difficult to be certain how late the supply continued.

Catalogue

11. Splayed rim, shallow lid-seating, and cream granular fabric (Fig 296).
   MIL 4, *256*, Period 4A/B, Road **7645**, road surface

12. Drooping rim with pronounced lid-seating (Fig 296).
   MIL 5, *2805*, Period 5B, Road **4662**, road surface; also unstratified

13. Amphora lid in a Gauloise 4 fabric (Fig 296).
   MIL 5, *6878*, Period 3C, Building **7200**, floor

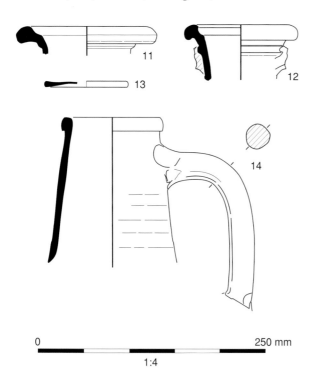

0   250 mm

1:4

Figure 296: Gaulish and 'black sand' amphorae

'Black sand' amphorae: Dressel 2-4, Camulodunum 139
This distinctive light-coloured fabric with black volcanic grits, which is known to have originated in Campania, around the Bay of Naples, comprised 3.1% of the total weight of amphorae, 3.5% of the total sherds, and 10.9% of the total EREs (Table 22).

It was mainly represented by the Dressel 2-4 wine amphora (beaded rim and bifid handles), but the other certain form in this fabric was a rare example of the jug-amphora, Camulodunum 139 (Hawkes and Hull 1947), which retained most of its internal pitch with remarkable clarity, including the marks of the brush with which it had been applied (Pl 193). It is now evident that viticulture around the Bay of Naples was all but wiped out by the eruption of Vesuvius in AD 79 (Williams 2004), so the 'black sand' amphorae are likely to have been deposited during Period 3A. Those from Periods 3B-6C are thus likely to represent the Period 3A supply, and are therefore clearly residual in later contexts.

The bulk export of 'black sand' wine amphorae to Britain seems to have re-emerged in the early third century (Arthur and Williams 1992; Williams 1997, 973), originating from northern Campania (perhaps including Ischia), on the northern side of the Bay of Naples. However, these later forms are less common and slightly different from Dressel 2-4, being characterized by distinctive 'almond-shaped' rims and oval handle-sections. Examples appear at South Shields in contexts dated from AD 222/35 to the late third/early fourth century (there, period 6; Williams 1997, 217-19). At Carlisle, there is an increase in the quantities of 'black-sand' amphora sherds associated with Period 6A (and a sudden drop thereafter: Table 21), but, except for one (typically early bifid) handle, all the examples in that phase are undistinguished body-sherds, and it is difficult to know whether or not they are contemporary, or residual from Period 3A. In support of the former, it is worth noting that although the construction of the stone fort in the first decade of the third century (Period 6A) caused significant disturbance to earlier deposits, far from an increase in early residual amphora fragments, there was a major decrease in the other mainly first-century types (such as the South Spanish Camulodunum 186, *p 577*). In Period 6A, all 14 indeterminate 'black sand' sherds occurred in the earliest levels of that phase (*ie* in the primary make-up of a road, and in external deposits) and might, therefore, have been discarded by the Severan builders of the stone fort. This impression tends to be reinforced by the incidence of the eight indeterminate 'black sand' sherds associated with Period 5B; all are from external or road deposits, which were open at the time that construction of the Period 6A fort began, and thus could well have been trodden in by the builders. Indeed, a sherd of a North African amphora (of a type only occurring in deposits associated with the building of the stone fort) was found in the same Period 5D road deposit as a 'black sand' sherd, and had almost certainly been trampled into the surface during building work, as were several other fragments of this type. 'Black sand' vessels and the Severan North African amphorae are both absent in Period 6B. A possible interpretation of this is that, because both were in use only at the beginning of Period 6A, and then only in small quantities, they were not lying about in significant amounts to be incorporated in the deposits of the following phase. In short, it is likely that at least some of these 'black sand' sherds derive from late Campanian vessels, which reached the site with, or at the same time as, the first North African amphorae supplied to the Severan building gangs, and may have been shipped with them (*pp 578-9*).

Catalogue

14. Jug-amphora with single handle (Camulodunum 139), pitched on interior and over top of rim (Fig 296; Pl 193); pre-AD 79; residual in Period 4B.

    MIL 5, *6374*, Period 4B, Road **7217**, fill of robber trench *7471*

Cadiz and allied Southern Spanish amphorae (Peacock and Williams Classes 17 and 18; Camulodunum 186 A and C)

This group of amphorae in brownish-yellow fabrics, with small ceramic lids, was made mainly in the Cadiz region of southern Spain, and contained fish-based products. They comprised 5.2% of the total weight of amphorae, 7.5% of the sherds, and 6.9% of EREs (Table 22). Though many of the Carlisle sherds were too featureless to distinguish the various forms, a number still retained their pitch lining, and the anaerobic conditions also facilitated the preservation of a sherd with a fine series of panels with *tituli picti* in pen and ink (*16*). It would seem that such provisions arrived with, or at the same time as, the builders of the first fort, the base of a Camulodunum 186C vessel having been trodden into the old ground surface (*15*; Period 1).

Catalogue including titulus pictus

15. Hollow spike of Camulodunum 186C/Pélichet 46/Beltràn IIA (Fig 297).

    MIL 5, *4000*, Period 1, soil layer (old ground surface)

16. Sherd from the wide neck and shoulder of an internally pitched Camulodunum 186C, with a series of inscribed panels on the exterior (Fig 297). An examination of the sherd indicated that these were achieved by coating an area of the lower neck with

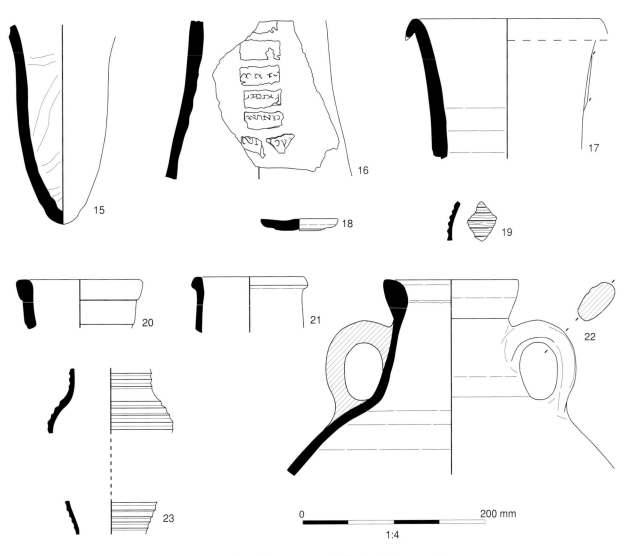

Figure 297: Spanish, carrot, and North-African amphorae

a thick slip or clay slurry (perhaps after drying or firing, since it had not adhered well), and when the vertical sequence of labels had been written on the area, the remainder of the slip had been chipped away around each word or phrase, leaving a series of slightly raised panels. This high-grade product was found in a Period 3A context, the external area between the *principia* (Building **7400**) and the presumed *praetorium* (Building **7392**), and would almost certainly have been waste from the household of the commanding officer, in the AD 70s or early 80s.

Roger Tomlin comments (2002b, 360-1, no 7, fig 6). 'This cursive text, on the series of rectangular panels of pale slip, has been neatly inscribed in black ink with a pen:

CO[.]T[.]NGV[.]
PENVA<u>R</u>
EXSCEL[.]
[..]MA<u>V</u>R
[...]
[...]
COD Ting(itanum) v[e(tus)] penuar(ium) | exscel[l(ens)] | [SV]MAVR | [...] | [...]

"Old Tangiers tunny relish, 'provisions' quality, excellent, top-quality [...]."

For the contents see Tomlin and Hassall (2000, 441, n56). They were COD (or CORD), a preserved fish-product made by chopping up young tunny (*cordula*) and digesting them in their own juices. *PENVAR* and *SVMAVR* were grades of COD, of uncertain meaning, but evidently derived from *penus* ('provisions') and *summus* ('top'). Now lost (line 5) is a note of the age in years; (line 6), a numeral, presumably a note of capacity; (line 7, not part of this sherd), one or two names in the genitive case, presumably of the manufacturer(s). Other British examples (*RIB* II.6, 2492.11 (Chester), 2492.19 (Colchester) [Collingwood and Wright 1994]; Tomlin and Hassall (2000, 440), no 32 (London)) are inscribed directly onto the surface of the amphora, but for the same use of rectangular panels of white slip see *CIL* iv 9370 (Pompeii) [Zangemeister and Schoene 1871] and probably *RIB* II.6, 2492.32 and 33 (London) [Collingwood and Wright 1994]. Camulodunum 186 amphorae with labels in this particular style are rare (perhaps less than 25 are known) and seem to be confined to the early Flavian period (there is another example from Masada; D B Casasola *pers comm*). It is now known that after manufacture in the Cadiz region, these containers were shipped across the Straits of Gibraltar to be filled with fish-based provisions from production centres on the North African coast; *Tingi* (Tangiers), as here, is one of several cities named on the labels. These factories exploited the seasonal migration of tunny fish through the Straits of Gibraltar, as did other coastal centres on the southern tip of Spain'.

MIL 5, *7431*, Period 3A, external layer

17. Typical hooked rim and neck of Camulodunum 186C with traces of pitch on the interior (Fig 297).
    MIL 5, *6414*, Period 4B, Building *5689*, possible floor

18. Amphora lid, in coarse burnt fabric, almost certainly of southern Spanish origin (Fig 297); glossy black pitch covers the interior and is dribbled over part of the exterior.
    MIL 5, *1967*, Period 3B, Building *2061*, R3.1, floor

Small carrot amphorae (Peacock and Williams Class 12)

These small carrot amphorae (as distinct from carrot-bodied amphorae; *p 579*) have a small rim and little or no neck, and usually a reddish granular fabric. A single sherd was recorded, in Period 3A. A detailed classification of their forms was first published in the 1990s (Vipard 1995), but until relatively recently, their region of production was unknown, thought to lie either in Egypt, or possibly in the Eastern Mediterranean. Petrological thin-sectioning (Carreras Monfort and Williams 2002), and further research by Reynolds (2005, 567, 571-2, fig 135, 567-8), have now shown that these containers were produced in Beirut, probably in the south of Lebanon, and perhaps elsewhere in Palestine, mainly for export markets. Widely distributed in the northern provinces and parts of the Mediterranean, from the Augustan period until the mid/late second century, they probably contained dates or other dried fruit.

Catalogue

19. Body-sherd with sharply rilled rounded shoulder, probably of Vipard Form Bb (Fig 297).
    MIL 5, *7411*, Period 3A, Building *7392*, R5.2, fill of pit *7525*

North African amphorae in Tunisian lime-poor fabrics (Peacock and Williams Class 34-5)

These amphorae, in brick-red fabrics with sparse lime inclusions and a cream to buff saline coating, probably contained olive oil, but fish-products are also a possibility. The quantities recorded at Carlisle were very small, accounting for little more than 2% of the total number of sherds, and 5% of EREs (Table 22). Their appearances, briefly in the early third century, and then, after a break, in the mid-late fourth century, seem to relate to two separate and distinctly different episodes in the history of the site. The first examples (*20*) appear in external deposits of Period 5D, which almost certainly comprised the old ground surface, disturbed and trampled by the builders of the Period 6A stone fort. North African amphorae are scarce throughout Britain before the early to mid-third century (Williams and Carerras 1995), and it seems likely that these reached Carlisle with the building-vexillations, which are known to have included men from the York legion, *Legio VI Victrix* (*see Ch 21, p 873*, for a *Legio VI* inscription in the wall of the Carlisle *principia*). At this period, the legion evidently contained North African reinforcements, initially brought to York c AD 208-9, by the Emperor Severus in the course of his northern campaigns (Swan 1992; 1997). At the York fortress, the apparent arrival of these drafts coincides with an exceptionally early surge of North African amphorae in York's ceramic record (Williams and Carerras 1995, 237); for example, they were found in an alley between barracks under the present York Minster, where they are associated with North African culinary vessel types, made locally for the Severan troops (Perrin 1995, fig 132-8, no 56, 167, 197; B Heywood *pers comm*). Some of these North African-style products also occur at Carlisle (*pp 604-5*). The possibility that these North African amphorae were used only by *Legio VI* building-vexillations, and were not subsequently part of the normal supply to the garrison of the Carlisle fort, tends to be supported by the contextual evidence: they are found only in Period 5D deposits, where they had a possible association with late 'black sand' amphorae and could well have been discarded by construction gangs. Their absence from later occupation deposits within Periods 6A and 6B (early third to early/mid-fourth century) suggests that they were not subsequently part of the normal institutional supply to the Carlisle garrison.

The second period of deposition for late North African amphorae (represented by a container of uncertain type, an unusual variant of an African IID wine amphora (*21*), and small quantities of unidentifiable body sherds) is attributable to Period 6C, when abundant small coinage and other evidence suggest the existence of a market in the centre of the fort (*Ch 9; p 463*), just outside the *principia*. The distribution of these containers (including *22*, residual in a Period 6E pit), and of the contemporary carrot-bodied amphorae (residual in Periods 6D and 7), is coincident with the concentrations of small change, and suggests temporary market stalls (perhaps lean-to structures) just outside the central buildings of the fort. Such material is very unlikely to represent institutional military supply, but presumably arose from commercial activities. It is likely that these vessels were being opened on the spot and their contents sold 'on draught', perhaps decanted into smaller containers. The large size of these North African cylindrical amphorae (and perhaps the carrot-bodied containers too) would have precluded their being sold as whole units complete with contents, and presumably explains why they were seemingly discarded *in situ* (*22* was large, freshly broken, and not abraded). The associations of these North African amphorae confirm the dating implied by the coins (after *c* AD 388/92 or later; *Ch 17*), as one of their contexts also contained three sherds of Crambeck Parchment ware (dated after *c* AD 370/80), and another contained a local copy of a Huntcliff jar (after AD 360/70).

Catalogue

20. Africana IIB type (Peacock and Williams Class 34), with quadrangular rim (closest to Bonifay Type 23), in a dark red-brown fabric with a buff saline skin (Fig 297). Bonifay (2004, 111, fig 59) suggests a date not earlier than the third century for this particular form.
MIL 5, *5900*, Period 5D, external layer

21. Slightly burnt, but probably North African (Fig 297).
MIL 5, *2228*, Period 6C, external layer

22. Large unabraded fragment (Fig 297) close to Bonifay types 26 and 27, and probably dating to the second half of the fourth century; unabraded but residual.
MIL 5, *5358*, Period 6E, fill of pit *5357*

Eastern Mediterranean amphorae (including Palestinian carrot-bodied amphora Agora M334)

Only a very small number of sherds can be attributed to the Eastern Mediterranean generally, and only one vessel can be assigned to a broad production region: a carrot-bodied amphora (Agora M334), in a hard, moderately rough, sandy buff to light salmon-coloured fabric, with abundant fine quartz and sparse larger lime particles protruding through the surface; the gap in the rilling at the neck/shoulder is characteristic of the type. Ultimately related to the early so-called 'carrot amphora' from approximately the same region (Carreras Monfort and Williams 2002, 138), this probable wine amphora has recently been shown (Reynolds 2005, 567, 570-2, figs 104-14) to have been made in north-west Palestine, particularly in the region of Akko (*Ptolemais*) and up to the Lebanese border (*ie* in the southern part of the late Roman province of *Phoenice*); the Carlisle example seems likely to be in an Akko fabric, but is not closely datable. This vessel almost certainly carried wine and its contents were presumably being sold in the same market (and perhaps at approximately the same time) as the mid-late fourth-century North African amphorae; indeed, they might both have been shipped together in a mixed load from the Mediterranean. Amongst the unsorted material there were several other rilled sherds in two fine micaceous fabrics, which seem likely to have had an origin on the Aegean littoral, but cannot be further identified.

Catalogue

23. Two sherds from the neck/shoulder and body (Fig 297); the gap in the rilling at the neck/shoulder junction is characteristic of the type.
MIL 5, *5329*, Period 6D, Building *5200*, R4, fill of robber-pit *5328*; also *5259*, Period 7, post-Roman 'dark earth'

Mortaria and mortarium stamps

In total, 47.418 kg of mortaria were recovered, of which about 86% came from stratified Roman contexts (Table 23). There are still relatively few quantified assemblages of mortaria from well-stratified military sites in northern Britain, and the fluctuations in the sources of supply seen at Carlisle will provide interesting comparanda for other northern sites (Table 24). Details of the stamped and unstamped mortaria have been integrated within the coarseware catalogue (*pp 608-60*). Summary fabric descriptions are found in *Appendix 2*.

Periods 1-3A (pre-AD 72/3–83-4)

Of the mortaria used in the first decade of the fort, 72-3% (by total weight and EREs) originated in

Period	Weight (g)	Sherds	EREs
3A	4468	31	1.98
3B	6554	46	1.82
3C, 3D, 3E	1148	28	0.25
4A	4742	50	1.25
4B	3928	63	1.48
4A/B	3273	41	1.19
4C	449	6	0.12
5	2044	36	0.27
5A, 5B	2265	43	2.08
5C, 5D	1958	32	0.84
6A	3490	79	0.75
6B	2701	48	1.28
6C	2425	48	1.54
6D, 6E	1510	26	0.87
7, 8, 9, US/Not closely phased	6463	159	2.25
Total	**47,418**	**736**	**17.97**

Table 23: Quantities of mortaria by period

the Verulamium region (including Brockley Hill; Table 24), which was also a significant supplier for many other contemporary forts in the North (*eg* Hartley 1984, 292). These mortaria were particularly sturdy and it is highly likely that a considerable number of vessels arrived in military baggage when the fort was founded.

This over-provisioning created an exceptionally large temporary resource, presumably intended to support the needs of the garrison until local production was well established (by Period 4A). Also constituting part of the initial military provisioning were imports from northern France and the Oise-Somme region (over 15% by weight and almost 18% EREs), which occur in some of the earliest deposits, but steadily decreased in quantity in the course of the first century.

The local pottery workshop at Carlisle had already begun to make mortaria of 'military' type by this time, presumably alongside other local coarsewares (*pp 589-90*); a burnt and heavily worn example was found in a post-pit of a primary building (**7657**), and should, therefore, date to *c* AD 72/3. However, quantities for this period were relatively small (less than 10% of the total by EREs), contrasting strongly with the strong emphasis on local cooking and tablewares at this time.

Period 3B (AD 83-4 - *c* 93-4)

A very significant drop in the quantities of mortaria from the Verulamium region, more than might be expected of normal trade or institutional provisioning at this period, serves to emphasise the exceptional 'one-off' nature of the supplies that accompanied the foundation of the fort in Period 3A. This, together with a slight reduction in the imports from *Gallia Belgica* (to about 12-13%), was balanced by a significant increase in the supply of mortaria probably made at Carlisle

Fabrics	Periods 1-3A	Period 3B	Periods 3C-3E
Carlisle	358 g (8.0%) R 0.19 (9.6%)	1325 g (20.2%) 0.33% (18.1%)	381 g (33.2%) R 0.16 (64.0%)
North-West	034 g (0.8%)	37 g (0.6%)	133 g (11.6%)
Old Penrith	123 g (2.8%)	-	-
Verulamium region	3233 g (72.4%) R 1.44 (72.7%)	794 g (12.1%) R 0.22 (12.1%)	355 g (30.9%) R 0.09 (36.0%)
North France	175 g (3.9%)	672 g (10.3%) R 0.09 (5.0%)	76 g (6.6%)
Oise/Somme	497 g (11.1%) 0.35 (17.7%)	193 g (2.9%) R 0.12 (6.6%)	184g (16.0%)
Wroxeter	-	898 g (13.7%) R 0.43 (23.6%)	-
Corbridge	-	-	19 g (1.7%)
Elginhaugh	-	2635 g (40.2%) R 0.63 (34.6%)	-
Indeterminate	48 g (1.1%)	-	-
Total mortaria	**4468 g (47.7%)** **R 1.98% (25.3%)**	**6554 g (66.5%)** **R 1.82 (25.9%)**	**1148 g (19.7%)** **R 0.25 (4.6%)**

Table 24: Stratified mortaria for Periods 1-3: weights and EREs (=R) and percentages of totals for each period or grouped periods

itself (over 20% by weight and 18% EREs; Table 24). Evidently, the potters of the second garrison (*Ch 13*) were manufacturing mortaria on a regular basis. A significant number of them were probably being made in the Fisher Street workshop (*pp 593-4*), close to the fort, which probably began production during this period. Some of these products were so close in style to those made in the Verulamium region (including the distinctive method of attaching the spout) that it is possible that a potter from there could have been working in Carlisle.

The overall picture of mortarium usage is distorted by the presence of large fragments of two mortaria from sources which do not represent normal supplies, and were presumably carried to the site by individual soldiers or groups of military personnel. Both have important implications for the history of the fort and military dispositions elsewhere. A vessel from Wroxeter, stamped by the potter Decianus was found in a construction trench for the *principia* (Building **7391**). This had presumably arrived with *Legio XX* detachments, who may have been engaged in the rebuilding of the interior of the fort at the beginning of Period 3B (see *p 586*, Stamp 2). Wroxeter mortaria of the mid/late Flavian-early Trajanic period rarely spread beyond Wales and the West Midlands, and were certainly never traded as far as the Tyne-Solway region (*2*; Hartley 2003). A stylus tablet found in the ditch of the putative fort annexe, in a context thought to date to *c* AD 83-4 (Caruana 1992, 104), records the presence of two men of *Legio XX* on 7 November AD 83 (Tomlin 1992, 146-7), the very time when the putative fort refurbishment seems to have been in progress, and it is highly likely that the men belonged to legionary detachments sent from Wroxeter to aid in the building work. Almost without doubt, these men would have brought some of their own mess equipment with them, including the heavily worn mortarium, broken and discarded shortly after.

The second vessel of note was a stamped mortarium (3) from the fort at Elginhaugh (Pl 197), near Edinburgh, found in a layer outside a barrack in the south-west quadrant (Building **2058**), and another Elginhaugh product, with an identical stamp, was recorded in the late Dorothy Charlesworth's 1973-7 excavations in an area south of the same barrack, near the fort's defences (unstratified but perhaps derived from one of the cook-houses with ovens recorded behind the rampart in that area (Caruana in prep)). These mortaria are known to have been in production in the AD 80s, but do not appear to have been traded beyond the Elginhaugh fort, the only other two outlying examples recorded being from Camelon (K Hartley *pers comm*). This might thus reflect the presence of a soldier in transit, in view of Camelon's probable role as a port and springing-off point for campaigning (Swan and Bidwell 1998). Both mortaria were probably brought to Carlisle by troops who had been based in Scotland, either at Elginhaugh or at a nearby establishment receiving Elginhaugh products. Such men might have been among those transferred to Carlisle in *c* AD 83-4 following the battle of *Mons Graupius* (Swan 2008, 53), or subsequently evacuated to Carlisle in the late AD 80s, in the first stage of the abandonment of Agricola's conquests (Daniels 1989, 34; Hobley 1989, 69-70). Although Building **2058** and its twin, **3772**, are slightly larger than usual (*Ch 4*), there is no evidence that these were occupied by legionary detachments, as suggested by Tomlin (1992, 152-3, n59), and indeed there is slight evidence that they could have been cavalry barracks (*Ch 4*). The excavator of Elginhaugh has recently concluded that this was most probably a cavalry fort (Hanson 2007). This raises the possibility that the *turmae* in Carlisle's garrison (probably, but not certainly, the *ala Gallorum Sebosiana*; *Ch 12*), which occupied these barracks, may have previously been based at Elginhaugh, since, although that fort was not large enough for a whole *ala*, there is no reason why the unit could not have been split. The garrison of Newstead is thought to have included a cavalry detachment, and if part of the *ala Gallorum Sebosiana* had been based there and re-united at Carlisle, this might explain the address ('at *Trimontium* or *Luguvalium*') recorded on a *stylus* tablet at Carlisle (Tomlin 1992). However, this can be no more than informed speculation.

Periods 3C-3E (*c* AD 93-4 - *c* 105)
The unexpected fluctuations in the quantities of mortaria from various sources during this period may reflect both the relatively small amount recovered and also the variable nature of activity on the site at this time, which involved refurbishment, demolition, and

Plate 197: The stamped mortarium from Elginhaugh

abandonment. In addition, these deposits may also have suffered from disturbance by the builders of the Period 4 fort. Thus, any attempt at interpretation must be tentative, needing to take into account the levels of supply in the following period, as well as the possibility of residuality from Period 3B. That said, the strength of local supply is very clear (Carlisle products comprise 33% by weight and 64% by EREs; Table 24), but this might represent levels of supply that pertained in the early AD 90s, before the fort was demolished and the garrison departed. The relatively high numbers of Verulamium mortaria (30% by weight, 36% by EREs) are less easily explicable, given their declining levels in the previous decade (Period 3B). All derived from demolition deposits and could represent old stock removed from buildings which were being demolished and levelled. Another, perhaps less likely, explanation is that they were brought to the site by various detachments engaged in demolishing and building at a time when local production had ceased (there are similar discrepancies in the finewares at

this period; *see pp 615-16*). The presence, for the first time, of a Corbridge mortarium (in demolition debris) may also reflect similar factors, though this might be intrusive from Period 4A.

Period 4A (*c* AD 105-25)

The interruption in military occupation in the early years of the second century, *c* AD 103-5, (see *Ch 5*) is both supported and amplified by the mortaria (Table 25). Typologically, the local mortaria of Period 4A are significantly different from those of Period 3, and their quantities are relatively small (less than 9% EREs), though they increased slightly in Period 4B. The evidence, with that of the coarsewares, suggests that manufacture had ceased during Periods 3C-3E, and had restarted on the Fisher Street site, the designated area for the fort's pottery workshop, where earlier production is evidenced, almost as soon as rebuilding began (*pp 593-4*). However, the availability of other mortaria, perhaps partly due to advances in general security and the construction of roads, meant that,

Fabrics	Period 4A	Period 4B	Periods 4C-4D
Carlisle	628 g (13.3%) R 0.11 (8.8%)	849 g (21.6%) R 0.21 (14.2%)	124 g (27.6%)
North-West	335 g (7.1%)	187 g (4.8%)	133 g (29.6%) R 0.12 (100.0%)
Old Penrith	135 g (2.9%)	135 g (3.4%) R 0.05 (3.4%)	-
Verulamium region	585 g (12.3%) R 0.05 (4.0%)	59 g (1.5%)	-
North France	162 g (3.4%)	-	-
Oise/Somme	1720 g (36.3%) R 0.62 (49.6%)	437 g (11.1%) R 0.38 (25.7%)	-
Wroxeter	147 g (3.1%) R 0.10 (8.0%)	27 g (0.7%)	-
Corbridge	297 g (6.3%) R 0.10 (8.0%)	-	78 g (17.4%)
North-East forts	-	501 g (12.8%) R 0.21 (14.2%)	114 g (25.4%)
Mancetter-Hartshill	-	3 g (0.1%)	-
Aldborough	-	143 g (3.6%) R 0.13 (8.8%)	-
Northern	-	16 g (0.4%)	-
Indeterminate	-	50 g (1.3%)	-
Residual	733 g (15.5%) R 0.27 (21.6%)	1521 g (38.7%) R 0.50 (33.8%)	-
Total mortaria	4742 g (27.7%) R 1.25 (7.3%)	3928 g (11.9%) R 1.48 (4.0%)	449 g (7.6%) R 0.12 (1.8%)

Table 25: Stratified mortaria for Period 4: weights and EREs (=R) and percentages of totals for each period or grouped periods (excludes MIL 1)

from then on, the fort depended less on the supply of local mortaria than had been the case in the first two decades of its existence. New types of mortaria made locally during this period included several impressed with the name-stamps of potters who are known to have had workshops at Wilderspool and Wroxeter (*11, 12*), and who may have been civilian contractors working for the military (*p 589*). This workshop continued in production until at least AD 160 (*p 594*), around 20 years after the garrison departed and the fort had been demolished (probably in the early AD 140s; *Ch 6, pp 241-2*), suggesting that the workshop was wholly civilian rather than military by that time.

Numerically, the most significant feature of this period is the exceptionally large quantity of mortaria from the Oise-Somme region (almost 50% EREs), but not from other producers in Northern France. This surge, at a time when the importation of Oise-Somme mortaria to Britain was running down, requires some explanation. It is generally thought that these mortaria are more common on sites near the coast (particularly in the South and South East), and their transportation to Carlisle in quantity does not fit the normal pattern. One possible explanation could be that pottery production had ceased when the previous garrison left and that the incoming garrison brought a stock of these mortaria to Carlisle to bridge the gap until local production was re-established. The name of the new unit is unknown; it is possible that it was the previous garrison returning, as at Vindolanda (Birley 2002, 70), but a number of the contemporary tablewares suggest that it had been in northern *Gallia Belgica* (*p 618*), and this might explain a bulk shipment of mortaria from that region, contrasting with the normal trend for Britain. It might also explain the presence of a single mortarium from the Rhineland or adjacent *Gallia Belgica* (*163*; *p 625*).

Overall, during the course of Period 4A, the range of mortaria diversified only slightly, with the addition of very small quantities from workshops at Wroxeter and Corbridge. As is normal for the period, supplies of Verulamium mortaria continued to decline (12% by weight, 4% EREs), and although their workshops continued to operate into the Antonine period, imports did not reach the fort from the Hadrianic period (Period 4B; Table 25).

Periods 4B-4D (*c* AD 125 - *c* 140/50)

Relative to the length of occupation, there are fewer mortaria in these periods. This may be connected with the seemingly industrial nature of many of the buildings erected in Period 4B, replacing structures hitherto used for accommodation and administration, presumably meaning that food-preparation (involving the use of mortaria) was taking place elsewhere. The manufacture of Carlisle mortaria had evidently increased (over 14% EREs; Table 25) and was supplemented by North Western mortaria (in Periods 4B, 4C, and 4D), some of which could have been made at Carlisle, and products from the vicinity of Old Penrith (over 3%). Oise-Somme and Verulamium mortaria were probably residual towards the end of this period. Other supply-sources were, however, recorded for the first time, including the products of potters working at one or more forts in the North East (Binchester (Evans and Ratkai in press), Bainesse-Catterick (Hartley 2002a), or Corbridge (Bishop and Dore 1988, 265-6)). The single item from Aldborough (Stamp 7) would almost certainly have been carried to the fort by an individual or a group of soldiers. One possible agency might have been building-detachments of legionaries from York (where at least three Aldborough stamps are known). The scrap from Mancetter-Hartshill came from a fill and might have arrived after *c* AD 140.

Periods 5A-5D (*c* AD 140/50-early third century)

Parts, at least, of the fort seem to have been unoccupied at this time (*Ch 7*) and thus the mortaria could reflect civilian trade, or even vessels carried to the site (Table 26). Although the quantities of mortaria are too small to provide really secure data, and there is considerable residuality, they are relatively diverse (including Corbridge, Wroxeter, the North Eastern forts, Colchester (these perhaps arriving in tandem with small numbers of Colchester colour-coated beakers), and Mancetter-Hartshill), and a continued military presence on the site cannot be discounted. The Colchester mortaria are of interest, being extremely unusual or completely absent at Carlisle and other sites in the North West, although more normally part of the assemblage in the eastern sector of the Antonine Wall. Thus it is possible that this example was carried to the site by a detachment which had been stationed in eastern Scotland, and other unexpected types of pottery were recorded in the same part of the site, perhaps supporting this hypothesis. Whilst production in the Fisher Street workshop seemingly continued until the early AD 160s at least (*p 594*), it seems not to have done well in the Antonine period, and, indeed, it is just possible that some of the potters, such as Austinus and Docilis, had opened another workshop in western Scotland, rather than attempting to supply the Antonine Wall from their Carlisle centre, and that the latter was allowed to run down (K F Hartley *pers comm*). Production on the English Damside site may well have commenced *c* AD 150/60 (*p 594*), although its contribution to the mortarium supply was not large at that time, being confined to Raetian types with distinct red-painted flanged rims.

The emergence, at this time, of Mancetter/Hartshill at a significant source (*p 638*) might be of significance (2.65 EREs in Periods 5C-5D). As Kay Hartley has observed (*pers comm*), these Midlands kilns had become serious suppliers to Carlisle by the last third of

Fabrics	Periods 5A-5B	Periods 5C-5D	Period 5
Carlisle	451 g (19.9%) R 0.63 (30.3%)	668 g (34.1%) R 0.38 (45.2%)	147 g (7.2%)
North West	640 g (28.3%) R 0.36 (17.3%)	449 g (22.9%) R 0.15 (17.9%)	-
Raetian	-	25 g (1.3%)	-
Wroxeter	346 g (15.3%) R 0.25 (12.0%)	-	38 g (1.9%)
Corbridge	307 g (13.6%) R 0.26 (12.5%)	83 g (4.2%)	315 g (15.4%)
North East forts	214 g (9.5%) R 0.14 (6.7%)	-	127 g (6.2%) R 0.10 (37.0%)
Mancetter-Hartshill	21 g (0.9%)	245 g (12.5%) R 0.22 (26.2%)	-
Midlands or Corbridge	-	46 g (2.4%)	-
Colchester	135 g (6.0%) R 0.14 (6.7%)	-	-
Indeterminate	9 g (0.4%)	-	-
Residual	142 g (6.3%) R 0.30 (14.4%)	442 g (22.6%) R 0.09 (10.7%)	951 g (46.5%) R 0.17 (63.0%)
Total mortaria	2265 g (20.3%) R 2.08 (10.9%)	1958 g (14.5%) R 0.84 (4.7%)	2044 g (37.0%) R 0.27 (5.6%)

Table 26: Stratified mortaria for Period 5: weights and EREs (=R) and percentages of totals for each period or grouped periods (excludes MIL 1)

the second century, if not before, although no stamps are earlier than AD 145, and they could all be later than AD 150 or even AD 160. The occurrence of these products in such an outlying location, apparently with no formal garrison at this time, might suggest that there was some sort of military impetus behind the workshop's expansion.

Period 6A (early-late third century)

Relative to the length of occupation, the mortaria from Period 6 are few (Table 27). Drawn from at least six sources, the quantity is too small to be of statistical significance and it is likely that 50-86% of the material is probably residual, having been disturbed by the construction of the stone fort. Locally produced mortaria, particularly of north-western Raetian type, are present, but of relatively little significance. Small quantities of vessels came from Mancetter-Hartshill and perhaps Corbridge, which might just have still been in operation early in the third century (Bishop and Dore 1988). The first Nene Valley mortarium appears towards the end of the period, perhaps arriving with finewares from the same source, but they were never common in Carlisle (*p 606*). Although Crambeck cooking-wares arrived in very small quantities at the end of Period 6A, there were no mortaria from this source until Period 6B, and they remained scarce until Period 6C.

Period 6B: (late third to mid-fourth century)

Although even fewer mortaria can be attributed to this period, from only four sources, there seems to be considerably less residuality (about 22-31%; Table 27). Mancetter-Hartshill mortaria appear to peak, although it is possible that the figures reflect some residuality and that their zenith should in fact be attributed to the latter part of the previous century. The other sources, of slightly less significance, are the Lower Nene Valley and Crambeck; the products of a relatively new pottery at Catterick make a very small showing, in comparison with the total quantity from this source.

This period saw the first appearance of Crambeck mortaria on the site, but only in contexts towards the end of the period. The quantities were minute, representing no more than two or three vessels. The forms represented are, however, of particular chronological interest. It has long been appreciated from Corder's classification (Corder and Birley 1937) that his type 6, and the sub-types (6a-d) defined by Hartley (1995), were the earliest group of Crambeck mortaria, perhaps beginning in about AD 280/300. All were made in the variable, but slightly sandy, fabric (Fabric 322), which preceded the use of the finer Parchment ware (Fabric 323). Crambeck type 6a, in its classic form, with a plain, out-splayed, hooked flange (typologically

Fabrics	Period 6A	Period 6B	Periods 6C-6E
Carlisle	855 g (25.3%)	-	-
North West and north-west Raetian	150 g (4.4%)	-	9 g (0.2%)
Corbridge	335 g (9.9%) R 0.10 (13.3%)	-	-
Mancetter-Hartshill	241 g (7.1%)	551 g (20.4%) R 0.35 (27.3%)	263 g (6.7%) R 0.04 (1.7%)
Lower Nene Valley	25 g (0.7%) -	475 g (17.6%) R 0.28 (21.9%)	-
Crambeck	46 g (1.4%)	782 g (29.0%) R 0.27 (21.1%)	1570 g (39.9%) R 0.99 (41.1%)
Catterick	-	53 g (2.0%) R 0.09 (7.0%)	136 g (3.5%) R 0.13 (5.4%)
Indeterminate	34 g (1.0%)	-	-
Residual	1699 g (50.2%) R 0.65 (86.7%)	840 g (31.1%) R 0.29 (22.7%)	1957 g (49.7%) R 1.25 (51.9%)
Total mortaria	**3385 g (19.0%)** **R 0.75 (3.7%)**	**2701 g (22.9%)** **R 1.28 (9.5%)**	**3935 g (13.5%)** **R 2.41 (7.5%)**

Table 27: Stratified mortaria for Period 6: weights and EREs (=R) and percentages of totals for each period or grouped periods

the earliest in the series and perhaps produced from *c* AD 280/300 onwards), was well-represented in the York Minster excavations (Hartley 1995), but was absent from this and other sites in Carlisle. It is possible that the distribution of these earlier products was mainly confined to sites closer to the kilns, in the Malton/York area (Tyers 1996, 188). A single example of the form, catalogued as a variant on type 6a, was recovered from a Period 7 'dark earth' deposit, clearly residual, and could be considerably later than the classic type 6a. The only Crambeck mortarium of identifiable form was a single fully developed version of type 6b (almost a type 6c; *475; p 653*). Thus it can be seen that, despite the appearance of Crambeck greywares from the late third or very early fourth century, the evidence suggests that very few Crambeck mortaria reached Carlisle until the end of the second third of the fourth century.

Period 6C (*c* mid- to late fourth/early fifth century)
The sources of mortaria had, by this point, narrowed to no more than three producers at the beginning of the period, and probably only two for the remainder. At the beginning of the period, supplies from Mancetter-Hartshill potteries were barely a trickle and were probably drawing to a close. Mortaria from the Lower Nene Valley workshops had already ceased to arrive, probably driven out by competition from closer sources such as Crambeck, which was imitating some of their forms; even mortaria from the Catterick workshop were relatively few. At least 50%, and probably more, of the

mortaria were residual, and taking this into account it is likely that the Crambeck workshops were providing over 80% of the contemporary mortaria. These may have been sold in the putative market alongside other types of pottery (*Ch 9*).

The range of the Crambeck mortarium types in this phase (both present and absent) is also of particular interest, as they now occur in greater variety, and appear to have a typologically later emphasis than the single diagnostic example recorded in Period 6B. The relatively early dating of Corder type 6 mortaria (Corder and Birley 1937) is clear, but the stratigraphic evidence from the site provides chronological support for Kay Hartley's (1995) proposed sequence of sub-types. Of the 14 vessels for which the form was distinguished, all are variants of type 6; they include: type 6b; one example; type 6c: seven examples; type 6d: three examples; one York Minster form 66 (perhaps related to type 6c or 6d), and two examples of type 6 not attributable to a sub-type; type 6a is absent. Presumably type 6c was at its peak, with type 6d a newer innovation. The latter may have had a shorter life, having emerged only shortly before (or at the same time as) the introduction of Parchment ware mortaria. Evidence from the Yorkshire signal stations, probably founded *c* AD 383-8 or even AD 390 (Casey 1980, 51-2; Brickstock 2000), tends to accord with this suggestion, as, apart from a single type 6d from Scarborough, type 6 vessels are absent there.

All the type 6 mortaria from this period are in the sandier Crambeck fabric (Fabric 322), but the finer Parchment ware fabric (Fabric 323) was evidently introduced for mortaria relatively early in the period. Just two forms in the Parchment ware fabric were represented: a Corder type 5 flanged bowl-like form (loosely imitating samian form Dr 38); and a Corder type 7 wall-sided vessel (ultimately related to samian mortarium form Dr 45). The former was stratigraphically early in the period, and the production of both may have just overlapped with type 6c and possibly type 6d vessels. Kay Hartley (*pers comm*) has long held the opinion that the production of the gritted mortarium version of the Corder type 5 bowl may have been one of the earliest mortaria made in Parchment ware (emerging by AD 370/80 at least). Both this and Corder type 7 are forms known to have been produced without grits in the paler Parchment fabric, and were being made in reduced greyware and in orange-slipped fabrics from an earlier date; there is a reduced example in Period 6A and a red-slipped one in Period 6B (*419; p 649*). Notably absent in this period were any examples of Corder type 8 or any mortaria with painted decoration. An oddity amongst the mortaria from this period was a mortarium (*453; p 652*) in the Crambeck reduced grey culinary fabric, a rare York Minster type M66, a Swanpool-influenced form, perhaps also related to Corder type 6d.

Period 6E (late fourth-fifth century)

There were no identifiable mortaria in the demolition deposits of Period 6D, but Period 6E produced four (one type 6c, one type 6d, and two type 5). The type 6 vessels were probably residual by this date, but as one of the type 5 vessels had painted decoration, this might hint at a later date.

Period 7 (early post-Roman 'dark earth')

It seems that the latest Crambeck mortaria (some painted) did reach Carlisle, appearing in the earliest deposits of Period 7, and concentrated above the remains of barrack-like structure, Building **2302**, and the minor road (**2303**) to the south (Fig 274). Despite some residuality, demonstrated by the presence of type 6 mortaria, there were four of type 5 (two with painted decoration), four of type 7 (three painted), two of type 8 (both painted), and two unidentified types, again both painted. Thus the incidence of painted decoration was much higher than hitherto. This, and the first appearance of type 8, seems to suggest that, even as occupation within the fort was declining, new supplies of mortaria continued to arrive, reflecting innovations at the Crambeck potteries which were taking place in the fifth century. The Carlisle assemblage seems to suggest, albeit very tentatively, that type 8 mortaria could have been a very late addition to the Crambeck Parchment ware repertoire (perhaps early in the fifth century), and that at a similarly late date, the

practice of painting rather than slipping mortaria may have been added to the longer-established tradition of painting tablewares. Worthy of remark is the extraordinary character of Corder type 8 bowls and mortaria (Gillam's 'General de Gaulle' type). Such profiles are unparalleled in any other mortarium in Roman Britain, and the independent development of the type at Crambeck would not be incompatible with a pottery industry steering its own course in isolation at the end of its working life.

The stamps

K F Hartley

These are arranged in chronological order of manufacture, with indications of residuality, where appropriate.

1. Fabric 320, Brockley Hill (Fig 298). Heavily burnt and worn, the whole rim of a mortarium stamped once only on the left side with the partial impression of a stamp of Secundus (SECV[....]), small V inside C; AD 55-85.
    MIL 5, *4306*, Period 3A, Building *4653*, R1.1, fill of pit/trench *4305*; also unstratified

2. Fabric 364, Wroxeter (Fig 298). Worn and slightly singed; left- and right-facing stamps survive, both complete, reading DECA.F, with small blind A inside C; it is from one of at least seven dies of the potter Decanius (see Hartley 2003, fig 7.12, no 9 for a stamp from the same die) and *op cit*, 249, no 9 for some further details of this potter, who was active in the workshop which supplied Wroxeter with mortaria in cream fabric. Its *floruit* was in the first half of the second century, though some rim-profiles have previously suggested production as early as AD 90. This mortarium is entirely exceptional in rim form, both for this potter and for the Wroxeter workshop in general, and must be one of its earliest mortaria. It cannot be later than Trajanic, and could very well be mid- to late-Flavian. In type it compares most closely with Flavian mortaria made in the Verulamium region. Fortunately, this example was found in a construction trench of Building *7391*, the rebuilt *principia* of the first fort (Period 3B: AD 83-4 from dendrochronological dating). The internal surface shows much wear and the slip has been worn from the underside of the base. The primary markets of the workshop in question were in the west Midlands and Wales, with some reaching sites as far north as Chester and Wilderspool; north of this area they are rare, and it is uncertain whether normal dispersal was involved or whether they were outliers carried by troop movements. The extremely early date of this example almost certainly means that it reached Carlisle in the baggage of a soldier coming from Wroxeter in the Flavian period. It also provides a date of *c* AD 80 for the setting up of the Wroxeter workshop.
    MIL 5, *7350*, Period 3B, Building *7391*, fill of construction trench *7385*

3. Fabric 362, Elginhaugh (Fig 298). This mortarium was barely used before breakage; the slip is intact on the outside and is minimally scuffed on the inside. The slightly diagonally

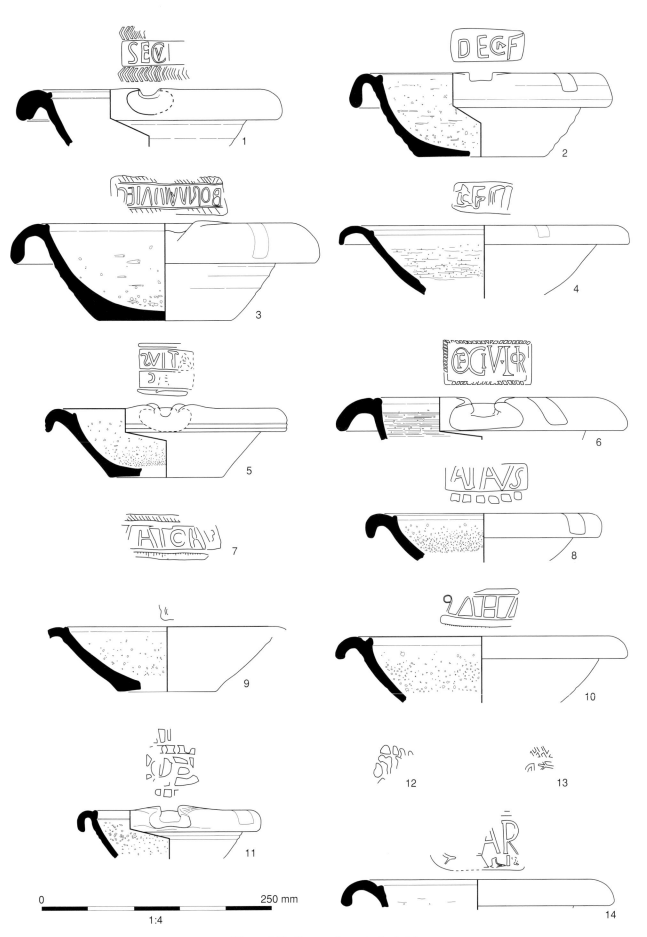

Figure 298: Stamped mortaria, 1-14

impressed, right-facing stamp is retrograde. The name begins in BOR… and the stamp ends with EC; either FE is ligatured or the preceding downstroke may represent F, a normal enough version of *fecit*. RSO Tomlin has suggested BORINIANFEC as a possible reading; unfortunately, stamps from a second die would be necessary to provide any certainty. The stamp is, however, easy to recognise. Three mortaria of this potter are now known, two from Carlisle and a third from Elginhaugh. The fabric undoubtedly indicates manufacture at Elginhaugh, which was occupied within the period AD 79-86 (Hanson 2007). The second Carlisle stamp, from the Annetwell Street excavations (Caruana in prep), is on a vessel complete enough to show that it had been stamped only once. This mortarium is not complete enough to show any second stamp. The Elginhaugh mortarium shows that practice varied, as it is stamped to each side of the spout. It is virtually unknown for mortaria made in Scotland to appear at sites in England; they were certainly not sold or distributed there in any normal way, so that it is reasonable to believe that the two Elginhaugh mortaria at Carlisle were carried there by military personnel; for further discussion of the stamp and the potter, see Hartley (2007, 353)

MIL 3, *999/1011*, Period 3B, external layer; also residual in *819*, Period 9, fill of post-medieval cellar *841*

4. Fabric 364, Wroxeter (Fig 298). There is no sign of use on the sherd; probably a Wroxeter product, though Carlisle Fabric 302 is a possibility. The stamp is intended to be a FECIT stamp, but it cannot yet be attributed to a known potter. Trajanic.
    MIL 1, *222*, Period 4A/B, but presumably in use in Period 4A, Road **7645**, external layer

5. Fabric 363 (Fig 298), very little use. A poorly impressed, retrograde, two-line stamp, reading ATTIVS on the upper line and FEC on the lower line; the stamp could have *ansae* which might indicate a military connection. Three of his mortaria are now recorded from Carlisle, two of them from the northern Lanes, and also from Milecastle 79 (Richmond and Gillam 1952, 33, no 21, misread as MATT). All of his mortaria are similar and not later than Hadrianic; the attempt at concentric scoring would fit better with a Trajanic date.
    MIL 2, *555*, Period 5B, fill of pit *567*, where it is residual

6. Fabric 313, Noyon (Oise) Somme (Fig 298). Hard, fine-textured, pale brown version fired to cream at the surface. Well-worn. A curved Gillam 238, stamped once only. The right-facing stamp is probably slightly obscured by clay added to form the spout; it reads OF CIVLPRI[.], F inside O, I inside C, PRI ligatured; in complete stamps, S follows with small C in its upper loop. His full name was G Iulius Priscus, whose workshop can be confidently attributed to Noyon (Oise), where six of his mortaria have now been recorded (Hartley 1998, 203–4). AD 65-100.
    MIL 1, *337*, Period 4A/B, Road **7645**, road surface, probably just residual

7. Fabric 359, Aldborough (Fig 298). Left-facing stamp reading [.]ATOR, probably for Viator; see Hartley 1971, fig 18, nos 1-4

and 66 for details of the potter who worked at Aldborough, Yorkshire, AD 100-40 (there was probably more than one potter called Viator and most dies giving Viator were not used at Aldborough).
MIL 5, *6381*, Period 4B, Road **7477**, road surface

8. Probably a variant Fabric 360 or Bainesse/Catterick Fabric MB16 (Hartley 2002a, 358; Fig 298); it has a much greyer, more prominent core than is normal for Fabric 302, which is the nearest in the Carlisle fabric series. No sign of wear on the sherds. A broken stamp of Anaus survives; Anaus was active at Corbridge at some point in the period AD 140-60, but it is likely that he had worked in the period AD 120-40 in the Binchester-Catterick area (see Hartley 2002b, 467-8 and fig 213 for further details). He therefore has several variations of fabric (*ibid*), few of which are easy to source. Stamped mortaria of other potters who worked in both areas are found at Carlisle, but in small numbers. Probably Binchester-Catterick area rather than Corbridge.
    MIL 1, *169*, Period 4A/B, Road **7645**, external layer; also Period 5, *245*, external layer

9. Fabric ?360, unidentified, ?Corbridge (Fig 298). Heavily worn; second century.
    MIL 1, *245*, Period 5, external layer

10. Fabric 364, Wroxeter (Fig 298). Some wear; two sherds, not joining. Incomplete stamp, one of a series of semi-literate stamps produced by a group of potters at Wroxeter AD 100-50, but this profile is probably not earlier than AD 110. See Hartley 2003, 249, no 11 for details of the group. This example is highly unusual.
     MIL 5, *2569*, Period 5A, fill of gully *2712*

11. Fabric 301, Carlisle (Fig 298). No wear on sherds. The right-facing stamp is from the same die of Doc(e)ilis 3 as one from Hardknott (Hartley 1999, fig 42, no 1). For details of his varied activity see *op cit*, 99, no 1, and for up-to-date information on his workshop at Carlisle, see Johnson and Anderson (2008). AD 115-55, but primarily Hadrianic. Possibly residual.
     MIL 5, *2492*, Period 5B, Road **4662**, external layer

12. Fabric 301 (Fig 298). A second mortarium of Doc(e)ilis, with some wear; the fragmentary stamp is from the beginning of a stamp from the same die as *11*. Residual.
     MIL 5, *5647*, Period 6A, Building **5200**, fill of construction trench *5193*

13. Fabric 360 (Fig 298), slightly burnt. Fragmentary stamp, unidentified; Corbridge; primarily Hadrianic.
     MIL 1, *327*, Period 4A/B, Road **7645**, road surface; also residual in *234*, Period 6B, Road **7646**, fill of hollow *233*; and *209*, Period 6C, Road **7646**, fill of robber trench *208*

14. Fabric 301, North of England, ?Carlisle (Fig 298). Two joining sherds with a broken left-facing, two-line stamp of Martialis, which reads MAR/TIALIS, with blind A on lower line. His mortaria are now recorded from Birrens, Carlisle (two),

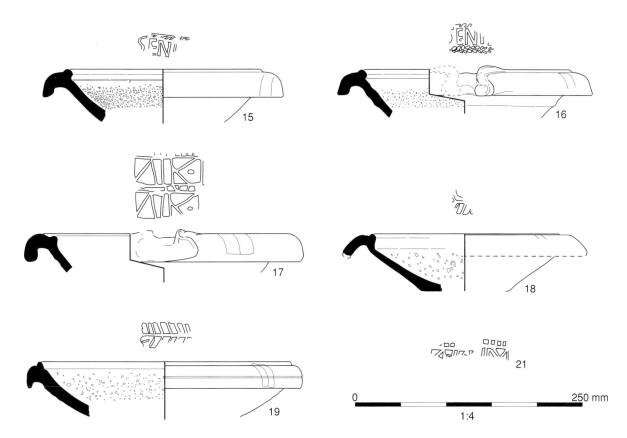

Figure 299: Stamped mortaria, 15-19, 21

and Corbridge (*pers obs*). Made in the north of England, the fabric would fit well with a source in Carlisle. Hadrianic-Antonine.

MIL 5, *5928*, Period 5B, external layer; also residual in *5991*, Period 5C, Structure **7473**, fill of ?construction trench *5990*

15. Fabric 324 (Fig 299). Fragmentary stamp of Sennius, who worked at Mancetter (Hartley 1959, 11). His dating rests largely on the gutter deposit at Wroxeter, where 17 of his mortaria were found with an even larger deposit of samian which is dated AD 160-80; the latest coins (worn) are dated AD 155 (Atkinson 1942, 127-9, 279-80). Sennius belongs to the latest generation of potters to stamp their mortaria at Mancetter. Optimum date AD 150-70. Residual.
   MIL 5, *2166*, Period 6C, Road **2303**, road surface

16. Fabric 324, Mancetter (Fig 299), burnt. A second mortarium of Sennius (see *15* above for comments). Optimum date AD 150-70.
   MIL 5, *2358*, Period 5C, fill of hollow *2359*

17. Fabric 303, probably Carlisle (Fig 299). Burnt after breakage; there are two stamps impressed close together to the left side of the spout, of which only the one to the right survives. The stamp is easily recognisable, but the reading is uncertain. Only one other mortarium is known with the same stamps (arranged in exactly the same way), from Annetwell Street, Carlisle (Caruana in prep). Carlisle is a likely source, *c* AD 130-70.
   MIL 5, *2510*, Period 5C, external layer; also residual in *2463*, Period 5D, Road **4662**, fill of roadside ditch *2466*

18. Fabric ?360, ?Corbridge (Fig 299), heavily worn. Fragmentary stamp, possibly the end of a small herringbone stamp. Distribution and fabric indicates that at least four such dies were in use in the Corbridge workshop in the Antonine period (see also *19*). Residual.
   MIL 5, *2400*, Period 6A, Road **2303**, surface

19. Fabric 360 (Fig 299). A partially impressed stamp, probably from one of at least four herringbone-type dies used at Corbridge in the Antonine period. The rim-profile of this mortarium would fit well with production in the workshop of Bellicus (Birley and Gillam 1948, fig 1, nos 5ii-5vi). Residual.
   MIL 5, *2484*, Period 6A, Building **2302**, R4.1, floor

20. Fabric 350 or 302, perhaps Carlisle (not illus). Broken, unidentified stamp, second century. The context, Period 4B (*c* AD 125-45), provides greater dating precision.
   MIL 5, *2767*, Period 4B, Road **4659**, road surface

21. Fabric 301 (Fig 299). Probably the North West, Carlisle possible. Unidentified stamp, probably AD 130-70. Residual.
   MIL 4, *1676*, Period 8ii, fill of medieval ditch **1231**

The coarse pottery
Local production: Carlisle and its environs
The local coarsewares of Carlisle and its environs have received little petrological investigation. The only relevant fabrics described in the *National Roman Fabric Reference Collection Handbook* (Tomber and Dore

1998) derive from mortaria in the so-called Carlisle/ Scalesceugh white-slipped ware (CSA WS; *op cit*, 124), which is thought to have been made in the Carlisle-Scalesceugh-Old Penrith area (including the valleys of the rivers Petteril and Eden), in the first and second centuries AD. Two different fabrics were discussed in the handbook, but only one was thin-sectioned (*op cit*, 124 and figs 97a and b); neither can be equated exactly with the other coarseware fabrics of probable local origin that were identified in the Millennium assemblage.

Three kiln sites are now known to have been in operation in the Carlisle area during the first and second centuries AD, producing both coarsewares and mortaria. Scalesceugh, in the Petteril valley, lies about 9 km south-west of Carlisle (Bellhouse 1971; Richardson 1973) and Brampton is approximately 14 km to the east of the city (Hogg 1965). More locally, kilns are known from Fisher Street, Carlisle, only 100 m to the east of the south-eastern corner of the earliest fort (McBride and Hartley forthcoming). A fourth kiln site, operating in the late second and early third centuries, is suspected at English Damside, also in Carlisle; represented by wasters recovered during a watching brief (Frere 1988, 438), this site is *c* 500 m to the south of the south-east corner of the fort.

Because the potters were probably drawing on similar clays and tempering, there are significant difficulties in distinguishing many of the fabrics macroscopically, and in consequence details of the forms are of paramount importance, particularly for the first and second centuries. Conveniently, the forms of known Scalesceugh and Brampton products do not overlap significantly, so that rim sherds formed the most reliable indicator of probable origin for this study. It is, however, highly likely that the vessels recovered to date from the two kiln sites do not cover the whole range of vessels produced.

Scalesceugh

A single kiln was excavated at Scalesceugh, and though the structure was published (Richardson 1973), none of the associated pottery was illustrated or described,

although drawings of a type-series of vessels from the excavations are archived in Tullie House Museum and Art Gallery. Geophysical survey in 1971, by the Ancient Monuments Laboratory, revealed a number of significant anomalies, several of which indicate the presence of further kilns or related inductrial activity (A David *pers comm*), some of which seem have to been relatively large and were most probably used for firing tiles. Tiles stamped by *Legio IX* and *Legio XX* recovered during field walking (I Caruana *pers comm*; *RIB* II.6, 2462.2, 2462.4; 2463.2; Collingwood and Wright 1994), together with the distinctive range of vessel types from the excavated kiln, suggest that the site was essentially a military works-depot and that it had started production by the Trajanic period (before the departure of *Legio IX Hispana* after AD 108), perhaps supplying tiles for the construction of the Period 4A fort at Carlisle (Swan 2008, 59), and reaching a peak in production during the construction of Hadrian's Wall.

The range of vessel types recorded in the Millennium assemblage, and those seen in previously published assemblages from Carlisle, for example Castle Street (Taylor 1991), seem to suggest that Scalesceugh products (or at least the forms and fabrics known to date) were not being supplied to the fort. This might be accounted for in a number of ways: Scalesceugh could have started production later than Brampton and concentrated mainly on tile production; or it could have been intended to supply military sites elsewhere, possibly using the Petteril and access to the sea to export its products to the north and west.

Brampton

Seven pottery and tile kilns, alongside evidence for other industrial activity, including iron-working (Manning 1966), were excavated at Brampton in 1963, under rescue conditions (Hogg 1965). The kiln structures were published, but like Scalesceugh, none of the pottery was described or illustrated. A series of later drawings of the pottery, again archived in Tullie House Museum and Art Gallery, was made available for this research and, in addition, annotated drawings

Plate 198: Examples of products from the Brampton kilns

of a type series of most of the main Brampton kiln products, made by the late John Gillam, were also available. The range of probable Brampton products noted in the Millennium assemblage (Pl 198) is, however, broader than that known from the kiln sites, and it is probable that other kilns producing similar fabrics existed at Brampton.

The Brampton kiln site lies in the Irthing valley, south of the Stanegate military road, and 1.3 km east of the fort at Brampton Old Church (Breeze 2006, 456); its foundation almost certainly preceded both. The site has been described as an auxiliary works-depot and certainly the morphology of some of its kilns and the nature of its products suggest military control, under either legionary or, less certainly, auxiliary, authority. None of its tiles appear to have been stamped, but when production started on the site in the early AD 80s it had yet to become normal practice to do so.

No doubt the need for a major depot for the manufacture of ceramic and metal products, within the western zone of what was to become the Stanegate frontier, was appreciated at an early stage, and Brampton's early development can be traced within the Millennium pottery assemblage. During Period 3A, when the first fort was built, Brampton products are, unsurprisingly, absent from the assemblage, but evidence from the construction deposits of Period 3B has, for the first time, shown that Brampton was probably in production by AD 83-4. For the first two decades of its production, however, the supply of Brampton products (mainly cooking wares) to Carlisle was of only minor significance (2.2% by weight and 5.8% by EREs; Table 28), and quantities did not increase significantly until after the construction of the second fort in about AD 105 (Period 4A). This perhaps suggests that Brampton was at first intended primarily as a tilery, supplying tiles for the construction of new forts being built within the Tyne-Solway isthmus, and supporting the units transferred there from campaigns in Scotland, being the first stage in the build-up of troops which culminated in the development of the so-called Stanegate frontier. Perhaps in support of this, it appears that forts further to the east of Carlisle, for instance Vindolanda, were receiving more Brampton pottery earlier (perhaps in association with tiles; *pers obs*). The early start-date for production might explain why the Brampton kilns are neither on the Stanegate road, nor close to the Trajanic fort at Brampton Old Church (Breeze 2006, 456).

Between the construction of the second timber fort at Carlisle in *c* AD 105 (Period 4A) and its demolition in *c* AD 140/50 (Period 4C), Brampton became a major supplier of kitchen wares to the fort. In the Trajanic period (Period 4A), it supplied between 13.3% (by weight) and 15.7% (by EREs) of the coarsewares, in comparison to 43.8% (by weight) and 57.5% (EREs) from the more local Carlisle workshops (mortaria excluded; Table 28). It must be noted that the amount of material supplied by the latter is probably substantially inflated by residual material, as it had already been the fort's dominant supplier for over 30 years. Brampton's share of supplies increased significantly in the Hadrianic period (Period 4B), to 23.1% (by weight) and 24.8% (EREs), whilst the supply of more local wares diminished to 35.1% (by weight) and 39.9% (EREs); again, the quantities of local wares are probably inflated by residual material. By the time the second fort was demolished (Period 4C), perhaps in the AD 140s (*Ch 6, pp 241-2*), evidence suggests a decrease in Brampton's supply to 17.6% (by weight) and 18.7% (EREs), and a significant increase in local products to 58.9% (by weight) and 65% (EREs). The relatively small group of material from these periods reflects pottery usage immediately before the end of Period 4, and the significant reduction in supply from Brampton seems to suggest that supplies from the Brampton depot had almost certainly ceased a few years before the fort was demolished; as a result, Carlisle had fallen back on its local workshops as principal suppliers. Until the analysis of the Millennium assemblage, it was assumed that the Brampton works-depot had been closed down *c* AD 125 (*pers obs*), at the time of the construction of the forts on Hadrian's Wall, and the recognition of its continued production (to *c* AD 140) represents a major revision of the understanding of the logistics of the frontier.

In addition, the influx of Dorset Black-burnished ware Fabric 1 (BB1) at the time of the construction of Hadrian's Wall (*p 601*) had been regarded as another, indirect, factor in the presumed cessation of production at Brampton in the early AD 120s. The arrival of Black-burnished ware Fabric 1 was thought to represent a significant change in military provisioning (*eg* Gillam 1976, 57), whereby future pottery supplies were to be obtained from civilian contractors. It appears, however, that, despite any such official change of policy, supplies in the region continued, for the next century at least, to be drawn from a pragmatic mix of military and civilian producers. Indeed, evidence from Carlisle now seems to suggest that, rather than flooding into the North in the AD 120s, Black-burnished ware Fabric 1 first arrived in relatively small quantities, perhaps because of limited availability, and did not make a significant contribution to Carlisle's pottery supply until the Antonine period (*p 602*; Table 29). To compensate for this, Brampton produced quantities of imitation BB1 jars and bowls, as well as other products, until the end of the Hadrianic period (Table 28), when the frontier was moved north to the Antonine Wall.

Period	Black-burnished and allied	Brampton	Local	East Yorkshire	Coarse gritty	Unknown greywares	Other pottery	Period Total
3A	169 g (1.8%)	-	3928 g (42.1%)	-	-	260 g (2.8%)	4976 g (53.3%)	9333 g
	R 0.26 (3.4%)		R 4.66 (60.1%)			R 0.30 (3.9%)	R 2.53 (32.7%)	R 7.75
3B-3E	-g	346 g (2.2%)	6888 g (43.9%)	-	-	426 g (2.7%)	8040 g (51.2%)	15,700 g
		R 0.72 (5.8%)	R 7.49 (60.2%)			R 0.37 (3.0%)	R 3.86 (31.0%)	R 12.44
4A	67 g (0.4%)	2277 g (13.3%)	7498 g (43.8%)	-	-	1350 g (7.9%)	5920 g (34.6%)	17,112 g
	R 0.22 (1.3%)	R 2.70 (15.7%)	R 9.92 (57.5%)			R 2.05 (11.9%)	R 2.35 (13.6%)	R 17.24
4B	2352 g (7.1%)	7627 g (23.1%)	11,585 g (35.1%)	-	-	4100 g (12.4%)	7306 g (22.2%)	32,970 g
	R 2.40 (6.4%)	R 9.26 (24.8%)	R 14.90 (39.9%)			R 5.45 (14.6%)	R 5.32 (14.3%)	R 37.33
4C-4D	252 g (4.3%)	1036 g (17.6%)	3472 g (58.9%)	-	-	368 g (6.2%)	769 g (13.0%)	5897 g
	R 0.04 (0.6%)	R 1.24 (18.7%)	R 4.31 (65.0%)			R 0.50 (11.2%)	R 0.54 (8.1%)	R 6.63
5	106 g (1.9%)	608 g (11.0%)	1833 g (33.2%)	-	4 g (0.1%)	691 g (12.5%)	2287 g (41.4%)	5529 g
	R 0.32 (6.6%)	R 0.47 (9.7%)	R 1.68 (34.6%)			R 1.69 (34.8%)	R 0.70 (14.4%)	R 4.86
5A-5B	2160 g (21.6%)	864 g (8.6%)	3434 g (34.4%)	-	-	839 g (8.4%)	2700 g (27.0%)	9997 g
	R 3.25 (18.0%)	R 1.50 (8.3%)	R 7.59 (42.0%)			R 1.20 (6.6%)	R 4.54 (25.1%)	R 18.08
5C-5D	3039 g (24.1%)	736 g (5.8%)	2958 g (23.5%)	-	-	2498 g (19.8%)	3369 g (26.7%)	12,600g
	R 4.09 (24.4%)	R 1.40 (8.4%)	R 4.13 (24.7%)			R 3.35 (20.0%)	R 3.77 (22.5%)	R 16.74
6A	2697 g (15.0%)	955 g (5.3%)	3716 g (20.7%)	1338 g (7.5%)	50 g (0.3%)	4533 g (25.3%)	4642 g (25.9%)	17,931 g
	R 4.60 (22.4%)	R 0.48 (2.3%)	R 5.06 (24.6%)	R 1.20 (5.8%)		R 7.02 (34.1%)	R 2.20 (10.7%)	R 20.56
6B	1641 g (13.9%)	164 g (1.4%)	1894 g (16.0%)	1233 g (10.4%)	691 g (5.9%)	2538 g (21.5%)	3646 g (30.9%)	11,807 g
	R 1.89 (14.0%)	R 0.26 (1.9%)	R 2.39 (17.7%)	R 1.70 (12.6%)	R 0.79 (5.9%)	R 3.34 (24.8%)	R 3.10 (23.0%)	R 13.47
6C	939 g (5.2%)	371 g (2.1%)	1368 g (7.6%)	3044 g (17.0%)	2734 g (15.3%)	5601 g (31.2%)	3875 g (21.6%)	17,932 g
	R 1.04 (5.9%)	R 0.57 (3.2%)	R 1.32 (7.5%)	R 2.20 (12.4%)	R 1.59 (9.0%)	R 7.83 (44.2%)	R 3.18 (17.9%)	R 17.73
6D	481 g (8.2%)	45 g (0.1%)	644 g (11.0%)	1161 g (19.7%)	516 g (8.8%)	1942 g (33.0%)	1091 g (18.6%)	5880 g
	R 0.91 (9.9%)		R 0.94 (10.2%)	R 0.94 (10.2%)	R 1.02 (11.1%)	R 3.48 (37.9%)	R 1.89 (20.6%)	R 9.18
6E	137 g (2.6%)	49 g (0.9%)	173 g (3.3%)	829 g (15.6%)	772 g (14.5%)	2045 g (38.5%)	1309 g (24.6%)	5314 g
	R 0.08 (1.5%)		R 0.29 (5.5%)	R 0.99 (18.6%)	R 0.64 (12.1%)	R 2.19 (41.2%)	R 1.12 (21.1%)	R 5.31
Post-Roman and unstratified	2101 g (7.7%)	1156 g (4.2%)	4393 g (16.1%)	3303 g (12.1%)	2184 g (8.0%)	5362 g (19.6%)	8841 g (32.3%)	27,340 g
	R 1.42 (7.6%)	R 0.44 (2.3%)	R 2.73 (14.5%)	R 2.87 (15.3%)	R 2.56 (13.6%)	R 4.50 (23.9%)	R 4.28 (22.8%)	R 18.80

Table 28: Stratified major coarse wares by period: weights and EREs (=R) and percentages of each ware or category (excludes MIL 1 from Period 4 onwards)

Period	Dorset BB1	South-west BB1	Rossington Bridge BB1	BB2 (S-E and N Kent)	Other pottery	Period Total
3A	169 g (1.8%) R 0.26 (3.4%)	-	-	-	9164 g (98.2%) R 7.49 (96.7%)	9333 g R 7.75
3B-3E	-	-	-	-	15,700 g (100%) R 12.44 (100%)	15,700 g R 12.44
4A	67 g (0.4%) R 0.22 (1.3%)	-	-	-	17,045 g (99.6%) R 17.02 (98.7%)	17,112 g R 17.24
4B	1644 g (5.0%) R 1.60 (4.3%)	708 g (2.2%) R 0.80 (2.1%)	-	-	30,618 g (92.9%) R 34.93 (93.6%)	32,970 g R 37.33
4C-4D	92 g (4.2%) R 0.04 (1.8%)	160 g (2.7%)	-	-	5645 g (95.7%) R 6.59 (99.4%)	5897 g R 6.63
5	106 g (1.9%) R 0.32 (6.6%)	-	-	-	5423 g (98.1%) R 4.54 (93.4%)	5529 g R 4.86
5A-5B	2115 g (21.2%) R 3.25 (18.0%)	13 g (0.1%)	32 g (0.3%)	39 g (0.4%)	7798 g (78.0%) R 14.83 (82.0%)	9997 g R 18.08
5C-5D	2884 g (22.9%) R 3.94 (23.5%)	-	155 g (1.2%) R 0.15 (0.9%)	160 g (1.3%) R 0.09 (0.5%)	9401 g (74.6%) R 12.56 (75.0%)	12,600 g R 16.74
6A	2616 g (14.6%) R 4.16 (20.2%)	17 g (0.5%) R 0.10 (0.1%)	64 g (0.4%) R 0.34 (1.7%)	11 g (0.1%) R 0.05 (0.2%)	15,223 g (84.9%) R 15.91 (77.4%)	17,931 g R 20.56
6B	1603 g (13.6%) R 1.73 (12.8%)	10 g (0.1%) R 0.04 (0.3%)	25 g (0.2%) R 0.12 (0.7%)	11 g (0.1%)	10,158 (86.0%) R 11.58 (86.0%)	11,807 g R 13.47
6C	911 g (5.1%) R 0.92 (5.2%)	-	28 g (0.2%) R 0.12 (0.9%)	1 g (<0.1%)	16,992 g (94.8%) R 16.69 (94.1%)	17,932 g R 17.73
6D	465 g (7.9%) R 0.91 (9.9%)	-	- -	16 g (0.3%)	5399 g (91.8%) R 8.27 (90.1%)	5880 g R 9.18
6E	137 g (2.6%) R 0.08 (1.5%)	-	-	10 g (0.2%)	5167 g (97.2%) R 5.23 (98.5%)	5314 g R 5.31
Post-Roman and unstratified	2101 g (7.7%) R 1.42 (7.6%)	-	-	16 g (0.1%) R 0.08 (0.4%)	25,223 g (92.3%) R 17.30 (92.0%)	27.340 g R 18.80

Table 29: Stratified Black-burnished wares by period (weights and EREs (R)), with percentages of total weights and EREs (in brackets) for each fabric or group of fabrics excluding amphorae); excludes MIL 1 from Period 4 onwards

Two characteristic Brampton fabrics were recorded within the Millennium assemblage: the more common oxidised fabric and a corresponding reduced ware. Both are particularly distinctive, being loaded with coarse white grit, having a prickly feel and a pustular surface (except where deliberately smoothed). A potential difficulty in attribution might arise from the fact that the oxidised fabric can sometimes be only slightly more coarse than the coarsest versions of the North West gritty oxidised ware made at the Fisher Street kiln site, and care must be taken to use form and fabric in conjunction in the identification of these wares.

Carlisle: Fisher Street kiln site
It is clear from pottery in the earliest deposits associated with the fort (Period 3A) that pottery was produced locally (presumably by the occupants of the fort) from the moment troops arrived. It is, however,

difficult to link this earliest material with the kilns at Fisher Street (just 100 m east of the south-eastern corner of the fort), though it would seem likely that these or related kilns were the source. Two kilns were examined in advance of redevelopment in 2002, and are dated to c AD 72-117 and c AD 117-50 (Johnson and Anderson 2008; McBride and Hartley forthcoming). Most of the material from the excavated kilns would appear to be contemporary with that seen in Periods 4A and 4B, but there were also some earlier vessel types, including kiln wasters, which suggest that there could have been Flavian workshops in the immediate vicinity. From their location, it is highly likely that the kilns would, from the outset, have constituted part of a military, and possibly defended, industrial annexe.

The evidence (Table 28) indicates that production continued into the third quarter of the second century at least (until the end of Period 4), perhaps to supply the remaining veterans and other civilians. Whether this area would still have been under direct military control by this time is far from clear, particularly since the putative annexe on the south side of the fort was apparently absorbed into the expanding civilian settlement around this time (*Ch 1, p 9*).

Over 60.1% (by EREs) of the pottery (excluding samian and amphorae) from Period 3A (AD 72-3/83-4) was locally made (Table 28). This may be a slight underestimate, as some of the undiagnostic greywares and the 'other wares' might be local products. These local products also included over 80% of the fine tablewares (Pl 199). In the early fort, the total numbers would be affected by the fact that the army brought with it large quantities of mortaria (over 90% by EREs), and perhaps some other coarsewares, on its advance into hostile territory. For this reason, though mortaria were made locally from Period 3A onwards, their production appears relatively modest at first (less than 9% EREs) before the early AD 80s, but increased significantly until the fort was abandoned in the early AD 100s. Thus local contribution to Carlisle's supply was still at least 61% EREs, and probably more if undistinguished greywares are included.

It is almost certain that local pottery production ceased when the garrison departed in the opening years of the second century, but that there was a resumption on the Fisher Street site in *c* AD 105, in tandem with the reoccupation of the fort. The local products constituted almost 58% of the total in Period 4A (57.5% EREs), and included almost 48% of the finewares, but less than 9% of the mortaria, the last being depressed by a huge influx of mortaria imported from the Oise-Somme region (probably arriving with the new garrison (see *p 583*)). Another factor affecting the total of local wares at this period was a surge in the supply of kitchen wares from the Brampton works-depot (almost 16%); it seems likely that this may have influenced the repertoire of the Fisher Street workshop, meaning that cooking-wares did not constitute a very significant part of their production in the Trajanic period, flagons, mortaria,

tablewares, and special items for use in the fort seeming to have been more important.

By the Hadrianic period, the local production of coarsewares (almost 40% EREs) and finewares (36%) had declined even further, though local mortaria had a higher profile (over 14%) now that fewer imports were reaching the site (Table 28). Several factors were affecting these totals, including a significant increase in the supply of Brampton products, and the arrival of the first Black-burnished ware Fabric 1, accompanied by large quantities of imitations. Some of these last could well have been made on the Fisher Street site, but they are not included in the totals of local products.

The 60-year period following the end of Period 4, during which Carlisle seemingly survived as a largely civilian centre (Period 5), is reflected by smaller quantities of pottery generally in Periods 5A-5D. Although there was a major increase in Dorset Black-burnished ware Fabric 1, the relative amount of locally produced pottery continued at similar levels in Periods 5A-5B (only slightly raised to 41% and perhaps more, if some of the Black-burnished ware Fabric 1 imitations and 'unknown greywares' are included), partly because the Brampton works-depot (*p 591*) had ceased production. However, there was a large reduction in local products in Periods 5C-5D, stemming from the closure of the Fisher Street workshop (probably *c* AD 160-70), the quantities of local coarsewares being steady at about 24%, partly because of the opening by now of another Carlisle workshop at English Damside, and partly through residuality.

Carlisle: English Damside kiln site (Borough Street)
The English Damside kiln site lies some 500 m south of the fort, beyond the known area of civilian settlement, but close to the Roman road that headed south-westwards towards Old Carlisle. No formal excavation has taken place there, and its existence is known only from dumps of pottery, including wasters, recorded during a watching brief (Frere 1988, 438). All are unpublished, but evidence suggests the commencement of production in the second half of the second century (perhaps *c* AD 150/60), presumably to cater for a civilian population during Period 5, when the nature of the fort site had changed significantly (*Ch 7*).

The products of the English Damside workshop seem to have comprised mortaria (including Raetian-type forms with zones of slip-painting), and a very basic and limited range of cooking-wares, mostly undecorated burnished greyware vessels, the majority of which imitate Black-burnished ware Fabric 1 forms. Small quantities of oxidised pots in similar forms were also found on the site, and may again be kiln products (though of minor significance). The

Plate 199: Fine rouletted beakers from Carlisle

mid-grey burnished fabric is not distinctive and was rarely decorated. Occasionally, when the rim and upper part of certain types are present, it is possible to recognise probable English Damside products; for example, some of the bowls and dishes which imitate Black-burnished ware types have external burnishing which starts 20-30 mm below the rim. The detail of some of the rounded rims of undecorated dish or bowl forms which loosely imitate Black-burnished ware types (such as Gillam (1970) forms 223, 224, 225) can be diagnostic, as is a gradual rounded junction between the interior of the wall and the top of rim, the rim having been formed by gently rolling over the top of the vessel wall (*352; p 642*). From this it will be clear that the majority of English Damside reduced ware sherds in the assemblage will not have been distinguished, and will have been quantified as 'unidentified greywares'. Allowance, therefore, needs to be made for this in the interpretation of the figures for the 'local' products (Table 28).

The typological dating of mortaria from English Damside suggests that production began soon after the middle of the second century, and the quantified data tend to support this. It may even have started at about the same time that the Fisher Street kiln closed. Although the data appear to indicate a continuous decline in 'local' wares from about the third quarter of the second century (Periods 5A-5B: 42% EREs) to about the last quarter of the second century (Periods 5C-5D: 24.7% EREs; Table 28), this partly reflects the probable closure of the Fisher Street kiln in the early AD 160s, and the significant rise in Black-burnished ware Fabric 1 imports in Periods 5C/5D. Of particular relevance is a very large rise in 'unknown greywares', from 6.6% (EREs) in Periods 5A-5B to 20% (EREs) in Periods 5C-5D. Most of this increase probably reflects the appearance of the less easily distinguished English Damside kiln products and should be viewed as a component of local production. It is therefore quite possible that, in the last quarter of the second century, local production (in the form of the English Damside greywares) may have actually increased, accounting for perhaps about 30% of pottery supply in Carlisle.

Such typological dating may also be applied to an examination of the quantitative data for Period 6A. In this relatively long period (approximately the early-late third century), it is evident from the stratified groups that there were significant changes towards the end that have a slightly distorting influence on the quantified data which (ideally) need to be split into shorter sub-phases. Local wares continue at a level similar to that of the late second century (24.6% EREs), but the 'unknown greywares' peak at 34.1% (EREs). Again, this total is likely to include significant amounts of English Damside products and could also include some of the less distinctive East Yorkshire greywares, which

appear at the beginning of this phase (Table 28). English Damside copies of Black-burnished ware forms were certainly in use in the stone fort in the early decades of the third century, but the date at which the workshop ceased production is unknown, although it is likely to have been earlier than the middle of the century, possibly as a result of increased competition from the East Yorkshire producers. There is no evidence of locally produced pottery within the fort from then on.

Non-local pottery: finewares
The code after a fabric name indicates that the fabric has been described in the *National Roman Fabric Reference Collection Handbook* (Tomber and Dore 1998). As far as possible the fabrics are described in chronological sequence.

General discussion
The most important point to note about the appearance of non-local finewares in the Flavian and early Trajanic forts is their very small quantities and their very limited range, which did not begin to widen until the AD 90s. Set alongside this is the very marked dominance of the locally produced finewares from the foundation of the fort until well into the Hadrianic period, apart from the AD 90s to *c* AD 105 (Period 3A: 80%; Period 3B: 78-86%; Period 4A: at least 48%; Period 4B: at least 35%; percentages of EREs, Tables 30 and 31). This balance in favour of local products is undoubtedly a reflection of the isolation of Carlisle at the time of its foundation and in the following two or three decades, which can be accounted for in a number of ways. It is reasonable to suggest that there would have been problems with the security of supply-lines in a newly conquered territory, and, in addition, Carlisle's distance from the East Coast shipping routes was presumably a hindrance in gaining access to goods shipped down the Rhine. Moreover, roads may have frequently been in a poor state of repair, a fact mentioned in one of the Vindolanda documents (Bowman and Thomas 1994, 343), and, unlike more substantial vessels like mortaria, finewares were rather fragile to transport by road. These problems must have encouraged the army to produce the bulk of its own finewares alongside the standard range of culinary wares that normally characterise the output of military potteries.

Although there was an increase in the range of imported and other finewares in the Trajanic and Hadrianic periods, it is debatable whether this represents a genuine expansion of trade. There is very little duplication in the individual imported fineware forms, which might be expected in bulk orders, and in consequence there must be a strong suspicion that at least some, and perhaps a substantial number, of these vessels had been brought to the fort as personal possessions, or in the baggage trains of groups transferred from other regions. In Periods 3C-3E, a significant proportion of the finewares which appear for the first time was from contexts that could have contained material deposited by those demolishing the first timber fort and building the second. Both groups may have been legionaries, since the vacating garrison will have moved out before the demolition of the fort, and the construction of the new fort, after a short period with no occupying force (Periods 3D-3E; between *c* AD 103 and *c* AD 105), could have been undertaken before the new occupants arrived. Such a break in formal occupation would best explain the relative scarcity of local finewares at this time, and the slight expansion in the range of non-local wares available immediately before Period 4A.

It seems unlikely that the same garrison (probably the *ala Sebosiana Gallorum*; *Ch 12*) returned to occupy the new buildings in Period 4A, and where the new garrison had been stationed previously remains unknown. However, a significant increase in the range of finewares from North Gaul (white, grey, and mica-dusted fabrics) might suggest a transfer from *Gallia Belgica* or the Lower Rhine, and this tends to be confirmed by major changes in the pottery being made at the Fisher Street workshop (*p 594*). In addition, the passage of time and the presence in Carlisle during the Trajanic period of the *centurio regionarius* (Bowman and Thomas 1994, 250) might have encouraged the availability of a better range of finewares. This apparently gradual opening-up of supply continued into the Hadrianic period, when there was a concomitant decline in locally made tablewares. Some of the Hadrianic finewares can be associated with the presence of men from *Legio VI* (Ebor wares), and

probably also *Legio XX* (Wilderspool finewares), who were involved in the construction of Hadrian's Wall (Breeze and Dobson 2000). For the Antonine period (Period 5), when there seems to have been no resident unit (*Ch 7*), many of the finewares (including the local products) may have been residual, although the Colchester and Cologne beakers (the latter appearing for the first time) suggest the continuance of some long-distance trade. There is no indication that the contemporary local kiln made any tablewares after the AD 160s (*p 594*).

There was a significant change in the pattern of supply of finewares at the beginning of Period 6A, with the arrival of Nene Valley colour-coated wares; from then onwards, other imports had little or no significance. By the last decades of the third century, when Crambeck grey tablewares first arrived, all the imports were residual and Romano-British products constituted the sole tablewares. The range of these Romano-British finewares expanded in the mid-late fourth century, seemingly in connection with the establishment of a market in the middle of the fort (*Ch 9*); Oxfordshire red-coated wares and other less distinctive red-slipped wares (probably including Swanpool), as well as Crambeck painted Parchment wares, appeared. They may have disappeared again once coinage ceased to arrive, but this is not certain.

Lyon colour-coated ware
The quantities were very small and many sherds were residual (Table 30); vessel types were confined

Fabrics	Periods 1-3A	Period 3B	Periods 3C-3E
Lyon	1 sherd (7.7%)	4 sherds (7.4%) R 0.17 (21.3%)	1 sherd (3.6%)
Central Gaulish colour-coated 1 and 2	3 sherds (2.3%) R 0.05 (7.0%)	2 sherds (3.7%)	1 sherd (3.6%) R 0.16 (13.1%)
Argonne	-	-	1 sherd (3.6%)
Terra Nigra	-	1 sherd (1.9%)	-
North Gaulish greyware	-	-	5 sherds (17.9%)
Imported fine white tableware	-	-	5 sherds (17.9%) R 0.71 (58.2%)
East Anglian fine reduced	-	-	1 sherd (3.6%)
Other fine tablewares	1 sherd (7.7%) R 0.09 (12.7%)	-	3 sherds (10.7%)
Local barbotine	-	12 sherds (22.2%)	3 sherds (10.7%) R 0.14 (11.5%)
Other local finewares	8 sherds (61.5%) R 0.57 (80.3%)	35 sherds (64.8%) R 0.63 (78.8%)	8 sherds (28.6%) R 0.21 (17.2%)
Total of finewares	**13 sherds (3.3%)** **R 0.71 (9.1%)**	**54 sherds (18.1%)** **R 0.80 (11.4%)**	**28 sherds (8.1%)** **R 1.22 (22.6%)**

Table 30: Stratified fine tablewares for Periods 1-3: sherd numbers and EREs (=R) and percentages of totals for each period or grouped periods

Fabrics	Period 4A	Periods 4B-4D
Central Gaulish colour-coated 1 and 2	8 sherds (7.5%) R 0.36 (18.6%)	33 sherds (14.4%) R 0.13 (2.8%)
Argonne	-	9 sherds (3.9%) R 0.11 (2.3%)
Colour-coated unsourced	-	4 sherds (1.8%) R 0.26 (5.5%)
Mica-dusted	1 sherd (0.9%) R 0.10 (5.2%)	37 sherds (16.2%) R 0.45 (9.5%)
Imported fine white tableware	1 sherd (0.9%)	4 sherds (1.8%) R 0.08 (1.7%)
Gallia-Belgica greyware	15 sherds (14.0%)	4 sherds (1.8%) R 0.58 (12.3%)
North Gaulish greyware	3 sherds (2.8%) R 0.55 (28.4%)	6 sherds (2.6%) R 0.04 (0.9%)
Wilderspool fine	-	12 sherds (5.2%) R 0.65 (13.8%)
Colchester fine	1 sherd (0.9%)	2 sherds (0.9%) R 0.14 (3.0%)
East Anglian fine reduced	6 sherds (5.6%)	4 sherds (1.8%)
Local finewares	55 sherds (51.4%) R 0.93 (47.9%)	97 sherds (42.4%) R 1.69 (35.8%)
Other unsourced finewares	5 sherds (4.7%)	15 sherds (6.6%) R 0.59 (12.5%)
Residual Flavian imports	12 sherds (11.2%)	2 sherds (0.9%)
Total of finewares	**107 sherds (9.2%)** **R 1.94 (11.3%)**	**229 sherds (8.3%)** **R 4.72 (10.7%)**

Table 31: Stratified tablewares for Period 4: sherd numbers and EREs (=R) and percentages of totals for each period or grouped periods (excludes MIL 1 from Period 4 onwards)

to globular or indented beakers, and cups seem to have been absent (commensurate with a site starting after AD 70). Willis (2003, 126-7) has argued for a more extended dating for the occurrence of the ware in Britain, into the mid AD 80s, and the Carlisle Millennium Project evidence tends to support this. Three unabraded fragments of a beaker (*31*; 17% EREs) in layer *960*, outside a Period 3B barrack, and more joining sherds residual in later deposits, suggests that this vessel had probably still been in use after AD 83-4.

Central Gaulish colour-coated 1 and 2
Very few sherds in the white ware (Fabric 1) were recorded (Tables 30 and 31). Most of the Central Gaulish colour-coated Fabric 2 wares comprised beakers in pale buff fabrics with dark brownish slips, all occurring in relatively small quantities, but, nonetheless, they spanned the early Flavian to at least the Hadrianic period. Such thin-walled vessels are relatively fragile and were frequently broken before they could become heirlooms, so large sherds are not wholly residual.

This, and the narrow and secure dating of the phases, makes the typological development of these beakers of particular importance. It is possible to track the change from the early Flavian small everted-rim (Period 3A; *28*), to the Trajanic and Hadrianic simple dished cornice rim (Period 4A; *120*; Period 4B; *262*); from the early Flavian high-shouldered globular form (Period 3A; *28*) to the more ovoid Trajanic (Period 4A; *120*), and then the bag-shaped Hadrianic profile; also the appearance of the grooved cornice rim (Period 3C; *54*). The quantified data suggest that these vessels were residual by the beginning of the Antonine period (Period 5A).

Argonne colour-coated ware (Exeter Group 1 rough-cast colour-coated beakers)
This group of colour-coated, rough-cast, cornice-rim, bag-shaped beakers was first distinguished at Exeter (Swan 1979), and recent publications suggest that these vessels should probably be attributed to workshops in the Argonne region of France (Tomber and Dore

1998, 47). They usually have a grooved cornice rim (often with traces of diagonal wiping on the interior), and clay rough-cast decoration, sometimes below a shoulder-groove. Apart from a single body-sherd in a Period 3C construction trench of *c* AD 93/4, these beakers first appear in the Hadrianic period (Tables 30 and 31), though the earliest may be residual Trajanic on typological grounds (the profile is more rounded). However, their occurrence seems to be mainly Hadrianic, when they tend to become more bag-shaped, and they are likely to be residual by the last quarter of the second century or perhaps earlier. An Argonne attribution would explain why such products were more common than comparable contemporary beakers at Exeter (Swan 1979), and also why they were among the relatively few imported finewares at Carlisle, as they were not dependent on Rhine shipping, and transport down the Seine and its tributaries, and thence up the west coast of Britain, would have been relatively straightforward (*236, 398, 409*).

Terra Nigra and related fine grey imports from Gallia Belgica
Only a single sherd of *terra nigra* was found (Table 30), in a deposit of Period 3B (where it was possibly residual); extremely low levels of *terra nigra* are characteristic of the rest of Carlisle (V Rigby *pers comm*). Vessels in fine polished greywares, almost certainly derived from *terra nigra*, were, however, slightly better represented. None of the vessels in this group (rouletted beakers and bowls) can be attributed to the similar (and probably related) London fine reduced wares (Tomber and Dore 1998, 137; Seeley and Drummond-Murray 2005, 128-9), East Anglian stamped greywares (Rodwell 1978), or Nene Valley greywares, and the forms cannot be paralleled in Britain. They are thus most probably imports from *Gallia Belgica*, produced in the *terra nigra* tradition which survived there after *terra nigra* had ceased to be imported to Britain (they are therefore referred to as 'Gallia Belgica' greywares' in Table 31). At Carlisle, they occur mainly in the Trajanic period (Period 4A) and are residual by the Antonine period at the latest (*124, 203, 325*).

North Gaulish greyware and allied wares
This imported range of slightly granular fabrics, which might superficially be seen as a 'coarseware', nevertheless qualifies as a tableware, by reason of the forms, which are mainly large beakers ('*vases tronconiques*') and table-bowls; beakers, though occasionally used for cooking, were essentially drinking-vessels. At Carlisle, only large beakers were present, in small quantities and very diverse fabrics (Tables 30 and 31), suggesting that they had probably reached the site as personal possessions. They first appear in minute amounts in Periods 3C-3D (perhaps reaching the site with demolition or building gangs), but are mainly Trajanic and probably residual

thereafter. Their distribution in southern Britain is primarily coastal, particularly at cosmopolitan ports such as London, and sites connected with the *Classis Britannica* (Richardson and Tyers 1984), although quantities are never very large. Their distribution pattern is much more uneven in the North, and the circumstances underlying the presence of North Gaulish greyware at sites distant from the East Coast, such as Carlisle, Binchester (J Evans *pers comm*), and Vindolanda (Richardson and Tyers 1984, 139), require special explanation. Current research suggests that the use of these large vessels for drinking (most probably for beer) was an ethnic trait, possibly indicative of the presence of men from North Gaul and the mouth of the Rhine. This evidence is compatible with historically known patterns of recruitment in the late first and second centuries (Swan 2009; *106, 121, 206*).

Imported fine white tablewares (North Gaul or Lower Rhineland)
A range of white or cream wares is known to have been exported to Britain from North Gaul and the Lower Rhineland in the late first and early second centuries (Tomber and Dore 1998, 22-4, 74-8). From the Flavian period onwards the best known comprised Oise-Somme and North French mortaria (including Groups 1 and 2) and flagons (including the so-called pipe-clay flagons). However, the latter have been excluded from the present discussion, as their large size tends to suggest a use that focused on the collection and storage of the wine ration, although they might also have occasionally been used at table. At Carlisle, the range of these imported fineware vessels is very restricted, mainly comprising small beakers with an everted-rim (at least one with red-painted lines on the exterior), and a flanged bowl. Although they first appear in Periods 3C-3E (again, perhaps, brought to the site as the personal possessions of demolition or building gangs), they are uncommon thereafter and probably residual by the Antonine period (Tables 30 and 31; *42, 52*).

Mica-dusted wares: probably from Gallia Belgica
Just two mica-dusted vessels were distinguished, from different production sources, but both probably in use in the Trajanic-Hadrianic period (Periods 4A-4B; Table 31). The first, a beaker (*241*), is very similar in surface appearance and technique to vessels made near Braives (northern *Gallia Belgica*), but the fabric is not identical. The neat, slightly cupped rim, the use of multiple grooves on the shoulder, and the extremely thin wall suggest a close relationship to these and other products made in the region (Pl 200). Several workshops were making such mica-coated wares in this part of northern *Gallia Belgica* and the immediately adjacent Lower Rhineland, sometimes in association with 'Belgic' (Gallo-Belgic) wares; both traditions shared some of the same forms, including flanged and collared segmental bowls. Production of mica-dusted wares seems to have

Plate 200: A mica-dusted indented beaker

peaked in the Flavio-Trajanic period (Deru 1994; 1996, 190). This high-quality, expensive vessel had, almost certainly, originated from the *praetorium* in Period 4B, and had presumably belonged to the commanding officer's household. The other mica-dusted vessel (*60*) is in a completely different fabric, but its 'silky' surface (not dissimilar to Gallo-Belgic wares) might, nevertheless, suggest an origin in *Gallia Belgica*, the general form being a common one in that region.

Mustard-coloured tableware (probably imported)
This unusual and distinctive fineware, with a mustard-coloured, silky surface, was represented by at least two bowls (one segmental and carinated) and a beaker. It first appears in Period 3C, and is residual, or not closely phased, thereafter. Vessels in this fabric have not previously been recorded in Britain and their source is unknown; they are most likely to be imports (*74*).

Cologne colour-coated ware
Only 14 sherds were recorded (EREs 51%; Tables 32 and 33); most were plain, and too small to determine whether any of these cornice-rim beakers had barbotine decoration. A single beaker was rouletted from the shoulder downwards. All the contexts were Antonine or later (residual), and since there was seemingly no conventional garrison at this period, they should, presumably, be viewed as civilian supply (*388*).

Fabrics	Periods 5A-5B	Periods 5C-5D
Central Gaulish (1 and 2)	6 sherds (12.8%)	-
Cologne	3 sherds (6.4%) R 0.25 (15.2%)	4 sherds (7.0%) R 0.12 (22.6%)
Colour-coated unsourced	1 sherd (2.1%) R 0.34 (20.6%)	13 sherds (22.8%) R 0.12 (22.6%)
Imported fine white tableware	14 sherds (29.8%) R 0.29 (17.6%)	6 sherds (10.5%) R 0.21 (39.6%)
Gallia Belgica greyware	1 sherd (2.1%) R 0.11 (6.7%)	-
North Gaulish greyware and related	6 sherds (12.8%) R 0.40 (24.2%)	4 sherds (7.0%)
Wilderspool fine	1 sherd (2.1%) R 0.13 (7.9%)	-
Colchester	1 sherd (2.1%)	8 sherds (14.0%)
East Anglian reduced	-	15 sherds (26.3%)
Local finewares	10 sherds (21.3%) R 0.05 (3.0%)	2 sherds (3.5%)
Other unsourced fine	3 sherds (6.4%) R 0.05% (3.0%)	4 sherds (7.5%) R 0.08 (15.1%)
Residual fine	1 sherd (2.1%) R 0.03% (1.8%)	1 sherd (1.8%)
Total of finewares	**47 sherds (5.9%)** **R 1.65 (8.7%)**	**57 sherds (4.8%)** **R 0.53 (2.9%)**

Table 32: Stratified tablewares for Period 5: sherd numbers and EREs (=R) and percentages of totals for each period or grouped periods

Fabrics	Period 6A	Period 6B	Periods 6C-6D
Cologne	2 sherds (2.7%) R 0.14 (10.4%)	2 sherds (3.2%)	2 sherds (1.0%)
Central Gaulish black slip	1 sherd (1.3%)	-	1 sherd (0.5%) R 0.14 (3.2%)
Crambeck reduced tableware	2 sherds (2.7%) R 0.07 (5.2%)	12 sherds (19.0%) R 0.92 (39.3%)	50 sherds (25.8%) R 1.92 (44.2%)
Moselkeramik	-	7 sherds (11.1%) R 0.20 (8.6%)	18 sherds (9.3%) R 0.16 (3.7%)
North Gaulish greyware	-	1 sherd (1.6%)	-
Nene Valley colour-coated	30 sherds (40.0%)	20 sherds (31.8%) R 0.32 (13.7%)	90 sherds (46.4%) R 0.91 (21.0%)
Nene Valley Parchment	-	5 sherds (7.9%) R 0.17 (7.3%)	-
Crambeck Red slip	-	1 sherd (1.6%) R 0.10 (4.3%)	1 sherds (0.5%)
Crambeck Parchment	-	2 sherds (3.2%)	12 sherds (6.2%) R 0.38 (8.8%)
Late 'brown varnish' ware	-	-	1 sherd (0.5%) R 0.25 (5.8%)
Oxfordshire red slip	-	2 sherds (3.2%) R 0.13 (5.6%)	5 sherds (2.6%) R 0.07 (1.6%)
Unidentified tablewares	2 sherds (2.7%) R 0.05 (3.7%)	3 sherds (4.8%) R 0.06 (2.6%)	3 sherds (1.6%) R 0.29 (6.7%)
Residual fine	38 sherds (50.7%) R 1.09 (80.7%)	8 sherds (12.7%) R 0.44 (18.8%)	11 sherds (5.7%) R 0.22 (5.1%)
Total of finewares	**75 sherds (5.3%)** **R 1.35 (6.6%)**	**63 sherds (6.8%)** **R 2.34 (17.4%)**	**194 sherds (8.9%)** **R 4.34 (13.5%)**

Table 33: Stratified tablewares for Period 6: sherd numbers and EREs (=R) and percentages of totals for each period or grouped periods

First- and second-century Romano-British tablewares
Again, the fabrics, particularly colour-coated wares, are listed in the chronological order of their first appearance. See also the pottery from sources with British military connections (*pp 603-5*).

East Anglian fine reduced wares
These products are all characterised by a relatively fine/semi-fine mid/light-grey fabric containing much fine silver mica, and are smoothed, or sometimes burnished, on the surface. Most cannot be sourced precisely, but probably emanated from either the Wattisfield industry of Suffolk (Tomber and Dore 1998, 184), or various kiln sites with similar micaceous fabrics in Norfolk (Swan 1984). The quantities are relatively small (Tables 31 and 32), but include a small jar with

a constricted girth (*486*), and a sherd with a panel of barbotine dots, probably from a poppy-head beaker (perhaps from Wattisfield). The earliest example (that with barbotine dots) occurs in a very late Flavian or very early Trajanic context, but most material was in Trajanic-Hadrianic deposits (Periods 4A-4B), and was almost certainly residual by the late Antonine period onwards, although this material occurs on a number of military sites in the north-eastern military zone (*eg* Malton, Newstead, and Camelon (Swan and Bidwell 1998)). It is difficult to accept that such small quantities would have reached Carlisle as the result of trade, particularly since the emphasis of the imports to Carlisle was essentially on western sources. The possibility that these vessels might have reached the site with recruits or transfers from the east or south-east of Britain cannot be totally dismissed.

Colchester (late) colour-coated ware 2

Quantities were extremely small, and none seems to be earlier than the late Hadrianic (or possibly the early Antonine) period; most are Antonine (Tables 31 and 32). All vessels appeared to comprise beakers with a grooved cornice rim (where surviving) and clay rough-cast decoration. These colour-coated Colchester products need to be considered with the probable Colchester jug and the single Colchester mortarium from the site. Taken together, the evidence seems to imply that Colchester had little significance for Carlisle, contrasting with contemporary sites on the eastern side of England, including the eastern sector of the Antonine Wall (Swan 1999). The scarcity of Black-burnished ware Fabric 2 at Carlisle, and the near absence of other coarsewares produced in the Thames Estuary and the South East, adds to this and serves to emphasise how little reached Carlisle via East Coast shipping routes throughout the Roman period (*281*).

First- and second-century Romano-British coarsewares

The fabrics are again described in the chronological order of their first appearance. See also the wares from sources with British military connections (*pp 603-5*).

Black-burnished wares (BB1 and BB2)

Because there is an unbroken sequence of stratified deposits in the fort from the Trajanic period until the end of the Hadrianic period, the quantified data from the Millennium assemblage provide the first secure evidence for the beginning of the supply of Dorset BB1 to military sites on the Tyne-Solway isthmus (Table 29). There has been considerable controversy as to whether Dorset BB1 arrived in this region at the time of the construction of Hadrian's Wall (Gillam 1973, 54-5), or in the Trajanic period (Simpson 1974, 324-5). Holbrook and Bidwell (1991, 91-3) have summarised the arguments, and emphasised a possible link between the introduction of the ware and the arrival (for the construction of the Wall) of large detachments of *Legio II Augusta* from its Caerleon fortress, who were already familiar with the ware through supplies crossing the Bristol Channel to forts in South Wales during the Trajanic period. As they pointed out, however, unequivocal data from well-stratified sequences have hitherto been lacking in the Wall region itself.

It is, of course, important to differentiate between the occurrence of individual items of Dorset BB1 and its appearance as institutional supply, a distinction which can only be made with any certainty through the quantification of ceramic assemblages. This is particularly well demonstrated by the Carlisle Millennium sequence. Dorset BB1 first appears in the fort in the latter part of Period 3A (AD 72-3 - 83-4), in the form of a lid (*17*; not in a primary context), and a small fragment of a cooking-pot (in a demolition deposit),

but no other items are present. These should not be seen as indicative of direct institutional provisioning, but are most likely to represent items carried to the site by troops transferred from other locations. One possibility is that they had been brought by troops from the South West, the Exeter fortress having been evacuated in *c* AD 74/6 (Holbrook and Bidwell 1991, 6-8). Other garrisons were removed from the region during the AD 70s; some of these are known to have been sent to support military activities in the North. Long-distance transfers from the South West are evidenced at Camelon (Swan and Bidwell 1998), which, if the earlier chronology for the Flavian advance into Scotland is correct, will have been occupied shortly after the foundation of Carlisle. Another possibility is that these vessels may have been brought to Carlisle by legionary detachments from *Legio II Augusta* (*c* AD 83-4).

There is no further occurrence of Dorset BB1 in the fort until Period 4A (*c* AD 105-*c* 125), and just two vessels occur in this phase (together 0.067 kg, 0.22 EREs): a fragment of bowl or dish (*122*) from the second of three road surfaces (road **4659**), and a cooking-pot, found in the fill of a ditch sealed by a Period 4B road surface, and possibly derived from it. Again, the first could have been brought by an individual, and the second was probably deposited during building at the beginning of Period 4B. Set against the significant quantities of pottery found in Period 4A contexts (some 17.112 kg; 17.24 EREs, excluding amphorae: see Table 29), the amounts found do not suggest formal military supply to the Tyne-Solway isthmus in the pre-Hadrianic period. Also probably reaching the fort by a similar mechanism is an imitation BB1 jar (*61*), found in deposit *6630* (associated with road **7476**) at the end of Period 3C, perhaps, on this occasion, brought by a demolition or building party from outside the region.

It was thus not until Period 4B (beginning *c* AD 125) that Dorset BB1 was present at Carlisle in quantities that are large enough to indicate that it had become part of the institutional provisioning of the army of the region (Table 29). The amounts are statistically significant (in a deposit of almost 33 kg constituting almost 4.9% of the total weight and 4.3% of total EREs), but still cannot be described as a huge influx, and quantities increase more markedly in the second half of the second century (see *p 625*). However, at the beginning of Period 4B, a large number of close imitations of BB1 also appear, some of which were almost certainly being manufactured near the fort, at the Fisher Street kiln site, a workshop whose products included items specially targeted at the fort (*eg* crucibles; *pp 593-4*; *263*).

This production of close imitations of BB1, in an institutional context, at the very beginning of

Period 4B, might suggest that the authorities had already appreciated that the availability of BB1 from south-western Britain was unlikely to be sufficient to fulfil the requirements of such a large force at such short notice. Indeed, it is very likely that, in the early Hadrianic period, the Dorset potters making BB1 were struggling to increase their production in order to meet the demand from the army of the North for a very limited range of vessels selected from their normally wider repertoire. This could well explain why several of the Dorset BB1 forms recorded in Periods 4B or 5A were vessel-types exported relatively rarely (eg two early flanged bowls with a relatively upright wall; *240* and *315*; and an undecorated bead-rim bowl with a rather slack carination; *253*), and why the Dorset products needed to be supplemented by supplies of South Western BB1 from neighbouring potteries.

The fact that demand for Dorset BB1 outstripped supply may also partly account for the presence in Period 4B of the relatively rare South Western BB1, a finer sandier fabric than Dorset BB1, sharing some of the same forms (Holbrook and Bidwell 1991, 114-38), but which was not commonly exported. It accounted for almost a third of the total BB1 in the Hadrianic period (2-3% of total pottery, excluding amphorae, in Periods 4B/4C), and comprised mainly jugs and jars (no more than three or four vessels stratified in that phase, and about six *in toto*). The ware is probably residual after the middle of the second century.

During the second half of the second century, there was a steady increase in the amount of BB1 reaching the fort (Periods 5A-5B: about 18-21%; Periods 5C-5D: almost 23-4%; see Table 29). Its strong showing after the early AD 140s, when the fort seems to have been no longer occupied by a conventional garrison (*Ch 7*), is of particular interest, suggesting that what had been a bulk purchase-system initiated by the military may now have been continued by civilians, and it was perhaps due to its intrinsically efficient heating properties that the demand for this import continued. The cessation *c* AD 140 of production by the Brampton pottery (*p 591*), which had been an important supplier of cooking-bowls and jars (including imitations of BB1), must have further contributed to the relative increase in BB1. However, though the production of mortaria and flagons at Carlisle's Fisher Street workshop evidently continued, it is not known whether it was now making BB1 imitations, and it may have been in general decline (K Hartley *pers comm*).

It was in the Antonine period that Dorset BB1 was supplemented by very small quantities of Rossington Bridge BB1 (Table 29). About eight to ten items, including jars, bowls, and dishes, were distinguished (*350, 383, 408*), initially from Periods 5A-5C, perhaps

arriving with a 'Parisian' fineware beaker, probably from the same general source (Buckland *et al* 2001). Thereafter, the occurrence of Rossington BB1 sherds in Periods 5D and 6A-6C almost certainly results from the disturbance of earlier Antonine deposits by the Severan builders of the stone fort.

BB1 was also supplemented by BB2 in the second half of the second century, but in very small quantities, forming just 2-5% of the total supply of Black-burnished wares in Periods 5C-5D (Table 29). There is a single sherd in Period 5A, but most (including a bowl/dish with a sub-triangular rim: Gillam (1970) form 223) are slightly later. A dish with a rounded rim (Gillam (1970) form 225) in Period 6A dates either to the end of the second or the early third century, but most, by that period, is likely to be residual. Just two sherds of the slightly later related products from South Essex or North Kent were found in Periods 6B and 6D (both probably residual).

Dorset BB1 continued as a major component in the supply of cooking wares throughout the third century, and into the fourth, but its quantities were already declining in the third century (about 14-20% of all coarsewares), principally because there were other rival sources of cooking wares at or closer to Carlisle. The kiln at English Damside was making greyware imitations of BB1 forms in the early third century (although many are not particularly distinctive). In addition, the introduction of East Yorkshire greywares, which were dominated by imitations of Black-burnished forms, probably in the Severan period (perhaps by *Legio VI*), and steadily increasing thereafter, also provided a challenge to the Dorset BB1, as many of them imitated Black-burnished forms. There was a further decline from the end of the third to shortly before the middle of the fourth century, in Period 6B (little more than 12-13%), which coincided with the arrival of East Yorkshire calcite-gritted vessels (nearer to Carlisle and probably with lower transport costs), together with Crambeck reduced wares (*pp 606-7*). By the end of this period, BB1 was probably no longer reaching the North. This was followed by a sudden drop (to about 5%) in Period 6C (spanning the mid-fourth to early fifth centuries). In fact, none of the BB1 forms from the fort are likely to be later than the mid-fourth century. The apparent rise in its quantities in Period 6D (see Table 29) stems from the disturbance of earlier deposits during the demolition of the fort buildings.

From the Claudio-Neronian period, when Dorset BB1 first began to be acquired by the Roman army in southern England, the production of wheel-thrown imitations seems to have followed immediately. This was even the case in southern Dorset itself, where wheel-thrown copies were made at the Corfe Mullen

Plate 201: Locally produced dish imitating a Black-burnished ware form

kiln site, presumably for the nearby fort at Lake Gates (Calkin 1935). It follows, therefore, that copies of BB1 (usually wheel-made) were almost certainly produced at, and supplied to, other military sites already using Dorset BB1 (*eg* Caerleon and other forts in South Wales); such imitations will have been equally available to troops involved in transfers. This almost certainly explains the occurrence of a wheel-thrown gritty grey imitation BB1 jar with lattice decoration in a Period 3C context which appears to have been disturbed during the construction of the second timber fort in Period 4, *c* AD 105. It is highly likely that it arrived on the site with a detachment engaged in demolition or building work. A simple everted-rim-profile of this type (not a precise copy of a BB1 profile) would not be out of place in the late Flavian or early Trajanic period on many other types of coarseware beaker or jar.

There is no doubt that, once Dorset BB1 began to be supplied to Carlisle, its imitation by local potters followed immediately (Pl 201). At least two or possibly three local workshops were involved. The Brampton works-depot (*p 591*) made BB1-type jars with incised lattices, as well as dishes and bowls in its traditional coarse fabrics, in oxidised and, increasingly, in reduced fabrics. Decoration had not, hitherto, been intrinsic to the Brampton material, and the lattice on these jars was finely incised instead of burnished.

Another, probably local, workshop, with two successive or overlapping potters, also made jars (BB1 imitation A, and BB1 imitation B). These may have been made in the Fisher Street workshop (*pp 593-4*), but whether they represent new blood in the existing military pottery, innovations by existing craftsmen, or a new workshop is uncertain. Contemporary undecorated versions of BB1 jars were also made simultaneously in the traditional North West gritty oxidised ware, presumably by the existing local potters. An example of these (*87*) occurs in a demolition deposit

of Period 4A, whilst a jar of BB1 imitation A type was found in a Period 4A context sealed immediately by a road surface of Period 4B. The immediate response to the appearance of BB1, in the form of local copying, suggests that the available quantities of BB1 were inadequate in the AD 120s and perhaps later. While it is clear that jars of BB1 imitation A-type appeared *c* AD 122/5, and were more common in Periods 4B and 4C, jars of BB1 imitation B-type do not appear until towards the end of Period 4B and continue into Period 5, when they appear to be more frequent, perhaps lasting as late as Periods 5C or 5D. In Britain as a whole, from the Antonine period onwards, most potteries were copying Black-burnished ware forms in reduced, mostly grey fabrics (*eg* English Damside, Carlisle (*p 595*)). Few of these fabrics resembled the texture of BB1 itself as closely as the earliest copies at Carlisle.

Verulamium Region white ware
Although Verulamium mortaria were very significant from the foundation of the fort (Period 3A), probably having been transported there in bulk by the builders or the first garrison (*p 580*), other Verulamium products did not appear until at least three decades later, in Period 4A, and did not outlast the Hadrianic period. They are confined to large flagons or *lagenae*, narrow–mouthed jars (presumably for storage), and a small lid (perhaps for use with the latter). The absence of other Verulamium products (including vessel types appropriate to military use, such as ring-necked flagons and carinated cooking-bowls, which were sometimes exported to northern forts) is significant. In the early decades of the second century, Carlisle's local pottery was producing quantities of flagons and cooking bowls, and the Brampton works-depot was making large amphora-like flagons, so it is difficult to see why the fort would need to purchase relatively coarse flagons and jars from such a distance, unless they were filled with a commodity that was more important than the vessels themselves. London was a trans-shipment point for many items destined for the army of the North, and it is possible that provisions arriving in bulk (such as wine in barrels) may have been decanted into the amphora-like Verulamium white-ware jars (manufactured in both London and the Verulamium region; Seeley and Drummond-Murray 2005), and then shipped on to the military.

Pottery from sources with British military connections
Eboracum fine and coarse oxidised and reduced wares
Eboracum wares were made at York over an extended period, from the foundation of the fortress *c* AD 71 until the early third century, episodically in the legionary pottery/tilery within the *canabae*, and also, in the Trajanic-Antonine period, in a workshop at Heworth near York, which was closely linked to the military

and might have involved veteran potters (Swan 2002; Swan and McBride 2002). Apart from minute amounts found at sites close to York, this pottery does not seem have been traded over long distances. Thus, its occurrence on military sites elsewhere in the North is likely to indicate the presence of detachments of the York legion, arriving either as personal possessions or as casual supplies, and this may be corroborated at some sites by historical or epigraphic evidence. By implication, a building site would usually be unoccupied; forts built on virgin sites might have no local pottery production, and the workshop serving a fort which had been demolished might have declined or closed down on the departure of the previous garrison. Legionary building gangs thus needed to ensure that their short-term ceramic needs were met by carrying essentials with them.

The quantities of the various Ebor wares were quite small (only 15 items; *30, 309, 338, 360, 364, 374, 438, 536, 582*), and the contexts from which they were recovered fit such circumstances. Although some occur residually, most probably relate to major episodes in the structural history of the site. Except for the fine red-slipped and polished Ebor 3 wares, none of these wares is macroscopically distinctive, and most rely on the forms for their recognition. This difficulty is exacerbated by the fact that there is significant variation in the colour of the fabrics, which have a much wider range than indicated by Tomber and Dore (1998, 199), and may be as pale as cream or as dark as brick red. In addition, reduced versions of the basic Ebor 1 fabric (sometimes in the same forms as the oxidised products) are far from uncommon at York, and may be expected elsewhere, but are virtually impossible to recognise, except where the rim profiles and other details are distinctive. It is therefore likely that more Ebor products were present at Carlisle than have been recognised in present and past analyses.

Two Ebor ware vessels probably reflect Flavian activity in the fort. A reduced grey carinated bowl with a reeded undercut rim of distinctive profile (*30*) came from a Period 3A demolition deposit, and could be associated with work-gangs replacing interior buildings in the fort in AD 83-4. A late Flavian or early Trajanic lamp of York origin (*338*) occurred residually (in Period 5B), having been displaced from earlier buildings. One possible explanation for its presence is that it belonged to a detachment from *Legio IX*, which may have been either demolishing the first fort (Period 3D) or building the second fort (Period 4A) in the early years of the second century. A fine beaker or bowl with cut-glass-style faceted decoration, and a second bowl probably imitating Dr 18/31, both in fine polished Ebor 3 orange fabric, dating to the early Hadrianic period, may have arrived with detachments from *Legio VI*, which are known to have been involved in the construction of

Hadrian's Wall (Swan 2002, 52-5; 2004). This short-lived ware is not known to have been traded, and scarcely ever occurs outside York, so is probably best linked to detachments from this legion.

At least seven of the Ebor ware vessels found relate to Severan production (including four lids and part of a bowl, all of North African type). They occur in deposits of Periods 5C and 5D (probably disturbed by the builders of the stone fort) and residually. The background to this pottery of North African type has been fully discussed (Swan 1992; 1997; 2002), and it seems that reinforcements from the North African legion (*III Augusta*) were brought to York by Emperor Severus, in connection with his *expeditio* in the North. Cooking-vessels of North African type were made in the *canabae* of the York fortress, presumably to kit out these men for their traditional cooking practices before they moved north for the campaigning season. When Severus died in AD 211 and his Scottish conquests were abandoned, the distribution of Severan Ebor ware vessels suggests that at least some of his North African troops were dispersed to various forts along Hadrian's Wall and elsewhere in the North. These distinctive round-bottomed casseroles, domed lids, and convex-walled platters are present at Carlisle in significant quantities, as evidenced by other excavations, mostly on sites in the extramural settlement, having been recorded at Blackfriars Street (Swan 1992, fig 3, nos 48-52; from unpublished drawing archive, *per* M McCarthy), the northern and southern Lanes (M McCarthy, L Hird *pers comms*), under the Cathedral, in Fisher Street (L Hird, I Caruana *pers comms*), particularly Castle Street (Taylor 1991, nos 426-7, 463, 528-9 (lids), 531-5, 627-8, 761-2, 791 (lid)), and Annetwell Street (I Caruana, L Hird *pers comms*). It is likely that these vessels (together with the North African amphorae (see above, *pp 578-9*) indicate the presence of men from *Legio VI* (probably at least one vexillation), who were involved in the construction of the stone fort (*Ch 8*; Tomlin and Hassall 2001, 390-1, no 16).

The overall distribution of this type of pottery is of particular significance. It is not common within the fort, perhaps unsurprisingly, as presumably construction gangs were unlikely to be living on precisely the site where they were engaged in building. However, the plentiful and widespread distribution of these vessels within the extramural settlement, presumably in the area where they were living (and depositing their rubbish), raises the intriguing question of how accommodation in the town became available to house such detachments. Were the troops billeted with the civilian inhabitants? It is difficult to see how this would have provided accommodation at short notice. Perhaps, as probable tenants of the military, within a zone that was the official *territorium* of the fort, the *vicani* were removed from their homes or workshops to make room for the troops. The dating of this activity should fall within the period AD 208–12/13. Either Severus decided, on his arrival, to build a new fort at Carlisle in c AD 208+, as part of an ongoing programme of reconstruction of military establishments in the North and to support a route northwards into his area of campaigning, or, more probably, troops evacuated from the orbit of Severus' campaigns (following his death and on Caracalla's abandonment of Severus' initiative) were sent to build the Carlisle fort in AD 211/12 as part of a plan to revive Hadrian's Wall as the northern *limes*. Whatever the case, the distribution of the Ebor wares in the fort and town suggests that *Legio VI* building detachments never became the permanent garrison, and that the fort was intended for another unit (*Ch 12*).

Wilderspool red-slipped ware
As has been discussed (Swan 2004, 272-3; Swan and Philpott 2000, 60), Wilderspool had a significant role in the supply of mortaria to the military in the North Midlands and the North West, and the Twentieth Legion, in Chester, in particular. Until the discovery of the kilns at Fisher Street, Carlisle (K Hartley *pers comm*), it was thought that Wilderspool was a major contributor to the supply of Carlisle. It now seems unlikely that Wilderspool mortaria (and presumably other products) reached Carlisle as institutional supplies, and the presence at Carlisle of small quantities of finewares from Wilderspool therefore requires another explanation.

Only seven oxidised Wilderspool vessels, all finewares, were recorded (*212, 237, 239, 291, 326, 553*; Tables 31 and 32), comprising three rough-cast beakers with darker slip, two red-slipped tableware vessels imitating samian or Italianate *sigillata*-derived forms (one with red-painted stripes; Pl 202), and another vessel with white slip-painting over the red slip. Such items are not types known to have been traded and occur only in

Plate 202: A red-slipped Wilderspool vessel

very small quantities outside their production source. In fact, their distribution is confined to a few military sites in the North West. The introduction of unusual forms and painted finishes at Wilderspool in the early Hadrianic period has been linked to the transference to the region of troops (and with them potters) from outside the province, perhaps from Upper Germany (Hartley 1981; Swan 2004), and the Hadrianic context of the vessels at Carlisle (Period 4B, or later residually) is wholly compatible with the chronology recently proposed for these wares (Swan 2004, 272-3, 278-9). Thus, they most probably reached Carlisle with personnel involved in the construction of Hadrian's Wall or supporting activities (perhaps men in *Legio XX* or units within its command).

Third- and fourth-century imported tablewares
The following colour-coated wares are described in the chronological order of their first appearance.

Central Gaulish black-slipped ware: formerly 'Rhenish'
The quantities were minute (Table 33), just three sherds of indeterminate form. The fabric appears first in Period 6A, probably in the first decade or two of the third century, and is residual thereafter.

Moselkeramik black-slipped ware: formerly 'Rhenish'
Again, quantities are very small (39 sherds), and few forms were identifiable (Table 33). They included the standard globular and indented funnel-mouth beakers, and just one sherd had traces of barbotine dots and lines. The fabric first occurs in Period 6B, which probably implies that the material is residual.

Third- and fourth-century Romano-British tablewares
Again, the following colour-coated and other wares are described in the chronological order of their first appearance.

Lower Nene Valley colour-coated ware and Lower Nene Valley Parchment ware
It seems that no Lower Nene Valley products reached Carlisle before the construction of the stone fort (Period 6A, *c* AD 208/12), possibly confirming the hitherto relatively imprecise evidence suggesting that Nene Valley colour-coated wares were not traded to the North before the early third century, and that their production might not have commenced long before that date. Whilst far from abundant (*415, 417, 430, 457, 466, 469, 479, 493, 504, 517, 551* (colour-coated), *424* (Parchment); Table 33), the chronological evidence for the arrival of Nene Valley-ware in Carlisle is relatively secure. A Nene Valley sherd was recorded in the foundation trench of the buttress of a probable granary (*216*; Building **1196**) in the south-west quadrant of the site and, if the date of its construction coincides with that of the construction of the rest of the stone fort, then the Nene Valley-ware sherd has a *terminus*

ante quem of AD 212/13. Marginally later contexts included a primary occupation deposit (*540*) in a barrack (Building *669*) containing a single Nene Valley beaker sherd, and a primary make-up layer in R3 of the putative *principia* (*5630*; Building *5200*) with three Nene Valley sherds. Other Period 6A contexts containing Nene Valley sherds include the construction trenches of Buildings *2301* and *2302*, both barracks or barrack-like structures, in the south-west quadrant.

The relatively small quantities of Nene Valley colour-coated wares during the first half of the third century (or even slightly later) suggest that only small amounts were reaching the site, but that the quantities gradually increased, particularly in the fourth century, and peaked in Period 6C, probably about the mid-late fourth century. This high-point may have been exaggerated to some extent by concentrations of material from the commercial activity in the centre of the fort, where such products are likely to have been sold (*Ch 9*). Significant amounts of residual sherds, in post-Roman deposits of Period 7 (*Ch 10*), are likely to derive from such activities, and it seems likely that the supply of Nene Valley wares continued until the end of the Roman period in the fifth century.

The vast majority of the Nene Valley colour-coated vessels represented were beakers, almost exclusively in Period 6A, with the exception of part of a castor box. To these were added, in Period 6B, a plain-rimmed colour-coated 'dog dish' (towards the end of the period), a Parchment ware flask with painted stripes (the sole example of this form and ware), and an indeterminate colour-coated flagon, although the context from which this derived may well relate to Period 6C. By Period 6C, the range of colour-coated products had diversified to include imitations of Dr 38 bowls, pentice-moulded beakers (the most common identifiable beaker type), and also colour-coated versions of flanged bowls or dishes of BB1 type. These latter did not figure as prominently as might be expected for the period, perhaps a result of competition from rival versions in fine reduced Crambeck ware. The Crambeck producers, being closer, must have had lower transport costs, a factor that had also affected the supply of contemporary Nene Valley mortaria. However, Nene Valley beakers significantly outnumbered those made at Crambeck (Table 33), and this suggests that they were preferred for their intrinsic attractions, regardless of their probable higher price.

The question of whether applied-scale decoration on Nene Valley colour-coated beakers continued to be used into the fourth century, after barbotine under-slip decoration in general had ceased, has long been a matter of uncertainty (Howe *et al* nd, 18); in the Millennium assemblage, no vessels decorated in this style were seen until Period 6C, but it is possible that all were residual. Of particular note is a fragment of a probable Nene Valley funnel-mouth beaker (from a post-Roman context) with three letters executed in white slip over the red colour-coat on the neck. In the past, such white slip lettering was assumed to be unique to *Moselkeramik*, originating in the Trier region, and, although the majority of published motto-beakers are probably correctly attributed, this find presents an opportunity for a reconsideration of such material from unusual locations (*eg* another example in Nene Valley ware from Lincolnshire; M Darling *pers comm*).

Oxfordshire red-slipped ware
Oxfordshire red-slipped ware is always relatively scarce on sites in the North, and Carlisle is no exception, there being just ten sherds from no more than seven vessels (Table 33). The earliest, a single beaker, can be placed in Period 6B, but there is little doubt that the majority were associated with the putative market of Period 6C (and residual material derived from it) and were being sold alongside Nene Valley and Crambeck tablewares into the early fifth century (*Ch 9*). The forms included the more common imitations of Dr 18/31, Dr 38 bowls, and also a wall-sided bowl with an impressed wheel-like stamp, not hitherto recorded.

Swanpool colour-coated ware and Brown 'varnished' ware
A single probable Swanpool sherd occurred in a residual context. A flanged bowl with a glossy slip, imitating a Dr 38 bowl, may be from the same source, but its origin is uncertain. Its context may suggest that it was also a product sold in the putative market in the centre of the fort (*Ch 9*).

Crambeck reduced tableware and other vessels
Crambeck reduced wares were among the most significant products in the late third and fourth centuries at Carlisle (*82, 414, 418, 420, 428, 470, 481, 507, 511, 529, 532, 533, 537*). They first appeared at the end of Period 6A (probably in the AD 280s), increasing sharply in quantity in Periods 6B and 6C (Table 33). Many seem to have been associated with the putative commercial activity in the centre of the fort at the end of the Roman period (*Ch 9*).

For the purposes of quantified comparison, they have been divided into two principal groups. Crambeck reduced ware is usually relatively fine-textured, and it has been noted on several occasions (Evans 1989, 70-80) that many of the vessels were probably treated as fine tablewares, despite the fact that many of them were bowls and dishes which imitated Black-burnished ware forms normally used for cooking (for instance, conical flanged bowls and dishes, and plain-rimmed dog-dishes, both frequently sooted from use on cooking fires). At Carlisle, however, none of the Crambeck reduced bowls and dishes were sooted, which also seems to be the case with comparable vessels from other sites. Another argument in favour of these vessels as tableware is the presence of internal decoration (in the form of a burnished wavy line) on some of the flanged bowls of the AD 370s and later; this would seem pointless on a cooking vessel. Indeed, no internal decoration (apart from burnishing, which has non-stick properties) is ever present on the interior of Black-burnished ware prototypes.

The products of a number of other late Roman potteries in Britain also seem to indicate that the forms normally associated with Black-burnished ware cooking-vessels were being adopted for tablewares. For instance, the Nene Valley potteries began to make colour-coated versions of 'dog-dishes' in the second half of the third century (Perrin 1999, 102-3), and these were followed by colour-coated flanged bowls in the early fourth century. Similarly, the Oxfordshire and Hadham (Hertfordshire) industries also produced conical flanged bowls in red-slipped fabrics, some from the latter centre with an internal wavy line. For these reasons, it seems logical to class the Crambeck reduced ware bowls and dishes as fine tablewares in the quantification tables, alongside beakers, jugs, narrow-mouthed flagons or flasks, and more obvious tableware forms in the same reduced fabric.

If these arguments are accepted, the question remains as to how to classify other forms in Crambeck reduced wares (*ie* the jars, S-shaped bowls, and large flagons similar to *lagenae*). It seems most likely that these vessels were primarily for the storage and preparation (but not usually cooking) of food (the widespread use of jars for collecting water is attested from their frequent association with wells (*eg* Evans 1989, 79)). Of the Crambeck reduced ware jars from Carlisle, only one showed any signs of sooting. The emergence and rapid uptake of East Yorkshire calcite-gritted ware jars and, to a lesser extent, cooking dishes and bowls, was virtually coincident with that of the Crambeck reduced wares. As they would probably have travelled together from production sites in the same region, they should probably be viewed as complementary, the Crambeck wares being intended primarily for the table and, in certain cases, for storage, whilst the calcite-gritted wares were primarily suited to cooking, but may also have been suitable for some sorts of storage. The importance of Crambeck reduced wares as tablewares might, in part, explain why Crambeck painted Parchment ware developed late and never became frequent, since there were plenty of cheaper alternatives in Crambeck fine reduced ware.

Crambeck red-slipped ware
At Carlisle, such products were typically scarce, there being only three vessels, two bowls and a beaker, only two of which were in stratified contexts (*419, 524*; Table 33). One was in an external deposit dated to the end of Period 6B, and the other in Period 6C. Evans (1989) has pointed out that this ware was never very successful, because problems with the iron-bearing clays used caused it to laminate, whereas Crambeck reduced wares were of better quality and more durable, being made of a mixture of two local clays (iron-free and iron-laden). It seems that the production of these oxidised vessels at Crambeck (perhaps not before the later fourth century) was stimulated by the enduring and widespread popularity of red-slipped imitations of samian forms such as Dr 38 and Dr 18/31 or Dr 31, which had been produced at other centres, such as the Nene Valley and Oxfordshire since the previous century.

Crambeck Parchment ware
The recent reassessment of the dating of this material (Bidwell 2005) has reaffirmed that it was not added to the Crambeck repertoire until at least *c* AD 370. Apart from two sherds attributed to contexts dated to the end of Period 6B, but which may nevertheless be intrusive from disturbance associated with Period 6C, most Parchment wares can be associated with Period 6C (38% of the finewares), perhaps belonging to the putative commercial activity in the centre of the fort (*464, 459, 534*; Table 33). They appear alongside reduced and oxidised Crambeck tablewares, and other finewares from potteries such as the Nene Valley, Oxfordshire, and probably Swanpool, and at least one unsourced workshop. In fact, painted Parchment wares were added to the Crambeck repertoire at a time when reduced Crambeck tablewares had already secured a major share of the market. Being painted, and usually slipped and burnished, it is likely that they were more expensive than the reduced wares and were probably treated with more care than cheaper vessels, potentially reducing the amount of breakage, and perhaps explaining in part why so little was found. However, they had probably only been available for no more than two or three decades before the end of formal occupation of the site.

Third- and fourth-century Romano-British cooking, storage, and other culinary wares
These fabrics are again described in the chronological order of their first appearance.

East Yorkshire greywares
These hard-fired grey burnished wares (*377, 392, 402, 452, 456, 463, 468, 485, 495, 502, 510, 516, 518, 521*) were made at Norton (Hayes and Whitley 1950) and perhaps other kiln sites in the vicinity. They first appear at the very beginning of Period 6A, being

present in the construction trenches of Buildings *2301* and *2302* (Table 28), where they may, however, have been intrusive (*Ch 8, p 303*). The sudden appearance of this product in some quantity (almost 6%, by EREs, of all coarsewares in Period 6A) may be connected with the arrival of detachments of *Legio VI* involved in the construction of the stone fort. The legion, which came from the region in which the pottery was produced, may have instigated its supply in circumstances broadly comparable with those surrounding the introduction of BB1 in the Hadrianic period. Whatever the case, East Yorkshire greywares increased in quantity in Period 6B, but began to decline in Period 6E, presumably as a result of competition from East Yorkshire calcite-gritted wares.

East Yorkshire calcite-gritted wares
Although scraps of East Yorkshire calcite-gritted ware first appear in the late third century (the end of Period 6A), it made little impact on pottery supplies to the site until the fourth century (Period 6B; almost 6% EREs), and increased in the fifth century (*427, 462, 472, 477, 478, 494, 500, 506, 514, 515, 535, 549*; Table 28). However, it was never as dominant as on sites on the north-eastern side of Britain.

Dales shelly ware
Only two examples of Dales shelly ware were recorded (*542*), the earlier in a Period 6B context (early-mid-fourth century) and the other in a post-Roman context. This is as would be expected in the North West.

Discussion and illustrated catalogue
The catalogue of vessels (excluding amphorae and stamped mortaria) is grouped by period, then entries are arranged by context and, where appropriate, by building and room number. Numbers following the room number refer to the local structural phase within that room. Gillam numbers, with no further qualification, refer to Gillam 1970, Corder types are those given in Corder and Birley 1937, and Norton types are from Hayes and Whitley 1950.

Periods 1 and 2: earliest Roman activity (*c* AD 72-3)
Without a doubt, the Roman builders of the fort brought container-borne supplies with them, along with pottery for cooking and use at table. Inevitably, some of this was broken and trodden into the extant ground surface during the early days of their arrival, and whilst the fort was under construction. It seems likely that the construction gangs lived in close proximity to the buildings upon which they were working, and the Period 2 distribution of pottery in early features resembles that seen in primary features at Blake Street, York (Hall 1997, 308-10, 377), and at Silchester (Swan 2009).

Although the quantities of pottery seen in Periods 1 and 2 were small, they are of significance. The presence of an Iberian fish-sauce amphora (*p 577*) in a Period 1 deposit (effectively trodden into the old ground surface) indicates that even before the construction of the fort (and presumably while still in tents), the army had already brought with it comestibles that exceeded the most basic levels of necessity. Similarly, the presence of distinctive non-local tablewares, such as cup *1*, serves to illustrate the range of material probably reaching the site as personal possessions.

Catalogue
1. Cup imitating samian form Dr 24/25 (Fig 300). Unsourced semi-fine oxidized pale orange fabric (Fabric 806); no other examples are known from the site. In Britain, most examples of the samian prototype of this form are pre-Flavian, as small bowl-like cups of this class were rapidly going out of fashion by then; an imitation such as this would be unlikely to post-date the very early Flavian period. For a similar early Flavian coarseware form at Hayton, East Yorkshire, see Johnson 1978, fig 25, no 57.
   MIL 1, *1150*, fill of depression/hollow

Period 3A: AD 72-3 - 83-4
Local products: sources and supply
Local products made up at least 60% (by EREs) of the coarsewares (Table 28), 80% of the finewares (Table 30), and almost 10% of the mortaria (Table 24) in use at this time, although production of the latter may have started later than that of the coarsewares. The Roman army almost certainly began to make pottery immediately on its arrival at Carlisle, even whilst the fort was under construction; vessels in the local gritty oxidised ware, North West fine oxidised ware, and semi-coarse reduced ware occur in the construction trenches of Buildings *4652, 4654*, and *7393*, and under the main east to west road (*7476, Ch 3*). The army was in a vulnerable advance location, in a possibly hostile region that was effectively aceramic, so it clearly planned to cater for all its basic needs. This can be paralleled in the early days of the construction of the fortress at York (Hall 1997), where the production of Ebor wares and local greywares had begun whilst the first fortress was still under construction, supplementing the range of vessels brought to the site from elsewhere (Monaghan 1993, 773-4).

The range of local products in Period 3A is quite narrow, comprising the traditional military staples for cooking (carinated cooking-bowls with lids: *9, 15, 16, 30*; rusticated jars: *13*), for food-preparation (mortaria: *26*), and for the storage and the issue of rations (lid-seated and bead-rimmed jars: *2, 21, 22, 23*, and flagon: *24*), but notably tablewares (polished rouletted drinking-beakers: *5, 10-11*, and semi-fine bowls imitating samian and allied forms: *14*); several of these were also present in Castle Street and Annetwell Street

(Taylor 1991, Caruana in prep). Several vessel types have idiosyncratic details which are characteristic of this period alone, and their recognition could provide date-markers for future pottery analysis in Carlisle. They include a ring-necked flagon with a 'beaked' rim (*12*), also seen in an early Flavian context at Annetwell Street (I Caruana *pers comm*); rusticated jars with an undercut, almond-shaped, everted-rim (*4*); jars with an upright neck and flat-topped everted-rim (*21, 55*); carinated cooking-bowls with a rectangular reeded rim with a diagnostic upturn at the tip (a potting feature also seen on some locally-made jars (*3, 18, cf* jar *29*)), and the lids used with these vessels, which had a plain, squared-off rim with no expansion at the tip (*9*).

The tablewares, in particular small rouletted beakers and bowls imitating samian forms, are of outstanding quality, and may suggest that the expectations of the garrison were very high, perhaps indicative of a legionary element (an impression also supported by some of the coins attributable to this period; *see Ch 17*). Such local products may account for the relative dearth of imported finewares, and the nature of the samian at this period (*see p 541*). Comparison may be made with the situation at Colchester at the very beginning of the conquest of Britain, when the first garrison, from the Lower Rhineland, provided for almost all its ceramic necessities, even to the extent of making colour-coated tablewares, and where the celebrated finewares of Lyon, and other high-quality imports, and even much of the available range of decorated samian, were absent or scarce until the following phase (J Timby *pers comm*).

Several fabrics characterise the earliest products of probably local origin (North West very fine oxidised wares, North West gritty or semi-coarse oxidised wares, reduced gritty and semi-coarse fabrics, some of a type used for rusticated wares). Whilst it is not certain whether they all derive from the same kilns, the divisions between the fabrics are not clear-cut, and the textural and colour differences within individual fabrics might represent variations in the processing and mixing of clays from a single source, one or two workshops or potters working on the same site. Unlike potteries trading commercially, the army craftsmen did not have to aim for conformity in the colour or texture of their fabrics; they presumably used whatever clays were currently available, and mixed them to less uniform standards.

A consideration of the forms (in conjunction with the coarse texture of the fabrics) produced at this period, from both the present excavation and earlier excavations in the city, suggests a Lower Rhineland origin for the potters and, by implication, the first garrison. The rouletted bowls reminiscent of samian ware (*246*) were also being made at the Hunerberg

workshop at Nijmegen (Heimberg and Ruger 1972), and the small rouletted oxidised beakers (*5, 10*) resemble orange and grey beakers made elsewhere in the vicinity of the same military complex (Holwerda 1941, pl II, no 61, pl IV, no 141, pl X, nos 477-9). A face-pot from the ditch of the first fort at Carlisle recovered during an earlier excavation (Hird 1992, fig 7, no 1; and *inf* G Braithwaite), is another local product that points quite specifically to that region.

Non-local vessels: supply and acquisition
The army involved in the building the fort seems to have brought with it a range of essential amphora-borne provisions as well as staple vessels for culinary uses. Dressel 20 oil-amphorae occur in the construction levels, and there are huge quantities of the relatively robust mortaria from the Verulamium region (almost 73% EREs), and to a lesser extent mortaria from sources in *Gallia Belgica* (almost 18%). Mortaria were more sturdy and less prone to breakage in transit than other vessel types and this may explain why huge stocks were almost certainly brought to Carlisle at its foundation (*p 580*), and why, initially, the emphasis at the local workshop resided much more in the production of less robust culinary wares and relatively fragile vessels, such as tablewares, as well as why locally produced mortaria were not of great significance until the following phase (from AD 83-4 onwards: Period 3B).

Apart from this, other vessels brought from outside the region do not appear to be very numerous; two 'pipe-clay' flagons (*19*) belong to a group of products that were already being supplied to other military sites in Britain (for instance Exeter; Holbrook and Bidwell 1991), probably from *Gallia Belgica*. Fine tableware imports (mainly Lyon and Central Gaulish beakers), were very scarce and are most likely to have constituted the personal possessions of soldiers in the garrison (see Table 30 and *pp 596-7*).

At the end of Period 3A, the demolition levels of the internal buildings produced two particularly noteworthy items, a Dorset Black-burnished ware lid (*17*) and a fragment of cooking-jar from the same source. These most probably arrived with troops involved in the demolition process (or less certainly in the construction of buildings for the next phase), perhaps from the South West or South Wales (see *p 601*).

Almost all the amphorae belonged to a standard 'package' of products supplied to the forts of northern Britain (Table 22; *pp 592-3*). The early Flavian period was the time of greatest variety, because Italian wine imports ceased after AD 79 (Williams 2004). The only amphora-borne food-stuff of particular note was the top-quality tunny-fish relish manufactured in *Tingi* (Tangiers), North

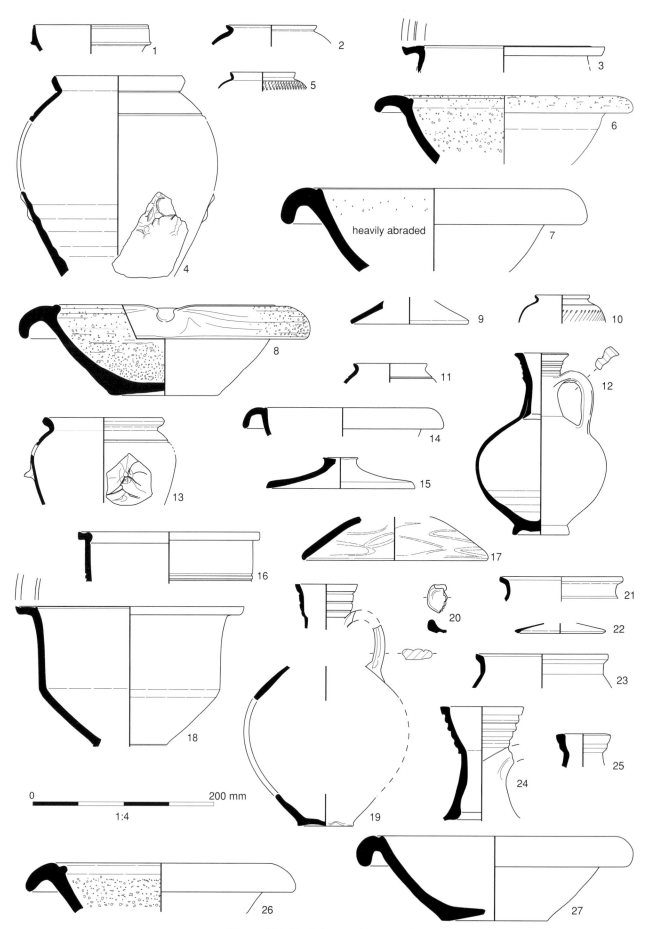

heavily abraded

0   200 mm

1:4

Figure 300: Periods 2 and 3A vessels

Africa. From its location, the container had probably been discarded from the house of the commanding officer (Building *7392* (*see pp 577-8*)).

Spatial aspects of the ceramics

The greatest abundance and variety of amphorae occurred in and around the putative *praetorium* (Building *7292*) and the presence of containers for Palestinian dates / dried-fruit and top-quality fish relish, in addition to containers for the normal basics of wine, oil, and fish sauce, and a high-quality imported flagon, together suggest that the life-style of the commanding officer was commensurate with his rank. Mortaria and other culinary vessels indicate that R5 of Building *7292* could have been a kitchen (though there is also evidence of metalworking there; *Ch 17*), and that R3 may also have had some connection with food.

The intervallum area, where ovens backed onto the rampart, was the zone for food preparation and cooking in most forts, and the presence of mortaria there, especially outside Building *1194*, seems to accord with this. Mortaria were, however, mainly concentrated in the barracks and associated buildings, and attest to food preparation within (Building *4652*, R1; Building *4653*, R1 and R5; and Building *1222*).

Catalogue (see also amphorae and stamped mortaria)

2. Everted-rim jar. North West gritty oxidised ware (Fig 300); burnt on rim and interior (Fabric 750).
    MIL 1, *472*, Building *1194* , occupation layer

3. Carinated bowl with reeded rim (Fig 300); North West semi-fine oxidised ware (Fabric 754).
    MIL 1, *472*, Building *1194*, occupation layer; *cf 18*

4. Everted-rim jar with rustication (Fig 300); local semi-fine reduced ware (Fabric 3).
    MIL 1, *1123*, Building *166*, R1.1, floor

5. Everted-rim beaker with judder-rouletting (Fig 300); fine North West gritty oxidised ware.
    MIL 3, *963*, Building *1222*, floor

6. Mortarium, Gillam 238 (Fig 300); Oise-Somme region.
    MIL 1, *1075*, Building *1222*, fill of pit *1089*

7. Mortarium, well worn and heavily burnt (Fig 300); Verulamium region; Flavian.
    MIL 5, *4414*, Building *4652*, R1.1, floor; also residual in *3401/3404*, Period 3B, Building *4651*, fills of gullies *3375* and *3405*

8. Mortarium, Northern France (Fig 300); Q Valerius Veranius-type, barely worn but very heavily burnt; Flavian.
    MIL 5, *4105*, Building *4653*, R5.1, fill of pit / trench *4104*; also residual in *3878/3961*, Period 3B, Building *4006*, floor and fill of construction trench *3500*

9. Lid with cut-off rim (Fig 300); North West fine oxidised ware; burnt on edge of interior and exterior.
    MIL 5, *4105*, Building *4653*, R5.1, fill of pit / trench *4104*

10. Everted-rim beaker with judder-rouletting (Fig 300); very fine-textured North West fine oxidised ware.
    MIL 5, *4566*, Building *4654*, R3.2, fill of pit *4565*

11. Everted-rim beaker or small jar (Fig 300); North West fine oxidised ware; burnt.
    MIL 5, *4279*, Building *4654*, R3.2, floor

12. Flagon. North West fine oxidised ware (Fig 300); mid-Flavian form.
    MIL 5, *4012*, Building *4658*, fill of gully *40112*

13. Everted-rim jar with high nodular rustication (Fig 300); local reduced semi-coarse fabric.
    MIL 5, *4012*, Building *4658*, fill of gully *4011*

14. Segmental flanged bowl (Fig 300); North West semi-fine oxidised ware, burnt and abraded on interior.
    MIL 5, *4088*, Building *4658*, fill of construction trench *4087*

15. Lid (Fig 300). North West gritty oxidised ware, burnt on knob.
    MIL 5, *3967*, Building *4658*, floor R1.2; also residual in *3952*, Period 3B, Building *4006*, fill of pit *3951*

16. Carinated bowl with grooved rim (Fig 300), North West semi-fine oxidised ware, slightly burnt on interior and exterior.
    MIL 5, *3967*, Building *4658*, R1.2, floor

17. Lid. South-east Dorset BB1 (Fig 300), with burnished line above rim and squiggles on interior and exterior; Exeter 2, type 64 (Holbrook and Bidwell 1991, fig 33).
    MIL 5, *3969*, Building *4658*, R1.2, fill of possible gully *3968*

18. Carinated bowl with reeded rim (Fig 300); North West semi-fine oxidised ware; *cf* form CP3.
    MIL 5, *7545*, Building *7392*, R3.1, fill of hollow *7544*

19. Ring-neck flagon (Fig 300), smoothed on exterior in hard 'pipe-clay' fabric (*cf* Exeter, Holbrook and Bidwell 1991, fabric 405, fig 49, but typologically slightly later); possibly from Northern France.
    MIL 5, *7505*, Building *7392*, R5.3, fill of pit *7506*; *7546*, Building *7392*, R5.2, occupation layer; *7569*, Building *7392*, R5.1, fill of pit *7570*; *7573*, Building *7392*, R5.1 ?floor; also residual in *3933*, Period 3B, Building *3772*, R2.1, floor

20. Crucible (Fig 300), probably local North West reduced ware.
    MIL 5, *7498*, Building *7392*, R5.3, occupation layer

21. Jar with upright neck (Fig 300), in fine North West gritty oxidised ware.
    MIL 5, *7318*, Building *7392*, demolition layer

22. Lid with expanded squared-off rim (Fig 300); North West fine oxidised ware; burnt.
MIL 5, *7115*, Building *7393*, occupation layer

23. Jar with upright neck (Fig 300); North West gritty oxidised ware.
MIL 5, *6638*, Road *7476*, external layer

24. Ring-neck flagon (Fig 300); North West semi-fine oxidised ware, with red-brown self-coloured slip; partly burnt on exterior.
MIL 5, *6638*, Road *7476*, external layer; also *7628*, Road *7476*, construction layer

25. Flask or flagon (Fig 300). North West semi-fine fabric with self-coloured slip on exterior.
MIL 5, *6638*, Road *7476*, external layer

26. Mortarium (Fig 300). Carlisle military Fabric 312; burnt, concentric scoring on interior and flange; heavy wear; Flavian.
MIL 5, *7294*, Building *7657*, fill of post-pit *7293*

27. Mortarium (Fig 300), Fabric 320, Verulamium region. Heavily worn with traces of concentric scoring; the form is typical of Secundus; *c* AD 55-85.
MIL 5, *7587*, Road *7476*, fill of drain *7630*

28. Beaker in hard, fine, light buff fabric with a lustrous, dark brown colour-coat, which thins to an orange colour (Fig 301). This appears to be a Central Gaulish product (CNG CC1), and typologically early Flavian, but the rather blunt end to the rim is unusual.
MIL 5, *7407*, fill of external gully *7188*

29. Lid-seated jar (Fig 301); in North West gritty oxidised ware; the rim detailing suggests this to be a product of the same workshop as carinated bowls *3* and *18*.
MIL 5, *7454*, demolition layer adjacent to Building *7392*

30. Carinated bowl with reeded rim (Fig 301); North West semi-coarse reduced ware (Fabric 3).
MIL 5, *7334*, demolition layer adjacent to Building *7392*

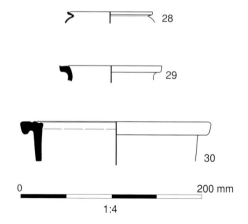

Figure 301: Period 3A vessels

Period 3B: AD 83-4 - *c* 93-4
Local products: sources and supply

Local coarse and finewares continued to form the major component in the pottery supply, providing over 60% of the coarseware (Table 28) and almost 79% of the fineware (by EREs; Table 30), and the local mortaria appear more frequently (over 18% by EREs; Table 24). The refurbishment at the beginning of Period 3B has been associated with preparation for a new garrison, perhaps *ala Gallorum Sebosiana* (Ch 12, p 439). It is thus a good point at which to consider whether the local military pottery production and supply changed completely or retained a significant element of continuity. The answer seems to lie somewhere between the two extremes.

All the local fabrics recorded in the previous phase appear to have continued, although this probably reflects the availability of similar or identical clay supplies. Even making allowances for residuality, a number of the staple military forms appear to continue in the same traditions, these including oxidised ring-neck flagons and mortaria (both more developed typologically; *37, 39, 48*), and a new and unusual type of flagon (*43*), possibly derived from the earlier Hofheim type. Reduced jars with a thick, blunt-ended lid-seated rim appeared for the first time (*34, 107*). Reduced jars with an everted-rim and/or rustication continued in production (the rustication now being less nodular and more linear), as did shallow lids with cut-off rims (*38*); whether or not the same individuals were working, the potters were clearly aiming at the same range of standard forms. However, new culinary forms augmented the standard range at this time, perhaps suggesting different potters, but not necessarily a different unit; they include reduced jars of uncertain affinities (*36, 47, 53*), convex-walled cooking dishes (*44*), lids with bi-lobed rims (*57, 76*, see also Castle Street, no 27 (Taylor 1991)), oxidised tazze with knife-cut frilling (*58*), and an extraordinary upright barrel-like costrel, a rare type more appropriate to a legionary pottery (*33*), and rouletted bowls imitating samian forms (*51*; see also Taylor 1990, fig 196, no 10; Taylor 1991, fig 305, no 1).

The fine rouletted beakers of Period 3A were no longer in production, being replaced by a series of large beakers (or small jars) with a distinctive everted-rim and smoothed surface, which are decorated with barbotine dots in a contrasting darker reddish-brown clay (*46, 133*). Residual sherds in later contexts suggest that the same potter may have been using a hybrid appliqué/barbotine technique to make leaves (*194, 208*) and other motifs, such as the fine depiction of the god Silenus (*341*). Similar vessels were also recorded at Castle Street (Taylor 1991, nos 66-7, 1-3-6, 180, 256). Such sophisticated pottery may suggest influences from outside the province, perhaps military craftsmen with a background in the Lower/Middle Rhineland or North Gaul, as beakers with barbotine dots appear to have been a tradition particular to the Strasbourg region. This would not be improbable, given the background of the *ala Gallorum Sebosiana* (Tomlin 1988), which may have continued to recruit from Gaul after its transfer to Britain (probably with Cerialis in AD 71; *Ch 12, p 439*).

The first reliable dating evidence for the commencement of production at the Brampton pottery is particularly valuable (*p 613*). The distinctive, very gritty oxidised and reduced products of this workshop are poorly represented at Carlisle at this period, by fragments of no more than five vessels, including a cooking-dish (*32*). They nevertheless suggest that the establishment of the works-depot may have been coincident with the rebuilding of Period 3B. Carlisle was never the main market for Brampton wares (although they were to play a more significant role in Period 4), and Brampton's location was more appropriate for the supply of forts (such as Vindolanda, where the Brampton wares are prominent; *pers obs*) at the central-western end of the Tyne-Solway isthmus, which were built possibly from about AD 83, and certainly after the partial evacuation of Scotland in AD 87.

Non-local vessels: supply and acquisition

The fineware imports (including Lyons ware (*31*) and possible Central Gaulish beakers) show little change at this period (with the addition of a single item in *terra nigra*, and a white beaker, perhaps from northern France or the Lower Rhineland), and remained at a relatively low level, probably because the local finewares were fulfilling the needs of the unit. Similarly, the mortaria were now dominated by local products, although there seems to have been a rise in imports from northern France relative to those from Verulamium, which had predominated in the previous phase (Table 24). The presence of two mortaria of unexpected origin is of interest for the interpretation of the site, one perhaps denoting the presence of legionary building parties from Wroxeter, and the other, from Elginhaugh, indicative of troops evacuating forts in Scotland (*Ch 13, pp 451-2*).

Supply of amphora-borne products

There were few major changes in the amphora assemblage, but the overall range narrowed (Table 21).

Spatial aspects

The quantity of pottery in Building *4006*, interpreted as a possible workshop/store (Fig 267), again suggests that this was an area where the preparation and consumption of food and drink took place, particularly the latter, which is also reflected in barrack Building *3772*, and the adjacent road (*4661*; *Ch 4*). A local beaker with barbotine dots was found in R2 of the *principia* (Building *7391*), perhaps

belonging to an officer, and one or two of the soldiers in the barracks were clearly able to afford high-class imported drinking vessels (*31, 42*).

Catalogue (see also amphorae and stamped mortaria)

31. Rough-cast cornice-rim beaker in Lyon ware (Fig 302).
    MIL 3, *960*, external layer

32. Dish with inturned rim and grooved wall (Fig 302); Brampton reduced gritty ware.
    MIL 5, *3726/3807*, Building *3772*, fill of construction trench *3725/3806*

33. Large costrel in the form of an upright barrel with suspension loops at the top (Fig 302); North West semi-fine oxidised ware; a rare type mostly occurring in legionary contexts.
    MIL 5, *3634*, Building *4006*, floor; also residual in *3749*, Period 3E, fill of posthole *3748*; *3722, 3626, 3240*, Period 4A, Building *3376*, fill of construction trenches *3724, 3448, 3241*; *2792*, Period 5A external surface

34. Lid-seated jar, sooted on exterior (Fig 302); semi-coarse reduced ware (Fabric 3).
    MIL 5, *3763*, Building *4006*, fill of gully *3762*

35. Everted-rim jar (Fig 302). North West gritty reduced ware.
    MIL 5, *3763*, Building *4006*, fill of gully *3762*

36. Everted-rim jar with grooved beaded rim (Fig 302); North West semi-fine oxidised ware (Fabric 751).
    MIL 5, *3802*, Building *4006*, occupation layer

37. Ring-neck flagon, slightly burnt (Fig 302); North West semi-fine oxidised ware; typologically mid-late Flavian.
    MIL 5, *3878*, Building *4006*, floor

38. Lid with cut-off rim (Fig 302); North West gritty reduced ware, burnt on rim.
    MIL 5, *3971*, Building *4006*, fill of construction trench *3970*

39. Ring-neck flagon (Fig 302); North West semi-fine oxidised ware; a mid-late Flavian form?
    MIL 5, *3835*, Building *4006*, floor

40. Flat-rimmed dish (Fig 302); local grey sandy ware, black coating on rim and interior, partially burnt on exterior. Typologically at end of phase?
    MIL 5, *3805*, Building *4006*, floor

41. Ring-neck flagon (Fig 302); North West fine oxidised ware with self-coloured slip; possibly residual.
    MIL 5, *3404*, Building *4651*, fill of gully *3405*

42. Small everted-rim beaker with girth constriction (Fig 302); fine white 'Watercrook-type' fabric.
    MIL 5, *3503/3516/3517*, Road *4661*, make-up layers; also residual in *3476, 3483*, Period 4A, Building *4655*, fill of construction trench *3410*, and R4.1, floor

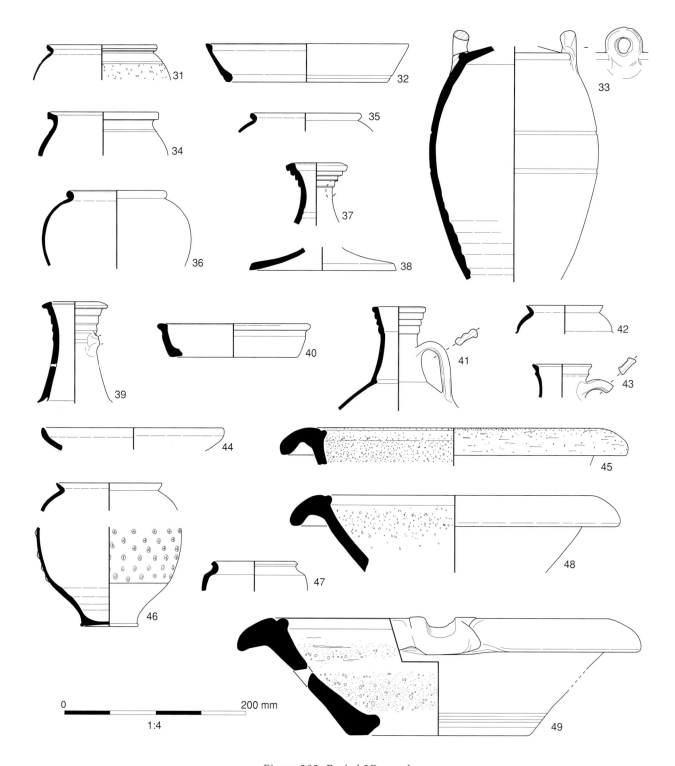

Figure 302: Period 3B vessels

43. Collared flagon, Hofheim-related type (Fig 302); North West fine oxidised fabric, possibly residual.
MIL 5, *3518*, Road *4661*, make-up layer

44. Concave-walled dish, burnished on exterior (Fig 302); North West coarse gritty reduced ware.
MIL 5, *3358*, Road *4661*, external deposit

45. Mortarium, *cf* Gillam 238 (Fig 302); Oise-Somme region.
MIL 5, *3536*, Road *4661*, fill of gully / drain *3470*

46. Everted-rim jar (Fig 302); fine, pale buff, slightly sandy North West oxidised ware, with barbotine dots in reddish-brown slip. Burnt.
MIL 5, *7174*, Building *7391*, R2.1, occupation layer; also *7322*, Building *7391*, R2.2, floor; residual in *7156*, Period 3E, external layer

47. Everted-rim jar with concave shoulder (Fig 302); local semi-coarse reduced ware (Fabric 3), burnished or slipped on exterior.
MIL 5, *7215*, Building *7394*, R1.1, floor

614

48. Mortarium (Fig 302); Carlisle, Fabric 312; well-worn, Flavian.

MIL 5, *7215*, Building *7394*, R1.1, floor

49. Mortarium with matt-brown slip (Fig 302); Carlisle military, Fabric 310, probably Flavian, heavy wear.

MIL 5, *7215*, Building *7394*, R1.1, floor

Periods 3C-3E: (*c* AD 93-4 - *c* AD 103-5)

Local products: sources and supply

The alterations to the fort which heralded Period 3C do not seem to have been accompanied by any very significant changes in the ceramic repertoire. Local production continued to dominate supply, with essentially the same basic fabrics and variations of the same military vessel types: flat-rim jars; carinated bowls with a reeded rim; lids with an almost bi-lobed rim; tazze; rusticated cooking-jars (much more common than in the previous phase); and also mortaria (more common and typologically more developed). The barbotine and appliqué-decorated beakers, however, went out of production. These changing emphases, and subtle changes in the forms, suggest the addition of a new potter in the military workshop, but no overall change.

Although difficult to distinguish from some of the coarser local fabrics, the oxidised products of the Brampton workshops (*pp 590-3*) were reaching the fort in a gently increasing trickle throughout these years. The range is limited to a very small number of forms, particularly reeded-rim bowls and convex-walled dishes, cooking-jars, and also an imitation of a samian bowl, form Dr 37.

Non-local vessels: supply and acquisition

There is some increase in the variety of non-local wares during these phases, but insufficient to indicate a significant opening-up of trade in the frontier zone. How many of the imports reached Carlisle in the course of trade, or as personal baggage, is uncertain. Some are clearly not vessels known to have been regular components of trade or supply, and at least some of them probably ought to be linked to the arrival of recruits or transfers from outside the region. Attested at Carlisle from sometime within the governorship of Agricola (*c* AD 77-83), the *ala Gallorum Sebosiana* may have remained in garrison until the end of Period 3C (*Ch 12, pp 440-1*). Having been stationed near Worms in the Rhineland in the AD 60s, *Gallia Belgica* would have constituted its prime recruitment area, and the Carlisle evidence seems to indicate that it had continued to recruit from that region after its departure to Britain (Jarrett 1994, 41). This would explain the small but significant showing of pottery imported from *Gallia Belgica* during Periods 3B-3E (for example, mica-dusted bowl *60*; and beaker *241*, residual in Period 4B). Of particular interest among the finewares is a small drinking beaker in a fine pale fabric with red-painted decoration (in Period 3C),

likely to have been made in the Rhineland or North Gaul. It is unparalleled elsewhere in Britain, apart from two virtually identical vessels recorded in the fort at Watercrook (Lockwood 1979, 253, nos 198, 206). All three were undoubtedly produced in the same workshop, but if they had been objects of trade or institutional supply, a more widespread distribution might be expected. That the owners may have all come from the same part of Gaul is quite likely, as there are several North Gaulish greyware vessels from the site (*see below*), and the possibility of a link between men in the two units is of potential interest.

The other significant indicators for the presence of Gauls are North Gaulish greyware beakers and other vessels in the same tradition, in Period 3D and also in Periods 4A and 4B. Being relatively coarse-textured and intrinsically unattractive, such products would not be expected as normal luxury imports to the site (though they would have been treated as tablewares), but are more likely to have constituted personal possessions brought in the baggage of recruits. These biconical beakers (so-called '*vases tronconiques*'), in rough granular fabrics, often with horizontal burnishing on the neck, were made and used in northern *Gallia Belgica*, in the tribal territories of the Atrebates, Menapi, Morini, Nervii, and perhaps the Tungri. Their relatively large capacity means that they were inappropriate for wine, and they must surely have been intended for the consumption of beer (though occasional sooting suggests that they might sometimes have been used for cooking). These territories coincide with the modern beer-drinking regions of Belgium and northern France (Swan 2009), and their use may have been integral to the lifestyle of people in the region. The Carlisle examples are in more than one fabric, and their presence is almost certainly a reflection of recruitment or transfers (on more than one occasion and from more than one location) of men from within those tribal territories.

Imports from other parts of Britain include minute amounts of the distinctive grey micaceous ware (including part of a beaker with barbotine dots) made in East Anglia, a region where pottery production was burgeoning at this period. The mechanism for their arrival is uncertain. Probably belonging to the late Flavian or early Trajanic period, but residual in Period 4A/B, there are two vessels (*139* and *155*) which have their origins in Humberside or North Lincolnshire. These are not the only examples of such imports, because a range of forms produced in this region was recorded in the Castle Street excavations, in contexts from deposits dated to AD 92/3-105 and *c* AD 105 (Taylor 1991, fig 312, no 87; fig 314-6, nos 127, 134, 190, and probably no 160). They include a native coarseware form (*op cit*, no 190), which can hardly have been an object of trade, and there is a real possibility of the presence of recruits or transfers from that region. Although found residually in a third-century context, an Ebor ware lamp (*338*) is likely to have been produced in the AD 90s or 100s. Made in the legionary workshop at York (Bailey 1993), it is highly unlikely that such vessels were traded, and it is thus probable that it had been brought to Carlisle by an individual, perhaps a member of a building-detachment from *Legio IX Hispana* involved in the demolition of the first fort, and/or its reconstruction in the early AD 100s.

Supply of amphora-borne products

Supply was now confined to a very limited range of products, Pélichet 47 (for wine) and Dressel 20 containing olive oil (Table 21).

Spatial aspects

Evidence for eating and drinking in the buildings bordering on the main east to west road (Buildings **4657** and **7200**) continued to be strong.

Catalogue: Period 3C

50. Body-sherd of large storage-vessel (Fig 303); North West fine oxidised ware, partially burnt; ownership graffito of at least two six-pronged 'stars' on shoulder.
MIL 5, *4220*, Building **4657**, fill of construction trench *4221*

51. Bowl imitating samian form Dr 37, with judder rouletting (Fig 303); Brampton gritty oxidised ware.
MIL 5, *3190*, Building **4657**, R1.3, occupation layer

52. Small everted-rim beaker (Fig 303), in a fine, pale cream fabric with light brownish-red, slip-painted stripe and wavy lines. Two very similar beakers, recorded from Watercrook (Lockwood 1979, 252-3, fig 105, nos 198 and 206), were almost certainly made in the same workshop; all were probably imported; *Gallia Belgica* seems the most likely production-source.
MIL 5, *4144*, Building **4657**, R1.3, fill of pit *4130*

53. Jar with concave neck and square-ended rim (Fig 303); reduced rusticated-type fabric.
MIL 5, *6655*, Building **7200**, R1.1, floor

54. Beaker with a grooved cornice rim (Fig 303); light buff fabric, dark brown slip, and clay-pelleted rough-casting. Probably Central Gaulish. This is a relatively early example of a grooved cornice rim, but the body is less globular than related Flavian beakers (*eg 28*), and a production date in the early–mid AD 90s would seem appropriate.
MIL 5, *6877*, Building **7200**, R2/3.1, floor

55. Bead-rim dish or possibly a bowl (Fig 303); North West fine oxidised ware, polished on exterior.
MIL 5, *6396*, Road **7476**, fill of drain *6399*

56. Convex-walled dish (Fig 303); North West semi-fine oxidised ware, thoroughly burnt and reduced.
MIL 5, *6396*, Road **7476**, fill of drain *6399*

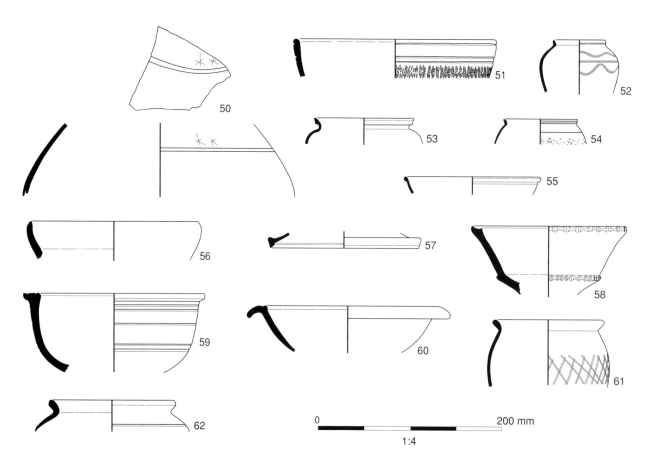

Figure 303: Period 3C vessels

57. Lid with bipartite rim (Fig 303); North West gritty reduced ware; wasters of this form occur (probably redeposited) in Carlisle at the Fisher Street kiln site (McBride and Hartley forthcoming).
MIL 5, *6396*, Road **7476**, fill of drain *6399*

58. Tazza, with knife-cut notches on rim and carination, and three random knife notches on the wall (Fig 303). Slightly sandy North West fine oxidised ware, with a thin self-coloured slip on interior; intense sooting on rim and patches of burning on the interior.
MIL 5, *7193*, Road **7476**, fill of robber trench *7252*

59. Hemispherical bowl with flat reeded rim (Fig 303); Brampton oxidised ware.
MIL 5, *6675*, Road **7476**, fill of drain *6399*; also residual in *6895*, Period 4B, fill of pit/posthole *6894*

60. Flanged segmental bowl (Fig 303); fine pinkish-orange silky-textured fabric with a greenish grey core and mica-dusting on surface. Unsourced, but perhaps North Gaulish; the fabric does not appear to resemble known Gaulish or Romano-British products, *cf* Deru 1994, fig 1, no 13 for a closely similar form.
MIL 5, *6630*, Road **7476,** external layer

61. Jar imitating BB1 form with burnished lattice, slightly burnt on rim (Fig 303); indeterminate reduced ware; see discussion of BB1 and allied wares (*pp 601-3*).
MIL 5, *6630*, Road **7476**, external layer

62. Everted-rim jar (Fig 303); reduced rusticated-type fabric; probably residual.
MIL 5, *4505*, Road **7478**, fill of drain *4466*

Catalogue: Period 3D

63. Mortarium; Carlisle military (Fig 304); Fabric 304, Flavian. A slight effort has been made to effect concentric scoring on the flange.
MIL 5, *3377*, Building **3772**, demolition layer

64. Everted-rim jar, slightly burnt (Fig 304); North West gritty oxidised ware.
MIL 5, *3447*, Building **3772**, demolition layer

65. Narrow-mouthed jar, burnt (Fig 304); North West fine slightly sandy oxidised ware.
MIL 5, *3447*, Building **3772**, demolition layer

66. Convex-walled dish with slight groove on rim (Fig 304); sooted on exterior; Brampton reduced gritty ware.
MIL 5, *3447*, Building **3772**, demolition layer

67. Jar with flattened rim and short neck (Fig 304); North West gritty oxidised ware.
MIL 5, *3326*, Building **4006**, demolition layer

68. Probable spout of strainer or jar (Fig 304); North West fine oxidised ware.
MIL 5, *3326*, Building **4006**, demolition layer

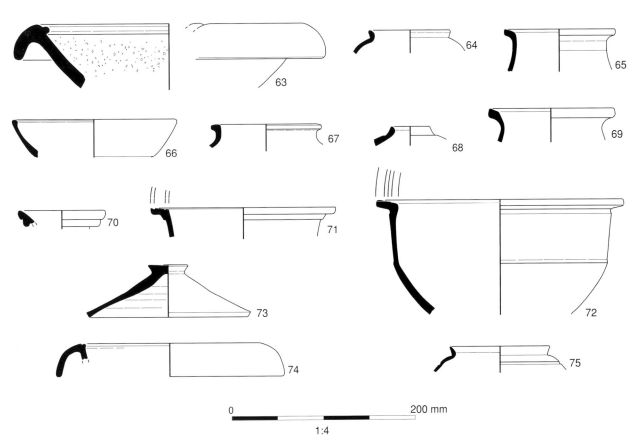

0   200 mm

1:4

Figure 304: Periods 3D-3E vessels

617

69. Narrow-mouthed jar (Fig 304); Brampton gritty oxidised ware.
   MIL 4, *1798*, Building **2058**, demolition layer

70. Flask or flagon (Fig 304); North West fine oxidised ware with a smooth surface.
   MIL 5, *7336*, Building **7394**, fill of robber trench *7333*

71. Bowl (Fig 304); North West semi-fine gritty oxidised ware; slightly sooted on tip of rim.
   MIL 5, *7336*, Building **7394**, fill of robber trench *7333*

Catalogue: Period 3E

72. Carinated bowl with reeded rim (Fig 304); North West gritty reduced ware.
   MIL 2, *620*, external layer

73. Lid with squared-off rim (Fig 304); burnt at tip; North West gritty reduced ware, oxidised in core; burnt on tip of rim.
   MIL 2, *620*, external layer

74. Collared segmental bowl (Fig 304); mustard-coloured fabric with smoothed surface; probably an import.
   MIL 5, *3744*, root disturbance; also residual in *3569*, Period 4A, Building **3376**, fill of construction trench *3568*; *3216*, Period 4B, Building **4660**, fill of construction trench *3215*; *3315*, Road **4659**, fill of roadside ditch *3314*

75. Everted-rim beaker (Fig 304); North West gritty oxidised ware; probably residual.
   MIL 5, *7156*, external layer

Period 4A: (*c* AD 105 - *c* AD 125)

Local products: sources and supply

The ceramic evidence combines to suggest that, after a possible break in military occupation, there was a new garrison, which had probably been based in *Gallia Belgica* immediately before its transfer to Carlisle, and that a new ceramic workshop had opened on the site of the previous (Fisher Street) military pottery (*p 594*). As there is by this time a considerable amount of residual material as a result of renewed building, the evident reduction in the level of local wares could actually have been even greater than is apparent from the tables (Tables 22, 27-30). Products local to Carlisle, or nearby Scalesceugh (*p 590*), now constituted almost 57.5% of the total (by EREs), and represented almost 48% of the tablewares, but less than 9% of the mortaria, the latter reflecting a huge influx of imports from the Oise-Somme region (Table 25), probably arriving with the new garrison. Certainly, there seem to have been significant changes in the range of vessels made, although not surprisingly most of the staple types popular with the army (such as ring-necked flagons and later versions of everted-rim jars with longer, more curved rims) continued to be produced. New vessel types included pinched-mouthed jugs (*182, 259, 265*); jars with a rilled neck and shoulder (*119, 125, 224, 227*); burnished convex-walled dishes with internal combing (*103*); lids with an up-turned rim (*78, 81*); tazze with a frilled rim (*130*); triple vases (*100*); flanged segmental bowls (*211*); and segmental dishes with a groove inside the lip (*88*). The suggestion of new ceramic traditions in a new workshop is confirmed by the mortaria (*pp 582-3*), which show a complete break with previous types. The mortarium potters include some who stamped their names (*eg 4, p 588*); perhaps, having links with Wroxeter and Wilderspool traditions, they might have been working under military contract.

There was also a very significant increase in the Brampton products supplied to the site, both in the quantity and in the variety of forms and fabrics, and this was set to escalate in the Hadrianic period (Period 4B). This increase might well reflect the construction of the Stanegate road, facilitating the bulk transportation of pottery.

Non-local vessels: supply and acquisition

The level of fineware imports remained much as before, with only a slight increase. Rough-cast beakers continued to be imported, mainly from sources in Gaul, but there were significant changes in the morphology; high-shouldered globular/ovoid forms were replaced by the first bag-shaped beakers, with carefully formed, often grooved, cornice rims, forms that were to last with only slight change until the late second century.

The connections and probably the origins of the unit are reflected in the imported pottery. North Gaulish greyware beakers are again present in small quantities, and several other vessels (perhaps fewer than previously) seem likely to have come from *Gallia Belgica* (*eg* fineware beaker *124*, and large coarseware lid-seated jar *128*). The contribution of potteries in other parts of Britain remained minimal: a few flagons and a possible transport jar from the Verulamium region; and a trickle of greywares from East Anglia. It is possible that one or two vessels in Dorset Black-burnished ware may have reached Carlisle in the late Trajanic period, but they were clearly not part of regular institutional supply until later.

Supply of amphora-borne products

The supply of amphorae remains restricted, and identical to that of the preceding period (*ie* Dressel 20 oil and Pélichet 47 wine amphorae).

Catalogue: Period 4A

76. Lid (Fig 305); North West gritty reduced ware; burnished on outer flange and wall; the burnishing is not dissimilar to North Gaulish greyware.
   MIL 4, *1639*, Building **2059**, R2.1, possible floor

77. Flagon (Fig 305); North West fine oxidised ware; self-coloured slip on exterior.

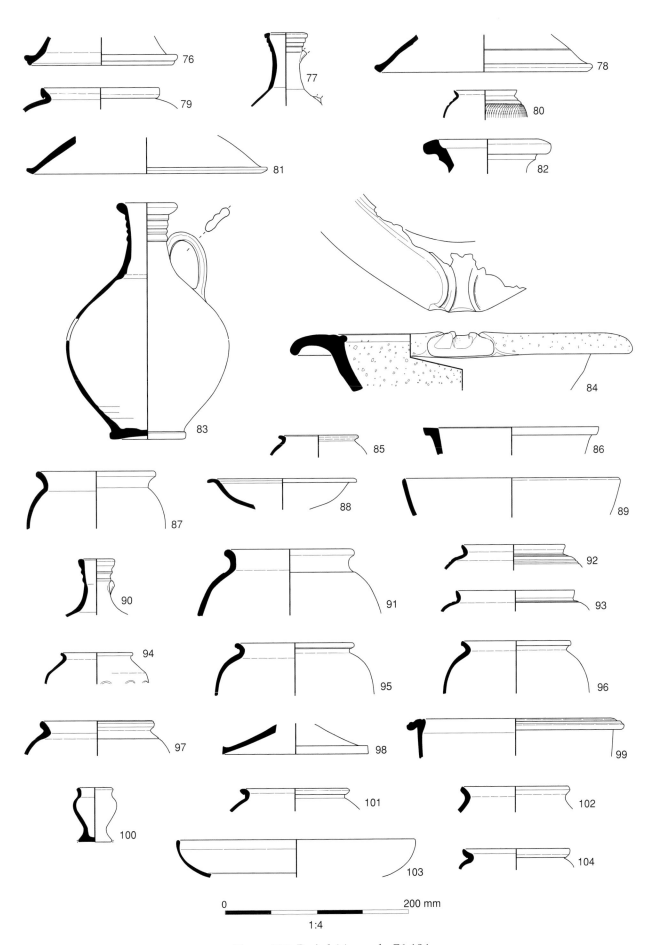

76

77

78

79

80

81

82

83

84

85

86

87

88

89

90

91

92

93

94

95

96

97

98

99

100

101

102

103

104

0   200 mm

1:4

Figure 305: Period 4A vessels, 76-104

619

MIL 4, *1821*, Building **2059**, fill of construction trench *1822*, also *1781*, fill of robber trench *1752*

78. Lid (Fig 305); North West fine oxidised ware, thoroughly burnt.
    MIL 4, *1756*, Building **2059**, R3.2, fill of posthole *1757*

79. Everted-rim jar (Fig 305); possibly, but not certainly, local slightly sandy reduced (pale grey) fabric.
    MIL 4, *1641*, Building **2059**, R3.3, demolition layer

80. Beaker (Fig 305); local / North West very fine oxidised ware, nicely burnished on rim and exterior.
    MIL 4, *1709*, Building **2059**, fill of robber trench *1718*

81. Lid (Fig 305); North West semi-fine oxidised ware.
    MIL 5, *2999*, Building **4655**, fill of construction trench *2922*

82. Amphora, Gauloise 3 (Fig 305); Southern Gaul.
    MIL 5, *3272*, Road **4659**, road surface

83. Ring-neck flagon (Fig 305); local North West fine gritty oxidised ware.
    MIL 5, *3272*, Road **4659**, road surface; also residual in *3315*, Period 4B, Road **4659**, fill of roadside ditch *3314*

84. Mortarium, Gillam 238 (Fig 305); Oise-Somme region.
    MIL 5, *3272*, Road **4659**, road surface

85. Everted-rim jar (Fig 305); Brampton reduced ware, burnished bands on exterior and top of rim.
    MIL 5, *3018*, Road **4659**, fill of roadside ditch *3168*

86. Dish with thick, rectangular rim (Fig 305); Brampton gritty oxidised ware.
    MIL 5, *3018*, Road **4659**, fill of roadside ditch *3168*

87. Jar (Fig 305); imitation BB1 type A, fine burnished mid-grey fabric (?slip on rim and exterior).
    MIL 5, *3018*, Road **4659**, fill of roadside ditch *3168*

88. Segmental Dish (Fig 305); probably North West fine oxidised ware (*cf* cream import in the same form).
    MIL 5, *3018*, Road **4659**, fill of roadside ditch *3168*

89. Plain-rim dish, smoothed on interior and exterior (Fig 305); Brampton oxidised ware.
    MIL 5, *3626*, Building **3376**, fill construction trench *3448*

90. Ring-neck flagon with three simplified rings (Fig 305); North West fine oxidised ware.
    MIL 5, *3211*, Building **3376**, demolition layer

91. Jar imitating BB1 form, with patches of sooting on rim and exterior (Fig 305); slightly sandy version of North West gritty oxidised ware.
    MIL 5, *3211*, Building **3376**, demolition layer

92. Everted-rim jar (Fig 305); Brampton oxidised ware, or coarse version of North West gritty oxidised ware.
    MIL 5, *3211*, Building **3376**, demolition layer

93. Jar (Fig 305); possibly coarse version of North West gritty oxidised ware.
    MIL 5, *3211*, Building **3376**, demolition layer

94. Everted-rim jar or beaker with trace of rustication or applied decoration on concave, angular shoulder (Fig 305); reduced granular fabric; *cf* Gillam 67 for generally similar, but typologically slightly earlier form; source uncertain.
    MIL 5, *3211*, Building **3376**, demolition layer

95. Everted-rim jar, mid-grey (Fig 305); finely sandy fabric.
    MIL 5, *3211*, Building **3376**, demolition layer

96. Everted-rim jar (Fig 305); mid-grey, probably finely sandy version of North West reduced ware.
    MIL 5, *3211*, Building **3376**, demolition layer; and *3240*, Building **4655**, fill of construction trench *3241*

97. Everted-rim jar (Fig 305); reduced gritty local fabric.
    MIL 5, *3211*, Building **3376**, demolition layer; also residual in *3234*, Period 4C, Building **4660**, demolition layer

98. Lid with cut-off rim, sooted at tip (Fig 305); North West gritty oxidised ware.
    MIL 5, *3211*, Building **3376**, demolition layer

99. Reeded-rim bowl (probably carinated), sooted at tip of rim and patches of sooting on exterior (Fig 305); Brampton ware.
    MIL 5, *3240*, Building **4655**, fill of construction trench *3241*

100. Miniature jar with everted-rim (probably from triple-vase or ring-vase) (Fig 305); the whole edge of the base is chipped, presumably where this component has become detached; North West gritty reduced ware; probably residual from Period 3.
     MIL 5, *3240*, Building **4655**, fill of construction trench *3241*

101. Everted-rim jar (Fig 305); North West gritty oxidised ware.
     MIL 5, *3244*, Building **4655**, fill of construction trench *3241*

102. Everted-rim jar (Fig 305); North West semi-fine oxidised ware.
     MIL 5, *3422*, Building **4655**, fill of construction trench *3459*

103. Dish (Fig 305); Local fine oxidised, heavily burnished on interior and exterior.
     MIL 5, *3285*, Building **4655**, R1.1, occupation layer

104. Lid-seated jar (Fig 305); Brampton gritty reduced ware.
     MIL 5, *3422*, Building **4655**, fill of construction trench *3459*

105. Bowl, probably imitating a Gallo-Belgic form (Fig 306); Brampton oxidised ware.
     MIL 5, *3250*, Building **4655**, demolition layer

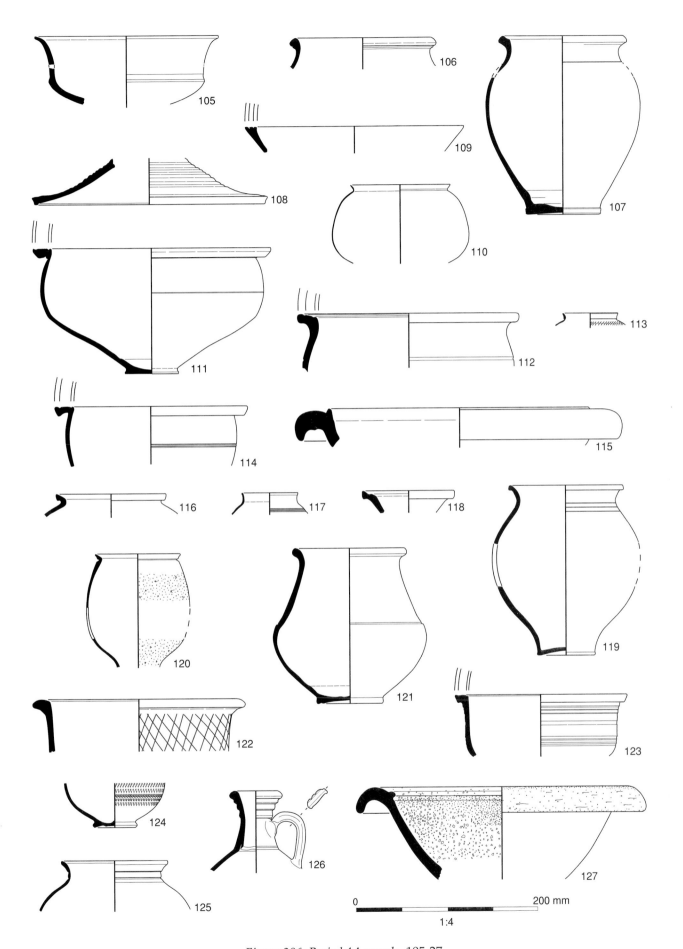

Figure 306: Period 4A vessels, 105-27

621

106. Jar (Fig 306); reduced finely sandy fabric usually associated with rusticated ware at Carlisle.
MIL 5, *3422*, Building *4655*, fill of construction trench *3459*

107. Lid-seated jar (Fig 306); semi-coarse reduced ware *cf 34* (Fabric 3).
MIL 5, *4460*, Structure *4664*, floor

108. Lid with cut-off rim (Fig 306); North West gritty oxidised ware; burnt.
MIL 5, *6188*, Building *5688*, fill of construction trench *6600*

109. Dish with reeded rim (Fig 306); North West fine oxidised ware; probably a Brampton product.
MIL 5, *6188*, Building *5688*, fill of construction trench *6600*

110. Bag-shaped, everted-rim beaker (Fig 306); very fine, probably North West gritty oxidised ware; random burning on exterior.
MIL 5, *6277*, Building *5689*, fill of construction trench *6966*; also residual in *6558*, Period 4B, floor; *6564*, occupation deposit, same building

111. Reeded-rim bowl (Fig 306); an early product in Brampton oxidised ware.
MIL 5, *6825*, Building *5688*, fill of construction trench *6600*

112. Reeded-rim bowl (Fig 306); North West fine oxidised ware, with self-coloured brownish slip.
MIL 5, *6869*, Building *5688*, fill of construction trench *6866*

113. Beaker, rouletted (Fig 306); finer variant of Fabric 750.
MIL 5, *7159*, Building *5688*, fill of construction trench *7158*

114. Reeded-rim bowl (Fig 306); Brampton oxidised ware, upper tip of rim sooted.
MIL 5, *6845*, Building *5688*, R1.1, occupation layer; Building *5688*, R1.2, floor

115. Mortarium (Fig 306); Carlisle, Fabric 303, with self-coloured slip, second century.
MIL 5, *6873*, Building *5689*, fill of construction trench *7069*

116. Everted-rim jar or large beaker (Fig 306); North West fine oxidised ware with brownish slip on exterior; burnt; probably residual.
MIL 5, *7024*, Building *5689*, fill of gully / slot *7090*

117. Beaker with combed shoulder (Fig 306.117); fine North West gritty oxidised ware.
MIL 5, *6708*, Building *5689*, fill of pit *6706*; also residual in *6587*, Period 4B, Building *5689*, floor

118. Jug (Fig 306); Brampton oxidised ware, abraded; Gose (1950) type 237.
MIL 5, *6658*, Road *7477*, fill of drain *6781*

119. Jar with grooved neck and warped rim; burnt on rim and exterior (Fig 306); Brampton oxidised ware.
MIL 5, *6405*, Road *7217*, fill of drain *6375*

120. Cornice-rim beaker with clay rough-cast decoration (Fig 306); Central Gaulish (CNG CC2); slightly burnt.
MIL 5, *6651*, Road *7217*, external layer; also residual in *6374*, Period 4B, fill of robber trench *7471*

121. Beaker-like jar (Fig 306); light grey semi-fine sandy fabric with dark grey surface. The form is identical to the North Gaulish '*vase tronconique*', but the fabric is less granular and unburnished, though probably from the same region; sooted on exterior and probably used for cooking.
MIL 5, *6511*, Road *7217*, road surface

122. Bowl (Fig 306); Dorset BB1: *cf* Gillam 1976, type 34.
MIL 5, *6514*, Road *7217*, road surface

123. Reeded-rim bowl (Fig 306); Brampton oxidised ware; sooting on rim-tip and exterior.
MIL 5, *5816*, Building *7396*, R1.2, occupation layer

124. Globular beaker (Fig 306); hard fine blue-grey fabric with black surface (lustrous on exterior), bands of deep rouletting (probably executed with a roulette); source unknown, probably *Gallia Belgica*.
MIL 5, *6660*, Building *7396*, R2.2, occupation layer

125. Jar with grooved neck (Fig 306); slightly sooted on underside of rim; Brampton oxidised ware; *cf 227*.
MIL 5, *6565*, Road *7477*, external layer

126. Ring-neck flagon (Fig 306); North West gritty oxidised ware with brownish self-coloured slip; possibly residual.
MIL 5, *6565*, Road *7477*, external layer

127. Mortarium (Fig 306); Corbridge fabric 511.
MIL 5, *6565*, Road *7477*, external layer

128. Large lid-seated jar (Fig 307); unsourced, coarse dark grey granular fabric, with ill-sorted inclusions of white quartz and limestone.
MIL 5, *6678*, Road *7477*, external layer

129. Jar with curved everted-rim (Fig 307); unsourced dark grey granular fabric, with white quartz inclusions (local BB1 imitation), burnished on rim and shoulder.
MIL 5, *6678*, Road *7473*, external layer

130. Tazza with frilled rim (Fig 307); North West fine oxidised ware; tip of rim burnt.
MIL 5, *6516*, Road *7477*, fill of robber trench *6610*

131. Lid with expanded blunt-ended rim (Fig 307); Brampton oxidised ware, burnt on tip of rim.
MIL 5, *6565*, *6543*, Road *7477*, external layers

132. Lid (Fig 307); North West gritty reduced ware; residual?
MIL 5, *5714*, Road *7479*, fill of drain / gully *5702*

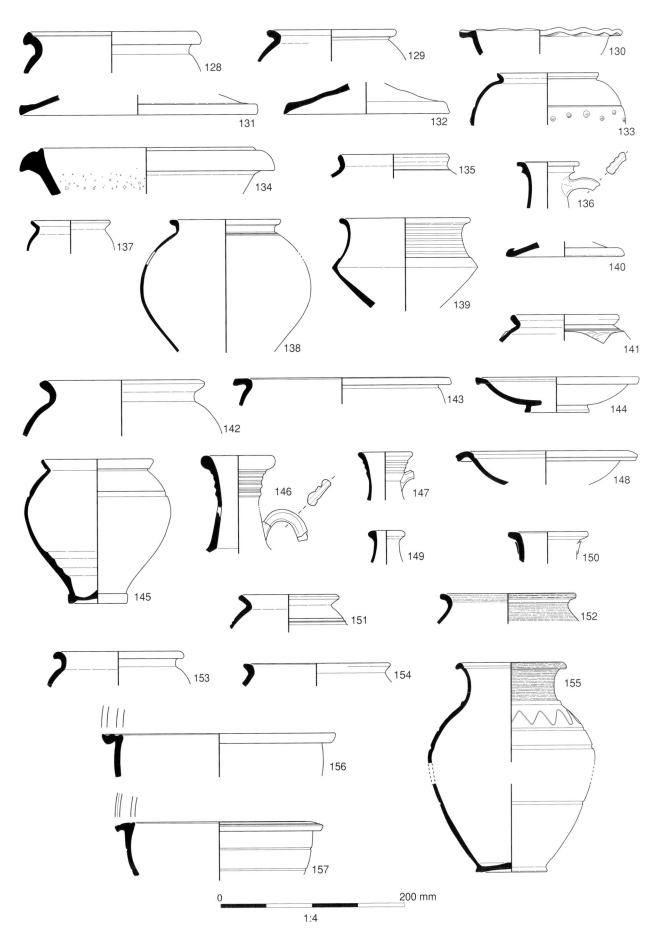

128
129
130
131
132
133
134
135
136
137
138
139
140
141
142
143
144
145
146
147
148
149
150
151
152
153
154
155
156
157

0   200 mm

1:4

Figure 307: Periods 4A and 4A/B vessels

623

133. Everted-rim beaker with barbotine dots in darker (orange-brown) clay (Fig 307); local semi-fine oxidised ware; the shoulder is uneven, probably where the potter has held the vessel when adding the barbotine dots.

MIL 5, *3211*, Building *3376*, demolition layer; also residual in *3149*, Period 4B, Building *4660*, R4.1, fill of hollow *3150*

Catalogue: Period 4A/B

134. Mortarium (Fig 307); North West fabric 552, perhaps from Old Penrith.

MIL 1, *333*, Road *7645*, fill of gully *332*

135. Jar, rilled neck (Fig 307); North West semi-fine oxidised ware.

MIL 1, *1172*, Road *7645*, fill of possible pit *1170*

136. Collared flagon (Fig 307); North West fine oxidised ware

MIL 1, *222*, Road *7645*, external layer

137. Small jar. Slight lid seating (Fig 307); unidentified fairly fine mid-grey fabric.

MIL 1, *338*, Road *7645*, external layer

138. Jar (Fig 307); North West gritty oxidised ware.

MIL 1, *1169* Road *7645*, external layer

139. Biconical bowl with burnishing on neck (Fig 307); fabric not unlike North Gaulish greyware. Similar forms were made at Dragonby and probably other Humberside sites; *cf* Dragonby: May 1996, kiln-pit 2567, fig 20.34, nos 1472, 1476.

MIL 1, *1169*, Road *7645*, external layer

140. Lid (Fig 307); Brampton oxidised ware. Badly made and laminated.

MIL 1, *221*, Road *7645*, external layer

141. Jar (Fig 307), *cf* Castle Street 109 (Taylor 1991); local reduced semi-coarse rusticated ware.

MIL 1, *361*, Road *7645*, external layer

142. Large jar with upright neck and everted-rim (Fig 307); North West gritty reduced ware; imitation BB1?

MIL 1, *1169*, Road *7645*, external layer

143. Bowl (Fig 307); semi-coarse local reduced ware.

MIL 1, *222*, Road *7645*, external layer

144. Dish (Fig 307); probably fine grey local fabric with black surface, heavily burnished on interior, lightly burnished on exterior; *cf* similar form in oxidised fabrics; Fabric 776 *terra nigra* imitation?

MIL 1, *222*, Road *7645*, external layer

145. Large beaker or jar with distinctive everted-rim (Fig 307) (*cf* 4, Period 3A); fine sandy local oxidised ware; burnt on lower exterior.

MIL 1, *355*, Road *7645*, fill of pit *319*

146. Ring-neck flagon (Fig 307); North West fine oxidised ware. The treatment of this form is unusual in having combing

between the rings; possibly a Fisher Street product; late Trajanic or early Hadrianic.

MIL 1, *256*, Road *7645*, road surface

147. Flagon (Fig 307); ?North West fine oxidised ware; thin white slip on interior and exterior.

MIL 1, *320*, Road *7645*, fill of pit *319*

148. Dish, possible import (Fig 307); Northern France.

MIL 1, *318*, Road *7645*, fill of pit *317*; also residual and abraded in *326*, Period 5, external layer

149. Flagon (Fig 307); local oxidised.

MIL 1, *327*, Road *7645*, road surface

150. Narrow-mouthed jar (Fig 307); North West fine oxidised ware.

MIL 1, *327*, Road *7645*, road surface

151. Jar (Fig 307); unidentified grey fabric; rough and granular, variety of North Gaulish greyware.

MIL 1, *327*, Road *7645*, road surface

152. Jar (Fig 307); unidentified light grey fabric; perhaps in Gallo-Belgic tradition, semi-fine horizontal burnishing on rim and exterior.

MIL 1, *327*, Road *7645*, road surface

153. Jar (Fig 307); North West gritty reduced ware, possibly Brampton; imitates BB1.

MIL 1, *327*, Road *7645*, road surface

154. Jar (Fig 307); North West gritty oxidised ware, slightly burnt.

MIL 1, *327*, Road *7645*, road surface

155. Narrow-mouthed, lid-seated jar (Fig 307); slightly granular grey fabric; horizontal burnishing in pronounced horizontal facets on rim and neck, smoothed on rest of exterior body and on interior. This vessel is probably an import from North Humberside, where the rim form is characteristic (*cf* Winterton: Rigby and Stead 1976, fig 82, no 62); and where similar arrangements of neck- and shoulder-cordons with wavy line decoration also occur (*cf* Dragonby kiln 3: *op cit*, fig 64, no 9).

MIL 1, *327/360*, Road *7645*, external metalled surface and fill of pit *359*

156. Bowl (Fig 307); Brampton oxidised ware, burnt on tip and underside of rim.

MIL 1, *256*, Road *7645*, road surface

157. Bowl (Fig 307); Brampton oxidised ware.

MIL 1, *256*, Road *7645*, road surface

158. Bowl (Fig 308); Brampton oxidised ware.

MIL 1, *256*, Road *7645*, road surface

159. Dish (Fig 308); Brampton oxidised ware; patchy burning of exterior.

MIL 1, *256*, Road *7645*, road surface

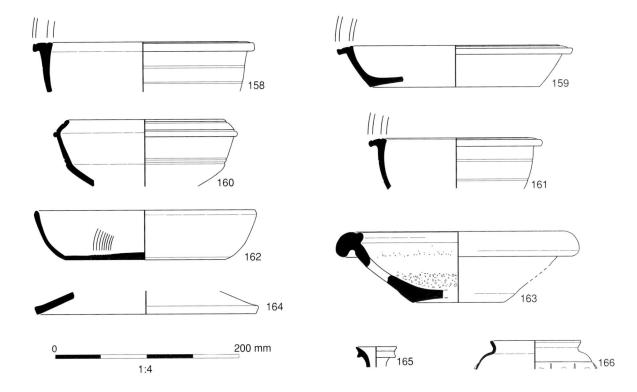

Figure 308: Period 4A/B vessels

160. Dish (Fig 308); North West gritty reduced ware.
MIL 1, *256*, Road **7645**, road surface

161. Reeded-rim bowl (Fig 308); Brampton oxidised ware.
MIL 1, *256*, Road **7645**, road surface

162. Cooking-dish (Fig 308); North West fine oxidised ware. Traces of burning on underside and lower wall.
MIL 1, *327*, Road **7645**, road surface

163. Mortarium (Fig 308); Rhineland or adjacent area of *Gallia Belgica*, Fabric 314; for an example from the same source in a Flavio-Trajanic context at Verulamium, see Wilson 1972, no 355.
MIL 1, *327*, Road **7645**, road surface

164. Lid (Fig 308); tip of rim burnt.
MIL 1, *327*, Road **7645**, road surface

165. Flagon (Fig 308); in slightly sandy oxidised fabric with thin pale cream slip, possibly from York; Gillam 17; mid/late second century.
MIL 1, *283*, possible Rampart **7658**, rampart layer

166. Everted-rim jar (Fig 308); reduced semi-coarse rusticated ware, burnished on rim and shoulder; probably Trajanic.
MIL 1, *283*, possible Rampart **7658**, rampart layer

Periods 4B-4D: (*c* AD 125 - *c* 140/150)

Local products: sources and supply

By the Hadrianic period, the local production of coarsewares (almost 40% EREs) and finewares (36% EREs) had declined even further, although a slight rise in the representation of locally-made mortaria probably reflects the decline in imports reaching the site (Tables 25, 29, 21). This decline can be accounted for in part by the sudden expansion of trade in BB1 (Table 29), and also by the significant increase in the amount of pottery supplied by the Brampton works-depot during this period, the quantity of which almost rivalled that of the workshop just outside the Carlisle fort (allowing for residuality). In general, the ranges of vessels supplied by the two producers seem to have been complementary. The coarser Brampton fabric was evidently best suited for cooking wares, and supplies to Carlisle comprised mainly cooking-bowls, with reeded rims and matching lids, and jars, whilst the Carlisle workshop, with its finer fabrics, concentrated more on flagons, jugs, table-bowls, dishes, and mortaria, as well as specialist items such as crucibles. It may also have made copies of Black-burnished wares. When the fort entered a period of decline *c* AD 140/50, possibly as a result of troop movements (*Ch 7*), the Carlisle workshop continued in production for several decades (perhaps because it was run by civilian contractors), presumably to supply the remaining civilian population. In contrast, Brampton, being an entirely military enterprise, appears to have gone out of production *c* AD 140 (*p 591*). The Brampton pottery is generally assumed to have been shut down when the transfer of garrisons from the Stanegate installations to the newly constructed forts on Hadrian's Wall coincided with an influx of Black-burnished cooking wares from Dorset (*p 602*), which was to become central to pottery supply arrangements in the military North.

However, the quantities of Brampton products seen in the Hadrianic deposits preceding the demolition of the Carlisle fort seem to suggest that it was in fact the move from Hadrian's Wall into Scotland that ended production at Brampton. Moreover, rather than immediately swamping the market at this time, it seems to have been the case that local imitations of BB1, made at Brampton and probably Carlisle, outnumbered the imported products until at least the second half of the second century.

Non-local vessels: supply, acquisition, and impact on local production
There was a significant increase in the quantity of non-local pottery, both fine and coarse, at this time. The modest growth in the quantity and range of sources for the fineware beakers in particular (most of which were likely to have been private purchases) suggests an expansion of wider trade in the frontier zone. This could have been a consequence of increased security on supply-routes, possibly concomitant with improvements to the road system, both of which would have accompanied the development of Hadrian's Wall and its environs; in addition, the associated build-up of troops, including legionary vexillations with their greater purchasing-power, must surely have enabled markets to flourish.

The most significant development seen amongst the coarsewares was the establishment of Dorset BB1 as a component of the institutional supply to the army of the North. Holbrook and Bidwell (1991, 92), following Boon (1974, 184-5), have associated this with the arrival of vexillations from *Legio II Augusta* (which was already using the ware), who were involved in the construction of Hadrian's Wall. It is important to emphasise that the quantities for the Hadrianic period at Carlisle are not large (see Table 29), but are sufficient to indicate bulk purchase rather than items brought in by individuals. They included cooking-jars, bowls, and dishes (*202, 204, 253, 256, 277, 335*) from south-east Dorset, and also very small quantities of South Western BB1 probably from Devon (such as jug *251*), which presumably arrived with the same shipments.

Perhaps even more important was the impact of the arrival of BB1 on the potteries at Carlisle and Brampton, which evidently began their copying immediately. The Brampton military works-depot started by producing rather imprecise versions of BB1 jars and bowls in oxidised and reduced wares. However, the potters working at Carlisle were quick to appreciate the superior cooking properties of the fabric, and carefully imitated its granular texture (laden with coarse quartz sand), as well as the superficial appearance of the forms. Their copies had heavily burnished facets on the rim and exterior, and were coated on the exterior and rim-top with a thick black slip, as well as having burnished lattice decoration. In fact, the main difference between these imitations and the Dorset imports was that the latter were handmade and the copies are not, although it is also possible to distinguish them from the detailing of the rim. BB1 was, of course, fired in a reducing atmosphere, and this may have encouraged the Carlisle and Brampton potters to reduce some of their other products, including some that were normally oxidised.

A number of other non-local vessels (some residual in later deposits) add significant details to the interpretation of this period. A fine red-slipped and polished dish (*212*) and two sherds with 'cut glass'-style decoration (*309 a/b*, residual in Period 5) are in Ebor 3 ware, a type of pottery that was made immediately outside the York fortress in the pottery/tilery of *Legio VI Victrix* in the AD 120s, and was not normally traded (Monaghan 1993, 706). These had presumably been brought to Carlisle with detachments from that legion, involved in the construction of the Wall. A fine red-painted cup from Wilderspool is in a related tradition, coming from a kiln complex working in a military milieu and possessing strong links with *Legio XX*, whose products tend to be confined to military sites.

In addition, there are two vessels (*139, 155*) which have their origin in Humberside or North Lincolnshire. Such imports are also known from Castle Street (Taylor 1991, fig 312, no 87, fig 314-6, nos 127, 134, 190). As these include a native ware form (*op cit*, no 190), they are unlikely to have been objects of trade, and there is a real possibility that they reflect the presence of recruits or transfers from that area.

The supply of mortaria is not significantly different from that in the later Trajanic period, but it is worth noting the first appearance in this phase of a Mancetter-Hartshill product, a source that was to become increasingly important until its decline in the early fourth century.

Supply of amphora-borne products
The supply of amphorae remains restricted and identical to that of the preceding phase (*ie* comprising Dressel 20 oil and Pélichet 47 wine amphorae; Table 21).

Spatial aspects
Of particular interest was an unused crucible (*263*) with a pouring spout, in a local fabric, found in a context associated with the putative central-range workshop (Building *5689; Ch 6*).

Catalogue: Period 4B
167. Amphora, Dressel 20 (Fig 309); South Spanish.
    MIL 2, *582*, Building *546*, occupation layer

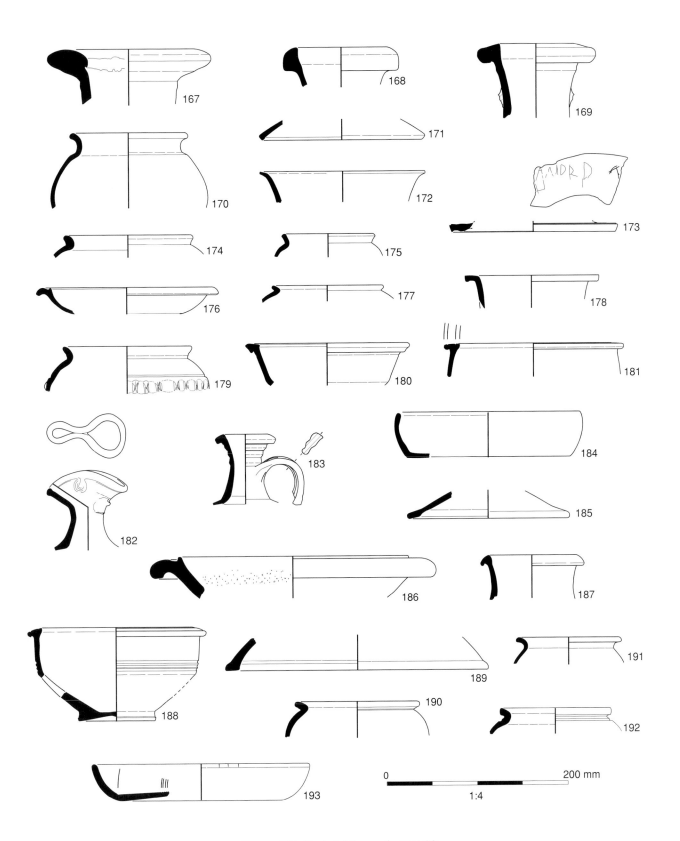

Figure 309: Period 4B vessels, 167-93

168. Amphora, Gauloise 4 (Fig 309); Southern Gaul.
MIL 2, *575*, Building *546*, floor

169. Amphora, Gauloise 5 (Fig 309); Southern Gaul.
MIL 2, *596*, Road *7668*, fill of possible pit *597*; *613*, Building
7644, occupation layer

170. Jar imitating BB1 form (Fig 309); gritty grey, possibly
Brampton, fabric.
MIL 3, *988*, fill of posthole *989*

171. Lid, with cut-off rim (Fig 309); North West gritty oxidised ware.
MIL 4, *1561*, external layer

172. Bowl, probably campanulate-type (Fig 309); Brampton oxidised ware.
MIL 5, *3053*, Building *2765*, R2.1, possible floor

173. Lid with cut-off rim (Fig 309); North West gritty oxidised ware, burnt and reduced; *post-cocturam* graffiti scratched around edge on upper side.
MIL 5, *3056*, Building *2765*. R3.1, possible floor

174. Everted-rim jar (Fig 309); North West gritty oxidised ware.
MIL 5, *3056*, Building *2765*, R3.1, possible floor

175. Jar (Fig 309); North West gritty reduced ware.
MIL 5, *3097*, Building *2765*, R2.1, fill of pit *3098*

176. Segmental flanged dish (Fig 309); North West gritty oxidised ware, or Brampton oxidised ware with cream slip.
MIL 5, *3132*, Building *2765*, R4.1, cut and fill of pit

177. Everted-rim jar, rim slightly sooted (Fig 309); Brampton oxidised ware.
MIL 5, *3228*, Building *2765*, R1.1, fill of slot *3229*

178. Flat-rim bowl, probably carinated (Fig 309); ?local oxidised, with self-coloured slip on rim and exterior; sooting on rim tip and exterior.
MIL 5, *3116*, Building *2765*, R4.1, fill of pit *3132*; also *4462*, Road *7479*, fill of pipe-trench *5712*

179. Everted-rim jar with rustication (Fig 309); in local granular reduced fabric; residual.
MIL 5, *3000*, Building *2765*, R4.2, occupation layer

180. Bowl (Fig 309); Local gritty reduced ware.
MIL 5, *3000/3106*, Building *2765*, R4.2, occupation layer and fill of gully *3143*

181. Bowl with reeded rim (probably carinated) (Fig 309); fine, mid-grey, slightly micaceous fabric.
MIL 5, *3000*, Building *2765*, R4.2, occupation layer

182. Pinched-mouth jug (Fig 309); North West fine oxidised ware; probably a Fisher Street product.
MIL 5, *2714*, Building *2765*, R5.2, fill of pit *2716* ; also residual in *2709*, Period 5A, fill of gully *2712*

183. Ring-neck flagon (Fig 309); North West fine oxidised ware; probably a product of the Fisher Street kiln.
MIL 5, *2714*, Building *2765*, R5.2, fill of pit *2716*, also residual in *2709* Period 5A, fill of gully *2712*

184. Concave-walled dish (Fig 309); Brampton oxidised ware.
MIL 5, *2800*, Building *2765*, R4.3, occupation layer

185. Lid with flattened rim (Fig 309); ?North West fine oxidised ware.
MIL 5, *2800*, Building *2765*, R4.3, occupation layer

186. Mortarium (Fig 309); Old Penrith fabric 1, with gold mica in the grit; unused; first half of the second century.
MIL 5, *2800*, Building *2765*, R4.3, occupation layer

187. Transport-vessel, perhaps a narrow-mouthed jar (Fig 309); unsourced granular mid-grey fabric with lightly burnished bands, probably from North Lincolnshire.
MIL 5, *2913*, Building *2765*, R4.3, fill of pit *2914*

188. Bowl (Fig 309); unidentified grey fabric.
MIL 5, *2913*, Building *2765*, R4.3, fill of pit *2914*

189. Large lid (Fig 309); Brampton oxidised ware.
MIL 5, *2981*, Building *2765*, R4.3, fill of possible posthole *2982*

190. Everted-rim jar (Fig 309); Brampton oxidised ware.
MIL 5, *3315*, Road *4659*, fill of roadside ditch *3014*

191. Jar, curved everted-rim (Fig 309); BB1 imitation, local type B.
MIL 5, *3315*, Road *4659*, fill of roadside ditch *3014*

192. Everted-rim jar, slightly sooted on exterior (Fig 309); Brampton oxidised ware.
MIL 5, *3015*, Road *4659*, fill of roadside ditch *3014*

193. Convex-walled dish with internal groove at wall/base junction, and internal combing on base (Fig 309); three *post-cocturam* notches, incised on the rim, presumably denote ownership (?? the third *contubernium*); residual.
MIL 5, *3015*, Road *4659*, fill of roadside ditch *3014*

194. Jar with appliqué leaves and barbotine dots; the basic outline of the leaves was probably applied, and then further shaped and incised *in situ* (Fig 310); North West fine oxidised ware; smoothed on surface.
MIL 5, *2767*, Road *4659*, road surface

195. Amphora-like transport-vessel with reeded rim, probably originally double-handled (Fig 311); Brampton oxidised fabric.
MIL 5, *2767*, Road *4659*, road surface

196. Large everted-rim jar (Fig 311); North West gritty oxidised ware, probably residual.
MIL 5, *2767*, Road *4659*, road surface

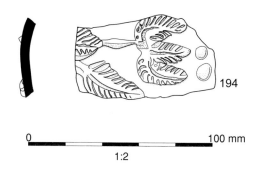

Figure 310: Fragment of jar (194) with appliqué leaves

628

197. Everted-rim jar (Fig 311); Brampton oxidised ware; burnt on tip of rim and exterior.
MIL 5, *2767*, Road *4659*, road surface

198. Reeded rim bowl (Fig 311); Brampton oxidised ware.
MIL 5, *2767*, Road *4659*, road surface

199. Convex-walled dish with trace of internal groove at wall / base junction, slight ridging on underside; smoothed on interior (Fig 311); imitation of Pompeian red ware form Fabric 782 (*cf 74/117*; *cf* Antonine Wall North African non-local fabric).
MIL 5, *2828*, Road *4659*, road surface

200. Large beaded-rim bowl (Fig 311); Brampton oxidised ware.
MIL 5, *2828*, Road *4659*, road surface

201. Possibly a local, shallower, version of Gillam 349 ('wine-cooler') (Fig 311); the beginning of the transverse (perforated) membrane is broken at the springing point from the wall of the vessel; North West gritty oxidised ware.
MIL 5, *2828*, Road *4659*, road surface

202. Flanged dish (Fig 311); Dorset BB1, with fine, acute-angled, burnished lattice. Though rarely exported to the military North, this basic type (which normally had a chamfer) has been recorded in the South West from the late first century onwards (Holbrook and Bidwell 1991, 98, South East Dorset BB1 type 44.1), and in an Antonine context at Birrens (Robertson 1975, fig 83, no 18; mis-identified as BB2); it should not be confused with the late third- and fourth-century conical flanged bowls, which never have fine acute-angled lattice burnishing. For another example see *315*.
MIL 5, *2828*, Road *4659*, road surface

203. Segmental dish, with elaborate flange, internal basal 'peak', and carefully formed foot-ring (Fig 311); very fine mid-grey fabric, with finely polished surface; the rouletting is deep and well-defined, having been executed with a proper toothed roulette-implement. The source is unknown, but the fabric texture and finish may be in a Gallo-Belgic tradition, and a source in northern *Gallia Belgica* seems most probable. Another vessel, probably from the same source (*325*; residual in Period 5B) may have constituted a matching lid, or a bowl in the same tableware set.
MIL 5, *2720*, Building *4660*, R4.1, occupation layer

204. Jar (Fig 311); Dorset BB1 (*cf* Gillam 1976, type 1, but no wavy-line under rim), heavily sooted on exterior.
MIL 5, *2721*, Building *4660*, R4.1, fill of possible scoop *2722*

205. Lid with squared-off dished rim, sooted around the tip (Fig 311); North West fine oxidised ware.
MIL 5, *2917*, Building *4660*, R4.1, possible floor

206. Jar; '*vase tronconique*', with horizontal neck burnishing (Fig 311); North Gaulish greyware.
MIL 5, *2919*, Building *4660*, R4.1, possible floor

207. Jar (Fig 311) with flattened rim and short neck (*cf 67*); North West gritty oxidised ware; residual.
MIL 5, *3149*, Building *4660*, R4.1, fill of hollow *3150*

208. Fragment of beaker or jar with leaves and stem in barbotine (Fig 311); North West semi-gritty oxidised ware; residual.
MIL 5, *3710*, Building *4660*, fill of construction trench *3217*

209. Jar (Fig 311); in mid-grey finely sandy fabric, with darker surface, not certainly local.
MIL 5, *2770*, Building *4660*, R1.1, possible make-up layer

210. Reeded-rim bowl, probably carinated (Fig 311); Brampton oxidised ware.
MIL 5, *3170*, Building *4660*, fill of construction trench *3169*

211. Segmental flanged bowl (Fig 311); North West gritty oxidised ware.
MIL 5, *3170*, Building *4660*, fill of construction trench *3169*

212. Concave-walled, lid-seated dish (Fig 311); fine burnished fabric with a reddish slip; made in the Wilderspool potteries (Hartley and Webster 1973, no 62; Hartley 1981, fig 29.1, no 11; Swan 2004 for dating); early Hadrianic; residual.
MIL 5, *3216*, Building *4660*, fill of construction trench *3215*

213. Everted-rim jar (Fig 311); North West gritty reduced ware; residual.
MIL 5, *3029*, Structure *4665*, fill of posthole *3030*

214. Lid-seated jar (Fig 311); dark grey, slightly sandy fabric with sparse white quartz, and almost black exterior; source uncertain, but possibly local.
MIL 5, *3032*, Structure *4665*, possible floor

215. Convex-walled dish, with slight faceting on exterior (Fig 311); North West fine oxidised ware.
MIL 5, *3032*, Structure *4665*, possible floor

216. Hemispherical bowl imitating samian form Dr 37, with judder-rouletting (Fig 311); Brampton oxidised ware.
MIL 5, *3032*, Structure *4665*, possible floor

217. Plain-rim, convex-wall dish, with trace of internal groove at wall/base junction, and broad band burnt on edge of rim indicating its use as a lid (Fig 311); Brampton oxidised ware.
MIL 5, *6208*, Building *5688*, R5.2, floor

218. Cooking-dish, smoothed on interior, slightly burnt on lower exterior (Fig 311); North West fine oxidised ware.
MIL 5, *6273*, Building *5688*, R5.3, occupation layer

219. Reeded-rim bowl (Fig 311); Brampton oxidised ware.
MIL 5, *6273*, Building *5688*, R5.3, occupation layer

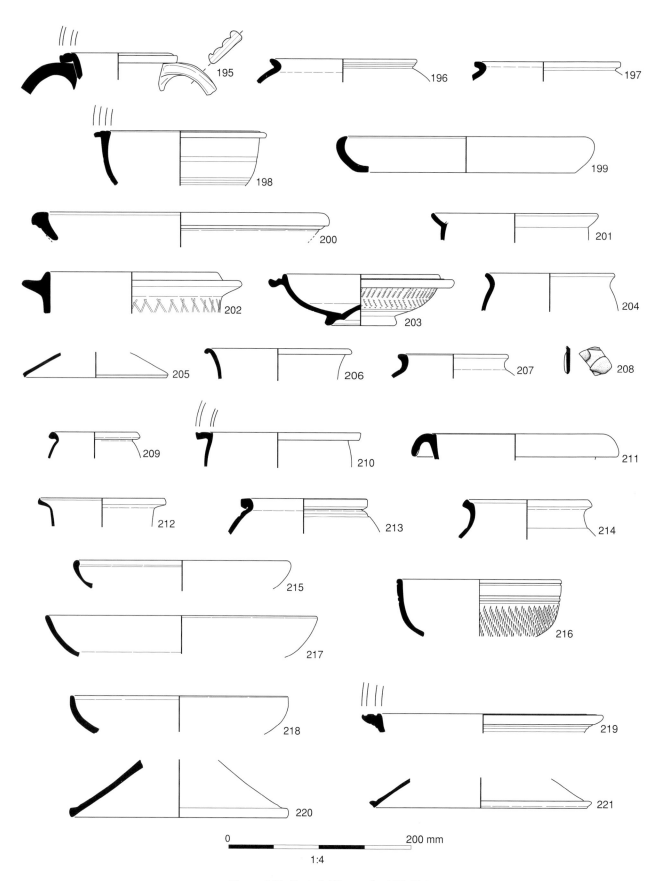

Figure 311: Period 4B vessels, 195-221

220. Lid (Fig 311); North West very gritty oxidised fabric close to Brampton oxidised ware; *cf 222*.
MIL 5, *6328*, Building *5688*, R5.1, floor

221. Lid with cut-off rim (Fig 311); North West gritty oxidised ware; rim-tip burnt and deposit on interior; *cf 222*.
MIL 5, *6328*, Building *5688*, R5.1, floor

222. Lid with cut-off rim (Fig 312); North West fine oxidised ware.
MIL 5, *6328*, Building *5688*, R5.1, floor

223. Segmental flanged bowl (Fig 312); moderately fine, slightly sandy, brownish-orange, slightly micaceous fabric, probably an import; evenly burnished on interior and exterior.
MIL 5, *6328*, Building *5688*, R5.1, floor

224. Everted-rim jar (Fig 312); North West gritty oxidised ware; residual.
MIL 5, *6328*, Building *5688*, R5.1, floor

225. Lid, reduced core, oxidised surface (Fig 312); North West gritty oxidised ware.
MIL 5, *6341*, Building *5688*, R4.5, floor

226. Plain-rim, straight-sided dish, with random burning on exterior of rim (Fig 312); North West fine oxidised ware.
MIL 5, *6312*, Building *5688*, fill of construction trench *7151*

227. Jar with rilled neck (Fig 312); North West gritty oxidised ware, *cf 125*.
MIL 5, *6293*, Building *5688*, R4.7, occupation layer; also *6183*, Building *5688*, R4.8, floor

228. Mortarium (Fig 312); Carlisle or the North West; Trajanic-Hadrianic.
MIL 5, *6314*, Building *5688*, R4.7, occupation layer

229. Amphora, Cam 186 (Fig 312); Southern Spain.
MIL 5, *6330*, Building *5688*, R5.1, occupation layer

230. Reeded-rim bowl, top of rim burnt (Fig 312); sandy North West oxidised ware.
MIL 5, *6568*, Building *5689*, fill of pit *6566*

231. Small lid with cut-off rim, possibly for a transport- or storage-vessel (Fig 312); dirty cream fabric, too burnt for recognition.
MIL 5, *6572*, Building *5689*, fill of pit *6521*

232. Lid with plain, slightly inturned rim, burnt on exterior wall (Fig 312); Brampton oxidised ware; *cf 293*.
MIL 5, *6429*, Building *5689*, occupation layer

233. Reeded-rim bowl (Fig 312); probably Brampton oxidised, but slightly finer than usual, sooted on rim.
MIL 5, *6429*, Building *5689*, occupation layer

234. Beaded-rim jar, burnished in facets on rim and shoulder, above heavily burnished lattice (Fig 312); Brampton reduced ware; probably a loose imitation of a BB1 beaker; ?Gillam 1976, types 30/32.
MIL 5, *6414*, Building *5689*, possible floor

235. Amphora, Dressel 20 (Fig 312); Southern Spain.
MIL 5, *6419*, Building *5689*, occupation layer

236. Cornice-rim beaker with pelleted clay, rough-cast decoration; diagonal wiping inside rim (Fig 312); heavily fired, grey core, brownish fabric with matt brown slip; Exeter group 1?? Argonne (Holbrook and Bidwell 1991).
MIL 5, *6419*, Building *5689*, occupation layer

237. Beaker with grooved cornice rim, clay rough-cast decoration (Fig 312); fine orange-brown fabric, with sparse small white inclusions and dark brown slightly glossy slip on exterior, and on interior of rim; source uncertain, perhaps Argonne.
MIL 5, *6280*, Building *5689*, occupation layer; also residual in *6205*, Period 4C, external layer

238. Mortarium (Fig 312); North West, local.
MIL 5, *6281*, Building *5689*, possible floor

239. Beaker with grooved cornice rim (Fig 312); orange-brown fabric, with ill-sorted white quartz and rough-casting, and a bubbly surface appearance; dark brown slip on exterior and rim (?painted on); *cf 291*; source uncertain, possibly Wilderspool.
MIL 5, *6282*, Building *5689*, hearth construction

240. Jar imitating BB1 type (Fig 312); mid-grey finely sandy, slightly micaceous fabric with black slip, applied on wheel, ending abruptly just inside rim; knife-trimming facets on shoulder.
MIL 5, *6289*, Road *7217*, fill of gully *6290*

241. Indented beaker with everted-rim (Fig 312); light brown fabric with self-coloured mica-dusted slip on exterior; import, probably from *Gallia Belgica*; *cf* Deru 1994, fig 3, no 20.
MIL 5, *6289*, Road *7217*, fill of gully *6290*; also *6424*, Building *5689*, occupation layer

242. Probable crucible (unused); base detached from wheel with cord (Fig 312); Brampton oxidised ware.
MIL 5, *6289*, Road *7217*, fill of gully *6290*

243. Jar imitating BB1 form (Fig 312); local imitation BB1 type A.
MIL 5, *6289*, Road *7217*, fill of gully *6290*

244. Jar (Fig 312); Brampton gritty reduced ware with black slip (?local BB1 imitation).
MIL 5, *6289/6401*, Road *7217*, fills of gully *6290* and robber trench *7471*

245. Jar (Fig 312); Brampton gritty reduced ware with black slip (?local BB1 imitation).
MIL 5, *6289*, Road *7217*, fill of gully *6290*

246. Bowl, loosely imitating samian form Dr 29 (Fig 312); North West fine oxidised ware; residual.
MIL 5, *6288*, Road *7217*, fill of gully *6290*

247. Dish imitating BB1 type (Fig 312); patchy burning on exterior.
MIL 5, *6288*, Road *7217*, fill of gully *6290*

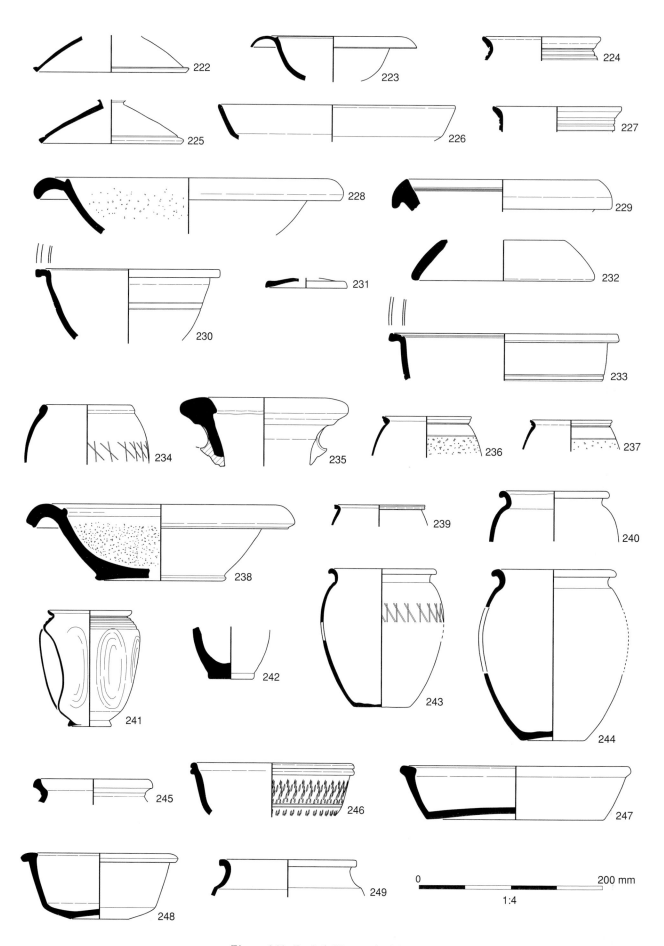

Figure 312: Period 4B vessels, 225-49

248. Bowl imitating BB1 type (Fig 312); Brampton oxidised ware.
MIL 5, *6288/6374*, Road **7217**, fills of gully *6290* and robber trench *7471*

249. Jar with concave neck, heavily sooted on exterior, and burnt (Fig 312); Brampton oxidised ware.
MIL 5, *6288/6374*, Road **7217**, fills of gully *6290* and robber trench *7471*

250. Ring-neck flagon, almost complete (Fig 313); North West gritty oxidised ware.
MIL 5, *6288/6374*, Road **7217**, fills of gully *6290* and robber trench *7471*

251. Pinched-mouth jug (Fig 313); South Western BB1.
MIL 5, *6289*, Road **7217**, fill of gully *6290*

252. Double-handled flagon (Fig 313); Brampton oxidised ware, with self-coloured slip on exterior; pale greenish-yellow deposit on lower part of interior.
MIL 5, *6374*, Road **7217**, fill of robber trench *7471*

253. Chamfered bowl with grooved rim (Fig 313); Dorset BB1, heavily sooted on exterior; Gillam 1976, type 50.
MIL 5, *6374*, Road **7217**, fill of robber trench *7471*

254. Everted-rim beaker with judder-rouletting (Fig 307); North West gritty oxidised ware, probably residual from Period 3A?
MIL 5, *5715*, Road **7479**, fill of pipe-trench *5712*

255. Large everted-rim beaker with judder-rouletting (Fig 313); North West fine oxidised ware; residual.
MIL 5, *6374*, Road **7217**, fill of robber trench *7471*

256. Flat-rimmed bowl with burnished lattice (Fig 313); Dorset BB1; Gillam 1976, type 34; early-mid-second century.
MIL 5, *6374*, Road **7217**, fill of robber trench *7471*

257. Mortarium (Fig 313); Oise/Somme Fabric 313, Bushe-Fox (1913a, 77) types 26-30, heavily worn and burnt; AD 70-150.
MIL 5, *6374*, Road **7217**, fill of robber trench *7471*

258. Jar imitating BB1 (Fig 313); local semi-fine sandy greyware burnishing on shoulder and rim, and with black slip, semi-incised lattice; heavily sooted.
MIL 5, *6374/6401*, Road **7217**, fills of robber trench *7471*

259. Pinched-mouth jug (Fig 313); local semi-fine reduced fabric, with thin black slip on exterior; the wall has bubbled and cracked in the kiln-firing and the firing is patchy; probably a local waster.
MIL 5, *6401/6288*, Road **7217**, fills of robber trench *7471* and gully *6290*

260. Jar imitating BB1 form (Fig 313); finely sandy version of North West reduced mid-grey fabric, with thick black coating on interior and exterior (worn away on underside of base); burnished immediately above lattice and on tip of rim.
MIL 5, *6401*, Road **7217**, fill of robber trench *7471*

261. Jar, imitating BB1 form, with uneven burnished lattice (Fig 313); mid-grey ??North West reduced fabric with black slip on exterior, petering out unevenly on interior of rim (type B; *cf* rim *260*).
MIL 5, *6401*, Road **7217**, fill of robber trench *7471*

262. Beaker, with dished cornice-rim, clay rough-casting on exterior and underside of base (Fig 313); light buff fabric with sparse red, black, and white inclusions, and brown colour-coat; slightly burnt on exterior; Central Gaulish (CNG CC2).
MIL 5, *6401*, Road **7217**, fill of robber trench *7471*

263. Crucible with pouring spout (Fig 313); coarse version of North West gritty oxidised ware.
MIL 5, *6401*, Road **7217**, fill of robber trench *7471*; also non-joining rim sherd, possibly from same vessel, in *6429*, Building **5689**, occupation layer

264. Plain-rim dish, probably imitating BB1 form; burnt on tip of rim (used as a lid) (Fig 313); North West gritty oxidised ware.
MIL 5, *6381*, Road **7477**, road surface

265. Pinched-mouth jug (Fig 313); Brampton gritty oxidised ware.
MIL 5, *6574*, Road **7477**, external layer

266. Large beaker with beaded rim (Fig 313); Brampton reduced ware, burnished on exterior.
MIL 5, *6418*, Road **7477**, fill of drain/channel *5920*

267. Plain-rim dish, burnished on rim and interior (Fig 313); ??North West fine oxidised ware, slightly micaceous fabric, not certainly local.
MIL 5, *6381*, Road **7477**, layer

268. Beaker, probably local (Fig 314); light-coloured fine oxidised ware with traces of very thin reddish-brown slip, judder rouletting.
MIL 5, *5909*, Road **7477**, fill of gully *5917*

269. Jar (Fig 314); local imitation BB1 type A; facet burnished on exterior and interior of rim and neck.
MIL 5, *5918*, Road **7477**, fill of drain *5925*

270. Lid, burnt on rim and exterior (Fig 314); Brampton oxidised ware.
MIL 5, *5918*, Road **7477**, fill of drain *5925*

271. Storage-jar (Fig 314); slightly sandy oxidised fabric, possibly, but not certainly, local.
MIL 5, *6000*, Road **7477**, road surface

272. Reeded-rim bowl, probably carinated (Fig 314); local oxidised ware? with brownish self-coloured slip.
MIL 5, *6000*, Road **7477**, road surface

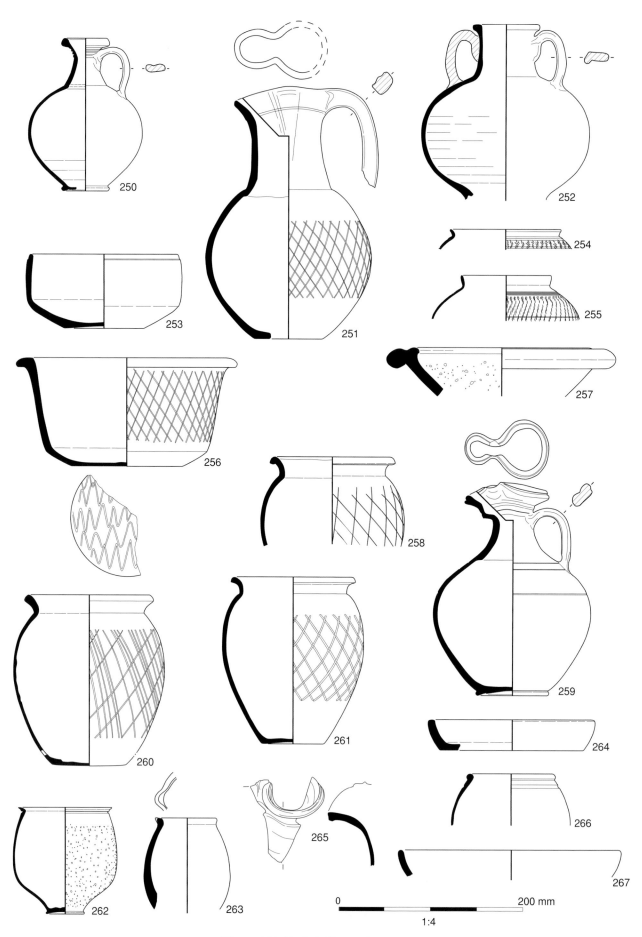

250

251

252

253

254

255

256

257

258

259

260

261

262

263

264

265

266

267

0   200 mm

1:4

Figure 313: Period 4B vessels, 250-67

634

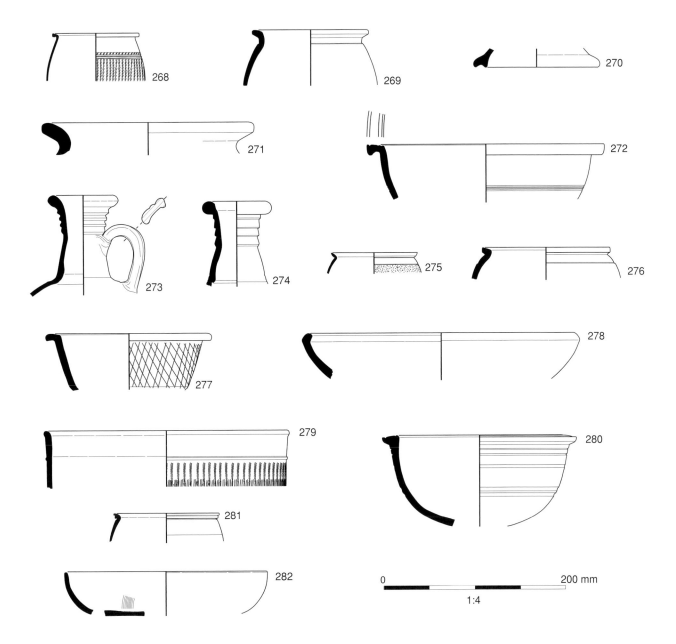

Figure 314: Period 4B vessels, 268-82

273. Ring-neck flagon (Fig 314); North West fine oxidised ware, slightly sandy with self-coloured slip.
MIL 5, *6321/6352*, Road **7477**, external layers; also residual in *6096*, Period 5B, fill of gully / hollow *6095*

274. Ring-neck flagon (Fig 314); North West fine oxidised ware, with light brown self-coloured slip.
MIL 5, *4462*, Road **7479**, fill of pipe-trench *5712*

275. Cornice-rim beaker with rough-casting of fine grit (Fig 314); hard-fired orange-brown fabric with grey core and sparse ill-sorted white and black iron-rich grits and cavities; mottled red slip on top of rim (probably painted on) and exterior; source uncertain, probably Wilderspool, or a North Western workshop such as Carlisle, working in a Wilderspool tradition; probably Hadrianic.
MIL 5, *4462*, Road **7479**, fill of pipe-trench *5712*

276. Everted-rim jar (Fig 314); Brampton oxidised ware, burnt.
MIL 5, *4462*, Road **7479**, fill of pipe-trench *5712*

277. Carinated bowl, with fine burnished lattice (Fig 314); Dorset BB1 (Gillam 1976, types 34/37).
MIL 5, *5701*, Road **7479**, road surface

278. Convex-walled dish (Fig 314); Brampton oxidised ware, burnt.
MIL 5, *5705*, Road **7479**, road surface

279. Hemispherical bowl with judder-rouletting, imitating samian form Dr 37 (Fig 314); local oxidised; residual; *cf 361*.
MIL 5, *6604*, Structure **7475**, fill of pit/posthole *6603*

280. Reeded-rim bowl (Fig 314); Brampton oxidised ware.
MIL 5, *6604*, Structure **7475**, fill of pit/posthole *6603*

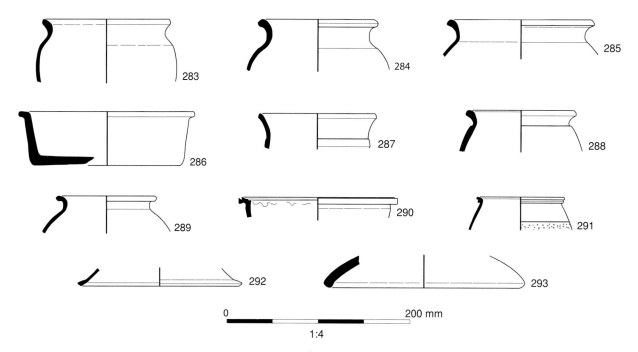

Figure 315: Period 4C vessels

281. Colour-coated beaker with grooved cornice-rim, and trace of rough-casting (Fig 314); Colchester (late) fabric.
MIL 5, *6604*, Structure **7475**, fill of pit/posthole *6603*

282. Convex-walled dish (Fig 314).
MIL 5, *6895*, Structure **7475**, fill of pit/posthole *6894*

Catalogue: Period 4C

283. Jar imitating BB1 form (Fig 315); Brampton reduced ware.
MIL 5, *2794*, Building **4660**, demolition layer

284. Jar imitating BB1 form, Gillam (1970) 122/124 (Fig 315); Brampton oxidised ware or North West oxidised sandy ware.
MIL 5, *3234*, Building **4660**, demolition layer

285. Jar imitating BB1 form, Gillam (1970) 122/124 (Fig 315); ?fine reduced local fabric with oxidised core.
MIL 5, *3234*, Building **4660**, demolition layer

286. Dish, imprecise imitation of BB1 form, Gillam (1970) 308/309; the rim is distorted and the body has hair-line cracks, suggesting a local waster (Fig 315); sandy North West fine oxidised ware.
MIL 5, *3234*, Building **4660**, demolition layer

287. Bowl with slight hint of lid-seating on interior; probably handmade (Fig 315); grey granular fabric, with ill-sorted quartz and abundant mica; burnished on rim and exterior.
MIL 5, *5998*, Building **5688**, demolition layer

288. Jar imitating BB1 form (Fig 315); local imitation BB1 type A.
MIL 5, *6258*, Building **5689**, external layer

289. Jar imitating BB1 form (Fig 315); local imitation BB1 type A.
MIL 5, *6248*, Building **5689**, external layer

290. Reeded-rim bowl, roughly-made with untrimmed surplus clay on angles (perhaps a waster; Fig 315); North West gritty oxidised ware.
MIL 5, *6175*, Building **5688**, demolition layer

291. Beaker with grooved cornice rim, with internal wipe-marks and clay rough-casting (Fig 315); fine orange-brown fabric with sparse ill-sorted white quartz inclusions, dark brown slip, with bubbly surface appearance; *cf* 239; source uncertain, possibly Argonne.
MIL 5, *6242*, Building **5689**, external layer

292. Lid with cut-off rim (Fig 315); North West fine oxidised ware.
MIL 5, *6268*, Building **5688**, fill of possible robber trench *6269*

293. Domed lid with slightly inturned rim, lightly burnt on exterior (Fig 315); Brampton oxidised ware; *cf 232*.
MIL 5, *6278*, Building **5689**, external layer

Catalogue: Period 4D

294. Flanged bowl (Fig 316); fine cream fabric of slightly speckled appearance, containing sparse, ill-sorted white and grey quartz, and red sandstone; smoothed on surface with thin self-coloured slip; possibly local.
MIL 5, *2790*, external layer; also residual in *2789*, Period 5A, fill of posthole *2788, 2806*, external layer

295. Bowl imitating samian form Dr 30, with impressed ovals imitating the style of cut-glass technique decoration (Fig 316); fine yellowish-cream fabric with thin light brown slip on exterior. Bowls with generally (but not precisely) similar decoration were made in the Nene Valley, but the fabric is normally grey and unslipped, and the detailing of the moulding is quite different, being much less prominent (Perrin 1999, fig 65, no 294); the

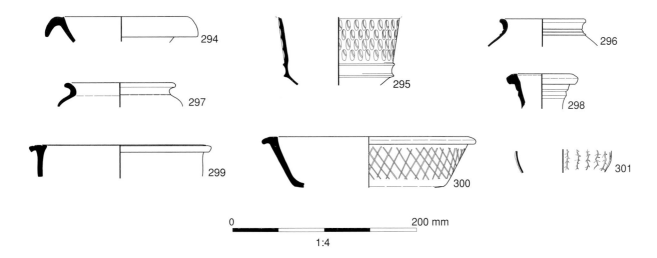

0   200 mm

1:4

Figure 316: Period 4D vessels

source of the present example is uncertain: this general style of 'cut-glass' decoration on pottery (but not the execution) also occurs at the York legionary pottery in the early Hadrianic period (*p 638*) and may represent a contemporary fashion; probably Hadrianic.

MIL 5, *2790*, external layer

296. Narrow-mouthed jar with everted-rim (Fig 316); North West gritty oxidised ware.

MIL 5, *2823*, fill of hearth *3159*

297. Jar (Fig 316); reduced local sandy-gritty ware.

MIL 5, *3163*, fill of hearth *3159*

298. Ring-neck flagon (Fig 316); North West fine oxidised ware.

MIL 5, *3214*, fill of possible construction trench *3213*

299. Reeded-rim bowl (probably carinated) with sooting on tip (Fig 316); Brampton gritty oxidised ware.

MIL 5, *3214*, fill of possible construction trench *3213*

300. Dish with burnished lattice (Fig 316); Dorset BB1 (Gillam 1976, type 57).

MIL 5, *3214*, fill of possible construction trench *3213*

301. Body-sherd of jar with linear rustication (Fig 316); North West fine oxidised ware reduced on surface; residual.

MIL 5, *3214*, fill of possible construction trench *3213*

Period 5 (second half of the second century)

Supply of locally produced vessels

Pottery from this phase includes a considerable amount of residual Brampton and North West oxidised ware (Table 28), mainly arising from the large-scale disturbance of earlier deposits. The Brampton works-depot had almost certainly shut down by this time (*p 591*), but the Fisher Street kilns continued making North West oxidised wares (particularly mortaria and flagons) into Period 5B (closing *c* AD 160-70; *p 594*). It is, however, likely that production of the close

imitations of BB1 ceased. By Periods 5C-5D, though, the evidence indicates the emergence of another producer at Carlisle. Significantly, the workshop was not located on the site of the old military pottery, but much further to the south, beyond the area of civilian occupation, at English Damside (*pp 594-5*). Production was dominated by grey burnished copies of BB1 types, but mortaria of devolved Raetian-style (with a slip on the rim) were also produced. The morphology of both the BB1 imitations and the mortaria implies a starting date towards the end of the second century. Unfortunately, the BB1 imitations are not always clearly distinguishable from other reduced burnished wares of the period, so quantification cannot be entirely reliable, but there is a distinct impression that they dominated the culinary supply of Carlisle at the end of the second century, and for at least two or three decades into the third century.

Supply of non-local vessels

There was a significant increase in the amount of BB1 reaching the site, and sources diversify, with very small quantities of Rossington Bridge BB1 present, and similarly, BB2 appears. Though the quantities are not large, the emphasis changes within the sources of the fineware beakers; the products of Cologne and Colchester are more prominent (Table 32), accompanied by small quantities of mortaria from the same workshops. Significantly, Nene Valley colour-coated wares do not arrive until the following period, and this provides additional support for the recent view that production did not start there until at least the late second century (*pers obs*).

Corbridge products are an interesting new arrival among the mortaria during Periods 5A-5C (Table 26); there seems to have been a garrison in residence at Corbridge until the early AD 180s (Bishop and Dore 1988), providing a continued market for such products. It may, therefore, be significant that they appear to be absent in the Millennium assemblage from Period 3D. From Period 5B onwards, supplies of Mancetter-Hartshill mortaria increase steadily, presaging their dominance in the third century (Table 26).

Supply of amphora-borne products
The supply of amphorae remains restricted and identical to that of the preceding phase (comprising Dressel 20 oil and Pélichet 47 wine amphorae (Table 21)).

Catalogue: Period 5
302. Jar, imitating BB1 form (Fig 317); unidentified light grey, semi-fine fabric, with silky burnish on rim and exterior, and under lattice.
MIL 1, *245*, external layer

303. Narrow-mouthed, flat-rimmed storage-jar (Fig 317); Verulamium region white ware.
MIL 1, *267*, external layer

304. Probably mortarium (Fig 317); ?North West fine oxidised ware.
MIL 1, *267*, external layer

305. Mortarium, Gillam type 238 (Fig 317); Oise-Somme.
MIL 1, *267*, external layer

306. Hemispherical bowl with rouletted zone, imitating samian form Dr 37 (Fig 317); North West fine oxidised ware with thin light brown slip.
MIL 1, *326*, external layer

307. Body-sherd of probable beaker (Fig 317); perhaps Parisian or more probably a Gallo-Belgic form related to Deru (1996) types P30/P32; residual.
MIL 1, *326*, external layer

308. Bowl with grooved rim, and wide-spaced burnished lattice (Fig 317); Dorset BB1 (Gillam 1976, type 42); *c* AD 180+.
MIL 1, *326*, external layer

309. Two body-sherds of beaker (possibly conical) with 'cut-glass'-type faceted decoration (Fig 317); York Ebor 3 fine fabric; *cf* Perrin 1990, nos 1243-5; Hadrianic, residual.
MIL 1, *326*, external layer

310. Crusey (open lamp; Fig 317); North West gritty reduced local, sooted on rim and interior. Unidentified greyware.
MIL 1, *326*, external layer

311. Flanged bowl (Fig 317); North West gritty oxidised ware, burnished on exterior, uneven patchy burning over interior and exterior; probably mid-late second century.
MIL 1, *330*, fill of pit *329*

Catalogue: Period 5A
312. Flanged bowl, imitating BB1-type bowl (Fig 318); burnished on rim and interior. Unidentified greyware.
MIL 2, *560*, external layer

313. Convex-walled dish, with internal groove at wall-base junction (Fig 318); Brampton oxidised ware.
MIL 2, *560*, external layer

314. Collared flagon (Fig 318); probably local semi-fine oxidised ware with thin cream slip on exterior.
MIL 5, *2673*, external layer

315. Flanged dish (Fig 318); Dorset BB1, with fine, acute-angled, burnished lattice. For a discussion of this type, see *202*, with which it may have arrived simultaneously, and may therefore date to the late Hadrianic period.
MIL 5, *2709*, fill of gully *2712*

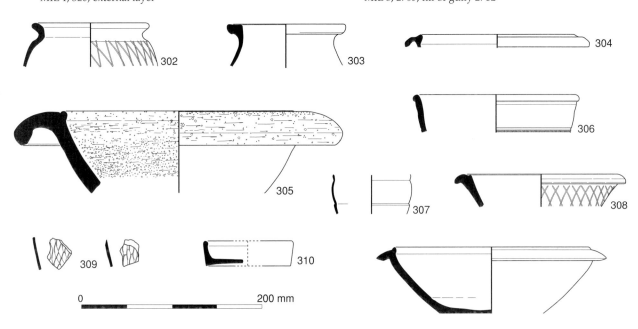

Figure 317: Period 5 vessels

638

316. Unguent flask, with roughened surface (Fig 318); North West fine oxidised ware.
MIL 5, *2782*, external layer

317. Everted-rim jar (Fig 318); Brampton, reduced gritty fabric, sooted on tip and under rim.
MIL 5, *2782*, external layer

318. Lower part of unguent flask (Fig 318); North West fine oxidised ware.
MIL 5, *2893*, external layer; also residual in *2710*, Period 5B, external surface

319. Convex-walled dish with internal grooving (Fig 318); North West fine oxidised ware, burning/sooting on interior and exterior of wall suggests its use as a lid.
MIL 5, *2955*, fill of possible posthole *2956*; also residual in *2952*, Period 5B, external layer

320. Large lid (Fig 318); Brampton oxidised ware.
MIL 5, *5997*, external layer

321. Bowl imitating BB1 dish (Fig 318); grey sandy fabric with black slip and semi-incised lattice, probably local.
MIL 5, *6229*, external layer

322. Ring-neck flagon (Fig 318); North West fine oxidised ware.
MIL 5, *6229*, external layer

Catalogue Period 5B

323. Everted-rim jar, burnt on exterior (Fig 318); Brampton oxidised ware.
MIL 2, *555*, fill of pit *567*

324. Mortarium (Fig 319); Colchester.
MIL 5, *2655*, Building *2764*, fill of posthole *2657*

325. Bowl (or possibly a lid; Fig 319); unsourced very fine, silty-textured mid-grey fabric, with polished surface, possibly an import from *Gallia Belgica*; the rouletting is deep and well-defined and will have been executed with a proper toothed roulette-implement; the vessel is in the same fabric as *203*, and may have constituted a matching lid; whether a bowl or a lid, it would almost certainly have come from the same pottery or perhaps from the same dining set; residual from Period 4A.
MIL 5, *2784*, Road *4662*, fill of possible posthole *2783*

326. Cup, probably imitating samian form Dr 33 (Fig 319); Wilderspool fine oxidised fabric; traces of red slip-painting on interior and exterior with vertical brush-marks; Hadrianic, residual.
MIL 5, *2492*, Road *4662*, external layer

327. Mortarium (Fig 319); Binchester-Catterick or Corbridge, Fabric 360/Catterick MB 16, with thick cream slip; possibly a product of Anaus; *c* AD 120-60.
MIL 5, *2492*, Road *4662*, external layer

328. Amphora, Dressel 20 (Fig 319); Southern Spain.
MIL 5, *2518*, Road *4662*, external layer

329. Mortarium, Fabric 360, from the workshop of Bellicus of Corbridge; worn, AD 160-200.
MIL 5, *2572*, Road *4662*, external layer

330. Convex-walled dish (Fig 319); Brampton oxidised ware.
MIL 5, *2624*, Road *4662*, external layer

331. Lid with flattened rim (Fig 319); North West gritty oxidised ware with thin cream slip.
MIL 5, *2628*, Road *4662*, external layer

332. Everted-rim jar, possibly a storage-jar (Fig 319); local North West grey gritty reduced ware, dark grey slip painted on

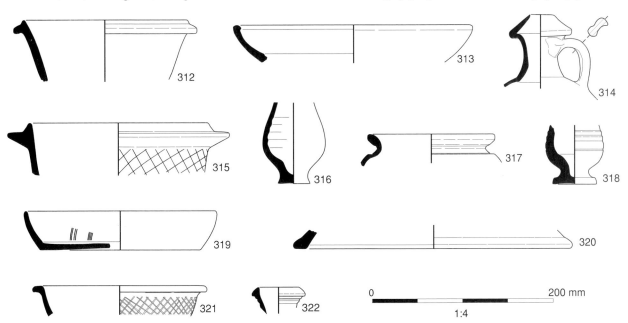

Figure 318: Period 5A vessels

639

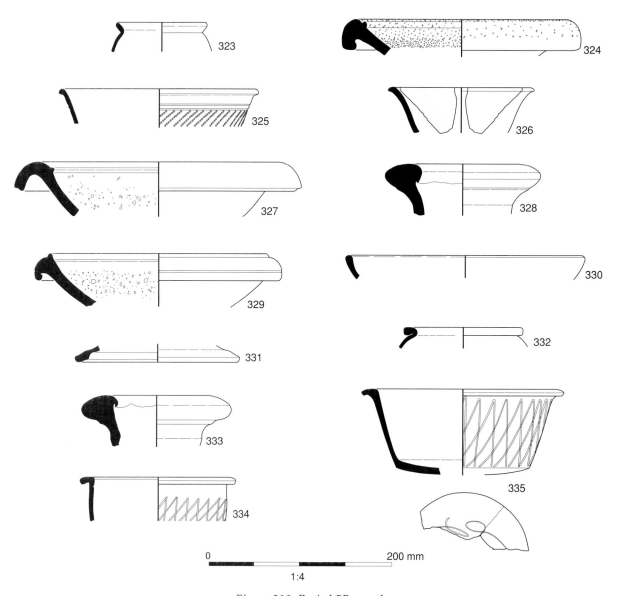

0   200 mm

1:4

Figure 319: Period 5B vessels

exterior and on interior of rim.
MIL 5, *2804*, Road **4662**, external layer

333. Amphora, Dressel 20 (Fig 319); Southern Spain.
MIL 5, *2805*, Road **4662**, road surface

334. Flat-rimmed bowl imitating BB1 type (Fig 319); local reduced
semi-fineware, black slip painted on rim and exterior.
MIL 5, *2833*, external layer

335. Bowl, with heavily burnished inverted chevron decoration
(Fig 319); Dorset BB1; *cf* Gillam 1976, type 35; there are small
notches at intervals on the underside of the rim, perhaps to
aid the setting-out of the decoration.
MIL 5, *5928*, external layer

Catalogue: Period 5C

336. Large jar (Fig 320); black granular fabric, containing abundant
coarse white quartz; similar to BB1 but wheel-thrown and
more micaceous; heavily burnished in facets on exterior;

perhaps a native North Gaulish product.
MIL 5, *2421*, Road **4662**, external layer

337. Mortarium (Fig 320), Raetian Type E (Hartley in prep a);
Fabric 308 with mixed grit; the form is unusual in having a
cream slip on the exterior; Hadrianic-Antonine.
MIL 5, *2437*, Road **4662**, road surface; also residual in *5869*,
Period 5D, external layer

338. Lamp, fragmentary, lightly sooted around the spout (Fig 320);
Loeschcke (1919) type X, with a vestigial lug and impressed
circles on the shoulder and a ring-handle (broken); the base
is flat and defined only by a distinct angle with the side-wall.
This lamp is closely paralleled by examples from a dump of
early / mid Flavian (pre-AD 85/90) samian (mainly unused
and probably from a store) and lamps, found in the legionary
fortress of York (Blake Street; Bailey 1993, fig 285, nos 2783-4).
It is in an Ebor 1 fabric and Bailey (*op cit*, 733-4) independently
suggested a York origin for this distinct lamp-group (*op cit*,
fig 285, nos 2775-84), now confirmed by evidence from wasters

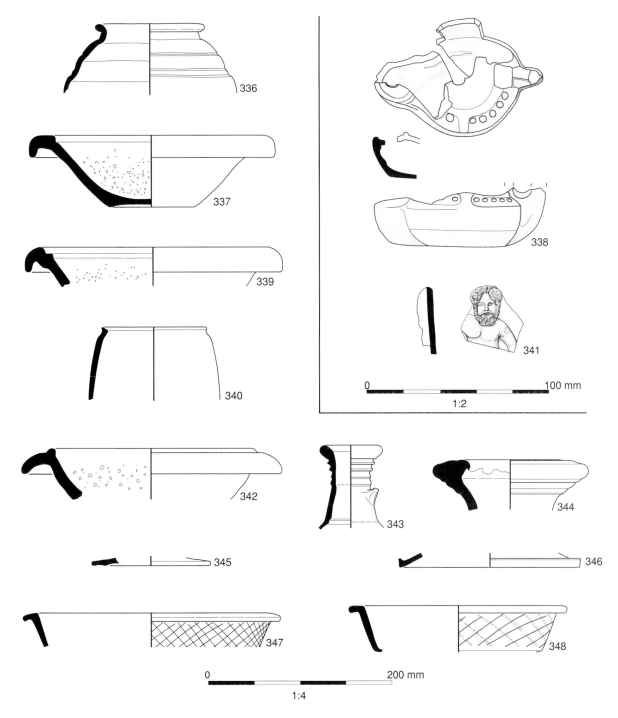

Figure 320: Period 5C vessels

found on the site of the legionary pottery in the *canabae* (Swan and McBride forthcoming). This lamp would almost certainly have reached Carlisle from York in Period 3; residual.
MIL 5, *2444*, Road *4662*, fill of drain *2550*

339. Mortarium (Fig 320). Raetian type Ch (Hartley in prep a); Fabric 301, with patches of slip; Antonine.
MIL 5, *2442*, Road *4662*, external layer

340. Jar (or water-pipe) (Fig 320); unsourced semi-fine micaceous oxidised fabric.
MIL 5, *2512*, external layer

341. Body-sherd of ?beaker or flagon, with an appliqué figure of a bearded Silenus, with moustache, lips, and slit-like eyes; the knobs on the head are most likely intended to represent bunches of grapes, and there is a hint of ?horns at the centre-top of the head (Fig 320); a local product, North West fine oxidised ware; residual, probably Period 3B.
MIL 5, *2587*, Road *4662*, fill of drain *2550*

342. Mortarium (Fig 320); Carlisle Fabric 308, with a hard-fired self-coloured slip; burnt; Antonine.
MIL 5, *2635*, fill of possible posthole *2636*

641

343. Ring-neck flagon (Fig 320); local semi-fine oxidised fabric; probably product of Fisher Street kiln; late Trajanic or early Hadrianic; residual.
MIL 5, *5825*, fill of robber trench *5824*

344. Amphora, Dressel 20 (Fig 320); Southern Spain.
MIL 5, *5958*, external layer

345. Shallow lid (Fig 320); fine brownish fabric with thin white slip on upper side; the form is similar to that used with amphorae, but the diameter is rather large; probably used for sealing a transport vessel; unsourced.
MIL 5, *5958*, external layer

346. Lid (Fig 320); probably local fine oxidised ware.
MIL 5, *5991*, Structure **7473**, fill of possible construction trench *5990*

347. Dish, with fine lattice (Fig 320); Dorset BB1 (Gillam 1976, type 58), early/mid second century.
MIL 5, *6096*, fill of gully/hollow *6095*

348. Dish with lightly executed, fine obtuse-angled lattice (Fig 320); Dorset BB1 (Gillam 1976, type 59), mid-second century.
MIL 5, *6096*, fill of gully/hollow *6095*

Catalogue: Period 5D

349. Dish with pronounced groove below rim (Fig 321); Rossington BB1 (Gillam 1976, type 69); although the burnished lattice is obtuse (and might be interpreted as mid-third century or later), the Rossington BB1 potters seem to have been less particular than the Dorset BB1 potters about

the angle of their lattice on dishes (Buckland *et al* 2001, 49, *cf* fig 40, no 33); mid-late second century.
MIL 5, *2274*, Road **4662**, external layer

350. Plain-rim dish (Fig 321); probably Rossington BB1, abraded; mid-late second century.
MIL 5, *2415*, Road **4662**, fill of drain/ditch *2409*

351. Tazza with frilled flange (Fig 321); North West gritty oxidised ware with thin cream slip; sooting on tip of rim and flange suggests its use a lid.
MIL 5, *2410*, Road **4662**, fill of ditch/drain *2409*

352. Bowl imitating BB1 type (Gillam 1976, type 41), burnished on rim, and on exterior to a short distance below rim (Fig 321); local greyware, probably from English Damside workshop; late second-early third century.
MIL 5, *2541*, Road **4662**, external layer

353. Bowl, loosely imitating BB1 type (Fig 321); North West gritty oxidised ware; patchy burning on exterior.
MIL 5, *2541*, Road **4662**, external layer

354. Lid with flattened beaded rim (Fig 321).
MIL 5, *2546*, Road **4662**, fill of hollow *2549*

355. Jar with short curved rim (Fig 321); Dorset BB1 (*cf* Gillam 1976, types 31/2); the right-angled lattice suggests that this should be dated to the late second century.
MIL 5, *2576*, external layer

356. Beaker, imitating cornice-rim type, but with simple everted-rim (Fig 321); cream fabric with pale orange-buff slip on rim

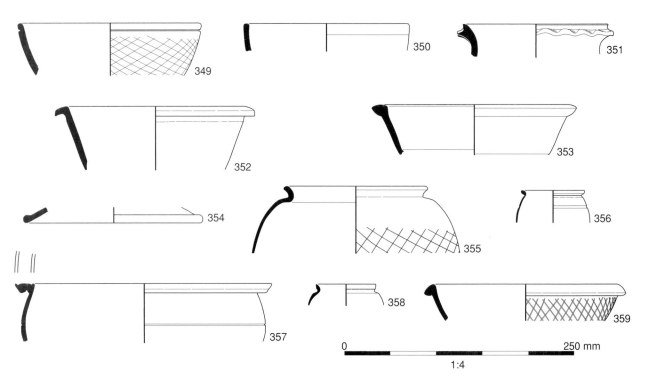

Figure 321: Period 5D vessels

and exterior; ?local North West fineware.
MIL 5, *5842*, external layer

357. Reeded-rim bowl (Fig 321); Brampton oxidised ware.
MIL 5, *5868*, external layer

358. Small everted-rim jar (Fig 321); North West gritty reduced
ware, burnished on exterior; possibly an imitation of a BB1
beaker of cooking-pot form (Gillam 1976, type 19).
MIL 5, *5967*, fill of possible gully *5969*

359. Dish with sub-triangular rim (Fig 321); a rare example of BB2
at Carlisle.
MIL 5, *5975*, external layer

Period 6A: early-late third century
Sources, supply, and acquisition: coarseware
By this time, the amount of residual material is very
large (probably at least 50% of the assemblage),
but there is clear evidence that the construction of
the new fort (*Ch 8*) heralded the major changes in
supply that can be observed at many military sites
in northern Britain (Tyers 1996). Though the English
Damside kiln site still played a significant role in
the provision of cooking wares at the beginning of
this phase (*p 595*), it is unlikely to have continued
in production after *c* AD 230/40, as there are no
imitations of BB1 flanged bowls among its products.
With its demise, the pottery supply to Carlisle lost
its individuality, and resembles that of other military
sites in northern Britain. BB1 continued to arrive
in quantity, along with minute amounts of BB2,
and allied products from South Essex/North Kent
(Table 29). These were probably outnumbered by
greyware copies, important among which were the
products of the East Yorkshire potteries (including
Norton; Table 28). It is possible that the arrival of
these greywares, early in the period, could be linked
with the presence of *Legio VI Victrix* (from the same
region), which was demonstrably involved in the
construction of the new stone fort (*Ch 8*).

The pottery dating for the construction of the fort
depends on the presence of Ebor ware vessels imitating
North African types (*364, 404, 438, 439*; also candle-stick
374), and although their numbers within the fort are
relatively low, considerable amounts have been recorded
in the extramural settlement, perhaps suggesting that
much of the accommodation for incoming troops lay
beyond the fort (Swan 1992, 24, fig 3, 48-62; Swan 2008,
19, fig 14, n 20). These vessels were manufactured in
the York legionary pottery to serve the culinary needs
of North African reinforcements drafted into *Legio
VI* to participate in Severus' campaigns in Scotland
(*c* AD 208-11; Swan 1992). At the death of Severus in
AD 211, Caracalla decided to abandon his father's
conquests and to withdraw to the Tyne-Solway frontier,
and many of these men seem to have been dispersed

to other northern military establishments, including
Carlisle (Swan 1992, fig 5.11, map).

It was not until towards the end of Period 6A (probably
in the last quarter of the third century), that Crambeck
greywares began to appear in the fort (Table 33),
occurring in only four contexts at that time. Likewise,
the occurrence of East Yorkshire calcite-gritted wares in
only four contexts (not the same ones as the Crambeck
wares) suggests that these too did not arrive until the
end of the century.

Finewares
There was a significant change in the pattern of
supply for finewares at the beginning of this period,
with the appearance of Nene Valley colour-coated
wares, which from then on dominated the supply
of finewares (Table 33). They were supplemented by
very small quantities of Central Gaulish black-coated
ware and *Moselkeramik* (residual in Period 6B), both of
which probably arrived early in the first third/half of
Period 6A. By about the AD 280s, the first Crambeck
greywares were reaching the site.

By this time, Romano-British producers were supplying
all the fine tablewares, with the possible exception of very
small quantities of *Moselkeramik*. Their range expanded
in the mid-late fourth century, perhaps reflecting the
establishment of a marketplace in the centre of the fort
(*Ch 9*). As a result, Oxfordshire red-coated tablewares
and other less distinctive red-slipped wares (including
possible Swanpool products) appear for the first time, as
do Crambeck painted Parchment wares, all apparently
sold alongside the latest Nene Valley products.

Supply of amphora-borne products
It is uncertain whether the considerable numbers of
Dressel 20 oil amphorae present at this time are all
residual, since recent research suggests that supply
may have continued well into the third century
(Williams 1997). Of particular interest is the presence
of fragments of at least one North African amphora
(probably for olive oil). Williams and Carreras
(1995) have discussed the incidence of these vessels
in Britain, and, from comparative evidence at York,
these are likely to have arrived with (or for) the North
Africans in *Legio VI*. This tends to be confirmed by
the contexts of the two sherds from the site, which
were evidently trampled into final Period 5D contexts
at the beginning of Period 6A.

Catalogue
360. Dish (Fig 322); fine York Ebor 3; early Hadrianic; residual.
MIL 1, *106*, Wall **118**, fill of construction trench *105*

361. Bowl imitating samian forms Dr 29/37, with judder-rouletting
(Fig 322); North West fine oxidised ware; Flavian, residual; *cf 279*.
MIL 1, *133*, Road **7646**, external layer

362. Amphora, or large flagon, perhaps a Gauloise 4 variant (Fig 322); Southern Gaul.
MIL 1, *234* and *240*, Road **7646**, fill of hollow *233* and fill of drain *238*

363. Mortarium (Fig 322); Corbridge fabric 360, with brown matt slip, and heavy wear; Hadrianic, residual.
MIL 1, *242*, Road **7646**, road surface

364. Lid with beaded rim (Fig 322); Ebor 1/2; North African type; Severan/Caracallan.
MIL 1, *216*, Building **1196**, fill of construction trench *173*

365. Jar, sooted on underside of rim (Fig 322); Dorset BB1; Gillam 1976, type 5; late second-early third century.
MIL 1, *259*, fill of pit *258*

366. Jar, with short rim (Fig 322); Dorset BB1; Gillam 1976, type 31, mid-second century; residual.
MIL 2, *544*, Building **669**, R2.1, possible make-up layer

367. Carinated bowl with reeded rim (Fig 322); North West gritty reduced ware (not very coarse); burning on exterior; residual.
MIL 5, *1850*, Building **2063**, fill of construction trench *1842*

368. Ring-neck flagon (Fig 322); North West fine oxidised ware; residual.
MIL 4, *1852*, Building **2063**, fill of construction trench *1842*

369. Base of jar (Fig 322); mid-grey fabric with dark grey surface, perhaps local, but abraded; the underside has been inscribed after firing with an 'X' ownership mark.
MIL 5, *2150*, Building **2302**, fill of construction trench *2297*

370. Dish, imitating BB1 type (Fig 322); fabric similar to semi-fine North West gritty oxidised ware; burnishing on interior and exterior except immediately below rim; the form and treatment suggest an English Damside product, though these are usually reduced; late second-early third century.
MIL 5, *2150*, Building **2302**, fill of construction trench *2297*; also residual in *2147*, Period 6C, fill of posthole *2146*

371. Amphora, Dressel 20 (Fig 322); Southern Spain.
MIL 5, *2177*, Building **2302**, fill of construction trench *2178*

372. Jar (Fig 322); Dorset BB1; Gillam 1976, types 7/8, early mid-third century; the profile of vessel looks towards the late second century, but the lattice, only just wider than right-angled, is among the earliest examples of obtuse-angled lattice, in this construction context of the early third century (*cf* Holbrook and Bidwell 1991, 96).
MIL 5, *2177*, Building **2302**, fill of construction trench *2178*

373. Bowl imitating form Dr 37, with judder-rouletting (Fig 322); North West gritty oxidised ware, residual.
MIL 5, *2179*, Building **2302**, fill of construction trench *2187*

374. Candlestick (Fig 322); orange fabric with thick cream slip; probably Ebor 1 ware; zone of sooting on the interior and exterior of the rim; the flange as been filed off (presumably following breakage to aid the balance of the object; probably early third century.
MIL 5, *2179*, Building **2302**, fill of construction trench *2187*

375. Bowl with grooved rim and burnished intersecting arcs (Fig 322); Dorset BB1; Gillam 1976, 42; late second to early third century.
MIL 5, *2191*, Building **2302**, fill of construction trench *2190*

376. Flanged bowl, imitating BB1 type (Fig 322); unsourced grey, slightly sandy fabric, burnished on the rim and interior; two rivet-holes suggest that the vessel had been mended; *c* AD 230/40+, and more probably at least AD 250 or later.
MIL 5, *2205*, Building **2302**, R1.1, possible floor

377. Bowl, imitating BB1 type (Fig 322); light grey English Damside fabric, burnished on rim, interior, and sporadically on exterior; late second to early third century.
MIL 5, *2273*, Building **2302**, fill of construction trench *2178*

378. Tazza with slightly frilled flange; line of burning just inside rim suggests that the vessel had been used as a lid (Fig 322); Brampton gritty oxidised ware; residual.
MIL 5, *2275*, Building **2302**, R3.1, floor

379. Dish (Fig 322); North West semi-fine oxidised ware, burnished on rim and interior; possibly English Damside product.
MIL 5, *2354*, Road **2303**, external layer

380. Flanged bowl, perhaps a loose imitation of samian form Dr 38 (Fig 322); local grey slightly sandy ware; sooted on rim and exterior and perhaps used as a lid; probably second half of second or early third century.
MIL 5, *2355*, Building **2301**, fill of construction trench *2178*

381. Bowl imitating BB1 type (*cf* Gillam 1976, type 41) (Fig 322); grey sandy fabric burnished on rim and interior and on lower part of exterior; probably English Damside product; late second to early third century.
MIL 5, *2355*, Building **2301**, fill of construction trench *2178*

382. Small globular jar, almost certainly part of a triple vase (Fig 322); North West gritty oxidised ware; residual.
MIL 5, *2355*, Building **2301**, fill of construction trench *2178*

383. Jar (Fig 322); pale grey Rossington BB1; sooted on underside of rim; mid-late second century, possibly residual.
MIL 5, *2400*, Road **2303**, road surface

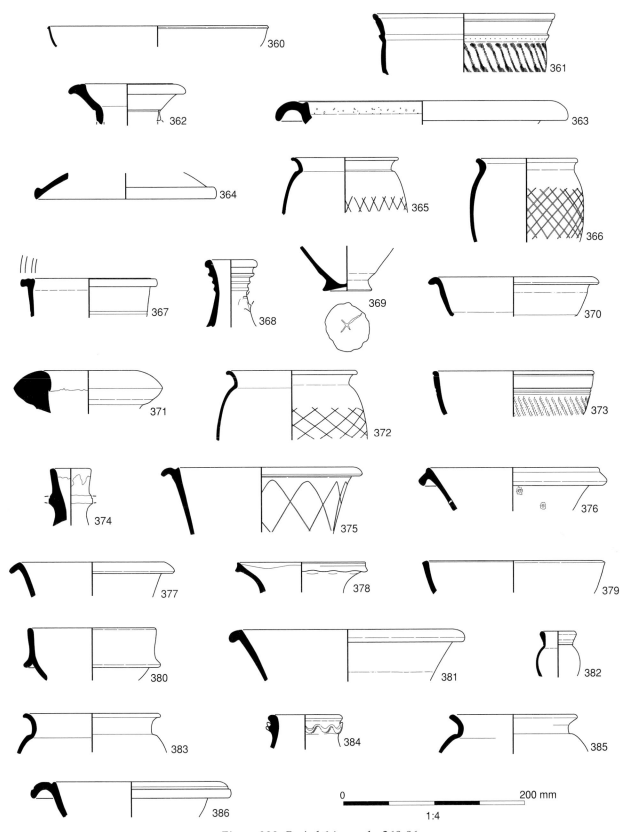

Figure 322: Period 6A vessels, 360-86

384. Narrow-mouthed jar with frilled collar (Fig 322); ?residual. MIL 5, *2400*, Road **2303**, road surface

385. Jar imitating BB1 type, with marked groove at neck/shoulder junction (Fig 322); probably East Yorkshire

greyware; third century. MIL 5, *2400*, Road **2303**, road surface

386. Mortarium or mortarium-like bowl, a multi-reeded hammer-headed form with a dished bead rim (Fig 322); Corbridge fabric

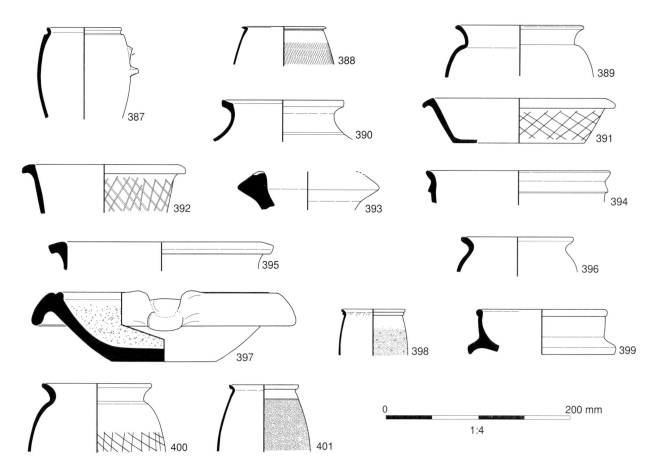

Figure 323: Period 6A vessels, 387-401

360 with cream fabric and orange slip; Hadrianic, residual.
MIL 5, *2484*, Building *2302*, R4.1, floor

387. Tankard imitating BB1 form; Gillam 1976, type 24 (Fig 323); hard-fired semi-coarse dark grey fabric, burnished on exterior and rim; possible East Yorkshire greyware (*cf* Norton Type 17).
MIL 5, *2578*, Building *2301*, R1.1, make-up layer

388. Cornice-rim colour-coated beaker with judder-rouletting (Fig 323); Cologne fabric; probably residual.
MIL 5, *2578*, Building *2301*, R1.1, make-up layer

389. Jar imitating BB1 type (Fig 323); unsourced grey semi-coarse fabric, smoothed on rim and exterior.
MIL 5, *2581*, Building *2301*, fill of construction trench *2187*

390. Narrow-mouthed, lid-seated jar (Fig 323); North West gritty oxidised ware; random burning on exterior; residual.
MIL 5, *3145*, Building *2301*, fill of construction trench *3146*

391. Dish, with burnished lattice (Fig 323); BB1; the light fabric and obtuse lattice suggest a Rossington Bridge product; mid-late second century.
MIL 5, *2365*, Building *2302*, R3, floor

392. Bowl imitating BB1 type (Fig 323); East Yorkshire greyware.
MIL 5, *2392*, Road *2303*, fill of pit/hollow *2391*

393. Amphora, ?Dressel 23 (Fig 323); Southern Spain.
MIL 5, *2690*, Road *2303*, fill of posthole *2688*

394. Bowl with collared rim and rouletted wall, probably intended to imitate samian form Dr 29 (Fig 322); North West fine oxidised ware; probably Flavian; residual.
MIL 5, *5506*, Road *7652*, road surface

395. Flat-rimmed bowl probably imitating BB1 type (Fig 323); North West gritty oxidised ware; first half of second century; residual.
MIL 5, *5503*, Road *7652*, road surface

396. Jar, generally imitating BB1 type, but with groove on tip of rim (Fig 323); Brampton gritty reduced ware, burnished on rim and exterior; Trajanic-Hadrianic; residual.
MIL 5, *5687*, Building *5200*, R2.1, make-up layer

397. Mortarium (Fig 323); Raetian Type F (Hartley in prep a); Carlisle, possibly from English Damside workshop, *cf* Fabric 301; burnished on exterior.
MIL 5, *5691*, Road *7652*, external layer

398. Beaker with grooved cornice rim and clay rough-casting (Fig 323); probably Argonne; residual.
MIL 5, *5774*, Road *7652*, fill of linear feature *5773*

399. Flanged bowl imitating samian form Dr 38 (Fig 323); hard fine, deep brownish-orange fabric with small sparse white

inclusions and brownish-orange, varnish-like slip; *cf 465*.
MIL 5, *5786*, fill of drain *5784*

400. Jar imitating BB1 type (Fig 323); local imitation BB1 type B;
Hadrianic; residual.
MIL 5, *5787*, Building *5200*, R1.1, make-up layer

401. Cornice-rim beaker, with fine dense sand rough-casting
(Fig 323); source uncertain, but likely to be Romano-British
and possibly local North West fine oxidised ware; residual.
MIL 5, *6616*, Road *7652*, fill of drain/channel *6615*

Period 6B: early-mid-fourth century
Coarsewares: sources and supply
Again, there is considerable residuality as a result of
disturbance, and a number of the vessels are burnt.
However, Dorset BB1, East Yorkshire greywares,
Crambeck greyware, and calcite-gritted wares all
continued to arrive at the site (Tables 28, 29, 33),
the last two in significantly increased quantities.
Interestingly, calcite-gritted ware is by no means as
dominant as it was in York at this period, perhaps
indicating that shipping BB1 from the South West
to Carlisle was an easier option than land-transport
for the relatively heavy cooking wares from East
Yorkshire. Dales ware jars (possibly residual)
and the handmade North Pennine gritty wares
(source unknown) also supplemented the supply
of cooking-jars.

In chronological terms, the most important
element of the assemblage during this period is
the appearance of Crambeck painted Parchment
ware (Table 33), which (following doubts raised
by evidence from Birdoswald (Hird and Perrin
1997, 236)) can now be reconfirmed as dating to
at least *c* AD 370 (Bidwell 2005). The appearance
of Crambeck painted Parchment ware in several
contexts is of importance, as this fabric was never
common on any site, and the presence of several
vessels must extend the end-date for Period 6B
from *c* AD 360 (based on coin evidence) to at least
the AD 370s. Mancetter-Hartshill products continue
to be the dominant mortaria, although there are at
least two of the early Crambeck types (first classified
at York Minster as type M6; Hartley 1995), a Nene
Valley, and a Catterick product (Table 27).

Finewares
Nene Valley colour-coated beakers continue to
dominate the finewares (Table 33), though an
Oxfordshire red-slipped bowl and a Nene Valley
Parchment ware beaker are also present. Also of
interest is the appearance of the first Nene Valley
colour-coated kitchenware form (*417*).

Supply of amphora-borne products
There are no amphorae from this phase.

Catalogue

402. Flask or narrow-mouth jar (Fig 324); Crambeck light reduced
fabric with bands of burnishing; late third century or later.
MIL 1, *167*, Road *7646*, fill of robber trench *168*

403. Jar (Fig 324); semi-fine grey fabric, burnished on rim and
exterior; possibly Crambeck.
MIL 1, *304*, Road *7646*, fill of drain *309*

404. Lid-seated, casserole-type cooking-bowl (Fig 324); unsourced,
finely sandy, micaceous, reddish-brown fabric, with grey core;
a North African type, not Ebor ware and possibly an import;
Antonine or Severan/Caracallan; residual.
MIL 1, *304*, Road *7646*, fill of drain *309*

405. Flanged bowl imitating BB1 type (Fig 324); fine burnished
Fabric 798; mid-third to fourth century.
MIL 5, *2219*, Road *2303*, R4.2, possible make-up layer

406. Bowl or dish imitating BB1 type, burnished on interior and
top of rim (Fig 324); North West gritty oxidised ware, possibly
an English Damside product.
MIL 5, *2350*, Road *2303*, road surface

407. Pinched-mouth jug (Fig 324); probably local North West grey
slightly sandy ware; abraded, residual; second century.
MIL 5, *2350*, Road *2303*, road surface

408. Jar (Fig 324); pale BB1 fabric, possibly from Rossington
workshop; *cf* Buckland *et al* 2001, fig 47, no 182; mid-late
second century; residual.
MIL 5, *2384*, Building *2301*, R1.2, floor

409. Beaker with grooved cornice rim (Fig 324); probably an
Argonne product; second century; residual.
MIL 5, *2384*, Building *2301*, R1.2 , floor

410. Bowl (Fig 324); grey semi-coarse fabric, burnished on rim and
interior, ?English Damside; late second-early third century.
MIL 5, *2399*, Road *2303*, external layer

411. Everted-rim jar (Fig 324); unsourced, mid-grey sandy fabric,
lightly burnished on rim and exterior; ?local reduced; probably
early second century; residual.
MIL 5, *2691*, Road *2303*, external layer

412. Mortarium, York Minster type 38 (Fig 324); Crambeck
Parchment ware.
MIL 5, *5319* and *5323*, Road *7652*, fill of posthole *5322*, and
road surface

413. Bowl imitating samian form Dr 38 (Fig 324); Oxford fine
red-slipped ware; abraded.
MIL 5, *5399*, Building *5200*, R3.6, possible floor

414. Plain-rim dish with grooved wall (Fig 324); Crambeck reduced
ware, G 160/1.
MIL 5, *5399*, Building *5200*, R3.6, possible floor

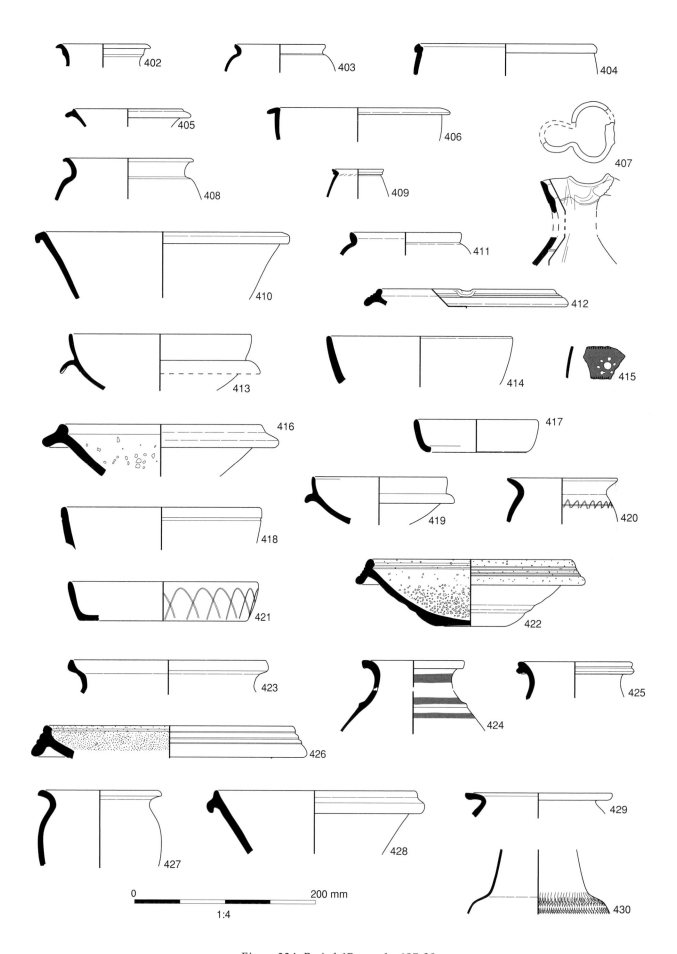

Figure 324: Period 6B vessels, 405-30

648

415. Beaker with white-painted dots centred on shallow indentation (Fig 324); Lower Nene Valley colour-coated ware.
MIL 5, *5399*, Building *5200*, R3.6, possible floor

416. Mortarium (Fig 324); Lower Nene Valley Fabric 328; concave-hammerhead form; AD 250-400.
MIL 5, *5474*, fill of pit *5530*

417. Dish (Fig 324); Lower Nene Valley colour-coated ware; late third-early fifth century.
MIL 5, *5478*, Road *7652*, road surface

418. Plain-rim dish with grooved wall (Fig 324); Crambeck reduced ware.
MIL 5, *5478*, Road *7652*, road surface

419. Bowl imitating samian form Dr 38 (Fig 324); red-slipped and burnished Crambeck ware (Corder type 5).
MIL 5, *5496*, external layer

420. Jar; the rim imitates that of BB1 jar types, but the shoulder-groove and running chevron decoration are more reminiscent of Gillam 41 (Fig 324); Crambeck reduced ware; late third century or later.
MIL 5, *5531*, fill of gully *5546*

421. Plain-rim dish with shallow intersecting-arc burnishing (Fig 324); Dorset BB1; Gillam 1976, type 80; burnished on underside; mid-late third century.
MIL 5, *5538*, external surface

422. Mortarium with reeded hammer-head rim (Fig 324); Mancetter-Hartshill.
MIL 5, *5561*, Road *7652*, road surface

423. Lid-seated bowl or wide-mouthed jar (Fig 324); North West fine oxidised ware; sooted under rim; second century; residual.
MIL 5, *5564*, fill of pit *5563*

424. Flask (Fig 324); Lower Nene Valley Parchment ware; (buff fabric, white slip, orange-brown paint; Gillam 34; partly burnt; late third-mid/late fourth century.
MIL 5, *5567*, Building *5200*, R3.4, floor; also *5690*, fill of ditch *5836*

425. Narrow-mouthed jar (Fig 324); North West fine oxidised ware; probably a local Carlisle product as there is a waster from the site; second century, residual.
MIL 5, *5570/5571*, external layer and fill of ditch *5572*

426. Mortarium (Fig 324); Catterick Fabric 500.
MIL 5, *5575*, external layer

427. Proto-Huntcliff jar (Fig 324); East Yorkshire calcite-gritted ware; sooted on underside of rim; late third century or later.
MIL 5, *5575*, external layer

428. Flanged bowl imitating BB1 type (Fig 324); Crambeck reduced ware; fourth century.
MIL 5, *5578*, external layer

429. Jar with sharply everted, elongated rim (Fig 324); North Pennine gritted ware (Fabric 799).
MIL 5, *5589*, external surface

430. Pentice-moulded beaker (Fig 324); brownish-orange fabric, with grey core and dark grey lustrous slip; ?Nene Valley colour-coated ware; late third-fourth century.
MIL 5, *5590/5638*, external surfaces

431. Mortarium (Fig 325); Lower Nene Valley Fabric 328; some burning; AD 250-400.
MIL 5, *5690*, fill of ditch *5836*

432. Conical bowl or cup with flanged rim, and sharply rilled wall (Fig 325); buff fabric with yellowish core and self-coloured slip; probably an import, but source unknown, perhaps North Africa.

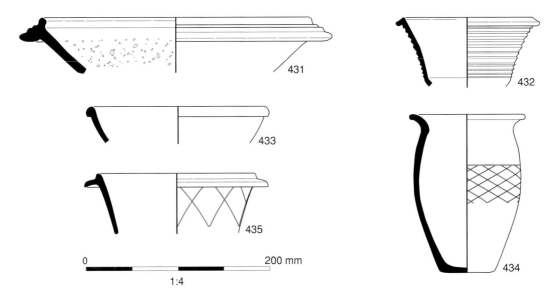

Figure 325: Period 6B vessels, 431-5

MIL 5, *5690*, fill of ditch *5836*; also residual in *5252*, Period 6E, fill of pit *5251*

433. Beaded-rim bowl imitating samian form Dr 18/31 (Fig 325); fine brownish-orange fabric with sparse ill-sorted white quartz and mid-brown varnish-like slip; source uncertain; possibly Swanpool.
MIL 5, *5726*, fill of pit *5668*

434. Jar (Fig 325); Dorset BB1 with obtuse lattice (Gillam 1976, type 11); heavily sooted on exterior, thick deposit of lime on interior; late third-early fourth century.
MIL 5, *5727*, fill of pit *5668*

435. Flanged bowl, with intersecting-arc burnishing (Fig 325); Dorset BB1; Gillam 1976, type 48; early-mid-fourth century.
MIL 5, *5727*, fill of pit *5668*

Period 6C: mid-fourth-fifth century
Coarsewares: sources and supply
There was a very large increase in calcite-gritted wares during this period, and an accompanying impression that BB1 was no longer being shipped to the North (Table 28). Small quantities of North Pennine gritty wares were also present, but it is uncertain whether they are residual. A few gritty handmade vessels might be local.

Finewares: sources, and supply and acquisition
Despite relatively little choice in the cooking wares, the finewares show considerable variety, though apart from the surprisingly common Crambeck Parchment wares, none are present in any quantity (Table 33). They are presumably among the products that were being traded in the putative market which is evidenced within the fort (Ch 9). They include not only Nene Valley beakers, and colour-coated ware culinary vessel types from the same source, but also several Oxfordshire red-slipped ware bowls (rare on the northern frontier), and Swanpool red-slipped wares, as well as rare Crambeck red-slipped wares. Crambeck mortaria monopolise the mortarium market. Chronologically, the frequency of the Crambeck Parchment wares leaves little doubt that most of this phase spans the last quarter of the fourth century and presumably runs into the fifth.

Supply of amphora-borne products
Sherds of North African amphorae occur in no less than six contexts (Table 21). These could have been associated with retail trade in the putative market, probably being opened there and their contents decanted. Their implications for continued long-distance trade are highly significant.

Spatial aspects
The distribution of the finewares and the amphorae suggests the presence of lean-to stalls along the edge of the main street (Road *7652*) in the vicinity of the *principia* (Building *5200*; *Ch 9*).

Catalogue
436. Body-sherd (Fig 326); unsourced, semi-fine, brownish-orange fabric, with sparse fine white quartz, rare fine dark reddish inclusions, and slightly rough surface; an impressed lozenge is linked to an incised line.
MIL 1, *207*, Road *7646*, fill of drain construction trench *206*

437. Mortarium of Crambeck type 7 (Fig 326); Crambeck Parchment ware.
MIL 1, *236*, Road *7646*, road surface

438. Lid (Fig 326); brownish-orange fabric with mustard-colour slipped pustular surface, probably Ebor 2; beaded rim suggests North African affinities; probably Severan/Caracallan.
MIL 2, *518*, Building *669*, R2.3, floor

439. Bowl or large jar, burnt on exterior (Fig 326); perhaps Ebor 2; residual.
MIL 2, *523*, Building *669*, R2.3, make-up layer

440. Jar copying BB1 form, unevenly burnished on exterior and top of rim (Fig 326); North West gritty oxidised ware, possibly an oxidised English Damside product.
MIL 5, *2147*, fill of posthole *2146*

441. Jar, imitating BB1 type (Fig 326); grey semi-fine fabric; burnished on rim and shoulder; black slip painted on rim and exterior; probably East Yorkshire; third-fourth century.
MIL 5, *2166*, Road *2303*, road surface

442. Jar imitating BB1 form (Fig 326); mid-grey sandy fabric lightly burnished on rim and exterior; source uncertain.
MIL 5, *2166*, Road *2303*, road surface

443. Jar imitating BB1 type (Fig 326); unsourced hard dark grey finely sandy fabric, burnished on rim and exterior.
MIL 5, *2166*, Road *2303*, road surface

444. Jar imitating BB1 type (Fig 326); unsourced, mid-grey slightly sandy fabric, with black slip on interior of rim; third-fourth century.
MIL 5, *2166*, Road *2303*, road surface

445. Jar imitating BB1 type (Fig 326); unsourced, very hard dark grey fabric, with moderate amounts of fine white quartz, burnished on rim and exterior.
MIL 5, *2166*, Road *2303*, road surface

446. Dish imitating BB1 type (Fig 326); unsourced, sandy mid-grey fabric, burnished on interior and exterior.
MIL 5, *2166*, Road *2303*, road surface

447. Dish or bowl imitating BB1 type (Fig 326); mid-grey, semi-fine fabric, with silky burnishing on rim and interior; probably English Damside product.
MIL 5, *2166*, Road *2303*, road surface

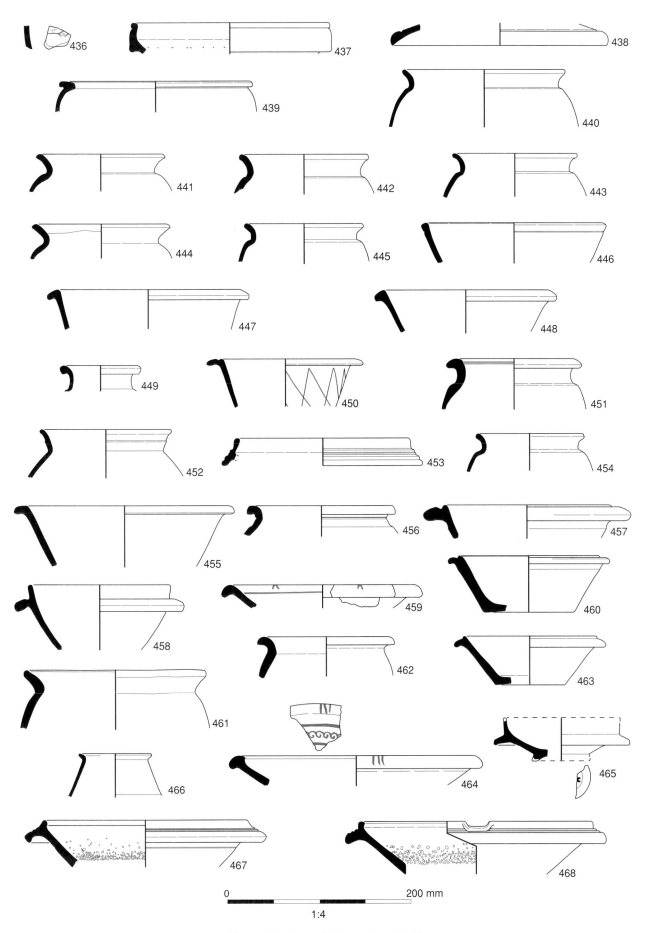

436 437 438 439 440 441 442 443 444 445 446 447 448 449 450 451 452 453 454 455 456 457 458 459 460 461 462 463 464 465 466 467 468

0   200 mm

1:4

Figure 326: Period 6C vessels, 436-68

651

448. Bowl imitating BB1 type (Fig 326); mid-grey, semi-fine fabric, with light grey exterior, silky burnishing on rim and interior; probably English Damside product.
MIL 5, *2166*, Road *2303*, road surface

449. Narrow-mouthed jar (Fig 326); unsourced, fairly micaceous, finely sandy, dark grey fabric, with narrow bands of burnishing; probably East Yorkshire.
MIL 5, *2186*, Building *2301*, clay sealing layer

450. Bowl with grooved rim (Fig 326); Dorset BB1; as Gillam 1976, type 42, late second-early third century, but with inverted chevron decoration.
MIL 5, *2186*, Building *2301*, clay sealing layer

451. Jar, copying a Huntcliff-type cooking-pot (Gillam 18) (Fig 326); non-calcitic fabric; handmade, the fabric is micaceous, dark grey, granular with abundant quartz; possibly a local or North Pennine origin; *c* AD 360 or later.
MIL 5, *2228*, external layer

452. Jar with grooved, almost upright rim (Fig 326); hard-fired mid-grey fabric with brown-grey core, probably East Yorkshire greyware.
MIL 5, *2238*, Road *2303*, fill of gully/slot *2271*

453. Mortarium (Fig 326) imitating York Minster type M66 in Crambeck reduced grey fabric.
MIL 5, *2307*, Building *2302*, fill of slot *2308*

454. Jar imitating BB1 type (Fig 326); grey semi-coarse fabric, burnished on exterior of body and interior of rim; source unknown.
MIL 5, *2377*, Road *2303*, fill of pit/hollow *2376*

455. Bowl (Fig 326); semi-coarse, mid-grey, burnished on rim, interior, and lower part of exterior, probably English Damside product; burnt on exterior.
MIL 5, *2407*, Road *2303*, external layer

456. Jar, with undercut rim (Fig 326); hard grey burnished fabric, probably East Yorkshire greyware, perhaps from Throlam.
MIL 5, *5235*, external surface

457. Flanged bowl (Fig 326); Nene Valley colour-coated ware; fourth century.
MIL 5, *5286* external surface; also *5410*, Road *7652*, road surface

458. Bowl, imitating (approximately) samian form Dr 38 (Fig 326); Crambeck reduced fabric; fourth century.
MIL 5, *5286*, external surface

459. Dish (Fig 326); Crambeck Parchment ware, with light orange-red painted decoration; burnt and abraded Corder 10; Evans (1989, 53) dec E:015.
MIL 5, *5310*, Road *7652*, road surface

460. Flanged bowl, probably approximately imitating BB1 third-century type, but with extra grooves on rim and flange (Fig 326); grey semi-coarse fine fabric, burnished overall except under the flange.
MIL 5, *5310*, Road *7652*, road surface

461. Lid-seated handmade jar (Fig 326); North Pennine gritty ware; abraded.
MIL 5, *5372*, Building *7651*, fill of pit *5378*

462. Proto-Huntcliff-type jar (Fig 326); East Yorkshire calcite-gritted ware; end of third-mid-fourth century.
MIL 5, *5383*, Building *5200*, R3.7, make-up layer

463. Flanged bowl imitating BB1 type (Fig 326); East Yorkshire greyware; mid-third-fourth century.
MIL 5, *5380*, Building *5200*, R3.7, make-up layer

464. Segmental bowl (Fig 326); Crambeck Parchment ware, with brownish-red painted scroll and line decoration.
MIL 5, *5380*, Building *5200*, R3.7, make-up layer

465. Flanged bowl, a shallow imitation of samian form Dr 38 with traces of a barbotine arc on tip of rim (Fig 326); hard, fine, deep brownish-orange fabric with small sparse white inclusions and with brownish-orange, varnish-like slip; probably Swanpool; *cf* Darling 1977, no 33; probably late fourth century.
MIL 5, *5333*, Building *5200*, R5.2, floor

466. Funnel-mouth beaker (Fig 326); Lower Nene Valley colour-coated ware.
MIL 5, *5334*, Building *5200*, R5.2, make-up layer

467. Mortarium, York Minster type 35 (Fig 326); Crambeck Parchment ware.
MIL 5, *5377*, Structure *7651*, fill of pit *5378*

468. Mortarium, Crambeck type 6d, *cf* York Minster type 38 (Fig 326); Crambeck Parchment ware.
MIL 5, *5377*, Structure *7651*, fill of pit *5378*

469. Mortarium; the profile is close to that of a late BB1 flanged bowl, but the slight in-turn/groove just inside the rim is a mortarium characteristic; abraded and worn, only a few black grits and pitting survive on the interior (Fig 327); Nene Valley colour-coated ware, probably late third-mid/late fourth century.
MIL 5, *5401*, external layer

470. Plain-rim dish (Fig 327); coarse East Yorkshire reduced ware; heavily sooted on exterior and abraded.
MIL 5, *5401*, external layer

471. Mortarium, Crambeck type 6d, *cf* York Minster type 39 (Fig 327); Crambeck Parchment ware.
MIL 5, *5404*, Structure *7651*, fill of pit *5378*

472. Dish (Fig 327); East Yorkshire calcite-gritted ware.
MIL 5, *5404*, Structure *7651*, fill of pit *5378*

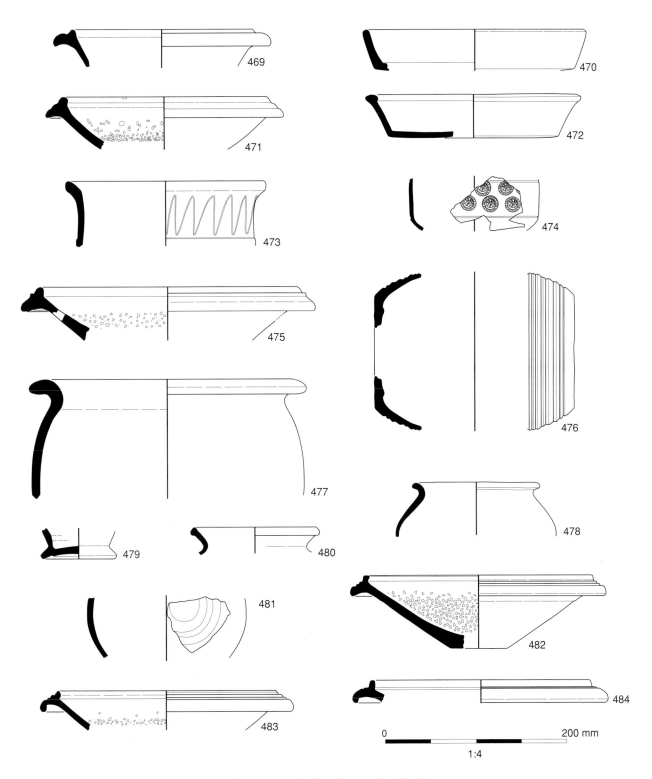

Figure 327: Period 6C vessels, 469-84

473. Everted-rim bowl (probably carinated) with running chevron burnishing on exterior wall and area of burnishing on rim and interior (Fig 327); mid-grey, moderately granular fabric, with moderate amounts of ill-sorted white and grey quartz and mica; source unknown; probably early-mid-second century, residual.
MIL 5, *5408*, Structure **7662**, fill of foundation trench *5409*

474. Wall-sided bowl (Fig 327); Oxfordshire fine red-slipped ware, with an impressed stamp not previously recorded, perhaps representing a spoked wagon wheel; *c* AD 340 or later.
MIL 5, *5410*, Road **7652**, road surface

475. Mortarium (Fig 327); Crambeck fabric 322, Corder type 6B, York Minster M32; burnt; AD 280-400.
MIL 5, *5410*, Road **7652**, road surface

476. Barrel-like costrel with rough combing and surplus clay on the flat end (Fig 327); North West gritty oxidised ware; much abraded, residual; probably late first or second century. This was probably a rare form in Carlisle's local military repertoire and not an import like those recorded on the Antonine Wall (Swan 1999), which have a different fabric.
MIL 5, *2192*, Period 6C, Building *2301*, clay sealing layer

477. Large proto-Huntcliff jar (Fig 327); East Yorkshire calcite-gritted ware.
MIL 5, *5413*, Building *5200*, R3.7, fill of pit *5412*

478. Proto-Huntcliff-type jar (Gillam 159) (Fig 327); East Yorkshire calcite-gritted ware; late third-mid-fourth century.
MIL 5, *5435*, Structure *7651*, occupation layer

479. Base of beaker (or a flagon; Fig 327); Lower Nene Valley colour-coated ware; this is a late base-form, probably mid-late fourth century.
MIL 5, *5440*, Building *5200*, make-up layer

480. Lid-seated jar (Gillam 158) (Fig 327); North Pennine gritty ware, Fabric 799.
MIL 5, *5494*, Structure *7651*, possible floor

481. Globular jar or flask, with deeply burnished concentric circles (Fig 327); ?Crambeck reduced ware; no parallels known.
MIL 5, *5494*, Structure *7651*, possible floor

482. Mortarium (Fig 327); Crambeck Fabric 322, variant of York Minster type M6; some burning; fourth century.
MIL 5, *5450*, external surface

483. Mortarium (Fig 327); Crambeck Fabric 322; Corder type 6 variant, York Minster M35/37 burnt; fourth century.
MIL 5, *5443/5494*, Structure *7651*, possible floor

484. Mortarium (Fig 327); Crambeck Fabric 322; Corder type 6 variant, burnt; fourth century.
MIL 5, *5404*, Structure *7651*, fill of pit *5378*

Period 6D: end of fourth-fifth century
These deposits were limited, and much of the pottery would have been residual.

Catalogue
485. Flanged bowl imitating BB1 form, burnished on rim and interior (Fig 328); East Yorkshire Greyware.
MIL 2, *512*, Building *669*, demolition layer

486. Jar with constricted girth (Fig 328); fine sandy, mid-grey fabric loaded with silver mica. The fabric and use of a girth constriction suggest a source in Suffolk, perhaps Wattisfield (Rogerson 1977, fig 76, no 73); residual, probably Trajanic-Hadrianic.
MIL 5, *2114*, Building *2301*, fill of robber trench *2113*

487. Bowl, with hooked-over rim loosely imitating BB1 type (Fig 328); mid-grey, semi-coarse, burnished fabric (Fabric 791), probable English Damside product; late second–early third century.
MIL 5, *2140*, Building *2301*, demolition layer

488. Bowl with burnished lattice (Fig 328); Dorset BB1, abraded; Gillam 1976, type 39/41, late second century.
MIL 5, *2154*, Building *2302*, fill of pit/robber trench *2153*

489. Mortarium (Fig 328); Mancetter-Hartshill fabric 324; the thin wall, small size, and neat rim all point to a fourth-century date, perhaps as late as the middle of the century; this will have been one of the latest mortaria to reach the site from this source.
MIL 5, *2161*, Road *2303*, demolition layer

490. Bowl imitating BB1 type (Fig 328); mid-grey, semi-fine fabric, with silky burnishing on rim and interior, and in random bands on exterior; probably English Damside product.
MIL 5, *2162*, Road *2303*, demolition layer

491. Flagon with under-cut rim (Fig 328); unsourced semi-fine, very hard orange-brown fabric with thick grey core.
MIL 5, *2165*, Road *2303*, demolition layer

492. Bowl/dish probably imitating BB1 (Fig 328); North West gritty oxidised ware; second century, residual.
MIL 5, *2185*, Building *2301*, demolition layer

493. Beaker or flagon (Fig 328); Nene Valley colour-coated ware, with white-painted vegetable or scroll decoration.
MIL 5, *2185*, Building *2301*, demolition layer

494. Jar with semi-hooked rim and slight shoulder (Fig 328); East Yorkshire calcite-gritted ware, proto-Huntcliff type; Gillam 160, probably early-mid-fourth century.
MIL 5, *2204*, Building *2302*, demolition layer

495. Dish (Fig 328); light grey burnished granular fabric; East Yorkshire greyware; Norton 1a.
MIL 5, *2204*, Building *2302*, demolition layer

496. Flask or narrow-mouthed jar with beaded rim (Fig 328); burnished; probably East Yorkshire greyware.
MIL 5, *2216*, Building *2302*, demolition layer

497. Flanged bowl imitating BB1 type (Fig 328); fine burnished, Fabric 798.
MIL 5, *2216*, Building *2302*, demolition layer

498. Flanged bowl with burnished intersecting-arc decoration (Fig 328); Dorset BB1; Gillam 1976, type 48/9; fourth century.
MIL 5, *2216*, Building *2302*, demolition layer

499. Handmade jar (Fig 328); light grey North Pennine gritty ware, *cf* Gillam 158.
MIL 5, *2216*, Building *2302*, demolition layer

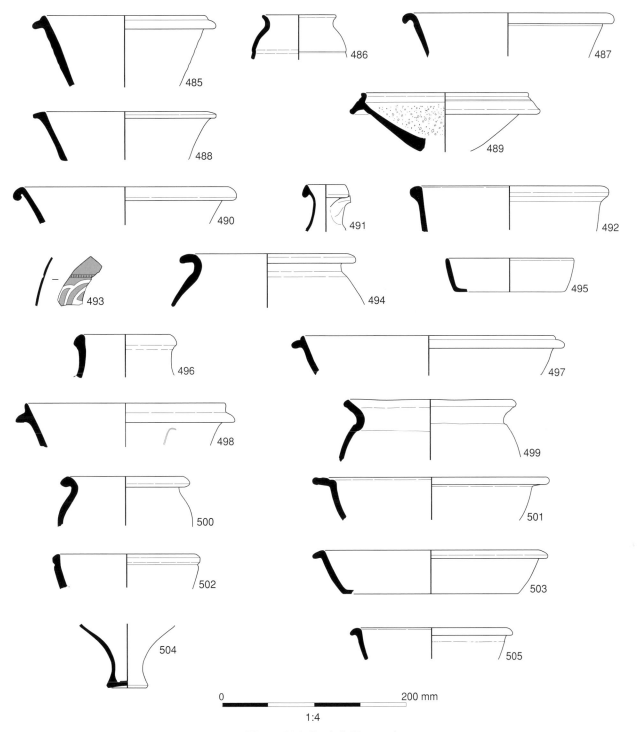

485

486

487

488

489

490

491

492

493

494

495

496

497

498

499

500

501

502

503

504

505

0   200 mm

1:4

Figure 328: Period 6D vessels

500. Jar, proto-Huntcliff type (Fig 328); East Yorkshire calcite-gritted ware; Gillam 158, late third-mid-fourth century. MIL 5, *2216*, Building *2302*, demolition layer

501. Bowl with reeded rim (Fig 328); probably North West fine oxidised ware, but the rim form is unusual. MIL 5, *2216*, Building *2302*, demolition layer

502. Dish imitating BB1 type (Fig 328); probably abraded East Yorkshire greyware. MIL 5, *2230*, Building *2302*, demolition layer

503. Bowl imitating BB1 type (Fig 328); light grey English Damside fabric, burnished on rim, interior, and lower part of exterior; abraded; late second-early third century; residual. MIL 5, *2286*, Road *2303*, demolition layer

504. Base of beaker (Fig 328); Nene Valley colour-coated ware, a late form lacking any foot-ring; possibly mid-fourth century. MIL 5, *2313*, Building *2302*, fill of robber trench *2312*

505. Dish, imitating BB1 type (Fig 328); grey semi-coarse, burnishing on interior and exterior, except immediately below rim, English

Damside product; late second-early third century, residual.
MIL 5, *2313*, Building **2302**, fill of robber trench *2312*

Period 6E: fifth century
All the material in this deposit is residual and much has derived from the disturbance of deposits connected with Period 6C, including amphorae.

Catalogue

506. Large jar or bowl (Fig 329); East Yorkshire calcite-gritted ware; fourth century.
MIL 5, *2134*, Building **2302**, possible floor

507. Flanged bowl with internal burnished wavy line (Fig 329); Crambeck reduced ware; AD 350/60 or later.
MIL 5, *2134*, Building **2302**, possible floor

508. Bowl, imitating BB1 type (Fig 329); light grey English Damside fabric, burnished on rim and interior; abraded; late second-early third century; residual.
MIL 5, *2263*, Road **7652**, fill of robber trench *2264*

509. Jar with slightly beaded upright rim (Fig 329); hard mid-grey fabric, burnished on rim and exterior; ? East Yorkshire greyware, perhaps a later version of Norton type 4b; third century, residual.
MIL 5, *2280*, Road **2303**, fill of gully *2279*

510. Indented beaker (Fig 329); East Yorkshire greyware; *cf* Norton type 9; early third century; residual.
MIL 5, *2280*, Road **2303**, fill of gully *2279*

511. Flanged bowl (Fig 329); Crambeck reduced ware; late third-fourth century.
MIL 5, *2287*, Road **2303**, fill of pit *2285*

512. Straight-sided dish loosely imitating BB1 type, abraded but traces of burnish on lower exterior (Fig 329); North West fine oxidised ware.
MIL 5, *2287*, Road **2303**, fill of pit *2285*

513. Funnel-mouthed beaker with flattened beaded rim (Fig 329); very hard, dark grey fabric with lustrous (almost vitrified) grey-buff colour-coat; source uncertain, possibly New Forest.
MIL 5, *2164*, Road **2303**, fill of pit *2285*

514. Jar, proto-Huntcliff type (Fig 329); East Yorkshire calcite-gritted ware; Gillam 161.
MIL 5, *2290*, Road **2303**, fill of pit *2285*

515. Huntcliff-type jar (Fig 329); East Yorkshire calcite-gritted ware; mid-late fourth century.
MIL 5, *5306*, Road **7652**, fill of robber trench *7650*

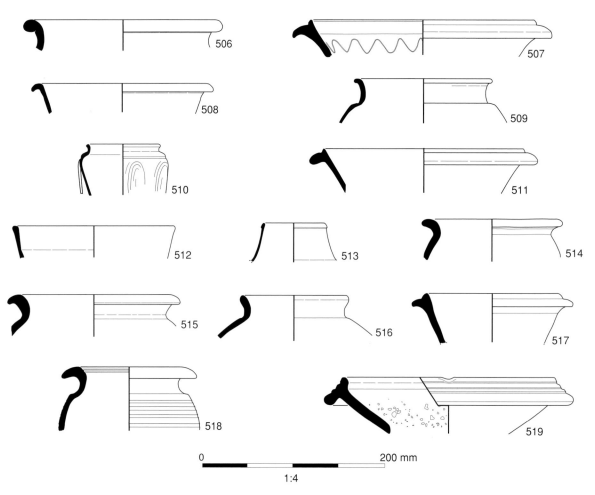

0   200 mm

1:4

Figure 329: Period 6E vessels

656

516. Jar (Fig 329); East Yorkshire greyware; probably residual.
MIL 5, *5306*, Road **7652**, fill of robber trench *7650*

517. Flanged bowl imitating BB1 type (Fig 329); Nene Valley colour-coated ware; fourth century.
MIL 5, *5306*, Road **7652**, fill of robber trench *7650*

518. Huntcliff-type jar (Gillam 163) with double-grooved lid seating (Fig 329); East Yorkshire calcite-gritted ware; *c* AD 360 or later.
MIL 5, *5349*, fill of posthole/hollow *5350*

519. Mortarium (Fig 329); Catterick fabric MB12 (Hartley 2002a, 357), with cream slip on rim and upper internal sides; matt slip on outside; AD 250-400.
MIL 5, *5382*, fill of pit 5381

Period 7: post-Roman 'dark earths'

Whilst most of the pottery is residual, the emphasis on painted decoration in the mortaria gives the material a chronologically later flavour than that of Period 6C, suggesting activity and even new supplies of pottery even as occupation inside the fort declined.

Catalogue

520. Mortarium (Fig 330); Mancetter-Hartshill multi-reeded hammerhead rim, Fabric 324; second half of third century, residual.
MIL 5, *2105*; post-Roman 'dark earth'

521. Narrow-mouthed jar (Fig 330); East Yorkshire greyware.
MIL 5, *2105*, post-Roman 'dark earth'

522. Jar with rim rolled over internally (Fig 330); North Pennine gritty ware (Fabric 799); late third-fourth century.
MIL 5, *2105*, post-Roman 'dark earth'

523. Reeded-rim bowl (Fig 330); semi-fine mid-grey fabric; ?local reduced; late first-mid-second century; residual.
MIL 5, *2105*, post-Roman 'dark earth'

524. Bowl imitating samian form Dr 38 (Fig 330); Crambeck oxidised ware.
MIL 5, *2110*, post-Roman 'dark earth'

525. Domed lid with beaded rim; North African type (Fig 330); light orange-brown fabric with grey core and thick smooth light orange-brown slip; source uncertain, perhaps an Antonine Wall (?Bar Hill) product or ?Ebor ware; mid-second or early third century; residual.
MIL 5, *2110*, post-Roman 'dark earth'

526. Mortarium, Crambeck type 6c (Fig 330); Crambeck Parchment ware.
MIL 5, *2110*, post-Roman 'dark earth'

527. Bowl probably imitating BB1 type (Fig 330); North West gritty oxidised ware; probably early-mid-second

century; residual.
MIL 5, *2115*, post-Roman 'dark earth'

528. Bowl (Fig 330); Blaxton or Doncaster region.
MIL 5, *2119*, post-Roman 'dark earth'

529. Bowl (Fig 330); Crambeck reduced ware.
MIL 5, *2112*, post-Roman 'dark earth'

530. Narrow-mouthed jar; with bi-lobed rim (Fig 330); North West fine oxidised ware; local product; late first- early second century; residual.
MIL 5, *2112*, post-Roman 'dark earth'

531. Narrow-mouthed jar (Fig 330), a mostly reduced, over-fired and distorted waster (with sagging neck and warped rim); local form that is normally found in North West fine oxidised ware, Hadrianic; residual.
MIL 5, *2112*, post-Roman 'dark earth'

532. Jar, imitating Huntcliff-type cooking-pot (Fig 330); mid-grey sandy fabric, probably East Yorkshire; mid-fourth century or later.
MIL 5, *2112*, post-Roman 'dark earth'

533. Bowl (Fig 330); Crambeck reduced ware.
MIL 5, *2120*, post-Roman 'dark earth'

534. Bowl (Fig 330); Crambeck reduced ware.
MIL 5, *2120*, post-Roman 'dark earth'

535. Jar (Fig 330); East Yorkshire calcite-gritted ware.
MIL 5, *2120*, post-Roman 'dark earth'

536. Lid of North African form (Fig 330); York Ebor 2; tip of rim is burnt; early third century.
MIL 5, *2227*, post-Roman 'dark earth'

537. Funnel-mouthed beaker (Fig 330); Crambeck reduced ware, heavily burnished on exterior; *cf* Corder 12; probably mid-late fourth century.
MIL 5, *2227*, post-Roman 'dark earth'

538. Mortarium, Crambeck type 7 (Fig 330); Crambeck Parchment ware.
MIL 5, *2117*, post-Roman 'dark earth'

539. Mortarium, Crambeck type 8 (Fig 330); Crambeck Parchment ware.
MIL 5, *2117*, post-Roman 'dark earth'

540. Lid-seated flagon with bifid rim (Fig 330); probable reduced local fabric, perhaps an English Damside product; Gillam 16; late second- early third century; residual.
MIL 5, *5259*, post-Roman 'dark earth'

541. Transport-vessel or storage jar, perhaps a larger version of Gillam type 7 (Fig 330); North West gritty oxidised ware; late

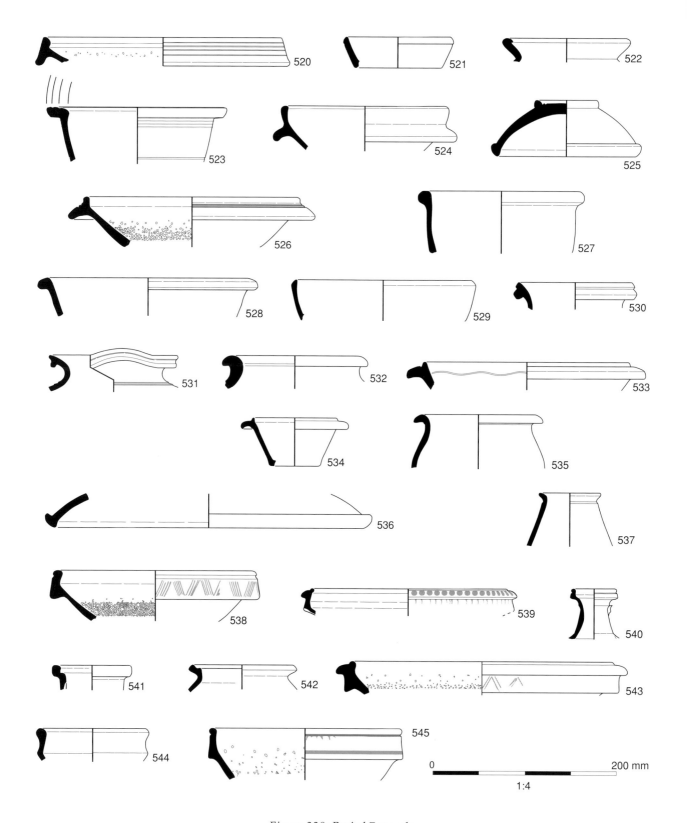

Figure 330: Period 7 vessels

first-early second century; residual.
MIL 5, *5276*, post-Roman 'dark earth'

542. Lid-seated jar (Fig 330); shell-gritted fabric; Dales-related/
devolved; similar to Swanpool/Rookery Lane, perhaps from
North Lincolnshire.
MIL 5, *5296*, post-Roman 'dark earth'

543. Mortarium, Crambeck type 8 (Fig 330); Crambeck Parchment
ware.
MIL 5, *5296*, post-Roman 'dark earth'

544. Concave-walled bowl (Fig 330); possibly local reduced ware;
late first-early second century.
MIL 5, *5304*, post-Roman 'dark earth'

545. Mortarium, Crambeck type 7 (Fig 330); Crambeck Parchment ware.

MIL 5, *5305*, post-Roman 'dark earth'

Periods 8 and 9: medieval and post-medieval
Catalogue: Period 8

546. Dish imitating BB1 type; burnished overall except for band below rim (Fig 331); local reduced ware, probably English Damside; late second-early third century.

MIL 1, *203*, Period 8A/B, fill of construction trench *150*

547. Handmade jar with roughly flattened rim (Fig 329); granular black fabric with abundant coarse black quartz and grog (Fabric 801); the rim may ultimately imitate (very approximately) that of Dales-type jars.

MIL 5, *5375*, Period 8A, Road **7654**, fill of pit *5376*

548. Reeded-rim bowl (Fig 331); Brampton oxidised ware; partly burnt; probably Trajanic-early Hadrianic.

MIL 5, *5257/5258*, Period 8A, cut and fill of posthole *5258*

549. Tankard, handmade (Fig 331); East Yorkshire calcite-gritted ware; late fourth century.

MIL 5, *5288*, Period 8A, external layer

550. Mortarium (Fig 331), variant of Crambeck type 6, *cf* Catterick type M43 (Hartley 2002b, 385, 387).

MIL 5, *5102*, Period 8C, external layer

551. Body sherd of probable funnel-mouth beaker (Fig 331); Lower Nene Valley ware, with brush-painted white slip lettering on shoulder. In the past, it has been assumed (*eg* RIB II.6, 89; Collingwood and Wright 1994) that lettering

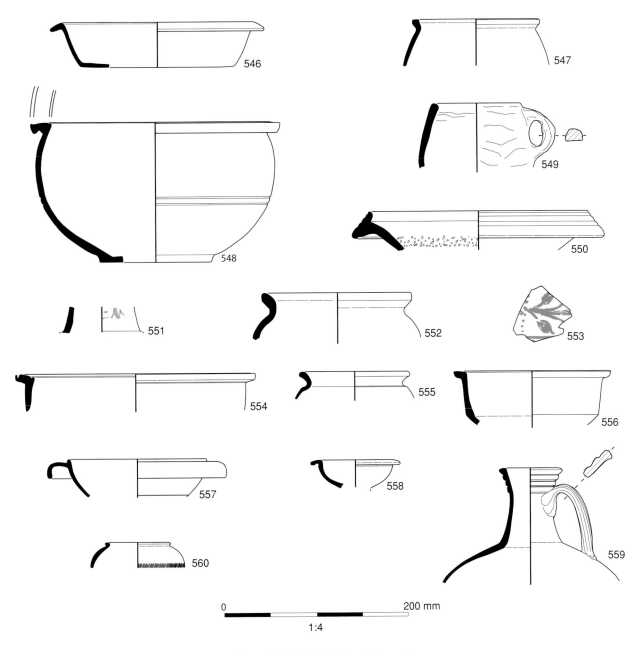

Figure 331: Periods 8 and 9 vessels

in white slip was only executed on so-called 'Rhenish ware' (originating from the Trier/Moselle region). This is one of the first Nene Valley examples to be both recognised and published, and two other published examples may now be assigned to this source (RIB II.6, 2498.3, and 22; Collingwood and Wright 1994); probably second half of third or early fourth century; residual.
MIL 5, *5042*, Period 8D, fill of pit *5038*

552. Jar with heavy rim (probably for storage; Fig 331); North West gritty oxidised ware; residual.
MIL 4, *1698*, Period 8iii, fill of ditch **1231**

553. Jar or bowl (Fig 331); Wilderspool red-slipped fabric with cream-painted horizontal ?wreath of leaves/buds on stem, and vertical dots above groove; probably Hadrianic; residual.
MIL 4, *1729*, Period 8ii, fill of ditch **1231**

554. Reeded-rim bowl (Fig 331); North West fine oxidised ware; late first or early second century.
MIL 4, *1300*, Period 8iii, Tenement **1234**, external layer

555. Jar, imitation BB1 (Fig 331); unidentified pale grey fabric.
MIL 4, *1409*, Period 8iii, fill of ditch *1403*

556. Flat-rim bowl imitating BB1 type (Fig 331); heavily burnished in facets; local reduced ware; Hadrianic.
MIL 3, *810*, Period 8iii, Tenement **1235**, external layer

Catalogue: Period 9
557. Segmental flanged bowl, finely burnished (Fig 331); fine reduced fabric probably local, but usually oxidised.
MIL 5, *2103*, fill of subway construction trench *2104*

558. Miniature segmental bowl (Fig 331); local fine oxidised fabric.
MIL 5, *2103*, fill of subway construction trench *2104*

Catalogue: Not closely phased
559. Flagon (Fig 331); North West gritty oxidised ware; Flavian.
MIL 1, *343*, external layer

560. Everted-rim beaker with judder-rouletting on shoulder (Fig 331); North West gritty oxidised ware; Flavian.
MIL 5, *9993*, unstratified

The Medieval and Post-medieval Pottery

J Bradley and I Miller

The paucity of good assemblages of medieval pottery from archaeological excavations in the North West has been highlighted by English Heritage (Mellor 1994), whilst evidence for pottery production in the region is extremely poor (Newman 2006, 136). Although there have been several excavations within

Cumbrian towns that have produced reasonable assemblages in recent years, and especially in Carlisle, medieval ceramic traditions in the region are still not understood sufficiently to provide close dating of archaeological deposits. In many cases, this is due to the absence of a secure stratigraphic sequence, or because the pottery does not occur in close association with dated buildings or events. The Millennium assemblage, however, together with the pottery recovered from another excavation of the northern defences of medieval Carlisle at Rickergate (Zant *et al* forthcoming), is both large and well-stratified, and close dating of specific contexts has been provided by other classes of material, affording a significant opportunity to refine and enhance earlier, and future, work on medieval pottery in the region. The bulk of the assemblage, which dates from the twelfth to fifteenth centuries, is also significant in the identification of periods within a relatively undifferentiated sequence of activity (Period 8).

Close dating of these pottery assemblages remains difficult, however, especially when compared to those from the North East. There, in towns such as Hull or Beverley, the local pottery traditions were augmented by regional, national, and international imports, which can be used to refine the chronology of what were large and well-stratified assemblages (see for instance Armstrong and Ayers 1987; Armstrong *et al* 1991). This large range of imports is, sadly, effectively absent from Carlisle and other North Western towns, and it is this absence that hampers dating, and marks a clear difference between the two regions. Nevertheless, significant advances have been made in refining the dating of pottery assemblages from the Millennium and Rickergate sites through the use, firstly, of dendrochronological evidence (*Appendix 16*) and, secondly, of large groups of well-preserved and relatively closely dated leather shoes (*Ch 20*; Zant *et al* forthcoming). The contribution of the leatherwork towards refining the dating of the pottery sequence can be seen especially in the pottery from the outer ward ditch of the castle (*Ch 11*).

Methodology
The post-Roman pottery was analysed in accordance with guidance provided by English Heritage in *Management of Archaeological Projects* (English Heritage 1991) and the guidelines provided by the Medieval Pottery Research Group (2001). All the material was examined and recorded by sherd count, weight (to the nearest gram), and minimum numbers of rims, handles, and bases, in order to determine the vessel forms and estimated vessel numbers. The fabrics were analysed through the use of macroscopic examination and a hand lens (x10) and any surface treatment or decoration was also

Site	Sherd Totals	Weight (g)	Unstratified Pottery sherd totals	Unstratified Pottery by weight (g)
MIL 1	403	4545	9	88
MIL 2	58	1111	6	196
MIL 3	261	5128	27	831
MIL 4	796	1484	20	409
MIL 5	1911	25467	6	224
Total	**3429**	**51096**	**68**	**1748**

Table 34: Quantification by sherd count and weight of the medieval pottery

Site	Sherd Totals	Weight (g)	Unstratified Pottery sherd totals	Unstratified Pottery by weight (g)
MIL 1	28	363	14	401
MIL 2	5	47	3	22
MIL 3	4	34	2	2
MIL 4	10	41	4	14
MIL 5	104	1312	4	104
Total	**151**	**1797**	**27**	**543**

Table 35: Quantification by sherd count and weight of the post-medieval pottery

noted. The broad grouping of fabrics was undertaken with reference to the collections of medieval pottery from previous excavations in Carlisle (McCarthy and Taylor 1990; Brooks 1999; McCarthy 2000; Zant *et al* forthcoming).

Quantification

The pottery (3580 fragments; 52.893 kg) was divided into broad medieval and post-medieval groups, with 3429 sherds (51.096 kg; *c* 96%) being medieval and only 151 sherds (1.797 kg) being post-medieval. Quantification of the medieval pottery produced from each of the excavation trenches is presented by sherd count and weight (Table 34), as is the post-medieval pottery (Table 35).

As might be expected, the majority of the fragments were vessel body sherds, although a range of diagnostic rims, handles, and bases was also retrieved (the relative proportions are shown in Figure 332). The amount of post-medieval pottery was small and, as it largely comprised small and abraded sherds, it adds little to the interpretation of the site.

The fabrics

All the medieval sherds were assigned to fabrics defined in the extant Carlisle type-series (McCarthy and Taylor 1990). Four main fabric groups were identified within the assemblage: Gritty wares; Lightly Gritted wares; Partially Reduced wares; and late medieval

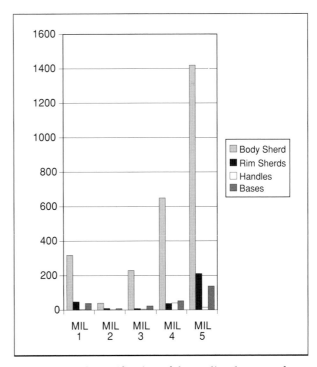

Figure 332: Quantification of the medieval pottery from each excavation trench

Reduced Greywares. Detailed descriptions of these fabrics have appeared previously in the *Transactions of the Cumberland and Westmorland Antiquarian and Archaeological Society* (*eg* Brooks 1999). A summary of the main types is, however, presented here.

661

Red Gritty wares: Fabrics 1 and 2

These wares are generally hard and coarse, with numerous sub-angular to sub-rounded inclusions. Gritty wares were the dominant type in circulation throughout the North during the twelfth century, and, in broad terms, appear to have continued until the mid-thirteenth century (McCarthy and Brooks 1992, 22).

These hard, coarse gritty wares have a dense clay matrix, and are usually oxidised to red or reddish brown. The fabric division is based on the size of the quartz inclusions: Fabric 1 incorporates grains from 0.5 mm to 1 mm, and Fabric 2 has grains from 0.1 mm to 0.5 mm in size. Vessels are often given a dipped or splashed brown, or occasionally olive-green, lead glaze. Forms are mainly jugs and jars, with occasional bowls.

In addition, 33 sherds (199 g) in a reduced gritty fabric were described during the initial assessment and identification stage as being an unusual gritty ware and given Fabric code 502. It would appear likely that, rather than being a hitherto unrecognised fabric, they are simply a reduced variant. Jars were the only forms represented.

White/Buff Gritty ware: Fabrics 3–6

Fabrics 3 and 4 are hard, coarse, gritty wares, usually off-white, buff, or pale grey, with yellow to olive-green glaze. Referred to as White Gritty wares, the main forms are jugs and jars. The production centres for these fabrics are unknown, although the white fabric suggests that it may not be local, and broad parallels may be drawn from Scotland (particularly Kirkcudbright) and Ulster (Jope and Hodges 1955).

Other, less common, coarse gritty wares (Fabrics 5 and 6) are orange to reddish-buff, or reduced grey, with olive-green to brownish glazes. The main forms are jugs and cooking pots.

Partially Reduced Greywares: Fabrics 15, 17, 18, 19

These form a group of closely-related sandy fabrics, which are thought to have been produced locally (McCarthy and Brooks 1992). They usually have a dark grey core and the surfaces are oxidised externally and reduced internally. It is noteworthy that some of the vessels within this fabric type exhibit a lighter grey, almost white, margin below the glaze. The glaze is usually olive-green, but occasionally has copper speckles. Main forms tend to be jugs, sometimes decorated, with occasional cooking pots and pipkins.

Lightly Gritted wares: Fabrics 11, 13, 14, 51, 52

Less common sandy fabrics, usually completely oxidised, range in colour from orange (Fabric 11) to buff/reddish-buff (Fabric 13), with the main forms being jugs. Whilst present in other ceramic assemblages from excavations in Carlisle, such as that from Rickergate (Zant et al forthcoming), these fabric types are similar to the dominant thirteenth- and early fourteenth-century fabrics in Penrith (Brooks 2000, 124), and it is likely that they originated in the Vale of Eden; similar fabrics have also been recovered from excavations at Dacre (McCarthy and Brooks in prep).

Late medieval Reduced Greywares: Fabrics 41, 43, 44, 46

These fabrics form part of a widespread northern 'Reduced Greenware' tradition, which has historically been seen as being introduced during the fourteenth century, becoming the dominant ware during the fifteenth and sixteenth centuries (McCarthy and Brooks 1992). The wares comprise dark grey, hard, smooth, fine sandy fabrics, often with a pale grey margin below the glaze. The smooth, sometimes flaking, glaze is usually drab olive green, but occasionally brownish. The main forms include plain jugs, although decorated examples are known, bung-hole cisterns, urinals, and bowls (White 2000a, 285-91).

Regional imports

A total of seven discrete fabric types could not be related to those from the existing Carlisle fabric series; all were present in only small quantities. None could be identified or provenanced with any certainty, and it was assumed that they were probably imports from outside the region. The existence of a trade network centred on the Irish Sea, and in particular south-west Scotland, has been recognised since the 1950s as an important factor in the study of Carlisle pottery (Jope and Hodges 1955, 79–80). Sequences of numbers were allocated to these fabrics starting at 500, so that they would not be confused with the more thoroughly studied Carlisle fabric series, with the intention that they could, at some later date, be integrated.

Fabric 500 comprised 15 sherds (208 g) of brown-glazed oxidised ware. A single 7 g sherd in a green-glazed buff fabric represented Fabric 501 and was thought to be a Scottish import, based on its similarity to material recovered from Caerlaverock Castle near Dumfries (Hall 2004). Three sherds (51 g), all from the same context and likely to be from the same vessel, were again highlighted as being unusual, and possible imports. The fabric (Fabric 503) was hard-fired and sandy, partially reduced and brownish-buff in colour. The glaze was a drab brownish-green, and all three sherds displayed leaf decoration resembling that of a Fabric 15 vessel from earlier excavations in Carlisle (McCarthy and Brooks 1992, fig 5, 13).

Fabric 504 was represented by a single sherd, weighing 21 g. The fabric was hard fired, with poorly-sorted gritty inclusions and was whitish-buff in appearance.

The exterior had a purple slip and a green glaze. Four sherds (20 g) were allocated to Fabric 505, which was a fine oxidised ware with a brown glaze. There were also 13 sherds weighing 145 g of a buff ware (Fabric 506). Fabric 507 (two sherds; 10 g) was green-glazed, partially reduced, and was considered to be an import from the East Coast.

Forms
There were 433 bases, 348 rims, and 61 handles from the excavations. The bases were classified as sagging, flat, concave, or ring-foot. Some 241 sagging and 76 flat bases came from the trenches (MIL 1, MIL 5) within the outer ward of the medieval castle, whilst in the outer ward ditch (MIL 3, MIL 4) there were 79 sagging, nine flat, six concave, and one ring-foot. To the south, in MIL 2, there were six sagging and one flat base. The evidence suggests that sagging bases were by far the most common form, representing 75% of those present. This type of base is typical of medieval cooking jars from Carlisle, and supports the data from previous excavations (eg Jope and Hodges 1955, 102). Flat-bottomed cooking jars tend to date to around the late thirteenth century (op cit, 81).

Several different rim types were evident, such as squared, bevelled, and clubbed. In the outer ward of the castle, where Gritty ware predominated, clubbed and squared forms were in the majority, followed by everted examples. Collared rims predominated in the outer ward ditch, probably reflecting the change in fabric types, rather than having any other significance; squared rims were a common form on both sides of the Pennines from the twelfth century onwards (Jarrett and Edwards 1964, 42; Jope and Hodges 1955, 82). Most handles represented were straps, with a smaller number of rod handles.

A range of vessel forms has been identified, including jars, jugs, bowls, and bottles. In addition, fragments of at least two lamps were recovered from Period 8C deposits within the outer ward. Jars were the dominant form in the twelfth and thirteenth centuries, with a minimum of 119 identified from the outer ward of the castle, again reflecting the preponderance of Gritty wares in that part of the site. The outer ward ditch produced 45 jars, with the majority coming from the northern side and, by extension, the castle kitchens. Six jars were also found in MIL 2.

Jugs were also relatively common (32), with the majority from the later deposits in the southern half of the outer ward ditch; this might be expected in an assemblage comprising largely Partially and Reduced Greywares, in which jug forms were more common. The outer ward ditch produced cylindrical and globular jugs, and a single baluster was recognised from the northern part of the ditch. Globular jugs

tend to be dated to the late thirteenth century and are common on Scottish and Northumbrian sites, but not in the Carlisle area (Jarrett and Edwards 1964, 42). Other forms include bowls, one each from MIL 1 and MIL 4; bottles were found solely in the outer ward.

Its is perhaps worth considering briefly some absences from the assemblage, such as urinals, drinking vessels, and large three-handled glazed pitchers with bung holes, typical of the fifteenth century. The absence of urinals, which first appear in the northern potters' repertoire in the fourteenth century (Armstrong and Ayers 1987, 98), may simply be because diagnostic sherds have not survived; three-handled pitchers, however, genuinely appear to be absent.

Evidence of function and use
The exteriors of 109 vessels were extensively sooted, pointing to their use for cooking purposes. The majority was recovered from MIL 5 (69 vessels), and most are Gritty-ware vessels (Fabrics 1–5), the one exception being a Reduced Greyware vessel (Fabric 41).

Surface treatments and decorations
In broad terms, the assemblage is notable for the limited decorative treatments on vessels and a paucity of applied ornamentation, such as thumbed strips and motifs, which was a trademark of British pottery in general, and particularly in the North, between the mid-thirteenth and early fourteenth centuries. Such material does occur in Carlisle, a notable example being recovered from English Street in 1951 (Hogg 1953, 207-9), but does not appear to be widespread. There is some evidence of fingernail or fingertip impressions, and some more elaborate features, such as rouletting. One interesting form of decoration is square rouletting, previously recognised at Carlisle (McCarthy and Brooks 1992, 24), which occurs on eight yellow/green-glazed sherds, perhaps representing five vessels. All the vessels are in White Gritty wares (Fabric 3), giving a date range of the twelfth to early thirteenth centuries (Brooks 1999, 102). Glazes are fairly common and tend to be olive-coloured, although some have splashed copper.

Dating
It is widely accepted that the Northern Gritty-ware tradition represents the earliest post-Conquest pottery in the region (McCarthy and Brooks 1992, 22). Previous excavations have suggested that Red Gritty wares (Fabrics 1 and 2) were the dominant twelfth-century fabric in Carlisle, and these were almost certainly produced locally (Jope and Hodges 1955). Alongside these, the White Gritty wares (Fabrics 3 and 4) are considered to be of twelfth- to early thirteenth-century date. In broad terms, these fabrics were then superseded by the Partially Reduced wares and Lightly Gritted wares, a group of closely-related sandy fabrics,

Site	Medieval			Post-medieval		
	No	Wt (g)	No vessels	No	Wt (g)	No vessels
MIL 1	403	4545	216	28	636	5
MIL 5	1911	25467	1084	104	1312	86
Total	**2314**	**30012**	**1300**	**132**	**1948**	**91**

Table 36: Amounts of medieval and post-medieval pottery in MIL 1 and MIL 5

which are thought to have been introduced during the late twelfth century, and to have dominated late thirteenth- and fourteenth-century assemblages in the region (McCarthy and Brooks 1992; Brooks 2000; Zant *et al* forthcoming).

The Millennium Project and earlier excavations at Rickergate (Zant *et al* forthcoming) have both produced well-stratified assemblages which, to an extent, confirm this view, although both also highlight the apparent persistence of Gritty wares into the fourteenth century. Crucially, the dating of pottery from both of these excavations has been aided by independently dated leather shoe assemblages (*Ch 20*), and a good series of dendrochronology dates (*Appendix 16*). Similarly, a fourteenth-century date has been ascribed traditionally to the introduction of Reduced Greywares, although confirmation has been hampered by a paucity of vessel sherds recovered from well-dated contexts (McCarthy and Brooks 1992, 29). The opportunity to use independent sources of dating at the Millennium and Rickergate sites, however, has allowed a late fourteenth-century date to be postulated for the inception of Reduced Greywares, whilst secure stratigraphic sequences demonstrate that these wares were the dominant Carlisle fabric type in the fifteenth century.

The outer ward (MIL 1 and MIL 5)

As there are clear spatial links between MIL 1 and MIL 5, which were situated within the outer ward of the medieval castle, their pottery assemblages are considered as a single unit (Table 36). It should be noted that Periods 8A and 8B were only distinguished in MIL 5 (*Ch 11*), so discussion of these relates only to that area.

Period 7

The earliest medieval pottery was recovered from the Period 7 post-Roman 'dark earths' in MIL 5 (approximately fifth to late eleventh centuries). The principal layers, 2227 and 2112, above the south-west quadrant of the Roman stone fort, and 5296, 5237, and 5242 from the former central range, all produced Red and White Gritty wares (Fabrics 1, 2, 4; 11 vessels) and three vessels of Lightly Gritted ware (Fabric 11; Pl 203), indicating a twelfth-century date for the top of the 'dark earth' horizon, with the presence of Lightly

Gritted ware suggesting that the ground was possibly open until the later twelfth century.

The pottery fragments from soils 2112 and 2227 were neither small nor abraded, and did not look like the result of trampling, raising the possibility that the fragments were relatively undisturbed. Whether the presence of the William II penny (AD 1087-1100) in layer 2227 (*Ch 17, p 686*) might imply a slightly earlier introduction for Gritty wares than hitherto thought is open to debate, as the evidence for this period is somewhat contradictory. It can, however, be suggested that the castle erected by William Rufus in 1092 (Earle and Plummer 1892), and the concomitant plantation of men from the south (McCarthy *et al* 1990, 7, 118), heralded the arrival of medieval pottery production in Carlisle, although whether this was produced by the incomers, or was a demand-led response to their arrival, cannot as yet be determined.

Period 8A

Period 8A yielded an assemblage of 211 sherds (2.981 kg), of which 72% was in Red Gritty ware Fabrics 1 and 2, indicating a twelfth-century date for their deposition. A small number of sherds in the Lightly Gritted-ware tradition suggests that activity was continuing into the later part of the century. Forms

Plate 203: Gritty-ware rims

represented were predominantly jars, with only one jug identified, and would appear to be exclusively domestic in origin. Although the majority of the pottery was in the local Red Gritty-ware tradition, the white or buff fabrics (18%) are thought to be a regional import, although whether from the Cumbrian plain, Scotland (Kirkcudbright), or possibly Ulster (Zant *et al* forthcoming) remains to be determined.

The principal feature of this period was a roughly metalled road or trackway, *7654* (*Ch 11*; Fig 278), which may be associated with the construction of de Ireby's Tower in the mid-twelfth century (McCarthy *et al* 1990, 7, 121). The trackway was flanked on the east by a timber structure (*7653*), and further to the west there was a probable palisade trench (*2125*). Deposits and features sealed below the road produced typical twelfth-century pottery, which included Fabric 11, indicating a date later in the century. The road surfaces (*5181* and *5241*) contained Red and White Gritty wares (Fabrics 1, 2, and 3; 14 vessels), and Structure *7653* and its associated features and deposits all produced Fabrics 1, 2, and 3. The external area east of the road, which included an area of rough cobbling (*5234*) and pits (*5162*, *5173-4*, and *5258*), yielded several sherds of Red Gritty ware (Fabrics 1 and 2). In the vicinity of the palisade trench (*2125*), although not directly connected with it, a layer of cobbles (*2226*) produced the only pottery (ten sherds), which was all Fabric 1.

Period 8B

In total, 112 sherds (1580 g) were recovered from stratified contexts allocated to this period. Fabrics 1 and 2 were dominant, accounting for 74% of the total. Jars were the only vessel form represented, and included fragments of sooted body sherds, pointing to their use in cooking. It is notable that very small quantities of Fabrics 11 and 15 (Lightly Gritted ware and Partially Reduced Greyware) were both present within the assemblage, which would again suggest a late twelfth-century date for their deposition. Fabric 505, a fine oxidised ware, from the fill of a posthole (*5248*), is thought to be an import from elsewhere in the region. It possibly joined with another sherd from Period 8D pit *5006*.

This period was characterised by the presence of a substantial timber building, *7399* (Fig 278), constructed over Period 8A trackway *7654* and Structure *7653* (*Ch 11*). Nearly all of the 18 massive post-pits associated with this structure yielded Red Gritty-ware pottery, with lesser amounts of white and buff fabrics, but only in modest quantities (11 sherds or less per context). As might be expected, few, barring posthole *5168*, produced large sherds, probably indicating that this was not their primary place of deposition. The presence of Fabrics 11 and 15 (one sherd each), in the fills of post-pits *5119* and *5158* respectively, would indicate a late twelfth-century date for deposition.

Period 8A/B (MIL 1)

The most notable feature within this period in MIL 1 was the foundation for the western city wall, *110*, which was almost certainly begun in the first half of the twelfth century (McCarthy *et al* 1990, 7, 119–20). The fill, *112*, found within wall construction trench *150*, produced ten sherds (170 g) of pottery, which included a single jar. All the sherds were in Fabrics 1 and 2 or a variant thereof (Fabric 502), with the exception of a single fragment of Lightly Gritted ware. The remaining feature, *176*, a spread of sandstone rubble (*Ch 11*), produced a further seven sherds (86 g) of Red Gritty ware, including jars, some with evidence of sooting. Although a *terminus post quem* of the late twelfth century would be appropriate on the basis of the single Lightly Gritted sherd, the probable date of the construction of the town wall in the AD 1120s and 1130s (*ibid*) would indicate that the pottery was probably deposited in the first half of the twelfth century. Thus, the activity recorded in this trench may have been broadly contemporary with Period 8A in MIL 5.

Period 8C

Period 8C saw a distinct change, from the intensive occupation seen previously to an open environment, and was characterised by the accumulation of extensive spreads of soil (*Ch 11*). In the eastern part of MIL 5, these dark brown loamy deposits (*5051*, *5054*, *5058*, *5086*, and *5102*) sealed all the remains of Periods 8A and 8B. There was a significant increase in the amount of pottery being deposited, with 933 sherds (11.186 kg) recovered. Despite this increase in the rate of deposition, the relative proportion of fabric types remained the same, with 76% of the assemblage being in Fabrics 1 and 2; there were, however, nearly twice as many sherds of less gritty Fabric 2 than of Fabric 1. Fabrics 3 and 4 (White/Buff Gritty wares) accounted for 16% of the assemblage. Interestingly, there were fewer sherds of Fabric 11 than earlier, accounting for only 6% of the total, as compared to 17% in Period 8B. This change is difficult to account for, unless, as noted by Brooks (1999, 103), the fabric was generally scarce in Carlisle at this time.

Once again, the main vessel forms were jars, although jug forms were noted for the first time, exclusively in Fabrics 1 and 2. Quite large numbers of vessels were heavily sooted, again indicating their domestic origin. The appearance of a range of jug forms, perhaps implying increased high-status activity, combined with the high-status food remains found within the same deposits (*Ch 22*), would suggest that much of this material had its origins in the castle kitchens. Deposits *5058* and *5102* both yielded fragments of probable oil lamps in Fabric 1 (*17 and 23*, pp 672-4), representing an unusual form in the assemblage.

Large sherds in Fabric 1 from layers *5086* and *5102* might indicate primary deposition, although the same context produced a single (undoubtedly intrusive) sherd of post-medieval brown-glazed red earthenware, and had probably been disturbed by modern landscaping. Strap handles were the commonest form found at this time (Pl 204), but *5086* also produced a single twisted or plaited handle (*22, p 674*). Given the dating of Period 8B and the general make-up of the assemblage, a *terminus post quem* of the late twelfth to early thirteenth century would suggest itself; however, this must be tempered by the findings from Period 8D.

Contemporary soils (*2109, 2111, 2155*) were examined on the northern edge of the western half of MIL 5; elsewhere in this area they had been removed by modern landscaping. These contained the same range of medieval wares, along with another sherd of brown-glazed red earthenware. A similar and probably contemporary soil (*149*) was also noted along the northern edge of MIL 1. This, too, contained a mixed assemblage, including Red Gritty ware, White Gritty ware, Lightly Gritted ware, Partially Reduced, and late medieval Reduced Greywares, along with a sherd of white-glazed earthenware of eighteenth- to twentieth-century date. The presence of Reduced Greywares, given their lack in the succeeding period, together with the post-medieval sherd, suggests a degree of disturbance, again probably the result of late landscaping (*Ch 11*).

The significant increase in the rate of deposition of pottery in Period 8C suggests that there was a considerable amount of dumping on what may have been open ground at this time. It seems most likely that the pottery derived ultimately from the castle kitchens, but whether it was dumped directly, or accrued as a result of the clearance and spreading of midden deposits on land used for horticulture, remains open to debate.

Period 8D
This period was characterised as a localised phase of activity in the central part of the site (MIL 5), represented by several large pits and a group of possible hearths. Some 284 sherds, weighing 4.414 kg, were recovered from this phase. Fabrics 1 and 2 accounted for 83% of the whole, with a much reduced presence of Fabric 3 (10%) compared with the preceding period. Again, there was little evidence of Fabric 11, which was represented by only five sherds (1.5%).

Intercutting pits *5036* and *5038* (*Ch 11*) both produced large assemblages of pottery and, as would be expected, these were mainly Fabrics 1 and 2. Fill *5039* from pit *5038* produced 64 sherds of pottery, from only two vessels, including a complete profile (*28, p 674*). The

northern pit group, comprising *5005*, *5072*, *5125*, and *5134*, produced, on the whole, a fairly unremarkable assemblage of Fabrics 1 and 2, and Fabrics 3 and 4. Fabric 11 was present, but only in small quantities, for instance, a single sherd in fill *5006* of pit *5005*. Sooting on some of the sherds would again indicate a domestic origin for the pottery. Pit *5005* also yielded a single sherd of an imported medieval fineware (Fabric 505) in a fine oxidised fabric with a brown glaze, which joined a sherd in Period 8B posthole *5248*, and was thus demonstrably residual. The group of hearths produced very little in the way of pottery, apart from a sherd in Fabric 2 with rouletted decoration, and there were certainly no specialised forms of the kind that might be expected in an industrial area.

The small quantities of Fabric 11, combined with the overwhelming predominance of Fabrics 1 and 2, suggest that the assemblage was largely twelfth century in origin. A coin of Stephen, found in the upper fill of pit *5036* (*Ch 17, p 686*), was broadly contemporary, and reinforces the proposed dating.

Period 8E
A total of 391 sherds (4.755 kg) of medieval pottery was retrieved from deposits ascribed to this period. Fabrics 1 and 2 were again the largest component of the group (76.5%), followed by Fabrics 3 and 4, which made up 13% of the total. Lightly Gritted (Fabrics 11, 13, 14, and 20) and Partially Reduced wares accounted for 4% and 5% respectively. The range of forms represented include jars and an increasing number of jugs, with strap handles. Sooting on some of the vessels again suggests that they had been used in the preparation of foodstuffs.

The principal feature assigned to this period was linear earthwork **7655**, which seemingly ran from east to west, broadly parallel with the castle's outer ward ditch (Fig 278). In MIL 1, the earthwork was formed from dumped layers (*108–9, 111,* and *144–5*) comprising mixed material, with Red Gritty wares, White Gritty wares, Lightly Gritted wares, Partially Reduced, and Reduced Greywares present. Given the date and make-up of the rest of the assemblage, the latter were probably intrusive, but could alternatively have been the result of later trampling on a long-lived feature.

Only the extreme southern edge of the earthwork deposits was examined in MIL 5 (*2152, 5026, 5032*). These deposits contained Red and White Gritty wares, although *5032* also produced a sherd of Lightly Gritted ware and an intrusive sherd of brown-glazed red earthenware (late seventeenth to twentieth centuries). To the east of the earthwork in MIL 5, *5017, 5043,* and *5055* were layers of compacted cobbling, possibly the remains of a road or track (*Ch 11*). These contexts contained mainly Red and White Gritty wares, although there were two Partially Reduced-ware vessels in *5017*.

The character of the pottery from this period suggests a date range in the twelfth and thirteenth centuries for the most part, with the presence of Partially Reduced wares, and the increase of jug forms, consistent with a date in the earlier thirteenth. The small numbers of fourteenth- to fifteenth-century sherds and post-medieval material were all likely to be intrusive.

Period 8F

In total, 172 sherds (2.362 kg) were assigned to this period. As before, the dominant fabrics were Red Gritty wares (Fabrics 1 and 2), which accounted for 70.3% of the assemblage; of these, over half the sherds (by weight and number) were in the more gritty Fabric 1. Fabric 4 accounted for 10% of the assemblage, while Fabric 11 accounted for only 4%; partially Reduced wares (Fabrics 15 and 17) were once again noted in small quantities (6%). Two sherds from a Partially Reduced vessel (Fabric 507) bore an unusual glaze and were thought to be imports from the East Coast. Although still dominated by Red Gritty ware, the assemblage saw a small but possibly important representation of Partially Reduced ware, which might indicate a late twelfth- to early thirteenth-century date for deposition, as was noted for Period 8E.

Jars and jugs were both present within the assemblage, with the former showing evidence of sooting. The latter, all Partially Reduced-ware vessels, had strap handles (Pl 204), but there was a single rod handle. A Partially Reduced-ware plate/bowl was also noted.

This period comprised the latest medieval deposits recorded within MIL 1 and MIL 5. In MIL 5, it was marked by an extensive accumulation of earth (*5002*), blanketing earlier deposits, while in MIL 1 cobbling (*142*) and a few pits were noted (*Ch 11*). Cobbling *142* contained two sherds of Red Gritty ware, including one which had been shaped into a rough disc and had most probably been used as a gaming piece. Soil layers seen in a deep foundation pit in the northern part of the trench were also tentatively attributed to this phase; two of these (*122–3*) yielded a mixture of pottery, including Red Gritty ware, Partially Reduced ware, and an intrusive sherd of late eighteenth- to twentieth-century white-glazed earthenware.

In the eastern part of MIL 5, soil *5002* produced Red, White, and Lightly Gritted wares, and fragments of five Partially Reduced-ware vessels. There were also six sherds (one vessel) of an unusual white fabric (Fabric 506). There was also another unusual vessel (Fabric 507) that perhaps originated on the East Coast, as broadly comparable wares have been recovered from excavations in Hull, Hedon, and Beverley in Yorkshire (Cumberpatch 1997). Two intrusive sherds of post-medieval brown-glazed red earthenware were also noted. It has been suggested that *5002* was a cultivated or 'garden' soil that had been accumulating, perhaps, since the thirteenth century (*Ch 14*). It should, however, be noted that no Partially Reduced fabrics or Reduced Greywares were noted within this layer, which might indicate that there was little or no later medieval deposition in the area. Modern topsoil directly covered most of this deposit, and could explain the presence of post-medieval pottery in it. The apparent lack of late medieval activity in the outer ward can probably

Plate 204: Large fragments of green-glazed jugs

	Medieval			Post-medieval		
Site	No	Wt (g)	No vessels	No	Wt (g)	No vessels
MIL 3	261	5128	146	4	34	1
MIL 4	796	14845	317	10	41	6
Total	1057	19973	463	14	75	7

Table 37: Amounts of medieval and post-medieval pottery in MIL 3 and MIL 4

be related, at least in part, to the use of the area as gardens by the late fourteenth century (McCarthy *et al* 1990, 150), and if the pottery evidence is taken at face value, then the beginning of this usage can be placed much earlier (*Ch 14*).

The outer ward ditch (MIL 3 and MIL 4)

MIL 3 and MIL 4 both examined the large ditch (*1230/1231*; Fig 278) that formed the southern boundary of the outer ward, and of the entire castle complex. The material from them can be considered together (Table 37).

Period 8i

Period 8i represents the primary phase of the outer ward ditch (*1230*; *Ch 11*). Although the precise date of its creation is not recorded, it can be deduced that it was probably at about the same time as the castle and city walls were linked together, in the second half of the twelfth century (McCarthy *et al* 1990). The earliest features associated with this period did not produce any pottery. Enigmatic features within MIL 4, possibly the remains of a timber structure within the ditch (including fill *1993* of slot *1796*), produced only a single sherd of Red Gritty ware (15 g), which cannot be relied on for dating the feature. The ditch fills of Phase 3 may have been deposited over a long period of time: pottery was recovered only sporadically and principally from the upper fills, although it should be noted that a large part of the Period 8i ditch was removed when it was recut in Period 8ii (as *1231*). On the south side of the ditch, and quite high in the sequence, fills *821* and *790* produced seven sherds of Red Gritty ware, for which a twelfth- or thirteenth-century date would be appropriate. However, beneath these, fill *857* yielded White/Buff and Lightly Gritted wares, and three sherds of Partially Reduced ware, which conventionally appears in the Carlisle sequence in the late twelfth century (Brooks 1999, 103). On the north side of the ditch, only one fill, *1442*, produced pottery, which included three sherds of Partially Reduced ware (Fabric 15) and a single sherd of Fabric 502, a reduced version of Red Gritty ware.

The lack of pottery deposition within this period might be accounted for by the lack of activity around the edges of the ditch. To the north, within the castle's outer ward, activity probably decreased in the early part of

the thirteenth century, and it seems clear that the outer ward ditch had not yet been encroached upon from the south, as happened later (*Ch 11*). It is also significant that the small amount of Partially Reduced ware that appears in Periods 8E and 8i would connect activity within the castle to the time of the construction of the outer ward ditch. Ceramically speaking, however, all that can be said is that the infilling of ditch *1230* took place in the twelfth or thirteenth century, with the weight of evidence perhaps pointing toward the latter.

Period 8ii

The recut ditch of Period 8ii (*1231*) produced 350 sherds (5.414 kg). Some 91% of the assemblage was represented by Partially Reduced wares (Fabrics 15 and 17); Gritty wares made up 8% of the total. This was in stark contrast to both Period 8i and the final phase of medieval activity (Period 8F) in the outer ward, which were, particularly in the case of the latter, dominated by the Gritty-ware tradition. Furthermore, if the dating of the leather from this ditch can be used to refine the pottery chronology (shoes from this period were all considered to be of fourteenth-century date (*Ch 20*)), then the Gritty-ware fabrics were largely residual. This impression is further reinforced by cross-context joins between two sherds of reduced Gritty ware (Fabric 502), one of which was from Period 8A. Such cross-joins highlight the way material was being moved around on the site. Other cross-context joins were more local, with joining Partially Reduced sherds found within fills *1765*, *1755*, and *1495*, on the northern edge of the outer ward ditch. The predominant forms were jug types (Pl 204), with both rod and strap handles. Jars were occasionally present in the assemblage, although very few retained any indication of sooting, reflecting the move away from ceramic to metal cooking vessels in the fourteenth century (Jennings 1992, 12).

Phase 1

Phase 1 saw the recutting of the outer ward ditch, *1231*, and its subsequent filling. As in Period 8i, several features were noted at the base of the ditch, though their significance is unclear (*Ch 14*). Pits *1428* and *1431* produced only Partially Reduced wares, while a slightly earlier pit, *1433*, yielded four sherds of Partially Reduced ware and one of Fabric 4, which was likely to be residual. A mid-thirteenth- to mid-fourteenth-century date would be appropriate for deposition, especially in the light of the recovery of a shoe of similar date from a context in this phase (*Ch 20*).

Phase 2
This phase yielded the majority of the pottery recovered from Period 8ii, reflecting the substantial dumping which characterised the deposits. However, it should be noted that the pottery distribution on the south side of the ditch contrasts sharply with that to the north. In MIL 3 (to the south), only 16 sherds were recovered, of which 12 were in Partially Reduced-ware fabrics, the others probably residual Fabric 2. This strongly suggests that most of the pottery and other rubbish being dumped into the outer ward ditch at this time came from the castle, and therefore entered from the north side of the ditch. The presence of a baluster jug within fill *1755* is of note, as it is of a style that appears in the south of England in the second half of the thirteenth century (Rackham 1947). A slightly later date for the deposition of this vessel is evidenced by dendrochronology (*Appendix 16*) and analysis of the leather shoes (*Ch 20*), which both suggest a fourteenth-century date for Period 8ii.

Period 8iii
A total of 230 sherds (4.202 kg) of medieval pottery was recovered from this period. Partially Reduced wares were the most abundant (77.5%); two sherds of Reduced Greywares within the assemblage would appear to herald the later fourteenth century, if it is assumed that this staple of the later medieval period was first introduced in the later rather than the earlier part of the century (Zant *et al* forthcoming). Nearly 20% of the pottery was from the Gritty-ware tradition, of which a third were from the fabrics (Fabrics 11 and 13) that survived longest. There would appear to be a large residual element, presumably deriving from reworked deposits elsewhere.

Jugs were the dominant form, with jars perhaps over-represented because of the relative abundance of Gritty wares. The Partially Reduced jug forms tended to be cylindrical with strap handles, although rod handles were evident. Very little in the way of decoration was recorded, except a single example of fingertip impression on a Partially Reduced ware vessel from a ditch (*1403*, fill *149*; Fig 280*)*.

This phase was characterised by the construction of wooden fences, marking tenement boundaries, and a timber building over partially infilled ditch *1231* (*Ch 11*). Clay layers that had been placed as consolidation on top of the ditch fills (*1581* and *1728*) contained five sherds of Partially Reduced ware. The northern boundary ditch, *1788*, of tenement *1234* produced a few sherds of Partially Reduced ware. Wooden Building *1492* in the same tenement yielded a further ten Partially Reduced-ware sherds

from floors *1668* and *1671;* the sherds from *1668* were small and abraded, as would befit a floor. Other layers inside the building, for instance surface *1421*, sealing drain *1694*, produced assemblages of a reasonable size (32 sherds), where over two-thirds of the pottery was Partially Reduced ware, but the rest was still made up of Gritty wares; the abraded nature and small size of the sherds would again be consistent with a floor rather than a layer associated with the disuse of the building. This does, however, raise a question as to whether the Gritty wares in this layer can all be residual. Dendrochronological dates from Building *1492* have produced a date range of between AD 1283–1328 and AD 1296–1341, suggesting a construction date in the early to mid-fourteenth century, though much of the timber within this building had probably been reused (*Ch 11*). This would be consistent with the fourteenth-century date of the pottery. North of Building *1492*, a group of layers (*1727*, *1724*, and *1301*), with little stratigraphic relationship to the building, again had pottery consistent with a fourteenth-century date. These layers produced six vessels in Fabrics 17 and 19.

To the south, only a few silt layers could be assigned to this phase, including *791*, which produced single sherds of Fabrics 17 and 5. These were the only ceramic dating evidence, but shoes from this area date from the mid-thirteenth to mid-fourteenth century (*Ch 20*), thereby corroborating the proposed date for this phase.

Following the demolition of Building *1492*, the subsequent accumulation of deposits (*1300, 1317–18*) above the structure again demonstrated that Partially Reduced wares were still the dominant fabric. Layer *1300* did, however, produce sherds in Fabric 501, and Fabric 500, in the form of an oxidised strap handle. Again, a mid-thirteenth- to mid-fourteenth-century date would be appropriate, confirmed by the leather assemblage (*Ch 20*).

In the adjacent tenement (*1235*), the earliest phase of activity, which included the fill of a large but shallow feature (*1578*), contained approximately eight vessels in Fabric 17, including several large sherds from a single vessel. Later layers (*739*, *738*, and *719*) contained a mixture of wares, including Gritty wares (Fabrics 1, 2, 5, and 6; nine vessels), Lightly Gritted (Fabrics 11 and 13; three vessels), Partially Reduced (Fabrics 15 and 17; 15 vessels), and Reduced Greywares (Fabric 41; two sherds). Fabric 15 yielded evidence of jars, whilst Fabric 5 had some sooting. The intervening fenceline (*2064*) also produced a mix of Gritty wares (Fabrics 1, 2, 5, and 6; five vessels), Partially Reduced wares (Fabrics 15 and 17; 17 vessels), and an intrusive post-medieval sherd (Blackware, seventeenth-twentieth centuries), incorporated into a layer of dark organic silt, *750*. One Fabric 15 sherd represented a cylindrical jug.

To the north of the tenements, there was a ditch or drain (*1403*), the fills of which (including *1585, 1493, 1409, 1481, 1414,* and *1402*) contained Red Gritty ware (Fabric 2; two vessels), Lightly Gritted ware (Fabric 11; two vessels), Partially Reduced ware (Fabric 17; ten vessels), and an early post-medieval and presumably intrusive vessel. Among these were a globular jug of Fabric 11, cylindrical jars in Fabric 17, including one with fingertip impressions, and a jar in Fabric 2. A large assemblage of leather was also recovered from this ditch, which included shoes in styles suggesting a late fourteenth- to early fifteenth-century date (*Ch 20*).

Thus it appears likely that the encroachment over the fills of the outer ward ditch began in the late fourteenth century, with much of the pottery from associated features being residual, as might be expected. The group of leather shoes from this period can be dated from the presence of styles fashionable in the late fourteenth and early fifteenth centuries (*Ch 20*). The dendrochronology demonstrates that the activity was clearly of the fourteenth century, with a bias toward the end of the century (*Ch 11; Appendix 16*). However, a felling date of AD 1385 from a probably reused timber might imply a very late fourteenth-century date; there is nothing in the pottery sequence that need be later than the end of the fourteenth century. Significantly, however, there is a real absence of Reduced Greywares, normally held to have been introduced in the fourteenth century (McCarthy and Brooks 1992, 29). It might, therefore, be possible to place the introduction of Reduced Greywares in the later fourteenth century, a revision supported by evidence from Rickergate, where their first appearance was associated with a later fourteenth-century dendrochronological date (Zant *et al* forthcoming).

Period 8iv
Period 8iv yielded a total of 378 sherds of medieval pottery, weighing 8.329 kg. By sherd count, the Partially Reduced fabrics (279 sherds; 5.320 kg) dominated, in comparison with only 57 sherds of Reduced Greywares. By weight, however, it should be noted that those 57 sherds weighed 2.479 kg and accounted for 29% of the assemblage by weight, suggesting that they were a more significant element of the assemblage, and were much more prominent in this period than in Period 8iii. Fabrics 503 and 504 are probably imports.

Jugs were the commonest form within the assemblage, in Fabrics 15 and 17, and 41, with cylindrical jugs in Fabric 41, and at least one globular jug represented within the Fabric 17 material. Leaf decoration was also noted on this jug rim. Strap handles were dominant among the jugs, as would be expected in late fourteenth- or fifteenth-century forms. A bowl was

also present in Fabric 41. Large sherd sizes, indicative of relatively undisturbed contexts, were evident in Fabrics 17 and 41.

This period was characterised by several changes in tenements **1234** and **1235** (*Ch 11*). This included the repair of the fence dividing the plots, a poorly preserved timber building (Structure **1233**) in tenement **1234**, and the replacement of ditch *1403* by timber-lined channel *1499*. In tenement **1234**, the remains of foundation trench *811* produced a small amount of Fabric 17 with raised rouletting as decoration. A rectangular feature (*727*), that appeared to cut foundation trench *811* in Structure **1233**, again only produced a small quantity of Fabric 17.

The northern part of the tenement (MIL 4) was covered by layers that included *1312–14, 1362, 1580, 1589, 1687,* and *1696*. These produced the first substantial group of Reduced Greywares on the site. All were large sherds, many indicating sagging bases, and appeared to be from jug forms. Deposits lying over the remains of Structure **1233** again produced Fabric 41, but in larger quantities than seen previously, whilst the Partially Reduced fabrics were reduced to little more than single sherds per context. This interesting group included a cylindrical jar/jug with internal sooting, fragments of which were recovered from layers *714, 732,* and *707*.

In the eastern tenement, **1235**, the deposits accumulated over the area (*1320, 1383–6, 1407,* and *1501*) yielded 51% (by fragment count) of the sherds from the period, all in Partially Reduced ware. Deposit *1407* alone produced 110 sherds (21% by weight). The leather-working debris from the same contexts comprised a fairly large group of shoes of late fourteenth- to early fifteenth-century date (*Ch 20*). If these two groups of deposits are contemporary, then the dominance of different types of fabric is interesting.

In the southern half of the tenement (MIL 3), a possible cut feature (*1225*: fills *722, 737, 705, 726,* and *712*) produced small amounts of Gritty wares, four vessels in Partially Reduced ware, and six Reduced Greyware vessels. A later fourteenth- to early fifteenth-century date can be ascribed to this assemblage, particularly in the light of the associated shoe fragments of the same date (*Ch 20*).

If it is accepted that Period 8iii dated to the late fourteenth century, the addition of a moderate quantity of Reduced Greywares (15% by sherd count, 29% by weight) suggests that an early fifteenth-century date might be appropriate for Period 8iv. This can be corroborated by leather-working debris, comprising shoes, predominantly of late fourteenth- to early fifteenth-century date (*Ch 20*), while

Plate 205: Zoomorphic jug handle

dendrochronological samples gave felling dates of between AD 1322–67 and AD 1368–1403 (*Ch 11*).

Period 8 (MIL 2)
In all, 58 sherds (1.111 kg) of medieval, and five (47 g) of post-medieval, pottery were recovered from MIL 2, representing an estimated 49 medieval and three post-medieval vessels. Excavation showed that in this area there had been extensive disturbance, and the only medieval remains to survive were two heavily truncated intercutting pits (*501* and *503*). An estimated 27 vessels, including jars and jugs in Gritty ware Fabrics 1, 2, and 5, were identified from these features, while there were only a single vessel of Lightly Gritted ware and eight of Partially Reduced ware. A very fine zoomorphic jug handle (Pl 205), of a probable thirteenth- or early fourteenth-century date, was also recovered from the fill (*504*) of pit *503*.

Period 9
Very few post-medieval features and deposits were encountered anywhere on the site, which is thought to reflect a genuine absence of activity, at least within the castle. In addition, extensive modern truncation was responsible for the removal of all post-medieval deposits within MIL 2, MIL 3, and MIL 4. The lack of post-medieval remains within the outer ward (MIL 1 and MIL 5), due in part to modern truncation, also appeared to reflect the continued use of that area as gardens from the fourteenth century, if not earlier.

A layer of mixed earth and mortar (*107*), immediately adjacent to the inner (east) face of the western medieval curtain wall, covered the whole of the northern arm of MIL 1. The layer contained Mottled

ware, brown-glazed oxidised and white Salt-Glazed Stoneware, and residual Gritty-ware sherds, with a date range spanning the late seventeenth to mid-eighteenth centuries. A gravel-filled trench (*5063*), in MIL 5, contained residual medieval wares. Topsoil (*2108* and *5001*) in this part of the site also yielded post-medieval pottery, including some English stoneware, brown-glazed red earthenware, and white-glazed white ware, with a date range spanning the seventeenth to mid-late eighteenth centuries.

Catalogue of illustrated vessels
The catalogue is presented in chronological order of the vessels.

1. Red Gritty ware jar (Fig 333), with everted square rim (Fabric 1).
   MIL 5, *5296*, Period 7, post-Roman 'dark earth'

2. Red Gritty ware jar (Fig 333), with everted rim (Fabric 1).
   MIL 5, *5227*, Period 8A, Structure **7653**, external deposit

3. Red Gritty ware jar (Fig 333), with simple rim (Fabric 1).
   MIL 5, *5241*, Period 8A, Road **7654**, road surface

4. Red Gritty ware jar/cooking pot (Fig 333), with everted rim (Fabric 1).
   MIL 5, *5091*, Period 8B, Building **7399**, fill of posthole *5029*

5. Red Gritty ware jar (Fig 333) (Fabric 1).
   MIL 5, *5120*, Period 8B, Building **7399**, fill of posthole *5119*

6. Red Gritty ware jar (Fig 333), with thickened rim (Fabric 1).
   MIL 5, *5244*, Period 8B, Building **7399**, fill of posthole *5243*

7. Red Gritty ware jar (Fig 333), rounded or shouldered (Fabric 1).
   MIL 5, *5058*, Period 8C, external layer

8. Red Gritty ware vessel? Jar? (Fig 333), with everted rim (Fabric 1).
   MIL 5, *5058*, Period 8C, external layer

9. Red Gritty ware jar (Fig 333), with thickened rim (Fabric 1).
   MIL 5, *5058*, Period 8C, external layer

10. Red Gritty ware jar (Fig 333), with clubbed rim (Fabric 1).
    MIL 5, *5058*, Period 8C, external layer

11. Red Gritty ware jug (Fig 333), with thickened rim (Fabric 1).
    MIL 5, *5058*, Period 8C, external layer

12. Red Gritty ware jar (Fig 333), with everted rim (Fabric 1).
    MIL 5, *5058*, Period 8C, external layer

13. Red Gritty ware large storage vessel (Fig 333), with straight rim (Fabric 1).
    MIL 5, *5058*, Period 8C, external layer

14. Red Gritty ware jar (Fig 333), with everted rim (Fabric 1).
    MIL 5, *5058*, Period 8C, external layer

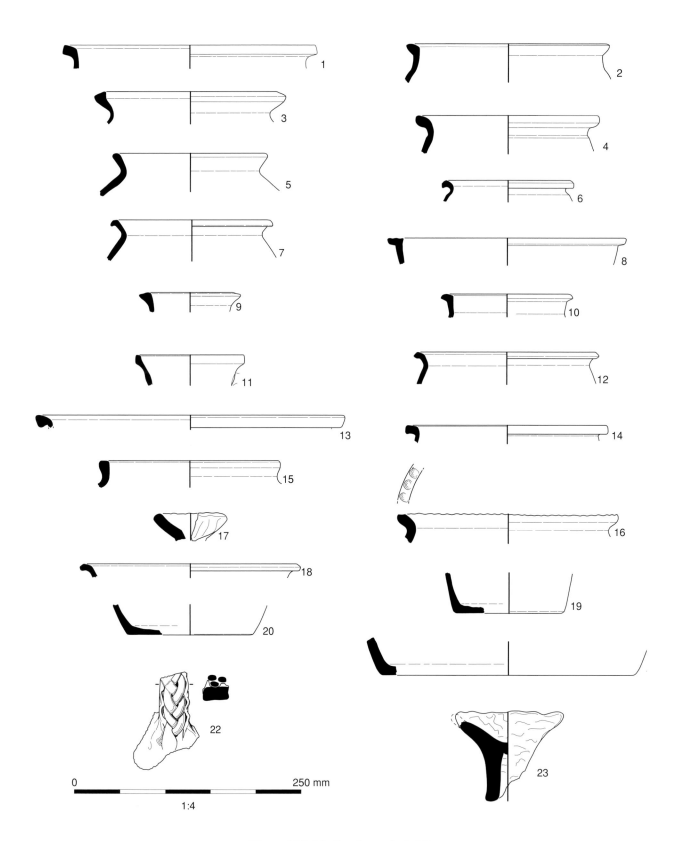

Figure 333: Medieval vessels, 1-23

15. Red Gritty Ware jar (Fig 333), with upright rim (Fabric 1).
MIL 5, *5058*, Period 8C, external layer

16. Red Gritty ware jar (Fig 333), with everted and thumbed rim (Fabric 1).
MIL 5, *5058*, Period 8C, external layer

17. Red Gritty ware lamp (Fig 333), (Fabric 1).
MIL 5, *5058*, Period 8C, external layer

18. Red Gritty ware jar (Fig 333), with everted rim. (Fabric 1).
MIL 5, *5058*, Period 8C, external layer

672

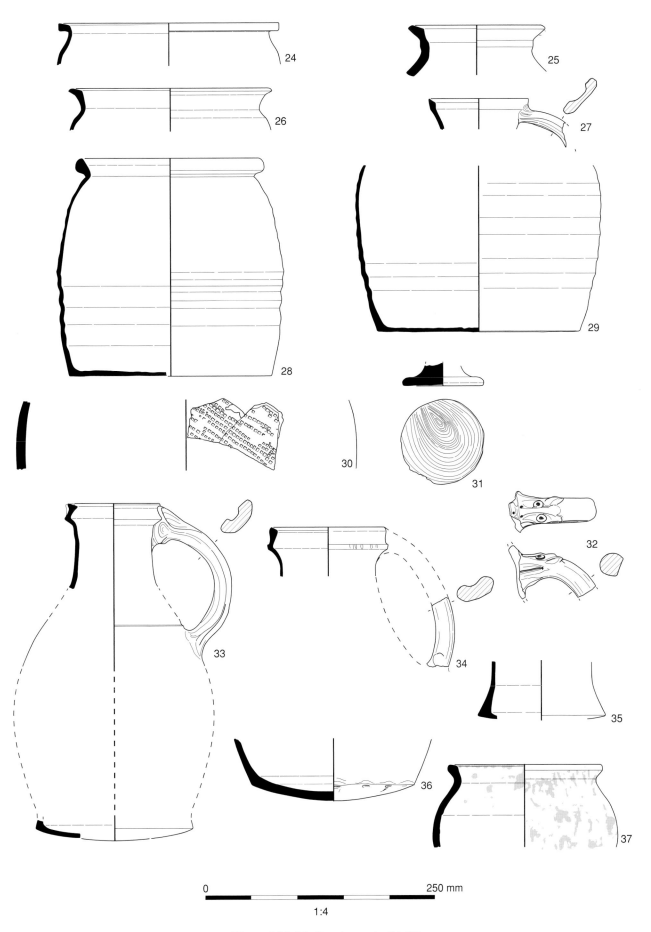

Figure 334: Medieval vessels, 24-37

19. Red Gritty ware jar (Fig 333), with flat-bottomed base (Fabric 1).
    MIL 5, *5058*, Period 8C, external layer

20. Red Gritty ware jar (Fig 333), with acute-angled flat-bottomed base (Fabric 1).
    MIL 5, *5058*, Period 8C, external layer

21. Red Gritty ware large storage jar (Fig 333), with flat base (Fabric 1).
    MIL 5, *5058*, Period 8C, external layer

22. Red Gritty ware composite strap handle (Fig 333), with plaited strip (Fabric 1).
    MIL 5, *5086*, Period 8C, external layer

23. Red Gritty ware lamp (Fig 333), (Fabric 1).
    MIL 5, *5102*, Period 8C, external layer

24. Red Gritty ware jar / cooking pot (Fig 334), with squared rim (Fabric 1).
    MIL 5, *5115*, Period 8D, fill of possible hearth *5111*

25. Red Gritty ware jar (Fig 334), with everted rim (Fabric 1).
    MIL 5, *5089*, Period 8D, fill of possible hearth *5090*

26. Red Gritty ware jar (Fig 334), with everted rim (Fabric 1).
    MIL 5, *5052*, Period 8F, external layer

27. Red Gritty ware jug (Fig 334), with strap handle (Fabric 2).
    MIL 5, *5054*, Period 8C, external layer

28. Red Gritty ware cylindrical jar (Fig 334), flat-based, with clubbed rim (Fabric 2).
    MIL 5, *5039*, Period 8D, fill of pit *5038*

29. Red Gritty ware cylindrical jar (Fig 334), flat based (Fabric 2).
    MIL 5, *5039*, Period 8D, fill of pit *5038*

30. White / Buff Gritty ware body sherd (Fig 334), with squared rouletting (Fabric 3).
    MIL 5, *5051/5082*, Period 8C / Period 8D, external layer and fill of possible hearth *5080*

31. Complete pedestal (Fig 334), (Fabric 11).
    MIL 2, unstratified.

32. Partially Reduced Greyware (Fig 334; Pl 205), with zoomorphic rod handle (Fabric 17).
    MIL 2, *504*, Period 8, fill of pit *503*

33. Partially Reduced Greyware jug (Fig 334), with strap handle and inturned rim (Fabric 17).
    MIL 4, *1697*, Period 8ii, fill of ditch **1231**

34. Partially Reduced Greyware jug (Fig 334), with collared rim and strap handle (Fabric 17).
    MIL 4, *1427*, Period 8ii, fill of ditch **1231**

Plate 206: Reduced greyware jar base

35. Partially Reduced Greyware baluster jug (Fig 334), with sagging base (Fabric 17).
    MIL 4, *1765/1495/1755*, Period 8i / Period 8ii, fill of ditch **1230**, fill of ditch **1231**

36. Late Medieval Reduced Greyware cylindrical jar (Fig 334; Pl 206), with sagging base (Fabric 41).
    MIL 3, *707*, Period 8iv, tenement **1234**, external deposit

37. Globular jar (Fig 334), with everted rim (Fabric 506).
    MIL 5, *5002/5012*, Period 8F, external layer and fill of gully *5013*

Discussion

Studies of medieval ceramics in the North West have focused traditionally on two principal urban centres, from where the most significant assemblages of medieval pottery in the region have been found: Chester, the largest city and the major port for the North West; and Carlisle, which has been a nexus for the study of medieval ceramics since the 1950s, when Jope and Hodges (1955) first published a detailed study of the pottery from excavations on Castle Street. Indeed, Carlisle is the only large urban centre to the north of the river Mersey, with the possible exception of Lancaster, for which a ceramic sequence for the medieval period has been defined.

Throughout the medieval period, Chester and Carlisle both served an extensive hinterland, and had wider connections with trade in the Irish Sea, yet there are striking contrasts in the ceramic assemblages recovered from these two cities. Notably, the medieval pottery from Chester, as in towns east of the Pennines, appears to follow traditions based on pre-Norman wares, and / or were linked into a much wider trade network (Davey 1977, 6; Armstrong et al 1991, 101-2). Further north, the Northern Gritty wares of the later twefth century characterise the inception of medieval ceramics, as is seen clearly in Carlisle. In broad terms, the production of Gritty wares appears to have been highly localised, although it is becoming evident that there are variations in the supply of medieval pottery on a sub-regional level, and Carlisle certainly differed from other Cumbrian towns in several ways. Excavations at Kendal and, in a rural setting, at Dacre (McCarthy and Brooks 1992, 29-33), for instance, have shown that trade links with the North East were more apparent.

The Millennium excavations, like those at Rickergate (Zant *et al* forthcoming), have refined the relative chronology of certain fabric types within the Carlisle fabric series. Both excavations have demonstrated that Gritty wares had a longer life than previously thought (*ibid*) and, moreover, comparison with other assemblages has determined that late medieval Reduced Greywares were in more prominent use in some parts of the city than in others during the same period.

The Millennium excavations themselves have highlighted several points of interest in the study of the area between the castle and medieval town. In broad terms, medieval activity in the outer ward of the castle has been shown to have been intensive and short lived, with six periods of activity spanning the twelfth and thirteenth centuries (Periods 8A-8F), which included earthfast-post buildings and associated cobbled surfaces, superseded by an earthwork aligned parallel to the outer ward ditch. The cessation of this activity appears to coincide with the historically and cartographically attested development of gardens within the outer ward (*Ch 14*). These events also appear to coincide with ceramic changes in Carlisle. The pottery assemblage from the outer ward is dominated by Gritty wares, whereas the material from the backfill of the outer ward ditch (**1231**), recut seemingly at the end of the thirteenth century (*Ch 14*), is largely Partially Reduced wares. It was also apparent that until the encroachment of the tenements over the ditch in Period 8iii, much of the material being dumped into the outer ward ditch came from the northern side, and thus ultimately from the castle itself. There, both the pottery and animal bone assemblages (*Ch 22*) denote high-status activity, which was particularly apparent in the outer ward in Period 8C. It is also notable that jugs, thought to be an indicator of status during the twelfth and thirteenth centuries, were more common in the assemblage from the outer ward. Only the northern half of the outer ward ditch produced more jugs, and this was partly because the pottery there was of a later date, when jugs tended to predominate.

In terms of other excavations in Carlisle, for instance that at Blackfriars Street (McCarthy and Taylor 1990), similar fabrics and forms have been identified. This is to be expected, as most of these wares were probably manufactured locally and therefore likely to be widely distributed throughout Carlisle. The same is also true of other sites in the region, such as Penrith (Brooks 2000) and Dacre (Newman and Leech forthcoming), which have very similar fabrics and forms, that can

be easily incorporated into the extant Carlisle fabric series. It is interesting to note that, at these sites, there is a greater amount of Lightly Gritted ware (Fabrics 11 and 13 for Carlisle) than at Carlisle, perhaps suggesting local production and subsequent trade/exchange with Carlisle.

The outer ward - Periods 8A–8F

The combined pottery assemblages from Periods 8A-8F represent a remarkably short chronological phase of activity, probably spanning the twelfth to early thirteenth centuries, with nothing in the assemblage that need be later than the thirteenth century. The assemblage is dominated by Red Gritty wares, which account for 75% of the material. Lesser amounts of White/Buff Gritty ware (Fabrics 3 and 4) and other Lightly Gritted wares (Fabrics 11, 13, 14, and 20) formed small but significant groups, but were never above 20%. The Partially Reduced fabrics were first noted within Period 8E, but never in great quantities (6% or less).

The outer ward ditch
Periods 8i and 8ii
It may be possible to see a connection between Periods 8E and 8i. Both produced little in the way of Partially Reduced wares, and therefore it would be appropriate to suggest a late twelfth- to early thirteenth-century date for both Period 8E, and for the filling of ditch **1230**. If only the sparse pottery assemblage from Period 8i is used as an indicator, then doubt might be cast over the validity of the date, were it not for the leather assemblage, which also suggests a date in the first half of the thirteenth century (*Ch 20*). This would seem to indicate that the Partially Reduced wares were not widely available until the mid-thirteenth century.

Period 8ii marks the recutting of the outer ward ditch. Within this period, Partially Reduced wares became dominant. Based on the ceramic evidence, dendrochronology, and the leather-working evidence (*Ch 20*), it is suggested that the recut outer ward ditch began to fill in the early fourteenth century. This in turn would concur with the suggestion (*Ch 14*) that the ditch was recut at the start of the Scottish wars in *c* 1296, when there are references to the cleaning out of the castle's ditches. Further references indicate that by 1304 the castle was once again in a state of disrepair, principally because the threat from Scotland had dissipated (McCarthy *et al* 1990, 133). By extension, it may be inferred that the castle played less of a military role, and that there would be no bar to dumping rubbish into the outer ward ditch.

Periods 8iii and 8iv
Encroachment over the part-filled outer ward ditch, indicated by the tenements (**1234** and **1235**) laid out in Period 8iii, can be dated to the late fourteenth century by felling dates obtained from the timber structures within the tenements (*Ch 11*). This tends to confirm the

suggestion by McCarthy and Brooks (1992, 29) that Reduced Greywares, present in only small quantities in Period 8iii, were really a phenomenon of the later fourteenth and fifteenth centuries in Carlisle. This also seems to be the situation at Rickergate, where large sherds of Reduced Greywares were associated with a wooden tub made of timbers with a felling date of after 1358 (Zant *et al* forthcoming). Thus, the availability of secure dendrochronological dates from both sites has allowed the introduction of Reduced Greywares to be dated more precisely but, as was noted at Rickergate (*ibid*), caution should be exercised when ascribing dates without taking account of potential socio-economic factors. It may be possible, therefore, to demonstrate that the market for different pottery types varied from one part of the city to another, perhaps reflecting a demographic difference. In addition, there is a real contrast between Carlisle and Cockermouth, to the south-west, where fabrics in the Reduced Greyware tradition were dominant in fourteenth-century contexts (Leech forthcoming).

Pottery from the tenements over the outer ward ditch, and from the ditch fronting the medieval city's north wall at Rickergate, demonstrated similar trends. At Rickergate, it was observed that there was an apparent persistence of Gritty wares into the fourteenth century, alongside an absence of Partially Reduced Greywares (Zant *et al* forthcoming). Although the Millennium excavations did not provide an exact parallel, it can be noted that, during Period 8iii, 20% of the assemblage was Gritty ware Fabrics 11 and 13, whilst the majority were Partially Reduced-ware vessels. This might suggest, once again, that there was still a market for these vessels, perhaps amongst the poorer inhabitants of Carlisle.

The final phase of activity (Period 8iv) associated with the tenements, which had spread over the outer ward ditch, saw the appearance of a small but significant component of Reduced Greywares, with many large sherds suggesting primary deposition. It might be possible to suggest that, because this phase of activity saw the demolition of the tenement buildings, the material deposited above them derived from the more affluent parts of Annetwell Street. The felling dates for various timbers from this period and the leather assemblage both indicate a date not later than the early fifteenth century for this activity (*Chs 11* and *20*).

The origins of Carlisle pottery

Carlisle has no recognised pre-Conquest pottery tradition, only a few sherds of what was termed 'Anglian' pottery having been tentatively identified from Blackfriars Street and Annetwell Street (McCarthy and Taylor 1990, 303). Gritty wares

then make a widespread appearance in the twelfth century, perhaps as a result of the arrival of Norman influence in the late eleventh century. In Scotland, which saw a comparable situation during the twelfth and thirteenth centuries, it has been suggested that the influx of southerners provided the impetus for the appearance of a native medieval pottery tradition (Cox *et al* 1984, 395–6). The same process might be suggested for Carlisle, which lay, it could be argued, in the Scottish sphere of influence (McCarthy and Brooks in prep). It is asserted that monastic influence was a driving force behind the setting up of various craft industries in Scotland, potting amongst them (Cox *et al* 1984, 395), but how much this could be argued for Carlisle remains open to debate.

Recent examination of medieval pottery from Cockermouth has drawn attention to the presence of sherds very similar in appearance to Norman Gritty ware (Leech forthcoming). Elsewhere, an eleventh- to twelfth-century date has been ascribed to this fabric, and it is possible that the Cockermouth sherds were imported. Such a discovery could not only reinforce the idea that the potters formed a part of Norman plantation, monastic or otherwise, but might also raise the possibility that the medieval ceramic tradition in the North West was partly attributable to the Normans. It was, however, pointed out by Jarrett and Edwards (1964, 42) that, whilst the Carlisle material compared fairly closely to south-west Scottish examples, it was also heavily influenced by the more extensive English Northern Gritty-ware tradition.

The Millennium site in its wider context

In broad terms, the pottery sequences from various urban and rural sites in Cumbria, for instance Dacre (Newman and Leech forthcoming) and Cockermouth (Leech forthcoming), are the same. Generally speaking, the chronology of the Carlisle fabric sequence, with Red Gritty wares dominating in the twelfth and thirteenth centuries, being replaced by Partially Reduced wares in the fourteenth century, and the latter superseded by Reduced Greywares in the fifteenth, holds true for those sites.

At Penrith, where excavation took place in the core of the medieval town, it was possible to compare the assemblage directly with those from Carlisle and, to a lesser extent, Dacre, with which it had close affinities (Brooks 2000, 119–24). At Cockermouth (Leech forthcoming), an urban site examining two burgage plots, the sequence started in the thirteenth century. Gritty wares were not dominant but Sandy wares were. Unusually, it appeared possible to see the nature of the medieval pottery change from phase to phase, with the Sandy wares developing into Partially Reduced wares. Reduced Greyware made an early appearance at Cockermouth, in the fourteenth century. For Dacre (McCarthy and Brooks 1992, 30–31; McCarthy and Brooks in prep), the story is similar.

Two factors differentiate these sites from Carlisle: the local source of the ceramics; and a small but significant presence of trans-Pennine imports. For instance, at Cockermouth, the Sandy wares were quite distinct from those found in either Carlisle, Penrith, or southern Scotland. The Penrith and Dacre affinities were clear, but, above all, this was because the products were local, and in consequence the fabrics were different. One obvious reason for this is the isolated nature of the region, where, unless there was access to the sea, an individual producer would have had a relatively limited market physically. Wider trade seems to have been restricted to south-west Scotland and the Irish Sea areas, in considerable contrast to the towns of the East Coast, distinguished by long-established river and seaborne trade routes, linking them to Continental markets. As a result, local pottery assemblages there have a wealth of well-dated pottery types from the Low Countries, France, Germany, and occasionally as far south as Spain (Armstrong and Ayers 1987).

Scottish and Irish imports into Carlisle were noted by Jope and Hodges (1955, 79–80) and subsequently by Jarrett and Edwards (1964, 42), and a sherd of French green-glazed pottery from St Nicholas Yard was noted by Brooks (1999, 103). These are, however, extreme rarities in a city that has seen a considerable number of excavations in the last 30 years, and the situation bears little comparison with the quantities found, for instance, in Hull (*eg* Armstrong and Ayers 1987). What appears to be significant for sites outside Carlisle, and in particular Kendal and Dacre, is that they produced small quantities of Humber ware, other North Yorkshire wares, and some Cistercian wares (McCarthy and Brooks 1992, 29–30, 32). Cistercian wares in Yorkshire appear in the late fifteenth century and are abundant in Hull in the sixteenth century (Armstrong and Ayers 1987, 114). It can be argued that these finds were from fifteenth-century or later levels and in the Millennium excavations these levels were missing, but, in general, such wares are conspicuous in Carlisle by their absence. It must be borne in mind that even in Kendal and Dacre they occurred only in small quantities, but it should also be noted that both also produced trans-Pennine imports. Thus it is access to trade eastwards and thence access to wider markets, that distinguishes Kendal and Dacre, only some 20 miles south of the city, from Carlisle.

17

THE COINS, MILITARIA, AND OTHER METALWORK

Introduction

Every metal object, including coins, was examined and recorded, but the size of the assemblages has meant that detailed catalogues appear in *Appendices 3, 5-7*. As might be expected, data recorded included material, identification, quantity (fragment count and, where relevant, weight and estimated number of objects represented), condition, completeness, basic dimensions, outline description, dating, and conservation undertaken, including a cross-reference to x-ray plates and other conservation information.

In the case of the metalwork, the project departed from standard practice (Fell *et al* 2006) in that, with the consent of Tullie House Museum and Art Gallery, it was not x-rayed by default. Material from the smaller elements of the project (MIL 1-MIL 4) had been x-rayed during the course of the fieldwork, as had some of the more important pieces from MIL 5. The bulk of the ferrous and non-ferrous metalwork from the latter had not been x-rayed by the assessment stage, and it was decided not to undertake this procedure on the unusually well-preserved material from waterlogged stratigraphic units, unless the complexity of the individual object warranted it, and thus the process was only undertaken on objects where identification would otherwise have proved difficult, if not impossible. The excellent preservation of most of this material would suggest that little information regarding surface decoration or manufacturing technique was lost by this decision.

The Roman Coins

DCA Shotter

Roman coins were recovered in unequal numbers from the various sites forming the Millennium Project. In the southern part of the fort, where survival was poor, only two coins came from MIL 3, and four from MIL 2. Nine coins were recovered from MIL 4, and in the area of the western rampart, in MIL 1, 11

were found, together with a further 'group' of seven Flavian *aes*-issues. The vast majority, 510 coins and a 'group' of five *denarii* found corroded together in a column, came from the largest area excavated, MIL 5.

The multiple coin-finds

In the course of the excavations, two multiple finds were recovered. A group of seven Flavian *aes*-issues was found in occupation layer *472* within Building *1194* (Period 3A; *Ch 3*), close to the western rampart. Their condition in terms of corrosion and wear was reasonably similar, the wear not being great, suggesting that the coins had been lost/deposited not long after the date of the latest (AD 77–8). From the nature of the findspot, it appeared that the coins represented a multiple casual loss rather than a hoard. The numerical superiority of coins of AD 77–8 points to the possibility that this loss took place very close to the date of issue, a time when Agricola will have been conducting his third campaign, for which, on the evidence of writing-tablets, Carlisle was a base (Tomlin 1998). Although of slightly earlier date, this group is reminiscent of that found in 1962, a little to the north, at Edenbridge (Shotter 1979, 11). The seven coins are issues of Vespasian or of Titus as Caesar. It may not be without significance that the coins represent exactly one *denarius*, a logical amount perhaps for a soldier to carry in his purse for the day.

A group of five *denarii* (Pl 207) was found in Period 3D demolition layer *3447* (*Ch 4*), which overlay Buildings *3772* and *4006* in the south-west quadrant. When found, the coins were corroded into a column, and analysis of the corroded material revealed the presence of decayed linen, in which, presumably, the coins had been wrapped. As they came from a demolition deposit, it is impossible to say whether they represent a complete find or had become separated from others, nor is it possible to be certain whether the coins should be regarded as a multiple casual loss or as the whole or part of a hoard.

The coins consist of three very worn Republican issues and one each of Augustus and Tiberius; the fact that all of the coins are pre-Neronian strongly suggests their connection with legionary activity:

Plate 207: Group of five denarii *from layer 3447, overlying Buildings* **3772** *and* **4006**

five *denarii* would have represented a little less than a week's pay for a legionary soldier. It is worth noting that this group contains one of the earliest Roman coins recorded as a site-find in north-western England. The sites excavated at the southern end of the fort between the 1970s and 1990s produced 15 Republican *denarii*, but no pre-Neronian imperial issues (*cf* Shotter 1990a, 85).

Casual losses
The vast majority of coins were clearly casual losses, since they came from a wide variety of contexts from both the timber and stone forts (Periods 3-6) as well as being residual in post-Roman contexts (for a complete list, see *Appendix 3*).

Chronological and spatial distribution
The total number of 536 Roman coins from these excavations is of approximately the same order as those excavated at the various Annetwell Street sites, in the southern part of the fort in the 1970s, 1980s, and early 1990s, which was 715 (Shotter in prep). The profiles of the two groups, however, are markedly different. The coins throughout have been divided by periods, based upon those defined by Reece (1988).

Although a number of factors no doubt contributed to this difference, one major consideration is that the largest trench, MIL 5, investigated an area in the central part of the fort, occupied mostly by the *principia* and early workshops (*fabricae*), where smaller amounts of money might be expected to have been carried when the fort was in full use; the Annetwell Street sites, on the other hand, were characterised by the southern gateway-complex and the front-ends of barrack-blocks. A further factor may be the fact that when investigating the lowest, and therefore the earliest, levels, the extent of MIL 5 was considerably smaller than its equivalent amongst the Annetwell Street sites, and also smaller than that concerned with the later deposits.

It should be noted that, of the 536 (526 legible) coins recovered, no fewer than 326 derive from periods XIII (AD 259–75) and XVII (AD 330–46). Such high figures must exercise a distorting effect on the proportions of coins belonging to other periods.

The first century AD, and the establishment of Roman Carlisle
Although Carlisle had long been accepted as a foundation of Agricola's governorship (AD 77–83; Campbell 1986), doubts had often been expressed, suggesting that it might in fact have been earlier, during the governorship of Quintus Petillius Cerialis (AD 71–4; Bushe-Fox 1913b; Ogilvie and Richmond 1967). The issue was finally settled in favour of the earlier date as a result of dendrochronological analysis of timbers recovered in the 1973–84 excavations on Annetwell Street, the site of the fort's southern rampart and gateway-complex (*Ch 12*). As a result, it has been possible to identify a coin-profile that might point to such early occupation (Shotter

2000a; 2001). Three criteria appeared significant, either singly or in combination: the presence of pre-Flavian coinage, particularly *aes*-issues; a strong dominance of Flavian coins over Trajanic; and, within coins of Vespasian's reign, a strong showing of coins of the early AD 70s.

The present group of coins contains a number of Republican *denarii*, no coins of Claudius, and a few of Nero and/or the emperors of AD 68–9. First, Republican *denarii*: these coins enjoyed an extremely lengthy circulation-life, being well-represented in two multiple finds from Birdoswald on Hadrian's Wall (Shotter 1990a, 179f and 201). Dio Cassius (*Roman History 68*, 5, 3[1]-*Xiphilinus* (Cary and Foster 1925)) reports that, in *c* AD 107, Trajan recalled 'old silver', which appears to have embraced *denarii* issued prior to Nero's coinage reform of AD 64, although it evidently did not include *denarii* issued by Marcus Antonius, probably because of the (false) allegation, perhaps originally made by Octavian (later, the emperor Augustus), that they were made of base silver (Pliny, *Natural History* xxxiii, 132 (Rackham 1952)). The latter appear to have remained in circulation until the demise of the *denarius* (AD 230s/40s), often virtually worn smooth. Reece (1988, 92) has shown, however, that Trajan's decree probably took until some time into Hadrian's reign to become effective in Britain. These early coins, therefore, do not provide much help in the discussion of the earliest activity at Carlisle, although it is possible that their presence might point to the involvement of legionary soldiers at the site. In this connection, the small column of Republican and early *denarii* from MIL 5 (*pp 679-80*) may take on a special significance. A legionary presence will have been particularly likely if Carlisle was used as winter-quarters for troops operating further north.

Pre-Neronian *aes*, save for the very occasional pieces, appear to have been lost from circulation by the early years of Vespasian's reign. It is for this reason that the appearance of such coins in the North West (Shotter 1994) probably points to pre-Flavian military activity. The present sample contains just two pre-Flavian *aes*-coins, both of them issues of Galba (AD 68–9).

The coin-series commences in earnest with issues of Vespasian, many of them in exceptionally fine condition. Tacitus records (*Agricola 7*, 3 (Mattingly 1948)) that in AD 70 Vespasian appointed the young Agricola to take charge of the still-recalcitrant *Legio* XX: this, and the decision to send his own relative (perhaps his son-in-law), Petillius Cerialis, as governor as soon as he was free of the Gallo-German uprising, indicates the importance that Vespasian attached to Britain in the matter of his own 'image-building' (Shotter 2004a). The immediate dominance of coins of the new regime may point in the same direction, and is clearly indicated both in the present sample and in that from the southern end of the fort. The numerical superiority of Flavian coins from Annetwell Street (Shotter in prep) could be, in part, explained by the fact that the dendrochronology implies that the rampart and gate may have been in place in advance of the fort's internal buildings.

The period proportions from both parts of the fort are similar; particularly striking is the fact that, in both cases, Flavian coins outnumber Trajanic by approximately 3:1 (Table 38). In north-west England, only Ribchester shares this pattern of distribution (Shotter 2000b). It is likely that it derives from the fact that these sites were active throughout the *entire* Flavian period, that is, from the early 70s until the mid-90s. This can be demonstrated in a more detailed distribution of early Flavian coins (Table 39).

The dominance of coins of the early years of Vespasian, corresponding to the governorships of Vettius Bolanus and Petillius Cerialis, is very clear, and can hardly be explained by any factor other than the occupation of the site in the early

Coin period	Millennium Project		Annetwell Street sites	
	No	*%*	*No*	*%*
I (- AD 41)	5	6.41	15	6.94
II (AD 41-54)	-	-	-	-
III (AD 54-68)	2	2.56	3	1.39
IV (AD 69-96)	51	65.38	130	60.19
V (AD 96-117)	15	19.23	44	20.37
VI (AD 117-38)	5	6.42	24	11.11
Totals	**78**		**216**	

Table 38: Roman coins until the death of Hadrian

Dates	Millennium Project %	Annetwell Street sites %
AD 69–73	51.16	46.55
AD 74–6	4.65	2.59
AD 77–9	20.93	28.45
AD 69–79	20.93	21.65
AD 79–81	2.33	0.86

Table 39: Carlisle: early Flavian coins

70s: the similarity of proportions in the two groups of sites leaves little doubt that these results can be regarded as reliable. In this way, the coin-evidence which, on its own, would have been more difficult to interpret, can be seen as confirming the results of dendrochronology (Shotter 2001). Although the total numbers of Flavian coins differ markedly between the two areas, the distribution of the coins (in percentage terms) from both between periods of the reigns of Vespasian and Titus, and between periods I and VI overall, are very similar (Table 38).

It is also striking that coin-loss was so prolific in the later first century. This may to some extent have been caused by a predominance, in a turf-and-timber fort, of unmetalled surfaces which would have made the loss of coins less easy to detect and their recovery much more fortuitous (Casey 1988, 40). Beyond this, it should be regarded as an indication of the significance of Carlisle at this early stage of conquest. It will have been a pivotal site in the North West, not only for the conquest of Brigantian and Carvetian territory, but also for the advance into Scotland (Shotter 2000a). This importance has recently been confirmed by the indication that the main gate of the earliest fort at Newstead faced westwards, that is, towards Carlisle (RFJ Jones *pers comm*); further, writing-tablets discovered at Carlisle (Tomlin 1998) demonstrate the site as a hub of activity in the Flavian period, a base for forward-activity, and providing winter-quarters for troops operating further north.

Again, the late-Flavian coins (reign of Domitian) show a chronological distribution similar to that from the Annetwell Street sites (Shotter in prep): the substantial majority of both groups are *aes*-issues of AD 86–7; whilst this to some extent mirrors issue-patterns, it was a period whose significance in the history of Carlisle and the northern frontier-zone was momentous (Hobley 1989; Jones 1990). With the changes in frontier-strategy, it is certain that Carlisle would have seen, even if temporarily, an enlarged military population. Thus, the pattern of first-century coin loss both mirrors the results from the other areas sampled within the fort, and what is now taken as orthodoxy in the early years of the Roman occupation of the North West.

The second century

The history of the second century in the North is, unsurprisingly, dominated by developments and changes in frontier-policy, but whilst this is becoming better understood in broad outline, the quality of the documentary sources (literary and non-literary) is such that the detail is still poorly understood. Besides this, the second century appears to have been a time of growing uncertainty, militarily, economically, and socially.

The coinage itself mirrors this uncertainty, with the progressive debasement of the *denarius*, so that, by the close of the century, it contained only 50% (or even less) silver (Boon 1974; 1988). In addition, there had been a progressive loss from circulation of the smaller *aes*-denominations, as inflation rendered them increasingly redundant. By the end of the second century, the coinage in normal usage consisted of *denarii, sestertii*, and *dupondii*. It is also probable that the loss of such higher-value coins would have prompted a more diligent search; further, with the increase of construction in stone, and of metalled surfaces, the loss of coins was probably more easily noticed. Thus, in interpreting the coin-loss of the second century, one has to be alert to the working of economic factors. It may be that the peak of hoarding of *denarii* in the Antonine period, so often cited as evidence of military difficulties and even 'Brigantian revolts' (Shotter 2000b, 186), may in fact have had more to do with the decline in the quality of the coins and with people attempting to safeguard the value of their savings by retaining earlier coins of higher intrinsic value. In north-west England, the second century generally shows a steady decline in recorded coin-loss from period V (the reign of Trajan) to period IX (the reign of Commodus). Whilst some sites, for example, Watercrook and Hardknott, certainly do have erratic second-century coin-loss pointing to erratic occupation-patterns, a steady decline in coin-loss is noted at sites which evidently enjoyed unbroken occupation through the period (Shotter 1993).

Of the Millennium sites, only MIL 5 has yielded any coins of periods VI–IX (AD 117–92); as a percentage of the whole sample, these coins represent 2.05%, whereas the coins of the same period from the

Annetwell Street sites represent 4.36% (Shotter in prep). If, however, this is expressed as a percentage of losses of the first and second centuries, the Millennium sites show 13.25% compared with 15.03% from the Annetwell Street sites. The two pictures differ largely in the comparative effect of coins of the third and fourth centuries.

The Millennium sample shows the Flavian period (IV) dominating the Trajanic (V) by approximately 3:1. Whilst this reflects the long period of accumulation of Flavian coin-loss, it may also have been affected by factors within and beyond the Trajanic period itself. It has been shown (Jones 1990) that Stanegate forts witnessed changes and complex developments. This certainly involved reductions, if not actual loss, of garrisons on a temporary basis. Carlisle's pattern of use could well have been more complex, particularly if the Stanegate was re-routed to bypass Carlisle through Cummersdale (Shotter 2004b, 61). However, in view of the current state of evidence from Cummersdale, this must remain entirely speculative. A further factor which may have acted to depress the total Trajanic coin-loss may lie in events of the Hadrianic period, as this would normally be expected to have seen substantial loss of the coins of Hadrian's predecessor. The building of Hadrian's Wall may, in fact, have caused local emphasis to shift from Cummersdale to Stanwix. It should, however, also be noted that the presence in the Carlisle sample of some little-worn coins of Trajan's later years might reflect the difficulties alluded to by Hadrian's biographer (*Scriptores Historia Augusta, Hadrian 5*,2 (Magie 1921)) as causing concern at the opening of his reign.

Several military sites in the North West display sharply-depressed Hadrianic-period samples (for example, Lancaster: Shotter 1993; 1995, 6). This may be connected with troop-loss associated with the construction of the Antonine Wall. Whilst this is less noticeable at the Millennium sites than elsewhere, the fact that most Hadrianic coins show a considerable degree of wear suggests that they should be regarded as losses of later than the Hadrianic period itself. Similarly, with the exception of a fresh coin of Faustina II (issued in the reign of Antoninus Pius), the small number of Antonine coins had seen some circulation before loss. In all, therefore, the coin-loss of the second century AD poses rather more questions than it answers, leaving the nature and density of activity in this period very uncertain.

The third and fourth centuries

Issues from the first half of the third century are poorly represented: four Severan coins (period X, AD 192-222); and one each of Pupienus and Valerian (period XII, AD 235-59). Severan coins are rarely well-represented on North Western sites, and it is not uncommon for

there to be a complete absence of coins of periods XI and XII. The low coin-loss in these periods need not, therefore, occasion comment. In any case, the fact that the *principia* was rebuilt in stone in the Severan period (*Ch 8*) indicates activity and a time of considerable change. The milestone recently discovered near Penrith, dated to AD 223 and mentioning the *Civitas Carvetiorum*, suggests that Severus may, during his time in Britain (AD 209–11), have been responsible for initiating major changes in Carlisle (Edwards and Shotter 2005).

From the middle of the third until the late-fourth century, however, coin-loss shows a sharp increase, providing in excess of 80% of the overall sample, with two clear peaks in periods XIII (AD 259-75) and XVII (AD 330-46). All of the coins from periods X-XXI (AD 192-388+) have derived from MIL 5, with the exception of three from XIII (AD 259-75) and one from XVII (AD 330-46), which came from MIL 1. A general ignorance of the workings of the money-system through these periods makes interpretation of coin-loss difficult.

The third and fourth centuries were a time of fluctuating, but often great, uncertainty; in particular, the changes brought about to military and, as a consequence, social organisation, by the Severans, led to extreme economic problems. Especially dangerous was the ease with which men might 'bid' for imperial power and subsequently 'print money' to buy support for themselves. The money-system had already been in difficulties at the turn of the second and third centuries, with the decline in the silver content of the *denarius* and the disappearance from circulation of the lower denominations, giving clear signals of developing inflation. During the first half of the third century, the situation worsened: the double-*denarius* (*antoninianus*) was introduced by Caracalla (Reece 1987, 9) and the double-*sestertius* in the AD 240s; the same period saw both the disappearance of the *denarius* and the progressive debasement of the *antoninianus*, to the point where, by the AD 260s, it was a small copper coin of poor quality, with the radiate head on the obverse side providing the only reminder of its prototype.

It is clear that, in a situation of hyperinflation, the mints could not cope with demand: the only way to produce coinage on the unprecedented scale required was by having recourse to local copying of radiates; the quality of these was variable, and at worst execrable, possibly pointing to a local copying-centre in Carlisle. This is supported by the discovery of what appear to be two examples of forgers' blank flans (*302* and *336*; *Appendix 3*), which may suggest that the copying of coins was being carried out *within* the fort. Six of the recorded coins of periods XII (AD 235-59) and XIII (AD 259-75) may be regarded as regular issues, whilst 113 are copies of varying quality. Such figures are not, however, greatly at variance with those recorded from other sites in Carlisle: both military and non-military sites have produced approximately 35% of their coin-loss from period XIII (Shotter 1990a, 72f; 1990b; *Appendix 3*).

A problem, however, attends the interpretation of such figures, concerning the period over which these coins circulated. It has often been noted that legitimate coins of *c* AD 275–310 are relatively uncommon as site-finds in northern Britain; the Millennium Project provides no exception to this. It may, therefore, be reasonable to extend the circulation-period of radiates and copies into the early years of the fourth century, and perhaps also their production (Mattingly 1963). Indeed, it is worth noting that they continue to appear in hoards of the later fourth century (Shotter 1978), suggesting that their circulation-life extended that long. Another factor of possible significance is the (unjustified) claim of Constantius I and his family that they were descended from Claudius II (AD 268–70) (*Panegyrici Latini 6* (Nixon and Saylor Rodgers 1994)); this may have led to an extended life for, and perhaps, revived manufacture of, coins of that emperor, especially those of the DIVVS CLAVDIVS series.

The uncertainties of the mid-third century descended into anarchy and breakaway movements: in AD 259, Postumus took the western provinces (including Britain) into the rebellion known as the *Imperium Galliarum* (Independent Empire of the Gauls), which lasted until the removal of the Tetrici by the armies of Aurelian in AD 273. There is no doubt that this led to internal strife in provinces between 'loyalists' and 'rebels' (Shotter 2003); this is sometimes reflected in the distribution of coinage: although 37 coins of period XIII (AD 259-75) (31.09%) cannot be related to a certain prototype, 37 (31.09%) of the remainder are regular or irregular issues of legitimate emperors, and 45 (37.82%) of rebel rulers. The strength of the rebels in the territory of the *Civitas Carvetiorum* is well-illustrated by the milestone of Postumus found at Frenchfield (Edwards and Shotter 2005).

Although there are no regular coins of the period AD 275–94, the sample does include 16 of Carausius and Allectus (3.04%). Similarly poorly represented are pre-Constantinian tetrarchic issues; it is possible that, as the size of these began to deteriorate after *c* AD 303, many of the earlier tetrarchic issues found their way into savings' hoards, such as those from Kirksteads (Casey 1978; Shotter 1990a, 193) and Cliburn (Shotter 1990a, 188f).

The second quarter of the fourth century, however, saw a further major increase in coin-loss; 49.05% of all the coins from the Millennium Project were issues of AD 324 and later, 39.55% comprising regular issues

and copies of period XVII (AD 330-46). It might be expected that the upgraded status of Carlisle, associated previously with major building work as the town became the *civitas*-capital of the Carveti (Higham and Jones 1985), would have led to more obvious manifestations of economic vibrancy. Indeed, Carlisle must have taken on twin roles as a garrison-town in the frontier zone and as a flourishing market centre for local communities. Coin-loss, however, provides little indication of this in the first half of the third century, although activity strengthens markedly from the AD 260s. It is noticeable that all Carlisle sites share not only the large loss of coins of period XIII (AD 259-75), but also those of period XVII (AD 330-46).

Overall, Carlisle sites have yielded 20.90% of their coins of periods XVII-XXI (AD 330-88+) from military activity, and 30.98% from non-military sites with, respectively, 14.29% and 18.84% from period XVII (AD 330-46) alone (Shotter 1990a, 74-5). The Millennium Project, in contrast, has a far higher showing.

The bulk of the fourth-century coins came from an area adjacent to the *principia*, and along the main east to west road (Fig 258). Whilst it could possibly be suggested that some of these coins represent hoard material, their distribution over such a large area and the fact that a similar spatial distribution has been noted in excavations of the fort at Newcastle upon Tyne (Brickstock 2002) appears as persuasive evidence against such an interpretation. It seems much more likely that the fort, and especially its principal building, was assuming a function akin to that of an *emporium*, perhaps accompanied by roadside gambling. This mirrors the evidently much closer relationship between military and civilian populations that has been noted in the context of the fort at Birdoswald (Wilmott 2001).

A strong showing continues into the Valentinianic period: as elsewhere in Carlisle, the wear of several of these coins, together with the inclusion of a few issues of periods XX (AD 378-88) and XXI (AD 388+), indicates that local people continued to feel involved in the Romano-British way of life throughout the fourth and into the fifth centuries, and indeed, longer still, if the evidence of Bede in his *Life of St Cuthbert* (Colgrave 1940), can be trusted. Indeed, the coin evidence from the Millennium sites (and especially MIL 5) tends to point to the continuing strength and importance of the idea of being Romano-British in the chief town of the Carvetii.

Denominational analysis (Periods I-IX)
It is evident that the denominational distribution of coins in circulation changed through the first and second centuries as a mirror of changing economic conditions (Table 40). Whilst to some extent such

Coin period	Den	Ses	Dp	As	Qd	No coins	As-value
I	5	-	-	-	-	5	80
II	-	-	-	-	-	-	-
III	-	1	-	1	-	2	5
IV	3	6	7	34	1	51	120.25
V	6	6	1	1	-	14	122
VI	2	3	-	1	-	6	45
VII	-	1	-	2	-	3	6
VIII	-	2	-	-	-	2	8
IX	-	-	-	-	-	-	-
Totals	16	19	8	39	1	83	386.25

Den=*denarii*; Ses=*sestertii*; Dp=*dupondii*; As=*asses*; Qd=*quadrantes*

Table 40: Distribution of coins by denomination

figures reflect the vicissitudes of the coinage itself, there are some notable comparisons to be made. In particular, the low '*as*-value' of coins of period IV throughout the fort, combined with the low percentage of *denarii* in the same period, prompts the suggestion that legionary troops were not barracked in the fort on a long-term basis during the Flavian period. Indeed, writing-tablets (Tomlin 1998) possibly indicate the presence in Carlisle during Agricola's governorship of a unit of auxiliary cavalry (*ala Gallorum Sebosiana*), although by the early-second century this unit had probably moved south to Lancaster (Shotter and White 1990). Whilst the rise in '*as*-value' in periods V and VI may be in part due to economic factors, this may be a pointer to the arrival of troops of higher status in connection with frontier duties.

Mints of origin of fourth-century coins

Although the mint-marks were illegible on a very large number of the fourth-century coins (40.4%), the remainder display a distribution that is normal for sites in north-west England. Until the middle of the century, the dominant mint was Trier, with London making a significant impact at the turn of the third and fourth centuries (Table 41). The contributions of other western European mints become more significant in the second half of the fourth century, with Arles playing a major role in the Valentinianic period.

Coin-loss related to Periods

There is a considerable degree of residuality throughout (*Appendix 3*), with Flavian coins appearing in almost every phase of the site. Until the first half of the third century, there is no reason why such residuality should not have been due to coin-circulation: both *denarii* and *aes*-denominations (especially *sestertii*) could well have circulated into the AD 240s and AD 250s. Thereafter, residuality of such coins is more likely to have been a result of their incorporation in demolition rubbish. The long-term residuality of radiates and copies (period XIII (AD 259-75)) is also demonstrated; various causal factors may account for this, but there is every reason to believe that they continued to circulate as usable money into the later years of the fourth century. In contrast, no doubt, for political reasons, radiate coins of Carausius and Allectus appear to have made little impact on circulating money beyond the early years of the fourth century. Further, whilst it may be unsound to base propositions about activity in the late fourth century on the presence of worn coins of the earlier years of the century unless late fourth-century coins are also present, this situation (*Appendix 3*) demonstrates how resilient coins of the earlier fourth century in fact were. One cautionary note should be sounded regarding these apparent trends: evidence from this project shows that Castle Gardens has experienced considerable physical disturbance of various kinds over the centuries (*Ch 14*). It would

Mints	Period XV	Period XVI	Period XVII	Period XVIII	Period XIX	Period XX	Period XXI
London	16	-	-	-	-	-	-
Trier	10	1	88	9	-	-	1
Lyons	7	-	18	1	2	-	-
Arles	1	-	6	1	9	-	-
Rome	1	-	1	-	-	-	-
Amiens	-	-	-	3	-	-	-
Aquileia	-	-	-	-	2	-	-
Siscia	-	-	1	1	-	-	-
Cyzicus	-	-	1	-	-	-	-
Uncertain	10	-	92	13	4	3	-
Total	45	1	207	28	17	3	1

Table 41: Originating mints of the fourth-century coins

be surprising if this has not led to some disturbance of the sites of archaeological interest, particularly in the later levels.

The Post-Roman Coins

A Gannon and J Zant

Four post-Roman coins were recovered by a combination of hand retrieval and the use of a metal detector. All came from deposits within MIL 5.

Catalogue

1. *Styca*, Eanred?, *c* AD 810–40? Obv. +(?)EANRED... around annulet, with pellet or cross within. Rev illegible.
   MIL 5, *2110/2149*, Period 7, post-Roman 'dark earth'

2. Penny, William II, 1087–1100 (North 1959, 853).
   MIL 5, *2227/2000*, Period 7, post-Roman 'dark earth'

3. *Styca*, Eanred, by the moneyer Wulfred, *c* AD 810–40 (Pirie 1996, type II, Ci, b). Obv +EANREDREX around cross. Rev. +VVLFRED around cross.
   MIL 5, *5058/3517*, Period 8C, external soil layer

4. Penny, Stephen, 1135–54 (North 1959, 908).
   MIL 5, *5037/3487*, Period 8D, fill of pit *5036*

Two of the coins were recovered from the Period 7 post-Roman 'dark earth' (Northumbrian *styca 1* and the penny of William II (*2*)). Both can be regarded as being securely stratified rather than residual or intrusive (*Ch 11*). The coin of William II came from the surface of the dark soil that represented the old ground surface at the beginning of the Norman period. The second *styca* (*3*) was residual within a later medieval soil layer of Period 8C. The penny of Stephen (*4*) was found in the uppermost fill of medieval pit *5036* (Period 8D; *Ch 11*), and is likely to have been broadly contemporary with that deposit.

Medieval coins of any date are relatively uncommon finds from excavations in Carlisle, and those of the twelfth century and earlier are rarer still. This small assemblage therefore represents a useful addition to the corpus of post-Roman coins from the city. Northumbrian *stycas* of the ninth century are not infrequent finds from sites within the city centre (over 50 are known) and as such represent an important source of evidence for activity during this period. Their distribution shows a marked concentration on the western side of the city, north and south of the medieval cathedral, which seems likely to have been the focus of settlement at this time (McCarthy 1993, 36–7); the Millennium excavations were at the northern periphery of this

area. The penny of William Rufus would seem to be the first to have been found in Carlisle. Its discovery close to the medieval castle is noteworthy, in view of William's known association with the castle, as recorded in the *Anglo-Saxon Chronicle* (Earle and Plummer 1892). The penny of Stephen may also represent a first for the city, at least in terms of coins recovered by archaeological excavation.

The Goldwork

C Howard-Davis

Two fragments of gold were recovered. Both were ornate decorative links (*1, 2*; Fig 335), presumably from a single necklace; one was complete, the other damaged. They were found in association with a shattered blue glass cylinder bead (Glass *192*, *Ch 18*), which may well have been a component of the same piece of jewellery. Evidence seems to suggest that the blue glass bead was originally threaded on thin copper-alloy wire, and may even have represented a repair, as originally the entire necklace would have been of gold. The goldwork and associated bead were recovered from occupation deposit *2309*, within Period 6A stone building *2302* (*Ch 8*).

The links would have formed part of a necklace similar to the mid-third-century example from Obfelden in Switzerland (Drack and Fellman 1988, pl 20), where links identical to the Carlisle examples alternated with plain ones, some or all of which were originally threaded through beads. A slightly earlier, second-century example from Çorum in modern Turkey, has the ornate links separated by orange agate beads (Bingöl 1999, 131). As part of a necklace with almost identical links has been found at Kirkby Thore (Pl 208; T Padley *pers comm*), it might suggest local manufacture, or perhaps more probably, supply. Similar, but not identical, links are to be seen in a necklace from London, dated to *c* AD 200 (Higgins 1961, pl 57A).

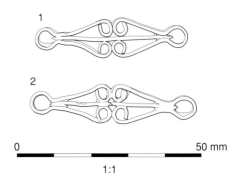

Figure 335: The goldwork

The juxtaposition of gold with what to the modern mind are relatively worthless glass beads is common in Roman jewellery, where the bright colours offered by glass were valued as an important design element (Johns 1991, 29). Allason-Jones (1989a, fig 2, no 37) illustrates an earring from Godmanchester which is identical in design, and also notes its similarity to a necklace terminal from the hoard found at Wincle, in Cheshire (Johns *et al* 1981). A gold necklace link found during excavations at the Lanes, Carlisle, is similar, but not identical, the links in that case being in the form of a Hercules knot (reef knot), regarded by the Classical world as having apotropaic powers (Johns 1996, 36). Necklaces of this kind seem to have been produced in reasonable quantities in the Cologne area (Johns 1991) and a continental origin is perhaps corroborated by the bead, as Guido (1978) notes a predominantly southern distribution for the type, suggesting that they could be imports.

Such a necklace obviously implies the presence of at least one woman of wealth and status within the stone fort during Period 6. Evidence from a number of artefact groups (for instance, hairpins and coins) seems to imply that the focal areas of the fort were much more public during this period than earlier, and there are several mechanisms by which such a valuable and essentially feminine object could have entered the fort. The most obvious, however, is as the possession of a woman within, or visiting, the household of a senior officer.

The Roman Militaria

M C Bishop and C Howard-Davis

The excavations produced a large assemblage of metalwork, both copper alloy and iron, which included many day-to-day objects alongside a significant collection of militaria, which comprises a large and important group of armour, projectile weapons, and horse gear. Whilst not unexpected, as a significant number of military objects were found during the Annetwell Street excavations (Caruana in prep), the amount recovered, and the extent of its

contribution to Roman military studies, is unusual. Most obviously, the deposit of body armour has added important information regarding the construction, maintenance, and dating of various styles of scale and plate armour, and the group is of international significance. In addition, there is a large collection of weaponry, including arrowheads, spearheads, and other projectiles. Over and above this, a large collection of fittings intended for horse tack reflects the sustained use of the fort by cavalry units. This is mirrored in the leatherwork, where fragments of several saddles and bardings were recorded (*Ch 20*). There was also a considerable amount of material associated with metalworking, and probably more particularly the repair of arms and armour. Whilst less spectacular, this group of off-cuts and part-made objects, such as rivets, allows insight into the wear and tear of legionary and auxiliary kit, and its routine maintenance.

In general, the importance of the metalwork was much enhanced by its excellent state of preservation, a persistent feature of artefact groups from Carlisle, where extensive waterlogging has ensured that many objects have remained in a condition similar to that on the day when they were lost or discarded, giving some indication of the importance of colour and pattern in the lives of both legionary and auxiliary soldiers.

The body armour
M C Bishop
It is demonstrably the case that nearly all significant advances in the study of Roman armour have come about as the result of the study of major assemblages or hoards, the best known probably being the Corbridge Hoard and its role in allowing Charles Daniels and H Russell Robinson to make the definitive functional analysis of Roman segmental body armour (Allason-Jones and Bishop 1988). Indeed, such assemblages tend to be pivotal in our impression of the Roman army, with major new finds often changing perceptions of the army as we think we understand it. Thus there was always potential for the Carlisle armour to make an important contribution to knowledge of Roman warfare, and to add something to an understanding of the nature of the military presence in Britain, and it has not disappointed these expectations.

The material upon which this report is based was examined in the conservation laboratories at the University of Durham before (in some cases) and during the conservation process (*Appendix 4*). In addition, numerous digital photographs and x-rays were made available, providing a valuable subsidiary source of information, adding to what could be gained by examination of the artefacts themselves.

The principal group of armour came from Building *5689* in the central range of the Period 4B fort

*Plate 209: Layer **6419**, containing armour, during excavation*

(*c* AD 125-40/50), immediately next to (and on the other side of a road from) the headquarters building (*5688*; *Ch 6*). The key deposit, *6419* (Pl 209), overlay three small wooden boxes or tanks (*6521*, *6566*, and *6597*) set into the floor of the building. Layer *6419* accumulated during the penultimate phase of the building (Phase 6), whilst the floor into which the tanks were set was ascribed to Phase 4, Phase 5 being a resurfacing of the floor. The spatial (if not direct temporal) association of similar finds of military equipment with those tanks might be thought to suggest that there is a link between them and the deposit of armour, and that it was not in any way an alien introduction. It is of importance to note that the objects within the assemblage were sufficiently distinctive that, had the stratigraphic context not been sufficient to date the collection, the collection could have supplied a date for the context. In addition, the quality of the stratigraphic data was good enough to offer some new insights into the introduction of certain types of armour, as well as posing some intriguing historical questions.

The principal deposit of armour was, as is so often the case with Roman military equipment, abandoned scrap (Bishop 1985, 5–9). The scarcity of raw materials, especially metals, meant that the Roman army exercised an aggressive recycling policy hand-in-hand with their repair and maintenance regime. This meant that if an item of armour could not be repaired, it would be cannibalised to repair other pieces or, failing that, turned back into raw material by melting (in the case of copper-alloy) or re-forging (for ferrous metals). Thus every unit would have had an accumulated stock of damaged equipment (Bishop and Coulston 1993, 184–5) that ranged in quality from (on the one hand) easily reparable objects, to (on the other) those of no

use except as scrap. When the time came to abandon a site, even temporarily, it became necessary to decide, by a process of triage, how much of this stock was to be taken with them, and how much abandoned, the latter usually buried (in order to deprive any potential enemy of its use). Thus it is that most deposits of armour from the Roman world show signs of repeated repair, often of a very rudimentary nature, and this group is no exception. What makes it particularly interesting, however, is its date and the frequency with which some elements appear to have been repaired.

Form and function
Deliberate deposits of military equipment tend to be associated with times of upheaval and change (Bishop and Coulston 1993, 37), when units were being transferred as a result of conflict (and not necessarily in the immediate vicinity: for example, it is held that the Flavian withdrawal from Scotland was a result of military demands elsewhere in the empire (Breeze and Dobson 2000, 9–10)). The mid-second-century date of this group places it at a time of transition in Roman arms and armour coincident with the advent of the Antonine emperors, and this is reflected in the constituents of the assemblage, and the fact that both 'old' and 'new' equipment is represented. The material from deposit *4619* can therefore be taken to indicate change in the middle of the second century, significant enough for the unit concerned to have had to triage its scrap; what it left behind almost certainly bears the scars of battle, and thereby tells a tale.

The body armour
In order to facilitate comparison amongst items of the same type, the following is organised by category of artefact, rather than by material, since many objects

are composite in nature, whilst other items with the same function are made of different materials (see *Appendices 5* and *6* for catalogues). In the case of the arm-guards, the nature of the remains means that they have been described, in the main, from x-radiographs, and their fragile condition has meant that only the better preserved parts of arm-guards A and C could be illustrated (*pp 694-700*).

Scale armour

There were two main types of scale armour (Bishop and Coulston 1993, 117), the flexible form (used throughout the Roman period), formed from rows of ferrous or copper-alloy scales wired together horizontally and stitched to a textile backing, and the semi-rigid type (only found from the second century AD onwards), where scales were not only wired to their neighbours horizontally, but also vertically. Flexible scale overlapped quincunx fashion (like fish scales), whereas semi-rigid overlapped vertically in columns. The basic scale forms were defined by von Groller (von Groller 1901, Taf XV) as a result of his excavations in the *Waffenmagazin* at *Carnuntum*.

The largest fragment recovered was a curving patch of three rows of 21 shaped, semi-rigid scales (Iron *2722*; Pl 210; Fig 336), found lying face down in Period 4C layer *6205*, within Building *5689*; it was approximately 111 mm deep and 292 mm wide. All of the 1 mm-thick scales are ferrous, except for a column of three 0.5 mm-thick scales, which are of copper alloy, as are all of the wire ties. Viewed from the front, there are eight scales to the left of the copper-alloy column and 12 to the right in each row; they have been set to overlap left over right. Each of the scales in the middle row is intended to be wired to its neighbours, and those above and below, and so has eight holes (von Groller type VII). Each scale in the top row is wired to its neighbour on either side and below, and has a single hole in the centre of the top edge, thus having seven holes (modified von Groller type VII). Each of the bottom row is wired to its neighbour on

either side and above, but has no hole on its lower curved edge, having six holes (von Groller type V). The scales taper towards the top in each of the rows and are between 44 mm and 46 mm in height (see *Appendix 6* for detailed dimensions).

Many of the copper-alloy wire ties (which range between rectangular- and oval-sectioned) bear linear marks showing them to have been drawn, although they give the impression of several different wires being used. The ties are secured by each end being passed through from the front and then bent down to lie side by side, the end from the top hole to the right and that from the bottom to the left (as viewed from the rear), and this suggests one (fairly careful) craftsman fastening the ties (for details of separate fragments of iron and copper alloy adhering to the inner face of the scales, see *Appendices 5* and *6*). All of the copper alloys in this assemblage are brasses of slightly differing types. Scales 1–5 on the bottom row are noticeably bent downwards towards their lower end, possibly as a result of a blow when being worn, or perhaps as a result of something heavy, for instance the foot of the person dumping the material, being placed on top of the patch when it was lying face downwards in the ground.

A second patch of scales (Iron *2885*) was found lying face up in a marginally earlier layer (*6419*) within the same building (*5689*). It comprised three rows of shaped semi-rigid scale, measuring approximately 380 mm wide and 170 mm deep. The right-hand portion of the patch, approximately 14 scales wide, is best preserved (only this has been illustrated; Fig 337). All the 1 mm-thick scales are ferrous, but some have an additional copper-alloy sheathing (cut exactly to shape, with no overlap, and with matching wiring holes) added on the outer face. They have been set to overlap right over left, as viewed from the front, and the patch as a whole contains two 0.5 mm-thick copper-alloy sheathed scales in the bottom row, one in the middle, and two in the top. The left-hand copper-alloy scale in the bottom row has had its lower curved edge folded back on itself obliquely, whilst the top of the copper-alloy sheathing in the top row has been folded down. The scales on the top row are distinguished by having a single central hole *c* 3 mm in diameter (with two smaller (*c* 2 mm) holes on either side and at the bottom of the scale (modified von Groller type VII), whilst those from the other rows have two smaller ones at the top, bottom, and on either side (von Groller type VII). The exception is one of the bottom row copper-alloy sheathings, which has a single larger hole at the bottom. Ferrous wire ties *c* 1 mm in diameter have been used for fixing, except in two cases, where the x-ray shows copper-alloy ties. As with Iron *2722* (Pl 210), the scales taper towards the top in each of the rows (see *Appendix 6* for detailed dimensions).

Plate 210: Fragment of scale mail, from Building **5689**

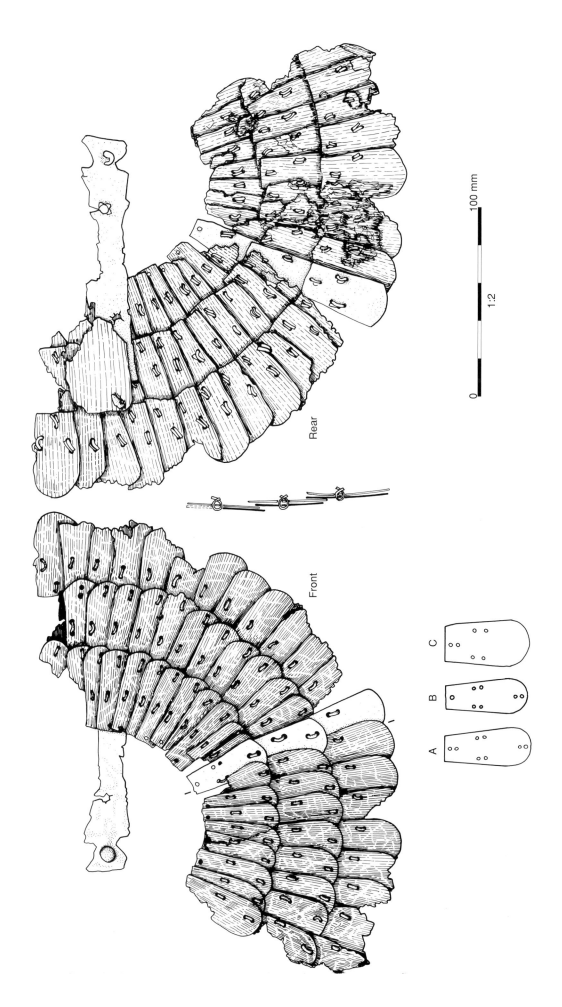

Rear

Front

A B C

100 mm

1:2

0

Figure 336: Scale mail fragment 2722

690

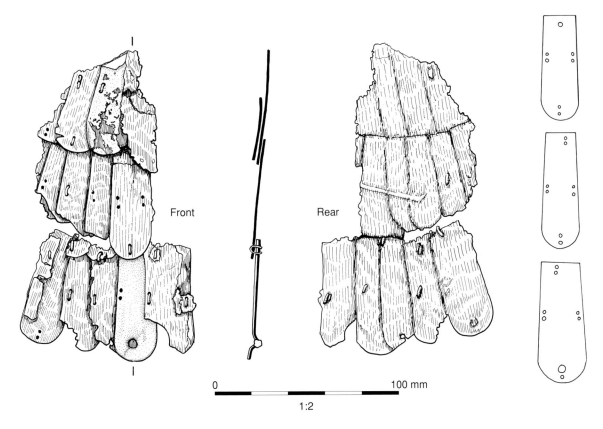

Figure 337: Scale mail fragment 2885

A third large patch of scales was found in Period 5D layer *5866*. Measuring some 130 mm in height, and 90 mm deep, it comprised seven rows of ferrous and copper-alloy scales with copper-alloy ties from flexible scale armour (Iron *2657*; Fig 338), folded over behind an embossed(?) ferrous breastplate (66 mm wide and at least 134 mm high), which retains its upper copper-alloy turning pin. This would have served to fasten it to its neighbour, thereby closing the neck aperture. Each scale has two holes on either side arranged vertically, and two horizontally along its top edge (von Groller type V), and each measures 25 mm high by 15 mm wide. The scales are arranged so that rows of exclusively ferrous scales alternate with ones containing a recurring sequence of three ferrous scales and one copper alloy. The breastplate

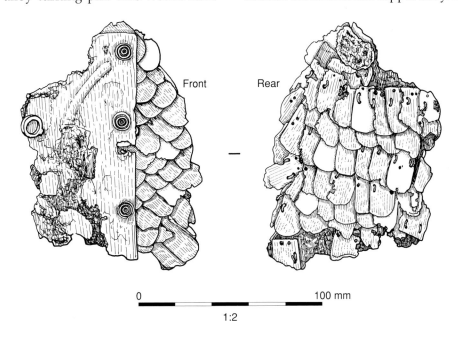

Figure 338: Scale mail fragment 2657

691

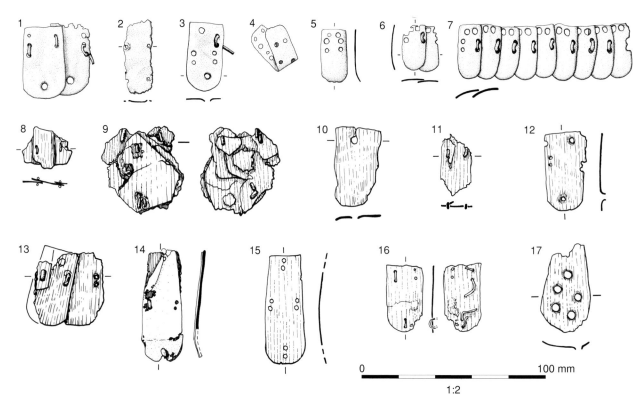

Figure 339: Iron and copper-alloy scales from mail

retains its curving neck opening, and its inner and outer sides, although the bottom edge is missing. Three copper-alloy disc-headed rivets attach the breastplate to the scales, each rivet being 10 mm in diameter, with three concentric rings on its upper surface. Traces of embossed decoration survive on the surface of the plate.

Several more small patches of scale mail, and individual scales, both ferrous and copper alloy, were recovered from a range of contexts from Periods 4 and 5 (Fig 339; see *Appendices 5* and *6*).

Plate armour
Three principal forms of segmental body armour (*lorica segmentata*) are recognisable from the archaeological record: the Kalkriese type of the late first century BC to the mid-first century AD (Bishop 2002, 23–9); the Corbridge type of the mid-first to the mid-second century AD (*op cit*, 31–44); and the Newstead type of the mid-second to the late-third century AD (*op cit*, 46–59). An additional composite form, the *Alba Iulia* type, has been suggested on the basis of one sculptural relief (*op cit*, 62–6).

Corbridge-type armour is only represented on the site by its distinctive copper-alloy fittings. It is not, however, impossible that some of the many fragments of ferrous sheet recorded are from body armour of this kind. The fittings include copper-alloy lobate hinges (*308, 682*, and *813*; Fig 340.1-3), hinged fittings and buckles (*170* and *683*;

Fig 340.4-5), and fasteners and tie loops (*347, 738, 784, 925*, and Iron *2739*; Fig 340.6-10; see *Appendix 5* for detailed descriptions).

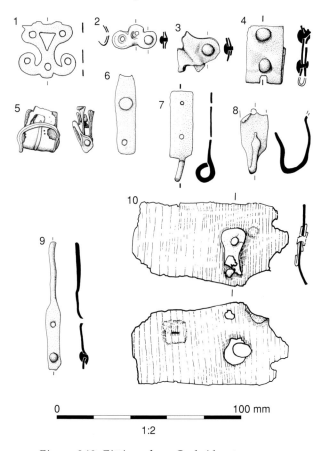

Figure 340: Fittings from Corbridge-type armour

692

Plate 211: Newstead-type backplate 2721

Newstead-type armour is better represented, the most important find being a ferrous backplate (Iron *2721*;

Pl 211), retaining its shoulder hinge and several other fittings. A second hinge (Copper Alloy *559*) is in a different style, resembling examples from *Carnuntum*.

The right-hand ferrous backplate was found in the Period 4A fill (*6405*) of roadside drain *6375*. It is almost complete (some 227 mm high and 152 mm wide) and still retains a large-format copper-alloy lobate shoulder hinge; two copper-alloy aperture borders also remain *in situ* (Fig 341). In addition, small fragments of both of the vertical fasteners survive, attached by rivets towards the bottom of the plate, although its whole lower edge is missing. The upper right-hand corner of the plate is rounded and neither of the surviving edges are very straight, features that are shared with other such plates. Each of the horizontal fastening slots would originally have been held in place with four rivets, the lower being intact, the upper missing two sides and one rivet. In common with other such lobate hinges, the fitting is secured to the plate by means of five rivets and is only doubled over at the hinge (top) end. Analysis shows the copper-alloy fittings to be of brass, and extensive traces of mineralised leather were identified on both the front and rear faces of the object

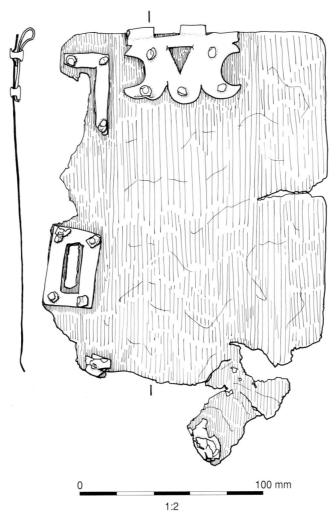

0   100 mm

1:2

Figure 341: Newstead-type backplate 2721

(*cf* Thomas 2003, category L; category Fviii (although its adaptation of the lobes into a lunate form is not exactly paralleled by any published examples)).

The similar large-format lobate hinge was found in Period 5A layer *6241*. Although now distorted, it is of similar size to that seen on the backplate (Iron *2721*), being 62 mm wide and 44 mm deep. It is now somewhat distorted, with a tear near the top lobe, and one of the volutes is missing (*559*; Fig 342.1). Four of the original five rivet holes survive, punched through from the upper surface. The hinge barrel has been formed by doubling over part of the body, evidently before the triangular aperture was cut out, as the doubling was cut at the same time. The object retains a brassy patina (*cf* Thomas 2003, category Fviii (this example is closer in shape to examples published from *Carnuntum* than the piece attached to the backplate)). The remainder of the group are again copper-alloy fittings (*164*, *1253*; Fig 342.2-3), or fragments of ferrous plate (Iron *2759*, Iron *2893*, Iron *3356*; see *Appendices 5* and *6* for descriptions).

There are, in addition, at least 14 fragments of ferrous plate, which can be identified as body armour, but are of uncertain type (*2757, 2759, 2767, 2764, 2890, 2893, 2943, 2965, 3026, 3033, 3356,* and *3455*; Fig 343.1-11; *2740, 2937, 2938, 2949, 2950,* and *3451*; *Appendix 6*). At least two of these (Figs 343.1, 343.3), possibly from a shoulder guard, have been pierced by a square-sectioned projectile (possibly a bodkin arrowhead or *pilum*), indicating that the armour had seen some use. None add significantly to the conclusions drawn except for a few fragments where conservation seems to suggest that some of the armour could have been painted black (see, for instance *Appendix 4*, Iron *2757*, one of two fragments from deposit *6272*, associated with Building *5689* in Period 4C).

Limb defences
Segmental arm defences, or *manicae,* could be made of copper-alloy or ferrous plate (Bishop 2002, 68–71) and first occur in a Roman military context during the latter part of the first century AD. Arm-guards were articulated on internal leather straps, by means

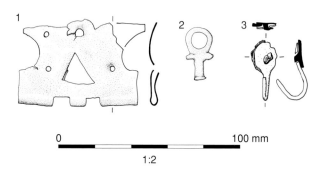

0 _____ 100 mm
1:2

Figure 342: Fittings from Newstead-type armour

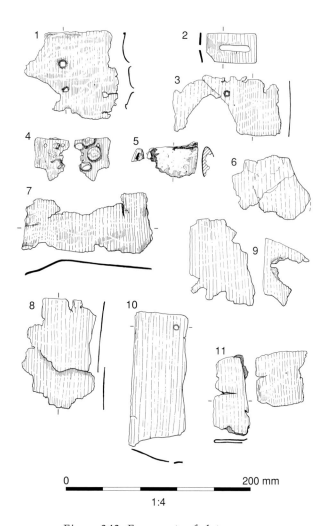

0 _____ 200 mm
1:4

Figure 343: Fragments of plate armour

of rivets, the plates overlapping upwards from wrist to shoulder, and were sewn to some sort of backing using holes at either end of each plate (or lame). Three well-preserved examples (Iron *2883 A-B; 2886*) were found together in a Period 4B occupation layer (*6419*) within Building *5689*, and have added considerable detail regarding their construction, and the manner in which they were repeatedly repaired.

Arm-guard A (Fig 344) comprises a series of articulated laminated ferrous plates with copper-alloy rivets and, as it survived, was 365 mm from shoulder to wrist, and a maximum of 180 mm wide (dimensions are of the x-rayed artefact, before conservation). It does not appear to have been complete at the time of deposition, as the lowest surviving lame (A1) is not a wrist terminal plate, a fact which is betrayed not only by its length, but also by the rivet holes on its lower edge. It can be estimated, by comparison with Arm-guard C (*p 697*), that between five and seven plates (including the wrist plate) are missing from the lower end of this defence.

Individual lames vary between 31 mm and 36 mm in width and, as is usual, their ends are oblique,

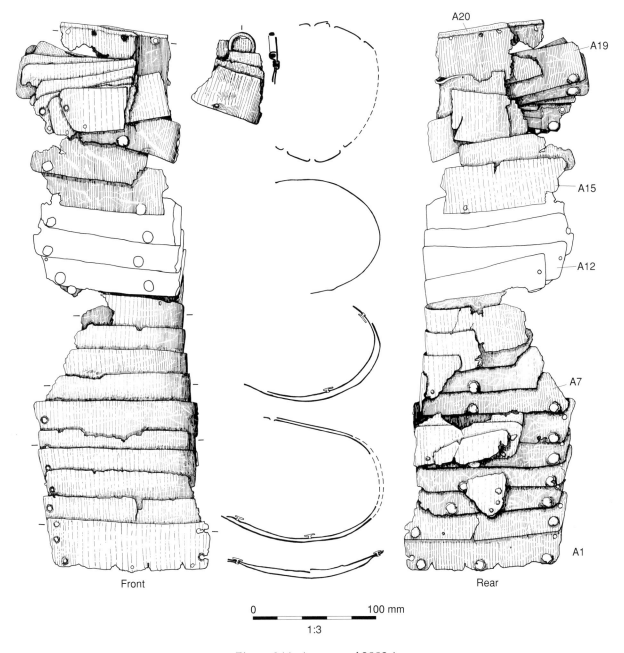

A20
A19
A15
A12
A7
A1

Front

Rear

0   100 mm

1:3

Figure 344: Arm-guard 2883A

being wider towards the top than the bottom; the lames overlap from front to back, and the rivets are located along the lower edge of each lame (concealed beneath the overlap of the lame in front). Towards the middle of the sides of each lame, there is a circular hole, punched from the upper surface, presumably to accommodate the system of fastening and/or padding. Where original corners survive, they tend to be finished off obliquely (presumably in order to avoid any sharp points, this being common in segmental limb and body armour). The edges are slightly irregular (lame A19 varies between 33 mm and 35 mm in width, A15 between 33 mm and 36 mm), but not overly so in the case of most plates, by comparison with, for instance, the Eining body armour (Bishop forthcoming). The whole defence was

deposited with its outer face uppermost (in contrast to Arm-guard C) and whilst the lower lames have tended to splay outwards, those towards the top have bent back under themselves as a result of the inherent weakness of the structure.

Lame A1 is riveted directly to A2, using the rivets of lame A2, and is clearly a repair; this has obviously required some adjustment to the placing of the rivets as there are now four holes at one end of A1 (two of which contain rivets), and three at the other end (two of which contain rivets). Lame A2 is lacking one leathering rivet, that for an oblique internal leather (one leather runs up either side, another passes obliquely up the inside, crossing the centre line of the defence; *p 704*) although the hole for it is visible. Lame A1 may in fact be an

695

alien introduction, since its central internal rivet does not fit in with the leathering regime of those above it, and this would be supported by the riveting together of lames A1 and A2, indicating a hasty repair and possibly the joining of two different donor arm-guards (the remainder of the part to which A1 originally belonged being now absent, perhaps as a result of it having been used elsewhere). Lames A1–A7 form a coherent group resting at one angle, whereas those of A8–A11 are resting in a different position, evidently more compressed, and different again from A12 onwards. One explanation for this might be the fact that the defence is reflecting the most common point of flexion (and thus greatest wear on the internal leathers) in the region of the elbow.

One fragment of plate, clearly visible on the x-ray (although its relation to the surrounding lames is not clear; Pl 212), has a D-sectioned copper-alloy ring, 21 mm in diameter (4 mm wide, 2 mm thick), hinged to it by means of a looped copper-alloy hinge plate, which is in turn riveted to the inside of lame A19 (just below the top plate) with the domed head of the rivet to the outside. Where lames A12–A19 have been folded over themselves, the underlying group of highly concertinaed lames was retrieved and consolidated in one clump. A second copper-alloy ring, 18–19 mm in diameter (now distorted to an oval shape) and of much flimsier construction (only 3 x 2 mm), was found within the upper portion of the arm-guard, but no obvious means of attachment survived, so its function (or even whether it belonged with the defence) is unclear. Similarly, a diamond-shaped piece

of leather with a rectangular slot in its centre (30 mm wide, 38 mm long) need not have had anything to do with the armour (*Ch 20*).

The top plate itself (lame A20) is 45 mm wide and has been turned outwards before being rolled inwards (rather unevenly) along its top edge. This edge is punctuated with holes approximately 25 mm apart (except where an extra one appears to have been inserted). This lame has been dented obliquely, possibly by a sharp blow to the internal face of the plate; it is thus unlikely to be battle damage. It also retains an 18 mm-long mineral-preserved fragment of the central leather terminal, 18 mm wide, *c* 1.5 mm thick, and projecting 12 mm beyond the point at which the rivet attaches it. Elsewhere, all of the rivets on the arm-guard retain traces of the original leathers, in the form of a thin ring of mineral-preserved organic material around the head of each. A short section of the end of one 32 mm-wide plate from the lower end (possibly from lame A3) contains two leathering rivets side-by-side, an obvious and rather clumsy repair.

Arm-guard B (Iron *2883B*; Fig 345) is again made from articulated laminated ferrous plates, but this time with both ferrous and copper-alloy rivets. From wrist to shoulder it measures 430 mm, and is 215 mm at its widest. The upper part of the defence was lying on its side with the ends of the lames to the south, whilst the wrist end had been rotated through 90° and twisted, and was resting with the inside of its plates uppermost. This arrangement may be due to its having been disturbed in the ground after deposition but prior to excavation,

Plate 212: X-ray of arm-guard 2883A

but it could also reflect the fact that the defence had been discarded when broken and that it was thrown to the ground in this state, perhaps due to a leathering failure between lames B6/8 and B7. The top plate and some of those below it (probably at least six) are missing (but may conceivably be represented by iron fragments *2749-50, 2752,* and *2754-6; Appendix 6*). The plates vary quite considerably in width, between 28 mm and 33 mm, even over the length of an individual plate, suggesting less care in manufacture than is evident in Arm-guards A and C. Some plates (*eg* B7 and B8) show signs of multiple re-leatherings, one leathering point retaining one copper-alloy and two ferrous rivets (one large, one small) for the same strap. Lame B1 has both large-headed ferrous and truncated (snipped-off then hammered flat?) copper-alloy leathering rivets. The lames have two or in some cases three holes at their ends.

Lames B7 and B8 have been riveted together with a large-headed ferrous rivet. This defence gives the impression of having been originally manufactured with copper-alloy rivets (and repaired with them at least once), then repaired using large-headed ferrous ones. The end of lame B8 has multiple piercings, some of them evidently fairly forceful. No internal leathers survive.

Arm-guard C (Iron *2886*; Fig 346) again comprises a series of articulated laminated ferrous plates, this time with exclusively ferrous rivets. It appears to have been complete at the time of deposition, in as much as the terminal wrist plate and the upper plate are present with 28? lames between them. However, because it was folded over on itself, the uppermost portion (corresponding to that part between the middle and one end) has at some time been removed

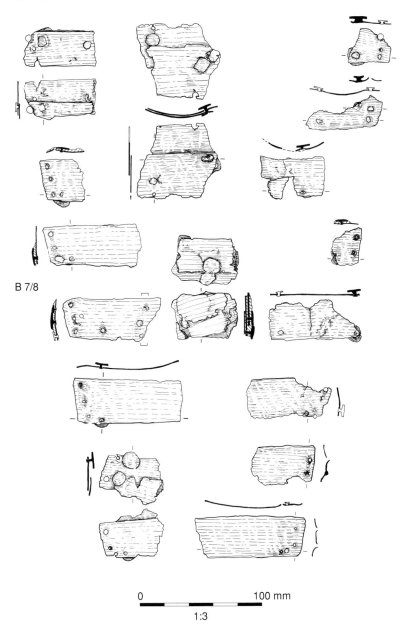

B 7/8

0   100 mm

1:3

Figure 345: Arm-guard 2883B

by truncation. The surviving fragment is 622 mm from wrist towards the shoulder, and a maximum of 137 mm wide. The lames of this arm-guard vary between 28 mm and 34 mm in width. The arm-guard has been folded over on itself along its length, so that one edge rests against the interior of the plates between lame C9 and the top plate (C30). Lame C16 is clearly bent back upon itself and there is a sharp

crease suggestive of pressure being applied (with the blade of a tool?) to compact the assemblage. Lames C16 and C17 have been compressed within C15, perhaps indicating that this is the elbow area. On the first six lames (C1–C6) it is clear that there are rivets for three internal leathers: one running up either side; and one towards the middle, which runs obliquely up the east side, more or less parallel to (and, on C2, 37 mm away

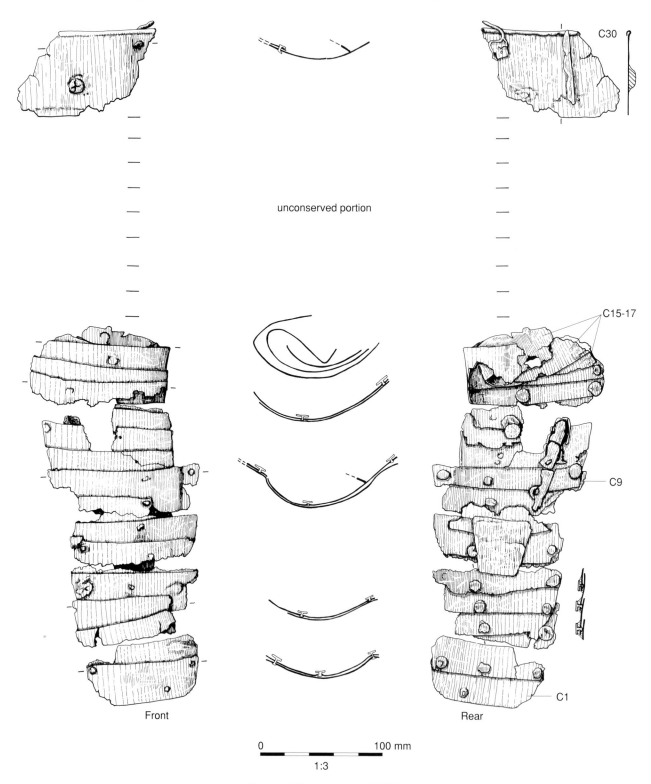

Figure 346: *Arm-guard* 2886

698

from) the eastern end. The eastern ends of lames C6 and C7 rest flat against their own interiors approximately 30 mm from their west ends; the southern side of the eastern edge of lame C9 is considerably higher than its northern side, this lame appearing to have been twisted laterally. Plates C23 and C24 overlap at an angle, but are virtually complete, folded double, and have not been truncated. Lame C8 is apparently riveted through C9, and likewise C9 through C10. The edges of the lames are reasonably straight, but far from perfect (although not as crude as some examples). The top plate (which is 68 mm wide and 125 mm long) has an outward-turned, inward rolled edge and there is a

vertically-aligned ferrous fastening hook (similar to a vertical fastener on segmental body armour) riveted to the inside, the hook now being distorted. The top plate does not appear to have any perforations along its upper edge.

No internal leathers survive (although their presence is indicated by the articulation of the defence), but the internal leathering regime appears to change at lame C11, with the introduction of broad-headed rivets on the same alignment, but shifted some 20 mm to the west of the line of those on lames C1–C10. The rivets suggest a thickness of 3–4 mm for the internal leathers.

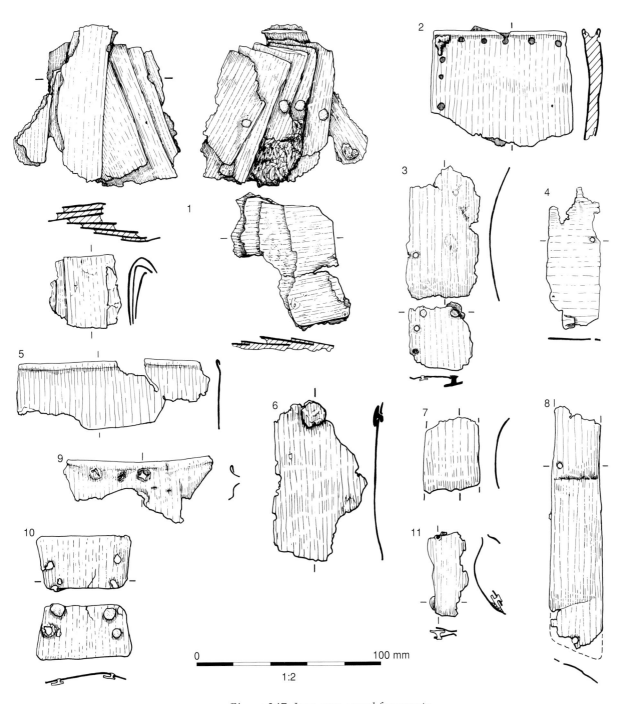

Figure 347: Iron arm-guard fragments

There were, in addition, a number of disarticulated plates, and fragments of plates, clearly from arm-guards, but whether they came from the three largely complete examples described above, or from others, could not be determined (*61, 2750, 2754, 2756, 2768, 2780, 2861, 2862, 2882, 2891, 3453; Fig 347.1-11; 2749, 2752, 2753, 2755, 2863, 2878, 2936; Appendix 6*). Of note were the plates (*61*) from Period 6A deposit *242*, the primary surface of intervallum road **7646**; these are clearly later than the three arm-guards from the main deposit, and derive from a different part of the site (MIL 1), but it is not clear whether or not they were residual.

Greave

A rare example (*cf* Garbsch 1978, Taf 39; Born and Junkelmann 1997, 128–31) of a plain ferrous greave (*2724; Fig 348*) came from Period 4C external layer *6205*, associated with Building *5689*. It was represented by two substantial (but not joining) fragments indicating an undecorated greave, originally in excess of 350 mm long, and a maximum of 147 mm wide. Both fragments have been flattened from their original shallow V-shaped section, but the central ridge is still visible on both, as is an embossed border line. As was usual, the greave was narrow at the knee, broadened lower down to match the shape of the shin and calf, and then narrowed again towards the ankle. One of the six peripheral rivets used to secure the tie rings that once bordered the vertical edges survives *in situ* on the larger fragment, and likewise one survives on the smaller piece. These tie rings originally served to lace the greave around the back of the leg. Plain greaves such as this example were designed to be used with hinged knee protectors (as was also the case with decorated examples), and are indicative of cavalry use. Exceptions to this latter feature are some greaves from Künzing (Robinson 1975, pl 510).

Helmets

Fragments of one ferrous helmet cheekpiece and the copper-alloy binding of another were noted, the former found in the same layer (*6205*) in Building **5689** as ferrous scale armour fragment *2722* (*p 689*). Other evidence for helmets was confined to copper-alloy fittings.

The ferrous cheekpiece (*2723; Fig 349*) can be assumed to be closely associated with the scale armour fragment. The surviving fragment is some 85 mm in length and 160 mm wide, with a thickness of *c* 1 mm. There is a flat-headed copper-alloy rivet near one curved edge, which retains fragments of silver on the outer face, whilst (by means of a bent-over shank) securing a rectangular loop for a tie ring on the reverse. The surviving S-shaped edge is the tip and lower cusp of the front edge, whilst a fragmentary

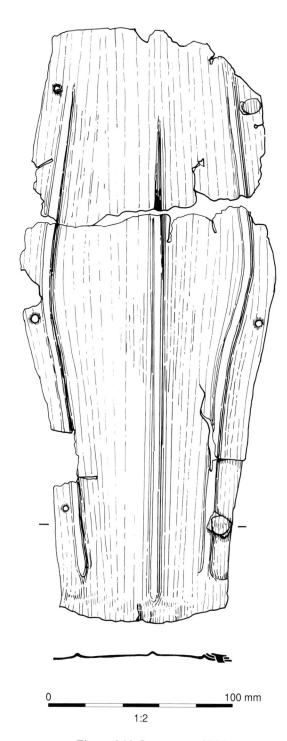

0   100 mm
1:2

Figure 348: Iron greave 2724

straight edge at the other end of the object represents the rear. The original shape of the cheekpiece has been lost, and although obviously silvered, there are no traces of embossed decoration.

The other evidence for helmets is copper-alloy fittings or edge bindings. A cheekpiece hinge (*773; Fig 350.1*) came from a layer associated with Building **7200** in Period 3C. Some 34 x 29 mm, and only 0.5 mm thick, it is pierced to receive the two rivets that would have secured it to the

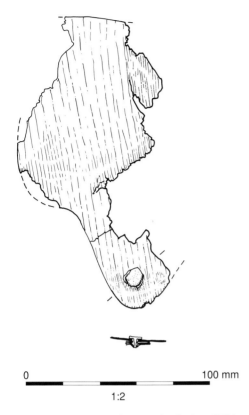

0   100 mm

1:2

Figure 349: Iron helmet cheekpiece 2723

helmet bowl. The cheekpiece would have had two corresponding barrels of the hinge at the top, through which a spindle would have passed, as in an example from Xanten (Schalles and Schreiter 1993, Taf 29, Mil 19). Object *283*, from the fill (*3971*) of a construction trench for Period 3B Building *4006*, is probably a helmet cheekpiece tie-loop hinge, made from a copper-alloy plate 31 mm wide, with a ferrous loop attached to it by means of a single copper-alloy rivet (Fig 350.2). The tie ring is missing (see Xanten (Schalles and Schreiter 1993, Taf 27, Mil 12), for a similar example). The right-hand copper-alloy ear guard (*752*; Fig 350.3) from an infantry helmet of Robinson's (1975) Imperial-Gallic/Italic types came from a Period 3C clay floor (*6877*) within Building *7200*. Unlike the Coolus and Montefortino types of helmet, which restrained the ears within the helmet bowl, the Weisenau (or Imperial-Gallic/Italic) types forced

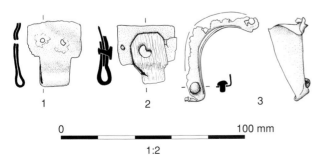

0   100 mm

1:2

Figure 350: Copper-alloy helmet fittings 1

them to protrude, thus introducing the need for protection. One rivet is still present to the rear, whilst a further (torn) hole is visible at the front.

An almost complete copper-alloy cheekpiece binding came from *6280*, a Period 4B occupation layer within Building *5689*. The outline of the flanges for the chin and cheekbone are present, with the cusps for the mouth and eyes; thus the binding is almost complete, allowing it to be identified as probably coming from a cheekpiece of Robinson's (1975) Imperial-Gallic/Italic type (Fig 351), indicating that the cheekpiece was originally 149 mm long and *c* 100 mm wide, although the strip itself is only between 3 mm and 5 mm in width (see also fragments from South Cadbury (Bishop 2000, figs 120, 6–13; 121, 14–22)). Interestingly, conservation suggests that it bound leather rather than iron. Finally, fragment *1254* (*Appendix 5*), found unstratified, is probably part of a copper-alloy brow band strip with incised longitudinal decoration and two surviving rivet holes (see Robinson 1975, fig 82, for a more complete example).

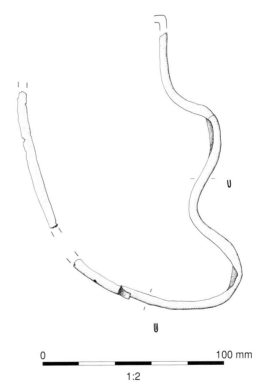

0   100 mm

1:2

Figure 351: Copper-alloy binding for cheekpiece

In addition to these, a few less securely identified fragments were noted. A curved and now badly deformed piece of copper-alloy sheet with a marked bead along one edge, from Period 3B external layer *3777* (*240*; Fig 352.1), could be seen as the edge trim for the neck guard of an infantry helmet. A riveted fastening loop (*647*; Fig 352.2) came from another occupation layer within Building *5689*.

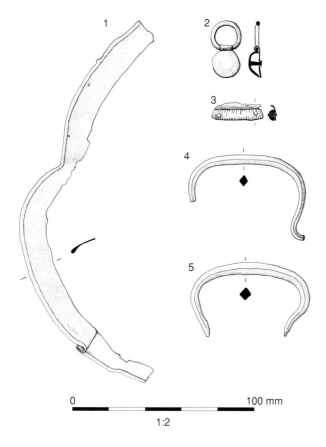

0   100 mm

1:2

Figure 352: Copper-alloy helmet fittings 2

Several other smaller fragments of U-profiled edge binding similar to the cheekpiece were also recovered. None is large enough to be confident that they derived from helmet trim, but it seems very likely that some did, and that all were associated with armour. Almost all of the fragments derive from Building *5688* during its occupation and subsequent demolition (Periods 4B and 4C; *Ch 6*), and a lesser

amount from Building *5689*. It also seems likely that the two fragments from Period 6, both from the fill of a construction trench for Building *5200* (*Ch 8*), are residual. A small section of a beaded D-sectioned bar, still pinned to an irregular fragment of sheet (*811*; Fig 352.3), was clearly intended as reinforcement, and presumably also comes from a helmet rather than other elements of armour.

Two small drop handles, *73* and *81* (Fig 352.4-5), both from Period 6 contexts associated with Building *2303*, have been tentatively identified as helmet-carrying handles. It is, however, equally possible that these items came from furniture rather than helmets, especially as the amount of military material from Period 6 is much smaller than from earlier phases.

A final fragment of ferrous sheet is of interest (Fig 353). It appears to have a decorative device, or complex fixing riveted to one side. Although no parallels have been found for the piece, the ferrous sheet suggests an origin in armour.

Discussion
The scale armour
One of the most noticeable second-century innovations in Roman military equipment was the introduction of semi-rigid scale mail (Bishop and Coulston 1993, 117), in which scales were no longer just wired to their horizontal neighbours and sewn to a fabric backing, but were also wired to the rows above and below. There are innate drawbacks to this new type of armour, less flexibility for the wearer being the most obvious, and today its advantages are less clear, but they must have mattered to the Romans. The changes might well have been intended to reduce the efficacy of upward thrusts, which parted

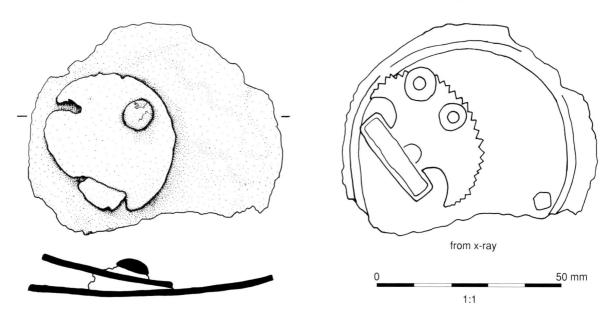

from x-ray

0   50 mm

1:1

Figure 353: Complex fitting (Copper Alloy 223)

the rows in conventional scale mail. Its manufacture undoubtedly demanded greater skill from the armourers, as scale shirts now had to be very carefully fitted to the shape of the human form, whereas before it had been possible to be more slapdash. It is clear that the neck opening patches (Figs 336 and 337) were carefully shaped, one of them (Iron 2722) even going to the lengths of using progressively tapering scales to assist in the formation of the aperture (Pl 210).

The Carlisle assemblage is significant for the use of ferrous metal for scale armour, which, although not unknown in the Roman world, is considerably less often found than copper alloy, although also prevalent amongst the Carnuntum assemblage (p 705). Striking amongst the more run-of-the-mill material is a small parcel of ferrous and copper-alloy scales wrapped around a decorated ferrous breastplate (Pl 167). Copper-alloy breastplates are comparatively common finds, for a long time, probably incorrectly, associated with cavalry 'sports' equipment (op cit, 117), but they are virtually unknown in ferrous metal, and the Carlisle find is a revelation.

The use of plated scale is of particular interest, in one case (Iron 2885) presumably a decorative device. The tinning (and occasionally silvering) of alternate scales had been used since at least the first century AD (op cit, 85), but this item employed a thin skin of copper alloy to sheath the outer face of some scales. As this can have had no practical purpose, it seems reasonable to suggest that it must have been for aesthetic reasons. In fact, it will have led to bimetallic electrolytic corrosion between the copper-alloy and ferrous metals, a problem that had dogged lorica segmentata (segmented armour) since its inception, but to which the Romans appear to have been oblivious. Patch 2657 (Appendix 6) also shows systematic decoration, mixing copper-alloy and ferrous scales in a deliberate pattern (alternate rows of all ferrous, then three ferrous scales and one of copper-alloy, repeating):

fe	fe	fe	fe	fe	fe	fe	fe
ae	fe	fe	fe	**ae**	fe	fe	fe	**ae**
fe	fe	fe	fe	fe	fe	fe	fe

Similarly, Iron 2722 uses a single column of copper-alloy scales, which can only have had a decorative effect, to mark the centre line of the wearer's shoulder, like an epaulette.

The segmental body armour
It was also during the second century AD that Corbridge-type segmental body armour began to be replaced by the Newstead variety. The fact that both types occurred together in the Waffenmagazin at Carnuntum (von Groller 1901, Taf XVII–XIX) hinted

that this change took place during the Antonine period, although unfortunately the deposits at Carnuntum were largely undated. The Corbridge-type armour in the Corbridge Hoard is late Hadrianic to early Antonine in date (Allason-Jones and Bishop 1988, 5–6), indicating that there was a fairly lengthy transitional period, an assertion that now seems to be supported by finds of both types in late third-century contexts from León (Aurrecoechea and Muñoz Villarejo 2001-2). The occurrence of both types in approximately contemporary deposits at Carlisle is probably attributable to the same process of change.

The Newstead-type backplate (Iron 2721) is particularly significant (Pl 211) in that it proves conclusively that this type of cuirass continued the tradition of using lobate hinges, seen earlier in the Corbridge type (Bishop 2002, 47). An earlier find from Carlisle was the first indication that this might be so (Caruana 1993), although at the time it was thought that it might be a late modification. Subsequent finds have reinforced the possibility, but none are as categorical in their proof as this new example. Although Robinson first speculated that the Newstead type was Trajanic in date (1975, 180), the evidence that its main period of use was in the second half of the second century AD has been accumulating (Poulter 1988, 38–9; Bishop 2002, 49). This new example appears to be the earliest datable find yet, and it must be remembered that this piece of armour, like all the others, was probably not new when deposited, and thus the possibility of a Hadrianic, rather than Antonine, origin for this form of lorica segmentata must now be given serious consideration.

The segmental arm-guards
The prominence of segmental arm-guards (Iron 2883 A-B; 2886) amongst this group is another element that might once have seemed surprising. The realisation that this form of limb defence was more widespread than once thought has been gradually dawning on scholars, who had once thought it the exclusive preserve of the troops fighting in Trajan's Dacian wars, primarily as a defence against the Dacian falx, a sickle-like single-edged bladed weapon (Sim 2000). However, finds from a number of sites, such as Newstead (Bishop 1999), Eining (Bishop forthcoming), Carnuntum (von Groller 1901), Corbridge (pers obs), and most recently León (A Morel pers comm), have presaged the discoveries in Carlisle, although until now an as yet unpublished find from Ulpia Traiana Sarmizegetusa (L Petculescu pers comm) has remained the most complete known example. Limb protection was evidently not confined to the arms, as fragments of a greave (Fig 348) show that one or both legs could be protected if the need arose, and this detail once again recalls the Adamklissi metopes, where legionaries are shown wearing greaves (Richmond 1982, 49).

At an early stage in the examination of the arm-guards from deposit *4619*, it was hoped that they might provide detail of the internal leather straps upon which they were articulated, and any padded undergarment that might have been worn on the arm beneath the metal plates (all body armour requires padding to work effectively: Bishop and Coulston 1993, 59). Although no obvious trace of any such padding was found, a significant discovery was made in relation to the internal leathers. The arm-guards were clearly articulated at the time of deposition, but the only traces of their internal leathers were mineral-preserved fragments around the rivets holding them in place. This is despite the fact that conditions of preservation were such that tanned leather survived well. There is thus a clear implication that the leather used for the internal straps was not tanned, oiled leather perhaps being used instead. Coincidentally, where internal leathers have been preserved on segmental body armour (as in the Corbridge Hoard), it, too, is as a mineral-preserved organic material. Tanned leather appears to have been a Roman introduction to Britain (Q Mould *pers comm*), so it seems that there might have been a distinct advantage to be gained by using oiled leather for internal articulation straps on segmental armour, although what it might have been is currently unclear.

Composite armour

One of the more intriguing possibilities suggested by this group of armour is that the various components might conceal composite armour of the *Alba Iulia* type, named from a sculpture from the Romanian legionary fortress of *Porolissum* (Coulston 1995), which depicts a legionary with segmental armour on the torso, scale with small breastplates on the shoulders, and a laminated arm defence (Bishop 2002, 62–6). This of course cannot be proved on the basis of only one relief, and all the pieces may in fact represent cuirasses of their own particular type.

Damage

A final, but in many ways perhaps the most significant, observation can be made about the evidence of damage and repair. Most Roman military equipment usually shows signs of repair, often of only mediocre competence. Indeed, it is thought that one of the prime vectors by which it entered the archaeological record was discard after it had been put aside for repair. The arm-guards were not only in need of repair when deposited, but detailed examination also shows that each had been repaired several times, and that at least one was a 'cut'n'shut', put together from cannibalised elements of more than one defence. This can be seen in the types of rivets used, and the lines of leathering, working from the not-unreasonable assumption that, when a defence was first made, the same type of rivets would have been used throughout, and that the leathers would run in single continuous lines from wrist to

shoulder; once cannibalised, different rivet types and discontinuous leathering would be found (Fig 354). Inevitably, the more often it was repaired, the more styles of riveting it would accumulate.

Once damage has been identified, however, it is not unreasonable to wonder how it may have occurred. Modern reconstructions confirm that, even in everyday use, segmental armour is demonstrably fragile (although arm-guards had fewer vulnerable fittings to come adrift), but the amount of repair evidenced by these arm-guards may be indicative of some cause more violent than everyday use. A significant proportion of the damage might have been inflicted as a result of vigorous training, although the Roman style of combat (and combat training) eschewed the sort of strong slashing blows dealt by the *falx* or similar bladed weapons. Nor was it the Roman style to imitate or simulate the style of combat of potential opponents during training, so this can probably be ruled out as a major contributory factor leading to the damage. This leads to the inevitable conclusion that the arm-guards (and presumably the other damaged equipment) seem to have been used in combat. Whether

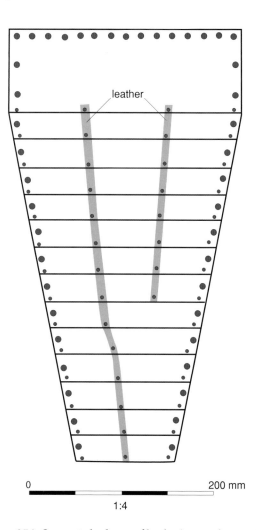

Figure 354: Suggested scheme of leathering on the manicae

this was high-intensity battlefield conflict or low-intensity counter insurgency operations is difficult to tell, but the impression given by these repairs is one of pressure to repair hurriedly and effectively, rather than elegantly and correctly. Thus minor repairs, such as parts of the arm-guards that did not move much (only the lames around the elbow required flexion), could be (and were) riveted together directly, bypassing the internal leathers completely, whilst cut'n'shut repairs could supply complete working arm-guards from the salvaged sections of other badly damaged examples. The impression gained is of a compelling need to maintain as many serviceable arm defences as possible.

The circumstances of the find

There is little doubt that this armour was material awaiting repair. Moreover, most of it shows signs of previous repair, in some cases several times. It is also obvious that the quality of the repairs can only charitably be described as adequate, effected with only that skill necessary to maintain serviceability. In this there are considerable similarities, beyond that of dating, between the Carlisle material and items of armour in the Corbridge Hoard, encompassing the indications of damage, frequent repair, and a process of triage prior to disposal (Allason-Jones and Bishop 1988, 110). That the other items in the Corbridge chest are also reminiscent of the variety of objects in deposit *4619* might be indicative of similar processes in action at both sites, in terms of repair, disposal, and the proximity to conflict.

The assemblage can be compared with a number of similar deposits. The first to be discovered, from the *Waffenmagazin* of the legionary base at *Carnuntum*, might be thought to be the most similar. This assemblage, from a rampart-back store building identified as an armoury (different types of equipment were stored in each of the four rooms, apparently on shelves), included segmental body armour of both Corbridge and Newstead types, as well as segmental arm defences, scale, and various weapons. Although undated as a result of the excavation techniques used at the time, it is probably best placed in the second century (von Groller 1901). Excavations at Prysg Field at Caerleon (Nash-Williams 1931) also examined a rampart-back building that produced an important group of second- and third-century military equipment.

These rampart-back deposits can, however, be contrasted with those from central-range structures, like the material from pit I (the well) in the *principia* at Newstead (Curle 1911, 47–9) or the Corbridge Hoard, buried just outside the building immediately east of the period 2 *principia* (Allason-Jones and Bishop 1988, 109). In addition, the deposition of weaponry has been associated with the central range within

fortifications at Housesteads, Künzing, and *Lambaesis* (Bishop and Coulston 1993, 199), so Carlisle fits in with the association of arms and armour with this area of a military base, rather than the rampart-back structures seen elsewhere (the *Waffenmagazin* building at *Carnuntum* was clearly used for storage rather than manufacture or repair).

Conclusions

The armour from deposit *4619* in Building **5689** suggests that during the second century the Roman army in Britain was more concerned about the protection of limbs than had previously been the case. The presence of segmental body and limb armour is strongly suggestive of the employment of legionary, and not just auxiliary, troops at this time. Moreover, the condition of the armour when abandoned points towards its use in combat on a regular and persistent basis, rather than being damaged through over-enthusiastic training, or the occasional scuffle. The group is particularly notable for its similarities with the near-contemporary Corbridge Hoard, and recalls how the two sites can often be seen to have more general similarities. The possibility of conflict involving troops from both sites is intriguing, but as yet remains unilluminated by known literary, sub-literary, or epigraphic sources.

Other military equipment

C Howard-Davis

Inevitably, in an assemblage as large as this, with such a distinctly military origin, military items in addition to the armour were recorded. These range from smaller fragments of armour to high-quality horse gear of the kind used not only by cavalry, but also by legionary officers.

Suspension loops and split pins

A few suspension loops were recorded (Copper alloy *404*, *606*, *664*, and *672*; Fig 355.1-4), all made from folded copper-alloy sheet and intended to be riveted

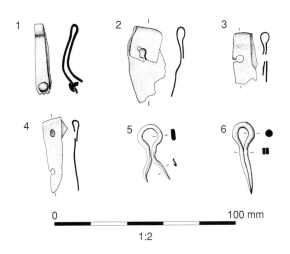

Figure 355: Copper-alloy suspension loops and split pins

onto a second object. Many must have served to attach buckles and other fittings to the plates of *lorica segmentata*, others to fix harness fittings, but this cannot now be determined. A group of small split pins (Copper Alloy *695* and *772*; Fig 355.5-6) is also most likely to have been associated with armour.

Shield fittings?
Three fragments of U-shaped copper-alloy binding strip were substantially larger than those thought to be associated with helmets (*p 702*). It seems likely that they were intended to protect the edges of shields rather than thinner armour plates, the width across the open arms of the 'U' suggesting a thickness of up to 14 mm. One (*529*) came from Period 4C demolition layer *5998*, which also produced a fragment of iron shield grip (Iron *2696*), adding weight to this interpretation.

Amongst the ironwork, two long fragments of narrow, sub-rectangular-sectioned bar were identified as parts of shield grips, on the basis of

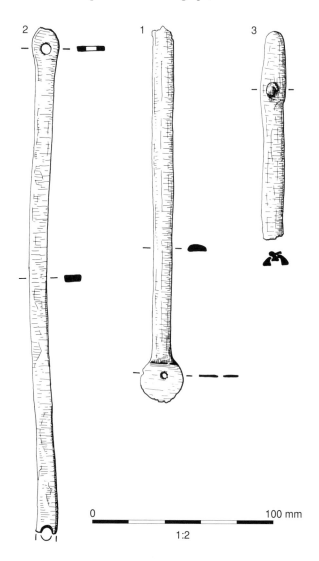

Figure 356: Iron shield fittings

their resemblance to that seen on the first-century shield from Doncaster (Buckland 1978a) and other examples from Newstead (Curle 1911). Nailed or riveted to rectangular wooden shields, the grip ran vertically down the centre of the back, crossing the hollow of the *umbo* and thereby creating a space for the hand. Evidence from Doncaster suggests that, where it ran across this space, the grip was wrapped with leather. The complete examples from Doncaster and Newstead are around 0.8 m in length, whilst the two fragments from Carlisle, from road *7478* (Period 3C) and Building *5689* (Period 4C), are 225 mm and 268 mm respectively (Iron *1774* and *2720*; Fig 356.1-2). A third, smaller fragment, with a D-shaped cross-section (Iron *2696*; Fig 356.3), came from a Period 4C demolition layer associated with Building *5688*, and a fourth fragment (Iron *1440*) came from Period 5C layer *2605*.

Military belts and aprons
Object *846* (Fig 357.1), a hinged dagger frog in copper alloy from Period 3A external layer *7192*, is clearly first-century in date, and can be paralleled amongst material from Hod Hill (Brailsford 1962, pl 1, A97), where a Tibero-Claudian date is suggested on the basis of examples from *Vindonissa*. Such a date would imply that this object had been in use for some time when it was lost at Carlisle. Evidence from the armour and horse tack seem to suggest that a make-do and mend attitude prevailed in the early days of Roman occupation at Carlisle, and this would not therefore be particularly unreasonable. Copper-alloy object *26* (Fig 357.2) is badly damaged and fragmentary, but might be a second example from a broadly similar and contemporary context (*342*).

Two enamelled copper-alloy belt plates can be dated to the second century, when such decoration was probably at its most popular. One, with dark red and turquoise enamels (*704*; Fig 357.3), can be paralleled by an identical example from an Antonine context at Strageath (Grew and Frere 1989, 145, fig 73.48), whilst the other, *125* (Fig 357.4), hinged for a buckle and decorated in green and turquoise, is identical to an example from Caerleon (Lloyd-Morgan 2000, 377, fig 91.157). Both, again, are from external layers, perhaps suggesting items lost in day-to-day wear.

In addition, two fragmentary examples of open-work belt plates were noted, one from a Period 6D robber trench associated with Building *2301*, where it is almost certainly residual (*98*; Fig 357.5), and the second (*409*; Fig 357.6) from Period 7; again, this is likely to be residual. Both are common and widespread types, probably second-century or later in date. Antonine examples are illustrated by Bishop and Coulston (1993, 120, fig 80.1–3), and examples are known, for example, from South Shields

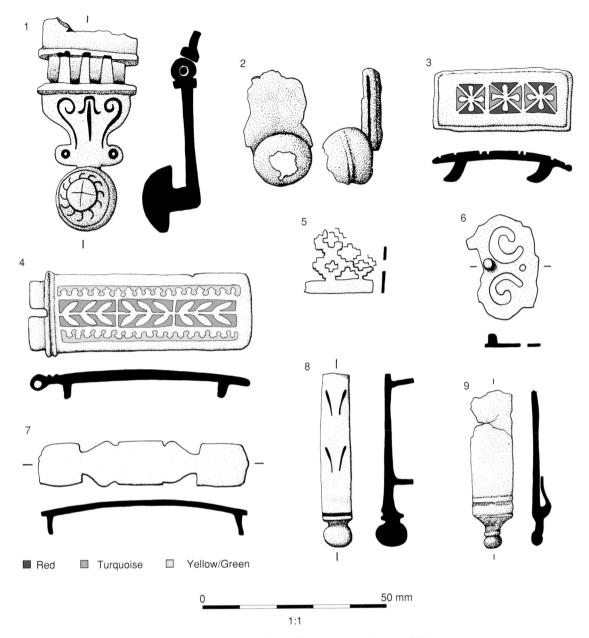

Figure 357: Copper-alloy military belt and apron fittings

■ Red ■ Turquoise □ Yellow/Green

0   50 mm

1:1

(Allason-Jones and Miket 1984, figs 3.771 and 3.772) and Corbridge (Bishop and Dore 1988, fig 86.173). Small fragments, tentatively identified as belt or strap mounts, were noted from external layer *2781* (Period 5B) and demolition layer *2306* (Period 6D).

A silvered or tinned apron mount (Copper Alloy *228*; Fig 357.7) came from the fill (*3572*) of a construction trench associated with Period 4A Building *3376*. The object is probably decorated with niello, in typical fashion (see, for example, Crummy 1983, fig 151.4219), but the surface is very worn and this has been lost. These mounts are regarded as first-century in date, and are common and widespread. The amount of wear on this example suggests that, again, it could have been relatively old when lost. An apron or strap terminal with niello decoration (*888*; Fig 357.8) is

closely related to this mount, and again is likely to be of first-century date. A second, more fragmentary, example (*6*; Fig 357.9) is broadly similar, but has a different method of fixing, suggesting it to be from horse harness. Both are from Period 3A contexts.

Two small copper-alloy studs with niello decoration (*341, 1260*; Fig 358.1-2), one from the floor of Period 3A Building *4654*, the other unstratified, are also likely to have been elements of the decoration of a military apron. Niello decoration was in particular vogue in the first century AD (Bishop and Coulston 1993, 192). A third stud, a well-known type with repoussé decoration (*697*; Fig 358.3), in this case a radiate head, is thought to have been used as decoration on the military uniform or military belt (Feugère 2002, 178). Common on the western *limes*, and thought to have

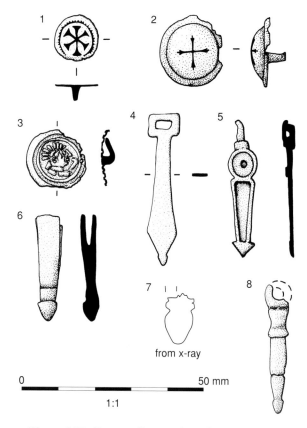

Figure 358: Copper-alloy studs and strap terminals

Davis 2000a, fig 67.233), normally in first-century contexts. The largest known example, however, from York (Cool *et al* 1995, 1536, fig 716.6312), was from a considerably later context. A second similar, but by no means identical, object (*365*; Fig 359.2) was recovered from a medieval layer (Period 8F). Finally, although it has no obvious purpose, a decorative object in the form of an eagle (*1245*; Fig 359.3), made from thin sheet, seems unlikely to be anything other than military in origin.

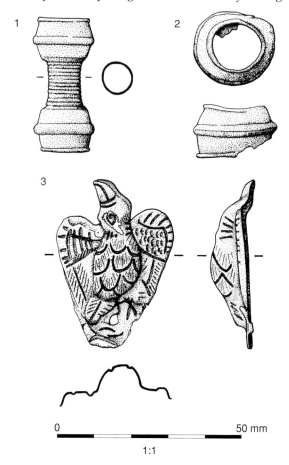

Figure 359: Other copper-alloy military fittings

been made in some quantity in Besançon, in modern France, it has been suggested that these could have served in some way as campaign medals or badges of rank (*ibid*). Its context, a Period 4A occupation deposit (*6672*) within Building *7396*, might reinforce its potential association with an individual soldier.

A teardrop-shaped strap terminal from *6000* (*530*; Fig 358.4), part of main east to west road *7477* in Period 4B, is a common and widely distributed military type with numerous examples known from Hadrian's Wall and other forts throughout the North. An enamelled example (*484*; Fig 358.5) was lost on the same road in a later period (*7652*, Period 6A). Strap terminal *492* (Fig 358.6) is probably of Antonine or later date, being lost on the main east to west road in Period 6B. It differs in form, the strap being inserted into the split end rather than through a loop, but it is otherwise similar to *477* (Fig 358.7) and *454* (Fig 358.8), both from Period 6C, the former from the same road, the latter from Structure *7651*.

Other fittings of copper alloy

As always, there are a few objects which, whilst enigmatic in purpose, consistently appear in a military context, and thus must be regarded as closely associated with soldierly activity. Object *1255* (Fig 359.1) is one such, seen on a number of demonstrably military sites, for example Castleford (Cool 1998a, 61, fig 28.343), or Ribchester (Howard-

Weapons
Sword handles

Although no blades were recovered, there was a group of five bone or ivory sword handgrips, two (*24* and *69*; Fig 360.1-2), from floors associated with Period 3 buildings, whilst the other three (*48-50*; Fig 360.3-5) are from external layer *6321*, associated with the Period 4B main east to west road (*7477*). All belong to the well-known series of Roman sword grips with four depressions for the fingers, which were present in Britain and elsewhere by the first century AD (MacGregor 1985, 165) and continued for several centuries. Sword grips are usually made in animal bone, but the use of ivory is well attested, and not unusual. A bone example is known from Castle Street (Padley 1991a, 173), where the high polish was noted, a feature particularly of *24*. A sixth fragment, from floor or make-up deposit *7573* (*70*; Fig 360.6) is similar, but seems to have come from a rather smaller item.

708

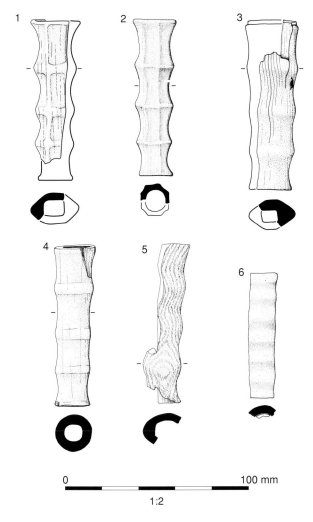

Figure 360: Bone and ivory sword grips

Iron arrowheads

A group of 32 certain and possible arrowheads was recovered from contexts belonging to Period 4B and later, and it is possible that the activity which resulted in their deposition on the site was confined to Period 4 (*Chs 5* and *6*). This contrasts significantly with the ceramic slingshots (*pp 717-18*), which were probably all originally deposited in Period 3, and thus might allow some inference with regard to the nature of the garrison occupying the successive timber forts. Although they must have been in common use, arrowheads are regarded as uncommon finds in Roman Britain (Bidwell 1985, 136; Manning 1985, 177), but on rare occasions they are found in substantial quantities, as for instance the group of about 800 from the *principia* at Housesteads (Manning 1976, 22).

The most common form represented within the group is the 'tanged bodkin' type (Coulston 1985, 265). These can be either three- or four-sided; nine and ten examples respectively were recorded (Fig 361.1-9; Fig 361.10-19). Although some are barbed whilst others are not, there does not seem to be any real difference between the two types. Those with triangular sections seem to

vary in size, from 43 mm to 70 mm, but whether this implies any difference in use, or is simply a reflection of different manufacturers, is not clear. Three of this type (*2716, 2731*, and *2888*; Fig 361.1-3) were found in occupation layers within Period 4B Buildings **5688** and **5689**; most of the remainder (*2698, 2699, 2725*, and *2758*; Fig 361.4-7) came from external layers or demolition deposits (*6103, 6205, 6272*) associated with the same buildings in Period 4C, and one from Period 5 external deposit *245* (*106*; Fig 361.8). A final example (*2495*; Fig 361.9), found within the layers making up the main east to west road of the stone fort (Period 6A), is likely to be residual.

The four-sided examples were generally longer, between 70 mm and 80 mm in length, being smaller and less substantial than tanged, four-sided ballista bolts (*pp 711-12*), although the two do, to an extent, grade into each other. This type overlaps chronologically with the three-sided examples, being from Period 4C external and demolition layers (*2711* and *2746*; Fig 361.10-11), but they continued to be found in Period 5A (*2732*; Fig 361.12), on road **7646** in Period 6B (*29* and *54*; Fig 361.13-14), and layer *2161* (*838*; Fig 361.15) in Period 6D. Two examples were recovered from Period 7 post-Roman 'dark earths' *2139* and *5304* (*784* and *2269*; Fig 361.16-17). The latter was fragmentary, identified only from x-ray. Two other examples were unstratified (*3443* and *3445*; Fig 361.18-19).

A similar bodkin-type arrowhead, but with a socket rather than a slender tang and a rather stumpier head (*83*; Fig 361.20), came from a Period 5 external layer (*245*). It appears that the socket was secured to its wooden shaft in some way that necessitated a rectangular slot in the socket rather than the round rivet hole seen in some other socketed weapons, for instance artillery bolt heads.

The trilobate tanged arrow is thought to have had its origin in the East, but was in common use throughout the Empire from the late Republic onwards. It appears that their use in Britain and on the German-Raetian *limes* declined severely from the late Antonine period (Coulston 1985, 264) and this might account for their almost complete absence from Period 6 contexts, although equally, this might imply a change in the composition of the garrison. They are known from a considerable number of military sites in Britain, including forts on Hadrian's Wall; a single example has been published from Vindolanda (Birley 1996, 19, fig 7.33). Five were recovered from this site, associated in the main with Period 4. One (*2714*; Fig 361.21) came from surface *6198* within Building **5688** (Period 4B), and a second (*2712*; Fig 361.22) from an associated demolition layer (Period 4C, *6175*). Two more derived from layers *6242* and *6258* (*2738, 2748*; Fig 361.23-24) associated with the

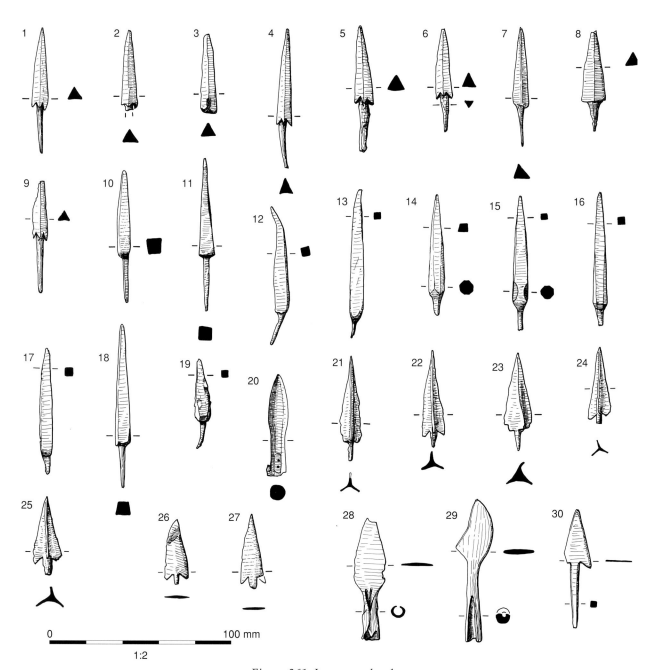

Figure 361: Iron arrowheads

demolition of Building *5689* (Period 4C), and another one came from Period 5 layer *6229* (*2734*; Fig 361.25), and is thus possibly residual. A single arrow of this type was identified amongst the poorly preserved ironwork from Blackfriars Street (Caruana 1990, 148). A similarly sized group from Watercrook, Kendal, has been used to argue for the presence of a unit of archers (Potter 1979, 223), following the suggestion by J L Davies (1977, 260–1) that this arrow type was characteristic of units of *sagittarii* recruited mainly in the eastern provinces. This seems unlikely at Carlisle, although it is not impossible that a few specialists, possibly acting as instructors, visited the fort.

In addition, two flat tanged and barbed arrows were recovered from Period 4B Building *5688* (*2715, 2763*;

Fig 361.26-27). Easy to make, if compared especially to the trilobate type, they are regarded as an almost *ad hoc* form, requiring little skill, and made on site as required (Sim 1995, 2). A flat-bladed but socketed example (*991*; Fig 361.28) was found in a Period 6A posthole associated with road *2303*, again raising the likelihood that it was residual.

Three flat arrowheads (*2020, 2193*; Fig 361.29-30; *354; Appendix 6*) came from medieval contexts. Although similar in appearance to those recovered from Roman layers, they are likely to be of medieval date rather than residual, as flat barbed and unbarbed arrows remained in use throughout the medieval period (Jessop 1996) and an archer's wristguard was amongst leatherwork from the medieval tenements (Period 8; *Ch 20*).

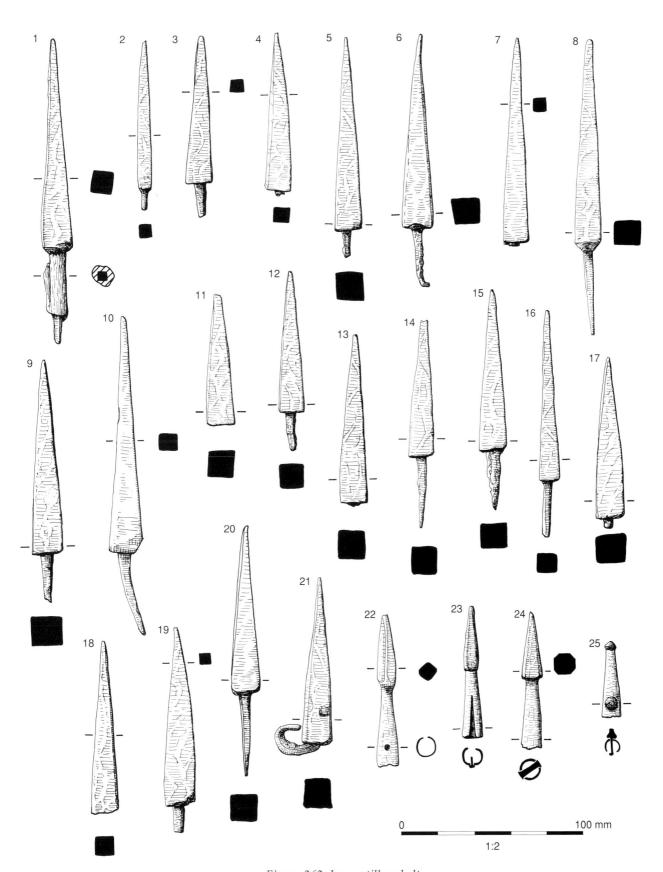

Figure 362: Iron artillery bolts

Artillery bolt heads

In all, 27 artillery bolt heads were recovered, all but four being large pyramidal points with a short tang (*Appendix 6*; Fig 362.1-21). Complete examples appear to be around 120–30 mm in length, with the tang comprising 25% or so of the overall length. They are distinguished from four-sided bodkin-type arrows by their length and much less gracile appearance, although it seems likely that the two forms grade into one another. There is no doubt that in the past these have often been confused with *pilum* heads, with the tang seen as the stump of the thin iron shaft typical of these weapons (see, for instance, Bishop and Coulston 1993, fig 34), which was intended to bend or break on impact. One amongst this group, however, retains sufficient of the ash-wood shaft to show that the short tang was in fact driven into a round-sectioned shaft, with apparently no other form of fixing (*2880*; Fig 362.1). Like the arrowheads, these are confined to Period 4B Buildings *5688* and *5689*, and later deposits associated with their demolition (Period 4C), stratigraphic evidence suggesting that all those from contexts later than Period 4B could be residual. There was, in addition, a single example of the more common socketed version of this form of bolt head, which was unstratified (*3444*; Fig 362.22).

Two socketed examples have sub-conical rather than pyramid-shaped heads. Both are similar, with a socket some 12 mm in diameter, and appeared to have been fixed to the shaft, part of which survives in one case, by a small pin. One bolt head (*1650*; Fig 362.23), from the fill of a Period 3B construction trench and thus possibly originally associated with Period 3A, has had its point blunted and burred, presumably by use and impact. The second example (*3230*; Fig 362.24) retains part of its wooden shaft, but the wood was too poorly preserved for identification.

Finally, Building *5688* also produced one example of the small conical-tipped socketed type (*3184*; Fig 362.25) that has been the subject of some debate as to its function, often being identified as a ferrule rather than a bolt head. This interpretation has been challenged (Birley 1996, 23; Howard-Davis 2000b, 267), raising the possibility of their use as specialised arrowheads. The fact that this particular example was fixed rather clumsily with a relatively large, dome-headed pin, might, however, undermine this suggestion, as presumably it would have caused a somewhat erratic flight. Elsewhere, for instance at Ribchester (Howard-Davis 2000b), they can be shown to have been rather more neatly fixed,

and the Millennium example could be an isolated aberration, perhaps a repair. Examples of both socketed bolt heads and these 'ferrules' were found during the Castle Street excavations (Padley 1991b, 151, fig 132).

A storage rack?

Wooden object 25 (Fig 363) cannot be identified with certainty. Now badly damaged, it is a thin board, perforated by at least nine pairs of holes, all around 15 mm in diameter. It has been suggested (J Zant *pers comm*) that its close association with the projectile weaponry found in Building *5688* might identify it as a storage rack for, perhaps, *ballista* bolts, and the diameter of a surviving fragment of ash wood shaft on one (*2880*; Fig 361.1) would fit comfortably within the holes in this object. There is, however, a second potential identification, as one element of a large brush or broom, with the holes intended to accommodate bundles of bristles, in the manner of a modern yard broom.

Parts of a possible *ballista* mechanism

Two large iron-bound D-shaped blocks of oak (Wood 26 and 27; Fig 364.1-2) came from Period 4C demolition layer *6175*, associated with Building *5688*. These have been tentatively identified as elements of the mechanism of a *ballista* or other projectile machine, and possibly represent the first known from Britain (M Bishop *pers comm*). Slight differences between the two objects (Pl 213) suggest that they could derive from different machines, but as there is mounting evidence that parts of Building *5688* was used as a store and maintenance area (*Chs 12* and *15*), it is possible that the two objects were spares or recycled parts, rather than the remnants of complete machines. Thus far, no parallels have been found, either for the complete objects or for the substantial and distinctive iron bands which surround them. A review of the considerable literature concerned with the reconstruction of the artillery in use by the Roman army has not proved helpful, except in perhaps disqualifying some types. A recent attempt, however, to reconstruct the Vitruvian *ballista* (Wilkins 2003, 55–60) produced similar (but not identical) objects serving as hole carriers (*op cit*, pl 42).

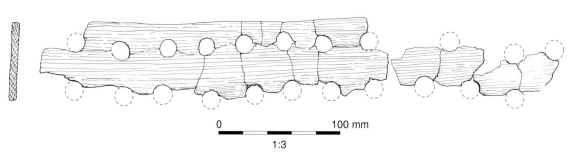

0   100 mm

1:3

Figure 363: Wooden rack 25

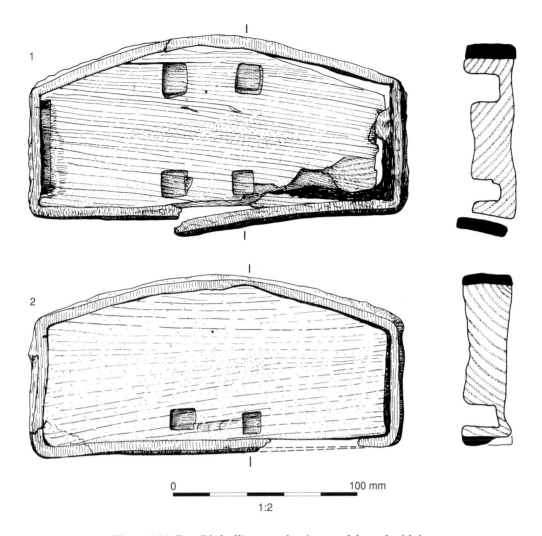

Figure 364: Possible ballista mechanisms, oak bound with iron

Plate 213: Possible ballista mechanisms

Pilum?

Nothing within the assemblage can be identified with complete confidence as a *pilum* head. There are, however, two fragments (Iron *1747* and *2445*; Fig 365.1-2) which seem likely to derive from these weapons. Both

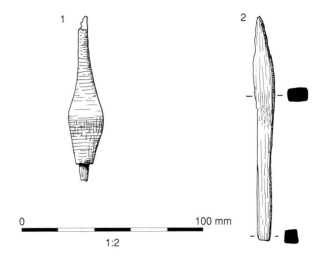

Figure 365: Possible pila

can be separated from the pyramidal bolt heads (*p 711*) by the length of the shaft, its more substantial cross-section in comparison with the tangs of the bolt heads (in one case round), and the fact that both are most definitely broken across the shaft. Indeed, the difficulty in recognising incomplete *pila* is not new, and is mentioned by Curle (1911, 189) with regard to the weaponry from Newstead.

Spearheads

Eleven spearheads were identified, a relatively large number, although Castle Street produced two (Padley 1991b). There is still no definitive typology

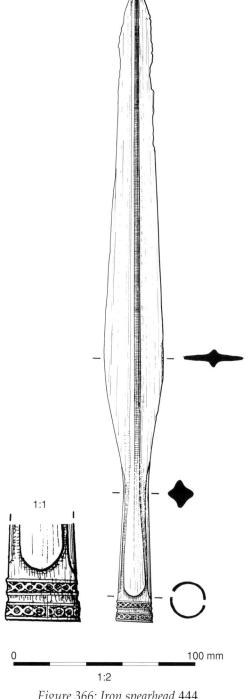

1:1

1:2

0   100 mm

Figure 366: Iron spearhead 444

of spearheads (Manning 1976) and the divisions used are those defined by Manning (1985), based largely on first-century material from Hod Hill. As the form is so closely dictated by the intended use of these objects, there was little change through time, and thus little scope for dating (Bishop and Coulston 1993, 69). Most of those from the site fall into Manning's groups 3 and 4, narrow leaf-shaped blades which seemed to have been equally suitable for use as cavalry lances or hand-to-hand weapons. It is of significance that a document (Tomlin 1998) recovered from the southern part of the fort (Caruana in prep) is an inventory of lost and missing lances and spearheads. Dating to before AD 105, it slightly pre-dates the group from the Millennium excavations, but is close enough to be effectively contemporary.

The spearheads vary slightly in size and shape, as well as in quality of manufacture, with the best-made coming from a demolition layer associated with Period 4A Building *2059* (*444*; Fig 366). This exceptional weapon, a leaf-shaped spear with pronounced central rib, has punched decoration around the mouth of the socket and is an excellent example of the quality of workmanship available, which is also shown by the copper-alloy horse trappings (*pp 719-24*). Only its deposition in anaerobic conditions has enabled such fine detail to survive, and it is perhaps the case that many spearheads were originally decorated, although none of those from similar conditions at Newstead, which are illustrated by Curle (1911), appear to have borne similar decoration.

A plain long slender spearhead (Iron *2972; Appendix 6*) was recovered from the Period 4A fill of a robber trench associated with the main east to west road (*7477*). This raises difficulties with regard to its dating, but there is no reason that it should not be roughly contemporary with *490*. Other leaf-shaped spearheads from Periods 4A/B and 4B came from intervallum road *7645* (*190*; Fig 367.1) and a feature associated with Building *2765* (*1596*; Fig 367.2); the same building also produced an ogival blade (*1597*; Fig 367.3). Two more are from Period 4C demolition layers associated with Building *5688*. One of these (*2704*; Fig 367.4) retains part of an ash-wood shaft, and conservation of the other (*2717*) provided evidence that the blade had been wrapped or sheathed in leather (*Appendix 6*).

Although of similar form, the spearheads from later contexts are generally more fragmentary, suggesting that they were residual and thus subject to more disturbance, perhaps especially that from Period 5D (*1345*; Fig 367.5). A significant exception to this is *2656* (Fig 367.6), from the fill (*5846*) of the foundation-pit (*5843*) for a column-base associated with the Period 6A *principia*, Building *5200*. Although complete, this example has been deliberately bent and twisted

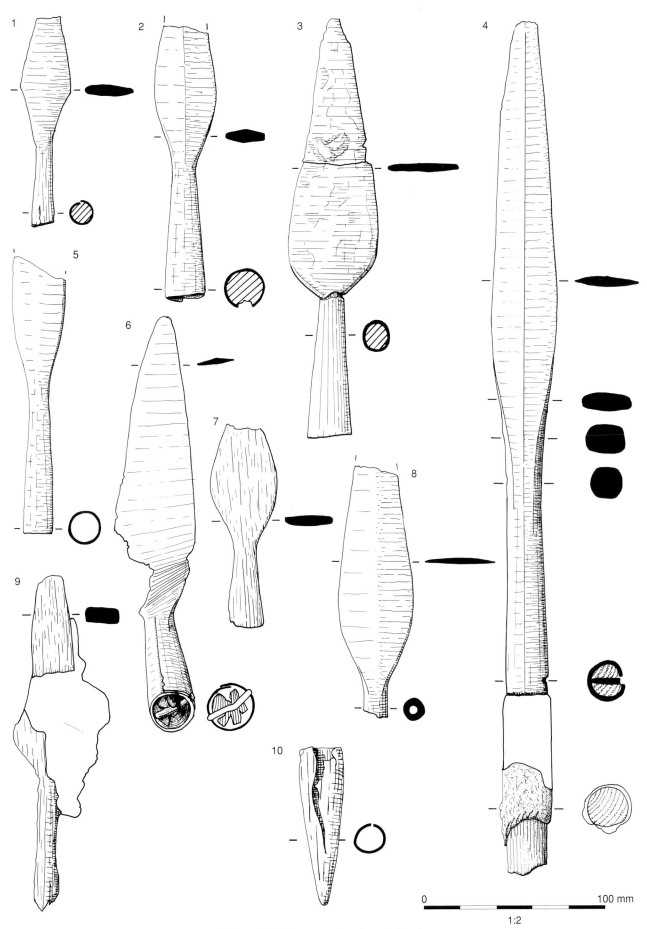

Figure 367: Iron spearheads and ferrule

715

beyond use, and it is tempting to see it as a foundation deposit associated with the renewed *principia*. Other spearheads from this period (*949* and *2622*; Fig 367.7-8) are in a similar state to *1345*. Object *179* (Fig 367.9) from road **7645** also appears to be a spearhead of ogival form, although it is in poor condition and no evidence remains to indicate that it was ever hafted.

In addition, a single well-preserved spear butt ferrule of simple conical form was recovered from Period 3B construction trench fill *7427* (Iron *3326*; Fig 367.10). It is quite likely that most spear shafts were protected with such ferrules, providing a counterbalance to the weight of the head and, *in extremis*, a secondary weapon. Other poorly preserved examples came from Period 4B occupation layer *6419* in Building **5689** (Iron *2931*), Period 6A floor *2365* in Building **2302** (Iron *1198*) and Period 6C stone feature *2323* in road **2303** (Iron *1123*). All were identified from x-ray.

A possible standard
A large socketed object (Iron *2898*; Fig 368) was found in occupation layer *6419*, within Period 4B Building **5689**. It is difficult to parallel, but is tentatively identified as part of a standard, like that illustrated by Feugère (2002, 50, figs 38 and 40). The socket makes it clear that it was intended to be mounted on a shaft, although arguments could be made for it being either at the top or the bottom. An alternative, though entirely speculative, identification might link it with the deposit of armour that was found nearby (*pp 687-8*), suggesting that it might have served in some way as a stand for storage or display.

Caltrops
In all, 13 caltrops (*Appendix 6*; Fig 369) were recognised, all more or less complete. It is possible, however, that individual arms, detached from more such objects, remain unrecognised and there might possibly have been more. All but one of those recovered was from a Period 6 context. As these unpleasant devices were used as a protection against cavalry, it might be the case

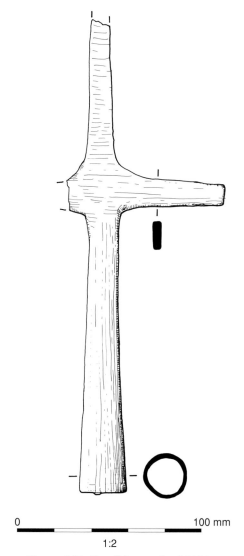

0   100 mm
1:2

Figure 368: Possible standard 2898

that by Period 6 mounted troops were not common within the fort, their use presenting a problem for Roman and other cavalry alike. Again, they are not common finds (Manning 1985, 178), and a group as large as this is unusual, although they are found in ones and twos on a number of sites.

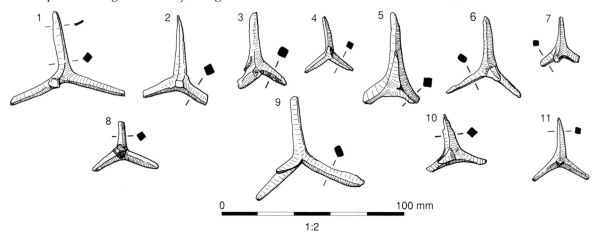

0   100 mm
1:2

Figure 369: Caltrops

716

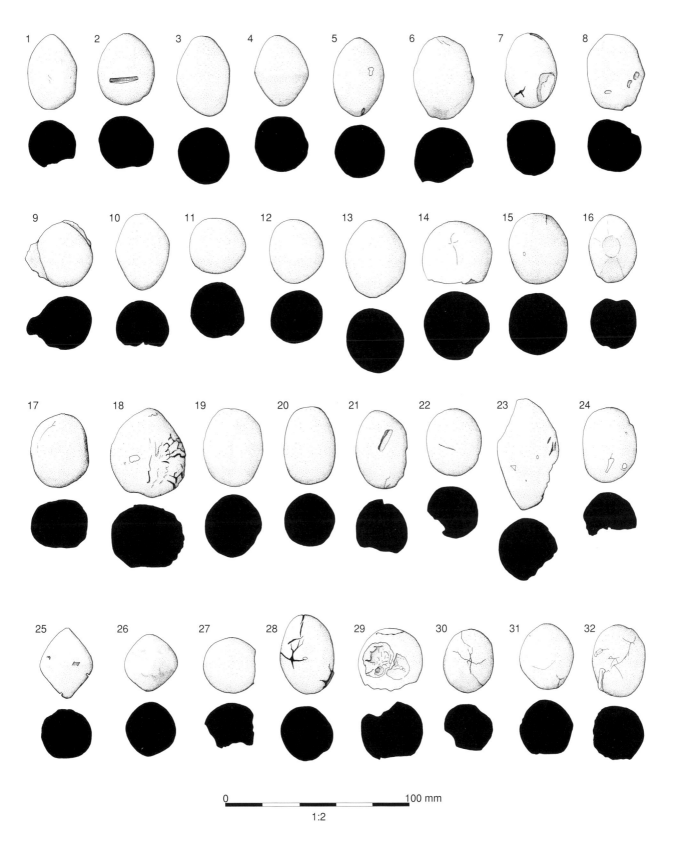

Figure 370: Ceramic slingshot

Ceramic and lead slingshot

In total, 47 fired clay slingshots were recovered (*Appendix 8*), and although from several successive phases of activity, it seems likely that most originated in the vicinity of Period 3B Building *4006* (Fig 370). The remainder, from Period 3D demolition layers associated with this building and with clearance and the subsequent construction of its successor, *3376* (Period 4A), seem likely to be residual.

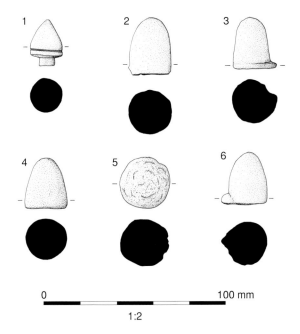

Figure 371: Lead slingshot

The shape of the slingshot varied between spherical and elliptical. There seems to have been no deliberate pattern, although more of the surviving examples could be described as elliptical, a shape easy to form in the hand, assuming that such objects were made on an *ad hoc* basis by the slingers who used them. Being extremely low-fired, it seems reasonable to assume that they were in fact baked in domestic fires or on hearths in a fairly unsystematic manner. It also seems reasonable to assume that these objects were made and cached (rather than made as needed) in order to have a readily accessible supply. It is likely that this group actually represents one such cache, now highly disturbed and dispersed through a number of later deposits. Even if this were not the case, the concentration of sling shots in this single place is of significance and might indicate a practice area, or even somewhere where they were used in earnest.

Three examples of lead slingshot were recovered from Period 6B contexts (*32, 240, 242*; Fig 371.1-3), a further three from Period 7 contexts (*27* and *162*; Fig 371.4-5; Lead *179; Appendix 7*), and one from Period 9 (*140*; Fig 371.6). Acorn-shaped slingshot (Greep 1987, type 2), like *32*, from a make-up layer (*2219*) associated with Building *2302*, seem more typical of the Antonine period, and are known from sites in Scotland at that date (Bishop and Coulston 1993, 115), even though in general the use of lead slingshot was falling out of favour by this time. Its deposition in a putative make-up layer might suggest that it is in fact residual, and should be more closely linked with the ceramic shot known from Periods 3 and 4.

The remainder of the slingshot from Period 6B seems more likely to be contemporary with its context, whilst that from Period 7, very similar in shape and weight (all sub-cylindrical, with one exception between 70 g and 80 g), seems likely to be of Roman origin. Although direct evidence for the use of lead slingshot is not common in the later third and fourth centuries (*op cit*, 166), examples are known from fourth-century contexts at Vindolanda (Birley 1996, 11).

It has been noted that the use of lead slingshot had declined throughout the empire by the end of the first century AD (Greep 1987, 190-1), with Britain proving unusual in the persistence of the use of lead shot throughout the Roman period. The same appears to hold true for fired clay shot, and it is of interest that Greep (*op cit*, 198) also points out a strong bias in the distribution of clay slingshot towards auxiliary establishments, although it appears that there is no particular association with specific types of unit. The large group from these excavations seems most likely to be of first-century date, especially if its origins lie entirely in Period 3, rather than Periods 3 and 4. In contrast, the lead examples are all from Period 6 or later.

Other military equipment
Evidence from the leather (*Ch 20*) makes it clear that tents and (presumably) wooden tent pegs were common on the site. These are, of course, closely associated with the accommodation of soldiers in the field. Only a single iron tent peg (*1374*; Fig 372) was noted, however, and the type is considerably less common than its wooden counterpart; it can be closely paralleled amongst the group from Vindonissa (Feugère 2002, 181, fig 243). It is perhaps of interest that no wooden examples were recovered from this part of the fort, although some have been found at Annetwell Street (T Padley *pers comm*), and they have been relatively

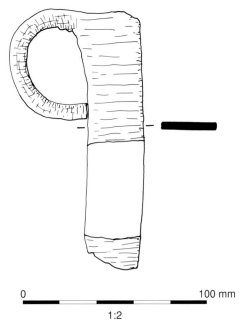

Figure 372: Iron tent peg 1374

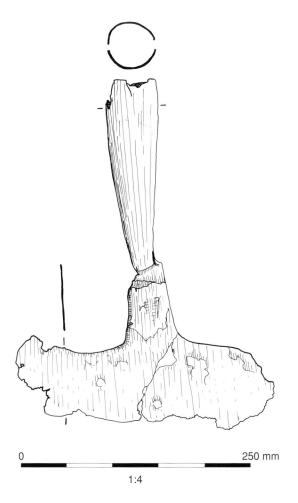

0 _____ 250 mm

1:4

Figure 373: Iron turf cutter 2706

common finds elsewhere, for example at Ribchester (Howard-Davis 2000c), the second-century fort at Kirkham, on the Lancashire Fylde (Howard-Davis 2000d), and amongst currently unpublished material from Wigan (OA North 2006).

Turf cutter

An almost complete, but poorly preserved, socketed turf-cutter (Iron *2706*; Fig 373) was recovered from a demolition layer associated with Building *5688* (Period 4C). These tools, associated almost exclusively with military sites, are thought to have been specialised equipment for digging ditches and cutting the turf blocks for defences.

Cavalry equipment

C Howard-Davis

Horse tack

A substantial proportion of the copper-alloy objects from the site derive from horse harness and saddlery. These clearly indicate the presence of a considerable number of horses within the fort, especially during Periods 3 and 4. It is not clear, however, and cannot be determined with certainty, whether they represent cavalry or the horses of officers from legionary or other infantry units.

Plate 214: Object 340, *showing the clumsy repair*

Perhaps the most impressive object is *340* (Pl 214), a breast or shoulder junction of the kind typically used in horse harness of the Flavian period, although the use of high-relief decoration makes this a very special piece. Both the central *phalera* and the strap junction clips are decorated with eagles (Fig 374), suggesting that this object might, originally, have adorned the horse of a soldier of considerable rank. The piece has, however, been mended on a number of occasions, and not always in a manner sympathetic to its high quality, for instance the hole driven through the left leg of the eagle and, like a lot of the military equipment, there is an air

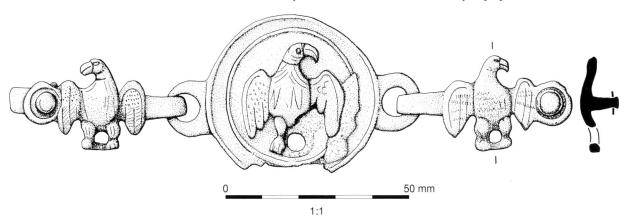

0 _____ 50 mm

1:1

Figure 374: Copper-alloy horse harness 340

of make-do and mend, suggesting that it had been passed from hand to hand for some time before being lost. The dating of this object is not clear, except that its position in a Period 3A construction trench for possible workshop Building *4654* makes it early Flavian at the latest. Few pieces of this quality are known and, therefore, comparison is difficult. The silvered trappings from Xanten (Jenkins 1985) provide no close parallels and the closest likeness for the central plate adorned with an eagle comes from the much later silver horse tack within the Esquiline Treasure (Shelton 1981, pl 46), regarded as mid-fourth century, which is impossible to be the case for the Carlisle piece. A similar eagle can be seen on an unprovenanced roundel from Augst (Deschler-Erb 1999, 167, Taf 27.551) and a less substantial example, resembling those on the harness clips, and also from Augst (*op cit* 177, Taf 37.695), is dated to the late first century.

Several less spectacular strap junction clips were recovered, all but one from contexts of Periods 3 or 4, the exception being from Period 5. Object *1064* (Fig 375.1) is of unusual form, most closely resembling Bishop's type 10 (1988, fig 51), although the box-like arrangement of the attachment plates

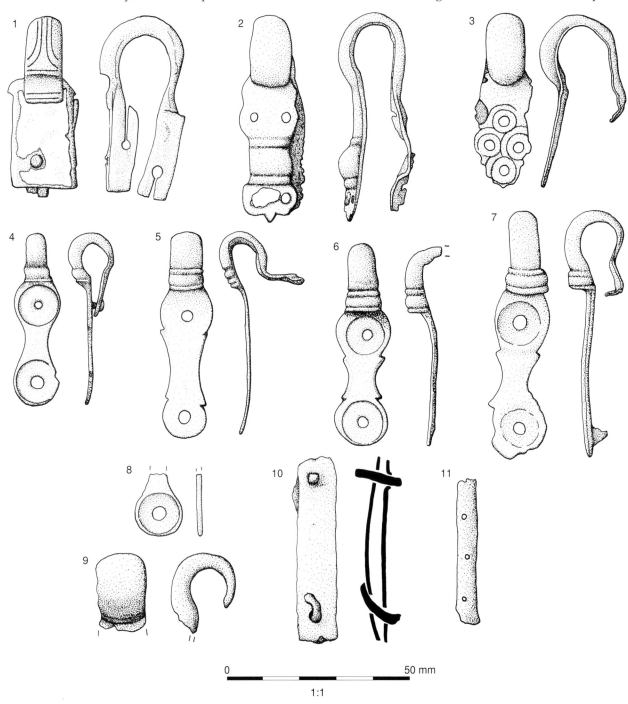

0   50 mm

1:1

Figure 375: Copper-alloy harness clips

seems unusual. Its context, occupation layer *7537* within Period 3A Building **7392**, implies a first-century date. Bishop suggests that this type could be associated with draught or civilian harness rather than riding (*op cit*, 100); in this case draught harness might seem more likely. A single 'double-spectacle'-type loop (*231*; Fig 375.2), perhaps Bishop's (1988) type 3b, was recovered from fill *3632* of a construction trench associated with Building **3772** (Period 3B). A second example of this type was unstratified (*1256*; Fig 375.3). Fragments of four 'spectacle'-type loops (*47, 190, 659, 666*; Fig 375.4-7), probably all Bishop's type 1j (1988, fig 50), were from Period 4 contexts, with *659* coming from a deposit within Building **5688** (Period 4A). A fifth fragmentary example, possibly of this type, was from Period 3A floor *3954*, within Building **4653** (Fig 375.8). This style of junction loop appears to have been current between the Julio-Claudian and Hadrianic periods, being common in Germany and Britain (*op cit*, 100). An undiagnostic loop (*147*; Fig 375.9) probably derives from a similar harness clip, as do *155* and *785* (Fig 375.10-11), both probably detached backplates.

Period 3 also produced a single example of the male element of a Bishop type 1 (1988) bar and keyhole strap fastener (*269*; Fig 376.1) from the fill of a construction trench associated with Building **3772**. Only a single, somewhat damaged *phalera* (*220*; Fig 376.2) was recovered, again from Building **3772** (Period 3D). Its size suggests that it could be from the bridle. These are also used to connect and distribute elements of harness, and it is possible that the amount of harness elements from this particular building is of significance. A pierced disc, *840* (Fig 376.3) from an external layer (*7156*) associated with the Period 3B *principia* (Building **7391**), is probably a second example.

A single petal-headed strap slider (*368*; Fig 376.4) was residual in Period 8. In recent years, evidence has begun to suggest that these objects could have military links, being in use from the Flavian to the Antonine periods (Bishop 1998, 64).

Harness pendants

A group of 11 harness pendants was noted (Fig 377), deriving from all phases of activity within the fort. Most are from Period 4, however, and the presence of at least three in occupation layers within Building **5688** might suggest that they were associated in some way with its use.

One large and four small lunate pendants were noted. These seem to have served a largely decorative purpose, perhaps apotropaic, the symbolism of the crescent moon frequently being used to ward off evil. Lunulae of this type (Bishop 1988, type 9) are common from the Augustan to the Antonine periods. The largest (*353*; Fig 377.1; Bishop type 9d), can be paralleled amongst the assemblage from Blackfriars Street (Caruana 1990, fig 109.49). It came from a construction trench associated with Period 3C Building **4657**, suggesting a Flavian date, whereas all of the smaller examples (*588, 594, 645, 646*; Fig 377.2-5) are marginally later, all coming from Period 4B contexts. The close similarity of three of the four small pendants strongly suggests that they were part of a set, or possibly that they were being produced in the vicinity.

Another small pendant (*544*; Fig 377.6) was recovered from a construction trench for Building **5689**. Its size, and the fact that it resembles none of the others excavated, could point to this coming from a military apron rather than harness.

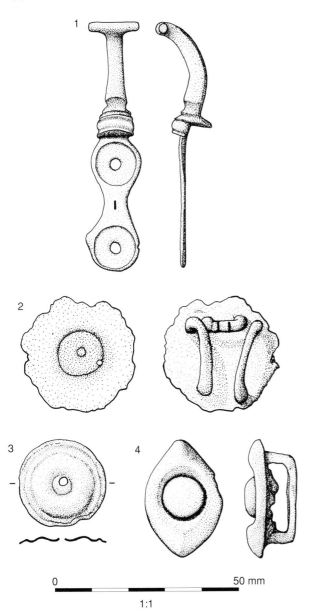

0   50 mm

1:1

Figure 376: Copper-alloy harness decorations

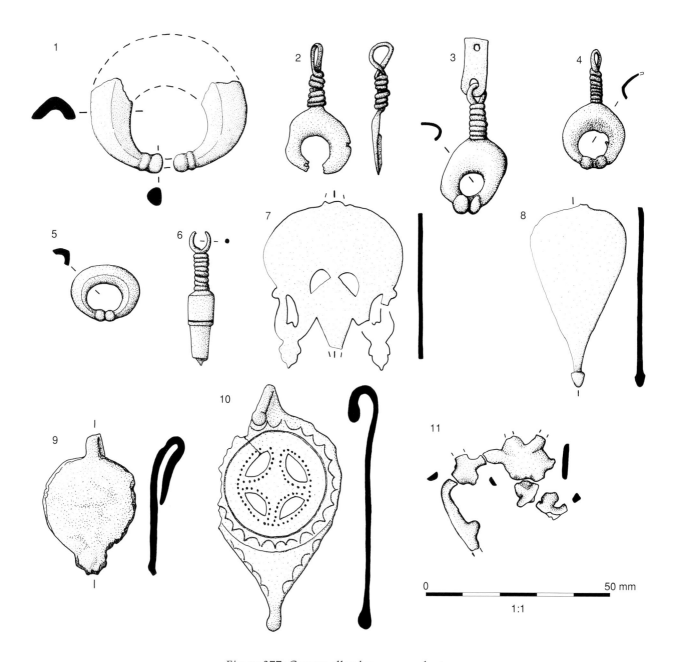

Figure 377: Copper-alloy harness pendants

Five larger harness pendants came from a range of contexts, two from Period 5 external layers. The earliest of the five (*346*; Fig 377.7) is an example of Bishop's type 1l (1988, fig 43) and can probably be securely dated to the first century AD. A second example (*643*; Fig 377.8), Bishop's type 5e (*op cit*, fig 45), was recovered from an occupation layer associated with Period 4B Building **5689**, which has produced a great deal of military equipment and could have been used as a store (*Ch 15*).

Two examples were from Period 5 external layers; *183* (Fig 377.9) is crudely made, and conforms to no particular type, but *36* (Fig 377.10), teardrop-shaped, is a carefully made and decorated version of type 5. A heart-shaped openwork example, *494*, now badly damaged (Fig 377.11) was found in an external layer

of Period 6B. Pendants of this type can be dated to the third century (Bishop and Coulston 1993, fig 112.13) and an example of this type is known from the amphitheatre at Chester (Thompson 1976, fig 26.11), where it was recovered from a potentially fourth-century context. A twelfth pendant might be represented by a badly damaged fragment from Period 4A (*828; Appendix 5*), deriving from a construction trench (fill *7152*) for Building **5688**.

Dome-headed studs
In addition, 27 of the small dome-headed studs used to fix harness and other military fittings to leather were recovered from a range of contexts covering the entire life of the site; two examples are illustrated, (*39* and *243*; Fig 378.1-2; for others, see *Appendix 5*). These studs were usually treated as rivets, the end of

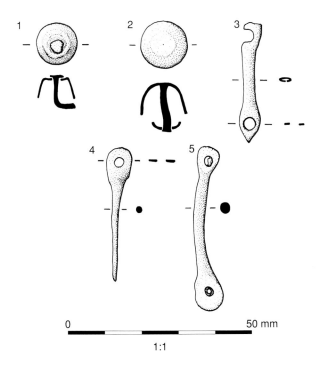

Figure 378: Dome-headed studs

the shaft passing through a small rove, before being spread by hammering. This, of course, prevented the shaft from pulling through the soft leather. As a typically Roman object, it seems likely that those from Periods 7 and 8 are residual, and the fall-off in numbers from Period 4A to Period 6B might also suggest that the three examples from Period 6 are also residual. Three small objects (Copper alloy *309*, *436*, *654*; Fig 378.3-5) are probably fixing plates intended to secure any one of a number of fittings.

Saddle plates

Four saddle plates were recovered, and should be considered alongside the other evidence for saddles (*Chs 19* and *20*). Again, evidence is concentrated in Periods 3 and 4, but the finest example was residual in Period 8, and thus technically unstratified. A fixing strip (Copper alloy *848*; Fig 379.1) came from the fill of a pit associated with main east to west road *7476*, where it was possibly residual. A small fragment of an openwork plate (*217*; Fig 379.2) of indeterminate form (possibly type 6; Bishop 1988, fig 38) was again found in a robber cut, associated with the demolition of timber Building *4006* (Period 3D).

A plain, possibly silvered/tinned saddle plate (*737*; Fig 379.3) of Bishop's type 2 (1988, fig 37) came from *6869*, the fill of a construction trench associated with Period 4A Building *5688*. One of a small group of unusually fine horse or cart trappings from the site, saddle plate *363* (Fig 380.1) was residual in Period 8F. It is a plate of Bishop's type 3b, originally silvered or tinned, and inlaid with floral motifs in niello. Although now slightly distorted, the piece is in excellent condition and gives an idea of the elaborate and showy nature of the harness used by officers and elite cavalry troops during the first century AD. A second highly ornate saddle plate (*1258*; Fig 380.2) of Bishop's type 5b (1988, fig 38), was unstratified, and is badly deformed, although it is, again, silvered and inlaid with niello. The purpose and disposition of these objects, comparatively rare finds, is discussed in detail by Bishop. He suggests (1988; Bishop and Coulston 1993, 105) a close link between the use of Bacchic motifs, such as grapes and vine tendrils, and cavalry, presumably reflecting the god's association with horses. The decoration on these saddle plates does not conform to that norm, perhaps hinting, although it must remain speculation, that they adorned the mount of an infantry officer.

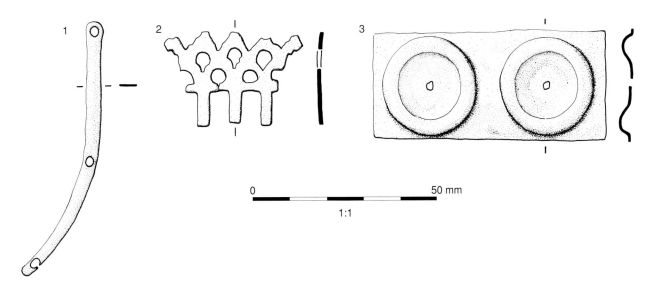

Figure 379: Copper-alloy saddle plates

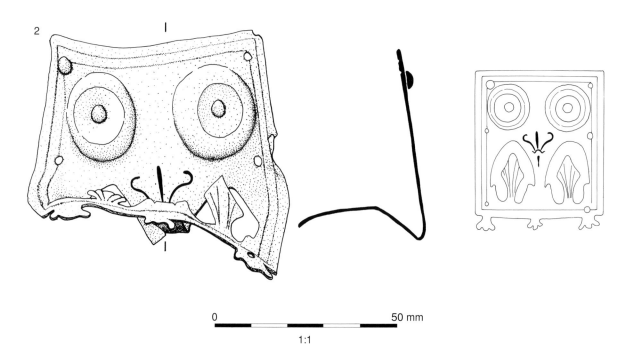

0   50 mm

1:1

Figure 380: Saddle plates 363 and 1258

Other Copper-alloy Objects

C Howard-Davis

Brooches

Only 21 brooches were recovered, displaying a considerable variation in type over the site (Table 42). This group of brooches seems relatively small in comparison with the size of the copper-alloy assemblage as a whole, but is similar to assemblages from elsewhere in the town (15 from Castle Street (Padley 1991b) and 28 from Blackfriars Street (Mackreth 1990)), or further afield, for example that from the auxiliary fort at Ribchester, where 22 brooches were recovered (Olivier 2000).

In all, there were ten bow brooches. Interestingly, there was only one each from Periods 3 and 4, encompassing the late first to mid-second centuries, during which more might have been expected, their use being in severe decline by the end of the period (Hattatt 1985, 128; Cool 1998b, 32). It must, however, be borne in mind that other types were being lost in the lifetime of the first timber fort, if not the second. Bow-brooch loss seems to have increased during the latter part of the second century, reaching a peak during Period 6.

The single headstud brooch (*311*; Fig 381.1) was from Period 3C pit *4130*, associated with Building *4657*. This is a predominantly second-century type, though its origins lie in the Flavian period (Cool 1998b, 30). The form mainly has a northern distribution (Snape 1993, 14), although this has been challenged by Mackreth (1990, 107), who sees it as a considerably more widespread type. The hinged pin and fixed headloop would place it late in the typological sequence, probably after about AD 135 (Snape 1993), although this is at slight odds with the stratigraphic evidence.

Only one example of a fully developed trumpet brooch (*154*; Fig 381.2) was recovered, from Period 4C demolition layer *4801*. It is similar, but not identical, to an example from Castle Street (Padley 1991b, 105, fig 63.7) from a mid-late second-century context. This type again has a Flavian origin (Cool 1998b, 31) and seems to go out of use between AD 150 and AD 175 (Mackreth 1990, 109). A distinctive Alcester-type brooch (*129*; Fig 381.3), decorated with spirals of silver wire, was found in a layer associated with Period 5B road *4662*. Regarded by Hattatt as a trumpet derivative (1987, fig 190.980), it appears to have the same general range, appearing to date, in the main, from the first half of the second century. An uncommon type, thought to have had native origins, Hattatt (1989, 95, fig 49.1539) lists only 37 examples, mainly from south of the Midlands, and around Hadrian's Wall. An example is also known from Corbridge (Allason-Jones 1988, 161, fig 76.12).

Only one of the three knee brooches was recovered from a contemporary military context, a semi-circular-headed example (*112*; Fig 381.4) coming

Period	Headstud	Trumpet	Alcester	Knee	Crossbow	Plate	Figure of eight	Penannular	Total
3A							*	*	2
3B						*		*	2
3C	*								1
4A						*			1
4C		*							1
5B			*						1
5C				*				*	2
6A								*	1
6B					*			*	2
6C					*			**	3
6D					*				1
7				*				*	2
8C					*				1
U/S				*					1
	1	1	1	3	4	2	1	8	21

Table 42: The chronological distribution of brooch types

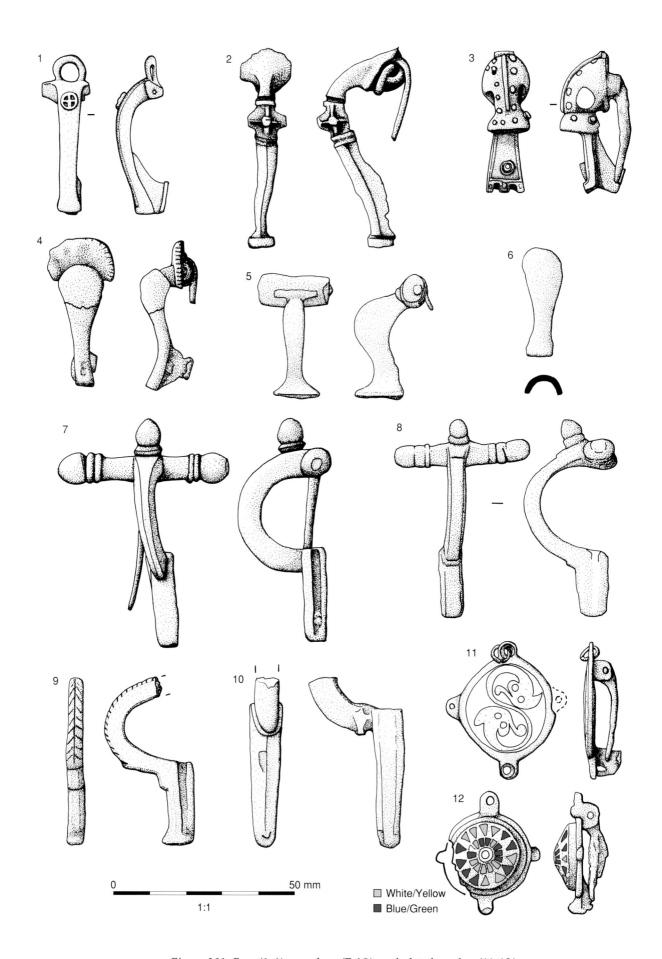

Figure 381: Bow (1-6), crossbow (7-10), and plate brooches (11-12)

White/Yellow
Blue/Green

0   50 mm
1:1

726

from a Period 5C wall foundation (fill *2442*). A second example (*69*; Fig 381.5) was residual in layer *2139*, regarded as a post-Roman 'dark earth', and the third was unstratified (*1257*; Fig 381.6). Dating to *c* AD 125–225 (Cool 1998b, 32), these brooches have a strong military distribution, being seen in the Rhineland, along the Danube, and in Pannonia (Hattatt 1989, 194); many were apparently imported, but it is likely that the type was soon copied in Britain (Olivier 2000, 239). Brooch *112* is the inverted baluster type most common in Britain (Cool 1998b, 32), and an example is also known from Blackfriars Street (Mackreth 1990, 111, fig 101.13). The distinctive shape of brooch *69* is confined to Britain and Germany, being seen at the Saalburg and Zugmantel (Hattatt 1989). The third example (*1257*) is fragmentary.

Not surprisingly, the crossbow brooches all come from Period 6 or later contexts, two from road **7652** (*446, 478*; Fig 381.7-8), and a third (*79*; Fig 381.9) from Period 6D demolition layer *2204*. The fourth, fragmentary, example (*385*; Fig 381.10) is from a medieval layer (*5135*). The two brooches from road **7652** are very similar, the marginally earlier, complete, example being slightly larger, whilst the other two are less well preserved. The bow of that from demolition layer *2204* is decorated with chevrons. Again, crossbow brooches are typically associated with military activity, dating to the third and fourth centuries (Hattatt 1989).

There were only two plate brooches within the group, from Periods 3 and 4 respectively. The earlier of the two (*867*; Fig 381.11) is flat, with a flowing naturalistic design, reminiscent of a dragonesque brooch. Although they were presumably intended to hold enamel, none now remains in the deep cells, raising the possibility that the brooch was in fact unfinished. The second plate brooch is a common umbonate form (*181*; Fig 381.12), enamelled in blue and white. A similar example was recovered from Blackfriars Street (Mackreth 1990, 112, fig 101.22) and both brooches can be dated to the second century, when enamel decoration was at its most popular, although it has been suggested (Bateson 1981, 36) that the type first appeared in the late first century and persisted into the early third.

Brooch *923* (Fig 382.1) is clearly a variant on the more common penannular brooch, being nipped in at the middle, and encircled by a moulded band to form a

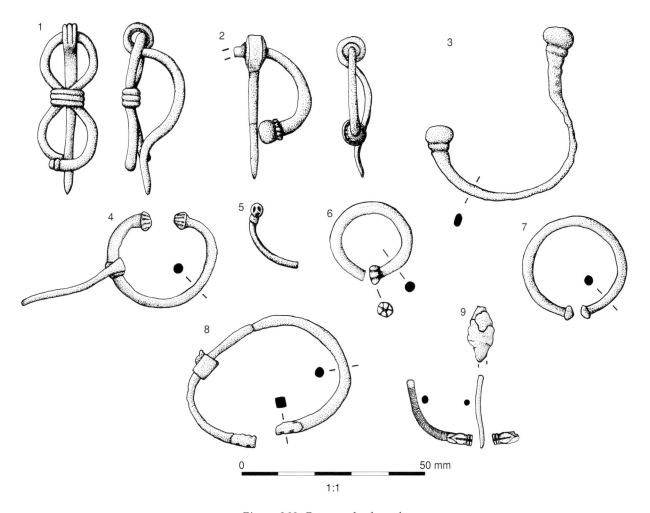

0   50 mm

1:1

Figure 382: Penannular brooches

figure of eight. It is an unusual form, and few parallels can be cited. It seems likely to be related to the wire spiral and other brooches made at Victoria Cave, near Settle (Olivier 2000, 240), suggesting a native origin. Its presence in Period 3A might add to this, being in an occupation layer associated with timber Building **7400**, the putative *principia*. Hattatt (1985, 657) illustrates a related example.

Eight penannular brooches were recovered, those from Period 3 (*32* and *997*; Fig 382.2-3), being Fowler's

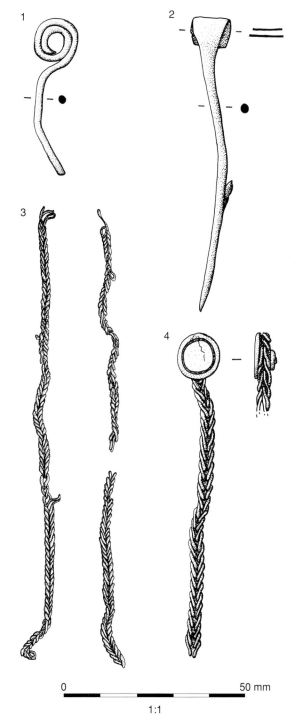

0   50 mm

1:1

Figure 383: Brooch or buckle pins and chains

type A3 (1960), and three of those from Periods 5 and 6 being type A2 (*107, 134, 457*; Fig 382.4-6), along with a fourth from Period 7 (*84*; Fig 382.7). The fifth is Fowler's type E (*8*; Fig 382.8). All of these have a long date range, being effectively current throughout the Roman period. The eighth example, again from Period 6 (*397*; Fig 382.9), is also Fowler's type E, and can be dated to the mid-late fourth century (see, for instance, Allason-Jones and Miket 1984, 3.113). A single iron example was also noted (Iron *3134; p 745*).

In addition to the more complete examples, a number of small fragments might have been parts of brooches. Fragments *22, 30, 374, 407, 417, 444, 519, 679, 686*, and *1235* (*Appendix 5*) are likely to be fragments of bow brooches, although neither x-ray nor conservation could further their identification. Fragments *226* and *916* (Fig 383.1-2) are brooch or buckle pins.

In addition, two fragments of relatively fine loop-in-loop chain were recovered (*644* and *749*; Fig 383.3-4). Although these could have been parts of necklaces or intended for the suspension of elements of military dress, copper-alloy chains of this sort were often used to join pairs of brooches (Johns 1996, 149), worn one on each shoulder. One (*749*), from a construction trench for the *principia* (Building *5688*), has a round-headed stud riveted through one end.

Bracelets and anklets

Fragments of nine bracelets and a single anklet were recognised, only the latter being complete. All derived from Period 6 floors or external surfaces, or were presumably residual in Period 7. Cool (1998a, 61) notes that 'copper-alloy bracelets are predominantly a late Roman phenomenon' and this chronological distribution does not challenge her observation.

Four fragments of cabled wire bangle were noted. Two were extremely fine, both with three wires twisted together (*445, 471*; Fig 384.1-2); in the case of *448*, the ends were bound together with even thinner wire, in order to form a neat terminal. The other two (*456, 458*; Fig 384.3-4), again made from three wires twisted together, were rather more substantial. It is perhaps of significance that three of the four examples were recovered from the surface of **7652**, the main east to west road of the Period 6 fort, and presumably a fairly public thoroughfare at that time. Examples of this type are known from first- and second-century contexts, but the type was clearly at its most fashionable during the third and fourth centuries (Lentowicz 2002, 46).

Five of the remaining six fragments were from narrow bangles bearing multiple motifs (*9, 11, 414, 415*, and *424*; Fig 384.5-9), again a common type, seen at South Shields (Allason-Jones and Miket 1984, type 1; see, for example, 3.223). These bracelets are typified by punched decoration arranged symmetrically around a central panel, but few if any are precisely similar. Again, these have a broad third- to fourth-century date.

The size of *426* (Fig 384.10) suggests it to have been worn around the ankle rather than the wrist. It is made from a single square-sectioned strand, twisted, the ends lapped over to form an expanding fastening. Close parallels from Catterick (Mould 2002a, 126, fig 292.6; 2002b, 109, fig 282.8) were found around the lower legs of the deceased in two separate fourth-century burials, and a similar armlet from Butt Road cemetery, Colchester (Crummy 1983, 1590, fig 41), derived from a burial dated to *c* AD 320–450.

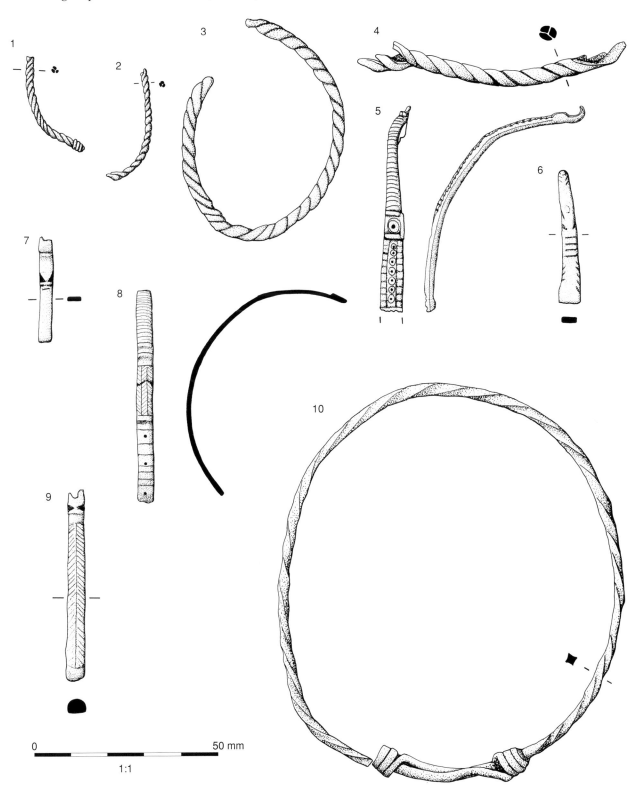

Figure 384: Bangles and an anklet

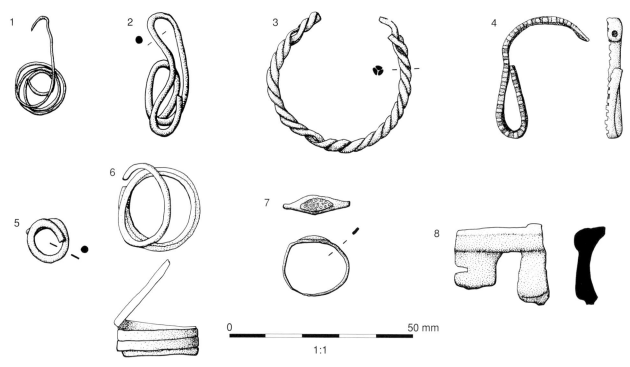

Figure 385: Earrings and finger rings

Earrings

Only four earrings were recognised amongst the metalwork, probably reflecting their apparently strong association with women in the Roman period, and the suggestion from the rest of the assemblage that women were not frequent visitors to those parts of the fort investigated, until Period 6 (*Ch 15*). It does not appear, from contemporary illustrations and documentary evidence, that Roman or Romanised men habitually wore earrings (Allason-Jones 1989b, 16–17; 1995), although it is possible that auxiliary troops or foreign individuals maintained their own ethnic traditions, and thus might have worn them in one or both ears.

Two of the examples (*156, 467*; Fig 385.1-2) were Allason-Jones type 9 (*op cit*, 8, fig 1.9), thought to have been an early type, effectively confined to the first century, and thus probably residual in their contexts. This might imply that women were in fact present within the fort from the beginning, but perhaps of lower status, or less Romanised in their apparel.

The third earring (*430*; Fig 385.3) is Allason-Jones type 5 (*op cit*, 7, fig 1.5), made from three wires plied together. It is easy to confuse damaged or incomplete examples of this kind of earring with finger rings or bracelet fragments made in the same manner, but the diameter of this example, at *c* 39 mm, seems somewhat large for a finger ring. A fourth fragment (*83*; Fig 385.4) has been tentatively identified as an earring of Allason-Jones type 2d (*op cit*, 4, fig 1.2d), although in its present state it has no pointed end and would be difficult to insert into a pierced ear, unless

the small hole at one end was intended for a thinner wire, which would have passed through the ear. It was recovered from a post-Roman deposit.

Finger rings

Five finger rings were recovered, four of copper alloy, the fifth of iron (*p 745*). Two of these (*304* and *435*; Fig 385.5-6) were simple spirals, the former made from four or more twists of wire, which cannot be dated except by their context. These are so simple as to have probably been made on an *ad hoc* basis, from whatever was to hand, and possibly not worn for any protracted period. The third example (*851*; Fig 385.7), from a Period 3E external layer, was also insubstantial and must never have been more than a cheap trinket. Nonetheless, the form, with a lozenge of repoussé dots representing a faux bezel, is common and widespread. An example from Castle Street (Padley 1991b, 108, fig 69.28) was dated to the AD 90s, and two identical examples from the cavalry fort at Ribchester can be dated to the Hadrianic period (Howard-Davis 2000a, 242, fig 54, 4 and 5). The fourth copper-alloy example (*401*; Fig 385.8), this time from a Period 6C external layer, is part of a typical key-ring, common throughout the Roman period.

Hairpins

In all, ten metal hairpins were recovered, all of them of copper alloy, which should be considered alongside the seven bone examples (*Ch 20*). They vary considerably in date and style. Pin *990* (Fig 386.1) from Period 3A Building **7400**, lacks part of its decorative terminal and gives the impression of being incomplete rather than broken, which might perhaps suggest

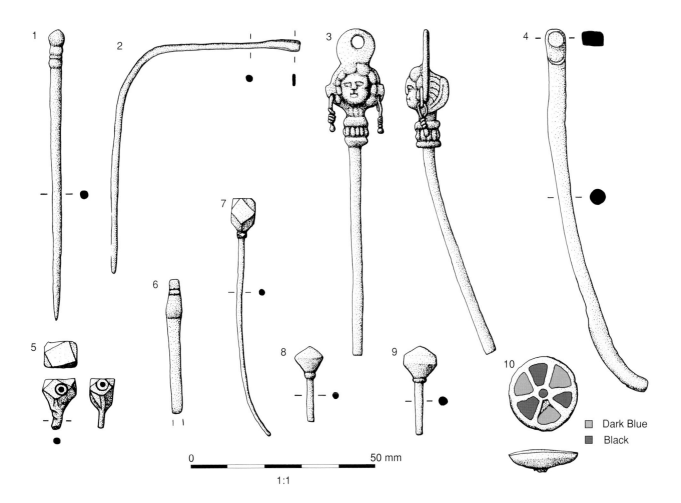

Figure 386: Hair pins

that it was unfinished or a failed casting. Pin *1115* (Fig 386.2), from the Period 3A *praetorium*, Building *7392*, lacks its terminal and is badly bent. Both are *c* 80-90 mm in length, and were probably originally around 100 mm, which corroborates their position in Period 3 deposits. Hairpins generally became shorter through time (Allason-Jones 1989b, 137) as the fashions in hairstyles changed, the hair being brought tighter to the head.

Pin *868* (Fig 386.3) was recovered from a construction trench of Building *7394* (Period 3B), which presumably implies that it could pre-date that building, making it first-century in date. The plain tapering shaft is topped by a female head above three narrow collars. The figure has a complex hairstyle and her exaggeratedly large ears were pierced to accommodate earrings made from thin wire. A third hole, at the top, also presumably held another item originally, perhaps beads. A second, less well-preserved example came from Annetwell Street (T Padley *pers comm*). These have proved difficult to parallel, although a similar example, possibly with the face being made of a separate inset gemstone, has been recovered from Westcott, near Dorking, Surrey (Bird 2004, fig 1.1); broadly similar objects

were recovered from Richborough (Wilson 1968, 100, obj 166, pl 42) and Colchester (Crummy 1983, fig 31 no 503), although both these heads were identified as male, which is certainly not the case with the Carlisle example. It obviously bears a close relationship to the series of bone pins with female busts (see, for instance, Murdoch 1991, 175, obj 491), which seem to date from the later first and second centuries, and the elaborate and presumably expensive pins, such as those with standing figures of Venus and Fortuna, from London (Brailsford 1958, fig 14, nos 10 and 11). None of these, however, have free-swinging additions. A series of ornate crescentic pins (Cool 1990, type 27), such as those from London (Wheeler 1930, fig 32.3; Brailsford 1958, fig 14, no 13) and Richborough (Wilson 1968, obj 167), all have dangling droplets not dissimilar to this example's earrings, but otherwise bear little resemblance. There is little doubt that hairpins such as these were regarded as a decorative ornament in their own right, and would have stood out from the hair (Cool 1990, 164), as can be seen on Egyptian mummy portraits of wealthy women painted in the second century AD (Walker and Bierbrier 1997, 57–9, nos 33 and 34), or might even have held a veil or other headgear in place. In the case of this example, the freely swinging earrings would, presumably, have become

731

tangled in, and pulled at, the wearer's hair, unless it was worn protruding by some distance.

Three pins were associated with minor road **2303** in the latter part of Period 6 and the demolition and decay of the adjacent buildings (**2301** and **2302**). One (*105*; Fig 386.4) has a simple spherical head and might reasonably be placed alongside similar bone examples, dating to the third and fourth centuries AD. Pin *91* (Fig 386.5) is incomplete, with only a short stump of the pin surviving. The head is of faceted cuboid type (Crummy's type 4; 1983, 29, fig 20), with ring and dot decoration on the larger faces. It is very similar in appearance to bone and metal examples from Colchester (*op cit*, nos 393 and fig 29, no 490). The faceted cuboid head seems to have been widely adopted during the later third century, continuing in use into the fourth; it was, however, rarely decorated during this period (Cool 1990, 164), unlike post-Roman examples. Cool notes (*ibid*) that, unlike the later examples, Roman pins have no collar beneath the head, and this example lacks a collar. Finally, a third hairpin fragment (*99*; Fig 386.6) has a sub-conical or baluster-shaped head which is without doubt Roman, but cannot otherwise be dated.

A second, almost complete example of a pin with a faceted cuboid head (*389*; Fig 386.7), this time with a marked collar, was recovered from a Period 7 layer. It seems likely to be of post-Roman date, possibly having a date range from the seventh to ninth centuries (see, for example, those from Fishergate, York (Rogers 1993, fig 662, nos 5352, 5354), and is thus of particular interest, adding to the small corpus of early medieval artefacts from Carlisle.

The three pins from Period 8A contexts are all unlikely to be Roman in date, although the biconical head of *386* (Fig 386.8) might point to it being a residual Roman example. However, a similar pin from Fishergate, York, regarded as residual in a later medieval context, has been dated broadly to the seventh to ninth centuries AD (*op cit*, 1363, fig 662, no 5358), whilst an example from Castle Street, Carlisle (Padley 1991b, fig 73 no 39), which would seem to lie midway between pins *386* and *390*, was recovered from a context suggesting it to be ninth-century or later.

Pin *390* (Fig 386.9), with a relatively large biconical head, flattened and faceted around the circumference, can again be paralleled amongst material from Fishergate, York (Rogers 1993, fig 662, no 5362), and this example was also regarded as residual within its context. Similar examples were recovered at Whitby, strongly suggesting that pins of this type are of post-Roman date (Peers and Radford 1943, fig 39, no 3). Finally, what appears

to be the head of a pin, enamelled in turquoise and black (*393*; Fig 386.10), came from layer *5234* (Period 8A). It remains unparalleled and thus undated other than by its context, which suggests a medieval date, anywhere between the ninth and the twelfth centuries.

Other pins
Another 17 fragmentary pins were noted, most comprising only slender round-sectioned shafts or fragments of shaft (*Appendix 5*). Without heads, their original purpose cannot be identified with certainty, but some at least were probably hairpins, whilst others could have been needles. In all, five came from Period 3 contexts, three from Period 4, three from Period 5, and two from Period 6.

Interestingly, two of the Period 3 pins (*133* and *769*; Fig 387.1-2) appear to be unfinished; both

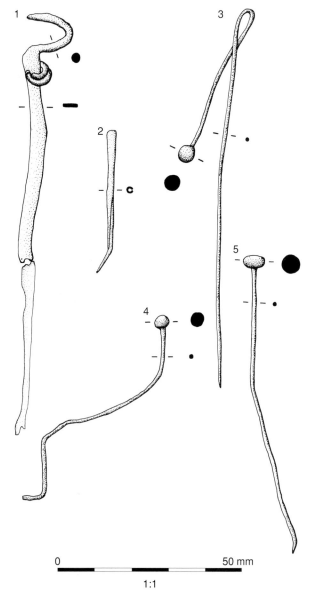

Figure 387: Other pins

derive from contexts associated with the possible *praetorium* (Building **7392**) and might reflect the suggested association of the excavated part of that building with metalworking (*Ch 3, pp 98-9*). Clearly, they would not have had elaborate cast heads, and may have served some other purpose. Two methods of manufacture are evident amongst this group, the shafts either being rounded by hammering from a square-sectioned bar, or being rolled from thin sheet; neither method would have been used to make hairpins, which must have been cast. The shaft of pin *126* (*Appendix 5*), which clearly has a cast head, is broken close to the head and could have been a round-headed stud.

In addition, three small pins (*42, 43,* and *45*; Fig 387.3-5) came from medieval contexts. All three appear to have wound rather than cast heads, making them typical of dress pins of the medieval period, used to pin veils, headdresses, and other items of clothing.

Buckles
Outside of the material directly associated with arms and armour (*p 692*), very few buckles were recognised, and of these none was complete. Indeed, most were represented only by large, but relatively insubstantial, pins, made by rolling sheet metal into a tapering tube and forming a tag at the wider end. Two of these came from the floor of Period 3A Building **4658** (*277,*

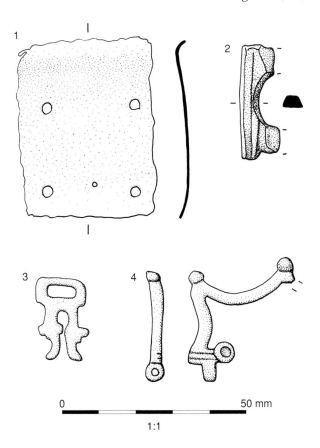

Figure 388: Elements of buckles

278; Appendix 5). A plain buckle plate (*55*; Fig 388.1) came from Building **2061** (Period 3B); incomplete, it has been identified as a part of a belt buckle on the basis of its similarity to one illustrated by Crummy (1983, fig 144.4179), with the reservation that it could come from armour. A small part of the bar of a buckle, probably where it hinged with a decorative belt plate (*245*; Fig 388.2), was recovered from the floor of another Period 3B building, **4006**. It has been deliberately cut up, presumably for recycling, and possibly offers a small amount of evidence for metalworking within that building. A third example of the rolled sheet pins, first seen in Building **4658**, came from a demolition deposit in Building **7200** (*670*, Period 3D).

Only two fragmentary buckles were found in Period 4 contexts: a small D-shaped buckle loop (*832*) from the fill of a construction trench for the Period 4A *principia*, Building **5688**, and a buckle pin from the fill of a gully associated with Period 4B Building **4660** (*178*). A third fragment, a plain buckle plate (*170; Appendix 5*), was recovered from a Period 5C external layer.

Again, buckles associated with Period 6 contexts were extremely fragmentary. A plain D-shaped loop (*10*) came from the surface of the probable intervallum road, **7646** (Period 6B). A small part of a more ornate buckle, of a widely found type, predominantly associated with the second or third centuries AD (Brewer 1986, 175, obj 32, fig 57), came from Period 6C layer *2254* (*85*; Fig 388.3). Examples are known from Blackfriars Street, Carlisle (Caruana 1990, 138, fig 122.115), from Old Penrith (Austen 1991, fig 93.660, 93.661) and from Birdoswald (Summerfield 1997, 310, fig 227.253); as well as from other sites on Hadrian's Wall, the type is very common on the German-Raetian *limes* (Brewer 1986). Another, equally fragmentary, buckle (*97*) was recovered from a robber trench associated with Building **2302** (Period 6D). A fragment from a Period 5 external layer in MIL 1, *245* (*12*; Fig 388.4), is, like *85*, a common second- to third-century type, although it appears earlier than this. It is well represented in the military North, relevant examples coming from Corbridge (Allason-Jones 1988, 177, fig 84.142) and Castleford (Bishop 1998, 80, fig 27.325). A plain trapezoidal plate (*380*), from medieval layer *5102* (Period 8C), again cannot be dated with any precision, and could be either residual Roman or medieval in date.

Button-and-loop fasteners
Three examples of button-and-loop fasteners were recovered. The earliest (*15*; Fig 389.1), is a poorly preserved example of Wild's class I (1970a, 138, fig 1), thought by him to be an early form more closely associated with late Iron Age native contexts.

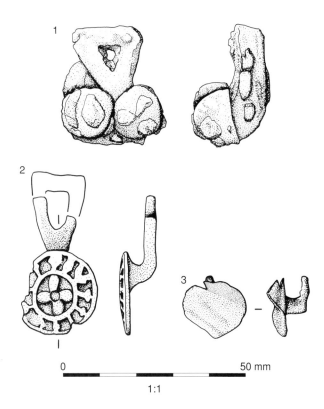

Figure 389: Button-and-loop fasteners

shafts with a small spatulate tip or scoop. These implements are thought to have been used to extract cosmetics or other valuable substances from small or narrow-necked containers (Crummy 1983, 59), and are often regarded as gender-specific because of the association with cosmetics, but could equally have been used in a medicinal context. They continued in use throughout the Roman period. Example *669* (Fig 390.1), from occupation layer *6617* (Period 3C, Building *7200*), is relatively delicate, and the straight edge of its scoop could mean that it was used in a different manner, perhaps for spreading or erasing, in the same manner as a *stylus*, although the very slender point seems unlikely to have stood up to use as a writing implement, as well as being rather too small to grip. Object *705* (Fig 390.2), from Period 4A

Interestingly, the only example cited by him which came from an unequivocally Roman context is from Brough under Stainmore, which policed an early trans-Pennine crossing, but a second example is known from Corbridge (Allason-Jones 1988, 175, fig 83.134), making it fairly certain that this class continued in use into the Flavian period at least. This particular example came from Period 5 external layer *267* in MIL 1. A second-century enamelled example (Wild's class Vb) came from Period 4A workshop *7396* (*696*; Fig 389.2). Wild (1970a) notes that the type is found in the forts of both Hadrian's Wall and the Antonine Wall, and on the Upper German *limes*. Allason-Jones and Miket (1984, 186) cite a number of parallels for the type and discuss alternative suggestions for its function. The third example (*815*; Fig 389.3) is more tentatively identified, being a plain round-headed stud with only the stump of a right-angled shank remaining. If correctly identified, it is an example of Wild's class Vc, again restricted to the second century.

Toilet, surgical, or pharmaceutical instruments

Neither toilet nor surgical instruments were well represented within the group, again probably reflecting the focus of the excavations on the administrative and logistical heart of the fort, rather than important but peripheral buildings such as the *valetudinarium*. Four or possibly five *ligulae* or toilet spoons were recovered, all with plain tapering

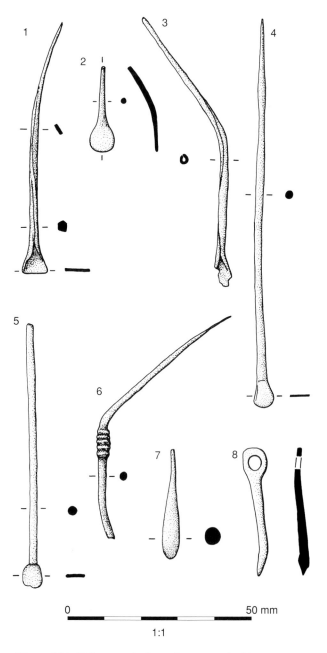

Figure 390: Toilet, surgical, or pharmaceutical instruments

734

Building **5689**, is a smaller and yet more delicate version of the same type of instrument, and a third, probably similar, example was from posthole **6082** (*535*; Fig 390.3; fill *6083*, Period 5C). Two *ligulae* of common type (*113, 116*; Fig 390.4-5), with small round spatulate heads, were found in the build-up of soils over road **4662** (Period 5B).

Object *596* (Fig 390.6), from Period 4B robber trench *7471*, lacks its tip, but has a moulding towards the centre of the shaft, intended to improve the user's grip, and perhaps suggesting a more vigorous use than the extraction of small amounts of unguent or powder. It is thus likely to be a surgical probe of some sort. Object *537* (Fig 390.7) appears to be the swollen tip of a spoon probe, again used either for some cosmetic purpose, or surgically.

Fragmentary nail cleaner *204* (Fig 390.8) is of the type found on chatelaine sets of personal grooming implements, and *148*, from Period 5C layer *2782* (*Appendix 5*), is a small fragment of a polished metal mirror, possibly coated with a white metal on one side.

Interestingly, examples of finds from this group were restricted to contexts in Periods 4 and 5, the latter a point when it might be expected that the numbers of women in or about the fort may have been reduced. Period 6, however, when there would probably have been more women resident in, or visiting, the fort on a frequent basis (*Ch 15*), produced nothing.

Objects used in the manufacture or working of textiles

A small triangular plate with holes at its corners (*924*; Fig 391) can be identified as a weaving tablet, used in the production of ribbons and cords, often decorative in nature (MacGregor 1985, 191). These objects are more usually made of bone, and one such example was also recovered (*Ch 20*). Although such

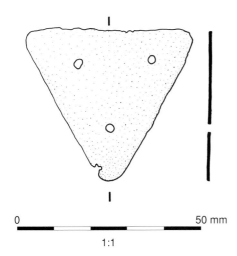

Figure 391: Weaving tablet

objects were used in sets, it is usual to find single tablets, this one coming from occupation layer *7442*, associated with Building **7400** (Period 3A). These are relatively common objects and other examples are known from Castle Street in Carlisle (Padley and Winterbottom 1991, fig 175, no 764).

Household utensils and furniture

Surprisingly few items relating to the household were found. Household utensils were confined to a single spoon (*480*; Fig 392.1) from the main east to west road in Period 6B, and several small fragments of vessel rims. The former, with a lute-shaped bowl, is a type associated with the mid-third century and later (Cool and Philo 1998, 196), and numerous examples are known from South Shields (Allason-Jones and Miket 1984, 3.221-3.341). Evidence of moulds from Castleford, West Yorkshire, suggests that they were produced there (Cool and Philo 1998, 373). A bone spoon with round bowl was also found (*Ch 20*).

Small fragments from the rims of open vessels came from five contexts, spanning Periods 3–6, with one residual in the topsoil (Period 9). All are too small for the original shape of individual vessels to be determined, although all appear to have been cast rather than raised by hammering; *362* (Fig 392.2), is the only illustratable example. A small cylindrical box (*305*; Fig 392.3), raised from sheet metal, was recovered from Period 3A (*4088*, fill of *4087*, a foundation trench of Building **4658**). Despite the lid surviving in place, the nature of the original contents remains unknown. Part of the lid of a flagon was found in Period 4A demolition layer *1628* (*46*; *Appendix 5*). The lid is of a common type, with a thumbstop to help raise it in pouring.

Object *77* (Fig 393) is a large disc, decorated in millefiori enamels. The decoration is of a frequently seen type, with a chequer of black, yellow, white, and blue. Neither the purpose nor the dating of these objects is clear, but one suggestion is that they were used as applied decoration on open bowls, a use certainly seen in the post-Roman period (Bateson 1981). It came from *2186*, a possible floor within Period 6C Building **2301**, suggesting a date in the third or fourth century. A similar example was found at Uley in a context dated to *c* AD 200 (Woodward and Leach 1993, fig 126.1), where it was also suggested that these discs were soldered onto other objects. It must, however, be noted that identical objects have also been seen used as harness decoration in the late second century (Rajtár 1994, fig 8.10), or even as scabbard chapes (Feugère 2002, fig 115, an example from an early fourth-century burial at Severinstor, Cologne), and a whole range of decorative uses could be possible.

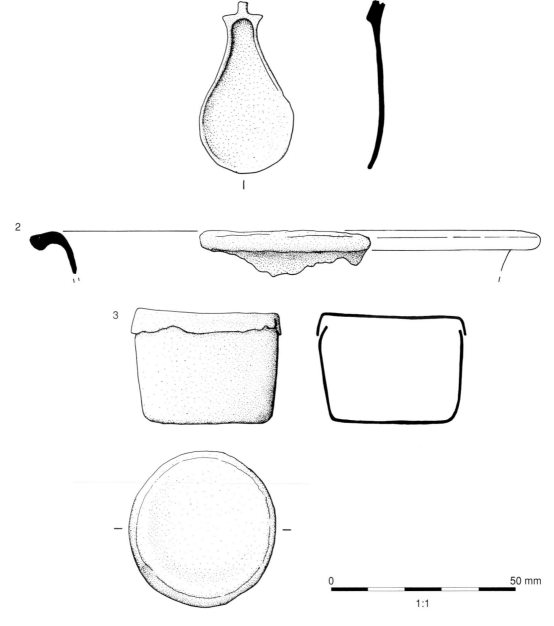

Figure 392: Spoons and vessels

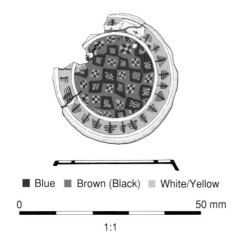

Blue ■ **Brown (Black)** ▨ **White/Yellow**

0 ————————————— 50 mm

1:1

Figure 393: Enamel disc 77

Locks and keys

The remainder of the objects associated with household items are probably associated with furniture and their closure. Object *920* (Fig 394.1) is an elaborate hasp, part of the locking mechanism for a smallish box or cupboard. The type is well-known, with examples from a range of sites, including the cavalry fort at Ribchester (Howard-Davis 2000a, 255, fig 64.200). A second, smaller example (*757*; Fig 394.2) came from a construction trench associated with Building **5689** (Period 4A) and is again a well-known type.

Although fragmentary and in very poor condition, *193* (*Appendix 5*) appears to be a barrel lock, coming from within Period 4A Building **4655**. Two keys and a bolt came from simple slide lock mechanisms (*485*,

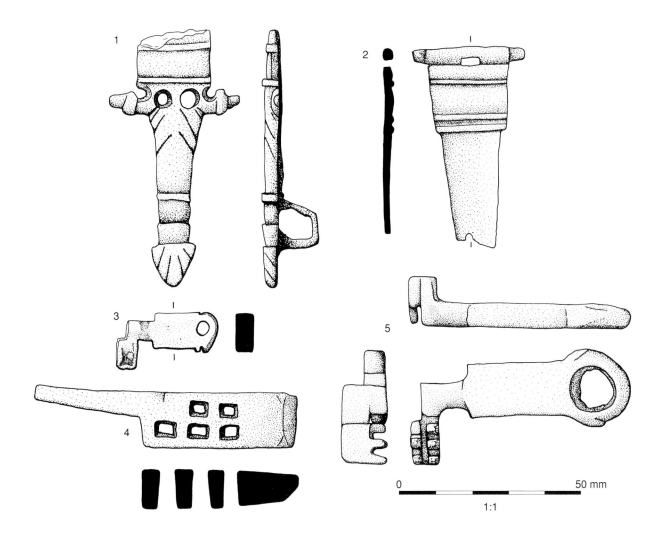

Figure 394: Locks and keys

798, and 859; Fig 394.3-5). The size of that from road surface 5506 (485) makes it clear that this must have been used in an extremely small lock, probably no larger than that opened by key-ring 401 (p 730).

Furniture fittings

Baluster-shaped knobs (151, 533, and 794; Fig 395.1-3) are common finds, and were probably used on a range of furnishings and fittings. Their findspots, however, associated with the Period 4B main east to west road (7477; layer 6000), the Period 4 *principia* (5688), and a Period 5 external layer (2792), have little in common. A fourth object (60; Fig 395.4), from Period 7 layer 2110, is similar enough in appearance to be considered another, presumably residual, example.

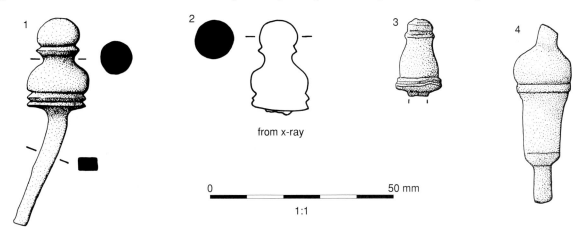

Figure 395: Baluster-shaped knobs

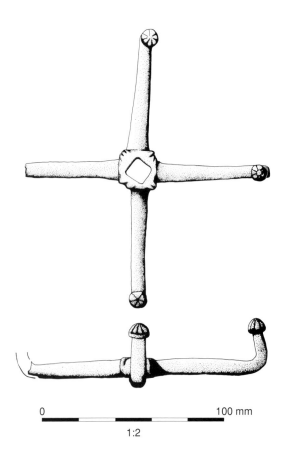

Figure 396: Possible candlestick 509

Possible candlestick

The identification of object *509* (Fig 396) remains uncertain, but it bears some resemblance to, admittedly simpler, iron tripod candlestick bases, for instance that from Uley (Woodward and Leach 1993, 201, fig 149.1), and, whilst the identification is tentative, it was obviously intended to serve as the raised base of a complex object. Nothing else from Building *7396* (Period 4A) gives any clue as to any specialised activity within it.

Objects used for or associated with written communication

Despite the large number of iron *styli* (*see pp 751-3*), there were few other metal objects associated with

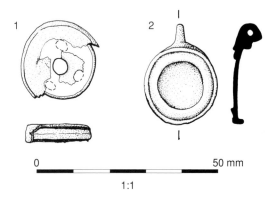

Figure 397: Seal boxes

written communication. Two round seal boxes were found, one just the base (*41*; Fig 397.1), from a Period 4B posthole, the other a lid (*383*; Fig 397.2), although there is nothing to link the two, and the latter was residual within a Period 8 context (*5118*). The lid was once, as is commonly the case, decorated with enamel inlay. Both examples are probably Bateson type 2 (Bateson 1981, 49, fig 7c), in use throughout the Roman period, but, as with seal boxes in general, most common in the second century AD. Although several seal boxes are known from Carlisle (Caruana 1990, 115-17), none of those published are of type 2.

Buildings and services

A single copper-alloy nail (*716; Appendix 5*) was recovered from pit *6808* (fill *6809*), associated with Period 3C Building *7200*.

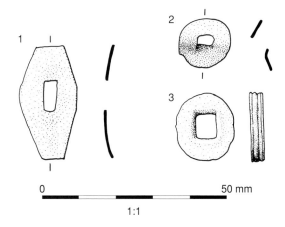

Figure 398: Knife guards

Tools

By far the majority of tools from the site were made of iron (*see pp 756-8*), and the knife guards are probably more rightly discussed alongside the iron blades. Three small such guards (*589, 754, 839*; Fig 398.1-3), which fit between blade and hilt, were all recovered from Period 4A contexts associated with the construction and occupation of Buildings *5688* and *5689* in the central range. The knives are unlikely to have been weapons; rather they were small personal possessions.

Fasteners and fittings

Finds which fall into the group of fasteners and fittings are disparate, and some could derive from more complex items. Amongst these are the 29 small flat, round-headed studs or rivets (*Appendix 5*), which are often used (as *749, p 728*) to secure the ends of fragments of chain, ensuring that they do not unravel. Others, like the repoussé decorated example *697* (*see pp 707-8*), are well-known as military objects. Most of the examples from the site are small, between 9 mm and 20 mm in diameter, with only three falling

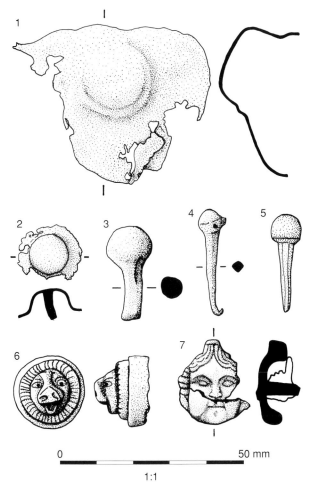

through a small circular rove. These objects have no particular distribution.

Bell-shaped studs vary considerably in size, although there must be some doubt as to whether object *54* (Fig 399.1) could actually have served as a stud. The six examples from the site (*52*; Fig 399.2; *481, 500, 852, 857*, and *973*; *Appendix 5*) are a common type, found extensively in the North, and elsewhere (*eg* Allason-Jones 1985). Similarly, spherical-headed studs or pins, of which 11 were noted amongst the assemblage, have a characteristically short shaft and seem likely to have been used decoratively on wooden items such as chests (*eg 198, 598,* and *1234*; Fig 399.3-5).

Lion-headed studs like *29* (Fig 399.6) have on occasion been found on relatively small lockable boxes of the kind sometimes found in graves (see, for instance, Borril 1981), but they undoubtedly served a number of purposes. A similar stud, with a human face rather than the lion mask (*337*; Fig 399.7), was recovered from a floor in Period 3A Building **4652**. It was probably used in the same sort of context, but similar examples can also be seen used as decoration on a leather chamfron from Vindolanda (van Driel-Murray 1993, 11, fig 5) and would fit in well with the considerable amount of horse gear from Period 3 (*see Ch 20*).

Whilst serving a similar function, the appearance of the head of a small stud can vary quite considerably, presumably depending on their purpose and context. Four (*836*; Fig 400.1; *359, 597,* and *730*; *Appendix 5*) have a thin round cap with a single groove running round the periphery, whilst *276* (Fig 400.2) has two concentric grooves.

Figure 399: Studs and pins

outside this range, two being smaller, the third larger (26 mm diameter). Again, all seem to have been used as rivets, with the pointed end of their shank passed

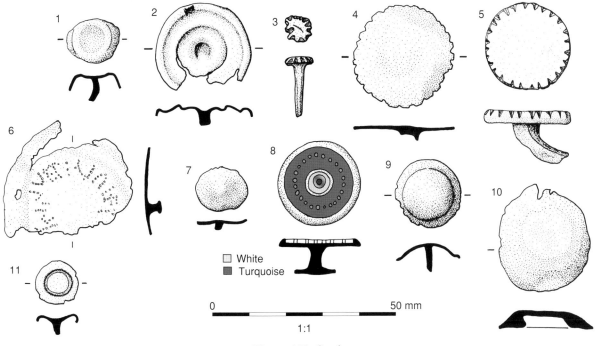

Figure 400: Studs

739

Studs with flat round, or irregular-shaped, heads, the edges of which are decorated with a series of shallow nicks, are not uncommon. The site produced one small, possibly leaf-shaped example (*690*; Fig 400.3) from a Period 3C hearth (*6657*; Building *7200*) and two round ones, both from Period 4 contexts, one (*599*; Fig 400.4) from drain fill *6405* (drain *6375*, road *7217*), and the other (*667*; Fig 400.5) from hearth fill *6588*, in Building *5689*. The latter example was tinned. A second leaf-shaped stud, without the nicked edges (*837*; *Appendix 5*), came from *7152*, the fill of a construction trench for Period 4A Building *5688*. Object *583* (Fig 400.6) was a large flat, round, stud bearing a punched but largely illegible inscription (*Appendix 5*).

Two small enamelled studs presumably served originally to decorate leather straps or belts; although not necessarily with military connections, they are often found in such contexts. Enamelling reached its height of popularity in the second century AD, but first-century examples are known. The original colour scheme of *919* (Fig 400.7) is lost, but *488* (Fig 400.8) is apparently turquoise and white.

Many of the studs had slightly domed heads and probably served a decorative purpose, the fragility of their heads perhaps suggesting that they were unlikely to have been under any particular stress. In all, some ten round and one oval example were noted in the assemblage (*eg 713*; Fig 400.9). One (*520*; Fig 400.10) shows signs of having been lead-filled, possibly as the result of a repair. Three other examples with a slight central depression (*eg 1237*; Fig 400.11) were also seen. A further 14 studs were

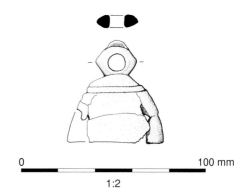

0   100 mm

1:2

Figure 401: Copper-alloy bell 225

too badly damaged or too fragmentary to establish their original appearance (*Appendix 5*).

Objects associated with agriculture, horticulture, and animal husbandry

As might be expected, there were few items which could be directly linked with agriculture or animal husbandry, except for an antler hoe (*Ch 20*), and an iron reaping hook or brushwood cutter (*p 759*). Bearing in mind that a considerable number of horses would have been closely associated with the fort, as is evidenced by the large amount of harness fittings, saddles, and other items of tack (*p 753*), it is perhaps surprising that there is so little evidence for their management, be they draught animals or mounts for officers and men. The two copper-alloy bells, *104* (*Appendix 5*) and *225* (Fig 401), and a third iron example (*2947*; *p 759*), could have served a number of purposes, one of which world have been as an audible warning, attached to a collar, although Webster (1995, 55)

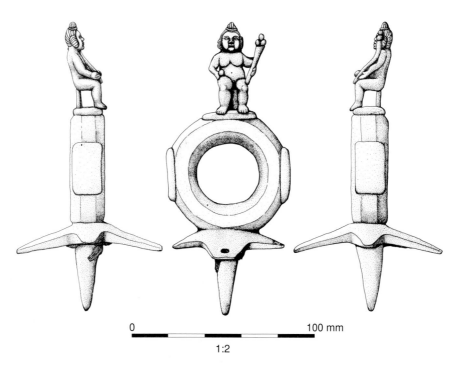

0   100 mm

1:2

Figure 402: Rein trace 580

notes that bells often played an important role in religious ceremony.

Equestrian objects

Rein trace

Amongst the items recovered from Period 4 Building *5689* was a large and ornate rein trace (*580*; Fig 402). Whilst not strictly a cavalry item, it seems most likely, from its classical appearance, that this object would have been set on a cart put to military or political use. The trace is surmounted by a seated boy, with a cornucopia in one hand and what appears to be a pomegranate in the other. The fleshy nature of the child suggests Cupid, but Harpokrates cannot be ruled out: whilst not depicted with a finger to his lips, as is often the case, the cornucopia is often shown as an attribute of his mother, Isis. Henig has noted some degree of syncretism between the two deities (Henig 1984, 114), and it does not imply an eastern origin for either the cart fitting or its owner, as Pliny (*Natural History* xxxiii, 41 (Rackham 1952)) notes the frequent appearance of Harpokrates on signet rings. Whilst rein traces are not unknown, one of this richness appears unparalleled.

Medieval horse tack

A single object (*40*; Fig 403) of clearly medieval date seems most likely to derive from horse tack. It is a small decorative fitting in the form of a six-petalled flower, riveted to a short metal strip. The context, an external deposit within tenement *1234* (Period 8iii) suggests a fourteenth-century date.

Tools and other objects associated with metalworking

Finds associated with metalworking are confined to a small amount of solidified spills of molten copper alloy, which could suggest the melting and casting of the metal, and a large number of small fragments of what appear to be metalworking off-cuts and scraps, either being collected for recycling or simply accumulating in the workplace.

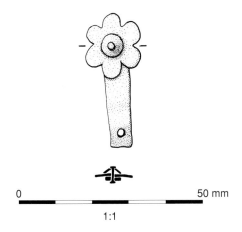

Figure 403: Medieval harness fitting 40

The 16 small spills represent only a very small amount of metal, and little if any of this material can be linked directly with metalworking hearths. In addition, only a few fragments of crucible were noted amongst the ceramic finds (*Ch 16*), and mould fragments were absent. Together, this suggests that high-temperature processes involving the melting and casting of copper alloy were not being carried out in those parts of the fort that have been excavated. Object *927*, from an occupation layer (*7442*) within Building *7400* (Period 3A), appears to be a casting sprue, trimmed from a newly cast artefact, and *427*, from Period 7 layer *5305*, appears to be an unfinished casting (*Appendix 5*). Whether it is of residual Roman or later date cannot now be determined.

Thin sheet metal has been divided into cut strip, defined as elongated fragments with two deliberately cut parallel sides, and other cut fragments, subdivided into triangular, square, lozenge-shaped, rectangular, and irregular polygonal. Fragments of sheet with one or no surviving cut edges are not included in these groups. All of these items have been catalogued as off-cuts, but it is obvious that some have been used to make rivets of the kind used to repair plate armour (*eg p 696*), whilst others have been intended for use as roves and patches.

In all, 161 fragments of deliberately cut strip were recorded (*Appendix 5*). These fragments are relatively small, with only four or five exceeding 80 mm in length, and none being in excess of 170 mm. This presumably reflects the likelihood that these fragments were regarded as without further potential for use, and had been set aside for disposal or melting down. All are between 0.25 mm and 1 mm in thickness, with little evidence for the means of manufacture; edges appear to have been cut with a bladed tool, and the thinness of the sheet suggests that this might have been a knife or shears rather than a chisel, which would have caused considerable deformation (for example, *236*; Fig 404.1). All fragments were relatively narrow, being between 2 mm and 25 mm in width, the range coinciding quite well with that of fragments of U-shaped binding strips seen in association with arms and armour in Periods 3 and 4 (*p 706*).

Some of the strip appears to have been collected for reuse, having rivet holes, or on occasion having been torn down the line of a row of rivets. Again, it is possible that these were being stock-piled for reuse, or were the trimmings from the recycling of larger fragments, for example, *863* (*Appendix 5*).

As an indicator of metalworking, the distribution of these and other off-cuts is significant; only 22 fragments were not directly associated with a specific building. It is obvious that there was a concentration

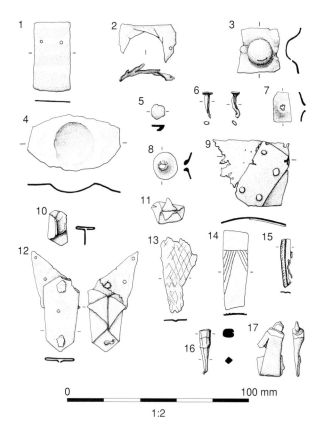

Figure 404: Metalworking scrap

Only some 27 fragments were not associated with buildings, and the distribution of other fragments, even at a relatively gross level, gives some insight into the nature of activity within specific structures. It is of note that deposition of this material was almost entirely limited to Periods 3 and 4, tailing off through the remainder of the Roman period to such an extent that many of the fragments from Period 5 onwards are likely to be residual, deriving from disturbed earlier deposits. It seems a marked enough distribution to suggest that the type of metalworking indicated by these fragments was particularly important in Period 3A, and was not carried out, at least in the areas excavated, after Period 4B at the latest.

Most of the fragments are very small, but there appears to be some evidence for their use, without particular modification, for the production of simple folded rivets of the type seen on the plate armour from the site, and also on other scrap fragments where sheet metal has been torn along a line of weakness, often a row of rivets. The rivets seem to have been formed by rolling an irregular fragment of sheet into a cone, which was then inserted into a hole running through the items to be joined, and hammered flat, sometimes with the addition of an equally irregular rove on the underside. The hammering presumably drove the rivet firmly into the hole, further crushing the top and bottom to form a secure join. It is clear, however, that such rivets were frequent victims to wear and tear, and evidence from the armour (*eg p 696*) suggests that they needed frequent renewal.

of material in Period 3A Building **7392**, thought to be the *praetorium* (*Ch 3, pp 98-9*), where the excavated evidence suggests that a considerable amount of metalworking took place.

In addition to these strips, 462 fragments of sheet were recorded, the majority being small triangular, lozenge-shaped, or polygonal fragments (*Appendix 5*). It has been suggested at other sites (*eg* Howard-Davis 2000a, 256) that the presence of large numbers of small pieces of sheet metal could indicate the manufacture or repair of scale mail, substantial fragments of which have been found at Carlisle (*pp 689-92*). There is a small amount of evidence to suggest that scales were manufactured (*1102*; Fig 404.1), which would not be surprising, even if only for *ad hoc* patching and repair to existing mail shirts. It seems, however, that most of the surviving off-cuts are too small to be intended for that purpose, but it is not impossible that they in fact represent waste from the process.

At least one fragment (*237*; Fig 404.2) indicates the cutting of small discs of sheet. An obvious suggestion is that these represent the blanks from which dome-headed studs were raised. An alternative is that the heads of such studs were raised from squares or ovals of sheet and then trimmed round (for instance, *209* and *255*; Fig 404.3-4). Such studs were used in large numbers in fixing the wide range of harness fittings to leather harness straps, and might indeed represent the repair and refurbishing of harness.

Nineteen unused rivets and six roves were noted amongst the large group of metalworking scrap (for example, rivets *991* and *1226*; Fig 404.5-6), and roves *660* and *1252* (Fig 404.7-8); eight of the rivets were from *7569*, the fill of a pit within Period 3A Building **7392**, and the majority were from Period 3A contexts. The remainder could have been residual in disturbed contexts.

In addition, there is a small amount of evidence for the patching of larger items, presumably vessels, or other objects which might be made of sheet, and these must be examined within the wider metalworking context. Two of the items are rectangular patches, riveted onto a second object using the irregular rivets (*1023*; Fig 404.9; *1037*, *Appendix 5*), and the remainder (six items) are so-called paper-clip patches (for example, *1050*, *1057*, and *1119* (Fig 404.10-12), probably unused, again suggesting a workshop. All but one are from Period 3A contexts. Three small fragments of decorated sheet, all from Period 3A Buildings **7392** and **7400**, are also probably off-cuts (*963*, *1113*, and *1223*; Fig 404.13-15).

Fragments of bar (rectangular or square section) or rod (round or oval section) were also recovered from numerous contexts (*Appendix 5*). Some of these fragments are undiagnostic elements of items such as pins, *ligulae*, and so on. Most, however, are almost certainly off-cuts from metalworking, but it is difficult, if not impossible, to be certain where to draw any division between such finds.

In all, 48 fragments of bar of varied dimensions were recorded. Most were relatively small, their length falling within a range from 20 mm to 50 mm, and their width and depth between 2.5 mm and 8 mm. Many had extensively hammered surfaces, suggesting their method of manufacture might have involved reduction, by hammering, from a larger block (for example, *781*; Fig 404.16). Indeed, in one example, the original rectangular section was tapering down to a round-sectioned rod, presumably indicating that some of the round-sectioned rod was produced in this manner (for instance, fragment *1236*, from a possible floor in Period 3A Building **7392**). In addition, 11 fragments of rod and 15 of wire (diameter <2 mm) were recognised. One of these (*1036*, Period 3A Building **7392**) seems to indicate that thin rod, perhaps wire, or for pin-making, was made by twisting and stretching thicker examples; other fragments suggest that wire could have been formed by rolling strip longitudinally into cylinders (*eg 677*) or, more frequently, by twisting strip into a tight spiral (*eg 691*; *Appendix 5*). A single fragment of beaded wire (*167*) was found in a Period 3A construction level of the main east to west road (**7476**), and may have served a more decorative purpose.

Finally, a single fragment of (originally) rectangular-sectioned bar, now twisted and cut (*958*; Fig 404.17) was partially coated with a white metal (presumably silver or tin). Again, it seems likely that this object was generated by metalworking, being possibly the sprue by which an object being coated in white metal was held during the process, which was subsequently trimmed away.

Objects of unknown or uncertain function or purpose

Inevitably, in an assemblage of this size, a substantial proportion of the fragments and objects remain enigmatic as to their function or purpose. A few are obviously objects of significance, but the remainder, such things as cast rings, which could have served any number of purposes, and literally hundreds of fragments of sheet, wire, or square/rectangular-sectioned bar are listed in *Appendix 5*.

Several objects are clearly of importance; *185* (from demolition layer *3211*, Period 4A Building **3376**) is a large and highly decorative escutcheon (Fig 405), possibly intended to incorporate a drop handle or suspension loop. If intended for a metal or wooden stave-built vessel, it would have to have been of considerable size. Clearly intended to latch over the side of a second object (possibly of wood), an alternative identification might be as chariot or cart furniture, although it is in a completely different style to the highly classical rein trace (*580*) from Building **5689** (*p 741*).

Two objects (*903* and *1103*; Fig 406.1-2), both from Period 3A contexts, are clearly related. Both are tubes, made from rolled sheet, and have a flat, spatulate head (one much larger than the other), with a small round hole in the tube just above the head. These remain unidentified, although, to the modern eye, their form seems to suggest a surgical purpose, possibly as catheters. A review of the literature (see, for

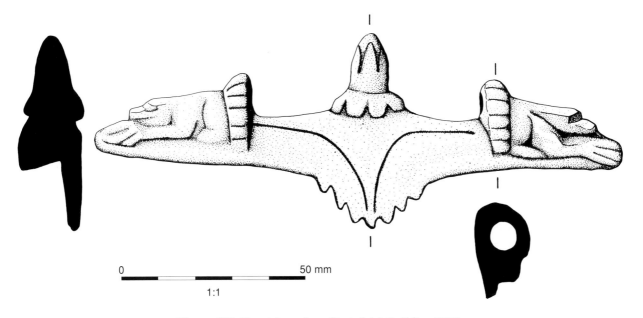

Figure 405: Escutcheon from Period 4A Building **3376**

743

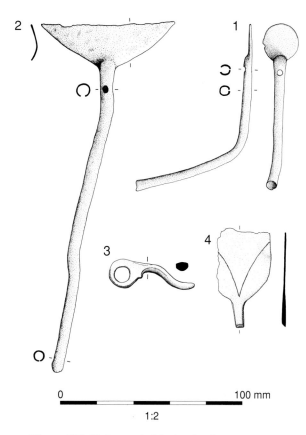

Figure 406: Tubes and objects of unknown purpose

Fig 406.3-4; *56, 364, 384, 541, 658, 707, 828, 1150, 1151, 1238*; Fig 407.1-10), but they obviously derive from significant objects.

Undiagnostic items
In all, 28 plain rings were noted, almost entirely restricted to Roman contexts. Sections ranged from lozenge-shaped (*501*; Fig 408.1) to oval (*44, 103, 142, 343, 399, 505; Appendix 5*) to D-shaped (*34, 218, 570,* and *814*; Fig 408.2-5; *67, 106, 109, 123, 127, 545, 595, 630, 694; Appendix 5*), but, in general, they did not vary significantly in size, being in the main between 19 mm and 30 mm in diameter. These simple objects must have been used in a wide range of circumstances, none of which can now be identified.

Nine plain and one decorated discs (*497*; Fig 408.6) were noted; again, no function can be assigned to these objects. Along with these were two small pierced discs or washers. Completely unidentifiable fragments (125 in all) were recovered from numerous contexts (*Appendix 5*).

Discussion
It can be seen that the enormous assemblage of copper alloy from the site was generated almost exclusively by Roman activity, the greater part during Periods 3 and 4. Only a single harness fitting can be assigned with confidence to a medieval context, from Period 8ii (tenement *1234*), other fragments from Period 8 being unidentifiable or probably residual Roman.

instance, Jackson 2002) provides no enlightenment, but the size of the tubes raises the possibility of a veterinary use, perhaps, in view of the large amount of horse harness.

A group of material, from Periods 3–5, and Period 8, have also eluded identification (*310* and *939*;

Within the Roman period, the greatest emphasis is on metalworking, probably for the most part the

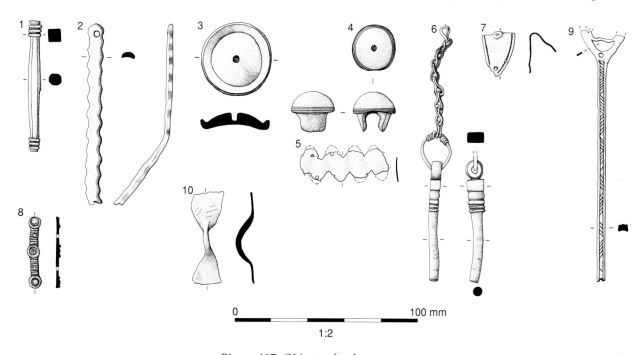

Figure 407: Objects of unknown purpose

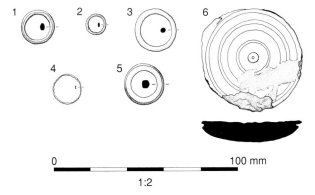

0   100 mm

1:2

Figure 408: Undiagnostic objects

repair and maintenance of armour, and on other military objects, like horse tack. Surprisingly little is associated with day-to-day living, despite the fact that other classes of finds suggest that, in Periods 3 and 4 at least, standards of living were good, and expectations high. Although there is considerably less demonstrably contemporary metalwork from Period 6, there is a greater feminine element, with bangles and other items of jewellery forming a significant part. This probably reflects the reforms of the late second century, which allowed more women to have a role in fort life (Goldsworthy 2003, 102), and the changing purpose of the garrison, which at this point was presumably very different from that of the invading force of Period 3.

Other Objects of Iron

C Howard-Davis

A large assemblage of iron was recovered, some 5364 fragments; by far the majority of the material was recovered from MIL 5 (Table 43). As with other material groups, the state of preservation varied considerably, with material from the waterlogged contexts of MIL 5 in considerably better condition than that from later periods in the same trench or from other trenches.

Apart from a predictably large number of nails (3926, 73% of the assemblage; *Appendix 6*), many of the

MIL 1	300
MIL 2	69
MIL 3	77
MIL 4	104
MIL 5	4814
Total	**5364**

Table 43: Distribution of ironwork between trenches

identifiable objects can be quite closely linked with military activity, and include considerable numbers of arrowheads, spearheads, and other projectiles, as well as the collection of armour from Period 4 (deposits *6419* and *6205, pp 687-705*).

Most of the datable objects were Roman, although a significant group of 'wavy edge' horseshoes and fiddle-key horseshoe nails were recovered from Periods 7 and 8, suggesting activity in the vicinity from perhaps the tenth century onwards. A large number of the recognisable blade fragments derived from Period 8, and there is no reason to suggest that they are not medieval in date. A delicate pair of shears, small enough to have been used for fine needlework, was also recovered from a medieval context (*p 749*).

Objects of personal adornment or dress

Apart from hobnails, very few other items of dress or adornment were noted amongst the ironwork. An almost plain penannular ring (*774*; Fig 409) has been identified as a possible brooch, as the terminals appear larger than the remainder of the ring, although in the absence of a pin, this must remain tentative. Iron brooches of this type are well known, and have a wide date-range, covering the entire period.

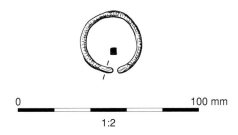

0   100 mm

1:2

Figure 409: Brooch 774

A single, poorly preserved, iron finger ring (*3113, Appendix 6*) came from a Period 3C occupation layer within Building **7200**. Originally incorporating a gemstone which is likely to have had an intaglio device, its form suggests a first/second-century date. In addition, it is possible that a small rectangular object (*995; Appendix 6*) is a belt loop, intended to hold the loose end of a leather belt in position.

Hobnails

Dome-headed hobnails are typical of Roman footwear from the first century onwards and must have been produced and used in huge quantities by the army (van Driel-Murray 1987, 40). A considerable proportion of civilian footwear was also nailed, however, presumably reflecting a desire for more substantial and hard-wearing shoes as metalled roads became a more common element of daily life. There is little appreciable variation in the form of these simple but distinctive objects, and in consequence they cannot be used for dating. A single hobnail was recovered from Period 1 layer *354*, seemingly the pre-Roman ground surface, and it is a tempting if speculative conclusion to see it lost from the shoe of one of the first Roman arrivals at the site in the first century AD. In subsequent periods there was an occasional loss of hobnails in the course of day-to-day life, both in occupation layers within the buildings and on metalled roads. This should be considered in conjunction with the distribution of evidence for shoemaking drawn from the leather assemblage (*Ch 20*).

About 366 loose hobnails were recovered, over and above those remaining in the leather shoe soles (*Ch 20*). All have an almost hemispherical head, *c* 12 mm in diameter, with a tapering shank *c* 12-16 mm long. In several instances, the nails were recovered in corroded clumps, implying that they had entered the archaeological record whilst still fixed to shoe soles (*Appendix 6*).

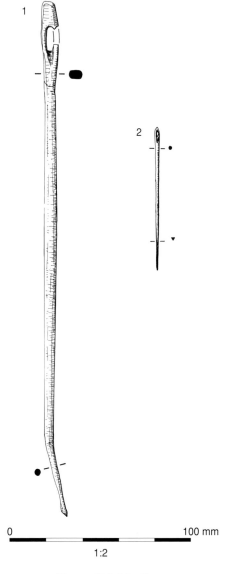

0   100 mm

1:2

Figure 410: Needles

Objects used in the manufacture or working of textiles

Very few items associated with working textiles were present in the ironwork assemblage, despite there being a scatter of objects in other materials (bone artefacts especially, *Ch 20*) and, in medieval layers (Period 8), preserved textile (*Ch 20*). It is possible that the large needle (*1767*; Fig 410.1) from Period 3A Building **4654**, a possible workshop, was used for sewing something more substantial, like leather, or was perhaps used as a baling needle. A second fragment of fine tapering round-sectioned rod (*3216*; *Appendix 6*) from Period 4A Building **5688** is possibly also part of a needle. A third example, *384* (Fig 410.2) from medieval tenement **1235** (Period 8iv), is a common type, of which several are known from Carlisle, especially from Castle Street (Padley 1991b), and could be of either Roman or medieval date.

Two more fragments of fine round-sectioned rod, both possibly with the remnant of a split or eye at one end, are also possibly needles, but their identification remains less certain. Both date to Period 4B and are associated with Buildings **5688** and **5689** respectively (*2785*, *2809*; *Appendix 6*).

Household utensils and furniture
Razors and knives

In all, 36 fragments, representing 35 blades, were recovered, less than half (15 examples) from secure Roman contexts. Blade fragments are relatively easy to identify, having a distinctive triangular cross-section, but, lacking other diagnostic features, they are difficult to date.

All of the knives recognised, both Roman and medieval, are relatively small and were probably personal possessions used in day-to-day living, including being used as eating implements. It is interesting that four of the Roman blades are of types which can be identified with relative certainty as razors, reflecting both the concentration of men within the fort, and the first- and early second-century fashionable preference for being clean-shaven (Croom 2002).

Ivory-handled razor or toilet knife *3415* (Fig 411.1) is of a well-known and distinctive type (Manning 1985, type 1c, 110, fig 28), probably the product of specialist cutlers rather than the local blacksmith, as is suggested by a grave relief from Rome, where knives of this type can be clearly seen (Kemkes *et al* 2002, 220, fig 254). Found in a roadside drain, it raises the possibility that the fort was visited by professional barbers of the kind envisaged by Boon (1991), who would most likely have set up in the open air, where light was better. A similar example, but possibly with a metal-bound wooden handle, was found at the Blackfriar's Street site (Caruana 1990, fig 113, 74) in a late first-century context.

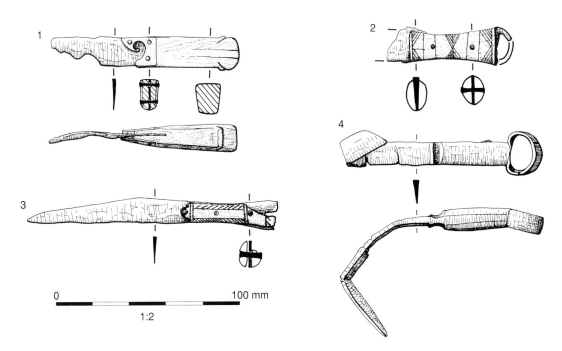

Figure 411: Razors and knives

Two more knives (*1601* and *2650*; Fig 411.2-3), probably both Manning type 7 (1985, 112, fig 28), are both small enough to have served as razors, the angled back of the blade being particularly suited to this use. This is regarded as an early type (*op cit*, 112), although only one (*486*) came from occupation deposits within a building (Period 4A Building *7396*). The nature of activity associated with Period 5 is ambiguous and it thus seems likely that the second example is residual.

Several similar knives were noted in the Castle Street assemblage (Padley 1991b, fig 120), two bearing makers' marks. The consistency of design suggests a specialist use, and Manning's suggestion that they served as razors seems appropriate (Manning 1985, 110). A fourth knife (*344*; Fig 411.4) can also be identified as a razor of Roman type (Manning 1985, type 4), although it was found within the fills of medieval ditch *1230* (Period 8i).

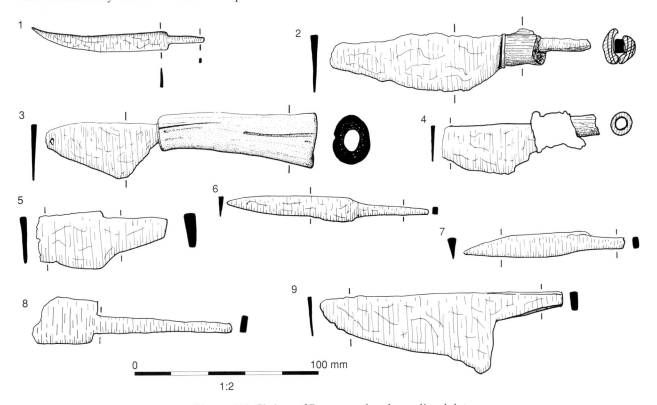

Figure 412: Knives of Roman and early medieval date

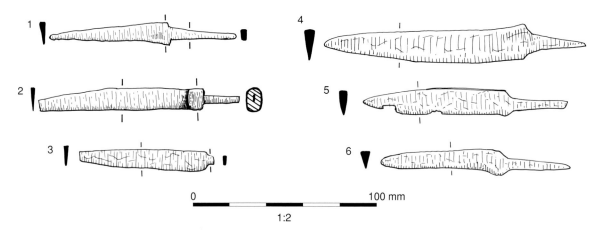

Figure 413: Knives of medieval date 1

A small upwards-curving whittle-tang blade, found in a Period 3C pit fill within a workshop, **4657** (*1729*; Fig 412.1), could have been used for any number of purposes. A larger blade with fragmentary wooden handle is a common, all-purpose type (Manning 1985, type 15; *2999*; Fig 412.2). Found in Building **7396**, it could have been used by the leatherworkers thought to have used the building as a workshop during Period 4A (*Ch 20, p 819*). A well-worn antler-handled knife with short triangular blade (*420*; Fig 412.3; Manning 1985, type 12) was from a Period 4A demolition layer associated with Building **2059** (*Ch 5*). Larger versions of this knife are regarded as cleavers (*op cit*, 114), but, again, this small example could have been used for a number of purposes. A socketed blade, possibly large enough to be used as a cleaver, was, however, found in layer *283* (*131*; Fig 412.4), part of the possible west rampart of the Period 4 fort, although little of the blade remains.

Blades from Period 6 are undiagnostic, and again small enough to have been used for any number of purposes. Examples (*1197* and *2344*; Fig 412.5-6), were associated with floors in Buildings **2302** and **5200** in Periods 6A and 6C respectively, and thus are likely to reflect contemporary activity. Two similar blades came from Period 7 contexts (*609* and *2033*; Fig 412.7-8). Their forms are not helpful for dating

and they could be either residual Roman examples or early medieval blades contemporary with the 'dark earth' deposits. A third short triangular example (*2165*; Fig 412.9) was recovered from Period 7 layer *5242*, and again could be Roman or later in date.

The remainder of the well-preserved blades (*405, 413, 1842, 1877, 1921, 1959,* ; Fig 413; *386, 387, 395, 3499*; Fig 414) are all likely to be medieval in date, coming from the outer ward ditch or other medieval deposits. All are typically long triangular blades, often quite worn, mainly with whittle tangs. This is a common form throughout the medieval period, not losing popularity until the fifteenth century (Cowgill 1987, 25). Evidence from one (*413*; Fig 413.2) suggests a horn or bone handle was once held in place by an iron hilt band.

Three knives have makers' marks, two inlaid with copper alloy (*386*; Fig 414.1; Pl 215; *395*; Fig 414.3), the third struck (*387*; Fig 414.2; Pl 216). The latter had a whittle tang, whilst the other two probably both had scale tangs with bone plates attached by copper-alloy rivets. Although the handle of knife *395* is missing, it does have a copper-alloy shoulder plate. Scale tangs are virtually unknown on medieval knives until the fourteenth century (Cowgill 1987, 26), which suggests that two of the

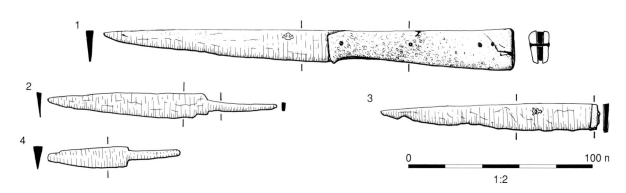

Figure 414: Knives of medieval date 2

Plate 215: The blade of knife 386, showing an inlaid maker's mark

Plate 216: X-ray of knife 387, showing struck maker's mark

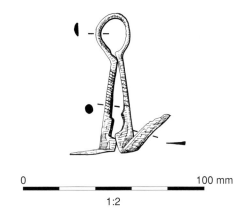

Figure 415: Shears 316

three marked blades must date to this period or later, and stratigraphic evidence would suggest that the third was contemporary. Finally, an unstratified blade of long-lived and thus undatable form (*3499*; Fig 414.4) provides evidence of a leather sheath, presumably similar to those seen amongst the medieval leatherwork (*Ch 20*).

A single small pair of shears (*316*; Fig 415) came from a Period 8iv fill of a possible landscaping feature (*1225*), and are most likely to be medieval. The shears, with decorated arms, are too small to have been used for anything like shearing fleece, and were probably intended for use in needle-working or even trimming hair (de Neergard 1987, 59). Although there is little typological change, de Neergard suggests that these small examples are of late fourteenth- to early fifteenth-century date and are a precursor to the elaborate needlepoint scissors of the sixteenth century and later (*ibid*).

Flesh hooks, bucket handles, and possible suspension chains

Undoubtedly some of the knives would have been used in the preparation of food, and relatively large-scale cooking would have been undertaken in some of the Roman buildings, although at what scale is a matter for speculation. Flesh hooks were used to manipulate meat during cooking and their appearance did not change appreciably over a very long period, possibly into the early post-medieval period. Manning defines two types seen in Roman Britain (Manning 1985, 105) and the example (*2373*; Fig 416.1) from a make-up layer associated with Period 6 Building *5200* falls into his type 1, having two teeth on the same side. Although broken, it is clear that the shaft was twisted to produce a decorative effect and it is quite possible that there was a large shallow ladle at the other end, as is shown on examples from Castle Street (Padley 1991b, 133, fig 107). Two other similar toothed objects (*3272* and

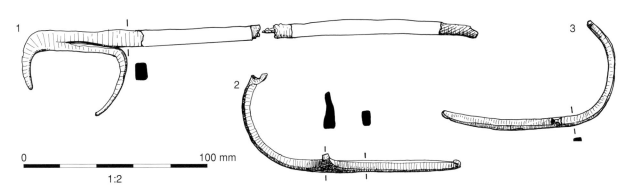

Figure 416: Flesh hooks

749

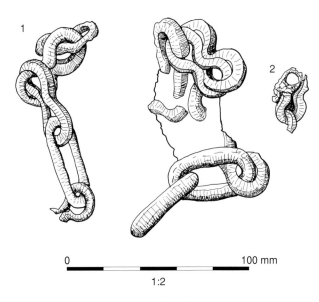

Figure 417: Chain fragments

Three large handles are probably from stave-built buckets (*1768, 2766,* and *3355*; Fig 418.1-3), and fragment *3407* (Fig 418.4) appears to be a plain escutcheon. Two of the three handles were found within buildings, where buckets would have been used for a range of purposes.

Lamp

An open lamp holder was associated with Building **7394** in its earliest phase (Period 3B). Evidence for means of lighting Roman buildings is surprisingly uncommon, and it would not seem unlikely that any suitable container was used. Iron lamp holders like *3262* (Fig 419) were intended to facilitate suspension.

3357; Fig 416.2-3) have been tentatively identified as flesh hooks.

A few fragments of large chains were noted. The largest (*82*; Fig 417.1), from Period 5, comprised alternating oval and figure-of-eight links, an arrangement typical of Roman iron chains. These could have been used for a number of purposes, including suspending cooking vessels over a fire. The second, highly corroded, fragment was seen in x-ray only (*1274; Appendix 6*), with little or no metal remaining; it again appeared to have figure-of-eight links. The final fragment, just two links (*554*; Fig 417.2), was from Period 7.

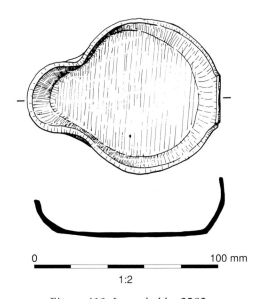

Figure 419: Lamp holder 3283

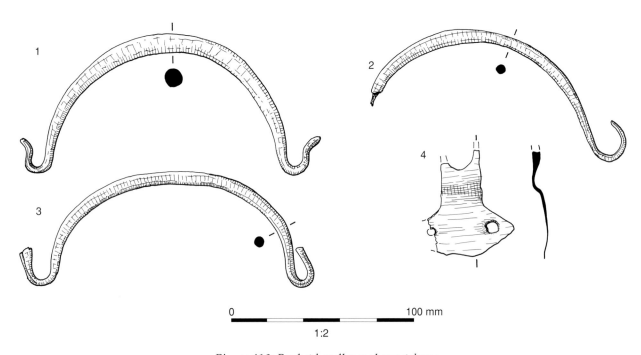

Figure 418: Bucket handles and escutcheon

750

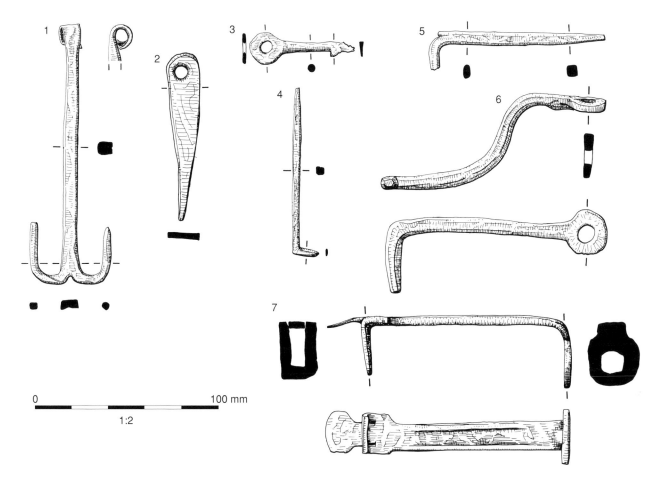

Figure 420: Latch lifter, elements of locks, and keys

Locks and keys

Only one latch lifter (*3048*; Fig 420.1) and two possible keys were identified. The earliest key (*3364*; Fig 420.2), from an occupation layer within Period 3A Building **7400**, is only represented by a plain handle, whilst the second (*1943*; Fig 420.3), probably from a mortise lock, is from a medieval context (layer *5058*). As the dating of medieval keys is largely reliant on the shape of the loop and the ward, and as the loop is plain and the ward missing, this cannot be dated more closely. Three L-shaped objects, probably door catches or slide bolts, were also found; two are from Period 3 contexts (Period 3A gully fill *7450*, and Period 3C pit fill *4144*, Building **4657**; *1731* and *3350*; Fig 420.4-5), and the third example was from an occupation layer within

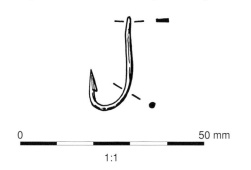

Figure 421: Fish hook 3285

Period 4 Building **5689** (*2897*; Fig 420.6). In addition, part of a barrel padlock of Roman type came from road **7217** (*2840*; Fig 420.7).

Objects used for recreational purposes

A remarkably well-preserved barbed fish hook was recovered from a construction trench for Period 3B Building **7394** (*3285*; Fig 421). These are not common finds, but are known from other Roman sites, their size and fragile nature probably meaning that they do not survive well.

Objects used for or associated with written communication

Considerable numbers (23) of iron *styli* were recognised (Fig 422.1-18; *Appendix 6*), coming almost entirely from Periods 3 and 4. Almost all are Manning's type 1 (1985, 85, fig 24), the exceptions being *2676* and *3226* (Fig 422.15-16), examples of type 3, and *3185* and *3237* (Fig 422.17-18), both of type 4. The differences between the types is slight, with both 3 and 4 being marginally more decorative than type 1. There seems to be no chronological division, and it is possible, in a highly regulated context such as a fort, that the difference between the incidence of type 1 and the other types reflects that between 'standard issue', being plain, functional, and probably cheap, and personal

751

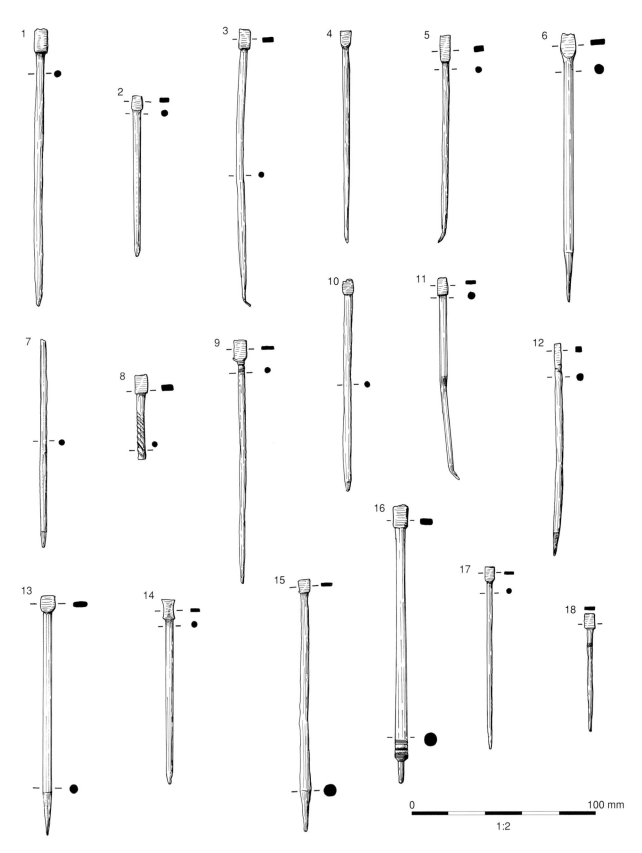

Figure 422: Styli

possessions, which might perhaps be more elaborate. *Styli*, used for writing on wax writing tablets, are not uncommon finds and considerable numbers have been recovered from other sites in Carlisle, such as Castle Street (Padley 1991b). A few fragments of wax writing tablet were recovered from contexts of Periods 3A and 4A (*Ch 19*), as well as a few samian inkwells (*Ch 16; p 552*).

Two of the four examples from Period 3A came from contexts associated with a probable workshop, *4654*, and it is easy to see them used in administrative tasks associated with activity within. Similarly, both of those from Period 3B came from internal surfaces, as did those from Period 3C, and again it is likely that they reflect the need for record-keeping and administration within the fort. In contrast, all those from Period 4 were from potentially disturbed fills, perhaps suggesting that the administrative activity associated with Period 3 had moved elsewhere in the fort.

Objects associated with transport
Horse tack
Metalwork giving evidence for the use of horses in Period 6 is not copious, especially if compared with that from Periods 3 and 4. Apart from a few caltrops (*p 716*), there was only a single equestrian object of iron, part of the two-link bar of a typical snaffle bit (*293*; Fig 423), of common form, came from Period 6C Building *669*.

Horseshoes
There is a continuing debate as to whether the Romans used horseshoes. Some researchers are confident that on occasion Roman horses were shod (Manning 1985, 63; 1995, 42), whilst others are equally confident that the use of nailed iron shoes is a post-Roman phenomenon (Clark 1995, 78–9). At least some of the 23 fragments of horseshoe (representing probably 17 shoes) from the Millennium Project were recovered from what appear to be securely stratified Period 6 Roman contexts. The earlier of the two (*1272*; *Appendix 6*) was poorly preserved and was thus identified from x-ray alone. It is small, the relatively narrow web, almost smooth outer edge, and more-or-less square nail holes being reminiscent of the possibly Roman example from Dowgate, London (Clark 1995, 80, fig 57). It came from the fill of a drain associated with intervallum road *7646* in Period 6A. The second example (*1049*; Fig 424.1) is in all ways identical to Clark's type 2A, which he places after *c* 1050, although there are

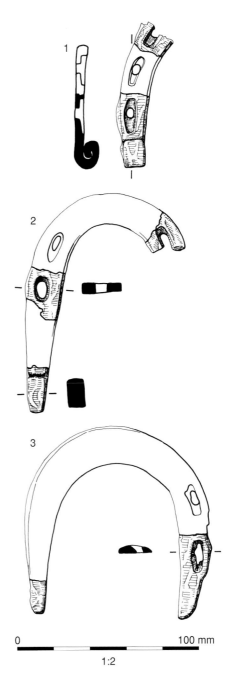

Figure 424: Horseshoes

earlier, possibly intrusive, examples known from London (1995, 92, fig 75). In addition, it should be remembered that Ward-Perkins, writing some years earlier (1941), suggested an Iron Age origin for the type.

The fact that all the horseshoes from medieval contexts were of the same type as that from Period 6C, so-called 'wavy edge' horseshoes, with a conventional date range from the eleventh to the thirteenth centuries, must raise some doubt as to the provenance of the earlier examples, but it remains possible that it was a long-lived type (*1948* and *1977*; Fig 424.2-3). Most of the horseshoes were identified from x-ray only.

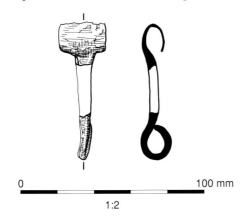

Figure 423: Snaffle bit 293

In addition to those surviving within horseshoes, another 73 horseshoe nails were recovered, the majority of fiddle-key type (Clark 1995, 86, fig 64). A small number could have been the later L-shaped type, but all were identified from x-ray only (*Appendix 6*).

Buildings and services
Nails
Iron provided a cheap and easily available material for the small fittings associated with Roman and later structures, not least for the huge number of small nails that must have been employed in basic carpentry. Inevitably, hand-forged nails formed a huge part of the assemblage of ironwork, some 3926 fragments in all. Not all were complete, but the assemblage showed an overall consistency, with most being Manning's broad type Ib (Manning 1985), with an approximate length of between 40 mm and 65 mm. Darrah has noted (*Ch 19*) that few of the surviving timbers show evidence for nailing, and thus it can be assumed that these nails were not intended to join major structural timbers. The survival, however, of a fragmentary panel of nailed weather-boarding (*Ch 19, p 802*) gives a clue to the kind of uses to which medium-sized nails would have been put, and to this it is possible to add their use in other architectural detail, for doors, windows and shutters, furniture, and so-on. The principal interest of this group lies in a consideration of the distribution of nails between buildings (*see Appendix 6*).

Holdfasts and other structural ironwork
Holdfasts are essentially large-headed nails, used to fix the larger elements of woodwork or masonry. They can be found on most sites where there have been substantial buildings. The fort has, however, produced surprisingly few (seven, two of which are illustrated: *1064* and *2666*; Fig 425.1-2), and the medieval deposits none.

Carpenters' dogs are large and distinctive staples used to join timbers. Only one was substantially complete (*1677*; Fig 425.3), from the fill of a Period 3B

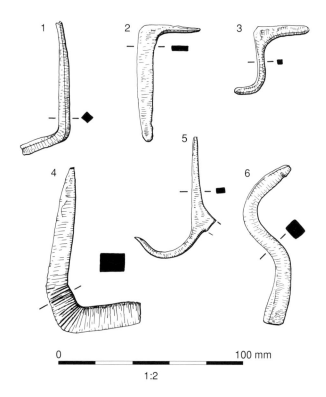

Figure 426: Iron wallhooks

construction trench for Building *4006*. A second poorly preserved example (*1135*, *Appendix 6*) was incorporated in a make-up layer for Period 6 Building *2302*, and thus was probably residual.

Wallhooks are common finds, and eight were recovered from contexts from Period 3 onwards, including Period 8 (medieval contexts). They served a number of purposes within buildings, with L-shaped examples likely to have been hinge pivots, whilst others were used to suspend a range of objects, including hanging lamps. Only the earliest (*3249*; *Appendix 6*) was associated with activity within a building (from floor *7203* in Period 3B Building *7391*), the remainder being from demolition layers (*422*; Fig 426.1; *934*, *Appendix 6*), pits (*1862, 2341*, and *2367*; Fig 426.2-4), and external surfaces (*1875*; Fig 426.5; *2658*; *Appendix 6*). In addition, smaller, less well-preserved examples were recovered from intervallum road *7645* (Period 4A/B) and Building *2302* (Period 6B), both from disturbed contexts (*205, 1134*; *Appendix 6*).

A more sinuous object (*327*; Fig 426.6) could be a specialised form, perhaps intended to support something with a rounded profile, such as a pipe or gutter. It was associated with medieval tenement *1235* (Period 8iii), and could well derive from a contemporary structure.

Hinges
The simple strap hinge was in common use during the Roman period (Manning 1985, 127). Many of

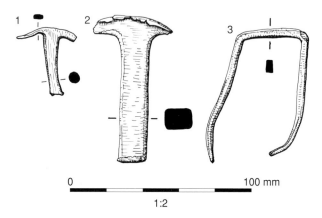

Figure 425: Holdfasts and a carpenter's dog

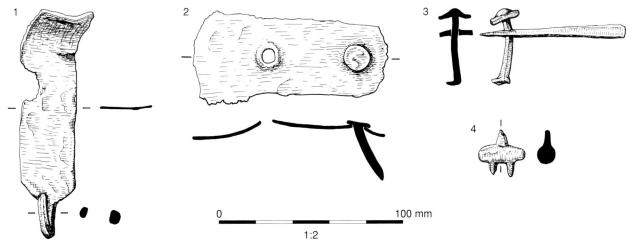

Figure 427: Hinges

the fragments of nailed strap found on sites such as the this are probably fragments of hinges from doors and possibly window shutters. The hinges were mounted on a simple L-shaped pivot driven into the door or window frame, and were often indistinguishable from other wall hooks. Other hinges could be fitted to storage items, such as chests, whilst smaller and often more ornate examples were used in finer furniture. Their form has remained essentially unchanged since the Roman period. An unstratified example from MIL 5 shows the typical looped form used on chests with relatively loosely fitted lids (*3502*; Fig 427.1). Other fragments are less diagnostic, but nailed strap *2947* (Fig 427.2), from

an occupation layer (*6424*) attributed to Period 4B Building *5689*, is probably part of a hinge assemblage, as is a later fragment (*2802; Appendix 6*) from a robber trench over Building *5688* (Period 4C), and a probably medieval fragment (*1912*; Fig 427.3) from Period 8C. Although much smaller, object (*2285*; Fig 427.4) could be a more decorative example, probably from furniture or a small lidded box.

Spiked loops
Double-armed spiked loops also served a wide range of structural purposes. Eight were noted within the assemblage (*306, 948,* and *2127; Appendix 6*; *1038, 1065, 1728, 3132,* and *3301*; Fig 428.1-5), and

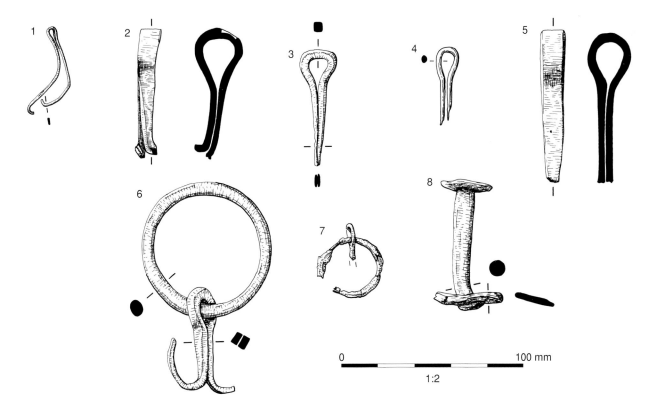

Figure 428: Spiked loops and rove bolt

755

a ninth, medieval example, incorporating a ring (*339*; Fig 428.6), shows how they could be used to form such things as simple handles. Object *2309* (Fig 428.7), from Period 6D, although much smaller, could well have served the same purpose. It is quite likely that some of the small rings (*p 760*) were used in the same manner.

Rove bolts

Two substantial rove bolts were also noted (*602*; Fig 428.8; *2396*, *Appendix 6*), from an external surface dated to Period 6C and the Period 7 'dark earths'. It is unclear whether they have come from structural timbers or from a large timber construction, like a cart.

Tools

Evidence from other classes of finds seems to suggest very strongly that there was a considerable amount of metalworking and leatherworking going on in the successive timber forts (Periods 3 and 4). This is not particularly surprising if it is accepted that army units in the North, especially in the early years of conquest, were expected to be largely self-sufficient. Indeed, leather goods and metal items accounted for a substantial part of a soldier's equipment. Many of the tools associated with both activities are difficult to identify and are often missed, as the finer items, such as awls, are easily confused with nails, styli, and so on. The excellent preservation afforded by widespread waterlogging, with x-radiography and careful conservation, has allowed a number of items to be identified as tools. As there is little difference in appearance between the finer awls and punches used in metalwork and those of a leather worker or a carpenter, it is almost impossible to differentiate them. In consequence, all tools are discussed together.

In all, 35 items have been recognised as possible tools, almost half of them (15) coming from Periods 3 and 4, three from Period 5, and seven from Period 6. The remainder, from Periods 7 and 8, could well be residual, but simple functional objects change little over time, their form being determined by their purpose rather than by fashion, and they could equally well be medieval in date.

Awls and punches

The earliest identifiable tool from the site appears to be a fine awl with a wooden handle (*3278*; Fig 429.1). Such implements were used in leatherwork, and could also be used in fine metalwork, for instance for making rivet holes in thin copper-alloy sheet. The purpose of the second tool from within the same building (**7392**) remains unidentified (*3383*; Fig 429.2).

Two punches (*3186*; Fig 429.3; *3282*; *Appendix 6*), both with heads burred by use, were from

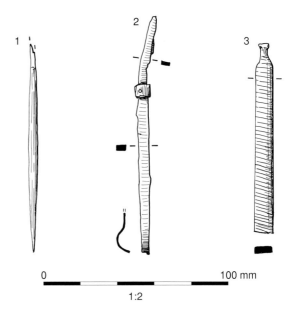

Figure 429: Tools, Period 3

Period 3B contexts. Although punches are used in leatherworking, the size of both implements suggests that they are more likely to have been used in metalworking.

Two cold chisels (*2978* and *2992*; *Appendix 6*) from occupation layers within Building **7200** point to metalworking. A third tool of unidentified purpose was associated with Building **4657** (*1751*; *Appendix 6*).

Although there is not a wide range of tools present in any period, the group from Period 4 is perhaps more general. A file (*3220*; Fig 430.1) and part of a saw blade (*3215*; Fig 430.2) both come from the fills of construction trenches for Building **5688**, and would seem most likely to have been lost or discarded during the construction of that building. A second fragment of saw (*3012*; Fig 430.3) came from an occupation layer within Building **7396**. A punch or awl-like tool (*2997*; Fig 430.4) was lost on road **7477** during the same period.

A square-sectioned, tapering tool, set in a whittled wooden handle (*2951*; Fig 430.5), came from the fill of one of the drains associated with the main east to west road (**7477**) during Period 4B; again probably an awl of some kind, the tip of the tool has been lost. Another tapering, rectangular-sectioned object, probably a punch, but possibly a file (*2964*; *Appendix 6*), came from a floor within Building **5689**. Although badly bent, a third tool (*2810*; Fig 430.6), this time from the floor of Building **5688**, is more distinctive, being a modelling tool of well-known form (Manning 1985, type 3). A very similar example was found at Castle Street to the south (Padley 1991b, 140, fig 118) in an early second-century context. Manning (1985, 32)

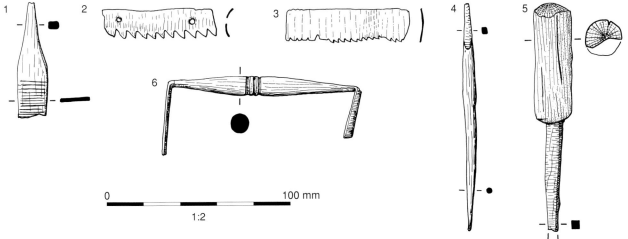

Figure 430: Tools, Period 4

notes that these tools were used for a number of purposes, from sculpting to pottery, and a link to metalworking might be seen through their use to mould the clay and wax originals used in the 'lost-wax' casting process, in common use to produce three-dimensional copper-alloy objects.

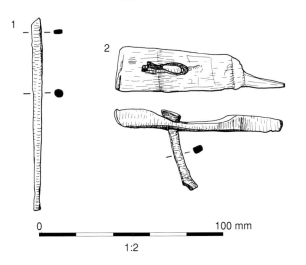

Figure 431: Tools, Period 5

Two of the three examples from Period 5 were from cobbled area *4662* (*1358*; Fig 431.1; *1448*; *Appendix 6*). The former, like many of the other tools, a slender bar with a round-sectioned point at one end, and wedge-shaped at the other, was probably intended for relatively fine work of some kind. Object *2659* (Fig 431.2) is more difficult to identify, but, with a steep chisel-shaped blade at one end, it could be the blade of a woodworking plane.

Two distinctive and obviously complete objects were recovered from Period 6A cobbled surface *244* (intervallum road *7646*). Both have a sub-rectangular cross-section at the centre, and taper to a point at both ends. It seems likely that they, too, are tools, perhaps again punches of some sort (*71* and *72*;

Fig 432.1-2). Other tools from this period include a possible cold chisel (seen only in x-ray) from fill *282* (*126, Appendix 6*) and a punch from the floor (*2554*) of Building *2301* (*1392*; Fig 432.3). A second possible modelling tool of less common type (Manning 1985, 32, type 1) was found in the fill *5515* of a drain associated with main east to west road *7652* of the Period 6A stone fort (*2499*; Fig 432.4).

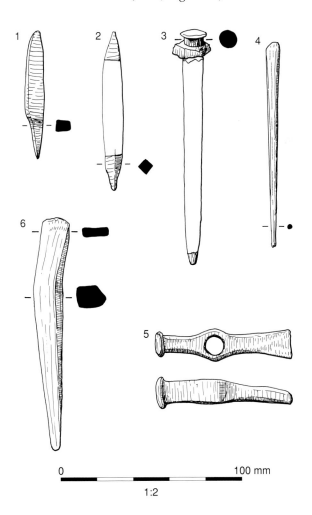

Figure 432: Tools, Periods 6 and 7

A possible awl (*1068; Appendix 6*) came from occupation layer *2278* within Building **2302** (Period 6B). Another possible cold chisel (*14, Appendix 6*) was found in a Period 6B external layer (*187*), and well-used hammer *2352* (Fig 432.5) was from Period 6C external layer *5406*. A single incomplete example of a possible awl (*613*; Fig 432.6) was from Period 7 layer *2112*. It seems likely to be residual, but this cannot be stated categorically.

In all, five objects tentatively identified as tools were recovered from medieval contexts. Like many of the iron finds, they could be either residual Roman objects or medieval ones contemporary with the layers in which they were discovered. A round-sectioned tanged tool (*2040*; Fig 433.1) came from Period 8A Structure **7653**, and a possible tanged file (*1876*; Fig 433.2) from metalled surface *5043* (Period 8E).

A long, square-sectioned bar from a fill of ditch **1230** (*453*; Fig 433.3) comes to a fine, neatly made point at one end. The square section precludes it being a needle, and it is probably an awl or similar tool. Another possible awl came from Period 8iii tenement **1234** (*376*; Fig 433.4), as did a more triangular fragment (*380; Appendix 6*), probably a tool, although its purpose remains obscure. A small tanged object, possibly a chisel blade (*311*; Fig 433.5), was from Period 8iv tenement **1235**.

Unstratified finds include an axe (*3504; Appendix 6*), and two well-preserved sockets, which could derive either from tools of some kind, or spearheads, came from the fill of a Period 6D robber trench (*139, Appendix 6*) or were unstratified (*3498*; Fig 434.1).

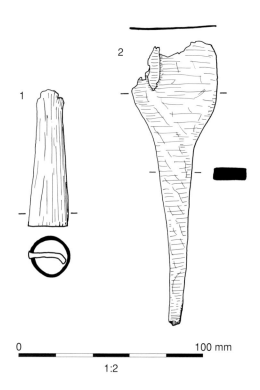

Figure 434: Unstratified tools

A tanged object (*3505*; Fig 434.2) can also be regarded in this group, but again its purpose cannot be determined.

Fasteners and fittings

Although small, there is a distinctive group of six U-shaped suspension loops (of which two are illustrated: *3148* and *3279*; Fig 435.1-2). It is quite likely that these were associated with armour or horse harness, but they must have been used in a number of circumstances.

Two small but distinctive looped pins were noted, both around 100 mm in length (*2778* and *2896*; Fig 436.1-2). It is possible that these served as lynch pins, although they do not resemble other kinds Roman lynch pin in either size or form. Alternatively, both were found in occupation layers within Period 4B Building **5689**, which might suggest a link with armour also found there (see *Ch 6*).

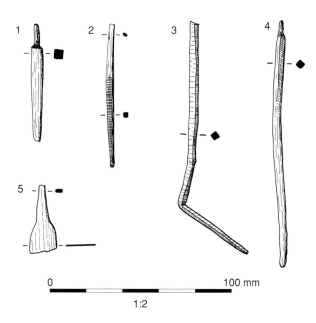

Figure 433: Tools, Period 8

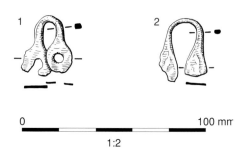

Figure 435: Suspension loops

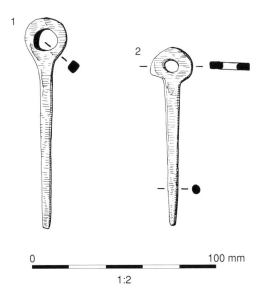

Figure 436: Looped pins

Objects associated with agriculture, horticulture, and animal husbandry

A well-preserved and almost complete reaping hook, or perhaps a tree-pruning knife (possibly a *falx arboraria; 3000*; Fig 437), was recovered from occupation debris within Period 4 Building **7396**. White (1970, 239) suggests that the latter were likely to have been used for cutting bracken or brushwood. A small fragment of a sharply curving blade (*1976*; Fig 438.1) was from Period 8C layer *5102*, and could have been from a similar tool or from something larger, like a sickle.

A single excellently preserved example of an 'ox goad' (*1734*; Fig 438.2) was found in a Period 3C pit (*4130*) in Building **4657**, which also produced horse bardings (*Ch 20*). Some have suggested that these objects were in fact dip pens (*1734*; Birley 1999, 29), and this possibility must be borne in mind.

Whilst not exclusively associated with animal husbandry, the copper-plated bell (*2927*; Fig 438.3) from an occupation layer within Period 4B Building **5689** is of a size suitable for an animal and

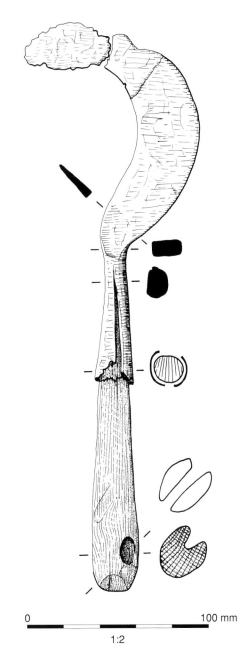

Figure 437: Reaping hook 3020

is indistinguishable from modern examples still worn by sheep and goats in many parts of Europe.

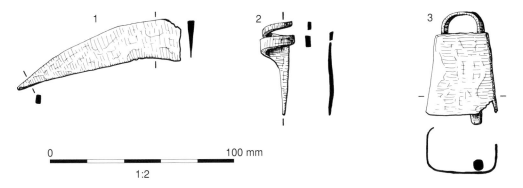

Figure 438: Agricultural objects

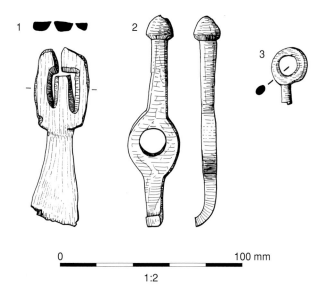

0 ───────────── 100 mm

1:2

Figure 439: Unidentified objects

Objects of unknown or uncertain function or purpose

Inevitably, some of the assemblage remains unidentified, either because they are fragmentary, or they are such common objects that the range of uses to which they might have been put is so wide that tying them to any one is impossible. Only two complex objects remain unidentified (*62* and *2984*; Fig 439.1-2).

Plain rings

Small, wrought rings are a common find on Roman and later sites, and must have served a wide range of purposes. In all, 18 fragments were noted, probably representing 16 objects (*Appendix 6*). They were spread throughout the stratigraphic sequence, and it is unlikely that their distribution has any significance. The smallest (*874*) is only 7 mm in diameter, and might have been from chain mail, and a slightly larger example, possibly with a short tag on one side (*3321*; Fig 439.3), is possibly a fastener from plate armour.

Square or rectangular-sectioned bars and round-sectioned rods

Fragments of deliberately formed bars, with square and rectangular sections, are common finds within any large assemblage of ironwork. In all, 32 fragments were noted; none can be further identified. Similarly, there were also fragments of deliberately formed round-sectioned rod. Their chronological distribution is shown in *Appendix 6*.

Sheet fragments

Several fragments of sheet (34) were also noted (*Appendix 6*). In addition, there were 24 fragments of relatively narrow parallel-sided strip, which could have served a number of purposes. It has been suggested (M Bishop *pers comm*) that most of this sheet is likely to have originated in armour. These fragments are too small or too damaged to be identified.

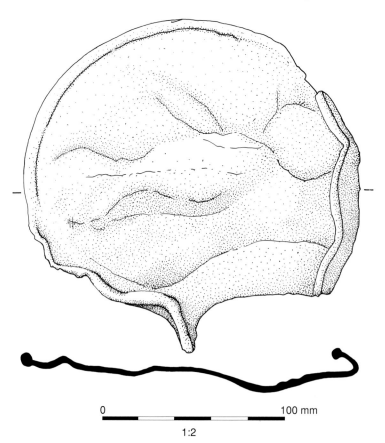

0 ───────────── 100 mm

1:2

Figure 440: Vessel (or lid) 91

The Lead Objects

C Howard-Davis

Although a large amount of lead was recovered from the excavations (414 fragments), very little derived from recognisable objects. This can be accounted for by the widespread use of lead in building, with lead sheet frequently being used as waterproofing, either to keep water in (cisterns, tanks, *etc*) or to keep water out (principally as an element of roofing). In addition, the low melting point of lead makes it easy to reuse, and without a doubt much of the large amount of lead, which must have been present within the fabric of a large and long-established fort, was scavenged, and must have been melted down and reused time and again.

Most of the lead was securely stratified, although it is likely that some of the objects from Period 7 onwards are residual and represent later disturbance and scavenging. That does not, however, rule out the likelihood that some objects from Periods 7 and 8 are in fact contemporary with their context. The lead is perhaps predictably distributed through the successive periods, with 58% coming from Periods 3 and 4, only 5% from Period 5, and only a little more, 15.5%, from Period 6.

If considered at a context by context level, there were few obvious concentrations within the assemblage, but if considered building by building, it is notable that half of the formal weights came from the *principia*, Building *5688*, and Building *5689* (Period 4), both thought to be linked in some way to centralised control and distribution of resources (*Ch 15*). An unusually large amount was recovered from the Period 6 main east to west road, *7652*, mainly drips and spills, probably the debris from the ongoing repair of neighbouring buildings.

Excavations in Botchergate, Carlisle (Zant *et al* in prep), have demonstrated that lead was in fact being smelted from ore on the edge of the contemporary Roman civil settlement, and it would seem reasonable to assume that some of the products of that process found their way to the fort. The extremely functional nature of most lead objects means that there was little morphological change through time.

Household utensils and furniture

A single fragment of a vessel or lid (*91*; Fig 440) was recovered from a Period 4A demolition layer, *3250*, associated with a barrack, Building *4655*. It appears to be a large shallow bowl, now badly deformed, and no function or purpose is indicated.

Objects employed in weighing and measuring

What appears to be a scale pan (Fig 441), and nine weights were recovered. They show no particular distribution, except that all but one of the formal weights came from Period 3 or 4, the exception

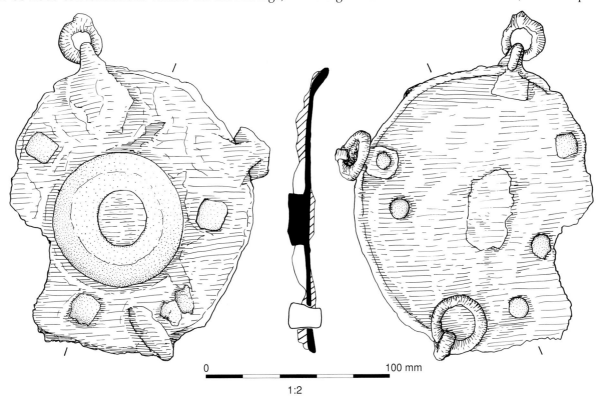

0   100 mm

1:2

Figure 441: Scale pan 286

761

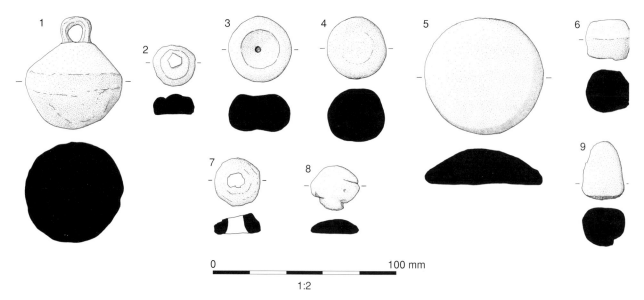

Figure 442: Lead weights

being from Period 8. The scale pan (*286*; Fig 441) is in fact of iron, with a large annular lead weight attached to it, presumably as a tare, to allow for the weighing of relatively heavy objects. The pan is, however, only 150 mm in diameter, and a maximum of 22 mm deep, suggesting that, although heavy, whatever was weighed was not of great bulk. Presumably the pan was intended for use with a large steelyard, of the kind seen until recently in the markets of Britain and Europe. It was recovered from an occupation layer within Period 4A Building *7396*, where leatherworking may have been undertaken.

A single biconical steelyard weight (*304*; Fig 442.1), of typical Roman form, was recovered from Period 3B

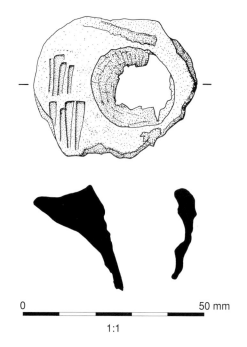

Figure 443: Gallet 7

external layer *7109*. These are common finds and would be expected in most, if not all, Romanised contexts.

Typical cheese-shaped weights were recovered from Period 3A gully fill *7459* (*329*; Fig 442.2) and from Period 4B occupation layer *6273* (*262*; Fig 442.3), within Building *5688*; a second, sub-spherical weight (*261*; Fig 442.4) came from the same context. A third weight (*255*; Fig 442.5), this time a flattened hemisphere, but weighing the same as *261*, was recovered from a later demolition layer (Period 4C) associated with the same structure. A third cheese-shaped weight (*270*; Fig 442.6), marked with three dots, probably indicating a weight of three Roman ounces, came from an occupation layer within neighbouring Building *5689*.

Two possible weights were recovered from Period 7 contexts, although, neither can be identified with certainty as formal weights. Object *18* (Fig 442.7) could equally be a spindle whorl, or some sort of counterweight, whilst *33* (Fig 442.8) could be a neat plug for a ceramic or other vessel. A small sub-conical weight (*147*; Fig 442.9) was also recovered from fill *5041* of Period 8D pit *5036*. There is no reason to believe that it is other than medieval in date.

Buildings and services

Lead was frequently used, especially in masonry, to secure inserts, for instance door pivots or other hinges, in stonework. Only nine such objects were recovered (*7, 31, 138, 146, 152, 214, 222, 248,* and *322; Appendix 7*), four, as might be expected, from Period 6, by which time the fort had been rebuilt in stone. It is perhaps of significance that the two largest examples (*eg 7*; Fig 443) were both found in robber trenches, perhaps suggesting that lead was amongst the materials being scavenged during the life of the fort.

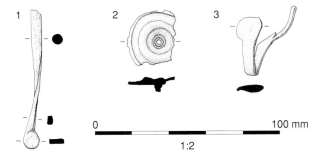

Figure 444: Tools and fasteners

Tools

A single object, from the fill (*7152*) of a Period 4A construction trench for Building *5688* (*306*; Fig 444.1), can perhaps be identified as a spatula of some sort.

Fasteners and fittings

Although any fine metal cap has gone, object *294* (Fig 444.2) appears to be the lead infill of a copper-alloy stud. The lead could have been intended to fix the cap (a repair?), or to give weight to what was probably a somewhat flimsy object.

Object *271* (Fig 444.3) is a tie of some kind, but cannot be further identified. The remainder of the objects which fall within this group are rolled ties. Sixteen examples (*34, 37, 45, 68, 102, 148, 154, 157, 164, 176, 188, 200, 215, 217, 347,* and *348*; *Appendix 7*) were noted amongst the assemblage, all but two of which came from contexts associated with Period 7 or later. These small objects, essentially a tightly rolled strip of lead, must have served a wide range of purposes, including the securing of the base of storage nets, or *ad hoc* weights (Howard-Davis in prep). Simple artefacts such as these cannot be dated with any confidence, but they do appear regularly on Roman sites.

Tools and other objects associated with metalworking

Lead-working on the site was only represented by a few fragments of galena, an ore, which could have been brought accidentally or for other purposes, although there is evidence for lead smelting from other sites in Carlisle (Zant *et al* in prep). Unless these can be specifically linked with industrial structures, they cannot be taken as evidence for the primary production of metallic lead in the fort. Single fragments of galena were recovered from Period 3A floor *3967* (Building *4658*), and Period 4A make-up layer *3343* and deposit *3366* (road *4659* and Building *4655*). Layer *3343* is notable for containing much redeposited slag, and it seems reasonable to link the origin of the galena with that of the slag.

Object *87* (*Appendix 7*) from Period 4A demolition layer *3211*, associated with Building *3376*, is a cast fragment reminiscent of a slide lock bolt, and could be a trial piece. Object *152* (*Appendix 7*) could be a second example, although the form of the intended object is not clear and the context from which it was recovered is medieval in date (Period 8C) rather than Roman. Object *6* (*Appendix 7*) appears to be part of a small ingot and could thus be associated with metalworking during the medieval period (fill *1493* of ditch *1403*; Period 8iii).

The largest part of the evidence for the use of molten lead comes in the form of solidified spills (151 fragments; *Appendix 7*). As lead was widely used in building, however, it is possible that at least some of these spills originated in accidental fires, which would have melted structural lead. The fact, though, that some of the larger spills had apparently been collected up and twisted together for further recycling might suggest that they were the debris from the deliberate use of molten metal, rather than any more accidental occurrence.

The distribution of solidified molten lead between buildings does not appear to have any particular significance. A considerable amount does, however, derive from Period 7 and could indicate subsequent disturbance of the latest Roman layers, possibly in the search for recyclable materials, or that burnt waste was also being dumped during that period (*Appendix 7*).

Objects of unknown or uncertain function or purpose

Although no function can be attributed to them, several fragments have clearly been deliberately cut and shaped, either as rectangles (tablets) of sheet (seven examples, perhaps intended as labels or even curse tablets, or *ad hoc* weights), a single small block, and discs (again seven examples, two possibly seals or seal blanks, although neither bear any sign of inscriptions). In addition, three fragments appear to be leaden plugs for ceramic or copper-alloy vessels. All three are from Period 3 contexts (*331*; Fig 445.1; *76, 130*; *Appendix 7*); a fourth, from Period 6E, resembles a rivet (*44*; Fig 445.2), and may again have been intended to plug a small hole in a vessel or similar object. Two small rings (*137* and *321*; *Appendix 7*), one made from round-sectioned rod, the other cast, with a D-shaped section, both come from Period 3 contexts, and a crudely-formed tube (*142*; *Appendix 7*), made from rolled sheet, was from a medieval context (Period 8F).

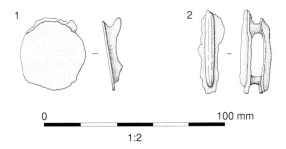

Figure 445: Unidentified lead objects

A large proportion of the assemblage of lead cannot be identified except as fragments of sheet (171 fragments) or deliberately cut strip (29 fragments). These almost without doubt derive from the use of sheet lead in buildings and other structures, and are in some sense working off-cuts. In addition, five fragments of rectangular-sectioned bar and three of round-sectioned rod were recovered (*Appendix 7*). Again, these are likely to be remnants and off-cuts from the use of lead in construction. A small number of fragments (five) remain completely unclassifiable.

A small fragment of what appears to be modern split shot (*78*), of the kind used for weighting fishing line, was recovered from Period 6A fill *3138*, associated with Building *2301*. The strong possibility arises that this is intrusive.

The Iron Slag

L Keys

An assemblage of *c* 158.4 kg of slag was examined, the bulk of which came from four large concentrations of smithing slag and related debris from within Building *2765* (Period 4B) and adjacent road *4659* (Periods 4A and 4B), from within Building *5689* (Period 4B), and from deposits associated with medieval outer ward ditch *1231*. The slag was recovered by hand and from bulk soil samples, and this was examined visually and categorised on the basis of morphology. Each category of slag in each context was weighed to within 2 xg, and the smithing hearth bottoms were weighed individually, their dimensions being recorded. Additionally, a magnet was run through the soil in bags to detect micro-slags such as hammerscale.

Context and date
Period 3
During Period 3A, small amounts of slag began to appear on the site (1.197 kg). Most is vitrified hearth lining and cinder, both of which could be produced by domestic as well as industrial hearths. One fragment of vitrified hearth lining from Building *7400* has a tuyère hole, which implies the use of bellows in whatever activity generated the fragment; this could include metalworking.

Buildings *7394* and *4006* in Period 3B each produced a smithing hearth bottom and, in addition, slag from the fill of construction trench *7218* had hammerscale adhering to it. This evidence is interesting, given the amount of ironworking debris from Period 4, but not, of its own, sufficient to indicate that ironworking was taking place on any significant scale at this time (only 4.523 kg was found).

Period 3E external layer *3342* produced seven smithing hearth bottoms, a quantity of flake and spherical hammerscale, a small amount of undiagnostic slag, and some cinder (3.743 kg in total). The smithing hearth bottoms indicate that ironworking was taking place in the vicinity, either in Period 3E itself or at the beginning of Period 4A.

Period 4
The large group of material from Period 4A (43.665 kg) precedes the main period of ironworking activity (in Period 4B). It indicates that a substantial amount of slag had already accumulated, either within the fort or nearby, which was available to be used as metalling on road *4659*. The road incorporated a considerable amount of redeposited slag, including 85 smithing hearth bottoms, mixed with cobbles. It is curious that no other road examined in the fort had any quantity of slag as part of its make-up, despite the fact that adding slag would produce a well-bonded, hard-wearing surface. It seems reasonable to assume that if, as its use in road *4659* seems to suggest, slag was available in large amounts, it would have been used on major as well as minor thoroughfares. The demolition deposits associated with Building *3376* incorporated a spread of very mixed burnt clay, which contained two smithing hearth bottoms, some undiagnostic slag, and some vitrified hearth lining, all of which could have been deposited after the building was demolished. Road *4659* was resurfaced in Period 4B but the amount of slag used was very small (a total of 5.722 kg) compared with the Period 4A surface.

Building *2765* produced a substantial amount of iron slag, indicating that it had been used as a smithy. The focus of activity appears to have been R4, producing 22 smithing hearth bottoms and almost all the hammerscale recovered by sampling (*Ch 6*). The latter consisted of both flake and small spheres, some concreted into lumps (as in square *2800*/1). Material from the grid of samples taken from the floor is not conclusive; squares *2800*/1 and *2800*/10 contained large amounts of both types of hammerscale, whereas *2800*/9 contained many flakes but very few spheres. There was a hearth (*2907*) in R5, which produced broken flake hammerscale, vitrified hearth lining, and some undiagnostic slag, suggesting that it could have been used at least once for smithing. Nearby, occasional slag fragments, including two smithing hearth bottoms, cinder, and fired clay, were also recovered from Building *4660* (Phase 1). It is not, however, thought that smithing was taking place there, with the material probably representing redeposited waste.

Central range Building *5689* also appears to have served as a smithy during this period. Phase 5 deposits produced compacted wood, charcoal, and hammerscale lumps from floor and occupation deposits. The slag was generally very flaky, and was often hammerscale which had not quite fused together, while the smithing hearth bottoms were quite friable, and liable to break up during handling. The slags and the deposit from which they came were black, with fine charcoal dust, suggesting that this was probably not a pleasant place in which to work. Articulated arm-guards (*manicae*) came from Phase 6 deposits within this building (*pp 694-9*), and another sheet of perforated iron plate was found during examination of the slag assemblage, adhering to a lump of loosely concreted hammerscale. The temperature at which a smith would work on such a thin iron plate would almost certainly produce flaky slags, as it was not high enough to fuse the different waste elements together. This seems to suggest quite strongly that a smith or smiths were shaping or repairing armour plates at low temperatures within this building.

In Phase 7 (*Ch 6*), of this building, a stone structure (*6282*) with a flue-like feature was created in its south-west corner. Its appearance (*Ch 6, pp 221-2*) suggests a hearth with raised firebed, allowing the smith to work standing up. The hearth was probably *c* 1.6 m square, formed from an outer box of stone or wood, into which crushed sandstone was packed above a T-shaped (at ground level) flue. The flue came in from the north side (where a bellows could have been inserted to provide oxygen), reached the centre of the stone mass, and then turned upwards to the top of the hearth. It is possible that the flue utilised an air draft, rather than bellows, thereby producing a lower fire temperature. The lack of burning at ground level implies that the firebed was raised well above the ground. The identification of this feature as a hearth is confirmed by the charcoal-rich deposits dumped immediately to the south of it, on the opposite side to the air source (which needed to be kept clear), and away from the working area of the smith (on the east side of the structure, since the west side was against the wall). It can be assumed that when the outer casing of the hearth decayed or was removed, the inner rubble collapsed across the floor towards the north-east; the amount surviving on excavation suggests that some may have been cleared away.

The evidence for ironworking drops dramatically after Period 4B (only 3.151kg came from contexts of Periods 4C to 5A), although two contexts in Period 5A (*2673* and *2894*) produced very small amounts of hammerscale (in the case of *2673*, 6 g).

Period 5
Although the quantity of slag from Period 5B nowhere near matches that from Periods 4A and 4B, there was a concentration on road *4662* and in Building *2764*, both in the same area as earlier smithing activity and slag dumping. The slag from Period 5B is either residual (certainly the case with regard to that in *2764*) or indicates the continuation of smithing elsewhere in

the fort. Slag on the road almost certainly represents deliberate dumping, as was the case with Period 4A road *4659*. Dumping on the road appears to have continued through Periods 5C and 5D, although there was no archaeological evidence for a smithy in the vicinity at this time. It might well, however, have been relatively close by, and it is perhaps worth recalling that no slag was dumped on the main roads during this period.

Period 6
With the exception of the apparently deliberate deposition of slag on the main east to west road (*7652*) and minor road *2303*, slag in the other buildings associated with Period 6A (Buildings *2301* and *2302*) is probably residual (1.288 kg). The slag types recovered from Periods 6B-6E do not indicate that any ironworking activity was taking place in the vicinity during this period (1.871 kg).

Period 7
The disturbed nature of the deposits ('dark earths') of Period 7 means that it was impossible to tell whether the slag was residual, or reflected contemporary activity (not necessarily metalworking) in the surrounding area (3.5 kg).

Period 8
The slag from Period 8A (540 g) consists mainly of vitrified hearth lining, which could be domestic in origin. Neither Periods 8B nor 8C (934 g and 338 g) had any evidence for ironworking. Although the evidence from Period 8D is slight (1.162 kg), there are some hints that mixed metalworking may have been taking place using at least one of the hearths (*5111*). The fills of pit *5005* contained two smithing hearth bottoms and a fragment of crucible.

Some 26 smithing hearth bottoms were recovered from outer ward ditch *1231* in Period 8ii (28.243 kg). This quantity implies that the forge producing them was nearby, with their being dumped to the rear of a property, presumably on Annetwell Street (*Ch 14*), into the ditch.

In Period 8iii, nine smithing hearth bottoms were found in tenement *1235*, whilst in tenement *1234*, Building *1492*, Phase 1, produced one smithing hearth bottom, some undiagnostic slag, and a little vitrified hearth lining. Whether this represents limited ironworking activity cannot be determined. The debris weighed 9.96 kg in total.

A similar picture is indicated in Period 8iv in tenement *1235*. In Phase 2, there were two smithing hearth bottoms, whilst in Phase 3, there was one (in total, 2.761 kg). Whether these are residual or represent metalworking somewhere nearby cannot be ascertained.

Nature of the assemblage

Activities involving ironworking can take two forms: smelting and smithing. The former comprises the manufacture of iron from ore in a smelting furnace, the resulting products being a spongy mass (an unconsolidated bloom) consisting of iron with a considerable amount of slag still trapped inside, and slag (waste). There is no smelting slag in the Carlisle assemblage and, without a doubt, iron production was carried out elsewhere.

Smithing can be divided into two distinct processes. Primary smithing, usually undertaken near the smelting furnace, is intended to remove excess slag from the bloom by hot working by a smith using a hammer. By this process the bloom becomes a rough lump of iron ready for use. The slags from this include smithing hearth bottoms and micro-slags, in particular tiny smithing spheres. Secondary smithing transforms the rough iron into a usable artefact, or is intended to repair an extant object (again the iron is hot-worked by a smith and strikers). As well as bulk slags (including smithing hearth bottoms), this will also generate micro-slags: hammerscale flakes from ordinary hot working; or tiny spheres from high-temperature welding to join two pieces of iron. All the slags recovered from the site derived from smithing.

Perhaps the most readily identifiable smithing debris is the plano-convex hearth bottom, formed as a result of high-temperature reactions between the iron, iron-scale, and silica from either a clay furnace lining or the silica flux used by the smith. The predominantly fayalitic (iron silicate) material produced by this reaction drips down into the base of the hearth, forming an accumulation of slag which, if not cleared out, develops into the characteristic smithing hearth bottom. It seems to have been common practice on removal to dump the hearth bottoms in the nearest convenient pit or ditch, and the association of a building with dumps of smithing hearth bottoms is often a good indication that the structure may have been a smithy.

Both the Roman and medieval smithing hearth bottoms are within the expected statistical range for their respective periods (Table 44). The low standard deviations on the dimensions can be taken to indicate that a standard size of hearth was being used by Roman smiths working on the site.

Much of the slag could be said to be undiagnostic, most often because its production could not have been attributed to a specific process without supporting evidence. In addition, slags could have been broken up during deposition, redeposition, or excavation, and may have to be assigned to the undiagnostic category because the original morphology cannot be determined. Other types of debris encountered in

	Range	Average	Standard Deviation
Roman (149 examples)			
Weight (g)	42–1768	263	269
Length (mm)	40–170	88	25
Width (mm)	40–140	68	19
Depth (mm)	15–100	42	14
Medieval (48 examples)			
Weight (g)	82–2329	703	542
Length (mm)	55–180	114	27
Width (mm)	50–160	92	25
Depth (mm)	20–90	51	18

Table 44: Roman and medieval smithing-hearth bottom statistics

iron slag assemblages may be the result of a range of other kinds of high-temperature activities (including domestic fires) and cannot, on their own, be taken to indicate that ironworking was taking place. This includes materials such as fired clay, vitrified hearth lining, cinder, and fuel ash slags. If they are found in association with diagnostic iron slag, however, they can be considered as possible products of the ironworking process. Hearth lining can vary considerably in appearance, from highly vitrified nearest to the tuyère (the region of highest temperature in an industrial hearth) to burnt clay further away (only a little of the latter was recovered). By itself it is not diagnostic of ironworking activity, but its association with other diagnostic material strengthens evidence for identifying the process. Cinder is a very porous, vitrified material, formed at the interface between the alkali fuel ashes and siliceous material of a hearth lining.

Except for a tiny amount of coal in Period 4B, charcoal is the fuel best represented during the Roman period (see also *Appendix 14*). Subsequent to this (Periods 7 and 8), charcoal was much less prevalent and coal appeared. Fuel ash slag is a very lightweight, highly porous, light-coloured (grey-brown) residue, produced by a high-temperature reaction between alkaline fuel ash and siliceous material such as a clay lining or surface. It can be produced by any high-temperature activity where these two constituents are present, including domestic hearths, accidental fires, and even cremations. Very little was recovered.

Ferruginous concretion is made up of a redeposition of iron hydroxides (rather like iron panning) but is enhanced by surrounding archaeological deposits, particularly if there is iron-rich waste present as a result of ironworking. The amount of ferruginous concretion from the site was greatest in the Roman period, when ironworking was taking place and deposits of ironworking slag were particularly prevalent.

18

THE GLASS AND OTHER FINDS

C Howard-Davis

Introduction

The glass was recorded following standard formats (Price and Cottam 1998) in order to ensure compatibility with data from other sites in Britain and Europe. Data recorded included material, identification, quantity (fragment count, and, where relevant, weight and estimated number of objects represented), condition, completeness, basic dimensions, outline description, dating, and conservation undertaken. Other artefact groups follow a similar format (catalogues appear in *Appendix 8)*.

The Roman and Later Vessel and Window Glass

In all, 576 fragments of vessel and 96 fragments of window glass were recovered from the excavations. Of these, 536 fragments were recognisably of Roman date, two very small and heavily mineralised fragments were probably medieval, and the remainder can be dated to the mid-late eighteenth century or later. As usual in Carlisle, the Roman glass was in outstanding condition. In comparison with other assemblages from excavations in the city, it appeared to represent a relatively restricted range of common vessel types, dating predominantly to the later first to third centuries AD.

Material was recovered by stratigraphical unit and is discussed where possible within its stratigraphical context. The fragments were generally quite small and often largely featureless, meaning that many of the blown vessels are represented only by thin, undiagnostic body sherds. Identification of vessel type and estimation of vessel numbers are both generally reliant on the presence of rims and bases, which were not particularly common within the material. All references to vessel form cite Isings (1957) or Price and Cottam (1998).

Context and date of the Roman glass

The assemblage dates principally to the later first to third centuries, with no forms later than the third century identified with confidence. It is thus likely that much of the glass recovered from Period 6 is in fact residual, a likelihood borne out by its frequent presence in recut features and, on occasion, in what might be termed a kick zone, over the surface of roads. In general terms, the bulk of the Roman vessel glass (*c* 60%) was recovered from Periods 3 and 4, a single tiny chip being the only evidence for the use of glass during Period 2. Together, Periods 5 and 6 produced *c* 25.8% of the vessel glass, and the remainder (*c* 14.2%) was residual in post-Roman contexts.

Nature

The assemblage is similar in composition to other published groups from Carlisle, with a noticeable element of first-century fine tablewares. It is, however, considerably smaller than those from Blackfriars Street (Price 1990a) and the southern Lanes (Price and Cottam in prep). There is a limited range of early tablewares, represented principally by strongly coloured pillar-moulded bowls, and a small number of other items of late first- and second-century tableware, principally flagons and cups, the latter in surprisingly small quantities. Evidence also suggests the presence of at least one collared jar. The remainder of the vessel glass unsurprisingly comprises storage bottles of various kinds, principally square mould-blown examples.

First-century tablewares

Ten fragments of pillar-moulded bowl (Isings form 3) were noted (*103, 396, 633,* and *656;* Fig 446.1-4), representing at least four vessels. The distinctive nature of these exclusively first-century vessels (Price and Cottam 1998, 44) means that they can be recognised from very small fragments. The fragments represented bowls in dark brown (four fragments), dark blue (three fragments), and natural blue-green (three fragments). Vessels of this form in strong colours seem to have gone out of production soon after the middle of the first century, whilst those in natural blue-green glass continued in use, if not production, to the end of the first century (*ibid*), and as relatively robust objects are often found residually in later contexts, which is probably the case with regard to several of the fragments from this site. Pillar-moulded vessels have been noted on other sites in Carlisle, including Blackfriars Street (Price 1990a, 167), and Castle Street (Cool and Price

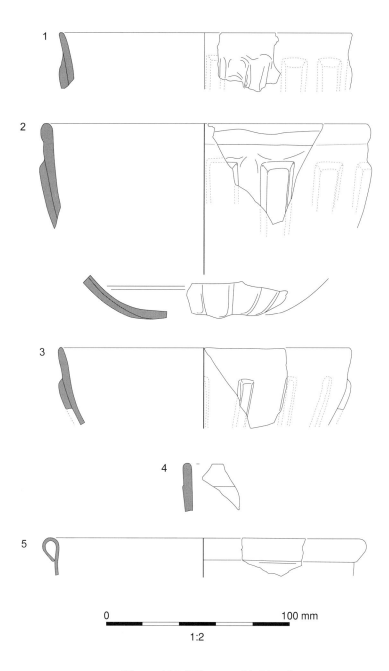

Figure 446: Pillar-moulded bowls

1991, 165), where vessels in the same three colours were noted, and the putative Flavian annexe (Cool 1992, 65), which produced fragments of two blue-green examples.

The remainder of the strongly coloured glass (yellow-brown and dark blue) derived from monochrome blown vessels, the only recognisable form being the ribbed conical jug (Price and Cottam 1998, 152-4; Isings form 55a), of which there is at least one, and possibly as many as three, dark blue examples. In all cases, the fragments are small, and from the neck or upper body. Dark blue flagons, especially conical examples, were not common after the third quarter of the first century. None of the yellow-brown fragments give any indication of the vessel

form, being completely plain. The use of yellow-brown glass continued well into the second century, which would accord with the proposed dates of the stratigraphic sequence, with yellow-brown glass being restricted to Period 4 and later, and coming from the construction trenches of Building **4660**, and the floors within Building **5688** (*Chs 5* and *6*). Fragments from Period 5 are regarded as residual. A single small fragment of dark green glass from Period 6C layer *2228* is also likely to be residual.

A single fragment of a tubular-rimmed bowl (*48*; Fig 446.5) in olive green (Isings form 44) was also noted, from Period 4A Building **7644**. Such bowls are generally dated to the late first- to early second-century (Price and Cottam 1998, 78-9) and other

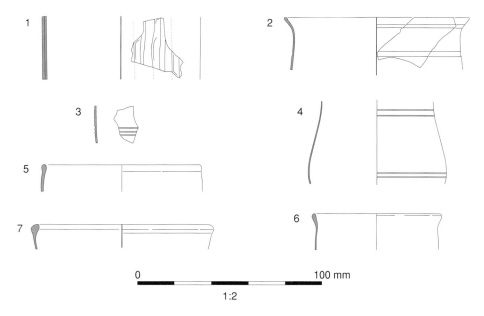

Figure 447: Colourless vessels, cups

examples (*ibid*) are known from Carlisle in natural blue-green (Blackfriars Street) and yellow-brown (The Lanes).

Colourless vessels
Colourless glass is rare in Britain before the Neronian period (Cool and Price 1995, 11), coming into popularity in the late first century and being the predominant colour for fine tablewares throughout the second century and into the third (Price and Cottam 1998, 16). To this end, the amount of colourless glass from the Millennium Project is surprisingly small, there being only 49 fragments, including eight small chips, very few with a maximum dimension in excess of 30 mm. Colourless Roman glass was recovered from all periods, being probably residual in Period 6, and definitely thereafter.

Although lacking the vessel walls which would make its identification conclusive, vessel *67* (*Appendix 8*) seems to be the base of a mould-blown cylindrical cup of first-century date (third quarter). Although not common, these were a relatively widely distributed form, bearing a range of sporting and other motifs, including chariot racing and scenes of gladiatorial combat. In this case, nothing of the scene on the vessel wall survives. Examples from Carlisle include a dark blue cup from contexts of slightly later date at Annetwell Street, and small fragments in blue-green from The Lanes (Price and Cottam 1998, 63-4). It was recovered from a possible floor within Period 3A Building *166*. A second mould-blown fragment (*130*; *Appendix 8*) was from a ribbed vessel, but insufficient survives to determine the form; again, such forms are generally confined to the first century and the fragment is probably residual, being from a Period 7 context.

Fragment *32* (Fig 447.1) is clearly from a facet-cut vessel, the size suggesting a cup. Facet-cut vessels are found in Britain over a long period, from the mid-first to the fourth century (Price and Cottam 1998). The colour, style of cutting, and the stratigraphical context not surprisingly suggest a first-century date for this fragment from the floor of Period 3B Building *1195*. Few of the other colourless fragments are diagnostic as to form. Two fragments (*17*; *Appendix 8*) clearly derive from a small, narrow-necked vessel but this is not otherwise identified.

Vessel *635* (Fig 447.2) is represented by the cracked-off and ground rim of a cup *c* 100 mm in diameter. The rim and body are decorated with wheel-cut horizontal lines. It could derive from one of several forms decorated with such lines, common from the first to the fourth centuries AD, but the stratigraphical context suggests a first-century date. A second, very small, and badly abraded, rim fragment (*13*; *Appendix 8*), was recovered from layer *236* (Period 6B), where it seems likely to have been residual.

Body fragments with one (*617*), three (four fragments (not joining) of a single vessel, *eg 634*; Fig 447.3), and four (*616*; Fig 447.4; *3, Appendix 8*) abraded horizontal lines were also recovered from contexts ascribed to Periods 3 and 4, or residual in Period 7. Although otherwise undiagnostic, the thinness of the glass and the curvature of individual fragments suggests that all are from cups.

Fragments of three upright fire-rounded rims (six fragments, *167, 472, 489*; Fig 447.5-7) were also recovered, each too small for confident identification of the form. It seems, however, from the estimated curvature of the rims, that they are most likely to be of Isings form 57, a cylindrical cup with fire-rounded rim (Price and Cottam 1998, 99-101). In addition, fragment *207* (*Appendix 8*) is a well-known variant with applied self-coloured trail (Isings form 85; *op cit*, 101-3). Such cups were in widespread use, and date generally from the third quarter of the second century to the mid-third (Isings 1957).

A single, extremely small fragment of a colourless blown vessel, with an opaque blue unmarvered trail (*469, Appendix 8*), came from a Period 8D pit fill. This has been tentatively identified as coming from a snake-thread decorated vessel, a distinctive style of decoration which is found on a range of late second- and early third-century vessels, all probably imports from Köln and the lower Rhineland. Although complete vessels are rare in Britain, small fragments are relatively frequent finds (Cool and Price 1995, 61-2), and fragments are known from Blackfriars Street, Carlisle, and a number of northern military and civilian sites (Price 1990a, 170 and fig 17a). Undiagnostic body fragments of colourless vessels were also recovered from Period 6D robber trench fill *2143* (*152; Appendix 8*) and Period 8D pit fill *5151* (*470; Appendix 8*).

Blue-green blown vessels

Although numerous fragments (174) of free-blown natural blue-green glass were recovered, few were diagnostic as to form, although the presence of two small fragments of handles (*252, 320; Appendix 8*) corroborates the identification of some at least as flagons. Fragments of the rims of two collared jars (Isings form 67c), dating to the late first to early/mid-second century, were recovered from Period 4A layer *6674* (*623*; Fig 448.1), and (presumably residual) in the fill of a Period 6A construction trench for Building *2301* (*165*; Fig 448.2). The rim of a tubular-rimmed bowl, probably Isings form 44, dating to the period from AD 60-5 to the third quarter of the second century, was recovered from the fill of a construction trench for Building *4655* (*327*; Fig 448.3).

Several open pushed-in base fragments (*26, 389*; Fig 448.4-5; *349, 416*, and *427; Appendix 8*) seem likely to be from bowls or jugs of late first- to early/mid-second-century date, for instance Isings form 67c, Isings form 52, or Isings form 55b, one at least (*389*) being a spiral-ribbed vessel. In addition, a ribbed body fragment, possibly from the same vessel, came from Period 4A Building *3376* (*358; Appendix 8*). A small fragment of another pushed-in base (*318*) is of uncertain form. Other base fragments came from Period 4A Buildings *4655* (*334, 349*) and Building *3376* (*338; Appendix 8*). A small vessel with a pushed-in base, probably of Roman date, was residual in a Period 8D pit (*471*; Fig 448.6).

Undiagnostic rim or shoulder fragments, probably of first- to second-century date, were also recovered from Period 3A Building *7200* (*639*; Fig 448.7), and Period 3B Building *4656* (demolition layer *4556* (*439, Appendix 8*)). A very small fire-rounded rim fragment

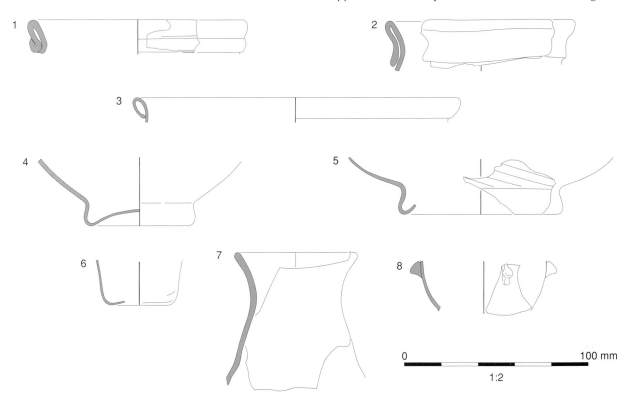

Figure 448: Blue-green blown vessels

came from Period 6A road **2303** (*199, Appendix 8*). A small body fragment from Period 6D robber trench fill *2322* (Building **2301**, *193*) has applied self-coloured trails typical of the third century, and fragment *490* (Fig 448.8), from the fill of Period 6E pit *5376*, had pinched decoration.

Mould-blown bottles
Natural blue green storage bottles
Blue-green storage bottles were manufactured in enormous quantities from the Neronian or early Flavian period onwards (Price 1990b, 101) and were widely used as containers for liquid or semi-liquid substances. There is ample evidence, in the form of wear patterns, to suggest that they were normally transported in wicker or wooden containers, which must have significantly prolonged the life of individual vessels. The commonest

forms are cylindrical (Isings form 51) or square (Isings form 50) bottles, although hexagonal and rectangular forms were also produced, the latter absent from this assemblage. Of these, square bottles were employed over the longest period, continuing in widespread use until the end of the second century, whilst the other forms had fallen from popularity much earlier in the century. It was common practice to reuse storage bottles, especially the larger examples, as burial containers for cremated bone (Price and Cottam 1998, 8). Nothing from the site suggests the presence of burials, however, and indeed it would be highly unlikely in the centre of a functioning fort.

Cylindrical bottles
Very few fragments (20) of cylindrical bottles were recovered, all being from the vessel body. Cylindrical

Figure 449: Square storage bottles

771

bottles were generally free-blown, with a concave base (Cool and Price 1995, 179). The neck and rims of these vessels are effectively identical to those of square and rectangular bottles, and the vessel is often recognised from the distinctive scratches indicative of wicker or wooden outer sleeves. Whilst it is difficult to draw conclusions from relatively undiagnostic body fragments, the vessels present would seem to fall within the small- to medium-sized range, comparable with three vessels from Castle Street (Cool and Price 1991, 166). These bottles were particularly common in the first century, but went rapidly out of use early in the second (Price and Cottam 1998, 191). Significantly, 50% of the fragments from the Millennium Project derive from Period 3 contexts.

Hexagonal bottles
Only three fragments of hexagonal bottles were recognised, partly as a result of the small number of base fragments within the group of bottles as a whole, and also the lack of larger body fragments, those from hexagonal vessels being most easily recognised by the obtuse angle between the walls. Like cylindrical vessels, these are most common in the first century, passing out of use only a little later than cylindrical bottles, in the early second century (Price and Cottam 1998, 199). Examples of this form were seen amongst the Castle Street material (Cool and Price 1991, 166), and the southern Lanes (Price and Cottam in prep), but were absent from Blackfriars Street (Price 1990a). Further afield, an unusually large group of nine vessels was recovered from Ribchester (Price and Cottam 2000).

Square bottles
In all, 197 fragments of square mould-blown bottles (Isings form 50; Price and Cottam 1998, 194-8) were noted. Of this total, 195 fragments were blue-green and two, unusually, were in a greenish-tinged colourless metal. This form, common in the later first and second centuries, is widespread in its distribution. The extremely robust nature of the vessels also means that many examples, unless deliberately recycled, remained in use well beyond the period of production (Price 1990b, 101). The amount of residual material seen amongst this group, from Period 6 on, reflects that circumstance.

Most of the fragments recorded are from the featureless walls of the vessel, but the form of the neck and rim is indicated by *47, 190, 375,* and *419* (Fig 449.1-4), as well as *10, 197, 225, 233, 415, 499, 553,* and *612* (*Appendix 8*); typically combed handle fragments are represented by *79* (Fig 449.5), and *4, 126, 139, 142, 283, 322, 357, 390, 426, 494,* and plain handles by *363, 405, 653* (*Appendix 8*). Bases are represented by *70, 88, 89, 174, 212, 274,* and *487*

(Fig 449.6-12), as well as *72, 84-6, 92, 94-5, 163, 269,* and *589* (*Appendix 8*).

Characteristically, the bases of square storage bottles bore simple designs, the most frequently occurring pattern amongst this group being one or more raised concentric circles (in this group, up to five), occasionally with a central pellet (one example), which is regarded as the most commonly occurring design (Price 1990b, 101). As variations on this theme occur throughout the Empire (Cool and Price 1995, 181), there is little chance of using it to identify a common production centre. Only three bases provide evidence for other designs; *212* (Fig 449.10) has at least one ring and bracketed corners, *174* (Fig 449.9) has a distinctive, complex design, and *487* (Fig 449.12) has a curvilinear geometric design.

Medieval and post-medieval vessels
As might be expected, as medieval glass was not particularly durable, evidence for the use of glass during the medieval period was almost absent. Only two, very small, completely demineralised vessel fragments were recovered from ditch fill *1404* and layer *1407*, Periods 8iii and 8iv respectively (*Ch 11*). There was also little late glass, reflecting the situation with regard to post-medieval and later pottery (*Ch 16*). The dark olive-green wine or beer bottle typical of the post-medieval period was only represented by 17 fragments; all are relatively small, none exceeding 64 mm in maximum dimension. Most were otherwise undiagnostic body fragments, but can be placed in a broad date-range from the later seventeenth to the early nineteenth centuries, and a mould seam surviving on fragment *446* (*Appendix 8*) places it in the latter part of the nineteenth century. Fragment *16* seems highly likely to be intrusive within *244*, a Period 6C layer, as are fragments *467, 2,* and *454*, from Periods 8C, 8E, and 8F respectively (*Appendix 8*). A restricted range of later nineteenth- and twentieth-century glass was also recovered.

Window glass
In all, 96 fragments of window glass were identified, all but a few being the well-known matte-glossy type characteristic of the first to third centuries AD. Only 11 fragments were identified as modern. All the Roman glass was natural bluish-green in colour; like Roman glass all over the North West, most has survived in excellent condition, being almost completely unweathered, and in the specific case of contexts associated with Building *5688* (*Chs 5* and *6*), in relatively large fragments.

The earliest use of window glass must have been in Period 3, but as only three fragments can be assigned to this (from Period 3A pit/gully *1075* (*65, Appendix 8*) and road surface *6629* (*611*), and

Period 3B road surface *3358* (*343*), it seems likely that it was not used widely in the parts of the fort examined during that period. Over half of the window glass (52 fragments) was from Period 4, by far the majority from contexts associated with the use (Period 4B) and subsequent demolition/decay (Period 4C) of Building *5689* (22 and 21 fragments respectively; *Ch 6*). This appears to establish, fairly conclusively, that the building was glazed, although, bearing in mind the possibility that it also seems to have been used as a store for a range of objects, it is not impossible that panes of glass were amongst the items stored.

Period 5, as might be expected, produced only a few fragments of window glass (eight), some at least probably residual from the preceding phase, and it seems likely that the 13 fragments from Period 6 are also residual, the use of matte-glossy window glass having gone into decline by this time (Price and Cottam 2000, 292). Roman-type window glass from Periods 7 and 8 (three and seven fragments respectively) is also regarded as residual.

A single completely mineralised fragment of medieval window glass (*68*; *Appendix 8*) was recovered from layer *1313* (Period 8iv). The six fragments of modern blown or sheet window glass, all very small, are from Period 9 contexts, as are two joining fragments of Roman type.

The three largest fragments of window glass (*574-6*; *Appendix 8*), with maximum dimensions of 118 mm, 155 mm, and 170 mm, all came from *6374*, a fill of Period 4B robber trench *7471*. This disturbed the road (*7217*) which flanked Building *5689* (*Ch 6*). Glass of all sorts was regarded as a valuable and frequently recycled resource, and was often collected or scavenged (Price and Cottam 1998, 7). The presence of such large fragments in this context might give a clue to the sort of robbing being carried out, glass possibly being amongst the materials sought. The maximum dimensions of most other fragments fell within a range from 20 mm to 50 mm, making them considerably more difficult and time-consuming to collect.

Matte-glossy window glass was intended to admit light, but was far from transparent. It was probably made by pouring molten glass into wooden trays (Boon 1966, 43-4) and is characterised by its smooth upper surface, in contrast to the rough lower one, which was in contact with the tray. The glass was pushed manually into the corners of the tray whilst molten, in order to form square or rectangular panels, and tooling marks are visible on three large fragments from fill *6374* (*574-6*; *Appendix 8*). Roman window glass is not an uncommon find, and

published material from Carlisle includes some 30 fragments from excavations at Blackfriars Street (Price 1990a, 179), 74 from Castle Street (Cool and Price 1991, 169), and 55 from the southern Lanes (Price and Cottam in prep).

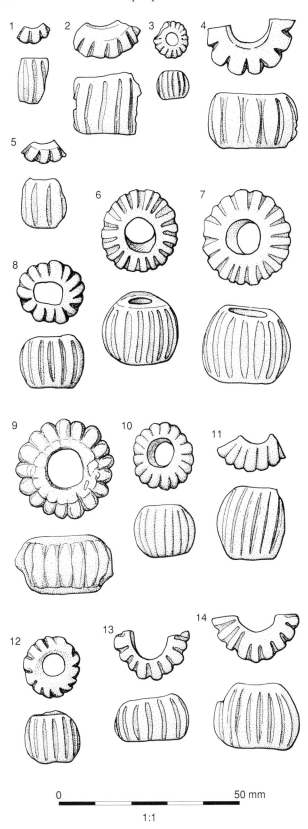

Figure 450: Melon beads, Period 3

773

Other Objects of Glass

Beads

In all, 41 glass beads were recovered (Figs 450 and 451). By far the majority were turquoise frit or dark blue glass melon beads, the latter being particularly associated with the second century AD (Guido 1978, 100), and thus not out of place in either Periods 3C-3E or 4. Melon beads of both kinds are common finds on Roman military sites and must thus be regarded as in some way associated with male dress or uniform accoutrements, possibly even cavalry harness.

Thirty-one melon beads were found, ten of which were made from dark blue translucent glass (*60, 63, 391, 436, 437;* Fig 450; *254, 510, 513;* Fig 451; *332, 341; Appendix 8*), the remainder being turquoise frit (*22, 36/37, 44, 61, 66, 337, 351, 362, 399, 400, 429;* Fig 450; *216, 226, 275, 299, 365, 518, 527;* Fig 451; *33, 331, 339;*

Appendix 8). Melon beads are very frequently found on first- and second-century sites (Price and Cottam 2000, 291), especially those of the first century with a military origin (Cool and Price 2002, 259), and this group from Carlisle is of considerable size. The 42 beads found in the cavalry fort at Ribchester, Lancashire (Price and Cottam 2000), 80 from Vindolanda (Birley and Greene 2006, 39), a similarly-sized group of 83 from the legionary fortress at Usk (Price 1995a), and the 99 from the fort and extramural settlement at Castleford, Yorkshire (Cool and Price 1998, 181), are all exceptionally large groups. The group of ten glass melon beads from the Millennium excavations is also similar in amount to these sites, the last-named possibly being a production centre (Guido 1978, 229). It is of note that few if any other excavations in Carlisle have produced comparable quantities. Roman glass melon beads were made in a range of sizes, although none appear to be as small as some of the smallest frit beads. The Carlisle glass melon beads do not differ significantly in height, all being between 10 mm and 17.5 mm. Some beads can be rather larger,

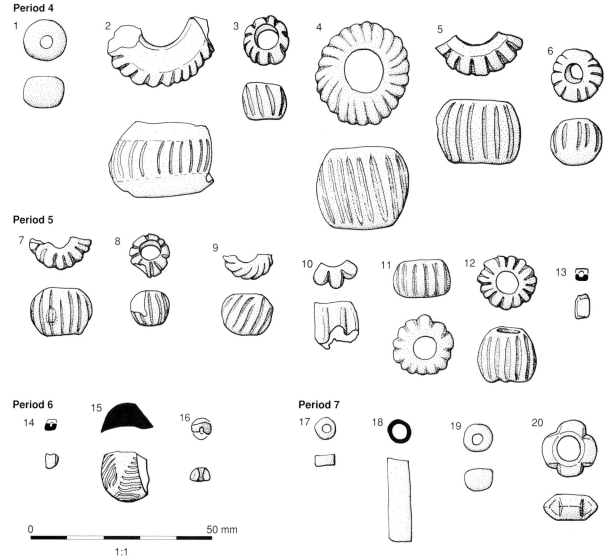

Figure 451: Beads, Periods 4-7 and unstratified

such as a complete example from Usk (21-23 mm high; Price 1995a, fig 31, no 35).

Frit melon beads are always more abundant than their glass counterparts, and 21 examples were noted amongst the assemblage. All but one was probably turquoise, the exception being an unusually small example in black (*61*; Fig 450.3). Several are now distinctly greyish in colour, probably the result of prolonged burial in an anaerobic environment rather than a deliberately produced colour. All but one of the turquoise examples were between 12 mm and 20 mm in height, the exception being rather smaller, at 9 mm, and the black bead is smaller still, at only 8 mm in height.

Melon beads, both glass and frit, were the only types recovered from Periods 3 (Fig 450) and 4, and also predominated in Period 5 (Fig 451). Glass examples were most common in Periods 3B and 4A. Although the range of available bead types is somewhat restricted in the first and second centuries, the almost complete absence of other types before Period 5 is of interest. Although it is recognised that the presence of melon beads has a close association with military activity (Price and Cottam 2000, 291), the function of these objects is still a matter of debate. The beads, particularly those of glass, appear to be rather large and heavy to be worn around the neck, and it has been suggested that they were used as decoration for horse harness (*ibid*), which would not be out of place considering the probable presence of *ala Gallorum Sebosiana* during the late first and early second centuries (*Ch 13*; also reflected in the high-quality harness decorations recovered during these excavations; *Ch 17*). In all, 42 melon beads were found at Ribchester (a cavalry fort) and 28 beads were found at Oberstimm, in Germany, where a cavalry unit is believed to have been stationed (Garbsch 1978, 286-9, nos F28-55, Taf 113). Ritterling has compared melon beads from Hofheim with the beads portrayed on a decorative strap around the neck of the horse on the tombstone of T Flavius Bassus, found at Cologne (Ritterling 1912/13, 179-80, Abb 35), and they were perhaps used in the manner illustrated by Kemkes *et al* (2002, 105, pl 108).

Only two (*46, 166*; Fig 451.13-14) of the small green cuboid beads (Guido 1978, type 7) characteristic of the later Roman period (third-fourth centuries) were recovered, one from Period 5A, the other from Period 6B. These are thought to imitate emeralds, which were a fashionable gemstone throughout the period, and seem far more likely to have been lost from women's jewellery than from horse harness. A small fragment of what appears to be a dark blue glass bead with marvered white *reticella* trails (*189*; Fig 451.16) came from fill *2282* (pit *2283*) associated

with Period 6B Building *2302* (*Ch 9*). It is likely to be an exotic import, but the remaining fragment is too small for comment. In addition, amongst the later groups (Periods 6 and 7), there were three cylindrical beads (Guido 1978, 94-5; types 4 and 5); two in emerald green were both recovered from post-Roman 'dark earths' (*144, 146*; Fig 451.17-18), the third being in blue (*192*; *Appendix 8*), found with links from a gold necklace (*Ch 17*). Again, these are later Roman types, the former common, the latter less so. A small annular bead in dark blue translucent glass came from a posthole associated with the same building, but in Period 6C (*176*; Fig 451.16), and a small globular bead in a natural blue-green metal was unstratified (*669*; Fig 451.19) and could thus be of any date.

Finally, a dark blue gadrooned or multi-lobed bead (*131*; Fig 451.20) was recovered from post-Roman 'dark earth' deposits. Although reminiscent of glass melon beads, this is not a common Roman form (Guido 1978, 99). It shows considerable variation (Rogers 1993, 1381) and this relatively small, four-lobed example would not look out of place in the post-Roman groups from Fishergate, Coppergate, and Pavement, in York (Rogers 1993, 1381-2; Hall, 1984, 104, fig 124; Waterman 1959, 104, fig 25, 17).

Bangles

Two small fragments of spun glass bangles were recovered, one (*64*; Fig 452.1) from possible barrack, Building *1222* (Period 3A), and the other (*478*; Fig 452.2), from a Period 7 'dark earth' (*5296*). The former is natural blue-green, with an unmarvered

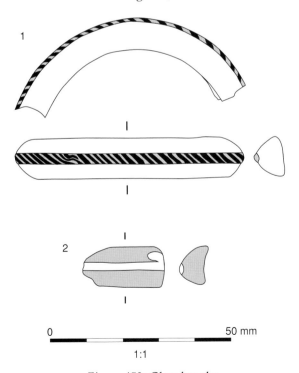

Figure 452: Glass bangles

opaque white and blue twisted cord at the apex (Kilbride-Jones 1938, type 2). Its internal diameter is estimated at around 70 mm. Price (1995b) has defined a group of these bangles, which are associated with early activity (Claudian, Neronian, and early Flavian) on the basis of their size (an internal diameter of 70 mm plus), and it would seem that this example falls within this group, although most examples have a more southerly distribution. Smaller versions of this type continue to be found in contexts dating up to the end of the first century, but appear to be restricted to Britain, with very few Continental examples known (*ibid*).

The second example (*478*, Fig 452.2), in dark blue, with marvered opaque white 'pot hook' decoration, falls within Kilbride-Jones type 3i (1938), current in the late first–early second centuries (Price and Cottam 2000, 292). Other examples of this type are known from The Lanes (Worrell and Price in prep, no 126) and Annetwell Street (Cool and Price 1993, 292), and other sites in north-western England.

Objects used for recreational purposes

Recreational objects were confined to gaming counters. In all, there were 20 of bone (*Ch 20*) and 29 of glass (*57-8, 105, 298, 369, 379, 393, 398, 401-2, 428, 435, 440-3, 453, 501, 600, 610, 625, 628-30, 636-7, 641-2, 657; Appendix 8*). They are not uncommon

finds on Roman military sites and could have served a number of purposes, the bone ones possibly being used as much as accounting tallies as gaming pieces. The glass examples, however, predominantly in black and white, seem more likely to have been used for specific board games, amongst them *ludus latrunculorum*, a war game similar to draughts, which is discussed by Turner (1979) with regard to a hoard of bone and glass counters from Ravenglass, on the Cumbrian coast. The number of counters needed to make up a complete set remains unknown, but is thought to have been around 15 of each type. A group of 54 recovered with the hoard of armour from Corbridge (Allason-Jones and Bishop 1988, 82) probably gives some indication of the number required for a range of board games of this kind. Ancient sources suggest that the game of *ludus latrunculorum* was played with black and white counters (*op cit*, 77).

The glass counters are all roughly plano-convex, ranging from round to oval (Fig 453). It seems that such counters were formed by simply dropping a blob of molten glass onto a hard, flat, but not particularly smooth, surface, and the variation in shape is far more likely to reflect the simplicity of the production method than any deliberate act. In all, eight were made from a dirty-looking opaque white metal, six from opaque blue, and the remaining 16 were opaque

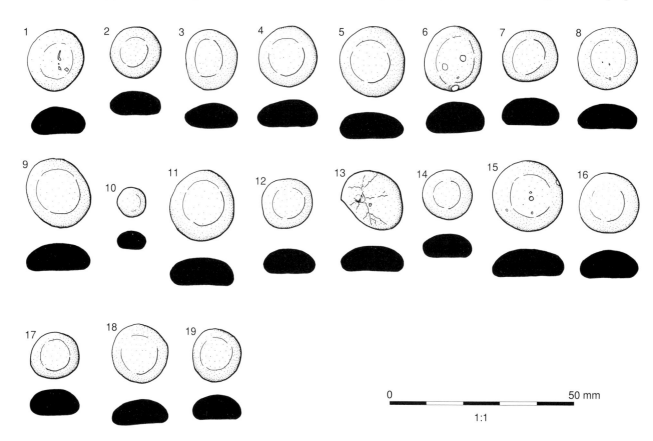

Figure 453: Glass gaming counters

black. Whether the six opaque dark blue counters reflect a third type or are merely an alternative to black cannot be determined.

The Ceramic Objects

The ceramic objects formed an extremely limited group, confined almost entirely to the large collection of fired clay slingshot (discussed with other militaria in *Chapter 17*), and a number of small discs and spindle whorls made from reused samian sherds (*Ch 16*, *pp 565-6*). There was, in addition, a single medieval spindle whorl (*1*; Fig 454), which came from the fill of a posthole associated with outer ward ditch *1231* (Period 8ii, *Ch 11*). It was made from a fragment of Fully Reduced green-glazed pottery, suggesting a date somewhere in the fourteenth to sixteenth centuries (*Ch 16*).

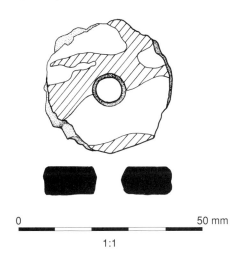

0   50 mm

1:1

Figure 454: Medieval spindle whorl

Jet and Amber Objects

As might be expected, only small numbers of amber and jet/shale objects were recovered. Amber was confined to a single bead, whilst perhaps five, possibly more, items of jet or shale were recorded. Amber and shale have not survived well, the amber having shattered and the shale objects laminated. The jet, however, is in excellent condition, and both items in this material are of exceptional quality.

As might be expected from such a small group, there were no marked concentrations of finds, either physical or chronological. It is, however, of interest that both objects of jet were recovered from the same context (Period 3A occupation layer *7548*

in Building *7392*; *Ch 3*), suggesting that they could have been deposited simultaneously, and might represent the possessions of a single individual.

Nature

Although the most likely source of amber is the Baltic (Strong 1966, 1), mentioned by both Pliny and Tacitus (*op cit*, 4), small fragments of sea-washed amber are frequent finds on the east coast of England, and it is likely that the raw material for this single bead came from this source. Although not a popular material during the Roman period, it was used for jewellery and other prestige goods, and is thought to have been regarded as having some amuletic virtues (Johns 1996, 15), being particularly associated with the well-being of women (McCarthy *et al* 1982, 89; Allason-Jones 1989b, 127) and possibly also children (Swift 2003, 37).

Recent analysis has made it clear that the principal attraction of jet and shale was their colour, and that in fact a relatively wide range of materials was used, from true jet, shales, and cannel coals, to burnt bone (Allason-Jones 2002). These are not easy to differentiate by eye, and there is reason to believe that, if the Roman craftsman did differentiate, it was probably on the basis of the differing mechanical properties, choosing that most suitable to the task in hand (*op cit*, 127). In the case of this small group, shale objects have been separated on the basis of the strong tendency of shale to split in a laminar fashion, whilst jet or cannel coal both have a conchoidal fracture. York is now recognised as a centre of production for jet objects (*op cit*), but undoubtedly simple turned objects, such as the bangles, were made at a number of sites.

Objects of personal adornment or dress
The amber bead
A single amber bead (*1, Appendix 8*) came from layer *1110*, a floor within Period 3A Building *1194* (*Ch 3*). It is too fragmentary for confident reconstruction, but appears to be an annular bead similar to one recovered during excavations at Castle Street (Padley 1991b, fig 151.619). That example, however, came from a context dated to the Anglian/Anglo-Scandinavian or medieval periods, whilst that from the Millennium Project is clearly associated with the Flavian fort. Several amber beads have been recovered from Carlisle, for example the four small examples from Antonine contexts at The Lanes (Padley 2000a, 96, fig 57, H1-4), and two were recovered from Annetwell Street (*ibid*).

Small amber beads such as these have an extremely wide date range, appearing more or less unchanged in form from the Bronze Age (Johns 1996, 15) to recent times. The use of amber is not particularly common in Britain during the Roman period (*op cit*, 70), but other finds from Carlisle include a carved finger ring, again from excavations at The Lanes (McCarthy *et al* 1982, 88). The trade in amber seems to have flourished from the Flavian period until about AD 200 (Strong 1966, 10), which would accord well with the recovery of this object from the Flavian fort.

Shale bangles

Two fragments of turned shale bangles (*3*, *4*; Fig 455.1-2) were recovered from Period 6B external layer *5500* (*4*) and Period 7 'dark earth' *2227* (*3*) respectively. They are common objects, often found on military sites in the North (see Allason-Jones and Miket 1984, 7.121–39), and there is reason to suggest that there is some specific military connection. Both examples have plain oval sections, an extremely common type, and are as a result impossible to date with precision. The widespread use of jet and shale is normally associated with the later Roman period, but there are numerous earlier examples of these bangles, for example, those from late first-century contexts at Ribchester (Howard-Davis 2000c, 295). Parts of two were recovered from Castle Street (Caruana 1990, 154), and they are known both from military sites on Hadrian's Wall and within the military hinterland to the south (see Birley and Greene 2006, 151; Bishop and Dore, 1988, 212–3; Allason-Jones and Miket 1984, 7.121–39).

Figure 455: Shale bangles

Objects used in the manufacture or working of textiles

Shale spindle whorl *2* (Fig 456) is amongst the earliest stratified Romano-British objects from the site, coming from a Period 1 ground surface (*354*). It is in poor condition, but appears turned and decorated, with the central perforation apparently lined with lead. Such objects cannot be dated with precision, and it is not impossible that the loss of this object pre-dates the foundation of the fort.

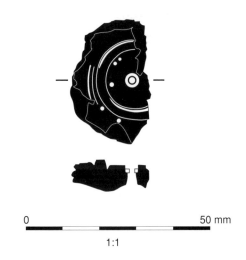

Figure 456: Shale spindle whorl

Military equipment

Two extremely fine jet objects were recovered: a large ring, and a possible sword pommel (*5*, *6*; Fig 457.1-2). Both derive from the same context (*7548*), an occupation layer within Building **7392**, possibly the *praetorium* of the primary fort (Period 3A; *Ch 3*).

The ring (*5*) is 40 mm in diameter, with a sub-oval central perforation *c* 18 mm across, making its identification as a spindle whorl unlikely. An almost identical example from South Shields (Allason-Jones and Miket 1984, object 7.171) is tentatively identified as a spindle whorl, but the identification is hedged by alternatives. Lawson (1976, fig 7.59) suggests that an example from Silchester might have served as a hair ring or clothes' fastener. Dating is imprecise, as identical examples have been produced from sites as early as the late Iron Age to as late as the fourth century AD.

Although there is some evidence to suggest that the use of jet was gender-specific, being associated almost entirely with objects conventionally used by women (Allason-Jones 1989b, 128), object *6* has been tentatively identified as part of a sword pommel, or a complete handguard, on the basis of its similarity to wooden examples from Ringonheim (Bishop and Coulston 1993, fig 36.1) and Vindonissa

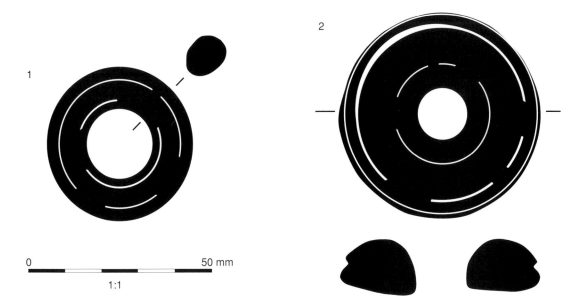

Figure 457: Jet objects

(*op cit*, fig 37.1 and 37.4). The object might equally be a damaged spindle whorl, although in that case the strong ridge running around the maximum circumference seems unusual. Similarly, if the roughly finished, but worn, underside of this object implies that it was not intended to be seen, then it would seem more likely to have been part of a sword handgrip than a spindle whorl. In addition, spindle whorls from the relatively large collection published from South Shields (Allason-Jones and Miket 1984) seem almost entirely to have a low cylindrical profile.

There seems little doubt that both jet and amber were regarded as objects of considerable value and, to that end, were not in widespread use. The discovery of the two large jet objects within the suggested *praetorium* of the Period 3 fort is thus of significance in linking it with relatively high-status and thus (presumably) wealthy individuals.

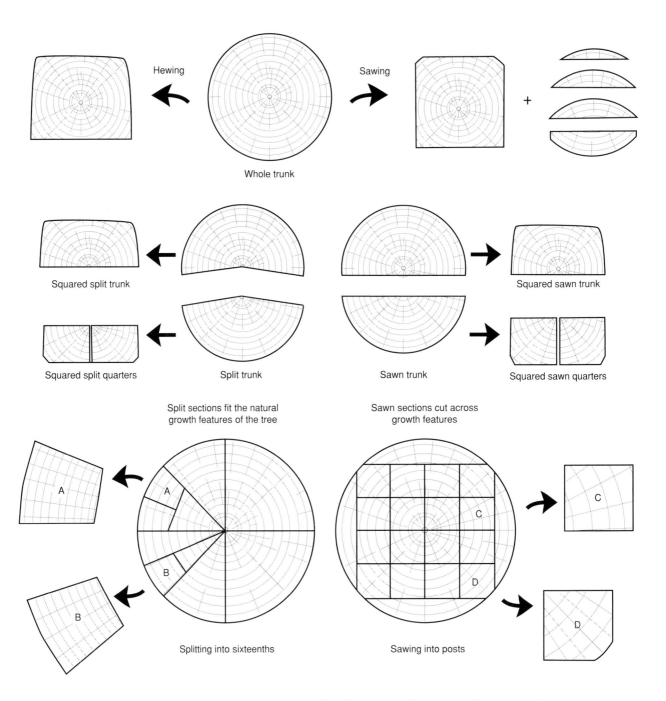

Figure 458: Techniques for the conversion of oak by splitting, hewing, and sawing to shape

19

THE STRUCTURAL WOOD AND OTHER WOODEN ARTEFACTS

The Structural Wood

R Darrah

In all, some 2000 large fragments of well-preserved timber were recovered, from contexts ranging in date from the first to the nineteenth century AD. Circumstances meant that much of it was stored in adequate, but not optimal, conditions for a considerable amount of time before being recorded. As a result, most of the timbers showed some surface deterioration and a decision was therefore made to preserve the assemblage by record, rather than to attempt a large-scale programme of conservation. The data recorded, and a series of detailed drawings, form the basis of the site archive, and the timbers have been discarded. In addition, a substantial programme of sampling was undertaken for the purposes of dendrochronological dating (*Appendix 16*),which has formed a framework for dating the site, especially in its earlier phases.

The results of the detailed analysis of the structural wood are summarised (see *Appendix 9* for greater detail), offering a substantial insight into the woodland and timber resources available locally in the first and second centuries AD; they also illustrate the Roman army's criteria for the selection and use of timber within the Carlisle fort. The analysis has also shown the range of tools used in woodworking, the techniques used by Roman military carpenters, and the appearance of timber buildings within the fort in the late first and second centuries AD. To a lesser extent, the analysis has allowed a consideration of medieval timber use from the twelfth to fifteenth centuries, by examining the remains of simple structures on the site at that time, and of discarded wood dumped into the castle's outer ward ditch.

The type and quantity of woodland exploited during the Roman period

The earliest buildings excavated by the Millennium Project (Period 3A; *Ch 3*) were built mainly from alder and ash, suggesting that these were, at the time, the most easily available species, growing locally in valley and wet valley alderwoods, like those which still thrive in Cumbria (Peterken 1981, 150–2). It is likely that the fort site and a surrounding *cordon sanitaire* were clear-felled (every tree cut down) for defensive purposes immediately before building work started, and pollen evidence (*Ch 22*) suggests that alder had been a significant component of the local vegetation, the nearby river banks, and presumably the damp ground of the fort itself, providing a suitable habitat. This might well explain the use of a wider range of woods in the earliest buildings (Period 3A), with most of the timber generated by local clear-felling.

The pollen evidence (*Appendix 15*) makes it clear that there was very little oak growing in the vicinity of the site when the Romans arrived, but from Period 3B (*Ch 4*) onwards, oak was the predominant wood used, presumably reflecting a systematic reconnaissance for suitable building timber. The often high-quality straight-grained, knot-free oak used on the site suggests that large trees were being selected with an individual task in mind, and a clear understanding of how they could be converted into specific constructional components (Fig 458). The area of woodland needed to produce enough timber to build a fort has been discussed by Hanson (1978), with numerous *caveats* with regard to the different volumes of timber that may be produced by any given acre. The Carlisle timbers provide new information, in that some of the trees used were very large indeed, being over 1 m in trunk diameter. Such large, slow-grown trees, probably growing in dense woodland for several hundred years, provided immense amounts of timber and, if suitable individuals were selected for felling, draw felled from a relatively large area of woodland, no significant acreage would have had to be cleared in order to provide sufficient timber. Individual trees would probably have been selected and felled in response to specific demands for wall posts, tie beams, or rafters, with experienced native or Roman woodsmen choosing straight-grained and knot-free timber, with the potential to be split easily, and leaving the majority of trees standing (less suitable individuals, without straight grain, or knotty).

Seasonality

The dendrochronological evidence points to some summer felling (for example timber W994 (Period 3B,

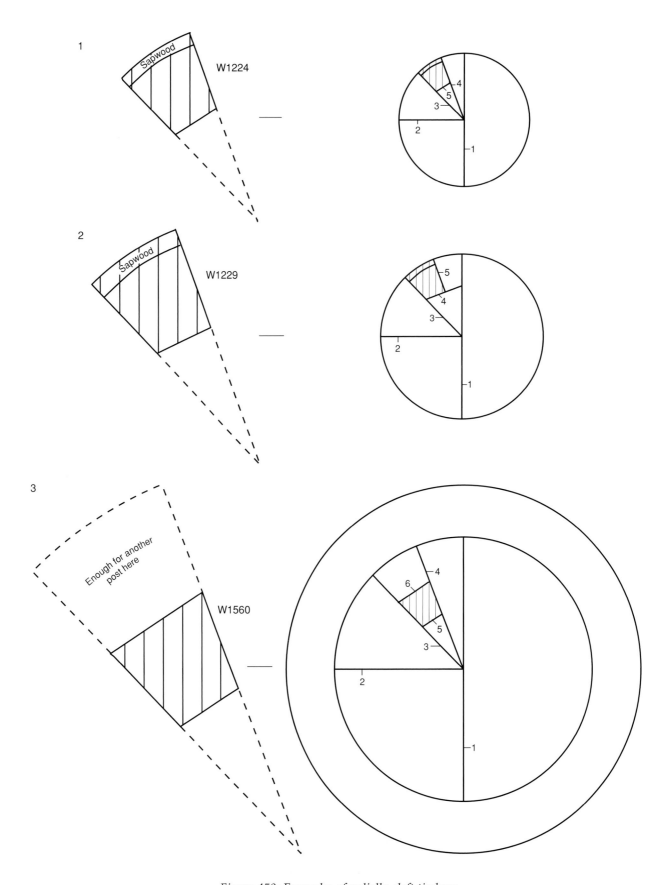

Figure 459: Examples of radially cleft timbers

Building **4656**, **4595**) cut down in the summer of AD 83), as well as the more usual winter felling (timbers in the same building were felled in the winter of AD 83-4).

Winter, and preferably close to the solstice, was regarded as the best time for felling by the Romans (Latham 1957, 19, citing Pliny, *Natural History XVI*) and it is difficult to account for this difference. Perhaps it was busy-work for bored troops, or local labour was being used out of season, or it might simply reflect the opportunist collection and use of wind-felled trees. It might also point to a limited element of stockpiling, but whether of dressed timber within the fort, or part-converted timber at the felling site, cannot now be determined.

The conversion of trees into structural components

The trees selected can be shown to have varied considerably in size (from 0.12 m to 1.1 m in diameter). Although their original height cannot be determined, the largest were likely to have had trunk lengths of over 10 m (based on the usual tree canopy height of broad-leaved woodlands in the Northern Hemisphere today). Where evidence survives, it seems they were felled, trimmed, and dressed with axes. Given that freshly-felled oak weighs 1.073 tonnes per cubic metre, such a tree trunk would weigh about 8 tonnes and would have been very difficult to transport entire. Thus, it is most likely that they were converted to posts and boards at the felling site (much reducing the weight of wood to be transported) before it was carried to the fort. This suggestion is supported by the marked lack of wood chips in the construction trenches of the fort buildings (although larger off-cuts, where posts were cut to the exact lengths required in the buildings, do survive (*Appendix 9*). Skilled woodsmen would have optimised the conversion, producing posts and boards as required. For example, a long trunk might have produced a range of timber, the bottom 4 m being split into radial planking, the next part of the trunk into pieces that could be hewn into posts, and so on.

Various techniques were available for converting trunks into squared building timbers: shaping from a whole trunk length by hewing or sawing; splitting or sawing in half, then hewing or sawing to shape; splitting or sawing into quarters or smaller sections, then being left as sawn, or redressed with an axe. Each of these procedures produced distinctive cross-sections (Fig 458). A short off-cut (W1301, *4442*) from Period 4B Building *4660* seems to suggest that, in fact, timbers were quite carefully dressed at the felling site, reducing the weight of the timber yet further. A high-quality, radially-cleft timber, from a trunk of over 1 m diameter, the off-cut is likely to have been the outer part of a radial sixteenth that had been split across tangentially. Whilst this piece had been carefully finished, being axe-hewn, it had not been squared, and retained its markedly trapezoid section. It is likely that this was the original surface finish of timbers brought from the felling site.

Splitting

Most of the oak used in the buildings was split. Although requiring some considerable skill, timber can be split, both radially and tangentially, in a controlled manner, with very simple tools. For instance, an oak trunk of 1.2 m diameter can be split into usable boards and posts using just wooden wedges and a mallet, and other species such as alder and ash can be split almost as easily. Splitting is a basic technique in the preparation of timbers, and, using good quality timber, can be much faster than sawing, even with modern power tools (*pers obs*). As split (or cleft) surfaces follow the natural planes of growth of a tree, or tear from one to the next, they are more easily identified than any other method of conversion, unless subsequently hewn with axes to provide a smooth surface.

Post W1224 (Period 4A, Building *3376*) was broadly typical of the posts surviving from buildings of Periods 3 and 4, being 0.73 m long, and rotted at one end. It was radially-cleft oak, with a trapezoidal cross-section of 90 x 70 mm (Fig 459.1), but unusually, none of the faces were hewn. The original end, set on the base of the construction trench, was cut straight across. Its outer face comprised the interface between the sapwood and bark, the inner face was a tangential split, and both sides were radial splits. Oak has well-marked medullary rays, which allow the diameter of the trunk to be estimated, by extrapolating the lines of the rays converging on the notional centre of the tree. Thus the original diameter of the trunk from which W1224 was taken could be estimated at *c* 0.4 m, and the outer face of the post represented one sixteenth of the circumference. The tangentially-split inner face showed that the trunk was split radially, and then individual timbers sub-divided tangentially, to produce suitably-sized posts. Thus, a trunk of *c* 0.4 m diameter could have produced 16 posts, and 16 inner radial pieces. A skilled woodsman can split lengths of over 10 m, but it is unlikely that a piece of this cross-section would have been more than 7 m, and was more likely to have been 3-4 m in length. A slight variation in technique can be seen in post W1229 (in fill *3657* of robber pit *3659*, Period 3D Building *4006*; Fig 459.2), where the trunk was originally split radially into eighths, with each eighth divided tangentially into two, and the outer piece then halved radially, giving 16 outer, but only eight inner, pieces.

Evidence for sawing and the use of axes

The lack of knots is a feature of most of the timber examined. This might suggest the deliberate selection of more efficiently splitable timber. Knots do, however, survive in several sections, and there is rare evidence showing how the Roman wood-worker overcame the problem. On timber W1426 (Fig 460), a radially-split eighth from Period 4 road *7477* (*6444*), the outer face was tangentially split, but had a 50 mm diameter knot in it. There were saw marks visible, running across the face of the knot, suggesting that the workman converting this timber

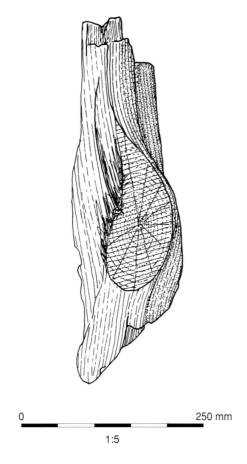

0   250 mm

1:5

Figure 460: W1426, showing the sawn knot

had split it up to the knot, sawn through it, and then carried the split on.

Pile W1665 (*7325*; Period 3E) was an inner radial split, triangular in section, with the outer face tangentially cleft, and unusual in being complete and not rotted at one end (Fig 461). Only 0.72 m long, it was probably an off-cut from the top of a considerably longer timber. One end had been cut to a point, and at the other it had been cross-cut with an axe. The cross-cut was made at the point where the timber branched and thus became unsplitable, suggesting that the converters endeavoured to maximise the lengths of timber they were producing from each individual trunk, rather than cutting to standard lengths.

Oak sill-beam fragment W1013 (*6245,* in Period 4B Building *5688*, the *principia* (*Ch 6*)), also had knotty wood at one end. Although only 1 m survived, the beam could be expected originally to have been between 3 m and 7 m long. One of the original ends was extant, comprising a saddle lap joint, which was cut through a large knot (Fig 462). The timber was a cleft outer radial section, but as the knot was of sufficient size to prevent it being split any further, it can be assumed that it was cleaved as far as the knot, and the knot hewn away. As such a large knot would have made the saddle lap more difficult to cut, and weakened the joint, it is not clear why knotty wood was selected for this timber, unless a specific length was required and no other suitable timber was available.

Although most of the posts and boards excavated had been broken in antiquity, or had rotted *in situ*, those from drain *4463* (Period 3C) were better preserved, and widths were available from 55 planks and boards used in its construction. These ranged between 70 mm and 300 mm, and their distribution (Fig 463) does not seem to indicate any 'standard widths' that might imply the systematic production of standardised timbers. Rather, it appears that those converting the timber were aiming to make the widest possible boards from each available trunk.

Timber selection and use in the first and second timber forts (Periods 3 and 4)

The timber resource drawn upon for the posts and studs used in the buildings of Periods 3 and 4 is set out in Table 45. As posts can be made from either a whole trunk squared up, or a smaller section of a large tree (when large trees are freely available, this is the easiest method), they are a good indicator of the range of tree sizes selected and exploited. Thus, when posts are routinely made from small sections of large trees, it may be assumed that there are reasonable numbers of large straight-grained trees readily accessible.

In some cases, it can be shown that trees of around 400 years old were being used to provide timber for the fort buildings. When split, planks and posts from the inner parts of such a tree appear to be

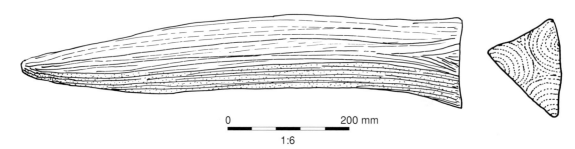

0   200 mm

1:6

Figure 461: W1665, inner radially split section of oak, surviving as a complete pile

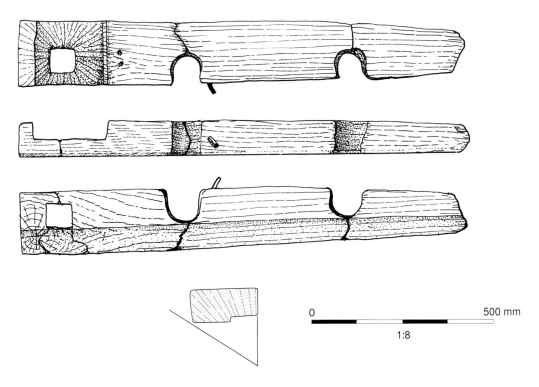

Figure 462: Sill-beam fragment W1013, probably from a long timber

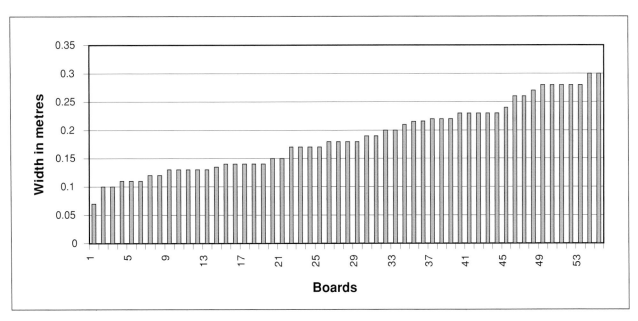

Figure 463: Widths of the planks and boards used in Period 3 drain 4463

much older (when dated dendrochronologically) than the building of which they are part (Table 46). For example, the dendrochronological evidence shows that post W1071 and board W1024 (both from Period 3A Building **4654**) came from the interiors of trees with at least 180 years of further growth (*ie* 180 missing rings).

The buildings of Period 3

In the earliest timber buildings excavated in the Millennium Project (Period 3A), the posts were made almost entirely from alder and ash, with only limited use of oak. The posts were either small tree trunks used whole, or split into halves or quarters; in all cases the timbers were squared up. Although alder is easy to hew with an axe, ash is actually slightly more difficult to work than oak; this seems to imply that the builders were willing, or obliged, to use inferior timber that was harder to shape. By extension, this suggests that alder and ash were, at the time, the only easily available species. Indeed, the easy availability of alder probably accounts for

Building	Period	Section of tree				Species		
		Whole trunk	Halved trunk	Quartered trunk	Radially spit	Oak	Other than oak	Not identified
4653	3A	7	4	2	5	1	14	3
7392	3A	1		3	3		6	1
3772	3B	1		2	26	14	1	14
4656	3B				6	6		0
4657	3C	1		1	5	6	1	0
7200	3C	1		4	2	6		1
3376	4A			4	15	12		7
5688	4A	3	3	9	9	16		8
5689	4A			3	12	11		4
4660	4B				13	5		8
Total no		14	7	28	96	77	22	46

Table 45: The sections and species used to make posts for buildings in Periods 3 and 4

Wood number	Context	Earliest ring	Latest ring	Cross-section area (m²)	Width (m)	Average ring width (mm)	Estimated tree diameter (m)	Description
W449	*2030*	~150 BC	64 BC	0.009	0.13	>1	~0.9	Wall post
W1014	*4236*	~180 BC	104 BC	0.006	0.12	1.5	~1.0	Stake
W1024	*4238*	~230 BC	151 BC	0.007	0.14	1.5	~1.1	Wall post
W1071	*4575*	~230 BC	112 BC	0.0168	0.14	1	~0.8	Wall post
W1560	*6922*	?	164 BC	0.0132	0.12	1	~1.1	Post-size off-cut

Estimates of diameter should be treated with caution as they are based on two estimates: the distance of the inside of the piece from the notional centre of the tree; and the assumption that the rate of growth of the outer piece was the same as that of the inner piece.

Table 46: Size and function of timbers made from inner sections of large trees in AD 83 or later

its continued use throughout the life of the fort; for instance, the floor planks in R5 in the second phase of Building **4653** (Period 3A) were of alder. Neither alder nor ash is particularly durable and the timbers would probably have rotted at ground level within five to ten years (HMSO 1956, 8), perhaps prompting the Period 3B rebuild (*Ch 4*). There is evidence that some timbers deteriorated swiftly; the post and stake grouping in the external west wall of Building **4653**, for example (Fig 464), could reflect a repair, with pointed timbers hammered in, for support, alongside rotting timbers. Although alder and ash were the main timbers used for the buildings excavated, this does not preclude the use of oak elsewhere, and, indeed, it was used almost exclusively in the primary rampart on the south side of the fort and in the adjacent gate (Caruana in prep). It is also possible that any more durable oak posts were subsequently reused, a possibility raised by the dendrochronological evidence (*see Appendix 16*).

This early use of alder and ash can be seen in forts elsewhere; for instance, alder was used widely in period 2 structures at Vindolanda (Birley 1994, 128), continued to be used for floor planking in the late first century (*op cit*, pl 7.1), and was still being used for wattle sails, set into oak sill beams, in a barrack block constructed *c* AD 103-4. Further afield, squared-up small alder trunks were used for buildings in the first and second forts at the Valkenburg in the Netherlands, dated to the first century (Glasbergen 1972, 128).

Within a few years, the fort buildings were demolished and rebuilt (Period 3B; *Ch 4*). This time the posts used were exclusively oak, being squared-up,

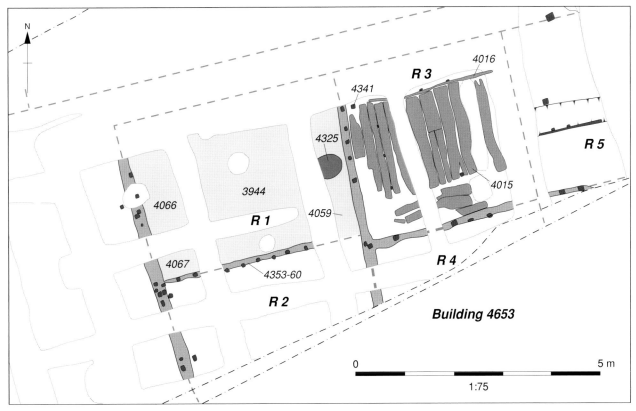

*Figure 464: Period 3A Building **4653**, the west wall of which may have been a rebuild*

radially-split eighths or sixteenths of very large and long-lived trees. Similar oak timbers continued in use during Period 3C. Although the source of this timber is not known, dendrochronological evidence (*see Appendix 16*) indicates that many of the timbers had growth patterns similar to those of trees used at Vindolanda, 20 km to the east (albeit at a later date, probably not until *c* AD 104/5; Birley 1994). This seems to imply that both were drawing on a substantial, relatively local resource, and common sense might suggest that it lay between the two forts. It must, however, be noted that buildings at Vindolanda contemporary with the fort buildings of Periods 3B and 3C in Carlisle used a wider range of timber, including birch and other small species (A R Birley *pers comm*).

The buildings of Period 4

Oak continued to be used extensively in Period 4 buildings (*Chs 5* and *6*). Although the types of conversion used were similar, the timber quality probably decreased somewhat, as did the size of trees used. Detailed examination of the timber used in drains dated to Periods 4A and 4B has allowed some observation on the size, appearance, and growth rate of the trees from which it derived. The growth rate of oak is influenced by a number of factors, but in general terms these can be summarised as follows: trees from dense woodland have a growth rate of less than 2 mm per year; standards from 'coppice with standards' have growth rates of 2-4 mm per

year; hedgerow trees, or trees growing in other open conditions, may grow at up to 10 mm per year.

Individual posts and beams used in the construction of drain *6781* (Period 4A, road *7477*) show appreciably different rates of growth (Table 47) and can be divided into two distinct sets: those of <2 mm *per annum* (slow grown); and those of >2 mm (up to 6 mm or 7 mm) (fast grown). This suggests that, by the time the drain was built, timber was being taken from a range of habitats, including open woodland and more densely stocked areas. All the wood was, however, of good quality, implying that, whatever the source, trees were being selected for their size and straightness of grain. However, two of the posts used in drain *6781* were clearly reused, so that it cannot be assumed that the criteria governing their original choice had any relevance to their subsequent use in the drain.

Period 4B drain *5925* ran below *6000*, the final surface of road *7477* (*Ch 6*). It appears to have been made from a mixed group of timbers; most of the wood with which it was capped was slow-grown oak (<2 mm *per annum*; Table 48), most of very poor quality (knotty and twisted) with the bark left *in situ*, being small trunks and branches, either unworked or halved by cleaving. The quantity of branch wood used in the structure was less than would have been produced by one large slow-grown tree (James 1982, 81). In addition, there was a relatively small group (19 out of 90) of better-quality timber, fast-grown oak, with few knots and a

Wood no	Width (m)	Thickness (m)	Growth rate per year (mm)	Tree diameter (m)	Conversion	Similar pieces from 1 m trunk length	Age at felling (years)	Notes
W1571	0.09	0.085			Radial eighth	8		
W1566	0.1	0.9		0.45	Outer radial eighth	8		
W1551	0.11	0.07	1	0.2	Halved	2	100	AD 98 winter
W1576	0.16	0.1	1	0.16	Roundwood	1	80	Not oak
W1559	0.09	0.07	1	?	Radial			
W1575	0.12	0.09	1–2	0.12	Roundwood	1	40	Not oak
W1570	0.125	0.07	2		Outer radial eighth	2		
W1577	0.1	0.06	2–5	0.12	Halved	2	20	Not oak
W1565	0.13	0.11	5	0.4	Quartered	4	25	
W1561	0.135	0.09	4–6	0.35	Quartered	4	30–40	
W1599	0.1	0.08	7		Radial			Rebate suggests reused

Table 47: Growth rates and average annual ring widths of posts from drain 6781

Wood no	Conversion	Branch wood = B	Width (m)	Thickness (m)	Annual ring width (mm)	Trunk diameter (m)	Comments
W1389	Radial eighth	B	0.1	0.06	2	>0.2	
W1418	Rad/tan		0.085	0.07	2		
W1421	Radially cleft		0.055	0.03	2		Planking-quality oak
W1448	Tangential		0.06	0.045	2		
W1424	Rad/tan		0.07	0.06	2.5		
W1417	Quartered	B	0.06	0.9	2–1	0.12	
W1386	Radial eighth	B	0.08		2–1	0.16	
W1423	Quartered	B	0.08	0.1	2–1	0.16	Pulp quality
W1436	Rad/tan		0.09	0.08	2–1	~0.8	
W1381	Radial		0.05	0.035	2–1		
W1382	Radial eighth		0.06		2–1		Spiral grain
W1385	Quartered		0.1		2–0.5		Band of very slow growth 0.12 mm
W1390	Radial eighth		0.065	0.05	2–0.3	0.15	
W1393	Roundwood	B	0.08		1	0.08	
W1380	Halved	B	0.08		1	0.08	
W1446	Quartered	B	0.06	0.09	1	0.12	
W1387	Quartered	B	0.075	0.075	1	0.15	Curved firewood quality
W1427	Rad/tan		0.07	0.06	1		
W1419	Rad/tan		0.08	0.035	1.5	0.16	Gatepost quality
W1425	Quartered	B	0.06	0.09	1.5–1	0.12	Curved firewood quality

Rad/tan = radially and tangentially cleft section

Table 48: Characteristics of the slow-grown timber from drain 5925

Wood no	Conversion	Branch wood = B	Width (m)	Thickness (m)	Annual ring width (mm)	Trunk diameter (m)	Comments
W1441	Radial sixteenth outer tangential section		0.12	0.05	1–2	0.24	Poor planking quality
W1437	Radial outer tangential section		0.12	0.02	1–2	~0.7	
W1444	Halved	B	0.085	0.04	1–0.5	0.085	
W1432	Radial/ outer tangential section		0.1	0.03	0.75	0.32–0.40	Epicormic growth, gatepost quality
W1449	Radial quarter		0.08	0.06	<2		
W1431	Quartered		0.045	0.045	<1	0.09	Canker on stem
W1383	Radial		0.1	0.1	1		Spiral grain

Rad/tan = radially and tangentially cleft section

Table 48: Characteristics of the slow-grown timber from drain 5925 (contd)

Wood no	Conversion	Branch wood =B	Width (m)	Thickness (m)	Annual ring width (mm)	Trunk diameter (m)
W1579	Radial eighth inner tangential section		0.1	0.05	8	~0.6
W1440	Radial sixteenth inner tangential section		0.15	0.05	7	~0.6
W1420	Radial thirty-second section		0.08	0.06	7 to 1	~0.6
W1439	Radial tangential section, cleft		0.1	0.06	6	~0.5
W1429	Radial eighth inner tangential section		0.1	0.05	6	
W1438	Radial outer tangential section		0.08	0.06	5	~0.4
W1434	Tangential section		0.1	0.07	4	0.4
W1445	Radial eighth	B	0.08	0.05	4	0.16
W1428	Radial eighth inner tangential section		0.07	0.5	4	
W1435	Radial eighth inner tangential section		0.07	0.05	4	
W1392	Radial thirty-second		0.17	0.07	4 to 1	0.6
W1391	Quartered	B	0.07	0.1	4 to 1	0.14
W1426	Radial eighth inner tangential section		0.1	0.08	4 to 3	
W1433	Roundwood		0.03	0.03	3	0.03
W1447	Roundwood		0.07	0.07	3	0.07
W1442	No data		0.12	0.08	3.5	
W1422	Quartered		0.1	0.12	3 to 1, last ring 3 mm	0.6
W1443	Quartered	B	0.06	0.06	3 to 1, last two years 2 mm	0.12
W1430	Halved		0.09	0.05	2 and increasing	0.2

Table 49: Characteristics of the fast-grown timber from drain 5925, ordered by growth rate

straight grain. Most were from large trunks (Table 49), and could represent small parts of only the trunks of two or three larger trees. Vigorous trees such as these also have fast-grown branch wood, but this does not appear to have been used in the drain. The varied nature of the timbers might suggest that there was

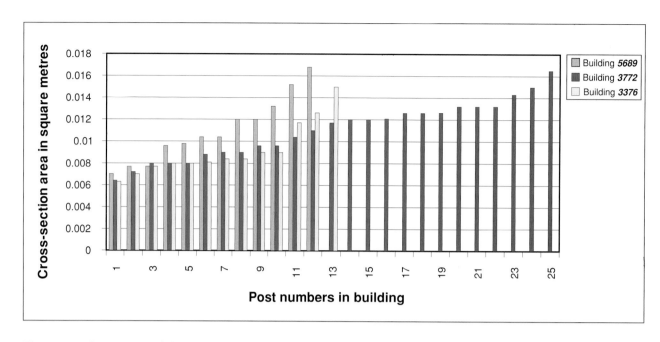

*Figure 465: Comparison of the cross-sectional areas of posts in Buildings **3772** (Period 3B), **3376**, and **5689** (Period 4A)*

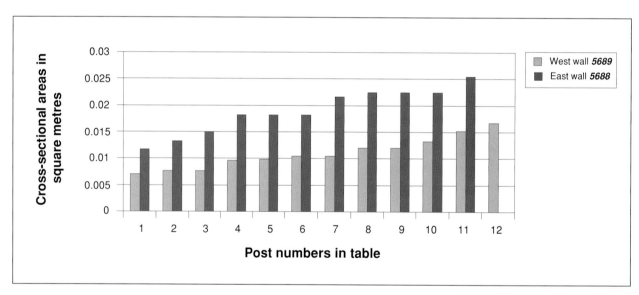

*Figure 466: Comparison of cross-sectional areas of posts in adjacent Period 4 buildings, **5688** and **5689***

Building no	Wall	Period	Building type	Post size (m²)	Post spacing (m)	Maximum post spacing (m)	Minimum post spacing (m)	Construction
3772	North	3B	Barracks	0.012	0.85	0.95	0.7	Post-in-trench
5688	East	4A	*Principia*	0.019	0.98	1.1	0.55	Post-in-trench
5689	West	4A	?	0.011	0.65	0.07	0.55	Post-in-trench
7200	North	3C	?	0.019	0.98	0.6	1.2	Sill beam
7392	West	3A	Barracks	0.009	1.01	0.85	1.25	Post-in-trench

*Table 50: Sizes and spacings of post centres for Buildings **3772**, **5688**, **5689**, and **7392** (walls where there are significant runs of posts)*

little deliberate selection of timber for the construction of this drain, with the capping, at least, using whatever was to hand, with no consideration of its quality.

Constructional components

Posts provide the vertical and horizontal supports within any timber building. Some 51 posts were well-enough preserved to provide information with regard to their relative size. In all discussion of post sizes, unless stated otherwise, the minimum dimensions allowing definition of a timber as a post are 80 x 80 mm. The cross-sections of the various timbers were not particularly substantial, with half of them (Fig 465) less than 0.1 x 0.1 m (four inches square) in cross-section. None were even as large as 0.15 x 0.15 m (six inches square), and despite comprising significant uprights in important military structures, they can only be described as small posts.

If the surviving posts from buildings of probably similar functions from Periods 3B (Building *3772*) and 4A (Building *3376*), both putative barrack blocks, are compared, it can be seen that the average Period 3B post (0.011 m^2) was larger that of Period 4A (0.009 m^2), perhaps reflecting a slight diminution in the quality of the timber available. A second Period 4A building, *5689*, however, had similar-sized posts to those of the Period 3B barracks (Fig 465). This seems to suggest a systematic difference between individual Period 4 buildings, perhaps indicating that relatively subtle post-size changes might reflect differences in status between buildings, which is supported by the comparison of two contemporary Period 4A buildings, the *principia*, Building *5688*, and its neighbour, Building *5689*. For example, posts in the east wall of *5688* had almost twice the cross-section area of those in the west wall of Building *5689* (Fig 466).

It is possible that post cross-section had a direct relationship with post-spacing, with larger posts being more widely-spaced, as they would have been able to carry more weight. This does not, however, seem to have been the case; Buildings *7200* and *5688* had large, widely-spaced posts, whilst those of Building *7392* were the smallest recorded, but were nonetheless more widely spaced than those of other buildings (Table 50). It is also worth noting the irregular spacing of posts. Although this can, on occasion, be caused by modification, or the removal of uprights, those in Building *7200* were irregularly spaced (0.6–1.2 m separation). As this building was of sill-beam construction, and the upright posts would have been inserted into mortises cut into the beam, missing or removed uprights would be indicated by empty mortises, and there were none.

Of course, posts can vary in size according to their placement within a building, as demonstrated by the cross-sectional areas of the posts in the south and east walls of the Period 4 *principia* (Building *5688*), and an internal wall in the same building (Fig 467). The posts in the south wall are on average larger in cross-section (0.027 m^2) than those in the east wall (0.019 m^2), although there are some small posts in the south wall. Interestingly, the internal posts are also large (0.024 m^2 on average), which might reflect their visibility within the building, or that they were required to support the roof ridge, as seems to have been the case in Building *3376*, a Period 4A barrack in the south-west quadrant of the fort, where it appears that the posts in the internal walls were at least as large, and sometimes larger, than those in the external walls (Fig 468). The internal wall in this building lay centrally, running the length of the long, narrow building, and may have been a more

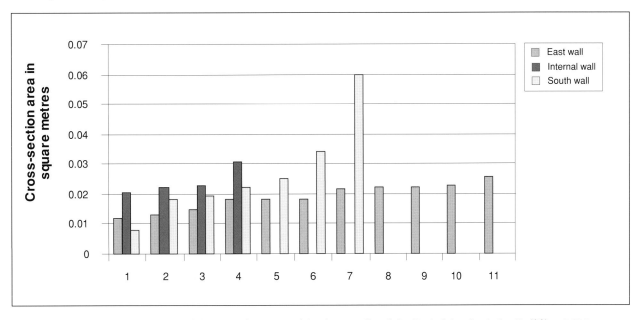

Figure 467: Comparison of the size of posts used in three walls of the Period 4 principia, *Building* **5688**

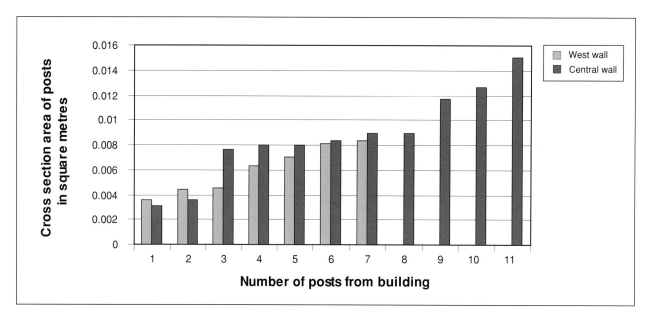

Figure 468: Comparison of post sizes used in Period 4 Building **3376**

important structural element than other internal (partition) walls, possibly supporting the roof ridge (Fig 469). Many internal walls were, however, built out of small-diameter wood, and seem to have been secondary additions, as their construction trenches do not join those of the main walls. They may thus have been partitions added after the main building was completed.

Stakes (smaller than posts, and with a pointed rather than flat-bottomed base) were also used within individual buildings. In Building **4653**, for example, there was a line of multifacet-pointed roundwood stakes, all 70 mm in diameter, which ran from the west wall to the central wall in the second phase of the building, probably replacing an earlier trench-set wall (*Ch 3, p 87*). Rather than being set in the extant

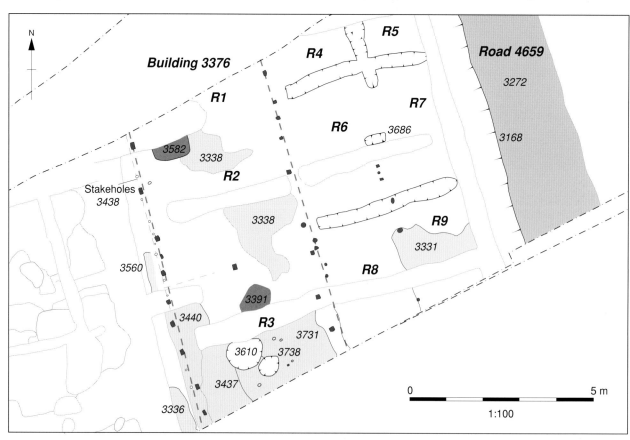

Figure 469: The internal wall of Building **3376**, which may have supported the roof ridge

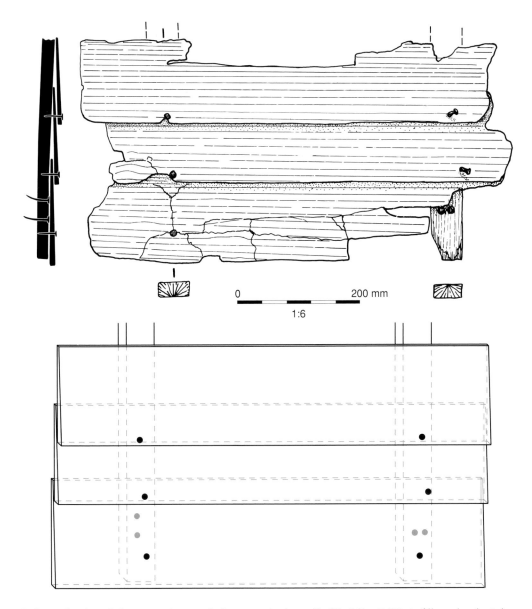

*Figure 470: Oak weather-board shutter, perhaps nailed to a gap in the wall of Building **5688**, to fill a redundant door or window*

construction trench, they were driven into the ground, some 0.33 m apart. This would probably have been impossible without removing the roof covering if they had been long enough to reach the roof, so it seems likely that they formed only a low partition, possibly of wattle similar to that in Period 3B Building *4656* (*4391; Ch 6, p 133*).

A good-quality finish seems to have been the expected norm in Roman timber buildings (*pers obs*), and many of the timbers had smooth, hewn faces. For example, post W1205 (*3252*), discarded in the construction trench of Building *4660* (*Ch 6*), was made from a radial section (probably an eighth split) of very high-quality timber, and had been carefully and accurately worked into a rectangular post with right-angled corners and flat-hewn faces. Most timbers were not, however, finished to quite such a high standard: corners were left waney; some pieces had bark left on; and most were left 'as split'. For example, post

W1209 (*3387*), from Period 3 Building *3772* (*Ch 3*), was made of high-quality straight-grained oak, split and hewn into an approximately squared post, but only two sides were hewn at right-angles, sapwood was left on the third face, and the fourth was left 'as split' (see Fig 459). It could well be the case that only those faces intended to be seen were dressed, and that others were hidden within the structure.

Evidence suggests that most of the buildings had a timber frame, with uprights either set directly into construction trenches, or mortised into horizontal sill beams. The latter were joined at the corners with saddle lap joints. A good example was noted on sill-beam fragment W1013 (Fig 462), found in a layer associated with the final phase of occupation of the Period 4B *principia* (Building *5688*; *Ch 6, pp 216-18*). The spaces between uprights were infilled with wattle panels, and the whole wall then daubed over, for the most part completely hiding the wooden structure, at least at ground level. There was, however, some evidence for different wall treatments. An incomplete weather-boarded panel (6136: W1348; Fig 470) was recovered from the destruction phase of Building 5688 (Period 4C; Ch 6). It appeared to have been battened to a wall, either to cover an opening, or over the wattle and daub to add extra weatherproofing and insulation.

Building construction techniques
Post-in-trench construction
With the exception of Buildings 7200 and 4657 (both Period 3C; Ch 4), the timber buildings were all of post-in-trench construction. This was a common Roman technique, probably because digging trenches is physically easier than digging individual postholes (Hanson 1982, 170). In the case of buildings in the central and southern part of the fort, most of the trenches had flat bottoms, and the flat bases of the posts rested directly on them. The space between posts was filled with wattle panels, the ends of which were inserted into sloping mortises cut into the uprights. In Building 3772 (barrack), it was possible to measure or estimate the distance from the bottom of the lowest mortise (two slots were cut into each post to house the lowest sail or stave of the wattle infill panels) to the bottom of the post. When plotted (Fig 471), it is clear that the slots, which might be expected to have been at floor level, or at a fairly regular height just above floor level, were not at a standard distance from the bottom of the posts, and their height did not increase or decrease regularly along the length of the wall. This seems to suggest, if the slots were cut after the posts were erected, that the bottoms of the trenches were uneven, or that posts were erected with level tops, the bases being packed-up as necessary. If the latter, it would seem reasonable to expect some stone or wooden post-packing, similar to that found in Building 4656 (W994; 4595; Ch 4). Timbers W973 and

W975, both from Period 4C demolition debris (6271) over Building 5688, were also typical of Roman post pads, but as they were not in situ, their use remains uncertain. Both were 0.24 m lengths of squared alder (150 x 80 mm) with sawn ends; both had a square mortise cut in the centre of their faces and could have been sole plates (post pads with a jointing system for keeping them in place) for posts with stub tenons, 40 mm long, on their bases.

Sill-beam construction
Building 7200 (Period 3C; Ch 4) was built using a combination of earthfast posts and long sill beams, or shorter sill beams with a post at each joint. At the corners of the building, the sill beams butted up to corner posts, rather than having saddle lap joints as might be expected, and in the north wall, shorter beams butted up to a central post. The sill beams had a set of almost square blind mortise holes, between 70 mm and 50 mm wide, 50 mm long, and 50 mm deep, cut in their upper surfaces. These held studs with stub tenons at their ends, and with angled rectangular slots for the sails of wattle infill panels. The surviving slots were up to 0.12 m from the face of the beam, suggesting roughly how far below the slots the vertical wattlework was expected to extend. This building was similar to that in London described by Goodburn (1991), in that the wall studs had slots to hold wattle panels in place prior to the application of daub. It did, however, differ in one important aspect, not being framed, but relying on the earthfast posts to provide rigidity. There is a clear distinction between the two methods of construction, in that post-built structures have to be built in situ, whilst rigidly framed structures can be almost entirely prefabricated.

The north wall of Building 7200 was c 9 m long and comprised three posts and two sill beams. The central post was met by an outside lap from one sill beam, and

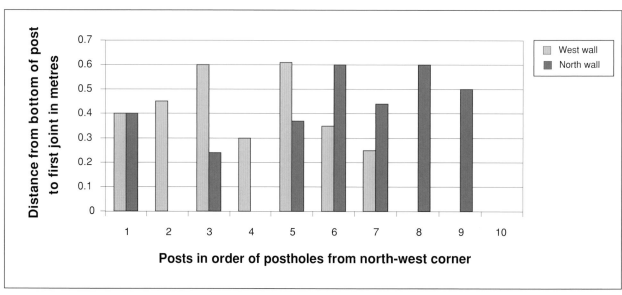

Figure 471: Distance between the lowest slot and the bottom of the posts in Building **3772**

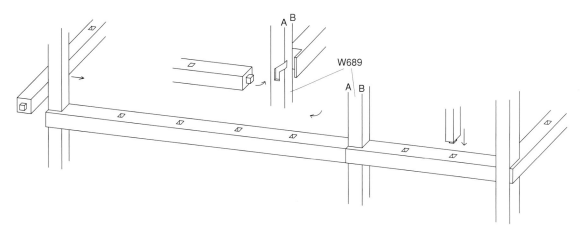

*Figure 472: The construction of the north wall of Period 3C Building **7200***

by a stub tenon on the other (Fig 472). The joint on post W689 (*6891*) suggests that the sills were fitted after the uprights were in position, and from outside the building, by forcing the stub tenon into the dog-leg mortise on the side of the post. The junction between the stub tenon in the left sill beam at the dog-leg mortise of the central post and its entrance corner (Fig 472) indicates that the dog-leg mortise could serve as normal in timber construction, as well as holding the end of a sail in a wattle panel. Care must thus be taken in identifying whether a dog-leg mortise functions as a mortise and tenon joint, holding an oak timber in place, or as a notch to hold the end of a piece of wood in a wattle infill.

In London (Goodburn 1991), Valkenburg (Glasbergen 1974), rural Scole (Ashwin and Tester forthcoming), and Ribchester (Buxton and Howard-Davis 2000, 108 and pl 7), the corner would have comprised a saddle lap joint, the corner post, with a square central tenon at its base, being inserted into a square mortise passing through the centre of the saddle lap joint. Later, in second-century Carlisle (McCarthy 1991, 58–60), a combination of saddle lap joints and posts clasped by the sill beams seems to have been used. A fragment of beam with a saddle lap joint of this type was recorded from Building *5688*, but was not in its original location.

Sill-beam construction can be seen in surviving timber structures elsewhere. At Valkenburg (castle 1; Glasbergen 1974), the early fort was built mainly in alder and oak, using a style in which the sill beams were jointed at the corners and most other intersections. The sills had square through-mortise holes spaced irregularly along their length, into which the studs were set, with long square tenons that went right through the sill beams. The sill-beam constructions seen in London were similar to those from Valkenburg, but made from oak (Goodburn 1991). A single sill-beam structure was found at Scole, with saddle lap corners and through mortises similar to those at Valkenburg, but it was without mortise holes to support upright studs (Ashwin and Tester forthcoming).

Wattle infill panels

Whether the buildings were of post-in-trench construction or used studs on sill beams, the infill between the main uprights was vertical panels of wattle, coated with daub, and probably made to fit the gap, rather than being ready-made to a standard size. The external walls of all the excavated buildings retained evidence for slots in the sides of the surviving upright posts, which were probably intended to hold the panels, and in some cases still had the horizontal sails *in situ*. The woven rods also survive, and can be seen in cross-section in the east wall of Building *3772* (Pl 217). This vertical wattle panelling is also

*Plate 217: The remains of wattle panelling in the east wall of Building **3772***

known from Valkenburg, Colchester, and London (Glasbergen 1974; Crummy 1984; Goodburn 1991). In London, the evidence suggests that the panels were over 2 m tall (Goodburn 1991). A woven panel, similar to those that must have been used between the wall posts of most of the buildings, survived in the destruction debris of Building **5688**.

Doorways and doors

Two internal door thresholds survived within the *principia* (Building **5688**, Period 4; *Ch 5*), complete with holes for harr-hung doors. The narrower example (W670) was 0.83 m long by 0.17 m wide, and had a lip along one edge, against which the door closed. No evidence was seen for the method of fitting the threshold to the doorpost at the harr-hinge end, but the latch end had a short stub tenon that presumably fitted into the face of the latch post. The second threshold (W675) was 0.84 m long by 0.14 m wide, and also had a lip along one edge; it had a stub tenon at the harr end. There is good evidence for harr-hung doors (doors which pivot about a vertical wooden axis) at Valkenburg (Glasbergen 1974).

A fragment of wattle woven through a slot and back round the next timber (from Building **7392**, Period 3A) may have been part of an internal door. If this were so, then it raises the question of whether, if there were woven but undaubed doors, the internal walls were also undaubed. Elsewhere, at Vindolanda (Birley 1994, pl 4.2) and at Papcastle (C Howard-Davis *pers comm*), plank-clad doors have been recorded.

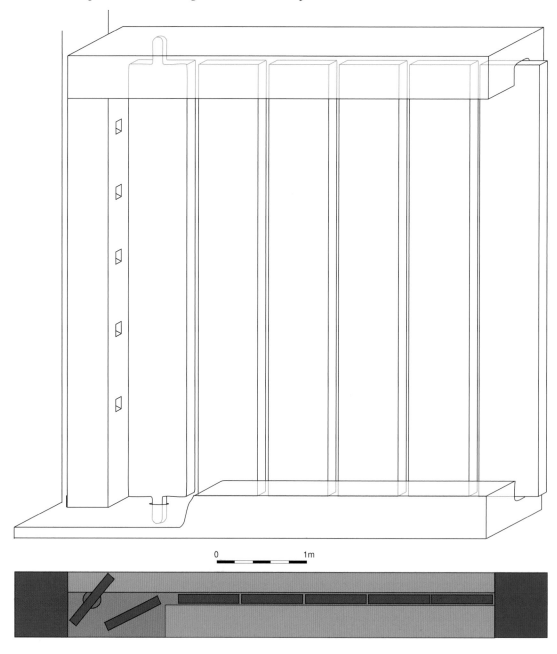

0   1m

Figure 473: Reconstruction of proposed shutter system on the south wall of Building **5689**

A third threshold beam (W660; *6765*) was noted in the south wall of Building *5689*, facing onto the main east to west road. It was more than 1.82 m long (0.31 x 0.19 m in cross-section), and had a slot cut along the entire length of its upper face, with an oval hole, which together might have formed part of a shutter system. The oval hole could have held a hinged plank that closed against (and thereby locked in) movable vertical boards that were fed into slots in the sill and lintel (Fig 473). A similarly positioned slot survived on the wall of Building *4656*, which also faced the main east to west road, suggesting that they might represent open fronts. Similar thresholds in stone survive along the fronts of the shops at Pompeii, and casts of the carbonised wooden doors give some indication of their appearance (Beard 2008, 78, pl 30).

Drain construction

In addition to the buildings of Periods 3 and 4, there were also wooden drains, adjacent to, and sometimes running beneath, roads and buildings. In all cases, the sides of the drain were revetted, either by wooden boards held in place by stakes, or with wattlework behind the stakes, or by frames backed by boards or wattlework; the tops were covered with partially removable wooden lids. Two of these structures were examined in detail (*see Appendix 9*).

A large drain, *6781* (0.56 x 0.56 m), ran along the northern edge of main road *7477* in Period 4A. Its sides were revetted with wattle, and braced at intervals with mortised frames, presumably to prevent collapse (Fig 474). This drain was then covered by a series of carefully constructed plank lids or 'bridges' (Fig 475). Similar drain covers were encountered in a period 5 *fabrica* at Vindolanda, erected after AD 112 (Birley 1994, pl 7.2).

Drain *6362* (Period 4B; Fig 476) lay under the floor of the *principia* (Building *5688*) and was of a different construction. Timber-lined, it was covered by a plank more than 3.8 m long and up to 0.36 m wide, which would have weighed more than 60 kg. The sides of the structure were formed by planks set on edge and held *c* 0.2 m apart at the top by cross struts, creating a drain *c* 0.2 x 0.2 m.

Drain *5925* was a large wood-lined, sub-surface drain between 0.9 m and 1 m wide, located on the northern edge of road *7477* (Period 4B). It was spanned by a large number of curved and knotty timbers, possibly originally supporting a cover. Drain *5920*, which was a contemporary surface drain situated on the southern edge of road *7477*, was completely different in design. For most of its excavated length it was lined with horizontal withies woven around stakes, but where it crossed the north end of north to south road *7479* (at the junction of that road with road *7477*), it comprised a 4.6 m length of oak trunk (*5922*) with a slot (0.2 x 0.2 m) cut

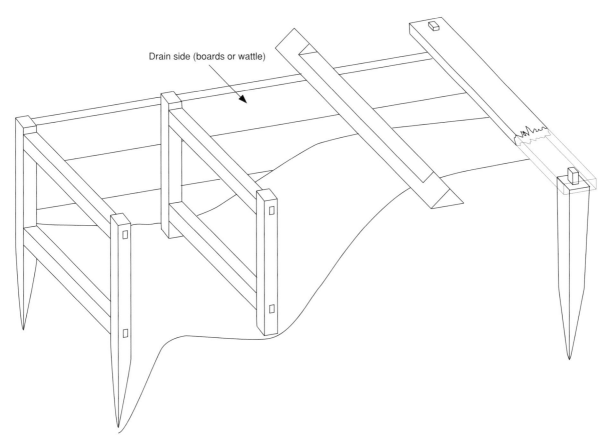

Drain side (boards or wattle)

Figure 474: Frame forming the structure of Period 4A drain 6781

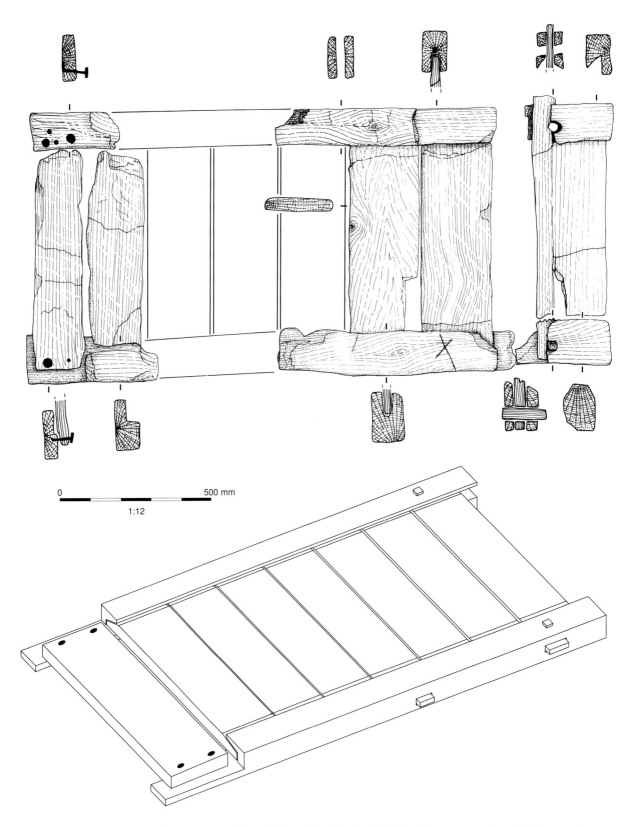

Figure 475: Framed drain cover of drain 6781, with nailed planks allowing access to the drain beneath

down its length to form a channel, through which water flowed. It is unclear whether this was a covered drain designed to withstand the heavy traffic at this major road junction, or an open gutter intended to trap surface water.

Water pipes

Several wooden water pipes were found during the excavation, from Periods 3, 4, and 6. No complete lengths were recovered from Period 3, and there was only one, 1.5 m long, from Period 4 (Table 51). Several complete examples were found in Period 6

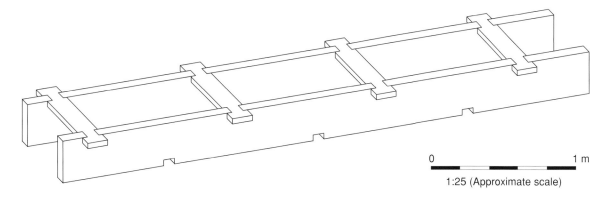

Figure 476: Part of Period 4B plank drain 6362, made from high-quality oak

Wood no	Period	Pipe length (m)	Pipe diameter (m)	Bore diameter (m)	Junctions	Notes
W622	3C	>1.07	0.15	0.06	Iron strip	Bore diameter not recorded, but estimated from drawing
W623	3C	>1.02	0.16	0.08	Iron strip	
W610	4B	1.5	0.18	0.04	Oak block, 90° turn upwards	
W602	4B	>0.7	0.165	0.08	Oak block, straight	
W602	4B	>0.8	0.16	0.075	Oak block, straight	
W602	4B	>1.2	0.19	0.07	Oak block, straight	
W609	6B	1.15	0.25	0.07	Butt joint	Bore diameter not recorded, but estimated from drawing
W613	6B	1.15	0.02	0.07	Butt joint	
W614	6B	1.46	0.02	0.07	Butt joint	

Table 51: Details of complete water pipes, and those with a recorded bore diameter

Plate 218: Water pipe of alder, the originally circular bore having been flattened by the weight of soil above

contexts, being between 1.15 m and 1.46 m in length. Other pipes were recorded on site, but not retained; they appear to have been between 0.85 m and 1.75 m in length. Where the species was determined, it was consistently alder, the pipes being made from roundwood, 0.15–0.25 m in diameter. The bore of the pipes was usually *c* 70 mm (except pipe W610 (*6531*), from Period 4B road **7477**, which was *c* 40 mm). It was, however, difficult to measure with accuracy, as they

had been distorted by the weight of soil above, creating a flattened oval in cross-section (Pl 218). In all cases, the hole was bored using an auger (the profile of that used to bore a pipe section (W1333) being shown in Figure 477 A). In Period 6B, several broken lengths of pipe were used as sleeper beams in order to level the pipe runs (Fig 477 B). W1333 (from Period 6B drain *5610*) appeared to have been broken whilst being manufactured, as it was only partly bored, and it

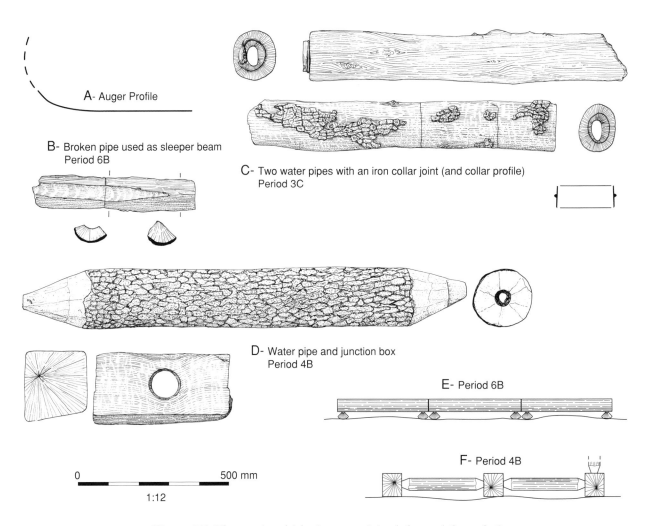

A- Auger Profile

B- Broken pipe used as sleeper beam
Period 6B

C- Two water pipes with an iron collar joint (and collar profile)
Period 3C

D- Water pipe and junction box
Period 4B

E- Period 6B

F- Period 4B

0   500 mm

1:12

Figure 477: The way in which pipes were joined changed through time

is possible that it was abandoned when the auger jammed as, in practice, when boring a trunk, the auger has to be extracted frequently in order to clear the cut wood from the hole. If this is not done often enough, the auger will jam, and it is more cost-effective to split the log and retrieve the auger, than to break the tool, which was presumably more expensive to replace.

There appeared to be a distinct chronological difference in the manner in which pipe lengths were joined. In Period 3C, the ends of the pipes were cut straight across and joined with a circular iron collar (this had a central rib up to which the pipes were forced; Fig 477 C). Pipes from Period 4B had their ends tapered and jammed into holes (chiselled rather than augered) cut in large blocks of oak (Fig 477 D), which acted as junction boxes (Pl 219). During Period 6B, the pipes were butted up to each other (Fig 477 E; *Ch 9*). It is not clear whether they were formally joined, but an iron concretion was seen over one joint, which might imply the former presence of an iron collar, as can be seen in contemporary drains in Colchester (Crummy 1984, 115). The Period 4B pipeline (*Ch 6*), consisting of alder pipes and oak junction boxes, would undoubtedly have been watertight, and thus could have carried

Plate 219: Period 4B pipes and junction boxes in situ

water under pressure (Fig 447 F). Most of the junction boxes formed straight joints, but W594 (*6532*), at the corner of the *principia* (Building **5688**), made a right-angled turn from horizontal to vertical, and could thus have carried pressurised water up into a water trough, spigot, or fountain, or if not under pressure, could have drained a downspout from the roof. An identical drain can be seen in essentially contemporary deposits at Vindolanda (Birley 1994, pl 11.2).

The reuse of timber

There is little doubt that significant amounts of timber were salvaged and reused when any particular building was remodelled or demolished, with some appearing in later buildings, and others in new structures, like the various drains. This can be demonstrated by the dendrochronological evidence (*Appendix 16*), where timbers felled during Period 3 were reused in new buildings alongside timbers felled in Period 4.

The Roman carpenter's toolkit
R Darrah and C Howard-Davis

Evidence from the site has enabled a carpenter's toolkit to be reconstructed, in part at least. With identifications based on toolmarks seen on the wood, and tools found on the site, it covers most of the activities associated with construction (Table 52). While not directly associated with the structural wood, antler hoes, probably used in digging construction trenches, were recovered from Periods 4A and 6C (*Ch 20*).

Tool	Blade width	Context no	Wood no	Comments
Auger or awl	6 mm diameter holes	*6746*	586	Board base of wicker box
Auger	8 mm	*6419*	1407	For edge pegs to join together board from a coopered vessel
Auger	12 mm	*4373*	1294	Spacing of holes along length (in mm): 130; 125; 132; 241
Auger	15 mm	*6136*	1364	Perforated board
Auger	15 mm	*6472*	1081	Drain cross piece
Auger	19.5 mm	*4472*	1305	Countersunk nail
Auger used as a pipe borer	~70 mm	*5700*	614	1.5 m shaft (Period 4B), and 1.75 m shaft (Period 6B)
Axe	>68 mm	*6922*	1560	Off-cut
Axe	~80 mm	*6187*	671	Angled entry makes this an axe
Axe	>80 mm	*3428*	1213	
Axe	>98 mm	*4442*	1301	
Axe	Signature not at right-angles to blade edge	*6923*	1562	On four-sided point
Chisel	~15 mm blade width	*6922*	1561	Within mortise
Chisel	16 mm blade width	*6944*	1575	Mortise, species other than oak
Chisel	16.5 mm blade width	*6549*	1462	Species other than oak, through mortise
Chisel	~20 mm blade width	*6906*	1546	Grooves in beams from drain
Chisel	25 mm blade width	*6911*	1549	Grooves in beams from drain
Chisel	26 mm blade width	*7020*	1599	Within mortise
Saw	2.5 mm kerf	*6922*	1560	Off-cut
Saw	3 mm kerf	*3268*	1207	
Saw	3.5 mm kerf	*4472*	1305	7 mm overcut
Saw	180 mm from blade edge to frame	*7412*	1677	Board sawn from both edges and last 10 mm broken
Saw	1.5 mm cut per stroke	*6935*	1570	Drain post
Saw	2.2 mm cut per stroke	*6922*	1561	Drain post
Saw	At angle across timber	*6312*	810	Off-cut
Saw	Cutting knot in cleaving	*6444*	1426	Branch on split surface
Rip saw		*6601, 6767, 6642*	633, 718, 719	

Table 52: Evidence for the carpenter's toolkit

Axe marks were clearly visible on a number of the timbers, in the main the result of felling and hewing. Despite this, no complete blade profiles or even blade widths were identified, the widest blade seen being over 98 mm. A small iron axe was unstratified, and it remains uncertain whether it was a Roman or medieval implement; the blade was *c* 43 mm wide (*Ch 17, p 758*). There was no surviving evidence for the use of adzes, all the hewn faces being consistent with axe use.

A range of other tools has been identified or postulated from analysis of the surviving toolmarks seen on the surfaces, and within the joints of the timbers used on the site. Well-preserved toolmarks within joints imply the use of chisels of ~15 mm, 16 mm, 16.5 mm, ~20 mm, 25 mm, and 26 mm width. No woodworking chisels were noted amongst the ironwork, however. A range of several auger sizes was noted, indicating the use of tools that bored holes of 6 mm, 8 mm, 12 mm, 15 mm, and 19.5 mm diameters. The 8 mm holes were from coopered vessels which could have arrived at the site ready-made, so, unlike the other tools, this size of auger was not necessarily used on site. A special auger must have been used to bore out the water pipes. The longest of the pipes was 1.75 m, which suggests that the tool used (including an iron handle) would have been at least that long and probably longer, as it is not usual practice to auger holes from opposite ends of a pipe, since it will tend to break (R Darrah *pers obs*). The hole it produced was mostly *c* 70 mm in diameter.

Evidence for the use of cross-cut saws survived on the ends of boards and posts, although decay at the bottom ends of *in situ* posts can sometimes make it impossible to identify the method of skilful cross-cutting, which can also be achieved using an axe. It is clear that cross-cut saws were being used to cut timbers to length. They were also being used to cut joints in planks and beams, which have enabled the identification of the kerf (width of cut) of the saws at 2.5 mm, 3 mm and 3.5 mm. A conserved iron blade fragment has a thickness above the teeth of *c* 1.5 mm (*Ch 17*, Fig 432.2). These were undoubtedly framed saws, and the depth of the cut made when cross-cutting wide boards (where the cut was made from both edges to the centre) showed the distance from the blade edge to the frame to be over 180 mm (board W1677, Period 3A Building *7392*). The rate of sawing, dependent on factors such as the hardness and thickness of the timber, was recorded from two timbers as being 1.5 mm and 2.5 mm per stroke. The evidence for rip sawing (sawing along the grain of the timber instead of across it) was limited, but three pieces (less than 1% of the sample) had clear evidence of such sawing. The best of them (board W633, in Period 3C drain *6399*) had evidence of sawing at right-angles to the length, with the last 0.3 m being split. This suggests that the sawing was done with

two trestles rather than the see-saw method with a single trestle (Garton and Salisbury 1995).

A hammer, used for nailing, was recovered (*Ch 17*, Fig 434.5), together with large numbers of nails. There were, in addition, several fragments of saw blades (*Ch 17*, Fig 432). Several punches and awls, all relatively small, were also found (*Ch 17*, Figs 431-5), although these could have been used in carpentry, metalworking, or leatherworking, all of which are known to have been undertaken on the site during the Roman period (*Ch 15*). A short fragment of an extremely fine-quality wooden ruler (*p 812*) was found in a Period 4B deposit in Building *5689*, where its accuracy might well associate it with the production and repair of armour (see *Ch 15*), rather than woodworking, as none of the timbers seemed to have been measured to the inch. In addition, a wooden tool, identified as a possible plasterer's float (*pp 813-14*), was recovered from Building *4653* (Period 3A), and could have been used in the application of daub, or a finer surface render.

Clearly, a range of other tools must have been used, including wedges and mauls for splitting timber, claw irons for extracting nails, large wooden mallets for driving water pipes, ladders, plumb lines, and strings for marking out buildings (although the irregularity of joint and post spacing suggests that much measuring was done by eye), but there is no direct evidence for the use of these tools. Where countersunk nails are reported (only one is recorded on this site) this implies the use of a metal punch to drive the nail home.

The medieval timber

Although timber was recovered from several medieval contexts, the great similarity between many of the medieval timbers and those from Roman features strongly suggests that, in mixed or isolated contexts, both around the castle and elsewhere in the city, dating on appearance or woodworking technique cannot be regarded as entirely reliable, without supplementary evidence.

Several of the medieval timbers were very much like Roman cleft timber in appearance, and small post W96 (dated AD 1368–1408; *Appendix 16*) was remarkably similar to posts used by the Romans. The medieval material included the reused remnants of a framed building, all of which appear similar to Roman examples (for example, a small-diameter medieval beam with rectangular through mortises is very similar to a Roman timber from Building *5688*).

The conversion of trees into structural components
Fragmentary timbers from ditch *1230* (Period 8i; *Ch 11*) comprised roundwood and cleft baulks that may have been stakes. Few of them were oak. Little

evidence for growth rate survived and almost all of the pieces could have been cut from trees under 0.3 m in diameter. Exceptions include plank W103 (over 0.34 m wide), and radially cleft board W288 (both from fills of Period 8i ditch *1230*), both of which must have come from oaks of at least 0.4 m diameter. This use of smaller trees is quite is distinct from the large-diameter oak used in the Period 3 Roman fort.

Building construction techniques

Only one medieval timber building survived. Somewhat flimsy, Building *1492* (Period 8iii) was of sill-beam construction. The timbers were not joined at the corners and the upright structure of the walls seems to have been supported by stakes.

Fence *2064* marked the boundary between tenements *1234* and *1235* in Period 8iii. Made from timbers up to 0.05 m thick, several were clearly reused boards, whilst others were radially cleft sections of oak from a tree with a diameter of 0.3 m. Most had been chamfered at the end to drive them into the ground, or were pointed; timber W334 shows clear axe marks on its point.

Discussion

C Howard-Davis

The large collection of Roman and medieval timbers from these excavations has produced a considerable amount of information on a wide range of aspects of the provision and use of wood in construction.

Woodland management

It is thought that the alder and ash used widely in the first buildings erected within the fort (Period 3A) derived in large part from the initial clearance of the site and its locale, and was from entirely unmanaged woodland. From Period 3B on, however, the use of large, straight-grained oak timber from mature trees must point to the existence of relatively large stands of ancient forest in the vicinity, at least to the end of the first century AD, when they were apparently being exploited by woodsmen from the forts at Carlisle and Vindolanda, and presumably elsewhere. Whether this timber was freely available to all, or was regarded by local populations as untouchable, perhaps because they formed sacred groves, as attested elsewhere in Britain and Europe (see Cunliffe 1999, 197–8), or was ignored as a resource by the late Iron Age building traditions of the area, remains unknown, but it is clear, since many were over 400 years old, that they had hitherto been allowed to grow unchecked. It seems unlikely that there would have been a great need to manage woodland for building timber until this resource had been severely depleted, which, if trees were selected individually, rather than larger-scale felling, could have taken some time. It is likely,

however, that considerable amounts of woodland, probably in closer proximity to the fort, would have been managed for roundwood from early on, the methods used including coppicing, as coppiced wood not only produces the resource for woven wattle (McCarthy 1986, 342) and the numerous other poles and stakes required, but also provides wood for fuel and charcoal production, the demand for which would have been considerable.

Exploitation of the high forest would not have destroyed it completely, although the size of the biggest trees available may well have decreased over time, and there would have been a greater tendency to fell poorer-quality trees, as seen in Period 4. If the first major felling of large oaks took place in AD 83, regenerated woodland would have been producing viable roundwood in a few years, and timber standards suitable for large poles or small posts by about AD 120. For example, the very fast-grown oak, from which a sill beam in Building *5689* was cut, could easily have been a dominant tree growing through the canopy of regenerating woodland. Although there was a slight reduction in the quality of the timber used during Period 4, there does not seem to have been significant pressure on the resource until some years after the arrival of the Roman army. A shortage of good-quality timber can lead to the use of sub-standard wood, as indicated by the widespread use of large numbers of small trees for studs or posts seen in London (Goodburn 1991), or the conversion by sawing of fast-grown knotty timber, as seen during the second century at Scole (Ashwin and Tester forthcoming), but neither practice is evident at Carlisle in the earlier phases.

The timber resource

Whilst it seems likely that the outer appearance of Roman buildings on the site did not change particularly, it is clear that the materials from which they were constructed, and the way they were used, did, with the available forest resource changing considerably through time, and the method of construction varying from building to building. In addition, comparison between the Carlisle buildings and those of the fort at Valkenburg (Glasbergen 1974) show some marked similarities and contrasts. For instance, both at Carlisle and Valkenburg, the earliest buildings show a heavy reliance on alder and ash, neither a particularly durable timber. The fact that both sites were subsequently waterlogged presumably suggests that conditions were more or less identical prior to the arrival of the Roman army, with alder woods relatively close by, if not on the site. Thus it seems reasonable to suggest that the use of alder and ash reflects pragmatic use of the locally available resource, with the stress on the rapid erection of military buildings a paramount requirement, principally, it might be assumed, for accommodation and weatherproof storage. Relatively small trees provided much of the timber, including squared whole trunks, and squared half or quarter trunks. Again, this might reflect an emphasis on speed, rather than the considered or economical choice of timbers, and it might also be the case that much of this wood derived from an inferred practice of clear-felling not only the site of the fort, but also a substantial *cordon sanitaire*, perhaps including the banks of the nearby rivers.

In later periods, both at Valkenburg and in Carlisle, oak was favoured overwhelmingly, much deriving from large, straight-grained trees, hundreds of years old. The economy inherent in the manner in which the trees were converted, and the resulting timbers used, points to specialist woodsmen selecting specific trees for specific projects, and there is strong evidence from the dendrochronological study (*Appendix 16*) to suggest that, wherever the woodland from which these trees were drawn was located, it was also exploited by those building at Vindolanda, to the east. Evidence seems to show, not surprisingly, that trees were converted at the felling site, with the trunks and larger branches split and hewn into a range of boards and posts. In the main, the trunks were split radially, with the distinctive triangular-sectioned baulks of timber created by this process being sub-divided across the grain when the size of the piece allowed. This process much reduced the weight of timber to be transported from the felling site, and the marked lack of woodworking debris (bark, chips, and so on) has led to the conclusion that on some occasions the riven faces of timbers were even axe-hewn and squared at the felling site, being brought to the site in a condition more-or-less ready for use (just needing to be cut to size). Economy of materials seems to have led to the frequent reuse of timbers, both in comparable buildings and as auxiliary pieces in different structures, for example structural timbers used as levelling in a drain.

Wooden buildings and structures
Most of the buildings were of post-in-trench construction, and the timbers used in what were, for the most part, long rectangular structures were roughly squared posts with surprisingly small cross-sections, although there is evidence for larger posts in some of the more important buildings. In general terms, larger posts were found in the front walls and in central longitudinal internal walls (where they might have been taller and more substantial in order to support the roof). Usually the posts stood in rectangular-profiled trenches, and their irregular spacing seems to be a constant feature, seen also at Valkenburg (Glasbergen 1974) and other Roman buildings in Britain, like those at Vindolanda (Birley 1994), Ribchester (Buxton and Howard-Davis 2000), and elsewhere in Carlisle

(McCarthy 1991; Caruana in prep). It does not appear that it was particularly important for the trench to have a level base, and it seems that some posts were raised up, presumably to achieve a level on the tops, by the insertion of wood and stone packing, or post pads, within the trench before it was backfilled, though this was rarely seen *in situ*. This certainly seems to indicate that timbers were not supplied cut into standard lengths, and that, on occasion, some of those available were almost too small for the job in hand, perhaps again hinting at some stockpiling, alongside the choice and use of wood felled and converted for the specific job.

Some buildings were constructed on ground-laid sill beams, but rather than being a rigid-framed structure with saddle lap joints at the corners, as has commonly been the case elsewhere, they butted, or were jointed to, corner posts and centre posts in the longer walls. This is a building technique seen elsewhere in Carlisle, at Castle Street (for example, period 6A building 806), where it was combined with saddle lap joints at some corners (McCarthy 1991, 33 and fig 23). The sill beams were mortised to support upright studs. The evidence from the site does not appear to indicate the mixture of both techniques in a single building, as can be seen at Ribchester (Buxton and Howard-Davis 2000) and was noted by Hanson (1982) at a number of other sites. In all cases, the space between studs was filled with custom-made woven wattle panels, either inserted ready-made, or, perhaps more likely, woven *in situ*, after horizontal sails had been set into slots in the sides of the studs. The wattle panels were then daubed and rendered. The irregularly shaped, and sometimes poorly dressed, timbers used as studs might suggest that the daub was carried across the entire wall, so that all the timbers were hidden. There is evidence for the use of weather-boarding in Period 4, specifically on Building *5688*, which might well mark it out as of higher status than others on the site, unsurprising given its interpretation as the *principia*. Evidence from elsewhere (Goodburn 1991) suggests that such buildings were around 2 m high to the top of the wall. Despite the presence of several angled off-cuts, the pitch of the roofs remains unknown, and would presumably have depended on the roofing material chosen.

The internal partitions within buildings seem on the whole to have been added subsequent to the erection of the shell. They seem to have been of wattle, possibly daubed, and either set in trenches or with vertical sails driven into the floor. This must have lent versatility to the division and use of space, and must presumably have meant that many of the partitions did not reach the roof, especially if they were stakes, although tall partitions could have been inserted before the buildings were roofed. Nothing is known of the fenestration of the buildings, although the amount of window glass (*Ch 18*) indicates that some at least were glazed. There is, however, evidence for the position of internal doors in the form of lipped thresholds, and a possible wattle door fragment. A single outside threshold seems to imply that some of the buildings had vertically shuttered frontages facing the main east to west road, which would seem to be a sensible solution for providing extra light in workshops, or providing an open frontage that could be secured overnight.

The naturally wet site seems to have been extensively drained, and several different styles of drain were noted, suggesting that the design changed with the size, and perhaps the intended permanency, of the drain. Many were simply plank-lined, often made with reused or high-quality wood, whilst others were wattle-lined and braced with custom-made frames. In the latter case, evidence seems to show that no less than three styles of frame were used over a distance of 15 m, which, if it does not point to frequent renewal and repair, would seem to suggest that the style of frame was of no particular import, and individual carpenters working on the construction each found their own solution to the problem of bracing the drain's wicker sides. Until the end of Period 4, and again in Period 6, wooden pipes were vital to the distribution of (presumably) clean water within the site, with bored alder trunk pipes capable of carrying water under pressure. Identical drains have been found at Vindolanda (Birley 1994), and both used oak block junction boxes to link the alder pipes.

Conclusions

The results of this analysis have served to emphasise the wealth of evidence that can be gained from a waterlogged site, where organic materials, and especially wood, have survived in quantity. Whilst the survival of Roman wooden structures is relatively common in Carlisle, as a result of the widespread existence of waterlogged deposits within the city centre, it is still uncommon in Britain, and beyond. Thus the data gained from the site have added significantly to the body of knowledge concerning the construction and appearance of Roman military buildings in the first and second centuries AD, and have, by comparison with surviving structures elsewhere in Roman Britain, begun to establish the variety of materials and techniques used, perhaps on a regional basis, or reflecting the ethnic origins of the troops engaged in the construction. This has also emphasised the small size of the timbers used, indeed, the total lack of standardisation in building timbers and the absence of military precision in the finishing of the wood. The analysis has also suggested that changes in building techniques and external finishes might even reflect status, and that, far from being permanent, the internal divisions within buildings could have been changed relatively easily, suggesting that although the size and external

conformation of buildings such as barracks might have been relatively standardised, internal arrangements could be altered to suit the needs of the inhabitants, or the range of activities carried out within.

In addition, the analysis has added to the broader picture of the environs of the fort and the hinterland from which it drew its timber supplies. There is nothing to suggest that ready-cut timbers or prefabricated buildings were brought to the site; rather, the evidence provides a picture of specialist woodsmen selecting the timber needed for a particular project, almost on a tree-by-tree basis. Analysis also suggests that there was a relatively constant supply of timber, although with a number of military establishments likely to have been drawing on the same resource, it is unsurprising to note that there was a slow, but general, decline in the quality of timber available. In addition, it is clear that military carpenters and builders were pragmatic enough to reuse scrap timbers in a number of circumstances.

Although less medieval timber survived, it too provides some indication of the nature of structures and construction techniques, the latter, where surviving, remarkably similar to their Roman predecessors. Sadly, timbers did not survive in most of the medieval buildings excavated, deposits by that time having risen above the water table. Again, the surviving wood allowed some speculation on the nature of the locally available timber supply, suggesting that although substantial trees were still to be found within an acceptable distance of the site, they were no longer the ageing giants that had been available to the Romans.

The Wooden Artefacts

C Howard-Davis

Over and above the huge assemblage of structural wood from the site, there were a few wooden artefacts of other kinds (c 50 fragments, representing approximately 45 objects). They form a disparate group, their survival reliant entirely on depositional circumstance. Most were preserved as a result of the widespread waterlogging, others, notably the fragment of furniture, by slow carbonisation, possibly as a result of burning rubbish.

Extensive waterlogging was confined to Periods 3 and 4, the Roman timber forts, and it is not surprising that the chronological distribution of wooden artefacts reflects this. In addition, the fills of the medieval castle's outer ward ditch (Period 8) were also waterlogged, and at least one wooden item was recovered from there. With regard to the latter, there is some evidence for residual Roman material; the turned bowl from this period is, however, impossible to date.

The species of wood used for small artefacts is often dictated by the nature of the artefact and the particular qualities of the wood. Thus boxwood is commonly used for hair combs and small turned items, as its fine, dense nature is particularly suited to their production. Pugsley (2003, 15) notes that boxwood (*Buxus* sp) was so commonly used for combs that *buxus* in fact became a common Latin synonym for a comb. Ash seems to have been particularly favoured for larger turned vessels.

Objects of personal adornment or dress

Part of a wooden-soled sandal or patten came from *4117*, the fill of a construction trench for Building *3772* (Period 3B), where it was probably residual. This is discussed with the rest of the Roman footwear (*Ch 20, p 840*).

Combs

Four plain, double-sided boxwood combs of typical Roman form were recovered (*4, 8, 31*, Fig 478.1-3; *41, Appendix 9*). These appear to have been common day-to-day objects, and one, from deposits associated with a Period 3A barrack, Building *1222*, seems likely to have been the personal property of a resident, whilst those from Period 3B were probably residual, appearing in construction trenches. These are common finds on Roman sites in Carlisle (Padley 1991c, 204, fig 179) and elsewhere, suggesting a fairly widespread interest in hygiene and appearance. As often noted, these combs closely resemble the nit combs of today, whose fine, close-set teeth are used to rid hair of lice. It is growing increasingly common for analysis to show the presence of evidence for human head lice in such combs (Fell 2000), as is the case here (*Ch 22*), and their long, closely set teeth make them ideal for the removal of both the live louse and its egg cases (nits). Evidence from Vindolanda, however, suggests that their use was not confined to humans, with animal hair and varieties of lice associated

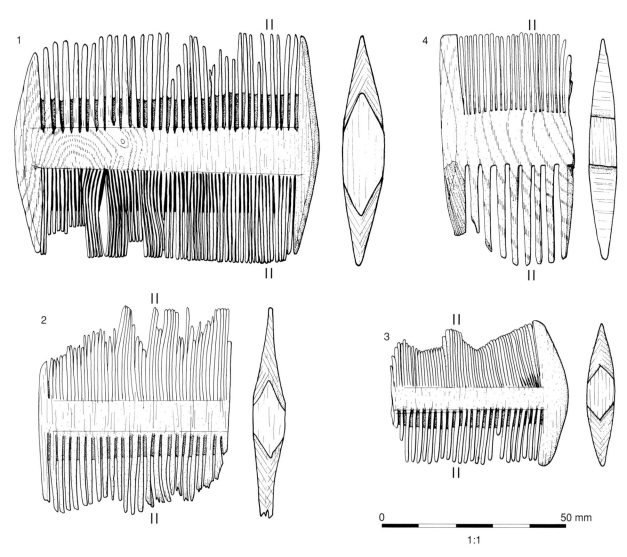

Figure 478: Roman, and possibly medieval, combs

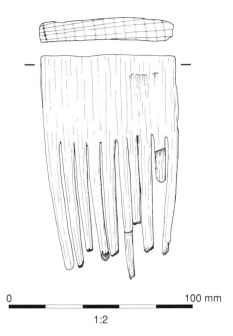

Figure 479: Coarser combs, perhaps for grooming horses

with other animals retrieved from their teeth, one suggestion being that they were possibly being used to remove the hairs from cow-hide (Birley 1977, 123-4). A fifth, slightly coarser comb (7; Fig 478.4) was recovered from the construction fill (1785) of a medieval tenement boundary (2065). Boxwood combs are a long-lived type, and their form changed little. It is thus not possible to ascertain whether this example is a residual Roman object or a contemporary medieval example. The more complete examples clearly show the manner in which the comb blank was scored and laid out prior to cutting. During the Roman period, production seems to have been a specialised occupation, working from roughly shaped blanks (Ferrarini 1992), and it is possible, although perhaps unlikely, that most were imported.

A second, much coarser, type of comb (3; Fig 479) was found in a Period 3B external layer (999). At the contemporary cavalry fort of Ribchester to the south, these coarse combs seem likely to have been associated with horse management (Howard-Davis and Whitworth 2000, 335), possibly serving to groom the long hair of horses' tails and manes. This must also have been a consideration at Carlisle, where horse trappings of outstanding quality (Ch 17) suggest a concern with good management and the presentation of horses. It must be borne in mind, however, that Wild (1970b, 154, obj 12) suggests that such combs have a link with textile production, and were used for combing flax fibres after retting, in order to free them, and align them for spinning. Waxed linen thread must have been extensively used for sewing leather goods and could well have been spun as needed (see below). Although later in date, Period 4A Building 7396 has been identified

as a possible leather-working workshop, and there is no reason to believe that the soldiers of Period 3 had any less need for leather goods.

Objects used in the manufacture or working of textiles

A turned wooden spindle whorl (35; Fig 480.1) came from what might well have been a leatherworking workshop, Period 4A Building 7396. It is possible that it was used for the production of relatively coarse thread, perhaps linen, of the kind that might have been used for sewing leather. A second fragment from the same context, clearly originating from a turned plano-convex disc (36; Fig 480.2), has been tentatively identified as a second whorl, although whether or not it was originally perforated is not clear.

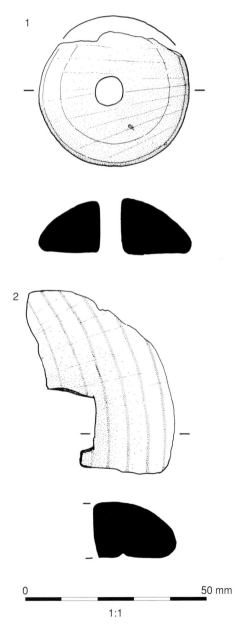

Figure 480: Wooden spindle whorls

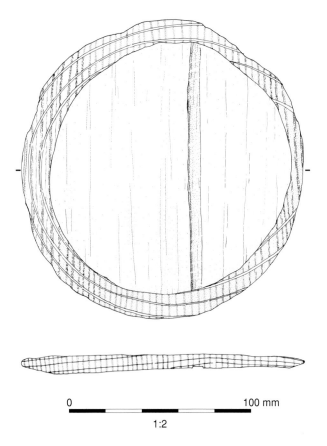

Figure 481: Round oak base of a stave-built vessel

0   100 mm

1:2

Household utensils and furniture

Household utensils and furniture form a disparate group, most being relatively common finds. Object *9* (*pp 810-12*), a carbonised decorated table leg, is of some importance in illustrating the levels of luxury and comfort expected by at least some of the inhabitants of the fort.

Stave-built and coopered vessels
(with a contribution by R Darrah)
The round oak base of a relatively small stave-built vessel (*13*; Fig 481) was found within Building **4653**. Its size (158 mm in diameter) suggests a small bucket or tankard, like that known from the Corbridge hoard (Allason-Jones and Bishop 1988, 83–6), and, like that example, it could have been a personal possession of a soldier billeted in the building. These vessels seem to have had their origins in the late Iron Age (*ibid*) and to have continued in use throughout the first century AD at least. Their handles and other metal escutcheons are relatively common finds and often hark back to flowing native designs for their decoration, but it is interesting that none were found during these excavations.

Fragments of a large barrel or cask (*24*; Pl 220) were found in Period 4B metalled surface **7475**. In all, fragments of seven staves and a base were recovered, and can be partially reconstructed (Fig 482), being some 0.91 m in diameter. The wood is silver fir (*Abies alba*),

Plate 220: Base of barrel 24

as seems most commonly the case. It is thought that large containers such as this were closely associated with the Rhine wine trade (White 1975, 143), but obviously empty barrels have many uses, including as pit and well linings (Earwood 1993, 79), and were often reused, as this example appears to have been. Conservation suggests that the outside of the barrel was branded, presumably with a description of the contents, or the shipper, but all that is legible is a letter O (Pl 221).

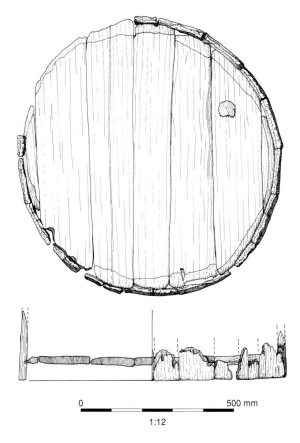

0   500 mm

1:12

Figure 482: Partial reconstruction of barrel 24

Plate 221: Brand on barrel 24

Several of the timbers reused in buildings have been identified as originating from the bases of barrels or tubs (Table 53). These were all softwood boards that were edge-pegged together. Two have been identified as silver fir (*Abies alba*) and appear to be from the base and wall of a small barrel or tub, with an estimated diameter of 0.36 m (from boards W1407 and W1413, both from occupation layers within Building *5689*), much smaller than that of wine barrel 24. The rural settlement at Scole produced evidence for the production of oak tubs of about 0.8 m diameter, and there were also silver fir tubs of 0.6 m diameter (R Darrah *pers comm*). In London, evidence was found for barrels of 0.66 m, 0.68 m, and 0.93 m diameter, again all probably silver fir (Goodburn 1991). That of 0.66 m was estimated to have a capacity of 80–90 gallons, equivalent to about 15 amphorae.

Object W596 (from *7053*, an external layer associated with the Period 3B-3D *principia* (Building *7391*; *Ch 4*) was semi-circular, but without edge pegs for the

other half, and might originally have been a single disc of 0.16 m diameter (*Appendix 9*). This would be rather small for a coopered vessel, and, as bases are generally made up of a number of narrow boards, edge-pegged together, this may not be from such a vessel but something else, perhaps a pot lid.

Turned vessels and basketry

The only turned vessel of Roman date was a small cylindrical boxwood pyx (*40*; Fig 483) from occupation layer *6897* within Period 3C Building *7200*. These are not uncommon finds in Carlisle, and several are known from Castle Street, Blackfriars Street, The Lanes, and Annetwell Street (Padley 1991c, 204–5, fig 180; 1990, 156–7; 2000a; Caruana in prep); this example lacks its lid. Whilst any comment on distribution must necessarily be skewed by the circumstances of preservation, it is perhaps significant that, north of the Alps, these small boxes seem to be concentrated at military sites (Pugsley 2003, 81). A similar but plainer container in copper alloy (*Ch 17*, Fig 392) came from construction trench *4087* (fill *4088*; Period 3A Building *4658*). There is no direct evidence for the contents of these finely-made containers, but the consistency in their size makes it clear that they were intended for a relatively restricted range of substances. Cosmetics or medicinal ointments seem obvious suggestions, the latter perhaps more likely on a military site.

Description	Barrel size	Species	Wood no
Stave	Incomplete	silver fir	W1108
Base board	Incomplete	silver fir	W565
Baseboard complete	0.91 m diameter	?	W574
Base board/ pot lid	Halved, 0.16 m diameter	?	W596
Base board	0.18 m radius	?	W1407
Base board	0.365 m diameter	?	W1413

Table 53: Details of evidence of coopered vessels

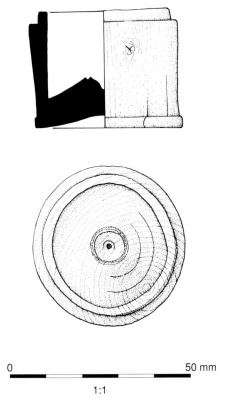

0   50 mm

1:1

Figure 483: Boxwood pyx, 40

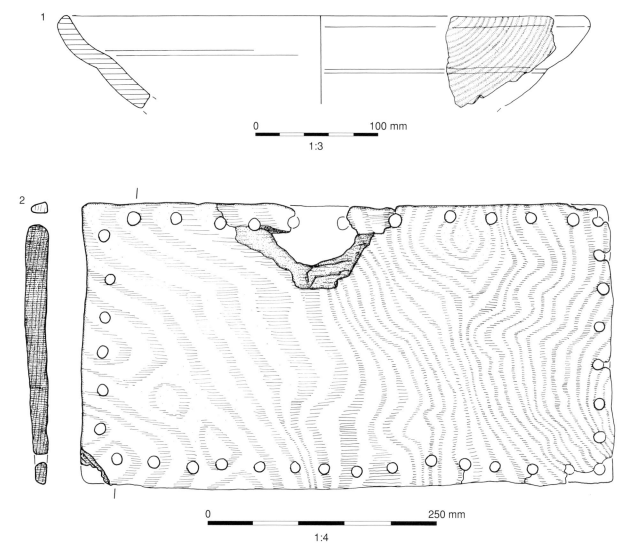

Figure 484: Turned bowl and the base of a basket

No other turned vessels were recovered from the Roman levels, although a larger turned vessel in ash (*5*; Fig 484.1) was recovered from fill *1587* of medieval ditch *1403* (Period 8iii). Again, this reflects the widespread use of turned wooden vessels throughout the medieval period. A large rectangular object, with evenly-spaced holes around its edges, is likely to be the base of a large basket, although nothing remains of its withy sides (*39*; Fig 484.2). It had been reused as part of a floor in Period 4A Building *5689*.

Other utensils

A baker's peel (*38*; Fig 485.1) was also reused in the floor within Building *5689*. A carefully-made scoop or scraper (*33*; Fig 485.2) also came from an occupation layer within Building *5689* (Period 4B) and a second, less carefully made example (*30*; Fig 485.3) came from the fill of a gully associated with road *7217*, which ran alongside the same building; both should be compared to the later bone scoop (*Ch 20, p 863*) from a Period 6C pit fill associated with Building *5200*. All three objects could have been associated

with the measuring of ingredients and preparation of food.

Two handles were noted, one (*10*; Fig 485.4) the plain handle of a tanged iron tool. The other, a tapering barrel-shaped object (*11*; Fig 485.5), bears a round tenon at one end, and was clearly intended to be attached to a second, larger object.

Three-legged table

Finally, object *9* (Fig 486), from floor *3802* in Building *4006* (Period 3B), appears to be the top of a relatively small, carefully carved, possible cabriole table leg, decorated with a band of ring-and-dot motifs. The top terminates in what appears to be part of a dovetail joint. Most evidence for furniture in this country is based on examples carved from Kimmeridge shale, but small fragments of wooden furniture are also known from Brough on Humber (Wacher 1969, fig 47.6), and London (Weeks and Rhodes 1986, 231, fig 10.6). The present piece most closely resembles the ornate legs of shale tripod tables and their plainer counterparts in

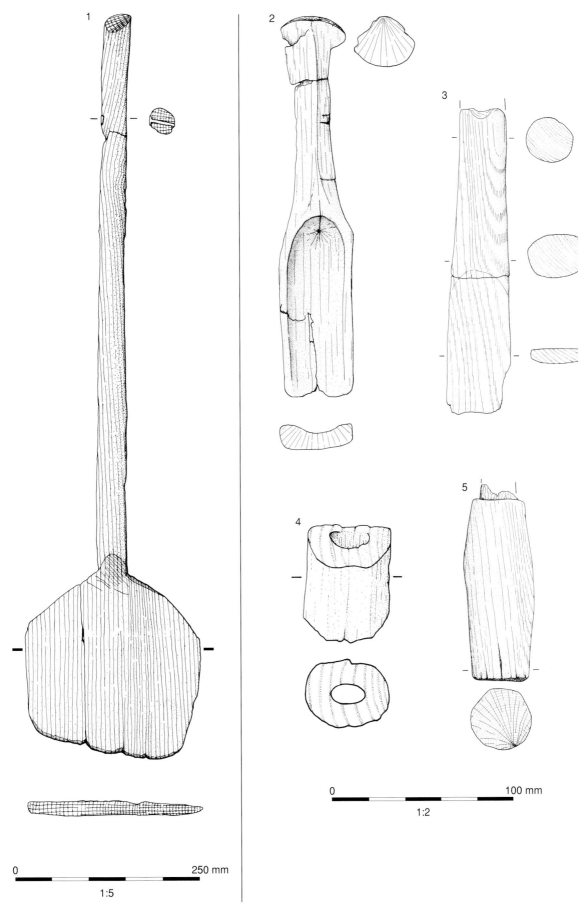

Figure 485: Other utensils

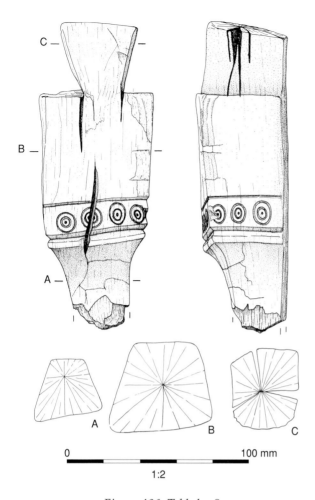

Figure 486: Table leg 9

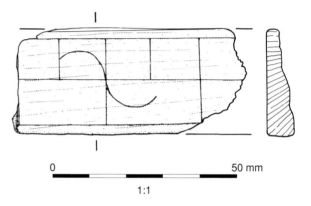

Figure 487: Ruler 28

wood, seen at the *Casa del Mobilio Bruciato*, Herculaneum (Liversidge 1955, 47, pl 16). There is no doubt that wooden examples must have been very common, most of them relatively plain; all known examples have the same distinctive appearance, with a small round top on three curved legs with hooved or clawed feet. The disposition of the decoration on the present example suggests that it was intended to be seen from several angles, which seems to confirm this interpretation. Apart from shale examples like that from Colliton Park, Dorchester (*op cit*, 37–8), the corpus of wooden and shale furniture from this country is too small to allow meaningful comparisons, except to note that the almost complete shale leg from Colliton Park has some incised circle decoration. The type seems to have been long-lived, the wooden examples from Herculaneum obviously having a date no later than AD 79, and therefore more or less contemporary with this fragment from Carlisle, whilst the Colliton Park example is dated to the second century, and other more fragmentary examples to the third and fourth centuries.

Objects employed in weighing and measuring

Object *28* (Fig 487) resembles nothing more than a ruler. It is a carefully made rectangular-sectioned fragment, both sides being smooth, possibly planed. One face was divided in two longitudinally, and is sub-divided laterally every 25 mm (approximately one inch). To one side of the longitudinal line, the primary sub-divisions are divided again; two of these are linked by an S-curve. Although not resembling the well-known Roman folding rulers (see, for instance, Wheeler 1930, 84, fig 21.1), its resemblance to a modern wooden ruler or even a surveying staff is inescapable, although no direct parallels have been found, and it does not resemble the ten-feet long surveyor's ranging pole (*pertica*) described by White (1975, 42–3). It was found within a floor layer (*6256*) in Building *5689* (Period 4B).

Objects used for, or associated with written communication

Fragments of three (possibly four) stylus-writing tablets were recovered (*16, 22*; Fig 488.1-2; *17, 34*; *Appendix 9*). All are typical single-sided examples, but only *16*, from Period 3A layer *4083* (Building *4653*), is anywhere near complete. None of the fragments bears decipherable inscriptions, although faint markings on the outside of *16* could be the remnant of an address. All three examples are made from silver fir (*Abies alba*). Writing tablets are a relatively common find in the waterlogged levels of Roman Carlisle and several have been published (see, for instance, McCarthy *et al* 1982; Tomlin 1992).

Objects associated with transport

Although only tentatively identified, object *20* (Fig 488.3), from occupation layer *4120* in Building *4653*, could be a small fragment of a wheel spoke, possibly the nave end. It bears considerable resemblance in size and shape to the spoke fragment from Castle Street (Padley 1991c, 218, fig 192). Wheeled vehicles are also indicated by an ornate rein trace and other copper-alloy fittings (*Ch 17, p 741*).

Buildings and services

Notwithstanding the large collection of structural wood, only one other wooden artefact gives any indication of the appearance of the buildings. Object *2*

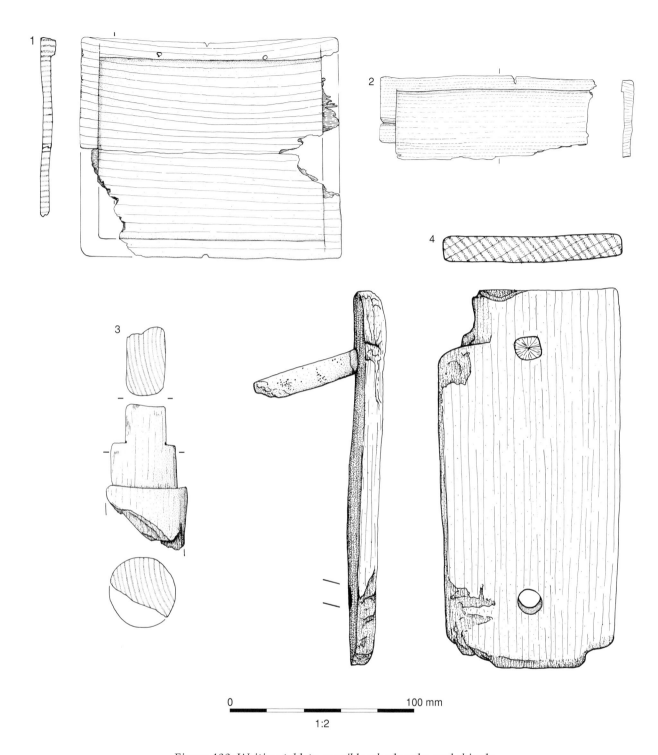

Figure 488: Writing tablets, possible wheel spoke, and shingle

(Fig 488.4) appears to be a sub-rectangular shingle made from tangentially split oak. Two peg-holes retain fragments of apple/pear roundwood pegs. Little is known of the use of shingles for roofing during the Roman period, although possible examples occasionally appear, and a substantial dump of *c* 100 oak shingles was associated with the Period 3 *praetorium* at Vindolanda (Birley 1994, 77 and fig 23).

A second object (*18*; Fig 489); from layer *4083* (Period 3A Building *4653*), is clearly intended to be fixed to a second, larger object, possibly by countersunk nails or rivets. Whilst difficult to identify with confidence, it bears a strong resemblance to a modern lock housing, and it seems reasonable to suggest that it served a similar purpose, accommodating the mechanism of a small slide lock, probably for a door.

Tools

Object *15* (Fig 490), from Period 3A layer *4083* in Building *4653*, bears a strong resemblance to a modern

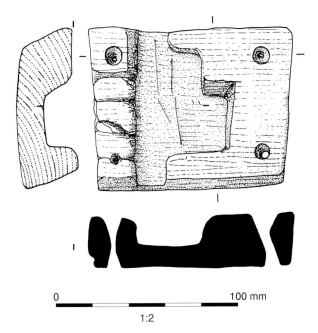

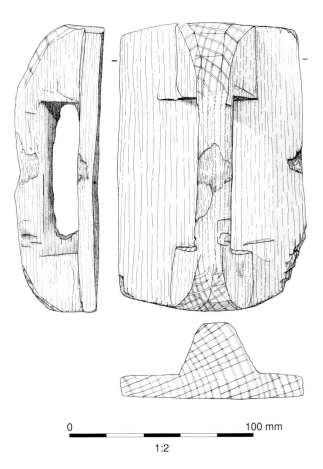

Figure 489: Lock housing 18

float for smoothing plaster or render, and perhaps served the same purpose, although to modern eyes it might seem a little small. Contemporary wall-paintings from Sens in Northern France (Ling 2000, fig 54) show plastering floats like this in use for applying the fine top-coat of plaster, prior to painting, and a broadly similar example, of wood and iron, was found at *Viturdurum* (Hedinger and Luizinger 2003, 90).

Military equipment

Although not strictly military in origin, it seems likely that *21* (Fig 491), from occupation layer *4165* within Period 3A Building *4658*, is possibly part of the wooden frame of a saddle, and presumably derives

Figure 490: Plasterer's float 15

from one of those noted amongst the sheet leather assemblage (*Ch 20*), although the saddle casings recorded were not from the same building. Again a rare and unusual item, there are few parallels, although the appearance and structure of Roman saddles has been much discussed (see also *Chapter 17* for other objects of a military nature).

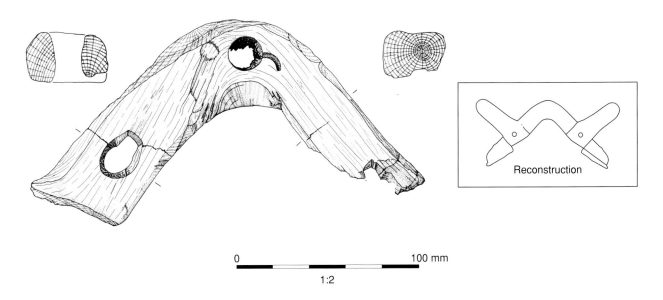

Figure 491: Fragment of saddle frame 21

814

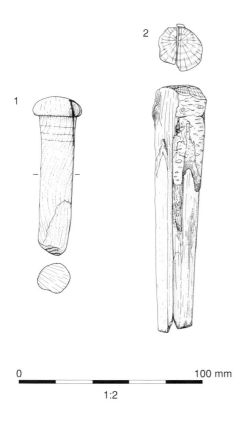

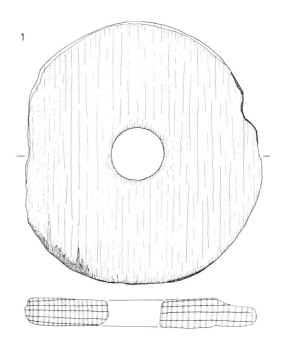

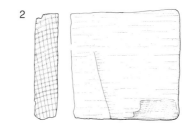

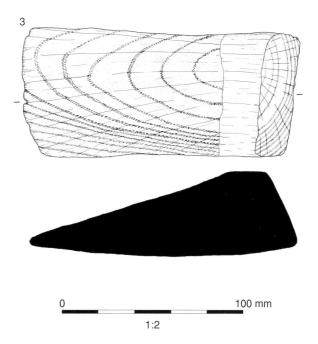

Figure 492: Wooden pegs

Objects of unknown or uncertain function or purpose

Three pegs were noted in contexts associated with the timber forts (*23, 32, 42; Appendix 9*). They vary from carefully (*42*; Fig 492.1) to somewhat roughly made (*32*; Fig 492.2), and no indication of their original purpose can now be determined. One, however (*42*), shows clear signs of having been coated in a red pigment (Pl 222).

Object *14* (Fig 493.1) is a large, deliberately made disc with a central perforation. The edges lack the chamfer which might suggest that it was the head of a small barrel, but no other purpose can be suggested, unless it served as a lid, the central perforation providing scope for a rope handle. A small block of oak (*12*; Fig 493.2),

Plate 222: Red pigment on peg 42

Figure 493: Wooden objects of unknown purpose

and a deliberately-made wedge (*37*; Fig 493.3), could originate in woodworking, although the latter could equally have served to keep a door open!

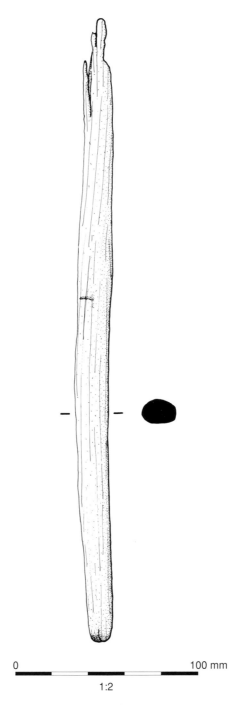

Figure 494: Possible bow 1

Object *6* (*Appendix 9*) appears to be a roll of birch bark. There is considerable evidence for the use of birch bark resin as a glue, and many ethnographic examples demonstrate the widespread use of sewn birch bark to form containers (Earwood 1993, 164–8). Other examples are known from Carlisle, and it is suggested that they might have served as firelighters (T Padley *pers comm*). The roll appears unused, having been deposited in medieval ditch **1230** during Period 8i (*Ch 11*). A second object (*1*; Fig 494) was recovered from Period 8iii layer *750*. Its function is unknown, although, as it is of yew, there is a possibility that it was part of a bow.

20

THE LEATHER AND OTHER ORGANIC ARTEFACTS

The Roman Stitched Sheet Leather

S Winterbottom

Some 586 items of stitched leather were recovered, most of which had formed parts of larger, complex constructions, but no single piece of equipment survived complete. The relative completeness of saddle cover *43* (*Appendix 10*), where 20 out of an estimated 27 original components survived, was outstanding, and many items were found to join others to which they had probably still been stitched when deposited. Although thread did not survive intact, it was not uncommon for pieces still to be held together by vestigial stitching, particularly short sections of tent gable seams. Overall, some 33% of panel pieces showed secondary cutting, making it likely that the recycling or repair of damaged equipment was taking place within the area excavated.

Preservation of most of the finds from Periods 3 and 4 (first and second centuries AD) was good to excellent, with poorly preserved material being confined to areas disturbed by later activity. Material from Period 5 onwards was relatively sparse, no doubt due to the absence of waterlogging, particularly on the west of the site. Much of what comes from contexts dated to later than AD 150 was recovered from cut features; it was often degraded and could well be residual.

The range of equipment that could be recognised includes tents, saddle covers and horse bardings, shield covers, bags or cases, and straps, but as is usual in comparable assemblages, the origin of a significant number of items could not be determined. This was either because they were too fragmentary, or because, despite their distinctive appearance, there are still many items of Roman military leatherwork whose use is unknown. Tent leather occurred in all periods and accounted for some 60% of the finds. Horse gear accounted for 14%, shield covers, bags, and items judged likely to come from an individual soldier's equipment accounted for a further 6%, leaving 20% of unknown origin. Though this seems a high figure, it is comparable to the 18% of unidentified items recorded for the adjacent excavations at Annetwell Street

(Winterbottom 1992). Periods 3B, 3C, and 4B produced particularly large amounts of stitched leather and, while the proportion of tent leather overall was 60%, this varied considerably between periods (Table 54).

The Annetwell Street excavations produced over 700 closely comparable leather items which still await publication (Caruana in prep); further collections from Castle Street and Abbey Street are published (Padley and Winterbottom 1991; Caruana 1992). All this material must be seen against a backdrop of the, now, vast quantities of Roman military leatherwork recovered from waterlogged sites across northern Britain since the 1970s, from Vindolanda, York, Castleford, Ribchester, and more recently Newstead. Assimilation of the data provided by these assemblages is by no means complete, particularly as regards the identification of unfamiliar objects and the reconstruction of large items. Attempts to understand manufacturing and supply processes and how the equipment ended up where it did, often in a systematically dismantled state, are also still in progress. The conclusions presented here should be viewed as an attempt to contribute to the emergence of a larger, clearer picture (see *Appendix 10* for a catalogue of illustrated items).

Period	Amount	Tentage component
3A	7%	2%
3B	21%	15%
3C	17%	7%
3D-3E	3%	2%
All of Period 3:	*48%*	*26%*
4A	9%	9%
4B	28%	16%
4C	1.5%	1.5%
All of Period 4:	*38%*	*26%*
5	2.5%	1.5%
6	4.5%	4%
Residual	6.5%	2%
Totals:	**100%**	**60%**

Table 54: Approximate distribution of Roman stitched leather by period (total number of finds = 586)

Context and date

Around 94% of the leather finds were well stratified, the remaining 6% being clearly residual, for example Roman military items in fills of the medieval outer ward ditch. The relative amount recovered from each period has been calculated in terms of the total number of discrete items, the largest number being from Period 4B (Table 54). It should be borne in mind, however, that many pieces from Period 4B were small, and that quantification using another measure, for example weight or surface area, would produce rather different results. Nevertheless, Periods 3B, 3C, and 4B are identified as being those where the most significant concentrations occurred, and in each of those periods it is possible to point to one area or building, even to a particular context, which accounts for the bulk of the finds. However, there was no obvious general location for material of this type; it was found in quantity both inside and outside buildings, and different periods show different tendencies in this respect (Table 55).

Period 3A

Period 3A produced relatively little stitched leather, which is in strong contrast to Annetwell Street, where 40% of the total recovered came from the earliest occupation. Many of the finds there were associated with workshops south of the intervallum road and backing onto the turf rampart (Winterbottom 1992).

A possible floor in Building *4654* (Fig 262), which fronted onto the main east to west road, contained small cut pieces of stitched leather mixed with off-cuts from shoemaking, and this has led to its interpretation as a workshop (*Ch 3*). What is thought to be part

Period	I	E	C	D	R
3A	33	4	0	5	0
3B	19	100	3	0	0
3C	88	11	1	0	0
3D-3E	0	10	0	5	2
All of Period 3:	*140*	*125*	*4*	*10*	*2*
4A	16	27	12	1	2
4B	101	31	3	0	29
4C	0	5	0	1	0
All of Period 4:	*117*	*63*	*15*	*2*	*31*
5	0	13	0	0	0
6	0	7	16	0	3
Totals:	**257**	**208**	**35**	**12**	**36**

I= Inside buildings; E= external contexts; C= construction trenches and postholes; D= demolition spreads; R= robbing

Table 55: Distribution of stratified stitched leather finds according to context type (n=548)

of an oak saddle tree was found in the adjacent building, *4658* (*Ch 19*, Fig 491), although there was no sign of an accompanying leather casing. Building *7392*, particularly R5 and R6, also showed clear evidence of leatherworking in their third occupational phase: over 100 pieces of shoemaking waste were recovered, but there was no significant component of stitched material.

The largest concentration was associated with the second phase of a barrack, Building *1222* (Fig 262), and came mainly from its drain and gully fills. It consisted mostly of small, single fragments but with some articulated groups of two or three joining pieces. The material seemed to come from tents and possibly a horse barding, otherwise it could not be identified. Broadly similar finds came from another barrack, Building *4653*, and from beside another possible workshop, *7393*, on the south side of the main east to west road. One feature which helped to distinguish between these groups was that the 'workshop' material showed more evidence of secondary cutting.

Period 3B

Material from Period 3B came predominantly from external contexts (Table 55) and contained many more large, recognisable items. The two factors may not be unrelated, as it would seem sensible to dismantle or repair large equipment such as tents outside, rather than in a confined space. Since the amounts of waste generated were more than could be easily lost on a floor or in a drain, disposal in open areas might be anticipated too.

A mass of discarded leather, 83 separate components in all, came from soils which had probably accumulated beside Building *2058* (a barrack), to the east of the main north to south road. There were numerous joining pieces from tent corners and sides (*1–15; Appendix 10*), and also a very tattered section of a horse barding (*47*). Another external deposit, adjacent to Structure *7474* in the angle between the main north to south and east to west roads, contained the reinforced top of a tent gable, together with part of the adjacent roof ridge panel (*23, 24*). These showed particularly crude attempts at repair.

As in Period 3A, a number of buildings had small quantities of stitched leather in their floor or occupation levels, or in the fills of features. Of particular interest is part of a wide composite strap (*60*), conceivably part of a baldric (*balteus*), which came from a floor in the possible *principia*, Building *7391*.

Period 3C

Some 86 of the 100 items recovered from this period came from 4144, the fill of a shallow pit (4130) dug through the floor of R1 in Building *4657* in its final phase of occupation. The pit also held a variety of other rubbish, ranging from copper-alloy waste to an iron needle and a knife (*Ch 17*). The leatherwork included large portions of two saddle covers (*43, 44*), parts of one or more horse bardings (*48, 50*), and material which seems to relate to the manufacture or repair of bardings (*49*). There was a small flat case (*68*), a rectangular piece cut from a shield cover (*55*), and five groups of tent pieces, all of which had been cut across or had pieces cut out of them (*27, 28*). The disposal of all this material by burying it may reflect on the nature of the activities taking place at the time; there is certainly a contrast with Period 3B, where similar deposits were allowed to accumulate in the open.

A patch of soil, *6630*, on the southern edge of the main east to west road (*7476*) produced a fragmentary panel with three applied patches (*29*). The origin of this group is uncertain, though in some respects they resemble tent pieces. One patch has a small, serifed stamp, 'S D V', in one corner, an inscription recorded at Newstead as well, also apparently on a reinforcing patch (McIntyre and Richmond 1934, 88). Such stamps are believed to have been used to mark batches of hides with the name of the owner of the tannery which supplied them (van Driel-Murray 1985, 61–2) and it is of great interest to know that the same source may have supplied the leather for equipment in use both at Carlisle and Newstead in this period.

Periods 3D and 3E
The material consisted mostly of smallish fragments, with the exception of a group of joining pieces (*30*) from *7156*, the soils overlying the demolished *principia*, Building *7391*. These came from a panel with a strongly reinforced free-hanging corner, perhaps a tent door flap, though there is some uncertainty as to what type of tent is represented by these objects (*Appendix 10, p 1398*).

Period 4A
Finds from this period were almost exclusively of tent leather and were thinly spread across the eastern part of the site. Buildings to the west of the main north to south road produced next to nothing, perhaps partly on account of the freer-draining subsoil that underlay the western half of this area, and partly because this part of the site was largely occupied by barracks (*Ch 5*). The largest concentration (20 pieces) was in *901*, external to the east wall of Building *2059*. This was on the same spot where sheet leather had been dumped in quantity in Period 3B (*999*). No stitched leather was associated with the large dump of shoemaking waste within a putative workshop, Building *7396* (R1, *5816*).

Period 4B
The finds in Period 4B were more diverse than in the preceding period, and their spatial distribution was

also different. With few exceptions, all the material came from the central range and adjacent roads, including five pieces of shield cover, out of a total of only seven from the site. This could support an hypothesis that the area was one where weapons and / or armour were kept or maintained. The largest piece (*56*), apparently from the cover for a rectangular shield, is itself a significant find, since these are rare in the archaeological record (van Driel-Murray 1988, 58). Two oddly-shaped reinforcing pieces (*62, 63*) have no clear parallels and may also come from rarer items, such as clothing or personal possessions.

Leather associated with the articulated armour finds
Within Building *5689* (Phase 6), layer *6419* contained sections of plate and scale armour (*Ch 17*) with quantities of sheet leather both above and below them. Altogether, 130 discrete items were identified, though many were fragmentary, and all were examined closely to see whether they were related to the structure of the armour itself (for instance straps holding the plates together), to the manner in which it was worn, or to its packing and storage. None of it was strap-like, although evidence for the strapwork survived as mineralised deposits adhering to the metal (*Appendix 4*). The fragments seemed unrelated to the armour, and the stitched pieces were quite diverse in nature, appearing to derive from a range of objects: *34, 59, 69, 70, 71,* and *75* all come from this deposit. Some had secondary cutting and were no different from workshop waste found elsewhere. Some was almost certainly tent leather, which makes any functional relationship with the metalwork unlikely. One fragment, *69*, is interpreted as coming from the edge of a bag, but if this had been anywhere near complete, as might be expected if the armour was stored or deposited in a leather bag, it would seem reasonable to have found many more fragments. The largest pieces recovered had torn edges without stitching. In places these extended around and below the armour sections, so there remains the possibility that they were wrapped in a sheet of scrap leather. With the stitched leather, too, parts of the same object were found lying both above and below the metalwork, and thus it does appear that both were dumped together.

Periods 4C, 4D, and 5
Nothing of significance was recovered in Periods 4C or 4D. Only 13 pieces of stitched leather were recovered from Period 5, and five of these had been used as packing in the sole layers of shoe *13* (*Appendix 10*). An unusually shaped reinforcing patch (*38*) closely resembles one from the Castle Street excavations, which was also of mid- to late second-century date (Padley and Winterbottom 1991).

Period 6
Fifteen of the 24 pieces came from the construction trenches of the *principia*, Building *5200*, and could well

have been redeposited. No stylistic or technological differences were observed that would distinguish the small amount of Period 6 material from that of earlier date.

Nature of the assemblage

Where identification of species has been made, the stitched sheet leather equipment has proved to be overwhelmingly of sheep/goat skin. This is also the case at Vindolanda and Newstead (van Driel-Murray 1990, 118) but it cannot be assumed that all assemblages in northern Britain are the same. At Ribchester, for instance, about half of the tent panels were of calf skin (Howard-Davis 2000e, 307), while calf skin predominated in early second-century Catterick and, later, at York (Hooley 2002, 339). The reasons for these differences are obscure and likely to remain so, while it is still not known where any of the equipment was made, whether in Britain itself, Gaul, or even in Italy.

Within MIL 3 and MIL 5, most notably in Periods 3B, 3C, and 4B, the finds were not randomly scattered but tended to occur in small dumps of related material. Many of the pieces from Period 3B layer *999*, for example, came from tent corners; pit fill *4144* contained a large proportion of horse gear, layer *6419* produced many small hemmed fragments, and so on (Table 55). These are certainly not casual losses but appear to be part of a process which had stitched leather as its object, or for which it was one of the raw materials. That process may have involved one or more of the following: manufacture; repair; recycling/reuse; and disposal as unserviceable or surplus to requirements.

Manufacture

No context provided substantial evidence for the manufacture of stitched leather equipment in the form of primary off-cuts, though small quantities of sheep/goat skin off-cuts were recovered from both the Millennium excavations and Annetwell Street and Castle Street (S Winterbottom *pers obs*). Manufacture would not necessarily generate large quantities of waste; much of the surplus left after cutting out would be used to make the numerous bindings, patches, and ties. Fragment *29A* (*Appendix 10*) shows that pieces with edge of hide could also be used as main components (perhaps when leather was in short supply), so long as the irregularity was hidden from view. Nevertheless, unusable portions of skin should accumulate if manufacture using new materials was a regular activity. It still seems likely that equipment with multiple components, such as tents, horse bardings, and saddle covers, was made by specialist craftsmen working in dedicated centres (van Driel-Murray 1985, 55–8), though the position for less complex items, such as shield covers, purses,

and cases, is less clear. Manufacture using recycled materials is another possibility.

Repair

Repairs to the equipment are described in the catalogue where they occur (*Appendix 10*). They included patching, either from the outside or inside, additional thread or thong stitching along damaged seams and hems, whipping together the edges of tears, and in one case (*36*) apparently adding a wider reinforcing strip to a seam that had proved not to be wind- or waterproof. The same assessment as that made for repair techniques in the Ribchester leather assemblage (Howard-Davis 2000e, 309) can be made here: the degree of skill displayed by repairers is generally less than that of the original makers of the equipment, and often markedly so (see for instance, *23A* or *44A*). The work is aptly described as 'field repairs' and it is worth asking who was carrying them out, since the skills and tools needed, while basic, may not have been possessed by every soldier. It can be assumed that such repairs were being carried out within the fort at Carlisle, though the activities themselves generate little evidence. A Period 4C context, however, associated with Building *5689*, produced a neat oval of leather looking like the blank for a repair patch. Other sites have produced similar pieces, or pieces of reused leather from which such blanks appear to have been cut, for example, Castle Street (Winterbottom 1991).

As at Ribchester and elsewhere, a proportion of the discarded leather at Carlisle is characterised by secondary cutting, which has sometimes neatly removed strips of the stitched edge (examples are *7, 9, 20, 35, 46*, and *48E-G, Appendix 10*). At other times, panels have been cut or torn in half, or have had a corner removed, with any applied or joining pieces still attached (*27, 28, 41, 48, 71*). Howard-Davis (2000e, 309) interprets this waste as the product of 'the professional repair of extensive damage by removal of all or part of an individual panel or panels', although it is questionable whether such surgical repairs would have been attempted often, as tents, for example, were a jigsaw of interlocking pieces, which would perhaps be difficult to disassemble in part. Internal evidence suggests they were assembled in strict order, the panels being first stitched end to end into wallpaper-like strips, which were then joined side to side to make roof and wall sections (Fig 495). After joining the side-wall sections to the roof, the final stage was the attachment of the end walls (van Driel-Murray 1990, 118; this order of assembly is borne out by the Carlisle evidence). Removing and replacing worn panels, other than by simply cutting them out, would be a very painstaking and skilled job. Doing the latter would only create large holes which had to be patched over, and would further weaken the whole structure. Furthermore, it is rare to find evidence, on the panels themselves, of replacement sides or corners having been

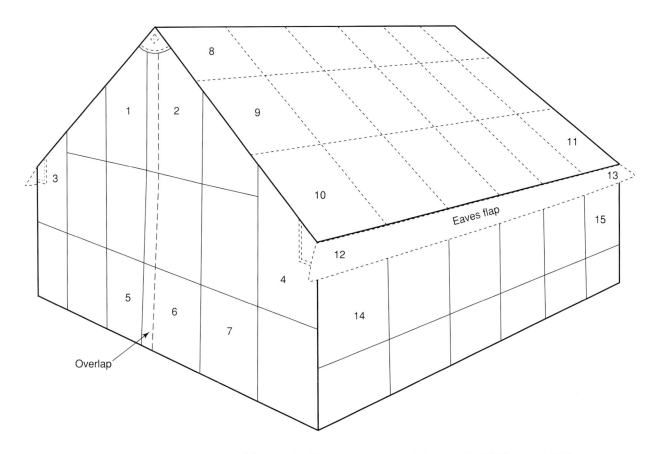

Figure 495: Reconstruction of the standard Roman army tent (after van Driel-Murray 1990)

inserted (though *2A* provides a possible example). The preferred option seems to have been to bury any damage under successive layers of patches, and sometimes these would need to be quite large (*1C* is an example; *72*, as big as half a tent panel, may be another). If *72* is part of a repair, then it was quite neatly executed, using a simple running stitch. Skills were also available within the field unit to re-stitch the side seam of a saddle cover in the manner of its original construction (*43A, 43B*) and to devise a means of protecting the torn tops of saddle horns from further damage (*43J, 43K, etc*). Whether they extended to the replacement of whole tent panels or sections is uncertain.

Reuse
Since it cannot be assumed that the cut and discarded pieces were produced during precision repairs to equipment, it must be asked how else they can be accounted for, and probably there are as many answers as there are uses for old leather. A collection of leatherworking debris from Period 3A Building *4654* contained equal amounts of both shoemaking waste and cut stitched pieces (*73*), raising the possibility of reuse in shoemaking or repairing. Likewise, the construction of a nailed shoe from Period 5D (Shoe *13, Appendix 10*) included five pieces of stitched leather as packing material between its sole layers. The same practice was recorded at Castle Street (Padley and Winterbottom 1991, 302, 1212). In Period 3C

Building *4657*, pit fill *4144* produced not only part of a dismembered horse barding (*48*) but also what may be blanks for replacement pockets / horns for a barding (*49*). Comparison of the leather suggests they could have been cut from *48*, providing a nice example of new kit being cobbled together from old.

The largest surviving piece of a shield cover, *56*, has had two large curved shapes removed from its lower-edge, and the centre of *41*, a tent door flap, supplied a large sub-rectangular piece. While it cannot be known what the leather removed was used for, it is possible that it provided uppers for new or repaired shoes, a practice that Hooley (2002, 340) found evidence for at Catterick.

When a large item such as a tent was no longer fit for its original purpose, it was still a rich quarry for leather. If a large piece was required, stitched areas could be cut off to obtain it; if only small repair patches were needed, then half a panel would do and the rest could be thrown away. All depended on purpose: for instance, an articulated tent side from Vindolanda had been used just as it was to line a pit (van Driel-Murray 1990, 110).

Disposal as waste
According to this recycling model, material would only be discarded when no use remained for it. In

Period	Number of panel pieces	Proportion with secondary cutting
3A	24	50%
3B	61	34%
3C	29	59%
3D-3E	3	0%
4A	28	21%
4B	84	24%
4C	3	0%
5	6	0%
6	16	31%

Table 56: Variation in levels of the reworking of stitched leather

most cases there is no difficulty in interpreting the finds in this light. Extensively damaged and frequently repaired items, however large, will not tend to display secondary cutting (*43A, 44A, 47A*). When whole components, with little or no damage, were thrown away (*11, 12*, and *15* in Period 3B) it must be supposed that it was because they were not required. Either nothing was being made or mended, or, more likely, supply of the material outstripped demand.

Pieces such as *28A* (Period 3C) and *71* (Period 4B) pose more of a problem. These were smallish sheets of dismembered stitched leather, which had been carefully folded and stored for future use, either in a workshop or by an individual soldier. Such folded wads have been found at several sites. At the moment of hoarding they were valuable: perhaps the supply of this material, used for example for patching, could not be guaranteed. Later, they were no longer of worth to the individual, and some change in circumstances is needed to explain why. Interestingly, researchers often interpret the jettisoning of quantities of reworked stitched leather as part of the process of refurbishing equipment before a campaign. It might be argued, on the contrary, that chopping up worn-out tents and even throwing out one's survival sewing kit are activities more suggestive of the end of a campaign than its beginning. The excavated material does not show discernible change, over time, in the nature of the repair and reuse. Nevertheless, the proportion of pieces which had been cut up before being discarded does vary from one period to another, suggesting there were times when reworking was more intensive (Table 56).

Form and function
Tents
Around 60% of the stitched leather can be attributed to tents (Table 54). This figure may be somewhat inflated, since it includes incomplete components which, though resembling tentage, could have other origins.

Tent types
The reconstructions proposed by van Driel-Murray in her seminal article, *New light on old tents* (1990), are now widely accepted, and the evidence from Vindolanda is indispensable to any discussion of Roman army tents. There, what is believed to represent the basic eight-man sleeping tents used by legionary or auxiliary troops were identified in two separate finds, one of late first-century and the other of Hadrianic date (Fig 495). The numbering serves to indicate where individual panels would belong in a tent of that type, but it is in no sense intended as an exact reconstruction (not being drawn to scale). No large articulated tent sections were found during the Millennium Project, but smaller associations, which can be associated with van Driel-Murray's positions 2, 3, 4, 7, 8, 10, and 12 (Fig 495) were identified (*41, 2, 4, 15, 23, 1* and *8, 10*, and *17* respectively). The range of hem and seam types is shown in Figures 496 and 497 (see *Appendix 10* for cross-referencing with previous numbering systems).

Both the Millennium Project and Annetwell Street (Winterbottom in prep a) have produced pieces which, according to the evidence from Vindolanda (van Driel-Murray 1993), constituted the edges of an entrance flap, and the bottom of a side and an end wall (*1-42, Appendix 10*). All were finished with a simple folded hem. This is the simplest to execute (hem I; Fig 496), quite unostentatious and wholly appropriate to equipment for the rank and file. At Carlisle and elsewhere, however, there are also hemmed panels finished in a more elaborate manner, with the conspicuous use of applied pieces and requiring more labour to produce (*30, 34*, and *37* are examples). Characteristic of these is use of a bound hem (hem IV; Fig 496) and the placing of circular reinforcing patches, both on the inside and the outside, at points where seam ends meet the hem (Padley and Winterbottom 1991, 292, 294; van Driel-Murray 1998, fig 143, 48).

It seems increasingly likely that these come from tents of a different type. The arrangement is very like that which appears along the edges of the roof overhang on the marquee-like structures depicted in Trajan's Column (scene XXI reproduced in McIntyre and Richmond 1934, 66, fig 3). On those tents, roundels at the seam ends appear to be points from which curtains or other detachable sides were suspended. Suspension circles (or rings?) also appear along a roof overfall in scene XVIII (Rockwell 1999, scene no 18). This is particularly interesting, given the clear evidence of piece *34* (Fig 498) and comparable finds (van Driel-Murray 1998, 315–16), that the circular patches along the hem were indeed attachment points. Larger sections will need to be recovered if the form of this second tent type is to be better understood, but it seems likely, given its larger size and more elaborate construction, that it was either intended as officer's quarters or was used for official business.

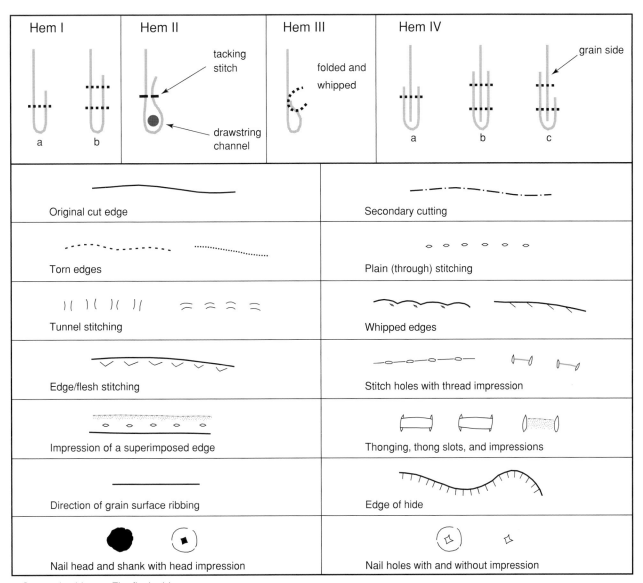

Hem I	Hem II	Hem III	Hem IV
a b	tacking stitch / drawstring channel	folded and whipped	a b c grain side

Original cut edge	Secondary cutting
Torn edges	Plain (through) stitching
Tunnel stitching	Whipped edges
Edge/flesh stitching	Stitch holes with thread impression
Impression of a superimposed edge	Thonging, thong slots, and impressions
Direction of grain surface ribbing	Edge of hide
Nail head and shank with head impression	Nail holes with and without impression

Gr = grain side   Fl = flesh side

Figure 496: Hem types and other conventions used (Appendix 10)

The different tent forms shown on Trajan's Column have always been seen as the product of status and function, and it seems reasonable to attribute differences in the excavated material to similar distinctions. There is some evidence from the Millennium Project that differentiation according to status may also be detected in the constructional detail of other stitched leather equipment, notably horse bardings and saddle covers.

Tent panel sizes and method of assembly
Some 15 tent panels with one or more complete dimension were identified (Table 57); all measurements were taken after conservation. All could derive from tents of the Vindolanda type, though other types are not ruled out.

The method of construction of waterproof tent seams dictates that the upper edges of rectangular panels will have 'b' stitching, and the lower edges 'a' stitching

(Fig 497; seams II-IV). This rule can help determine the orientation of isolated panels, and another clue is the direction of the grain-side ribbing (see for instance, *11* and *12*, shown by the double-headed arrow; *Appendix 10*); where present on panels of known orientation, this is usually horizontal (van Driel-Murray 1998, 312). An interesting exception is eaves flap panel *16*, where it runs vertically. Where a panel's orientation is known, it is usually possible to determine, at any intact corner, the order of completion of the horizontal and vertical seams. Evidence of this kind, supplied by *1A, 15, 25, 27*, and *41*, supports the 'wallpaper' strip model of tent assembly put forward by van Driel-Murray (1990).

Roof detail
Panels *1, 8, 23*, and *27* come from tent roofs (*Appendix 10*). Panel *1* is from a roof corner and has a large quarter-circle reinforcement at the point where the roof, side, and end walls all meet (*cf* Caruana 1992, 80, 1; van Driel-Murray

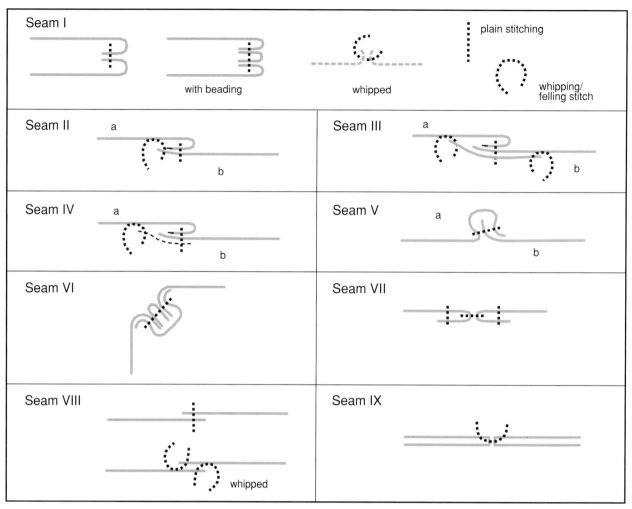

Seam I

plain stitching

with beading

whipped

whipping/
felling stitch

Seam II a
b

Seam III a
b

Seam IV a
b

Seam V a
b

Seam VI

Seam VII

Seam VIII

whipped

Seam IX

Figure 497: Seam types (Appendix 10)

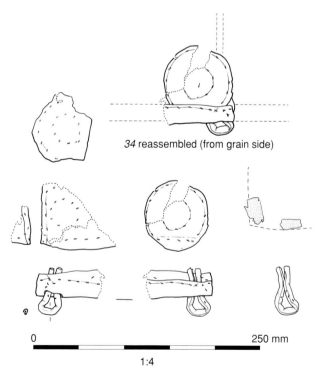

34 reassembled (from grain side)

0   250 mm

1:4

Figure 498: Attachment points on leather 34

1990, 136, V12). Panel 8 is from the same position. There is evidence from 1 and 27 for further reinforcement at the upper corners of these panels, where they joined the gable edge seam (Fig 495, junction of 9 and 10). This has not been observed before, and suggests a regular series of patches along the inside of the gable seam, though these were not necessarily attachment points for guys.

Panel 23 (Fig 499.1) is from position 8 at the roof ridge (Fig 495). Both ends have 'a' seam stitching (Fig 497), confirming that the uppermost panels spanned the ridge and there was no seam running along it. It is closely comparable to find 1200, panel 4, from Vindolanda (van Driel-Murray 1990, 121, fig 7): both are torn and distorted at the point corresponding to the apex of the gable. The whole panel has clearly been under tension, with the gable seam being pulled outwards. The leather there would have rested on a vertical pole, or on a ridge pole, but there is no evidence on 23 for any reinforcement to protect the area from wear.

Fragment 24 (Fig 499.2), along with several others (4, 40, 41, and 42; Appendix 10), provides some

Catalogue no	IRF no	Period	Length (mm)	Width (mm)	Shape/ origin
11	823.11	3B	450	165	Rectangular, eaves flap
12	823.49	3B	420	160	Rectangular, eaves flap
13	823.50	3B	inc.	162	Rectangular, eaves flap
-	825.01	3B	inc	150	Trapezoidal, eaves flap
10A	823.17	3B	inc	140	Trapezoidal, eaves flap
16	8107	3B	620	140	Trapezoidal, eaves flap
15	833.01	3B	640	490	Rectangular, end wall?
-	8173	4B	650	inc	Rectangular, end wall?
1A	823.02	3B	770	530	Rectangular, roof
14A	823.34	3B	inc	475	Rectangular, roof?
23	8117.01	3B	630	inc	Rectangular, roof ridge
25	8172	3B	inc	505	Rectangular, roof or end wall?
-	8153	4B	495	inc	Rectangular, side wall?
-	8196.01	5D	595	inc	Rectangular?
41	8004.01	u/s	600	520	Trapezoidal, doorway

inc= incomplete dimension

Table 57: Tent panels with complete length or width preserved

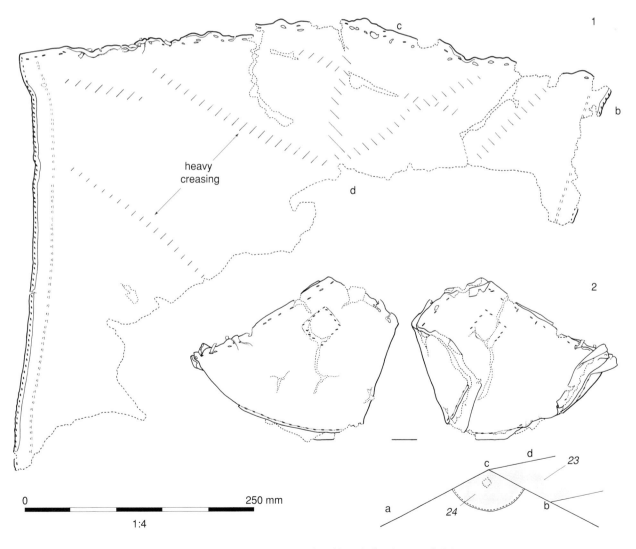

Figure 499: Panel 23 and gable reinforcing patch 24

825

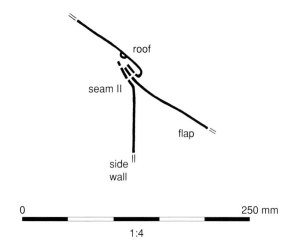

Figure 500: Reconstruction of the insertion of the eaves flap

Period	Seam II	Seam III	Seam IV
3A	7	0	6
3A*	24	6	8
3B	38	4	4
3C-3D	10	8	5
4A	18	7	6
4B-4C	11	12	13
5	1	2	0
6	3	4	0

*= 3A at Annetwell Street

Table 58: Number of instances of the three main seam types

evidence for the angle between the roof and side-walls. Something between 115° to 130° is suggested, with three measurements very close to 125°. Nine pieces from the eaves flap at the base of the roof (Fig 495) were recovered; fragments *11–13* (*Appendix 10*) formed an articulated section just over 1 m long (Fig 500). In all cases the lower edge was a folded Ia hem; the ends of the flaps were either Ia or a bound hem IVa (Figs 496 and 497).

The entrance
Panel *41* comes from a doorway formed by two overlapping flaps, and closely resembles door panels dated to *c* AD 92–7 at Vindolanda (van Driel-Murray 1990). This is the only type of entrance for which good evidence currently exists. The top was reinforced inside and out with large applied patches like *24* (Fig 499.2) and *40*. In another example from Annetwell Street (Winterbottom 1986, C167–172, L294), the patches still had parts of two overlapping hemmed panels sandwiched between them. By contrast, the central layer in *24* was a single uninterrupted sheet of leather. One explanation for the apparent lack of any flap there

is that *24* comes from the back wall of a tent and that these had no entrance.

Changes over time
There is insufficient material to detect any development in the types of tent in use, or in the form of individual components. Changing methods of manufacture, on the other hand, can possibly be observed in the choice of three stitching types for the main joining seams (Table 58) lists the number of instances of each seam type in each period. These have been converted to percentages (Fig 501), and for Period 3A, where finds were sparse, the figures for Annetwell Street have been added. During Period 3, seam II was by far the most commonly used, but by the end of Period 4 all three types were occurring in equal proportions. seam II shows a gradual decline in frequency, while seam III arguably shows an equally gradual rise; seam IV occurs at more or less consistent rates over the period. The situation is therefore not clear cut: Seam II remains the most frequent type until the end of Period 4A (*c* AD 125), yet data from nearby Castle

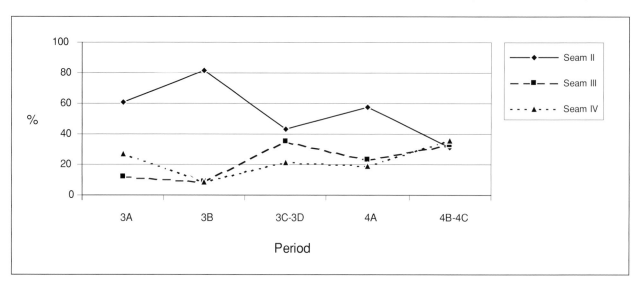

Figure 501: Percentage of different seam types over time

826

Street show seam III as predominant from *c* AD 105 onwards (Padley and Winterbottom 1991, 261).

Horse gear - saddle covers

Substantial parts of four saddle covers were recovered (*43-46; Appendix 10*). A substantially complete cover for a four-horned saddle (*43*, from Period 3C; Fig 502) has greatly helped to clarify the form of these objects, as well as adding to an understanding of the method of construction. In essence, the seat and horn coverings are as described in earlier publications (van Driel-Murray *et al* 2004). It is the form of the sides and ends, however, that were previously not well understood, and for which these finds provide important new evidence. Rather than being joined underneath, to produce an enclosed casing, the sides were extended by the addition of fringed panels, which hung down on either side of the saddle. Further side panels can now be recognised among the finds from Vindolanda and Ribchester (van Driel-Murray 1993, 22, 1; Howard-Davis 2000e, 315, 245). Similarly, the V-shaped ends of the cover (previously described as darts) were not stitched to other components but hung down as small flaps.

Method of assembly
The excellent preservation of thread impressions and those of overlapping edges make it possible to reconstruct the order of assembly of many of the components of cover *43* (*Appendix 10*). The first

stage was the attachment of the side panels to the central piece, following which the leading edges were hemmed as far as the bases of the horn pockets (from *q* to *a* and *p* to *k* in Figure 502, together with corresponding sections on the other side of the cover). The edges of the V-shaped projections were also folded and hemmed, with about 25 mm at either end being left unstitched at this stage.

The next step was the construction of the horn pockets, using facing pieces previously constructed from two layers of leather connected by a circle of stitching at the base (*43*, *I, M, P,* and *S*; Fig 503). Working inside out, the edges of the facings were sewn to the horn projections on the main panel, using seam I (Fig 497). At the end closest to the centre of the saddle, one radial edge of a three-quarter circle reinforcing patch was incorporated into this seam: the corresponding edge of the patch is folded as a result (*43*, *C, E, F*; Fig 503). The cover was then turned right side out again, and binding strips were sewn along the bottom of each horn facing to prevent its two layers from separating. Their ends ran onto, and were fixed to, the main body of the cover. At the end adjacent to the V-shaped flap, each strip was sewn over the second radial edge of the three-quarter circle patch, thus anchoring it to the upper arm of the V, previously left unstitched.

With the horn pockets now complete, the last stage was to fix the reinforcing patches at their inside corners

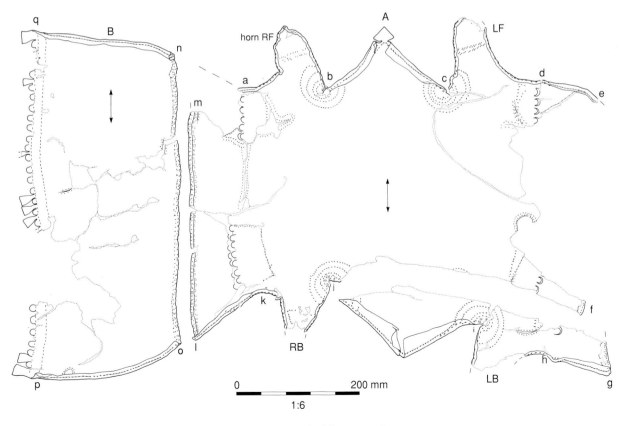

Figure 502: Saddle cover 43

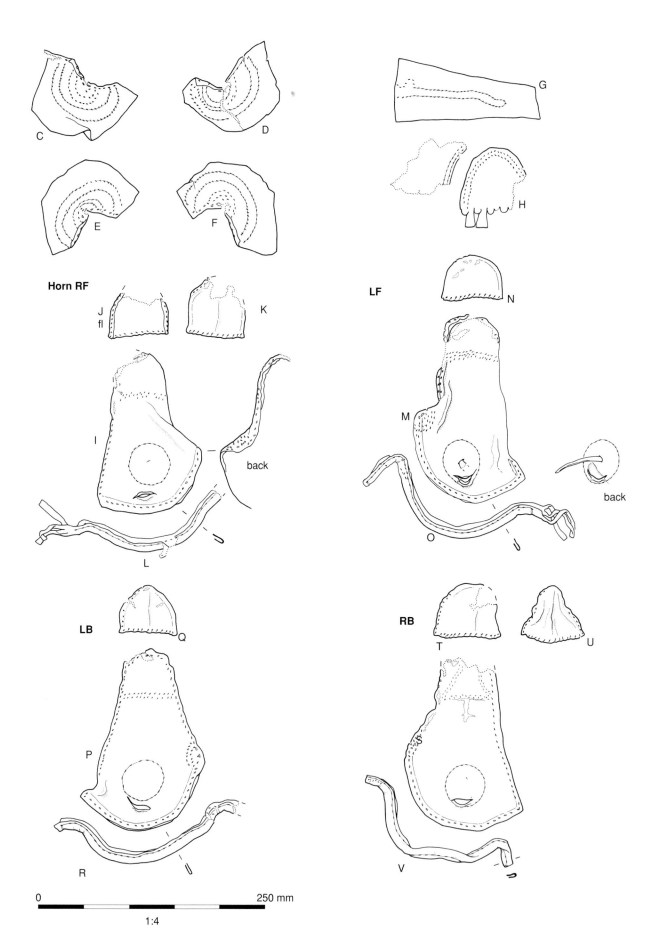

Horn RF

LF

LB

RB

0   250 mm

1:4

Figure 503: Elements of saddle cover 43

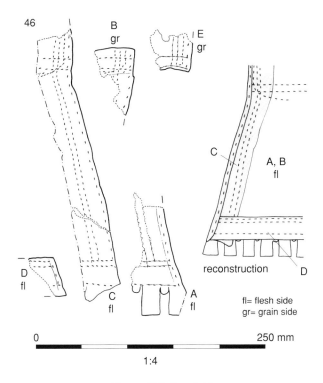

Figure 504: Panel 46

firmly in place with four concentric circles of stitching. Arcs of stitching also pass through the corners of the facings and their bindings. In addition, it seems that patches were sewn to the outside of the cover, though these are now lost. The cover could now be fitted onto the saddle for which it was intended, and from which it could, in principle, subsequently be removed if necessary, to carry out repairs. A tight fit was certainly desirable, or the cover would slip about when in use. Peter Connolly (*pers comm*) has suggested this may have been achieved by wetting and shrink fitting.

An alternative form
Panel 46 (Fig 504), though tantalisingly fragmentary, has a pelleted fringe at one end, which suggests it may also belong to the side panel of a saddle cover. The height of the assembly compares closely to that of *43B* (Fig 502), but the construction is altogether more elaborate, consisting of three thicknesses of leather, with additional binding along the edges. It is tempting to see another example of the differentiation of equipment according to status or purchasing power. With its double and triple rows of stitching, *46* would have taken longer to produce and would have had a more robust, 'armoured' appearance than *43*.

Horse gear - bardings
Pieces from large, draped coverings for a horse's head, back, and sides come from Periods 3B, 3C, and 6A (*47, 48;* Fig 505.1-2; *49-52, Appendix 10*). Generally known as bardings, they are characterised by a pointed brow piece, circular holes for the ears, and

a rectangular arrangement of four upstanding flat pockets in the middle of the horse's back. The basic form was established following a substantial find from Vindolanda (van Driel-Murray 1993, 49–51), although it is still not clear in what circumstances they would be used, or whether they could be combined with a pack saddle or riding saddle (van Driel-Murray *et al* 2004, 5–8).

Though no more than 20 years can separate them, there are significant differences between bardings *47* and *48* (Fig 505). The latter was constructed using the stronger seam III (Fig 497) and its edges, before being bound, were strengthened by the addition of continuous flat strips of leather on the outside. The treatment of the edges is similar to that on the presumed saddle panel (*46*); once again, the degree of elaboration could indicate a higher status item. In contrast, the edges of *47* lack any external stiffening and were simply bound with narrow strips of leather, thus resembling those of an Agricolan barding from Ribchester (Howard-Davis 2000e, 318, fig 101). A short length of sewn strap (*53*) is probably from horse harness of some sort.

Shield covers
Seven pieces of shield cover were identified (*54-59, Appendix 10*), five coming from the central range in Period 4B. Only one piece, *56*, is large enough to indicate the shield type: a straight segment 430 mm long which has the beginnings of a rounded corner at either end, suggesting a rectangular shield with a width of no more than 600 mm. A very similar piece from excavations at Law's Lane, Carlisle, preserved the full 90° corner angle (Winterbottom in prep b). Taken together, these two finds are of some importance since, despite the repeated illustration of rectangular shields on Trajan's column, most archaeological evidence has been for shields with rounded or pointed ends (van Driel-Murray 1988, 58).

Other equipment
As well as the shield covers, the central range in Period 4B produced two unusual pieces (*62, 63; Appendix 10*), which could derive from other items of personal equipment or possibly clothing. Fragment *60*, from the Period 3B *principia* (Building **7391**), may be part of a baldric.

Bags and cases
Among the sheet leather from the Flavian forts at Castleford, West Yorkshire, van Driel-Murray identified large rectangular bags, possibly tool or saddle bags, constructed using a narrow version of seam VI (1998, 289, 308–12). A very similar item was found during Dorothy Charlesworth's 1976 excavation at Annetwell Street (Winterbottom 1986, C174–188,

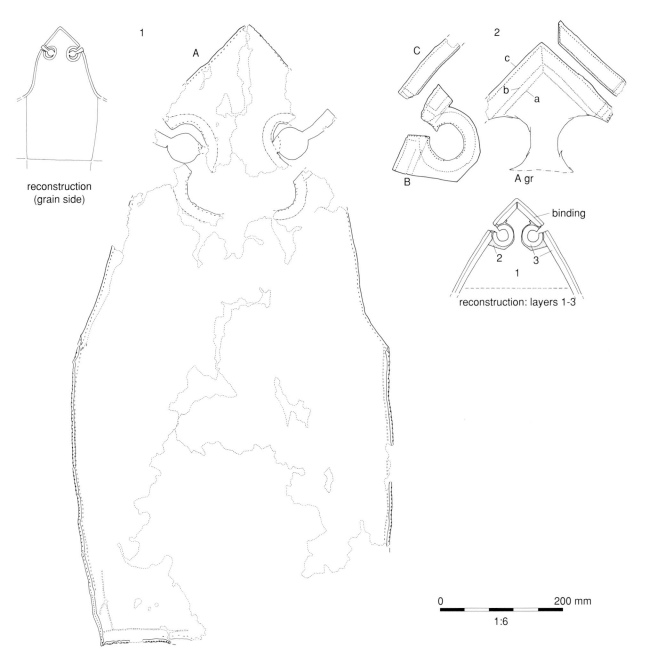

reconstruction
(grain side)

C

B

c
b
a

A gr

binding

2   3

1

reconstruction: layers 1-3

0   200 mm

1:6

Figure 505: Bardings 47 and 48

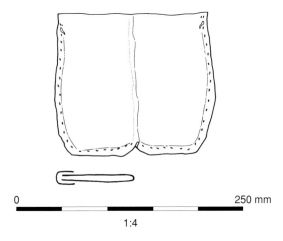

0   250 mm

1:4

Figure 506: Pouch 68

context C76/51). These bags measured some 750–850 mm across, and when relatively complete, their sides can be distinguished from tent panels by the presence of seam VI stitching (Fig 497) on adjacent or opposing edges, an arrangement that would not occur on a tent. Smaller pieces can be only tentatively identified from the narrowness of their bindings and beadings when compared to those from tents. On these grounds, *65, 66,* and *67* (*Appendix 10*) are cautiously attributed to such bags. Fragment *69*, with similar stitching but a curved edge, may come from another type of bag or casing, whilst *68* (Fig 506) is more obviously a small flat pouch, and the fastenings from a long narrow case or wallet from Valkenburg (Groenman-van Waateringe 1967, 171–3) provide the best parallel for *70* (*Appendix 10*).

Inscriptions and a stamp on leather fragments

D Shotter

Three of the sheet leather fragments bore inscriptions or stamps, presumably indicating the tanner or the supplier of the original hides (van Driel-Murray 1985, 61), rather than the manufacturer or owner of specific objects. A small off-cut of shoe-leather, from Period 4A robber trench *6610* (fill *6606)* on east to west road **7477**, bears the letters **C C M** (Pl 223); the off-cut is 103 mm long and no more than 47 mm wide, the 'letter-panel' itself being much smaller, at 23 x 4 mm. It is likely to represent a tanner's or supplier's mark, consisting of three names, such as **C**(aius) **C**(.......) **M**(.......), on the analogy of RIB 2445.3 (Collingwood and Wright 1992), also from Carlisle. The letters are incised with a knife, but the degree of proficiency of execution that they exhibit differs individually; in particular, whilst there are signs of attempted serifs on both of the letters **C**, there are indications of rather crude workmanship around the **M**. This particular set of initials has not been previously recorded. There is no sign that this off-cut was reused.

A second small off-cut (125 mm long by 27 mm wide), from the fill (*6402)* of Period 4B robber trench *7471*, associated with road **7217**, bears a poorly-cut inscription (Pl 223), probably the same initials (**C C M**) or possibly **C V M**. Again this should

presumably be restored to **C**(aius) **C** or **V**(.......) **M**(.......), the name of the tanner or supplier. The way in which the letters have opened up suggests that they may have been incised (or stamped) on the hide prior to tanning (Rhodes 1987; Van Driel-Murray 1993, 62ff). The inscription is slightly truncated at both ends, but was *c* 34 mm in length, with its letters 8 mm in height. There is no previous record of this inscription, and the second letter poses a problem: it is too truncated vertically and too square at the base for a normal **C** or **V**, but if it is to be read as **C C M**, it is in a completely different style from the previous example. The same off-cut also bears a portion of a second crudely-scored inscription, **C C[**; the letters are 12 mm in height and what survives is 15 mm in length. There are also signs on this inscription of the letters having opened up, again suggesting that it was cut before the tanning process began.

A third small off-cut of what is thought to be tent-leather (Pl 223) from a Period 3C external deposit (*6630*), was evidently reused as a patch, either to repair damage or strengthen a potentially weak area of the tent. Approximately 129 mm long and 94 mm wide, it bears the stamp **S D V**, which should presumably be restored to **S**(extus) **D**(.......) **V**(.......), indicating the name of the tanner or supplier. The same set of initials appears on what was interpreted as a patch of tent-leather excavated at Newstead in 1905–9 (*RIB* 2445.12; Collingwood and Wright 1992). The Carlisle stamp measures 17 x 5 mm, the same as the Newstead example. However, the stamps appear to represent different dies, for although both have stops in similar positions between the letters, the Carlisle stamp is of superior execution, with serifs to all three of the letters. It has been suggested (S Winterbottom *pers comm*) that, given the use made of this piece, the stamp is much more likely to have been that of the tanner or supplier than of an owner, and that the nature and condition of the piece indicates that leather may have been in short supply at the time, prompting the use of reuse of scrap material. The link between Carlisle and Newstead has added interest because of the fact that it is now known that the main gate of the earliest fort at Newstead faced west, that is, in the direction of Carlisle (Shotter 2000a; R F J Jones *pers comm*).

Plate 223: Inscriptions and stamp C C M (top left, and perhaps top right); S D V (bottom)

The Roman Shoes

Q Mould

The shoes come from deposits dating from AD 72 / 3–83 (Period 3A) through to the third century (Period 6A). A very small quantity of highly fragmentary shoe parts

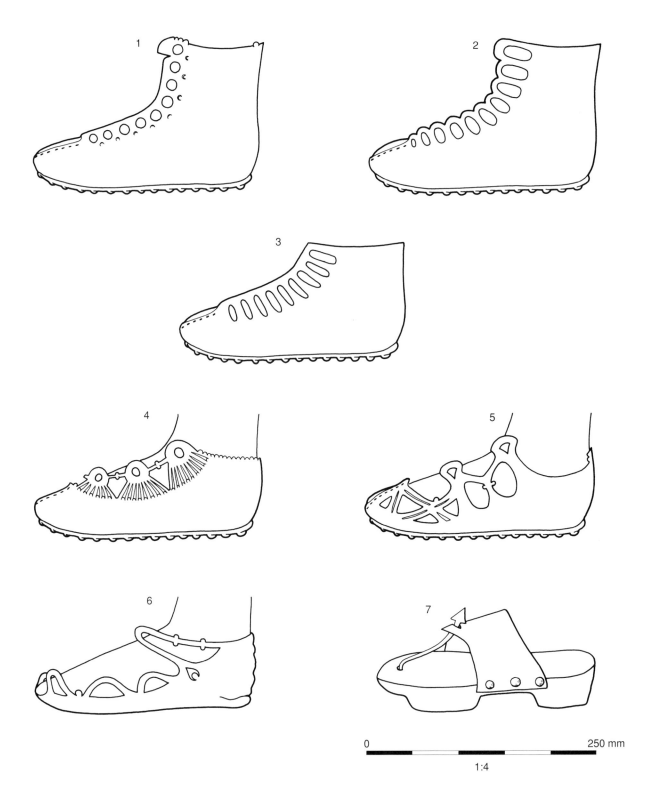

Figure 507: Styles of shoes from the forts at Carlisle

were also found in mid-fourth- to early fifth-century contexts (Periods 6C and 6E), where they are probably residual, as the shoe styles date no later than the third quarter of the second century.

Although the majority are fragmentary, at least 69 individual shoes are represented, with an estimated maximum of 97, over 75% being found in deposits dating to the first, or the first half of the second, century. The assemblage comprises mainly shoes of nailed construction, but there was also a single fragmentary sandal, four one-piece shoes, a wooden shoe sole, and a possible toe strap from a wooden-soled shoe (these types are shown in diagrammatic form in Figure 507, 1–5 being nailed shoes, 6 a one-piece shoe, and 7 a shoe with a wooden sole). No complete shoes were recovered and few had sufficiently well-preserved uppers to allow their style to be recognised with any certainty (see *Appendix 10*, for a catalogue of the illustrated items).

Methodology and terminology
The shoes and waste leather were examined after conservation, being recorded on *pro forma* sheets, accompanied by working drawings where necessary, in order to be consistent with records from previous excavations in Carlisle. Whenever it could be determined, all the components of a shoe were recorded on a single sheet. The highly fragmentary nature of many of the shoes made a total count of shoe parts irrelevant, but the minimum and maximum numbers of shoes represented have been estimated from a consideration of the shoe parts recovered from each context. Only one instance of parts of a single shoe being recovered from two separate contexts was noted (*1*, from deposits *6424* and *6429*). However, this is not particularly significant, as both contexts were spreads of silty soil overlying a floor in Period 4B Building *5689* (Phase 5), and may well have been part of the same general occupation deposit.

The terminology used is that most recently summarised by van Driel-Murray (2001a). The seams and stitch types use an expanded classification system, based on the earlier work of Groenman-van Waateringe (1967), Winterbottom (Padley and Winterbottom 1991), and van Driel-Murray (1993). The drawing conventions used in the illustrations are based on those advocated by Goubitz (1984), with modifications to accommodate the new classification, where appropriate.

Leather species were identified by examination of the hair follicle pattern under low-power magnification, but where the grain surface of the leather was heavily worn, identification was not always possible. The grain patterns of sheep and goat skins are difficult to distinguish, and these have been grouped together as sheep/goat when the distinction could not be made. Similarly, the distinction between immature (calfskin) and mature cattle hides is not always easy to determine, and the term bovine leather has been used when in doubt.

All shoes are of adult size unless otherwise stated, the shoe sizing being calculated according to the modern English shoe-size scale, with the insole measurement rounded up to the nearest size (continental sizing is provided in brackets in *Appendix 10*). Sizing was calculated from measurement of conserved leather, the shrinkage of thick 'shoe leather' following conservation being estimated at 3.5%, although the thin, flexible sheep/goatskin appears to have undergone no appreciable shrinkage (J Watson *pers comm*).

Context and date
Roman shoe parts were recovered from 69 stratified contexts and were also unstratified; for the most part, they were found in small numbers in a relatively large number of contexts. In the first century and the early part of the second (Periods 3A-4A), the majority of the shoe leather (between 66% and 88% according to the period) was found inside buildings. Most came from secondary deposits: construction cuts; the fills of pits and postholes; or incorporated in make-up or demolition layers; but *c* 25% came from occupation layers and floors. A small group was found in Building *7200*, associated with activity during Period 3C (Fig 269), and another was associated with Building *2059*, perhaps barracks, during Period 4A (Fig 270). Later in the second century (Period 4B), the situation changed, shoes being found in and around central range Building *5689*, a small number being in occupation layers and floors inside the building. In this period, however, 52% of the shoe leather was found outside buildings, principally in the backfill of gully *6290* and in a robber trench (*7471*) along road *7217*, adjacent to Building *5689*, with a small group from the surfaces of the main east to west road (*7477*). The small number recovered from later periods (Periods 5 and 6) came from the same area.

Nature of the assemblage
Despite its fragmentary nature, it was obvious that most of the footwear had been heavily worn, but its generally poor condition made it impossible to gauge the extent of repair. One shoe had the tread area of its nailed sole completely worn away. The majority of shoe parts were made of cattle hide, although occasional examples were found to be of thinner leathers, upper fragments of calfskin (*eg 8; Appendix 10*) and sheep/goatskin, and a multi-layered bottom unit of goatskin (*14*), being noted.

The condition of the footwear, and its overall distribution, suggests that it was deposited as a result of general rubbish disposal, rather than reflecting the dumping of material stripped of anything that might be usefully retained or recycled. There had, for instance, been no obvious, systematic removal of hobnails for recycling. Indeed, in contrast to the sheet leather, Roman footwear provides few opportunities for salvaging reusable materials. Despite this, some shoe parts (*eg 7, 5, 13; Appendix 10*) had been cut up before being thrown away, and the shoemakers had occasionally used salvaged material in nailed soles. A fragmentary bottom unit from an early second-century context (Period 4A road *7217*, layer *6651*) was found with five pieces of secondary waste, which may have been used as middle packing (see *Appendix 10* for a discussion of the waste leather). Other possible examples of reuse were noted; a shoe (*13*), from a later second-century deposit (*5900*), had small pieces of tent seam apparently reused as middle packing. Similar instances

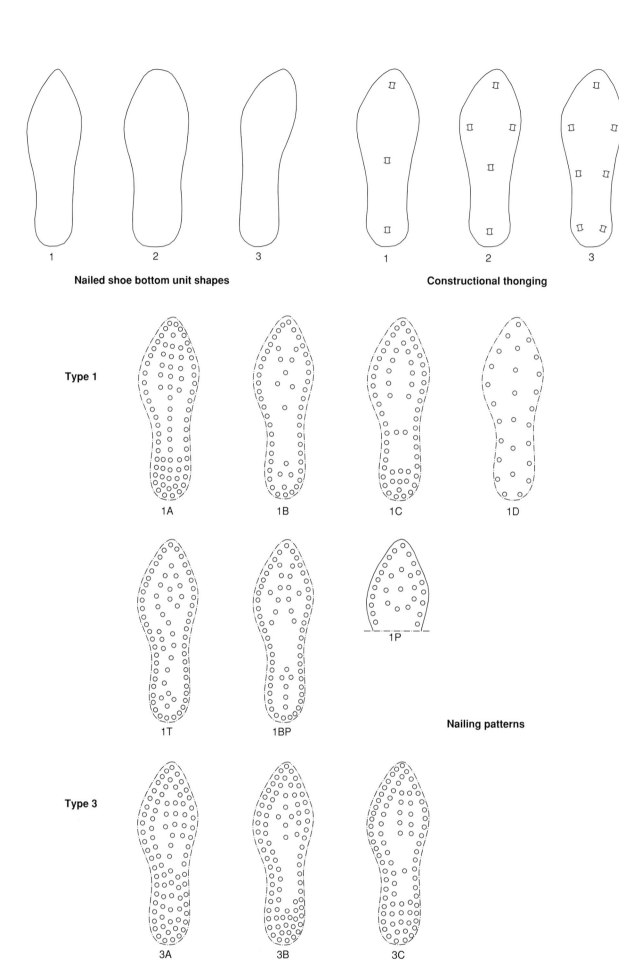

Nailed shoe bottom unit shapes

Constructional thonging

Type 1

1A   1B   1C   1D

1T   1BP   **Nailing patterns**

1P

Type 3

3A   3B   3C

Figure 508: Sole types, thonging, and nailing patterns

834

of cutting up shoe parts and the reuse of salvaged sheet leather in nailed footwear have previously been found in Carlisle (Padley 2000a, 99).

Nailed shoes

There were at least 65 nailed shoes. Only a small number (a minimum of six) came from first-century deposits (Periods 3A and 3B), and the majority (a minimum of 47) came from contexts dated to the late first century and first half of the second century (Periods 3C, 3E, 4A, and 4B). As no significant differences could be seen between the two groups, all the nailed shoes have been considered together, with constructional variations noted where appropriate.

Shoes of nailed construction have soles made of several layers of leather, held together principally by nailing. These layers, usually comprising an insole, a middle sole, middle laminae or small pieces of middle packing, and an outer sole, are known collectively as the bottom unit. As is generally the case with Roman nailed shoes, it is the bottom units that have survived. The uppers are generally poorly preserved and highly fragmentary, with only two notable exceptions, both of which survived almost intact.

Bottom units
Shape

The bottom units were all of adult size, with a 'natural foot' shape with a gently pointed or oval toe, the tread tapering to a wide waist and seat of similar size (Fig 508.1). Some examples were slightly wider and rather shapeless, with a blunt, more rounded toe (Fig 508.2). Five, from deposits of second-century date, had a swayed forepart with the tread area displaced inward (Fig 508.3).

Nailing patterns

Since previous work undertaken on the nailed shoes from Carlisle (Padley 1991d; in prep a, in prep b) and other sites along Hadrian's Wall (Mould 1997), a single scheme of classification for nailing patterns has been suggested and generally adopted (van Driel-Murray 2001a, 350–1, fig 21) and is used here. Thirty-six bottom units have a nailing pattern that could be classified, and are divided equally between those with a single line of nailing around the edge, with infilling at the tread and seat (Type 1, Fig 508), and those with a double line of nailing around the outer edge, and a single line at the inner edge, with similar infilling (Type 3, Fig 508). No certain examples with a continuous double line of nailing around the edge (Type 2) could be identified. Nailing of Types 1 and 3 was found in equal numbers (17 examples of Type 1, 18 examples of Type 3), the most popular variant being Type 3C (11 examples; Fig 508), with a single nail at the waist. This conforms to the distribution of nailing patterns seen in late first- and second-century assemblages elsewhere (van Driel-Murray 2001a, 351).

Decorative nailing patterns are found on soles with a single line of nailing around the edge. Two tread patterns recognised at Carlisle, a tendril design (Type 1T, Fig 508) and a circular pattern with a single nail at the centre (Type 1P, Fig 508), are commonly found in the northern provinces, and have been noted previously at Carlisle (Padley 1991d) and Birdoswald (Mould 1997). Another shoe (Fig 509.1), dating to the second quarter of the second century (Period 4B), has a distinctive nailing pattern that falls within Type 1B (Type 1BP, Fig 508). Whilst the nailing found at the tread and seat of soles, with a double line of nailing around the exterior edge (Type 3), usually takes the form of vertical lines, more decorative arrangements of crosses or circles may also occur at the tread. One shoe (509.2), from a deposit dating to AD 72/3–83 (Period 3A), with a Type 3B nailing pattern (Fig 508) with no nailing at the waist, has the tread filled with a cruciform pattern.

Constructional thonging

The majority of the nailed footwear had thonging joining the insole to the middle sole or laminae; only four bottom units had not been thonged. The distribution pattern conforms with that noted at Castleford (van Driel-Murray 1998, 293), with no thonging in shoes from the very earliest levels, but used extensively from AD 83–93/4 (Period 3B) onward. The three common arrangements of thonging (Mould 1997, 328–31) are all found in this assemblage, Type 2 being twice as common as Types 1 and 3 (Fig 508). At least four bottom units (*eg* Fig 509.3) have preserved lengths of thong 5–7 mm wide, while others (*eg* Fig 509.4) have the impression of thonging visible. The survival of thonging is a feature of shoes from Carlisle, being noted in assemblages from several excavations (*eg* Padley 1991d).

Shoe uppers

In all, 29 of the nailed shoes retained traces of their uppers. Most were represented by parts of the upper lasting margin, which had been protected by the bottom unit components, or areas around the heel protected by their proximity to a more robust heel stiffener; 21 heel stiffeners were found. Few uppers survived sufficiently well for the shoe style to be recognisable, but some had uppers that preserved characteristic features. In addition, some indication of the styles of shoe uppers can be gained from the shoemaking waste recovered (*Appendix 10*).

First/early second-century styles

The back part of a closed ankle boot (Fig 509.5), fastening up the foot with a series of circular lace holes, and made from cattle hide, was unstratified

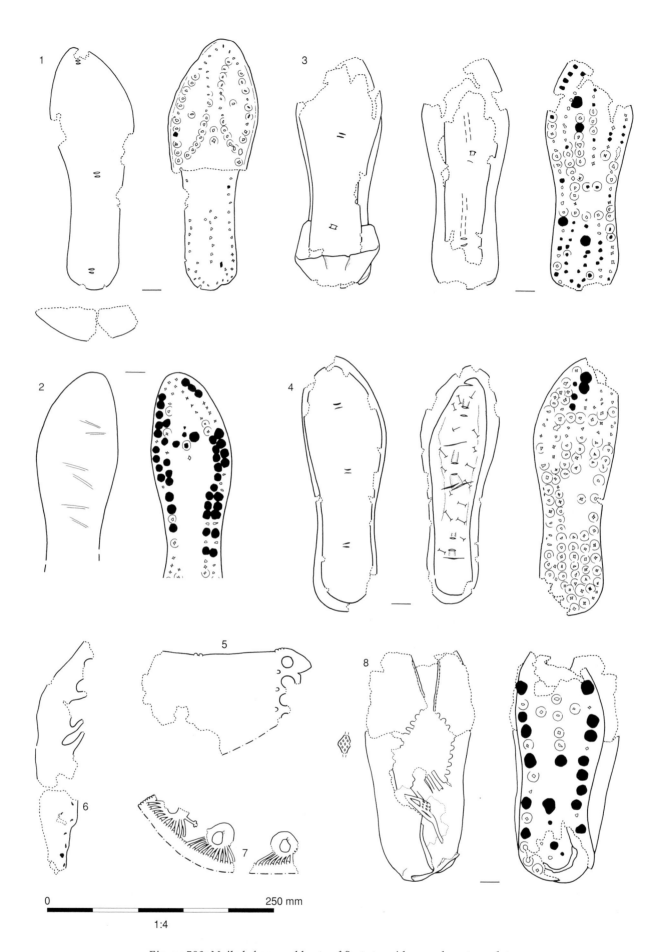

0   250 mm

1:4

Figure 509: Nailed shoes and boots of first- to mid-second-century date

(*eg* Fig 507.1). Soldiers' boots of this style (van Driel-Murray 2001b, fig 1.5) were worn at Vindolanda *c* AD 97–102/3, where the style was named the 'Fell boot' (van Driel-Murray 1993, 32, fig 17.1); the style remained popular to *c* AD 120 (van Driel-Murray 2001a, 364). A well-preserved ankle boot of similar style, but with longer, elliptical fastening holes (Pl 165; Fig 507.2-3), was found in soil layer *1639* in R2 of Building *2059* (Period 4A), and can be dated to *c* AD 105-25 (van Driel-Murray 2001b, fig 1.6). A fragment torn from the left side of what appears to be a third example (Fig 509.6) was found in the fill (*4088*) of post trench *4087* in Period 3 Building *4658*. A narrow lace, found with it, appears to have been torn from the top edge of the centre back of a soldier's boot; a pair of thin laces, often with decorative terminals ('dangles'), was a feature of military footwear at this time (*see* van Driel-Murray 1998, fig 131.10).

Mid-second-century shoe styles

Fragments of a cattle hide upper from a shoe of second-century date (Fig 509.7) were found in the fill (*7288*) of Period 3A pit *7287*, part of Structure *7657*. The pit was badly disturbed, and it is likely that the shoe was in fact intrusive within the later first-century deposit. The upper, with circular fastening loops and radiating narrow straps (*eg* Fig 507.4), had been deliberately cut away from the bottom unit, above the lasting margin, before being thrown away. It is comparable with a better-preserved example, made in one-piece with a central toe seam, found at Castle Street (Padley 1991d, no 895, 236 fig 209) in a context dated to *c* AD 105-80. This general style of shoe (van Driel-Murray 2001b, fig 1.18) was popular in the middle of the second century, and is commonly found at Antonine Wall sites (van Driel-Murray 2001a, 365); the general style was classified as 'calceus type C' when found at the Bar Hill fort (Robertson *et al* 1975, fig 23, nos 25-9). One of the better-preserved nailed shoes (Fig 509.8), found in Building *5689* on Period 4B floor *6426*, dating to the second quarter of the second century, appears to be another example of the type (*op cit*, particularly fig 23, no 25). The shoe, for the left foot, had a closed upper of calfskin, with a central toe seam and the remains of a series of narrow straps. Small, pierced, lozenge-shapes found with the shoe might also have been part of the upper strapwork.

A few other nailed shoes, with rather more fragmentary uppers (Fig 510.9-12) were found in contexts dating to the first half of the second century (Periods 4A and 4B), and one (Fig 510.13) in a late second-century deposit. The remaining uppers have characteristics seen on better-preserved shoes of mid-second-century date found elsewhere. A fastening loop on one example, *9*, suggests it comes from a style of shoe (van Driel-Murray 2001b, fig 1, style 11)

popular during the Antonine period (Fig 507.5) and seen at Bar Hill (Robertson *et al* 1975, fig 22, 5, 'calceus type A') and Birdoswald (Mould 1997, 335, fig 244, style 2). Other fragments of upper found with this shoe have narrow divided straps and a butted seam, probably from the central seam running down toward the toe. Narrow divided straps also occur on upper fragments (Fig 510.10) from an occupation layer in R2 within Building *7396*. The apparent back seam present on these two fragments suggests a shoe back part comparable with that on a shoe of one-piece construction from the Southern Lanes (Padley 2000a, 101, fig 61 M87) and others at Catterick (Hooley 2002, fig 395 no 94, and fig 396 no 100).

Another shoe (Fig 510.11) had a line of decorative roundels along the top edge, a feature again found on nailed shoes from Bar Hill (Robertson *et al* 1975, fig 23 nos 28, 30, fig 24 nos 42, 44). A single fragment of sheep/goatskin (from Period 4B robber trench fill *6373*, associated with road *7217*) was covered by regularly spaced, stabbed holes, and may possibly be cut away from a shoe upper of 'fishnet' design. Such uppers are more usually decorated by a series of tiny cut-outs or punched holes, rather than stabbed or awl-made holes, and the identification is far from certain.

A multi-layered shoe of nailed and stitched construction

Goatskin components from the bottom unit of a multi-layered shoe sole with nailing (Fig 510.14) were found in the fill (*1075*) of a gully (*1089*) associated with Period 3A Building *1222*, probably barracks, in the southern part of the fort. The elegant shape suggests it came from a stylish shoe of high quality. The middle laminae have tunnel stitching to attach the shoe upper, and lengths of upper lasting margin are preserved around the edge. Although the bottom unit was clearly nailed, it could come from a shoe with an essentially stitched construction, the nailing being added purely to make the sole more hard-wearing. This cannot now be confirmed, as the shoe lacks both the sole and insole. A second piece of goatskin, found in the same context, may be another component of its bottom unit. A bottom unit of this sort is likely to come from a 'dress' shoe not intended for heavy wear, though the addition of hobnails suggests it was worn out of doors. Shoes with multi-layered bottom units and a single shoe of nailed and stitched construction have been found at Castle Street (Padley 1991d, 234, nos 1013–6 and fig 216, and 233, fig 214, no 987). Shoes of stitched construction have been found previously in the fort (Annetwell Street, Padley in prep b, C572–4) and elsewhere in Carlisle, at the northern end of The Lanes (Padley in prep a, L135, L137) and Castle Street (Padley 1991d, 233 and fig 214). No shoes of exclusively stitched construction were found during these excavations.

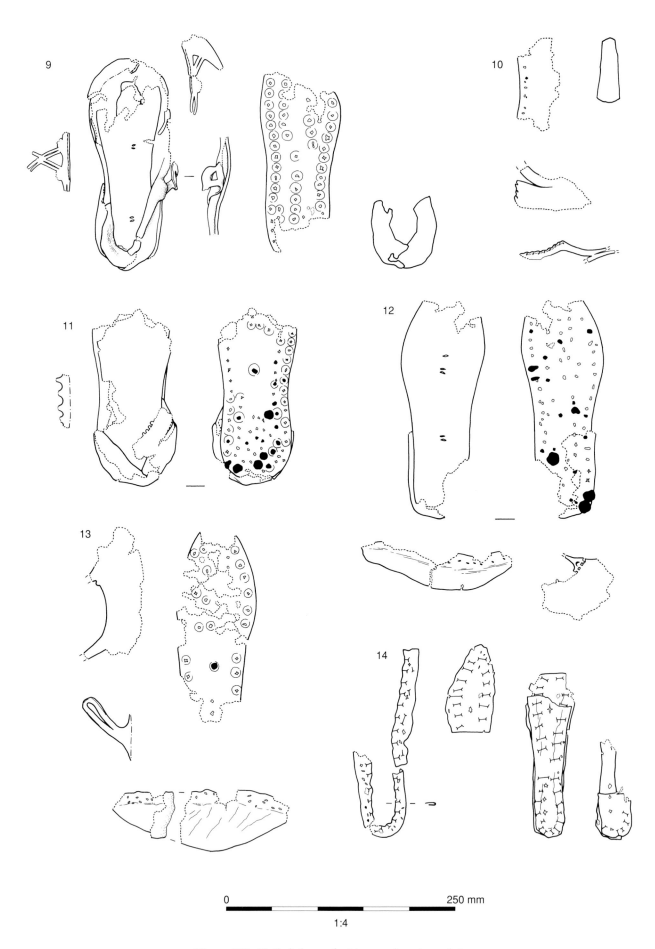

0   250 mm

1:4

Figure 510: Nailed shoes of mid-second-century date

Sandals

Sandals have the components of the bottom unit held together by thonging around the edge; the sole may also have hobnails to make it more hard-wearing. Fragments from a single example of a nailed sandal were recognised, the left side of the sole having been deliberately cut away from the rest of the bottom unit, which suggests that it was cobbling waste. It was found in a make-up layer (*6818*) in Building **7200** and is likely to date to the turn of the second century (Period 3C).

One-piece shoes

Only four shoes of one-piece construction were found (Fig 511.15-18), all coming from contexts dating to the first half of the second century (Periods 4A and 4B). Very small fragments, possibly broken from other examples, were also noted. All four were of adult size and made of cattle hide, with tooling giving a 'rounded' appearance to the cut edges (Fig 507.6). In each case, the seam around the seat was sewn with an edge/flesh seam, but the back seams differed. Two examples (Fig 511.17-18) had a closed back seam sewn with grain/flesh stitching, *18* with a running stitch, the other (*17*) with whip stitching. A third example (Fig 511.16) had a butted back seam with an edge/grain stitch on one side and a grain/flesh stitch on the other, again sewn with whip stitching. The fourth (Fig 511.15) had an edge/grain seam that had been repaired with edge/flesh and grain/flesh stitching.

Three of the one-piece shoes are of similar style. Two came from central range Building **5689**: one (*15*) from Phase 3 pit *6706*; the other (*16*) from a possible floor of Phase 6. The third example (*17*) came from

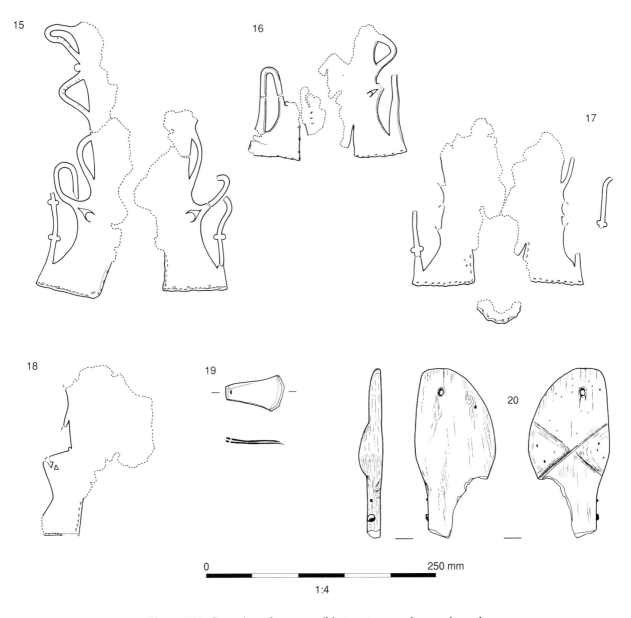

Figure 511: One-piece shoes, possible toe strap, and a wooden sole

a possible gully (*930*) in the south-east quadrant. They are of similar general design to those found in previous excavations in Carlisle. The lower fastening loops are plain and the ankle loops are decorated with small roundels (or lobes), with small triangular cut-outs with roundels at the base of the loop; these small decorative features being paralleled on one-piece shoes from both the southern (Padley 2000a, fig 61) and the northern Lanes (Padley in prep a, L149-150).

The fourth one-piece shoe ((Fig 511.18)) was found on an external surface of compacted cobbles (*1490*) attributed to Period 4B. Though little detail of the upper is preserved, a small cut-out triangle is present at the base of the ankle fastening loop; small triangular cut-outs were also a feature on an example from Castle Street (Padley 1991d, fig 215 no 1001).

Other types of footwear

A wooden shoe sole (Fig 511.20) was found in fill *4117* of a construction trench (*4118*) of Building *3772* (a Period 3B barrack). The sole is broken, but is of adult size (estimated Adult 5 (38)). It has a single hole for a toe strap, or possibly a toe peg of leather, wood, or bone. A fragment of iron shank close to the hole suggests that a toe strap of leather or textile may have been nailed in place; alternatively, a large knot may have been used. Iron nails in the side of the sole at the waist mark the former position of a strap across the instep. Wooden clogs (Fig 507.7) were worn in the bath-house to protect feet from the hot floors, and may well have been worn outdoors as overshoes to raise them above mud in the streets. This example, having a toe strap, was obviously worn barefoot, suggesting it had been used in the bath-house. A text from Vindolanda refers to *balnearia*, shoes for bathing, and large numbers of wooden soles and their leather straps have been recovered from that fort (van Driel-Murray 2001a, 359 and footnote 36).

A possible toe strap (Fig 511.19) of cattle hide, for a similar wooden-soled shoe, was found amongst a large amount of shoemaking waste (*Appendix 10*) in occupation layer *5816* in R1 of Building *7396* (Period 4A), interpreted as a workshop. The strap appears to have laminated into two pieces, one with the grain surface scored in two places, the other with no grain surface present. The pieces differ slightly in size, apparently due to differential shrinkage, and it is possible, though unlikely, that a pair of straps is represented. The shape is reminiscent of toe straps found on pattens and overshoes worn throughout much of the post-medieval period. This example, being found in a well-stratified context, is certainly of Roman date, though of a style rarely, if ever, previously found. The awl-made hole at the tip might suggest that it had been intended to tie

with a thong or cord across the toes. The toe strap has neither nail holes from nailing to a wooden sole nor stitch holes from stitching to a leather sole. This presents two possibilities: either it was unused, or had been cut away above the line of nailing or stitching so it could be attached to a new sole. The tie hole appears unused, suggesting it might had been cut from salvaged leather and subsequently rejected. The identification is only tentative, however, and it may well be a piece of secondary waste that superficially resembles a toe strap.

Shoe sizes

Shoe size is calculated from measurements of the complete insole (van Driel-Murray 1994, 344, note 3), but as there were only ten shoes that retained complete insoles, no valid analysis of shoe size and its implications for gender was possible. A further six shoes had complete soles, and many other shoe parts survived sufficiently well to allow a basic distinction to be made between adult and small child. Male sizes predominated, but examples of complete insoles corresponding to women's or adolescent male sizes were also present. Shrinkage of thick 'shoe leather' following conservation has been estimated at 3.5% for this assemblage (J Watson *pers comm*). It is possible to compare the actual measurement of relevant complete shoe parts with the corresponding equivalent modern shoe size, and the addition of this 3.5% allowance for shrinkage serves only to raise the estimate by a single shoe size; therefore, the presence of smaller foot sizes amongst the late first- and first half of the second-century military footwear appears to be a valid observation. Also of interest in this regard is the multi-layered bottom unit of goatskin (Fig 510.14) from an elegant, high-quality shoe (*Appendix 10*). Whilst the middle laminae would be of slightly smaller size than the insole that lay above, its size and shape all suggest a shoe for a female foot. No shoes of a size suitable to fit young children were recovered. A similar size distribution was found in previous excavations within the fort, and at Annetwell Street only a single possible insole to fit the foot of a small child was noted (Padley in prep b, C586, 130 mm in length, child size 4 (20)), in a second-century deposit.

Discussion

Shoes from the site show only a rather limited range of styles, comprising late first- to early second-century military footwear and second-century shoes worn by soldiers and civilians alike. Considering the date of the construction of the Period 3 fort (AD 72/3), it would be reasonable to expect to find military footwear of *caliga* type, at least in the earliest levels. None have ever been recovered from excavations in Carlisle, although they have been recognised in assemblages from a contemporary midden deposit at

Castleford, in West Yorkshire (fort I; AD 71/4-*c* AD 86; Cool and Philo 1998, 6; van Driel-Murray 1998, 289–91). Five shoes from excavations at Annetwell Street, Carlisle (Padley in prep b, C461–5, table 75), share certain characteristics, but do not appear to be examples of the true military *caliga*, but rather to be in styles that probably derive from them. The limited evidence from surviving shoe uppers from the Millennium excavations shows that soldiers' boots with closed uppers were being worn; ankle boots of this sort replaced the *caliga* as military wear in the late first century, probably as early as the AD 80s (Hooley 2002, 324).

The Medieval Leather

Q Mould

The medieval leatherwork comprised nearly 390 shoe parts (representing at least 64 shoes), 35 other items, including decorated straps, panels, and sheaths, an archer's bracer, fragments of a sword belt, and possible bellows-leather. There were, in addition, 327 pieces of waste, and 45 pieces of scrap. It came from the outer ward ditch (*1230* and recut *1231*), from features associated with tenements *1234* and *1235*, built over the partially infilled ditch at a later date, and spreads that accumulated over both properties after their abandonment.

Only 9% of the medieval material came from fills associated with the primary phase of the outer ward ditch (*1230*, Period 8i), with considerably more (23%) from the thirteenth- to fourteenth-century recut (*1231*, Period 8ii). More than half the assemblage derived from contexts dating from the second half of the fourteenth century onward, associated with tenements *1234* and *1235* (31%, Period 8iii; 36%, Period 8iv). None was found within the castle's outer ward itself, which was not waterlogged.

Methodology and terminology
The methodologies employed during quantification, identification of leather species, and estimation of the equivalent modern shoe size are the same as that employed for the Roman assemblage (*p 833*). Shoe soles and repairs are assumed to be of cattle hide unless stated otherwise. The estimation of modern shoe size of examples with long, pointed toes has been calculated from measurement of the sole from the seat to the estimated extent of the big toe, the latter based on consideration of the wear pattern and toe width. The definitions of categories of waste leather (primary and secondary) and scrap leather are those used for the Roman assemblage. Cobbling waste refers to shoe parts cut up for reuse (see *Appendix 10* for a discussion of the waste leather and for a catalogue of the illustrated items).

Condition
The leather was generally in good condition but, having been stored wet for several years prior to conservation, a small amount had suffered bacterial attack, causing small holes and areas with a pitted surface.

Context and date
Leather was recovered from 68 medieval (Periods 8i–iv) and five post-medieval deposits (Period 9). All the leather can be dated to the medieval period, with the exception of a very small quantity of residual Roman material (Table 59; *Appendix 10*). The medieval material can be divided into five main stratigraphic groups, with a small amount recovered residually in a modern context (*700*), and the fills of Period 9 cellar *841*.

Group 1: Primary fills of the first outer ward ditch (*1230*; Period 8i)
This group can be divided in two: a small amount of waste leather, scrap, and fragments of stitched sheet panel likely to be of Roman date (all from MIL 3); and a small group of medieval leather comprising at least six shoes (from MIL 4). The shoes are a mixed group; sole *21* (*p 845*) could be of late eleventh to the first half of the twelfth century in date, whilst the style of two uppers from the fills date from the (early to mid-thirteenth century onward, with one possibly being as late as the second half of the fourteenth century. In addition, cobbling waste (deriving from the repair rather than the manufacture of shoes) was identified in ditch fill *1754*.

Trench	Period	Context	IRF No	Species	Quantity	Comments
MIL 3	8i	*817*	656.01	Sheep/goat	13	Found with tent binding 656.02
MIL 3	8i	*852*	687	Sheep/goat	2	-
MIL 3	8i	*857*	664.01	Sheep/goat	1	Worn/abraded
MIL 5	8A	*5258*	8344	Sheep/goat	1	-

Table 59: Roman scrap/waste (sheet) leather in medieval contexts

Group 2: Recut of the outer ward ditch (*1231*; Period 8ii)

Two toggle-fastening ankle shoes (*eg 23; Appendix 10*), dating to the mid-thirteenth to mid-fourteenth century, were found in pits *1428* and *1433*, cut into the natural clay at the base of ditch *1231*. Above these, the lowest fills produced a large group of items, including a knife sheath, possible bellows'-leather, a disc, a girdle, straps, and at least 16 shoes. The latter were in styles popular in the thirteenth and fourteenth centuries and could, indeed, all date to the fourteenth. The wide range of items and the number of nearly complete shoes suggest that the group was mainly domestic rubbish, although there was also cobbling waste. The shoe parts in fill *1387* had been cut up in order to salvage reusable leather for cobbling.

Group 3: Features associated with tenement *1234*, built over ditch *1231* (Period 8iii)

This is a small group, from the open area to the north of tenement *1234*, comprising three shoes, along with fragments of plain and decorated leather panels (*49, 50, 51; p 855*). An archer's bracer (*52*) and the remains of two shoes (*eg 32*) were found in a fill of the construction trench (*1788*) for wooden fence *2065*, which marked the northern boundary of the property. A post in this fence had a felling date of spring/summer AD 1385 (*Appendix 16*). The style of the shoes suggests a mid-thirteenth- to mid-fourteenth-century date.

Group 4: Ditch *1403* (Period 8iii)

At least seven shoes, two panels, a strap, and a group of waste leather were found in ditch *1403* at the northern boundary of the tenements, immediately beyond fence *2065*. It probably represents domestic rubbish and a dump of shoemaking and/or cobbling waste that included a rough-out for a sole seat for a two-part shoe sole, or a clump seat repair (from fill *1420*). Shoe styles suggest a late fourteenth- to early fifteenth-century date for this group.

Group 5: Spreads accumulated over tenements *1234* and *1235* (Period 8iv)

At least 23 shoes, waste leather, and a small number of other leather items were found in these deposits. A similar range of material was found on each property, but that from the easternmost (*1235*) was more extensive and better preserved. At least part of the assemblage appears to be a small dump of cobbling waste. Shoes from deposits over *1235* were chiefly of styles dating to the late fourteenth and fifteenth centuries, with a single toggle-fastening shoe from layer *1384* (tenement *1235*) probably belonging earlier in the fourteenth century. The shoes from above *1234* suggest a similar date.

Nature of the assemblage

The medieval leather comprises a mixture of domestic rubbish and waste leather from shoemaking and

cobbling, with the majority generated by cobbling (*Appendix 10*). Characteristically, this comprises worn shoe parts, cut up in order to salvage leather for reuse, and in the main reflects the repair of worn shoes and the remodelling and refurbishing of old shoes for resale. Cobbling waste was present in the primary fill (*1754*) of the original outer ward ditch (*1230*; Period 8i) and two fills (*1387, 1764*) of recut *1231* (Period 8ii). It was also found in layer *791* to the north of tenement *1234* and the fills (*1420, 1481*) of ditch *1403* (Period 8iii), as well as layers *1320, 1384*, and *1580*, which accumulated over the properties during Period 8iv. Old shoes cut down and remodelled for further wear (known as translated shoes) were also present in the assemblage, *30* being an example (*p 845*). In contrast, a shoe from fill *1424* of recut ditch *1231* had the vamp cut in half down the centre, rendering it unusable and impossible to cut down to make a shoe of smaller size.

Types of leather used

The majority of the leather used at this time was bovine (98% of waste leather), with most of the shoe uppers of either cattle hide or calfskin. A few were made of sheep/goatskin, and uppers in this material were noted in Periods 8i–8iii: coming from fill *1754* in ditch *1230* (*21*, Period 8i); fill *1764* in recut *1231* (Period 8ii); and deposits *791* and *1785*, associated with the tenements (*eg 32*, Period 8iii). A single patch repairing a stitched sheet panel, found in fill *817* of ditch *1230*, was tentatively identified as deerskin, but may be of Roman date. The sheaths and other decorated items (*p 855*) were made of cattle hide or calfskin, and the archer's bracer and the straps were of cattle hide. A possible bellows-leather (*54*) and fragments from four panels were of sheep/goatskin. There were also small numbers of hide edges, trimmings, and other secondary waste pieces in sheep/goatskin.

The shoes
Construction

At least 64 shoes were represented by the shoe parts recovered, 40 being complete or near complete (with half or more surviving) single-piece shoe soles; a few soles were made in two parts, joined with a butted edge/flesh seam at the waist. Of the latter, two were complete (*24* and *30*), and five foreparts and three seats were found separately. Two-part soles were found from Period 8ii onward, the majority in recut outer ward ditch *1231*.

All the shoes were of turnshoe construction. The soles were sewn to the uppers with an edge/flesh seam, usually with a rand incorporated; rands were found in contexts from Period 8ii onward. The uppers were either one-piece, with additional inserts where required (at least nine examples were noted), or had separate vamps and quarters. Some styles, principally toggle-fastening shoes and front-fastening shoes, had been made in both cutting patterns. The upper components were joined with butted edge/flesh seams, and occasionally insert pieces were attached with whip stitching. This stitch was also used to attach tongues, top bands, heel stiffeners, and linings. Some shoes had stitching on the interior (flesh side) in areas subject to particular strain. On occasion, it clearly resulted from the attachment of a strengthening cord (*eg 34*), and a few others (*eg 38*) had small tabs attached to strengthen points of weakness. Two shoes (*30, 32*), both dating to the later fourteenth century (Period 8iii), had integral linings, cut in one piece with the shoe component, then folded over and stitched to the inside of the shoe. Two ankle boots of differing styles had heel stiffeners worn flesh side towards the foot (*eg 25*), rather than the more usual grain side out. Both these unusual features were seen in contemporary shoes from excavations at Rickergate, also in Carlisle (Mould 2004).

Two shoes, both from ditch **1231**, had incised marks on their interiors. Toggle-fastening ankle boot *25* had an arrow cut into the heel stiffener, and side-lacing ankle boot *31* had a cross in the same position. The meaning of the marks is unknown, although they might represent a sizing system, or be a mark of ownership, or possibly even determine a right from a left foot.

Toe shapes varied as fashions changed through time. Shoes from the original outer ward ditch (**1230**, Period 8i) were mixed, with oval toes, short-pointed, and long-pointed toes all present. There were two shoes with long-pointed toes, but little remained of the upper of *21* (*p 845*), and, consequently, its style cannot be identified, but the shape of its long, outward curving toe was popular at the end of the eleventh and into the first half of the twelfth century (Grew and de Neergaard 1988, 11). The other (*33*) was of a style popular in the later fourteenth century and seems likely to be intrusive in what appears to be a late twelfth- to thirteenth-century context. Shoes in the later recut of the ditch (**1231**, Period 8ii) mainly had oval toes, only two having short-pointed toes. Long-pointed toes were predominant in Period 8iii, with only single examples of short-pointed and oval toes. In Period 8iv, shoes with pointed toes, both long and short, were fashionable for adults, whilst children's or adolescent sizes had oval toes or short points.

The long-toed shoes had exaggerated points extending well beyond the end of the wearer's foot. Several of the 14 shoes had their long toe broken off, but eight complete examples were recorded, measuring between 43 mm and 100 mm. Lack of wear at the ends of two of the longest examples (*33, 34*; *p 849*) showed clearly that the toes had curled upward.

Moss toe-stuffing

Two shoes from Period 8iv deposits *1383* and *1384* provided evidence of stuffing in the toes. From the former, a long, pointed toe torn from a low shoe fastened with a divided strap over the instep, was stuffed with a species of moss (*Eurhynchium* spp), which grows on banks, or in woodland on calcareous or moderately nutrient-rich soil (A Hall *pers comm*). The latter, the sole of a shoe with a short, pointed toe, had staining marking the former position of stuffing.

Repairs

Many of the shoes were heavily worn, and about 17% of the soles and sole fragments had evidence of tunnel stitching to attach a repair. Three soles had been repaired several times before finally being discarded. One, from fill *1764* in ditch **1231** (Period 8ii), had been repaired at least three times at the seat ('re-heeled'), whilst the seat and tread of another (*22*) had been repaired twice ('heeled and soled'), and the third, from tenement **1235** (layer *1386*, Period 8iv), had had the tread repaired on two separate occasions. It may well be the case that the two-part shoe soles found were the result of replacing areas of heavy wear during the refurbishment of old shoes for resale.

Four shoe uppers had been repaired. An ankle shoe tying at the instep (*28*) had three small slashes or nicks on the interior of the vamp repaired with whip stitching; made during the tanning process, the slashes had been repaired before the shoe was assembled. Poor-quality leather was used in the construction of toggle-fastening ankle boot *26* (*p 845*), the heel stiffener having been made of belly skin, with a teat clearly visible. It is notable that whilst the most heavily repaired shoe soles were found in the later deposits (Period 8iv), in general terms fewer shoes from those deposits had been repaired. This, together with the number of exaggeratedly long toes found, might suggest that, at this time, part of the footwear assemblage derived from a more affluent sector of the population.

Foot pathology

Many of the shoes were heavily worn, but on two it was sufficiently pronounced to suggest that the wearer had problems with their feet. The pattern of wear on *27*, being heaviest at the toe, great toe joint, and inner heel area of the upper, as well as being distorted overall, suggests that the young child who wore this shoe might have been 'pigeon-toed'. Boot *40* had an unusual cutting pattern which, together

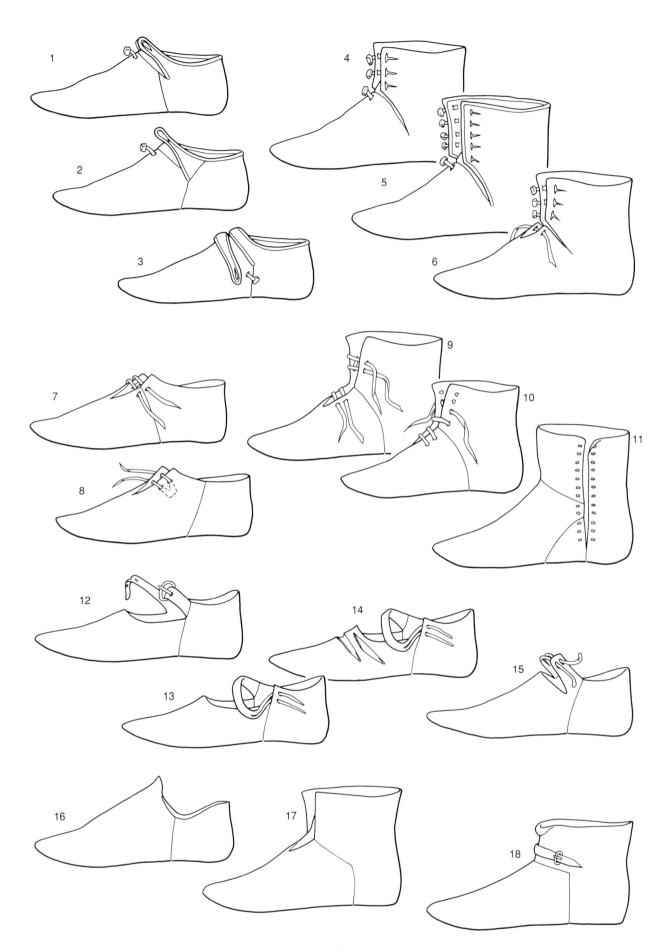

Figure 512: Shoe styles from the medieval deposits

with the deep impression made by the ball of the foot at the forepart of the sole, and the extent of wear at the vamp, indicated the wearer had a foot deformity. Two more soles had their foreparts heavily swayed inward, one showing particularly heavy wear, which could also indicate a foot problem, although in the absence of the upper, this could not be confirmed.

Styles
The range of shoe styles (Fig 512) can be dated to the mid-thirteenth-mid fourteenth, mid-late fourteenth, and early fifteenth centuries by comparison with shoes from the well-dated waterfront dumps in the City of London (Grew and de Neergaard 1988). Inevitably, styles and fashions overlap, and it is possible that the range of the entire assemblage could be reduced to a period of *c* 75 years between the middle of the fourteenth and the early fifteenth centuries.

Toggle-fastening shoes and boots
Seven shoes or boots were fastened with rolled toggles (as in styles 1-6; Fig 512), and other shoe parts are likely to represent a further five examples in this style; all were made of bovine leather. Toggle-fastening shoes and ankle boots were popular in England from the middle of the thirteenth to the middle of the fourteenth century. In London, the earliest are found in deposits of the early thirteenth century (Grew and de Neergaard 1988, 21), whilst in Europe, the style appears to have been popular during the fourteenth century (Goubitz *et al* 2001, 161).

Four shoes were recorded, all from Period 8ii contexts: two (*eg 23*; Fig 513) from pit *1433*, at the base of ditch *1231*, and two more (*eg 24*) from the fills above. All were similar, being fastened across the instep with a pair of narrow straps, which buttoned over a rolled toggle at the centre of the vamp throat. A tongue was sewn to the throat, a narrow top band sewn along the top edge of the uppers, and the back of the quarters supported by a heel stiffener. Cutting patterns varied, however; one (*23*) had a one-piece upper, the others had a separate vamp and quarters. The two better-preserved examples (Fig 513.23-24) are variants on the standard type. Shoe *24* had no holes on the fastening straps, the loops being formed by the top band, and the other, *23*, with a one-piece upper, lacked the toggle at the centre of the vamp, but had a toggle to each side, suggesting that the two fastening straps crossed over the instep (as in style 3, Fig 512). Both shoes were of adult size 3 (35), a size normally appropriate to women or adolescents; other shoes of this style were of adult size.

Two taller ankle boots (styles 4 and 5, Fig 512), in the same general style, were found in ditch *1231*.

One (*25*; Fig 514) fastened with three toggles up the leg, the other (*26*) with four. A third, fragmentary, example in cattle hide (associated with Building *1492*; Fig 280) also fastened with three toggles up the leg, but had a lace, rather than a toggle, at the instep (as in style 6, Fig 512).

There were vamps from three other shoes with a rolled toggle (or holes marking its former position), at the centre of the throat, a characteristic of this style, one from ditch *1230*, a second from recut *1231*, and the third from Period 8iv spread *1384* in tenement *1235*. Other fragments of shoe upper with remains of thongs from broken 'toggle-type' fastenings are likely to come from similar shoe styles, though they might have fastened with either toggles, tailed toggles, or tailed laces (knotted laces).

Ankle shoes and boots fastening through paired lace holes at the instep
There were at least ten shoes in this style (7-9; Fig 512), popular from the middle to the end of the fourteenth century. The majority were cut at or below the ankle, but at least one (style 9) extended to just below the calf. Most (six) shoes of this style were found in ditch *1231*, one was from ditch *1403*, and the remainder from deposits that accumulated over tenements *1234* and *1235*.

Of the four examples in which laces survived, two (Figs 514.27 and 515.29) had a divided (split) lace threaded through the pair of lace holes on one side of the instep and tied through the pair in the other. The other two (*eg* Fig 514.28) used a single lace apparently threaded in the same manner. Two distinct cutting patterns shared this type of fastening: those with one-piece uppers; and those with separate vamps and quarters. Four, ranging from adult size 3 (35) to adult size 6 (39), were made with separate vamp and quarters. A near-complete shoe for a young child, child size 6 (23) (Fig 514.27), had a one-piece upper.

Ankle shoes and boots lacing through multiple lace holes
There were parts from six or possibly seven shoes fastening through multiple lace holes (styles 10 and 11; Fig 512). Side-lacing shoes and boots were worn throughout the thirteenth and fourteenth centuries, and those with closely spaced multiple lace holes being popular in London during the early fifteenth century (Grew and de Neergaard 1988, 43). Front-lacing shoes were fashionable in the middle and later fourteenth century (Goubitz *et al* 2001, 187; Grew and de Neergaard 1988, 28, figs 55–8),

A single child's ankle shoe (Fig 515.30), from ditch *1403* (fill *1493*), laced up the instep via a series of six

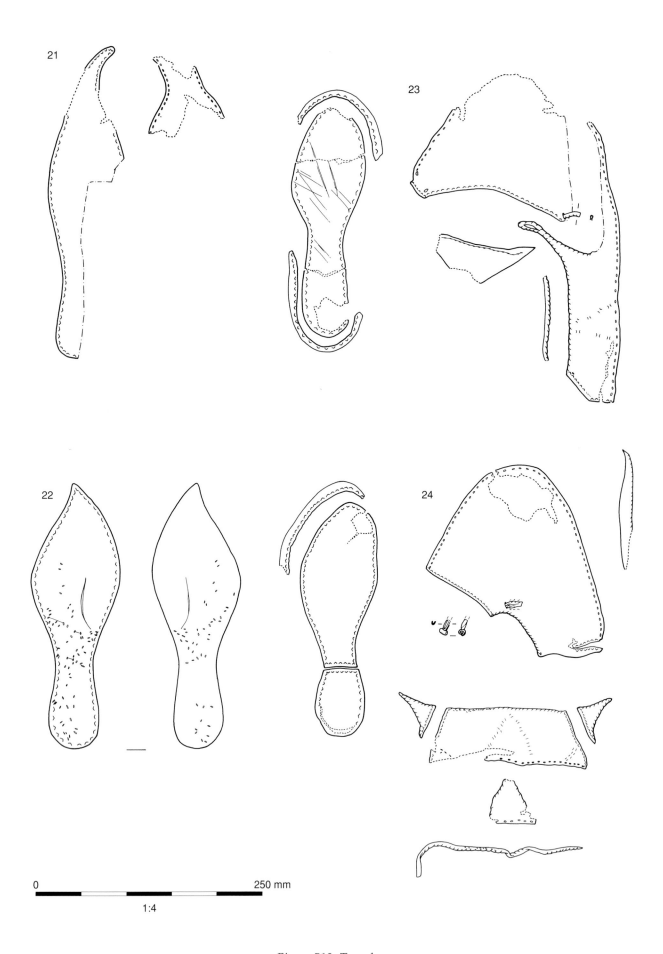

21

23

22

24

0   250 mm

1:4

Figure 513: Turnshoes

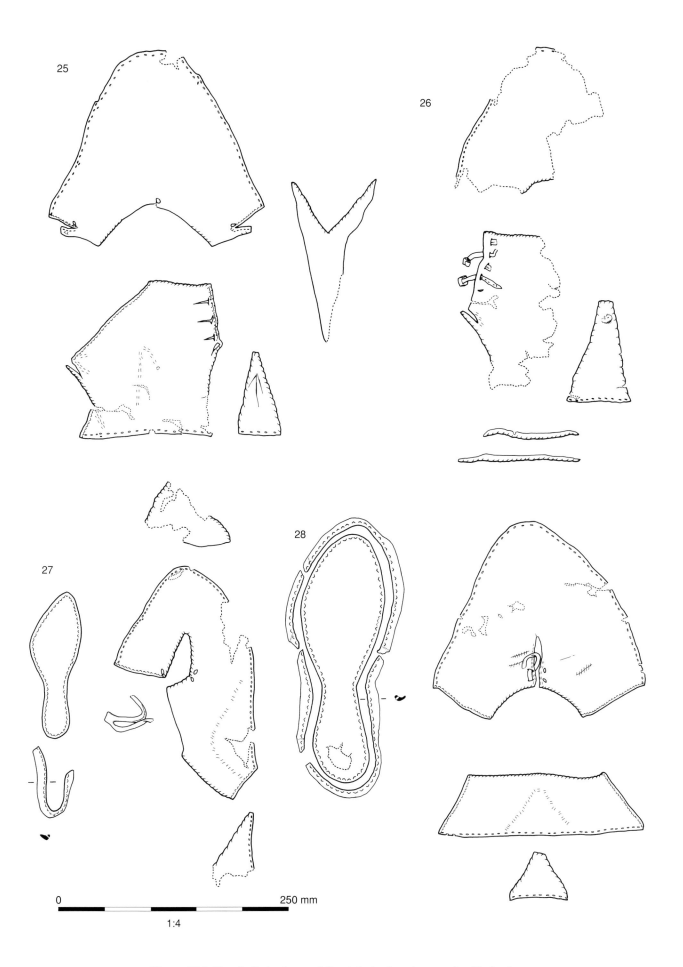

25

26

27

28

0   250 mm

1:4

Figure 514: Toggle-fastening and front-fastening shoes and ankle boots

847

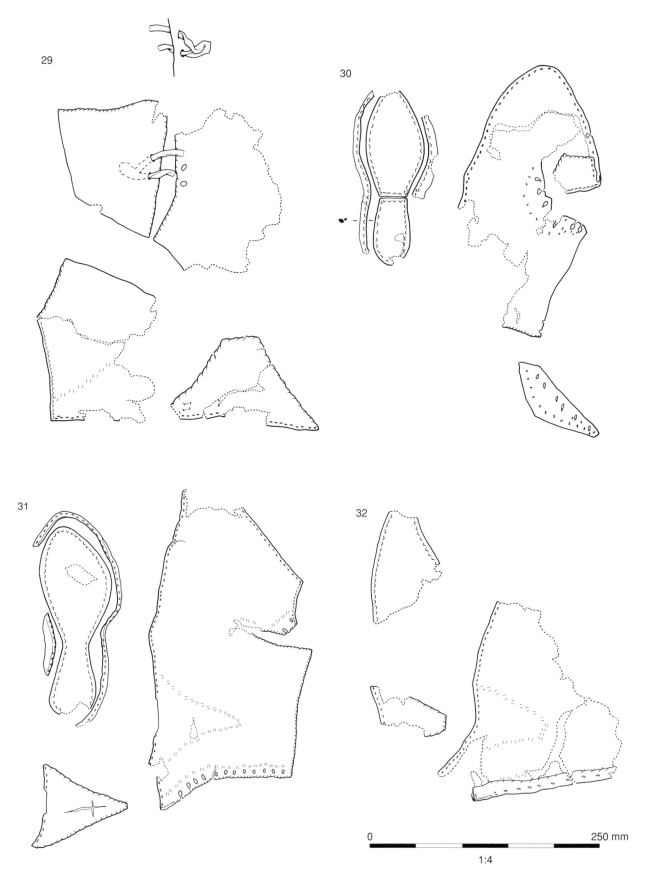

29

30

31

32

0   250 mm

1:4

Figure 515: Front-fastening and side-lacing boots and shoe

lace holes (style 10, Fig 512). It appears to have been refurbished and remodelled, presumably from an adult shoe, and in consequence the lace holes were irregularly spaced and the lining rather crudely stitched to the interior. In addition, the sole was in two parts, joined across the tread, suggesting that the seat had been replaced. The cattle hide upper was made mainly in one piece, and the single side-seam had an integral lining made by folding back a flap of leather, sewing a seam along the fold so created, and whip stitching the edges to the interior of the upper. Integral linings such as this are uncommon, but another was found in this assemblage (Fig 515.32) and they were also noted on three shoes with one-piece uppers from the excavations at Rickergate (Mould 2004). The technique appears to be particular to the late medieval shoemakers of Carlisle, and could be a distinctive regional feature.

At least three shoes laced at the side (style 11, Fig 512). A child's ankle boot of calfskin (Fig 515.31), lacing through 13 holes, was found in fill *1310* at the base of ditch *1231*. A fragmentary example in sheep/goatskin came from an external area to the south of tenement *1234*, at a time when Building *1492* was in use. Sheep/goatskin boot *32*, extending well above the ankle and fastened through a series of small, closely-spaced lace holes, was found in the fill (*1785*) of the construction trench (*1788*) for fence *2065* (Period 8iii). The position of the lacing could not be determined for the remainder of this group; pieces of leather lace were also found separately.

Low-throated shoes with long vamp wings and long-pointed toes
At least four shoes (Fig 516.33-4) had long-pointed toes and low-throated vamps with long wings (styles 12-14, Fig 512), but as in no case did their corresponding quarters survive, the method of fastening, if any, remains unknown. All were of bovine leather, and of adult size. One (*33*) was found in ditch *1230* (fill *1790*, Period 8i) but, as it appears to be of a later fourteenth-century style, it would seem to be intrusive. Another was found in fill *1480* of ditch *1403*, and the other two (*eg 34*) came from Period 8iv deposits *1383* and *1385*. Its size suggesting a woman's shoe, *34* (Fig 516), had long vamp wings and decorative horizontal slashing at the throat. With such a low throat it is likely that the shoe was held onto the foot by a narrow strap and buckle, or a divided lace that tied across the instep (as those below).

Low-throated shoes fastening with a divided tie-strap across the instep
Shoes with instep tie-straps were popular in the City of London during the late fourteenth and early fifteenth centuries (Grew and de Neergaard 1988, 37–8). There were at least five examples, each fastening with a divided strap that passed across the instep and tied through a pair of holes in the one-piece quarters (styles 13-14; Fig 512). All

were of bovine leathers and of adult size, the two measurable examples being probably of women's size 3 (35). The surviving toes were long and pointed; one, over 40 mm long, had been stuffed with moss (*p 843*). Two of the five were from Period 8iii ditch *1403*; three (*eg* Fig 516.35) were found in Period 8iv layers *1383* and *1384*. An additional tie-strap came from *1384*, but could not be matched to any one shoe with certainty. A shoe of comparable style, differing only in having a single hole in the quarters, came from a similar context (*1385*).

Shoes with vamps with higher throats and integral straps to tie across the instep
Four shoes had a higher throat (style 15; Fig 512) but were otherwise of a comparable style to that described above, fastening across the instep with a divided strap tying through a pair of holes on the opposite side. Two (*eg* Fig 516.36) had an integral strap for the fastening holes, extending from the side seam of the vamp. The other two (*eg* Fig 517.37) had the fastening holes on separate straps, although one had a broken vamp, and so it was not possible to be sure whether the separate straps had been attached to the vamp or the quarters. All four were made of bovine leathers and varied in size from child size 12 (30), intended for an adolescent, to adult size 7 (41), suitable for a man. In addition, the latter had the vamp throat irregularly cut away, a secondary modification, probably made by the wearer to relieve pressure across the instep.

All four shoes came from layers attributed to Period 8iv (*1383, 1385, 1502, 1580*) and dating to the late fourteenth to early fifteenth centuries. In the Netherlands, this style was popular between *c* 1325 and *c* 1390, being discarded in numbers at the turn of the fifteenth century (Goubitz *et al* 2001, 111, 167).

High-throated slip-on shoes
The remains of at least four slip-on shoes (style 16; Fig 512) were found, all being made with vamps and separate one-piece quarters; two had a straight throat, whilst the others were gently peaked. All were in Period 8iv layers (*1314, 1386, 1687*). The best-preserved example (Fig 517.38) had tunnel stitching to attach a small separate tab to the interior of the shoe, in order to reinforce the left side-seam. Stitching to attach a small tab to each side seam was present on another one-piece quarters, suggesting that it might come from a shoe of similar style.

Boots with two-piece quarters
There were two cattle-hide boots with two quarters joining in a straight back seam, a feature that indicates that they can be no earlier in date than the early fifteenth century. Both were from Period 8iv deposits, one from ditch *1403* (fill *1404*), and the other (*19*;

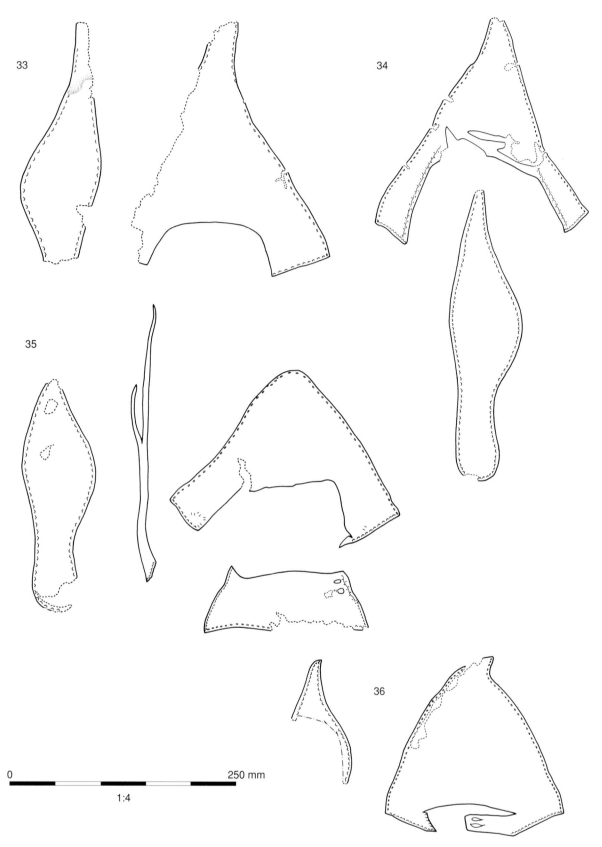

33

34

35

36

0   250 mm

1:4

Figure 516: Shoes with low throat, and divided tie-strap fastening

Fig 517.39) from layer 1384. The boots extended above ankle height and had plain-cut top edges (style 17; Fig 512), and both had a heel stiffener at the back seam, of which that in 39 was notable in being worn flesh outward to the foot. The boot from ditch 1403 had curved front seams like those on examples from the City of London (Grew and de Neergaard 1988, 73, fig 107).

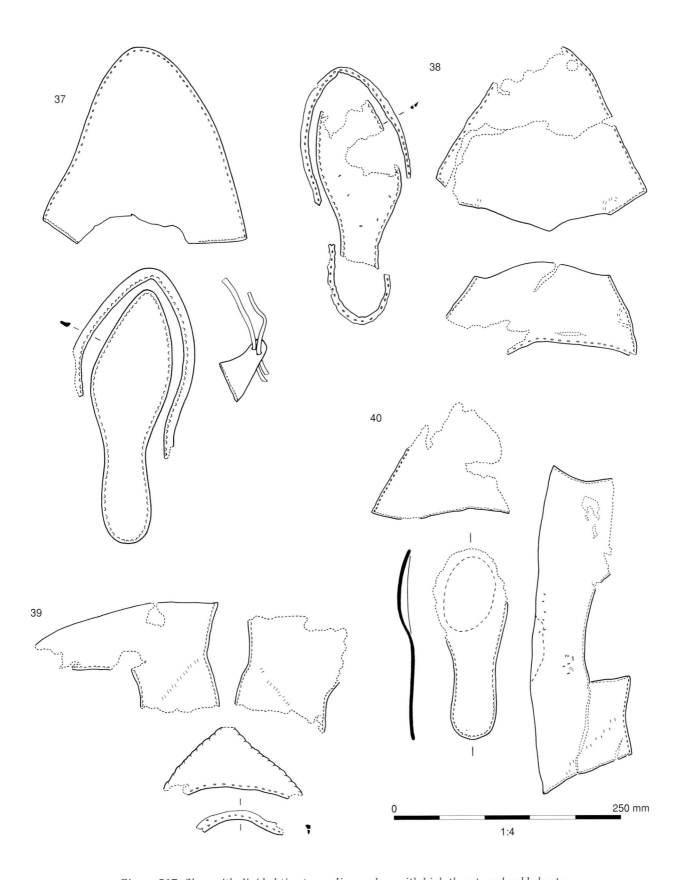

Figure 517: Shoe with divided tie-strap, slip-on shoe with high throat, and ankle boots

In addition, calfskin ankle boot *40* (Fig 517), from the final phase of activity recorded in tenement **1235**, had an unusual cutting pattern. Apparently made to accommodate a foot deformity, it comprised a separate, high-throated vamp, and quarters that extended to wrap around the front of the ankle, joining with a seam at the back of the heel. Stitching to attach a strap suggests that the shoe could have fastened with a buckled strap (style 18, Fig 512). In addition, the forepart of the sole was abnormally worn. The boot was of a size appropriate to a child or adolescent but, bearing in mind the shortening of the foot caused by conditions such as club foot, might have been worn by an adult.

Other boots were represented by parts with few characteristics helpful to dating. A panel from the leg of a boot cut to just above the ankle was found in layer *1385* (Period 8iv), and a small number of other parts came from footwear of similar height, but had no other diagnostic features.

Sandals and overshoes
A fragment of deer or goatskin was reused as a patch on a stitched sheet panel in the primary fill of ditch *1230* (Period 8i). It appeared to be the toe strap for a sandal or overshoe, but it is possible that its shape was coincidental. Whatever its use, as fine, supple leather it is likely to have started life as part of an expensive item, subsequently salvaged for use in a repair. Its dating is not clear, and as other leather from the ditch (as seen in MIL 3) was thought to be of Roman date

and thus residual, this panel might be of similar date. A small fragment torn from an ankle strap of a sandal was found in ditch *1403* (Period 8iii).

Items other than shoes
Straps
Fourteen straps, all of bovine leather, were found, principally in *1231*, the recut of the outer ward ditch (Period 8ii), but also in Period 8iv deposits spread over tenement *1235*. The majority were plain with parallel knife-cut edges, but a single example had an incised line along each edge, simulating a line of stitching. A variety of items was represented (Table 60). In addition, a wide strap that had fastened with a buckle (Fig 518.47) came from ditch *1403*.

Girdle
Joining pieces of a girdle (Fig 518.41) were found in fills *1698* and *1764* in the recut of the outer ward ditch (*1231*, Period 8ii). The wide strap, probably of calfskin, had a line of rouletted, vertical slits along each edge, marking the former position of decorative stitching. Surviving thread in similar slits on girdles from the City of London has been found to be of silk (Pritchard

Period	Context	IRF no	Length (mm)	Width (mm)	Thickness (mm)	Species	Mounts	Buckle/ mount holes	Comments
8ii	1792	8427	180	59	3	cattle	no	no	
8ii	1387	1251	500	12	4	cattle	imp	three	mock stitching, knotted
8ii	1387	1252	250	33	1.5	bovine (calf)	no	no	lining, suspension holes, knotted
8ii	1426	1286	128	16	1.5	bovine (calf)	imp	yes	-
8ii	1495	1301	149	12	2	bovine	no	yes	-
8ii	1698/ 1764	1316/ 1330	557	55-58	4	bovine	no	yes	rouletted slits along sides
8ii	1698	1316	138	50	4	bovine	no	yes	same item as 1316/1330, not joining
8ii	1698	8478	70	18	3.5	cattle	no	yes	central slit and ?mount hole
8ii	1729	1323	156	13-17	4	cattle	no	no	knotted
8ii	1764	1335	345	15	5	cattle	no	no	central slit, ends cut into thongs
8ii	1764	1336	346	8	3	cattle	yes, *c* 15	yes	three domed copper-alloy mounts, slashed end
8iv	1386	1001	58	7	5	cattle	yes, 35	yes	35 lead-alloy rivets with double domed heads
8iv	1386	1240	335	18-23	4	cattle	no	yes	-
8iv	1406	1264	397	15-33	4	bovine	no	no	two slots present
8iv	1406	1265	330	37-39	3	cattle	no	no	-

imp= impression

Table 60: Leather straps from medieval contexts

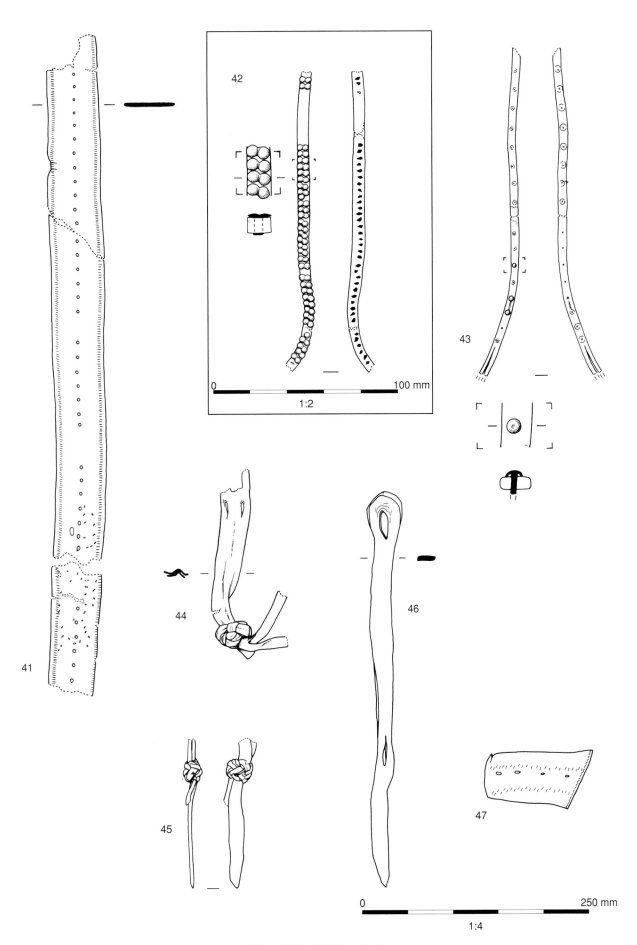

41

42

0   100 mm

1:2

43

44

45

46

47

0   250 mm

1:4

Figure 518: Girdle and straps

853

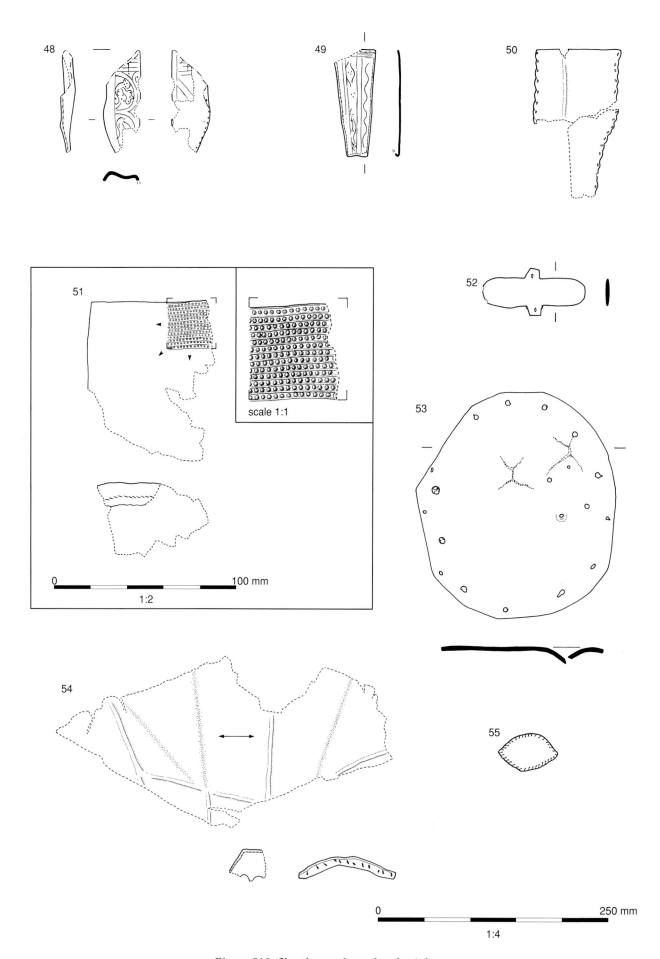

Figure 519: Sheath, panels, and archer's bracer

1991, 39). A line of small holes runs down the centre of the strap, possibly buckle or rivet holes from the attachment of decorative metal mounts, removed before the girdle was discarded. A piece cut from a girdle of similar type was also found in the defensive ditch fronting the medieval city wall at Rickergate (Mould 2004).

Straps with metal mounts
Two narrow straps (7–8 mm wide) were decorated with metal mounts. One (Fig 518.43), with widely-spaced, domed copper-alloy mounts, was found in *1231* (fill *1764*; Period 8ii). The other (Fig 518.42), with closely-spaced lead-alloy mounts with small, paired, domed heads, was recovered from Period 8iv deposit *1386*. The length of *43* suggests it could have come from horse harness or a long, narrow girdle; the dome-headed mounts are commonly found, for example in London (Egan and Pritchard 1991, 174, no 856–88). The other strap (*42*) could be from horse harness or a spur leather. The double-headed mounts decorated the suede (flesh) side of the strap, a feature also seen on straps from London (*op cit*, 37). Similar mounts, but of tin, ornamented a narrow strap from a later fourteenth-century context at Baynard's Castle (*op cit*, 205, no 1108, and fig 128). Two other straps, both from fills of ditch *1231*, retained the impressions made by the heads of metal mounts.

Straps for the suspension of sheaths
Straps that might have been used to suspend a sword scabbard or a knife sheath from a belt were found in fills *1387*, *1729*, and *1764* of ditch *1231* (Period 8ii), and late medieval spread *1406* (Period 8iv). A lined calfskin strap (Fig 518.44) with a characteristic pair of suspension holes at one end, and elaborately knotted to attach a narrow strap at the other, appears to be from a sword belt of a type popular in England in the twelfth and thirteenth centuries. These belts were divided into two narrow straps or thongs at one end, which tied through a pair of slots at the opposite end; a knot attached a narrow strap from which the scabbard was hung. This is a rare find, apparently only the second example to be recognised from this country, and comparable to that from a late eleventh-century context at Coppergate, York (Cameron 2003, 3367, no 15611, fig 1691). A second interwoven knot encircling two straps of cattle hide (Fig 518.45), which were possibly originally a single strap folded over to form a loop, could come from a second example. A suspension fastening (Fig 518.46), with a slotted terminal and a second slot toward the pointed end, was found in a late medieval deposit over tenement *1235*. Again, an example can be seen in material from Coppergate in York, but in a tenth-century context (Mould *et al* 2003, no 15729, 3401, and fig 1722). This type of fastening could have been used to suspend a knife sheath, or other accessory, from a belt. A slotted strap from fill *1764* of recut outer ward ditch *1231*, cut horizontally into narrow straps or thongs at the broken ends, could also be associated with a suspension fastening, but it is possible that the ends had simply been cut into thongs, which might rather suggest it to be an old strap reused to make thongs and laces. If this were the case, however, it seems odd that the entire strap was not cut up in this way. It is perhaps more likely that the ends of the strap were originally fringed, as seen in fragments elsewhere, for instance at Coppergate (Mould *et al* 2003, no 15612, fig 1691).

Sheaths
Fragments of a calfskin knife sheath with tooled decoration (Fig 519.48) came from a fill of recut ditch *1231* (*1495*). The sheath had been deliberately cut across at an angle; it seems to have been common practice for sheath leathers to be slighted, perhaps to render them unsaleable, before being thrown away. The tooled decoration, a foliate motif infilled with impressed dots within a double-bordered arch, suggested the sheath to be of thirteenth- to mid-fourteenth-century date. Sheaths with similar decoration are relatively common finds in thirteenth- and early-mid-fourteenth-century contexts elsewhere (*eg* York, Cameron 2003, type E, fig 1710; London, Cowgill *et al* 1987, 41–2, fig 88, no 417, fig 89, no 419-21). Recently, Cameron (2003, 3388 and table 383) has suggested that they might be more precisely dated to the thirteenth century.

Other decorated items
A tapering panel of calfskin (Fig 519.49), from layer *1319* in the northern part of tenement *1234* (Period 8iii), had tooled linear decoration and impressed dots similar to sheath *48*. Although superficially it resembled a knife sheath, it was made of more rigid leather, had two seamed edges, and was deliberately moulded at one end, and is likely to be from a different item, possibly a tool holder or case. An undecorated panel (Fig 519.50), also possibly from a tool holder or a sheath lining, was found in a similar context (*1317/1318*); fragments from a panel decorated with a linear pattern of raised dots and ribs (Fig 519.51) were found in another (*1706*). Again, the decoration is comparable to that found on knife and sword sheaths, but the dimensions of the surviving fragments indicate that these were elements of neither.

Archer's bracer
An archer's bracer (Fig 519.52) was found in the fill (*1785*) of the construction trench for a fourteenth-century wooden fence (*1788*) that formed the northern boundary of tenement *1234*. The bracer was small, plain, and utilitarian, with a pair of pierced tabs through which it was tied to the wrist. It is comparable to a smaller, rectangular bracer found with thirteenth/fourteenth-century pottery in a cesspit in Greengate,

Manchester (Mould 2005) and another, oval, example from Micklegate, Selby, in Yorkshire (Mould 2001, TP3 3457). This bracer, like that from Selby, was heavily worn and both appear to have been made from reused shoe soles. Two other examples from York (Mould *et al* 2003, 3403–5) were clearly made from reused shoe parts, suggesting that it was common for bracers to be made from recycled materials, presumably to keep costs low.

Sheet panels

Fragments from nine panels were found (Table 61). Four of the panel fragments were of sheep/goatskin, one (6) being a lapped seam, trimmed from a panel during salvage. Panel 5 may come from the lining of a flap-closing purse.

Other items

A large disc of rigid cattle hide (Fig 519.53), found in ditch *1231* (Period 8ii), appears to be the base of a container. The disc seems to have been cut freehand rather than being compass-drawn, having three straight edges. It was nailed around the edge, the

impression from a circular nail or stud head being visible around one hole. The nailing may have served to raise the base slightly above the ground when in use, but implies that the container was not water-tight. The lack of any stitching might suggest that the disc had been cut from the base of a container, possibly a bucket or quiver, and that the nailing might relate to secondary use. Alternatively, the disc could have served as a lid rather than a base, as a group of four nail holes to one side could have attached a leather strap to act as a simple hinge.

Fragments of a thin sheep/goatskin panel (Fig 519.54; Table 61, 2), only *c* 1 mm thick, and a strip binding of bovine leather (2 mm thick) were found in the same fill (*1424*) as *53*. Wear lines showed that the panel fragment had folded, concertina-style, into sections 75–80 mm wide, suggesting that it might have come from a bellows. The binding strip could have been an internal welt, or an external binding, where the leather was attached to a second panel or to a wooden baseboard. It is possible that disc *53* was cut from an upper bellows board or could represent the upper

Panel no	Period	Context	IRF	No fragments	L (mm)	W (mm)	Th (mm)	Species	Comments
1	8i	*817*	657.01	1	345	90	1	sheep/goat	double line gr/fl stitching from a lapped seam and torn area repaired with a ?deerskin patch (IRF 657.02)
2	8ii	*1424*	8415	5	370	180	1	sheep/goat	folded into sections
3					40	32	1	sheep/goat	gr/fl seam, and two scraps broken from the rest
4					112	10	2	cattle	strip with gr/fl seam
5	8ii	*1698*	1318	2	220	125	2	sheep/goat	gr/fl seam around edges several with impression of whip stitch thong
6	8iii	*1404*	1260	1	294	38	2	sheep/goat	cut down gr/fl lapped seam
7	8iii	*1409*	1270	1	60	68	2.5	cattle	three circular holes close to a cut edge
8	8iii	*1706*	1320	3	80	65	1	bovine	with two cut edges meeting at a corner
9					53	37	1	bovine	folded, with mock seam of rouletted incisions
10					60	50	1	bovine	
11	8iii	*1727*	1322	2 (joining)	195	105	3.5		triangular piece, cut edges, widely spaced gr/fl stitching along edges
12	8iv	*1312*	1206	1	358	205	1	sheepskin	line of paired gr/fl stitches
13	8iv	*1384*	8401	4	145	97	delam	?	whip stitch seam

Fl= flesh side; Gr= grain side; L= length; W= width; Th= thickness; delam= delaminated

Table 61: Sheet leather from medieval contexts

board of a circular 'concertina-shaped' bellows. Bellows in contemporary medieval illustrations are consistently of the traditional funnel-shape (see for instance Geddes 2001, fig 81), familiar today, with a pair of wooden boards, and whilst boards of thick and inflexible leather would function successfully, no examples are known, and the disc and panel may not be associated.

A small elliptical panel of cattle hide (Fig 519.55), with whip stitching around the edge and a curved profile, came from late medieval deposit *1386* (Period 8iv). It is part of a ball cover, usually made of four or more similar panels sewn together and stuffed to form a sphere. Covers for balls of this type have been found in London, York, Lincoln, and Exeter, examples ranging in date from the tenth to the seventeenth centuries (Mould *et al* 2003, 3406–8), and were used, no doubt, for a number of outdoor games. The core could have been made from a variety of materials. Two ball covers recovered from a large group of mid-seventeenth-century material, from St Paul-in-the-Bail, Lincoln, had been stuffed with leather shavings, whilst a third had a spherical wooden core (Mould 2008).

Discussion

The group of medieval shoes from these excavations has contributed significantly to clarifying the dating of the castle defences, as well as adding detail to the picture of daily life in the medieval city. Many of the shoes were recovered from the outer ward ditch, defining the southern limit of the castle. This group included toggle-fastening shoes and boots of mid-thirteenth- to mid-fourteenth-century date, which suggest, together with a small number of other leather items, that the outer ward ditch began filling in the later thirteenth century. The greater part of the assemblage, however, appears to date from the mid-fourteenth to the early fifteenth centuries, and is directly comparable to material from the defensive ditch fronting the medieval city wall seen in excavations at Rickergate, to the east (Mould 2004). Low shoes and ankle shoes fastening with buckled straps, seen at Rickergate, were absent from the present assemblage, but most styles were seen in both groups, underlining their contemporaneity. Much of the footwear examined can be described as everyday working wear and was often very worn and heavily repaired before it was discarded. There was, however, a significant proportion of highly fashionable shoes from both sites, with excessively long toes and slashed or punched decoration, which strongly suggest that the ditches were also receiving rubbish from a wealthier section of the population. Some of the other items found, like the archer's bracer, were utilitarian objects of low value, but in contrast, fragments of sword belt, as well as sword

scabbards and a possible hanger from Rickergate, are considerably more costly items, as are the girdles and decorated straps. The combination again makes it clear that the ditches were receiving rubbish originating from more than one social group.

Other excavations in Carlisle have produced medieval leather, but until more is published, comparison between sites is difficult. Small assemblages have been recovered from Castle Street (Padley and Winterbottom 1991, 118-21) and The Lanes (Padley 2000b), and a considerably larger group derives from excavations at Rickergate (Mould 2004). A twelfth-century assemblage from Castle Street (Edwards nd) comprised drawstring-fastening ankle boots popular from the twelfth to the middle of the thirteenth centuries. These compare well with an assemblage of similar date from the city's defensive ditch seen at Rickergate (Mould 2004). Nine shoe parts and a sling are included in the summary of medieval leather finds from the southern Lanes (Padley 2000b, 119, 121, fig 87) and a larger group of shoes from the same site is also catalogued (Padley in prep c).

Most closely related is the medieval leather from successive excavations at Annetwell Street, to the immediate south of the present site. Again unpublished, it includes a small group from Area A (Padley in prep b), which comprised poorly preserved shoe parts with few diagnostic features remaining, likely to be of thirteenth- to fourteenth-century date. The earliest Annetwell Street excavations, conducted in 1973–9 by the late Dorothy Charlesworth, produced three decorated sheaths or scabbards, including a clearly expensive sword scabbard with stamped fleur-de-lys decoration. The obvious presence of high-status objects within this material presages the situation in the present assemblage.

There is as yet no comparable published material from the rest of north-western England, and this makes it difficult to recognise the existence of local or regional characteristics in footwear or other leather goods. Certain features of the shoes at Carlisle, however, such as the unusual occurrence of integral linings, hint that it might, in the future, be possible to identify localised shoemaking practices. Elsewhere, major groups of medieval leather from York, Beverley, and Hull to the east, and several towns and cities to the south, most notably the groups from the well-dated waterfront dumps in the City of London (Grew and de Neergaard 1988), provide important comparators. Indeed, the quantity, state of preservation, and variety of late medieval leatherwork from these excavations and other sites in the city, including Rickergate, makes it clear that the material from Carlisle is amongst the most important to be recovered from Britain to date.

The Textiles and Cord

C Howard-Davis

Only five fragments of plied cord were recovered, all from Roman deposits, and all but one came from Period 4B Building *5689* (*6424*). The fifth fragment was from an earlier demolition deposit (*1809*, Period 3D) associated with Building *2061*. Preservation conditions were so good on the site, and leather so well-preserved, that it seems likely that, if textiles had been present in the deposits, they would have been found.

In all cases, the cord was two-ply, its very fibrous nature (Pl 224) suggesting that it was made from twisted withy or even perhaps straw (though not confirmed). In every case, the two threads were *c* 3 mm in diameter, and were in three of the five examples effectively S-spun, the others being Z-spun. Similarly, three of the five are plied with a Z-twist, the others S-twisted. This fairly coarse material seems most likely to have been cord or string used, presumably, for securing wrappings for some of the large number of objects which seem to have been stored within Building *5689*. Two highly compressed pads of moss were recovered

Plate 224: Example of two-ply cord

from floor *6426* in the same building. It is likely that these were also packaging material, but there remains the possibility that they were used to pad garments associated with some of the large group of armour from the building (*Ch 17*).

The other Roman textiles from the site survived only as mineralised remains associated with coins (*Ch 17*). In one case (found in deposit *472* within Period 3A Building *1194*), seven small-denomination coins were wrapped in a piece of tabby (plain-weave) cloth, identified as linen (by Penelope Walton Rogers), with 9-10 threads to 10 mm in one direction, and 10-12 in the other. The yarn in both warp and weft was Z-spun (*Appendix 10*). The second example, this time wrapped round a column of five silver *denarii* found in Period 3C demolition layer *3447* (*Ch 17, pp 679-80*), was only tentatively identified as linen (*Appendix 10*), and the remains were too poorly preserved for the weave to be identified.

Two fragments of coarse-woven woollen fabric were recovered from fills *1494* and *1495* of the recut outer ward ditch (*1231*, Period 8ii). Both are S-spun, plain tabby weave, with four warp and four weft to 10 mm. One possibly retains a selvedge (*Appendix 10*). It seems quite likely that the two fragments derive from the same garment, which might have had a leather trim (*Appendix 10*). Medieval textiles are unusual finds, but little can be said of the original appearance of the garment, if that is what it was.

The Worked Bone

C Howard-Davis

In total, 75 fragments of worked or modified animal bone were recovered, including antler and ivory. The material derived in the main from waterlogged contexts and was thus in excellent condition, although requiring conservation to avoid lamination and cracking on drying out. Although not large, the assemblage contains artefacts which reflect activity over the entire life of the site, from Periods 2-8.

Nature
The bone used appears to derive from a limited range of domesticates, including bovids and ovicaprids. An appreciable amount of red deer antler was also recovered, used both for heavy-duty tools such as hoes, and possibly *ad hoc* hammers. In both cases, the inherent flexibility of antler was probably a factor in the choice of material. Sawn fragments of antler, especially from Period 5 layer *326*, might hint at specialised manufacture, as might the plain sawn bone plaque from Period 6C intervallum road surface

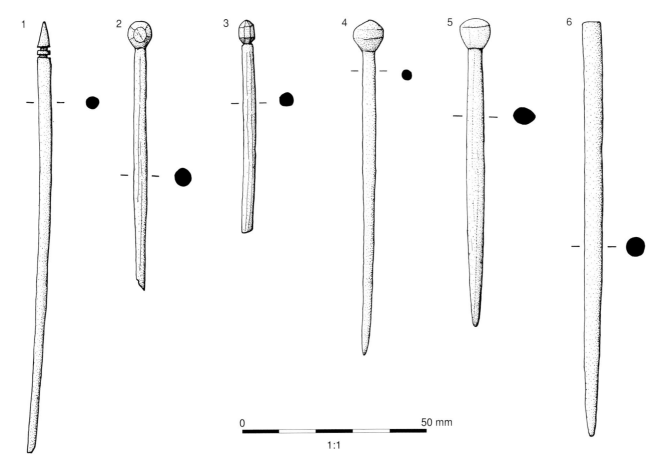

Figure 520: Roman hairpins

236 (Road **7646**). Ivory was used for sword and razor handles (*see Ch 17*), and probably indicates objects of considerable value or prestige, although any actual benefit in using an ivory rather than a bone sword grip are not obvious. With the exception of the ivory, which was probably imported as an element of ready-made objects, the raw materials were seemingly readily accessible locally.

Objects of personal adornment or dress
Hairpins
Seven bone hairpins were recovered, all but one from Period 6 contexts. The earliest, from Period 4C deposit *6248* (*47*; Fig 520.1), is an almost complete example of Crummy's Type 2 (1983, 21, fig 18), which she places in the first and second centuries. Four of the six remaining examples (*9, 42, 43, 45*; Fig 520.2-5) have spherical or oval heads on a baluster-shaped

shaft, which places them in Crummy's Type 3 (*op cit*, 21–2, fig 19) dated to the later third century and after. All are from Period 6 contexts, as is the single example of a Type 1 pin (*8*; Fig 520.6), plain with a flat or slightly conical top (*op cit*, 20, fig 17), current throughout the Roman period. The last example is fragmentary, lacking its head, and thus unidentifiable (*4*; *Appendix 10*). None of these hairpins is particularly unusual, and all can be paralleled widely in the north of England and beyond. It has been suggested that the use of hairpins was uncommon during the Iron Age (Allason-Jones 1989b, 137), and that their appearance during the first century represents a widespread change to more complex hairstyles, requiring greater artifice to support, and presumably owing their appearance to increased Roman influence. It is of interest that only two of the pins were found within buildings (both from the floor of Building **669**, a

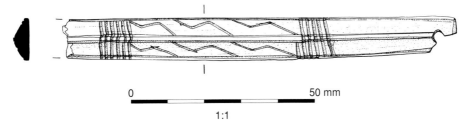

Figure 521: Probable early medieval comb case

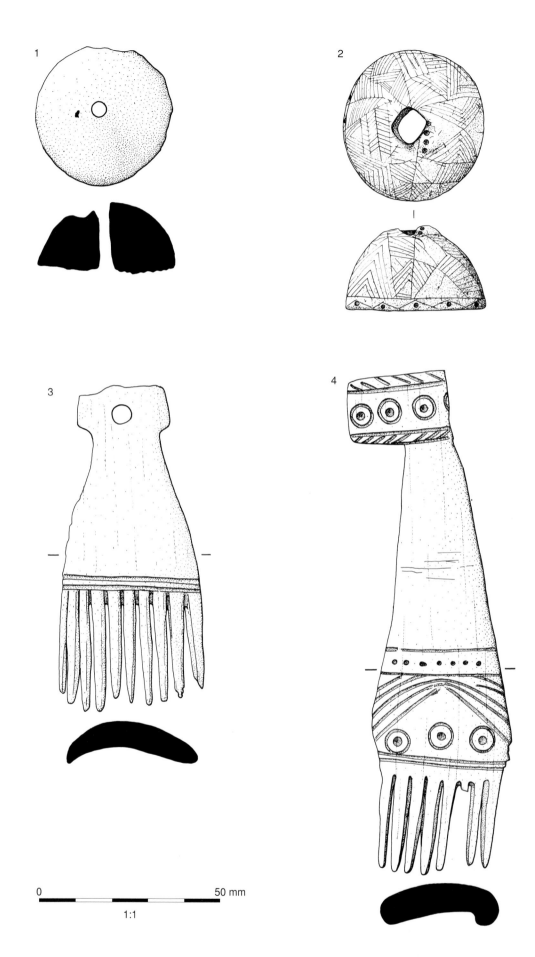

1

2

3

0 ───────── 50 mm

1:1

4

Figure 522: Spindle whorls and weaving combs

860

possible barrack block), the remainder coming from external deposits. As hairpins were a frequently lost item of women's attire, this pattern might reflect some restriction on access to parts of the area examined. Undiagnostic shaft fragments were also recovered from Period 6A external layer *257* and unstratified from MIL 5.

Toilet, surgical, or pharmaceutical instruments

Despite the recovery of several wooden combs, no bone examples were noted amongst the assemblage, although it seems likely that *32* (Fig 521) is part of a comb case, being similar to examples illustrated by MacGregor (1985, fig 54, particularly g, from Skaill on Orkney, which bears similar decoration). This would have been intended to protect a single-sided composite bone comb. No Romano-British comb cases are known (*op cit*, 97) and thus it is likely to be early medieval in date, a similar but not identical example from Northampton being dated to the Late Saxon period (Oakley and Harman 1979). It could, however, be more or less contemporary with its context, as the use of composite combs and their accompanying cases seems to have continued as late as the fourteenth century (MacGregor 1985, 98). It was recovered from fill *5075* of medieval pit *5072* (Period 8D).

Objects used in the manufacture or working of textiles
Spinning

Two bone spindle whorls were noted, both cut from the heads of femurs and thus relatively small and light. A plain example (*44*; Fig 522.1) was recovered from the fill of ditch *5572* (Period 6C), and is thus probably Roman. The use of specific animal bones (usually cattle) as a source of effectively ready-made whorls is noted by MacGregor (1985, 187), who suggests that, although first appearing in the Iron Age, at the Glastonbury and Meare lake villages, they had a particular currency during the Viking and Norman periods, thus allowing decorated whorl *33* (Fig 522.2), from a Period 8C layer, to be dated to between the ninth and twelfth centuries AD.

Weaving accessories

Two long-handled weaving combs were recovered (*25, 62*; Fig 522.3-4), both from occupation debris associated with buildings in the timber forts (Periods 3 and 4), Buildings *4658* and *5689* respectively. These distinctive and often highly decorated objects, thought to have been used to beat down the weft in textiles woven on an upright loom, are generally associated with Iron Age and later 'native' activity, and are thus regarded as an indication of local visitors or inhabitants, perhaps working to produce textiles for the flourishing Roman market (Wild 1970b; Greep 1998, 279). They appear with relative frequency on northern Roman sites,

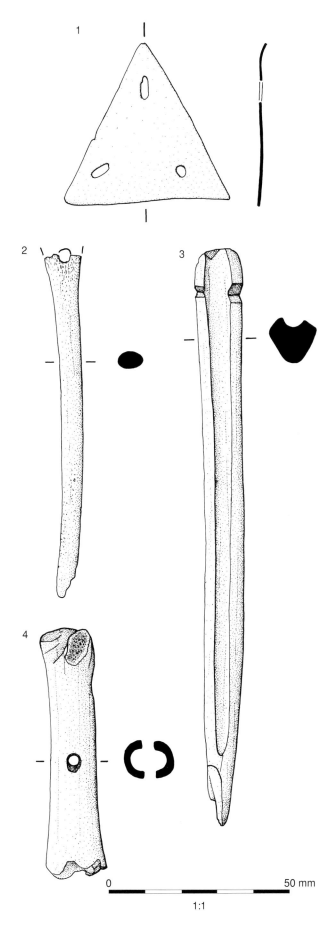

Figure 523: Possible weaving accessories

both military and civilian, during the first and earlier second centuries AD. The considerable demand for textiles of all kinds and for all sorts of purposes is well-illustrated by documentary evidence from Vindolanda to the east, which not only attests a trade in wool and possibly local production of textiles (Bowman 1994,

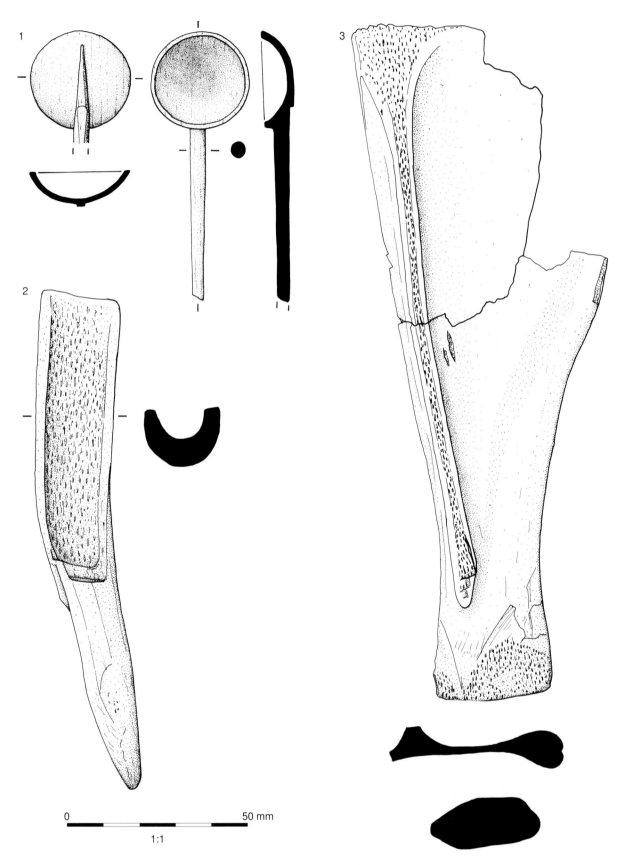

Figure 524: A spoon and scoops

44), but also lists a considerable range of garments, as well as other kinds and colours of textile (see, for instance, Birley 2002, 138-9).

In addition, a small triangular bone plate with holes at its corners can be identified as a weaving tablet (*26*; Fig 523.1), used in the production of ribbons and cords, often decorative in nature (MacGregor 1985, 191). Although such objects were used in sets, it is usual to find single tablets, this one coming from the fill of a construction trench for timber Building *4657* (Period 3C). These are relatively common objects, and other examples are known from Castle Street, Carlisle (Padley and Winterbottom 1991, fig 175, no 764). Examples in other materials are less common but not unknown, and a triangular tablet in copper alloy (*Ch 17, p 735*) was amongst finds from Building *7400* (Period 3A). Object *1* (Fig 523.2) appears to be a large bone needle of a kind described by Allason-Jones and Miket (1984, 2.260) as a weaving or netting needle.

The final two objects within this group are somewhat more enigmatic, but might have served as bobbins around which thread was wound. Both were recovered from medieval contexts, but their simplicity of form makes them effectively impossible to date. Object *29* (Fig 523.3) appears to be a pin or peg, being cut to a rough point at one end. It has two shallow nicks at the opposite end, as if to secure thread. Its small size suggests that it could not have served as a tethering peg or been used for any other more robust purpose.

Object *36* (Fig 523.4) is a more or less unmodified metapodial, with a single perforation approximately half way along the shaft. Obviously, such a simple object could have served a number of purposes, but Allason-Jones and Miket (1984, 2.24) suggest their use as bobbins, listing a number of examples from Iron Age and later sites, and they remain common into the medieval period (MacGregor 1985, 103). On the other hand, Crummy (1983, 105–6, fig 109.2537) suggests that an example made from a deer phalange might have served as an *ad hoc* cheekpiece in horse harness. Three examples are known from second-century deposits at Castle Street, Carlisle (Padley and Winterbottom 1991, fig 174.761–763).

Household utensils and furniture

Only three bone items can be thought of as household utensils: a spoon (*46*); and two scoops (*40* and *68*). The spoon (Fig 524.1) is a common Roman type, its form identical to copper-alloy and silver examples seen at sites throughout the Empire, and several copper-alloy examples are known from the Castle Street excavations (Padley 1991b, fig 76). Such round-bowled spoons are normally regarded as dating to

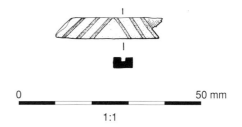

0   50 mm

1:1

Figure 525: Fragment of bone inlay

the second half of the first century and the second century AD. MacGregor, however, suggests that the dating of bone rather than metal spoons is less well-defined, and that they remained current over a longer period (MacGregor 1985, 181). Scoop *40* (Fig 524.2) is cut from antler and could have served a number of purposes, amongst them measuring small quantities of dry goods. A trimmed scapula (Fig 524.3) almost certainly served as a larger scoop.

A single small fragment of bone inlay (*39*; Fig 525) came from layer *5259* (Period 7). Whilst it cannot be dated with any certainty, recent evidence from the Brougham cemetery has highlighted the lavish use of bone inlay or veneer in furniture and larger objects, such as doors, during the Roman period (Greep 2004).

Objects used for recreational purposes

Objects from this group were almost entirely confined to counters; in all, there were 20 of bone, alongside a considerable number in glass (*Ch 18*). These objects are not uncommon finds on Roman military sites and could have served a number of purposes, possibly being used as accounting tallies as frequently as for gaming pieces.

The bone examples (*10, 15-17, 21, 27-8, 53-61, 63, 65-7, Appendix 10*) were all turned, many with a small central dimple, caused by centring on the lathe (see, for example, *63* and *67* (Fig 526.1-2). Most were plain on both surfaces, with a slightly undercut edge (Crummy's type 1; 1983, 91; Greep's type 1; 1986, 202). At Caerleon, Greep noted a predominance of this type in deposits of Flavian-Trajanic date, and at Carlisle their complete absence from deposits of Periods 5 and 6 might reinforce this dating. Whilst there is no doubt that these counters were used in board games, there is also evidence to suggest that they were used as gaming chips (MacGregor 1985, 133), as has been suggested for a group from Ewell in Surrey (Hassall and Tomlin 1977, 445), or tallies in the regulation of activities associated with the fort. Many seem to bear graffiti on the underside (see especially those from Ravenglass (Potter 1979, 75–6 and 79–87, figs 29-30)), which, although now meaningless, often seem to include numbers and letters, and suggest some other use. Caruana (1990, 156) suggests their

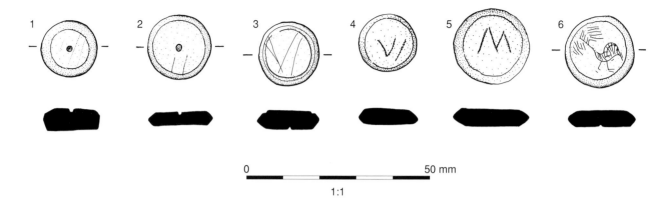

Figure 526: Bone counters

use in conjunction with abaci. Amongst examples from Mainz, one at least seems to refer to a military unit (Mikler 1997, Taf 18/18). The clear association of both bone and glass counters on this site with workshops (especially in Period 3), and the *principia* in Period 4A, might suggest that they served some organisational purpose. In Carlisle, small groups are known from Blackfriars Street (Caruana 1990, 154–6), Castle Street (Padley 1991b, fig 168), and the South Lanes (Padley 2000a, fig 73).

Amongst this group, *53* and *54* (Fig 526.3-4) are inscribed VI, *59* (*Appendix 10*) is inscribed IX, and *61* (Fig 526.5) is inscribed M. A fifth example, *66* (Fig 526.6), bears a lightly incised cross-hatched design, possibly a stylised depiction of a stag, or, less likely, a bird.

Medieval tuning peg

A single bone tuning peg was recovered from layer *1385* (*11*; Fig 527), associated with medieval tenement *1235*.

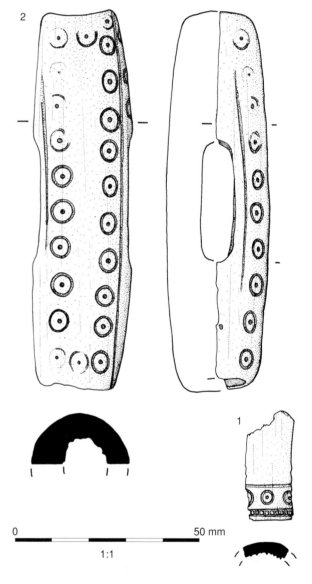

Figure 528: Toggles, possibly cheekpieces

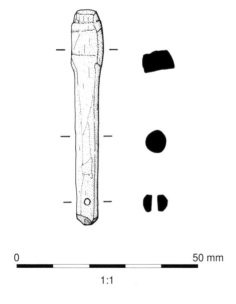

Figure 527: Tuning peg

These objects were used to fix and tension the strings of instruments such as harps, lyres, fiddles, or lutes, and are relatively common finds from medieval deposits (MacGregor 1985, 146–8).

Objects associated with transport

Two bone toggles of the kind often identified as cheekpieces from horse harness were noted from Roman deposits (Periods 3 and 4; *22, 51*; Fig 528.1-2). Greep (1998, 283) discussed the type briefly, noting that the function of such objects remain uncertain.

Tools

Two points, made from ovicaprid longbones, were noted, one (*71*; Fig 529.1) from the fill of a pit associated with the Period 3A *praetorium*, the other from a construction trench of a Period 6A barrack, Building *2063* (*13*; Fig 529.2). Like the weaving combs (*p 861*), they are a common Iron Age form that persisted into the Roman period. Greep (1998, 281) suggests that they are uncommon on military sites, but their presence in significant buildings within the Carlisle fort might suggest that this conclusion could be an artefact of recovery rather than a genuine difference. Their function is, like many simple objects, now uncertain, but they have been associated with textile production. Their presence in the fort, however, might militate against this. The earlier example (*71*) appears to have wood within the natural socket formed by the hollow centre of the bone (Pl 225), suggesting that they were originally hafted. If, as seems likely, they were intended as borers of some kind, a handle would have considerably increased

Plate 225: Wooden haft within bone tool 71

the amount of pressure that could be applied to them. Examples are known from Castleford (Greep 1998, fig 123.171–3), Corbridge (Bishop and Dore 1988, fig 97.40), and Castle Street, Carlisle (Padley and Winterbottom 1991, fig 178.776).

A metapodial, possibly from a sheep, incised with a ring-and-dot motif (*41, Appendix 10*), was recovered from a layer associated with road *7652*. Objects *34* (Fig 529.3) and *35* (*Appendix 10*) are also the handles of knives, or other hafted tools, the central perforation of *34* retaining evidence for an iron whittle tang. The simple ring-and-dot decoration seen on both is a common late Roman motif, used widely on handles and other day-to-day items, but is not useful in providing a date, remaining in use well beyond the Roman period. Its context, however, being the fill of a posthole associated with medieval Building *7399*, possibly suggests a relatively early post-Conquest date.

Fasteners and fittings

Object *52* (Fig 530) is clearly a cap or terminal of some sort, the hollow centre suggesting that it was fixed to a second object. It was associated with Period 4B Building *5689*.

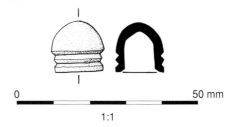

Figure 530: Small cap or terminal

Objects associated with agriculture, horticulture, and animal husbandry

Object *14* (Fig 531.1) has been identified as an antler hoe; again, it has been suggested that these objects represent the survival of a 'native' artefact (Allason-Jones and Miket 1984, 35, fig 2.1). This example differs

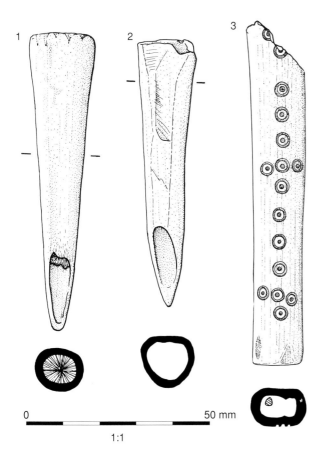

Figure 529: Bone tools and knife handle

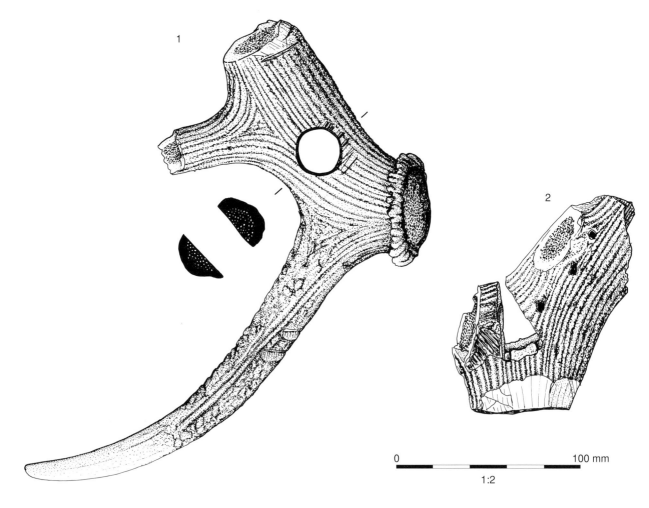

Figure 531: Antler tools

from that described by Allason-Jones and Miket in having a round, rather than square, socket for the shaft. The wear on it is identical to that described for an example from a mid-late second-century pit at Newstead (Stevenson 1950, 195); other examples are known from Wallsend and South Shields (Smith 1968b). Object *19* (Fig 531.2), although badly damaged, could be a second example. The fact that both were found in the fills of cut features might suggest that they were used in a manner similar to mattocks, to break up soil, rather than reduce it to a tilth.

Tools and other objects associated with metalworking

A sawn antler fragment, *20* (*Appendix 10*), with marked wear at both ends, came from Period 5B layer *2623*, associated with road *4662*. It is tentatively identified as a hammer-head, having some similarity to medieval example *31*. It is thought that soft, light hammers such as this were used in fine metalworking (MacGregor 1985, 172), an occupation well attested in the first/second-century fort.

A second, similar antler tool (*31*; Fig 532) was recovered from a medieval context (*5070*, a Period 8D pit fill). It seems to be a hammer-head, and is worn to a slight

concavity at both ends, suggesting it to be well-used. Inevitably, simple, easily made tools such as these hammers change little through time and both can be dated only by the context from which they derived.

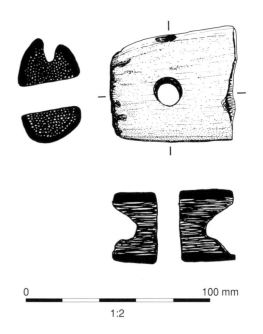

Figure 532: Medieval hammer-head

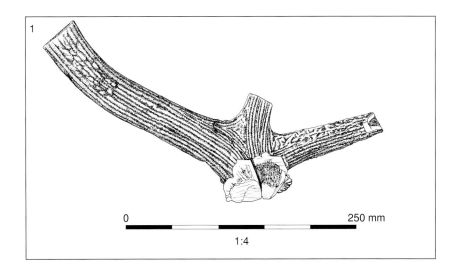

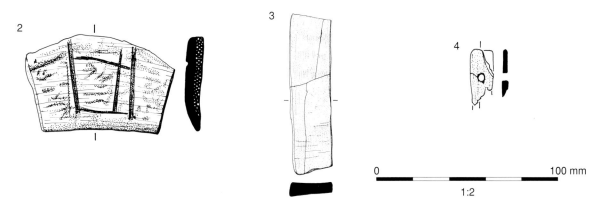

Figure 533: Off-cuts and plaques

Tools and other objects associated with working bone and other organic materials

A small group of what appear to be off-cuts from antlerworking was recovered. Two sawn fragments of trimmed antler beam were from Period 5 layer *326* (*5*, Fig 533.1; *6, Appendix 10*) and a third fragment (*30*; Fig 533.2) came from Period 8C layer *5058*. In addition, three rectangular plaques of bone are probably off-cuts from the production of bone objects, or perhaps the blanks for decorative inlay. Only one of the three (*3, Appendix 10*) derived from a Roman context, the other two being from Periods 7 and 8 respectively (*37, 2*; Fig 533.3-4).

Objects of unknown or uncertain function or purpose

Inevitably, some of the bone objects remain unidentified. A small ferrule or bead (*23*; Fig 534.1) was recovered from floor *3773*, within Period 3B Building *3772*. Its purpose remains obscure. Antler tines used as pegs or borers were recovered from demolition layer *1641* in Period 4A Building *2059* (*12*; Fig 534.2); Period 6A fill *2179* (*7, 18*; *Appendix 10*); and Period 6C floor *518*, in Building *669*. A bone peg (*38*; Fig 534.3) came from a Period 7 context. A rib fragment (*64*), originally thought to be worked, can be regarded as unmodified.

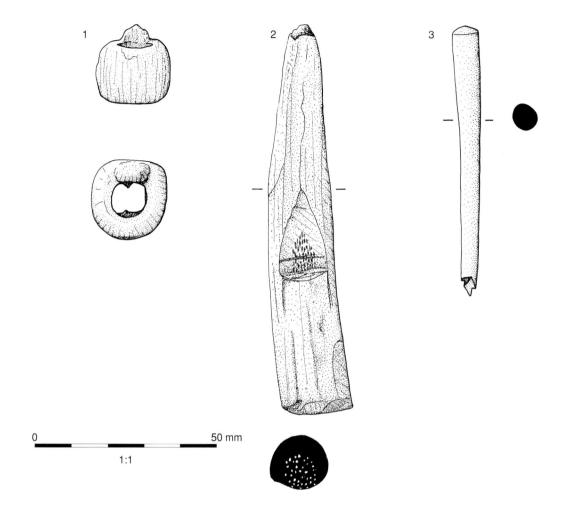

Figure 534: Objects of unknown purpose

0   50 mm

1:1

21

THE STONEWORK AND OTHER BUILDING MATERIALS

The Roman Sculptural Stone

M Henig

A few fragments of sculptural stone were recovered, in the main reused in the foundations of later structures. They have been catalogued (*Appendix 11*) following the conventions of the *Corpus Signorum Imperii Romani (Great Britain, 1)*, in which previous discoveries from Carlisle were published (Coulston and Phillips 1988, fascicule 6).

A relief-carved figure in white sandstone (*1*) was reused in Period 6B road **7652** (layer **5493**). It can be identified as a *Genius*, flanked by another figure (Pl 226), which might be a second *Genius*, or, more probably, a female personification such as *Fortuna*, as his consort. The head and feet of the male figure are now lost, and all that remains of his possible consort is a hand. The *Genius* stands to the front, and, although his head is lost, the ends of long locks remain on his shoulders; his upper torso is bare, with well-delineated musculature. His right arm is bent at the elbow and he holds his forearm horizontally across his body; this hand is clasped by that of the other figure. His left arm hangs by his side and he holds a *cornucopia* in that hand. For similar representations of *Genii* wearing the Greek *himation*, see the sandstone figure from the eastern Hadrian's Wall area (Phillips 1977, no 348), and especially another sandstone figurine of a long-haired *Genius*, from a well under the crypt of Southwark Cathedral, whose stylised drapery suggests association with the Carlisle school of sculpture (Goodburn 1978, 453, pl 29A). Other representations of *Genii* are known from Carlisle (Coulston and Phillips 1988, nos 469, 470), and from Burgh-by-Sands (*op cit*, no 26), but are stylistically inferior. The type of *Genius* represented here, with upper torso bare, and holding a *cornucopia*, is very common, and apart from British examples, it can be compared to several in Trier (Binsfeld *et al* 1988, nos 81–6).

A second white sandstone *Genius* (*2*) came from rubble foundation **5408** for the north wall of Period 6C Structure **7662** to the south of road **7652**. Again carved in relief, his head, feet, and left arm are all lost (Pl 227). This figure is also clad in an *himation*, and again holds his right forearm horizontally across his body. Thus, this sculpture would appear to be a smaller version of *1*, although there is now no trace of a consort.

Plate 226: Genius 1

Plate 227: Genius 2

Plate 228: Genius 3

Two fragments of a third *Genius* (*3*) were found in demolition debris *2216*, associated with Building *2302* (Period 6D). Again relief-carved in a grey/white sandstone, this figure lacks the head, right hand, and legs (Pl 228). He wears a square-cut tunic and holds a *cornucopia* in his left hand. His right hand would originally have held a *patera* over an altar.

Another fragment (*4*) was found in material (*5286*) used to repair a Period 6C metalled surface (to the east of the *principia*). Again in white sandstone, it represents either relief-carved pleating from a garment or, possibly, the mural crown from a figure of a *Genius* or *Fortuna* (Pl 229). The fragment has triangular notches along the upper edge, and eight grooves angled slightly inwards. There is possible tooling on the back of the stone. The identifications proposed are not very firmly based, but the pleating seen on this fragment might be compared with the dress of a goddess from Corbridge (Phillips 1977, no 115). Alternatively, three heads of *Genii* from early findspots in and around the fort at Carlisle (Coulston and Phillips 1988) sport mural crowns, making this interpretation equally likely.

The commanding grey/white sandstone head of a female (*5*; Pl 230), again carved in relief, was found reused in the rubble fill (*2317*) of a foundation trench for Building *2302* (Period 6C). Her almond-shaped eyes have well-defined lids, but the pupils are not

Plate 229: Fragment 4, *either a garment or mural crown*

indicated; the nose is triangular. There are bunched masses of hair on the crown of her head and ten small curls over the brow are held in place by a hair-band. Comparison may be made with the head of the well-known Carlisle-school statuette of *Fortuna* from Birdoswald (Coulston and Phillips 1988, no 15), as well as the head of a goddess from Bearsden on the Antonine Wall, whose eyes are very similar (Keppie and Arnold 1984, no 139), although these figures are

Plate 230: Female head 5

870

Plate 231: Male figure 6

obviously male, the gentalia are not shown in detail. The rounded head and undifferentiated genitals are those of a warrior god, similar to one from Maryport (*op cit*, 110-20, fig 8.13), and perhaps also represented by the similarly simplified horned deities from High Rochester (Phillips 1977, no 324) and Burgh-by-Sands (Coulston and Phillips 1988, no 373). It also bears comparison to a second figure from Maryport (Coulston 1997, 118, fig 8.12), although that figure's raised right arm, and an aureole of rays, suggest that it was intended to represent a sun-god.

A rectangular block, bearing a phallus carved in high relief (*7*, Pl 232), was set close to the corner of the south wall of the Period 6A *principia* (*5268*, Building **5200**; Fig 273), four courses above foundation level. Like the rest of the masonry in the wall, it is cut from red sandstone. A building stone inscribed **LEG VI** (*p 873*; Tomlin and Hassall 2001, 390-1, no 16) was set in a corresponding position in the east wall, at the south-east corner of the building. Representations of phalli are very common, intended as a protection against the Evil Eye (for others, see Coulston and Phillips 1988, 150–1, nos 458, 459 and 461, east of the fort at Birdoswald). Examples are also known from Wroxeter (Henig 2004, no 169) and Wall (*op cit*, no 170), all of which can be assigned to the second century, whilst this example is likely to date from the early third century (*Ch 8*; Tomlin and Hassall 2001, 391).

conceived as being in the round. More distantly, a head from Wroxeter should be noted; it has similar eyes, but S-shaped curls (Henig 2004, no 158).

A trapezoidal block of red sandstone (*6*, Pl 231) had been reused in a deposit (*5428*) associated with Structure **7651** (Period 6C). The shape and the roughly tooled sides of the block suggest that it was an architectural fragment, probably a keystone. A schematic representation of a male figure was carved in relief on the upper surface, and could well have had an apotropaic function. The figure, now lacking both arms and feet, has a circular head, with pecked eyes and mouth; although

Another red sandstone architectural fragment, this time clearly a pedimental stone or *aedicula* (*8*; Pl 233), came from a Period 6B external surface (*5590*), east of the *principia*, where it had been reused, face down. Clearly, the stone was intended to be seen only from the front, which is very well-finished, while the sides are rough, and, as the angle of the splay is over 90°, it is probably from a niche, rather than being one side of a rectangular window. There is a band of zig-zag chip-carved ornament along the edges of the pediment and the curve of the niche, and a six-petalled rosette is carved in relief at its centre. The petals are bifurcated, and there is a central stamen. A rosette seen on the left

Plate 232: Building stone 7

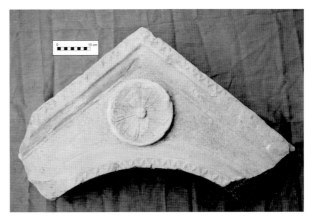

Plate 233: Pedimental stone or aedicula 8

Plate 234: Altar 9

side of the Jupiter Tanarus altar from Chester (Henig 2004, no 20) is somewhat similar in quality.

The top of a red sandstone altar dedicated to Asclepius (*9*; Pl 234) was found reused in the rubble foundations of Period 6C Structure **7662**, dating to the second half of the fourth century, and which encroached on the south side of the main east to west road, opposite the *principia* (*Ch 9*). The altar is broken in the die, below the first line of the inscription, and its lower part is lost. It is fairly plain, the top presenting a truncated pediment between bolsters, of which the surviving right-hand example has a sinking in the front, as has the pediment. There is a triple moulding below, continuing around the sides. The die is inscribed in large well-formed capitals, 480 mm in height: **ASCLE PI O**. The P and I are ligatured (Tomlin and Hassall 2001, 390 no 15, pl 16A).

Finally, one corner of decorative panel carved in sandstone (*10*) was found in a Period 5C pit (*2542*). Only part of one side remains, the frame being chip carved along its edges, and it would clearly have stood proud of the wall. The panel was not obviously inscribed, but there is part of a stroke which could have been part of a letter.

Discussion

Although the collection of sculptured stone from Periods 5 and 6 is not particularly impressive in terms of the quality of the pieces represented, the quantity of material recovered from a relatively small area of the stone-built fort does merit comment, seemingly indicating that carved figures and decorative architectural elements were relatively common within it, at least in the central range, around the *principia*. Viewed in conjunction with other figural carvings found in the city (Coulston and Phillips 1988), and the known existence of a Carlisle school of sculptors (Henig 1995, 51), this would seem to emphasise not

only the significance of Carlisle as a military site, but the prosperity of the settlement in general.

The concentration of the carved stonework on the *principia* is of significance, as, with, presumably, a *sacellum* at its rear, it would have represented a focus for the military and imperial cults which formed part of the day-to-day life of the fort (Goldsworthy 2003, 84). Whilst the presence of an altar (*9*) dedicated to Asclepius (the god of health) might most obviously suggest the proximity of a military hospital, the evidence (*Ch 22*) does not indicate any of the buildings examined to be identified as such. It should be noted that a veneration of Asclepius is most firmly attested in association with the *praetorium* and *principia* (Tomlin and Hassall 2001, 390 n20), presumably implying his responsibility for the notional well-being of the resident military units and the fort in general. This may be the explanation for the presence of the dedications at the legionary fortress of (*Legio XX*) at Chester (Henig 2004, no 3).

The presence of several *Genii*, and a possible representation of *Fortuna*, seems to reflect the concerns not only of the military establishment as a whole, but also of the ordinary soldier, for whom luck and good fortune were vital (Goldsworthy 2003). Although the bare-chested, *himation*-clad deity represented by fragments *1* and *2* could be identified with Asclepius, the long locks of the first figure, together with the *cornucopiae* which the first example carries, would appear to rule this out and suggests their identification as *Genii*, perhaps, bearing in mind the military context, and especially their proximity to the *principia*, *Genii Centuriae* or the like. The consort seen on fragment *1* is likely to have been a *Fortuna* figure, probably conceived as a territorial deity.

Other, more nebulous religious activity is suggested by the head of the goddess (*5*) and the apparently apotropaic figure carved on what appears to be a reused keystone (*6*), which should probably be seen as representing a local warrior god. Similarly, the apotropaic nature of the phallus, seen frequently on and around military buildings during the Roman period, most especially places where men might feel vulnerable, for instance the bath-house (Henig 1995, 116), as at Chesters (Breeze 2006, 208), again points to the need of the ordinary soldier to guard against ill-luck.

Although the workmanship of both the carved figures and the architectural fragments is not, on the whole, of high quality, part of a pedimented stone (*8*) is a significant exception. Its quality suggests that it was produced by a skilled sculptor, probably working for an influential patron, such as a legionary legate or similar high-ranking individual (Henig 1995, 49), and presumably suggests that such men were routinely in Carlisle.

The Building Stone

J Munby

Building stone was recovered from the excavations in large quantities, especially from the remains of the Period 6 *principia*; most of the pieces examined were of the locally available red sandstone prevalent in Carlisle. The foundation of the *principia* (Building *5200*) included large blocks about 1 m square, and long foundation slabs. The standard building blocks are of squared, but usually tapered, rubble stone, and have been recovered in large numbers. The later fourth-century alterations to the building (*Ch 9*) included long stones pierced with holes for railings, and stone *pilae* from the hypocaust.

The principal remaining items of architectural worked stone (*Appendix 11*) consist of fragments of columns and finials, but as individual and disassociated pieces, it cannot be seen how they may have featured

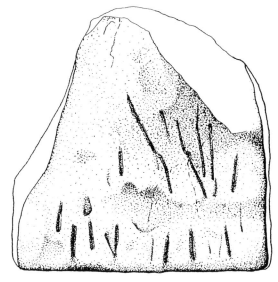

0 ⸻ 250 mm

1:4

Figure 535: Building stone from the Period 6 principia

on any building. Fragment *106* is clearly a column base (Pl 235), presumably indicating that there were typically classical buildings within the fort at this time (Period 6A).

Apart from minor and uncertain graffiti on some of the stone blocks and slabs, there are two inscribed stones. One is a fragment from an altar dedicated to Asclepius (*p 872*; Pl 234), the other a building stone from the east wall (*5191*) of the Period 6 *principia* (Fig 535). Inscribed **LEG VI**, it is a clear indication of the involvement of men from the Sixth Legion in the reconstruction in stone of the fort at this point (*Ch 8*). It was found in close association with the carved phallus seen in the south wall of the same building (*p 871*; Tomlin and Hassall 2001, 390-1, no 16).

The Other Worked Stone

R Shaffrey

In total, 153 items of non-architectural worked stone were retained from the excavations. These include 43

Plate 235: Column base, building stone 106

rotary quern fragments (36 separate examples), 45 whetstones, 32 projectiles, and 36 other items, including a loomweight, spindle whorl, tessera, counters, two possible lamps, two pot lids, and several items of indeterminate function. A petrological description of all objects was recorded with the aid of a x10 magnification hand lens, and dimensions were recorded with digital callipers. All significant characteristics of the rotary querns, whetstones, and other objects were recorded (see *Appendix 11* for a catalogue of the illustrated material).

Context and date

Although a disparate group, the worked stone objects can be divided into three groups of related objects (rotary querns, projectiles, and whetstones), with the remainder of the group discussed under a fourth, generalised, heading.

Rotary querns

Rotary quern fragments were recovered from a variety of contexts, mainly reused in features such as pits, floors or road surfaces, postholes, and structures. They were recovered from Period 3 onwards. Only two examples were found in contexts contemporary with their original use as querns: three adjoining fragments were found in *3377* and *3436*, demolition layers associated with Building *3772* (Period 3D); and one was found in a demolition layer (*2130*) relating to Building *2302* (Period 6D). Both querns had clearly been broken prior to discard and deposition, but the presence of the first example in an early second-century context in Building *3772* suggests it was probably used in this barrack building itself. The date of use of the

second example is not as clear, but this quern could well reflect activity in Building *2302*.

With the majority of the querns having been recovered from contexts where they were clearly reused, it is difficult to interpret differences in deposition between periods in any manner that reflects the original places of use of these objects. Analysis can nevertheless elucidate patterns of discard, and a plot of the quern fragments by period reveals a clear focus of deposition in the late fourth to early fifth century (Period 6C). When examined century by century, however, the distribution is more evenly spread, with ten quern fragments from the second, eight from the third century, and 15 from the fourth-early fifth century (Fig 536), the remainder being from medieval contexts, or unstratified.

Projectiles

In all, 32 projectiles were recovered, mostly from stratified contexts. Analysis of their distribution reveals that almost half of these were deposited during Period 5, although this is perhaps biased by the recovery of seven projectiles from a single external layer, *245*. There were no other marked concentrations, and projectiles were found in a variety of context types, including layers, postholes, ditches, road surfaces, and floors. Individual examples were found in several contexts that could have been related to their initial use, for example Building *669*, and other buildings such as *2301*, *4655*, and *5689*. The majority, however, came from road surfaces and layers, which might reflect either loss during use, accidental loss, or reuse, depending on depositional circumstance.

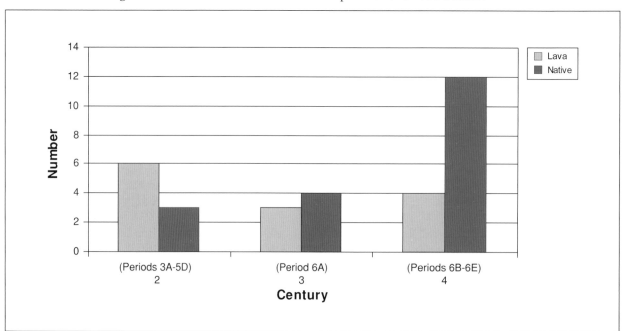

Figure 536: Histogram showing distribution of quern lithology by century

Whetstones

The 46 whetstones, largely stratified, were found in a variety of different context types, from Period 3 onwards. When analysed by phase, there are no clear concentrations of deposition, although analysis by date reveals that the greatest period of deposition was during the late first and early second centuries. No particular structure or individual context produced a large assemblage, although a substantial number came from barrack buildings, suggesting they may have been part of individual toolkits. Very few were retrieved from their original place of use, an exception being a large whetstone which probably belonged to a toolkit, rather than being for individual use. This was notably found on the floor of a building interpreted as a smithy (Period 4B Building *2765*). Two whetstones were associated with Building *4006*, which seems in part to have served an industrial purpose, as indicated by the remains of a furnace and metalworking debris (for example, *21*; *p 881*; *Chs 6* and *17*). A further eight whetstones were retrieved from medieval contexts: most were probably residual Roman examples and thus do not represent medieval activity.

Other items

The 35 other objects comprised 18 worked items, and a further 17 items which were either of indeterminate function or unworked. The former includes two probable pot lids, four pestles or hammer stones, three counters, two rubbers, a vessel fragment, a spindle whorl, a loomweight, a slate pencil, a tessera, and two possible lamps or moulds. These were mostly found in contexts which suggested that they were residual, such as the fills of postholes and foundation deposits. The single stone tessera was associated with floor *2401* in Period 6 Building *2301*.

Nature of the assemblage

The majority of the stone-types represented within the group are of local origin, the main exception being the rotary querns of Niedermendig Lava, which were imported from the Eifel region of Germany (Crawford and Röder 1955). The remainder of the assemblage comprises mainly pinkish-red, cream, and grey sandstones which, although they vary in grain size and in the presence or absence of mica, are fairly uniform and probably came from a very limited number of sources.

Pink/red sandstones were used to make both projectiles and rotary querns. Some of these may have had a source in the Permian sandstones to the south of Carlisle, where the reddish-brown Penrith Sandstone attains a thickness of up to 300 m (Arthurton and Wadge 1981, 70). An alternative, and perhaps more likely, source for the majority of the pink and dull red sandstones, especially those

used for the ballista balls, is in the Trias: the St Bees and Kirklinton sandstones. St Bees sandstone has been used in Carlisle as a building material (Dixon *et al* 1926) and would have been much more locally available than Penrith Sandstone. It may also have provided the source for a number of artefacts made from a cream-coloured sandstone of very similar mineralogy and structure. The colour of St Bees sandstone varies, and cream bands and patches have been well documented (Dixon *et al* 1926, 25; Arthurton and Wadge 1981, 73).

Perhaps surprisingly, Upper Carboniferous Millstone Grit is not common in the assemblage, although it was commonly used for the manufacture of rotary querns, and examples are widely distributed across Roman Britain. Only one rotary quern and one projectile in Millstone Grit were identified among this assemblage. Millstone Grit occurs in various places throughout the Pennines, with, in addition, limited sources in the Penrith area (Arthurton and Wadge 1981, 30). Given Carlisle's heavy reliance on local materials, it seems most likely that the small amount of Millstone Grit used was from a local source, and that the limited use was a result of its restricted outcrop. The single piece of haematite found probably also has its origins in the Upper Carboniferous deposits to the south-east of Carlisle, where nodules are common (*op cit*, 53). The grey sandstones, which seem to have been in common use for whetstones, are likely to have had a source in the Lower Carboniferous deposits which outcrop extensively to the south of Carlisle, where limestones are interspersed with grey sandstones (*op cit*, 30). The sandstone available is mostly fine-grained and occasionally micaceous, and would have been well suited to use as whetstones. A few rotary querns were made from coarser-grained grey sandstone. It is possible that some of these came from more distant sources, but the rock type is not distinctive enough to determine a precise origin.

There were a few other stone types in addition to the locally-sourced materials, including three rotary querns and a projectile made from granite. No attempt has been made to determine a precise source for this granite, but it could have come from south-west Scotland, like that used at Ravenglass (Potter 1979, 94), or equally could reflect the use of glacial erratics, many of which can be traced back to an original source in Scotland (Dixon *et al* 1926). Two of the whetstones might be made of Kentish Rag, a stone commonly used for whetstones in Roman Britain (Parkhouse 1997), and four other examples are made from a grey schist, the source for which has not been determined.

The range of stone used reflects that seen elsewhere in Carlisle and in the wider locality. At Castle Street and the southern Lanes, the querns were found to be

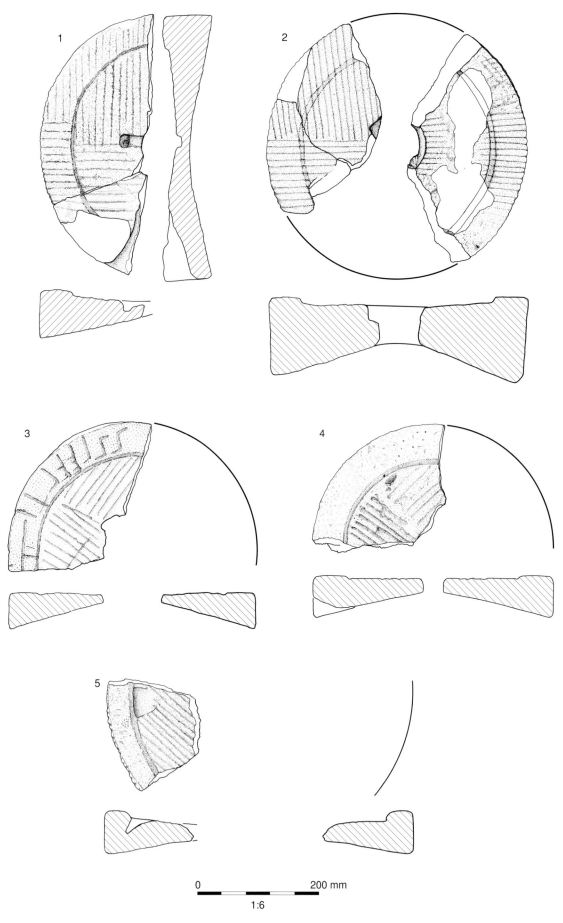

Figure 537: Imported style or 'kerbed' querns

a mixture of lava and local sandstones (Padley 1991a, 159; Padley 2000a). Unsurprisingly, given their close association, granite was also used at Annetwell Street (Caruana and Allnutt in prep), whilst at Blackfriars Street, objects of Penrith and St Bees sandstones, and of Carboniferous sandstones, were all identified (Caruana 1990, 158–61). A broader range of stone types (consistent with those seen at Carlisle) was also seen at the Roman fort of Ravenglass, with lava, Carboniferous sandstone, Permo-Triassic sandstone, Millstone Grit, and granite all being identified (Potter 1979, 94).

Rotary querns

In all, 36 fragments of rotary querns were recovered, some of them joining. They can be divided into a number of styles, according to their typological differences, although, obviously, the type of stone used can have a direct bearing on the typological form of the object. The group comprises five lower stones, 25 upper stones, and six items that were too small for the form to be determined. The number of upper stones represents a markedly higher proportion of the assemblage than seen at Annetwell Street (Caruana and Allnutt in prep), where there were 36 upper and 21 lower stones. The majority are between 300 mm and 500 mm in diameter, and 40 mm to 80 mm thick. There is, however, a small cluster of much thicker querns, in a variety of styles (disc, beehive, and kerbed) and stone types (both local and imported), but, with the exception of one, they are all from early second-century contexts.

Imported style or 'kerbed' querns

Of the 16 fragments of lava quern, two are from lower stones, eleven are upper stones, and three are small indeterminate fragments. The upper stones are all of 'kerbed' type, ten being Röder type 4 (Crawford and Röder 1955), which has an elbow-shaped handle socket running in from the outer edge to just inside the kerb. Only two fragments are from standard examples of this type (eg 15; Fig 537.1). Two others are of the same general type, but much more like beehive querns, being thicker (120 mm and 127 mm) and of smaller diameter (400 mm and 440 mm; for example 17, and 18; Fig 537.2). At Strageath, querns of appreciably greater thicknesses were found to be of earlier date (Flavian) than their thinner counterparts (Frere 1989, 181), and both the Carlisle examples are from very early second-century contexts. In addition, there are several querns with very shallow kerbs, barely distinguished from the upper surface, and there is one where the kerb is almost level with the upper surface, but separated from it by a groove (for example, 36 (Fig 537.3) and 38 (Fig 537.4)). A single quern of local stone was made in the Röder type 4 style and was certainly a copy of the imported type.

One of the lava querns could be Röder type 5, which, whilst similar to type 4 in all other respects, has a vertical handle socket just inside the kerb (8, Fig 537.5). Although this example has a socket just inside the kerb, it is not as deep as Röder's diagram suggests (Crawford and Röder 1955), and it is possible that it was not intended as a handle socket, but served some other purpose. This suggestion is perhaps supported by a lava quern found in 1892 and now in Tullie House Museum and Art Gallery (Acc: 1892.77), which has a socket like that seen on 8, but also has an elbow-shaped handle socket of type 4, positioned 90° further round the circumference of the stone. Thus, 8 could also be of Röder type 4 (ibid). Evidence suggests that lava querns arrived in the North with the Roman army in the late first century AD (Welfare 1985, 156), and examples from elsewhere in Carlisle, for example Blackfriars Street, have been dated to between c AD 79 and the end of the first century (Caruana 1990, 161).

Millstones

Six possible examples of mechanically-driven millstones were recovered, of which five were small, being between 540 mm and 590 mm diameter. Although the difference between a hand-operated rotary quern and a mechanically operated millstone is usually thought to be reflected in its diameter, the change being at between 550 mm and 600 mm, it is often very difficult to define with confidence. This problem is illustrated by 32 and 33 (Fig 538.1-2) and 10 (Fig 539.1); the former is 570 mm in diameter, but has a handle slot and must therefore have been hand-operated, whilst the latter has a diameter of 590 mm and a particularly wide central hole with a rynd slot fitting, which indicates, but does not prove, that it was mechanically driven. The evidence therefore suggests that there is one possible mechanical millstone (10) and one definite one (41, Fig 539.2), reused in a second-century road surface (6000; Period 4B road 7477). With a diameter of 800 mm, this is significantly larger than the biggest hand-operated querns, and is of a similar size to one found at Annetwell Street, which was 814 mm in diameter (Caruana and Allnutt in prep, ST 410). There are thought to have been two sizes of military mill, those around 400 mm in diameter, which were owned by each contubernium, and those of 660–810 mm diameter, owned by the whole century (Frere 1989; Moritz 1958, 116).

Native rotary querns

The majority of the 20 rotary querns of indigenous stone types are in a Romanised style, being heavily influenced by the design of imported lava querns. They fall into a number of groups and for consistency, where possible, the typology determined for material from Annetwell Street has been followed (Caruana and Allnutt in prep).

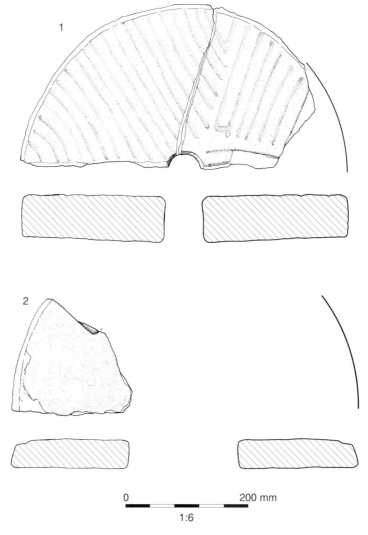

Figure 538: Possible millstones 32 and 33

'Cake Tin' querns

There are two upper stones of Caruana and Allnutt's 'cake tin' type (*eg 29*; Fig 540), having a flat top with concave grinding surface. Both are from Phase 6C.

Collared querns

A single example of a collared type (*10*; Fig 539.1), was recovered from a late third- to mid-fourth-century context, having been reused in floor *2214* (Period 6B Building *2302*). It was very similar to examples from Annetwell Street, being one of the largest querns recovered (590 mm diameter). It also provides evidence for a rynd-slot fitting, and this technological feature, along with the later date, supports the evidence from Annetwell Street, Chesterholm, and Ravenglass, which suggests that this design is of late Roman origin (Caruana and Allnutt in prep, 20; Welfare 1985, 162; Potter 1979, 94). Although many sites have produced querns of this design, they are not common, and do not occur in any great numbers in Carlisle: Annetwell Street produced only four examples, whilst Castle Street and Blackfriars Street produced only one each (Caruana and Allnutt in prep; Padley 1991b; Caruana 1990). Other military sites outside Carlisle reveal a similar pattern with few or no specimens; Ravenglass, for example, produced one, whilst Birdoswald produced none at all (Potter 1979; Summerfield 1997, 290-4).

Unpierced beehive

Two of the rotary querns are of the unpierced Beehive type (Caulfield 1977, 105). This type, distinguished by its thick, rounded top, and flat grinding surface, was first characterised by Curwen, who described it as the Hunsbury type, and regarded it as the Iron Age ancestor of the Roman Legionary type (Curwen 1937, 142). Philips (1950) later defined the Yorkshire or unpierced type, in which the handle socket does not pierce the feed pipe. Both examples from the site (*20* and *46*; Fig 541.1-2) are of typical beehive shape, with narrow cylindrical perforations. They both have radial rectangular-sectioned handle sockets which partially pierce the stone, and both were recovered reused in early second-century contexts. Indeed, one worn example was heavily burnt, before being used in construction, and it is thus likely that it was of some antiquity by the time it entered the archaeological record. A third quern, while not being distinctly of Beehive

878

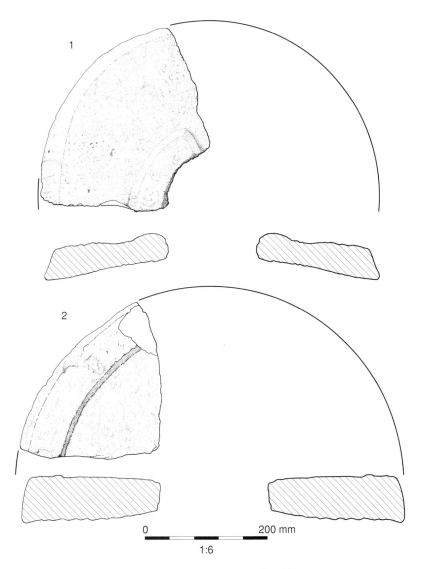

Figure 539: Possible millstone 10 *and millstone* 41

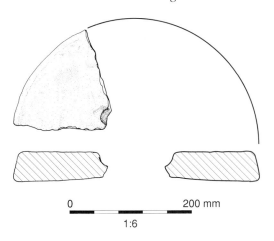

Figure 540: 'Cake tin' quern

shape, is reminiscent of this form, and is unusually thick, with a convex top (*3; Appendix 11*); this came from the fill (*189*) of a Period 6B pit (*188*).

The dating and period of use of the beehive quern remains unclear, although they were introduced during the Middle Iron Age, and in the South were beginning to be replaced by the thinner flatter querns, typical of the Roman period, well before the Roman Conquest. In the South, this transition was more or less complete by the start of the Roman period and beehive querns were not manufactured thereafter (Saunders 1998; Peacock 1987). In the North, however, there is an appreciable difference, and they appear to have remained in use well into the Roman period (Wright 1988, 66; Caulfield 1977, 107), a phenomenon particularly visible on domestic and rural sites, where they continued in use throughout the period. The villa at Dalton Parlours, near Leeds, for example, produced a large number of rotary querns, of which roughly half were of the beehive unpierced type, and which included *in situ* beehive-style lower stones (Buckley and Major 1990, 117) of Romano-British date. The most common form had a rounded top (*op cit*, 108) like those from Carlisle, although they were thicker (122-250 mm) and of smaller diameter (256–360 mm). This might suggest that the querns from the Millennium Project were

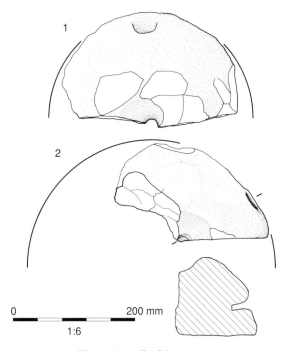

Figure 541: Beehive querns

Disc querns

The remaining 11 querns, both upper and lower stones, are of disc type (Caruana and Allnutt's flat thin and flat thick types (in prep)). These are mostly made in local stones, although there are two lower stones of lava which fall into this category. Both are grooved, as is typical for lava stones, but the first has a slightly raised lip around the perforation (*39*; Fig 542.1) and the second has a more rectangular profile, with straight sides and flat faces (*34*; Fig 542.2). As this is the most common design on military sites for rotary querns made from local stone, their presence is not a surprise.

Technology

Only ten of the fragments retain evidence of the way in which the quern was operated. Of these, four have handle sockets cut into the side of the quern, but not penetrating the eye. This arrangement is typically found on beehive and other querns with curved edges/upper surfaces, although two of those noted are on disc querns, both of which retain part of the iron handle within the socket. Four querns have elbow-shaped handle sockets, where the socket curves from the edge to the upper surface; this feature is exclusive to lava examples, being largely associated with the kerbed-style quern, where the handle was connected to the top of the kerb. Two examples have lateral handle sockets laid across the top, which of necessity requires the upper surface to be flat (*33-34*).

Although no quern stones showed markedly uneven wear to one side, lateral and side handle slots can be taken to indicate querns which were probably operated semi- rather than fully rotationally. Although some reconstruction drawings have inferred vertical handles

already somewhat influenced by contact with the Roman army, being thinner (98 mm and 140 mm) and of larger diameter (340 mm and 450 mm respectively). Indeed, evidence suggests that they fell out of use on northern military sites during the second century AD. An example was found at Newstead in a late first- to mid-second-century context (Curwen 1937, 147), and a further example was found in a mid-second-century context at Milecastle 54 (Randylands) (Simpson and Richmond 1935, 240, fig 19; Welfare 1985, 156).

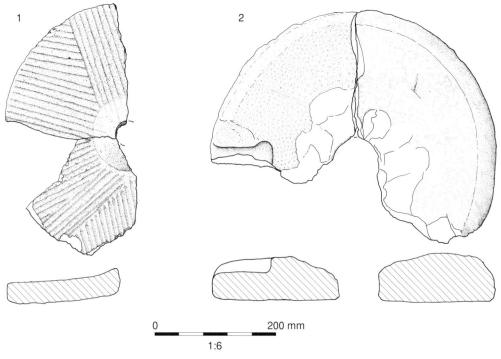

Figure 542: Disc querns

in these types of socket (Welfare 1985), a quern from Silchester, with surviving wooden handle, reveals a two-handled attachment which could only have been moved from side to side (Shaffrey 2003, 154, fig 6). The querns with elbow-shaped handle sockets are associated with Röder type 4 rotary querns, and were considered by him to be of an oscillating or semi-rotational type. Röder interpreted the transition to types 5 and 6 as a change to a vertically inserted handle, which would have made full rotation possible (Crawford and Röder 1955). The attachment on the type 4 quern, from a nineteenth-century excavation at Tullie House (Ferguson 1893), wrapped around the kerb to form a large band which would have held a cylindrical handle, probably wooden, in a vertical position. Type 4 querns with elbow-shaped sockets could therefore have been rotated fully.

Whetstones

A broad range of sizes, shapes, and materials was seen in the group of 45 whetstones. They have been divided into three broad categories according to their shape: primary; secondary; and natural. Within each category, variation in size and wear suggests that they were employed for different purposes.

Primary whetstones are those deliberately made as sharpening tools; they account for the majority of the whetstones found on site, 26 in total. Extensive variation in size, shape, and wear patterns indicates that they served a range of purposes. With the exception of two examples with one or more slightly concave face, there is a group of 12 with flat faces and squared edges, and rectangular or square cross-sections (*eg 22*;

Fig 543.1). These equate with the group D whetstones from *Leucarum*, used with the whetstone held firmly in one hand, while the blade was moved with the other (Parkhouse 1997, 421). They vary in size according to the size of the blades they were used to sharpen, and according to their overall purpose: larger whetstones may have been part of workshop toolkits, whilst smaller tools could have been personal belongings. The majority are between 20 mm and 40 mm wide and, where complete, approximately 100 mm long. There is one example of a very small rectilinear whetstone (*1*; Fig 543.2), which must have been used to sharpen very small blades, possibly surgical implements (*op cit*, 421). A second group was defined, comprising 11 primary whetstones. They have a more varied range of shapes and profiles, usually with one or more flat face or edge, and one or more curved face or bevelled edge. These equate with group C at *Leucarum* (*op cit*, 420). The varied wear patterns reflect use for a variety of purposes. One example (*2*; Fig 543.3) has very straight edges but the end has also been used, being rounded by wear. A smaller, more delicate version (*44*; Fig 543.4) has one very flat side, and all the others are curved, again suggesting that, despite its size, it was used in several ways. Two examples have pronounced bevelled edges (*eg 30*; Fig 543.5), and several have almost square or rectangular cross-sections and flat faces, but slightly rounded edges (*eg 6*; Fig 543.6). A further example of a rounded elongate whetstone has been utilised in such a way as to create a wedge shape at one end (*40*; Fig 543.7), whilst another has very angular edges, but the faces are concave. One whetstone was probably a shaft straightener or polisher and has been extensively used on all surfaces (*43*; Fig 544), forming extremely pronounced grooves.

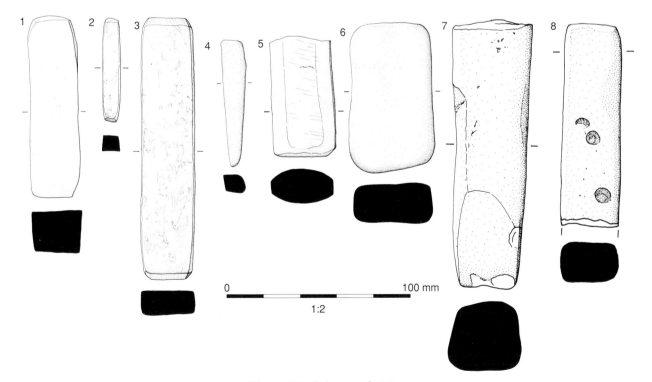

Figure 543: Primary whetstones

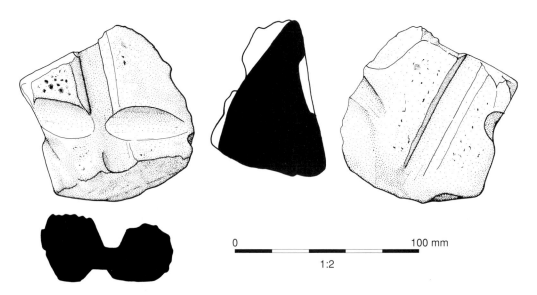

Figure 544: Possible shaft straightener

Secondary-use whetstones form only a small portion of the assemblage, accounting for only three tools; all are reused fragments of other stone objects. All are slab shaped, demonstrating wear on one of the main faces, one having grooves along one face, whilst another (5; Fig 545.1) has one face worn concave. They can be equated with the group A whetstones at *Leucarum*, which were probably used for the sharpening of smaller blades (Parkhouse 1997, 419). These whetstones contributed only a small proportion of the overall assemblage at both sites, despite the fact they are usually more commonly found, and it is likely that the military nature of the sites would have ensured that tools were in good supply, so that secondary reuse was not required.

The simplest type, natural whetstones, are pebbles used and collected on an *ad hoc* basis, probably locally, and characteristically their form has only been modified through use. Most are rounded with sub-circular cross-sections, and are comparable with the group B whetstones classified at *Leucarum* (*op*

cit, 418). The 15 whetstones of this type amongst the assemblage are amongst the larger examples, being mostly over 100 mm in length, for example, *16* and *35* (Fig 545.2-3). They mainly have curved surfaces, and would have been most appropriately used for sharpening long blades such as sickles (*op cit*, 420). Only one of the group (*25*, Fig 545.4) shows evidence of having been used for a different purpose, having a distinctive wear pattern, with one face flattened through use, and bevelled edges. Three other examples (*eg 26* and *31*, Fig 545.5-6) have one or more slightly flattened faces, putting them in Parkhouse's group C (1997, 42).

Only one whetstone can be identified as post-Roman in origin. A small, carefully made whetstone (*23*; *Appendix 11*) was recovered from Period 8C layer *5102*. Clearly small enough to be regarded as a personal object, it would probably have been worn suspended from a belt. As it lacks the typical perforation at one end, it is possible that originally it had a copper-alloy cap

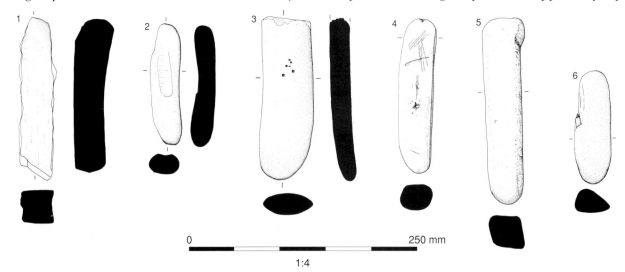

Figure 545: Secondary-use and natural whetstones

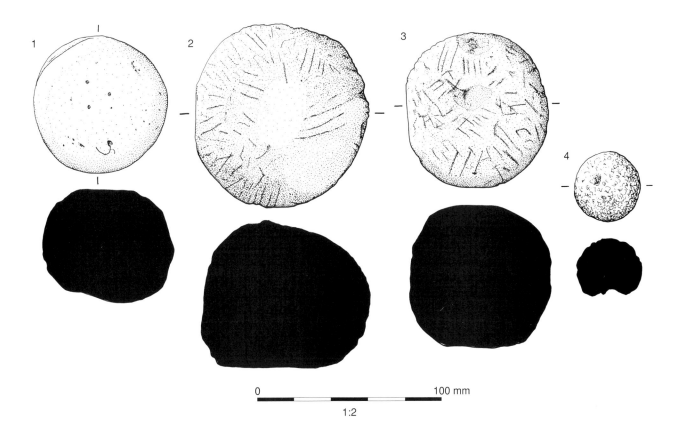

Figure 546: Projectiles

incorporating a suspension loop, which has been lost. Dating is not obvious, but a ninth- to tenth-century date is possible, reflecting the presence of a small number of other early medieval objects (including coins; *Ch 17*) in medieval deposits (Period 8).

Projectiles

In keeping with the military nature of the site, there are large numbers of stone projectiles (31), which should be considered alongside the many other clay and lead examples from the site (*Ch 17*). Of these,

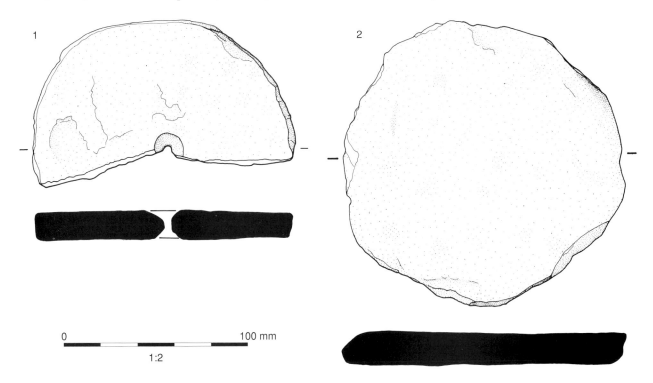

Figure 547: Pot lids

27 are spherical, having been carefully pecked into shape, albeit some more carefully than others, with many having one slightly flattened side (*eg 7, 13, 14, 48*; Fig 546.1-4). These objects are usually interpreted as *ballista* balls, although the suggestion that they may have been made for hand throwing seems equally plausible (Griffiths 1994, 205). Four of the projectiles are smaller ovoid objects, best categorised as sling-shot. They are not especially worked, but fit well with the known optimum dimensions for sling-shot of 20-50 mm in length (*op cit*, 204).

Other stone objects

There are two circular discs, one pierced and one unpierced (*4* and *50*; Fig 547.1-2). Of similar size (141 mm and 155 mm in diameter respectively), both show signs of burning around the edges, with *50* being particularly blackened. These objects are usually interpreted as pot lids, although the unpierced roundel had no obvious means of attaching a handle. Examples of pierced discs have been found at Vindolanda (Bidwell 1985, 152 and fig 58) and unpierced ones at Blackfriars Street, Carlisle (Caruana 1990, 161).

A single fragment of loomweight (*21*; Fig 548.1) was recovered from a late first-century deposit (*3536*) associated with road **4661** (Period 3B). The only other stone item associated with textiles is a beehive-shaped spindle whorl (*9*; Fig 548.2), found in post-Roman deposit *2112* (Period 7), in addition to a small number of copper-alloy and bone objects (*Chs 17* and *20*).

Four pestles were found, all being unmodified pebbles used for the purpose. All are elongated natural pebbles with rounded ends, which would have made useful pestles without alteration. Some are more extensively worn than others; *27* (Fig 548.3), in particular, has extensive wear at one end, including scars from the removal of several flakes, which suggests use for pounding rather than grinding. No stone mortars were found on the site, and the recovery of stone pestles is not common; it is often presumed that pestles were made from wood and thus are usually not preserved. Several of the natural whetstones also show wear patterns consistent with pounding, and may have been multi-functional tools (*eg 26*; Fig 545.5).

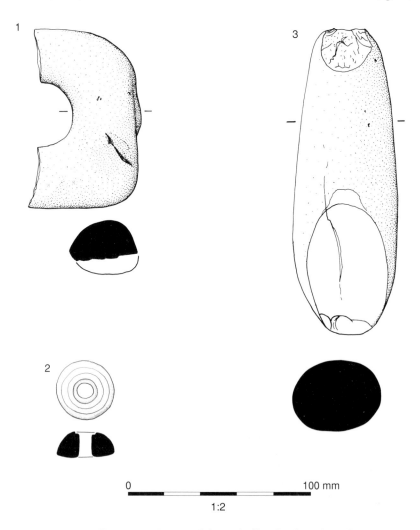

Figure 548: Loomweight, spindle whorl, and pestle

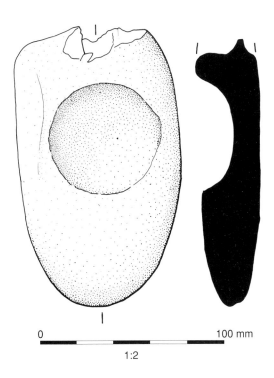

0   100 mm

1:2

Figure 549: Possible lamp or lampholder 49

Two additional items could be crude lamps. The first of them (*49*; Fig 549) is of a shape reminiscent of Roman open lamps, which come largely from military and/or northern contexts (Eckardt 2002, 243). Unfortunately, it does not have any precise parallels and was unstratified. The second lamp or probable lamp holder (*37*; Fig 550) was found in the late third- to fourth-century fill (*5727*) of Period 6B pit *5668* and is extensively burnt. It is slightly larger and, again, has no close parallels. Both are much simpler in form than the majority of open lamps, and of a substantially greater size (*op cit*, fig 107). Without the nozzle forming the typical figure-of-eight shape, it is difficult to identify either of these artefacts as lamps with confidence, and they may be better interpreted as lamp holders. The internal dimensions of both would have been appropriate for holding simple ceramic open lamps, and this could have led to the visible patterns of burning. Lamp *49* is made from a very micaceous rock, and is likely to have sparkled when lit by a naked flame.

Miscellaneous objects include three stone counters, a vessel fragment, and a crude writing implement.

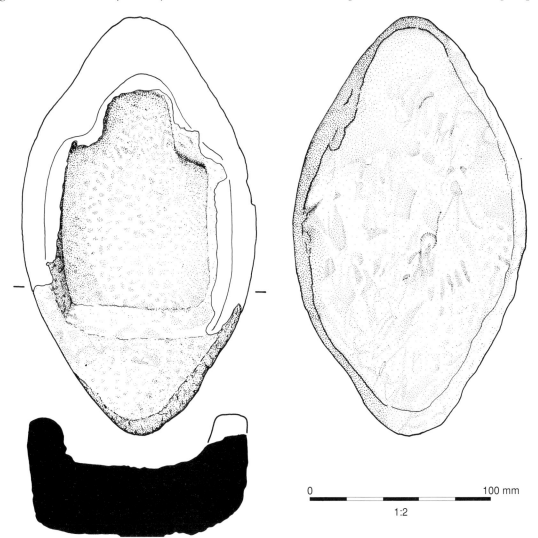

0   100 mm

1:2

Figure 550: Lamp or lampholder 37

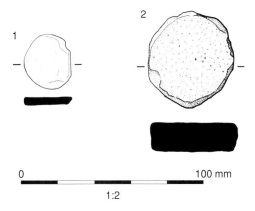

Figure 551: Counters

The three counters were recovered from contexts of late Roman (Period 6D) or post-Roman (Period 8A) date (*2313* and *5301* respectively). These are of very different design, with two being quite small (15 mm and 25 mm in diameter), with one (*11*; Fig 551.1) being very well finished; the third (*12*; Fig 551.2) is larger and more crudely made. The single vessel fragment (*45*; Fig 552) was recovered from a possible floor (*6587*) in Period 4B Building **5689**; it originally had a diameter of *c* 390 mm. The writing implement (*19*; Fig 553) is a tapered elongated piece of haematite, worn to a point by rubbing at one end, presumably using the red pigment like a pencil. It was found in a surface (*3516*) of Period 3B road **4661**.

Discussion
The worked stone is a disparate group, and in general terms there are no significant patterns in the spatial or chronological disposition of these items. The rotary querns, however, provide some evidence for temporal change in the use of different raw materials, which

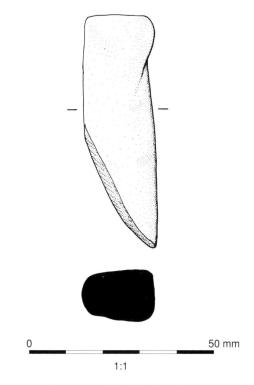

Figure 553: Writing implement

may be a reflection of supply patterns. Of the quern fragments found on the site, 16 were made of imported Niedermendig Lava and 20 were probably of locally available stone types. Comparison of the stratigraphic context of the two groups shows that the lava querns were deposited in greater numbers than other stone types in the first to early second centuries (Fig 536). Those querns of locally obtained materials were only discarded in small numbers during that period, but in much greater numbers in later phases, mainly during the fourth century.

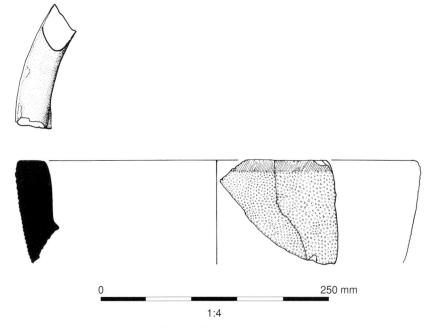

Figure 552: Stone vessel

Material	Weight (kg)	% of total weight	Count	% of total count
Roman ceramic building material	1059.131	75.26	10764	83.29
Post-medieval ceramic building material	3.933	0.28	10	0.08
Daub	4.596	0.33	139	1.08
Fired clay	0.448	0.03	25	0.19
Mortar	123.759	8.79	295	2.28
Opus signinum (flooring and other)	4.701	0.33	7	0.05
Plaster, including painted plaster	7.624	0.54	256	1.98
Stone	195.735	13.91	1247	9.65
Unidentified ceramic material	2.984	0.21	156	1.2
Unidentified calcareous material	4.368	0.31	24	0.18
Totals	1407.279	99.99	12,923	99.98

Table 62: Summary of the total building material assemblage

It is now generally accepted that there is a strong link between lava querns and military sites, where they are often the preponderant type, especially in the first and second centuries (Buckley and Major 1990, 117). This is not, however, entirely the case at Carlisle, where the representation of lava and other stone types is more balanced. The later change, with a greater representation of other stone types, is mirrored at other military sites, and particularly at Strageath, where querns of locally obtained rock were only found in later contexts (Frere 1989, 181). Interestingly, there is a difference in discard patterns between this part of the fort and that seen at Annetwell Street to the immediate south. At the latter, it appears that large numbers of querns made from locally obtained rocks were deposited in first-century contexts (Caruana and Allnutt in prep, table 94). Indeed, twice as many local fragments than lava fragments were recorded. This is a salutary warning, as the two excavations to a great extent investigated opposite ends of the same structures, and the differences presumably indicate very different practices in close proximity, perhaps suggesting that, even at an early date, some parts of the fort were used by individuals with more Romanised culinary habits than others. Whether or not this reflects a division of personnel is open to debate, but a difference of some kind is also to be seen in the distribution of stone projectiles, with only nine from Annetwell Street, compared to 31 from the Millennium Project, along with a large number of fired clay slingshot, and, in later contexts, lead slingshot (*Ch 17*).

In addition to the observably changing pattern in the supply of querns, the presence of a mechanically driven millstone fragment in a second-century road surface (*6000*), albeit reused, is of significance. Although in a considerably later context (mid-fourth century), a millstone of similar dimensions was found at Annetwell Street (Caruana and Allnutt in prep, 20, catalogue 1). The introduction and use of mechanically driven millstones has not been dated with precision, but mainly date from the second century onwards (King 1986, 110). The presence of a broken and clearly

reused example in a Period 4B context, dating to the second quarter of the second century, is clear evidence that millstones had been in use for some considerable time before this. The early date could be explained by the military nature of the site, although not all military sites have produced such millstones.

The Ceramic Building Materials

S Pringle

Almost 1.5 tonnes of ceramic and other building materials (excluding stone) were recovered from the excavations, most of which came from Roman deposits, with the exception of a few items from the nineteenth or twentieth centuries. The range of material recorded included ceramic building material, daub, fired clay, mortar, plaster, and stone, all being quantified by fragment count, type, and weight (Table 62). In addition, a large sub-section of the ceramic building material (644.33 kg) was also quantified by fabric. Where the form was not identifiable, fired ceramics were recorded as 'tile'. All stratified material has been quantified, and a small amount (6.772 kg) of unstratified building material was also recorded; this has not been included in the quantifications.

Context and date

The quantities of building materials excavated from the Roman phases varied widely, the least being associated with Period 3, the greatest amount with Period 6 (Table 63). Earlier periods (1 and 2)

Period	Weight (kg)	% of total
3	21.9	2
4	319.7	26
5	168.4	14
6	690.8	58
Total	1200.8	100

Table 63: Chronological distribution by weight

produced nothing, as did medieval Period 8. None of the material is closely dated.

Period 3
Period 3 produced the smallest amounts of fired ceramic and stone building materials and the largest amounts of daub and fired clay. Daub with impressions of flat timbers, probably studs, was noted from Buildings *1194* and *4657* (Fig 262); the outer surface of the latter was rendered with mortar 10–15 mm thick and was presumably part of an external timber and earth wall. Wattle impressions, sometimes clearly interwoven, as from Buildings *2061* (R3), *3772* (R2), and *4006*, are a feature of the daub from this period, making it likely that these buildings had wattle and daub internal partitions.

The earliest identifiable fired ceramics were fragments of water pipe from the main east to west road in Period 3A, although there is rather more evidence for the use of timber water pipes at this time (*Ch 3*), and in consequence the ceramic pipe could be intrusive from a later drain, cut through the road in Period 5 (*Ch 7*). In Period 3B, brick and a flat sooted tile, possibly a flue tile, were present in Buildings *4656* and *7394*, and by Period 3C, more bricks were found in Building *4657*, with brick and flue fragments from roadside drain *6399* (*Ch 4*). The only securely identified roofing tile from this phase was an *imbrex* from the robbing of drain *6399* (Period 3E).

Unsurprisingly, only 1.3 kg of stone came from Period 3 deposits. The predominant type was fine-grained red sandstone, several fragments of which came from the floor of Period 3B Building *4651* and a robber trench associated with the main east to west road in Period 3D. Slate was also in use at this time; a block from R5 or R6 of Building *7392* (*7573*), worn smooth in the middle of one face, suggests its use as a sharpening block or hone, and was perhaps associated with the copper-alloy-working activities for which there is some evidence (*Ch 3, pp 98-9*).

Period 4
There were considerably larger quantities of building materials from Period 4. Daub and fired clay were again fairly common, particularly in Building *3376* (timber and interwoven wattle impressions), and Buildings *4655* and *4660*. More significantly, the quantities of ceramic tile increased steeply. These were still mainly bricks and flue tiles, but *imbrices* and *tegulae* were by this time more abundant. Particularly good deposits came from central-range Buildings *5688* and *5689*, with brick, flue, roof-tile, and possibly water-pipe. However, the majority of the roof tile came from external areas, particularly road surfaces, and the probability that it represented make-up deposits rather than primary destruction material means it could not be attributed to specific buildings.

Similarly, there was more stone from Period 4. There seems to have been a greater variety of stone in use at this time, with coarser-grained, harder sandstones, probably used as paving or flagstones, supplementing the soft red sandstone used in Period 3. A quantity of soft, light grey, crinoidal limestone rubble was present in MIL 5, and continued to appear in later periods. It first appeared in demolition deposits associated with a possible barracks, Building *3376* (Period 4A), and in Period 4B was perhaps residual in the overlying smithy (Building *2765*), and a workshop, Building *4660*, and was found widely incorporated into the road surfaces.

Period 5
During Period 5, Building materials were less abundant than before. There was also a change in the character of the ceramic building material assemblage; the proportion of brick and flue tile fell, and that of roofing tile, particularly *tegulae*, increased (Table 64 shows the relative proportions of the main tile types in Periods 4, 5, and 6). Most of the tile in this period was associated with road *4662*, rather than with specific buildings, although a small quantity was associated with the external areas relating to Building *7397*. The most interesting

Form	Period 4		Period 5		Period 6	
	Weight kg (count)	% of total (count)	Weight kg (count)	% of total (count)	Weight kg (count)	% of total (count)
Brick	176.3 (420)	89.5 (66)	42.8 (97)	61.5 (41)	36.2 (78)	8.2 (3)
Flue	13.1 (164)	6.6 (26)	3.8 (28)	5.4 (12)	5.2 (46)	1.2 (2)
Imbrex	1.7 (29)	1 (5)	6.2 (48)	8.9 (20)	109.6 (967)	24.7 (36)
Tegula	6.0 (23)	3.1 (4)	16.8 (64)	24.2 (27)	292 (1570)	66 (59)
Total weight	197.1		69.6		443	
Total count	(636)		(237)		(2661)	

Table 64: The proportions, by weight, of the main tile types in Periods 4, 5, and 6 (fragment counts in brackets)

material was ceramic water-pipe *6044*, which was cut into the main east to west road. Period 5C saw the first appearance of tiles with legionary stamps, when a *tegula* with a stamp of either *Legio VI Victrix* or *Legio IX Hispana* (die RIB 2462.16; Collingwood and Wright 1992) was reused in the fill of a posthole (*2467/3447*). The composition of the building stone assemblage resembled that of Period 4, but the quantities were smaller.

Period 6

Deposits of the third and fourth centuries produced substantially more building material than any other period. Much of it came from the main east to west road and from external areas associated with the *principia*, which, between them, produced the largest roof tile assemblage from the excavations. More than 40 fragments of tile with legionary stamps came from this period, the majority from Period 6C. The legions represented by stamps were *II Augusta*, *XX Valeria Victrix*, and either *VI Victrix* or *IX Hispana*. There were also three examples of an incuse monogram stamp, RIB 2483 (Collingwood and Wright 1993), thought to be an imperial stamp.

In Period 6, the quantities of stone building materials increased. There were stone flags in both fine red sandstone and coarser quartzose sandstones, and what appear to be roofing tiles were present in both sandstone and grey slate. Crinoidal limestone rubble was present, some simply worked, and was particularly associated with Buildings *2301* and *2302*, where it may have been used as a wall-facing.

Periods 7 and 8

The ceramic and stone materials from Periods 7 and 8 were similar to those from Period 6, and much of the tile was residual. It seemed, however, to have been the case that Roman stone and tile was deliberately reused as road-surfacing, particularly in Period 8 Structure *7653* and road *7654*. There was also evidence for the use of stone paving in the same period. The range of stone types was the same as that seen in the Roman periods, although the material could not be positively identified as reused.

Nature of the assemblage
Tile fabrics

A large sub-section (644.33 kg) of the ceramic material was sorted by provisional fabric type, five main fabric groupings being identified. All are well-fired and hard, and all seem to contain monocrystalline quartz and reddish iron-rich inclusions. They also contain varying quantities of rock fragments, including polycrystalline quartz and sandstone. The main differences between the fabrics appeared, in the hand and under x10 magnification, to be in the grade of quartz silt within the matrix,

and the frequency and size of inclusions. They all seemed to reflect a similar geology, and the boundaries between groups were not always clear. This suggested that they were likely to have been made from similar clays, probably at the legionary tile works at Scalesceugh, a known source for Roman Carlisle (*Ch 16*). The colour range was light reddish-brown to reddish-brown (Munsell 2.5YR 6/4 to 5/4). The frequency of inclusions is described as being sparse, moderate, common, or abundant; the size categories for inclusions are fine (up to 0.25 mm), medium (0.25–0.5 mm), coarse (0.5-1 mm), and very coarse (greater than 1 mm). Where appropriate, the degree of angularity or rounding of inclusions is noted.

Fabric 1
The matrix contained fine quartz, with sparse, coarse to very coarse, rounded and angular quartz, and dark red to blackish iron-rich inclusions.

Fabric 2
A 'clean' matrix, with silt-sized quartz (with fine white or cream streaks in some examples), contained frequent medium quartz and sparse coarse to very coarse quartz, and moderate fine to coarse, reddish-brown iron-rich inclusions. Sparse, very coarse, polycrystalline quartz was present in some examples (Munsell 5YR 6/6, reddish-yellow).

Fabric 3
A 'clean' matrix contained silt-grade quartz, with common coarse to very coarse rounded quartz grains, and moderate fine to coarse reddish iron-rich inclusions. Some examples had inclusions of non-calcareous white rock fragments (less than 5 mm). The brick version of this fabric appeared to be sandier.

Fabric 4
The matrix contained fine quartz, with abundant medium quartz, common coarse to very coarse rounded quartz grains, and moderate, fine to very coarse, reddish-brown iron-rich inclusions.

Fabric 5
This had a harsh feel with a fine 'clean' matrix with silt-sized quartz, containing abundant, medium to very coarse, rounded and angular quartz (less than 1.5 mm), and moderate, coarse to very coarse, reddish-brown iron-rich inclusions and rock fragments.

Chronology of the fabrics on the site

The occurrence of each fabric type was quantified by period (Table 65). The distribution suggests that only tile fabrics 2, 3, and 4 were used in Period 3, but by Period 4 all fabric types were present.

Period	Fabric 1 weight kg (count)	Fabric 2 weight kg (count)	Fabric 3 weight kg (count)	Fabric 4 weight kg (count)	Fabric 5 weight kg (count)	Total weight (kg)	Total count
3	0	0.3 (5)	5.5 (22)	0.3 (1)	0	6.1	28
4	6.8 (42)	20.1 (93)	78.7 (333)	9.6 (19)	1.8 (7)	117	494
5	1. 4 (11)	13.2 (75)	84.8 (685)	2.4 (9)	9.0 (25)	110.8	805
6	8.3 (48)	133.7 (916)	78.4 (460)	9.9 (34)	54.5 (282)	284.8	1740
7*	1.8 (10)	18.3 (156)	9.5 (44)	6.6 (18)	3.5 (16)	39.7	244
8*	2.6 (14)	36.7 (238)	18.8 (123)	2.7 (18)	14.9 (57)	75.7	451
9*	0.2 (1)	1.3 (5)	0.7 (8)	0.3 (2)	0.6 (1)	3.1	17
Total weight	21.1	223.6	276.4	31.8	84.3	637.2	3779
Total count	(126)	(1488)	(1675)	(102)	(388)		

*Material in Periods 7, 8, and 9 is residual or reused in early medieval, medieval, and post-medieval deposits respectively

Table 65: Distribution of fabric types by period, giving weight in kilograms; the figures in brackets are fragment counts

Fabric	Brick	Flue	Imbrex	Tegula
1	4.8	3.3	2	3.3
2	16.2	22.4	56.2	46.8
3	69.3	63.3	23.1	23.8
4	8.4	9.3	2.3	4.3
5	1.3	1.7	16.4	21.8
Total %	100	100	100	100

Table 66: Percentage of main tile types in each fabric group (securely identified forms and fabrics only)

Fabric and form

The analysis used only that material for which tile type and fabric were securely identified, an assemblage of 484.639 kg. There are some indications that certain fabrics were preferred for certain tile types, and Table 66 shows the percentage, by weight, of the main forms in each fabric group. It appears that, within the group examined, over 60% of bricks and flue tiles were in fabric 3, whilst roofing tiles, *imbrices*, and *tegulae* were predominantly in fabric 2, essentially a less coarse version of fabric 3. None

Type	Fabric 1	Fabric 2	Fabric 3	Fabric 4	Fabric 5
Brick	42.3	13.1	53.7	47.6	3
Flue	4.4	2.7	7.4	8	1
Imbrex	10	26.2	10.4	7.6	21
Tegula	43.3	58	28.5	36.8	75
Total	100	100	100	100	100

Table 67: Main tile types as percentage of fabric groups 1-5 (securely identified forms and fabrics only)

of the fabrics, however, seemed to be associated with a single tile form. The same data can be re-arranged to present the tile types as a percentage of the total assemblage, by weight, for each fabric type (Table 67). This reinforces the impression that fabric 3 was primarily used for brick, and also suggests that fabric 5 was used mainly for roofing tile, particularly *tegulae*.

Roofing tile

Roofing tiles, both *tegulae* and *imbrices*, were the most abundant type recorded. The total weight of the *imbrices*, 146.946 kg, was approximately 38% of the total weight of the *tegulae*, 383.664 kg, which corresponds well to the ratio quoted by Brodribb for roof tiles from Beauport Park, where the average weight of an *imbrex* was approximately 40% that of a *tegula* (Brodribb 1987, 11). Thus the relative proportions of these roof tiles suggest that the two types were present in approximately similar numbers, which would have been the case if tile had been used primarily for roofing.

The *tegulae* were very fragmentary, with no complete length or breadth dimensions surviving. Several of the *tegulae* bore legionary stamps (Table 68), and other markings included signature (1, 2, 5; Figs 554.1-2; 555.4) and tally marks (Fig 554.3-5). Nail holes, made before the tile was fired, were seen in six examples, three of which also had a band of wavy finger-keying down the centre of the tile (*eg* 1; Fig 554.1), and a fourth was stamped, probably with the monogram IMP (die RIB 2483; Collingwood and Wright 1993). Of the remainder, one had the nail hole, 7 mm square, set diagonally. One example was recorded of a nail hole, centred at 50 mm from one end of the tile, bored through the tile after firing. Usually only a small percentage of *tegulae* were made with nail holes, as

RIB Die Type	Period	Type	Context	IRF No	Notes
2459.1	8	*Tegula*	504	9021	[.....]AVG
2459.1	7	*Tegula*	5199	2187	[....]IAVG; joins *5401/2186*
2459.1	6C	*Tegula*	523	759	[..]GIIAVG
2459.1	6C	*Tegula*	5235	3453	[..]GIIAV[.]; wooden stamp?
2459.1	6C	*Tegula*	5235	3454	[.]IIGIIAUG
2459.1	6C	*Tegula*	5287	3627	[.....]VG
2459.1	6C	*Tegula*	5401	2186	LIIGI[....]; joins *5199/2187*
2459.1	6C	*Tegula*	5408	3471	LIIGII[...]; two conjoin
2459.1	6C	*Tegula*	5410	3473	[.....]VG
2459.1	6C	*Tegula?*	5475	3997	[....]AV[.]; wooden stamp?
2459.1	6B	*Tegula?*	5478	3998	[.]IIGIIA[..]
2459.1?	6C	*Tegula*	5286	3468	[.......]G
2459.1?	6C	*Tegula*	5377	3959	Small part of stamp (raised area between 'L' and 'E')
2459.1?	6C	*Tegula?*	5472	3629	LE?[.....]
2459.1?	6B	*Tegula*	5690	9022	[........]G
2459.1??	6B	*Tegula?*	5478	3999	Small part of stamp - bar over II?
2462.16	6C	Brick	2146	9005	[.]EG[.....]
2462.16	6A	*Tegula*	2458	3446	LEG.VI[?], joins *2467/3447*
2462.16	5C	*Tegula*	2467	3447	LEG.VI[?], joins *2458/3446*
2463.1	6D	Brick	2185	2005	[...]XX.VV; two conjoin
2463.1	6D	*Tegula*	512	760	[.....]V
2463.1	6C	*Tegula*	5273	3451	[..]G.X[...]; joins *5401/2189*
2463.1	6C	*Tegula*	5286	3465	[..]G.X[...]
2463.1	6C	*Tegula?*	5325	3450	LE[......]
2463.1	6C	*Tegula*	5401	2189	[....]X.VV; joins *5273/3451*
2463.1	6C	*Tegula*	5435	3631	[...].XX.VV
2463.1	6B	*Tegula*	5496	4000	LEG.XX.VV; joins *5841/4073*
2463.1	6A	*Tegula*	5841	4073	Joins *5496/4000*
2463.1		*Tegula*	5475	9025	[....]X[..]
2463.1?	8A	*Tegula?*	5246	3633	LE[.....]
2463.1?	6C	*Tegula*	5475	9023	[.]EG[....]
2463.2	6D	*Tegula*	2216	2006	[..]GXX.V; two join
2463.2	6C	*Tegula*	2352	2036	[.]EG[....]
2463.2	6C	*Tegula*	5408	3472	LE[......]
2463.3	8B	*Tegula?*	5143	2188	[....]XVV
2463.3	8A	*Tegula?*	5181	3634	LE[.....]
2463.3	6C	*Tegula?*	5235	3449	[......]V
2463.3	6C	*Tegula*	5286	3467	[.....]VV
2463.3	6B	*Tegula*	5450	3630	[.....]VV
2463.3	6B	*Tegula?*	5557	4001	[.]EG[....]
2463.3?	6C	*Tegula?*	5235	3452	[......]V; Small part of stamp. ID not secure
2483	6B	*Tegula?*	5399	3626	Base of I or M
2483	6B	*Tegula*	5539	3996	Base of I or M
2483	6B	*Tegula*	5690	4074	IM
2483?	5D	*Tegula*	2537	9024	Probable P; has circular nail hole (diameter 8 mm) centred *c* 25 mm from end
?	6C	Brick?	5235	3636	LE?[...]
?	6C	*Tegula*	5286	3466	[...]E/F?; incuse, unframed
?	6A	?	5691	9006	LE?[...]

Table 68: The stamped tiles

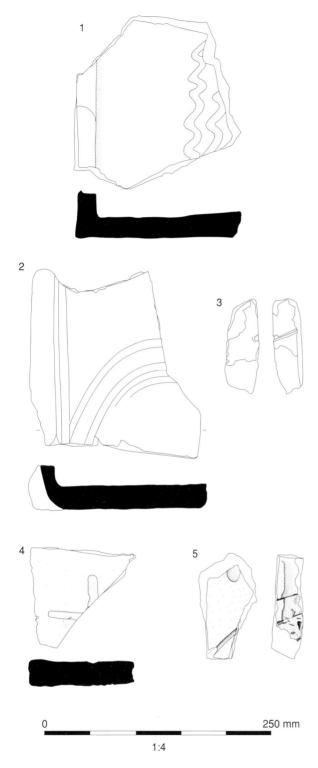

1

2

3

4

5

0   250 mm

1:4

Figure 554: Signatures and tally marks

was the case here. Brodribb, citing the *lex puteolana* of 105 BC, suggests that only the lowest tile course might ever have been nailed in position (*op cit*, 11), but there is some evidence from Britain that *tegulae* with nail holes were more common from the mid-second century AD on, implying that other factors, such as the use of smaller, and thus lighter, tiles (Betts 2003, 112–13), or a slight increase in the steepness of roofs, may have influenced this feature.

There were no complete *imbrices*, and only two complete ends were recorded. As *imbrices* tapered from one end to the other, their differing widths, 180 mm and 137 mm, presumably represent one example from each end. Some particularly thick fragments (*c* 28 mm) could have been fragments of ridge tile. Several *imbrices* had a reduced external surface. This could have been the result of subsequent burning, but it could alternatively have been a deliberate attempt to darken the colour, perhaps to provide a decorative contrast with lighter red *tegulae*.

Bricks

Again, the bricks were very fragmentary. Only two bricks with complete dimensions were recorded, a near-complete *pedalis*, 270 x 280 x 50 mm thick, with a curved signature mark and animal prints (*11*; Fig 555.1), and a *bessalis*, or *pila* brick, 221 mm long by 41 mm thick. Both are likely to have been used in a hypocaust system. Most of the bricks were between 30 mm and 68 mm thick, which suggested that a range of brick types was represented; the larger Roman bricks, the *sesquipedalis* and *bipedalis*, respectively one-and-a-half and two Roman feet square, were usually substantially thicker than the smaller types, probably because they were used in the construction of hypocausts, as bridging tiles between *pilae*, to form a suspended floor capable of supporting the weight of a substantial concrete or pebble-and-mortar make-up. Some bricks showed wear abrasion from having been used as paving or cobbles.

The presence of more specialised brick types is suggested by some fragments with unusual features. One exceptionally thick (73.5 mm) and two exceptionally thin (23.5 mm and 24 mm) fragments had scored lattice keying on one surface, on the sanded face in the case of the thin tiles (*13*; Fig 555.2). This type of keying was usually carried out to aid the bonding of a mortar render; the thinner keyed tiles (probably residual in deposits of Periods 5B and 6D, the latter in Building *2302*) may have been used as cavity walling in a hypocausted building, rendered and, probably, painted. The thick tile (*18*, from the post-Roman 'dark earths') was reduced and sooted on the unkeyed surface, suggesting its use in a suspended floor or as part of the structure of a furnace. Some fragmentary bricks from deposits of Periods 5 and 6 appeared to taper slightly along their length and might have been solid voussoirs, although the evidence is inconclusive. One example of a brick with one end cut at an angle to form a rough mitre was found in a Period 5A deposit: this may have been used for a cornice or other decorative feature. Fragments of two bricks bore legionary stamps (RIB 2462.16) (*7* and *8*) and RIB 2463.1 (*6*); Collingwood and Wright 1992).

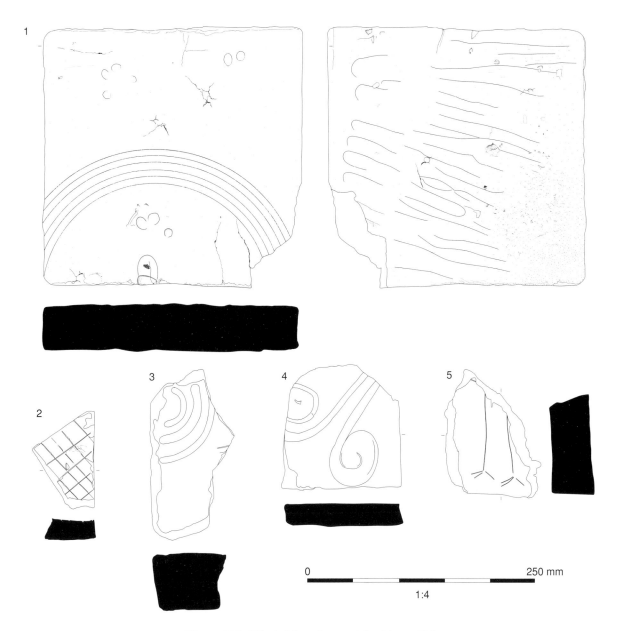

Figure 555: Pila *brick and material with graffiti*

Kiln flooring-block

This roughly made, rectangular clay brick (*16*; Fig 556), measuring approximately 260 x 80 mm, and up to 90 mm thick, had been hand-made of essentially unprocessed clay, containing inclusions of small stones and grit, and multiple laminations and air-pockets. The upper side is gently undulating, and there is evidence of trimming and smoothing during manufacture, presumably to create a relatively level surface. The narrow edges are roughly straight, and show a combination of knife trimming and hand-forming. All have a thin, but relatively even, covering of sand adhering to them, suggesting that each had been deliberately placed on a gritty surface following manufacture and while the clay was still pliable. The underside is flattened and had been treated similarly. Following this stage of manufacture, but while the clay was still flexible, two semi-vertical rectangular

holes (approximately 20 x 30 mm) had been made through the tile from the upper side. The clay displaced from this process protrudes on the underside, partly over the coating of sand, so the holes had evidently constituted the last stage of manufacture before firing. There is a third, very much smaller, hole at the edge of the block, but this does not penetrate the whole thickness and may be accidental. The surface of the underside of the block is reduced and slightly sooted; the narrow edges are superficially slightly reduced. In contrast, the remainder of the block (including the upper side) is oxidised.

This block most probably constituted part of the prefabricated floor of a tile or pottery kiln. This would explain why there is evidence of light reduction on the underside and narrow edges, the areas most exposed to the smoke in a kiln which was oxidising

0 ————————————————— 100 mm

1:2

Figure 556: Kiln flooring-block 16

the products stacked on the upper side of its block floor. Tiles or blocks of generally similar morphology and dimensions were used as flooring components at the legionary works-depot of Holt (Grimes 1930, figs 19, 24-5, 29), in kilns at Colchester (Hull 1963, 3-4, kiln 7), and other potteries or tileries. They would normally have been placed abutting one another, spanning the under-floor cross piers which protruded from either side of the kiln combustion chamber, and which supported the composite perforated raised oven floor of abutting blocks. The texture and appearance of the clay is generally similar to that found in kiln floors and prefabricated kiln furniture, and the deliberate gritting on the edges would have prevented the flooring-block from sticking to those placed adjacent to it. From a practical standpoint, the holes had most probably been perforated when this and the flooring-blocks were already *in situ* within the kiln, in order to locate them in the gaps between the under-floor piers.

Block 16 was found in R3 of Building **4655** (Period 4A). It had been deliberately set into the primary floor of the room, more-or less flush with it, and abutting a small bowl-like hearth, which had probably served for cooking or heating (*Ch 5, pp 191-2*). However, the very thick, sturdy nature of the brick, its large perforations, and uniform pattern of oxidation and reduction do not suggest that it had been made for, or used within, a domestic hearth. It more probably implies that it had come from an industrial kiln somewhere in the general vicinity of the fort, and had been reused in this barrack-block. Perhaps an earlier kiln in a nearby workshop (in Fisher Street) had been demolished when the Period 4A fort was built (*Ch 16, pp 593-4*), and an occupant of the barracks had spotted its suitability for use as a hob or kerb for the hearth. Whatever the precise circumstances of its reuse, it existence suggests that rectangular kilns, with prefabricated flooring components, in a style generally associated with the military, were being used for the manufacture of tile or pottery in the vicinity of the fort prior to, or at the very beginning of, Period 4A.

Flue tiles

Box flues, hollow rectangular tiles used in hypocaust systems to convey hot air and gases up through the walls to vents in the upper part of the building, are usually associated with bath-houses and domestic hypocausts. Fragments of unkeyed flue tile, and face fragments with scored and combed keying, were found, but no complete flue tiles were recovered.

Many of the box flue fragments appeared to be unkeyed but, as box flues often had both keyed and plain surfaces, the fragmentary condition of the tile made secure identification impossible. Apparently unkeyed flue tiles were noted with faces of two widths: 115–120 mm and *c* 155–160 mm, although it is possible that these may represent the breadth and depth of the same tile type. There was evidence of

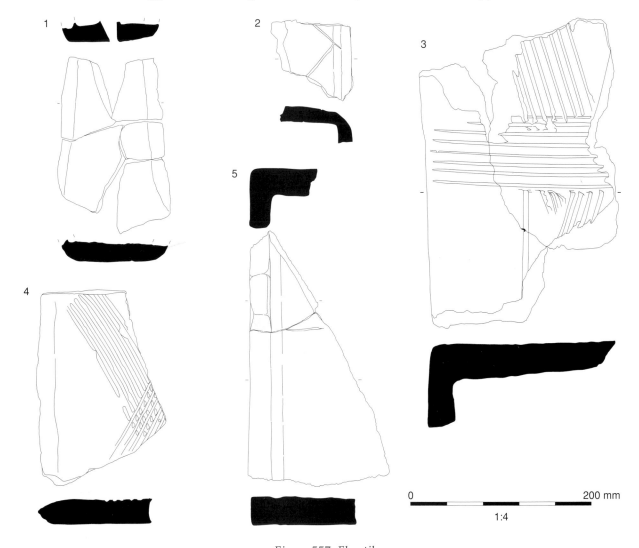

Figure 557: Flue tiles

both rectilinear and diagonal (probably triangular) vents (*17*; Fig 557.1), and a small fragment of an apparent double triangle or 'butterfly' vent, cut into the plain faces.

Several fragments were noted with knife-scored lattice keying on the outer face; some had rectilinear vent cuts, of which one is at least 65 mm long. The tiles were sanded inside, and, in some examples, on the outer surface (*18*; Fig 557.2).

Tiles with bands of four-, six,- and eight-toothed combing and rectangular vents were recorded (*19*; Fig 557.3). Others had bands of seven- and nine-toothed combing in the form of crossed diagonals (*20*; Fig 557.4); this pattern is often seen on hollow voussoirs, but the tiles were too fragmentary to enable secure identification of their type.

The earliest securely identified flue tile from the site was unkeyed and came from a Period 3C deposit, being residual in the main east to west road, its position perhaps suggesting that it could have originated in the Period 3A *praetorium*. The unkeyed tiles with triangular vents are also relatively early, the fragment with the butterfly vent coming from the western intervallum area in Period 4A/B. The tiles with larger triangular vents were first found in Period 4B, the majority reused in the floor of R4 of the *principia* (Building **5688**), the only building on the site with any quantity of flue tile (154 fragments) associated with it. These could, however, have been brought from elsewhere, as other flue tile from the *principia* (mainly R5) at this time is plain with rectilinear vents. Scored flue tiles were also first seen in Period 4 deposits, but were slightly more numerous in Periods 5 and 6; combed keying was noted from Period 5 on. Both scored and combed flue tiles occurred as residual material associated with roads and ditch fills, and could not be associated with any specific building or structure.

Flanged flue tile

An unusual flanged, or half-box, tile in coarse fabric 5 was found in a Period 5B external deposit. Superficially resembling a *tegula*, the tile had a sanded base with lattice-scoring, and a flange which had been cut away before the tile was fired, leaving a 45 mm-long section of flange with sloping sides (*21*; Fig 557.5) The side of the tile appeared to be notched at the base of one of the angled flange cuts, perhaps to allow the tile to be fixed in place with iron nails or T-shaped cramps. The design of this tile is similar to an example from Chester (Brodribb 1987, 66, fig 27b).

Water pipes

There were several different examples of Roman ceramic water pipes. The earliest appearance was in Period 3B, when three fragments were recovered from an early surface of the main east to west road (*Ch 3*). These were, however, similar to the pipe laid in the main east to west road during Period 5 (*Ch 7*), and might thus have been intrusive.

The most numerous and the most complete examples were from Period 5 deposits, found *in situ* in east to west pipe trench *6044*. Individual pipes were *c* 1.35 m long, made by luting together shorter wheel-thrown sections. They had an external diameter of between *c* 138 mm and 158 mm). One end had a narrow collar, which varied from square to triangular in section, whilst the other was chamfered for a distance of *c* 75 mm for insertion into the collared end of the adjacent pipe (*22*; Fig 558).

On excavation, some of the pipes had strips of leather adhering to them (Pl 236). There is no obvious reason for wrapping water pipes in leather, and it was not clear on excavation as to whether the leather was a deliberate addition, or simply dumped waste that had become wrapped around the pipes (S Winterbottom *pers comm*). The leather appeared, however, to have been deliberately cut into strips and bore no indication of reuse. Where original edges survived, these all lay at 90° to the pipe's length. One suggestion might be that the leather was used as a washer, sealing the joint between pipes, another that it was lagging, but it was attached to the main body of the pipe rather than the ends, and as the pipe was buried in a trench, insulation would seem to be unnecessary. There seemed to be some correspondence between tears

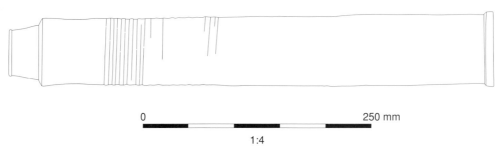

0   250 mm

1:4

Figure 558: Water pipe 22

Plate 236: Traces of leather wrapped around a water pipe

in the leather and the breaks in the pipe, suggesting that the relationship between the two was not accidental, although on some fragments the leather had wrapped itself around the broken edges. Some of it seemed to be stuck down, but this may have been due to the presence of a ferruginous deposit which had collected inside many of the pipes.

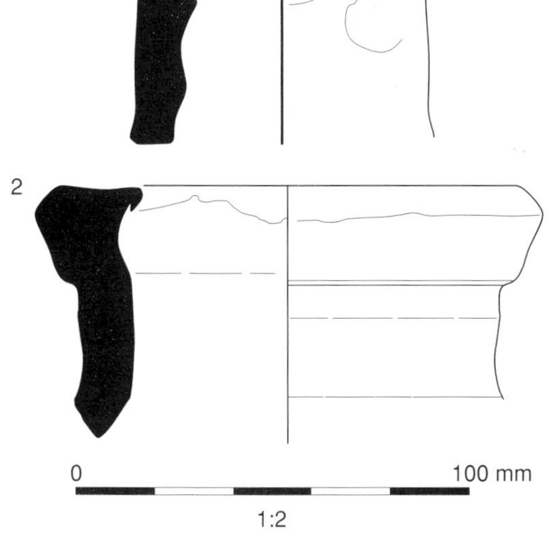

There were at least two smaller-diameter types of ceramic water pipe, both wheel-made. Four joining fragments from the end of a pipe with an external diameter of *c* 68 mm, widening to *c* 80 mm at the neck, and with an internal bore of *c* 40-50 mm, came from Period 6 deposits (*eg 24*; Fig 559.1), and several more small fragments of similar dimensions were noted. A wheel-turned fragment with a squared, flat-topped rim also appeared to be the neck of a pipe (*25*; Fig 559.2). These smaller pipes were similar in diameter to the ceramic vaulting tubes found in, or close to, bath-houses at three legionary forts, Chester, Caerleon, and York (Mason 1990, 218–20). However, there was no sign of either shouldered fragments, or the narrow 'nozzle' ends, and the external surfaces of the Carlisle pipes were smooth, unlike vaulting tubes, where the external wheel-formed ridges provided keying for the mortar or plaster into which they were set. On this evidence, it seems that they are more likely to have been used for conducting water rather than for the construction of roof vaults.

Chimneys
There were five fragments of chimney or louvre (*26-29*), all wheel-made, with curved and triangular knife-cut vents and bands of pie-crust decoration (Fig 560). All came from the area immediately east of Building **5200**, the Period 6 *principia*, and probably

Figure 559: Water pipes, or possibly vaulting tubes

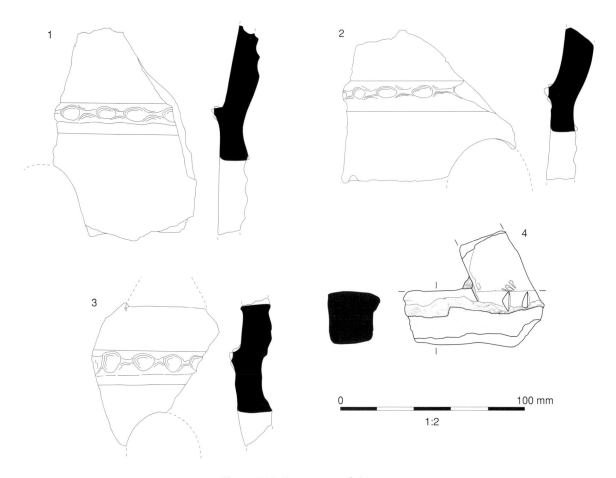

Figure 560: Fragments of chimney

represented two chimneys, although which building they came from remains uncertain.

Markings on tiles
Legionary stamps
In total, 44 tile stamps were recorded, of which two were on bricks, 28 on *tegulae* and the remainder on fragments of undifferentiated tile (Table 68). The majority of the stamps are those of legionary tile works; the die identification numbers used here are those of Collingwood and Wright (1992; 1993). The most frequent are the stamps of *Legio* XX *Valeria Victrix*, of which three types occur: stamp RIB 2463.1 (Collingwood and Wright 1992), ten definite or probable examples (12 fragments; *eg 6*; Fig 561.1); RIB 2463.2 (*ibid*), three examples (four fragments); RIB 2463.3 (*ibid*), seven definite or probable occurrences (seven fragments), a total of 20 stamps. Stamp RIB 2459.1 (*ibid*) of *Legio II Augusta* is also abundant, with 15 definite or probable stamps (17 fragments). Also present are four examples (three fragments) of the incuse stamp with the monogram, IMP (RIB 2483 (Collingwood and Wright 1993), which is thought to be an imperial stamp. All these stamps have previously been identified from Carlisle.

Two of the legionary stamps (RIB 2459.1 and RIB 2463.1 (Collingwood and Wright 1992)) and the imperial stamp (RIB 2483 (Collingwood and Wright 1993)) are unusual in that they produce incuse impressions. These dies are thought to have been made of metal, rather than the more usual wood block, although two impressions of RIB 2459.1 (Collingwood and Wright 1992) from this site (Table 68; *5235/3453* and *5475/3997*), appear to show wood grain, which could indicate that the die was in fact cut from a wooden block (*op cit*, 126). The use of this technique at Carlisle is interesting in view of a fragment of an unidentified incuse stamp with no frame, which appears to be a truncated letter E or F, the final letter in the stamp. This could be interpreted as a civilian stamp, as unframed incuse letters are not uncommon in such stamps (I M Betts *pers comm*), but the incidence of unframed, incuse legionary and official stamps in the Carlisle area might mean that it, in fact, forms part of an unidentified military stamp (*10*; Fig 561.2). Two other fragments of framed stamp could not be identified (*eg 9*; Fig 561.3).

Three of the stamped fragments, of which two join, are of die RIB 2462.16 (Collingwood and Wright 1992). This has been identified as a stamp of *Legio IX Hispana*, which is sometimes expressed as *Legio VIIII Hispana* (*op cit*, 174). Neither of the stamps shows the end of the inscription clearly; the larger fragment

898

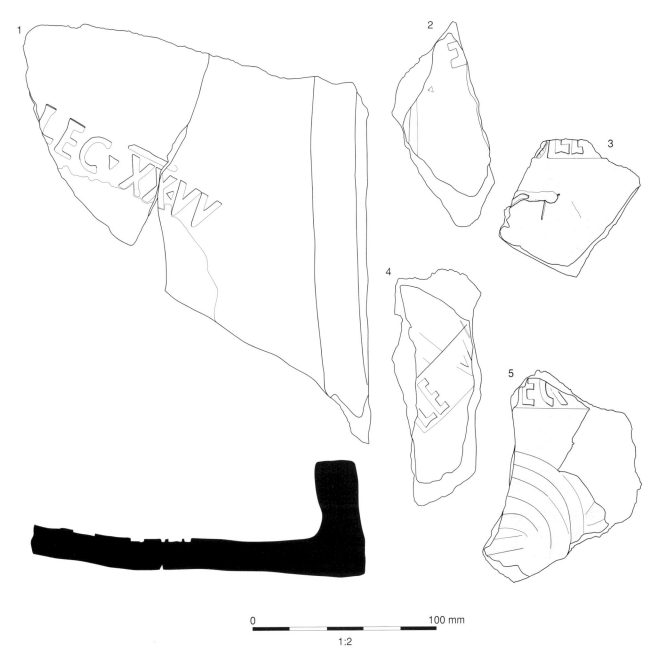

Figure 561: Legionary stamps

reads 'LEG.VI[…]' and the smaller, '[.]EG[…]' but the larger tile appears to show a return at the top right corner of the frame, where the tile is broken. If seen as a corner, it would represent a *Legio VI Victrix* stamp in the Scalesceugh fabric (7, 8; Fig 561.4-5).

Signatures and other administrative markings on tiles
Signature marks were observed on a number of tiles; all appear to have been made with the fingers, and most were curved. Bricks were recorded with curved marks made with two, three, and five fingers (*eg 11*; Fig 555.1; *12*; Fig 555.3). Of the 19 marks on bricks, all but two were three-finger curves. One-, two-, three-, and four-finger curved marks, more or less semi-circular, were also noted on *tegulae* (*eg 2*; Fig 554.2). The precise significance of these marks

is not known, but they are thought to have been made by the tiler, possibly as a personal signature (Brodribb 1987, 99–105).

Ten fragmentary *tegulae* had wavy vertical lines down the centre part of the tile, apparently made with the fingers; three of these had nail holes centred between 35 mm and 45 mm from the top edge. Similar wavy markings were seen on a *tegula* from the first-century legionary bath-house at Exeter, probably constructed by *Legio II Augusta* (Bidwell 1979, fig 50, 5). All *tegulae* with these markings are associated with Structure *7651* and road *7652* in Period 6C, or the external areas around Building *5200* (Period 6). They may have roofed structures that were demolished or altered at this time.

899

Knife-cut tally marks seen on the edges of *tegulae* were also made before firing. Three different marks were noted, two examples each of \ (3) and \\ (4), and one of / | (5). Again, the purpose of these marks is not known, but they might have represented numerals, perhaps to designate specific batches of material.

Several graffiti were recorded. One brick had a drawing of a phallus, apparently done with the finger (*14*; Fig 555.4); another had what appeared to be the legs and feet of a bird scored into the surface (15; Fig 555.5). Two joining fragments of waterpipe had a 'star' *graffito*, formed by a scored letter X with I superimposed (23; Fig 562); interestingly, a similar mark appeared on a *tegula mammata* from Exeter, although that example might have been made before firing, as it was catalogued as a possible tally mark (Bidwell 1979,149, fig 51, 10). Occasional animal paw-prints (*eg* Fig 555.1), probably of dogs, were noted on brick and *tegulae*, and one *tegula* had the tracks of a small mammal, possibly a weasel (A Pipe *pers comm*).

Unfired clay building materials
Other clay building materials comprised mud brick, daub, and accidentally fired clay. The daub was mainly of a hard consistency, fine in texture and with some organic inclusions. A few examples contained a small amount of coarse sand. Some fragments preserved impressions of other materials, the most common being wattle imprints. The better examples, such as those from Buildings *4006*, *3772* (both Period 3B), and *3376* (Period 4A), showed clear evidence of interwoven wattles. Also seen were flat impressions, probably of timber studs, such as that on a thick fragment from Period 3A rampart-back Building *1194*. Daub with a timber stud imprint on one side and mortar render *c* 15-20 mm thick on the other came from Period 3C Building *4657*. There were also examples of daub with a keyed surface, either to provide a base for mortar render or for decoration, from the fill of the construction trench

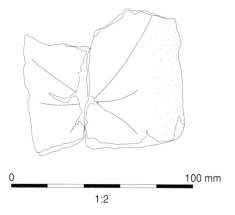

0   100 mm

1:2

Figure 562: Joining fragments of water pipe with star graffito

for Period 4A Building *4655*. As would be expected, most daub was associated with the timber buildings of Periods 3 and 4. Some fragments were vitrified, or had traces of slag, indicating a probable origin in some sort of hearth or industrial process. Daub with wattle impressions also came from Period 8iii tenement *1235*.

Flooring materials
In addition to the clay and stone flags, some evidence was noted for the existence of *opus signinum* and tessellated flooring. Four fragments of *opus signinum* flooring were recorded, only one of which, from demolition deposits in R5 of Period 4C Building *5688*, is likely to be primary material. Only four possible *tesserae* were noted, two of sandstone and two of reused tile. Of these, only one, in a quartzose sandstone, was associated with a Roman structure, a possible floor in R2 of Period 6A Building *2301*.

Discussion
As a whole, this large assemblage provided evidence for military involvement in the manufacture of tiles, and for the use of ceramic pipes in water distribution systems, for bricks and flue tiles that were used in under-floor heating systems, and for the use of ceramic roof tiles. However, the potential of the material to supply information on specific buildings, or on the sequence of tile use, was limited by the scarcity of primary demolition material, as a result of the extensive clearance and redeposition of building materials, which had destroyed many of the original relationships.

The chronological distribution of the material showed that fired ceramics were used in both the timber and stone forts. However, variations in the ratios of the various tile types in different periods reflected the different tile types that were used in association with timber and stone structures. Bricks and flue tiles were most common in the timber forts of the first and early second centuries, and were probably used primarily for the construction of hypocausted heating systems; no physical remains of early heated structures have been found, but the existence of a bath-house in the area was implied by the presence of wooden and ceramic water pipes. Such systems would have required, depending on the extent of the heating, masonry footings or walls.

The proportion of brick to roof tile fell in second-century deposits, suggesting either that more buildings had tiled roofs in the second fort than in the first, or that tile was not systematically collected for reuse when the second timber fort went out of use. The predominant types from the third-century stone fort are *tegula* and *imbrex* roofing tiles. There seemed to have been very little brick used in the

Plate 237: Stone pilae *in the hypocaust of the Period 6* principia, *obviating the need for brick*

later structures, probably because the hypocausts in the stone-built fort would have had stone *pilae*, as seen in the Period 6 *principia (Ch 9*; Pl 237). All the tile was made from clays which reflected a similar geology, and the legionary tile works at Scalesceugh (see *Ch 16*) was the probable source for most if not all of the material.

The daub was almost all from the timber forts in Periods 3 and 4, and concentrations of wattle and daub, and wall render from the area to the south-west of the principal roads, suggested that the barrack blocks in that area had wattle and daub internal partitions and daub-rendered walls, possibly with an external mortar render.

The presence of wooden and ceramic water pipes provided evidence of water supply and distribution systems on the site. The ceramic water pipes seen in deposits of Period 5 were of particular interest, as the pipes were of relatively wide bore (eg 22; *Appendix 11*) and may have carried substantial quantities of water, probably to supply a bath-house, for some distance. The building or complex that it served has not been identified, but it might have been associated with a broadly contemporary large courtyard building with substantial clay-

and-cobble foundations, built within the south-east quadrant of the earlier fort and excavated at Annetwell Street (Caruana in prep).

Two aspects of the assemblage provided evidence of the importance of tile as a resource to the Romans. Firstly, any brick and tile used in Period 3 structures seemed to have been cleared almost completely, suggesting that they were methodically dismantled and any fired ceramic materials retained for reuse, either in Period 4 structures, or as rubble for landfill and road construction. Secondly, much of the tile from Period 6 deposits was in small pieces which had been used for surfacing roads or levelling open areas, again suggesting that it was obtained from the deliberate demolition of standing structures.

Clear evidence for the role of the military in the manufacture of brick and roof tile was provided by the legionary stamps. *Legiones XX Valeria Victrix* and *II Augusta* seemed to have been particularly active in the manufacture of roofing tiles (Table 68). The dating of the stamps was not clear; only the *Legio VI Victrix* stamp on a brick (*8*; Fig 561.5), and the (probable) imperial monogram, *IMP*, came from Period 5 deposits, the others all being associated with Period 6 or later, and likely to be redeposited.

It is just possible, thought, that all could date to the early second century, and thus relate to the second timber fort; stamp RIB 2463.1 (Collingwood and Wright 1992), of *Legio XX*, has certainly been attributed to this period (*op cit*, 175). All the stamped tiles appeared to have been locally made, probably at Scalesceugh, with all the dies specific to the Carlisle area. An interesting and possibly unique feature of the stamps of the legionary tile-works at Scalesceugh (Bellhouse 1971) was the use of incuse or impressed letters for certain stamps of *Legio II* and *Legio XX* (*eg 6*; Fig 561.1) and for the *IMP* monogram. This suggests that Scalesceugh production was not overly influenced by practice at other legionary tile works; however, the striking similarity between half-box flue tiles from Carlisle (*eg 21*) and Chester (*p 896*) might support the suggestion of contemporaneity, perhaps through the agency of *Legio XX*.

22

PALAEOECOLOGICAL EVIDENCE

The Human Skeletal Remains

S Clough and A-S Witkin

Only ten disarticulated fragments of human skeletal material were found during the excavations, most of them badly weathered. It seems likely that most, if not all, were residual in their context and derive from highly disturbed earlier contexts (see *Appendix 12*).

Roman material

A heavily weathered adult human fibula came from a Period 3E external deposit (*620*). No pathology was observable, and it is perhaps not surprising that it was weathered, given its place of deposition.

Two heavily weathered fragments of adult human skull came from Period 6B pit *5495* (fill *5481*); their poor condition might well suggest that both were redeposited. One is a left anterior portion of parietal, thickened and with fairly open sutures. The other fragment is a right temporal posterior portion, with the suture closed enough to hold a small fragment of parietal; as it is appreciably thinner than the first fragment, it is possible that two different individuals are represented.

An occipital ossicle from the lambdoid suture, at the back of the skull, came from an external layer, *5287* (Period 6C), east of Building *5200*. It was from an adult skeleton, sex indeterminable, and had been cut on the left side. The fact that it was, again, much abraded suggests that it, too, was redeposited. Two joining fragments of adult human skull came from Period 6C deposit *5410*, associated with road *7652*. One is a left portion of occipital, with a slightly prominent nuchal crest, suggesting perhaps a male. The second is a left parietal, posterior portion, with an ossicle in the lambdoid suture. Both fragments are heavily weathered, and although roadside burial was common in the Roman period, it would have been extremely unusual within a fort (G Davies 1977, 17). It is therefore quite likely that these fragments are again far from their original place of deposition.

Medieval material

A fragment from an adult (unsexed) mid-shaft of femur was found in posthole *5119* (Period 8B Building *7399*) within the outer ward of the medieval castle. It was heavily weathered, suggesting that it had moved from its original place of deposition. No pathology was observable.

In addition, a well-preserved, but incomplete, cranial vault was recovered from the outer ward ditch (*1231*, Period 8ii, fill *1424*). It was that of an adult male aged between 40 and 50. The only pathology present was slight porosity on the superior part of the parietals; the lesions were healed and inactive at the time of death. This porosity is indicative of porotic hyperostosis, which is caused by iron deficiency (Roberts and Manchester 1995, 166-7).

There was also a complete radius from layer *1312*, an external deposit in tenement *1234* (Period 8iv). Again, its preservation was excellent, the diameter of the radial head indicating that this bone was also that of a male. The fused epiphyses indicated that the bone belonged to an adult aged over 18 years, with an estimated stature of 1.70 m tall. No pathological lesions were present.

Discussion

The obvious redeposition of many of the fragments, especially those from Roman contexts, means that no real conclusions can be drawn from their presence on the site. The very different state of preservation of two of the medieval fragments, and the position of one of them in the outer ward ditch, raises the possibility that they are in fact contemporary with the contexts from which they were recovered. It would be very unusual, by the medieval period, for bodies not to receive formal burial (Daniell 1997, 121), and thus it is possible that the skull, especially, might have been originally from a severed head, displayed on the battlements of the castle, and thus presumably that of an executed felon. It must, however, be emphasised that there is no skeletal evidence to support such an hypothesis.

The Animal Bone

E-J Evans, C Howard-Davis, and A Bates

In all, some 30,250 fragments of animal bone (*c* 500 kg) were excavated and analysed. Whilst assemblages

	Condition (%) after Lyman 1996						
Period	0	1	2	3	4	5	n
1	-	-	75.0	25.0	-	-	12
2	-	-	16.7	83.3	-	-	6
3	-	54.2	30.9	12.1	2.8	<1	1590
4	-	50.1	87.3	50.4	12.2	-	1514
5	-	10.4	50.4	36.7	2.4	<1	1835
6	-	2.7	34.4	60.7	2.1	<1	12,133
7	-	1.2	21.9	76.6	<1	-	6028
8	-	23.0	46.8	29.0	1.2	-	6914
Total	-	11.8	36.1	50.3	1.8	<1	30,032

Table 69: Condition of the animal bone, expressed as a percentage of the total number of fragments

were recovered from all five trenches, the majority was from MIL 5. Only 12 fragments could be associated with activity in Period 1 and six with Period 2, but the assemblages from the successive Roman timber and stone forts (Periods 3-6) comprised some 56% of the total assemblage (17,080 fragments), allowing a relatively detailed analysis of the material from the fort, particularly during Period 6, which produced the largest group (12,133 fragments). Rather more nebulous early medieval activity (Period 7), represented by dark silty-loam soils above the latest Roman deposits, also produced a relatively large quantity of bone (6028 fragments; 19%), although it is likely that a considerable portion of this group is residual. The medieval activity of Period 8 produced a comparable quantity (6914; 23%), providing a substantial amount of information about the use of domestic animals in and about the castle in the twelfth to fifteenth centuries. The amount in post-medieval contexts (Period 9; 180 fragments) was too small to sustain analysis.

The condition in which the bone has survived has an important bearing on its analysis, influencing the number of available measurements, estimation of tooth wear, and the visibility of surface modifications such as butchery, gnawing, and burning. The majority of the bone from the site has survived in fair condition, with an overall score of 3 according to Lyman's (1996) grading (Table 69). In Periods 3, 4, and 8, the bone was in generally good condition, but in Periods 6 and 7 it was noticeably poorer, raising the possibility that medium-sized and small mammals may be under-represented in these periods (see *Appendix 12* for a fuller presentation of the material).

Species representation

A relatively wide range of species was identified (*Appendix 12*). At a gross level, a simple fragment count makes it clear that cattle dominated the assemblage throughout, with other domestic animals, such as pig, sheep/goat, horse, and dog, present in lower numbers (Table 70). There was a limited range of wild species, with red deer being the principal game hunted at all times, and other species being represented by only a few individuals. Birds were dominated by domestic fowl, supplemented by mallard and greylag/domestic goose, which could have been wild or domesticated individuals, kept for eggs, meat, and feathers.

The principal stock animals

Cattle, pigs, and sheep/goat were, in both the Roman and medieval periods, as now, the main sources of meat. The large assemblage of bone, and its composition, makes it clear that animals arrived both as livestock (on the hoof) and as slaughtered and jointed meat (probably preserved in some way). The archaeological record can provide no evidence for filleted meat, perhaps bought and sold in small quantities to individuals, or pre-cooked dishes bought cheaply from local food sellers and bars (Wilkins and Hill 2006, 142), although such smaller transactions were without doubt a major supplement to the standard military provisioning (Davies 1971, 123-4). Thus, what is being examined, for the Roman periods (Periods 3-6), is the procurement and consumption pattern of the army units stationed at Carlisle between the first and early fifth centuries AD. Less directly, it allows an examination of possible stock-keeping regimes in the rural hinterland of the fort.

The later assemblages (Periods 7 and 8) present less well-defined evidence. Although radiocarbon dating (*Appendix 16*) makes it clear that deposition continued in Period 7, the group is likely to have been heavily contaminated by residual material from the latest Roman activity on the site (Period 6) and must be treated with circumspection. The Period 8 material was recovered from twelfth-century and later activity in the outer ward, its boundary ditch, and the later tenements that spread over this in the fourteenth century (Fig 278). The ditch (*1230*), cut and filled in the twelfth and thirteenth centuries, was recut (*1231*), perhaps, at the end of the thirteenth century, but then allowed to fill again, enabling fourteenth-century tenements to encroach on its line. The contents of the ditch appear to incorporate substantial amounts of domestic waste, dumped in the main from within the castle. Thus, the bone assemblage reflects meat procured for, and consumed by, both the elite households of the Constable and those of the soldiery stationed within the castle, and latterly, moderately well-to-do civilian households.

Metric analysis

The measurement of individual bones can provide valuable information regarding the demographic

Species	Period 1	2	3	4	5	6	7	8	Total
Horse			10	8	6	73	37	114	**248**
Cattle	3	1	318	293	274	2675	974	1477	**6015**
Pig		1	79	87	124	367	131	316	**1105**
Sheep/goat	1		128	70	69	253	140	430	**1091**
Sheep			5	5	8	7	3	53	**81**
Goat				1		2		6	**9**
Red deer			4	11	5	112	64	74	**270**
Fallow deer				1		1		4	**6**
Roe deer			1	4	2	6	1	2	**16**
Deer						1	1	3	**5**
Dog			12	3	1	24	8	82	**130**
Cat						1	4	43	**48**
Hare			18	2				3	**23**
Badger			1						**1**
Field vole						1			**1**
Water vole				1					**1**
Mouse			3						**3**
Medium mammal	1		183	133	209	498	217	547	**1788**
Large mammal	7	1	351	570	630	4072	1233	1956	**8820**
Small mammal			5			1	1		**7**
Unidentified mammal		3	456	306	506	3888	3231	1743	**10,133**
Bantam								2	**2**
Domestic fowl			3	1	2	10	8	83	**107**
Greylag/domestic goose			2	1		4		11	**18**
Grey heron						3		2	**5**
Pigeon				1					**1**
Raven								1	**1**
Rook				1					**1**
Swan						2		4	**6**
Buzzard			1					3	**4**
Mallard/domestic duck								5	**5**
Pink-footed goose				1				4	**5**
Barnacle goose			1	1	2	1		1	**6**
Greylag/pink-footed goose							1	4	**5**
Anserinae sp (goose)				2		5	2	6	**15**
Unidentified bird				2	1	11	1	25	**40**
Frog/toad			2			2			**4**
Total mammalian bone	12	6	1574	1495	1834	11982	6045	6853	**29,801**
Total avian bone	0	0	7	10	5	36	12	151	**221**
Total identified to a species level	4	2	586	492	493	3543	1371	2718	**9209**
Total bone	**12**	**6**	**1583**	**1505**	**1839**	**12020**	**6057**	**7004**	**30,026**

Table 70: Total number of fragments by species (articulated remains counted as 1)

profile of domestic animals, and is used to chart improvements in husbandry, and the possible introduction of new breeds. In addition, the dimensions of certain long bones of cattle, sheep/goat, horse, and dog can be used to estimate withers or shoulder heights, giving further data from which to estimate changes in the animal population over time (*Appendix 12*).

Throughout the Roman occupation (Periods 3-6), the height, at the withers, of cattle slaughtered or consumed at the fort fell within the range considered

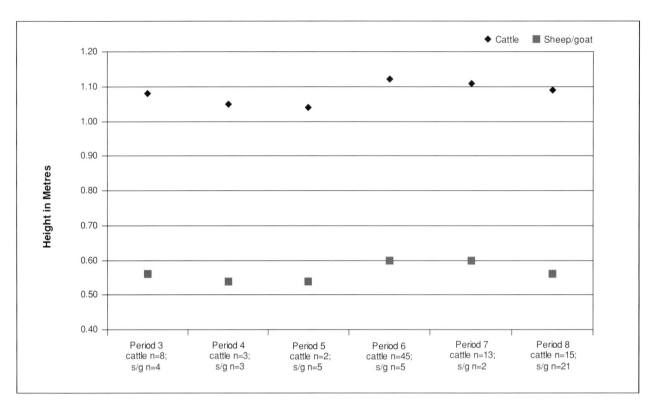

Figure 563: Average height at the withers of cattle and sheep/goat

normal for the relatively small 'Celtic shorthorn' cattle, thought to have been typical of the North West from the late Iron Age and throughout the Romano-British period (Stallibrass 1995, 127; Buxton *et al* 2000a, 46). There does, however, appear to have been a slight increase in the average height during Period 6 (Fig 563), although this might in part reflect the larger sample size for this period (*Appendix 12*). Such an increase might imply the introduction of larger breeds from elsewhere, or reflect an improvement in animal husbandry techniques, with selective breeding for increased size, as seen in southern Britain and some parts of Europe,

at least during the fourth century (Stallibrass 1995, 139). There was, however, a marked diminution in size by the medieval period, when cattle do not appear to have been any larger than their Celtic shorthorn predecessors, presumably indicating the loss, over a long period, of any larger Roman cattle breeds, as they merged back into unimproved native stock (*op cit*).

Because the sample sizes are small, considerations of the size of sheep/goat and pig are confined to a general comparison of the Roman and medieval assemblages. In both periods, the average height at the withers of

Plate 238: Natural holes in the parietal bone, a common trait in both ancient and modern cattle skulls

sheep/goat is the same, at *c* 0.56 m. Similarly, the biometric data suggest little difference in size between Roman and medieval pigs (*Appendix 12*).

Non-metric traits

Non-metric traits, which include minor non-pathological skeletal abnormalities due to variations in the developing skeleton, are thought to be largely genetic in origin, although this has yet to be confirmed by analysis. A few of the non-metric traits frequently seen in Roman and medieval groups have been observed in this assemblage.

The presence of one or more natural holes in the parietal bone is a trait seen often in both ancient and modern cattle skulls (Pl 238), and it appears in the Millennium assemblage, with examples from Periods 4, 6, and 8. The congenital absence of one or more teeth is also a condition commonly noted in the archaeological record (Baker and Brothwell 1980), but only a single example (a missing second premolar) was noted (in Period 6), from a sample of 62 mandibles retaining the relevant part. It has been suggested (Stallibrass 2000a, 381) that a high incidence of this trait could be a regional phenomenon, and an incidence of *c* 19% was noted in late first- and second-century deposits elsewhere in the fort (at Annetwell Street; Stallibrass 1991) and in contemporary deposits in the civilian settlement (Connell and Davis in prep), contrasting significantly with the evidence from the Millennium excavations. The absence of the hypoconulid (posterior cusp of the third molar) is a similarly common non-metric trait, and was recorded in small numbers on teeth from Periods 3, 6, and 7.

Another commonly seen non-metric trait is the presence of non-pathological depressions in the articular surfaces of a variety of post-cranial skeletal elements. There are three types: an oval facet on the articular surface; a narrow slit between articular facets; and a narrow slit running across the articular facet in a line slightly oblique to the medio-lateral axis (Baker and Brothwell 1980). Depressions of types 2 and 3 are most common in the Carlisle assemblage (*Appendix 12*), seen on both cattle and pigs. A final non-metric trait, the remnants of lateral metacarpals fused to the proximal shafts of the metacarpal, was observed on single cattle metacarpi from Periods 6, 7, and 8.

Health

Generally, the health of the stock in each period appears to have been quite good. Some pathological bones are present, but these are rare within the assemblage as a whole and their causes were often resolved during the life of the animal. Most of the pathological conditions noted affected cattle, but a few were also present in pigs and sheep/goats. These reflect the general health of the animals, the changes caused by old age, and, to a lesser

Plate 239: Deformation of the proximal articulations (left), in contrast to a normal bone of cattle (right)

extent, the uses to which they were put. Interestingly, only one instance of enamel hypoplasia, indicative of poor health or dietary insufficiencies in infancy, was recorded, whilst osteoarthritis, more common in older animals, was present in larger numbers, although still rare in the assemblage as a whole.

The majority of pathological conditions seen in cattle in the Millennium assemblage were associated with joints, and relate to both trauma and disease (arthropathies), affecting mainly the lower limbs; for instance, the proximal or distal ends of metapodials and the proximal articulations of phalanges showed evidence of deformation (splaying) through use of the animal for traction (Dobney *et al* 1996, 39). This was seen in both the Roman and medieval assemblages (Pl 239; *Appendix 12*), being most common in the former, comprising 3.7% of the Roman assemblage, compared to 1.8% of the medieval assemblage.

Osteochondritis dissecans, thought to be caused by small portions of the joint cartilage herniating through the articular surface as a result of joint trauma at a young age, was recorded on the distal articulation of a cattle humerus from Period 4. Grooving and osteoporosis in several Roman cattle foot bones (metatarsi, and first and second phalanges) probably indicate osteoarthritis (*Appendix 12*). Further examples of degenerative disease, again probably osteoarthritis, were seen in other parts of the cattle skeleton. A femur had porosity, eburnation, and new bone growth on the femoral head, and several cattle pelves had such symptoms on the acetabulum. The same changes were seen in medieval material (Period 8). Osteoarthritis and other degenerative problems, such as osteoporosis, osteophytes, and grooving in the articular surfaces, would normally be related to old age, but could be brought on earlier, or exacerbated, by use for traction, or habitually walking on metalled surfaces.

A number of bones, many of pigs, showed evidence of fractures and non-specific infections (*Appendix 12*); the often aggressive nature of the animals might possibly have led to more frequent damage. Ribs and lower limbs seem to have been particularly susceptible, and examples of healed fractures were seen in animals from Periods 3, 5, 6, and 8 (*Appendix 12*). Other problems included evidence for an open swelling, probably caused by an abscess, just under the tooth row of a probable cattle mandible from Period 6, whilst a pig mandibular canine from Period 8 has lines of enamel hypoplasia, an indication of ill health and/or poor diet in infancy.

Beef, pork, or mutton?

In considering the three important stock animals, it is clear that cattle predominated in all periods (*Appendix 12*; Table 71), comprising between 58% and 81% of the Roman assemblage (by fragment count). Although this must to an extent reflect the larger size and increased robusticity of cattle bones in comparison to those of sheep/goat and pigs, there was a known and demonstrable preference for beef in the Roman period, most marked on military sites (King 1984; 2005, 332), and this seems to hold true for elite medieval households, where often over half of the meat consumed was beef (Dyer 1989, 60).

The relative representation of the three species did, however, vary through time, with sheep/goat reaching a maximum of 25% in Period 3, but declining to 8% in Period 6. Pig comprised only 15% of the principal stock animals in Period 3, rising to a maximum of 27% of the assemblage in Period 5. In Periods 4-6, pig occurred in marginally greater numbers than sheep/goat. It has been suggested (King 2005, 331) that the consumption of sheep/goat reflects an indigenous tradition, most evident in the late Iron Age, but continuing into the Roman period, especially in rural communities. That Roman sheep/goat consumption at this military site was at a peak during Period 3 might be an indicator of necessity, with Rome moving into an area not yet geared to their preferences, and buying whatever meat was obtainable (Davis 1987, 183).

Period	Cattle (%)	Sheep/goat (%)	Pig (%)	n
3	60	25	15	530
4	64	17	19	457
5	58	15	27	473
6	81	8	11	3283
7	79	11	11	1220
8	64	22	14	2194

Note: In the sheep/goat category, the sum of sheep/goat, sheep, and goat fragments has been used

Table 71: Principal stock animals by phase, expressed as a percentage of the sum of cattle, sheep/goat, and pig fragments (n)

Pork was popular amongst the Gallic and Germanic auxiliary units (King 2005, 332), and the likelihood is that it was preferred more generally by the Romanised elite (Cool 2006, 82-3). In addition, it should be noted that a single pig (based on live weight) can weigh as much as 2.3 sheep (O'Connor 2003, 140) and produce commensurately more meat. It is also relatively easy to preserve, and bacon seems to have been an important element of military field rations (Davies 1971, 124), lard providing a more portable source of cooking fat than olive oil. Periods 6 and 7 show a higher relative abundance of cattle, in comparison to earlier periods.

Patterns of slaughter

Analysis of tooth wear and epiphysial fusion can indicate the age at death of individual animals (*Appendix 12*). The conformation of, and metrical data from, individual bones can be used to determine the sex of individuals and, in the case of males, whether or not they were castrates. Considered together, these can give a relatively clear indication of patterns of slaughter and, by extension, animal husbandry practices.

Such analyses rely on the availability of large samples of suitable skeletal elements, for instance mandibles and/or horncores (to provide an age at death profile), and long bones retaining their proximal and/or distal articular ends (for epiphysial fusion data). The amounts of these elements varied considerably between periods, with mandibles and horncores only being present in sufficient numbers in Periods 6 and 8, whilst bones suitable for epiphysial fusion analysis were present from Period 3 onwards.

Cattle

Evidence suggests that most of the cattle slaughtered and consumed on the site were adult (*Appendix 12*), many in excess of ten years old, and predominantly female. Very young specimens (less than 1-1.5 years) were present, but rare; whilst most obvious in the large group from Period 6, this appears to have been the case in every Roman period. Tooth wear indicates that there were very few animals under 1.5 years of age, and that 80% of the cattle were adult. This conclusion is supported by horncore and fusion data, indicating that 77% or *c* 80-5% respectively of the Roman cattle were older than 2-3 years of age at slaughter. As this correlates closely with data from Annetwell Street (Stallibrass 1991, 38), it can probably be regarded as an accurate representation of the range and quality of cattle procured for consumption in the fort, whether live or already butchered and preserved. Morphological data from 79 pelves suggest that 76-80% of the cattle were female; horncores give a broadly similar figure, identifying 74-90% as female. As might be expected,

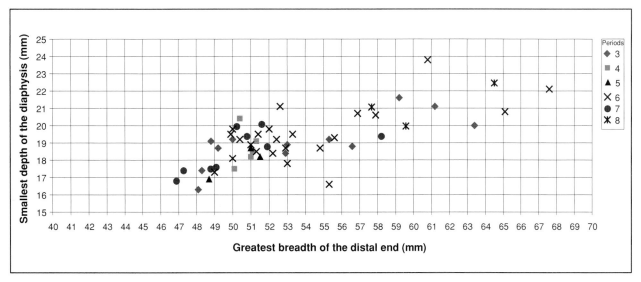

Figure 564: Scattergram of Roman and medieval cattle distal metacarpi (Periods 3-8)

bulls were not present in large numbers (4-11%), but the number of castrates was also relatively low, at 19-21%. These proportions are also suggested by a sexing technique relying on the dimensions of the distal metacarpal (Fig 564), which again identified most of the Roman cattle as female, with smaller numbers of bulls and castrates.

This pattern presumably results from the consumption, in the main, of older cows culled when their reproductive capacity was waning, and of traction animals at the end of their working lives, perhaps implying a local tendency towards dairying. The marked bias towards elderly cows appears to continue into the post-Roman period (Period 7), although the evidence for this period is probably skewed by high levels of residuality.

The same pattern, showing a significant preference for elderly female cattle, seems to persist during the medieval occupation of the site (Period 8; *Appendix 12*). Some very young individuals were represented, but were, again, rare. Both methods for the determination of sex, using pelves and horncores, again suggest that few bulls were being brought to the site for meat (2-11% respectively). The presence of castrates is not evident in the pelvic data, but horncore data suggests a considerably greater ratio of castrates to females, being 57-67% castrates to 19-21% females.

Sheep/goat
The quantity of suitable sheep/goat mandibles from any individual Roman period was too small for meaningful analysis of the tooth wear (*Appendix 12*). Considered together, however, there are suggestions of peaks in slaughter at 20-34 months and again at 3-5 years. Similarly, the epiphysial fusion evidence suggests that *c* 60% of the animals were slaughtered

before 2.5-3 years of age. Again, this corresponds well to evidence from the Annetwell Street excavations (Stallibrass 1991, 51-2), where it was suggested that very young lambs were brought in as a delicacy. Modern British preference calls for slaughter at around one year, whilst the Victorian taste, apparently closer to that of the Roman military, was for mutton of 3-5 years of age (Cool 2006, 87). In addition, sheep and goats were regarded as an important source of dairy produce. Of the few pelves (14) from which the sex could be determined, nine were female, one probably female, and four male. The mortality profile deduced from this data seems to suggest an emphasis on meat and dairy production rather than wool, with most animals producing only one or two fleeces before slaughter; it must, however, be noted that the quantities of milk produced per ewe would also be limited.

The medieval (Period 8) pattern of procurement and slaughter seems, again, to resemble that of the Roman period. Tooth wear indicates that only 37% of animals brought to the site had survived into adulthood. The fusion dataset, whilst small, seems to suggest that 53-69% of the sheep population had been slaughtered by, or was being slaughtered within, the 3-3.5-year age group (*Appendix 12*). Sex could be determined for a total ten pelves, and indicated a 50/50 split, although the sample is too small to be statistically valid.

Pigs
Again, the datasets from individual Roman periods were small and so they are considered together, demonstrating that the majority of animals to have been slaughtered before adulthood, at around 1-2 years (*Appendix 12*). The combined epiphysial fusion data concur, in that a far greater percentage of pigs were slaughtered before reaching skeletal maturity. A few very young individuals, seen in Periods 3, 6,

Period	Cattle	Sheep/goat	Pig
Dismemberment			
3	11	3	2
4	4		3
5	6	2	
6	25	2	5
3-6	46	7	10
7	11	2	
8	38	5	1
Filleting			
3	2		
4		1	
5	1	1	
3-5	3	2	0
Skinning			
3	1		
4	1		
5		1	
6	5		
3-6	7	1	
8	8	3	

Table 72: Quantification of cut marks identified as from the dismemberment, filleting, or skinning of animals

and 8, probably reflect a Roman and medieval liking for sucking pigs (White 1970, 318-20). Throughout the life of the site, the majority (85-6%) of the pigs were male, a pattern also noted at Annetwell Street (Stallibrass 1991, 55). This pattern, common in pig husbandry, is seen in all periods, and reflects the fact that pigs produce large litters of young and are not kept for secondary products, most being slaughtered for meat at a relatively young age, whilst maintaining a small breeding population.

Patterns of butchery

The preparation of a newly slaughtered carcass follows a fairly standard pattern; after skinning, the viscera are removed (which leaves no skeletal evidence) and the animal is either split in two along the line of the vertebral column, or dismembered by cutting through the joints (Vialles 1994, 41). The subsequent reduction of the carcass into joints, and the removal of flesh from the bones as necessary or required, was in the past, as it is today, the province of the butcher. Individual joints might then be further reduced in size, for cooking, by chopping through the bones. Large bones are often further reduced in size by chopping or splitting, primarily to gain access to the marrow. This process leaves distinct groups of butchery marks (Binford 1981), cut marks being associated with skinning, dismemberment, or filleting (Table 72). The condition of the bone from this site has affected the survival of butchery marks (Table 73), particularly in Period 7, which had a relatively high percentage of poorly preserved bone (*Appendix 12*), and, not unexpectedly, the lowest representation of butchered bone.

Cut marks associated with skinning are usually seen on the frontal portion of the skull, and on foot bones, around the lower (distal) diaphysis of metapodials, and the mid-shaft on the first phalanx. Evidence for skinning can be seen in cattle from Periods 3-6, and in Period 8, and in sheep from Periods 5 and 8 (Table 72; *Appendix 12*). Chop marks were by far the most abundant butchery marks found on the Roman animal bones, being seen on all three of the principal stock animals (Table 73). This reflects the use of a cleaver by Roman butchers, in order to reduce the carcass to smaller joints, as well as to fillet meat from the bones, although filleting marks *per se* were rare (Table 73). In addition, at least one pig skull had been split down the sagittal plane, presumably in order to recover the brain. Fat, tallow, or lard would also have been collected during butchery. Chop marks continue to be fairly common on all three species during the medieval period (Period 8),

Period	Cattle				Sheep/goat				Pig			
	% Chopped	% Cut	n	% of bone with butchery	% Chopped	% Cut	n	% of bone with butchery	% Chopped	% Cut	n	% of bone with butchery
3	66	26	116	35	68	37	19	15	36	64	11	13
4	66	22	77	25	80	20	5	7	64	36	14	16
5	69	20	54	19	75	38	8	11	67	33	9	7
6	70	26	224	8	82	9	22	9	80	25	20	5
3-6	68	25	471	13	76	24	54	10	65	37	54	8
7	55	40	47	5	60	40	10	7	100	0	3	2
8	66	36	231	15	63	52	52	12	58	58	12	4

n= total number of butchered bone

Table 73: Quantification of chop and cut marks in the three main species

but it is noticeable that they become more frequent on sheep/goat bone at this time (*Appendix 12*). In the Period 8 assemblage, the total sample size of butchered pig is too small for comment.

Representation of anatomical parts

Changes in the representation of body parts act as a guide to what stage in the butchery process the bone was discarded. The systematic presence or absence of specific skeletal elements could reflect dietary or social preferences, patterns of consumption, or the import of specific joints, as has been suggested for the marked over-representation of cattle scapulae in Period 3 (*Appendix 12*).

Interpretation of the presence and absence of anatomical parts during the Roman period at the site is complicated by the fact that in Periods 4A/B, 4B, 6B, and 6C significant amounts of the animal bone were recovered from layers which may well have contained imported material, possibly brought to the site during road construction: 51% of all animal bone from Period 4A/B; 40% of that from Period 4B; 40% from Period 6B, and 68% from Period 6C was recovered from road construction layers.

Cattle scapulae, many of them with hook damage, are the most frequently represented part (Fig 565), an abundance that was also noted at Annetwell Street (Stallibrass 1991, 32-4). This is most likely to reflect

the importance of ready-processed smoked or dried meat, the hook-damaged scapulae being discarded when all the meat had been cut from the bone for consumption (Dobney *et al* 1996, 26-7). Of the limb bones, the tibia appears relatively poorly represented. The distal end of the tibia, having a relatively high bone density, usually survives well in archaeological deposits (Brain 1981, 23; Lyman 1994, 241-8), and its absence is likely to be genuine. The same phenomenon was again noted at Annetwell Street (Stallibrass 1991, 33), where it was speculated that the distal ends of this bone were systematically removed for use as a raw material in bone-working.

The presence of large amounts of cattle bone in deposits associated with the principal roads during Periods 6A, 6B, and 6C (Fig 566) requires some discussion, as it shows a markedly different pattern of anatomical part selection to that of cattle bone from other contemporary deposits. Under normal conditions, the mandible would be expected to be the best-represented skeletal element, being a highly dense bone, more resistant to processes of attrition and, in non-road deposits this was the case. Within the road deposits of Periods 6B and 6C, however, metapodials, scapulae, and pelves were all very well represented, and astragali, calcanei, first phalanges, and distal radii were better represented than might be expected. Thus it appears that, within the road make-up deposits, there was a marked emphasis on

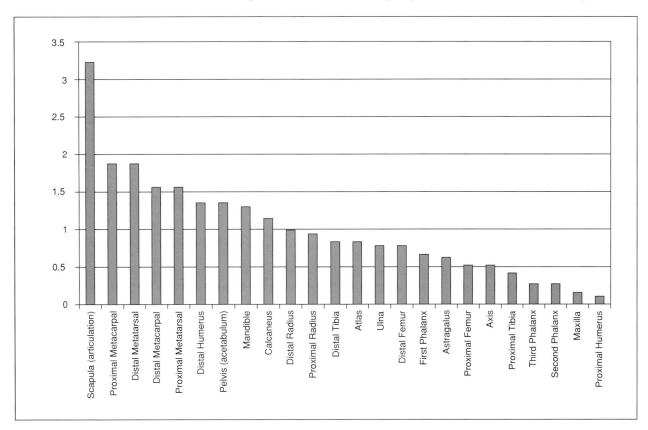

Figure 565: Anatomical part representation of cattle in rank order, Periods 3-5; n=914, SD=0.68, one sigma range=0.32-1.68

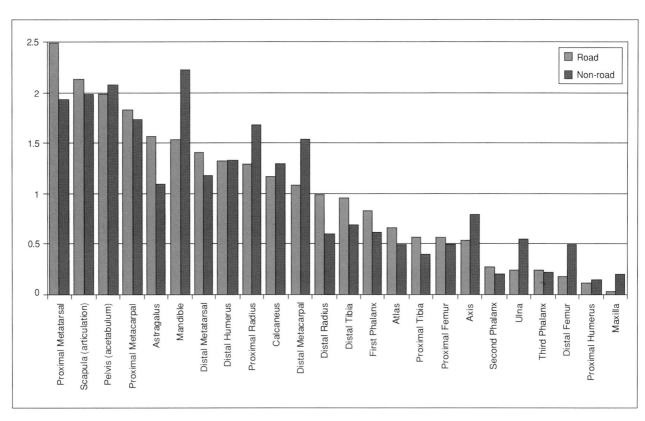

Figure 566: Anatomical part representation of cattle within road and non-road construction layers, Periods 6B and 6C (n=914, SD=0.67, one sigma range=0.32-1.67 (road)); Periods 6A-6C (n=242, SD=0.66, one sigma range=0.34 to 1.66 (non-road))

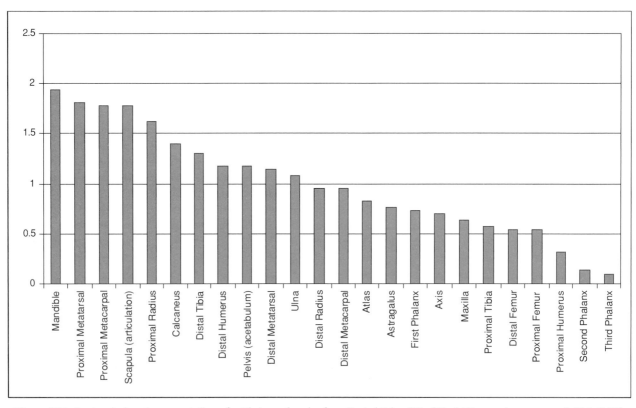

Figure 567: Anatomical part representation of cattle in rank order from Period 8 (n=821, SD=0.52, one sigma range=0.48 to 1.52)

cattle butchery waste, particularly foot bones, but also including pelves and scapulae, whilst the body-part representation in groups from the non-road deposits suggests that elements from the whole carcass were being deposited, although the apparent bias towards foot bones might point towards some admixture

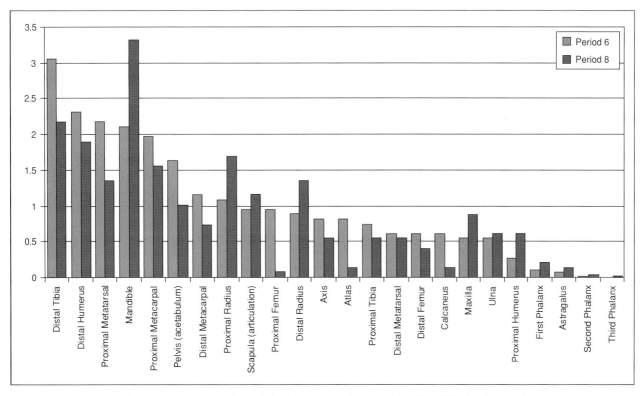

Figure 568: Anatomical part representation of sheep/goat from Period 6 (n=347, SD=0.79, one sigma range=0.21 to 1.79) and Period 8 (n=318, SD=0.91, one sigma range=0.09 to 1.91)

of material from the road deposits, or that some of the meat-bearing bones were being removed. The inclusion of this material, possibly brought onto the site from elsewhere, suggests that a large amount of butchery waste was available, either from within the fort or from the adjacent settlement. The latter might suggest a municipal system for the butchery of animals or the collection of butchery waste, as suggested in Roman Lincoln (Dobney *et al* 1996, 57-8).

For the medieval period (Period 8) mandibles were, as might be expected on taphonomic grounds, the best-represented skeletal element (Fig 567). It is also noticeable that distal tibia were well represented in this period, unlike during Period 6. Foot bones, represented by metapodials and calcanei, may be again somewhat over-represented, suggesting additional butchery waste in the assemblage.

Even considered as a single entity, the sheep/goat sample from Periods 3-6 is too small for detailed interpretation, but there is a trend towards the over-representation of distal tibiae (Fig 568). Metapodials also appear to be well represented, although this is possibly an artefact of the small sample size. A similar pattern was, however, seen in Period 3 at Annetwell Street (Stallibrass 1991, 49), albeit to a lesser degree. As at Annetwell Street, it may be that whole animals are represented, but with significant numbers of meat-bearing bones removed, leaving greater numbers of elements associated with butchery waste from the lower

limb. In Period 8, it appears that all skeletal elements are represented amongst the sheep/goat remains.

The representation of anatomical parts of pig during the Roman period (Fig 569) shows a similar pattern to that of sheep/goat in Period 8. It is thus thought that whole carcasses are represented, with mandibles being the most frequent element, because of their robustness.

Distinctive methods of preparation
A very distinctive Roman butchery technique is represented by the presence of elongated holes through the blades of cattle scapulae (Pl 240), which is generally thought to have been caused by hanging carcasses or part-carcasses on hooks for smoking, curing, or air drying. It has been recorded on many sites throughout Britain, including elsewhere in Carlisle, for instance at Castle Street (Rackham *et al* 1991), as well as at Ribchester (Stallibrass 2000a), Lancaster (Stallibrass in prep a), and Wigan (OA North 2006). In the Millennium Project, the majority were seen on cattle scapulae from Period 3, and the prevalence of hook-related damage decreased steadily through to Period 6, from 97% of all scapulae with blades surviving, to 23% (Table 74). This reduction would appear to reflect a genuine change in the method of processing cattle forelimbs, possibly beginning after Period 4.

At Annetwell Street and the southern Lanes, as well as at Ribchester to the south (Stallibrass 1991; in prep b;

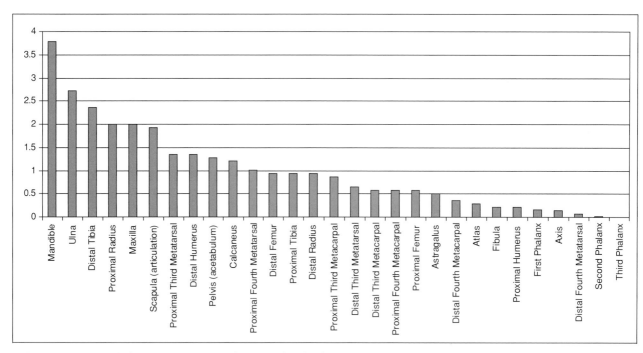

Figure 569: Anatomical part representation of pig in rank order from Periods 3-6; n=410, SD=0.91, one sigma range=0.09 to 1.91

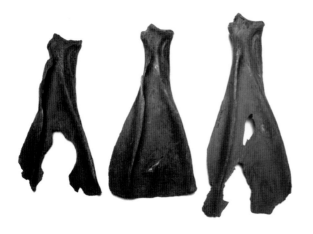

Plate 240: Cattle scapula, showing hook-related damage

2000a, 381), it has been noted that an abundance of cattle metapodials, especially if scorched, might reflect a distinct regional practice intended to extract marrow. Very few of the metapodials from the Millennium Project, however, show signs of being scorched or split. There is some evidence for longitudinal splitting from Period 3 and Periods 5-8, but with only one or two occurrences per period. Whilst this could be a technique employed to remove bone marrow, it is also associated with bone working, which favours the use of metapodia in the manufacture of artefacts such as pins (MacGregor 1985, 30; 2001, 360).

Horses

Artefactual and epigraphical evidence make it clear that the forts at Carlisle housed cavalry units at intervals (*Ch 12*), and, even in infantry units, the officers were mounted. This must mean that at times there were appreciable numbers of riding horses within the fort, alongside the significant numbers of pack animals that would have been required for day-to-day transport. The bone assemblage does not, however, appear to offer corroborative evidence, and horse bones were relatively scarce in all periods. In Periods 3-6, they comprise only 0.6% of the total fragment count, or 2% (248 fragments) of mammal bone identified to a species level, a level of representation not dissimilar to the 1% (or less) suggested by Stallibrass (2000a, 383) as the norm for Roman sites, both civil or military, although

Period	Total no scapulae	Total no scapulae with blade present	Total no scapulae with hook damage to the blade	Percentage of scapula blades with hook damage
3	35	30	29	97%
4	32	16	9	56%
5	21	11	3	27%
6	161	26	6	23%
7	46	4	0	0%
8	63	7	0	0%

Table 74: Incidences of hook-related damage to cattle scapulae

Plate 241: Glenoid of a horse scapula, with eburnation and pitting associated with osteoarthritis

the overall percentage is slightly greater than that calculated for Annetwell Street (Stallibrass 1991). This low representation seems somewhat at odds with the known cavalry fort at Ribchester, where horse bone comprised *c* 8% of the material identified to species, and included articulated partial carcasses (Stallibrass 2000a, 383). It can only be suggested that, when slaughtered, the carcasses of these animals were deposited outside those areas of the fort explored by excavation, or outside the boundaries of the fort altogether. Presumably, the medieval castle would also have housed a significant number of horses, intended both for riding and draught.

The heights at the withers could only be calculated for individuals from Period 8, with an average of 1.36 m, with minimum and maximum heights of 1.19 m and 1.52 m (up to 15 hands). There were few pathological specimens, and again these were from medieval deposits. They included a scapula showing widespread signs of osteoarthritis (Pl 241), and a first phalanx exhibiting evidence of an infection caused by trauma.

Age at death was calculated using a number of loose teeth from Periods 3, 4, 6, 7, and 8 (Table 75). All appear to be from adult horses over the age of 5.5 years; the majority seem to have reached 8-11 years, with one from Period 8 having reached the relatively advanced age of 16+ years. This age range is supported by the fusion data, with almost all the long bones coming from skeletally mature animals (*Appendix 12*).

Horseflesh was not normally consumed in the Roman period (Toynbee 1973, 185), eaten only in extremity

Period	Element	Age
3	mandibular molar/premolar	11.75 - 20 years
4	skull	8.5 - 11.5 years
6	mandibular molar/premolar	8 - 11 years
6	mandibular premolar	9.5 - 11.5 years
6	maxillary molars/premolars	5.5 - 8 years
6	maxillary molar	8.5 - 11.5 years
6	maxillary molar	8.5 - 11.5 years
6	maxillary molar/premolar	5.5 - 8 years
6	mandibular molar/premolar	8 - 11 years
7	mandibular molar/premolar	6.5 - 9 years
8	mandibular molar/premolar	8 - 11 years
8	maxillary molars	7 - 9.5 years
8	maxillary molar/premolar	5.5 - 8 years
8	mandible	16+ years

Table 75: Aged maxillary and mandibular teeth of horses

(Tacitus' *Histories* IV.60 (Wellesley 1975, 246)) or in a specific religious context (Cool 2006, 91-2). Nor was it a normal part of the diet during the medieval period (Wilson and Edwards 1993, 51). Nonetheless, there were a few instances of butchered bones within the assemblage. Cut-marks from dismemberment were noted on a pelvis from Period 6 and a pelvis and ulna from Period 8. A single first phalanx from Period 8 also bore skinning marks, indicating that the hide had been removed. Although in both cases the carcass might have been eaten, it is probably more likely that it was used for some other purpose, possibly cut up for dog meat, or for ease of disposal.

Dogs

Relatively few dogs were represented within the assemblage, although their remains were present from Period 3 onwards. Although the sample is small (only 130 fragments in all), epiphysial fusion data (*Appendix 12*) suggest that the majority of individuals were skeletally mature. Whilst tooth eruption and wear analysis is rarely considered for dogs, the eruption stages on a mandible from Period 8 suggest that the animal died before reaching three months, whilst an articulating skull and mandible, also from a medieval deposit, was that of quite an old individual, with the teeth very worn, and all but one of the maxillary incisors absent. The well-healed alveolar bone suggested that they had been lost some time before the animal's death. Another two dog mandibles were missing individual teeth, probably as a result of trauma or old age, as there was no sign of disease in the surrounding root sockets.

The average shoulder height for dogs in Period 6 was calculated as 0.41 m, broadly comparable with the dogs from Ribchester (Buxton and Howard-Davis 2000, 71), where, apart from a single small bandy-legged individual, they were mostly fairly gracile animals between 0.44 m and 0.47 m at the shoulder. During Period 8, the average shoulder height was slightly greater, at 0.55 m.

A single pathological specimen was recovered from Period 6, a tibia with signs of infection (periostitis), presumably the result of trauma. An articulated burial in Period 8ii recut outer ward ditch *1231* showed a misalignment of the first and second sacral vertebra, causing the slight displacement of the lower sacrum from the sagittal plane. A radius and a rib both showed healed breaks, and an associated radius and ulna had been broken, with a misalignment of the broken bones during the healing process shortening the damaged limb. In addition, the ulna showed signs of infection (osteomyelitis).

Dog bones from Period 3A Building *1222* (Fig 265) showed evidence of butchery. Dogs were, in fact, a common sacrifice to the goddess Hecate (Toynbee 1973) and the physician Galen makes it clear that they were, on occasion, bred for the pot and eaten (Garnsey 1999, 83). Thus, whilst unlikely, it is not impossible that dog was consumed by the inhabitants of the fort. Alternatively, unwanted or injured individuals could have been culled, and the corpses cut up and fed to other dogs. In addition, dog skin has been put to a number of uses, including drumheads (C Howard-Davis *pers obs*).

Cats

Unlike dogs, which were obvious inhabitants of the fort from Period 3 onwards, cats were not present in the assemblage until Period 6 (a single bone), and were at their most abundant in the medieval period (Period 8). In contrast to the dog remains, large numbers of the cat long bones were unfused, with approximately 53% being from skeletally immature animals. The evidence suggests that many of the cats died, or were killed, before reaching one year of age, with at least three younger than 8.5 months (*Appendix 12*).

The presence of cut marks on cat bones has been noted at a number of medieval sites, and Carlisle is no exception, several of the bones from the Millennium Project having cut marks consistent with skinning. This appears consistent with evidence from Broad Street, Reading (Norton forthcoming) and Exeter (Maltby 1979), where the skinning of young cats appears to have been a commonplace activity, presumably for the fur trade. Despite the evidence for skinning, none of the bones shows further evidence of the type of breakages or butchery marks associated with processing a carcass for consumption, which is again consistent with the findings at Broad Street and Exeter.

Domesticated and wild birds

The skeletal remains of domesticated and wild birds were noted in deposits from Period 3 onwards, although the number of bird bones and the range of species present are both very small in comparison to the total number of animal bones from the site. It is possible, however, that this reflects the lack of a dedicated sieving programme, rather than a real absence.

Domestic fowl was the most common species represented (by fragment count) with other possible domestic species (ducks and goose) present, but in much smaller numbers. The remainder of the species identified are wild, and present in very small amounts, often represented by a single bone, for instance the pigeon from Period 4, and a raven from Period 8 (Table 71).

Domestic fowl were introduced to Britain in the late Iron Age (Davis 1995, 182), and seem to have been widely consumed in Roman Britain, by civilian and soldier alike (Stallibrass 1995, 139), although they probably remained a relatively high-status foodstuff (Cool 2006, 100). All the bones from Periods 3-6 and on into Period 7 appear to be from adult birds, and only in Period 8 is there a small number of juveniles. Whilst this bias towards adults might be a result of preservation conditions, it also probably reflects the likelihood that birds would rarely have been killed before reaching maturity, in order to ensure they had reached their maximum meat potential. The presence of juveniles in Period 8 might well indicate that fowl were bred in small quantities, probably by individual households for both eggs and meat.

It is no surprise to find other domesticated bird species at the site, as agricultural writers such as Columella and Varro indicate that ducks, geese, and pigeons were all part of the customary diet, alongside wildfowl (Serjeantson 2000). Until the post-medieval period, however, it is virtually impossible to differentiate between domestic and greylag geese, or between mallards and domestic ducks on morphological grounds, and the examples from the site could be either.

The total fragment count suggests that, within the fort, domestic fowl, and geese, were the principal avian contributors to the Roman diet. Domestic/greylag geese could be either wild or domesticated, but the presence of barnacle goose, and, to a lesser extent, pink-footed goose, seems to suggest that wildfowling was supplementing the normal diet. Grey heron and swan bones from Period 6 both bore cut marks, indicating that both had been processed for consumption. Similarly, the pigeon from Period 4 could have been caught for eating, but could equally have been an accidental casualty, as pigeons, like the rooks and the raven, often live in or around human settlements. It is also likely that the buzzard bone is a result of a natural death, although there is occasional evidence of their consumption during the Roman period (Cool 2006, 115).

During the medieval period (Period 8), the numbers of domestic fowl, and wild and/or domestic duck and geese appear to increase greatly, although this may in part be due to the improved bone preservation in these deposits. A partially articulated domestic fowl was recovered from pit *301* (in MIL 1), with the remainder of the bones representing the disarticulated (and often butchered) remains of both adults and juveniles. Only one of the ten tibio-tarsi present had a spur, suggesting that it was unlikely that these birds were kept for cock-fighting. With the exception of three isolated bones, the mallard remains comprised an articulated skeleton, headless but otherwise almost complete, recovered from pit *1431* (in recut outer ward ditch *1231*).

The presence of cut marks on domestic fowl, geese, and swan bones in Period 8 deposits suggests that all these birds were consumed at or near the site during the medieval period. Swans, considered a high-status delicacy at this time, were bred in swanneries (Woolgar 1999, 114), as well as being taken in the wild. It is also likely that the grey heron was eaten, and was thought to have restorative properties, being hunted with specially trained heron hawks (Cummins 2001, 204). Whilst captive birds of prey were considered a status symbol in the medieval period, the buzzard was considered a low-status hawking bird (Dobney *et al* 1996, 52) and the three bones from pit *5036* (within the outer ward) could, just as easily, have been a natural fatality.

Game and other wild animals

The wild species present in the assemblage comprise deer, hare, badger, and a number of small mammals such as vole and mouse (Table 71). As with the birds, the bones of wild mammals were recovered in only small numbers. The majority were deer, with red deer greatly outnumbering the other species, but roe and fallow deer were both represented. Little could be said of the health of the live quarry, although a single roe deer pelvis

from Period 4 showed osteophytic lipping around the acetabulum.

Red deer was present from Period 3 onwards, and although the assemblage is small, a number of interesting observations can be made. In Period 6, for example, antler accounts for 80% of this assemblage, giving reason to believe that this was being collected as a raw material, perhaps even with shed antler brought to the site for use. Much of it appears to have been worked, representing waste from artefact manufacture, and several antler artefacts were noted within the Roman assemblage, including weaving combs, knife handles, and hoes (*Ch 20*).

Roe deer was also present from Period 3 onwards, but in considerably smaller quantities than red deer. There is only one antler fragment (from Period 6), suggesting that at all periods roe deer was better represented by butchery waste. It has been suggested (Cool 2006, 113-14) that there was a general Roman preference for roe deer meat, but it is clear that both were eaten, and the relative proportions noted in a number of assemblages from Britain may reflect availability rather than preference (*ibid*). Whilst only present in small quantities, the fallow deer is of interest. It appears in Periods 4, 6, and 8, and it is thought that the Romans introduced small numbers to Britain to hunt for sport, although they did not become common until the medieval period (Sykes *et al* 2006). Individual skeletal elements were recovered from Periods 4 and 6. One is an antler off-cut, the other a foot bone (first phalanx), which conceivably could have been brought to the site attached to a hide. The small number of fallow deer bones suggests that, as with roe deer, they made very little contribution to the customary diet of the local population.

During the medieval period (Period 8), deer hunting was a highly ritualised and socially stratified practice (Cummins 1988), and the relative importance of red deer to the diet of the nobility increased during this period. By this time, antler comprised only 31% of the deer assemblage, the increase in bone possibly reflecting the arrival of complete carcasses. In addition, the popularity of antler as a raw material seems to have been in decline (MacGregor 1985, 32), in part as a result of decreased availability. The carcass of the deer would traditionally, but not always, have been part-butchered at the site of the kill (the 'unmaking'), with specific joints distributed to specific individuals based on their social status and role in the hunt. Thus, the bone should reflect those elements, specifically the haunches, which would be consumed by elite groups. The left forelimb went to the forest parker as his fee, and the right to the best hunter or breaker of the deer, although the pelvis (the *corbyn* or crows' bone) was discarded (Sykes 2007; Cummins 1988, 42).

There seems to be a bias in the red deer bone from Period 8, towards haunches and possibly the right forelimb. It must, however, be borne in mind that the total sample size is small, and, looking at the femur and tibia, a less easily explained bias towards left hind limbs could also be suggested.

Other wild species present include the hare and badger (Table 71). Hare was hunted for food and fur during the Roman and medieval periods (Davis 1995, 194), and the remains of this animal probably found their way onto the site as food waste; butchery evidence on a single bone from Period 8 helps to confirm this. Badger is represented by only one bone from a demolition layer in Period 3, perhaps from an animal killed for its pelt.

The remaining wild mammals, water vole, field vole, and mouse, are all from Roman deposits. These small mammals, whilst not likely to have been exploited for food, can give us clues as to the local environment. The field vole inhabits damp ground, as well as open woods and grassland, as does the mouse. Frog/toad remains were also found in Roman deposits, and since again they are unlikely to have been eaten, their presence probably had a natural origin. Water voles today are closely associated with freshwater, such as rivers, lakes, and ditches, but it is evident that this has not always been the case (Stallibrass 2004, 42), and thus they are not particularly useful as an environmental indicator.

Discussion

The large quantity and generally good condition of the animal bones from these excavations has allowed a relatively detailed analysis of the ways in which animals and animal products were produced and used in the successive Roman forts and during the medieval occupation of the site. Considerable information has been gained with regard to the appearance and condition of the animals themselves, techniques of butchery and preparation of meat, and, of course, the diet of the contemporary inhabitants. Some insight has been acquired of changing patterns of procurement and provision, especially with regard to the Roman army, but also with regard to elite medieval households. In addition, it has been possible to consider possible changes in animal husbandry practices, reflecting local rural production.

Roman period

It is widely accepted that beef formed the largest component of the Roman soldier's diet (King 1984) and cattle bones are commonly found on Roman military sites in much greater quantities than those of other domestic animals (Alcock 2001). The fort at Carlisle is no exception, with cattle remains outnumbering sheep/goat or pig by a factor of about 6:1. Thus it

is clear that throughout several centuries of Roman military activity on the site, beef was the preferred meat. On the whole, it does not appear to have been of particularly good quality, the beasts slaughtered being older females, presumably past their reproductive best. Bulls and castrates appear to be represented in much smaller quantities. It is not impossible that the bulls reflect some of the many sacrificial animals that were required, the older castrates perhaps first having been used for traction, although younger animals might indicate that some prime beef was reaching the fort. The most obvious reason for this disparity could be a reflection of the social division and differing expectation of troops and their officers. It is thought that the two principal means of cooking meat were roasting and boiling (Davies 1971, 127, quoting Appian), and the general tendency of bones from the site to be split or chopped into smaller fragments might imply a fondness for stews, probably as a way of reducing tough meat to edibility.

The presence, especially in the earlier periods, of numbers of hook-damaged scapulae indicates that, on occasion, the front limbs were detached from the carcass and treated differently, presumably in a manner that required hanging. It is quite possible that these joints were preserved in some way, and methods of curing, such as brining, smoking, or even air-drying, would have extended the shelf-life of the meat considerably. It is of note that hook-damaged scapulae are most common in Period 3, but decrease in numbers over time, reflecting changes in treatment of these joints, or even in the procurement of supplies. Neither sheep/goat nor pigs show any physical evidence for systematic preservation, although pork is particularly easy to preserve, and bacon seems to have played an important part in field rations (Davies 1971).

It can be tentatively suggested, from the metrical analysis of the cattle bones, that the size of the cattle slaughtered increased in Period 6 (*Appendix 12*), possibly as a result of selective breeding and an overall improvement in animal husbandry techniques, or perhaps as a result of the deliberate introduction of larger breeds. This would appear to concur with the evidence for slaughter and butchery waste on external surfaces in Period 6 (Fig 566), and might imply that, during its later life, the fort was serving some sort of specialist role in provisioning.

Sheep/goat and pigs are also well represented amongst the bone assemblage, and doubtless played a large part in provisioning, although the consumption of pork and mutton or lamb appears to have declined by Period 6. It could be tentatively proposed that sheep/goat formed a larger proportion of the meat slaughtered and consumed on the site in its early days (Period 3), with pork being more common from Period 4 onwards. It has been suggested (King 2005, 331) that the consumption of sheep/goat is more closely associated with an indigenous Iron Age tradition, and although entirely speculative, as there is little evidence from rural sites in the surrounding area, it is possible that, in the early days of the Roman occupation, sheep and goats were easier to procure than pigs. This could well have changed as the local agriculture adapted in response to new markets opened up by the presence of the army.

Remarkably little is known about Romano-British stock-raising practices (Trow-Smith 1967, 40), but presumably, given the amount of meat required by the army, there must have been considerable herds of cattle and sheep/goats, kept for meat and dairy products. The use of oxen for traction was common during the Roman period and can be seen in numerous illustrations (see, for instance, Burke 1978, fig 51, for a model from Piercebridge, Co Durham, of yoked oxen pulling the plough). Indeed, the situation that can be inferred from the patterns of slaughter at the site is one of older dairy cows, culled at the end of their productive lives, and older traction animals. It is not clear whether better-quality beef cattle, such as castrates slaughtered at a young age, or animals not required in dairy herds, such as veal calves, were consumed within the fort or were being sold and consumed elsewhere, presumably in a civilian context.

Sheep and goats were also an important source of dairy products, with goats being much less common than sheep (Alcock 2001). Whilst evidence suggests that little fresh milk was consumed, not least because it goes off quickly (Frayn 1979, 40), cheese of one kind or another was an important, and above all, very durable and portable foodstuff. The slaughter of relatively prime young individuals would seem to imply a concentration on meat production, with fewer older animals from which larger quantities of wool and milk could have been obtained. It is possible that some older animals in the rural hinterlands were not sent to the urban market, but the lack of any comparative rural sites in the region precludes any comparison. The majority of pigs brought to the site were slaughtered at a relatively young age, at or before maturity. There were a few sucking pigs, but then, as now, these could have been regarded as something of a delicacy. Pigs are prolific breeders and grow relatively quickly, and as they are not a source of dairy products, most are slaughtered when they attain an acceptable size for meat production.

There is no doubt that all three principal stock animals were slaughtered on site, presumably having been bought in from the rural hinterland, although a significant quantity of the animal bone recovered was incorporated in the hardcore used in road construction in Periods 4 and 6, and could have been brought to the site from slaughter-sites elsewhere. Canid gnawing implies that some of it, at least, was left open to the elements for a while, rather than being buried immediately, and this could be taken to imply an organised municipal system of butchery, or at least the collection of cattle butchery waste, in the adjacent settlement.

There is no evidence for how the animals were slaughtered, but it is to be presumed that the blood vessels of the neck were severed, as in traditional methods seen today (Vialles 1994, 74), which facilitates bleeding. It is likely that an effort would have been made to utilise as much of the carcass and its by-products as possible. Offal and some of the fresh meat would have been used rapidly, whilst it seems that some specific cuts might have been preserved in any one of a number of ways. Fat would have been rendered, with lard especially favoured for cooking. The hides could have been used as rawhide, or salted and sold on for tanning, and suitable bones, for example cattle tibiae and metapodia, were used widely in the production of bone artefacts; horn was also collected (as indicated by sawn horncores) for horn-working, and there is evidence for the systematic collection of red deer antler, either shed naturally, or collected from hunted animals.

Despite the fact that the fort is known to have housed cavalry at certain times (Chs 12 and 15), there were relatively few horse bones. Evidence suggests that the majority of the horses survived well into adulthood, but otherwise little can be said about their size or appearance. It is not possible to determine their role, so they might have been used for riding, traction, or as pack animals. Whilst horsemeat would not generally have been processed for consumption, butchered bones were recovered from Roman deposits, the slaughtered animals having been skinned, dismembered, and defleshed. Presumably, like cattle, their hides were retained and their bone regarded as a raw material. It is unlikely, but not impossible, that some of the meat was used for human consumption, possibly during times of hardship, but it is more likely to have been fed to hunting and other dogs; or the animals were simply butchered for ease of disposal. The dog remains were primarily from adults, probably kept as working, hunting, and guard dogs. The few cat bones from Roman features were from adult individuals, possibly pets or kept for rodent control.

Whilst domestic fowl and, potentially, domestic geese contributed to the Roman diet, they were not present in large numbers and may represent luxuries acquired by soldiers on an individual basis. Several wild species of bird were also present, pink-footed and barnacle geese making it clear that wildfowling was an occasional pastime, or possibly that wildfowl were available for purchase. The pigeon (squab) could have been eaten, and butchered swan and grey heron bones were recovered from Period 6. The latter were perhaps more opportunist additions to the diet, although it is clear from the works of Apicius (Flower and Rosenbaum 1958) that the Roman attitude to potential food animals was considerably more catholic than that of today. Hare was also hunted and eaten, as were deer, with red deer the most popular quarry, but roe was also taken. The two fallow deer bones could conceivably have been brought to the site in a piecemeal fashion, the fragment of sawn antler to be used as a raw material, and the phalanx possibly attached to a hide.

Medieval period

Evidence from the medieval deposits paints a surprisingly similar picture. Beef remained the most popularly eaten meat, with most of the animals slaughtered being older females at the end of their reproductive lives. At this time, however, horncore evidence suggests a larger number of castrates, likely to be prime beef cattle. Most of the horncores derive from the outer ward ditch, filled with domestic and other waste dumped from the castle (*Ch 11*), and could well reflect the enhanced status of the castle's principal households.

The consumption of mutton and lamb continued to play a significant role. The number of younger (20-34 months) animals being slaughtered perhaps reflects a liking for younger meat amongst some of the castle's residents. It is possible that these individuals had been sourced from animals surplus to the wool-producing flocks of the rural hinterland, trade in wool being a significant part of the economy from the thirteenth century onwards (Trow-Smith 1967, 133). Pork again made a significant contribution to the medieval table. It is thought that most animals would have been brought in from the surrounding hinterland (Maltby 1979, 59), although a small number of animals may have been bred at the site.

Again, there were relatively few horse bones, although the medieval material included an individual of considerable age (more than 16 years). Whilst these could have been riding horses, it is unlikely, and they were probably the remains of pack animals, or kept for traction. As in the Roman period, there was evidence of skinning and butchery amongst the assemblage. Interestingly, this is confined to Periods 8ii and 8iv (within the outer ward ditch and the tenements). Speed (1997, 204), quoting an anonymous life of Edward II, notes a widespread and disastrous famine in 1316, the document recording that 'it was even reported that in Northumberland folk ate dogs, horses and other unclean meat'. Period 8ii has been dated

to the thirteenth to mid-fourteenth centuries and, although it cannot be more than speculation, perhaps horse was, of necessity, consumed in the castle at that time. There were a few articulated dog skeletons within the fills of the outer ward ditch, but whether they were dogs kept within the castle or simply strays cannot be determined. Cat bones were more common, the majority from kittens skinned for their fur, which was presumably used to trim garments.

Domestic fowl, geese, and ducks (both wild and domesticated) all contributed to the medieval table, as did a number of wild species of bird. Again, swan and grey heron were consumed, regarded at the time as game and destined only for the high table. The status of the latter might presumably be reflected in its price, and a medieval ordinance (*London Letter Book H*, fol xcix, cited in Speed 1997, 173) gives the price of roast heron as 18d, whilst roast pork was 8d and wild mallard 4½d. Buzzard bone from a medieval pit could originate from a bird kept in captivity for hawking. There was also evidence for the consumption of deer, the hunt being a significant aspect of high-status medieval social life at that time (Cummins 1988). Thus it can be seen that the animal bone assemblage from the site has not only elucidated the preferences and eating habits of its Roman and medieval occupants, but has also contributed in part to a recognition of status and social practice.

Fish Remains

C Ingrem

In total, 28 fragments were examined, of which 18 are identifiable (Table 76). Most of the remains came from Roman deposits, although fish bones were recovered from all phases of the site.

Roman period

At least three species of fish were recovered from deposits dated to Period 3, although it was only possible to identify bones belonging to cod (*Gadus morhua*) to their species. Salmonid and flatfish are also represented, the remains of the latter most probably belonging to plaice (*Pleuronectes platessa*), or flounder (*Platichthys flesus*). Apart from a basioccipital bone (layer *7573*, Building *7392*; Fig 265) belonging to salmonid and recovered by sieving, the other four identified specimens are vertebrae, recovered by hand from a single context (pit fill *1075*, Building *1222*). The eight unidentifiable fragments are fin spines (from layer *7202*, Building *7391*). It is of interest that Period 3B Building *7394*, a direct replacement for *7392*, produced an iron fish hook (*Ch 17*).

Type	Period					Total
	3	4	5	7	8	
Salmonid	2		7	1		10
Gadus morhua	1				4	5
Large Gadid					1	1
Flatfish	2					2
Unidentifiable fish	8				2	10
Total	**13**	**1**	**7**	**1**	**7**	**28**

Table 76: Representation of taxa according to phase (NISP)

Deposits dated to the second half of the second century (Period 5) produced seven fish bones, all belonging to small (150–300 mm total length) salmonids. All the bones are vertebrae and both the abdominal and caudal regions of the body are represented. As all the remains were recovered from a single context (occupation layer *6172*, Building *7397*; Fig 272), it is conceivable that the bones belonged to one, or perhaps two, individual fish.

Fish remains are frequently encountered in Roman deposits in Britain, albeit in relatively small numbers, thereby suggesting low-intensity exploitation of nearby estuarine waters (Ingrem nd). Occasionally, larger assemblages, comprising the remains of numerous small fish, are recovered and these have been interpreted as indicating local *garum* (fish sauce) production (Bateman and Locker 1982; Jones 1988). All the fish represented are extremely good to eat, and there is no reason to believe that they represent anything other than the occasional inclusion of fish in the diet. The sample size is too small to provide interpretative information concerning the representation of body parts, but it is probable that sea fish were caught locally, in the Solway Firth, and transported fresh to Carlisle.

Early medieval period
Pre-Norman deposit *5296* produced a single fish bone, a post-abdominal vertebra belonging to a large salmonid. These fish are anadromous and therefore their presence at Carlisle may result either from the exploitation of local freshwater or importation from the coast.

Medieval period
Five identifiable fish bones were recovered from medieval deposits, all belonging to large or very large cod or cod-family fish (*Gadidae*). Period 8iii produced a single post-abdominal vertebra belonging to a large cod (600–1200 mm in total length), from layer *1421* (within Building *1492*). All of the other specimens came from Period 8iv, including a quadrate (from *1313*, within tenement *1234*) and a caudal vertebra (from *1320*, from tenement *1235*), again both belonging to large cod. In addition, a cleithra belonging to a very large (>1200 mm in total length) gadid (probably cod), a caudal vertebrae belonging to cod, and two unidentifiable fragments were recovered from layer *1384* (also in tenement *1235*).

Large and very large cod-family fish are generally caught in offshore waters (Wheeler 1969). Their remains are commonly found on medieval sites, indicating that, by this time, fishing had become a commercial activity. Cod-family fish were often preserved by salting or drying and transported as fillets (Locker 2000), the fish having been decapitated at the landing site. The assemblage from the Millennium Project is clearly too small to provide conclusive evidence concerning body part representation, but the presence of a quadrate does suggests that at least one cod arrived at the site whole, and therefore probably in a fresh form, having been transported from the coast.

Insect Remains

D Smith and E Tetlow

Full analysis of insect remains was undertaken on 13 samples from contexts associated with early Roman activity (Periods 2 and 3) and one from the medieval outer ward ditch (Period 8), chosen as having the greatest potential for meaningful results (see *Appendix 13* for technical details).

The faunas
Period 2
Only one insect fauna was examined from the earliest Roman deposits (fill *1969* from pit *1961* (*Ch 2*), sample *138*). The assemblage was relatively small but, nevertheless, it is dominated by several species associated with rather decayed, foul organic matter. Examples of this are *Megasternum boletophagum*, and the *Philonthus*, *Cryptophagus*, and *Encimus* species are also present. *Laemophloeus ferrugineus* is the 'rust red grain beetle', usually associated with stored grain and other foodstuffs which have reached an advanced

state of decay (Hunter *et al* 1973). It is difficult to give a specific interpretation for such a small fauna; however, it is likely that it has a similar origin to many of those from later periods.

Period 3

Five insect faunas were examined from a range of contexts associated with the establishment of the timber fort in AD 72/3 and its early occupation: Period 3A pit fills *1075* (in Building **1222**, sample *64*) and *7604* (in the central range, sample *482*), Period 3B pit fill *3831* (in Period 3B Building **3772**, sample 220), and layers *7202* (in Building **7391**, sample *458*), and *7209* (Period 3E, in the central range, sample *452*). The majority of the deposits sampled were fills from shallow gullies, timber-lined channels, and pits, or occupation layers associated with buildings. In terms of insect remains, these are some of the earliest Roman insect fauna to be examined from England, the only directly comparable material being from One Poultry, London, which dates from before the Boudiccan revolt (Smith 2000; 2009).

The five assemblages are essentially similar in terms of both the range of insects (*Appendix 13*) and the ecology of these species (Fig 570). At least 20% consist of species associated with granaries and grain storage. Typically, this includes several individuals of *Sitophilus granarius,* which is the 'granary weevil'. This species of beetle attacks whole grain whilst it is relatively dry and unspoiled, and it can cause considerable damage, often being held responsible for much of the initial loss of stored grain. In addition, several other pests were found,

all species that are usually associated with grain in a relatively advanced state of decay. Examples are *Oryzaephilus surinamensis,* the 'saw toothed grain beetle', *Laemophloeus ferrugineus,* the 'rust red grain beetle', and a single individual of the 'rust red flour beetle', *Tribolium castaneum,* in layer *7209.*

Many of the other species of beetle from this period are sometimes associated with decaying grain or granary waste, although they are also found in a range of other decaying settlement wastes and rubbish. Examples of these species are *Typhaea stercorea, Xylodromus concinnus, Cryptophagus,* and *Enicmus minutus,* which are all associated with relatively dry organic materials around archaeological settlements (Hall and Kenward 1990; Kenward and Hall 1995). The various species of *Cercyon, Oxyleus,* and *Aphodius,* on the other hand, are associated with foul and wet decayed matter (Carrot and Kenward 2001). The latter type of material is also indicated by the large numbers of puparia of the common house fly, *Musca domestica,* and the stable fly, *Stomoxys calcitrans,* from a shallow gully (fill *1075* of gully *1089*) in Building **1222**, identified as a barrack. Both species commonly inhabit a range of foul and wet decaying organic materials, such as excrement or food waste around human settlements (D N Smith 1997; K G V Smith 1989). The stable fly is commonly associated with stable waste, but is also found in a range of other similar materials. Fill *1075* also contained the remains of the *Sepsis* fly, which is commonly associated with excrement and rather fluid organic rubbish, and the yellow dung fly, *Scathophaga stercoraria,* which is normally associated with herbivore dung (Smith 1989). In addition, several larvae of the *Psychoda* fly were recovered (M Robinson *pers comm*). These develop in organic-rich liquids in dark places, an environment shared by the small fly, *Telomerina flavipes* (Skidmore 1999; Smith 1989).

These fauna (Table 77; Fig 571) are dominated by members of Kenward's putative 'house fauna' (Hall and Kenward 1990; Kenward and Hall 1995) and by synanthropic species, although there is a relatively small proportion of the kinds of beetle which are normally associated with outdoor environments. In addition, the ground beetles and weevils present are also species typically associated with external areas of human settlement in the archaeological record. In particular, *Cidnorhinus quadrimaculatus* feeds on stinging nettles and *Gynetron* on plantains, which are both species of plants commonly found in waste areas around human settlement. Occupation layer *7202* in the possible *principia,* Building **7391** (Period 3B), produced one of the few human ecto-parasites found on site, a human louse (*Pediculus humanus*). Another was noted during conservation of the boxwood hair combs (*Appendix 9*).

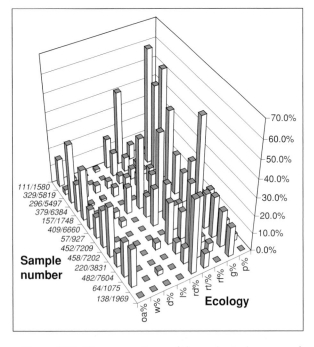

Figure 570: The proportions of the ecological groups of Coleoptera

	138/ 1969	64/ 1075	482/ 7604	220/ 3831	458/ 7202	452/ 7209	57/ 927	409/ 6660	157/ 1748	379/ 6384	296/ 5497	329/ 5819	111/ 1580
Total number of individuals	12	78	30	25	7	14	58	53	7	96	376	38	71
Total number of species	6	33	23	16	5	13	27	17	6	31	77	14	37
oa%	0.0%	21.8%	20.0%	8.0%	28.6%	21.4%	12.1%	11.3%	28.6%	15.6%	33.2%	2.6%	15.5%
w%	0.0%	0.0%	0.0%	4.0%	0.0%	0.0%	0.0%	0.0%	0.0%	1.0%	15.4%	0.0%	1.4%
d%	0.0%	2.6%	0.0%	0.0%	0.0%	0.0%	3.4%	3.8%	0.0%	1.0%	4.3%	0.0%	0.0%
l%	0.0%	0.0%	0.0%	4.0%	0.0%	0.0%	0.0%	15.1%	0.0%	5.2%	4.0%	0.0%	1.4%
rd%	41.7%	9.0%	6.7%	24.0%	0.0%	21.4%	12.1%	39.6%	0.0%	8.3%	4.5%	13.2%	16.9%
rt/%	8.3%	34.6%	36.7%	16.0%	14.3%	21.4%	44.8%	17.0%	0.0%	7.3%	5.9%	7.9%	40.8%
rf%	0.0%	5.1%	3.3%	0.0%	0.0%	7.1%	1.7%	0.0%	0.0%	8.3%	2.7%	2.6%	8.5%
g%	16.7%	20.5%	23.3%	20.0%	57.1%	28.6%	17.2%	22.6%	42.9%	60.4%	47.9%	63.2%	2.8%
p%	0.0%	3.8%	6.7%	0.0%	14.3%	7.1%	3.4%	1.9%	0.0%	4.2%	4.0%	0.0%	2.8%

Species: oa=those that will not breed in human housing, w=aquatic, d=associated with damp watersides and river banks, l=associated with timber, rd=primarily associated with drier organic matter, rt=associated with decaying organic matter, but not belonging to the rd or rf groups, rf= primarily associated with foul organic matter (often dung), g=associated with grain, p=phytophage species often associated with waste areas or grassland and pasture (after Kenward and Hall 1995).

Table 77: The proportions of the ecological groups of Coleoptera

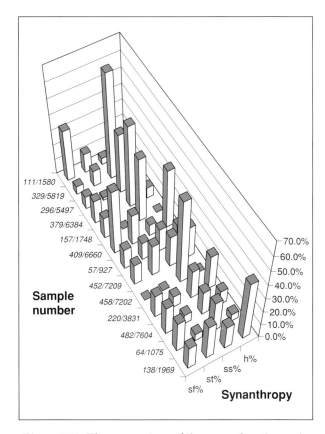

Figure 571: The proportions of the synanthropic species

Period 4

Four samples from Period 4 were examined, the contexts from which they derive dating from the beginning of the second century and continuing to around the middle of that century. Fill *927* (sample *57*) came from a small gully in the south-east quadrant of the fort. In terms of the beetles recovered, the fauna was essentially similar to that seen in Period 2, there being substantial numbers of grain pests. Judging from the range of species associated with decaying plant material and occupation waste, it also seems to have reached an advanced state of decay. This is most clearly indicated by the large numbers of the housefly, stable fly, and *Sepsis* flies recovered. Smaller, but essentially similar, insect faunas were also recovered from other deposits dating from this period: occupation layer *6660* in Building *7396* (Period 4A; sample *409*), fill *1748* (Period 4A; sample *220*) from a gully in a possible barrack, Building *2059*, and a Period 4B fill (*6384*; sample *379*) from a road drain associated with the main east to west road (*7477*).

Period 6

Only one sample from Period 6 was examined (fill *5497* (sample *296*)) from a stone-lined pit, possibly a latrine (seemingly associated with the *principia*, Building *5200*), which produced the largest insect fauna from the site (Table 78). Once again, the largest component was pests of stored grain (Fig 570). In addition to *Sitophilus granarius*, *Oryzaephilus surinamensis*, and *Tribolium castaneum*, which were recorded earlier, in Period 3, *Palorus ratzeburgi*, the 'small eyed flour beetle', was also present. Once again, the presence of these species clearly indicates that considerable amounts of mouldy and

	138/ 1969	64/ 1075	482/ 7604	220/ 38311	458/ 7202	452/ 7209	57/ 927	409/ 6660	157/ 1748	379/ 6384	296/ 5497	329/ 5819	111/ 1580
sf%	16.7%	21.8%	20.0%	16.0%	0.0%	14.3%	13.8%	43.4%	14.3%	15.6%	8.2%	5.3%	33.8%
st%	25.0%	5.1%	6.7%	8.0%	0.0%	21.4%	12.1%	20.8%	0.0%	3.1%	1.6%	10.5%	12.7%
ss%	16.7%	21.8%	16.7%	20.0%	57.1%	21.4%	15.5%	7.5%	42.9%	54.2%	39.4%	68.4%	4.2%
h%	41.7%	5.1%	10.0%	24.0%	0.0%	21.4%	12.1%	39.6%	0.0%	7.3%	4.3%	21.1%	15.5%

Synanthropes: sf=faculative: common in 'natural' habitats, but clearly favoured by artificial ones; st=typically: particularly favoured by artificial habitats, but believed to be able to survive in nature in the long term; ss=strong: essentially dependent on human activity for survival (after Kenward 1997); h=members of the 'house fauna', a very arbitrary group based on archaeological associations (Hall and Kenward 1990)

Table 78: The proportions of the synanthropic species

decayed grain entered the deposit. The insect fauna from this feature also contains a relatively large proportion of species derived from human habitation and settlement (Kenward's (1978) 'house fauna' and the synanthropic species in Table 78; Fig 571). Many of these taxa, such as the *Cryptophagus, Typhaea stercorea, Mycetea hirta*, and the 'spider beetles', *Ptinus fur* and *Tipnus unicolor*, are associated with a range of mouldering, but relatively dry, organic materials. They can, however, also occur as common pests of spoilt grain (Hunter *et al* 1973). Another pair of species that are commonly associated with habitation are the common woodworm, *Anobium punctatum*, and the powder post beetle, *Lyctus linearis*, both of which attack structural timbers. Once again, a relatively large proportion of the insects present suggest that this material may have reached an advanced state of decay. This is clearly indicated by the *Cercyon*, Histeridae, the majority of the staphylinids, and the *Aphodius* species present. The presence of the latter genus may be particularly significant. Though usually described as dung beetles, recent work by Carrot and Kenward (2001) has clearly indicated that the taxa found in the archaeological record for the Carlisle Millennium Project are probably associated with decayed and fluid settlement wastes and rubbish. Surprisingly, no fly pupae were recovered from this deposit, which is unfortunate, since the clearest indicator to establish that this feature contained human faeces, and was therefore a latrine, would be a range of flies thought to be particularly indicative of cesspit material (Belshaw 1989; Skidmore 1999; Smith 2000; 2009).

This pit also contained a relatively large proportion of species, such as ground beetles and weevils, which probably do not have their origin in the fort buildings. The ecology of the species present suggests that there was relatively clear scrubby land with stinging nettle, clover, dock, and plantains within the fort. This is also the only fauna examined which contains several species of water beetle, for example the dytiscid diving beetles, and the hydraenids. This might suggest that either a pool of standing water developed in the pit or that the pit was flooded.

Period 8
Only one insect fauna dates from the medieval period: from layer *1580* (sample *111*) in tenement **1234**. The fauna recovered again seems to be derived from a range of settlement wastes, and is dominated by many of the synanthropic and 'house fauna' species (Table 78) seen in earlier periods. However, though grain pests are present, there is neither the range nor the numbers encountered in the Roman periods. This material, therefore, represents assorted rubbish and settlement waste, and reflects other finds from the area.

Discussion
Pests of stored products
The most noticeable feature of the insect assemblages from samples of Roman date was the significant presence of species associated with spoilt grain and other stored products, which occur in the range of 20–30% of the total fauna recovered (Table 77; Fig 571). In terms of the grain pests, *Sitophilus granarius*, the granary weevil, was encountered frequently, and is a common pest in granaries, where both the larvae and the adults feed on whole grain in the early stages of spoilage (Coombs and Woodroffe 1963; Hunter *et al* 1973). It is a very destructive species and, if an infestation is allowed to get out of control, can cause a considerable loss of stored grain. Many of the other stored-product species present are considered to be pests of grain that has further decayed, having been broken and become wet and mouldy; often this is material that has already been attacked and damaged by *S granarius*. This second group is frequently regarded as 'secondary' in the natural succession of infestation of stored grain (Freeman 1980; Coombs and Freeman 1955; Hunter *et al* 1973) and includes species such as *Oryzaephilus surinamensis* (the saw-toothed grain beetle), *Laemophloeus ferrugineus* (the flat grain beetle), *Palorus ratzburgi* (the small-eyed flour beetle), and *Tribolium castaneum* (the rust-red grain beetle). They will also attack a range of other stored products, and, in the case of the latter two species, this can include flour and bran meal (Freeman 1980; Salmond 1956; Hunter *et al* 1973). *T castaneum* is not

believed to overwinter successfully in unheated warehouses in Britain today, and is often considered to be a pest of imported grain (Solomon and Adamson 1955). It has, however, now been found to be able to survive in large deposits of grain which, although not heated as such, do have an internal insulated microclimate which is above average temperature (*ibid*). Therefore, at a minimum, the presence of this species suggests substantial storage of grain on site, and might possibly indicate evidence of imported rather than 'native' grain.

Buckland (1978b) has examined the archaeological record of grain pests and has observed that they appear to be absent from Britain before the beginning of large-scale importation of grain by the Roman army and civil administration. He has suggested that this absence is primarily due to the minimal import of grain from the continent in the Iron Age, and because the storage of grain in sealed, and hence carbon dioxide-rich, pits would probably inhibit infestation. Roman above-ground ventilated granaries may have been more convenient and viable as a method of storage for large armies and civilian populations, but they appear to have been considerably more vulnerable to insect attack.

If Buckland (*op cit*) is correct that grain pests are a Roman introduction to Britain, then the results from this site and the pre-Boudiccan deposits at One Poultry, London (Smith 2000; 2009) clearly suggest that these species entered Britain almost immediately after the Roman invasion. This is probably the result of the import of large amounts of grain from southern Europe in order to support both the military and new civil administration.

Buckland (*op cit*) also suggests that the presence of these species is not just a low-level annoyance, but could account for a considerable loss of agricultural production once they became established. He also argues that a degree of agricultural intensification would have been needed in order to counterbalance this loss (*ibid*). Certainly, the vast majority of deposits examined from the early and later Roman periods suggests that disposing of infested grain must have been a common activity for the military and civil administrations alike.

Deposition of material
It is clear from the dominance of granary pests that the majority of deposits sampled must have an association with grain storage. However, there are several possible routes by which this material could become incorporated into the deposits in which it was found. Given that many of the buildings with which this material was associated appear to have been barracks, there is a distinct possibility that it may reflect

the use of spoilt grain as feed for horses or other stock animals. Osborne (1983) elegantly demonstrated that fragments of these species are able to pass through the human dietary tract without damage, and it seems logical to presume the same is true of herbivore dung. If this was, in fact, the case, it would suggest stabling waste and effluent must have been a common feature of life within the fort.

Kenward and Hall (1997) have refined the nature of the insect faunas thought to be particularly indicative of stabling, which has also been addressed by statistical work undertaken by Carrot and Kenward (2001). Though several parts of the stabling material 'indicator grouping' have been found in the fort, specifically the grain pests and the stable fly, other relevant species are ostensibly absent. In particular, there is a lack of any of the characteristic lice associated with horses or other herbivores. Equally, there does not appear to be a substantial 'hay fauna' present (*eg* Smith 1998), which could indicate the presence of fodder and bedding. Thus, though it is a fair supposition to argue that the material analysed may represent stabling, the evidence is not as clear-cut as that seen at a number of other sites (*eg* Kenward and Hall 1995; 1997; Smith 1997; Smith and Chandler 2004; Kenward *et al* 2004).

An alternative origin for the material present might be to suggest that it represents an attempt to dispose of spoilt grain in a variety of ways. Work on a number of other Roman sites has indicated that such piecemeal disposal may have been a common practice. It is noticeable that the systematic deposition of spoilt grain seems to have occurred at several military sites, for example, the infamous deposits of grain at the Roman fort at Malton (Buckland 1982) and the Coney Street warehouse in York (Kenward and Williams 1979), which probably represent an attempt to dispose of infested grain through burning. Equally, the large numbers of grain pests encountered in the fills of both the Roman Skeldergate and Bedern wells in York (Hall *et al* 1980; Hall *et al* 1983; Kenward *et al* 1986), and the well fill from Inveresk Gate (Smith 2004), all suggest that disused wells may also have been a common receptacle for spoilt grain. Similarly, some of the deposits associated with both military and civilian granaries and flour mills at the pre- and post-Boudiccan revolt site at One Poultry, London, might indicate that grain residues were disposed of in pits and into contexts associated with road maintenance and levelling (Smith 2000).

Health and hygiene
Some of the insects recorded would have had direct implications for human health. Kenward and Large (Kenward and Hall 1995, 762) have suggested that the flies and other insects breeding in such rubbish could potentially carry pathogens and the eggs of

internal parasites, such as *Trichuris* worms, into human housing. In particular, the two commonest species of fly present, the house fly, *Musca domestica*, and the stable fly, *Stomoxys calcitrans*, are seen as potential vectors for a range of detrimental pathogens, such as salmonellosis, typhoid, and diarrhoeal infections. It has also been suggested that they could be involved in the transmission of poliomyelitis (Oldroyd 1964; Smith 1973). The single human louse recovered suggests that the Roman military carried the usual infestations of ecto-parasites.

Waterlogged and Charred Plant Remains

E Huckerby and F Graham

Plant remains from the site included pollen, seeds, and vegetative fragments, preserved either by charring or waterlogging (see *Appendix 14* for fuller reports). Charred plant remains, which include deliberately or accidentally burnt grain, crop-processing waste, seeds, and vegetative remains (for example charcoal), herbaceous plant stems, rhizomes, and nut shells, survive in both wet and dry contexts. The survival of waterlogged evidence, however, depends heavily on taphonomic conditions; the contexts must be not only wet, but also anaerobic, for plant material to be preserved. In general terms, waterlogging preserves a more generalised range of plant matter than dry sites, and thus allows a better understanding of the site's environment. Pollen is usually only preserved under waterlogged conditions.

Results

The representation of charred plant remains in samples of all periods is relatively small, with only 57% of those analysed producing any cereal grains. Considered by period, however, the percentage of samples producing carbonised cereal grains varied considerably, being as high as 77% in Period 3B (Table 79). In addition, three samples produced crop-processing waste, although no cereal grains were identified in their flots. Contexts particularly rich in charcoal (*Appendix 14*) contained vegetative plant fragments, including rush and sedge stems, heather charcoal, leaves, and flowers, and weed seeds. In contrast, the waterlogged plant remains from some parts of the site were abundant and well preserved. This was most evident in contexts dating to Periods 3 and 4, and in Period 8, although there was a decline in the later Roman and immediately post-Roman periods (Periods 5-7).

Plants were assigned, where possible, to broad ecological categories, although in many instances this was difficult, as some plants can commonly be

Period	No of samples analysed	No of samples with charred cereal grains
1B	6	3 (50%)
2	2	2 (100%)
3A	23	15 (65%)
3B	9	7 (77%)
3C	3	0
3D	2	1 (50%)
3E	2	2 (100%)
4A	11	5 (45%)
4A/B	1	1 (100%)
4B	11	5 (45%)
4C	1	1 (100%)
5	1	1 (100%)
5A	1	1 (100%)
5B	1	0
5C	2	1 (50%)
6B	5	3 (60%)
6C	7	1 (14%)
8A	1	1 (100%)
8D	2	2 (100%)
8i	1	1 (100%)
8iii	6	3 (50%)
8iv	5	3 (60%)
Total	**103**	**59 (57%)**

Table 79: Samples producing carbonised cereal grains

found growing in several different communities. There are few obvious differences between the plant assemblages from different periods, although on occasion individual contexts stand out as being significantly different from the majority. Because of this overall similarity, changes in the archaeobotanical record are described by plant communities rather than by period.

Each individual plant species has been assigned to a single plant community, although many taxa are to be found growing in more than one type. This ordering of the data allows comparisons to be made more easily between the Millennium Project and other excavations in Carlisle, for example at The Lanes (Huntley 2000b), Castle Street (Goodwin 1991), Annetwell Street (Huntley 1989a), and elsewhere in north-west England, for example at Ribchester (Huntley 2000a). The ecological groupings are:

1. Cereals: mainly represented by grains and chaff;
2. Arable and cultivated weeds: these are annual plants found in arable fields and cultivated ground;
3. Ruderals: these are plants found growing on waste or fallow ground. The plants are usually

perennials or biennials, and inhibit the growth of annuals;

4. Grassland plants: found growing in open grassland or meadows;
5. Heathland / mire plants: found on dry heaths and blanket or raised mires (bogs);
6. Wet ground and aquatic plants: found growing on wet marshy ground, in water meadows, and on river, ditch, or pond banks;
7. Woodland communities: these comprise trees, shrubs, and their associated ground flora, and represent forest, woodland clearances, and hedgerows;
8. Food and economic taxa: imported and native taxa that may be used as food sources, for example blackberries and wild strawberry;
9. Plants belonging to broad ecological groupings, but not characteristic of any one, often being found in several.

Cereals (grains and chaff)

On the whole, cereals (Pl 242) were not found in abundance, although amounts varied from period to period. In the pre-Roman and Roman periods (Periods 1-6), hulled barley (*Hordeum*) and spelt/emmer wheat (*Triticum spelta / dicoccum*) were the most frequently identified cereal-types, although a little bread wheat (*Triticum aestivum*) and some oats (*Avena*) were also recorded (*Appendix 14*). There were also, in addition, significant numbers of grains and fragments which could not be identified to species in some of the richer contexts. In the medieval period (Period 8), bread wheat and oats both became more abundant.

There is little evidence to suggest that the early stages of crop processing were taking place at the site at any time, although there were small amounts of charred crop-processing waste and charred and/or waterlogged arable weeds, characteristic by-products of fine-sieving the processed grain to remove the glume bases and small weed seeds (van der Veen 1992, 81; Hillman 1981,123–62). In the Roman contexts in which cereal grains were abundant, there was often a large component of other charred material, usually from plants likely to have been present in hay, or used as flooring, for example the seeds of grasses, sedges, and sorrels, and also of burnt stems of plants, such as rushes, sedges, and grasses. At Annetwell Street, Huntley (1989a) refers to similar groups of carbonised material as a 'background assemblage' and notes the relative lack of cereals. This pattern seems to be repeating itself in all but a few contexts from the Millennium Project, and even features like ovens and hearths, which should have had a greater likelihood of producing charred grain (perhaps used as kindling or burnt accidentally (Hillman 1981), often produced very little.

Plate 242: Cereal grain, germinated (W Smith)

The paucity of preserved cereals from both sites is in marked contrast to the evidence from the insect remains, where grain beetles (*p 924*) were plentiful in many of the samples analysed, implying that cereals must have been stored in the fort in considerable amounts. The reason for this apparent discrepancy is not obvious, but a number of alternatives can be considered, although lack of evidence means that they remain conjectural. It is possible that the taphonomic conditions were unfavourable for the preservation of charred plant remains; for example, fluctuations in the water table over time have been shown to be detrimental to the long-term preservation of charred material (Campbell 1992; Hillman 1981; G Campbell *pers comm*). Over and above this, burnt grain represents a failure, the accidental spoiling of a valuable resource, and it is possible that, because of the relatively isolated position of the fort with regard to the military administration of the province, housekeeping was stringent, and waste of good grain avoided. The numbers of grain pests recorded seem to suggest a considerable problem with regard to long-term storage, and it is possible that this increased the need for careful handling of the grain still further, although elsewhere it seems to have been the case that spoiled grain was used as animal feed. Kenward and Hall (1997) suggest that large numbers of grain beetles may be more indicative of stable manure than grain storage or activities associated with cereal processing or dietary uses. *In extremis*, it is possible that the beetles were removed from the grain and that the best of it was still used for food.

Arable weeds and ruderals

Arable weed seeds were recorded in most samples, although why they should be so consistently recorded from a Roman military fort (see also Huntley 1989a for Annetwell Street), where little if any primary crop processing would have been undertaken, is puzzling. Huntley (*ibid*) suggests that they may have been brought into the fort in partly-processed cereals, and removed during fine sieving (Hillman 1981; van der Veen 1992). It is not impossible that these, and others that might have entered the fort on people's feet, were dispersed, and rapidly colonised areas of bare ground within the fort. Alternatively, it might be the case that there were some small gardens or allotments within the walls, where individuals might grow supplementary crops to augment their basic rations, or improve the range of foodstuffs available, perhaps to provide familiar herbs or vegetables. Literary and other evidence from *Mons Claudianus*, in the Egyptian desert, implies that this was taking place elsewhere (van der Veen 1998), and it has been postulated at Ribchester (Buxton and Howard-Davis 2000); certainly, there are many modern instances where small vegetable plots are cultivated on any available ground, for example in municipal gardens (C Howard-Davis *pers comm*), especially in times of social stress.

Arable weeds characteristic of drier sandy soils and of heavier wetter clay soils appear within the same contexts, suggesting that neither the Romans nor the local population were restricting their cultivation to one soil type. This seems to suggest that produce was brought from a range of local contexts and from further afield. Very specific and distinctive cornfield weeds, such as cornflower (*Centaurea cyanus*), corn marigold (*Chrysanthemum segetum*), and corncockle (*Agrostemma githago*), were recorded in many of the samples analysed, but in general they were rare, even in medieval contexts (less than five seeds or fragments in a litre, and seldom more than 25 per litre), and despite the fact that corn marigold is recognised as having been a serious pest in the late twelfth century (Huntley 2000b).

The presence of seeds of corn spurrey (*Spergula arvensis*), parsley piert (*Aphanes arvensis*), and fumitory (*Fumaria*) in many of the samples indicates that more acidic sandy soils were also cultivated. Evidence for heavier, damper soils comes from the presence of seeds from fat-hen (*Chenopodium album*), pale persicaria (*Persicaria lapathifolia*), redshank (*Persicaria maculosa*), and possibly the small nettle (*Urtica urens*). Wild radish (*Raphanus raphinistrum*), which is described by Stace (1997) as probably being imported, deliberately or otherwise, into this country, was ubiquitous in most contexts from the pre-Roman to the medieval periods, thus suggesting a very early introduction.

A further grouping of arable/cultivated/open-ground weeds is more tolerant in its ecological requirements. It includes such prolific plants as shepherd's purse (*Capsella bursa-pastoris*) and common chickweed (*Stellaria media*), and most gardeners are aware of how rapidly these plants germinate, flower, and set plentiful, small and easily dispersed seeds from early spring to late autumn, rapidly colonising any cleared or waste ground. Other plants, for instance knotweed (*Polygonum aviculare*), recorded in many samples, are

primarily arable weeds, but are resistant to trampling and so survive by roads and paths (Huntley 2000b, 71), and could easily have been growing within the fort in such contexts.

The boundaries between arable weeds and ruderals are not clear-cut, and if land is poorly cultivated or allowed to lie fallow, biennial or perennial ruderal plants gradually become established and ultimately out-compete the annuals. Once established, perennials, for example dandelion (*Taraxacum officinalis*), can survive for many years, making them very undesirable weeds in lawns, gardens, or fields, but also a useful salad ingredient. Significant numbers of taxa, such as black bindweed (*Fallopia convolvulus*), pale persicaria, and common hemp nettle (*Galeopsis tetrahit*), recorded in many of the samples, are found growing today on waste and cultivated ground (Stace 1997). Other plants, such as common nettle (*Urtica dioica*), burdock (*Arctium*), hemlock (*Conium maculatum*), and the perennial docks (*Rumex longifolius* and *Rumex obtusifolius*), which were identified in many of the samples, are clearly ruderals. Today, the common nettle is often found growing on nitrogen-rich soils beside ditches and streams, in drier areas, and on rubbish dumps, and is a good indicator of the former presence of animals and humans. Henbane, also found in many of the samples, suggests that the ground had been well manured by cattle. Several of the common native ruderal plants also have medicinal properties or are known to be toxic.

Grassland plants
Grassland taxa were identified in a large percentage of the samples from all periods. Some of those recorded are characteristic of more calcareous soils, and are found growing in traditional hay meadows, for example fairy/purging flax (*Linum catharticum*), self heal (*Prunella vulgaris*), hawkbit (*Leontodon saxatilis*), and yellow rattle (*Rhinanthus minor*). A second group includes those from more acidic conditions, such as sheep's sorrel (*Rumex acetosella*), a common plant of grassland, waste ground, heaths, and roadsides.

The contexts producing samples in which the seeds of grassland taxa were abundant are thought to have either contained animal dung, or been associated in some way with the storage of hay. The acquisition and storage of hay for fodder and bedding would have been an important part of the life of the fort, with horses (both riding and draught animals) and other livestock present in considerable numbers. The dung-producers may have been fed hay whilst stabled (for instance, the material from elongated pit *4305* in Period 3A Building *4653*), or have been allowed to graze outside the fort. Interestingly, the range of contexts in which seeds associated with hay were identified might also provide evidence for hay being used for mattresses in barracks.

The grassland taxa, like the arable weeds, also comprise a number of plants that are often recorded in other plant communities. These include the *Ranunculus repens*-type (which contains the three buttercup species *R bulbosus*, *R repens*, and *R acris*); all are described as grassland taxa, although the creeping buttercup (*R repens*) is a serious weed of good basic soils that are poorly cultivated (Huntley 2000b). Common stitchwort (*Stellaria graminea*), which was identified in many contexts, grows today in dry grassy areas or in woodland (Stace 1997). A further group of plants that are associated with grassy places and hedgerows, for example upright hedge parsley (*Torilis japonica*) and nipplewort (*Lapsanna communis*), was also recorded frequently.

Heathland/mire plants

Plants from dry heaths or damper moorland and mires were recorded in many of the Roman samples, suggesting that they were exploiting these communities, perhaps for roofing, animal bedding, fodder, or fuel. The use of heathland and mire communities was also obvious in some of the charred plant assemblages, with occasional seeds of heath grass (*Danthonia decumbens*), and charred rush and sedge stems.

Further evidence for the use of heath plants comes from waterlogged contexts, where large numbers of fragments of bracken fronds were identified. The shoots, leaves, and flowers of heather (*Calluna vulgaris*) and cross-leaved heath (*Erica tetralix*) were also identified in many contexts. Heather has, in the past, and until comparatively recently, been an economically valuable plant, being used for roofing, animal bedding, fodder, dyeing, and, in Scotland, to flavour beverages (Dickson and Dickson 2000, 260–2): in parts of Western Norway, the Lindås Project (S Peglar *pers comm*) recorded that it was still being regularly harvested in the second half of the twentieth century. It would have been a common plant on the fells of Cumbria (Pearsall and Pennington 1973) or on the drier areas of the large raised mires to the west and south-west of Carlisle (Wedholme Flow, Glasson Moss, and Bowness Common) and to the north and east, at Solway, Scaleby, and Bolton Fell Mosses (Hodgkinson *et al* 2000), to all of which the Romans would have had easy access. The fact that both leaves and flowers were identified suggests that the heather was being harvested in the late summer, when it flowers. Another series of plants very frequently recorded was tormentil-type (*Potentilla erecta*-type; this includes more than one species), and these are often found in heathland or mires, and have been used in the past both medicinally and in the tanning process. There is, however, little likelihood that this unpleasant and noxious process would have been carried out within the fort.

Bogmoss (*Sphagnum*) and cottongrass are characteristic plants of acid raised or blanket mires and may have come from similar habitats to the heather, which also comes from drier heaths. Bogmoss is recorded frequently on archaeological sites in northern Britain (Dickson and Dickson 2000) and because of its excellent water retention, and acidic qualities, may have been used as a dressing for wounds, as toilet paper, or for menstrual hygiene (*op cit*, 225–6), although the latter would seem less likely in a military establishment.

Wet ground and aquatic plants

Plants of wet ground were ubiquitous in most samples; in those from Periods 1 and 2, and Period 3A, they dominated the plant assemblages, becoming less dominant in Periods 5 and 6, but more common again in Period 8. Blinks (*Montia*), sedges (*Carex* lenticular and trigynous types), rushes (*Juncus*), bristle club-rush (*Isolepis setacea*), and spike-rushes (*Eleocharis*) were present in most periods.

Several plants from wet meadows and fens, such as meadowsweet (*Filpendula ulmaria*), marsh cinquefoil (*Potentilla palustris*), marsh pennywort (*Hydrocotyl vulgaris*), and ragged robin (*Lychnis flos-cuculi*), were recorded sporadically throughout all periods, and Huntley suggests, with regard to the southern Lanes (2000b), that the wet meadows may have been cut for fodder or used for grazing. Meadowsweet is frequently identified from archaeological sites of all periods and is another plant which has many uses, most notably as a flavouring, in mead, and medicinally (Dickson and Dickson 2000, 267–8).

Aquatic plants from more mineral substrates, the sides of ditches, ponds, and rivers, were also recorded, as at The Lanes (Huntley 2000b). In some samples, lesser spearwort (*Ranunculus flammula*), celery-leaved buttercup (*R scleratus*), and the crowfoots (*Ranunculus* Batrachium-type) were abundant. Large numbers of seeds of wild celery (*Apium graveolens*), a plant found today growing in damp, usually brackish places, often near the sea, were recorded in two fills from earthfast wooden-lined boxes or silos in Building **5689** in both Periods 4A and 4B. As the boxes were not large in volume, it would seem unlikely that the wild celery was actually growing in them, and it is perhaps more likely that this was part of the Roman diet, entering the boxes in cess.

Woodland taxa

Woodland taxa were present in some contexts but, except for hazel (*Corylus avellana*) and sloe (*Prunus spinosa*), their numbers were small, with only occasional seeds of rowan (*Sorbus aucuparia*), alder (*Alnus glutinosa*; Pl 243), bird cherry (*Prunus padus*), alder buckthorn (*Frangula alnus*), and buckthorn (*Rhamnus cathartica*) identified. There was no distinct

Plate 243: Alder seed (W Smith)

Plate 244: Fragments of hazelnut shell (W Smith)

pattern in their distribution, and only two contexts, fill *1075* (sample *64*, *Appendix 14*) from a gully in Building *1222* (Period 3A), and *800* (sample *52*), the fill of outer ward ditch *1230* from Period 8i, had significant numbers of woodland seeds in them. In both cases these were birch seeds, which are very light, easily dispersed, and rapidly become established on waste ground. A roll of birch bark was identified in wood from the outer ward ditch (*Ch19*), and birch might have been used for hurdles and wattle, not to mention as firelighters (T Padley *pers comm*). One frequently recorded woodland herb, hairy wood-rush (*Luzula pilosa*), can also be found growing amongst heather on heaths or moorland.

Food and economic plants

This group covers crop and wild food plants other than cereals. Fig (*Ficus carica*), grape (*Vitis vinifera*), coriander (*Coriandrum sativum*), and dill seeds (*Anethum graveolens*) were present in a number of contexts, but rarely in significant numbers, except for coriander. This relative dearth is in marked contrast to some contexts from Annetwell Street and the Lanes, when obvious cess pits were identified and sampled, and seeds of plants, such as grapes, figs, and olives (*Olea europaea*), and herbs like coriander and dill, were abundant (Huntley 1989a; 2000b). Walnut shells (*Juglans regia*) were identified in a few contexts, but again the numbers were small.

More mundane plant remains, such as hazelnut shells (Pl 244), were recorded in most samples from Periods 3A, 3B, 4A, and 4B. Their appearance in large numbers perhaps suggests that such fruits were a staple food or pleasant supplement in the military diet, whether as a source of protein and fat, or as a substitute for flour, much as poorer Corsicans used chestnuts until comparatively recently (Abram 2003, 312): there is a reference by John Lightfoot, writing in 1777 (Lightfoot 1777), to hazel being made into bread, and in Norway, the nuts were allowed to germinate in the spring, when the shells were easily broken in half

and the seedlings eaten (*op cit*). It is difficult to estimate exactly how many nuts were being consumed from the fragments of shell, but they are consistently present on the site. Sloes, elderberries, wild strawberries (*Fragaria vesca*), and bilberries are also likely to have featured in the Roman diet and possibly also the occasional flax seed (*Linum usitassimum*). In contrast, evidence from the medieval period (Period 8) indicates that economic taxa such as flax and hemp (*Cannabis*) were more common, and bilberry (*Vaccinium myrtillus* L) was found more frequently than before.

Many of the common native plants recorded are known to have been used, in the past, for culinary purposes. Plants such as common and sheep's sorrel add flavour to salads, and the young leaves and shoots of nettles are a nutritious vegetable, as well as being a source of a fine fibre (for textiles) and having medicinal properties. Others herbaceous plants used as vegetables include fat-hen, which may also have been an alternative to cereals for making flour, and wild radish was used as an oil or flavouring. Some plants may have been collected as fodder; as the name suggests, hogweed (*Heracleum sphondylium*), for example, was in the past collected for pigs (Stace 1997).

Medicinal, toxic, and more generally useful plants

Many of the plants recorded are known to have medicinal, culinary, or economic uses. It is, however, very difficult to determine whether they were present in the plant assemblages as natural occurrences or were specifically collected. It is perhaps worthwhile detailing the use of some, and exploring the reasons why they may have been a valuable resource in the Roman fort or the medieval castle.

Abundant seeds of shepherd's purse (*Capsella bursa-pastoralis*) were recorded in some contexts. This plant is known to have a number of different medicinal uses and is mentioned by herbalists both ancient (Culpeper *c* 1640) and modern (Grieve 1971); its properties are also described by Allen and Hatfield (2004). It has been used both in human and veterinary medicine as a haemostyptic (helping to stop bleeding), and as a cure for diarrhoea in people and calves. It is easy to see that on a military site such properties could be invaluable in the treatment of battlefield injuries, although no evidence is known for its use by the Romans.

Another commonly recorded plant is tormentil (*Potentilla erecta*-type), which is described as being a cure for diarrhoea, and in Cumbria there are folk records of it being used for cuts (Allen and Hatfield 2004, 145–6). It is also used in tanning, but this seems unlikely to have been its principal use within the fort.

Quite large numbers of charred seeds of hedge bedstraw (*Galium mollugo*) were recorded in a burnt layer (*3364*) under a hearth in Building *4655* (Period 4A; Fig 270). This is a native plant, which may easily have been growing within the fort or close by, and it is perhaps of interest to note that Grieve (1971, 91–2), in her modern herbal, describes many uses for lady's bedstraw (*Galium verum*) and comments that hedge bedstraw has many of the same properties. In the past, lady's bedstraw has been used with rennet to curdle milk for cheese, as a filling for pillows, and as a dye. Culpeper and Gerard both describe the medicinal properties of the bedstraws as a remedy for epilepsy and cutaneous eruptions (Gerard 1974), to stop inward bleeding and bleeding at the nose, and all inward wounds (Culpeper *c* 1640).

The seeds of other potentially medicinal plants identified include the common mallow (*Malva sylvestris*), burdock, henbane, and fairy/purging flax. The record of seeds from the common mallow is of interest, and Dickson and Dickson (2000, 242–3), who recorded pollen of the plant in a ditch at Bearsden on the Antonine Wall in Scotland, mention that Pliny described the important medicinal uses of the plant. Buurman (1988) notes the finding of a second-century earthenware vessel in Germany which was full of mallow seeds. Burdock, a plant of waste places and hedgerows, is mentioned by Culpeper (*c* 1640) and Grieve (1971) in their herbals as being valuable in the treatment of, amongst other symptoms, skin complaints, indigestion, and burns.

There was also a group of more or less toxic plants, with well-known medicinal uses. These include hemlock (seeds of which were abundant), with lesser amounts of deadly nightshade (*Atropa belladonna*), black nightshade, henbane, opium poppy, and common and small nettle seeds. The identification of seeds of black nightshade may again reflect a natural find within the plant assemblage or the deliberate collection of a plant thought to be toxic and with mild narcotic properties (Grieve 1971, 582–3). Henbane is a highly toxic plant known to have been used medicinally, and its presence in a pit adjacent to Building *5200* (Period 6B) might suggest that this building, the *principia*, had some

medical role by the early fourth century. Other plants with known medicinal qualities that were ubiquitous on the site include selfheal and hawkbit. It must, however, be stressed that these plants are common members of the native flora in north-western England (Halliday 1997).

The plant record and the chronological development of the site

Records from three periods in the development of the site are of particular importance to an understanding of the palaeobotanical development of Carlisle, and can be compared with other sites from the city (for instance Huntley 1989a; 2000b). They are the pre-Roman period (Period 1), the very earliest Roman activity (Period 2), and the medieval period (Period 8; *Appendix 14*).

Period 1
Only a few viable samples were available for the apparently pre-Roman activity: two from the old ground surface; and four from the pre-Roman buried soil (*Ch 2*). Those from the old ground surface had very few plant remains preserved in them, but there were indications of possible cereal use, although these could have been the result of later contamination. Samples from the pre-Roman buried soil all suggest that the environment around the fort site was one of wet ground interspersed with drier areas, some probably cultivated, as evidenced by the seeds of arable-type weeds. Hemp nettles and wild radish were widespread over the site when the Romans arrived. The general wetness, or possibly seasonally waterlogged nature, of the site is also borne out by soil micromorphology (*Appendix 15*), which confirms the earlier agricultural activity suggested by ard-marks (*Ch 2*). Although diatoms were recorded in the sections analysed, pollen was thought to be rare, but when concentrated by chemical preparation it was later established that it was present in sufficient amounts to allow some analysis (Pl 245). The pollen

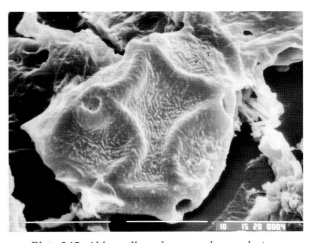

Plate 245: Alder pollen, shown under an electron microscope (P Barker)

Plate 246: Modern alder carr in Cumbria (T N Huckerby)

record (*Appendix 15*) was somewhat homogeneous, which is to be expected given the level of biological reworking noted. Even its presence and survival in the soils of Carlisle is, however, unusual. It suggests that when the soil was forming there were extensive areas of alder carr in the pollen catchment area (Pl 246), possibly by the River Caldew, with some hazel and more open grassland. This is possibly reflected in the preferential use of alder in the timber buildings of the Period 3 fort (*Ch 19*). Towards the upper part of the profile, cereal pollen was recorded, suggesting local arable cultivation (*Appendix 15*). A similar pollen record was identified from buried soils at Tarraby Lane, on Hadrian's Wall (Balaam 1978), some 1.5 km to the north-east, and, more recently, close to the fort at Stanwix (OA North 2005a).

Period 2

Again, the plant remains were very limited and only two samples were analysed, from a possible hearth (*7608*) and a pit fill (*1969*). Low levels of cereal grains and crop-processing waste were well represented. Relatively large concentrations of the charred stems of rushes, sedges, and grasses may represent the use of such plants for flooring, or hay. The other plant remains recorded suggest that conditions on the site continued to be very damp, with blinks, rushes, and sedges growing in the wetter parts. Arable weeds associated with damper soils were either

being brought onto the site, or there were areas of cultivation close by.

Periods 3 and 4

The local environment of the timber forts continued to be wet at this time, although the representation of plants from wet ground decreased in Period 4. The plant assemblages were mixed, coming from a number of different communities, with the seeds of arable weeds recorded consistently in most samples, together with obvious evidence for hay and ruderal plants. There were also small numbers of seeds from food plants in many samples, but exotic taxa, except for coriander, were only present sporadically. Spelt/emmer wheat and barley were the important cereal types, and whilst in Period 3 few cereal grains were identified, the number of samples in which they appeared increased in Period 4.

Fill *6708* of a wooden-lined box, associated with the third phase of Period 4A Building *5689* (Fig 270), produced a notable plant assemblage. Although the only charred plant remains were some hazelnut shell fragments, the waterlogged assemblage was diverse. Most notably, there were very large numbers of seeds from wild celery, possibly being used as a food flavouring. Other food plants in this context included sloe stones, as well as the hazelnut shells, perhaps suggesting, whatever the function of the box, that

Plate 247: Sedge rhizome bases (T N Huckerby)

some cess was entering the fills, a possibility perhaps reinforced by the presence of moss. Seeds of arable weeds, ruderal plants, grassland taxa, wet ground plants, and those from broad ecological groupings were also recorded.

Period 5

This period was poorly represented in the plant record, but produced a few samples with higher than average representations of charred plant remains, possibly reflecting its interpretation as a time of widespread demolition and clearance. One fill (*330*) of possible pit *329*, cut into the accumulated silt (*245* and *326*) in the western part of the fort, is of particular interest. It contained a considerable amount of charcoal (*Appendix 14*), unusually of heather, and a large quantity (in excess of 100 fragments) of sedge rhizome bases (the underground stems of the plants; Pl 247; A Hall *pers comm*). A single barley grain was also recorded in the sample. The fill appeared to have been deliberately deposited over half a flanged bowl of mid- to late second-century date (*Ch 7, p 246*), but the absence of burnt bone seems to rule out a cremation. It would, however, appear to be an unusual deposition, perhaps votive, possibly with the sedge rhizomes being burnt for their aromatic properties.

Period 6

The plant remains from the stone fort were in many ways similar to those of the timber forts (Periods 3 and 4), with a similar background flora of arable weeds, ruderals, grassland taxa, wet ground plants, with some food plants. However, there were three contexts which produced distinctive assemblages.

Two of them were fills of stone-lined pit *5668* (Period 6B), seemingly a latrine which was associated with a drainage channel (*5632*) that served the *principia* (Building *5200*; Fig 273). Fill *5726* produced a varied and interesting assemblage of waterlogged plant remains and included a group of plants which are known to be toxic and/or have medicinal uses.

These included significant numbers of hemlock seeds, with smaller amounts of deadly nightshade (*Atropa belladonna*), black nightshade, henbane, opium poppy, and common and small nettle seeds. Burdock, purported to have medicinal uses (Culpeper *c* 1640; Grieve 1971), was also recorded. There were also seeds and remains of food plants such as grape, walnut, dill, blackberry, and elderberry. The seeds of plants from wet ground or shallow ponds and ditches were also identified in the assemblage, and included many seeds of a group of water crowfoot species (*Ranunculus batrachium*-type), which are found in shallow ponds and ditches, or on damp ground (Stace 1997). Again, seeds of arable weeds, ruderals, and broad ecological groupings were recorded. The record of grape and dill seeds, and walnut shell fragments, suggests a more exotic diet, which is to be expected if the building was indeed the *principia*. There was also a small assemblage of charred plant remains, mainly weeds but with infrequent cereal fragments and processing waste.

The presence of a fragment of altar dedicated to Asclepius, the god of medicine, in close proximity (*Ch 21*) might suggest that the pit could have been a hospital latrine, although the altar was not in its original position. The presence of luxury foods seems more in keeping with the identification of the building as the *principia*, but it is not impossible that the commanding officer's household provided medical care, certainly for the family, and perhaps also for others.

A second fill, *5727*, from the same pit was also of interest. Charred plant remains in this sample were rare and no cereal grains were recorded. Evidence for potential food plants was infrequent, but included fragments of hazelnut shell, and seeds of blackberry, elderberry, and bird cherry. Seeds of arable weeds, ruderals, grassland, wet ground, and broad ecological habitat taxa were recorded, and of these, common nettle (a ruderal plant), common and sheep's sorrel (grassland taxa) were abundant. Seeds from plants of wet ground were present but, except for celery-leaved buttercup, were not as prolific. Unlike fill *5726*, this did not contain many plants with obvious uses, although the sorrels, nettles, and hemlock are all described in the herbals as having medicinal properties. Celery-leaved buttercup, a frequent plant of marshy fields, ditches, ponds, and stream sides, is described by Grieve (1971, 235) as 'raising a blister and creates a sore by no means easy to cure'. In Culpeper (*c* 1640, 105–6), another species, Goldilock's buttercup (*Ranunculus auricomus*), which is closely related to celery-leaved buttercup, is described as 'this furious biting herb', causing blisters, which is 'in no way fit to be given inwardly', but as an ointment is useful. Celery-leaved buttercup may have been a member of the site flora, or could have been accidentally brought into the fort, or perhaps the Romans valued it in some way.

In Period 6C, the fill (5497) of stone-lined pit 5378, again external to the *principia* (Building 5200), contained an assemblage of plant remains that included a suite of toxic or medicinal plants. These comprised abundant hemlock, common and small nettle seeds, and lesser numbers of deadly nightshade, black nightshade, henbane, and opium poppy seeds. There were large numbers of seeds from common sorrel and burdock, and swine-cress seeds were also recorded, as were arable and grassland weeds, ruderals, and plants from broad ecological groupings. The remains of possible dietary plants were, however, rare, although occasional blackberry and elderberry seeds were recorded, and there was some indication of bran. Plants of wet ground were also well represented, with large numbers of seeds from rushes, crowfoots (a group of plants of shallow water, ponds, ditches, and muddy ground), and celery-leaved buttercup. Perhaps water draining off the eaves caused the ground around the *principia* to become much wetter in Period 6C, allowing plants associated with wet ground or shallow water to flourish, the general wetness emphasised by the presence of the ephippia of *Daphnia*, an aquatic invertebrate (*Appendix 13*).

The assemblage of medicinal plant remains was similar to that from fill 5727, but without the indications of any exotic food plants. The presence of amorphous plant, moss, and insect remains, bran fragments, fly puparia, fish, and calcined bone suggests that cess had been incorporated into the fill, indicating, perhaps, a latrine.

Period 8
No significant plant assemblages were recovered from deposits associated with activity that occurred in Period 7, between the late Roman period and the eleventh century. Most medieval contexts analysed were associated with the outer ward ditch (Periods 8i and 8ii), and the overlying tenements (Periods 8iii and 8iv), with only a few from elsewhere. The plant assemblages were diverse in both taxa and the communities they represented, although it is obvious that by the medieval period flax was much more important in the Carlisle economy, with both seeds and seed capsule fragments being recorded.

Periods 8i and 8ii
Only a few charred cereal grains were recorded for Period 8i, but the assemblage of waterlogged plant remains was diverse, and included a number of food plants, including apple/pear, hazelnut, bilberry, and cereals. Arable and grassland weeds, ruderals, and plants of wet ground and broad ecological groupings

continued to be recorded. Large numbers of birch seeds and scales, and bracken fragments, were also identified. Birch seeds are easily dispersed by wind and may reflect the local presence of the tree, but a small roll of birch bark was recovered from the outer ward ditch (*Ch 19*), which might imply that birch branches were being brought to the site for a specific purpose. The impression gained was that the ditch was wet, with sedges, rushes, and other wet ground plants, including marsh marigold and ragged robin, present in the assemblage. In general terms, the waterlogged plant assemblage was similar to those from many of the Roman contexts. The large numbers of bracken fragments may have been associated with buildings, perhaps being used for flooring or bedding, for either humans or animals. The only evidence from Period 8ii was a few charred cereal grains.

Period 8iii
Fills 1481 and 1493, within the ditch (1403) to the north of the medieval tenements, produced sporadic evidence for dietary plants, with some wheat, barley periderm, and fig seeds identified. Flax and hemp seeds were also recorded, but there is nothing to suggest that the ditch was used for retting. The presence of bran suggests that some cess found its way into the ditch fills.

Arable weeds and ruderal seeds were present in significant numbers, including stinking chamomile, corn marigold, and corn cockle. Some seeds from these groups were abundant, for example fat-hen, pale persicaria, and the cabbage family; other abundant types include hairy buttercup (a plant of cultivated ground or grassland) and creeping buttercup-types. Seeds of common mallow, winter-cress, upright hedge parsley, and henbane were also recorded. There were a few heather remains and plants of wet ground were present, with significant numbers of sedges and lesser spearwort seeds.

A further three samples from this period were associated with Building 1492 in tenement 1234. One was from the fill (1421) of a shallow drain, another an organic layer (1668), and the third (1693) was from the fill of a drain (1694) cut into the floor of the building (*Ch 11*). Charred plant remains were not abundant, but there was a few of oats and barley. The waterlogged plant assemblages were very rich and diverse, with some food and economic taxa recorded. Hemp and flax seeds, and flax capsules, were identified, together with seeds of native plants, such as wild strawberry, blackberry, bilberry, and elderberry, that may have been used as food sources.

These samples, with a large number of seeds from arable weeds, suggest that tenement 1234 was associated with nearby cultivation. The record of heather, bog moss, bilberry, tormentil-type, and sheep's sorrel may indicate that mire or heather moorland was being utilised, either as a source of fodder, animal bedding, fuel, or roofing material. Petals from the flowers of the pea family (Fabaceae) were recorded, and, when considered alongside the large amounts of amorphous plant remains and abundant seeds, might indicate the presence of some horse manure. Again, seeds of plants from a range of ecological groupings were recorded, the most abundant types being hairy buttercup, creeping buttercup-type, and celery-leaved buttercup, a plant characteristic of marshy ground, ditches, stream sides, and ponds. A few seeds of henbane and hemlock were also recorded. Considered in its entirety, the assemblage suggests a mix of domestic activity, cultivation, and possible animal husbandry associated with the tenement, with the fills of the outer ward ditch by this time overgrown with plants, such as lesser spearwort and marsh marigold.

Period 8iv
Samples from *1405*, the fill of a timber-lined channel/drain north of tenements *1234* and *1235*, from *723*, the fill of drain/gully *727* in Structure *1233*, and a layer (*1580*) containing animal waste and fly puparia in tenement *1234* each produced only a few charred plant remains, with occasional oats, indeterminate cereal grains, and spelt/emmer glumes. The waterlogged plant remains from these contexts, however, contained a number of different taxa. Dietary and economic plants included grape, hemp, flax, and straw, whilst native taxa, possibly used as food sources, included hazelnut and seeds of blackberry, elderberry, and bilberry. Again, arable weed seeds were recorded, with many fragments of corn cockle, and seeds of other taxa, for example fat-hen, corn marigold, and corn spurrey. Sheep's sorrel and common nettle seeds were among the other plant remains that were plentiful, and both hemlock and henbane were also noted. The seeds of grassland and ruderal plants were recorded in significant numbers and many fragments of bell heather and cross-leaved heath were identified. Rushes, celery-leaved buttercups, and sedges, all wet ground plants, reflect the damp conditions. Insect evidence (*p 924*) characterised layer *1580* as general settlement waste, with the insect assemblage dominated by 'a house fauna', and the plant assemblage, and other material in the sample, supports this identification, the seeds of arable weeds and the remains of flax suggesting that some of the debris was specifically from cultivation. The presence of bran in the sample suggests some cess.

Discussion
The Millennium Project has produced exceptionally rich and diverse assemblages of plant remains from all periods, contributing significantly to modern knowledge and understanding of the local environment from the pre-Roman period onwards. The very large numbers of seeds from plants such as rushes, sedges, and blinks identified in Periods 1-4, and again in Period 8, are strongly indicative of prolonged and very wet conditions in some parts of the site. It was a result of this that anaerobic conditions prevailed, allowing organic finds (*Chs 19* and *20*) to survive in such excellent condition.

The results have confirmed many of the conclusions drawn from previous archaeobotanical research in Carlisle, notably at Annetwell Street (Huntley 1989a), Castle Street (Goodwin 1991), and The Lanes (Huntley 2000b). Evidence from the Millennium Project and Annetwell Street has shown that charred plant remains are often sparsely represented, and that there is a marked lack of evidence for the burning, accidental or otherwise, of grain. This physical lack is in considerable contrast to evidence from the insect fauna (*pp 924-5*), where the presence of several species of grain beetles suggests that there were, in fact, large quantities of cereals stored in the fort. This discrepancy is difficult to explain, although it seems most likely that the taphonomy of the site inhibited preservation even of charred grain, or alternatively that, for some reason, great care was taken in its handling.

Few of the contexts analysed yielded obvious faecal remains, except for pit *1089*, associated with Period 3A Building *1222*. In this, there were abundant wheat/rye and bran fragments, suggesting the presence of either human or animal excrement. Small numbers of grape pips and figs, together with seeds of coriander and dill, were identified in a few contexts, but in general the plant assemblages were more mundane, unlike those elsewhere in the forts, at Annetwell Street (Huntley 1989a), where large numbers of fig seeds, olive stones, and grape pips were recorded in some contexts. In this respect, the Millennium Project's plant assemblages resemble those from Ribchester (Huntley 2000a), within the military hinterland. Indeed, neither fort shows much change through time in the range of plants present.

It is a point of interest that, throughout the life of the forts, there was consistent and considerable evidence of arable cultivation, hay crops, and the use of heathland plants. Whether the cultivation was undertaken on or off site is difficult to ascertain, although it must be presumed that most took place outside the fort. The consistency with which arable weeds were recorded in so many contexts and in all periods does, however, seem to suggest that there might have been some small garden areas within the fort or very close by.

Throughout the twelfth and thirteenth centuries, the outer ward ditch dominated the site, although later, as it silted, properties encroached over its fills; again, the waterlogged preservation there was excellent. The flora recorded was similar to that in the Roman period, although flax and hemp became more important and the arable weeds more diverse. Interestingly, there was also considerable evidence for flax cultivation from elsewhere in the city's defensive ditch system, at Rickergate, from both plant macrofossil and pollen evidence (Bonsall 2005; OA North 2002a). Pollen from the Rickergate ditches also recorded changes in local agricultural regimes, with an alternating record of cereal, flax, and hemp cultivation. There was, in contrast, little evidence for aquatic plants in the samples from the Millennium Project, compared to those from Rickergate (Bonsall 2005), although plants of stream banks and ditch sides were fairly common. Unlike the ditches at Rickergate, there do not appear to have been fluctuations in the water level, nor of widespread dumping of waste (*ibid*).

Conclusions

It is clear that some parts of the Roman forts at Carlisle have always been damp. The land was wet when the Romans first built there, and it continued to be so throughout the occupation, although some areas became drier in the later Roman period, because the land was built up by use of successive buildings, and by the medieval period, only deep cut features were waterlogged. The ground continued to be sufficiently wet that the fills of the medieval outer ward ditch remained permanently wet, though, with continuing good waterlogged preservation. Whilst not necessarily the best conditions in which to live, the damp and boggy conditions have been of enormous benefit to studies of the foundation and development of Carlisle, and without it the archaeological and archaeobotanical record of Carlisle would be much the poorer.

936

BIBLIOGRAPHY

Abram, D, 2003 *The rough guide to Corsica*, London

Albarella, U, and Davis, S L M, 1994 *Medieval and post-medieval mammal and bird remains from Launceston Castle, Cornwall: 1961-1982 excavations*, Ancient Monuments Laboratory Rep, **18/94**, London

Alcock, J, 2001 *Food in Roman Britain*, Stroud

Allason-Jones, L, 1985 Bell-shaped studs?, in M C Bishop (ed), *The production and distribution of Roman military equipment: proceedings of the second Roman Military Equipment Seminar*, BAR Int Ser, **S275**, Oxford, 95-108

Allason-Jones, L, 1988 The small finds, in Bishop and Dore 1988, 159–218

Allason-Jones, L, 1989a *Earrings in Roman Britain*, BAR Brit Ser, **201**, Oxford

Allason-Jones, L, 1989b *Women in Roman Britain*, London

Allason-Jones, L, 1995 'Sexing' small finds, in P Rush (ed), *Theoretical Roman Archaeology: second conference proceedings*, Aldershot, 22–32

Allason-Jones, L, 1999a What is a military assemblage? *J Roman Military Equip Stud*, **10**, 1–4, 105–111

Allason-Jones, L, 1999b Health care in the Roman North, *Britannia*, **30**, 133–46

Allason-Jones, L, 2002 The jet industry and allied trades in Roman Britain, in P Wilson and J Price (eds), *Aspects of industry in Roman Yorkshire and the North*, Oxford, 125–32

Allason-Jones, L, and Bishop, M C, 1988 *Excavations at Roman Corbridge: the hoard*, Engl Heritage Archaeol Rep, **7**, London

Allason-Jones, L, and McKay, B, 1985 *Coventina's Well: a shrine on Hadrian's Wall*, Newcastle upon Tyne

Allason-Jones, L, and Miket, R, 1984 *The catalogue of small finds from South Shields Roman fort*, Soc Antiq Newcastle upon Tyne Monog, **2**, Newcastle upon Tyne

Allen, D E, and Hatfield, G, 2004 *Medicinal plants in folk tradition: an ethnobotany of Britain and Ireland*, Cambridge

Andersen, S T, 1979 Identification of wild grass and cereal pollen, *Danm Geol Unders Årbog* 1978, 69–92

Applebaum, S, 2002 Animal husbandry, in J Wacher (ed), *The Roman world*, London, 504–26

Armstrong, P, and Ayers, B, 1987 *Excavations in High Street and Blackfriargate*, E Riding Archaeol, **8**, Hull Old Town Rep Ser, **5**, Hull

Armstrong, P, Tomlinson, T, and Evans, D H, 1991 *Excavations at Lurk Lane, Beverley, 1979–82*, Sheffield Excav Rep, **1**, Sheffield

Arthur, P, and Williams, D F, 1992 Campanian wine, Roman Britain and the third century, *J Roman Archaeol*, **5**, 250–60

Arthurton, R S, and Wadge, A J, 1981 *Geology of the country around Penrith: memoir for 1:50,000 geological sheet 24*, London

Ashwin, T, and Tester, A, forthcoming *Excavations at Scole*, 1993–4, E Anglian Archaeol

Atkinson, D, 1914 A hoard of samian ware from Pompeii, *J Roman Stud*, **4**, 26–64

Atkinson, D, 1942 *Report on excavations at Wroxeter (the Roman city of* Viroconium*) in the County of Salop, 1923-1927*, Oxford

Aurrecoechea, J, and Muñoz Villarejo, F, 2001–2 A legionary workshop of the 3rd century AD specialising in *loricae segmentatae* from the Roman fortress in León, Spain, *J Roman Military Equip Stud*, **12–13**, 15–28

Austen, P S, 1991 *Bewcastle and Old Penrith, a Roman outpost fort and a frontier vicus: excavations 1977–78*, Cumberland Westmorland Antiq Archaeol Soc, Res Ser, **6**, Kendal

Bailey, D M, 1993 The lamps, in Monaghan 1993, 770–2

Baillie, M G L, and Pilcher, J R, 1973 A simple crossdating program for tree-ring research, *Tree Ring Bull*, **33**, 7-14

Baker, J, and Brothwell, D, 1980 *Animal diseases in archaeology*, London

Balaam, N, 1978 Pollen analysis of the buried soils, in G H Smith, Excavations near Hadrian's Wall at Tarraby Lane, *Britannia*, **9**, 54–6

Bateman, N, and Locker, A, 1982 The sauce of the Thames, *London Archaeol*, **4.8**, 204–7

Bateson, J D, 1981 *Enamel-working in Iron Age, Roman and sub-Roman Britain*, BAR Brit Ser, **93**, Oxford

Beard, M, 2008 *Pompeii: the life of a Roman town*, London

Beijerinck, W, 1947 *Zadenatlas der Nederlandsche Flora ten behoeve van de botanie, palaeontologie, bodemculture en warenkennis omvattende, naast de inheemsche flora, onze belangrijkste cultuurgewassen en verschillende adventiefsoorten*, Wageningen

Bellhouse, R L, 1971 The Roman tileries at Scalesceugh and Brampton, *Trans Cumberland Westmorland Antiq Archaeol Soc*, n ser, **71**, 35–44

Belshaw, R, 1989 A note on the recovery of *Thoracochaeta zosterae*, (Haliday) (Diptera: Sphaeroceridae) from archaeological deposits, *Circaea*, **6**, 39–41

Beltràn Lloris, M, 1970 *Las ánforas romanas en España*, Zaragoza

Bemmann, H, 1985 Eine neue Ware des Virtus von La Madeleine, *Saalburg Jahrbüch*, **40–41** (1984–85), 5–27

Betts, I M, 2003 Stone and ceramic building materials, in C Cowan (ed), *Urban development in north-west Roman Southwark*, Museum London Monog, **16**, London, 105–19

Bewley, R H, 1994 *Prehistoric and Romano-British settlement on the Solway Plain*, Oxbow Monog, **36**, Oxford

Bidwell, P T, 1979 *The legionary bath-house and basilica and forum at Exeter*, Exeter Archaeol Rep, **1**, Exeter

Bidwell, P T, 1985 *The Roman fort of Vindolanda*, Hist Build Monuments Comm Engl Archaeol Rep, **1**, London

Bidwell, P, 2005 The dating of Crambeck parchment ware, *J Roman Pottery Stud*, **12**, 15-21

Binford, L, 1977 *For theory building in archaeology: essays on faunal remains, aquatic resources, spatial analysis and systemic modelling*, London

Binford, L, 1981 *Bones: ancient men and modern myths*, New York

Bingöl, F R I, 1999 *Museum of Anatolian civilisations: ancient jewellery*, Ankara

Binsfeld, W, Goethert-Polaschek, K, and Schwinden, L, 1988 *Corpus signorum Imperii Romani. Deutschland. IV, 3, katalog der Römischen steindenkmäler des Rheinischen Landesmuseums Trier, 1, Götter und Weihedenkmäler*, Mainz

Bird, J, 1986 Samian, in L Miller, J Schofield, and M Rhodes, *The Roman quay at Saint Magnus House, London, excavations at New Fresh Wharf, Lower Thames Street, London 1974–78*, Spec Pap London Middlesex Archaeol Soc, **8**, London, 139–85

Bird, J, 1993 Third-century samian ware in Britain, *J Roman Pottery Stud*, **6**, 1–14

Bird, J, 2004 Two hairpins from Surrey, *Britannia*, **35**, 225–7

Birks, H J B, 1973 *Past and present vegetation of the Isle of Skye: a palaeoecological study*, Cambridge

Birley, A, 2002 *Garrison life at Vindolanda: a band of brothers*, Stroud

Birley, B, and Greene, E, 2006 *The Roman jewellery from Vindolanda, beads, intaglios, finger rings, bracelets and earrings*, Vindolanda Res Rep, n ser, **4**, Fasc 5, Greenhead

Birley, E, Birley, R, and Birley, A, 1993 *The early wooden forts: reports on the auxiliaries, the writing tablets, inscriptions, brands and graffiti*, Vindolanda Res Rep, **2**, Hexham

Birley, R, 1994 *The early Roman forts*, Vindolanda Res Rep, n ser, **1**, Bardon Mill

Birley, R, 1996 *The weapons, The small finds*, Vindolanda Res Rep, n ser, **4**, Fasc 1, Greenhead

Birley, R, 1999 *Writing materials, The small finds*, Vindolanda Res Rep, n ser, **4**, Fasc 4, Greenhead

Biró, M, 1975 The inscriptions of Roman Britain, *Acta Archaeologica Academiae Scientiarium Hungaricae*, **27**, 13-58

Bishop, M C, 1985 The military *fabrica* and the production of arms in the early principate, in M C Bishop (ed), *The production and distribution of Roman military equipment: proceedings of the second Roman Military Equipment Research Seminar*, BAR Int Ser, **S275**, Oxford, 1–42

Bishop, M C, 1988 Cavalry equipment of the Roman army in the first century AD, in J C Coulston (ed), *Military equipment and the identity of Roman soldiers*, BAR Int Ser, **S394**, Oxford, 67–196

Bishop, M C, 1998 Military equipment, in Cool and Philo 1998, 62–81

Bishop, M C, 1999 The Newstead *lorica segmentata*, *J Roman Military Equip Stud*, **10**, 27–43

Bishop, M C, 2000 The Roman military equipment, in J C Barrett, P W M Freeman, and A Woodward, *Cadbury Castle, Somerset: the later prehistoric and early historic archaeology*, Engl Heritage Archaeol Rep, **20**, London, 242–7

Bishop, M C, 2002 *Lorica segmentata, Vol I: a handbook of Roman plate armour*, J Roman Military Equip Stud Monog, **1**, Chirnside

Bishop, M C, forthcoming The Eining *lorica segmentata*, *J Roman Military Equip Stud*, **14–15**

Bishop, M C, and Coulston, J C N, 1993 *Roman military equipment from the Punic Wars to the fall of Rome*, London

Bishop, M C, and Dore, J N, 1988 *Corbridge: excavations of the Roman fort and town, 1947–80*, Engl Heritage Archaeol Rep, **8**, London

Blagg, T F C, 2002 *Roman architectural ornament in Britain*, BAR Brit Ser, **329**, Oxford

Boessneck, J, 1969 Osteological differences in sheep (*Ovis aries* Linné) and goat (*Capra hircus* Linné), in D Brothwell and E Higgs (eds), *Science in Archaeology*, London, 331–58

Boessneck, J, and von den Driesch, A, 1974 Kritische anmerkingen zur widerristhöhenberechnung aus längenmassen vor und frühgeschichtlicher Tierknochen, *Saugetierkdl Mitt*, **22.4**, 325–48

Bonifay, M, 2004 *Études sur la céramique romaine tardive d'Afrique*, BAR Int Ser, **S1301**, Oxford

Bonsall, S, 2005 *A comparison of waterlogged and charred plant remains from the medieval ditch at Rickergate, Carlisle, with the waterlogged and charred plant remains from the medieval ditch at Carlisle*, unpubl diss, Univ Sheffield

Boon, G C, 1966 Roman window glass from Wales, *J Glass Stud*, **8**, 41–5

Boon, G C, 1974 Counterfeiting in Roman Britain, *Sci American*, **231.6**, 120–30

Boon, G C, 1988 Counterfeit coins in Roman Britain, in P J Casey and R Reece (eds), *Coins and the archaeologist*, London, 102–88

Boon, G C, 1991 *Tonsor humanus*: razor and toilet-knife in antiquity, *Britannia*, **22**, 21–32

Born, H, and Junkelmann, M, 1997 *Römische Kampf- und Turnierrüstungen*, Sammlung Axel Guttmann, Bd **6**, Mainz

Borril, H, 1981 The casket burials, in C Partridge, *Skeleton Green: a late Iron Age and Romano-British site*, Britannia Monog, **2**, London, 304–8

Bowman, A K, 1994 *Life and letters on the Roman frontier*, London

Bowman, A K, and Thomas, J D, 1994 *The Vindolanda writing-tablets: Tabulae Vindolandensis II*, London

Bozarth, S R, 1992 Classification of opal phytoliths formed in selected dicotyledons native to the Great Plains, in S Mulholland and G Rapp Jr, *Phytolith systematics: emerging Issues*, New York, 193–214

Brailsford, J W, 1958 *Guide to the antiquities of Roman Britain*, 2nd edn, London

Brailsford, J W, 1962 *Hod Hill, Volume 1: antiquities from Hod Hill in the Durden Collection*, London

Brain, C K, 1981 *The Hunters and the hunted*, Chicago and London

Breeze, D J, 1977 The fort at Bearsden and the supply of pottery to the Roman army, in J Dore and K Greene (eds), *Roman pottery studies in Britain and beyond: papers presented to John Gillam, July 1977*, BAR Int Ser, **S30**, Oxford, 133-45

Breeze, D J, 2006 *John Collingwood Bruce's Handbook to the Roman Wall*, 14th edn, Newcastle upon Tyne

Breeze, D J, and Dobson, B, 2000 *Hadrian's Wall*, 4th edn, London

Brewer, R J, 1986 Other objects of bronze, in J D Zienkiewicz, *The legionary fortress baths at Caerleon, II: the finds*, Cardiff, 172–89

Brickstock, R J, 2000 Coin supply in the North in the late Roman period, in T Wilmott and P Wilson (eds), *The Late Roman Transition in the North*, BAR Brit Ser **299**, Oxford, 33-7

Brickstock, R J, 2002 The coins, in M Snape and P Bidwell, Excavations at Castle Garth, Newcastle upon Tyne, 1976–92 and 1995–6: the excavation of the Roman fort, *Archaeol Aeliana*, 5 ser, **31**, 175–209

Brodribb, G, 1987 *Roman brick and tile*, Gloucester

Bronk Ramsey, C, 2005 *OxCal version 3.10*, http://www.rlaha.ox.ac.uk

Brooks, C M, 1999 The medieval and post-medieval pottery, in C L E Howard-Davis and M Leah, Excavations at St Nicholas Yard, Carlisle, 1996–7, *Trans Cumberland Westmorland Antiq Archaeol Soc*, n ser, **99**, 89–115

Brooks, C M, 2000 The medieval and post-medieval pottery, in R M Newman, N J Hair, C L E Howard-Davis, C Brooks, and A White, Excavations at Penrith Market, 1990, *Trans Cumberland Westmorland Antiq Archaeol Soc*, n ser, **100**, 105–30

Brooks, D, and Thomas, K W, 1967 The distribution of pollen grains on microscope slides. 1. The non-randomness of the distribution, *Pollen et Spores*, **9**, 621–9

Brunning, R, 1995 *Guidelines for the recording, sampling, conservation, and curation of waterlogged wood*, Engl Heritage, London

Brunskill, R W, 1977 *Illustrated handbook of vernacular architecture*, London

Buckland, P, 1978a A first-century shield from Doncaster, Yorkshire, *Britannia*, **9**, 247–70

Buckland, P C, 1978b Cereal production, storage and population: a caveat, in S Limbrey and J G Evans (eds), *The effect of man on the landscape: the lowland zone*, CBA Res Rep, **21**, London, 43–5

Buckland, P C, 1982 The Malton burnt grain: a cautionary tale, *Yorkshire Archaeol J*, **54**, 53–61

Buckland, P C, Hartley, K F, and Rigby, V, 2001 The Roman pottery kilns at Rossington Bridge: excavations 1956–1961: a report on excavations carried out by J R Lidster on behalf of Doncaster Museum, *J Roman Pottery Stud*, **9**, 1–96

Buckley, D G, and Major, H, 1990 Quernstones, in S Wrathmell and A Nicholson, *Dalton Parlours. Iron Age settlement and Roman villa*, Yorkshire Archaeol, **3**, Wakefield, 105-19

Buikstra, J E, and Ubelaker, D H, 1994 *Standards for data collection from human skeletal remains*, Arkansas

Bullock, P, Federoff, N, Jongerius, A, Stoops, G, and Tursina, T, 1985 *Handbook for soil thin section description*, Wolverhampton

Bulmer, M, 1980a An introduction to Roman samian ware, with special reference to collections in Chester and the north west, *J Chester Archaeol Soc*, **62**, 5–72

Bulmer, M, 1980b Samian, in D J P Mason, *Excavations at Chester, 11–15 Castle Street and neighbouring sites 1974-8, a possible Roman posting house, mansio*, Grosvenor Mus Archaeol Excav Surv Rep, **2**, Chester, 87-9

Burke, J, 1978 *Life in the villa in Roman Britain*, London

Bushe-Fox, J P, 1913a *Excavations on the site of the Roman town at Wroxeter Shropshire, in 1912*, Rep Res Comm Soc Antiq London, **1**, London

Bushe-Fox, J, 1913b The use of samian pottery in dating the early Roman occupation of the north of Britain, *Archaeologia*, **64**, 295–314

Buurman, J, 1988 Roman medicine from Uitgeest, in H Küster (ed), *Der prähistorische Mensch und seine Umwelt, Festschrift für Udelgard Körber-Grohne zum 65. Geburtstag*, Forschungen und Berichte zur Vor- und Frühgeschichte in Baden-Württemberg, **31**, Stuttgart, 341-51

Buxton, K, and Howard-Davis, C L E, 2000 *Bremetenacum: excavations at Roman Ribchester 1980, 1989–90*, Lancaster Imprints, **9**, Lancaster

Buxton, K, Howard-Davis, C, Huntley, J, Stallibrass, S, and Kenward, H, 2000a Phase 1: the establishment of the Roman fort and settlement, in Buxton and Howard-Davis 2000, 25–49

Buxton, K, Howard-Davis, C, Huntley, J, Stallibrass, S, and Kenward, H, 2000b Phase 2: renewal of the fort, and arrangement of the extramural area, in Buxton and Howard-Davis 2000, 51–75

Calkin, J B, 1935 An early Romano-British kiln at Corfe Mullen, Dorset, *Antiq J*, **15**, 42-55

Callender, M H, 1965 *Roman amphorae*, London

Cameron, E, 2003 Sheaths of knives from post-Conquest York, in Mould *et al* 2003, 385–9

Campbell, D B, 1986 The date of Agricola's consulship, *Zeitschrift fur papyrologie und Epigraphik*, **63**, 197–200

Campbell, G V, 1992 Bronze Age Plant Remains, in J Moore and D Jennings, *Reading Business Park: a Bronze Age Landscape*, Thames Valley Landscapes Monog, **1**, Oxford, 103-10

Carreras Monfort, C, and Williams, D F, 2002 "Carrot" amphoras: a Syrian or Palestinian connection?, in J H Humphrey (ed), *The Roman and Byzantine Near East, 3*, J Roman Archaeol Suppl Ser, **49**, Oxford, 133–44

Carreras Monfort, C, and Williams, D F, 2003 Spanish oil trade in late Roman Britain: Dressel 23 amphorae from Winchester, *J Roman Pottery Stud*, **10**, 64–8

Carrot, J, and Kenward, H K, 2001 Species associations amongst insect remains from urban archaeological deposits and their significance in reconstructing the past human environment, *J Archaeol Sci*, **28**, 887–905

Caruana, I D, 1990 The small finds, in McCarthy 1990, 83–196

Caruana, I D, 1992 Carlisle: excavations of a section of the annexe ditch of the first Flavian fort, 1990, *Britannia*, **23**, 45–109

Caruana, I D, 1993 A third century *lorica segmentata* back-plate from Carlisle, *Arma*, **5**, 15–18

Caruana, I D, in prep *The Roman forts at Carlisle: excavations at Annetwell Street 1973–84*

Caruana, I D, and Allnutt, E R T, in prep Querns, in Caruana in prep

Cary, E, and Foster H B (trans), 1925 *Dio Cassius, Roman History, VIII, 61–70*, Harvard

Casey, P J, 1978 A further component of the Beaumont hoard, 1855, *Coin Hoards*, **4**, 50–5

Casey, P J, 1980 *Roman coinage in Britain*, Princes Risborough

Casey, P J, 1988 The interpretation of Romano-British site finds, in P J Casey and R Reece (eds), *Coins and the archaeologist*, London, 39–56

Caulfield, S, 1977 The beehive quern in Ireland, *J Roy Soc Antiq Ireland*, **107**, 104–38

Challinor, D, 2008 Wood charcoal, in P Booth, A Bingham, and S Lawrence, *The Roman Roadside settlement at Westhawk Farm, Ashford, Kent: excavations 1998-9*, Oxford Archaeol Monog, **2**, Oxford, 343-9

Charlesworth, D, and Thornton, J H, 1973 Leather found in Mediobogdum, the Roman fort of Hardknott, *Britannia*, **4**, 141-52

Clark, J, 1995 Horseshoes, in J Clark (ed), *The medieval horse and its equipment c.1150-c.1450*, Medieval Finds Excav London, **5**, London, 75–123

Clarke, S, 1997 Abandonment, rubbish disposal and 'special' deposits, in, K Meadows, C Lemke, and J Heron (eds), *TRAC 96, proceedings of the sixth Annual Theoretical Roman Archaeology Conference, Sheffield 1996*, Oxford, 73–81

Clarke, S, 1999 Contact, architectural symbolism and the negotiation of cultural identity in the military zone, in P Baker, C Forcey, S Jundi, and R Witcher (eds), *TRAC 98, proceedings of the eighth annual Theoretical Roman Archaeology Conference, Leicester 1998*, Oxford, 36–45

Coles, J, Orme, B, and Rouillard, S, 1985 Prehistoric woodwork from the Somerset Levels, *Somerset Levels Pap*, **11**, 39

Colgrave, B (trans and ed), 1940 *Two lives of Saint Cuthbert: a life by an anonymous monk of Lindisfarne and Bede's prose life*, Cambridge

Collingwood, R G, 1931 Roman objects from Stanwix, *Trans Cumberland Westmorland Antiq Archaeol Soc*, n ser, **31**, 69-80

Collingwood, R G, and Richmond, I, 1976 *The Archaeology of Roman Britain*, London

Collingwood, R G, and Wright, R P, 1983 *The Roman inscriptions of Britain*, **1**, R Goodburn and H Waugh (eds), Gloucester

Collingwood, R G, and Wright, R P, 1992 *The Roman inscriptions of Britain*, **2**, Fasc 4, S S Frere and R S O Tomlin (eds), Stroud

Collingwood, R G, and Wright, R P, 1993 *The Roman inscriptions of Britain*, **2**, Fasc 5, S S Frere and R S O Tomlin (eds), Stroud

Collingwood, R G, and Wright, R P, 1994 *The Roman inscriptions of Britain*, **2**, Fasc 6, S S Frere and R S O Tomlin (eds), Stroud

Collingwood, R G, and Wright, R P, 1995 *The Roman inscriptions of Britain*, **2**, Fasc 7, S S Frere and R S O Tomlin (eds), Stroud

Connell, B, and Davis, S J M, in prep The animal bones, in J Zant and C Howard-Davis (eds), *Roman and medieval Carlisle: the northern Lanes, excavations 1978-82, Volume 1, the Roman period*

Connolly, P, 1986 A reconstruction of a Roman saddle, *Britannia*, **17**, 353-5

Cool, H E M, 1990 Roman metal hairpins from Southern Britain, *Archaeol J*, **147**, 148–82

Cool, H E M, 1992 The vessel glass, in Caruana 1992, 65–8

Cool, H E M, 1998a Personal objects other than brooches, in Cool and Philo 1998, 57–61

Cool, H E M, 1998b The brooches, in Cool and Philo 1998, 29–56

Cool, H E M, 2000 The parts left over: material culture into the fifth century, in T Wilmott and P Wilson (eds), *The late Roman transition in the North: papers from the Roman Archaeology Conference, Durham 1999*, BAR Brit Ser, **299**, Oxford, 47–65

Cool, H E M, 2002 Craft and industry in Roman York, in P Wilson and J Price (eds), *Aspects of industry in Roman Yorkshire and the North*, Oxford, 1–11

Cool, H E M, 2006 *Eating and Drinking in Roman Britain*, Cambridge

Cool, H E M, Lloyd-Morgan, G, and Hooley, A D, 1995 *Finds from the fortress, the small finds*, Archaeol York, **17.10**, York

Cool, H E M, and Philo, C, 1998 *Roman Castleford: excavations 1974–85, Volume I, the small finds*, Yorkshire Archaeol, **4**, Wakefield

Cool, H E M, and Price, J, 1991 *Roman vessels and window glass*, in Padley 1991b, 165–76

Cool, H E M, and Price, J, 1993 *Roman glass from Annetwell Street, Carlisle*, unpubl rep

Cool, H E M, and Price, J, 1995 *Roman vessel glass from excavations in Colchester, 1971–85*, Colchester Archaeol Rep, **8**, Colchester

Cool, H E M, and Price, J, 1998 The vessels and objects of glass, in Cool and Philo 1998, 141–94

Cool, H E M, and Price, J, 2002 Beads, in P R Wilson (ed), *Cataractonium: Roman Catterick and its hinterland: excavations and research 1958–1997; Part II*, CBA Res Rep, **128**, York, 259–63

Coombs, C W, and Freeman, J A, 1955 The insect fauna of an empty granary, *J Entomol Res*, **46**, 399–417

Coombs, C W, and Woodroffe, G E, 1963 An experimental demonstration of ecological succession in an insect population breeding in stored wheat, *J Animal Ecol*, **32**, 271–9

Corder, P, and Birley, M, 1937 A pair of fourth-century Romano-British pottery kilns near Crambeck, *Antiq J*, **17**, 392–413

Coulston, J C N, 1985 Roman archery equipment, in M C Bishop (ed), *The production and distribution of Roman military equipment: proceedings of the second Roman Military Equipment Research Seminar*, BAR Int Ser, **S275**, Oxford, 220–339

Coulston, J C N, 1995 The sculpture of an armoured figure at Alba Iulia, Romania, *Arma*, **7**, 13–17

Coulston, J C N, 1997 The stone sculptures, in RJA Wilson (ed), *Roman Maryport and its setting: essays in memory of Michael G Jarrett*, Cumberland Westmorland Antiq Archaeol Soc, Extra Ser, **28**, Kendal, 112–31

Coulston, J C N, and Phillips, E J, 1988 Corpus signorum Imperii Romani. *Hadrian's Wall, west of the north Tyne and Carlisle*, **1**, Fasc 6, Oxford

Cowgill, J, 1987 Manufacturing techniques, in Cowgill et al 1987, 8–39

Cowgill, J, de Neergard, M, and Griffifths, N, 1987 *Knives and scabbards*, Medieval Finds Excav London, **1**, London

Cox, E, Haggerty, G, and Hurst, J G, 1984 Ceramic material, in C J Tabraham, Excavations at Kelso Abbey, *Proc Soc Antiq Scotl*, **114**, 381–6

Crawford, M H, 1974 *Roman Republican Coinage*, Cambridge

Crawford, O G S, and Röder, J, 1955 The Quern-quarries of Mayen in the Eifel, *Antiquity*, **29**, 68–76

Crone, B A, and Barber, J, 1981 Analytical techniques for the investigation of non-artefactual wood from prehistoric and medieval sites, *Proc Soc Antiq Scotl*, **111**, 510–15

Croom, A T, 2002 *Roman clothing and fashion*, Stroud

Crummy, N, 1983 *The Roman small finds from excavations in Colchester 1971–9*, Colchester Archaeol Rep, **2**, Colchester

Crummy, P, 1984 *Excavations at Lion Walk, Balkerne Lane, and Middleborough, Colchester, Essex*, Colchester Archaeol Rep, **3**, Colchester

Culpeper, N, c 1640 *Culpeper's complete herbal*, rev edn, London

Cumberpatch, C G, 1997 Towards a phenomenological approach to the study of medieval pottery, in C G Cumberpatch and P W Blinkhorn (eds), *Not so much a pot, more a way of life*, Oxbow Monog, **83**, Oxford, 125-52

Cummins, J, 1988 *The Hound and the Hawk: the Art of Medieval Hunting*, London

Cummins, J, 2001 *The Hound and the Hawk*, 2nd edn London

Cunliffe, B, 1999 *The ancient Celts*, 2nd edn, London

Curle, J, 1911 *A Roman frontier post and its people: the fort at Newstead in the Parish of Melrose*, Glasgow

Curwen, E C, 1937 Querns, *Antiquity,* **11**, 133–51

Daniell, C, 1997 *Death and burial in medieval England,* London

Daniels, C M, 1989 The Flavian and Trajanic northern frontier, in M Todd (ed), *Research on Roman Britain, 1960–89,* Britannia Monog, **11**, London, 31–5

Dannell, G B, 1978 The samian pottery, in A Down, *Chichester excavations, 3,* Chichester, 225–41

Dannell, G B, 1999 Decorated South Gaulish samian, in R Symonds and S Wade, *Roman pottery from excavations in Colchester, 1971–86,* Colchester Archaeol Rep, **10**, Colchester, 13–74

Dannell, G B, Dickinson, B M, Hartley, B R, Mees, A W, Polak, M, Vernhet, A, and Webster, P W, 2004 *Gestempelte südgallische Reliefsigillata, Drag 29 aus den Werkstätten von La Graufesenque,* Römisch-Germanisches Zentralmuseum, Mainz

Dannell, G B, Dickinson, B, and Vernhet, A, 1998 Ovolos on Dragendorff form 30 from the collections of Frédéric Hermet and Dieudonné Rey, in J Bird (ed), *Form and fabric: studies in Rome's material past in honour of BR Hartley,* Oxbow Monog, **80**, Oxford, 69–109

Darling, M J, 1977 *A group of late Roman pottery from Lincoln,* Lincoln Archaeol Trust Monog, **16-1**, London

Darling, M J, 1998 Samian from the city of London: a question of status?, in J Bird (ed), *Form and fabric: studies in Rome's material past in honour of BR Hartley,* Oxbow Monog, **80**, Oxford, 169–77

Davey, P J (ed), 1977 *Medieval pottery from excavations in the North West,* Liverpool

Davies, G, 1977 Burial in Italy up to Augustus, in R Reece (ed), *Burial in the Roman world,* CBA Res Rep, **22**, London, 13-20

Davies, J L, 1977 Roman arrowheads from Dinorben and the *Sagittarii* of the Roman army, *Britannia,* **8**, 257–70

Davies, R W, 1971 The Roman military diet, *Britannia,* **2**, 122–42

Davis, S J M, 1987 *The archaeology of animals,* London

Davis, S, 1995 *The archaeology of animals,* 2nd edn, Stroud

de Neergard, M, 1987 The use of knives, shears, scissors and scabbards, in Cowgill *et al* 1987, 51–61

Déchelette, J, 1904 *Les vases céramiques ornés de la Gaule romaine,* **2**, Paris

der Haroutunian, A, 1985 *North African cookery,* London

Deru, X, 1994 La deuxième génération de la céramique dorée, 50–180 après J-C, in M Tuffreau-Libre and A Jacques, La céramique du Haut-Empire en Gaule Belgique et dans les régions voisines: faciès régionaux et courant commerciaux, *Nord-Ouest Archéologie,* **6**, 81–94

Deru, X, 1996 *La céramique Belge dans le nord de la Gaule: caractérisation, chronologie, phénomènes culturels et économiques,* Publ d'Histoire de l'Art et d'Archéologie de l'Université Catholoque de Louvain, Louvain-la Neuve

Deschler-Erb, E, 1999 *Ad Arma! Romisches Militar des 1. Jahrhunderts n Chr in Augusta Raurica,* Forschungen in Augst, **28**, Augst

Deschler-Erb, S, 1998 *Römische Beinartefakte aus Augusta Raurica. Rohmaterial, Technologie, Typologie und Chronologie,* Forschungen in Augst, **27**, Augst

Dickinson, B M, 1984 The Samian Ware, in S Frere, *Verulamium Excavations,* **3**, Oxford Univ Comm Archaeol Monog, **l**, Oxford, 175-97

Dickinson, B M, 1990 The samian ware, in McCarthy 1990, 213–36

Dickinson, B M, 1991a The samian ware, in Taylor 1991, 344-65

Dickinson, B M, 1991b Samian pottery, in Austen 1991, 112–35

Dickinson, B M, 1992 Samian ware, in Caruana 1992, 51–8

Dickinson, B M, 1997 The samian ware, in T Wilmott, *Birdoswald: excavations of a Roman fort on Hadrian's Wall and its successor settlements: 1987-92,* Engl Heritage Archaeol Rep, **14**, London, 255-67

Dickinson, B M, 2000 Samian, in Buxton and Howard-Davis 2000, 202-24

Dickinson, B M, 2002a Catalogue of decorated samian ware, in P R Wilson (ed), *Cataractonium: Roman Catterick and its hinterland: excavations and research, 1958-1997. Part I,* CBA Res Rep, **128**, York, 418–38

Dickinson, B M, 2002b Selected decorated samian from the 1959 bypass excavations (site 433), in P R Wilson (ed), *Cataractonium: Roman Catterick and its hinterland: excavations and research, 1958-1997. Part I,* CBA Res Rep, **128**, York, 281-316

Dickinson, B M, forthcoming The Samian, in C Howard-Davis, I Miller, N Hair, and R M Newman, in prep, *Excavations at Mitchells Brewery and 39 Church Street, Lancaster*, Lancaster Imprints

Dickinson, B M, in prep The samian pottery, in Caruana in prep

Dickinson, B M, and Hartley, K F, 1971 The evidence of potters' stamps on samian ware and on mortaria for the trading connections of Roman York, in R M Butler (ed), *Soldier and civilian in Roman Yorkshire*, Leicester, 127–42

Dickinson, B M, and Hartley, B R, 2000 The Samian, in C Philo and S Wrathmell (eds), *Roman Castleford excavations: 1974–85. Volume III, the pottery*, West Yorkshire Archaeol, **6**, Leeds, 5–88

Dickinson, B M, Hartley, B R, and Pengelly, H, 2002 Samian ware from Catterick (site 434), in P R Wilson (ed), *Cataractonium: Roman Catterick and its hinterland: excavations and research, 1958–1997. Part I*, CBA Res Rep, **128**, York, 316–22

Dickinson, B M, Hartley, B R, and Pengelly, H, 2004 Inventory entry 107.7, in H E M Cool, *The Roman Cemetery at Brougham, Cumbria. Excavations 1966-67*, Britannia Monog, **21**, London, 124

Dickson, C, and Dickson, J H, 2000 *Plants and people in ancient Scotland*, Stroud

Dixon, E E L, Maden, J, Trotter, F M, Hollingworth, S E, and Tonks, L H, 1926 *The geology of the Carlisle, Longtown and Silloth district: memoirs of the Geological Survey of England and Wales. Explanation of Sheets 11, 16 and 17*, London

Dixon, K M, and Southern, P, 1992 *The Roman cavalry from the first to the third century AD*, London

Dobney, K M, Jaques, S D, and Irving, B G, 1996 Of butchers and breeds: report on vertebrate remains from various sites in the City of Lincoln, *Lincoln Archaeol Stud*, **5**, Lincoln

Drack, W, and Fellman, R, 1988 *Die Römer in der Schweiz*, Stuttgart

Dressel, H, 1899 *Corpus Inscriptionum Latinarum*, **15.1**, *Inscriptiones urbis Romae Latinae; Instrumentum Domesticum*, Berlin

Drummond, C, and Wilbraham, A, 1994 *The Englishman's food*, rev edn, London

Duncan, S, and Ganiaris, H, 1987 Some sulphide corrosion products on copper alloys and lead alloys from London waterfront sites, in J Black (ed), *Recent Advances in the conservation and analysis of artefacts: julbilee conservation conference papers*, London, 109-18

Dyer, C, 1989 *Standards of living in the later Middle Ages*, Cambridge

Earle, J, and Plummer, C (trans), 1892 *Two of the Saxon Chronicles*, Oxford

Earwood, C, 1993 *Domestic wooden artefacts in Britain and Ireland from Neolithic to Viking times*, Exeter

Eckardt, H, 2002 *Illuminating Roman Britain*, Monographies Instrumentum, **23**, Montagnac

Edlin, H L, 1949 *Woodland crafts in Britain: an account of the traditional uses of trees and timbers in the British countryside*, London

Edwards, B J N, and Shotter, D C A, 2005 Two Roman milestones from the Penrith-area, *Trans Cumberland Westmorland Antiq Archaeol Soc*, 3 ser, **5**, 65–77

Edwards, G, nd *The leather from The Cumberland Building Society, Castle Street*, unpubl doc

Egan, G, and Forsyth, H, 1997 Wound wire and silver gilt, in D Gaimster and P Stamper (eds), *The age of transition, the archaeology of the English culture 1400-1600*, Soc Medieval Archaeol Monog, **15**, Oxford, 217-38

Egan, G, and Pritchard, F, 1991 *Dress accessories c.1150-c.1450*, Medieval Finds Excav London, **3**, London

English Heritage, 1991 *Management of archaeological projects*, 2nd edn, London

English Heritage, 1998 *Dendrochronology: guidelines on producing and interpreting dendrochronological dates*, London

Evans, J, 1987 Graffiti and the evidence of literacy and pottery use in Roman Britain, *Archaeol J*, **144**, 191–204

Evans, J, 1989 The development of a major northern pottery industry, in P R Wilson (ed), *The Crambeck Roman pottery industry*, Yorkshire Archaeol Soc Roman Antiq Section, Leeds, 43–90

Evans, J, and Ratkai, S, in press The Roman pottery, in I Ferris, *The beautiful rooms are empty: excavations at Binchester Roman fort, 1976-81 and 1986-91*

Evans, J, and Ratkai, S, forthcoming The Roman pottery, in P Gibbons and C L E Howard-Davis, *Excavations at Walton-le-Dale, 1981-3 and 1996/7*

Faegri, K, and Iversen, J, 1989 *Textbook of modern pollen analysis*, 4th edn, rev K Faegri, P E Kaaland, and K Krzywinski, Chichester

Fell, C I, 1990 The prehistoric flint and stone material, in McCarthy 1990, 91-7

Fell, V, 2000 The nit combs, in Buxton and Howard-Davis 2000, 398–400

Fell, V, Mould, Q, and White, R, 2006 *Guidelines on the X-radiography of archaeological metalwork*, Swindon

Ferguson, R S, 1893 On a massive timber platform of early date uncovered at Carlisle: and on sundry relics found in connection therewith, *Trans Cumberland Westmorland Antiq Archaeol Soc*, 1 ser, **12**, 344–64

Ferrarini, F, 1992 Manufatti in legno e cuoio dall'area nord del Museo di Altino, *Quaderni di Archaeologia del Veneto*, **8**, 191–206

Feugère, M, 2002 *Weapons of the Romans*, Stroud

Flower, B, and Rosenbaum, E, 1958 *The Roman cookery book: a critical translation of 'the art of cooking', by Apicius, for use in the study and the kitchen*, London

Fock, J, 1966 *Metrische untersuchungen an metapodien einiger europäischer rinderrassen*, unpubl diss, Univ Munich

Fölzer, E, 1913 *Die Bilderschüsseln der ostgallischen Sigillata-Manufacturen*, Bonn

Fowler, E, 1960 The origins and development of the penannular brooch in Europe, *Proc Prehist Soc*, **26**, 149–77

Fowler, H W, and Fowler, F G (eds), 1974 *The concise Oxford dictionary of current English*, 5th edn, Oxford

Frayn, J M, 1979 *Subsistence farming in Roman Italy*, London

Freeman, P, 1980 *Common insect pests of stored products*, London

Frere, S S, 1988 Carlisle: (v) English Damside and Borough Street, in S S Frere, Roman Britain in 1987, *Britannia*, **19**, 438-9

Frere, S S, 1989 Hand mills, in S S Frere and J J Wilks, *Strageath: excavations within the Roman fort 1973–86*, Britannia Monog, **9**, London, 181–6

Fulford, M, 2001 Links with the past: pervasive 'ritual' behaviour in Roman Britain, *Britannia*, **32**, 199–218

Fulford, M, Sim, D, and Doig, A, 2004 The production of Roman ferrous armour: a metallographic survey of material from Britain, Denmark and Germany, and its implications, *J Roman Archaeol*, **17**, 197–220

Funari, P P A, 1996 *Dressel 20 inscriptions from Britain and the consumption of Spanish olive oil, with a catalogue of stamps*, BAR Brit Ser, **250**, Oxford

Gale, R, 1999 Charcoal [from Pomeroy Wood], in A P Fitzpatrick, C A Butterworth, and J Grove (eds), *Prehistoric and Roman sites in East Devon: the A30 Honiton to Exeter improvement DBFO, 1996-9. Volume 2: Romano-British Sites*, Salisbury, 372–82

Gale, R, and Cutler, D, 2000 *Plants in archaeology: identification manual of vegetative plant materials used in Europe and the southern Mediterranean to c. 1500*, Kew

Garbsch, J, 1978 Glasgefasse und Fensterglas, in H Schonberger, *Kastell Oberstimm, die Grabungen von 1968 bis 1971*, Berlin, 279–89

Gard, L, 1937 *Reliefsigillata des 3 und 4 Jahrhunderts aus den Werkstätten von Trier*, unpubl diss, Univ Tübingen

Garnsey, P, 1999 *Food and society in classical antiquity*, Cambridge

Garton, D, and Salisbury, C R, 1995 A Romano-British wood-lined well at Wild Goose Cottage, Lound, Nottinghamshire, *Trans Thoroton Soc Nottinghamshire*, **99**, 15–43

Geddes, J, 2001 Iron, in J Blair and N Ramsey (eds), *English medieval industries*, London, 167-88

Gerard, J, 1974 *The herball or generall historie of plantes*, rev T Johnson, Amsterdam

Gillam, J P, 1970 *Types of Roman coarse pottery vessels in Northern Britain*, 3rd edn, Newcastle upon Tyne

Gillam, J P, 1973 Sources of pottery found in northern military sites, in A P Detsicas (ed), *Current research in Romano-British coarse pottery*, CBA Res Rep, **10**, London, 53–62

Gillam, J P, 1976 Coarse fumed ware in north Britain and beyond, *Glasgow Archaeol J*, **4**, 57–80

Girouard, M, 1989 *Hardwick Hall*, London

Glasbergen, W, 1972 *De Romeinse castella te Valkenburg Z H vereniging voor terpenonderzoek*, Groeningen

Glasbergen, W, 1974 *The Pre-Flavian garrisons of Valkenburg Z H: fabriculae and bipartite barracks*, Amsterdam

Goldsworthy, A, 2003 *The complete Roman army*, London

Goodburn, D, 1991 A Roman timber framed building tradition, *Archaeol J*, **148**, 190–204

Goodburn, R, 1978 Roman Britain in 1977, *Britannia*, **9**, 404–72

Goodwin, K, and Huntley, J P, 1991 The waterlogged plant remains and woodland management studies, in M R McCarthy, *The stratigraphic sequence and environmental remains, the Roman waterlogged remains and later features at Castle Street, Carlisle*, Cumberland Westmorland Antiq Archaeol Soc Res Ser, **5**, Fasc 1, Kendal, 54-64

Gosden, C, 2005 What do objects want? *J Archaeol Method Theory*, **12.4**, 193–211

Gose, E, 1950 *Gefässtypen der römischen Keramik im Rheinland*, Bonn

Goubitz, O, 1984 The drawing and registration of archaeological footwear, *Stud Conserv*, **29.4**, 187–96

Goubitz, O, van Driel-Murray, C, and Groenman-van Waateringe, W, 2001 *Stepping through time*, Zwolle

Goury, G, 1939 L'atelier céramique Gallo-Romain de La Madeleine à Laneuveville-devant-Nancy, *Revue des Etudes Anciennes*, **41.4**, 1–16

Grant, A, 1982 The use of tooth wear as a guide to the age of domestic ungulates, in B Wilson, C Grigson, and S Payne (eds), *Ageing and sexing animal bones from archaeological sites*, BAR Brit Ser, **109**, Oxford, 91–108

Green, S H, 1980 *Flint arrowheads of the British Isles: a detailed study of material from England and Wales with comparanda from Scotland and Ireland, Part 1*, BAR Brit Ser, **75(i)**, Oxford

Greep, S, 1986 The objects of worked bone, in J D Zienkiewicz, *The legionary fortress baths at Caerleon: II, the finds*, Cardiff, 197-212

Greep, S, 1987 Lead sling-shot from Windridge Farm, St Albans, and the use of the sling by the Roman army in Britain, *Britannia*, **18**, 183–200

Greep, S, 1998 The bone, antler and ivory artefacts, in Cool and Philo 1998, 267–85

Greep, S, 2004 Bone and antler veneer, in H E M Cool, *The Roman cemetery at Brougham: excavations 1966–67*, Britannia Monog, **21**, London, 273-82

Grew, F, and de Neergaard, M, 1988 *Shoes and pattens*, Medieval Finds Excav London, **2**, London

Grew, F, and Frere, S S, 1989 The objects of metal, in S S Frere and J J Wilks, *Strageath: excavations within the Roman fort 1973–86*, Britannia Monog, **9**, London, 141–74

Grieve, M, 1971 *A modern herbal*, New York

Griffiths, W B, 1994 Throwing stones, in P Bidwell and S Speak, *Excavations at South Shields Roman fort*, **1**, Soc Antiq Newcastle upon Tyne Monog, **4**, Newcastle upon Tyne

Grimes, W F, 1930 *Holt, Denbighshire: the works depot of the Twentieth Legion at Castle Lyons*, Y Cymmrodor, **41**, London

Grimm, E C, 1991 TILIA and TILIA.GRAPH: PC spreadsheet and graphics software for pollen data. INQUA, *Working Group on Data-handling Methods, Newsletter*, **4**, 5-7

Groenman-van Waateringe, W, 1967 *Romeins lederwerk uit Valkenburg Z H*, Nederlandse Oudheden, **2**, Groeningen

Groves, C, 1988 *Tree-ring analysis of oak timbers from Castle Street, Carlisle, 1981-82*, Ancient Monuments Laboratory Rep, **161/188**, unpubl rep

Groves, C, 1990 *Tree-ring analysis and dating of timbers from Annetwell Street, Carlisle, Cumbria, 1981-84*, Ancient Monuments Laboratory Rep, **49/90**, unpubl rep

Groves, C, 1991 Absolute dating, in M R McCarthy, *The stratigraphic sequence and environmental remains, the Roman waterlogged remains and later features at Castle Street, Carlisle, Cumberland*, Westmorland Antiq Archaeol Soc Res Ser, **5**, Fasc 1, Kendal, 50-3

Groves, C 1993 *Dendrochronological analysis of timbers from the Lanes, Carlisle, Cumbria, 1978-82: Volume 1*, Ancient Monuments Laboratory Rep, **21**, unpubl rep

Groves, C, 1996a *Dendrochronological analysis of timbers from the northern area of 'The Lanes', Carlisle, Cumbria, 1978*, **1**, unpubl rep

Groves, C, 1996b *Dendrochronological analysis of timbers from the northern area of 'The Lanes', Carlisle, Cumbria, 1978*, **2**, unpubl rep

Groves, C, in prep Dendrochronology, in Caruana in prep

Guido, M, 1978 *The glass beads of the prehistoric and Roman periods in Britain and Ireland*, Rep Res Comm Soc Antiq London, **35**, London

Habermehl, K H, 1975 *Die alterbestimmung bei haus und labortieren*, Berlin

Haines, B M, 1982 *The Fibre Structure of Leather*, London

Hall, A R, and Kenward, H K, 1990 *Environmental evidence from the Colonia*, Archaeol York, **14.6**, London

Hall, A R, Kenward, H K, and Williams, D, 1980 *Environmental evidence from Roman deposits in Skeldergate*, Archaeol York, **14.3**, London

Hall, A R, Kenward, H K, Williams, D, and Greig, J R A, 1983 *Environment and living conditions at two Anglo-Scandinavian sites*, Archaeol York, **14.4**, London

Hall, D W, 2004 The Pottery, in M Brann, *Excavations at Caerlaverock Old Castle 1998-9*, Dumfriesshire Galloway Nat Hist Antiq Soc, Dumfries, 47-56

Hall, R A, 1984 *The Viking dig: excavations at York*, London

Hall, R A, 1997 *Excavations in the* Praetentura: *9 Blake Street*, CBA Res Rep, York

Halliday, G, 1997 *A flora of Cumbria*, Lancaster

Halstead, P, 1985 A study of mandibular teeth from Romano-British contexts at Maxey, in F Pryor, *Archaeology and environment in the Lower Welland Valley*, E Anglian Archaeol Rep, **27**, Cambridge, 219–24

Halstead, P, 1992 Demi & DMP: faunal remains plus animal exploitation in late Neolithic Thassaly, *Ann Brit Sch Athens*, **87**, 29-59

Hanson, W S, 1978 The organisation of Roman military timber supply, *Britannia*, **9**, 293–305

Hanson, W S, 1982 Roman military timber buildings: construction and reconstruction, in S McGrail (ed), *Woodworking techniques before AD 1500*, BAR Int Ser, **S129**, Oxford, 169–86

Hanson, W S, 2007 *Elginhaugh: a Flavian fort and its annexe*, 2 vols, Britannia Monog, **23**, London

Harcourt, 1974 The dog in prehistoric and early historic Britain, *J Archaeol Sci*, **1.2**, 151-75

Harrison, S G, Masefield, G B, and Wallis, M, 1981 *The Oxford book of food plants*, Oxford

Hartley, B R, 1972a The Roman occupation of Scotland: the evidence of the samian ware, *Britannia*, **3**, 1–55

Hartley, B R, 1972b The samian ware, in S S Frere, *Verulamium Excavations*, I, Rep Res Comm Soc Antiq London, **28**, Oxford, 216–62

Hartley, B R, and Dickinson, B M, 1985 The samian ware in Anglo-Saxon contexts, in S West, *West Stow, the Anglo-Saxon village*, E Anglian Archaeol Rep, **24**, Ipswich, 82

Hartley, B R, and Dickinson, B M, 1990 Samian ware, in J R Perrin, *Roman pottery from the Colonia 2: General Accident and Rougier Street*, Archaeol York, **16.4**, London, 275–303

Hartley, B R, and Dickinson, B M, 2008a *Names on terra sigillata: an index of makers' stamps and signatures in Gallo-Roman terra sigillata (samian ware)* 1 *(A to AXO)*, Bull Inst Classical Stud Suppl, **102-1**, London

Hartley, B R, and Dickinson, B M, 2008b *Names on terra sigillata: an index of makers' stamps and signatures in Gallo-Roman terra sigillata (samian ware)* 2 *(B to CEROTCUS)*, Bull Inst Classical Stud Suppl, **102**, London

Hartley, B R, and Dickinson, B M, forthcoming *Index of potters' stamps on samian ware*

Hartley, B R, Pengelly, H, and Dickinson, B, 1994 Samian ware, in S Cracknell and C Mahany (eds), *Roman Alcester series 1: Roman Alcester: southern extramural area, 1964–1966 excavations, part 2: finds and discussion*, CBA Res Rep, **97**, York, 93–119

Hartley, K F, 1959 The stamped mortaria, in R Hemsley, A Romano-British pottery kiln at *Manduessedum*, *Trans Birmingham Warwickshire Archaeol Soc*, **77**, 8-13

Hartley, K F, 1971 mortaria, in M U Jones, Aldborough, West Riding, 1964: excavations at the south gate and bastion and extramural sites, *Yorkshire Archaeol J*, **43**, 64-7

Hartley, K F, 1981 Painted fine wares made in the Raetian workshops near Wilderspool, Cheshire, in A C Anderson and A S Anderson (eds), *Roman pottery research in Britain and North-West Europe: papers presented to Graham Webster*, BAR Int Ser, **S123,** Oxford, 471-9

Hartley, K F, 1984 The mortaria from Verulamium: a summary, in S Frere, *Verulamium Excavations, 3*, Oxford Univ Comm Archaeol Monog, **1**, Oxford, 292-3

Hartley, K F, 1995 Mortaria, in D Phillips and B Heywood, *Excavations at York Minster 1: from Roman fortress to Norman cathedral*, Roy Comm Hist Monuments Engl, London, 304–23

Hartley, K F, 1998 The incidence of stamped mortaria in the Roman Empire, with special reference to imports to Britain, in J Bird (ed), *Form and fabric: studies in Roman's material past in honour of BR Hartley*, Oxbow Monog, **80**, Oxford, 199-217

Hartley, K F, 1999 The mortaria, in P T Bidwell, M Snape, and A Croom, *Hardknott Roman fort, Cumbria, including an account of the excavations by the late Dorothy Charlesworth*, Cumberland Westmorland Antiq Archaeol Soc, Res Ser, **9**, Kendal, 96-100

Hartley, K F, 2002a Mortarium fabrics, in P R Wilson (ed), *Cataractonium: Roman Catterick and its hinterland: excavations and research, 1958–1997. Part I*, CBA Res Rep, **128**, York, 355–60

Hartley, K F, 2002b Stamped mortaria from Catterick Bridge (Site 240), in P R Wilson (ed), *Cataractonium: Roman Catterick and its hinterland: excavations and research, 1958–1997. Part I*, CBA Res Rep, **128**, York, 467-8

Hartley, K F, 2003 Catalogue of stamped mortaria, in H James, *Roman Carmarthen excavations 1978-1993*, Britannia Monog, **20**, London, 247-54

Hartley, K F, 2007 Mortaria, in Hanson 2007, 326-78

Hartley, K F, in prep a *'Raetian' mortaria in Britain*

Hartley, K F, in prep b The mortaria, in J Zant and C Howard-Davis (eds), *Roman and medieval Carlisle: the northern Lanes, excavations 1978-82, Volume 1, the Roman period*

Hartley, K F, and Webster, P V, 1973 Romano-British kilns near Wilderspool, *Archaeol J*, **130**, 77–103

Hassall, M W C, and Tomlin, R S O, 1977 Inscriptions, *Britannia*, **8**, 426–49

Hather, J G, 2000 *The identification of northern European woods: a guide for archaeologists and conservators*, London

Hattatt, R, 1985 *Iron Age and Roman brooches*, Oxford

Hattatt, R, 1987 *Brooches of antiquity*, Oxford

Hattatt, R, 1989 *Ancient brooches and other artefacts*, Oxford

Hawkes, C F C, and Hull, M R, 1947 *Camulodunum*, Rep Res Comm Soc Antiq London, **14**, London

Hayes, R H, and Whitley, E, 1950 *The Roman pottery at Norton, East Yorkshire*, Roman Malton District Rep, **7**, Leeds

Hedinger, B, and Luizinger, U, 2003 Tabula Rasa. *Les Helvètes et l'artisanat du bois: les découvertes de Viturdurum et Tasgetium*, Avenches

Heimberg, U, and Rüger, C B, 1972 Eine Töpferei im Vicus vor der Colonia Ulpia Traiana, *Beiträge zur archäologie des Römischen Rheinlandes*, **3**, Rheinische Ausgrabungen, **12**, Bonn, 84-118

Henig, M (ed), 1983 *A handbook of Roman art: a survey of the visual arts of the Roman world*, London

Henig, M, 1984 *Religion in Roman Britain*, London

Henig, M, 1995 *The Art of Roman Britain*, London

Henig, M, 2004 Corpus signorum Imperii Romani, *Great Britain: Roman sculpture from the north west Midlands*,**1**, Fasc 9, Oxford

Hermet, F, 1934 *La Graufesenque, Condatomago*, Paris, repr Marseille 1979

Higgins, R A, 1961 *Greek and Roman jewellery*, London

Higham, C F W, 1969 The metrical attributes of two samples of bovine limb bones, *J Zool*, **157**, 63-74

Higham, N, 1986 *The northern counties to AD 1000*, London

Higham, N J, and Jones, G D B, 1985 *The Carvetii*, Stroud

Hill, P V, 1977 *The Coinage of Septimius Severus and His Family of the Mint of Rome*, London

Hill, P V, Carson, R A G, and Kent, J P C, 1960 *Late Roman Bronze Coinage*, London

Hillman, G, 1981 Reconstructing crop husbandry practices from charred plant remains of crops, in R Mercer (ed), *Farming practices in British prehistory*, Edinburgh, 123-62

Hird, M L, 1992 The coarse pottery, in Caruana 1992, 58–62

Hird, M L, forthcoming a The Roman pottery, in J Evans and S Ratkai forthcoming, in P Gibbons and C L E Howard-Davis (eds), *Excavations at Walton-le-Dale, 1981-3 and 1996/7*

Hird, M L forthcoming b Introduction and list of Roman fabrics, in M L Hird and C M Brooks, *Roman and medieval Carlisle: the Southern Lanes: excavations 1981–2, Fasc 3. The Roman and Medieval pottery*

Hird, M L, and Howard-Davis, C, in prep, in C Howard-Davis, I Miller, N Hair, and R M Newman, in prep, *Excavations at Mitchells Brewery and 39 Church Street, Lancaster*, Lancaster Imprints

Hird, M L, and Perrin, J R, 1997 The coarse pottery, in T Wilmott, *Birdoswald: excavations of a Roman fort on Hadrian's Wall and its successor settlements: 1987-92*, Engl Heritage Archaeol Rep **14**, London, 233-67

Hirschfeld, O, and Zangemeister, C, 1899-1943 *Corpus Inscriptionum Latinarum*, **13**, *Inscriptiones trium Galliarum et Germaniarum Latinae*, Berlin

HMSO, 1956 *A handbook of hardwoods*, London

Hobley, A S, 1989 The numismatic evidence for the post-Agricolan abandonment of the Roman frontier in northern Scotland, *Britannia*, **20**, 69–74

Hodgkinson, D, Huckerby, E, Middleton, R, and Wells, C E, 2000 *The lowland wetlands of Cumbria*, Lancaster Imprints **8**, Lancaster

Hodgson, J, and Brennand, M, 2006 The Prehistoric period resource assessment, in M Brennand (ed), *The archaeology of North West England: an archaeological research framework for North West England: Volume 1. Resource assessment*, Archaeol North West, **8**, 23-58

Hodgson, J, and Brennand, M, 2007 The prehistoric period research agenda, M Brennand (ed), *Research and archaeology in North West England: an archaeological research framework for North West England: Volume 2. Research agenda and strategy*, Archaeol North West, **9**, 31-54

Hodgson, N, and Bidwell, P T, 2004 Auxiliary barracks in a new light: recent discoveries on Hadrian's Wall, *Britannia*, **35**, 121–57

Hogg, R, 1953 Further accessions to the Carlisle Museum, *Trans Cumberland Westmorland Antiq Archaeol Soc*, n ser, **53**, 202-8

Hogg, R, 1965 Excavation of the Roman auxiliary tilery, Brampton, *Trans Cumberland Westmorland Antiq Archaeol Soc*, n ser, **65**, 133-68

Holbrook, N, and Bidwell, P T, 1991 *Roman finds from Exeter*, Exeter Archaeol Rep, **4**, Exeter

Holwerda, J H, 1941 *De Belgische Waar in Nijmegen, Beschrijving van de Verzameling van het Museum GM Kam te Nijmegen*, Nijmegen

Hooley, A D, 2002 Leather, in P R Wilson (ed), *Cataractonium: Roman Catterick and its hinterland: excavations and research 1958–1997; Part II*, CBA Res Rep, **128**, London, 318-80

Howard-Davis, C L E, 2000a Copper alloy, in Buxton and Howard-Davis 2000, 242–61

Howard-Davis, C L E, 2000b Ironwork, in Buxton and Howard-Davis 2000, 261–74

Howard-Davis, C L E, 2000c Other artefacts, in Buxton and Howard-Davis 2000, 295–300

Howard-Davis, C L E, 2000d Wood, in C L E Howard-Davis and K Buxton, *Roman forts in the Fylde, excavations at Dowbridge, Kirkham*, Lancaster, 59-61

Howard-Davis, C L E, 2000e Leather, in Buxton and Howard-Davis 2000, 301–23

Howard-Davis, C L E, in prep Lead, in Newman and Leech forthcoming

Howard-Davis, C L E, and Whitworth, A, 2000 Structural wood and wooden artefacts, in Buxton and Howard-Davis 2000, 323–35

Howe, M D, Perrin, J R, and Mackreth, D F, nd *Roman pottery from the Nene Valley: a guide*, Peterborough

Hull, M R, 1963 *The Roman potters' kilns of Colchester*, Rep Res Comm Soc Antiq London, **21**, London

Hunter, F A, Tulloch, B M, and Lamborne, M G, 1973 Insects and mites of maltings in the East Midlands of England, *J Stored Product Res*, **9**, 119–41

Huntley, J P, 1987 *Woodland management studies from Carlisle: Castle Street 1981*, Ancient Monuments Laboratory Rep, **119/87**, unpubl rep

Huntley, J P, 1988 Palaeoenvironmental investigations, in B Harbottle, R Fraser, and F C Burton, The Westgate Road milecastle, Newcastle upon Tyne, *Britannia*, **19**, 160-3

Huntley, J P, 1989a *Plant remains from Annetwell Street, Carlisle*, Ancient Monuments Laboratory Rep, **1/89**, unpubl rep

Huntley, J P, 1989b *Plant remains from excavations at the Lanes, Carlisle, Cumbria. Part I, CAL, OGL, OBL, LEL*, Ancient Monuments Laboratory Rep, **51/92**, unpubl rep

Huntley, J P, 1995 *Buddle Street, Wallsend: BS94, The pollen evidence*, Durham Environmental Archaeol Rep, **9/95**, unpubl rep

Huntley, J P, 1999 Environmental evidence for Hadrian's Wall, in Paul Bidwell (ed), *Hadrian's Wall 1989–1999*, Kendal, 48–64

Huntley, J P, 2000a Plant remains, in Buxton and Howard-Davis 2000, 349–58

Huntley, J P, 2000b The plant and wood remains, in McCarthy 2000, 71–81

Huntley, J P, in prep Synthesis of biological material, in Caruana in prep

Ingrem, C, nd *The fish bones recovered from Fishbourne Roman Palace, Sussex*, Univ Southampton, unpubl rep

Innes, J B, 1988 *Report on pollen analysis from Birdoswald Moss, Cumbria*, unpubl rep

Isings, K, 1957 *Roman glass from dated finds*, Groningen and Djakarta

Jackson, J (trans), 1937 *Tacitus: annals 13–16*, Harvard

Jackson, R P J, 1988 *Doctors and diseases in the Roman empire*, London

Jackson, R P J, 2002 Roman surgery: the evidence of the instruments, in R Arnott (ed), *The archaeology of medicine*, BAR Int Ser, **S1046**, Oxford, 87–95

Jacobs, J, 1913 Sigillatafunde aus einem römischen Keller zu Bregenz, *Jahrbüch für Altertumskunde*, **6**, Vienna, 172–84

James, N D G, 1982 *The forester's companion*, Oxford

James, S, 1999 The community of the soldiers: a major identity and centre of power in the Roman empire, in P Baker, C Forcey, S Jundi, and R Witcher (eds), *TRAC 98: proceedings of the eighth annual Theoretical Roman Archaeology Conference, Leicester 1998*, Oxford, 14–25

James, S, 2002 Writing the legions: the development and future of Roman military studies in Britain, *Archaeol J*, **159**, 1–59

James, S, 2004 *The excavations at Dura-Europos conducted by Yale University and the French Academy of Inscriptions and letters 1928 to 1937. Final report VII: the arms and armour and other military equipment*, London

Jarrett, M G, 1994 Non-legionary troops in Roman Britain: part one, the units, *Britannia*, **18**, 35–77

Jarrett, M G, and Edwards, B J N, 1964 The medieval pottery, in R Hogg, Excavations at Tullie House, Carlisle, 1954–56, *Trans Cumberland Westmorland Antiq Archaeol Soc*, n ser, **64**, 41–56

Jenkins, I, 1985 A group of silvered horse-trappings from Xanten, *Castra Vetera*, *Britannia*, **16**, 141–64

Jennings, S, 1992 *Medieval pottery in the Yorkshire Museum*, York

Jessop, O, 1996 A new artefact typology for the study of medieval arrowheads, *Medieval Archaeol*, **40**, 192–205

Johns, C, 1991 Romano-British jewellery, in Murdoch 1991, 28–37

Johns, C, 1996 *The jewellery of Roman Britain*, London

Johns, C, Thompson, H, and Wagstaffe, P, 1981 The Wincle, Cheshire, hoard of Roman gold jewellery, *Antiq J*, **60**, 48–58

Johnson, M, and Anderson, S, 2008 Excavation of two Romano-British pottery kilns and associated structures, Fisher Street, Carlisle, *Trans Cumberland Westmorland Antiq Archaeol Soc*, 3 ser, **8**, 19-36

Johnson, S, 1978 Excavations at Hayton Roman fort, 1975, *Britannia*, **9**, 145–51

Jones, A K G, 1988 Fish bones from excavations in the cemetery of St Mary Bishophill Junior, in T P O'Connor, *Bones from the General Accident site, Tanner Row*, Archaeol York, **15.2**, London, 61–136

Jones, G D B, 1990 The emergence of the Tyne-Solway frontier, in V A Maxfield and M J Dobson (eds), *Roman Frontier Studies, 1989*, Exeter, 98–107

Jones, W H S, 1951 *Pliny: natural history, VI, Books 20-23*, London

Jope, E M, and Hodges, H W M, 1955 The medieval pottery from Castle Street, in R Hogg, Excavations in Carlisle, 1953, *Trans Cumberland Westmorland Antiq Archaeol Soc*, n ser, **55**, 79–107

Juhász, G, 1935 *Die Sigillaten von Brigetio*, Dissertationes Pannonicae, **2/3**, Budapest

Jundi, S, and Hill, J D, 1998 Brooches and identities in first century Britain: material culture and the question of social continuity, in C Forcey, J Hawthorne, and R Witcher (eds), *Seventh Theoretical Roman Archaeology Conference, TRAC, Nottingham 1997–98*, Nottingham, 1–11

Karnitsch, P, 1959 *Die reliefsigillata von Ovilava*, Linz

Katz, N J, Katz, S V, and Kipiani, M G, 1965 *Atlas and keys of fruits and seeds occurring in Quaternary deposits of the USSR*, Moscow

Keeley, H, in prep, *Soil description profile 1*, in Caruana in prep

Kemkes, M, Scheuerbrandt, J, and Willburger, N, 2002 *Am Rande des Imperiums: der Limes. Grenze Roms zu den Barbaren*, Stuttgart

Kenward, H K, 1978 *The analysis of archaeological insect assemblages: a new approach*, Archaeol York, **19.1**, London

Kenward, H K, 1997 Synanthropic insects and the size, remoteness and longevity of archaeological occupation sites: applying concepts from biogeography to past 'islands' of human occupation, *Quat Proc*, **5**, 135–52

Kenward, H K, Engloua, C, Robertson, A, and Large, F, 1986 Rapid scanning of urban archaeological deposits for insect remains, *Circaea*, **3**, 163-72

Kenward, H K, and Hall, A R, 1995 *Biological evidence from Anglo-Scandinavian deposits at 16–22 Coppergate*, Archaeol York, **14.7**, London

Kenward, H K, and Hall, A R, 1997 Enhancing bio-archaeological interpretation using indicator groups: stable manure as a paradigm, *J Archaeol Sci*, **24**, 663–73

Kenward, H K, Hall, A R, and Jones, A K G, 1980 A tested set of techniques for the extraction of plant and animal macrofossils from waterlogged archaeological deposits, *Sci Archaeol*, **22**, 3–15

Kenward, H K, Hall, A R, and McComish, J M, 2004 Archaeological implications of plant and invertebrate remains from fills of a massive post-medieval cut at Low Fisher Gate, Doncaster, UK, *Environmental Archaeol*, **9**, 61-74

Kenward, H K, and Williams, D, 1979 *Biological evidence from the Roman warehouses in Coney Street*, Archaeol York, **14.2**, London

Keppie, L J F, and Arnold, B J, 1984 Corpus signorum Imperii Romani: *Great Britain I.4. Scotland*, Oxford

Kilbride-Jones, H E, 1938 Glass armlets in Britain, *Proc Soc Antiq Scotl*, **72**, 366–95

King, A C, 1984 Animal bones and the dietary identity of military and civilian groups in Roman Britain, Germany, and Gaul, in T F C Blagg and A C King (eds), *Military and civilian in Roman Britain*, BAR Brit Ser, **136**, Oxford, 187-217

King, A C, 1991 Food production and consumption – meat, in R F J Jones (ed), *Roman Britain, recent trends*, Sheffield, 15–20

King, A C, 2005 Animal remains from temples in Roman Britain, *Britannia*, **36**, 329–71

King, D, 1986 Petrology, dating and distribution of querns and millstones: the results of research in Bedfordshire, Buckinghamshire, Hertfordshire and Middlesex, *Univ London Instit Archaeol Bull*, **23**, 65-126

Knorr, R, 1905 *Die verzierten Terra Sigillata-Gefäße von Cannstatt und Köngen-Grinario*, Stuttgart

Knorr, R, 1907 *Die verzierten Terra-Sigillata Gefäße von Rottweil*, Stuttgart

Knorr, R, 1919 *Töpfer und Fabriken verzierter Terra-Sigillata des ersten Jahrhunderts*, Stuttgart

Knorr, R, 1952 *Terra-Sigillata-Gefäße des ersten Jahrhunderts mit Töpfernamen*, Stuttgart

Knorr, R, and Sprater, F, 1927 *Die westpfalzischen Sigillata-Töpfereien von Blickweiler und Eschweilerhof*, Speier

Latham, B, 1957 *Timber: an historical survey of its development and distribution*, London

Laubenheimer, F, 1985 *La production des amphores en Gaule Narbonaise*, Paris

Laubenheimer, F, 2003 Amphorae and vineyards from Burgundy to the Seine, *J Roman Pottery Stud*, **10**, 32-44

Lawson, A J, 1976 Shale and jet objects from Silchester, *Archaeologia*, **105**, 241–57

Leech, R, forthcoming *The excavation of three medieval and post-medieval burgage plots at 75–87 Main Street, Cockermouth, Cumbria*

Lentowicz, I, 2002 Copper alloy objects from Catterick bypass and Catterick 1972, Sites 433 and 434, in P R Wilson (ed), *Cataractonium: Roman Catterick and its hinterland: excavations and research 1958–1997; Part II*, CBA Res Rep, **128**, York, 46–78

Levine, M A, 1982 The use of crown height measurements and eruption-wear sequences to age horse teeth, in B Wilson, C Grigson, and S Payne, *Ageing and sexing animal bones from archaeological sites*, BAR Brit Ser, **109**, Oxford, 223–50

Lewis, N, and Reinhold, M, 1966 *Roman civilisation, sourcebook II: The Empire*, New York

Lightfoot, J, 1777 *Flora Scotia*, **1**, London

Ling, R, 2000 Working practice, in R Ling (ed), *Making classical art: process and practice*, Stroud, 91-107

Liversidge, J, 1955 *Furniture in Roman Britain*, London

Lloyd-Morgan, G, 2000 Other objects of copper alloy, in E Evans, *The Caerleon Canabae*, Britannia Monog, **16**, London, 344–84

Locker, A, 2000 *The role of stored fish in England 900–1750 AD: the evidence from historical and archaeological data*, Sofia

Lockwood, H, 1979 Coarse pottery [from Watercrook], in Potter 1979, 237-68

Loeschcke, S, 1919 *Lampen aus Vindonissa*, Zurich

Lucht, W H, 1987 *Die Kafer Mitteleuropas, katalog*, Krefeld

Ludowici, W, 1927 *Katalog V: Stempel namen und Bilder römischer töpfer aus meinen ausgrabungen in Rheinzabern, 1901-14*, Munich

Lyman, R L, 1994 *Vertebrate taphonomy*, Cambridge Man Archaeol, Cambridge

Lyman, R L, 1996 *Vertebrate taphonomy*, repr, Cambridge Man Archaeol, Cambridge

MacGregor, A, 1985 *Bone, antler, ivory, and horn: the technology of skeletal materials since the Roman period*, London

MacGregor, A, 2001 Antler, bone, and horn, in J Blair and N Ramsay (eds), *English medieval industries*, London, 355-78

Mackreth, D F, 1990 Brooches, in McCarthy 1990, 103–13

Macphail, R I, 1981 Soil and botanical studies of the 'dark earth', in M Jones and G W Dimbleby (eds), *The environment of man: the Iron Age to the Anglo-Saxon period*, BAR Brit Ser, **87**, Oxford, 309-31

Macphail, R I, 1994 The reworking of urban stratigraphy by human and natural processes, in A R Hall and H Kenward (eds), *Urban-rural connexions: perspectives from environmental archaeology*, Oxbow Monog, **47**, Oxford, 13-43

Macphail, R I, 2004 Soil micromorphology, in H Dalwood and R Edwards (eds), *Excavations at Deansway, Worcester, 1988-89: Romano-British small town to late medieval city*, CBA Res Rep, **139**, York, 558-67

Macphail, R I, Galinié, H, and Verhaeghe, F, 2003 A future for 'dark earth'?, *Antiquity*, **77**, 349-58

Macphail, R I, Romans, J C C, and Robertson, L, 1987 The application of micromorphology to the understanding of Holocene soil development in the British Isles: with special reference to early cultivation, in N Fedoroff, L M Bresson, and M A Courty (eds), *Micromorphologie des Sols*, Paris, 647–56

McBride, R M, and Hartley, K F, forthcoming The pottery from the Fisher Street kilns

McCarthy, M R, 1986 Woodland and Roman forts, *Britannia*, **17**, 339-43

McCarthy, M R, 1990 *A Roman, Anglian and medieval Site at Blackfriars Street*, Cumberland Westmorland Antiq Archaeol Soc, Res Ser, **4**, Kendal

McCarthy, M R, 1991 *Roman waterlogged remains at Castle Street*, Cumberland Westmorland Antiq Archaeol Soc, Res Ser, **5**, Kendal

McCarthy, M R, 1993 *Carlisle: history and guide*, Stroud

McCarthy, M R, 2000 *Roman and medieval Carlisle: the Southern Lanes*, Univ Bradford Res Rep, **1**, Bradford

McCarthy, M R, 2005 Social dynamics on the northern frontier of Roman Britain, *Oxford Archaeol J*, **24.1**, 47–71

McCarthy, M R, and Brooks, C M, 1988 *Medieval pottery in Britain AD 900–1600*, Leicester

McCarthy, M R, and Brooks, C M, 1992 The establishment of a medieval pottery sequence in Cumbria, England, in D Gaimster and M Redknap (eds), *Everyday and exotic pottery from Europe c 650–1900*, Oxford, 21–37

McCarthy, M R, and Brooks, C M, in prep The medieval pottery and tile, in Newman and Leech forthcoming

McCarthy, M R, Padley, T G, and Henig, M, 1982 Excavations and finds from The Lanes, Carlisle, *Britannia*, **13**, 79–88

McCarthy, M R, Summerson, H R T, and Annis, R G, 1990 *Carlisle Castle: a survey and documentary history*, London

McCarthy, M R, and Taylor, J, 1990 Pottery of the Anglo-Saxon to post-medieval periods, in McCarthy 1990, 301–11

McIntyre, J, and Richmond, I A, 1934 Tents of the Roman army and leather from Birdoswald, *Trans Cumberland Westmorland Antiq Archaeol Soc*, n ser, **34**, 62-90

Magie, D (trans), 1921 *Scriptores Historia Augusta*, I, Harvard

Maltby, M, 1979 *The animal bones from Exeter*, Exeter Archaeol Rep, **2**, Exeter

Maltby, M, 1981 Iron Age, Romano-British and Anglo-Saxon animal husbandry - a review of the faunal evidence, in G Dimbleby and M Jones, *The environment of man: Iron Age to the Anglo-Saxon period*, BAR Brit Ser, **87**, Oxford, 155-203

Maltby, J M, 1996 The exploitation of animals in the Iron Age: the archaeozoological evidence, in T C Champion and J R Collis (eds), *The Iron Age in Britain and Ireland: recent trends*, Sheffield, 17-27

Manning, A, Birley, R, and Tipping, R, 1997 Roman impact on the environment at Hadrian's Wall: precisely dated pollen analysis from Vindolanda, northern England, *Holocene*, **7**, 175-86

Manning, W H, 1966 A hoard of Romano-British ironwork from Brampton, Cumberland, *Trans Cumberland Westmorland Antiq Archaeol Soc*, n ser, **66**, 1-36

Manning, W H, 1976 *Catalogue of the Romano-British ironwork in the Museum of Antiquities Newcastle upon Tyne*, Newcastle upon Tyne

Manning, W H, 1985 *Catalogue of the Romano-British iron tools, fittings, and weapons in the British Museum*, London

Manning, W H, 1995 Horseshoes, in W H Manning, J Price, and J Webster, 1995 *Report on the excavations at Usk, 1965–1977: the Roman small finds*, Cardiff, 42–4

Marsh, G, 1981 London's samian supply and its relationship to the Gallic samian industry, in A C Anderson and A S Anderson (eds), *Roman pottery research in Britain and north-west Europe*, BAR Int Ser, **S123**, Oxford, 173–238

Martin-Kilcher, S, 1987 *Die Römischen amphoren aus Augst und Kaiseraugst*, Forschungen in Augst, **7**, Augst

Mason, D J P, 1990 The use of earthenware tubes in Roman vault construction: an example from Chester, *Britannia*, **21**, 215–22

Matolcsi, J, 1970 Historiche erforschung der Körpergrosse der Rinder auf Grund von Ungarischen Knochenmaterial, *Zeitschrift für Tierzüchtung und Züchtungsbiologie*, **87**, 89–128

Mattingly, H (trans), 1948 *Tacitus on Britain and Germany, a new translation of the Agricola and the Germania*, London

Mattingly, H, 1963 The Lightwood (Staffs) Hoard, *N Staffordshire J Fld Stud*, **3**, 19–36

Mattingly, H, Sydenham, E A, and Sutherland, C H V (eds), 1923-84 *The Roman Imperial Coinage*, London

May, J, 1996 *Dragonby: report on excavations at an Iron Age and Romano-British settlement in North Lincolnshire*, Oxbow Monog, **61**, Oxford

Medieval Pottery Research Group, 2001 *Minimum standards for the processing, recording, analysis and publication of post-Roman ceramics*, MPRG Occ Pap, **2**, London

Mees, A W, 1995 *Modelsignierte dekorationen auf südgallischer Terra Sigillata*, Forschungen und Berichte zur Vor- und Frühgeschichte in Baden-Württemberg, **54**, Stuttgart

Mees, A W, 2002 *Organisationsformen römischer töpfer-manufakturen am Beispiel von Arezzo und Rheinzabern, unterBerücksichtigung von Papyri, Inschriften un Rechtsquellen*, Römisch-Germanischen Zentralmuseum Forschungsinstitut für Vor- und Frühgeschichte Monogaphien, Bd **52.1–2**, Mainz

Meindl, R S, and Lovejoy, C O, 1985 Ectocranial suture closure ageing scheme, *American J Phys Anthropol*, **68**, 57–66

Mellor, M, 1994 *Medieval Ceramic Studies in England; a review for English Heritage*, London

Merrifield, R, 1987 *The archaeology of ritual and magic*, London

Mikler, H, 1997 *Die romischen funde aus bein im Landesmuseum Mainz*, Monographies Instrumentum, **1**, Montagnac

Miller, L B, and Rhodes, M, 1980 Leather, in D M Jones and M Rhodes, *Excavations at Billingsgate Buildings 'Triangle', Lower Thames Street*, London Middlesex Archaeol Soc Spec Pap, **4**, London, 95-8

Milner, N P (trans), 1993 *Vegetius: epitome of military science*, Liverpool

Monaghan, J, 1993 *Roman pottery from the fortress: 9 Blake Street*, Archaeol York, **16.7**, York

Monaghan, J, 1997 *Roman pottery from York*, Archaeol York, **16.8**, York

Moore, A, 2002 L'Hermione - recreating a c 1700 French Frigate, *Mortice and Tenon*, **14**, 6

Moore, C H, and Jackson, J (trans), 1931 *Tacitus: histories 4–5, annals 1–3*, Harvard

Moore, P D, Webb, J A, and Collinson, M E, 1991 *Pollen analysis*, 2nd edn, Oxford

Moritz, L A, 1958 *Grain-mills and flour in classical antiquity*, Oxford

Mould, Q, 1997 Leather, in T Wilmott, *Birdoswald: excavations of a Roman fort on Hadrian's Wall and its successor settlements: 1987–92*, Engl Heritage Archaeol Rep, **14**, London, 326-40

Mould, Q, 2001 *The leather from 241 Micklegate, Selby, Yorkshire, SDC97*, unpubl rep

Mould, Q, 2002a Copper alloy objects from Catterick Bridge, Site 240, in P R Wilson (ed), *Cataractonium: Roman Catterick and its hinterland: excavations and research 1958–1997; Part II*, CBA Res Rep, **128**, York, 126–31

Mould, Q, 2002b Copper alloy objects from Bainesse, Site 46, in P R Wilson (ed), *Cataractonium: Roman Catterick and its hinterland: excavations and research 1958–1997; Part II*, CBA Res Rep, **128**, York, 109–16

Mould, Q, 2004 *The leather from the defensive ditches at Rickergate, Carlisle*, unpubl rep

Mould, Q, 2005 *Leather from Greengate, Salford, Greater Manchester, GGS05*, unpubl rep

Mould, Q, 2008 The leather balls, in J Mann (ed), *Finds from the well at St Paul-in-the-Bail, Lincoln*, Archaeol Stud, **9**, Oxford, 54-9

Mould, Q, in prep The leather from Moor House London

Mould, Q, Carlisle, I, and Cameron, E, 2003 *Craft, industry and everyday life: leather and leatherworking in Anglo-Scandinavian and medieval York, the small finds*, Archaeol York, **17.16**, York

Müller, G, 1968 *Das Lagerdorf des Kastells Butzbach: die Reliefverzierte Terra Sigillata*, Limesforschungen Bd **5**, Berlin

Murdoch, T, 1991 *Treasures and trinkets: jewellery in London from pre-Roman times to the 1930s*, London

Murphy, C P, 1986 *Thin section preparation of soils and sediments*, Berkhamsted

Murphy, P, 2001 *Review of wood and macroscopic wood charcoal from archaeological sites in the West and East Midlands regions and the east of England*, Engl Heritage Centre Archaeol Rep, **23**, unpubl rep

Nash-Williams, V E, 1930 The samian potters' stamps found at Caerwent (*Venta Silurum*) in Monmouthshire, *Bull Board Celtic Stud*, **5**, 166-85

Nash-Williams, V E, 1931 The Roman legionary fortress at Caerleon in Monmouthshire: report on the excavations carried out in the Prysg Field, 1927–29, I, *Archaeol Cambrensis*, **86**, 99–157

Newman, C, 2006 The medieval period resource assessment, in M Brennand (ed), *The archaeology of North West England: an archaeological research framework for the North West region, Volume 1: resource assessment*, Archaeol North West **8**, Manchester, 115-44

Newman, R M, and Leech, R, forthcoming *Excavations at the early Christian site at Dacre*

Nieto, J, and Puig, A M, 2001 *Excavacions arqueològiques subaquàtiques a Cala Culip, 3. Culip IV: la terra sigillata decorada*, Monorgafies del Centre d' Arqueològia Subaquàtica de Catalunya, **3**, Girona

Nixon, C E V, and Saylor Rodgers, B (trans), 1994 *In praise of later Roman emperors: the* Panegyrici Latini: *introduction, translation, and historical commentary with the Latin text of R A B Mynors*, London

North, J J, 1959 *English hammered coinage*, **2**, London

Norton, A, forthcoming Excavations at 90–93 Broad Street, Reading, *Berkshire Archaeol J*

OA North 2002a *Rickergate, Carlisle, post-excavation assessment report*, unpubl rep

OA North, 2002b *Carlisle Millennium Project, post-excavation assessment report*, unpubl rep

OA North, 2005a *Ceramics Courtyard, Cumbria Institute of the Arts, Carlisle: archaeological excavation assessment report*, unpubl rep

OA North, 2005b *East bog, Northumberland: archaeological evaluation and palaeoenvironmental assessment report*, unpubl rep

OA North, 2006 *Grand Arcade, Millgate, Wigan, Greater Manchester: post-excavation assessment*, unpubl rep

Oakley, G E, and Harman, M, 1979 The worked bone, in J H Williams, *St Peter's Street, Northampton: excavations 1973–1976*, Northampton, 308–18

Oakley, G E, and Hunter, J, 1979 The glass, in J H Williams, *St Peter's Street, Northampton: excavations 1973–1976*, Northampton, 296-302

O'Connor, T P, 2003 *The analysis of urban animal bone assemblages: a hand book for archaeologists*, Archaeol York, **19.2**, York

Oddy, W A, and Bimson, M, 1985 Tinned bronze in antiquity, in G Miles and S Pollard, *Lead and tin: studies in conservation and technology*, UKIC Occ Pap, **3**, London, 33-9

Ogilvie, R M, and Richmond, I A, 1967 *Cornelii Taciti de vita Agricolae*, Oxford

Oldenstein, J, 1977 Zur ausrüstung römischer auxiliareinheiten, *Bericht der Römisch-Germanischen Kommission*, **57**, Mainz am Rhein, 49-284

Oldroyd, H, 1964 *The natural history of the flies*, London

Olivier, A C H, 2000 Brooches, in Buxton and Howard-Davis 2000, 234–41

Ollendorf, A L, Mulholland, S C, and Rapp Jnr, G, 1988 Phytolith analysis as a means of plant identification: *Arundo donax* and *Phragmites communis*, *Annals Botany*, **61**, 209–14

Orton, C, 1989 An introduction to the quantification of assemblages of pottery, *J Roman Pottery Stud*, **2**, 94–7

Orton, C, Tyers, P, and Vince, A, 1993 *Pottery in archaeology*, Cambridge

Osborne, P J, 1983 An insect fauna from a modern cesspit and its comparison with probable cesspit assemblages from archaeological sites, *J Archaeol Sci*, **10**, 453–63

Oswald, A, 1975 *Clay pipes for the archaeologist*, BAR Brit Ser, **14**, Oxford

Oswald, F, 1936 *Index of figure types on* terra sigillata, *'samian ware'*, suppl Annals Archaeol Anthropol Univ Liverpool, Liverpool

Padley, T G, 1990 The wooden objects, in McCarthy 1990, 156–8

Padley, T G, 1991a The bone objects, in Padley and Winterbottom 1991, 190–202

Padley, T G, 1991b *The metalwork, glass and stone objects from Castle Street, Carlisle: excavations 1981–2*, Fasc 2, Cumberland Westmorland Antiq Archaeol Soc Res Ser, **5**, Kendal

Padley, T G, 1991c The wooden objects, in Padley and Winterbottom 1991, 203–27

Padley, T G, 1991d The Roman shoes, in Padley and Winterbottom 1991, 228–43

Padley, T G, 2000a The other Roman material, in McCarthy 2000, 95–118

Padley, T G, 2000b The medieval material, in McCarthy 2000, 118–21

Padley, T G, in prep a The shoes, in J Zant and C Howard-Davis (eds), *Roman and medieval Carlisle: the northern Lanes, excavations 1978-82, Volume 1, the Roman period*

Padley, T G, in prep b The Roman shoes, in Caruana in prep

Padley, T G, in prep c Medieval leather, Caruana in prep

Padley, T G, and Winterbottom, S, 1991 *The wooden, leather and bone objects from Castle Street, Carlisle: excavations 1981–2*, Fasc 3, Cumberland Westmorland Antiq Archaeol Soc Res Ser, **5**, Kendal

Parker, A J, 2002 Trade within the Empire and beyond its frontiers, in J Wacher (ed), *The Roman world*, London, 635–57

Parkhouse, J, 1997 Objects of stone, in A G Marvell and H S Owen-John, Leucarum: *Excavations at the Roman auxilliary fort at Loughor, West Glamorgan, 1982-84 and 1987-88*, Britannia Monog, **12**, London, 411-26

Peacock, D P S, 1977 Ceramics and Roman and medieval archaeology, in D P S Peacock (ed), *Pottery and early commerce: characterisation and trade in Roman and later ceramics*, London, 21–34

Peacock, D P S, 1987 Iron Age and Roman quern production at Lodsworth, West Sussex, *Antiq J*, **67**, 61–87

Peacock, D P S, and Williams, D F, 1986 *Amphorae and the Roman economy: an introductory guide*, London

Pearsall, W H, and Pennington, W, 1973 *The Lake District: a landscape history*, London

Pearson, G W, 1987 How to cope with calibration, *Antiquity*, **61**, 98-103

Peers, C R, and Radford, C A R, 1943 The Saxon monastery of Whitby, *Archaeologia*, 2 ser, **89**, 27–88

Peglar, S M, 1993 The mid Holocene *Ulmus* decline at Diss Mere, Norfolk, UK: a year-by-year pollen stratigraphy from annual laminations, *Holocene*, **3.1**, 1–13

Pélichet, P E, 1946 A propos des amphores romaines trouvées a Nyon, *Zeit Schweiz Archaeol und Kunstgesch*, **8**, 189-209

Perrin, J R, 1990 *Roman pottery from the Colonia 2: General Accident and Rougier Street*, Archaeol York, **16.4**, York

Perrin, J R, 1995 Roman coarse pottery, in D Phillips and B Heywood, *Excavations at York Minster 1: from Roman fortress to Norman cathedral*, Roy Comm Hist Monuments Engl, London, 324–45

Perrin, J R, 1999 Roman pottery from excavations at and near the Roman small town of *Durobrivae*, Water Newton, Cambridgeshire, 1956–58, *J Roman Pottery Stud*, **8**, 1–141

Peterken, G, 1981 *Woodland conservation and management*, London

Philips, J T, 1950 A survey of the distribution of some querns of Hunsbury or allied types: Appendix 3, in K Kenyon, Excavations at Breedon-on-the-Hill, *Trans Leicestershire Archaeol Hist Soc*, **26**, 75–82

Phillips, E J, 1977 Corpus signorum Imperii Romani: *Great Britain. Hadrian's Wall east of the North Tyne*, **1**, Fasc 1, Oxford

Pirie, E J E, 1996 *Coins of the Kingdom of Northumbria, c 700–867, in the Yorkshire collections, the Yorkshire Museum, York, the University of Leeds, the City Museum, Leeds*, Llanfyllin

Polak, M, 2000 *South Gaulish* Terra Sigillata *with potters' stamps from Vechten*, Rei Cretariae Romanae Fautorum Acta Supplementum, **9**, Nijmegen

Potter, T W, 1979 *Romans in North-West England*, Cumberland Westmorland Antiq Archaeol Soc, Res Ser, **1**, Kendal

Poulter, A G, 1988 Certain doubts and doubtful conclusions: the *lorica segmentata* from Newstead and the Antonine garrison, in J C N Coulston (ed), *Military equipment and the identity of Roman soldiers: proceedings of the Fourth Roman Military Equipment Conference*, BAR Int Ser, **S394**, Oxford, 31–49

Powers-Jones, A, 1994 The use of phytolith analysis in the interpretation of archaeological deposits: an outer Hebridean example, in R Luff and P R Conwy (eds), *Whither environmental archaeology?* Oxford, 41–50

Price, J, 1990a Roman vessel and window glass, in McCarthy 1990, 163–79

Price, J, 1990b The glass, in S Wrathmell and A Nicholson, *Dalton Parlours: Iron Age settlement and Roman villa*, Yorkshire Archaeol, **3**, Wakefield, 99–105

Price, J, 1995a Glass beads, in W H Manning, J Price, and J Webster, *Report on the excavations at Usk, 1965–1977: the Roman small finds*, Cardiff, 105–12

Price, J, 1995b Glass bangles, in W H Manning, J Price, and J Webster, *Report on the excavations at Usk, 1965–1977: the Roman small finds*, Cardiff, 100–4

Price, J, and Cottam, S, 1998 *Romano-British glass vessels: a handbook*, CBA Practical Handbooks in Archaeology, **14**, York

Price, J, and Cottam, S, 2000 Glass, in Buxton and Howard-Davis 2000, 279–93

Price, J, and Cottam, S, in prep The Roman glass, in T G Padley, *Roman and medieval Carlisle: the Southern Lanes, Fasc 2, the Roman and medieval finds*

Pritchard, F, 1991 Girdles, in Egan and Pritchard 1991, 35-49

Prummel, W, and Frisch, H J, 1986 A guide for the distinction of species, sex and body size in bones of sheep and goat, *J Archaeol Sci*, **13**, 567–77

Pryce, T D, 1928 The decorated samian, in J P Bushe-Fox, *Second report on the excavations of the Roman fort at Richborough, Kent*, Rep Res Comm Soc Antiq London, **7**, Oxford, 160–83

Pryce, T D, 1932 The decorated samian, in J P Bushe-Fox, *Third report on the excavations of the Roman fort at Richborough, Kent*, Rep Res Comm Soc Antiq London, **10**, Oxford, 94–123

Pugsley, P, 2003 *Roman domestic wood: analysis of the morphology, manufacture and use of selected categories of domestic wooden artefacts with particular reference to the material from Roman Britain*, BAR Int Ser, **S1118**, Oxford

Rackham, B, 1947 *Medieval English pottery*, London

Rackham, H (trans), 1952 *Pliny, Natural History IX, Books 33–5*, Harvard

Rackham, J, Stallibrass, S M, and Allison, E P, 1991 The animal and bird bones, in M R McCarthy (ed), *The structural sequence and environmental remains from Castle Street, Carlisle. Excavations 1981–2*, Fasc 1, Cumberland Westmorland Archaeol Antiq Soc Res Ser, **5**, Kendal, 73–88

Rajtár, J, 1994 Waffen und Ausrüstungstele aus dem Holz-Erde-Lager von Iža, *J Roman Military Equip Stud*, **5**, 83–95

Raybould, M E, 1999 *A study of inscribed material from Roman Britain: an inquiry into some aspects of literacy in Romano-British society*, BAR Brit Ser, **281**, Oxford

Reece, R, 1987 *Coinage in Roman Britain*, London

Reece, R, 1988 Numerical aspects of Roman coin hoards in Britain, in P J Casey and R Reece (eds), *Coins and the Archaeologist*, London, 86-101

Reimer, P J, Baillie, M G L, Bard, E, Bayliss, A, Beck, J W, Bertrand, C J H, Blackwell, P G, Buck, C E, Burr, G S, Cutler, K B, Damon, P E, Edwards, R L, Fairbanks, R G, Friedrich, M, Guilderson, T P, Hogg, A G, Hughen, K A, Kromer, B, McCormac, G, Manning, S, Ramsey, C B, Reimer, R W, Remmele, S, Southon, J R, Stuiver, M, Talamo, S, Taylor, F W, van der Plicht, J, Weyhenmeyer, C E, 2004 IntCal04 Terrestrial radiocarbon age calibration, 0-26 cal kyr BP, *Radiocarbon*, **46** (3), 1029-59

Remesal Rodíguez, J, 1997 *Heeresversorgung und die wirtschaftlichen zwischen Bezeihungen der Baetica und Germanian*, Materialen zur Archäologie in Baden-Württemberg, **42**, Stuttgart

Reynolds, P, 2005 Levantine amphorae from Cilicia to Gaza: a typology and analysis of regional production trends from the first to the fifth centuries, in J Ma Gurt i Esparraguera, J Buxeda i Garrigós, and M A Cau Ontiveros (eds), *LRCW I: Late Roman coarse wares, cooking wares and amphorae in the Mediterranean: archaeology and archaeometry*, BAR Int Ser, **S1340**, Oxford, 563–611

Rhodes, M, 1987 Inscriptions on leather waste from Roman London, *Britannia*, **18**, 173–81

Richardson, B, and Tyers, P A, 1984 North Gaulish pottery in Britain, *Britannia*, **15**, 133-41

Richardson, G G S, 1973 The Roman tilery, Scalesceugh, 1970-1971, *Trans Cumberland Westmorland Antiq Archaeol Soc*, n ser, **73**, 79–89

Richmond, I, 1982 *Trajan's army on Trajan's Column*, London

Richmond, I A, and Gillam, J P, 1952 Milecastle 79 (Solway), *Trans Cumberland Westmorland Antiq Archaeol Soc*, n ser, **52**, 17-40

Ricken, H, 1934 Die Bilderschüsseln der Kastelle Saalburg und Zugmantel, *Saalburg Jahrbüch*, **8**, 130–82

Ricken, H, 1948 *Die Bilderschüsseln der römischen töpfer von Rheinzabern, Tafelband*, Speyer

Ricken, H, and Fischer, C, 1963 *Die Bilderschüsseln der römischen töpfer von Rheinzabern, Textband*, Bonn

Rigby, V, and Stead, I M, 1976 The coarse pottery, in I M Stead, *Excavations at Winterton Roman villa and other Roman sites in North Lincolnshire, 1958–1967*, Dept Environ Archaeol Rep, **9**, London, 136-90

Ritterling, E, 1912/13 *Das fruhromische lager bei Hofheim im Tausus, annalen des Vereins fur Nassauishe Alterumskunde und Geschichtforschung*, Wiesbaden

Roberts, C, and Manchester, K, 1995 *The archaeology of disease*, Stroud

Robertson, A S, 1975 *Birrens (Blatobulgium)*, Edinburgh

Robertson, A, Scott, M, and Keppie, L, 1975 *Bar Hill: A Roman Fort and its finds*, BAR Brit Ser, **16**, Oxford

Robinson, H R, 1975 *The armour of Imperial Rome*, London

Rockwell, P, 1999 http://www.stoa.org/trajan/buildtrajanpage.cgi?126

Rodwell, W, 1978 Stamp-decorated pottery of the early Roman period in Eastern England, in P Arthur and G Marsh, *Early fine wares in Roman Britain*, BAR Brit Ser, **57**, Oxford, 225–92

Rogers, G B, 1974 *Poteries sigillées de la Gaule centrale, I: les motifs non figurés*, Gallia suppl, **28**, Paris

Rogers, G B, 1999 *Poteries sigillées de la Gaule centrale, II: les potiers, I*, Lezoux

Rogers, N S H, 1993 *Anglian and other finds from Fishergate*, Archaeol York: the Small Finds, **17.9**, London

Rogerson, A, 1977 Excavations at Scole, 1973, *E Anglian Archaeol*, **5**, Gressenhall, 97–224

Romeuf, A-M, 2001 *Le quartier artisanale gallo-romain des Martres-de-Veyre, Puy-de-Dôme*, Les Cahiers du Centre Archéologique de Lezoux, Lezoux

Rosen, A M, 1992 Preliminary identification of silica skeletons from Near Eastern archaeological sites: an anatomical approach, in S Mulholland and G Rapp Jr, *Phytolith systematics: emerging issues*, New York, 113–23

Rosen, A M, 2001 Phytolith analysis in Near Eastern archaeology, in S Pike and S Gitin, *The practical impact of science on Near Eastern and Aegean archaeology*, Wiener Laboratory Monog, **3**, London, 9–15

Salmond, K F, 1956 The insect and mite fauna of a Scottish flour mill, *Bull Entomol Res*, **47**, 621–30

Saunders, R L, 1998 *The use of old red sandstone in Roman Britain: a petrographical and archaeological study*, unpubl PhD thesis, Univ Reading

Schalles, H-J, and Schreiter, C, 1993 *Geschichte aus dem Kies. Neue funde aus dem Alten Rhein bei Xanten*, Xantener Berichte, **3**, Köln

Schweingruber, F H, 1990a *Microscopic wood anatomy*, 3rd edn, Birmensdorf

Schweingruber, F H, 1990b *Anatomy of European woods*, Bern

Seeley, F, and Drummond-Murray, J, 2005 *Roman pottery production in the Walbrook Valley: excavations at 20–28 Moorgate, City of London, 1998–2000*, Mus London Monog, **25**, London

Serjeantson, D, 1996 The animal bones, in E S Needham and T Spence (eds), *Refuse and disposal at area 16, East Runnymede: Runnymede Bridge Research Excavations*, **2**, London, 194-223

Serjeantson, D, 2000 The bird bones, in M Fulford and J Timby, *Late Iron Age and Roman Silchester*, Britannia Monog, **15**, London, 484–500

Shaffrey, R, 2003 The rotary querns from the Society of Antiquaries' excavations at Silchester, 1890–1909, *Britannia*, **34**, 143–74

Shelton, K, 1981 *The Esquiline treasure*, London

Shotter, D C A, 1978 Unpublished Roman hoards in the Wisbech and Fenland Museum, *Coin Hoards*, **4**, 47–50

Shotter, D C A, 1979 Roman coin hoards from Cumbria, *Trans Cumberland Westmorland Antiq Archaeol Soc*, n ser, **79**, 5–17

Shotter, D C A, 1990a *Roman coins from North-West England*, Lancaster

Shotter, D C A, 1990b The coins, in McCarthy 1990, 98–104

Shotter, D C A, 1993 Coin-loss and the Roman occupation of North-West England, *Brit Numis J*, **63**, 1–19

Shotter, D C A, 1994 Rome and the Brigantes: early hostilities, *Trans Cumberland Westmorland Antiq Archaeol Soc*, n ser, **94**, 21–34

Shotter, D C A, 1995 *Roman coins from North-West England: first supplement*, Lancaster

Shotter, D C A, 2000a Petillius Cerialis in northern Britain, *Northern Hist*, **36**, 189–98

Shotter, D C A, 2000b *Roman coins from North-West England: second supplement*, Lancaster

Shotter, D C A, 2001 Petillius Cerialis in Carlisle: a numismatic contribution, *Trans Cumberland Westmorland Antiq Archaeol Soc*, 3 ser, **1**, 21–9

Shotter, D C A, 2003 The murder of Flavius Romanus at Ambleside: a possible context, *Trans Cumberland Westmorland Antiq Archaeol Soc*, 3 ser, **3**, 228–31

Shotter, D C A, 2004a Vespasian, *Auctoritas* and Britain, *Britannia*, **35**, 1–8

Shotter, D C A, 2004b *Romans and Britons in north-west England*, rev edn, Lancaster

Shotter, D C A, in prep Roman coins, in Caruana in prep

Shotter, D C A, and White, A J, 1990 *The Roman fort and town of Lancaster*, Lancaster

Silver, I A, 1969 The ageing of domestic animals, in D Brothwell and E S Higgs, *Science in Archaeology*, London, 283–302

Sim, D, 1995 Weapons and mass production, *J Roman Military Equip Stud*, **6**, 1–4

Sim, D, 2000 The making and testing of a *falx* also known as the Dacian battle scythe, *J Roman Military Equip Stud*, **11**, 37–41

Simpson, F G, and Richmond, I A, 1935 Randylands Milecastle, *Trans Cumberland Westmorland Antiq Archaeol Soc*, n ser, **35**, 236-8

Simpson, G, and Rogers, G, 1969 Cinnamus de Lezoux et quelques potiers contemporains, *Gallia*, **27**, 3–14

Simpson, M G, 1974 Haltwhistle burn, *Corstopitum* and the Antonine Wall: a reconsideration, *Britannia*, **5**, 317–39

Skidmore, P, 1999 The Diptera, in A Connor and R Buckley, *Roman and medieval occupation in Causeway Lane, Leicester*, Leicester Archaeol Monog, **5**, Leicester, 341-3

Smith, D J, 1968a Housesteads, *Archaeol Aeliana*, 4 ser, **46**, 284–91

Smith, D J, 1968b Two unpublished rakes of deerhorn, *Archaeol Aeliana*, 4 ser, **46**, 281–4

Smith, D N, 1997 *The insect remains from Mancetter Mill Lane, Roman well*, unpubl rep

Smith, D N 1998 Beyond the barn beetles: difficulties in using some Coleoptera as indicators for stored fodder, *Environment Archaeol*, **1**, 63–70

Smith, D N, 2000 *The insect remains from One, Poultry, London*, Univ Birmingham Environment Archaeol Serv Rep, **13**, unpubl rep

Smith, D N, 2004 The insect remains from the well, in M C Bishop, *Inveresk Gate: excavations in the Roman civil settlement at Inveresk, East Lothian, 1996-2000*, Scottish Trust Archaeol Res Monog, **7**, Loanhead, 81-8

Smith, D N, 2009 *Insects in the city: and archaeo-entomological perspective on London's past*, Lampeter

Smith, D N, and Chandler, G, 2004 Insect remains, in B Sloane and G Malcolm (eds), *Excavations at the Priory of the Order of the Hospital of St John of Jerusalem, Clerkenwell, London*, Mus London Archaeol Serv Monog, **20**, London, 389-94

Smith, K G V, 1973 *Insects and other arthropods of medical importance*, London

Smith, K G V, 1989 *An introduction to the immature stages of British flies*, Handbooks for the identification of British insects, **10.14**, London

Smith, W, 2001 *A review of archaeological wood analyses in Southern England*, Engl Heritage Centre Archaeol Rep, **00/01**, unpubl rep

Snape, M, 1993 *Roman brooches from Northern Britain*, BAR Brit Ser, **235**, Oxford

Solomon, M E, and Adamson, B E, 1955 The powers of survival of storage and domestic pests under winter conditions in Britain, *Bull Entomol Res*, **46**, 311–55

Speed, P (ed), 1997 *Those who worked: an anthology of medieval sources*, New York

Stace, C, 1997 *The new flora of the British Isles*, 2nd edn, Cambridge

Stallibrass, S M, 1991 *Animal bones from excavations at Annetwell Street, Carlisle, 1982-4, Period 3: the early timber fort*, Ancient Monuments Laboratory Rep, **132/91**, London

Stallibrass, S M, 1995 Review of the vertebrate remains, in JP Huntley and S Stallibrass, *Plant and vertebrate remains from archaeological sites in northern England: data reviews and future directions*, Architect Archaeol Soc Durham Northumberland Res Rep, **4**, Durham, 84-194

Stallibrass, S M, 2000a Animal bone, in Buxton and Howard-Davis 2000, 375–84

Stallibrass, S M, 2000b Cattle, culture, status, and soldiers in Northern England, in S Clarke and G Fincham (eds), *TRAC 1999: Proceedings of the Ninth Annual Theoretical Roman Archaeology Conference: Durham 1999*, Oxford, 64–73

Stallibrass, S M, 2004 Environmental evidence, in JH Williams and C Howard-Davis, Excavations on a Bronze Age cairn at Hardendale Nab, Shap, Cumbria, *Archaeol J*, **161**, 36-42

Stallibrass, S M, in prep a the animal bones, in C Howard-Davis, I Miller, N Hair, and R M Newman, in prep, *Excavations at Mitchells Brewery and 39 Church Street, Lancaster*, Lancaster Imprints

Stallibrass, S M, in prep b the animal bones, in M R McCarthy, in prep *Roman and medieval Carlisle: the Southern Lanes, excavations 1981-2*, Fasc 1, the stratigraphic sequence, absolute dating and the environmental remains

Stanfield, J A, 1935 A samian bowl from Bewcastle, *Trans Cumberland Westmorland Antiq Archaeol Soc*, n ser, **35**, 182–205

Stanfield, J A, 1936 Unusual forms of *Terra Sigillata*: second series, *Archaeol J*, **93**, 101–16

Stanfield, J A, and Simpson, G, 1958 *Central Gaulish potters*, London

Stevenson, R B K, 1950 Antler Rakes, *Antiq J*, **30**, 195

Stockmarr, J, 1971 Tablets with spores used in absolute pollen analysis, *Pollen et Spores*, **13**, 615–21

Stokes, P, and Rowley-Conwy, P, 2002 Iron Age cultigen?: experimental return rates for fat hen (*Chenopodium album* L), *Environmental Archaeol*, **7**, 95-9

Strong, D, 1966 *Catalogue of the carved amber in the Department of Greek and Roman Antiquities*, London

Summerfield, J, 1997 The small finds, in T Wilmott, *Birdoswald: excavations of a Roman fort on Hadrian's Wall and its successor settlements: 1987–92*, Engl Heritage Archaeol Rep, **14**, London, 269–320

Summerson, H R T, 1990 The history of Carlisle Castle from 1092 to 1962, in McCarthy *et al* 1990, 118-264

Swan, V G, 1979 Colour-coated wares (post Flavian), in Bidwell 1979, 189

Swan, V G, 1984 *The pottery kilns of Roman Britain*, Roy Comm Hist Monuments Engl, Suppl Ser, **5**, London

Swan, V G, 1992 *Legio VI* and its men: African legionaries in Britain, *J Roman Pottery Stud*, **5**, 1–33

Swan, V G, 1997 Vexillations and the garrisons of *Britannia* in the second and early third centuries: a ceramic view-point, in W Groenman-van Waateringe, B L van Beek, W J H Willems, and S L Wynia (eds), *Roman Frontier Studies 1995, Proceedings of the XVIth International Congress of Roman Frontier Studies*, Oxbow Monog, **91**, Oxford, 289–94

Swan, V G, 1999 The Twentieth Legion and the history of the Antonine Wall reconsidered, *Proc Soc Antiq Scotl*, **129**, 399–480

Swan, V G, 2002 The Roman pottery of Yorkshire in its wider historical context, in P Wilson and J Price (eds), *Aspects of Industry in Roman Yorkshire and the North*, Oxford, 35–79

Swan, V G, 2004 The historical significance of 'Legionary wares' in Britain, in F Vermeulen, K Sas, and W. Dhaeze (eds), *Archaeology in confrontation: aspects of Roman military presence in the Northwest: studies in honour of Prof Em Hugo Thoen*, Archaeol Rep Ghent Univ, **2**, Ghent, 259–85

Swan, V G, 2008 Builders, suppliers and supplies in the Tyne-Solway region and beyond, in P Bidwell (ed), *Understanding Hadrian's Wall*, South Shields, 49-82

Swan V G, 2009 *Ethnicity, conquest and recruitment: two case studies from the Northern military provinces*, J Roman Archaeol Suppl Ser, **72**, Portsmouth, RI

Swan, V G, and Bidwell, P T, 1998 Camelon and Flavian troop-movements in southern Britain: some ceramic evidence, in J Bird (ed), *Form and fabric, studies in Rome's material past in honour of B R Hartley*, Oxbow Monog, **80**, Oxford, 21–30

Swan, V G, and McBride, R M, 2002 A Rhineland potter at the legionary fortress of York, in M Aldhouse-Green and P Webster, *Artefacts and archaeology: aspects of the Celtic and Roman world*, Cardiff, 190–234

Swan, V G, and McBride, R M forthcoming The pottery from the Roman legionary kiln dumps excavated in 1995 at Peaseholm Green, York, in P Ware (ed), *Report on the 1995 excavations at Layerthorpe Bridge, York*

Swan, V G, and Philpott, R A, 2000 *Legio XX VV* and tile production at Tarbock, Merseyside, *Britannia*, **31**, 55-67

Swift, E, 2000 *Regionality in dress accessories in the late Roman west*, Monographies Instrumentum, **11**, Montagnac

Swift, E, 2003 *Roman dress accessories*, Princes Risborough

Switzur, V R, 1986 884BP and all that!, *Antiquity*, **61**, 241-61

Sykes, N J, 2007 Taking sides: the social life of venison in medieval England, in A Pluskowski, *Breaking and shaping beastly bodies: animals as material culture in the Middle Ages*, Oxford, 151-60

Sykes, N J, White, J, Hayes, T E, and Palmer, M R, 2006 Tracking animals using strontium isotopes in teeth: the role of fallow deer (*Dama sama*) in Roman Britain, *Antiquity*, **80/130**, 948-59

Tannahill, R, 1988 *Food in history*, rev edn, London

Taylor, J, 1990 The pottery, in McCarthy 1990, 197–311

Taylor, J, 1991 *The Roman pottery from Castle Street Carlisle: excavations in 1981-2*, Cumberland Westmorland Antiq Archaeol Soc Res Ser, **5**, Fasc 4, Kendal

Teichert, M, 1975 Osteometrische untersuchungen zur berechnung der widerristhöhe bei schafen, in A T Clason, *Archaeological Studies*, Amsterdam, 51-69

Terrisse, J-R, 1968 *Les céramiques sigillées gallo-romains des Martres-de-Veyre, Puy-de-Dôme*, Gallia Suppl, **19**, Paris

Thomas, M D, 2003 Lorica Segmentata, *Volume II: a catalogue of finds*, J Roman Military Equip Stud Monog, **2**, Chirnside

Thompson, F H, 1976 The excavation of the Roman amphitheatre at Chester, *Archaeologia*, **105**, 127–239

Tomber, R, and Dore, J, 1998 *The national Roman fabric reference collection: a handbook*, Mus London Archaeol Serv, London

Tomlin, R S O, 1988 Tabellae Sulis: *Roman inscribed tablets of tin and lead from the sacred spring at Bath*, Oxford

Tomlin, R S O, 1992 The Twentieth Legion at Wroxeter and Carlisle in the first century: the epigraphic evidence, *Britannia*, **23**, 141–58

Tomlin, R S O, 1998 Roman manuscripts from Carlisle: the ink-written tablets, *Britannia*, **29**, 31–84

Tomlin, R S O, 2002a Graffiti, in P R Wilson (ed), *Cataractonium: Roman Catterick and its hinterland: excavations and research, 1958–1997. Part I*, CBA Res Rep, **128**, York, 504–17

Tomlin, R S O, 2002b Carlisle, in R S O Tomlin and M W C Hassall, Roman Britain in 2000: II. Inscriptions, *Britannia*, **33**, 360-3

Tomlin, R S O, and Hassall, M W C, 2000 Roman Britain in 1999: II. Inscriptions, *Britannia*, **31**, 433–49

Tomlin, R S O, and Hassall, M W C, 2001 Roman Britain in 2000: II. Inscriptions, *Britannia*, **32**, 387–400

Toynbee, J, 1973 *Animals in Roman life and art*, London

Trow-Smith, R, 1967 *Life from the land: the growth of farming in Western Europe*, London

Tuohy, C, 1992 Long-handled 'weaving combs' in the Netherlands, *Proc Prehist Soc*, **58**, 385–7

Turner, R C, 1979 Identification of the game, in Potter 1979, 76–9

Twiss, P C, 1992 Predicted world distribution of C_3 and C_4 grass phytoliths, in S Mulholland and G Rapp Jr, *Phytolith systematics: emerging issues*, New York, 113–28

Tyers, I, 2004 *Dendro for Windows program guide*, 3rd edn, ARCUS Rep, **500b**, unpubl rep

Tyers, P, 1993 The plain samian ware, in W H Manning, *Report on the excavations at Usk 1965–1976: the Roman pottery*, Cardiff, 125–60

Tyers, P, 1996 *Roman pottery in Britain*, London

Ulbert, G, 1959 *Die römischen Donau-Kastelle Aislingen und Burghöfe*, Limesforschungen, **1**, Berlin van der Veen, M, 1992 *Crop husbandry regimes: an archaeobotanical study of farming in Northern England 1000 BC – AD 500*, Sheffield Archaeol Monog, **3**, Sheffield

van der Veen, M, 1998 A life of luxury in the desert? The food and fodder supply to *Mons Claudianus*, *J Roman Archaeol*, **11**, 101–16

van Driel-Murray, C, 1985 The production and supply of military leatherwork in the first and second centuries AD: a review of the archaeological evidence, in M C Bishop (ed), *The production and distribution of Roman military equipment*, BAR Int Ser, **S275**, Oxford, 43–81

van Driel-Murray, C, 1986 Shoes in perspective, in C Unz (ed), *Studien zu den Militärgrenzen Roms, 111, Vorträge des 13: Internationalen Limeskongresses, Aalen 1983*, Stuttgart, 139-45

van Driel-Murray, C, 1987 Roman footwear: a mirror of fashion and society, in D E Friendship-Taylor, J M Swann, and S Thomas (eds), *Recent research in archaeological footwear*, Ass Archaeol Illus Surv Tech Pap, **8**, 32–42, Northampton

van Driel-Murray, C, 1988 A fragmentary shield cover from Caerleon, in J Coulston (ed), *Military equipment and the identity of Roman soldiers*, BAR Int Ser, **S394**, Oxford, 51-66

van Driel-Murray, C, 1989 The Vindolanda chamfrons and miscellaneous items of leather horse gear, in C van Driel-Murray, *Roman military equipment: the sources of the evidence*, BAR Int Ser, **S476**, Oxford, 281-318

van Driel-Murray, C, 1990 New light on old tents: the evidence from Vindolanda, *J Roman Military Equip Stud*, **1**, 109-37

van Driel-Murray, C, 1993 The leatherwork, in C van Driel-Murray, P Wild, M Seaward, and J Hillam, *Vindolanda Volume III: the early wooden forts, preliminary reports on the leather, textiles, environmental evidence, and dendrochronology*, Vindolanda Res Rep, n ser, **3**, Bardon Mill, 1–73

van Driel-Murray, C, 1994 A question of gender in a military context, *Helinium*, **34.2**, 342–62

van Driel-Murray, C, 1995 Gender in question, in P Rush (ed), *Theoretical Roman Archaeology: Second Conference Proceedings*, Aldershot, 3–21

van Driel-Murray, C, 1998 The leatherwork from the fort, in Cool and Philo 1998, 285–334

van Driel-Murray, C, 2001a Footwear in the north-western provinces of the Roman Empire, in Goubitz et al 2001, 337–76

van Driel-Murray, C, 2001b Vindolanda and the dating of Roman footwear, *Britannia*, **32**, 185–97

van Driel-Murray, C, 2002 The leather trades, in P Wilson and J Price, *Roman Yorkshire and beyond: aspects of industry in Roman Yorkshire and the North*, Oxford, 109–23

van Driel-Murray, C, Connolly, P, and Duckham, J, 2004 Roman saddles: archaeology and experiment, 20 years on, in L Gilmour (ed), *In the saddle: an exploration of the saddle through history*, London, 1-20

van Driel-Murray, C, and Gechter, M, 1983 Funde aus der fabrica der Legio I Minervia am Bonner Berg, *Rheinische Ausgrabungen* **23**: *Beitrage zur Archaologie des Romischen Rheinlands*, **4**, 1-83

Vanvinckenroye, W, 1968 Naamstempels op *terra sigillata* te Heerlen, *Société Historique et Archéologique dans le Limbourg*, **103–4**, 1-33

Vaughan, L C, 1960 Osteoarthritis in cattle, *The Veterinary Record*, **72/N72**, 534-8

Vialles, N, 1994 *Animal to edible*, Cambridge

Vipard, P, 1995 Les amphores carottes, forme Schöne-Mau XV État de la question, *Société Français d'Étude de la Céramique Antique en Gaule, Actes du Congrès de Rouen, 25–28 Mai 1995*, **1**, Marseille, 51–77

von den Driesch, A, 1976 *A guide to the measurement of animal bones from archaeological sites*, Cambridge, Mass

von Groller, M, 1901 Römische waffen, *Der Römische limes in Österreich*, **2**, 85–132

Wacher, J S, 1969 *Excavations at Brough-on-Humber 1958–1961*, Rep Res Comm Soc Antiq London, **25**, Leeds

Walker, S, and Bierbrier M, 1997 *Ancient faces: mummy portraits from Roman Egypt*, London

Walters, H, 1908 *Catalogue of the Roman pottery in the Departments of Antiquities, British Museum*, London

Ward, M, 1989 The samian ware, in K Blockley, *Prestatyn 1984–5: an Iron Age farmstead and Romano-British industrial settlement in north Wales*, BAR Brit Ser, **210**, Oxford, 139–54

Ward, M, 1993 A summary of the samian ware from excavations at Piercebridge, *J Roman Pottery Stud*, **6**, 15–22

Ward, M, 1998 Some finds from the Roman works-depôt at Holt, *Studia Celtica*, **32**, 43–84

Ward, M, 2008 The samian ware, in H E M Cool and D J P Mason (eds), *Roman Piercebridge: excavations by D W Harding and Peter Scott 1969-81*, Architect Archaeol Soc Durham Northumberland Rep, **7**, Durham, 169-96

Ward, M, forthcoming a, The samian ware from excavation in 1999-2000 in C Howard-Davis, I Miller, N Hair, and R M Newman, in prep, *Excavations at Mitchells Brewery and 39 Church Street, Lancaster*, Lancaster Imprints

Ward, M, forthcoming b, The samian from Worcester Magistrates Court, excavations in 2000

Ward-Perkins, J B, 1941 The Iron Age horseshoe, *Antiq J*, **21**, 144–9

Waterman, D M, 1959 Late Saxon, Viking and early medieval finds from York, *Archaeologia*, **97**, 59–105

Watson, A (trans), 1985 *The digest of Justinian*, T Mommsen, and P Krueger (eds), Pennsylvania

Webster, J, 1995 Bells, in W H Manning, J Price, and J Webster, 1995 *Report on the excavations at Usk, 1965–1977: the Roman small finds*, Cardiff, 55–6

Webster, P V, 1996 *Roman samian pottery in Britain*, CBA Practical Handbooks in Archaeology, **13**, York

Weeks, J, and Rhodes, M, 1986 Wooden objects, in T Dyson (ed), *The Roman quay at St Magnus House, London. Excavations at New Fresh Wharf, Lower Thames Street, London, 1974–78*, Spec Paper London Middlesex Archaeol Soc, **8**, London, 230–2

Welfare, A T, 1985 The milling-stones, in Bidwell 1985, 154–64

Wellesley, K (trans), 1975 *Tacitus: the Histories*, London

Wheeler, A, 1969 *The fishes of the British Isles and North-West Europe*, London

Wheeler, R E M, 1926 *The Roman fort near Brecon*, Y Cymmrodor, **37**, London

Wheeler, R E M, 1930 *London in Roman times*, London Mus Catalogue, **3**, London

White, A, 2000a Pottery-making at Silverdale and Arnside, *Trans Cumberland Westmorland Antiq Archaeol Soc*, n ser, **100**, 285-91

White, A, 2000b The tobacco pipe, in R M Newman, N J Hair, C L E Howard-Davis, C M Brooks, and A White, Excavations at Penrith market, 1990, *Trans Cumberland Westmorland Antiq Archaeol Soc*, n ser, **100**, 126

White, K D, 1970 *Roman farming*, London

White, K D, 1975 *Farm equipment of the Roman world*, Cambridge

Widemann, F, 1987 Les effets économique de l'éruption de 79, nouvelles données et nouvelle approche, in *Tremblements de Terre, éruptions volcaniques et vie des hommes dans la Campanie antique*, Bibliothèque de l'Institut française de Naples **7**, Naples, 102–12

Wild, F, 1988 The samian ware, in B J N Edwards and P V Webster, *Ribchester excavations, part 3: excavations in the civil settlement 1968–1980 B, pottery and coins*, Cardiff, 9–50

Wild, J P, 1970a Button-and-loop fasteners in the Roman provinces, *Britannia*, **1**, 137–55

Wild, J P, 1970b *Textile manufacture in the northern Roman provinces*, Cambridge

Wilkins, A, 2003 *Roman artillery*, Princes Risborough

Wilkins, J M, and Hill, S, 2006 *Food in the Ancient World*, Oxford

Williams, D F, 1997 Amphorae, in Monaghan 1997, 967–73

Williams, D F, 2004 The eruption of Vesuvius and its implications for the early Roman amphorae trade with India, in J Eiring and J Lund (eds), *Transport amphorae and trade in the eastern Mediterranean: acts of the international colloquium at the Danish Institute at Athens, Sept 26–29, 2002*, Monog Danish Inst Athens, **5.5**, Aarhus, 441–50

Williams, D F, and Carreras, C, 1995 North African amphorae in Roman Britain: a re-appraisal, *Britannia*, **26**, 231–52

Williamson, G A (trans), 1972, *Josephus: the Jewish war*, London

Willis, S, 1998 Samian pottery in Britain: exploring its distribution and archaeological potential, *Archaeol J*, **155**, 82–133

Willis, S, 2003 The character of Lyon ware distribution, with particular attention to the evidence from the Midlands and the North of Britain, *J Roman Pottery Stud*, **10**, 125–38

Willis, S, 2005 Samian pottery, a resource for the study of Roman Britain and beyond: the results of the English Heritage-funded samian project, *Internet Archaeol*, **17**, http://intarch.ac.uk/journal/issue17/willis_index.html

Wilmott, T, 2001 *Birdoswald Roman fort*, Stroud

Wilson, B, and Edwards, P, 1993 Butchery of horse and dog at Witney Palace, Oxfordshire, and the knackering and feeding of meat to hounds during the post-medieval period, *Post-medieval Archaeol*, **27**, 43-56

Wilson, C A, 2000 *Processes of post-burial change in soils under archaeological monuments: a micromorphological study with particular reference to the processes of clay and iron redistribution*, unpubl PhD thesis, Univ Stirling

Wilson, K, and White, D J B, 1986 *The anatomy of wood: its diversity and variability*, London

Wilson, M G, 1968 Other objects of bronze, iron, silver, lead, bone, and stone, in B W Cunliffe (ed), *Fifth report on the excavations of the Roman fort at Richborough, Kent*, Rep Res Comm Soc Antiq London, **23**, Oxford, 93-110

Wilson, M G, 1972 Catalogue of the pottery, in S S Frere, *Verulamium Excavations I*, Rep Res Comm Soc Antiq London, **28**, London, 263–370

Wiltshire, P E J, 1997 The pre-Roman environment, in T Wilmott, *Birdoswald: excavations of a Roman fort on Hadrian's Wall and its successor settlements: 1987-92*, Engl Heritage Archaeol Rep, **14**, London 25–37

Winterbottom, S, 1986 *Leather from Dorothy Charlesworth 1976 Annetwell Street site*, unpubl rep

Winterbottom, S, 1989 Saddle covers, chamfrons and possible horse armour from Carlisle, in C van Driel-Murray, *Roman military equipment: the sources of the evidence*, BAR Int Ser, **S476**, Oxford, 319-36

Winterbottom, S, 1991 Waste from leatherworking, in Padley and Winterbottom 1991, 318-28

Winterbottom, S, 1992 Leather, in Caruana 1992, 45–109

Winterbottom, S, in prep a, Leather, in I D Cauana in prep

Winterbottom, S, in prep b, The stitched leather in J Zant and C Howard-Davis (eds), *Roman and medieval Carlisle: the northern Lanes, excavations 1978-82, Volume 1, the Roman period*

Woodward, A, and Leach, P, 1993 *The Uley shrines: excavation of a ritual complex on West Hill, Uley, Gloucestershire: 1977–9*, Engl Heritage Archaeol Rep, **17**, London

Woolgar, C M, 1999 *The great household in late medieval England*, New Haven and London

Woolley, L, 2002 *Medieval life and leisure in the Devonshire hunting tapestries*, London

Worrell, S, 2005 Finds reported under the portable antiquities scheme, *Britannia*, **36**, 447–72

Worrell, S, and Price, J, in prep The Roman glass, in J Zant and C Howard-Davis (eds), in prep *Roman and medieval Carlisle: the northern Lanes, excavations 1978-82, Volume 1, the Roman period*

Wright, M E, 1988 Beehive quern manufacture in the South-east Pennines, *Scottish Archaeol Rev*, **5**, 65–78

Zangemeister, C, and Schoene, R, 1871 *Corpus Inscriptionum Latinarum*, **4**, *Inscriptiones parietariae Pompeianae Herculanenses Stabianae*, Berlin

Zant, J, Miller, I, and Mould, Q, forthcoming *The northern defences of medieval Carlisle: excavations at Rickergate, 1998–99*

Zant, J, Miller, I, Murphy, S, and Hughes, V, in prep *Excavations on a Roman cemetery, industrial site and medieval suburb at 53-55 Botchergate, Carlisle*

INDEX

Please note that the Roman cohorts have been listed by their Latin names, but may be referred to differently in the text.

Aedicula   871, *see also* Sculpture
Agricola   490, 615, 679, 681
  governorship   680, 685
Agriculture   490, 511, 740, 919
  ard-marks   931
  dairying   524, 536, 909, 919
ala
  Gallorum Sebosiana   491, 500, 506, 509, 523, 581,
        612-13, 615, 685, 775
Aldborough   582-3, 588
Allectus   684-5
Altar   500, 523, 527, 870, 872-3, 933
Amber   502, 777-9
  beads   777
Anglo-Saxon Chronicle   530, 686
Animal bone
  assemblage   500, 514, 517, 519, 522-4, 528, 535-6,
     675, 904, 914, 918, 920
   burnt bone   777, 933
  carcasses   505, 521, 910, 912-13, 915-19
  cat   916, 919-20
  cattle   504, 517, 519, 536, 861, 904-8, 910-11,
    918-9, 928
   scapulae   504, 509, 514, 521, 911-14, 918
  deer   500, 514, 536-7, 863, 904-5, 917, 920
  dogs   500, 505, 905, 915-16, 920
  domestic fowl   502, 519-20, 523, 536, 554, 904-5,
    916-17, 919-920
  enamel hypoplasia   536, 907-8
  fish   920-1
  heron   520, 523, 905, 917, 920
  pigs   505, 517, 519, 522, 536, 904-10, 913-14,
    918-19, 930
  sheep   865, 905, 908-10, 919
  swans   505, 520, 523, 536, 905, 917, 920
  tooth wear   904, 908-9
Anklet   728
Antler   512, 740, 858, 863, 865, 917, *see also* bone/antler
  working
  hoe   512
  sawn   506, 920
Antonine Wall   583, 591, 601, 654, 657, 683, 734, 837,
    870, 931
Antoninus Pius   683
Antonius, Marcus   681
Apron
  military   707, 721
  mount   707
Archer's bracer   533, 841-2, 854-5, 857, *see also*
    Weaponry

Armour   491-2, 496-8, 503-4, 506, 508-10, 515, 519, 687-8,
    694, 702-3, 705-6, 733, 741-2, 745, 758, 819
  Alba Iulia-type   692, 704
  arm-guards   492, 497, 519, 689, 694-8, 700,
     704-5, 765
  body armour   496, 499, 687-8, 692, 694-5, 704
  breastplates   691-2, 704
  chain mail   760
  Corbridge-type   692, 703
  cuirasses   504, 528, 703-4
  greave   497-8, 700, 703
  helmets   498-9, 700-2, 706
   cheekpiece   498-9, 515, 700-2, 864-5
  Kalkriese-type   692
  lames   694-9, 705
  lobate hinges   692-4, 703
  lorica segmentata   496, 499, 692, 703, 706
  Newstead-type   496, 692-3, 703
   plate, ferrous   694
  scale   497, 492-3, 496-7, 499, 500, 506, 515-16,
    522, 547, 569, 687, 689-92, 702-5, 742, 749,
    764, 819, 822, 934
  shoulder guard   694
  tie hook   512
Asclepius   527, 558, 872-3, 933
Atrebates   615
Auger   799-802
Augst   574, 720
Aurelian   684
Awls   506, 519, 756, 758, 801-2
Axes   521, 758, 783-5, 801-2

Baker's peel   513, 810
Baldric   496, 818, 829
Ballista (bolts and mechanism)   *see* Weaponry
Bangle   528, 728-9, 745, 775-8, *see also* Bracelets;
  Jewellery
  glass   505, 528, 775-7
  metal/wire   728-9, 745
  shale   778
Bar Hill   657, 837
Barrels   573, 603, 694, 701, 808-9, 815
Basket   491, 513, 557, 809-10
Bath-house   486, 496, 526, 840, 872, 895, 897, 899-901
  Chesters   872
Beads   494, 528, 686-7, 731
  amber   *see* Amber, bead
  glass   *see* Glass, beads
  wooden   867

Bearsden 870, 931
Beer 509, 524-5, 598, 615
Bell 515, 741, 759
Bellows 532, 764-5, 842, 856-7
Belt plates 494, 496, 498, 706
Benwell 562
Besançon 708
Beverley 660, 667, 857
Bewcastle 561
Binchester 583, 598
Birdoswald 500, 523, 547, 566, 647, 681, 684, 733, 835,
        837, 870-1, 878
Birrens 588, 629
Blacksmith 494, 500, 746, 765-6, 866, 921-2, 924-7, 930
Blacksmithing 492, 508, 764-6, see also Ironworking;
        Metalworking; Smithy
Blades 511, 526, 533, 698, 708, 714, 738, 746, 748-9,
        756-7, 802, 881-2, 913-14
    scale tangs 748
    triangular 533
    whittle tangs 748, 865
Bolanus, Marcus Vettius 681
Bone/antler working 506, 520, 911
Boudiccan revolt 922
Boxwood 510, 806, see also combs, boxwood
Bracelets 728, 730, see also Bangles; Jewellery
Braives 598, see also Gallia Belgica
Brampton 513, 592, 627-30, 635-6, 638-9, 643, see also
        Pottery, Roman, Brampton
    kilns 510-11, 590-1
    works-depot 591, 594, 603, 625, 637
Bricks 488, 604, 888, 890-2, 895, 898-901
Brigantes 490
    revolts 682
Brockley Hill 580, 586
Brooches 505, 515
    bow 496, 725, 728
    crossbow 496
    figure-of-eight 494
    knee 528, 725
    penannular 496, 506, 520, 727-8
        ring 745
    plate 509, 726-7
Broom 712
Brough under Stainmore 734
Brougham cemetery 562, 863
Buckles 496, 501, 506, 510, 692, 706, 733, 849,
        852, 855
Burgh-by-Sands 869
Burials 729, 775, 903, 916
Butchery 500, 502, 505, 520-2, 536, 904, 910, 913, 916,
        918-20
    dogs 505
    waste 504, 519-20, 537, 913

Caerlaverock Castle 662
Caerleon 499, 603, 705-6, 863, 897

Caliga see Shoes, military boot
Caltrops 494, 512, 519-20, 716, 753
Camelon 581, 600-1
Campaign badge 511-12
Candlestick see Pottery, Roman, Ebor ware, candlestick
Cannel coals 777
Cannstatt 561-2
Caracalla 643, 683
Carausius 684-5
Carlisle
    city centre 686, 805
    Civitas Carvetiorum 683-4
    Guildhall Museum 553
    the Lanes 687, 769, 776-8, 809, 837, 857, 926,
        929-30, 935
        southern 604, 767, 772-3, 857, 864, 875,
            913, 929
    River Caldew 484, 526, 932
    River Eden 484, 590
    River Petteril 590
    Scalesceugh legionary pottery and tilery 486,
        590, 889, 901-2, see also Pottery
    St Nicholas Yard 677
    Streets
        Abbey Street 817
        Annetwell Street 488, 495, 533, 547-8, 680-1,
            776-7, 817-8, 826, 840-1,
            877-8, 887, 907-8, 910-11,
            913, 926-7, 935
            excavations 504, 528, 588, 680, 682-3,
                687, 817, 909
        Blackfriars Street 523, 539, 546-7, 559, 561,
            604, 675-6, 710, 721, 725,
            727, 733, 767, 769-70,
            772-3, 877
        Castle Street 484, 539, 541, 544, 546-8, 551,
            556-7, 612, 725, 746-7, 772-3,
            777-8, 820-1, 837, 857, 863-5
            excavations 504, 615, 712, 819, 863
        English Street 663, see also Pottery
        Fisher Street 502, 513, 516, 581, 583, 590, 593-6,
            601, 603-5, 617-18, 628, 637, 642,
            895, see also Pottery
        Rickergate 660, 662, 664, 670, 674, 676, 843,
            849, 855, 857, 936
Carlisle Castle
    castle ward 532
    curtain wall 671
    de Ireby's Tower 665
    kitchens 537, 663, 665-6
    medieval gardens 668, 671, 675
    outer ward 530, 535, 537, 663-4, 667-8, 671, 675,
        841, 903-4, 917
    palisade trench 665
    subway 540
Carlisle Cathedral 604, 686
Carlisle Roman fort 491, 500, 522, 524, 547, 561, 564,
        579, 591, 625-6, 781, 865

barrack blocks   484, 492, 504-6, 521, 680, 786, 861, 895, 901
barracks   485, 489, 491-4, 502, 508, 510, 519, 524-5, 566, 569, 581, 606, 790-1, 805-6, 818-19, 922-3
   cavalry   581
contubernia   513, 521, 525
garrison   496, 499, 511, 516, 521-2, 525, 568-9, 571-2, 579-83, 594, 596, 599, 601-4, 609, 615, 709
granaries   517, 524, 605
intervallum
   area   611, 896
   road   492, 542, 700, 714, 733, 753-4, 757, 818
praetorium   488, 492, 506, 513, 527, 573, 599, 731, 733, 742, 778, 813, 865, 872, 896
principia   488-9, 492-4, 512, 514-15, 519-20, 527-9, 578-9, 683-4, 791, 796-7, 818-19, 870-3, 896-7, 901, 922-3, 933-4
ramparts   581, 611, 681
rampart-back building   502, 506, 705, 900
water pipes   487, 641, 888, 900
   ceramic   487-8, 896-7, 900-1
   wooden   569, 798
workshops   488, 492, 501, 503-6, 511, 518, 520, 524-5, 527, 544, 564, 571, 588, 595, 748, 818
Carnuntum   689, 693-4, 703, 705
Carpenters' dogs   754
Castleford   555, 559, 708, 733, 735, 774, 817, 829, 835, 841, 865
Casurius   546-7, 561-2
Catterick   512, 559, 562, 564, 583-5, 729, 821, 837
Cattle *see* Agriculture, dairying; Animal bones, cattle; Husbandry; Stock-raising
Cavalry   492, 497, 499-501, 528, 703, 705, 716, 719, 723, 741
   fort   581, 730, 736, 774-5, 915
   harness   515, 774
   units   524, 687, 775
Cerialis, Quintus Petillius   505, 562, 613, 680-1
Cess pits   527, 929, 933-5
Chains   728, 738
Charcoal   764, 766, 926, 933
Charlesworth, Dorothy   829
Cheese   919, 931, *see also* Agriculture, dairying
   presses   524
Chester   499, 541, 546, 548, 578, 586, 605, 674, 722, 872, 896-7, 902
Chesterholm   878
Chimneys   489, 897-8
Chisel   510, 741, 801-2
Claudius   681, 684
Cockermouth   676-7
Coins   504, 530, 544, 549, 551, 569, 579, 589, 596, 609, 666, 679-87, 858, 883
   aes   679, 681-2, 685
   antoninianii   683

   asses   685
   circulation   681-4
   denarii   681-3, 685, 858
   dupondii   682, 685
   post-Roman
      penny   664, 686
      styca, Northumbrian   686
   quadrantes   685
   radiates   549, 683, 685, 707
   sestertii   682-3, 685
Colchester   516, 555, 559, 578, 583-4, 597, 599, 601, 609, 636-7, 639, 729, 731-2, 796, 800, 894
Cologne   516, 599, 600, 637, 735, 775
Column base   873
Combs   527, 806-7
   bone   533, 861
   boxwood   508, 807
   cases   533, 861
      composite   861
   wooden   501, 505, 861
Commodus   682
Constantius   684
Corbridge   496, 516, 559, 580, 582-5, 588-9, 622, 637, 639, 644-5, 687, 692, 703-5, 707, 725, 733-4
Corbridge Hoard   687, 703-5, 808
Cosmetics   734, 809
Counters   528, 565-6, 776, 863, 874-5, 886, *see also* Gaming, counters; Tallies
Cows   521-2, 524-5, 909, *see also* Animal bone, cattle; Agriculture, dairying; Husbandry
Crowfoots   929, 934
Cuirasses   *see* Armour, cuirasses
Cummersdale   683

Dacre   662, 674-7
Dagger frog   491, 498
Dark earths   528, 548, 551-2, 564, 575, 579, 586, 657-9, 664, 671, 686, 709, 727, 756, 765, 775
Daub   485, 488, 794-5, 804, 887-8, 900-1
Deer, *see* Animal bone, deer, *see also* Red deer; Venison
Diana   556, 558-9, 561
Dice   549-50, 559, 561-2, 586, 588, 872, 898
Dipinti   567, *see also* Pottery, Roman, amphorae; Tunny-fish sauce
Dolfin (lord)   530
Dorchester   812
Drain cover   797-8
Dress
  fastener   511
  pin   *see* Pins, dress
Ducks   see Animal bone, domestic fowl
Dye   931

Earrings   494, 508, 687, 730-1, *see also* Jewellery
Elginhaugh   580-1, 586, 588, 613
Enamel hypoplasia   *see* Animal bone

English Damside *see* Pottery, Roman
Exeter 526, 597-8, 609, 611, 857, 899, 900, 916
Extramural settlement 511, 516, 528, 548, 565, 570, 604, 643, 774

Farming, *see* Agriculture
Fastening loops 701, 837, 840
Faustina II 683
Ferrules 712, 715-16, 867
Festoons 553-4, 558-9, 561-2
Finials 873
Fish 509, 523, 537, 920-1, 934
      cod 523, 537, 920-1
      hook 751, 920
Fishing 528, 921
Fish-sauce 608
Flagon 508
Flesh hooks 520, 749-50
Flints 490
Flue tiles 489, 765, 888, 890, 895-6, 900
Fly
      house 527, 926
      stable 527, 922-3, 925-6
Fortuna 731, 869-70, 872
Frenchfield 684, *see also* Milestone
Funari 572-5
Furnace 875, 892
      smelting 766
Furniture 507, 509, 512, 520, 702, 735-6, 746, 754-5, 761, 805, 808, 810, 863, *see also* Knobs
      three-legged table 507, 810

Galena 503, 511, 763, *see also* Leadworking
Gallia Belgica 525, 580, 583, 596-9, 609, 615-16, 618, 622, 625, 629, 631, 639, 684
Gambling 527-8, 684
Gaming counters 504, 508, 511, 513, 566, 776
      bone 508, 512, 519, 527
Genii 520, 869-70, 872, *see also* Sculpture
      Centuriae 872
Girdle 842, 852-3, 855, 857
Glass 484, 504, 507-8, 511-13, 515, 519, 525-7, 530, 686-7, 767, 769, 772-3, 775-6, 863
      beads 774-5
            production centres 774, 777
            melon beads 494, 508, 514, 773-5
            turquoise frit 774-5
      bottles 506, 663, 771-2
      vessel glass 488, 490, 514, 767
Goad 759
Godmanchester 687
Gold 686-7, *see also* Necklace
Graffiti 513, 525, 539, 563-4, 572, 574-5, 863, 873, 893, 900, *see also* Pottery, mortaria; samian
Granite 875, 877

Gravestones 492, 521, *see also* Burials; Tombstones

Hadrian's Wall 513, 519, 527, 568, 571, 590-1, 596, 601, 604-5, 625-6, 681, 683, 708-9, 725, 733-4, 778
Haematite 875, 886
Hairpins 494-5, 508, 515, 520, 530, 533, 687, 730-3, 859, 861
      bone 520, 859
Hardknott 588, 682
Hare 502, 523, 536, 554, 557, 559, 905, 917-18, 920
Harness 492, 501, 504, 706, 721, 723, 742
      clips 720-1
      fitting 501, 504, 512, 533, 706, 740-2, 744
      pendants 492, 721-2
Hearth lining, vitrified 764-6
Hecate 916
Hedon 667
Hides 500, 506, 512, 521, 819-20, 831, 915, 917, 919-20, *see also* Leather; Leatherworking
High Rochester 871
Hinterland 547, 674, 778, 805, 904, 919-20, 935
Hobnails 484, 499, 504-5, 510, 512, 746, 833, 837, 839
      dome-headed 745
Hod Hill 498, 706, 714
Holdfasts 754
Horncores 908-9, 920, *see also* Animal bone; Antler
Horns 521, 559, 641, 748, 827, 919
Horse harness 501, 513, 707, 719, 744, 758, 775, 829, 855, 863, 865, *see also* Harness
Horses 485, 492, 494, 500-1, 503-4, 507-8, 520, 524, 528, 719, 723, 807, 904-15, 914-5, 919-20, 925
Horseshoe nails, fiddle-key 529, 745, 754
Horseshoes 529, 532, 745, 753-4
Household utensils 735, 746, 761, 808, 863
Housesteads 500, 527, 705, 709
Hull 573, 576, 660, 667, 677, 857, 894
Human bone 903
Human excrement 922
Hunting 500, 523, 528, 532, 536, 919, *see also* Animal bone; Meat
Husbandry 740, 759, 865, 905-6, 908, 910, 918, 935, *see also* Stock-raising
Hypocaust systems 486, 489, 873, 892, 895, 900-1, *see also* Pilae

Imbrices 488-9, 888, 890, 892, *see also* Roofing; *Tegulae*
Ink tablets 528, *see also* Writing tablets
Inkwells 519, 528, 544, 552
Inscriptions 578, 763, 831, 872, 898
Insects 921-5, 927, 934-5, *see also* Fly; Grain pests
Intaglio 745
Inveresk Gate 925
Ironworking 506, 510, 514, 519-20, 590, 706, 745, 754,

760, 764-6, 802 *see also* Blacksmithing; Metalworking; Smithy
  bloom 766
  hammerscale 508, 764-6
  slag 503, 763-6, 900
Ivory 708, 858-9

Jet 492, 506, 777-9
Jewellery 686-7, 745, 775, 777 *see also* Anklet; Bangles; Bracelets; Brooches; Earrings; Necklace

Kendal 500, 674, 677, 710
Keys 736-7, 751, 764, 801-2
Kilns 506, 516, 585, 590-1, 593, 602, 605, 609, 626, 893-5
Kirkby Thore 686-7
Kirkham 719
Kirksteads (hoard) 684
Knives 495, 509, 511-13, 518, 520, 526, 532-3, 535, 612, 617, 631, 738, 746-9, 855, 865, 896-7
  blade 509, 518, 520, 533, 749
  handles 495, 532, 865, 917
    antler 512
    bone 511, 748
  inlaid maker's mark 747-9
  sheath 533, 842, 855
Knobs 512, 520, 737, *see also* Furniture
Künzing 700, 705

Lamps 526, 528, 640-1, 663, 672, 674, 750, 754, 874, 885, *see also* Pottery, Roman, Ebor wares
Lancashire 525, 774
Lancaster 541, 544, 546-8, 564, 674, 683, 685, 913
Latrine 923-4, 933-4, *see also* Cess pits; Human excrement
  communal 527
Leadworking 763, *see also* Galena; Slingshot, Weights
Leather 496, 500-1, 504, 509, 514, 532-3, 537, 668, 695-9, 704-5, 817-21, 824, 829, 840-2, 855-6, 896-7
  bag 819
  ball 533, 535
  belt 745
  initials and stamping 831
  medieval 841-2, 857
  shoes, *see* Shoes
  tent, *see* Tents
Leatherworking 504, 506, 508, 511, 517, 532-3, 660, 670, 675, 687, 710, 756, 762, 802, 807, 818-9
  bovine leather 807, 833, 835, 837, 839-42, 845, 849, 852, 855-7, *see also* Hide
  scrap 512, 819, 841
  seam types 822, 824, 826
  sheep/goatskin 837, 842, 849, 856
  sheet leather 505-6, 741-3, 760-1, 763-5, 819,

829, 833, 841, 856
  waste 506, 511, 833, 841-2, *see also* Shoemaking, waste
Legions
  Legio II Augusta 604, 898-9, 902
  Legio III Augusta 604
  Legio IX Hispana 590, 604
  Legio VI Victrix 526, 578, 604, 901
  Legio XX Valeria Victrix 581, 590, 596, 605, 626, 681, 872, 889, 898, 901-2
  legionaries 497, 499, 500, 526, 568, 583, 591, 596, 681, 687, 703-5, 719, 822
Leucarum 881-2
Lezoux 544-5, 547-51, 559, 561, 564
  products 545, 549, *see also* Pottery
Lice 527, 806, 922, 926
Limes 605, 734
  German-Raetian 709, 733
  Western 501, 707
Lincoln 857, 913
Lincolnshire 606, 615, 626, 628, 658
Locks 736-7, 751, *see also* Keys
  barrel 736
  latch lifter 512, 751
  locking mechanism 736
  mortise 751
  slide bolt 512, 751
London 494, 561, 578, 598, 603, 685-6, 731, 753, 794-6, 803, 809-10, 845, 849-50, 855, 857
  One Poultry 922, 925
Loomweight 874-5, 884
Lot Valley 541
Lower Nene Valley 585, 605, 649, 652, 654, 659
Luguvalium 581

Mainz 864
Mancetter-Hartshill, kiln site 513, 516, 582-5, 649, 657, *see also* Pottery, Roman, mortaria
Manchester 856, 903
Manicae, *see* Armour, arm-guards
Manure and animal waste 527, 927, 935
Market 585, 606, 650
Maryport 871
Meat 521-4, 536, 749, 904, 908-11, 915-16, 918-20, *see also* Animal bone; Butchery; Stock-raising, Hunting
  beef 521-2, 536, 908, 918, 920
  ham 522
  horsemeat 500, 919
  mutton 521-2, 536, 908-9, 918, 920
  pork 521-2, 908, 918, 920
    fat 522
  venison 505, 523, 537
Medicinal plants
  burdock 928, 931, 933-4

common mallow 931, 934
fairy/purging flax 928, 931
hawkbit 931
hemlock 928, 931, 933-5
henbane 525, 928, 931, 933-5
mallow seeds 931
nightshade (deadly and black varieties) 931, 933-4
opium poppy 525, 931, 933-4
selfheal 931
Metalworking 504, 508, 511, 517, 528, 564-5, 611, 679, 687, 730, 733, 741-4, 756-7, 763-5, 819, 866, see also Blacksmithing; Ironworking; Leadworking; Smithy
crucible 506, 510, 571, 601, 611, 625-6, 631, 633, 741, 765
debris 506, 514, 875
hearths 505, 741
scrap metal 506, 510-11
smithing hearth bottoms 508, 764-6
Midden 504-5, 520-1, 666, 840
Milestone 683-4
Military
equipment 491-2, 506, 509, 513, 520, 688, 704-5, 718-9, 722, 778, 814, 817, 819-22, 829, see also Armour; Tent; Weaponry
fittings, niello-decorated 499, see also Niello
Milk 524-5, 536, 909, 919 see also Agriculture, dairying
Millefiori 735
Millstone Grit 875, 877
Millstones 524, 877, 879, 887, see also Querns
Minerva 555, 561
Mints 683, 685, see also Coins
Modelling tool 756
Mons Claudianus 928
Mons Graupius 581
Mortar 485, 671, 887-8, 892, 897, 900
Mortises 791, 795, 801-2
Mussels 504, 523

Nails 484-5, 489, 499, 504-5, 508, 510, 512, 514, 516, 518-20, 528-9, 533, 745-6, 802, 839-40
hand-forged 754
Necklace 494-5, 686-7, 728 see also Jewellery
Needle 504, 533, 535, 732, 745-6, 749, 758, 819, 863
Needlework 535, 745, 749
Nene Valley see Pottery, Nene Valley
Nero 681
Newcastle, fort at 684
Newstead 499, 509, 581, 600, 682, 703, 705-6, 714, 817, 819-20, 831, 866, 880
Niello 498, 500, 707, 723, see also Military, fittings
Nijmegen 609
Northampton 861

Oise-Somme see Pottery, Oise-Somme

Old Penrith 541, 556, 566, 580, 582-3, 628, 733
Olive oil 525, 578, 616, 643, 908
Osteoarthritis 907, 915, see also Animal bone
Ovens 506, 514, 524, 581, 611, 927, see also Kilns
Oysters 523, 537

Palaeoenvironmental evidence
alder 484-5, 781, 783, 785-6, 795, 799, 803, 929-30, 932
buckthorn 929
arable weeds 927-9, 932-6
ash 484-5, 781, 783, 785-6, 803, 806, 810
barley 524, 927, 932, 934
bedstraw 931
belladonna 933
bilberry 537, 930, 934-5
bindweed 928
birch 484, 787, 816
bark 930
seeds 930, 934
bird cherry 929, 933
bread wheat 524, 927
celery-leaved buttercup 929, 933-5
cereal grains 537, 926-7, 930, 932-6
chickweed 525
coriander 524
corn marigold 928, 934-5
corn spurrey 928
cornflower 928
dandelion 928
diatoms 931
dill 524, 930, 933, 935
fat-hen 525, 928, 930, 934
flax 930, 934-6
fairy/purging see Medicinal plants, fairy/purging flax
goldilock's buttercup 933
grain 524, 662, 787, 802, 804, 839, 922-7, 935
pests 923-5, 927, see also Insects
granary weevil 922, 924
spoilt 924-5
stored 524, 921-4
grapes 555, 559, 641, 723, 930, 933, 935
hay 525, 927-8, 932
hazel 484, 929, 932
hazelnut shells 930, 932-3
heather 486, 929-30, 933-5
hemp 928, 930, 934-6
mallow 525
nettles
common 928, 933
hemp 928
seeds 931, 933-4
oak 484-5, 487-8, 530, 712-13, 780-1, 783-8, 795, 799-804, 815
oats 524, 537, 927, 934-5
olives 930

parsley piert 928
plums 524
rowan 524, 929
ruderal plants 926-8, 932-5
rushes 926-7, 929, 932, 934-5
sedges 927, 929, 932, 934-5
silver fir 525, 808-9, 812
spearwort 929
spelt 524, 927, 935
wild celery 524-5, 929, 932
Parasites 527, 926
Penrith 541, 624, 662, 675-7, 683, 875, 877
Pestles 875, 884
Petillius Cerialis 681
Phalera 719, 721
Phallus 871-2, 900
Piercebridge 495, 548, 564-6, 919
Pilae 873, 892, 901, *see also* hypocaust
Pins 506, 712, 730-3, 739, 743, 745, 859, 863, 914, *see also* Hairpins
    bone 731
    buckle 503, 510, 728, 733
    dome-headed 712
    dress 533, 733
Plaster 814, 887, 897
Plasterer's float 505, 802, 814
Pliny 499, 681, 741, 777, 782, 931
Plough 919
Pollen 926, 931, 936
Pompeii 554-5, 578, 797
Postumus 684
Pottery
    Anglian 676
    lamps *see* Lamps
    Roman
        amphorae 523, 525, 566-8, 572-9, 593-4, 601-2, 608-9, 611, 613, 618, 626-7, 631, 638-40, 642, 644, 646-7
        Argonne wares 515, 548, 596-7, 631, 636, 646
        Beakers 509, 514, 516, 525, 597-9, 606-7, 612, 615-16, 620, 622, 631, 633, 638, 641-2, 646-7, 654-5
        Black-burnished ware 513, 516-17, 519, 570, 591, 593, 608-9, 617, 625-6, 633, 635, 637, 640, 642-7, 650, 652, 654-5
            Dorset 601-3, 622, 626, 629, 633, 637-8, 640, 642, 644, 647, 649-50, 652, 654
            imitations 602-3, 628, 637, 642-4, 646, 650, 654-7
                bowl 633, 642, 644, 646, 652, 654-5
                local 631, 633, 636, 647
                jar 617, 620, 627, 631, 633, 636, 645-7, 650, 652
        Brampton wares 506, 513, 592, 613, 616, 618,

620, 627-31, 633, 635-9, 643-4, 646
colour-coated wares 596-7, 599-601, 605-6, 637, 643, 649, 652, 654-5, 657
Crambeck 517, 579, 584-6, 596, 599-601, 602, 605-7, 643, 647, 649-50, 652, 654, 656-9
East Yorkshire calcite-gritted wares 519, 607-8, 643, 647, 649-50, 652, 654, 656-7, 659
Ebor wares 499, 517-18, 526, 596, 604-5, 608, 626, 640, 644, 647, 650, 657
    candlestick 499, 643
    lamp 499, 616, *see also* Lamps
    North African forms 604, 643, 657,
Eboracum wares 603, *see also* York
English Damside 516-17, 590, 594-5, 602-3, 637, 642-4, 646-7, 650, 652, 654, 657, 659
finewares 519, 571, 582, 584, 594-7, 599, 600, 605, 607-8, 612, 615, 625, 643, 647, 650
imported fine white tableware 596-9
mortaria 513, 519, 547-9, 552, 579-86, 588-91, 594-5, 608-9, 611-15, 617-18, 624-5, 637-41, 644-7, 649-50, 652-4, 657-9
    Elginhaugh 588
    Mancetter Hartshill *see* Mancetter Hartshill, kiln site
    Oise-Somme 580, 582-3, 594, 611, 614, 618, 620, 638
    stamped 548, 587-9, 608, 611, 613
Moselkeramik 600, 605-6, 643
Nene Valley 517, 519, 596, 598, 600, 605-7, 636-7, 643, 647, 649-50, 652, 654-5, 657
North African-type 509, 571, 596-600, 604, 615, 617-18, 622, 624, 629, 644, 647, 657
North Gaulish greyware 509, 596-600, 615, 618, 624, 629
Oxfordshire red-slipped wares 606, 650
oxidised ware 593, 603, 608, 611-12, 616-18, 620, 622, 624-5, 627-31, 633, 635-9, 642-4, 646-7, 654, 657, 659-60
    fine 608-9, 611-13, 616-18, 620, 622, 624-5, 628-9, 631, 633, 635-9, 641, 643-4, 646-7, 649, 655-7, 660
    semi-fine 611-13, 616, 620, 624, 644
proto-Huntcliff wares 654-6
reduced ware 593, 598, 600, 602, 606-7, 611, 613-14, 617-18, 620, 624-6, 628-9, 631, 643-4, 646-7, 649, 656-7

semi-fine wares   611-13, 616, 620, 624, 644
Samian 504, 508-9, 511-13, 519, 525-6, 538-40, 542-9, 552-8, 562-6, 569, 586, 607-9, 615-16, 635-6, 638-40, 646-7
  Central Gaulish   539, 544-5, 547, 551-2, 563, 596-7, 599, 600, 605, 609, 612, 616, 622, 633, 643
  East Gaulish   539-41, 547-9, 551-2, 566
  Heiligenberg   548, 561
  La Graufesenque   541, 549-50, 554-6, 558
  La Madeleine   546, 548, 551, 559
  Les Martres-de-Veyre   544-5, 548-52, 557-9
  Lezoux   544-5, 547-51, 559, 561, 564
  Montans   541
  Rheinzabern   548-9, 551, 561, 566
  Potters
    Attianus   559, 561
    Banassac   541
    Bellicus, workshop of   589, 639
    Cinnamus   546-7, 549, 559, 561-2
    Crestio   541, 549, 555-6
    Criciro   546-7, 551, 559, 561
    Docilis   491-2, 583
    Do(v)eccus   562
    Frontinus   542, 555, 557
    Germanus, school of   542, 554-5, 557
    Ioenalis   545, 549
    Mercator   541-2, 547, 549, 556-8
    Paternus   546-7, 559
    Reginus   546, 548, 561
    Roppus   541, 545, 550
    Secundinus   544-6, 550, 559
    Tasgillus   545, 550
   Stamps   541, 549
    name-stamps   583
  Swanpool   596, 606-7, 650, 652
  Wilderspool ware   499, 510, 541, 583, 586, 597, 599, 605, 626, 631, 635, 639, 660
Terra nigra   596, 598, 613
Trier   549
Verulamium 580-3, 586, 603, 609, 611-12, 618, 638, *see also* Brockley Hill
Wroxeter   506, 510, 580-4, 586, 588-9, 613, 871
  workshop   586
York Minster-type   586, 647, 652
Medieval 532, 537, 660-1, 666, 669-70, 674, 676
  Fully Reduced green-glazed   533, 777
  greywares   513, 618, 643, 645
    Partially Reduced   662-3, 665-71, 674, 676
    Reduced   586, 661-4, 666-7, 669-70, 674, 676
  Gritty wares   661-4, 668-70, 675-6
    Norman   676
    North Pennine   652, 654, 657
    red   530, 662-3, 666-7, 670-2, 674-6

    Reduced   613, 617
    white   662-7
   Humber ware   677
  Post-medieval   660-1, 664, 667-8
    red earthenware   666-7, 671
    Salt-Glazed Stoneware   671
    white-glazed earthenware   666-7
  Supplies   506, 509, 517, 519, 591, 595, 608, 612, 643
Prestatyn   558, 564
Preston   541
punches   506, 756-7, 802
Pupienus   664, 669-70, 675, 681-3
Purse   856
Pyx   809

Querns 519, 524, 874-5, 877-81, 886-7, *see also* Millstones
  beehive   877-80, 884
  'cake tin'   878
  collared-type   878
  fragments   874, 877, 886
  lava   877, 886-7
  rotary   874, 877
Quiver   500, 533, 856, *see also* Weaponry, arrows

Ravenglass   776, 863, 875, 878
Razors   526-7, 746-7, 859
  ivory-handled   527, 746
Reaping hook   511, 740, 759
Recipes   521, 523-4
Red deer   517, 520, 523, *see also* Animal bone, deer; Hunting; Meat, venison
Ribchester 487, 498, 500, 511, 521, 525, 540, 544, 546, 548, 551, 774-5, 804, 820, 913, 915-16
Richborough   551, 556, 731
Ring
  copper-alloy   516
  finger   510, 730, 745, 778
  jet   506
Rivets 497, 506, 510, 556, 564, 687, 693-6, 698-701, 704, 722, 738-9, 741-2, 763, 813
  disc-headed   692
Rod   663, 668-9, 742
  round-sectioned 743, 746, 760, 763-4
Roman army 490, 494, 570-2, 602, 608, 687-8, 712, 803, 877, 880, 918, 925
  officers in Carlisle   491
Roof/roofing   793, 801, 804, 820, 823, 825-6, 892
  materials   486, 804, 935, *see also* Shingles; Tiles, roofing; Thatch
  ridge   791-2, 824-5
  tiles   *see* Tiles, roofing; *see also* Imbrices; *Tegulae*
Roundels   561-2, 720, 822, 837, 840, 884
Rubbish dumping 509, 513, 520, 523, 528, 533, 566-8, 573, 604, 819, 857, 922, 924-5, *see also* Midden

Ruler   802, 812

Sacrifice   505, 522, 916
Saddle   501, 504, 509, 528, 687, 723, 740, 814, 817, 819-21, 823, 827-9
   bags   829
   plates   723-4
     niello-decorated   500-1
   seat covering   827
Saddlery   511, 719
Sagittarii   500, 710
Saw   511, 756, 801-2
   blade   511, 756, 802
Sawing   780, 783, 802-3
Scale pan   511, 761-2
Scissors   749, *see also* Needleworking; Shears
Scole   795, 803, 809
Scoops   629, 734, 810, 862-3, *see also* Animal bone, cattle, scapulae
Sculpture   520, 704, 869, *see also* Aedicula; Altar; *Genii*
Selby   856
Severus   578, 604-5, 643, 683
Shaft   712, 714, 716, 723, 732-5, 749, 801, 859, 863, 866
   ash wood   712
Shale   777-8, *see also* Jet
Shears   533, 535, 741, 745, 749, *see also* Scissors
Sheaths   703, 841-2, 854-5
Sheep/goat   505, 522, 524-5, 536, 759, 833, 841, 856, 865, *see also* Animal bone
Shingles   486, 813
Shoemaking   504, 506, 665, 667, 746, 818-19, 821, 835, 840, 842, 857
   shoemakers   496, 511, 833
   waste   504, 506, 533, 818-19, 821, 835, 839-42
   workshop   511
Shoes   495-6, 504, 510, 512, 532-3, 535, 668-70, 746, 753, 831-3, 835, 837, 839-43, 845, 848-52, 857
   adult size   833, 835, 840, 845, 849
   ankle boots   835, 837, 841, 843, 845, 847, 849, 851, 857
   boots   484, 535, 836-7, 841, 843, 845, 849-50, 852, 857
   children's   495, 535, 840, 843, 849
   heel stiffeners   835, 843, 845, 850
   laces   700, 845, 849, 855
   low-throated   849
   military footwear   496, 503, 837, 840
   moss toe-stuffing   843
   nailed   821, 832, 834-7
   one-piece   495, 832, 839-40
   overshoes   840, 852
   pointed toe   841, 843, 849
   sandal   510, 839, 852
   soles   533, 835, 842-3, 845
   reused   856
   thonging   834-5, 839
   tie-straps   849-51
   toes   840, 843, 849

   long-pointed   843, 849
     oval   843
   toggle-fastening   843, 845, 857
   toggles (leather)   845, 864
   wooden-soled bath   496, 526, 832, 840
Silchester   608, 778, 881
Silenus   525, 612
Sill beams   533, 786, 790, 804
   construction   791, 794-5, 803
Silos   505, 929
Sinew   521
Skinning   502, 910, 916, 920, see also Animal bone; Leather; Leatherworking
Slaughter   521, 908-9, 918-19, see also Animal bone
Slaves   491-2, 500, 507, 515, 526, 528
   ownership   494
Sloes   524, 929-30, 932
Smithy   514, 564, 764-6, 875, *see also* Blacksmithing; Ironworking; Metalworking
Solway Firth   921
South Shields   566, 576, 706, 728, 735, 778-9, 866
Southwark Cathedral   869, *see also Genii*; Sculpture
Spindle whorls   762, 875
   bone   860-1
   ceramic   533, 565-6, 777
   lead (possible spindle whorl)   762
   shale   778-9
   stone   874, 884
   wooden   511, 807
Spoons   863
St Cuthbert   684
Stables   494
Stanegate (Roman road)   683
Stanhope   523
Stanwix   683, 932
Stock-raising   490, 919, *see also* Husbandry
Strageath   706, 877, 887
Straps   499, 663, 666-70, 674, 697, 704, 817, 819, 832, 839-40, 842, 849, 851-3, 855
   hinge   754
   junction   513, 719-20
   mounts   707
   terminal   708
Studs   498, 508, 513, 722, 739-40, 742, 784, 794-5, 803-4, 888
   dome-headed   513, 722-3, 742
   repoussé   511-2
   round-headed   728, 733, 738
Stycas   see Coins
Styli   504, 508, 510, 515, 734, 752, 756
Stylus tablet   581, *see also* Ink tablet; Writing tablet

Tacitus, Publius Cornelius   490, 498, 500, 524, 681, 777, 915
Tallies   512, 528, 863, *see also* Gambling; Gaming counters
Tallow   521, 910

Tangiers (modern Morocco) 523, 578, 609
Tankard 659, 808
Tannery 512, 819
Tanning 521, 831, 919, 931, *see also* Skinning
Tarraby Lane 932
Taverns 528
Tegulae 888-90, 892, 896, 898-900
    mammata 900
Tenements 530, 533-5, 537, 660, 669-70, 674-6, 741, 758, 765, 841-3, 845, 851-2, 855, 903-4, 920-1, 934-5
Tents 484, 504-5, 508, 512, 532, 608, 718, 817-23, 826, 830-1, *see also* Leather; Leatherworking; Military, equipment
    army 484, 822
    leather 513, 817, 819
    peg 718
    pieces 819
Tessera 874-5
Tetrici 549, 684
Tetricus I 549
Textiles 491, 496, 511, 515, 689, 735, 746, 840, 858, 861-3, 865, 884, 930
    manufacture 511
    medieval 858
Thatch 486
Tiles 486, 488-9, 502, 569, 590-1, 887-90, 892-6, 898-901
    roofing 888-90, 901
Toilet, surgical, or pharmaceutical instruments
    ligulae 513, 734-5, 743
    nail cleaner 735
    surgical probe 735
Tombstone 500, 507, 521, 775, *see also* Gravestone
Tools 506, 511, 514, 518, 520, 698, 719, 738, 741, 756-9, 763, 781, 800-2, 813, 865-7, 881-2
Trackway 665
Trajan 544, 550, 681-3
Trier *see* Pottery, Roman
Trimontium 581
Tullie House Museum and Art Gallery 539, 590, 679, 877, 881
Tuning peg, bone 533
Tunny-fish sauce 609
Turf cutter 492, 719
Tyne-Solway isthmus 591, 601, 613

Usk 552, 774-5

Valerian 683
Valkenburg 786, 795-6, 803-4, 830
Vases tronconiques, see Pottery, beakers
Vegetius, Publius Flavius 484, 487, 497, 525
Venus 561, 731
Venutius 490
Vespasian 551, 681-2

Vessels, wooden
    coopered 802, 808-9
    turned 806, 809-10
Vesuvius 525, 576
Victory 556, 558
Vicus, see Extramural settlement
Vindolanda 486, 499, 505, 511, 522, 524, 583, 591, 598, 613, 709, 786-7, 796-7, 803-6, 820-2, 826-7
Vindonissa 706, 718, 778

Wall studs 794
Wallhooks 754
Wallsend 866
Watercrook 500, 541, 615-16, 682, 710
Waterlogging 483, 517, 532-3, 537, 687, 756, 805, 817, 926
Wattle 485, 488, 793-7, 804-5, 888, 901, 930
    infill 794-5
    panels 485, 793-5, 804
Weaponry 492-3, 500, 518, 687, 705, 714
    arrowheads 492-3, 500, 514, 532-3, 554, 559, 687, 694, 709-10, 712, 745, 843
      bodkin-type 694, 709, 711
    ballista 492, 712
      bolts 508, 512, 514, 519, 709, 712
      mechanism 712
    bolt heads 709, 711-12, 714
    bow 533, 816
    pilum 694, 712-13
    projectile 492, 511, 687, 694, 712, 745, 874-5, 883-4, 887
    storage rack 712
    shield 497-9, 509, 558, 566, 576, 706, 728, 735, 778-9, 817, 819-21, 829, 866
      covers 497, 509, 817, 820, 829
      grips 706
      rectangular 499, 819, 829
      wooden 706
    slingshot 884
      ceramic 492-3, 507, 511, 514, 709, 717-18, 777, 887
      lead 493, 519, 717-18, 887
    spear 492, 714
      butt ferrule 716
    spearheads 492, 500, 512, 514, 518, 687, 714, 716, 745, 758
    stone projectiles 511, 884
    sword
      bone collar 508
      chapes 519
      grip 492, 508
      handle 492
      hilt 738, 748
      pommel, jet 492, 506
Weather-boarding 485-6, 754, 794
Weaving
    combs 504, 860, 865, 917

bone 491, 513
    tablet 505, 735, 863
Weights *see also* Loomweights
    lead 511, 515, 761-3
Westcott 731
Wheel 504, 631, 812-13
Whetstones 874-5, 881-2
Wigan 719, 913
Windows 489, 515, 530, 533, 754
Wine 509, 572-3, 603, 609, 611, 615-16
    trade, Rhine 525, 808
Women 491, 494-5, 502, 515, 518-20, 533, 535, 537, 687, 730, 735, 745, 777-8, 840, 845
Wooden vessels *see* Vessels, wooden
Woodland 484, 781, 803-4, 843, 929

Woodworking 511, 781, 802, 815
Wool/woollen fabric and textiles 496, 498, 535-6, 858, 862, 909, 919-20, *see also* Textiles
Writing tablets 504, 528, 685, 752, 812-13, *see also* Ink tablets; *Stylus* tablets

Xanten 701, 720

York 499, 517-18, 526, 570-1, 578, 585-6, 603-4, 608, 625-6, 637-8, 640-1, 643, 647, 652-4, 732, 855-7
    legion, *see* Legion, *Legio VI Victrix*
    Minster 578, 585, 647